WASHINGTON

A Life

RON CHERNOW

PENGUIN BOOKS

PENGUIN BOOKS
Published by the Penguin Group
Penguin Group (USA) Inc., 375 Hudson Street, New York, New York 10014, U.S.A. •
Penguin Group (Canada), 90 Eglinton Avenue East, Suite 700, Toronto, Ontario,
Canada M4P 2Y3 (a division of Pearson Penguin Canada Inc.) • Penguin Books Ltd,
80 Strand, London WC2R 0RL, England • Penguin Ireland, 25 St. Stephen's Green,
Dublin 2, Ireland (a division of Penguin Books Ltd) • Penguin Books Australia Ltd,
250 Camberwell Road, Camberwell, Victoria 3124, Australia (a division of
Pearson Australia Group Pty Ltd) • Penguin Books India Pvt Ltd, 11 Community
Centre, Panchsheel Park, New Delhi–110 017, India • Penguin Group (NZ), 67
Apollo Drive, Rosedale, Auckland 0632, New Zealand (a division of Pearson New
Zealand Ltd) • Penguin Books (South Africa) (Pty) Ltd, 24 Sturdee Avenue,
Rosebank, Johannesburg 2196, South Africa

Penguin Books Ltd, Registered Offices:
80 Strand, London WC2R 0RL, England

First published in the United States of America by The Penguin Press,
a member of Penguin Group (USA) Inc. 2010
Published in Penguin Books 2011

1   3   5   7   9   10   8   6   4   2

Illustration credits appear on pages 869–72.

THE LIBRARY OF CONGRESS HAS CATALOGED THE HARDCOVER EDITION AS FOLLOWS:
Chernow, Ron.
Washington : a life / Ron Chernow.
p. cm.
Includes bibliographical references and index.
ISBN 978-1-59420-266-7 (hc.)
ISBN 978-0-14-311996-8 (pbk.)
1. Washington, George, 1732–1799. 2. Presidents—United States—Biography. I. Title.
E312.C495 2010
973.4'1092—dc22
[B]
2010019154

Printed in the United States of America
DESIGNED BY MARYSARAH QUINN

Praise for Ron Chernow's *Washington*

"Superb . . . The best, most comprehensive, and most balanced single-volume biography of Washington ever written. [Chernow's] understanding of human nature is extraordinary and that is what makes his biography so powerful."
—Gordon S. Wood, *The New York Review of Books*

"Chernow displays a breadth of knowledge about Washington that is nothing short of phenomenal. . . . Never before has Washington been rendered so tangibly in such a smart, tenaciously researched volume as Chernow's opus. . . . A riveting read."
—Douglas Brinkley, *Los Angeles Times*

"Until recently, I'd never believed that there could be such a thing as a truly gripping biography of George Washington. . . . Well, I was wrong. Ron Chernow's huge (900 pages) *Washington: A Life*, which I've just finished, does all that and more. I can't recommend it highly enough—as history, as epic, and, not least, as entertainment. It's as luxuriantly pleasurable as one of those great big sprawling, sweeping Victorian novels."
—Hendrik Hertzberg, *The New Yorker*

"*Washington* is a true achievement . . . that speaks to the triumph of Chernow's narrative structure, the depth of his research, and how alive he is to the emotional content of dry material. . . . Chernow's goal is to humanize Washington. He succeeds handsomely, depicting an irreducibly complicated figure."
—T. J. Stiles, *The Washington Post*

"Chernow's book rewards its readers with an epic tale of true greatness and enormous self-sacrifice."
—Alan Taylor, *The New Republic*

"[A] splendid achievement . . . grand." —*The Times Literary Supplement* (London)

"This book brings a lost world to light and skillfully places Washington—statesman, general, family man, lover—firmly in it. . . . If anyone wants to read about Washington, this book, rich in detail, meticulous in its research, sensible in its judgments, is the one to read." —*The Telegraph* (London)

"This is beautiful expository writing, a combination of detailed, spellbinding narrative, and zinging judgment. . . . This is a book for every American—a masterpiece of biography." —General Wesley K. Clark, *The Daily Beast*

"*Washington: A Life* keeps its distance from Washington mythology, and its narrative informs as much as it entertains. . . . Chernow lets the reader know he wants to give an accurate portrayal of an enigmatic historical figure. In this book's pages, he does it in a way that not even the most gifted portrait artist of Washington ever could." —W. Ralph Eubanks, NPR's *All Things Considered*

"Fascinating . . . Chernow's narrative is so rich, its scale so massive and epic, that what is new fits seamlessly into the wider picture. . . . Chernow has gone into Washington's world, almost into his mind, and inhabited it. Under his gaze, from the very first page, that world begins to speak and stir, and great Washington steps before us, as if on an enormous stage, distant but clear, breathing. If I have not said so already, this is far and away the best life of George Washington ever written." —Max Byrd, Salon.com / *Barnes & Noble Review*

"Riveting . . . Chernow has written award-winning biographies before tackling the 'Father of our Country,' but this is his best book to date. It will be considered the definitive biography of George Washington, and awards and accolades are sure to follow." —The Associated Press

"There were as many sides to George Washington as there are to a diamond, and in his epic and highly readable biography *Washington: A Life*, Ron Chernow holds each of them up to the light. Prepare to be dazzled." —*New York Post*

"Impossibly thorough and a damn good read." —GQ.com

"Vast and tenaciously researched . . . deeply rewarding . . . and it does genuinely amplify and recast our perceptions of Washington's importance. . . . This new portrait offers a fresh sense of what a groundbreaking role Washington played." —Janet Maslin, *The New York Times*

"Just as he resuscitated Alexander Hamilton in a heralded 2004 biography, Ron Chernow now resurrects Washington. . . . He makes excellent use of Washington's own voice—the man's angry letters are like thunderbolts—and turns constitutional debates and bureaucratic infighting into riveting reading." —*Entertainment Weekly*

"Chernow's great skill lies . . . in his ability to draw out hidden threads and find the man inside the legend. . . . The beauty of this biography is in the perfect pitch between the light and the dark, the enigmatic and the familiar. This is truly *A Life*."
—Amanda Foreman, *Mail on Sunday* (London)

"Hugely researched [and] engagingly written."   —*The Sunday Times* (London)

"*Washington: A Life* is a sweeping, compelling, and convincingly written story, a landmark accomplishment that embellishes Chernow's already distinguished reputation as a biographer."   —*St. Louis Post-Dispatch*

"Nearly every adult American carries his portrait with them wherever they go, but the man painted by Gilbert Stuart remains enigmatic. Ron Chernow, a renowned biographer and historian, looks beyond the myths to reveal a man much greater than all of the myths combined."   —*The Dallas Morning News*

"[A] marvelous, mammoth biography . . . The author has transformed the most marbled—or wooden—of presidents into flesh and blood."
—*The Christian Science Monitor*

"Chernow writes immensely readable books, thanks to a novelist's mastery of two techniques: telling a compelling story and creating unforgettable characters. Those skills are on full display in his new biography: *Washington: A Life*."
—*The Seattle Times*

"*Washington: A Life* is a prodigious biography, expertly narrated and full of remarkable detail."   —Jill Lepore, *The New Yorker*

"Today, books about Washington continue to appear at such an astonishing rate that the publication of Ron Chernow's prompts the inevitable question: Why another one? An obvious answer is that Chernow is no ordinary writer. . . . His *Washington* . . . is vivid and well paced . . . his understanding of psychology is acute and his portraits of individuals memorable. Most readers will finish this book feeling as if they have actually spent time with human beings."
—*The New York Times Book Review*

"[*Washington*] is so good in explaining the American Revolution, the founding of this country, and the complicated man who served as its first president that it could serve as a textbook for high school students. In fact, even history buffs who have put a dent in the mountain of books about the Founding Fathers should consider this one because of the quality of the writing and psychological insights. . . . The reader finishes this biography dazzled by Washington [and] grateful to Chernow."
—*USA Today*

"He really did have trouble with his teeth, but everything else most of us know about George Washington will need some readjustment now that Ron Chernow has produced his splendidly detailed biography of the first president of the United States." —Manuela Hoelterhoff, *Bloomberg News*

"Chernow has a crisp, clear style, and once again his depth of research helps him become a master of details—the small, vivid moments that bring the larger themes to life. . . . A single volume that shines a bright, clear light on the father of our country." —*Minneapolis Star Tribune*

"An enthralling account." —*The Kansas City Star*

"Now the brilliant biographer Ron Chernow . . . demonstrates in his magnificently written, richly detailed, and always compelling *Washington: A Life* just how and why his subject attained such an exalted status. . . . Chernow's latest accomplishment is historical biography at its best." —*BookPage*

"The massive yet briskly paced *Washington: A Life* is a rollicking read, sure to redefine perceptions and correct assumptions." —*Kirkus Reviews*

"[A] vastly enlightening, overwhelmingly engaging treatment of a great man . . . 'Another book on Washington?' is a question rendered pointless by this one, which happens to be the author's masterpiece. Definitive Washington is the point and effect of this biography." —*Booklist* (starred review)

"This broadly and deeply researched work is a major addition to Washington scholarship—every era should have its new study of him—and it should appeal to informed lay readers and undergraduates interested in stepping beyond the typical textbook treatment." —*Library Journal*

PENGUIN BOOKS

WASHINGTON

Ron Chernow is the prizewinning author of five previous books. His first, *The House of Morgan*, won the National Book Award. His two most recent books, *Alexander Hamilton* and *Titan: The Life of John D. Rockefeller, Sr.*, were both nominated for the National Book Critics Circle Award in biography. Chernow lives in Brooklyn, New York.

To Valerie, in Memoriam

Simple truth is his best, his greatest eulogy.

—ABIGAIL ADAMS, *speaking of George Washington after his death*

CONTENTS

PART THREE: *The General*

PART FOUR: *The Statesman*

PART FIVE: *The President*

PART SIX: *The Legend*

AUTHOR'S NOTE

Since I quote extensively from George Washington's vast correspondence, I have taken the liberty of modernizing the spelling and punctuation of the eighteenth-century prose. A biographer hesitates to forfeit the special period flavor that comes from preserving all the oddities of contemporary writing. But all too often, Washington's muscular style can seem awkward and stilted to modern readers because of the way he distributed his commas, for instance, whereas the writing suddenly becomes smooth and flowing with more familiar punctuation. Occasionally I retain the quirks of the original spelling in order to highlight the eccentricity or lack of education of the personality in question. Throughout the text, the actual wording has been exactly reproduced.

The Portrait Artist

IN MARCH 1793 Gilbert Stuart crossed the North Atlantic for the express purpose of painting President George Washington, the supreme prize of the age for any ambitious portrait artist. Though born in Rhode Island and reared in Newport, Stuart had escaped to the cosmopolitan charms of London during the war and spent eighteen years producing portraits of British and Irish grandees. Overly fond of liquor, prodigal in his spending habits, and with a giant brood of children to support, Stuart had landed in the Marshalsea Prison in Dublin, most likely for debt, just as Washington was being sworn in as first president of the United States in 1789.

For the impulsive, unreliable Stuart, who left a trail of incomplete paintings and irate clients in his wake, George Washington emerged as the savior who would rescue him from insistent creditors. "When I can net a sum sufficient to take me to America, I shall be off to my native soil," he confided eagerly to a friend. "There I expect to make a fortune by Washington alone. I calculate upon making a plurality of his portraits . . . and if I should be fortunate, I will repay my English and Irish creditors."[1] In a self-portrait daubed years earlier, Stuart presented himself as a restless soul, with tousled reddish-brown hair, keen blue eyes, a strongly marked nose, and a pugnacious chin. This harried, disheveled man was scarcely the sort to appeal to the immaculately formal George Washington.

Once installed in New York, Stuart mapped out a path to Washington with the thoroughness of a military campaign. He stalked Washington's trusted friend Chief Justice John Jay and rendered a brilliant portrait of him, seated in the full majesty of his judicial robes. Shortly afterward Stuart had in hand the treasured letter of introduction from Jay to President Washington that would unlock the doors of the executive residence in Philadelphia, then the temporary capital.

As a portraitist, the garrulous Stuart had perfected a technique to penetrate his subjects' defenses. He would disarm them with a steady stream of personal anecdotes and irreverent wit, hoping that this glib patter would coax them into self-revelation. In the taciturn George Washington, a man of granite self-control and a stranger to spontaneity, Gilbert Stuart met his match. From boyhood, Washington had struggled to master and conceal his deep emotions. When the wife of the British ambassador later told him that his face showed pleasure at his forthcoming departure from the presidency, Washington grew indignant: "You are wrong. My countenance never yet betrayed my feelings!"[2] He tried to govern his tongue as much as his face: "With me it has always been a maxim rather to let my designs appear from my works than by my expressions."[3]

When Washington swept into his first session with Stuart, the artist was awestruck by the tall, commanding president. Predictably, the more Stuart tried to pry open his secretive personality, the tighter the president clamped it shut. Stuart's opening gambit backfired. "Now, sir," Stuart instructed his sitter, "you must let me forget that you are General Washington and that I am Stuart, the painter." To which Washington retorted drily that Mr. Stuart need not forget "who he is or who General Washington is."[4]

A master at sizing people up, Washington must have cringed at Stuart's facile bonhomie, not to mention his drinking, snuff taking, and ceaseless chatter. With Washington, trust had to be earned slowly, and he balked at instant familiarity with people. Instead of opening up with Stuart, he retreated behind his stolid mask. The scourge of artists, Washington knew how to turn himself into an impenetrable monument long before an obelisk arose in his honor in the nation's capital.

As Washington sought to maintain his defenses, Stuart made the brilliant decision to capture the subtle interplay between his outward calm and his intense hidden emotions, a tension that defined the man. He spied the extraordinary force of personality lurking behind an extremely restrained facade. The mouth might be compressed, the parchment skin drawn tight over ungainly dentures, but Washington's eyes still blazed from his craggy face. In the enduring image that Stuart captured and that ended up on the one-dollar bill—a magnificent statement of Washington's moral stature and sublime, visionary nature—he also recorded something hard and suspicious in the wary eyes with their penetrating gaze and hooded lids.

With the swift insight of artistic genius, Stuart grew convinced that Washington was not the placid and composed figure he presented to the world. In the words of a mutual acquaintance, Stuart had insisted that "there are features in [Washington's] face totally different from what he ever observed in that of any other human being;

the sockets of the eyes, for instance, are larger than he ever met with before, and the upper part of the nose broader. All his features, [Stuart] observed, were indicative of the strongest and most ungovernable passions, and had he been born in the forests, it was his opinion that [Washington] would have been the fiercest man among the savage tribes." The acquaintance confirmed that Washington's intimates thought him "by nature a man of fierce and irritable disposition, but that, like Socrates, his judgment and great self-command have always made him appear a man of a different cast in the eyes of the world."[5]

Although many contemporaries were fooled by Washington's aura of cool command, those who knew him best shared Stuart's view of a sensitive, complex figure, full of pent-up passion. "His temper was naturally high-toned [that is, high-strung], but reflection and resolution had obtained a firm and habitual ascendency over it," wrote Thomas Jefferson. "If ever, however, it broke its bonds, he was most tremendous in wrath."[6] John Adams concurred. "He had great self-command . . . but to preserve so much equanimity as he did required a great capacity. Whenever he lost his temper, as he did sometimes, either love or fear in those about him induced them to conceal his weakness from the world."[7] Gouverneur Morris agreed that Washington had "the tumultuous passions which accompany greatness and frequently tarnish its luster. With them was his first contest, and his first victory was over himself . . . Yet those who have seen him strongly moved will bear witness that his wrath was terrible. They have seen, boiling in his bosom, passion almost too mighty for man."[8]

So adept was Washington at masking these turbulent emotions behind his fabled reserve that he ranks as the most famously elusive figure in American history, a remote, enigmatic personage more revered than truly loved. He seems to lack the folksy appeal of an Abraham Lincoln, the robust vigor of a Teddy Roosevelt, or the charming finesse of a Franklin Roosevelt. In fact, George Washington has receded so much in our collective memory that he has become an impossibly stiff and inflexible figure, composed of too much marble to be quite human. How this seemingly dull, phlegmatic man, in a stupendous act of nation building, presided over the victorious Continental Army and forged the office of the presidency is a mystery to most Americans. Something essential about Washington has been lost to posterity, making him seem a worthy but plodding man who somehow stumbled into greatness.

From a laudable desire to venerate Washington, we have sanded down the rough edges of his personality and made him difficult to grasp. He joined in this conspiracy to make himself unknowable. Where other founders gloried in their displays of intellect, Washington's strategy was the opposite: the less people knew about him, the more he thought he could accomplish. Opacity was his means of enhancing his power and influencing events. Where Franklin, Hamilton, or Adams always sparkled in print or in person, the laconic Washington had no need to flaunt his virtues or fill conversational silences. Instead, he wanted the public to know him as a public man, concerned with the public weal and transcending egotistical needs.

Washington's lifelong struggle to control his emotions speaks to the issue of how he exercised leadership as a politician, a soldier, a planter, and even a slaveholder. People *felt* the inner force of his nature, even if they didn't exactly hear it or see it; they sensed his moods without being told. In studying his life, one is struck not only by his colossal temper but by his softer emotions: this man of deep feelings was sensitive to the delicate nuances of relationships and prone to tears as well as temper. He learned how to exploit his bottled-up emotions to exert his will and inspire and motivate people. If he aroused universal admiration, it was often accompanied by a touch of fear and anxiety. His contemporaries admired him not because he was a plaster saint or an empty uniform but because they sensed his unseen power. As the Washington scholar W. W. Abbot noted, "An important element in Washington's leadership both as a military commander and as President was his dignified, even forbidding, demeanor, his aloofness, the distance he consciously set and maintained between himself and nearly all the rest of the world."[9]

The goal of the present biography is to create a fresh portrait of Washington that will make him real, credible, and charismatic in the same way that he was perceived by his contemporaries. By gleaning anecdotes and quotes from myriad sources, especially from hundreds of eyewitness accounts, I have tried to make him vivid and immediate, rather than the lifeless waxwork he has become for many Americans, and thereby elucidate the secrets of his uncanny ability to lead a nation. His unerring judgment, sterling character, rectitude, steadfast patriotism, unflagging sense of duty, and civic-mindedness—these exemplary virtues were achieved only by his ability to subdue the underlying volatility of his nature and direct his entire psychological makeup to the single-minded achievement of a noble cause.

A man capable of constant self-improvement, Washington grew in stature throughout his life. This growth went on subtly, at times imperceptibly, beneath the surface, making Washington the most interior of the founders. His real passions and often fiery opinions were typically confined to private letters rather than public utterances. During the Revolution and his presidency, the public Washington needed to be upbeat and inspirational, whereas the private man was often gloomy, scathing, hot-blooded, and pessimistic.

For this reason, the new edition of the papers of George Washington, started in 1968 and one of the great ongoing scholarly labors of our time, has provided an extraordinary window into his mind. The indefatigable team of scholars at the University of Virginia has laid a banquet table for Washington biographers and made somewhat outmoded the monumental Washington biographies of the mid-twentieth century: the seven volumes published by Douglas Southall Freeman (1948–57) and the four volumes by James T. Flexner (1965–72). This book is based on a close reading of the sixty volumes of letters and diaries published so far in the new edition, supplemented by seventeen volumes from the older edition to cover the historical gaps. Never before have we had access to so much material about so many aspects of Washington's public and private lives.

In recent decades, many fine short biographies of Washington have appeared as well as perceptive studies of particular events, themes, or periods in his life. My intention is to produce a large-scale, one-volume, cradle-to-grave narrative that will be both dramatic and authoritative, encompassing the explosion of research in recent decades that has enriched our understanding of Washington as never before. The upshot, I hope, will be that readers, instead of having a frosty respect for Washington, will experience a visceral appreciation of this foremost American who scaled the highest peak of political greatness.

PART ONE

The Frontiersman

*The earliest known portrait of George Washington,
dressed in his old uniform from the French and Indian War,
painted by Charles Willson Peale in 1772.*

CHAPTER ONE

A Short-Lived Family

THE CROWDED CAREER of George Washington afforded him little leisure to indulge his vanity or gratify his curiosity by conducting genealogical research into his family. As he admitted sheepishly when president, "This is a subject to which I confess I have paid very little attention. My time has been so much occupied in the busy and active scenes of life from an early period of it that but a small portion of it could have been devoted to researches of this nature."[1]

The first Washington to claim our attention was, ironically, the casualty of a rebellion against royal authority. During the English Civil War, Lawrence Washington, George's great-great-grandfather and an Anglican minister, was hounded from his parish in the Puritan cleansing of the Church of England under Oliver Cromwell. This shattered a cozy existence that intermingled learning with modest wealth. Lawrence had spent the better part of his childhood at the family residence, Sulgrave Manor near Banbury in Oxfordshire, before earning two degrees at Brasenose College, Oxford; he later served as a fellow of the college and a university proctor. Persecuted by the Puritans as one of the "scandalous, malignant priests," he was accused of being "a common frequenter of alehouses," which was likely a trumped-up charge.[2] His travails may have spurred his son John to seek his fortune in the burgeoning tobacco trade with North America. After landing in Tidewater Virginia in late 1656, John Washington settled at Bridges Creek, hard by the Potomac River in Westmoreland County. Less a committed colonist than a temporary castaway, John was stranded when heavy squalls grounded his ship and soaked its precious cargo of tobacco, prompting him to tarry in Virginia.

One marvels at the speed with which the young man prospered in the New

World, exhibiting certain traits—a bottomless appetite for land, an avidity for public office, and a zest for frontier combat—that foreshadowed his great-grandson's rapid ascent in the world. John also set a precedent of social mobility through military laurels after he was recruited to fight Indians in Maryland and was rewarded with a colonel's rank. In this rough-and-tumble world, he was accused of slaughtering five Indian emissaries and cheating tribes of land, activities that won him the baleful Indian nickname of Conotocarious, which meant "Destroyer of Villages" or "Town Devourer."[3] He also found time to woo and wed Anne Pope, whose well-heeled father favored the newlyweds with seven hundred acres of land. John piled up an impressive roster of the sort of local offices—justice of the peace, burgess in the Virginia assembly, lieutenant colonel in the county militia—that signified social standing in colonial Virginia. Most conspicuous was his omnivorous craving for land. By importing sixty-three indentured servants from England, he capitalized upon a British law that granted fifty acres to each immigrant, and he eventually amassed more than five thousand acres, with the single largest property bordering the Potomac River at Little Hunting Creek, the future site of Mount Vernon.

After his wife died, John Washington married, in quick succession, a pair of lusty sisters who had been accused, respectively, of running a brothel and engaging in adulterous relations with the governor. Coincidentally, both scandal-ridden women had appeared before him in his guise as justice of the peace. In 1677 John succumbed at age forty-six to a fatal disease, likely typhoid fever, setting an enduring pattern of shortened life expectancy for Washington males in America. By then he had struggled his way up to the second-tier gentry, an uncertain stratum that would endow George Washington with a modicum of money, while also instilling a restless yearning to advance into the uppermost ranks of Virginia grandees.

It was John's eldest son from his first marriage, Lawrence Washington, who inherited the bulk of his father's estate and became paternal grandfather of the first president. With the monarchy restored in England, Lawrence had been educated in the mother country before settling in Virginia, where he, too, collected an array of local posts—justice of the peace, burgess, and sheriff—that complemented his work as an attorney. If John furnished the family with a tenuous foothold in the gentry, Lawrence added a patina of social distinction by marrying Mildred Warner, daughter of a member of the prestigious King's Council. When he expired in 1698 at thirty-eight, Lawrence perpetuated the grim tradition of Washington men dying young.

Lawrence Washington's untimely death occurred when his second son, Augustine—the future father of George Washington—was only three or four years old. After his widow, Mildred, married George Gale, a British ship captain from Whitehaven, a port on the Cumberland coast, she sailed there with him and her three children in late May 1700. Already pregnant during the voyage, she died in January 1701, not long after her arrival in England, and her newborn daughter followed her shortly thereafter. For the next two or three years, Gale placed Augustine and his older brother John in the Appleby Grammar School in County Westmorland, a scenic spot east of the English Lake District. The school provided a classical education, with a heavy emphasis on Latin. When Mildred's three children were ensnared in a protracted legal tussle over their inheritance, they were shipped back to Virginia under a court order.

Raw-boned and good-natured, Augustine Washington remains a shadowy figure in the family saga, little more than a hazy but sunlit memory for his famous son. A strapping man, six feet tall with a fair complexion, he was favored with that brand of rustic strength that breeds backwoods legends. The sole contemporary description avers that he could "raise up and place in a wagon a mass of iron that two ordinary men could barely raise from the ground," yet he balanced this notable brawn with a mild-mannered demeanor that made his manly strength the more becoming.[4] No less community-minded than his Washington forebears, he was named a justice of the peace and sat on the county court.

From spotty early records, Augustine emerges as a remorseless, hard-driving businessman. He started with 1,100 acres that he inherited along the Potomac and augmented that with 1,750 acres from the dowry of his first wife, Jane Butler. He specialized in tobacco farming until he began snapping up properties rich in iron ore at Accokeek Creek, near Fredericksburg. In 1729 he traveled to England to seal a contract with the Principio Company, which owned iron operations in Virginia and Maryland. By the time he returned to Virginia, his wife had died, saddling him with the care of three small children: two sons, Lawrence and Augustine Jr. (often called Austin), and a daughter, Jane. Minding children on his own wasn't an option for a hard-pressed colonial widower, and Augustine may not have been overly fussy in his urgent quest to find a country bride. On March 6, 1731, the thirty-seven-year-old Augustine married Mary Johnson Ball, a pious, headstrong woman who would exert a profound formative influence on her son George. At twenty-three, Mary was already slightly old for marriage, which may say something about her feisty personality or about Augustine's hopeful conviction that he could tame this indomitable woman.

Mary Ball was born in 1708 into a situation that skirted the edge of local scandal. Her English-born father, Joseph Ball, a thriving businessman, had settled on the Potomac, married, and raised several children before his wife's death. Lonesome at fifty-eight, he then shocked propriety and threatened his children's inheritance by wedding an illiterate woman named Mary Johnson. Their daughter, Mary Ball, was only three when her elderly father died, leaving her with a bequest of four hundred acres, fifteen head of cattle, three slaves, and a sackful of feathers from which to fashion a bed. Her mother remarried but then died, converting Mary into an orphan at age twelve. The girl was farmed out to an obliging family friend, George Eskridge, who treated her so humanely that she would honor his memory by naming her first son George after him. It was probably Eskridge who acted as go-between in matching up Mary and Augustine Washington.

A crusty woman with a stubborn streak, Mary Ball Washington made few concessions to social convention. In a lesson internalized by her celebrated son, she didn't adapt or bend easily to others but stayed resolutely true to her own standards. We can only assume that her forlorn childhood, characterized by constant loss, left innumerable scars and insecurities, producing an anxious personality. With flinty self-reliance and iron discipline, she ran a thrifty household and was sparing in her praise and very definite in her opinions. A plain, homespun woman who may have smoked a pipe, she betrayed little interest in the larger world, confined her attention to the family farm, and shunned high society. Since her own mother was illiterate, Mary probably received scant education. Her few letters are replete with spelling errors, dispense with all grammar and punctuation, and confirm the impression of an unlettered countrywoman.

The thick family Bible at Mount Vernon records that George Washington was born around ten A.M. on February 11, 1732, at the family farm at Pope's Creek in Westmoreland County, an area of bucolic beauty less than a mile from the Potomac River. The modest birthplace later went up in flames. The newborn boy was reputed to be a baby of unusual heft. His original birthday derived from the Julian, or Old Style, calendar, which remained in effect in Britain and its colonies until the mid-eighteenth century, when the new Gregorian calendar deferred it by eleven days to February 22. Until the end of his life, some of Washington's admirers in Alexandria insisted upon celebrating his birthday on February 11.

Baptized in early April, the boy was reared amid the rich, open farmland of Tidewater Virginia, the eastern territory washed by four broad rivers: the James, York, Rappahannock, and Potomac. Broad tobacco fields flourished in tidal flats broken only by a scattering of tiny, isolated towns. George Washington entered a strictly hierarchical universe, ruled by simple verities and dominated by a distant monarch. That the commoner George could ever aspire to a life as richly consequential as that of King George II, then enthroned in royal splendor, would have seemed a preposterous fantasy in the 1730s. Hugging the eastern seaboard, the loyal British colonies were tightly lashed to the trading world of London by commerce and culture. The all-powerful planters in this provincial sphere strove to ape their English cousins, who remained the unquestioned model of everything superior and cosmopolitan. As the economic basis of this undemocratic world, slavery was commonplace and unquestioned, fostering an idle, dissolute existence for rich young Virginians. As one German visitor sniffed of the average Virginia adolescent, "At fifteen, his father gives him a horse and a negro, with which he riots about the country, attends every fox hunt, horse race and cockfight, and does nothing else whatever."[5]

As the eldest of Augustine Washington's second set of children, George straddled two families, perhaps forcing him to hone some early diplomatic skills. His older half brother, Lawrence, was sent to the Appleby Grammar School before George was born and was shortly followed there by his brother Augustine Jr. while George was still a toddler. Death first encroached on George's life when, right before his third birthday, his older half sister Jane died. As the eldest of Mary Washington's children, George probably helped to care for his gaggle of younger siblings, which grew to include Betty, Samuel, John Augustine, Charles, and Mildred. That only two of Gus Washington's nine offspring perished in an era of elevated mortality rates for children speaks to hardy family stock.

Later on, irked by the sanctimonious moralizing about Washington's perfections, Nathaniel Hawthorne wrote mockingly that Washington "was born with his clothes on and his hair powdered and made a stately bow on his first appearance in the world."[6] But there was nothing cosseted about his provincial boyhood, and he had little exposure to any pampered society that might have softened the rigors of his rural upbringing. Nor would the unforgiving Mary Washington have tolerated such laxity. She drilled habits of thrift and industry into her children, including rising early with the sun, a strict farmer's habit that George retained for the rest of his life.

The childhood was a roving and unsettled one. In 1735, when George was three, Augustine relocated his family sixty miles upstream to his 2,500-acre tract at Little Hunting Creek on the Potomac, an unspoiled area of pristine forests. Perched on a hilltop at a scenic bend of the river, the house he constructed was more ample than the earlier one, with four ground-floor rooms bisected by a central hallway and warmed by four fireplaces; a row of smaller bedrooms upstairs accommodated the growing clan. So sturdy was the new house that its downstairs rooms were later embedded into George's expanding mansion at Mount Vernon, turning the building into an archaeological record of his life.

In 1736 Augustine Washington sailed to England and negotiated a one-twelfth ownership share of the Principio Company. To aid his performance as manager of their iron furnace in Virginia, Gus uprooted his expanding family again in 1738 and moved them south to a sylvan 260-acre spread on the Rappahannock River, directly opposite Fredericksburg and a convenient ride away from Accokeek Creek. Poised on the brow of a hill and slightly recessed from the river, the farm had woods nearby for firewood; broad, level fields for growing tobacco, wheat, and corn; and several pure streams for drinking water. Since access to the ferry later ran straight through the property—to George's annoyance, crowds flocked gaily down the footpath during fair days or when courts were in session—the house would be dubbed Ferry Farm.

Touted in a newspaper advertisement as a "handsome dwelling house," the two-story clapboard residence was a dark reddish-brown color, roofed with wooden shingles and flanked by brick chimneys.[7] With its seven rooms—four downstairs and three upstairs—the house counted as a substantial affair for the time, and recent excavations have disclosed many unexpected touches of gentility. Among the artifacts unearthed have been wig curlers, bone-handled toothbrushes, and a Wedgwood tea set, betokening an unmistakable air of affluence. The Washingtons must have entertained a steady flow of visitors, for they had curtained beds sprinkled throughout the house. Other details of their home inventory—thirteen tablecloths, thirty-one napkins, twenty-six silver spoons—conjure up a sociable, highly prosperous clan. Having acquired nearly fifty slaves and ten thousand acres of land, Augustine Washington had planted his family firmly among the regional gentry. Though not born into great wealth, George Washington doesn't qualify for inclusion in the ranks of self-made Americans.

Ferry Farm provided George with his first treasured glimpses of a world beyond his boyhood haunts. The newly incorporated hamlet of Fredericksburg, with its courthouse and stone prison, was already an active port featuring rudiments of a more developed society. The young George Washington could peer across the river and see a perfect tableau of the British Empire in action. Moored at town wharves, ships bulging with tobacco, grain, and iron gave glimmers of the lucrative trans-atlantic trade with London that enriched the colony.

Around the time the Washingtons settled into their new home, changes occurred in the composition of the family. George's baby sister Mildred was born and soon died, and he also set eyes for the first time on his older half brother Lawrence, a quasi-mythical figure who suddenly materialized in Virginia, polished by years at the Appleby Grammar School. Tall and debonair, Lawrence must have radiated a mature, well-traveled air of worldly sophistication for George, who was fourteen years his junior. Since Lawrence had stayed at Appleby until age twenty, he had probably graduated to the status of an "usher," or assistant teacher, at the school. Lawrence would function as both a peer and a parental figure for his half brother, and his youthful adventures operated so powerfully on George's imagination that the latter's early life seems to enact a script first drafted by his older brother. When Augustine assigned Lawrence to superintend the Potomac River property recently vacated by the family, it immediately became the most desirable destination in George's eyes.

George's first exposure to war came vicariously through the exploits of his idolized brother. In 1739 Great Britain clashed with Spain in the Caribbean in a conflict styled the War of Jenkins' Ear—Robert Jenkins being a British ship captain whose ear was allegedly mutilated by the Spanish. To bolster an amphibious force the following year, the Crown enlisted colonial subjects into an American Foot Regiment, and Lawrence landed a coveted spot as the captain of a Virginia company. In the major offensive of this expeditionary force, Admiral Edward Vernon hurled nine thousand men against the Spanish at Cartagena, on the northern coast of South America, in what degenerated into a bloody fiasco. Lawrence and his men never disembarked from their ship, which was ravaged by yellow fever and other tropical diseases no less efficiently than their colleagues were mowed down by enemy bullets. Some perished from sunstroke in sweltering heat. In the gruesome account he sent home, Lawrence detailed how "the enemy killed of ours some 600 . . . and the climate killed us in greater number . . . a great quantity of officers amongst the rest are dead . . . War is horrid in fact but much more so in imagination." Amid the gloom, Lawrence struck a cavalier note that George mimicked years later: "We there have learned to live on ordinary diet, to watch much, and disregard the noise or shot of cannon."[8]

In these thrilling, if sanguinary, tales of war, Lawrence must have communicated mixed impressions of his British superiors. On the one hand, he had to brook the condescension of Brigadier General Thomas Wentworth, who sneered at colonial troops and kept them cooped up aboard the ship. At the same time, Lawrence retained clear affection for Admiral Vernon and, in a burst of Anglophilia, would rename the Little Hunting Creek estate Mount Vernon, hanging the admiral's portrait in an honored place there. Thus the name of a forgotten British admiral would implausibly grace America's secular shrine to the revolt against British rule. However frustrated with his British superiors, Lawrence earned the royal commission that would always elude George's eager grasp—a precedent that could only have sharpened the latter's keen sense of inequitable treatment at British hands. In his flourishing career, Lawrence was also named adjutant general of Virginia, which brought him the rank of major and entrusted him with the task of molding militia companies into an effective fighting force.

In June 1742 George's other older half brother, Augustine Jr., also returned from a lengthy stay at Appleby. George must have expected that he would shortly follow suit, but that dream was rudely dashed a year later, when he was summoned back from a cousin's home by news that his father was ill. On April 12, 1743, Augustine Washington died at forty-nine in a manner that eerily prefigured George's own demise at century's end: he had ridden out in a storm, gotten sick, and expired. This early death underscored a central paradox of George Washington's life: that although he was a superb physical specimen, with a magnificent physique, his family's medical history was blighted by truncated lives. He subsequently lamented, "Tho' I was blessed with a good constitution, I was of a short-lived family."[9]

The most significant bequest fell to Lawrence, who inherited Mount Vernon and the iron mine, while Austin received the family farm at Pope's Creek, where George was born and would spend much time after his father's death. George himself inherited Ferry Farm, a half share in an upriver parcel called Deep Run, and assorted lots in Fredericksburg. The eleven-year-old also found himself the juvenile owner of ten human beings. Since he could not claim this property until he reached maturity, George's newfound wealth was purely theoretical and placed him at the mercy of his strong-willed mother, who would not relinquish Ferry Farm for another thirty years. Augustine's early death robbed George of the classical education bestowed on his older brothers, leaving him with an enduring sense of stunted, incomplete schooling. His father's death threw the boy back upon his own resources, stealing any chance of a lighthearted youth. From then on, George grew accustomed to shouldering weighty family burdens. Because Mary never remarried—unusual in a frontier society with a paucity of women—George developed the deeply rooted toughness of children forced to function as adults at an early age. He discovered a precocious ability to perform many adult tasks, but he probably never forgot the sudden fright of being deprived of the protection of a father. One wonders whether he resented his mother for her failure to find a second husband, which imposed inordinate burdens on him as the eldest son. Quite naturally, George turned to older men as sponsors and patrons, cultivating the art of ingratiating himself with influential figures.

If Mary Ball Washington comes across as an unbending, even shrewish, disciplinarian, one can only imagine the unspoken dread that she, too, experienced at being widowed at thirty-five. She had to manage Ferry Farm, tend five children ranging in age from six to eleven, and oversee dozens of slaves. Gus's death forced Mary to eliminate any frills of family life, and her spartan style as a businesswoman, frugal and demanding, had a discernible impact on her son. "In her dealings with servants, she was strict," writes Douglas Southall Freeman. "They must follow a definite round of work. Her bidding must be their law."[10] With more than a touch of the martinet in her forbidding nature, Mary Washington displayed a powerful capacity to command, and one is tempted to say that the first formidable general George Washington ever encountered was his own mother.

This trying woman inspired a healthy trepidation among George's companions. "I was often there with George, his playmate, schoolmate, and young man's companion," said Lawrence Washington of Chotank, a distant relative. "Of the mother I was more afraid than of my own parents; she awed me in the midst of her kindness, for she was, indeed, truly kind."[11] There was nothing especially gentle about Mary Washington, little that savored of maternal warmth. Gus's death removed any moderating influence between mother and eldest son, who clashed with their similarly willful personalities. Always a dutiful but seldom a loving son, George treated his mother with frigid deference, taking refuge in polite but empty forms. His letters to her would be addressed to "Honored Madam" and end with distant formality, "Your most Dutiful and Obedient Son, George Washington." This studiously correct tone, likely laced with suppressed anger, only highlighted the absence of genuine filial affection.

There would always be a cool, quiet antagonism between Washington and his mother. The hypercritical mother produced a son who was overly sensitive to criticism and suffered from a lifelong need for approval. One suspects that, in dealing with this querulous woman, George became an overly controlled personality and learned to master his temper and curb his tongue. It was the extreme self-control of a deeply emotional young man who feared the fatal vehemence of his own feelings, if left unchecked. Anything pertaining to Mary Ball Washington stirred up an emotional tempest that George quelled only with difficulty. Never able to express these forbidden feelings of rage, he learned to equate silence and a certain manly stolidity with strength. This boyhood struggle was, in all likelihood, the genesis of the stoical personality that would later define him so indelibly.

On the one hand, the similarities between Mary Washington and her eldest son were striking. She was a fine horsewoman, enjoyed dancing, reputedly possessed enormous strength, was manic in money matters, tenaciously superintended her farm, and displayed a stubborn independence. Both mother and son exhibited supreme willpower that people defied at their peril. Both were vigorous, enterprising, and exacting in their demands. Yet in many other ways, George Washington defined himself as the antithesis of his mother. If his mother was crude and illiterate, he would improve himself through books. If she was self-centered, he would be self-sacrificing in serving his country. If she was slovenly, he would be meticulous in appearance. If she disdained fancy society, he would crave its acceptance. If she showed old-fashioned religious fervor, he would be devout in a more moderate fashion. And if she was a veteran complainer, he would be known for his stiff upper lip.

Unable to afford a fancy education for her children, Mary Washington did her best to pound moral precepts into them, reading daily portions from a volume entitled *Contemplations Moral and Divine* by Sir Matthew Hale. Many speculative theories have been floated about Washington's education. Before his father's death, he may have received a limited education in math, reading, and writing at a day school taught by a Mr. Hobby, one of his father's tenants, who boasted that he had "laid the foundation of [Washington's] greatness."[12] He may also have attended a school in Fredericksburg run by the Reverend James Marye, the rector of St. George's Parish. According to one classmate, George applied himself to math while the others played at field hockey, his sole indiscretion being that he was caught "romping with one of the largest girls."[13] Finally, when he stayed with Austin at the Pope's Creek farm, he may have been schooled in the rudiments of math and surveying by a schoolmaster named Henry Williams. Oddly for a towering personage in history, Washington never cited an early educational mentor, suggesting that his boyhood lessons were pretty humdrum. He left behind more than two hundred pages of schoolboy exercises that focused on geometry lessons, weights and measures, compound interest, currency conversions, and other skills necessary for business or surveying. Almost by osmosis, he absorbed law and economics by monotonously copying out legal forms for bail bonds, leases, and land patents, stocking his mind with a huge fund of practical information. The furnace of ambition burned with a bright, steady flame inside this diligent boy.

With painstaking effort, Washington learned to write in a round hand that lacked elegance but had great clarity. It took time for him to compose clean, declarative sentences—his teenage prose was often turgid and ungrammatical—but by dint of hard work, his powers grew steadily until he became a writer of considerable force, able to register his wishes with precision. It was in Washington's nature to work doubly hard to rectify perceived failings. Writing in 1807, the biographer David Ramsay said of the young Washington that "he was grave, silent, and thoughtful, diligent and methodical in business, dignified in his appearance, strictly honorable in his deportment."[14]

One can't help but surmise that Washington's life would have been vastly different had he attended college. He lacked the liberal education that then distinguished gentlemen, setting him apart from such illustrious peers as Jefferson, Hamilton, Adams, and Madison. He would always seem more provincial than other founders, his knowledge of European culture more secondhand. A university education would have spared him a gnawing sense of intellectual inadequacy. We know that he regretted his lack of Latin, Greek, and French—the major intellectual adornments of his day—since he lectured wards in later years on their importance. The degree to which Washington dwelt upon the transcendent importance of education underscores the stigma that he felt about having missed college. As president, he lectured a young relative about to enter college that "every hour misspent is lost forever" and that "future *years* cannot compensate for lost *days* at this period of your life."[15]

Without much formal schooling, Washington was later subject to condescension from some contemporaries, especially the snobbish John Adams, who disparaged him as "too illiterate, unlearned, unread for his station and reputation."[16] Washington has suffered from comparisons with other founders, several of whom were renowned autodidacts, but by any ordinary standard, he was an exceedingly smart man with a quick ability to grasp ideas. He seized every interval of leisure to improve himself and showed a steady capacity to acquire and retain useful knowledge. Throughout his life, he strenuously molded his personality to become a respectable member of society. As W. W. Abbot aptly expressed it, "More than most, Washington's biography is the story of a man constructing himself."[17]

As an adolescent, Washington dabbled in fiction, history, philosophy, and geography. An avid reader of periodicals, he sampled *The Spectator* by the age of sixteen. With the novel flowering as a literary form, he was to purchase copies of Henry Fielding's *Tom Jones* and Tobias Smollett's *The Adventures of Peregrine Pickle* in coming years, and he was especially drawn to military history. As he experienced the first stirrings of an abiding passion for theater, he read Joseph Addison's *Cato*, a paean to republican virtues that he quoted repeatedly throughout his life. It is often said, with truth, that Washington absorbed his lessons from action, not books, yet he came to own a vast library and talked about books as if he were a serious reader, not a dilettante. When his adopted grandson entered college, Washington lectured him thus: "Light reading (by this, I mean books of little importance) may amuse for the moment, but leaves nothing solid behind."[18]

Never an intellectual who relished ideas for their own sake, he mined books for practical wisdom and delighted in dredging up handy aphorisms. At seventeen, he possessed an English compendium of the principal *Dialogues of Seneca the Younger* and took to heart his stoic beliefs: "The contempt of death makes all the miseries of life easy to us." Or: "He is the brave man . . . that can look death in the face without trouble or surprise."[19] As his life progressed, Washington would adhere to the stoic creed of governing one's passions under the most adverse circumstances and facing the prospect of death with serenity.

In trying to form himself as an English country gentleman, the self-invented young Washington practiced the classic strategy of outsiders: he studied closely his social betters and tried to imitate their behavior in polite society. Whether to improve his penmanship or perhaps as a school assignment, he submitted to the drudgery of copying out 110 social maxims from *The Rules of Civility and Decent Behavior in Company and Conversation,* a handy guidebook of etiquette that traced its origins to a French Jesuit work of the sixteenth century. This humorless manual preached against assorted social gaffes that would have haunted the nightmares of an insecure youth who daydreamed of venturing into fashionable drawing rooms. Number four warned: "In the presence of others, sing not to yourself with a humming noise, nor drum with your fingers or feet." Number eleven: "Shift not yourself in the sight of others, nor gnaw your nails." Number twelve: "Bedew no man's face with your spittle by approaching too near him when you speak."[20] Number one hundred: "Cleanse not your teeth with the tablecloth, napkin, fork, or knife, but if others do it, let it be done with a pick tooth."[21]

Many of these rules, which talked about showing due respect for one's superiors, tread a fine line between self-abasement and simple humility. Number thirty-seven: "In speaking to men of quality, do not lean, nor look them full in the face, nor approach too near them; at least keep a full pace from them."[22] Or thirty-nine: "In writing or speaking, give to every person his due title according to his degree and the custom of the place."[23] This is a crib sheet for a world shot through with class distinctions and informed by a deep terror of offending one's betters. This guidebook "taught modesty, deference, and submission to authority," writes William Guthrie Sayen, who notes that it would have instructed Washington on how to control his temper and learn "the importance of managing his body, his facial expressions, his speech, and his moods."[24] The book must have spoken to some inborn sense of decorum in Washington, soothing his schoolboy fears of committing a faux pas. If thoroughly heeded, *The Rules of Civility* would have produced a cool, pragmatic, and very controlled young man with genteel manners—exactly the social facade Washington wished to project to conceal the welter of stormy emotions inside him.

Though respectful of education, George Washington was never a bookish boy. He loved to swim in the smooth, deep waters of the Rappahannock. He excelled in riding, liked to hunt, later learned fencing, attended a dancing school, played billiards, frequented cockfights and horse races, and experimented with his first flirtations. Despite a certain underlying roughness, he would perfect the social graces that prepared him to enter well-bred society. At the same time, he was an unusually sober and purposeful young man. In countless letters in later years, he advised young relatives that adolescence was a risky time when evil influences lurked nearby, ready to pounce: "You are now extending into that stage of life when good or bad habits are formed. When the mind will be turned to things useful and praiseworthy or to dissipation and vice."[25] He issued warnings against young male companions who "too often mistake ribaldry for wit and rioting, swearing, intoxication, and gambling for manliness."[26] The young George Washington seldom seemed to show a truant disposition, as if he were already preparing for bigger things.

CHAPTER TWO

Fortune's Favorite

IN THE ABSENCE OF A FATHER and with a mother who doled out criticism more freely than encouragement, George Washington turned naturally to his three younger brothers for recreation and to his two older brothers, Lawrence and Austin, for guidance. Of the younger brothers, John Augustine or "Jack" was decidedly his favorite, "the intimate companion of my youth and the most affectionate friend of my ripened age," as George remembered him.[1] It was his outgoing and older half brother Lawrence, however, who fired his ambitions and steered him firmly in the direction of a military career.

After his father's death, George found asylum from his difficult mother in periodic trips to stay with Lawrence at Mount Vernon, which would always beckon invitingly on the far horizon of his life. From time to time he also escaped to his brother Austin's place at Pope's Creek, though he was never as close to him. In a surviving portrait of Lawrence Washington by an unknown artist, he is clad in the uniform of a British Army officer but seems made of gentler stuff than George. He has boldly marked eyebrows, full lips, a cleft chin, and receding brown hair. The dark eyes are large and sensitive, evoking a poet or a scholar more than a bluff soldier. Indeed, the cultivated Lawrence presented an appealing model of urbanity for his younger brother. "For the enlargement of George's mind and the polishing of his manners, Lawrence was almost an ideal elder brother," writes Douglas Southall Freeman.[2]

After returning from the military debacle at Cartagena, Lawrence Washington appeared headed for a life of easy riches. Though a lackluster businessman, he was fortunate to marry Ann Fairfax in July 1743, three months after his father's death, a fateful match that catapulted him to the apex of Virginia society, a status certified by Lawrence's election to the House of Burgesses.

The bride was the daughter of the august Colonel William Fairfax, who wielded breathtaking power in Tidewater Virginia as land agent for the Northern Neck Proprietary, the long strip of fertile farmland between the Potomac and Rappahannock rivers. Through this land grant, dating back to the reign of King Charles II, the Fairfax family controlled a veritable duchy of five million acres that extended all the way west to the Shenandoah Valley. William represented his cousin, Thomas Fairfax, the sixth Baron Fairfax, in administering this princely domain. Through a maze of business dealings and social and marital ties, Fairfax power ramified into every corner of Virginia society.

Ann Fairfax grew up on the family estate, Belvoir, which shimmered like a radiant mirage on the Potomac River, four miles downstream from Mount Vernon. This luxurious realm encapsulated the youthful fantasies of George Washington, who later described it thus: "Within full view of Mount Vernon, separated therefrom by water only, [it] is one of the most beautiful seats on the river . . . there are near 2,000 acres of land belonging to the tract, surrounded in a manner by water." Of the two-story Georgian brick mansion that stood as its stately centerpiece, Washington recalled that it "stood on high and commanding ground."[3] The house was approached by a circular drive and a huge courtyard, with formal grounds, stables, a coach house, and lavish gardens laid out with the full grandeur of an opulent British country house.

By marrying Ann Fairfax, Lawrence Washington crossed a social chasm that segregated the merely comfortable from the fabulously rich, making George a welcome visitor at Belvoir at the impressionable age of eleven. When Lawrence and Ann lost four children in infancy, it only fortified their bond with George. Ushered into the rarefied milieu of Belvoir, George befriended the colonel's son, George William Fairfax, who was eight years his senior and rather snobbish; the latter faintly praised Belvoir as a "tolerable cottage" in a "wooded world."[4] A portrait of the fastidiously dressed George William shows a man with a long, narrow face and an alert, slightly suspicious glance. The Fairfax connection opened up a world of extraordinary magnificence for young Washington, who must have felt a rough country bumpkin in comparison. His amazing career would never have unfolded had his fortunes not meshed so neatly with the interests of this ruling clan.

George won more than grudging entree to the Fairfax estate, for Colonel Fairfax spied unusual potential in this capable youth, invited him on foxhunts, and took an active interest in furthering his career. The colonial world revolved around such pivotal connections. To secure a powerful patron was an indispensable prerequisite to advancement for a boy born outside the upper gentry. In the mid-1750s, while coaching his younger brother Jack, George exhorted him to spend more time at Belvoir: "I should be glad to hear that you live in perfect harmony and good fellowship with the family at Belvoir, as it is in their power to be serviceable upon many occasions to us as young beginners . . . to that family I am under many obligations, particularly to the old gentleman."[5] That old gentleman, Colonel Fairfax, seemed to dote on Washington and signed his letters to him "your assured and loving friend."[6] The Fairfax sponsorship lifted George above the mass of Virginia commoners and made the world of the highborn seem tantalizingly within reach. Perhaps he relived his own youth when he later instructed a young relative, "It is therefore absolutely necessary, if you mean to make any figure upon the stage, that you should take the first steps right."[7] From their letters, we can also tell that George and Colonel Fairfax shared copies of Caesar's *Commentaries* and a life of Alexander the Great and frequently swapped views on military heroes from antiquity. Since the colonel once boasted that he had trained himself to make no "outward show" of emotion, he may also have provided a model of restrained behavior for George as well.[8] Colonel Fairfax knew George thoroughly enough that, in writing to Mary Washington, he pinpointed her son's outstanding flaw, which he must correct: "I wish I could say that he governs his temper."[9] It should be said that the authenticity of this letter has been questioned.

In September 1746 Lawrence Washington and Colonel Fairfax concocted a plan to spring fourteen-year-old George from his mother's domination and launch him on a promising career in the Royal Navy. At a confidential meeting in Fredericksburg, designed to keep Mary Washington securely in the dark, Fairfax transmitted to George a letter from Lawrence telling of an open position for a midshipman aboard a royal frigate then anchored in Virginia. When George acquiesced in the idea, Fairfax reported back to Lawrence that his brother vowed to "be steady and thankfully follow your advice as his best friend."[10] As George later acknowledged, it was "the wish of my eldest brother . . . that this should take place."[11] From Lawrence, George received a letter endorsing the plan, which he was then to deliver to his mother, whose approval was hardly taken for granted.

At first, Mary Washington gave qualified approval to the move. Perhaps eager to flee from Ferry Farm, George indicated that he had his "baggage prepared for embarkation."[12] Then Mary consulted a family friend, Robert Jackson, who supported the plan, but she seized on passing statements that he made to confirm her growing reservations. As Jackson informed Lawrence, "She offers several trifling objections such as fond and unthinking mothers naturally suggest and I find that one word against his going has more weight than ten for it."[13] Mary also consulted her rich half brother in England, Joseph Ball, who sent back a canny analysis about naval discrimination against colonials. Advising that George be apprenticed instead to a tinker (a vendor of household utensils), Joseph noted that "a common sailor before the mast has by no means the common liberty of the subject; for they will press him from a ship where he has 50 shillings a month . . . and use him like a Negro, or rather, like a dog."[14] That his uncle wanted George to train as a tinker bespeaks low family expectations that would have struck terror into this upwardly bound young man. Mary finally vetoed the idea of George joining the navy and thereby performed a major service in American history, saving her son for a future army career.

Whether Mary was persuaded by reasonable arguments, or simply didn't wish to part with her robust eldest son around the farm, is impossible to know. One can say with certainty that it was the first of many times she seemed to measure her son's worth not by what he might accomplish elsewhere but by what he could do for her, even if it meant thwarting his career. She would always be strangely indifferent toward his ambitions, making decisions about him from a purely self-interested standpoint. On the other hand, she was a single mother, clearly valued George's abilities as the eldest son, and deemed him a necessary substitute for the missing father.

The following year, when George was fifteen, his family underwent a period of extreme financial stringency that ended his education. During a severe cash crunch in later life, he wrote that "with much truth I can say, I never felt the want of money so sensibly since I was a boy of 15 years old."[15] With his mother having ruled out a seaman's life, George opted to become a surveyor. Throughout his career, he would cherish real estate as an almost foolproof investment that always appreciated in value. Indeed, he could already see that most, if not all, of the major Virginia fortunes had arisen from rampant land speculation. Surveying was a well-trodden path for rising young men, and not only because surveyors could book rich fees as settlers sprawled into the western wilderness. While acting as agents for others, young surveyors with an eye on the main chance could scout choice properties for themselves. Such work could eventually elevate young men hampered by meager capital into the elite club of well-off planters.

Surveying suited Washington's talents perfectly. He was proficient in math, exacting in approaching problems, and fond of the outdoors. His father had left behind a complete set of surveying instruments, and George ran his first lines at Ferry Farm. By October 1747 he had netted three pounds and two shillings by apprenticing himself to a local surveyor, and he initiated the habit of recording his expenses and revenues with scrupulous care. George Washington was always a man who monitored his every move. He regarded his knowledge of math and surveying as preliminary steps toward becoming a top-notch planter, observing that nothing was more "necessary to any person possessed of a large landed estate, the bounds or some part or other of which are always in controversy."[16] For the rest of his life, Washington was stamped by his practical experience as a surveyor. At Mount Vernon, he had an irresistible penchant for carrying a compass and performing his own measurements. Even when he toured the thirteen states as first president, he methodically recorded the topographical features of places, as if he remained a working surveyor. Whether as planter or president, his study was liberally supplied with maps and charts.

Young Washington's emergence as a surveyor had a fortuitous start. In 1746 Baron Fairfax, the absentee proprietor of the Northern Neck, visited Virginia to canvass his vast domain and stayed at Belvoir. Portraits show a shrewd, worldly man with a jowly face and intelligent eyes. He had the ultimate power to sell and lease all lands in the Northern Neck. Apparently pleased by what he saw, this veteran foxhunter decided to erect a hunting lodge for himself, known as Greenway Court, in the Shenandoah Valley. This quickened the development of his western lands, producing a windfall for the surveyors he employed. George Washington was splendidly poised to benefit from this development. His stalwart patron, Colonel Fairfax—now head of the King's Council, the upper house of the Virginia legislature—hired the surveyors, and his son, George William, was assigned to sell the leaseholds.

Thus in March 1748 sixteen-year-old George Washington saddled his horse and joined his friend George William Fairfax on a surveying expedition across the Blue Ridge Mountains, plunging into the wilds of the Shenandoah Valley. Their mission was to carve up Lord Fairfax's acreage into salable leaseholds. To mark this rite of passage, George Washington set quill to paper and began a travel diary entitled "A Journal of My Journey over the Mountains." It represents his earliest piece of writing of any length. Here, beyond the pale of Virginia society, he told of pounding rains that swelled rivers and mountain winds that played havoc with his belongings. Overflowing waterways had to be forded, primitive roads traversed. Washington navigated canoes down whitewater streams in driving rain, shot wild turkey, and slept on bearskins under the stars or in smoky tents. This was a raw, violent world such as Washington had never experienced before, but he adapted to it with remarkable speed and aplomb and quickly grew inured to hardship.

This fastidious young man learned to deal with the many earthy surprises presented by frontier life. Early in the trip, when the group stayed with a Captain Isaac Pennington, George made the mistake of expecting clean, comfortable quarters. After he stripped off his clothes and climbed into the rustic bed, he found it to be "nothing but a little straw, matted together without sheets or anything else, but only one threadbare blanket with double its weight of vermin, such as lice, fleas, etc." He promptly got up and put back on his clothes. Worn out from a day of riding, he managed to fall asleep, but resolved henceforth "to sleep in the open air before a fire."[17] The next night at Fredericktown, he got a feather bed with fresh sheets and fumigated the lice he had picked up the previous night.

On March 23 Washington registered his first encounter with Native Americans, depicting his party as "agreeably surprised" by meeting thirty Indians fresh from battle who were dismayed to be bearing only a single scalp. Washington and his group plied the Indians with liquor, which prompted them to form a circle and leap about in a war dance, accompanied by a deerskin drum and the dry rattle of a gourd. George described how the "best dancer jumps up as one awaked out of a sleep and runs and jumps about the ring in a most comical manner."[18] Despite the martial nature of the dance, the gory detail of the scalp, and the fact that they had goaded the Indians into getting drunk, the young surveyor only saw something picturesque and outlandish in the spectacle. Still insular in his reactions, he chided one group of Dutch settlers as "ignorant" because they "would never speak English, but when spoken to, they speak all Dutch."[19] A patronizing streak in George later emerged when he derided some settlers as "a parcel of barbarians and an uncouth set of people."[20] Whatever his inner reservations about the frontier folk, George succeeded in handling them with uncommon finesse.

That George, tutored by Lawrence and the Fairfax family, was already a well-bred young man is reflected in his disdain for the crude existence he confronted. Yet a rugged side of his nature gloried in this unruly world. Possessed of unusual equanimity, he showed that he could shuttle gracefully between worlds of extreme gentility and roughness. He became accustomed to roasting food on sharpened sticks over open fires and dining on wooden chips instead of plates. Nothing appeared to faze him. One windy night in early April, George awoke to discover that the straw mat he was sleeping on had caught fire; luckily, one of the men woke up and stamped it out. The next night was even more blustery. "We had our tent carried quite off with the wind and was obliged to lie the latter part of the night without covering."[21] All this he took in stride.

On April 13, 1748, toughened by a month of adventures, Washington finished his surveying trip. He had shown sporadic traces of an aesthetic sense, rhapsodizing about the "beautiful groves of sugar trees" and the "richness of the land," but the trip had mainly alerted him to the extraordinary business opportunities that abounded in these virgin lands, commencing a lifelong fascination with westward expansion.[22] With extensive knowledge of these frontier outposts, Washington would emerge as the founder best able to visualize the ample contours of the American future, making the notion of a continental empire more than a mere abstraction.

Lawrence Washington helped to spark George's interest in distant settlements, having joined with Thomas and William Fairfax in a land venture called the Ohio

Company that ultimately gained the right to half a million acres of frontier land. The locus of settlement would be the so-called Ohio Country, west of the Allegheny Mountains, where the Allegheny and Monongahela rivers flowed together to form the headwaters of the Ohio River; the place was widely known as the Forks of the Ohio. It would be the competing claims of England and France to this bountiful territory that would shortly thrust George Washington into his first military confrontations and chart a direction for his future life.

BY THE LATE 1740S George Washington had his feet solidly planted in two worlds: while burnishing his social skills for polite Virginia society, he also readied himself for wilderness service. Now that he had found a professional footing, he needed to dress the part. He had already acquired a respectable wardrobe, taking along on one trip nine shirts, six linen waistcoats, four neckcloths, and seven caps.[23] Sometime in 1749–50 he jotted down, with impressive exactitude, a 152-word description of a frock coat he wanted made, which was to have "a lapel breast, the lapel to contain on each side six button holes and to be about 5 or 6 inches wide, all the way equal, and to turn as the breast on the coat does; to have it made very long-waisted and in length to come down to or below the bent of the knee, the waist from the armpit to the fold to be exactly as long or longer than from thence to the bottom, not to have more than one fold in the skirt etc. etc."[24] No tailor could have requested more specific instructions: Washington was designing his coat down to the smallest detail. Throughout his life, he exhibited a faultless precision in dress, regarding a person's apparel as the outward sign of inner order.

Still rather awkward in society—"He was a very bashful young man," one matron later recalled. "I used often to wish that he would talk more"—Washington was trying to acquire other social habits of the Virginia gentry.[25] He learned to dance, an activity in which he sparkled, and gambled at whist and loo, card games then voguish among the British aristocracy. But he remained trapped in an adolescent dependence on his mother, which cramped his social style, and he suffered from the spartan life at Ferry Farm. In one letter to Lawrence, he regretted that he could not join him on a trip to the colonial capital at Williamsburg: "My horse is in very poor order to undertake such a journey and is in no likelihood of mending for want of corn sufficient to support him."[26]

The young man was highly responsive to female charms. In December 1748 his friend George William Fairfax, twenty-four, had married eighteen-year-old Sarah Cary, who was to be immortalized under her married name of Sally Fairfax. The alluring daughter of Wilson Cary, an eminence in the House of Burgesses, Sally had grown up in a mansion on the James River near Hampton Roads. Her family was rich and cultured, boasting a well-stocked library, and Sally was fluent in French. A photograph of a lost portrait shows a comely young woman with smooth, creamy shoulders and a long neck, wearing a simple but glamorous décolleté dress that discloses an ample expanse of bosom. A woman of obvious beauty and sensuality, she has bright, sprightly eyes and an alluring personality. For an inexperienced youth like George, Sally, two years his senior, must have exuded a bewitching air of mystery. If his attraction to her blossomed into a full-blown infatuation, it probably started innocently enough.

Sometime around 1749–50 George became smitten with a young woman he coyly referred to as the "Low Land Beauty" and dallied with another he referred to as "very agreeable," who was likely Mary Cary, Sally's younger sister.[27] George found solace by copying out two banal poems about a man spurned by his lady love. In one poem, the poet is tortured by secret love: "Ah! woe's me, that I should Love and conceal, / Long have I wish'd, but never dare reveal."[28] In the second poem, the poet stands helpless beford his ardor. "Oh Ye Gods why should my Poor Resistless Heart / Stand to oppose thy might and Power / At Last surrender to cupids feather'd Dart / and now lays Bleeding every Hour / For her that's Pityless of my grief and Woes / And will not on me Pity take."[29] But Washington was not born to pine away as an idle, lovesick youth.

In the spring of 1749 he again profited from his connection with brother Lawrence when he helped to survey the new Potomac port of Alexandria, north of Mount Vernon; Lawrence served as a trustee of the town. A more momentous change occurred in July 1749, when George was appointed surveyor of Culpeper County. Even though the College of William and Mary, under a 1693 charter, retained the power to name the county surveyor, it proved susceptible to the blandishments of influential men. When seventeen-year-old George Washington captured this lucrative sinecure, becoming the youngest official surveyor in Virginia history, it reflected his privileged friendship with the omnipotent Lord Fairfax. Instead of starting out as a lowly, obscure apprentice, the young man was enabled by patronage to skip the preliminary steps. As Marcus Cunliffe has noted, the young Washington "was not an intellectual genius or the heir to a great fortune," but "he was evidently energetic, reliable, and canny."[30]

Two days after his appointment, George performed an obligatory survey of four hundred acres in eastern Culpeper County and proudly affixed his signature to the document with his new title. Apparently, this was the only survey George ever performed in the county for which he was the nominal surveyor. He then gladly turned his attention to more profitable opportunities awaiting him in the hinterlands beyond the Blue Ridge Mountains, where rich soil tempted hordes of settlers. As fortune's favorite, George received a steady stream of assignments that issued from the splendid portals of Belvoir as Lord Fairfax cashed in on the booming settlements in his domain. These surveys were often plum assignments, for they covered small, easily measured parcels that could be surveyed in a single day. Choosing to work in crisp spring or autumn weather, George avoided the summertime, when thick foliage impeded the sight lines of surveyors. Lord Fairfax pocketed one shilling per annum for every fifty acres of settled land and piled up a substantial fortune from the labors of George and his fellow surveyors. Within a year the busy young man shed his duties as surveyor of Culpeper County, most likely because he no longer needed the extra work.

In the spring of 1750 George Washington again mounted his horse, loaded up his surveying tools, and cantered off to the Shenandoah Valley. He laid out forty-seven tracts on that one trip alone, jotting notes for each survey in a tiny notebook he tucked into his pocket. He grew increasingly accustomed to the wilderness and was no longer too particular about changing his clothes. As he notified a friend, "The coldness of the weather will not allow my making a long stay, as the lodging is rather too cold for the time of year. I have never had my clothes off, but lay and sleep in them like a Negro."[31] An instant professional success, George toiled just a few months yearly and made his first significant land investment in October 1750, buying nearly fifteen hundred acres in the Shenandoah Valley. Thus began his continuing fixation on land speculation. As Dorothy Twohig, an editor of Washington's papers, notes, "No theme appears more frequently in the writings of Washington than his love for the land—more precisely, his own land."[32] Only eighteen, Washington already had his first plantation, on which tenants or hired help grew corn, wheat, and tobacco. He never stopped accumulating acreage and by age twenty had assembled 2,315 acres in the Shenandoah Valley. For a young man who could not afford corn for his horse a year earlier, it was a startling and nearly dreamlike elevation in status.

George's soaring success coincided with an alarming turn in Lawrence's health. In May 1749 the latter had to relinquish his seat in the House of Burgesses due to a hacking cough—a telltale symptom of tuberculosis. That winter at Mount Vernon, George had intermittently helped to care for his brother. On one occasion, he wrote tenderly to Lawrence, "Dear Brother, I hope your cough is much mended since I saw you last; if so, [I] likewise hope you have given over the thoughts of leaving Virginia."[33] Instead, the cough only worsened, and Lawrence sailed to England to consult doctors there. In his absence, George commiserated by mail with his sister-in-law Ann and did his best to cheer her up. He couldn't offer comfort in person at Mount Vernon because he himself had contracted a new ailment: malaria. "I am deprived of the pleasure of waiting on you (as I expected) by ague and fever which I have had to extremity," he informed her.[34]

While George recuperated, Lawrence returned from England still in the terrible throes of tuberculosis. In desperation, accompanied by his younger brother, Lawrence decided to test the medicinal powers of warm springs in western Virginia (later the town of Berkeley Springs, West Virginia). Infirm people had begun making pilgrimages to this natural spa to soak in the waters or drink them to regain their health. Later it was a fashionable place, but George found the warm springs dark, gloomy, and secluded and scarcely conducive to improved health. He grumbled that they "are situated very badly on the east side of a steep mountain and enclosed by hills on all sides, so that the afternoon's sun is hid by four o'clock and the fogs hang over us till nine or ten."[35] While Lawrence sampled the waters, George distracted himself with surveying trips in the surrounding countryside.

As Lawrence's condition deteriorated, he decided to gamble on a trip to Barbados, hoping the tropical warmth would revive him; at the time, people with consumption flocked to Barbados as an open-air sanatorium. Because Lawrence's wife had just given birth to a daughter, it again fell upon George, nineteen, to accompany his thirty-three-year-old brother, acting as both nursemaid and companion. So grave was Lawrence's prognosis that the brothers braved a season of severe hurricanes in the West Indies. On the boat to Barbados, George kept a ship's log, in which he documented heaving seas and blustery weather. After an exceptionally rough thirty-seven-day passage, the ship docked at Barbados on November 3, 1751. In short order, Lawrence was examined by a Dr. William Hillary, who delivered the hopeful opinion that Lawrence could be saved.

This reprieve provided a fleeting opportunity for George to relish his only trip outside of North America. As the two brothers rode outside of town in "the cool of the evening" to seek their new lodgings, George seemed enraptured by the profuse tropical flowers and foliage and extolled the "beautiful prospects which on every side presented to our view the fields of cane, corn, fruit trees etc. in a delightful green."[36] His senses came alive to the island's sights and sounds. He savored avocado and pineapple for the first time and marveled at the most gargantuan collection of fruits he had ever seen heaped on a dinner table. When he attended a melodrama by George Lillo entitled *The London Merchant,* it was probably his first taste of a professional stage production, marking the start of a lasting fondness for theater.

The two brothers rented rooms outside Bridgetown from a Captain Croftan, the commander of Fort James, who introduced them to island society. Aside from early morning rides with George, Lawrence was too debilitated to engage in much activity. In his despondent letters home, he bewailed their situation—"We soon tire of the same prospect. We have no bodily diversions but dancing"—even as George was enchanted by the social whirl.[37] From his window, the young man surveyed ships gliding by in Carlisle Bay and watched soldiers execute drills. He also appraised the island's fort with the critical eye of a future general. "It's pretty strongly fortified," he wrote in his diary, "and mounts about 36 guns within the fortifications."[38]

Even amid the trip's escapist pleasures, George had a conspicuous habit of improving himself, turning everything into an educational opportunity. He took copious notes on a multitude of topics. Curiously, the sole reference to slavery concerned the sensational trial of a slave owner, Colonel Benjamin Charnock, who was acquitted of raping his maid. George bore little sympathy for Charnock, as revealed by his reference to him as a man of "opulent fortune and infamous character."[39] The most intriguing diary entry contains shrewd observations on the leadership style of the Barbados governor, with George noting that "as he avoids the errors of his predecessor, he give[s] no handle for complaint. But, at the same time, by declining much familiarity, [he] is not overzealously beloved."[40] The proper degree of familiarity between governors and the governed would be an absorbing preoccupation throughout his career. George Washington, too, would decline familiarity and sometimes inspire more respect than outright love.

Just two weeks after arriving on Barbados, George started running a high fever and contracted a savage headache, evidence that he had been "strongly attacked with the smallpox," as he noted in his diary.[41] Within a few days ghastly red pustules erupted across his forehead and scalp. For three weeks the feverish young man, confined to bed, was nursed back to health by the "very constant" presence of Dr. John Lanahan.[42] Before long, the pustules turned to scabs, then dropped off altogether, leaving a smattering of reddish-brown spots. For the rest of his life, George's nose was lightly pitted with pockmarks, a defect discreetly edited from many sanitized portraits. The smallpox siege ended with his complete recovery on December 12, 1751. In retrospect, George's brush with a mild case of smallpox was a fantastic stroke of luck, furnishing him with immunity to the most virulent scourge of eighteenth-century armies.

Exactly one week after his recovery, George returned home to Virginia aboard a ship, the *Industry,* and endured yet another wrenching, storm-tossed journey. To compound his woes, as he succumbed to seasickness, a seaman filched his money while he lay dozing. By the time his ship made landfall in Yorktown in late January, George must have had an aversion to sea voyages, for he never essayed one again. He stopped off in Williamsburg, armed with letters of reference to Robert Dinwiddie, the new lieutenant governor, who invited him to dine and was to emerge as a prominent new mentor. George then hurried off to Mount Vernon to relay to Ann the dreadful news that Lawrence still languished in Barbados with no relief from his illness. Lawrence clung to one last wispy hope: that a stay in Bermuda would work the magic that had failed to materialize in Barbados, and he compared himself grimly to "a criminal condemned, though not without hopes of reprieve."[43]

With his brother marooned in Bermuda, George returned to surveying near his Bullskin Plantation in northern Frederick County and further supplemented his holdings there. Perhaps because his immune system was compromised after his bout of smallpox, George suffered yet another frightening illness, a "violent pleurisy" that must have petrified him with the prospect that he, too, had developed tuberculosis.[44] Though an exceptionally muscular and vigorous young man, he was susceptible to the many illnesses that ran freely in eighteenth-century Virginia.

In a bizarre piece of timing, George attempted a bit of courtship from his sickbed. He sought to win the hand of sixteen-year-old Elizabeth "Betsy" Fauntleroy, whose father was a luminary in Richmond County. The adolescent George seemed to daydream about one rich, unattainable girl after another. Having now recovered from the charms of the "Low Land Beauty," he was stalking bigger game. From a letter that he wrote to William Fauntleroy, Betsy's father, we can see that the girl had already rejected his advances. As George apprised the father, he intended "as soon as I recover my strength to wait on Miss Betsy in hopes of a revocation of the former, cruel sentence and see if I can meet with any alteration in my favor."[45] Unfortunately we do not have the father's response to this letter, leaving us to wonder whether Fauntleroy scoffed at George as a bumptious parvenu who aspired above his social rank.

Fate was about to hand George some advantages that would bring such a lofty marriage within his grasp. Lawrence's hope that Bermuda would rejuvenate him turned out to be his last illusion: returning to Virginia, he died at Mount Vernon on July 26, 1752. For George, his brother's death at age thirty-four was emotionally equivalent to the death of a second father and possibly more devastating. He had identified with Lawrence, shared in his professional life, and participated intimately in his terminal illness. Lawrence left his affairs in such a disorderly state that George, as an executor, bewailed their being in "the utmost confusion."[46] Luckily, the debts proved manageable, and Lawrence's death provided another bonanza for George, on whom windfalls showered at the most implausible moments. In his will, Lawrence bequeathed to him three parcels of land in Fredericksburg. Far more consequential was a clause stipulating that, if Ann and their infant daughter died without an heir, George would inherit the 2,500 acres of Mount Vernon and adjoining properties "in consideration of the natural love and affection" which Lawrence had borne "unto his loving brother George Washington."[47] At the time of Lawrence's death, this eventuality seemed a distant prospect, many decades away, if ever.

George had long hoped to emulate his admired brother, but now he would almost graft his life onto Lawrence's, as if George would extend his brother's short life and fulfill its golden promise. The older brother became a revered figure in

George's memory, "a young man of the most promising talents."[48] Though George was poorly equipped for such a post, lacking military experience, he vigorously pursued the position of adjutant general left vacant by his brother's death. Inspired by Lawrence's example, he decided to swap a surveyor's life for that of a soldier. The colony had now been divided into four districts, with an adjutant responsible for each. Naturally, George wanted to serve as adjutant in the district covering the Northern Neck. When he was awarded the Southern District instead, he seemed not thrilled by his assignment to an important post but dismayed by the low-prestige district.

At twenty, George already had enough powerful patrons in Williamsburg to jockey to alter the decision. When William Fitzhugh, who was named to the Northern Neck adjutancy, moved to Maryland, Washington saw an opening to lobby to replace him. "I am sensible my best endeavors will not be wanting and doubt not but by a constant application to fit myself for the office," he wrote to Dinwiddie. "Could I presume your Honour had not in view a more deserving person, I flatter myself I should meet with the approbation of the Gentlemen of the council."[49] The young Washington could be alternately fawning and assertive, appealingly modest and distressingly pushy. While he knew the social forms, he could never quite restrain, much less conceal, the unstoppable force of his ambition. In the end, Fitzhugh resigned his post and yielded the Northern Neck adjutancy to young Washington. In early February 1753, just before his twenty-first birthday, George Washington took the oath of office and became district adjutant, which paid one hundred pounds annually and crowned him with the title of Major Washington.

In his seemingly inexorable rise in the world, Washington proved no less resourceful in the social sphere. In September 1752 a new Masonic lodge was convened in Fredericksburg, and two months later Washington was inducted as one of its first apprentices. Within a year he progressed swiftly through the ranks to become a Master Mason. We don't know how Washington reacted to the fraternal group's arcane rituals and occult signs. Still a relatively young movement, Freemasonry had been founded in London in 1717, drawing its symbols from the squares and compasses of masons' guilds. While American Masons preached the Enlightenment ideals of universal brotherhood and equality, they discarded the anticlerical bent of their European brethren. Washington believed devoutly in the group's high-minded values. He attended lodge meetings sporadically, came to own two Masonic aprons, walked in Masonic processions, and was even painted in full Masonic regalia during his second term as president. Repeatedly throughout his career, he paid tribute to the movement. "So far as I am acquainted with the principles and doctrines of Free Masonry," he said toward the end of his life, "I conceive it to be founded in benevolence and to be exercised only for the good of Mankind."[50] On another occasion, he stated that the purpose of Freemasonry was to "enlarge the sphere of social happiness" and "to promote the happiness of the human race."[51] Whatever credence he gave to Masonic ideals, the young George Washington, a born joiner, was likely drawn to the group as a convivial place to hobnob and expand his social contacts.

What strikes one most about the twenty-year-old George Washington was that his sudden remarkable standing in the world was the result not so much of a slow, agonizing progress as of a series of rapid, abrupt leaps that thrust him into the topmost echelons of Virginia society. The deaths of those he loved most dearly had, ironically, brightened his prospects the most. Quite contrary to his own wishes, the untimely deaths of his father and his half brother had endowed him with extraordinary advantages in the form of land, slaves, and social status. Every misfortune only pushed him further along his desired path. Most providential of all for him was that Lawrence Washington had expired on the eve of the French and Indian War, a conflict in which George's newfound status as district adjutant would place him squarely at the forefront of a thunderous global confrontation.

CHAPTER THREE

Wilderness Mission

THROUGHOUT HIS CAREER, George Washington had the imposing face and virile form that suited a commanding leader. His most delicate feature was a complexion fair enough to sunburn easily; to shield him from sunlight in later years, he rode around Mount Vernon with an umbrella fastened to his saddle bow. The mild, deep-set eyes, of a pale grayish blue, seemed to glow with an inner fire whenever he grew excited. When Gilbert Stuart painted them a more brilliant blue, he explained that in a hundred years they would fade to the right color.

Washington's hair was reddish brown, and contrary to a common belief, he never wore a wig. The illusion that he did so derived from the powder that he sprinkled on his hair with a puffball in later life. He wore his long hair tied up in a black ribbon, knotted at the nape, in an arrangement called a queue. However formal it looks to modern eyes, the style was favored by military officers. Pulling the hair back also broadened the forehead and lent him an air of martial nobility. Once his hair was drawn into a queue (or sometimes a silk bag) behind him, the side hairs were fluffed out into twin projecting wings, furthering the appearance of a wig.

It is commonly said that Washington stood six foot two or three, an estimate that gained currency after a doctor measured his corpse at six feet three and a half inches. Even though dozens of contemporaries pegged his height at only six feet, there is no need for any guesswork. Before the Revolutionary War, Washington ordered his clothes from London each year and had to describe his measurements with great accuracy. In a 1761 letter, he informed his remote tailor that "my stature is six feet, otherwise rather slender than corpulent," and he never deviated from that formula.[1] Obviously, Washington couldn't afford to tell a fib about his height to his tailor. One can only surmise that when the doctor measured his cadaver, his toes were pointing outward, padding his height by several inches compared with his everyday stature.

Washington's weight fluctuated between 175 pounds as a young man and 210 and 220 during the war years. From the time of his youth, he was powerfully rough-hewn and endowed with matchless strength. When he clenched his jaw, his cheek and jaw muscles seemed to ripple right through his skin. Even though he was exceedingly graceful, his body was oddly shaped, with a small head in proportion to his general frame. He possessed strong but narrow shoulders and wide, flaring hips with muscular thighs that made him a superb horseman. It was the long limbs and big bones, not the pinched torso, that hinted at superhuman strength, and his hands were so gigantic that he had to wear custom-made gloves. But the massive physique was never matched by a stentorian voice. The pleurisy that Washington suffered as a young man left him hollow-chested. Never a superior orator, Washington spoke with a weak, breathy voice that only exacerbated the problem.

Washington's features were strong, blunt, and handsome. His nose was thick and flat and squared off at the bottom; it flamed a bright red in a wintry wind. Often easygoing with friends, he was praised by one companion for his "good nature and hatred of ceremony," yet people spotted that his outward tranquillity was deceptive and that he had trained his face to mask his emotions.[2] On the other hand, those potent emotions would repeatedly break through his well-composed facade at critical junctures throughout his career. In 1760 his friend and former aide George Mercer captured Washington's constant struggle between his dignified reserve and his underlying feelings: "His features are regular and placid with all the muscles of his face under perfect control, though flexible and expressive of deep feeling when moved by emotions. In conversation, he looks you full in the face, is deliberate, deferential, and engaging. His demeanor at all times [is] composed and dignified. His movements and gestures are graceful, his walk majestic, and he is a splendid horseman."[3] So perfect was his posture that he was described as "as straight as an Indian."[4] Very particular about his appearance, he dressed in style while avoiding ostentation. At twenty-three, he told his brother Jack, "As wearing boots is quite the mode, and mine are in a declining state, I must beg the favour of you to procure me a pair that is good and neat."[5] Even at this early age, Washington suffered from tooth decay, perhaps contributing to some self-consciousness. As Mercer noted, "His mouth is large and generally firmly closed, but which from time to time discloses some defective teeth."[6]

THROUGH HIS APPOINTMENT as district adjutant in February 1753, Washington was soon enmeshed in epochal events, as the British and French empires began to clash over their colonial possessions. In 1753 Britain's North American colonies, mostly clustered along the eastern seaboard, inhabited a corridor flanked by the Atlantic Ocean and the Allegheny Mountains. French colonial holdings followed a sweeping arc from New Orleans to the southwest, up through the Mississippi River, into the Great Lakes and the St. Lawrence River. When both major powers claimed control of the huge Ohio Country—covering present-day Ohio and Indiana, along with parts of western Pennsylvania and West Virginia—their imperial ambitions suddenly collided in ominous fashion.

On the British side, the impetus for this looming confrontation came from the huge royal grant to the Ohio Company. To encourage settlers and protect them from French encroachment, Lawrence Washington and his colleagues advocated establishing a fort and trading post at the Forks of the Ohio (the site of present-day Pittsburgh), which would act as the flash point of imperial conflict for many years. In 1752 the Marquis de Duquesne, governor general of French Canada, countered the British move by announcing plans to construct several forts between Lake Erie and the Ohio River system, buttressing French claims in a smooth crescent from Canada to the Mississippi. This aggressive move guaranteed a violent clash with British forces.

Lieutenant Governor Robert Dinwiddie, a portly, bewigged Scot, was a prime investor in the Ohio Company. Born in Glasgow and a former customs official in Bermuda, he had a beefy, well-fed face with a drooping chin, which one wag aptly described as the "face of a longtime tax collector."[7] He wanted to secure the Ohio Company's interests as well as the lucrative fur trade with the Indians, so he lobbied London for permission to erect forts in the Ohio Country. In August 1753 his superiors returned a dispatch that forever altered the life of George Washington. Dinwiddie was empowered to create a chain of forts in the disputed area and to send an envoy to the French to deliver a solemn ultimatum that they should vacate this territory claimed by England. It was a sure recipe for military conflict.

Washington likely learned of this directive from Colonel William Fairfax and in late October galloped off to Williamsburg to proffer his services as the special envoy. His prompt resolve demonstrated his courage and confidence and suggested no ordinary craving for success. Incredibly enough, on October 31, 1753, Dinwiddie and his council entrusted the twenty-one-year-old with this perilous mission. Three decades later Washington reflected on the extraordinary circumstance "that so young and inexperienced a person should have been employed on a negotiation with which subjects of the greatest importance were involved."[8] The instructions that Dinwiddie had received from London—and that Washington presumably stashed in his saddlebag—stated categorically that if the French were found to be building forts on English soil, they should be peacefully asked to depart. If they failed to comply, however, "we do hereby strictly charge and command you to drive them off by force of arms."[9] This order was signed by none other than King George II.

How could young George Washington have snared this prestigious commission? At the time, few Virginians were seasoned in frontier warfare, creating a simple lack of competitors. Washington confirmed that he was picked to go "when I believe few or none would have undertaken it."[10] Some practical reasons made Washington an excellent choice. He knew the western country from surveying; had the robust constitution to survive the winter woods; was mostly unflappable; had a mature appearance and sound judgment; and was a model youth, with no tincture of rowdiness in his nature. In certain ways, he was a very old young man. In London's *Gentleman's Magazine,* an approving author explained Washington's selection by stating that he was "a youth of great sobriety, diligence, and fidelity."[11] His friendship with leading personalities of the Ohio Company likely clinched the appointment. Four years later he admitted that there had been pervasive suspicions in other colonies that he represented only the interests of the company.

Such was the urgency of Washington's mission that he set out for the western country the same day he pocketed the assignment. He stopped in Fredericksburg to enlist the services of Jacob Van Braam, a Dutchman by birth and a fellow Mason who would serve as his French interpreter. A proficient swordsman, Van Braam had taught Washington how to fence. Two weeks later, at Wills Creek on the Potomac River in western Maryland, he also signed up Christopher Gist, a skilled guide and surveyor of the backcountry, who knew "more of Indians and of the nature of the country than any man here," as Washington was informed.[12] He also recruited four other men from the backwoods, including two Indian traders.

Even for someone with Washington's formidable stamina, this trip made incomparably daunting demands. Washington recalled how, "at a most inclement season," he had traveled 250 miles "thro[ugh] an uninhabited wilderness country" to "within 15 miles of Lake Erie in the depth of winter, when the whole face of the earth was covered with snow and the waters covered with ice."[13] It proved "as fatiguing a journey as it is possible to conceive, rendered so by excessive bad weather."[14] Starting in mid-November, he and his party spent a week crossing the Allegheny Mountains, slogging along a tortuous wilderness trail that twisted through impenetrable forest, forcing them to wade across streams and scale high ridges. They traveled through "excessive rains and [a] vast quantity of snow" that drenched them at every turn.[15] After a wretched week, they found warmth and comfort in the rough cabin of an Indian trader named John Fraser, at the junction of the Monongahela River and Turtle Creek.

The Monongahela was so swollen by incessant rain and snow that Washington found it "quite impassable." To lighten the heavy load on his packhorses, he had two men transport the baggage downstream by canoe, while he and others rode ahead on horseback. When they reached the Forks of the Ohio, Washington boldly showed the equestrian prowess that would later assume legendary proportions. Where others balked at crossing the frigid, fast-moving Allegheny on horseback, Washington showed no qualms. He vigorously urged his horse into the freezing current, sitting upright as it glided across the water—a magnificent image repeated many times later in his career. The more cautious group members went across by canoe.

Part of Washington's mandate was to evaluate this spot for a fort that would form a bulwark against French expansion. He gave the site his provisional approval and commended it as "extremely well situated for a fort, as it has the absolute command of both rivers."[16] But having traversed the Allegheny, Washington also worried that it was "a very rapid swift-running water," and he came to prefer the navigation of the Monongahela River, which would offer a calmer waterway for Virginia's frontier settlers.[17]

Washington had been directed to establish contact with the leaders of local Indian tribes—the "Sachems of the Six Nations" of the Iroquois—and extract intelligence from them about French operations.[18] He was also supposed to wheedle them into providing an escort to the French commander at Fort Le Boeuf, just south of Lake Erie. Winning over the Indians was no easy matter, since the Ohio Country had long been their hunting grounds and they reacted warily to European interference. On November 22 Washington made his initial contact with the Indians, meeting Chief Shingas of the Delawares, whom he invited along to a parley with other chieftains at the village of Logstown (today the town of Baden, Pennsylvania).

From these early dealings with Native Americans, Washington was later spared either a racist attitude toward them or a tendency to sentimentalize them. He seemed cynical but accepting about Indian diplomacy: "The Indians are mercenary—every service of theirs must be purchased—and they are easily offended, being thoroughly sensible of their own importance."[19] Once at Logstown, with an assurance that belied his years, Washington not only summoned the Seneca tribal leader, Tanacharison—known to the English simply as the Half King—who was then off on a hunting trip, but also distributed needed largesse to his deputy, Monacatoocha. "I gave him a string of wampum and a twist of tobacco and desired him to send for the Half King, which he promised to do by a runner in the morning."[20] From the outset, Washington conveyed an authoritative air that seemed instinctive. While awaiting the Half King, he quizzed four French deserters who had come up the Mississippi River. From them, he was able to corroborate the prevalent suspicion in Williamsburg that the French planned to encircle the British by uniting their Louisiana territory with Canada and the Great Lakes.

When the Half King, a man in his fifties, arrived in Logstown on November 25, he must have been taken aback to find a young envoy less than half his age inviting him into his tent. The previous year the chieftain had signed a treaty with the British, making him their nominal ally, and he had sternly warned the French against incursions in the region. He had a visceral dislike of the French, claiming that they had murdered, cooked, and consumed his father. He had bristled at high-handed treatment from Sieur de Marin, the French commandant, who referred to Indians as "flies or mosquitoes."[21] It soon became clear why the Half King preferred the British: they had come (or so he thought) simply to trade, whereas the French wished to seize their lands. (Other Indians, however, suspected the British of having designs on their homelands and sided with the French for the same reason.) Washington quickly discovered that the Half King was an artful diplomat who expected the British to respect Indian rights. It is clear that Washington believed devoutly in his mission and was incensed at French machinations to woo the chieftain. At this stage of his life, he trusted implicitly in the wisdom and benevolence of the British Empire.

By all indications, Washington handled his talk with the Half King smoothly. A cordial feeling arose between them, even though the Indian chief gave Washington the same predatory nickname, Conotocarious, that had been bestowed on his great-grandfather, John Washington. There's no evidence that Washington spurned the name as pejorative. In fact, he seemed proud of it, as if it were conferred with affection. After the Revolutionary War, he observed of the name that the Indians had "communicated [it] to other nations" and that it was "remembered by them ever since in all their transactions with [me] during the late war."[22]

The next day, when Washington addressed an Indian council, he slid deftly into the requisite high-flown style: "Brothers, I have called you together in Council, by order of your brother the governor of Virginia."[23] At this first meeting, Washington concealed the true nature of his mission, testing, for the first time, the diplomatic merits of evasion. He asked the Indians to provide an escort of young warriors for his journey to the French commandant. The Half King requested a few days' delay, so that Washington could receive ceremonial wampum from the Shawnee chiefs. Now a young man in a hurry, bearing the weight of an empire on his shoulders, Washington chafed at the notion, but his better judgment prevailed over his quick temper. "When I found them so pressing in their request . . . I consented to stay as I believed an offence offered at this crisis might have been attended with greater ill consequence than another day's delay," he wrote in his frontier journal.[24] In the end, the Indians mustered a paltry four escorts, including the Half King, then rationalized the small party as a way to prevent the French from suspecting hostile intentions. Washington penetrated this cover story to spy the true reason for the tiny convoy: deep-seated Indian ambivalence about their British allies.

After a five-day journey north in a pounding rain, Washington's party arrived at the trading post of Venango, located at the confluence of the Allegheny River and French Creek. Here he met a French officer, Captain Philippe Thomas de Joncaire, and had another chance to sharpen his diplomatic skills. The offspring of a French officer and a Seneca woman, Joncaire invited Washington to dine with some French officers. The Frenchmen drank freely and talked indiscreetly, while Washington never shed his steely self-control: "The wine, as they dosed themselves pretty plentifully with it, soon banished the restraint which at first appeared in their conversation and gave license to their tongues to reveal their sentiments more freely." To his amazement, the French bragged about "their absolute design to take possession of the Ohio" and even spilled military secrets about the location of their forts.[25] Washington's sense of triumph was premature. The next day the Frenchmen seduced the Indians with so much food and drink that they got roaring drunk and were reluctant to proceed. Joncaire was obviously a more slippery foe than the callow Washington had realized. The young envoy was still feeling his way in a disorienting new world that did not abide by the polite rules of Virginia drawing rooms.

After three days in Venango, Washington pushed on toward Fort Le Boeuf amid more inclement weather. Now fortified by both an Indian and a French escort, he traversed forty miles of treacherous terrain, punctuated by "many mires and swamps."[26] Even though he usually had an iron constitution and was accustomed to harsh weather, the temperature had turned intolerably cold. He and Christopher Gist decided to ride on ahead of the others through a snow-encrusted landscape, logging as many as eighteen miles per day in unending rain and snow.

When Washington reached Fort Le Boeuf after dark on December 11, he found a crude structure of four buildings, patched together from bark and planks. The next morning he received an obliging reception from the silver-haired, one-eyed commander, Captain Jacques Legardeur de St. Pierre, whom Washington described as an "elderly gentleman" with "much the air of a soldier."[27] Despite the civil reception, Washington carried a truculent message that the French should quit the Ohio Valley, and St. Pierre requested several days to respond. During this time Washington reconnoitered the grounds and scribbled detailed notes on the fort's military specifications. He noted the 220 birch and pine canoes lined up along the creek, which the French had assembled for military operations. St. Pierre made clear that he was not intimidated by the British and retained every right to arrest their traders poaching on French territory. "As to the summons you send me to retire," he told Washington, "I do not think myself obliged to obey it."[28] Clearly the British had not misread the hostile intent lurking behind French expansion into the Ohio Country.

As with Joncaire, Washington discovered that St. Pierre's elaborate courtesy masked a dense web of sinister intentions. On December 14 he summoned Washington, handed over a sealed message for Governor Dinwiddie, and then—ever the attentive host—said he had stocked Washington's canoe with supplies for the journey home. Only then did Washington discover that the crafty St. Pierre had waylaid his Indian guards by bribing them with guns and liquor if they stayed behind. Irate at such duplicity, Washington mentally accused St. Pierre of "plotting every scheme that the devil and man could invent to set our Indians at variance with us to prevent their going till after our departure."[29] In the end, Washington hotly confronted the Half King, accused him of patent betrayal, and got him to depart with the British party as promised.

Now eager to return to Williamsburg and sound the alarm about nefarious French designs, he set off toward a place called Murthering Town. By this point, his horses were so enfeebled that he decided to abandon them and hike with backpacks. Adapting to the woods, he stripped off his Tidewater costume and assumed "an Indian walking dress" of leather leggings and possibly even moccasins.[30] This return trip tested his wilderness skills. At first, he and Gist steered their canoe downstream in an icy, churning current that nearly dashed them against jagged rocks. At the first resting place, they found that their Indian guides, dining on roasted bears, wouldn't budge until they had consumed this feast.

With the cold weather having grown "scarcely supportable," Washington and Gist soldiered on alone to Murthering Town, where they picked up a "party of French Indians" who pledged to guide them on foot along the fastest route to the Forks of the Ohio.[31] The group trudged on for miles, with Washington so exhausted that he allowed one Indian guide to carry his backpack. Washington trusted this Indian, but Gist intuited something amiss as the woods suddenly grew unfamiliar. At one point, when they came to a meadow, the Indian hustled out into the clearing without warning, spun around, and fired at them point-blank from fifteen paces. Washington, unscathed, saw Gist race to disarm the Indian. "Are you shot?" the young man hollered, and Gist shouted back, "No." Gist jumped on the Indian, pinned him to the ground, and was about to execute him with his musket when Washington pleaded for his life. They kept the Indian bound and released him after dark. As he scuttled off into the woods, Washington and Gist, fearing he might return with others, dashed in the opposite direction. "As you will not have him killed," Gist upbraided Washington, "we must get him away and then we must travel all night"—which is exactly what they did.[32]

When these weary travelers arrived at an icy river, they expected to find it frozen solid. Instead, a large section of icy water swirled in the middle of the river. With "one poor hatchet," Washington remembered, he and Gist devoted an entire day to hacking out a rude raft to float them across.[33] Midway across the river, it became wedged in an ice floe, stuck so fast that Washington "expected every moment our raft would sink and we perish."[34] He tried to free the craft by pushing a pole against the river bottom: "I put out my setting pole to try to stop the raft that the ice might pass by, when the rapidity of the stream threw it with so much violence against the pole that it jerked me into ten feet [of] water."[35] Bobbing breathlessly in the current, Washington latched onto one log of the raft and heaved himself onto its surface. Unable to get ashore, he and Gist lay stranded on an island in the river. Although Washington had been submerged in the icy water, it was Gist who suffered frostbite in his toes and fingers. The pair withstood the elements on the island all night. By the next morning, the river having congealed into a sheet of ice, they were able to scramble across to safety. Clearly, to have survived these mishaps, Washington must have been a physical prodigy, made of seemingly indestructible stuff. In his first political assignment, he had overcome a punishing array of obstacles, both physical and psychological, without losing sight of his primary objectives.

After stopping briefly at Belvoir to regale the Fairfax family with tales of his wilderness saga, Washington beat a path to Williamsburg and on January 16, 1754, handed to Governor Dinwiddie the sealed letter from the French commandant, who refused to capitulate before British threats. Washington also supplied the governor with a map of Fort Le Boeuf and careful estimates of French military power. Impressed by the thoroughness with which Washington had tackled this complex task, Dinwiddie asked him to take the nearly seven thousand words of his frontier journal and convert them overnight into a coherent report for the council.

In presenting this narrative to the governor, Washington struck a note of servility: "I hope it will be sufficient to satisfy Your Honour with my proceedings, for that was my aim in undertaking the journey and chief study throughout the prosecution of it."[36] Washington had no time to buff his prose and prefaced his journal with a disclaimer: "There intervened but one day between my arrival in Williamsburg and the time for the Council's meeting for me to prepare and transcribe, from the rough minutes I had taken in my travels, this journal." Such a timetable "admitted of no leisure to consult of a new and proper form to offer it in or to correct or amend the diction of the old."[37] It was an early example of Washington being nagged by his sense of an inadequate education.

Published in colonial newspapers as far afield as Massachusetts, this report had repercussions beyond anything Washington could have envisioned. In late January, Dinwiddie alerted the Board of Trade in London to the prospect of a major French encroachment in the spring: the French would marshal fifteen hundred French soldiers and countless Indian warriors and commence a program to build more forts in the Ohio Country. To substantiate his case, Dinwiddie sent along Washington's report, which was published in London in pamphlet form as *The Journal of Major George Washington,* giving the obscure young man instant renown in the British Empire. The slim volume helped kindle a spark that eventually led to the conflagration of the French and Indian War. Washington had expected money as well as fame for his trouble and was not assuaged when the assembly voted him a measly fifty-pound reward. As he grumbled to his brother Augustine, "I was employed to go a journey in the winter . . . and what did I get by it? My expenses borne!"[38] It was Washington's first bitter lesson in politics.

Washington parlayed the governor's approval of his work into a central role in the colony's upcoming military campaign in the Ohio Country. Within a week of arriving in Williamsburg, he was authorized, as adjutant of the Northern Neck District, to raise and train one hundred militia. Joined by another hundred troops, they were to march to the Forks of the Ohio and construct a fort. On January 28 Washington contacted another Virginia official, Richard Corbin, and lobbied him for a promotion. Once again his style was both assertive and self-effacing: he tugged the forelock and pushed himself forward at once, as if he knew he was being boorish but couldn't contain himself. He started out by conceding that the "command of the whole forces" of Virginia would be "a charge too great for my youth and inexperience." Then he continued: "But if I could entertain hopes that you thought me worthy of the post of lieutenant colonel and would favour me so far as to mention it at the appointment of officers, I could not but entertain a true sense of the kindness." This dogged young man cited "my own application and diligent study of my duty," rather than his ability, as the best reason for his promotion.[39] As it turned out, Washington did not overstate his worth, and Dinwiddie presented him with a commission as a lieutenant colonel. Almost twenty-two, Washington was emerging as a wunderkind to be reckoned with in the world of Virginia politics.

CHAPTER FOUR

Bloodbath

FROM HIS HEADQUARTERS IN ALEXANDRIA, Lieutenant Colonel George Washington attempted to inject discipline into a group of raw recruits he had enlisted for the impending march. Scarcely the spit-and-polish outfit of his dreams, they were marginal figures who inhabited the fringes of colonial society, and his attitude toward these rank amateurs mingled sympathy with vague distaste. As he bemoaned to Dinwiddie, most of these soldiers were "loose, idle persons that are quite destitute of house and home and I may truly say many of them of clothes."[1] Throughout his career, Washington complained of his charges being too rambunctious; they never seemed mannerly enough for his tastes. These scruffy, underfunded troops lacked shoes, stockings, shirts, and coats, as well as cutlasses, halberds, pikes, and drums. Their tattered clothing was especially upsetting for Washington, who lobbied Dinwiddie for red uniforms, advancing the novel sartorial theory that among the Indians red "is compared to blood and is looked upon as the distinguishing marks of warriors and great men."[2] He went so far as to opine that the Indians ridiculed the French soldiers' shabby appearance, "and I really believe [that] is the chief motive why they hate and despise them as they do."[3]

To head the expedition, Dinwiddie named Joshua Fry, a former mathematics professor at the College of William and Mary; the English-born and Oxford-educated Fry was given command of the Virginia Regiment with the rank of colonel. Since Fry was already in his midfifties, Washington was stuck below a lumbering old man, as he likely perceived him. Most of all, however, he sulked about the inequitable treatment of colonial officers. Under the British imperial system, a captain from England with a royal commission could boss around Lieutenant Colonel Washington, even though the latter held a nominally higher rank—the sort of slight that rankled for many years with the proud young Virginian.

By mid-March, as intelligence reports filtered back from the Ohio Country of a French raiding party speeding toward the Forks of the Ohio, an apprehensive Dinwiddie ordered Washington "to march what soldiers you have enlisted immediately to the Ohio."[4] He furnished Washington with broadly elastic orders. In general, he was to maintain a defensive posture but could initiate hostilities if the French meddled with any military works or English settlements. Not mincing words, Dinwiddie granted him the power to apply deadly force, telling him that "you are to restrain all such offenders and in case of resistance to make prisoners of or kill and destroy them."[5] This open-ended mandate was crucial to the dramatic events shortly to unfold.

On April 2, 1754, Washington set out for the wilderness with 160 green recruits. For the first time, he must have felt like a true commander. Their supply-laden wagons progressed slowly, for the men had to carve out a frontier road. Three weeks later, at the junction of Wills Creek and the Potomac, a courier swept into Washington's camp with calamitous news: French troops had descended on the Forks en masse, forcing the surrender of British forces building a fort there; the French had renamed this pivotal outpost Fort Duquesne. It mattered little that the British had been aided by the Half King and his warriors, for the disparity in forces had been staggering: the French had assembled one thousand troops, 360 boats and canoes, and eighteen artillery pieces to subdue thirty-four helpless British soldiers. Not surprisingly, as the news percolated through camp, Washington had to cope with sinking morale and threatened desertions. He reassured the Half King that while his own detachment was too small to repel the French, it merely embodied the vanguard of "a great number of our warriors that are immediately to follow with our great guns, our ammunition, and our provision."[6] Washington evoked a phantom force, since Colonel Fry was bringing up the rear with little more than a hundred soldiers.

Far from being intimidated, the courageous Washington burned with what he called a "glowing zeal."[7] Once again he played the impromptu diplomat in the wilderness and dashed off spirited letters to Lieutenant Governor James Hamilton of Pennsylvania and Governor Horatio Sharpe of Maryland, rallying them to send reinforcements. He was achingly aware of his youthful presumption in doing so, saying apologetically to Sharpe, "I ought first to have begged pardon of your excellency for this liberty of writing, as I am not happy enough to be ranked among those of your acquaintance." He tried to stir the governors to action in ringing language, saying that the present contest "should rouse from the lethargy we have fallen into the heroic spirit of every free-born Englishman to assert the rights and privileges of our king."[8] An unknown young surveyor two years earlier, Washington was now penning admonitory letters to governors of neighboring colonies. Evidently he succeeded, because both Maryland and Pennsylvania dispatched more troops.

Strangely enough, at this moment of looming confrontation with the French, Washington wrangled bitterly with Dinwiddie over the mundane matter of pay. Washington and his men smarted over the inferior compensation colonial officers received compared with regular officers. In mid-May Washington expressed dismay to Dinwiddie over a decision by the House of Burgesses to fix their pay at a steep discount to royal British salaries, stating that he would rather serve without pay than suffer this indignity: "But let me serve voluntarily. Then I will, with the greatest pleasure in life, devote my services to the expedition without any other reward than the satisfaction of my country. But to be slaving dangerously for the shadow of pay through woods, rocks, mountains—I would rather prefer the great toil of a daily laborer and dig for a maintenance . . . than serve upon such ignoble terms."[9] From this letter, one can see how wholly Washington had imbibed the aristocratic ethos of the Fairfax family, since his own income scarcely entitled him to such grand, self-sacrificing gestures. Dinwiddie responded with irritation, expressing surprise that the young man for whom he had such "great expectations and hopes" should concur "with complaints in general so ill-founded."[10] He wrote in the impatient tone of an older man who had formerly found a young protégé quite sensible and was now shocked to find him far more headstrong than he had reckoned. The pay issue carried tremendous symbolic weight for the striving, hypersensitive Washington, who chafed at anything pertaining to inferior salary and status.

On the evening of May 24, Washington received disconcerting news that a French detachment had crossed the Youghiogeny River eighteen miles away. He decided to establish a defensive position at a place called the Great Meadows (near Uniontown, Pennsylvania, today), a remote, grassy area that was to figure prominently in the Washington saga. With little premonition of the disaster ahead, Washington told Dinwiddie of his plans and struck a note of juvenile bravado: "We have with nature's assistance made a good entrenchment and by clearing the bushes out of these meadows prepared a charming field for an encounter."[11] At the same time, Washington alluded to a disturbing episode: his sentries had heard rustling noises at night in the camp and didn't know whether it was French interlopers or six of their own deserters. The men had fired at this unseen menace, prompting Washington to keep his men by their guns until daybreak. This episode coincided with reports from Christopher Gist that fifty boisterous French soldiers had invaded his nearby wilderness cabin, vowing to kill his cow and smash "everything in the house."[12] Gist also told of suspicious tracks that presumably belonged to this shadowy band. The Half King confirmed that the French had set up camp about seven miles away.

At this jittery moment, Washington switched into a more aggressive mode and decided to hunt down the French contingent. Afterward he would evoke a nightmarish march in which he and forty men trudged through sheets of rain, "in a night as dark as pitch," along a path so narrow they had to travel single file. On this moonless night, they kept stumbling against each other in the black void, and seven soldiers went astray in the woods. This harrowing atmosphere is important in understanding Washington's hair-trigger response to the upcoming situation.

On the morning of May 28, Washington and the Half King decided to pounce on the French intruders. Washington was convinced of their hostile intentions by the stealthy way they had moved about. As he afterward explained, the French "came secretly and sought after the most hidden retreats . . . and remained hid for whole days together and that no more than five miles from us. From thence they sent spies to reconnoiter our camp."[13] Washington's sense of the situation, however faulty, likely predisposed him to launch a preemptive attack.

Early that morning the Half King led him to a "low obscure place" where thirty-five Frenchmen lay encamped in a secluded glen, surrounded by rocks. For Washington, this "skulking place" underscored the clandestine nature of the French mission. He marched bravely at the head of his column, placing himself in the most vulnerable position as they approached the sheltered hollow. With Washington's men in front of them and the Indians slipping behind them to block their escape, the French were encircled. According to Washington's version of events, the French soldiers, when they spied the British, instantly scurried for their arms and unleashed a brisk fire. Washington gave orders to fire in return, and his men ripped off two quick volleys. Trapped on low ground, the ambushed French soon threw down their arms and surrendered. The casualty count showed a lopsided contest in which ten French were killed and another twenty-one were captured, compared with only one dead and two or three wounded on Washington's side. Clearly, Washington and his men overpowered the French before they had a chance to respond, making it seem unlikely that the latter had fired first. The whole bloody affair was wrapped up in fifteen minutes.

What converted this local skirmish into a worldwide incident was the identity of one victim: Ensign Joseph Coulon de Villiers, Sieur de Jumonville, thirty-five, who bore an important diplomatic message to the British, demanding their evacuation from the Ohio Country. According to one account, as Jumonville read this ultimatum, the Half King stepped forward, split open his head with a hatchet, then dipped his hands into the skull, rinsed them with the victim's brains, and scalped him. What is beyond dispute is that Washington abruptly found himself presiding over atrocities, as his Indian allies swooped down on the remaining Frenchmen "to knock the poor, unhappy wounded on the head and bereave them of their scalps," as he wrote.[14] This was a curiously ironic way to describe a bloodbath, as if Washington wished to distance himself from the horror or pretend it was merely routine. The Indians' behavior placed him in an excruciating predicament, for he didn't wish to repudiate them after their victory or threaten their alliance. We don't know how many Frenchmen were murdered by Indian hatchets rather than British muskets.

In their radically different version of events, the French claimed that they awoke that morning to find themselves hemmed in by Indians and Englishmen, with the latter firing first. Through an interpreter, Monsieur de Jumonville beseeched the English to cease firing, and when they did, he read aloud his ultimatum. The French claimed that, while reading this message, Jumonville was shot through the head by a musket and that the remaining French would have been annihilated had not the Indians rushed between them and the English, averting further bloodshed.

Washington may have exaggerated the British role in killing the Frenchmen to establish his own military credentials. Whatever the exact sequence of events, he overstated his certainty that the French were spying on him and stalking his movements; his letter to Dinwiddie had admitted to doubts about the nocturnal spying incident. Afterward, when the French prisoners insisted that they had come only to deliver a warning, Washington scoffed at the claim. "*They informed me that they had been sent with a summons to order me to depart.* A plausible pretense to discover our camp and to obtain the knowledge of our forces and our situation!"[15] A genuine diplomat, he maintained, would have traveled straight to him and presented his message in a forthright manner. Washington was convinced that French espionage was merely the prelude to a murderous assault on his men. Still, the French party was so small that, whatever its true intent, it hardly seemed to constitute a dire threat to the British.

The French version likewise lacks plausibility in several particulars. It is hard to believe that Washington would have allowed a diplomatic messenger to be shot in cold blood, as the French insisted. After all, the previous fall he himself had been in an analogous situation, delivering a stiffly worded warning to the French. He was too cautious to jeopardize his career by murdering an ambassador. On the other hand, the French had already seized the Forks of the Ohio, and Washington may have felt the French and British empires were now at war in all but name. It also strains credulity that the Indians heroically thrust themselves between the French and the British. The Half King had recommended harsh measures against the French detachment, and in letters to Dinwiddie, Washington disclosed that the Indian chief circulated French scalps among friendly tribes as war trophies. The French version seems like a patent attempt to curry political favor with the Indians by exonerating them of blame for the savagery.

On May 29 Washington sat down in his camp at the Great Meadows to explain the apparent massacre to Governor Dinwiddie. Instead of turning straight to this fateful confrontation, he bizarrely devoted the first eight paragraphs to fresh complaints about colonial pay, which, he said, "debarred" him from "the pleasure of good living."[16] He informed Dinwiddie that he had told Colonel Fairfax that he intended to resign over the issue, but Fairfax had dissuaded him. Once again Washington feigned indifference to money and volunteered to serve without pay rather than accept meager compensation. When he finally got around to the Jumonville episode, he insisted that the French had flitted about likes spies and assassins. They had "sought one of the most secret retirements, fitter for a deserter than an ambassador to encamp in—stayed there two or 3 days [and] sent spies to reconnoiter our camp, as we are told, though they deny it."[17] For the next few weeks, Washington passed along to Dinwiddie every scrap of intelligence gleaned from French deserters that might strengthen his case.

To his younger brother Jack, Washington sent an account that showcased his leadership style in battle. Instead of hanging back in the rear, Washington had led by example and exposed himself unflinchingly to enormous risk. "I fortunately escaped without a wound, though the right wing where I stood was exposed to and received all the enemy's fire and was the part where the man was killed and the rest wounded." He also engaged in some youthful boasting. "I can with truth assure you, I heard bullets whistle and believe me there was something charming in the sound."[18] Instead of being traumatized by battle, he wanted to illustrate his coolness under fire. When King George II encountered Washington's blithe comments about the "charming" sound of bullets in a London periodical, he detected a false note of swagger. "He would not say so if he had been used to hear many," the king said acerbically.[19]

Aware that the large French army at the Forks would soon get wind of the massacre and retaliate swiftly in overwhelming numbers, Washington vowed not to "give up one inch of what we have gained."[20] He hastily ordered his men at the Great Meadows to dig trenches, drive in pointed stakes, and build a crude, circular, palisade-style stockade that he dubbed Fort Necessity. While the troops busily braced for an attack, Colonel Joshua Fry tumbled from his horse and died on May 31. Thus, at age twenty-two, George Washington took full command of the Virginia Regiment, in yet another case of his being promoted to higher things by events beyond his control.

Surely Washington must have wondered whether Governor Dinwiddie would applaud his encounter with the French or condemn it as violating his instructions. On June 1 Dinwiddie sent him a letter that removed any lingering doubt: he construed the clash as a famous victory. Warmly congratulating Washington for "the very agreeable account" of the episode, he labeled it a success on which "I heartily congratulate you, as it may give a testimony to the Ind[ian]s that the French are not invincible w[he]n fairly engaged with the English."[21] In the next letter, Dinwiddie heaped further praise on Washington's "prudent measures" and said he was sending four thousand black and four thousand white strings of wampum, fortified by three barrels of rum, for Indian diplomacy. At heart, however, Dinwiddie knew that Washington had acted rashly and exceeded instructions, for when he wrote to the Board of Trade in London, he converted Washington and his men into minor partners of their Indian allies. As he wrote, "This little skirmish was by the Half King and their Indians. We were as auxiliaries to them, as my orders to the Commander of our Forces [were] to be on the defensive."[22] While the folks at home embraced him as an improbable hero, Washington was denigrated in England as a reckless young warrior and in France as an outright assassin. He would have been crestfallen to know that, for some high-ranking folks in London, his behavior only confirmed that provincial officers couldn't be trusted. "*Washington* and many *such* may have courage and resolution," Lord Albemarle wrote to the Duke of Newcastle, "but they have no knowledge or experience in our [military] profession; consequently there can be no dependence on them!"[23] Destiny had now conferred upon Washington a pivotal place in colonial, and even global, affairs, for the Jumonville incident was recognized as the opening shot that precipitated the French and Indian War, known in Europe as the Seven Years' War. In the words of Sir Horace Walpole in London, "The volley fired by a young Virginian in the backwoods of America set the world on fire."[24]

AS HE STEELED HIMSELF at Fort Necessity for the enraged French onslaught, Washington squabbled with Dinwiddie over the unequal treatment of provincial officers. Despite his good fortune, he brooded on the penalties he suffered as a colonial. He had no quarrel, he told Dinwiddie, with the appointment of Colonel James Innes, a veteran Scottish officer leading a North Carolina regiment, as the new commander in chief to replace Joshua Fry. And he enjoyed cordial relations with Major George Muse, who brought two hundred men to Fort Necessity and deferred to Washington as leader of the Virginia Regiment. What nettled Washington was the imminent arrival of South Carolina Independents under James Mackay, a senior officer who held his captaincy by royal commission. Mackay's company was composed mostly of colonial soldiers, but it was part of the regular British Army. This renewed the thorny issue of whether a regular captain could lord it over Washington, who held a superior provincial rank. Washington assured Dinwiddie that he would "endeavor to make all my officers show Captain Mackay all the respect due to his rank and merit, but [I] should have been particularly obliged if your Honor had declared whether he was under my command or independent of it."[25]

When Captain Mackay arrived with one hundred men on June 14, he quickly asserted his prerogatives over Colonel Washington and staked out a separate camp-site. When Washington sent over the parole and countersign to be used, Mackay made it crystal clear that he wasn't bound by orders from a lowly colonial colonel. He also wouldn't allow his South Carolinians to join the Virginians in an important road-building operation, since Washington could pay only inferior colonial wages. This high-handed behavior dealt a stinging rebuke to Washington, who was fighting to protect a British Empire that insisted on consigning him to inferior status. Increasingly, he found himself fighting one war against the French and an equally acrimonious one behind the lines with his British brethren.

As it happened, Washington had much graver problems than his minor interpersonal drama with Captain Mackay. On June 18 he huddled with the Half King and other chieftains for three days to plot strategy against the French. In the end, the Indians concluded that Washington and his flimsy fortress couldn't shield them against the huge French force gathering at Fort Duquesne. This ended their short-lived alliance and threw young Washington back on his own resources. In his diary, he inveighed against the faithless Indians as "treacherous devils who had been sent by the French as spies" and could turn against his men at any time. The Half King, for his part, painted a portrait of Washington as a "good-natured" but naively inept young commander who "took upon him to command the Indians as his slaves" and refused to "take advice from Indians."[26] He derided Fort Necessity as "that little thing upon the meadow."[27]

On June 28 Washington ordered his exhausted men, who had been dispersed building roads, to retreat within the flimsy confines of Fort Necessity. At a war council that day, the outlook seemed pretty bleak. Intelligence reports, only slightly exaggerated, warned that the French would attack with eight hundred French soldiers and four hundred Indians, or several times Washington's own strength. And their army was commanded by a Frenchman with a fiercely personal mission. Captain Louis Coulon de Villiers was the older brother of the fallen Jumonville and was bent upon avenging his death. To worsen matters, Washington's depleted men had lacked meat or bread for six days and munched on withered corn as they dragged ponderous cannon across hilly terrain. Yet despite his vulnerable position, Washington remained sanguine that, with only three hundred men, he could defeat the superior French force. According to the Half King's mocking account, Washington thought the French soldiers would pop up conveniently in the open field and allow themselves to get shot.[28]

In choosing Fort Necessity, Washington opted for a spot poorly situated to withstand an incursion. He always refused to concede its demerits and years later still defended the Great Meadows as a place "abounding in forage" and convenient for a stockade.[29] An uncouth backwoods structure, covered with bark and animal skins, the fort was primarily defended by nine small cannon that spun on pivots. Because it could contain only sixty or seventy men, Washington had three-foot trenches dug around its perimeter to protect additional men and threw up earthen breastworks to bolster their position. Despite such precautions, Fort Necessity stood on low-lying grassland that was soft and boggy and would form stagnant ponds in the rain. It was also surrounded by woods and high ground that could protect marksmen within easy musket range of the fort. Significantly, the fort was open to the sky, affording no shelter from the elements.

On the morning of July 3, 1754, Washington and his men had hunkered down at the fort when frantic scouts reported that "a heavy, numerous body" of French soldiers had drawn within four miles of their camp.[30] They had stopped by the glen where Jumonville was killed and discovered the unburied bodies of dead compatriots, further inflaming their rage. Later that morning, while Washington's men scooped out trenches, this invisible force took on a sudden, terrifying shape, descending on Fort Necessity in three columns. Bullets rained down from everywhere. French and Indian soldiers "advanced with shouts and dismal Indian yells to our entrenchments," Washington recalled, but were greeted by a "warm, spirited and constant" fire that scattered them to the woods.[31] What Washington didn't recall was that the British regulars under Mackay had stood steadfast under French fire, while the ranks of his own Virginia Regiment had broken and dived for cover.

Washington received a costly lesson in frontier fighting as swarms of French and Indians kept up a scalding fire "from every little rising, tree, stump, stone, and bush."[32] Their well-protected marksmen took clear shots from woods as little as sixty yards away. Then late in the afternoon, a torrential rain began to fall—"the most tremendous rain that can be conceived," in Washington's words—and it soaked both his men and their weapons, turning the fort's floor into a treacherous mud bowl.[33] Worst of all, the water pooled in the ditches, trapping soldiers in their own defenses. Exposed to the sky, the men couldn't keep their cartridges and firelocks dry, rendering their muskets useless. By the end of the day, the rain-drenched stockade was a horrific swamp of mangled bodies, lying in blood and rain. The appalling casualty toll—a hundred men dead or wounded—represented a full third of Washington's soldiers. The pitiless French also butchered every cow, horse, and even dog in sight. So one-sided was the outcome that the French suffered only three dead and seventeen wounded. To put a better gloss on the bloodshed, Washington and Mackay magnified the scale of French casualties, pegging the figure as high as three hundred, as if the two sides had fought to an even draw.

The debacle was compounded by the surrender. It was nearly nightfall when the French commander signaled a willingness to talk. By that point, Washington's men had pounced on the fort's rum supply, and half of them had gotten drunk—perhaps leaving Washington with a lifelong detestation of alcohol, especially among soldiers. Lacking dry gunpowder and food, Washington and Mackay had no choice but to submit; their troops were down to their last bags of flour and a little bacon, with their fresh food spoiling in the summer heat.[34] The person picked to convey the terms of surrender was Jacob Van Braam, their French interpreter. The translation of those terms caused a brouhaha that engulfed Washington in yet another international controversy. As he shuffled between the two sides, Van Braam relayed an article of capitulation that said the French assault had been in retaliation for the *assassination* of Jumonville—a provocative word indeed. When Washington and Mackay signed the agreement around midnight, they imagined that the term used was the more neutral *death* or *loss* of Jumonville.[35] Their inadvertent confession supplied the French with a major propaganda victory.

How could this profound misunderstanding have arisen? The night of the negotiation was dark and rainy, and when Van Braam brought back the terms of surrender, Washington and the other officers strained to read the blurry words in a dim light. "We could scarcely keep the candlelight to read them," recalled one officer. "They were wrote in a bad hand, on wet and blotted paper, so that no person could read them but Van Braam, who had heard them from the mouth of the French officer."[36] Not expert in English, Van Braam might have used *death* or *loss* interchangeably with *assassination*, yet it's hard to imagine that he botched the translation deliberately. What is clear is that Washington was adamant that he never consented to the loaded word *assassination*. "That we were willfully, or ignorantly, deceived by our interpreter in regard to the word *assassination,* I do aver and will to my dying moment," Washington insisted.[37]

In other respects, the French treated Washington and his men more honorably. They wanted to characterize their military confrontation as an act of reprisal instead of war and to show due mercy to the vanquished after they had "confessed." Instead of being taken prisoner, the British soldiers would be allowed to retreat with the full honors of war, "our drums beating and our colors flying," as Washington phrased it.[38] Nevertheless, the next morning one hundred Indian allies of the French ransacked the British baggage, completing their humiliation. On the road back to Wills Creek, the Indians taunted and harassed Washington's men. The Virginia Regiment began to crumble from wholesale desertions, and the hapless Washington felt powerless to stop it.

In the rifled baggage, the French stumbled upon the diary that Washington had kept, and it was duly passed along to Governor Duquesne, who devoured its contents. "There is nothing more unworthy and lower and even blacker than the sentiments and the way of thinking of this Washington," Duquesne gloated after perusing the diary.[39] To Washington's mortification, it was published in Paris two years later to a jeering public. The French had a field day with the articles of capitulation, brandishing them as proof that Washington had murdered Jumonville, a man on a peaceful mission. In this manner, they cast the British as the first belligerents in the French and Indian War. The sudden celebrity that Washington had attained in Virginia turned to instant notoriety abroad. One English writer, in high dudgeon, lambasted the articles of surrender as "the most infamous a British subject ever put his hand to."[40]

The Fort Necessity debacle pointed up Washington's inexperience. Historians have rightly faulted him for advancing when he should have retreated; for fighting without awaiting sufficient reinforcements; for picking an indefensible spot; for the slapdash construction of the fort; for alienating his Indian allies; and for shocking hubris in thinking that he could defeat an imposing French force. Yet the major blame must lie with Governor Dinwiddie and the Virginia legislators, who had failed to fund the campaign properly and sent an insufficient force. Some Washington virtues stood out amid the temporary wreckage of his reputation. With unflagging resolution, he had kept his composure in battle, even when surrounded by piles of corpses. He had a professional toughness and never seemed to gag at bloodshed; a born soldier, he was curiously at home with bullets whizzing about him. Even in the wilderness, there was no doubt that he would faithfully execute orders. He was always tenacious and persevering and never settled for halfway measures. Utterly fearless, he faced down dangers and seemed undeterred by obstacles. Washington knew he had shown personal courage, contending that he had "stood the heat and brunt of the day and escaped untouched in time of extreme danger."[41]

It's also worth noting that Washington had received an invaluable education in frontier warfare. European conventional warfare stressed compact masses of troops, arrayed on open battlefields. In the New World, by contrast, the Indians had perfected a mobile style of warfare that relied on ambushing, sniping from trees, and vanishing into the forest. That June Washington noted that "the French all fight in the Indian method," and the Fort Necessity defeat demonstrated how lethal this could be.[42] Washington had seen how soldiers could defeat an enemy through speed and cunning. Two other lessons informed his later experience in the American Revolution. One was the futility of trying to hold posts that could become death traps for soldiers cooped up inside—a lesson Washington would have to relearn in the subsequent war. The other lesson, as President Washington repeated it to Indian fighters in his administration, was the resounding dictum "Beware of surprise!"[43] George Washington always demonstrated a capacity to learn from missteps. "Errors once discovered are more than half amended," he liked to say. "Some men will gain as much experience in the course of three or four years as some will in ten or a dozen."[44] It was this process of subtle, silent, unrelenting self-criticism that enabled him to rise above his early defeats.

When Washington rode into Williamsburg two weeks later, his exploits were the talk of the capital. At first he attracted criticism for his defeat and the seemingly scandalous admission that Jumonville had been "assassinated." To protect his own reputation, Dinwiddie alleged that Washington had disobeyed his orders not to engage with the French until "the whole forces were joined in a body."[45] But he couldn't denounce Washington without raising serious questions about his own judgment, and when he reported to London on the fiasco, he described it as a "small engagement, conducted with judgment by the officers and great bravery by our few forces."[46] Dinwiddie also condemned the "monstrous" failure of other colonies to shore up the Virginia forces—a failure that gave Washington his first powerful proof of the need for continental unity.[47]

In the coming weeks, condemnation of Washington gradually gave way to widespread acknowledgment that he had confronted terrifying odds at Fort Necessity. So sharp was the reversal of opinion that in early September the House of Burgesses paid special tribute to Washington and Mackay "for their late, gallant, and brave behavior in the defence of their country."[48] Governor Horatio Sharpe of Maryland, who had excoriated Washington for impulsive behavior, wrote to him and explained that, as the true story of Fort Necessity became known, public opinion had shifted in his favor, and he concluded with the reassuring words: "Your reputation again revived."[49] Thus, the ghastly frontier defeat came to be seen as a doomed but heroic defense rather than a military blunder that might have ruined Washington's budding career.

The aftermath of Washington's first military campaign was grievously disappointing to him. The Virginia Regiment, it was decided, would be divided into ten independent companies, with captain the top grade in each. For Washington, this would have meant an insulting demotion from his colonel's rank. Anyone who thought he would accept such a setback, he wrote indignantly, "must entertain a very contemptible opinion of my weakness."[50] Quite predictably, he decided to resign from the army in October rather than tolerate such a blow to his standing. But with his wilderness forays having confirmed his love of a military life, he said his resignation wasn't meant "to gratify any desire I had to leave the military line. My inclinations are strongly bent to arms."[51] If the whirlwind events had been hard on the tender ego of the ambitious young Washington, the carnage at Fort Necessity hadn't shattered his courage or altered his resolution to pursue a military career. For a young man without enormous inherited wealth, the military remained a sure path to colonial advancement. Washington must have had a premonition that his military retirement was only temporary, for in late October he ordered from London some costly items for a resplendent uniform: a gold shoulder knot, six yards of gold regimental lace, twenty-four gold embroidered loops, a rich crimson military sash, four dozen gilt coat buttons, and a hat adorned with gold lace.[52] The young officer seemed to know that the world had not heard its last of him.

CHAPTER FIVE

Shades of Death

EVER SINCE THE DEATH of Lawrence Washington, George had known he had an outside chance of someday becoming lord of Mount Vernon if Lawrence's widow, Ann, and daughter, Sarah, predeceased him. Then, in yet another of the improbable transformations that eerily propelled his life ever upward, the occupancy of Mount Vernon came unexpectedly within his grasp. Six months after Lawrence's death, Ann remarried and moved to Westmoreland County, and two years after that, on December 10, 1754, little Sarah Washington died. A week later Ann rented Mount Vernon to George Washington along with its eighteen resident slaves—a tremendous bonanza for the twenty-two-year-old. By the terms of the lease, he was required every Christmas to ship his sister-in-law fifteen thousand pounds of tobacco, packed in fifteen hogsheads, placing him under considerable pressure to manage the estate profitably.

The Mount Vernon house had not yet attained its later magnificence, so visitors singled out the natural setting for their poetic effusions. "The house is most beautifully situated upon a very high hill on the banks of the Potomac and commands a noble prospect of water, of cliffs, of woods and plantations," wrote one clergyman.[1] Unlike that of its later and more famous incarnation, the entrance stood on the river side, attesting to the extensive commercial traffic then churning along the Potomac down below. In those days, one could also see thousands of wild ducks gathering on the surface of the water.

As Washington had suspected, his respite from military service proved short-lived. On February 20, 1755, Major General Edward Braddock dropped anchor off Hampton Roads, soon to be accompanied by two smartly dressed regiments of

British redcoats. To this British Army veteran, an officer of the Coldstream Guards, had been assigned the task of ejecting the French from Fort Duquesne and blunting their thrust into the Ohio Valley. Washington rushed off a politic greeting to the general. After making inquiries, Braddock learned that Washington possessed an unmatched familiarity with the frontier. Whatever his misgivings about Washington's conduct at Fort Necessity, Braddock wanted him as an aide-de-camp. On March 2 Captain Robert Orme, a slim, dashing aide to the general, sent a letter to Mount Vernon, inviting Washington to join the general's personal staff. Judging from the latter's reply, it seems that his bruised feelings of the previous fall were quickly assuaged by the general's flattering attention. "To explain, sir," he wrote, "I wish earnestly to attain knowledge of the military profession," adding that no better chance could arise "than to serve under a gentleman of General Braddock's abilities and experience."[2]

Washington hinted that personal problems might hinder acceptance of the post. In fact, he was overwhelmed by the demands of planting his first spring crop at Mount Vernon and confided that the estate was "in the utmost confusion."[3] Aggravating matters was that he had nobody to whom he could entrust management of the place. As he contemplated service under Braddock, Washington struggled with his special bugaboo, the vexed matter of colonial rank. He still dreamed of a regular army commission, valid for life, but the best Braddock could award him was the temporary rank of brevet captain. Still balking at this demotion, Washington agreed to serve as a volunteer aide to Braddock, and the general, in turn, allowed him to devote time to his private affairs until the army headed west. To brother Jack, Washington explained that under this arrangement, he could "give his orders to all, which must be implicitly obeyed," while he had to obey only Braddock.[4] Already preoccupied with matters of honor and reputation, Washington feared that people might question his motives and suspect him of being a power-hungry opportunist—a recurring leitmotif of his career. Serving without pay would silence such potential naysayers. His sole desire, he told John Robinson, speaker of the House of Burgesses, was to serve his country: "This, I flatter myself, will manifestly appear by my going [as] a volunteer, without expectation of reward or prospect of attaining a command."[5] This theme of disinterested service—honored mostly in the breach when he was young and in the observance when he was older—would be one of the touchstones of his life.

To manage Mount Vernon in his absence, Washington wanted to recruit Jack, which sparked a family feud. Perhaps feeling bereft of family help at Ferry Farm, Mary Ball Washington arrived at Mount Vernon hell-bent upon preventing George from joining Braddock. George was supposed to meet with Captain Orme in Alexandria when Mary, appearing like the wrath of God, insisted upon settling her son's future plans on the spot. "The arrival of a good deal of company, among whom is my mother, alarmed at the report of my intentions to attend your fortunes, prevents me the pleasure of waiting upon you today as I had intended," George confessed to Orme.[6] This must have come as an extraordinary admission: Washington was canceling a vital military meeting to mollify his overwrought mother. As had happened when her son meditated going to sea, Mary had no qualms about thwarting his career for her own personal benefit. In the end, Jack Washington oversaw Mount Vernon, Ferry Farm, and the Bullskin Plantation for the next three years.

In early May, attended by his body servant, a Welshman named John Alton, George joined Braddock's army at Frederick, Maryland. At first, he didn't see much likelihood of a military engagement with the French and was there principally for career advancement. As he told Jack, he spotted a good chance "of forming an acquaintance which may be serviceable hereafter, if I shall find it worthwhile to push my fortune in the military line."[7] While Washington saw the cards stacked against him in the British military system, he warmed to the personal respect he received as a member of General Braddock's "family," or personal staff. He found a few other things to admire in the small, pudgy general with the long, sharp nose: a lack of pomp and ceremony in dealing with officers and physical courage in battle. "He was brave even to a fault and in regular service would have done honor to his profession," he was to write.[8]

At the same time, Braddock provided Washington with an object lesson in mistakes that any general should avoid, teaching him the virtues of patient moderation. Braddock was hotheaded and blustery, was blunt to the point of rudeness, and issued orders without first seeking proper advice. He also talked down to colonial governors "as if they had been infinitely his inferiors," said one observer, and was irate that the colonies failed to deliver two hundred wagons and 2,500 horses they had pledged.[9] Washington listened to Braddock drone on, spouting prejudiced views with a narrow-minded insistence. Once committed to an opinion, he refused to back down, "let it be ever so incompatible with reason or common sense," Washington noted.[10]

Schooled in European warfare, Braddock found it hard to adapt to the treacherous terrain of wilderness forests. As his army moved west, he wanted to level every hill and erect a bridge across each brook. Washington tried to impress upon him the improvisational tactics of the French and Indians, but the haughty general wouldn't deign to accept colonial advice. Benjamin Franklin also experienced firsthand Braddock's cocksure arrogance. When Franklin urged the general to beware of Indian ambushes, he retorted, "These savages may be a formidable enemy to your raw American militia, but upon the king's regular and disciplined troops, sir, it is impossible they would make any impression."[11] Braddock was deaf to Washington's argument that they should travel lightly across the steep mountains and rely on packhorses. Instead he relied upon cumbersome carriages that traversed mountain trails with difficulty, especially when transporting heavy siege guns.

In early May Washington wrote to his mother from the frontier town of Winchester. Probably because she had so hotly opposed his taking the post, he stressed his pleasure in serving on Braddock's staff: "I am very happy in the general's family, being treated with a complaisant freedom which is quite agreeable to me, and have no reason to doubt the satisfaction I hoped for in making the campaign."[12] Washington ended his formal note with the words, "I am Honored Madam Your most Dutiful and Obedient Son."[13] Mary Ball Washington had a knack for making unreasonable requests whenever her son went off on military campaigns, and she was known to say, "Ah, George had better have stayed at home and cultivated his farm."[14] The tacit accusation was always that he had deserted her for the military. She replied to George's letter by asking him to retain a Dutch servant for her and to buy her some butter. To this impossible request, George replied curtly that it wasn't in his power to get either the servant or the butter, "for we are quite out of that part of the country where either are to be had, there being few or no inhabitants where we now lie encamped and butter cannot be had here to supply the wants of the army."[15]

A far more pleasing distraction for Washington was his growing flirtation with Sally Fairfax, wife of his friend George William Fairfax. At the end of April, en route to linking up with Braddock's troops, Washington stopped by his Bullskin Plantation on the frontier and dashed off a letter to Sally that signaled a startling change in their relationship. Although he addressed the letter "To Mrs Fairfax— Dear Madam . . . ," he was clearly trying to deepen their intimacy, with nary a mention of George William. Washington promised that he would take "the earliest and every opportunity" of writing to her: "It will be needless to dwell on the pleasures that a correspondence of this kind would afford me."[16] This was an uncharacteristically bold and reckless move for Washington, who was playing with fire in seeking a private correspondence with a married woman, and a member of the toplofty Fairfax clan at that. Washington's dependence on that family was thrown into relief a week later when he wore out three horses and had to appeal to Lord Fairfax for an emergency loan of forty pounds for the forthcoming campaign.[17] The request, among other things, showed just how inappropriate it had been for Washington to volunteer his services, as if he were an independently wealthy man who could rise above petty monetary concerns.

When Braddock dispatched Washington to Williamsburg on an urgent mission to collect four thousand pounds, the latter made a detour to Belvoir to engage in some extemporaneous wooing. From a follow-up letter he sent to her, we can see that Sally was flirting with Washington, albeit within carefully prescribed limits. She told him to alert her to his safe arrival back at camp, but she also stipulated that he should communicate with her through a third party of her acquaintance—a clear sign that, at this point at least, she feared direct communication. To resort to this ruse, she must have regarded Washington's attention as something more than a mere schoolboy crush. Washington acknowledged her caution: "This I took as a gentle rebuke and polite manner of forbidding my corresponding with you and conceive this opinion is not illy founded when I reflect that I have hitherto found it impracticable to engage one moment of your attention." He ended by saying that he still hoped Sally would honor him "with a correspondence which you did once partly promise."[18] The coquettish Sally seemed to be feeding his amorous fantasies while simultaneously holding him rigidly at arm's length.

George Washington clearly had a much more active inner life than his reserved exterior might have suggested. In late May he confided to Jack his interest in obtaining a seat in the House of Burgesses. He said that he probably couldn't run in his home district because George William Fairfax might stand as a candidate, so he banked his hopes instead on Frederick County. His letter to Jack lays out in remarkable detail his canny political style, which served him well for the rest of his life. He instructed his brother to canvass the opinions of prominent men in the county "with[ou]t disclosing much of mine; as I know your own good sense can furnish you with means enough without letting it proceed immediately from me." If gentlemen seemed inclined to support him, "you then may declare my intentions and beg their assistance. If, on the contrary, you find them more inclined to favour some other, I w[oul]d have the affair entirely subside."[19] It is a highly revealing letter. Washington believed that ambitious men should hide their true selves, retreat into silence, and not tip people off to their ambition. To sound out people, you had to feign indifference and proceed only when convinced that they were sympathetic and like-minded. The objective was to learn the maximum about other people's thoughts while revealing the minimum about your own. Always fearful of failure, Washington wanted to push ahead only if he was armed with detailed knowledge and enjoyed a high likelihood of success. This cautious, disciplined political style would persist long after the original insecurity that had prompted it had disappeared.

As BRADDOCK AND HIS nearly three thousand men straggled toward Fort Cumberland (the former trading post at Wills Creek on the Potomac) in early June, the bullheaded general began to fathom the wisdom of Washington's advice to travel lightly across the mountainous territory. The pace of forward motion was so glacial, just two miles daily, that it seemed they would never penetrate to the Forks of the

Ohio. Braddock had insisted upon bringing along his complete artillery train and thousands of bushels of grain. Men and horses dropped dead from exertion as they crossed steep hills, and the frustrated Braddock, moody at the best of times, became increasingly testy. In this situation, he heeded Washington's advice and culled a division of eight hundred men to march ahead. With the French hourly strengthening their defenses at Fort Duquesne, time was now working against the British.

As it turned out, Washington could not pause to savor his influence, for he was "seized with violent fevers and pains in my head" in mid-June.[20] He proved the latest victim of an epidemic exacting a frightful toll on Braddock's forces: dysentery. This infection of the digestive system produces violent diarrhea, and Washington suffered cruelly from hemorrhoids. At first the stoic young aide tried to conceal the malady, but he soon found it so debilitating that he had to travel lying down in a covered wagon. On June 23 Braddock ordered him to accompany the slower-moving forces in the rear and gave him a patent medicine, Dr. James's Powder, which Washington pronounced "the most excellent medicine in the world."[21] (It consisted of phosphate of lime and oxide of antimony.) The young aide was so distraught at being left behind that Braddock solemnly pledged that he would be brought forward before Fort Duquesne was attacked. As Washington's condition worsened, he found it agonizing to lie in the wagon as it jolted along uneven country roads through impenetrable woods dubbed the "Shades of Death."[22] He told his brother on June 28 that he had barely enough energy to pen the letter and that a doctor had warned him that, if he persisted, he would risk his life.[23] Although the medicine helped Washington, his illness and frequent bleeding by doctors left him woefully depleted on the eve of a major battle. Even though he had recuperated sufficiently by July 8 to rejoin Braddock a dozen miles from Fort Duquesne, he was still so weak that when he mounted his horse the next morning, he had to strap on cushions to ease his painful hemorrhoids. He would require all the stamina he could muster for the extraordinary events in the offing.

Early on the morning of July 9, Braddock's advance force, which had grown to some fourteen hundred men, began to ford the Monongahela River in three groups. (The spot stands near present-day Braddock, Pennsylvania.) Each section was led by an officer who was to reappear in the American Revolution. The first party to cross was spearheaded by Lieutenant Colonel Thomas Gage, the son of a viscount and an officer much admired by young Washington. The second party was led by Captain Horatio Gates, said to be the illegitimate offspring of a duke's housekeeper. The last group to cross in the early afternoon was the five-hundred-man contingent led by Braddock himself, escorted by the weary Washington. All three groups crossed the river without the slightest intimation that a party of nine hundred soldiers from Fort Duquesne lay poised to attack on the other side.

As at Fort Necessity, the French and their Indian allies practiced a terrifying form of frontier warfare that unnerved the British. Letting loose a series of shrill, penetrating war whoops—"the terrific sound will haunt me till the hour of my dissolution," a shaken British soldier later said—the Indians swooped down suddenly and opened fire on the startled British.[24] Before British grenadiers could fire a retaliatory round, the enemy had melted nimbly into the woods. For a short interval, it seemed they had vanished. Then it became clear that they had split into two wings and encircled the British, releasing a hail of bullets from behind trees and well-protected elevated positions. The impressive miter caps of the grenadiers made them tall, conspicuous targets. In the rear with Braddock, Washington heard the ensuing panic, which he still couldn't see. The vanguard of British troops, he recollected, "were so disconcerted and confused" by the "unusual hallooing and whooping of the enemy" that they soon fell "into irretrievable disorder."[25] The British soldiers had never encountered this North American brand of fighting. "If we saw five or six [of the enemy] at one time," said one soldier, "it was a great sight and they [were] either on their bellies or behind trees or running from one tree to another almost by the ground."[26] Even as officers tried vainly to subdue the hysterical fears of their men, the latter threw down their muskets and fled helter-skelter. All the while, Indians scalped and plundered the British dead in what became a veritable charnel house by the river.

As Braddock and Washington rode toward this scene of helpless slaughter, panic-stricken redcoats streamed back toward them. After Braddock sent thirty men under Captain Thomas Waggener to climb a hillside and secure a high position, British troops fired at them in the smoky chaos under the mistaken assumption that they were French, while British officers fired at them thinking they were deserters. All thirty men under Captain Waggener were killed by French or British fire. For Washington, who had warned Braddock repeatedly about the unorthodox style of wilderness combat, the situation grimly fulfilled his worst premonitions. Braddock had clung to the European doctrine of compact fighting forces, forming his men into platoons, which made them easy prey for enemy marksmen. Washington now urged Braddock "before it was *too late* and the confusion became general" to allow him "to head the provincials and engage the enemy in their own way," Washington recalled years later. "But the propriety of it was not seen into until it was too late for execution."[27] Scholars have noted that Washington probably saw the superiority of Indian fighting methods much more clearly in retrospect than he had at the time.

Braddock handed Washington two directives: to send another party up the exposed hill and to retrieve two lost cannon. With exceptional pluck and coolheadedness, young George Washington was soon riding all over the battlefield.

Though he must have been exhausted, he kept going from sheer willpower and performed magnificently amid the horror. Because of his height, he presented a gigantic target on horseback, but again he displayed unblinking courage and a miraculous immunity in battle. When two horses were shot from under him, he dusted himself off and mounted the horses of dead riders. One account claimed that he was so spent from his recent illness that he had to be lifted onto his second charger. By the end, despite four bullets having torn through his hat and uniform, he managed to emerge unscathed.

One close observer of Washington's heroism was a young doctor and future friend, James Craik. Handsome, blue-eyed, and urbane, Dr. Craik had studied medicine in Edinburgh and was the illegitimate son of a wealthy man in western Scotland. He watched Washington's exceptional performance that day with unstinting admiration: "I expected every moment to see him fall. His duty and station exposed him to every danger. Nothing but the superintending care of Providence could have saved him from the fate of all around him."[28]

Even before the battle, Washington had suffered his fill of British condescension from Braddock. Now he was further embittered by his conviction that the Virginians had fought courageously and died in droves, while British regulars had fled to save their skins. "The Virginians behaved like men and died like soldiers," he insisted to Dinwiddie. By contrast, "the dastardly behavior of the English soldiers exposed all those who were inclined to do their duty to almost certain death . . . at length, in despite of every effort to the contrary, [they] broke and run as sheep before the hounds . . . And when we endeavored to rally them in hopes of regaining our invaluable loss, it was with as much success as if we had attempted to have stopped the wild bears of the mountains."[29]

So many intrepid British officers were killed or wounded—nearly two-thirds of the total—that it led to a complete collapse of the command structure. Among the wounded were Braddock's two other aides-de-camp. When Braddock was felled by a bullet that slashed through his arm and pierced his lung, only Washington was left to tend him. Braddock had fought with more valor than wisdom, having four horses shot from under him. Washington stretched out the general in a small cart and shepherded him back across the Monongahela. Henceforth Washington received orders from an intermittently lucid Braddock who lay groaning on a stretcher. "I was the only person then left to distribute the general's orders," Washington said, explaining that it was difficult to do so because of his own "weak and feeble condition."[30]

One order required Washington to relay a message to a Colonel Dunbar, whose division lay forty miles in the rear, to come forward with supplies, medication, and wagons to assist the moaning legions of wounded soldiers. By now Washington had been on horseback for twelve excruciating hours, yet he gathered up the energy to ride all night and execute Braddock's command. Thirty years later the horror of that night—the black woods, the ghastly cacophony of sounds, the unspeakable heaps of corpses—was still engraved on his memory. "The shocking scenes which presented themselves in this night's march are not to be described," he said. "The dead—the dying—the groans—lamentations—and cries along the road of the wounded for help . . . were enough to pierce a heart of adamant."[31] At this point, the fatigue experienced by the sleepless Washington must have been intolerable.

By his reckoning, three hundred soldiers died on the British side, with another three hundred wounded (the true number likely approached one thousand casualties); at least two-thirds, he thought, had been victims of friendly fire. He fulminated against the British soldiers as "cowardly regulars" who had shot down the men ahead of them, even if they happened to be comrades, and was outraged that the British had been routed by an inferior enemy force of nine hundred men.[32] "We have been most scandalously beaten by a trifling body of men," he complained to brother Jack.[33] In comparison, French and Indian casualties—twenty-three dead and sixteen wounded—were minuscule.

On the night of July 13, a shattered Braddock lay dying two miles from the Great Meadows, when he said memorably of his shocking defeat, "Who would have thought it?"[34] He praised his officers even as he damned his men, saying that "nothing could equal the gallantry and good conduct of the officers nor the bad behavior of the men."[35] Braddock displayed high regard for Washington and recommended that his body servant, Thomas Bishop, find future employment with him. He also gave the young Virginian a red silk sash and a pair of pistols that the younger man always treasured. Washington oversaw Braddock's burial, a task that fell to him by default as the only officer left standing to issue orders. After his men dug a trench in the road and lowered the blanket-wrapped body, Washington held an impromptu Anglican service by torchlight. Afraid that Indians might unearth the body and desecrate it, Washington had his wagons ride repeatedly over the grave to hide the freshly turned earth and "guard against a savage triumph . . . thus died a man whose good and bad qualities were intimately blended," he wrote.[36] This stratagem worked, and the French and Indians never located Braddock's grave.

One suspects that Washington knew that his fond hope of a Royal Army commission had been buried along with the general. The following year Dinwiddie speculated that if Braddock had survived, "I believe he would have provided handsomely for [Washington] in the regulars."[37] Nonetheless Washington's reputation grew in defeat. As he trotted homeward in late July, clutching his bullet-riddled hat as a battle souvenir, he knew that his well-publicized bravery had enhanced his image in the colonies. The governor of North Carolina congratulated the twenty-three-year-old "on your late escape and the immortal honor you have gained on the banks of [the] Ohio."[38] An admiring correspondent in Philadelphia informed him that Benjamin Franklin had paid tribute to his heroism and that "everybody seems willing to venture under your command."[39]

Perhaps the most gratifying response came from the rich, adoring family at Belvoir. The young war hero was lionized by William Fairfax, while Sally Fairfax sent him a sweet bantering note, cautiously cosigned by two friends, that chided him for not rushing to see her. "After thanking heaven for your safe return, I must accuse you of great unkindness in refusing us the pleasure of seeing you this night," she wrote. "I do assure you nothing but our being satisfied that our company would be disagreeable should prevent us from trying if our legs would not carry us to Mount Vernon this night. But if you will not come to us, tomorrow morning very early, we shall be at Mount Vernon."[40] An unabashed affection for Washington emerges from these Fairfax missives. Much more than merely a young favorite, he had been virtually adopted by the family, which expected great things from him.

In Braddock's crushing defeat, Washington had established an indelible image as a fearless young soldier who never flinched from danger and enjoyed a special intimacy with death. He had dodged so many bullets that he might have suspected he would escape the ancestral curse of his short-lived family. To Jack, Washington speculated that he was still alive "by the miraculous care of Providence that protected me beyond all human expectation. I had 4 bullets through my coat and two horses shot under and yet escaped unhurt."[41] In a stupendous stroke of prophecy, a Presbyterian minister, Samuel Davies, predicted that the "heroic youth Col. Washington" was being groomed by God for higher things. "I cannot but hope Providence has hitherto preserved [him] in so signal a manner for some important service to his country."[42]

Washington's derring-do even fostered a lasting mystique among the Indians. A folk belief existed among some North American tribes that certain warriors enjoyed supernatural protection from death in battle, and this mythic stature was projected onto Washington. Fifteen years later he encountered an Indian chief who distinctly recalled seeing him at the battle by the Monongahela and told how he had ordered his warriors, without success, to fire directly at him. The chief had concluded that some great spirit would guide him to momentous things in the future.

Perhaps the most enduring influence of Braddock's defeat was the altered colonial view of British power, formerly deemed to be invincible. "This whole transaction gave us the first suspicion that our exalted ideas of the prowess of British regular troops had not been well founded," said Benjamin Franklin.[43] Although Braddock had led the biggest British force ever to undertake an operation in the colonies, it had ended in a resounding failure. Washington had witnessed something hitherto unthinkable for loyal colonials: the British Empire could be defeated on a distant continent. For all of Braddock's derision of colonial troops, they had shown much more courage than the vaunted British regulars. It had been trained British soldiers who all too often had killed their brethren with misplaced fire. Washington was still imbued with the professional standards of the British military, but he had been exposed to the forest warfare perfected by their adversaries and had learned lasting lessons. One report published after the battle told of Washington urging Braddock to split up his troops while the general "obstinately persisted in the form of a field battle, his men standing shoulder to shoulder."[44] Braddock's defeat spawned a new awareness of the futility of European military practices on American soil, which later emboldened Washington and other colonists to believe that a ramshackle army of rough frontiersmen could defeat the world's foremost military machine.

CHAPTER SIX

The Soul of an Army

THE DISGRACEFUL DEFEAT of Edward Braddock exposed the vulnerability of western Virginia to attack. Every time the Indians staged a raid in the Shenandoah Valley, terrified British settlers streamed back across the Blue Ridge Mountains to the safety of older settlements. By mid-August 1755, the assembly in Williamsburg voted forty thousand pounds to protect the colony from such threats, and Washington's name was bandied about as the favored candidate to command a newly reconstituted Virginia Regiment. Evidently the mere prospect that Washington might be appointed elicited stiff resistance from Mary Washington, for George sent her a terse note, justifying his impending decision and holding his blazing temper in check, if barely. After his customary "Honored Madam," he went on: "If it is in my power to avoid going to the Ohio again, I shall. But [if] the command is pressed upon me by the general voice of the country and offered upon such terms as can't be objected against, it would reflect dishonour upon me to refuse it and that, I am sure, must, or ought, to give you greater cause of uneasiness than my going in an honourable com[man]d."[1] One notes the pointed rebuke tucked into that word "ought." Everyone in the colony seemed to cheer on George Washington as a bona fide hero except his own mother.

The same day Washington wrote to his mother—one suspects he already knew of his appointment—Governor Dinwiddie offered to make Washington, twenty-three, not only the colonel in charge of the Virginia Regiment but the supreme commander of all military forces in Virginia. In a measure of Washington's growing self-confidence, he bargained aggressively for a better deal, including the power to name field officers and recruit soldiers, plus an expense account of one hundred pounds yearly. As would be apparent later on, Washington was always reluctant to assume responsibility without the requisite powers to acquit himself honorably. As he put it, "No person who regards his character will undertake a command without the means of preserving it, since his conduct is culpable for all misfortunes and never right but when successful."[2] His hesitation at this moment of meteoric ascent also banished any appearance of an unseemly rush to power. Developing a mature instinct for power, Washington began to appreciate the value of diffidence, cultivating the astute politician's capacity to be the master of events while seeming to be their humble servant. Two weeks later, on August 31, 1755, a decent interval having elapsed, George Washington agreed to become commander in chief of all forces raised in Virginia. He was to remain extremely proud that the Virginia Regiment was the first to see service during the French and Indian War, a conflict not yet officially declared at the time of Braddock's defeat.

Determined to look every inch the new commander, Washington opened an account with a London agent to purchase clothing and other luxury goods. He selected a merchant named Richard Washington, mistakenly believing they were related, and told him, "I should be glad to cultivate the most intimate correspondence with you."[3] To defray his expenses, he sent ahead three hogsheads of tobacco. Washington was launching a new role as a country squire, seeking a social standing commensurate with his newfound military renown. He also took his first step to buy on credit, providing a bill of exchange to cover shortfalls in his account.

Among his first purchases, Washington ordered ruffles, silk stockings, and gold and scarlet sword knots to complete his elegant costume as commander. He had already sketched out uniforms for his officers, telling them in vivid terms what they should don: blue coats with scarlet cuffs and facings, scarlet waistcoats trimmed with silver lace, and "every one to provide himself with a silver-laced hat of a fashionable size."[4] From London, Washington also ordered two handsome livery suits, emblazoned with his coat of arms, for his servants. In several details, including the scarlet waistcoats and silver-laced hats, the livery suits matched the officers' uniforms, making it clear that Washington planned to ride about in high style, accompanied by fancily dressed servants and soldiers.

As chief of the Virginia Regiment, Washington confronted an awesome task, having to police a frontier 350 miles long against "the cruel incursions of a crafty, savage enemy," as he put it.[5] He had to supervise fifty officers and a few hundred men and groused about "indolent" officers and "insolent" soldiers.[6] As regimental commander, Washington received a comprehensive education in military skills, running the gamut from building barracks to arbitrating pay disputes. As he supervised every aspect of his operation, his phenomenal capacity for detail became apparent. A young man with a mission, Washington wanted to prove that he could transform colonial recruits into buffed and polished professionals on a par with anything England could muster. As always, he worked assiduously at self-improvement, perusing Humphrey Bland's *A Treatise of Military Discipline,* a manual popular in the British Army.

As he set up camp at Fort Dinwiddie on the western frontier, Washington ran into such a chaotic situation that he threatened to resign less than two months after taking the post. He told Dinwiddie that he couldn't commandeer a single horse in the area without threatening the inhabitants. The House of Burgesses had exempted property owners from the draft, leaving poor men to bear the common burden. Washington had a dreadful time raising troops in this rough, brawling area, where settlers resented coercive recruiting methods. In one letter, he gave a sharp tongue-lashing to a recruiting officer who had resorted to terror to collar men, chiding him for "forcibly taking, confining and torturing those who would not voluntarily enlist" and noting that this "not only cast a slur upon your own character, but reflect[ed] dishonour upon mine."[7] Despite such warnings, Washington inspired considerable fear in the region, although he vowed to Dinwiddie that he would persevere until the inhabitants "execute what they threaten, i.e. 'to blow out my brains.'"[8] When one captain informed Washington that, contrary to regimental rules, his company included two blacks and two mulattoes, the short-handed Washington allowed them to remain in an auxiliary capacity.

Once herded into service, the men deserted in droves, taking clothing and arms with them. Washington responded by clapping deserters into chains, throwing them into a "dark room," and flogging them vigorously. The only way to avert costly desertions, Washington avowed, was to "terrify the soldiers from such practices."[9] In October 1755 he and Dinwiddie lobbied the Virginia assembly for a bill to permit the death sentence for mutiny, desertion, and willful disobedience. Although Washington wasn't a martinet, neither was he squeamish about meting out harsh punishment. His policy was to be tough but scrupulously fair, and his inflexible sense of justice didn't shrink from applying lashes to deserters. In 1756 he decreed the death penalty for one Henry Campbell, whom he labeled "a most atrocious villain" who "richly merits an ignominious death."[10] Campbell had not only deserted but encouraged seven others to do so. Washington made a point of hanging people in public to deter others. His frontier experience only darkened his view of human nature, and he saw people as motivated more by force than by kindness. "Lenity, so far from producing its desired effects, rather emboldens them in these villainous undertakings," he told Dinwiddie.[11] Washington's methods, seemingly cruel to modern eyes, were standard practice in the British Army of his day.

Washington remained a stickler for discipline, which he identified as "the soul of an army," and he encouraged military discipline even in private matters.[12] Scornful of Virginia's licentious culture of gambling, whoring, and drinking, which was especially disruptive in an army, he set down strict moral standards for his men, and his use of corporal punishment gradually expanded. Unwilling to tolerate swearing, he warned that offenders would receive twenty-five lashes for uttering an oath, with more severe punishment reserved for second offenses. He was so upset by men "incessantly drunk and unfit for service" that he ordered fifty lashes for any man caught drinking in Winchester gin shops.[13] As an antidote to such behavior, Washington lobbied for the appointment of a regimental chaplain. "Common decency, sir, in a camp calls for the services of a divine," Washington informed the Governor's Council, stating that such an appointment "ought not to be dispensed with, although the *world* should be so uncharitable as to think us void of religion and incapable of good instructions."[14]

With a sovereign faith in leadership by example, Washington believed that courage and cowardice originated from the top of an army. As he wrote during the American Revolution: "This is the true secret . . . that wherever a regiment is well officered, the men have behaved well—when otherwise, ill—the [misconduct] or cowardly behavior always originating with the officers, who have set the example."[15] Like his mother, Washington tended to stint on praise, reflecting his stoic belief that officers didn't need encouragement since they were simply doing their duty. When he offered praise, he was careful to direct it not at individuals, but at the regiment as a whole.

In his correspondence at the time, Washington comes across as a young man who couldn't step back, laugh at himself, or leaven responsibility with humor. Nevertheless he proved popular among his officers, who valued his courage, dignity, and even-handed treatment. "Our colonel is an example of fortitude in either danger or hardships and by his easy, polite behavior has gained not only the regard but affection of both officers and soldiers," wrote one officer.[16] At the same time Washington's code of leadership stipulated that, for maximum effect, the commander should be cordial but not too familiar, producing respect instead of affection. As one writer later summed up this strategy: "Power required distance, he seems to have reasoned, familiarity and intimacy eroded it."[17] This view of leadership unfortunately had a way of distancing Washington from his subordinates and preventing relaxed camaraderie.

From a strategic standpoint, Washington was frustrated by the wartime role that the assembly had assigned to his regiment. While he advocated an offensive posture to end frontier raids by marching on Fort Duquesne, the assembly opted for a purely defensive stance, creating a string of frontier outposts. This, Washington noted cynically, was done "more with a view to quiet the fears of the inhabitants than from any expectation of giving security on so extensive a line to the settlements."[18] It thrust him into the untenable position of combating raids that never ended. In the meantime, the British shifted the major focus of the war to Canada and points north, leaving the Ohio Valley as a sideshow. This experience of being set up for failure, as he saw it, haunted Washington for the rest of his life.

While Washington was suffering from notoriety caused by tough recruiting methods, he stood for election to the House of Burgesses in Frederick County, which included Winchester. He was qualified to run there because his Bullskin Plantation lay in the region. Later in his career, the word *defeat* never appeared in the Washington lexicon, but he took a sound drubbing in this first election. His friends entered his name at the last minute, which may account for his poor show-ing. Already interested in running for office, Washington may not have known that his friends had placed him in contention. At the time it was thought unseemly for candidates to engage in electioneering, so they relied on proxies, professing all the while a saintly indifference to power. Luckily for Washington, the age frowned upon direct, backslapping politics, which would never have suited his reticent style.

At the time there were no secret ballots. While an open voting system was thought to prevent corruption, it enhanced the power of landowners who could personally monitor how their tenants voted. Voters stepped forward to announce their votes, which were then recorded by clerks seated at a table. At the election in Winchester on December 10, 1755, Washington was crushed by his two opponents; Hugh West re-ceived 271 votes, Thomas Swearingen 270, and Washington a mere 40. His friend and fellow officer Adam Stephen tried to soften the blow by blaming his eleventh-hour entry into the race. "I think your poll was not despicable, as the people were a stranger [to] your purpose until the election began," he wrote.[19] For future use, Washington pocketed a sheet with the voting tally, as if resolved to fare better next time.

As we recall, Washington had refrained from standing for election in Fairfax County because it would have pitted him against George William Fairfax, Sally's husband. According to legend, Washington attended the Fairfax County election and ended up in a heated exchange about George William with one William Payne, who favored an opposing candidate. Their confrontation grew so angry that Payne struck Washington with a stick, knocking him to the ground. When Washington got to his feet, he had to be restrained from assaulting Payne. In the prevalent honor culture of the day, Washington might have been expected to issue an invitation to a duel. Instead, he sent Payne an apology forthwith. Whether true or apocryphal, the story squares with the fact that Washington never fought a duel and usually tried to harmonize differences after even the most withering arguments.

FROM HIS LOFTY PERCH atop the Virginia Regiment, Washington kept bucking for a royal commission. His frustration crested in late 1755, when he clashed with a man named John Dagworthy at Fort Cumberland on the Maryland frontier. As a colonial captain from Maryland, Dagworthy held a rank that seemed inferior to Washington's, but he claimed superior authority based on an old royal commission. Writing to Dinwiddie, Washington threatened to resign if he had to truckle to the hated Dagworthy. Dinwiddie appealed to Governor William Shirley of Massachusetts, a barrister who had succeeded Braddock as supreme commander of British forces in North America. Aiming at deeper institutional change, Washington also wanted Shirley to absorb his regiment into the regular British Army, removing the two-tiered system that had bedeviled him. Governor Dinwiddie granted him permission to travel to Boston so that he could confront Shirley in person. When he set off for Boston in February 1756, Washington was accompanied by two aides and two slaves who sported the fine livery custom-made in London. In Philadelphia the young colonel, very dashing in his blue regimentals, enjoyed his first taste of a northern city and embarked on a shopping spree for clothing, hats, jewelry, and saddles. He was pleased by the clean, well-ordered town, which a friend was to tout to him as the peaceful home "of many nations and religions," while expressing admiration for "that great man Mr. Penn."[20] Christopher Gist had already notified him that his fame had spread to the city. "Your name is more talked of in Philadelphia than that of any other person in the army," he had written the previous fall.[21]

In New York, Washington socialized with his friend Beverley Robinson, son of the powerful speaker of the Virginia House of Burgesses, and he may have entered into a romantic dalliance with Robinson's sister-in-law, Mary "Polly" Philipse. The twenty-six-year-old Polly would have been a prime catch for an upwardly mobile young man: she was slim, dark-haired, beautiful, and heiress to a colossal fortune. Unsubstantiated legend claims that Washington proposed marriage; if so, he lost out to Major Roger Morris, son of an English architect, who had fought with Washington at Braddock's defeat.

By the time he moved on to Boston, Washington's triumphal journey attracted considerable interest. When he arrived, the *Boston Gazette* saluted him as "the Hon. Colonel Washington, a gentleman who has deservedly a high reputation of military skill, integrity, and valor, though success has not always attended his undertakings."[22] Aside from Washington's military renown, Governor Shirley may have had sentimental reasons for seeing him: his son had also acted as an aide to Braddock and was killed during the campaign. In presenting his grievances to the governor on March 5, 1756, Washington met with only mixed success. Although Shirley confirmed that he possessed superior rank to Dagworthy, he wouldn't budge on other matters and rebuffed a petition signed by Washington's officers for inclusion in the royal establishment. He also disappointed his young visitor by appointing Governor Sharpe of Maryland to lead the next campaign against Fort Duquesne—a military honor about which young George Washington already harbored a rich fund of fantasies. On his way home, the disappointed colonel stopped to confer with Sharpe, an interview that left him so dispirited that he "fully re-solved to resign my commission."[23] Upon arriving in Williamsburg, he was some-what assuaged by news that the assembly had decided to expand Virginia's forces to fifteen hundred men.

In these dealings with powerful older men, Washington hadn't yet developed the tact that would distinguish him in later life, and given his age, he seemed to bristle unduly at being assigned a subordinate position. His emotions were still raw, and he exhibited a naked, sometimes clumsy ambition that he later learned to cloak or conquer. This young careerist brooded interminably over the discrimina-tion leveled against colonial officers and betrayed a heightened sense of personal injustice—feelings that would assume a more impressive and impersonal ideologi-cal form during the American Revolution. Nevertheless there was a gravitas about the young Washington, a seriousness of purpose and a fierce determination to suc-ceed, that made him stand out in any crowd.

As soon as Washington returned to Winchester in early April, he confronted a fresh crisis. Indians had sacked so many settlements and slain so many inhabitants that the dazed surviving families looked to Washington as their savior. At first he could barely scrape up a few dozen men to mount a spirited defense and despaired of waging an equal battle with the Indians, telling Governor Dinwiddie that "the cunning and craft" of the Indians "are not to be equalled . . . They prowl about like wolves and, like them, do their mischief by stealth." He despaired of fighting them upon equal terms.[24] Feeling embattled, Washington issued a plea for intercolonial union that foreshadowed his later stress on national unity. "Nothing I more sin-cerely wish than a union to the colonies in this time of eminent danger," he told Pennsylvania governor Robert Hunter Morris.[25]

Even as a young man, the complex Washington seldom had a single reason for his actions. His pursuit of self-interest and selfless dedication to public service were often intermingled, sometimes making it hard to disentangle his true motives. Per-haps for this reason, he could always discern both the base and the noble sides of human nature. For Washington, the French and Indian War presented few elevating ideas beyond the moral superiority of the British side. Nevertheless, his indigna-tion about the savagery he purported to see practiced by his French and Indian foes seems heartfelt. He began to view himself as the self-styled champion of the backwoods people and was moved by their piteous plight. In a remarkable letter to Robert Dinwiddie on April 22, 1756, he made an impassioned statement about the murder of frontier families and his desire to alleviate their suffering.

> I am too little acquainted, sir, with pathetic language to attempt a description of the
> people's distresses, though I have a generous soul, sensible of wrongs and swelling
> for redress. But what can I do? If bleeding, dying! would glut their insatiate revenge,
> I would be a willing offering to savage fury and die by inches to save a people! I *see*
> their situation, *know* their danger, and participate [in] their *sufferings* without hav-
> ing it in my power to give them further relief than uncertain promises . . . The sup-
> plicating tears of the women and moving petitions from the men melt me into such
> deadly sorrow that I solemnly declare . . . I could offer myself a willing sacrifice to the
> butchering enemy, provided that would contribute to the people's ease.[26]

Here one can sense a flood of deep feeling welling up beneath the surface of Washington's tightly buttoned personality. A spark of idealism began to flicker intermittently through his sulking about his personal status—a spark that would someday
flare into a bright flame.

Faced with Indian raids that depopulated whole settlements, Dinwiddie issued
orders calling up the militia in western counties, and Washington suddenly found
himself at the head of a thousand temporary recruits who bridled at their treatment by highborn officers. Reflecting this resentment, the *Virginia Gazette* blasted
Washington's officers as "rank novices, rakes, spendthrifts, and bankrupts" who
"browbeat and discouraged" the militia and gave them "an example of all manner of debauchery, vice, and idleness."[27] Livid over this bad publicity, Washington
informed Dinwiddie of numerous warnings he had issued about these vices and
promised to "act with a little more rigor than has hitherto been practiced, since I
find it so absolutely necessary."[28] Washington presented the strange spectacle of a
young man chastising dissolute behavior, and Dinwiddie stood solidly behind him.
"He is a person much beloved here and has gone through many hardships in the
service and I really think he has great merit."[29]

Throughout the spring, Washington squawked about the fickle militia, who
disappeared whenever an Indian threat materialized. Apparently concerned by the
moods of his temperamental protégé, Colonel William Fairfax preached a stoic
calm in the face of adversity and wrote two letters invoking the military heroes of
antiquity. "Your good health and fortune is the toast of every table," he reassured
Washington. "Among the Romans such a general acclamation and public regard
shown to any of their chieftains was always esteemed a high honor and gratefully
accepted." Holding up Caesar and Alexander the Great as models to emulate, Fairfax said that Washington shouldn't be disturbed by unreliable militia but should
bear such hardships "with equal magnanimity [as] those heroes remarkably did."[30]

IN MID-AUGUST, Colonel Washington staged a small pageant in Winchester to mark the official start of the French and Indian War, announced in London three months earlier. Escorted by town worthies, he marched three companies to the parade ground and read aloud the declaration of war, urging his men to show "willing obedience to the best of kings and by a strict attachment to his royal commands [to] demonstrate the love and loyalty we bear to his sacred person."[31] With that, numerous toasts were drunk and muskets boomed. Nevertheless the absolute power of distant bureaucrats in London preyed on Washington's mind. Three weeks earlier he had conveyed greetings to John Campbell, Earl of Loudoun, the new commander of His Majesty's forces in North America. No longer a military novice, Washington touted himself as a war veteran and seasoned his welcome with self-promotion: "We humbly represent to your Lordship that we were the first troops in action on the continent on [the] occasion of the present broils and that by several engagements and continual skirmishes with the enemy, we have to our cost acquired a knowledge of them and of their crafty and cruel practices."[32]

Eager to please his new commander, Washington struggled to make his new recruits presentable. He had long been troubled by an inability to clothe them, but in March he procured for each man "a suit of thin sleazy cloth without lining" and some waistcoats of "sorry flannel."[33] No sooner had he accomplished this than he found men selling the miserable clothing he had obtained. Indignant, he threatened them with five hundred lashes. Where his men had once deserted two or three at a time, sixteen absconded into the woods in August, and the shortage of men grew more perilous. When a portion of the Augusta County militia was summoned to duty that October, fewer than a tenth even bothered to show up. From these early experiences, Washington came to believe devoutly in the need for rigorously trained, professional armies rather than hastily summoned, short-term militia.

All summer and fall Washington was exasperated by military arrangements on the western frontier. He objected in strenuous terms to Lord Loudoun's decision in early December to station Virginia troops at Fort Cumberland in Maryland, when it made more sense to keep them at Winchester, Virginia. Washington's tenacity on this issue led to a clash with Dinwiddie, who sided with Loudoun. Until this point Washington had prudently tended his relationship with the royal governor and was exemplary in bowing to civilian control. Now, in a terribly impolitic move, he bypassed Dinwiddie to lobby House of Burgesses speaker John Robinson, violating a cardinal rule of Virginia politics that the governor had final authority in such matters. The decision also smacked of disloyalty to someone who had consistently boosted Washington's career. The young man poured out his frustrations to Robinson, saying his advice to Dinwiddie had been "disregarded as idle and frivolous . . . My orders [from Dinwiddie] are dark, doubtful and uncertain: *today ap-*

proved, tomorrow condemned."[34] The same day Washington aggravated matters by telling Dinwiddie that Loudoun had "imbibed prejudices so unfavourable to my character" because he had not been "thoroughly informed."[35] Since Dinwiddie had been Loudoun's primary source of information, he would have interpreted this as a direct attack on his own conduct.

On January 10, 1757, throwing caution to the wind, Washington sent Lord Loudoun a letter so lengthy that it runs to a dozen printed pages in his collected papers. It provides a graphic picture of the twenty-four-year-old Washington's ambivalence about the British class system. On the one hand, he flattered Loudoun unctuously even as he denied doing so. "Although I have not the honour to be known to Your Lordship, yet Your Lordship's name was familiar to my ear on account of the important services performed to His Majesty in other parts of the world. Don't think My Lord I am going to flatter. I have exalted sentiments of Your Lordship's character and revere your rank . . . my nature is honest and free from guile."[36]

Washington then brashly declared his impatience with "chimney corner politicians" in Williamsburg and cited his failure to win a well-merited promotion in the British Army.[37] "In regard to myself, I must beg leave to say [that,] had His Excellency General Braddock survived his unfortunate defeat, I should have met with preferment equal to my wishes. I had his promise to that purpose."[38] Washington also mentioned that, after their brave stand at Fort Necessity, his men had expected inclusion in the regular British Army. In sending this letter, Washington knew that he had overstepped political boundaries and confessed in closing, "When I look over the preceding pages and find how far I have exceeded my first intention, I blush with shame to think of my freedom."[39]

Driven by thwarted ambition, the still-gauche Washington resolved to advise Loudoun in person and prevailed upon Dinwiddie to allow him to go to Philadelphia to consult with him. The governors of five colonies flocked there to see him too, but Lord Loudoun, a haughty Scot with a reputation as a martinet, was in no special hurry to see anyone, forcing Washington to cool his heels for six weeks. From an aide to Loudoun, Washington learned that the general had admired his long letter, but when he met with him, the commander seemed deaf to his opinions. It was clear that Virginia had been assigned a secondary importance in imperial war strategy and that any assault on Fort Duquesne had been postponed. The only victory that Washington could claim was Loudoun's decision that Maryland would take responsibility for Fort Cumberland, freeing the Virginia Regiment to man Virginia forts.

Before leaving Philadelphia, Washington wrote to Dinwiddie and vented his bitter outrage at the inferior status foisted upon the Virginia Regiment: "We can't conceive that being Americans should deprive us of the benefits of British subjects, nor lessen our claim to preferment. And we are very certain that no body of regular troops ever before served 3 bloody campaigns without attracting royal notice. As to those idle arguments which are often times used—namely, 'You are defending your own properties'—I look upon [them] to be whimsical and absurd. We are defending the King's Dominions."[40] This statement represented a huge intellectual leap: Washington was suddenly asserting that the imperial system existed to serve the king, not his overseas subjects. The equality of an Englishman in London and one in Williamsburg was purely illusory. In time, the Crown would pay dearly for Washington's disenchantment with the fairness of the British military.

When the bruised young colonel returned to Winchester—the "cold and barren frontiers," as he called them—he applauded one development: several hundred Catawba and Cherokee Indians had enlisted on the British side for the first time since the Fort Necessity debacle, an alliance that promptly embroiled Washington in a ghoulish commerce.[41] The Virginia assembly had agreed to pay the Indians ten pounds for every enemy scalp they brought into camp. When a party of Cherokees arrived bearing four scalps and two prisoners, Washington hadn't yet received the necessary gifts to reward them. "They are much dissatisfied that the presents are not here," he told Dinwiddie, labeling these new Indian allies "the most insolent, most avaricious, and most dissatisfied wretches I have ever had to deal with."[42] The Indians were about to terminate the alliance, when the gifts belatedly arrived.

During this humiliating period, Washington often felt helpless in dealing with his men. Despite being threatened with punishment, more than a quarter of new recruits deserted, and Washington's personal grievances fueled his rage at them. When a thousand lashes didn't stop the desertions, he upped the penalty to a draconian fifteen hundred lashes. The historian Fred Anderson has estimated that Washington administered an average of six hundred lashes in each flogging, putting him on a par with his most severe British counterparts.[43] With icy determination, he even constructed a gibbet tall enough to instill terror in anybody contemplating desertion. "I have a gallows near 40 feet high erected (which has terrified the *rest* exceedingly) and I am determined . . . to hang two or three on it as an example to others," he informed one officer.[44]

That summer Washington decided to hang fourteen men for desertion. Fortunately, even as a young man he never acted heedlessly, and he gave way to second thoughts. Knowing his own nature, he let his temper cool. In the end, he pardoned twelve of the men—they had been kept "in a dark room, closely ironed"—and executed only two repeat offenders. "Your honor will, I hope, excuse my hanging instead of shooting them," Washington told Dinwiddie. "It conveyed much terror to others and it was for example['s] sake we did it."[45] It should be noted that, while Washington didn't balk at naked terror, he had already warned that recidivists would be hanged.

Throughout the summer Washington grew quarrelsome in correspondence with

Dinwiddie, believing that his former patron was now hostile to him and opposed the regular commission he pursued. Indeed, Dinwiddie's letters were often carping and demeaning in tone. The young officer felt at the mercy of an incompetent governor, who for his part felt powerless in dealing with Lord Loudoun and arbitrary instructions from London. The experience gave Washington new insight into the problem of being ruled by people overseas who were ignorant of local conditions.

He ventilated his dismay to his admirer, Speaker Robinson: "I am convinced it would give pleasure to the governor to hear that I was involved in trouble, however undeservedly."[46] Dinwiddie must have heard that Washington was talking behind his back, because he scolded him that September. "My conduct to yo[u] from the beginning was always friendly, but you know I had g[rea]t reason to suspect yo[u] of ingratitude, which, I'm convinced, your own conscience and reflection must allow I had reason to be angry. But this I endeavor to forget."[47] The reason that Dinwiddie endeavored to forget was that he was now ailing and had decided to return to England. Washington responded to his accusation with hot-tempered indignation: "I do not know that I ever gave your Honor cause to suspect me of ingratitude, a crime I detest, and would most carefully avoid."[48] In the younger man's view, he was merely guilty of speaking openly about policy errors imposed by the governor. The correspondence with Dinwiddie degenerated into petty bickering. When Washington asked for a leave of absence to visit Williamsburg, Dinwiddie scoffed that he had already been indulged with too many leaves. Washington returned a stinging retort: "It was not to enjoy a party of pleasure I wanted [a] leave of absence."[49] Washington lost his other principal backer that September when Colonel Fairfax died and he made the melancholy journey to Belvoir to attend the funeral.

DOUBTLESS DISTURBING HIM that fall was a recurrence of the "bloody flux," or dysentery, which had started around midsummer. The symptoms stole upon Washington so gradually that he functioned more or less normally at first. With his staunch commitment to work, he kept Governor Dinwiddie in the dark about his condition. Then in early November he felt the full brunt of the illness. As fellow officer Captain Robert Stewart described it, Washington was "seized with stitches and violent pleuritic pains . . . his strength and vigour diminished so fast that in a few days he was hardly able to walk."[50] After Dr. Craik examined him, he warned Washington that his life was endangered and chided him for not seeking treatment sooner, saying that "your disorder hath been of long standing and hath corrupted the whole mass of blood. It will require some time to remove the cause."[51] Craik bled Washington several times, which only weakened him further. The doctor prescribed rest, fresh air, and water as offering Washington the best chance for recovery. His iron constitution having broken down, he relinquished command to Captain Stewart and set out for home.

Once at Mount Vernon in mid-November, he consulted Dr. Charles Green of Alexandria, who forbade him to eat meats and prescribed a diet of jellies and other soft foods, lubricated with tea or sweet wine. With a lifelong bias against medication, Washington preferred to let illness take its course. At first his sister (or possibly sister-in-law) came to nurse him, but when she left and he looked attractively helpless, he attempted to lure Sally Fairfax to his bedside. In a note, he asked if he could borrow a book of recipes to prepare jellies, noting that "my sister is from home and I have no person that has been used to making these kind of things and no directions."[52] It seems probable that Sally rose to the bait.

Every time Washington seemed to gain ground, the disease recurred with a vengeance. With some symptoms resembling tuberculosis, he grew terrified that he would follow in brother Lawrence's footsteps. In February he even had to deny reports of his death circulating in Williamsburg. "I have heard of letters from the dead, but never had the pleasure of receiving one till your agreeable favor came to hand the other day," his friend Robert Carter Nicholas told him wryly. "It was reported here that Colo. Washington was dead! As you are still alive, I must own myself obliged to the author of that report."[53] It said something about Washington's high standing in Virginia society that the capital hummed with these rumors. When he left for Williamsburg on February 1, he was soon overcome by fever and had to turn around and return home. The physicians again admonished Washington that he jeopardized his life by taking such a journey. On March 4 he described to Colonel John Stanwix the "great injury" already done to his constitution and the need for "the greatest care and most circumspect conduct" if he was to recover.[54] With only a slim chance of securing a regular army commission, the despondent Washington thought of "quitting my command and retiring from all public business, leaving my post to be filled by others more capable of the task."[55] The next day he left for Williamsburg, stopping en route to visit his mother. In the capital, Dr. John Amson assured him that his fears of consumption were unfounded and that he was indeed recuperating from the dysentery.

For someone with Washington's robust physique, the dysentery must have had a profound psychological effect. His body had suddenly lost the strength and resilience that had enabled him to cross freezing streams and ride through snowy forests. And it was not the first time he had experienced a sense of physical fragility. By the age of twenty-six, he had survived smallpox, pleurisy, malaria, and dysentery. He had not only evaded bullets but survived disease with astounding regularity. If these illnesses dimmed his fervor for a military commission, they may also have reminded him of the forgotten pleasures of domestic life.

CHAPTER SEVEN

A Votary to Love

AFTER HIS WOUNDING CONFRONTATIONS with the haughty agents of British imperial power—Dinwiddie, Shirley, and Loudoun—Washington could only have concluded that his dreams of a military career would always be foiled by deep-seated prejudice against colonial officers and that it made more sense to become an independent planter. While posted to the frontier in the summer of 1757, he daydreamed about Mount Vernon and compiled shopping lists of luxury goods to be shipped from London. Though he had never been to England, he tried to imitate the style of an English country gentleman, instructing Richard Washington that "whatever goods you may send me, where the prices are not absolutely limited, you will let them be fashionable, neat, and good in their several kinds."[1] The young man's social ambitions seemed boundless. He ordered a marble chimneypiece with a landscape painting above the mantel and "fine crimson and yellow papers" for the walls.[2] Such rich colors for wallpaper were then thought very fashionable. Though mahogany was an expensive imported wood, Washington opted for a mahogany bedstead and dining table and a dozen mahogany chairs. To entertain in regal style, he ordered a complete set of fine china, damask tablecloths and napkins, and silver cutlery whose handles bore the Washington crest—a griffin poised above a crown, set above an ornamental shield with three stars, the whole emblazoned with the Latin motto *Exitus Acta Probat* ("The outcome justifies the deed").[3] In his purchases, Washington instinctively trod the fine line between showiness and austerity, defining a characteristic style of understated elegance.

Mount Vernon would be George Washington's personality writ large, the cherished image he wished to project to the world. Had the estate not possessed profound personal meaning for him, he would never have lavished so much time and money on its improvement. It was Washington's fervent attachment to Mount Vernon, its rural beauties and tranquil pleasures, that made his later absences from home so exquisitely painful. He believed in the infinite perfectibility of Mount Vernon, as if it were a canvas that he could constantly retouch and expand. There he reigned supreme and felt secure as nowhere else.

In December 1757 he made his first additions to the property, buying two hundred acres at nearby Dogue Run and another three hundred acres on Little Hunting Creek. This proved the first wave of an expansion that would ultimately culminate in an eight-thousand-acre estate, divided into five separate farms. Since few professional architects existed at the time, Washington followed the custom of other Virginia planters and acted as his own architect. He worked from British architectural manuals, coupled with his own observation of buildings in Williamsburg and Annapolis. Drawing on popular classical elements, he melded ideas from various places and devised a synthesis uniquely his own.

In 1758 Washington doubled the size of the main house and began to convert Lawrence's farmhouse into an imposing mansion. He could have swept away the old foundations and started anew, making the house more symmetrical and architecturally satisfying. Instead, he built on top of earlier incarnations. Whether this stemmed from economy or family reverence is not known. But where Lawrence, a naval officer, had placed the entrance on the east side of the house, facing the water, George, an army officer and a western surveyor, switched the entrance to the west side, presenting an arresting view for visitors arriving by horse or carriage. First glimpsed from afar, the house would impress travelers with its grandeur. At this point, however, it was still boxy and unadorned and devoid of the elements that later distinguished it: the cupola, the piazza with the long colonnade, the formal pediment above the entrance. In a geometric pattern likely copied from Belvoir, Washington laid out a pair of rectangular gardens with brick walls in front of the house, allowing visitors to experience his magnificent grounds before alighting at his door. Washington also fleshed out the upstairs, making it a full floor, reworked most of the ground-floor rooms, and added a half-story attic, resulting in eight full rooms in all.

In 1758 Washington's aspirations still outstripped his means, and he resorted to ruses to make his abode seem more opulent. Unable to afford a stone house, he employed a method known as rusticated boards that created the illusion of a stone exterior. First plain pine boards were cut and beveled in a way that mimicked stone blocks. Then white sand from the Chesapeake Bay was mingled with white paint, which lent the painted wood the rough, granular surface of stone. In many respects, Mount Vernon is a masterpiece of trompe l'oeil. Washington used another sleight of hand on his study walls, a technique called "graining" that transformed cheap, locally available woods, such as southern yellow pine or tulip poplar, into something resembling expensive imported hardwoods, such as mahogany or black walnut.

Mount Vernon's history is inseparable from that of its resident slaves, who toiled in its shadows and shaped every inch of it. The mansion renovation absorbed a vast amount of human labor: sixteen thousand bricks were forged for two new chimneys that arose at either end of the house, and slaves scoured nearby woods for the white oak that underlay roof shingles. For more specialized work, Washington typically hired a white craftsman or indentured servant to supervise skilled slaves as assistants. By the late 1750s Washington had assembled an expert team of seven slave carpenters. During the remodeling, overseer Humphrey Knight assured Washington that he didn't hesitate to apply the lash, if necessary, to these enslaved artisans: "As to the carpenters, I have minded 'em all I posably could and has whipt 'em when I could see a fault."[4] It was a relatively rare example in Mount Vernon annals of an overseer confessing that he whipped slaves, a practice Washington grew to abhor, though he condoned it on rare occasions.

AS GEORGE WASHINGTON introduced new splendor at Mount Vernon, he needed a wife to complete the pretty scene, and Martha Dandridge Custis made her timely appearance. Their speedy courtship began in mid-March 1758, right after Washington journeyed to Williamsburg to consult Dr. John Amson, who allayed his medical fright by reassuring him that he was recovering from dysentery. Relieved and elated, Washington rode off to nearby New Kent County to stay with his friend Richard Chamberlayne, who introduced him to his neighbor, the widow Custis. Her husband, Daniel Parke Custis, had died the previous July, as had two of her children in early childhood. She now lived with her four-year-old son John Parke (called Jacky) and two-year-old daughter Martha Parke (called Patsy) in baronial splendor on the Pamunkey River at a bucolic mansion known, prophetically enough, as the White House. Family legend suggests a spontaneous romance between George and Martha, but the mutual attraction may well have been anticipated. Though this was their first documented meeting, their social circles must have crisscrossed in the small, clubby world of the Williamsburg elite.

On leave from the Virginia Regiment, Washington courted Martha with the crisp efficiency of a military man laying down a well-planned siege. He spent that first night at the White House before returning to Williamsburg—he tipped the servants liberally to strengthen his image as a wealthy suitor—and dropped by twice more during the first half of 1758. A brisk competition had already arisen to snare the wealthy widow. A prosperous tobacco planter and widower named Charles Carter, who was nearly twice her age, had grown enamored of the short, attractive woman with the "uncommon sweetness of temper," as he saw it.[5] Carter had sired a dozen offspring in his previous marriage, and Martha, twenty-six, may have been intimidated by the prospect of being stepmother to this numerous brood. Carter faced stiff competition from Washington, a tall, handsome, young military hero with room both in his heart and in his home for a wife and two children. To a solitary, anxious widow, George Washington could only have appeared manly, rock-solid, and utterly fearless.

We cannot pinpoint the precise moment when George and Martha agreed to wed, but we do know that within weeks of their first meeting, George was transformed into a giddy man of fashion, urgently ordering expensive fabric for what must have been his wedding outfit. He directed his London agent to ship "as much of the best superfine blue cotton velvet as will make a coat, waistcoat, and breeches for a tall man, with a fine silk button to suit it and all other necessary trimmings and linings, together with garters for the breeches."[6] He also ordered six pairs of tony shoes and gloves. A month later he ordered a gold ring from Philadelphia that he doubtless intended to slip on the diminutive widow's finger. Not to be outdone in brightening up a wardrobe, Martha ordered her London tailor to send her "one genteel suit of clothes for myself to be grave but not to be extrava[ga]nt and not to be mourning."[7] Throwing off her widow's weeds, she packed off a nightgown to London "to be dyed of fashionable color fit for me to wear."[8] Though such letters may give the unseemly impression of an overly lusty widow, it was then routine, as a matter of economic necessity, for the bereaved to remarry quickly. The prolonged mourning rituals that came with the Victorian era would have seemed like futile self-indulgence in the eighteenth century.

By marrying Martha Dandridge Custis, Washington swiftly achieved the social advancement for which he had struggled in the military. Almost overnight he was thrust into top-drawer Virginia society and could dispense with the servility that had sometimes marked his dealings with social superiors. Marriage to Martha brought under his control a small kingdom of real estate tended by dark-skinned human beings. She had a bountiful collection of properties, including thousands of acres around Williamsburg, nearly three hundred slaves, and hundreds of head of cattle, hogs, and sheep. The property came, however, with a significant catch. Inasmuch as Daniel Parke Custis had died intestate, English common law decreed that only one-third of his estate could be claimed directly by Martha during her lifetime. She thus owned only eighty-five slaves, referred to as "dower" slaves, who would revert to Jacky Custis after her death. The other two-thirds of the estate were pledged to the financial support of the Custis children. George would serve as custodian of this wealth, entangling him in legal complications for the rest of his life. It's worth noting that after her husband's death, the practical Martha hadn't thrown herself at the mercy of older male financial advisers but had had the pluck and fortitude to handle his business affairs by herself. Whether sending tobacco to England, placing orders with London merchants, or extending loans to neighbors, she gained an invaluable education in plantation management.

George and Martha Washington formed an oddly matched visual pair: she barely cleared five feet, and her hands and feet were as petite as George's were famously huge. A portrait of Martha done shortly before Daniel died displays nothing especially soft or alluring to set a young man's pulse racing. She wears a low-cut, satiny blue dress, shows a shapely figure and bosom, and wears her dark hair pulled back, adorned with pearls. The small head, set on its elongated neck, isn't especially pretty: the forehead is too low, the hairline receding, the nose too hooked, the mouth too short, the jaw too round. Her hazel eyes are serious and watchful. It is the portrait of a plain, sensible young woman who already seems a trifle matronly. All the same, one suspects that the artist failed to catch the irrepressible warmth and charm that animated her features. The sitter's soul is smothered by the stiff pose of a woman holding a blossom and staring at the viewer. It should also be said that Martha had the reputation of being a beauty in her youth. "She was at one time one of the most beautiful women in America and today there remains something extremely agreeable and attractive about her," recounted a Polish nobleman several years before her death.[9] From surviving artifacts, such as the purple satin shoes with high heels and silver sequins that she wore on her wedding day, we know that Martha Custis was a stylish young woman and even something of a clotheshorse.

In the eighteenth century, marriage was regarded more as a practical arrangement than as a vehicle for love, and the Washington marriage may never have been a torrid romance. But that aside, in selecting Martha Dandridge Custis, George Washington chose even better than he knew. She was the perfect foil to his mother: warm and sociable, always fun to be with, and favored with pleasing manners. She would give George the unstinting love and loyalty that Mary had withheld. By offering her husband such selfless devotion, she solidly anchored his life in an enduring marriage. Martha had the cheerfulness to lighten his sometimes somber personality and was the one person who dared to kid her "Old Man," as she teasingly referred to him. Despite the many people in his eventful life, George Washington lacked a large number of close friends or confidants, and Martha alone could cater to all his emotional needs.

In every respect, Martha turned out to be an immense social asset to his career. She was the perfect hostess, with a ready smile, overflowing goodwill, and a genuine interest in her guests. With company, she was convivial and welcoming, where

George tended to be more cordial and correct, and she worked her influence in a self-effacing style. "His lady is of a hospitable disposition, always good-humored and cheerful, and seems to be actuated by the same motives with himself, but she is rather of a more lively disposition," observed one visitor to Mount Vernon. "They are to all appearances a happy pair."[10]

Martha never craved wealth or status, perhaps because she already had it; nor did she feed her husband's ambitions. She was never dazzled by his later fame and never put on airs. Nevertheless she faithfully supported George's plans and bowed to the exorbitant demands of his career, if not always with unmixed enthusiasm. Direct, plainspoken, and free of frivolity, she lacked the feminine wiles that had so aroused George with Sally Fairfax. Abigail Adams captured Martha Washington perfectly when she said, "Her manners are modest and unassuming, dignified and feminine, not a tincture of hauteur about her."[11] In fact, she remained a bustling, hardworking housewife, occupied with domestic chores until the end of her life, and was fully equal to the administrative demands of Mount Vernon.

Eight months older than George, Martha Dandridge was born on June 2, 1731, in rural New Kent County, the eldest of eight children, three of whom died young. Her father, John Dandridge—a county clerk, militia colonel, and minor tobacco planter on the Pamunkey River—had married Frances Jones the previous year. Fifteen or twenty slaves worked the tobacco fields on their plantation, Chestnut Grove, which covered five hundred acres. Their agrarian household was fairly spartan, and Martha, or "Patsy," was raised as a domestic helpmate to her mother. She grew up in a proper though hardly genteel house and was never too superior to perform housework. The provincial world of Martha's girlhood didn't spoil young ladies. "She told me she remembered the time when there was only one single carriage in all of Virginia," said a later visitor to Mount Vernon. "Ladies invited to entertainment arrived on horseback."[12] As the eldest child, Martha Dandridge was occupied with domestic skills that she later taught to indentured servants and slaves at Mount Vernon. Her industrious nature must have pleased George Washington. Both of them were early risers, used every moment profitably, and stuck to the same daily routines.

Like her future husband, Martha Dandridge grew up in a world where slavery was taken for granted, as were illegitimate children sired by the master. A few historians (though by no means all) believe that she had a young half sister named Ann Dandridge who was the offspring of her father and a slave woman of mixed black and Cherokee Indian blood. The little girl, who was likely much younger than Martha, didn't know the true story of her identity. If the story is to be believed, Martha, to her credit, kept Ann Dandridge in the Custis family and brought her to Mount Vernon; to her discredit, she never emancipated her half sister, who wasn't freed until 1802, after Martha's death.[13] Helen Bryan, a Martha Washington biographer, believes that Ann Dandridge was free, although perceived to be a slave, while the historian Henry Wiencek thinks she was treated as a slave, albeit a privileged one.[14] George and Martha Washington never dropped hints in their letters about Ann Dandridge, who was all but expunged from their history and never listed in Mount Vernon records.

Martha Washington enjoyed a steady faith from the time of her childhood. Her father was a church vestryman, and she was an observant member of the Church of England until the Revolution. "After breakfast, she retired for an hour to her chamber, which hour was spent in prayer and reading the Holy Scriptures, a practice that she never omitted during half a century of her varied life," said her grandson.[15] As was palpable later on as she endured many family deaths, she retained a simple but intense belief in the afterlife. Her philosophic and religious outlook tallied well in most respects with George Washington's. They both believed in a world replete with suffering in which one muddled through with as much dignity and grace as one could muster. Neither George nor Martha ever reacted to grave setbacks in a maudlin, self-pitying manner.

Before she died, likely for privacy reasons and perhaps by prior agreement with her husband, Martha Washington committed to the flames their entire personal correspondence; only a handful of messages survived the bonfire. From two of her surviving letters—one addressed to "My Dearest" and the other to "My Love"—we can tell that she adored her husband, and George wrote in the same vein.[16] Martha had little, if any, formal schooling and had a habit of torturing the English language. Her grammar was poor, her spelling eccentric, her punctuation nonexistent. (She seemed to specialize in run-on sentences.) Nonetheless she was an avid newspaper reader and kept up with some of the best literature imported from London in the 1760s, including Oliver Goldsmith's *The Vicar of Wakefield* and Samuel Johnson's *Rasselas,* as well as gothic romance novels.

That Martha concealed a vein of steel behind her conciliatory manner—that she was much more than the sweet, grandmotherly little woman of popular legend—is manifest in the story of her marriage to Daniel Parke Custis. Daniel's father, Colonel John Custis IV, was a rich, tyrannical man who had made life sheer misery for his equally difficult wife, Fidelia, née Frances Parke. Their marital spats were the stuff of legend on the eastern shore of Virginia. When the couple rode by the shore one day, John became so enraged at Fidelia that he drove their carriage straight into Chesapeake Bay. When Fidelia asked where he was going, John replied with a sneer, "To hell, Madam." To which she retorted boldly, "Drive on, sir."[17]

The tightfisted Custis, an overbearing father, was appalled when he learned that his bachelor son Daniel, in his late thirties, was secretly engaged to the adolescent Martha Dandridge. He had already vetoed a series of potential brides and dismissed

Martha as a social-climbing commoner "much inferior in point of fortune" to his son, vowing that he would rather toss his silverware into the street than allow her to inherit it.[18] Adding to this combustible mix was a mulatto son named Jack that John Custis had fathered with a slave called Alice. Once before John had threatened to disown Daniel and leave all his money to "Black Jack." This seemed a distinct possibility if Daniel didn't shelve his plans to marry Martha Dandridge. Far from hiding Black Jack, the irascible John Custis doted on him, and when the little boy was five, he submitted a petition to the governor to free the boy "christened John but commonly called Jack, born of the body of his Negro wench young Alice."[19] To celebrate his emancipation, the boy was given four slaves as playmates.[20] Obviously John Custis didn't rate very highly as a child psychologist.

During the impasse over the proposed marriage, Martha made the courageous decision to appeal to John Custis directly at his Williamsburg mansion and beard the lion in his den. Somehow she reached into herself and found hidden reserves of strength. We don't know what she said to sweet-talk this cantankerous man into agreement, but she won him over completely. Although he now hailed her as "beautiful and sweet-tempered," he still didn't consent to the marriage. Nonetheless, soon after Martha's visit, a family lawyer named James Power gave a horse, bridle, and saddle to Black Jack and informed John Custis that this had been Daniel's doing. The touching display of brotherly love finally made John Custis submit to his son's marriage to Martha. As the lawyer told Daniel, "I am empowered by your father to let you know that he heartily and willingly consents to your marriage with Miss Dandridge—that he has so good a character of her, that he had rather you should have her than any lady in Virginia."[21] Power lauded the "prudent speech" that Martha made to her future father-in-law, but several scholars have speculated that Martha arranged the cunning gift to Black Jack, the master stroke of the drama. She had shown extraordinary coolness under fire, foreshadowing her ability to deal with incendiary situations later on. On May 15, 1750, Martha Dandridge, eighteen, at last wed Daniel Parke Custis, thirty-eight. Black Jack resided with the newlyweds at the White House until he died, probably from meningitis, eighteen months later.

BY EARLY APRIL 1758 George Washington was sufficiently recovered from his bout of dysentery that he traveled west to regain control of the Virginia Regiment. Due to his blossoming romance with Martha Custis, he had to deal with one piece of unfinished business: his lingering infatuation with Sally Fairfax. It seems likely that when her husband, George William, was detained in Great Britain on legal matters that winter, Sally frequented Mount Vernon and nursed George through his illness. We will never know whether their affair was consummated. Since Washington had retained the admiration of both his patron Colonel Fairfax and his son George William, it seems hard to believe he had ever lured Sally into outright infidelity. Both George and Sally would have recognized the forbidden, illicit nature of their bond, the fearful price they would pay in Virginia society for any major transgression. There was probably much saucy banter and teasing pleasantries—the stuff of eighteenth-century gallantry—mixed up with deep affection and flirtation in their relationship. At the same time, there is little doubt of George's passionate attachment to this woman or the lasting power she exerted on his feverish imagination. His feelings for Sally Fairfax belonged to that brand of impossible, unattainable love for an older married woman that has filled the amorous fantasies of ardent young men throughout history.

On September 12, 1758, George Washington sat down at Fort Cumberland and penned a letter to Sally Fairfax that was an eloquent valedictory, not so much to their friendship, which would continue unabated, as to their sentimental affair. He had just received a letter from Sally, relayed by George William, who was helping to supervise renovations at Mount Vernon. Flooded with emotion at seeing the letter, Washington told her "how joyfully I catch at the happy occasion of renewing a correspondence which I feared was disrelished on your part."[22] That Sally had suspended the correspondence suggests that she feared Washington might be straying into dangerous territory and had to be pointedly restrained. In his response, Washington was probably motivated by two impending events: his marriage to Martha Custis and a hazardous military campaign against Fort Duquesne that would naturally have awakened thoughts of mortality. The letter is written with the stilted syntax that Washington exhibited whenever he grappled with strongly conflicting emotions.

At the outset of this coded letter, he made glancing reference to "the animating prospect of possessing Mrs. Custis," leaving no doubt that he planned to proceed with the wedding. Then he went on to deliver a cunningly ambiguous love note in which he was obviously talking about Sally, while making it seem to prying eyes that he referred to Martha:

Tis true, I profess myself a votary to Love. I acknowledge that a lady is in the case and further I confess that this lady is known to you. Yes, Madam, as well as she is to one who is too sensible of her charms to deny the power whose influence he feels and must ever submit to. I feel the force of her amiable beauties in the recollection of a thousand tender passages that I could wish to obliterate till I am bid to revive them. But experience, alas!, sadly reminds me how impossible this is and evinces an opinion which I have long entertained that there is a destiny which has the sovereign control of our actions, not to be resisted by the strongest efforts of human nature.[23]

The reference to a "thousand tender passages" makes clear that Sally, not Martha, was the lady in question; George's acquaintance with Martha was too brief to have packed in so many tender memories. He seemed to be saying that their love, defeated by the practical circumstances of life, was simply not meant to be. She was married to a rich man, and he was about to marry a rich woman, and George Washington, for all his high-flown rhetoric, was an eminently practical young man, not cut out for doomed, quixotic affairs. He ended the epistle with a frank admission of love: "You have drawn me, my dear Madam, or rather have I drawn myself, into an honest confession of a simple fact. Misconstrue not my meaning—'tis obvious—doubt it not, nor expose it. The world has no business to know the object of my love, declared in this manner to you, when I want to conceal it . . . I dare believe you are as happy as you say. I wish I was happy also. Mirth, good humor, ease of mind and—what else?—cannot fail to render you so and consummate your wishes."[24]

This letter overturns the conventional image of a phlegmatic Washington and shows a much more passionate figure. It shocks as well because of his apparent betrayal of his friend and patron, George William Fairfax, and his fiancée, Martha. Any moral outrage must be tempered, however, by the overriding fact that George was honorably declaring an end to their amorous relationship on the eve of his marriage, which would call an irrevocable halt to such youthful folly. Sally Fairfax had always been somewhat coy and elusive with Washington, as evidenced by her recent discontinuance of their correspondence. Her coquetry, in the last analysis, was constrained by a self-protective instinct. She had also, as the letter makes clear, insisted that she was happy with her life. So why did Washington write such a daring letter? There is always the possibility that he was testing the waters with Sally one last time before he committed to marriage. Or perhaps, at the end, he wanted some final validation of his powerful longings for Sally, some recognition that she, too, had been deeply touched by taboo feelings. That he announced his love in such dramatic fashion confirms that he had never done so before and that he and Sally had left many things unsaid and probably undone. Whatever was the true situation, Sally must have recognized and treasured the frank admission of love, for she retained the letter until she died in 1811—a period of more than fifty years.

Although Sally's response has been lost, we can surmise its contents from Washington's September 25 reply. Apparently she either feigned ignorance of the mystery lady's identity, or pretended it was Martha. Washington stood his ground. "Dear Madam, do we still misunderstand the true meaning of each other's letters? I think it must appear so, tho[ugh] I would feign hope the contrary as I cannot speak plainer without. But I'll say no more and leave you to guess the rest."[25] Washington knew that any greater candor could wreck two marriages. That Sally refused to credit his love or openly reciprocate it suggests that she was an artful woman who had enjoyed having her vanity stroked by a handsome younger man. This would have made Washington the more appreciative of Martha, who was practical, honest, and straightforward. The youthful infatuation prepared Washington for the deeper joys of marriage, although the beguiling image of Sally Fairfax persisted in his memory. She would always be mixed up with recollections of Belvoir and an idyllic, sunstruck period of his youth. The Sally Fairfax saga may well testify to Washington's repressed romantic nature, buried beneath many layers of reserve. But it's even more a stoic tale of self-denial, previewing the supreme command he would attain over his unruly emotions. Washington's storied self-control was not something inherited but achieved by dint of hard work, making it all the more formidable an accomplishment.

In later years Washington liked to philosophize about love and marriage and became a veritable Polonius with young relatives as he peppered them with sage advice. In 1795 he received a letter from his adopted granddaughter, Eleanor Parke Custis, who had attended a Georgetown ball and boasted of her indifference to the advances of young men there. Washington warned her bluntly of the often-unstoppable force of passion. "Do not therefore boast too soon or too strongly of your insensibility . . . to its power. In the composition of the human frame, there is a good deal of inflammable matter [this meant flammable in the eighteenth century], however dormant it may lie for a time and . . . when the torch is put to it, *that* which is *within you* may burst into a blaze." Washington went on to say that this mighty blaze "ought to be under the guidance of reason, for although we cannot avoid first impressions, we may assuredly place them under guard."[26] The author of these lines seemed knowledgeable about ungovernable emotions and how to tame them.

Perhaps the best proof that the relationship between Washington and Sally Fairfax stayed deep but platonic is that the Washingtons remained intimate friends with George William and Sally Fairfax before the American Revolution and even traveled with them. In all likelihood, George confessed to Martha his longtime flirtation, which had cooled and receded to its proper place. The febrile yearnings of youth had made way for a more mature love. It speaks to the strength of the Washingtons' marriage that they were never threatened by the close proximity of Sally Fairfax, who remained a welcome guest at Mount Vernon and no less a friend to Martha than to George. There is something admirably grown-up, sensitive, and dignified about the way these two couples handled a most delicate situation.

CHAPTER EIGHT

Darling of a Grateful Country

IN THE SPRING OF 1758 George Washington entertained one last forlorn hope of a brilliantly climactic military campaign in the Ohio Valley. He was about to tender his resignation when he heard reports in March that the Crown planned to send a fleet with seven thousand men to North America and contemplated another operation against Fort Duquesne. The new commander, Brigadier General John Forbes, was a veteran Scottish officer who took a decidedly low view of colonial officers, maligning them as a "bad collection of broken innkeepers, horse jockeys, and Indian traders."[1]

Hoping to curry favor with Forbes, Washington wrote to Brigadier General John Stanwix and badgered him "to mention me in favorable terms to General Forbes," but "not as a person who would depend upon him for further recommendation to military preferment, for I have long conquered all such expectancies ... but as a person who would gladly be distinguished in some measure from the *common run* of provincial officers."[2] Perhaps a chastened Washington meant it when he now said that he expected no royal commission. Contrary to his bias against colonial soldiers, Forbes singled out Washington as "a good and knowing officer in the back countries."[3] To augment the chances for victory at the Forks of the Ohio, the Virginia assembly decided to raise a second regiment, doubling its armed force to two thousand men, with George Washington as the presiding senior officer.

In early July at Fort Cumberland, Washington showed how fighting in the hinterlands had tutored him in Indian-style warfare. When he ran short of uniforms, he outfitted both himself and his men in Indian hunting shirts and leggings, helping them to emulate the light, mobile style of their fleet-footed adversaries. While admitting to Forbes's chief aide that it was "an unbecoming dress" for an officer, he argued that "soldiers in such a dress are better able to carry their provisions, are fitter for the active service we are engaged in, and less liable to sink under the fatigues of a long march."[4] Even though Washington won permission to assume Indian dress, he still acknowledged the incontestable superiority of Indian warriors: "I cannot conceive the best white men to be equal to them in the woods."[5]

A victim of political wrangling in Williamsburg, Washington was eager to renew his bid for a seat from Frederick County in the House of Burgesses. He probably wished to erase the memory of his poor showing three years earlier and establish through public service his credentials as an aspiring gentleman. Learning from past mistakes, he gave plenty of notice for his candidacy this time and assembled a cadre of active, energetic friends who cheerfully drummed up support in Winchester in his absence. Nonetheless they pleaded with him to come and politick in person. His friend Colonel James Wood, the town's leading citizen, warned that there was "no relying on the promises of the common herd . . . There are many of us embarked on the same cause with you and a disappointment will sit heavy on us."[6] Leaving no stone unturned, Robert Rutherford told Washington that they were encouraging voters "with the greatest ardor, even down to Will the hatter and his oily spouse."[7] Washington secured permission to travel to Winchester to campaign, then chose to stay with his troops. This may have been from a sense of duty or from fear that he would miss a victorious battle. Washington had also begun to intuit the subtle art of seeking power by refraining from too obvious a show of ambition.

On election day, July 24, 1758, the absentee candidate engaged in the popular, if technically illegal, custom of intoxicating local voters. His campaign forwarded him an expense account for thirty-four gallons of wine, three pints of brandy, thirteen gallons of beer, eight quarts of cider, and forty gallons of rum punch, costing the candidate a sizable thirty-nine pounds in Virginia currency. Accepting this expense, Washington hoped that his backers had plied all voters impartially with strong beverages: "My only fear is that you spent with too sparing a hand."[8]

As voting for the two seats got under way in Washington's absence, it was clear how much power the young war hero wielded in this rustic area. He profited from the fact that one candidate was Thomas Bryan Martin, the nephew of Thomas, Lord Fairfax, proprietor of the Northern Neck. Since each voter cast two votes, Washington and Martin formed a ticket against the incumbents, with the latter's presence enlisting Fairfax support. Among those supporting Washington was Lord Fairfax himself, followed by a sterling list of local luminaries and his regimental surgeon, Dr. James Craik. Even George William Fairfax arrived in Winchester to endorse his wife's faithful admirer. The final vote sharply reversed Washington's crashing defeat of three years earlier as he garnered 309 of 397 votes cast and easily outpaced the other three candidates, including Thomas Bryan Martin, who, as runner-up with 240 votes, became the second burgess.

Washington's vote-getting prowess was only magnified by having trounced his opponents in absentia. Robert Rutherford credited his victory to his fair treatment of his men and "ardent zeal for the common cause."[9] Colonel Wood was hoisted aloft and carried about the town amid boisterous huzzahs for Washington. In thanking friends for their support, Colonel Washington sounded openly jubilant: "If thanks flowing from a heart replete with joy and gratitude can in any measure compensate for the fatigue, anxiety and pain you had at my election, be assured you have them."[10] He instinctively struck a generous tone, stating that his best way of thanking voters was by "making their interests . . . my own and doing everything that lies in my little power for the honor and welfare of the county."[11] With a thoroughness that previewed bigger things to come, Washington filed away the poll sheet so that he could form his own alphabetized list, showing how each person had voted.

Even as he thrilled to this electoral victory, he was entangled in a bitter imbroglio over the optimal route for the march to Fort Duquesne, a seemingly minor tactical dispute with major political overtones. Washington wanted the Forbes expedition to follow the road Braddock had charted through the wilderness, not only because he himself had originally blazed the trail but because it passed through Virginia and would consolidate the colony's commercial presence in the Ohio Country. Some assertive Philadelphians agitated for a road from Raystown, Pennsylvania, which would benefit their colony. After chatting with Colonel Henry Bouquet, an aide to General Forbes, Washington was aghast to discover that he favored the Pennsylvania road. "If Colo. Bouquet succeeds in this point with the general, all is lost! All is lost by Heavens!" Washington told Forbes's secretary, Francis Halkett.[12] In resorting to hyperbole, Washington may have thought he was claiming the moral high ground, but Forbes saw only a self-serving maneuver by a bumptious young Virginian. "By a very unguarded letter of Col. Washington that accidentally fell into my hands," Forbes told Bouquet, "I am now at the bottom of their scheme against this new [Pennsylvania] road, a scheme that I think was a shame for any officer to be concerned in."[13] At this stage of his life, Washington sometimes found it difficult to distinguish his own from the general interest. In selecting the Pennsylvania road, military historians have argued, Forbes may have selected the better route because it was shorter and bypassed treacherous water crossings. Conceding these advantages, an unyielding Washington countered that the Pennsylvania road had to span "monstrous mountains, covered with woods and rocks" and might not be finished before cold weather intervened.[14]

The willful Washington refused to let the matter drop. In late August he wrote a rude, hectoring letter to Bouquet, chiding him that, if only they had chosen Braddock's Road, they would now be undisputed masters of the Ohio Country.[15] Committing a mistake common among headstrong young people, Washington went behind his opponent's back to someone even higher. He hadn't yet acquired smooth political skills and could seem crudely insistent. With questionable judgment, he circumvented Forbes and Bouquet to lobby the new Virginia lieutenant governor, Francis Fauquier, who had replaced Dinwiddie. He also told Speaker Robinson that Forbes had squandered an egregious amount of time and money: "Will then our injured country pass by such abuses? I hope not. Rather let a full representation of the matter go to His Majesty. Let him know how grossly his [honor] and the public money has been prostituted."[16] All this heated rhetoric came from a man later renowned for his cool judgment. Perhaps, newly elected to the House of Burgesses, Washington felt entitled to issue blunt ultimatums to Williamsburg politicians. It should also be noted that his special pleading made him a folk hero in Virginia, where he was applauded for standing up for the colony's interests by proselytizing for Braddock's Road.

When General Forbes drew up plans for the assault on Fort Duquesne, he overcame his irritation with Washington and assigned him to lead one of three brigades spearheading the charge. The young Virginian was the only colonial officer thus honored. As he braced for a last chance to show his military mettle, Washington experienced one of the more harrowing moments in his career. The ghastly mishap began when scouts alerted Forbes to an enemy reconnaissance party, prowling the woods three miles away, who were seeking to grab livestock. To handle this threat, Forbes dispatched hundreds of Virginians under Lieutenant Colonel George Mercer. At camp, Washington heard distinct sounds of "hot firing," indicating to him and Forbes that Mercer's men were taking a terrible pounding from the enemy. Forbes sent Washington and several hundred men to relieve their fellow Virginians. They advanced through woods in a deepening twilight that was thickened by musket smoke, screening off any clear view of the fighting up ahead. Washington later insisted that he had sent a messenger to notify Mercer of his approach, lest his men be mistaken for the enemy.

No sooner did Washington's men glimpse the soldiers ahead than they reeled under the impact of repeated rounds of gunfire and began to fire back. It turned out that Virginians were firing at Virginians. As Washington fathomed the full horror of this mistake, he unsheathed his sword and slashed at his men's leveled muskets to stop their firing, but it was too late. The misadventure left behind staggering casualties: fourteen dead and twenty-six wounded. Even after the Revolutionary War, Washington said of this star-crossed episode that his life had been "in as much jeopardy as it had ever been before or since."[17]

This was now the fourth time that Washington had traversed the path to the

Forks of the Ohio, and each time his military aspirations had been foiled by unforeseen developments. For someone of Washington's dogged nature, the frustration must have been mortifying. The French and Indian War had humbled him with cruel ironies and unexpected setbacks, leaving him more philosophic and reflective. As he wrote a few years later, "Human affairs are always checkered and vicissitudes in this life are rather to be expected than wondered at."[18]

When the fall of Fort Duquesne finally came in late November 1758, it was almost anticlimactic. Forbes was about to defer the attack until the following spring when three prisoners disclosed that the French fort was now undermanned. An Indian scout then appeared and told of huge billows of smoke rising from the post. Forbes assembled 2,500 men to take the fort and gave Washington the "brevet," or honorary rank, of brigadier general for the operation. When this huge force arrived on the scene on November 25, 1758, they found only the charred, smoldering remains of Fort Duquesne. Deserted by their Indian allies, the French had deemed the fort dangerously indefensible, blown it up, and fled by night down the Ohio River. Fort Pitt—the new name paid tribute to William Pitt—would arise on the flaming wreckage of Fort Duquesne. Colonel Bouquet gloated that one reason for the triumph was Forbes's refusal to capitulate to Braddock's Road, "which would have been our destruction."[19]

The conquest rang down the curtain on Washington's military tenure after five years of devoted service. With the safety of Virginia's pioneers and traders temporarily assured, it was an auspicious moment for him to resign his commission and focus his energies on Martha Dandridge Custis and Mount Vernon. His upcoming marriage and service in the House of Burgesses offered a seamless transition into a promising new life. Health reasons also lay behind the resignation. Washington's dysentery had apparently flared up again, because he described his health as "precarious" that December, having worsened "for many months before, occasioned by an inveterate disorder" in his bowels.[20]

As word of Washington's resignation spread, his officers seemed genuinely crestfallen. He had done a superlative job of taking callow recruits, introducing discipline, and spurring them to function as more professional soldiers. His boon companion, Captain Robert Stewart, spoke for many when he wrote to Washington how he would miss "your constant company and conversation in which I have been so long happy."[21] Stewart's letter confirms Washington's high stature in Virginia, for he hoped that his friend would "continue the darling of a grateful country [i.e., Virginia] for the many eminent services you have rendered her."[22] Twenty-seven officers from the Virginia Regiment banded together to laud Washington in a farewell message. They extolled the same virtues that would be praised in the Revolutionary War and showed the same tender affection as their later counterparts. They hailed Washington's "steady adherence to impartial justice" and "invariable regard to merit," and they credited his "honor and passion for glory" as the source of his military achievements. They also eulogized him as "an excellent commander," "sincere friend," and "affable" companion.[23] These were mighty tributes to bestow on a twenty-six-year-old. So while Washington might have alienated assorted politicians and generals, he retained the unswerving fealty of his men and the Virginia public at large.

Beneath the hard rind, Washington was far more sensitive than he appeared, and this heartfelt message from his men "affected him exceedingly," he admitted.[24] He had a fine sense of occasion, displayed in this early response to his men. Already adept at tearful farewells, he exhibited the succinct eloquence that came to define his speaking style. He began by calling the officers' approval of his conduct "an honor that will constitute the greatest happiness of my life and afford in my latest hours the most pleasing reflections."[25] Unable to avoid a youthful dig at Dinwiddie and Forbes, he hinted at the "uncommon difficulties" under which he had labored. But it was the palpable affection he summoned up for his men that made the statement noteworthy. Washington thanked his officers "with uncommon sincerity and true affection for the honor you have done me, for if I have acquired any reputation, it is from you I derive it. I thank you also for the love and regard you have all along shown me. It is in this I am rewarded. It is herein I glory."[26]

Had Washington's military career ended with the French and Indian War, he would have earned scarcely more than a footnote in history, yet it is impossible to imagine his life without this important preamble. The British Empire had committed a major blunder by spurning the talents of such a natural leader. It said something about the imperial system that it could find no satisfactory place for this loyal, able, and ambitious young subject. The proud Washington had been forced to bow and scrape for a regular commission, and it irked him that he had to grovel for recognition. Washington's military career would be held in abeyance until June 1775, but in the meantime he had acquired a powerful storehouse of grievances that would fuel his later rage with England.

In the fullness of time, Washington would win a prize infinitely more valuable than the royal commission he had lost. As a member of the British forces, he had begun to articulate a comprehensive critique of British fighting methods in North America. For a young man, he had acquired an amazing amount of experience, and these precocious achievements yielded a lasting reservoir of self-confidence. He had proved his toughness and courage in the face of massacres and defeats. He had learned to train and drill regiments and developed a rudimentary sense of military strategy. He had shown a real capacity to lead and take responsibility for fulfilling the most arduous missions. Perhaps most important, his experience in the French and Indian War made him a believer in a strong central government and a vigorous executive. Forced to deal with destructive competition among the colonies, dilatory legislative committees, and squabbling, shortsighted politicians, he had passed through an excellent dress rehearsal for the prolonged ordeal of the American Revolution.

PART TWO

The Planter

The earliest known portrait of Martha Washington, painted by John
Wollaston in 1757, when she was still Martha Dandridge Custis.

CHAPTER NINE

The Man of Mode

ON JANUARY 6, 1759, coinciding with the celebration of Twelfth Night, George Washington and Martha Dandridge Custis, attired in the latest British fashions, were married at her White House residence. George was presumably resplendent in the blue velvet suit he had had specially shipped from London, while Martha made a fetching impression in a gown "of deep yellow brocade with rich lace in the neck and sleeves" accompanied by purple satin shoes.[1]

While never shrinking from a rich appearance, Martha, like George, shuddered at any hint of ostentation. We don't know what the Custis children, Jacky and Patsy, wore, but their dress probably conformed to that in an earlier painting by John Wollaston, which presents them in the pampered apparel of little British aristocrats. In that portrait, Jacky sports a shiny blue coat over a light-colored waistcoat, while Patsy wears a silvery gown edged with lace.

The newlyweds were by no means prudish. In his first postnuptial order to London, George ordered four ounces of Spanish fly, a popular aphrodisiac prepared from dried beetles. At some point that year, he also drew up a list of books inherited from the Custis estate that may disclose something of the amorous interests of Daniel and Martha Custis, or perhaps of Daniel's father. The couple possessed a copy of *Conjugal lewdness: or matrimonial whoredom* by Daniel Defoe and *The lover's watch: or the art of making love* by Aphra Behn.[2]

After the weak-willed Daniel Custis, George Washington must have struck Martha as the most commanding of men. Where Daniel had been cowed by a despotic father, George usually stood up to his forbidding mother. As best we can tell, Mary Ball Washington boycotted the wedding and, according to Martha's biographer

Patricia Brady, may not have met the bride until the year after the wedding.³ It is hard to resist the impression of a lasting coolness between Martha and her mother-in-law. Over the next thirty years, there is no evidence that Mary Washington ever visited Mount Vernon. The only time she saw her daughter-in-law was during obligatory stops that George and Martha made in Fredericksburg en route to Williamsburg. George routinely dropped in to see Mary and his sister Betty Lewis, who had married Fielding Lewis, a wealthy merchant, and lived nearby. (Betty bore an uncanny resemblance to George. Indeed, it was said that had she thrown on a military cloak and hat, battalions would have saluted her.) Washington kept his visits to his mother brief. During one snowy stay with her in January 1760, he recorded in his diary that after "getting a few things which I wanted out of the stores, [I] returned in the evening to mother's—all alone with her."⁴ That he jotted down this detail suggests that being alone with Mary was an effort. In all likelihood, George and Martha Washington treated Mary Ball Washington as a slightly dotty, difficult woman, a troubled oddball whom they had to put up with and never expected to reform.

Marriage came at a critical moment for George Washington, who went from a young officer at the mercy of the British military establishment to a prosperous planter who didn't have to truckle to anyone. He had married up in the world, as had Martha before him, and they both inherited a huge chunk of the Custis fortune. Once again an untimely death contributed immeasurably to Washington's burgeoning wealth. Martha's money made her husband one of Virginia's richest men, enabling him to issue his own declaration of independence. The marriage brought eighty-five dower slaves under his control, doubling his labor force. As the Washington editor Dorothy Twohig notes, "With his marriage, [Washington] was now in control of one of Virginia's largest and most profitable estates, including property in 6 counties amounting to nearly 8,000 acres, slaves valued at £9,000 Virginia currency, and accounts current and other liquid assets in England of about £10,000 sterling."⁵ Then on March 14, 1761, Ann Fairfax Lee, the widow of George's half brother Lawrence, died. Because she had no surviving child, George Washington suddenly graduated to full-fledged ownership of Mount Vernon, inheriting another five slaves. Once again he was the lucky beneficiary of a death in the family.

These sudden windfalls gave Washington new social standing and considerable freedom to maneuver. In time, this wealth would free up the better angels of his nature and give him the resources to back up his strong opinions. As John Adams later wondered, "Would Washington have ever been commander of the revolutionary army or president of the United States, if he had not married the rich widow of Mr. Custis?"⁶ Once he married, an air of contentment settled over Washington's restless life. From Mount Vernon, he wrote serenely to Richard Washington, "I am now, I believe, fixed at this seat with an agreeable consort for life and hope to find more happiness in retirement than I ever experienced amidst a wide and bustling world."[7] This was the first, but hardly the last, time that Washington nursed a pastoral fantasy of withdrawal from all worldly cares, a fantasy that would be repeatedly mocked by the imperious call of political events.

Civic duties formed an essential part of the ethos of a gentleman, so it was fitting that on his twenty-seventh birthday, one month after his marriage, Washington assumed his seat in the House of Burgesses. Four days later he enjoyed a heady moment when his new colleagues, in a glowing resolution, thanked him for "his faithful services to His Majesty and this colony" and his "brave and steady behavior."[8] A boisterous chorus of *ayes* roared their unanimous approval of the resolution. No longer a youthful protégé, Washington now stood forth as a social peer of these well-to-do planters. Such attention always brought out a certain awkwardness in Washington, who was ill at ease with public oratory and uncomfortable with flattery, perhaps because he secretly craved it. With a touch of embellishment, one burgess remembered Washington's flustered response: "He rose to express his acknowledgments for the honor, but such was his trepidation and confusion that he could not give distinct utterance to a single syllable." The man who faced bullets with sangfroid never conquered his terror of public speaking. "He blushed, stammered, and trembled for a second, when the speaker relieved him by a stroke of address . . . 'Sit down, Mr. Washington,' said he, with a conciliating smile, 'your modesty is equal to your valor, and that surpasses the power of any language that I possess.'"[9]

Washington was assigned to the Committee on Propositions and Grievances, which dealt with commercial and governmental matters. By the end of the year, drawing on his military experience, he sat on three committees that sorted through petitions from soldiers and army vendors. The taciturn Washington wasn't the kind of glib burgess who sprang to his feet and orated extemporaneously. He practiced a minimalist art in politics, learning how to exert maximum leverage with the least force. Thomas Jefferson, who was to serve with Washington and Franklin in the Continental Congress, spotted their economical approach to power. "I never heard either of them speak ten minutes at a time, nor to any but the main point," he later said of the two statesmen. "They laid their shoulders to the great points, knowing that the little ones would follow of themselves."[10] Later on Washington coached his stepson on how to be a Virginia legislator, reminding him to be punctual in attendance and "hear dispassionately and determine coolly all great questions."[11] Washington's experience as a burgess educated him in politics no less thoroughly than his combat experience on the western frontier groomed him for future military leadership, creating a rare combination of talents that endowed him with the ideal credentials at the time the American Revolution erupted.

From the outset, Washington demonstrated his conscientious nature as a legislator and attended sessions until early April to support a bill to sustain the Virginia Regiment. Then he, Martha, and her two children set off for Mount Vernon, with Martha and the children installed in the glamorous Custis coach and George trotting alongside them on horseback. Because he was still refurbishing Mount Vernon, Washington felt apprehensive about subjecting his bride and stepchildren to the dust and din, paint and plaster, of an unfinished house. He wrote ahead to have the rooms aired and cleaned and beds made up in two rooms. The nervous young husband, wanting everything just right for his new family's arrival, instructed John Alton to "get out the chairs and tables and have them very well rubbed and cleaned. The staircase ought also to be polished in order to make it look well. Inquire ab[ou]t in the neighborhood and get some eggs and chickens."[12] After Washington's lengthy frontier sojourn, the house was stirring to life again, and Martha would soon describe it as a place of "mirth and gaiety."[13]

If Martha's wealth lifted Washington into the top ranks of Virginia planters, it didn't emancipate him from all cares, for he was soon tangled in the legal complexities of the Custis fortune. Under the terms of the estate, George and Martha controlled one-third of the Custis property. The two children each received one-third of the income from the Custis assets, while only Jacky, as the male heir, would inherit eventually all the Custis land and slaves. In Williamsburg in late April, Washington won permission from the General Court to administer those portions of the estate vested in the two children. Being their legal guardian was a weighty, time-consuming task that required Washington to satisfy the court with annual reports on his fiduciary actions. Like every responsibility in his life, Washington executed this one with the utmost rigor, claiming that a stewardship demanded even more care from a stepparent than from "a natural parent, who is only accountable to his own conscience."[14] This arrangement, though it gave Washington extra wealth and power, also placed him in a curiously subordinate position vis-à-vis his stepchildren, making him effectively their employee and robbing him of the total paternal authority he might have wished.

Further complicating this strange situation was that while Washington adopted Jacky and Patsy, they retained the Custis surname. The children arrived at Mount Vernon with their own slaves—Jacky had a ten-year-old named Julius, Patsy the twelve-year-old Moll—who wore the formal uniforms known as livery, and it must have been annoying, if not demeaning, for Washington to have them sporting the Custis crest instead of his own. In ordering clothing for these servants from London, Washington always gave explicit orders to "let the livery be suited to the [coat of] arms of the Custis family."[15] Such details of everyday life reminded Washington of where the real financial power resided in his family. In his diary, he sometimes referred to his stepchildren as "Jacky Custis" and "Patsy Custis," as if they were temporary visitors.

Although Washington enjoyed children, his formal presence tended to freeze their jollity. "They felt they were in the presence of one who was not to be trifled with," said his adopted grandson.[16] Washington was a doting father to Patsy, a pretty girl with dark hair, who was very fond of music. Washington found it easy to spoil her and soon got her a spinet, an early form of the harpsichord, while Jacky studied the violin and flute. He also hired a dancing master at Mount Vernon for the two children. Washington had a more relaxed style with girls and used to say ruefully that he could govern men but not boys.[17] Jacky was to be a chronic problem. A foppish boy, lazy, wayward, and indulged by his mother, he shared few traits with his energetic stepfather, and their temperamental differences only aggravated matters. Forever wary of intruding upon Martha's relationship with her children, Washington was reluctant to apply discipline to Jacky and shielded her from knowledge of his many imperfections.

However genial as a hostess, Martha was a jittery mother, a mass of anxieties, much as her own mother had been. She had already endured so many deaths—her husband, two children, her father, a brother, a sister, and Daniel's half brother, Black Jack—that she flew into a panic at even trifling signs of illness in her children. Three years into the marriage, Martha experimented to see whether she could stand to be away from Jacky. She failed the test miserably. Every time a dog barked or some other noise occurred, Martha worried that it heralded the arrival of a messenger with dreadful news about her son. "I often fancied he was sick or some accident had happened to him," Martha said.[18] Henceforth she traveled with George only if both children came along.

Whatever the periodic tensions caused by Jacky's lax behavior, the marriage of George and Martha Washington proceeded happily, and they seemed united by strong desire and mutual need. Almost all observers found them exceedingly well matched. In later years the British ambassador's wife found something closer to friendship than romance between them—"Washington was a more respectful than a tender husband certainly"—but even she could identify no quarrels.[19] Something about this deep domesticity and respectability pleased Washington, who was never cut out for a gallivanting, footloose life. Martha gave him a secure, happy base for the myriad activities of a busy career. She was his dear companion, trusted adviser, and confidante long after lust faded, and they delighted in each other's company. When Washington was appointed commander in chief of the Continental Army, he wrote to Martha that "I should enjoy more real happiness and felicity in one month with you at home than I have the most distant prospect of reaping abroad, if my stay was to be seven times seven years."[20] Neither George nor Martha was tormented by a romantic striving after an impossible perfection, and both understood the compromises that accompanied a successful marriage.

While Washington left no direct comments about his marriage, he discussed marriage in general terms so often—he grew into something of a cracker-barrel philosopher on the subject—that we can readily infer his views about his own. He was an unabashed enthusiast for the institution and issued so many paeans to domestic felicity as to leave no doubt of his contentment with Martha. His advice to young relatives revealed that he had known the storms of passion as a young man but understood that they were fleeting and couldn't form the foundation of a lasting relationship; one had to enter into a match based upon practical factors, such as personality, character, temperament, and money. This seems to reflect accurately the progression of Washington's own feelings as he and Martha went from early love (albeit laced with realism about money) to the ripening friendship of later decades.

Many years later, writing to one of Martha's granddaughters upon her engagement, Washington warned that romantic love cooled in time. This letter may explain Washington's final preference for Martha Custis over Sally Fairfax.

> Do not then, in your contemplation of the marriage state, look for perfect felicity before you consent to wed. Nor conceive, from the fine tales the poets and lovers of old have told us of the transports of mutual love, that heaven has taken its abode on earth. Nor do not deceive yourself in supposing that the only mean[s] by which these are to be obtained is to drink deep of the cup and revel in an ocean of love. Love is a mighty pretty thing, but, like all other delicious things, it is cloying. And when the first transports of the passion begin to subside, which it assuredly will do and yield, oftentimes too late, to more sober reflections, it serves to evince that love is too dainty a food to live upon *alone* and ought not to be considered farther than as a necessary ingredient for that matrimonial happiness which results from a combination of causes; none of which are of greater importance than that the object on whom it is placed should possess good sense, good dispositions, and the means of supporting you in the way you have been brought up.[21]

Washington could never have married a poor woman, but neither could he have tolerated a cold and loveless marriage.

Throughout his life Washington was noticeably attracted to women, but his steely willpower and stern discipline likely overmastered any fugitive impulses to stray. Many people observed his gallantry with the ladies. One British officer described how women left his dining room after meals only to be squired right back in by Washington. As he recalled, Washington introduced "a round of ladies as soon as the cloth was removed by saying he had always a very great esteem for the ladies and therefore drank them in preference to anything else."[22] In corresponding with women, Washington frequently slipped into a breezily flirtatious tone. When the widow Annis Boudinot Stockton later sent him an ode in his honor, he encouraged her to produce more poetry: "You see, madam, when once the woman has tempted us and we have tasted the forbidden fruit, there is no such thing as checking our appetites, whatever the consequences may be."[23]

In a century of sterling wits, George Washington never stood out for his humor, but he had a bawdy streak and relished hearty, masculine jokes. In the 1920s the puritanical J. P. Morgan, Jr., destroyed some letters by Washington that he owned, claiming they were "smutty."[24] When breeding animals, Washington wrote about their couplings with dry, facetious mirth. In the 1780s, after the Spanish king sent him a male donkey nicknamed Royal Gift, he launched an experiment in breeding mules. Washington noted drolly that the donkey was at first indifferent to "female allurements" and that when he finally responded, he proceeded with "deliberation and majestic solemnity to the work of procreation."[25] At the same time he hoped Royal Gift would catch the democratic spirit in America and "that when he becomes a little better acquainted with republican enjoyments, he will amend his manners and fall into a better and more expeditious mode of doing business."[26]

Perhaps the earthiest comment Washington ever made about sex occurred when he learned of the marriage of forty-seven-year-old Colonel Joseph Ward. He seemed to find forty-seven a comically advanced age for matrimony. "I am glad to hear that my old acquaintance Colo. Ward is yet under the influence of vigorous passions," he told a correspondent. He supposed that Ward, "like a prudent general," had "reviewed his *strength,* his arms, and ammunition before he got involved in an action. But if these have been neglected . . . let me advise him to make the *first* onset upon his fair del Tobosa [Dulcinea del Toboso, the country girl in *Don Quixote*] with vigor that the impression may be deep, if it cannot be lasting or frequently renewed."[27]

The marriage thrived even though Martha and George lacked children. Many theories have been advanced to explain this barren marriage. Martha may have sustained injury during the birth of Patsy, her final child, making additional births impossible. Some scholars have speculated that George's early bout of smallpox or some other disease left him infertile. We know that George Washington didn't think he was sterile, because, in writing once to a nephew, he stated that if Martha died and he remarried, he "probably" wouldn't have children, but only because he would marry a woman suitable to his age—obviously implying that he could have children with a younger woman.[28] The historic stress on the childless marriage has obscured the fact that the Washingtons, far from being lonely, were always surrounded by children. In the early years at Mount Vernon, there were Jacky and Patsy Custis and then, in later years, two of Jacky's children, plus assorted other young relatives, perhaps numbering a dozen orphaned youngsters in all. This childless couple ran a household teeming with high-spirited children, which may have been their way of filling a perceived void.

Later on Washington's childless state helped him to assume the title of Father of His Country. That he wasn't a biological father made it easier for him to be the allegorical father of a nation. It also retired any fears, when he was president, that the nation might revert to a monarchy, because he could have no interest in a hereditary crown. In a draft of his first inaugural address, Washington (or his ghostwriter David Humphreys) wrote that "Divine Providence hath not seen fit that my blood should be transmitted or my name perpetuated by the endearing, though sometimes seducing, channel of immediate offspring. I have no child for whom I could wish to make a provision—no family to build in greatness upon my country's ruins."[29] Many contemporaries professed to discern heavenly influence in Washington's childless state—God's tacit way of protecting America. As Gouverneur Morris stated in his eulogy for Washington, "AMERICANS! he had no child BUT YOU and HE WAS ALL YOUR OWN."[30]

IN MARRYING MARTHA CUSTIS, George Washington inherited the posh commercial connection that Daniel Parke Custis had formed with the top-drawer London firm of Robert Cary and Company. That spring Washington sent an authenticated copy of his marriage certificate to this London agent and advised that "for the future please to address all your letters which relate to the affairs of the late Dan[ie]l Parke Custis Esqr. to me."[31] Like his previous London representative, Richard Washington, Robert Cary and Company were factors who received tobacco shipments from Virginia plantations, sold them at the best possible price, then used the proceeds to purchase wares from fashionable London purveyors. The firm had also collected dividends for Martha from her former husband's stock in the Bank of England. Robert Cary was a larger and more prestigious house than Richard Washington, providing further proof of Washington's swift ascent.

Washington's relationship with Robert Cary formed an integral part of his quest for refinement. A profligate spender, he promptly placed an order with Cary for a new bedroom set, complete with a four-poster bed, window curtains, a bedspread, and four chairs, all upholstered in matching blue and white fabric to give the "uniformly handsome and genteel" effect he desired.[32] From this first order, it was plain that the young couple planned to entertain in high style. They ordered a "fashionable set" of dessert glasses, special stands for sweetmeats and jellies, and silver knives and forks with ivory handles. In this first lengthy order, there was also an ominous hint of early dental trouble for Washington, who ordered from an apothecary on Ludgate Hill six bottles of a special brew concocted to cleanse teeth and cure toothaches.

In placing orders for goods from London, Washington often employed two adjectives that nicely sum up his taste: *neat* and *fashionable*. In the eighteenth century, the word *neat* differed subtly from its usage today. According to *The Oxford English Dictionary, neat* then meant "characterized by elegance of form without unnecessary embellishment; of agreeable but simple appearance; nicely made or proportioned." In other words, Washington preferred things that were stylish but subdued, denoting his worldly status without showily advertising it. Although he never lived to see England (he told one correspondent in 1760 that he "ardently desired" to go), this young provincial yearned to resemble the better class of London people.[33] In a typical order to his London agents, he wrote, "I have no doubt but you will choose a fashionable colored cloth as well as a good one and make it in the best taste."[34] The Virginia planter trusted blindly to the sartorial judgment of his London tailors. When he ordered "two pair of work[e]d ruffles at a guinea each pair," he added that "if work[e]d ruffles should be out of fashion, send such as are not."[35] After years of a rough soldierly life, Washington ordered breeches of black silk and crimson velvet. He was careful, however, to warn against lace or embroidery or anything that might stereotype him as a fop. Many of his clothing orders stressed practicality. When ordering a blue hooded greatcoat, he requested that it be made "of such cloth as will turn [away] a good shower of rain."[36]

Because he constantly sent his measurements to faraway artisans, Washington left many precise descriptions of his physique, but his somewhat oddly shaped body made him the bane of his tailors. His wide hips and powerful thighs caused the most trouble. In one of many letters about his ill-fitting clothes, he reproached the tailor in caustic terms: "I desire you to make me a pair of breeches of the same cloth as my former pair, but more accurately fitting. These breeches must be roomy in the seat, the buttons firmly sewn on . . . These breeches must be made exactly to these measurements, not to those to which you imagine that they may stretch after a period of use."[37]

Like her husband, Martha Washington went on a buying binge after their marriage and ordered a cornucopia of luxury goods, with George drafting the itemized list to London. She ordered silk stockings, white satin shoes, gold shoe buckles, beaver hats, and later on, purple kid gloves. She must have been proud of her hair, for she dressed it with "2 fine ivory combs" and "2 large tortoiseshell combs" as well as gauze caps and "2 pounds of fine perfumed powder."[38] Indeed, portraits of Martha Washington show that she often ornamented her brown hair with white beads or pearls.

As Colonel Washington evolved from regimental commander to tobacco planter, he felt pangs of envy as he watched a succession of British victories in the French and Indian War. Seventeen fifty-nine was the year, in Horace Walpole's words, that British bells were "worn threadbare with ringing of victories."[39] For Washington, those bells tolled with a somewhat mournful sound. "The scale of fortune in America is turned greatly in our favor and success is become the boon companion of our fortunate generals," he told Richard Washington, sounding a bit wistful.[40] That Washington still identified with the military life and retained some hope of future battlefield glory is evident in his ordering from Robert Cary six busts of great military figures in history: Alexander the Great, Julius Caesar, Charles XII of Sweden, Frederick II of Prussia, Prince Eugene of Savoy, and the Duke of Marlborough. When his London agents couldn't fill the order, they came up with an alternate proposal to supply busts of writers ranging from Homer to Shakespeare to Milton. For the young planter, these literary heroes didn't quite measure up to famous generals, and he vetoed the suggestion.

As time passed, a petulant tone crept into Washington's communications to his London factors, and he began to rant about the shoddy, overpriced goods fobbed off on him. The London factors had North American planters at their mercy and exploited the situation, reminding these consumers that, in the last analysis, they were powerless colonials. Washington wasn't the only Virginian grandee to feel resentful toward arrogant British merchants. Buying in London was a slow, tedious way to do business, hobbled by endless waits for deliveries. When Washington ordered plows from Robert Cary, for example, he found some essential parts missing and bemoaned that the parts already shipped were "entirely useless and lie upon my hands a dead charge."[41] Sometimes shipments from London wound up at the wrong river or arrived damaged. Even the wealthiest Virginians were simply captive customers.

By nature suspicious of people, Washington experienced a keen sense of injustice. He fretted that Robert Cary was padding his bills and charging exorbitant prices. Of one early shipment, he grumbled that the "woollens, linens, nails etc. are mean in quality but not in price, for in this they excel indeed far above any I have ever had."[42] By the second year of his marriage, his letters to London dripped with barefaced sarcasm, and he didn't bother to disguise his belief that he was being fleeced, telling Robert Cary that "you may believe me when I tell you that instead of getting things good and fashionable in their several kind, we often have articles sent us that could only have been us[e]d by our forefathers in the days of yore. 'Tis a custom . . . with many shopkeepers and tradesmen in London, when they know goods are bespoke for exportation, to palm sometimes old and sometimes very slight and indifferent goods upon us, taking care at the same time to advance 10, 15, or 20 p[e]rc[en]t upon them."[43] When the London factors blithely advised him to return unsatisfactory goods, Washington scoffed that nobody could go a full year without the required articles. His dealings with Robert Cary opened yet another chapter of disillusionment with the British whom he had once so admired.

One reason that Washington and other planters submitted to their London agents was that they offered easy credit unavailable in the colonies. Like many of his affluent neighbors, Washington was land rich and cash poor and spent a lifetime scrounging for money. Historians have often pondered the paradox of why rich Virginia planters later formed a hotbed of revolutionary ferment, and the explanation partly lies in their long, sullen dependence upon London factors. Of four million pounds borrowed by colonists by the outset of the American Revolution, half was owed by the prodigal farmers of Tidewater Virginia.[44] As they gorged on credit, their luxurious lives rested on a precarious foundation of debt. Virginia borrowers regularly blamed their London factors for this indebtedness rather than examining their own extravagant consumption. In piling up excessive debt, they repeated a vice then rampant among the spendthrift British upper class.

Almost immediately Washington stumbled into the same quagmire of debt that ensnared many fellow planters. After two years of marriage, he owed a sizable two thousand pounds sterling to Robert Cary. Eager to play the country squire to the hilt, he ordered goods from London with a free hand. In a letter to one of his former officers in April 1763, Washington complained of being hopelessly indebted to Robert Cary. In his defense, he pleaded the disorganized state of Mount Vernon when he returned from the war, the need to buy more land and slaves, and the expenses of a large family: "I had provisions of all kinds to buy for the first two or three years and my plantations to stock." Before he knew it, the money he spent on buildings and other things had "swallowed up . . . all the money I got by marriage, *nay* more."[45]

The situation deteriorated sharply the following year. Washington was congenitally prickly about money, and Robert Cary aggravated matters by being too quick to dun him for funds. In August 1764 Washington reacted to a call for more money by blaming "mischances rather than misconduct" for the repeated failures of his tobacco crops. He was outraged that Cary would pester him the second he lagged on his payments. "I did not expect that a correspondent so steady and constant as I have proved . . . would be reminded in the instant it was discovered how necessary it was for him to be expeditious in his payments," he complained. Unlike some patrician debtors, Washington was uneasy carrying so much debt, reminding his

London creditor that "it is but an irksome thing to a free mind to be any ways hampered in debt."[46] In subsequent letters to London, Washington's fury fairly exploded off the page. When he sent a large shipment of tobacco the following year, he was aghast at the poor prices that Robert Cary fetched for him and accused the firm of securing better deals for other Virginia planters. "That the sales are pitifully low needs no words to demonstrate," he wrote. "And that they are worse than many of my acquaintance upon this river Potomac have got in the outposts . . . is a truth equally as certain." Washington blustered that it might be "absolutely necessary for me to change my correspondence unless I experience an alteration for the better."[47]

For the rest of his life, Washington was vehement on the subject of debt and frequently lectured relatives about its dangers. Even though he scapegoated creditors for his own debt, it is clear from later letters that he searched his soul long and hard on the subject. Decades later he admonished one nephew that "there is no practice more dangerous than that of borrowing money . . . for when money can be had in this way, repayment is seldom thought of in time . . . Exertions to raise it by dint of industry ceases. It comes easy and is spent freely and many things indulged in that would never be thought of, if to be purchased by the sweat of the brow. In the mean time, the debt is accumulating like a snowball in rolling."[48] Washington spoke knowingly, as only a reformed sinner can do as he reviews past transgressions.

CHAPTER TEN

A Certain Species of Property

FOR THE FIRST SIX YEARS OF MARRIAGE, as he devoted mounting resources to growing tobacco, George Washington was a hostage to the fortunes of that fickle crop. As noted, he had returned from his military adventures to discover Mount Vernon, under brother Jack's supervision, in a scandalous state of disrepair. While off in the western hinterlands, he found it impossible to monitor business activities at home, which must have been profoundly distressing for someone of his meticulous work habits. As he worked to remedy matters, restocking the plantation and constructing new buildings, he ended up squandering part of Martha's fortune.

Though an inexperienced planter, the enterprising Washington was determined to produce high-quality tobacco, and to that end he expanded his acreage and revealed a scientific bent as he dabbled with different varieties. Always receptive to innovation, he pored over agricultural treatises and experimented with oats, wheat, and barley, planted in soil from various corners of his property. Only in retrospect did he perceive the folly of staking his future on tobacco. The soil at Mount Vernon, he duly learned, had "an under stratum of hard clay impervious to water," washing away the thin topsoil and leaving behind "eyesore gullies."[1] It posed insuperable challenges for a novice planter who had to contend with several seasons of drought and heavy rain, which only compounded the runoff problem. Besides poor topography, Washington also had to contend with fluctuating tobacco prices—under imperial law, all sales went through England—and he never knew what his crops would fetch until he heard back from London. With hindsight, it is easy to fault his emphasis on tobacco, but the crop was so omnipresent in Virginia that planters paid taxes with it and engaged in an intense rivalry to produce superior leaves.

In the 1760s Washington's letters on his tobacco trade often read like one long jeremiad. He started out with a bumper crop of 147,357 pounds in his first year of marriage, only to be repeatedly victimized by the vagaries of weather. "We have had one of the most severe droughts in these parts that ever was known and without a speedy interposition of providence (in sending us moderate and refreshing rains to mollify and soften the earth), we shall not make one ounce of tobacco this year," he reported to Robert Cary in 1762.[2] The next year his wheat crop was attacked by a fungus known as rust, while his Indian corn and tobacco were choked by weeds and grass spawned by incessant rains. The mediocre quality of his leaves further depressed the price his tobacco drew in London, making it impossible to pare down debt. At melancholy moments Washington sounded as if the elements conspired to punish his crops. In August 1765 he noted that the Mount Vernon soil had been parched since May because of drought, while a mere ten miles away the weather was "perfectly seasonable" and his neighbors had "promising crops of corn and tobacco."[3]

Perhaps the most pernicious aspect of tobacco culture was its labor-intensive nature, making it a natural match with slavery. No aspect of his life would so trouble Washington or posterity as his status as a major slave owner. Had he not started with tobacco, he might never have become so enmeshed with a reprehensible system that he learned to loathe. Slaves were ubiquitous in this rich, populous colony, making up 40 percent of Virginia's population. In fact, slavery had acquired such a firm grip on the colony that one minister maintained in 1757 that "to live in Virginia without slaves is morally impossible."[4]

Washington's opposition to slavery took the form of a gradual awakening over many decades. He seldom uttered the word *slavery,* as if it grated on his conscience, preferring polite euphemisms such as "servants," "Negroes," "my people," or "my family." Like other slaveholders, the young Washington talked about slaves as simply another form of property. He was cold-blooded in specifying instructions for buying slaves, telling one buyer, as if he were purchasing a racehorse, that he wanted his slaves "to be straight-limbed and in every respect strong and likely, with good teeth and good countenances."[5] He favored adolescent females who could maximize the number of slave children, urging one planter who owed him money to sell some slaves in the fall "when they are fat and lusty and must soon fall of[f] unless well fed."[6] In this savage world, planters posted slaves as collateral for loans, and Washington upbraided one debtor for asking him to rely upon "such hazardous and perishable articles as Negroes, stock, and chattels."[7] With another debtor, he threatened that, without speedy payment, "your Negroes must be immediately exposed to sale for ready money after short notice." In his diary, he often wrote of being "at home all day alone" when he was surrounded by slaves in the mansion and fields.

However horrifying it seems to later generations, abominable behavior toward dark-skinned people was considered an acceptable way of life. In 1767, when four slaves were executed in Fairfax County for supposedly colluding to poison their overseers, their decapitated heads were posted on chimneys at the local courthouse to act as a grim warning to others. Nobody protested this patent atrocity. At the same time, slave masters in the eighteenth century seldom rationalized or romanticized slavery as a divinely sanctioned system, as happened before the Civil War. Washington, Jefferson, Madison, and other Virginia planters acknowledged the immorality of slavery, while confessing perplexity as to how to abolish it without producing mayhem and financial ruin. When denouncing British behavior on the eve of the American Revolution, Washington made clear the degrading nature of the system when he said that, if the colonists tolerated abuses, the British "will make us as tame and abject slaves as the blacks we rule over with such arbitrary sway."[8]

The black population at Mount Vernon grew apace after Washington's marriage as he purchased slaves aggressively to keep pace with his widening economic activities. During the first year of his marriage, he acquired 13 slaves, then another 42 between 1761 and 1773. Since he paid taxes on slaves older than twelve years of age, we know that he personally owned 56 slaves of working age in 1761, 62 in 1762, 78 in 1765, and 87 in 1770.

Whether from humane considerations or merely from regard for property, Washington was tireless in his medical treatment of slaves; his diaries are loaded with references to doctors, and even to Washington himself, tending sick slaves. During the frosty first winter of his marriage, he grew alarmed by the death of four slaves by late January, three of them dower slaves from the Custis estate. As in the army, whenever trouble struck, Washington didn't shirk personal involvement. His direct management style became manifest that spring when smallpox cropped up at his western plantation on Bullskin Creek. At once he hastened off to Frederick County and was startled to find that two slaves, Harry and Kit, had already died, and that everything lay "in the utmost confusion, disorder and backwardness."[9] He rushed off to nearby Winchester to secure blankets and medical supplies, summoned a nurse, and instructed his overseer to quarantine slaves with smallpox. By the Revolutionary War, Washington made a regular practice of inoculating slaves against smallpox. The standard method was to scrape contaminated matter from the pustules of a victim with a mild case of smallpox, then slip it on a thread under the skin of the inoculated person. This produced a mild case of the disease, which prevented the more virulent form.

In written agreements with new overseers, Washington exhorted them to treat ailing slaves with a modicum of kindness. In 1762 a new overseer, Nelson Kelly, had to agree "that he will take all necessary and proper care of the Negroes committed to his management, treating them with humanity and tenderness when sick."[10] There seems little doubt that Washington was motivated by human sympathy as well as profit in caring for sick slaves. During his first term as president, he urged his estate manager to have overseers pay special heed to sick slaves, "for I am sorry to observe that the generality of them view these poor creatures in scarcely any other light than they do a draft horse or ox, neglecting them as much when they are unable to work, instead of comforting and nursing them when they lie on a sickbed."[11] Possibly because of his scrupulous care of sick slaves, Washington frequently complained about those who feigned illness. When he thought a slave named Sam was faking illness, he ordered his estate manager to "examine his case . . . but not by the doctor, for he has had doctors enough already of all colors and sexes and to no effect. Laziness is, I believe, his principal ailment."[12]

Another area of plantation life where Washington's behavior was comparatively humane, within the overall context of an inhumane system, was in his studious refusal to break up slave families. Although slave marriages were not sanctioned by law, Washington treated them as binding and sacrosanct. In time, he refused to sell slaves if it meant separating families. Slaves who wished to marry slaves from other plantations needed Washington's permission, but we have no evidence he ever denied it. That he felt a paternalistic responsibility toward his slaves was shown dramatically in his final years when a slave named Fanny was bedridden for a week after being beaten by her husband Ben, a slave on another plantation. Washington, livid, forbade Ben to set foot at Mount Vernon on pain of whipping. Four years later Fanny married another slave.[13] When Washington contemplated selling off slaves during the Revolution, he expressed reluctance to do so, then told his manager that "if these poor wretches are to be held in a state of slavery, I do not see that a change of masters will render it more irksome, provided husband and wife and parents and children are not separated from each other, which is not my intention to do."[14] Although he stopped buying slaves in 1772, his slave population swelled from natural increase so that he owned 135 able-bodied slaves when tapped to head the Continental Army. Ironically, his growing scruples about slavery and his refusal to break up families by selling them off saddled him with a fast-growing slave community.

Thanks to pioneering research at Mount Vernon in recent years, we have obtained a much more vivid sense of slave life there. The very design of the estate made it arduous for slaves to maintain families. Mount Vernon came to consist of five farms: the Mansion House Farm (what tourists think of today as Mount Vernon) and four satellite farms: Dogue Run, Muddy Hole, Union, and River. Many Mansion House slaves were either household servants, dressed in brightly colored livery of scarlet coats and white waistcoats, or highly skilled artisans; these last were overwhelmingly male, while the four distant farms held mostly field hands who, contrary to stereotype, were largely female. This sexual division meant that only a little more than a third of Washington's slaves enjoyed the luxury of living with their spouses and children. Since the slaves worked a grueling six-day week, from sunup to sundown, they had to tramp long distances on Saturday evening or Sunday to visit their far-flung families.[15] It speaks volumes about the strength and tenacity of slave families that two-thirds of the adults remained married despite such overwhelming obstacles.

We know that Mary Washington was tightfisted in treating slaves; one neighbor remembered her as "more given to housewifery, and to keeping their servants at their proper business and in their proper places than to any unnecessary forms of etiquette."[16] Thomas Jefferson thought that Washington had inherited that autocratic style. "From his childhood, [Washington] always ruled and ruled severely," Jefferson was later quoted as saying. "He was first brought up to govern slaves, he then governed an army, then a nation."[17] For the most part, Washington dealt with slaves through overseers whom he prodded to "be constantly with your people . . . There is no other sure way of getting work well done and quietly by negroes, for when an overlooker's back is turned, the most of them will slight their work or be idle altogether."[18]

Under Virginia law, slaveholders could freely abuse or even murder their slaves in punishing misbehavior and still avoid legal repercussions. Washington believed that whipping slaves was counterproductive and tried to restrain such brutality. As he lectured one estate manager, it "oftentimes is easier to effect [change] by watchfulness and admonition than by severity and certainly must be more agreeable to every feeling mind in the practice of them."[19] Overseers were required to issue warnings to wayward slaves before flogging them. In theory, they couldn't apply the lash to slaves unless they first secured written permission from Washington, but due to his extended absences from Mount Vernon, the rule wasn't always obeyed. "General Washington has forbidden the use of the whip on his blacks," a French visitor to Mount Vernon later averred, "but unfortunately his example has been little emulated."[20] He wanted his overseers to be strict, not cruel. Whether on the plantation, in the army, or in government, he stressed the need to inspire respect rather than affection in subordinates, a common thread running through his vastly disparate managerial activities.

Washington insisted that overseers track slaves closely during workdays that could stretch up to sixteen hours in summertime. He constantly reprimanded them for being drunk, lazy, or inattentive to their duties. Often feeling burdened by the expense and difficulty of dealing with white overseers, he turned to slave overseers, and at one point blacks supervised three of his five farms.

Washington prided himself on being firm but fair-minded, leading his adopted granddaughter to say later, "He was a generous and noble master and [the slaves] feared and loved him."[21] His presidential secretary, Tobias Lear, said of Mount Vernon, "The negroes are not treated as blacks in general are in this country. They are clothed and fed as well as any laboring people whatever and they are not subject to the lash of a domineering overseer—*but they are still slaves.*"[22] Several observers noted that Washington, with perfect self-control in public, could flare up with servants in private. During his presidency the wife of the British ambassador remarked that Washington "acquired a uniform command over his passions on public occasions, but in private and particularly with his servants, its violence sometimes broke out."[23] One cabinet secretary talked of Washington's reputation for "warm passion and stern severity" with his servants.[24] Another observer was taken aback by how gruffly the tactful president addressed his slaves, "as differently as if he had been quite another man or had been in anger."[25] Still another Mount Vernon guest noted how exquisitely attuned the slaves were to the master's moods: "His servants seemed to watch his eye, and to anticipate his every wish; hence, a look was equivalent to a command."[26] It should be said that if Washington displayed an irritable style with his slaves, he could also be short-tempered with his military and political subordinates.

Slavery presented special challenges to a hypercritical personality like Washington, for the slaves had no earthly reason to strive for the perfection he wanted. However illogical it might seem, he expected them to share his work ethic and was perturbed when they didn't follow his industrious example. Feeling entitled to extract the maximum amount of work from slaves, he advised one overseer that "every laborer (male or female)" should do "as much in the 24 hours as their strength, without endangering their health or constitution, will allow of."[27] Not surprisingly, his letters contain frequent references to slaves whom he saw as indolent or prone to theft, and he never regarded such behavior as rational responses to bondage. Reproaching his slave carpenters, he said, "There is not to be found so idle a set of rascals."[28] Of a slave named Betty who worked as a spinner in the mansion, he complained that "a more lazy, deceitful and impudent hussy is not to be found in the United States."[29] He talked caustically about malingering slaves as if they were salaried workers who had failed to earn their wages—a blind spot he never entirely lost.

Fond of system and efficiency, Washington was stymied by his slaves' inability to meet his high standards. Once in February 1760 he was dismayed to find that four slave carpenters had jointly hewn only 120 feet of poplar logs that day. Like a modern efficiency expert, he sat down, consulted his watch, and clocked them in a time-and-motion study. The master's presence instantly stimulated the slaves to *quadruple* their output to 125 feet of timber apiece. Once he had solved the motivational mystery, Washington wondered about the material being used. "It is to be observed here that this hewing and sawing likewise was of poplar," he wrote in his diary. "What may be the difference therefore between the working of this wood and [an]other some future observations must make known."[30] It is easy to see how the methodical Washington, with his excellent business mind, would have found infuriating an economic system that naturally discouraged hard work.

Male slaves at the Mansion House enjoyed accommodations superior to those of slaves at the outlying farms. They likely had better quarters because they were often trained artisans and lived within eyeshot of family members and visitors. At a later period many inhabited a large brick building with glazed windows that was divided into four rooms and fitted out like an army barrack, with bunks lining the walls. In the four remote farms, slaves were jammed into small, one-room log cabins, crafted flimsily from sticks cemented with mud. A Polish nobleman who admired Washington was taken aback by these squalid hovels. "We entered one of the huts of the blacks, for one cannot call them by the name of houses. They are more miserable than the most miserable of the cottages of our peasants. The husband and wife sleep on a mean pallet, the children on the ground; [there is] a very bad fireplace, some utensils for cooking, but in the middle of this poverty, some cups and a teapot."[31]

Each slave received one set of new clothes per annum—a woolen jacket, a pair of breeches, two shirts, a pair of stockings, and a pair of shoes—often made from a coarse brown linen called osnaburg. Slave women received an annual petticoat and smock. Some slaves also had Sunday outfits of dark coats with white vests and white breeches. Every day the slaves received approximately one quart of Indian cornmeal, and every month twenty salted herrings, which sounds like a terribly meager ration. "It is not my wish or desire that my Negro[e]s should have an ounce of meal more, nor less, than is sufficient to feed them plentifully," Washington told his estate manager.[32] Recent archaeological work at Mount Vernon has revealed that the slave diet was not entirely bleak. On Sundays Washington allowed slaves to borrow his large nets, or "seines," to fish in the Potomac. At least one elderly slave named Father Jack kept a canoe on the river and supplied fish to others. Archaeologists have identified bones from sixteen types of fish in the cellar of the main slave residence. Washington also distributed to the slaves meat left over from his table, innards of hogs slaughtered on the estate, surplus fish from his fishery, and buttermilk left after the milk was churned.

The most intriguing archaeological find has been the discovery of lead shot and gun flints, showing that Washington allowed selected slaves to keep firearms and hunt wild game in the woods. The remains of fifty-eight animal species have been identified in the slave cellar. The slaves could either eat the game or sell it to the master's table. Washington's adopted grandson remembered how a slave named Tom Davis hunted duck on the Potomac with his Newfoundland dog and brought down with his musket "as many of those delicious birds as would supply the larder for a week."[33] This made up part of a strictly limited market economy at Mount Vernon in which Washington allowed slaves to till their own garden plots, keep poultry, and sell eggs, chicken, fruits, and vegetables. On Sunday mornings he even permitted them to travel with passes to nearby Alexandria and peddle their wares in the open marketplace. This freedom of movement enabled Washington's slaves to meet and marry slaves on other plantations.

That the slaves at Mount Vernon could move about without supervision runs counter to the common view of slavery as a system enforced only by the daily terror of whips and shackles. Like other major planters, Washington owned more slaves than his overseers could effectively monitor, and so the only way to control a captive population was to convince them that runaways would be severely punished. Virginia had perfected a system of terror for capturing fugitive slaves. Under a 1748 law, a master could seek out two justices of the peace and have them issue a proclamation against runaways. To give the slaves fair warning, the proclamation had to be posted on church doors throughout the county. If the slave still didn't surrender, the law said that "it shall be lawful for any person . . . to kill and destroy such slaves by any ways or means, without accusation or impeachment of any crime for the same."[34]

If Washington, with few exceptions, avoided inflicting harm on captured runaways, he showed notable zeal in hunting them down, and the problem consumed considerable time. The scholar Philip Morgan has computed that Washington had forty-seven runaway slaves over the years, or 7 percent of the total population.[35] A year after his marriage Washington pursued a runaway named Boson and wound up paying a ten-shilling bounty to a slave from another plantation who recaptured him. Many slaves who fled were favorites of George and Martha Washington, who invariably reacted with a sense of shock and betrayal. In his diary for 1761, Washington recorded deep concern for the fate of a slave named Cupid, who had recently arrived from Africa, scarcely spoke English, and had contracted pleurisy. The master made a point of dropping in to inquire after Cupid's health and in one diary entry wrote anxiously that "when I went to bed, I thought [Cupid] within a few hours of breathing his last."[36] Notwithstanding this special care, Cupid subsequently ran away with three other slaves named Peros, Jack, and Neptune. On August 11, 1761, Washington placed a fugitive slave advertisement in the *Maryland Gazette*, noting that they had escaped "without the least suspicion, provocation, or difference with anybody, or the least angry word or abuse from their overseers."[37]

Washington's description of the four slaves showed that he didn't see them as an indistinguishable mass but as a collection of distinct individuals. Of Peros he said that he was thirty-five to forty years old, had a "yellowish complex[ion] with a very full round face and full black beard," and wore "a dark colored cloth coat, a white linen waistcoat, white breeches and white stockings."[38] He added that the runaway slave spoke decent English, had shed much of his African dialect, and was "esteemed a sensible, judicious Negro."[39] Of Cupid, Washington noted that "the skin of his face is coarse and inclined to be pimply."[40] Two of the slaves showed recent African ancestry, having been scarified by their tribes. Jack had "cuts down each cheek bearing his country marks," while Neptune had "his teeth straggling and filed sharp."[41] Washington offered a forty-shilling reward for the recovery of all four men.

Unless they proved repeat offenders, Washington usually forgave runaways who were brought back to Mount Vernon. He accepted the return of the "sensible, judicious" Peros without reprisals, only to have him flee again in 1770. In general, Washington didn't have the stomach for the more odious forms of punishment. On occasion, however, he resorted to the grisly penalty of selling refractory slaves in the Caribbean, where they faced hard labor and almost certain death as they toiled in sweltering sugarcane brakes. In July 1766 Washington meted out this unspeakable fate to a "healthy, strong" young slave named Tom whom he described as "both a rogue and runaway."[42] He assigned him to Captain Joseph Thompson, whose schooner *Swift* was sailing for St. Kitts. Washington told the skipper to keep Tom handcuffed until they got to sea and that if he was "kept clean and trimmed up a little when offered to sale," he might reap a good price.[43] From the proceeds, Washington hoped to receive one hogshead of molasses and one of rum, along with a barrel of limes and a pot of tamarinds. On at least two other occasions, Washington exported recalcitrant slaves to the Caribbean and brandished the threat of doing so to intimidate others.

In colonial Virginia the property of debtors, including slaves, was often sold at tavern lotteries, amid a jovial, high-spirited atmosphere, as a way of making partial repayment to creditors. In December 1769 Washington cosponsored a lottery in Williamsburg for the estate of one Bernard Moore, who had defaulted on a large loan from the Custis estate. For ten pounds, a sporting investor could purchase a chance to win parcels of Moore's land or some fifty-five slaves divided into thirty-nine lots. The most desirable male slaves were sold with their families intact, while other slave families were broken up indiscriminately. It is hard to imagine anything that more starkly contradicted Washington's stated policy of preserving slave families than raffling them off in this public manner. With some justice, Henry

Wiencek has written that Washington "reached a moral nadir" with the Bernard Moore lottery.[44] The editors of Washington's papers have noted that in the 1760s he "frequently bought tickets for lotteries," although the Bernard Moore case seems to be the only one in which he acted as an organizer.[45]

Fortunately, such notorious cases were the exception. George and Martha Washington worked in close proximity with their slaves and knew many of them individually. That George Washington acknowledged the humanity of some slaves is seen in his remarkably affectionate, long-standing relationship with his manservant William Lee. At a slave auction in 1768, Washington paid top dollar to a Mrs. Mary Lee of Westmoreland County for two mulatto brothers, William and Frank Lee, and then groomed William (also called Billy or Will) as his personal servant. A dark-skinned mulatto, Billy Lee was a short, compact, powerfully built young man with a gift for gab, a rich fund of anecdotes, and a wealth of opinions. A real daredevil as a horseman, he shadowed Washington in every major activity of his life and was an indispensable asset during the foxhunting season. Billy Lee combined in his person the job of Washington's valet, butler, and waiter. Whether Washington was trotting off to the House of Burgesses, the Continental Congress, or Valley Forge, Lee was the trusted aide in attendance. A New England visitor noted his singular place among Washington's slaves: "His servant Billy, the faithful companion of his military career, was always at his side."[46] Lee was one of the few slaves allowed the dignity of a last name, confirming his special standing.

Slavery was woven into every aspect of Mount Vernon life, even for visitors. "Everyone felt himself at home and had a negro servant to wait on him and supply his wants," wrote an admiring English visitor.[47] Often the first sight that greeted visitors was slave children playing near the front of the mansion, and Washington frequently grumbled that they disturbed his shrubs. He had a dozen house servants outfitted in livery ordered from Robert Cary in London. Breechy served dinner while Doll cooked it, assisted by the scullion Betty. Jenny and Mima washed and ironed, while Betty and Moll assisted Martha with sewing. Mulatto Jack served as general handyman. Never an idle mistress, Martha Washington oversaw a sewing circle of slaves who manufactured much of the estate's clothing. She kept this up even in later years, when one visitor painted this domestic scene: "Then we repaired to the old lady's room, which is . . . nicely fixed for all sorts of work. On one side sits the chamber maid with her knitting, on the other a little colored pet, learning to sew, an old, decent woman with her table and shears cutting out the negroes' winter clothes, while the good old lady directs them all, incessantly knitting herself."[48] Martha Washington treated the slaves well and became fond of many of them but tolerated no shirkers and expected loyalty and affection from her favorites.

A master of the profitable use of time, Washington listed his monthly doings in his diary under the rubric "Where and how my time is spent." Whether for business or social occasions, his punctuality was legendary, and he expected everyone to be on time. In his business dealings, he boasted that "no man discharges the demand of wages or fulfills agreements with more punctuality than I do."[49] Preoccupied with timepieces throughout his life, Washington aspired to stand at the center of an orderly, clockwork universe. He accorded the sundial a central spot on his mansion lawn, as if to suggest that everything hinged on the proper allotment of time; invariably he glanced at it when returning home from rides. As president, he loved to employ his leisure time by strolling over to see his Philadelphia watchmakers. "No one ever appreciated better than General Washington the value of time and the art of making use of it," recalled a French businessman.[50] His love of ritual, habit, and order enabled him to sustain the long, involved tasks that distinguished his life. "System in all things is the soul of business," he liked to say. "To deliberate maturely and execute promptly is the way to conduct it to advantage."[51]

Washington benefited from the unvarying regularity of his daily routine and found nothing monotonous about it. Like many thrifty farmers, he rose before sunrise and accomplished much work while others still slept. Prior to breakfast, he shuffled about in dressing gown and slippers and passed an hour or two in his library, reading and handling correspondence. He also devoted time to private prayers before Billy Lee laid out his clothes, brushed his hair, and tied it in a queue. Washington liked to examine his stables before breakfast, inspect his horses, and issue instructions to the grooms. Then he had an unchanging breakfast of corn cakes, tea, and honey.

After breakfast Washington pulled on tall black boots, mounted his horse, and began the prolonged circuit of his five farms, where he expected to find hands hard at work. Once again, he was a diligent boss, not a gentleman farmer. Each day he rode twenty miles on horseback and personally supervised field work, fence construction, ditch drainage, tree planting, and dozens of other activities. An active presence, he liked to demonstrate how things should be done, leading by example. One startled visitor expressed amazement that the master "often works with his men himself, strips off his coat and labors like a common man."[52] Washington couldn't bear anything slovenly. "I shall begrudge no reasonable expense that will contribute to the improvement and neatness of my farms, for nothing pleases me better than to see them in good order and everything trim, handsome, and thriving about them," he advised one estate manager. "Nor nothing hurts me more than to find them otherwise and the tools and implements laying wherever they were last used, exposed to injuries from rain, sun, etc."[53] No detail was too trivial to escape his notice, and he often spouted the Scottish adage "Many mickles make a muckle"— that is, tiny things add up.[54]

Washington made sure that he returned for dinner precisely at 2:45 P.M. when the first bell sounded for the large midday meal. According to legend, the clatter of his approaching hooves often coincided with the bell's loud clang. Washington then washed, dressed, powdered his hair, and appeared in the dining room by the stroke of three. He preferred a dinner of fish from the Potomac and typically ate with a hearty appetite. In this heavy-drinking era, he could polish off three or four glasses of an amber-colored wine known as Madeira without being thought a heavy drinker. The cloth was then removed, and Washington would lift his glass with his habitual toast to "All our friends." He then retired to his library before a light supper. Before going to bed at nine o'clock, he would often read aloud to the family from the newspaper or from sermons on Sunday evenings or join in a game of cards or backgammon.

To maintain a detailed grasp of his vast operations, Washington kept comprehensive records long before such bookkeeping was commonplace. Being a farmer, he scratched out a daily log of the weather, but his record keeping went far beyond such basics. "He also makes copious notes in writing relative to his own experiments, the state of the seasons, nature of soils, effect of different kinds of manure, and everything that can throw light on the farming business," wrote his later aide David Humphreys.[55] Everything was perfectly sorted, classified, and slotted in his compartmentalized mind and books. Washington's contemporaries recognized that this compulsive note taking, this itch to record his every action, went to the very essence of this well-regulated man. "You would be surprised to find what a uniform life he leads," wrote John Hancock's nephew after a visit to Mount Vernon. "Everything he does is by method of system . . . He keeps a journal where he records everything . . . he is a model of the highest perfection."[56]

CHAPTER ELEVEN

The Prodigy

LONG BEFORE he achieved great fame or renown, something about Washington's bearing and presence bedazzled people. In common with other well-bred boys of his day, he probably wore a corset as a small child, which pulled his shoulders back and thrust his chest out, giving him added dignity. Like a figure strutting on a stage, he never lounged or slouched and seemed as comfortable in a ballroom as on a battlefield. Properly appareled on all occasions, he never allowed people to see him in a neglected state, much less undressed, and ordered clothes that gave him elegance with freedom of movement. In ordering a suit from London, he admonished his tailor to "make it in the best taste to sit easy and loose, as clothes that are tight always look awkward and are uneasy to the wearer."[1] In the manner of European royalty, he never seemed to hurry. The impression fostered by his imposing physique, joined with his upright, virile carriage and natural aplomb, marked him out as a natural leader.

Much of the power of Washington's presence derived from his fluid gait, the antithesis of the stiff, wooden image Gilbert Stuart grafted on the American imagination. The quintessential man of action, he moved like a national icon long before he became one. The sculptor William Rush recalled his smooth, unruffled movements: "I have been in battle immediately under his command. I have viewed him walking, standing, sitting. I have seen him at a game of ball for several hours," and in all these activities he exhibited "the most manly and graceful attitudes I ever saw."[2] Washington was, quite simply, a sight to behold. "So tall, so straight!" one servant remembered. "And . . . with such an air! Ah, sire, he was like no one else!"[3] At Williamsburg, he exuded a special splendor with his ceremonial sword riding on his hip, while showing the light, confident tread of the military man. If much of this gracefulness came naturally to Washington, some of it likely came from strenuous youthful efforts to form himself for polite society as he acquired the easy manner and erect posture that distinguished a gentleman.

George and Martha Washington were a sociable couple who entertained an unending cavalcade of guests at Mount Vernon. During the seven years before the American Revolution, they fed (and frequently housed) an estimated two thousand guests.[4] One visitor murmured his approval at how cordially Washington had treated him "as if I had lived years in his house."[5] Washington was an excellent host of a certain sort. He was congenial without being deeply personal, friendly without being familiar, and perfected a cool sociability that distanced him from people even as it invited them closer. He never felt the urge to impress people. As John Marshall wrote, "He had no pretensions to that vivacity which fascinates, and to that wit which dazzles."[6] He knew the value of silence, largely kept opinions to himself, and seldom committed a faux pas.

Very concerned with winning the approval of others, Washington tended his image with extreme care, suggesting a self-conscious insecurity about how people perceived him. Peter Henriques has commented on Washington's "intense fear of failure" and the hundreds of times the word *approbation* crops up in his letters.[7] Since he struck people as stern and grave, pleasant and affable at once, he seemed to embody Benjamin Franklin's maxim "Let all men know thee, but no man know thee thoroughly." People sensed the turbulent, buried emotions within him and occasionally glimpsed their raw power. One stage actor who visited Mount Vernon said that Washington had "a compression of the mouth and [an] indentation of the brow . . . suggesting habitual conflict with and mastery over passion."[8]

During the American Revolution, some officers claimed that they never saw Washington smile. If he seldom submitted to belly laughs, he was never as dour as legend claims. Said one perceptive former slave: "I never see that man laugh to show his teeth—he done all his laughing inside."[9] If laughter didn't come readily to Washington, it could be coaxed out of him after several glasses of wine, when he fell into the uproarious spirit of a dinner party. James Madison later noted that while Washington didn't tell funny stories, he responded when others did: "He was particularly pleased with the jokes, good humor, and hilarity of his companions."[10] Washington was also more unbuttoned at the theater. "You would seldom see a frown or smile on his countenance, his air was serious and reflecting," wrote one observer, "yet I have seen him in the theater laugh heartily."[11]

Acutely aware of being a provincial subject in a remote corner of the British Empire, Washington sometimes sounded an apologetic, self-deprecating note when writing to London. When he invited his British factor, Richard Washington, to visit

Mount Vernon, he said, "We have few things here striking to European travelers (except an abundant woods) but a little variety, a welcome reception among a few friends, and the open and prevalent hospitality of the country in general."[12] With his emphasis on self-improvement, Washington trained himself to play the gentleman in polite drawing rooms and among the highly educated. People sensed something a bit studied about his behavior and suspected, correctly, that the manner was partly learned. The British ambassador's wife noted that he had "perfect good breeding and a correct knowledge of even the etiquette of a court," but how he had acquired it, "heaven knows."[13] Washington exemplified the self-invented American, forever struggling to better himself and rise above his origins.

While Washington cultivated friendships throughout his life, he didn't have many true intimates and his relationships were seldom of the candid or confessional type. His reserve, if not impenetrable, was by no means lightly surrendered. He was habitually cautious with new people and only gradually opened up as they passed a series of loyalty tests. "Be courteous to all but intimate with few," he advised his nephew, "and let those few be well tried before you give them your confidence. True friendship is a plant of slow growth."[14] Because Washington never invited people readily into his confidence, it had a nearly irresistible appeal when he did. He tended to be much more conversational among those he trusted and taciturn with strangers.

In a world not far removed from the frontier, Washington's physical strength and dexterity won many admirers. He knew that he was a physical prodigy and enjoyed displaying this with exhibitionistic flair. When he painted Washington in 1772, Charles Willson Peale observed an instance of Washington's herculean strength that he never forgot:

> One afternoon, several young gentlemen, visitors at Mount Vernon, and myself were . . . pitching the bar . . . when suddenly the colonel [Washington] appeared among us. He requested to be shown the pegs that marked the bounds of our efforts; then, smiling, and without putting off his coat, held out his hand for the missile. No sooner did the heavy iron bar feel the grasp of his mighty hand than it lost the power of gravitation . . . striking the ground far . . . beyond our utmost limits. We were indeed amazed, as we stood around, all stripped to the buff . . . having thought ourselves very clever fellows, while the colonel, on retiring, pleasantly observed, "When you beat my pitch, young gentlemen, I'll try again."[15]

A nice touch that he didn't bother to take off his jacket, as if to underscore his effortless feat. While Washington never threw a silver dollar across the Potomac, as legend asserts, he did hurl a rock to the top of the Natural Bridge in the Blue Ridge

Mountains, a height of 215 feet. Although boasting was always foreign to Washington's nature, after the Revolution he confided to David Humphreys that "he never met any man who could throw a stone to so great a distance as himself."[16]

In an age that gloried in horse racing and hunting as gentlemanly pursuits, Washington's virtuosity with horses excited comment throughout his life. Thoroughbred horses were especially prized in Virginia, where they literally elevated masters above their slaves. Jefferson extolled Washington as "the best horseman of his age and the most graceful figure that could be seen on horseback," an appraisal echoed by many others.[17] Ramrod straight and relaxed on horseback, he seemed taller in the saddle than anyone else, exhibiting perfect ease and projecting a magnetic air. Favored with long legs and broad, powerful hips, he could wrap himself around the smaller breeds of horses common in the eighteenth century. It is no coincidence that Washington has been commemorated by so many equestrian statues. "He is a very excellent and bold horseman," noted a French admirer, the Chevalier de Chastellux, "leaping the highest fences and going extremely quickly without standing upon his stirrups, bearing on the bridle, or letting his horse run wild."[18] Chastellux said Washington rode fast even when he was in no special hurry—something that added dash and drama to his movements. He broke and trained his own horses and retained mastery over them. One witness recollected how when Washington dismounted, he "gave a cut of the whip to his horse, which went off by itself to the stable."[19] Washington wrote with affection about horses, and when one man agreed to sell him his favorite horse, he responded gratefully. "The attachment which one feels for a good horse that has . . . been considered as a favorite, I know is very great."[20]

An avid hunter, Washington keenly stalked foxes, deer, ducks, quail, pheasant, and even occasional bears on his estate. He hunted in a handsome outfit, a blue riding frock and scarlet waistcoat threaded with gold lace and topped by a black velvet cap. He wore high boots and carried a smart-looking riding crop, decorated in a herringbone pattern. So much did Washington adore the sport that he papered his mansion with hunting prints. On hunting days, his ritual was to rise before sunrise, breakfast by candlelight, then ride off with his hounds while it was still dark outside. Invariably he was accompanied by Billy Lee, who got Washington to stop hunting black foxes and stick to gray ones after one black fox eluded them on an exhausting chase; Lee averred that there was something diabolical about the cunning black fox.

For a man of Washington's stern work ethic, it is striking how much time he dedicated to hunting, even in the dead of winter. Though he enjoyed fishing, it never matched his consuming interest in chasing animals. In January 1769, for example, he went foxhunting eight times in a twelve-day period even though the ground was packed hard with frost. During the foxhunting season, certain favored guests turned into semipermanent residents of Mount Vernon, staying for weeks at a time.

A lusty hunter, Washington often recorded in his diary the length of the chase and a description of the fox. It was not unusual for the hunt to occupy an entire day. "Hunting again," he wrote in March 1768, "and catched a fox with a bobbed tail and cut ears after 7 hours chase in w[hi]ch most of the dogs were worsted."[21] A month earlier, he recorded that he had killed five mallards and five bald eagles in one day—a curious triumph for the Father of His Country. Washington's fierce, relentless energy, cloaked in social encounters, emerged clearly in warfare and hunting. He liked to ride up ahead with the hounds and be present for the kill. Washington kept his hounds kenneled down by the Potomac and developed a breed that became known as the American foxhound. Protective of his hunting grounds, he was implacable when dealing with poachers. One day when out riding, he encountered a poacher who was furtively slipping away in a canoe. "Raising his gun," recounts a neighbor, the poacher "took deliberate aim at Washington, expecting to daunt him; but Washington dashed up to the culprit, and seizing his canoe, dragged it ashore. He then disarmed him and gave him a severe flogging, which effectually cured his thieving properties."[22]

Another area where Washington demonstrated uncommon agility was in dancing. Because colonial social life revolved around fancy balls and assemblies, gentlemen were expected to master reels, jigs, and minuets. An exceptionally graceful dancer, Washington flourished in such society, not only because he presented an image of strength and poise on the dance floor—one lady recalled that he was "a ceremonious and grave" partner—but also because it allowed some harmless interactions with the ladies.[23] It was the one venue where Martha permitted him to indulge his penchant for gallantry with younger women.

Among the chief diversions of Washington's social life was the theater. During stays in Williamsburg, he attended everything from concerts to waxworks to puppet shows, though nothing matched his sheer delight in a good play. Many scholars have noted the abundant theatrical imagery in his writings, as when he advised a young relative that he was about to "enter upon the grand theater of life."[24] The recurrence of such metaphors says something not only about Washington's love of theater but about his awareness of the dramatic nature of his life and the eventful times through which he passed. He would play many roles in his lifetime, always with consummate flair. That he turned to theater imagery when aiming at a high rhetorical pitch suggests that he saw himself as the protagonist of a great epic, dazzling an audience that had its eyes peeled on his every action.

Two touring companies, the American Company and the Virginia Company, performed at the Williamsburg theater and usually timed their visits to coincide

with meetings of the burgesses. They offered surprisingly rich and varied fare, running the spectrum from Shakespeare to Restoration comedy to Augustan drama
to contemporary plays. During one busy week in June 1770, Washington attended
the theater five nights out of seven. The unremitting emphasis on Joseph Addison's
Cato as being Washington's favorite play—partly because it was performed at Valley
Forge, partly because it fit the stereotype of Washington as the stoic Roman—has
obscured his love of many other plays, especially ribald and sophisticated comedies.
The play that he probably saw and savored the most was Richard Sheridan's racy
The School for Scandal. He also quoted Shakespeare frequently, and his letters are
filled with passing references to *Hamlet, Othello, The Merchant of Venice,* and *The
Tempest.* Not surprisingly, in wartime, he plucked timely quotes from the Roman
and history plays, including *Julius Caesar, Antony and Cleopatra,* and *Henry V.*

From Washington's correspondence with his London factors, what emerges
clearly is that he didn't relegate social duties to his wife, but took an active part in
ordering food, drink, and furnishings for all occasions. He wanted Mount Vernon
to conform to the highest standards of elegance, and he studied how other people
entertained. A telling diary entry, dated a year after his marriage, shows how observant he was of other people's parties and how scornful of anything that struck him
as slovenly or vulgar:

> Went to a ball at Alexandria, where music and dancing was the chief entertainment.
> However, in a convenient room detached for the purpose abounded great plenty of
> bread and butter, some biscuits with tea, and coffee which the drinkers of cou[l]d not
> distinguish from hot water sweetened. Be it remembered that pocket handkerchiefs
> served the purposes of tablecloths and napkins and that no apologies were made for ei-
> ther. I shall therefore distinguish this ball by the style . . . of the Bread and Butter Ball.[25]

Washington's diaries from the 1760s attest to a crowded social calendar and
show how George and Martha Washington absorbed Sally Fairfax into their lives as
a dear friend. Given her close proximity at Belvoir, it would have been difficult to
keep her at arm's length. Instead, Sally came and went freely at Mount Vernon, and
her husband remained one of Washington's favorite hunting partners. The Washingtons were likewise regular visitors at Belvoir. In January 1760 Sally came to visit
Martha, who was then recuperating from the measles. Three years later George
wrote to inquire about an illness that Sally had contracted and said Martha "was in
hopes of seeing Mrs Fairfax this morning," until she herself came down with a fever.[26] Martha Washington could never have befriended Sally Fairfax in this manner
unless she thought that the earlier romance with her husband had been an ephemeral, youthful infatuation that had now receded to a safe distance.

CHAPTER TWELVE

Providence

THE MOST SPLENDID STAGE on which George Washington paraded in his early years was the colonial capital at Williamsburg, now overseen by Lieutenant Governor Francis Fauquier—the "ablest man who had ever filled that office," in Jefferson's view—a charming man of eclectic interests who was a fellow of the Royal Society and had published papers on science and economics.[1] The town, which was characterized by "the manners and etiquette of a court in miniature," according to Washington, stood forth as a glittering symbol of British royalty, a showplace of surface brilliance whose major social priorities were "precedence, dress, imitation."[2] To jaded European eyes, Williamsburg might have appeared small and prosaic, but its handsome government buildings, formal gardens, and spacious streets with brick sidewalks surpassed anything seen in rural Virginia.

In October 1760 Martha asked her husband if she could join him for the upcoming session at the House of Burgesses, and they traveled there in the full regalia of rich tobacco planters—a coach and six, with uniformed slaves riding as coachman and postilion. Once at the capital, Washington lodged on the most fashionable thoroughfare, Duke of Gloucester Street. For ten years he stayed in the hostelry of a diminutive widow, Christiana Campbell, "a little old woman about four feet high and equally thick, [with] a little turn[ed] up pug nose, [and] a mouth screw[e]d up to one side," as one Scottish traveler sketched her.[3]

That October Washington arrived in Williamsburg amid much jubilation. In early September the French had surrendered to British forces at Montreal, bringing to a close the conquest of Canada and leading Fauquier to declare, somewhat prematurely, that "the war is gloriously brought to a happy end."[4] The festive tone proved transitory. On October 25, 1760, George II, the only king George Washington had ever known, died and gave way to a new monarch. On February 11 Fauquier announced the accession to the throne of George III, whose reign would be bedeviled by George Washington and an army of renegade soldiers. The tidings of a new king had immediate repercussions for Washington, since it meant that the old House of Burgesses would be dissolved and new elections held.

Four days later Washington learned of an unexpected challenge to his seat. Lieutenant Colonel Adam Stephen had fought with Washington at Fort Necessity and in the ill-fated Braddock expedition and wound up as second in command in the Virginia Regiment. More recently Washington and Stephen had sparred during an intense scramble for western lands. In 1754, to spur lagging recruitment, Governor Dinwiddie had promised bounty lands in the Ohio Country to war veterans, and Washington had formed a partnership with three veterans—Robert Stewart, George Mercer, and Nathaniel Gist—to accumulate such land. They competed with a rival partnership led by Adam Stephen, who in later years, in a conversation with Dr. Benjamin Rush, vilified Washington as a "weak man."[5] Washington, for his part, castigated his quondam friend Stephen as "designing" and unprincipled.[6]

On February 15, 1761, Captain Stewart relayed word to Washington from Winchester that Stephen was "incessantly employed" in campaigning for one of the two seats from Frederick County. For two years Washington and Thomas Bryan Martin had held those seats, but Martin had now decided to retire, prompting Washington's former aide and new partner, George Mercer, to run in his stead. Adam Stephen evidently denigrated Washington as the handpicked candidate of the wealthy landowners, for Stewart told Washington that "the leaders of all the patrician families remain firm in their resolution of continuing for you," while Stephen issued demagogic appeals for "the attention of the plebeians, whose unstable minds are agitated by every breath of novelty, whims, and nonsense."[7]

Washington was sufficiently alarmed by Stephen's election bid that, uncharacteristically, he stooped to an unscrupulous stratagem to win. The episode shows that at twenty-nine he still hadn't learned to curb his more assertive impulses. He urged the sheriff who oversaw the election, Captain Van Swearingen, to favor his candidacy with a blatantly unfair tactic. Because there was no secret ballot and people openly voiced their votes, it was hugely advantageous for candidates if the first voters favored them, stimulating a bandwagon effect. While disclaiming that he was doing this, Washington planted the idea in the sheriff's mind: "I hope and indeed make no doubt that you will contribute your aid towards shutting [Stephen] out of the public trust he is seeking." Then Washington suggested that if pro–Washington and Mercer voters were "hurried in at the first of the poll, it might be an advantage. But as sheriff, I know you cannot appear in this, nor would I by any mean[s] have you do anything that can give so designing a man as Colo. Stevens the least trouble."[8] If Washington took an ethical shortcut here, he wanted to keep up appearances and pretend that he wasn't.

Washington's trick seemed to work like a charm: of the first fifteen people to announce their vote, fourteen were Washington partisans and twelve also voted for George Mercer. The favoritism was so palpable that Washington's brothers Jack and Samuel were the first two people to vote, while his brother-in-law, Fielding Lewis, his friend Dr. Craik, and his brother Charles lagged not far behind. When the final count was tallied, Washington had 505 votes, Mercer 400, and Stephen 294. Washington, feigning aristocratic indifference to the outcome, told a visitor a few weeks later, "I deal little in politics."[9]

In mid-May 1761, about the time of this election, Washington came down with a "violent cold" and intermittent fever that he couldn't shake despite frequent doctor visits and doses of dried bark from the cinchona tree, called Jesuit's or Peruvian bark, then used to treat malaria. The disease was so widespread in Virginia that colonists spoke darkly of the "intermittent months" of late summer and early fall when epidemics grew commonplace. In late July Washington despaired of getting any useful advice from Virginia doctors, telling an English friend, "I have found so little benefit from any advice yet received that I am more than half of the mind to take a trip to England for the recovery of that invaluable blessing—health."[10]

In August Washington sought the therapeutic powers of the mineral waters at Berkeley Springs, where he had gone with his consumptive brother Lawrence. By this point Washington had likely assumed the classic look of a malaria victim: pale face with pinched features and dark circles beneath the eyes. At this uncouth spa, he found 250 men and women "full of all manner of diseases and complaints."[11] The long ride and sultry weather exhausted him and made his sleep fitful, but he responded well to the waters and hoped they would cure him. Nevertheless, back at Mount Vernon in late September, he again grew ill and complained that he hadn't been able to transact business since April. To Richard Washington, he confessed that the malady had nearly been fatal. "Since my last [letter] of the 14th July, I have in appearance been very near my last gasp. The indisposition then spoken of increased upon me, and I fell into a very low and dangerous state. I once thought the grim king would certainly master my utmost efforts and that I must sink in spite of a noble struggle, but thank God I have now got the better of the disorder and shall soon be restored I hope to perfect health again."[12] In November the conscientious Washington dragged himself off to Williamsburg to attend the House of Burgesses, only to skip an important session because he was too weak. Although he overcame the malaria after a gruesome six or seven months, the parasites were never fully eradicated from his system and flared up again repeatedly in later years.

No sooner had Washington rebounded from his illness than he had to bury his half brother Augustine, who at forty-one perpetuated the mournful tradition of Washington men dying young. Augustine had never been as close to George as Lawrence had been, but he had always written warmly to his younger half brother. Although he had suffered terribly from gout for years and had traveled to England in a vain quest to regain his health, Augustine had reassured George two years earlier that "I am at this time in a better state of health than I have been for the last seven years" and that he hoped to visit Mount Vernon in warm weather "such as will suit my gouty joints."[13] The early deaths of his father and two older half brothers, none of whom reached fifty, could only have heightened Washington's already considerable sense of mortality after he celebrated his thirtieth birthday.

In October 1762 Washington became a vestryman of Truro Parish, a post he held for twenty-two years. The twelve-man vestry oversaw the temporal affairs of the church at Pohick, which formed part of the Anglican, or "established," Church. During the next decade Washington performed standard vestry duties, such as helping to pay the minister, balance the church budget, choose a site for a new church, scrutinize its construction, and select furnishings for the communion table. When the new church was completed, he bought two pews and contributed funds to buy gold leaf for religious inscriptions emblazoned across the altarpiece. Washington also served three terms as churchwarden, a post in which he helped to care for poor people and orphans. Because Mount Vernon sprawled into Fairfax Parish as well, Washington bought another pew at Christ Church in Alexandria and joined the vestry there too. Washington's extensive church activities schooled him in self-government and provided him with plenty of administrative experience.

Many mysteries have surrounded George Washington's religious beliefs. A pair of notable acquaintances raised questions about his faith. Thomas Jefferson once remarked cynically that Washington "has divines [ministers] constantly about him because he thinks it right to keep up appearances but is an unbeliever."[14] Jefferson contended that when Washington stepped down as president, a group of clergymen presented him with a list of requests to bolster public faith in Christianity; they noted he had refrained from public endorsements of the tenets of Christianity and beseeched him to declare openly his beliefs. According to Jefferson, "the old fox was too cunning" for the preachers and replied to all their points except the one about his personal faith.[15] (It should be said that Jefferson's source, Dr. Ashbel Green, later insisted that Jefferson had garbled the story.) Bishop William White of Pennsylvania, Washington's pastor during his presidency in Philadelphia, also stated, "I do not believe that any degree of recollection will bring to my mind any fact which would prove General Washington to have been a believer in the Christian revelation."[16]

From family recollections, it seems indisputable that Washington grew up in a household steeped in piety. Mary Ball Washington was extremely devout and did not hesitate to invoke the aid of Jesus. "She was in the habit of repairing every day to a secluded spot, formed by rocks and trees near to her dwelling, where, abstracted from the world and worldly things, she communed with her Creator in humiliation and prayer," Washington's adopted grandson wrote.[17]

A stalwart member of two congregations, Washington attended church throughout his life and devoted substantial time to church activities. His major rites of passage—baptism, marriage, burial—all took place within the fold of the church. What has mystified posterity and puzzled some of his contemporaries was that Washington's church attendance was irregular; that he recited prayers standing instead of kneeling; that, unlike Martha, he never took communion; and that he almost never referred to Jesus Christ, preferring such vague locutions as "Providence," "Destiny," the "Author of our Being," or simply "Heaven." Outwardly at least, his Christianity seemed rational, shorn of mysteries and miracles, and nowhere did he directly affirm the divinity of Jesus Christ.

Numerous historians, viewing Washington as imbued with the spirit of the Enlightenment, have portrayed him as a deist. Eighteenth-century deists thought of God as a "prime mover" who had created the universe, then left it to its own devices, much as a watchmaker wound up a clock and walked away. God had established immutable laws of nature that could be fathomed by human reason instead of revelation. Washington never conformed to such deism, however, for he resided in a universe saturated with religious meaning. Even if his God was impersonal, with scant interest in individual salvation, He seemed to evince a keen interest in North American politics. Indeed, in Washington's view, He hovered over many battlefields in the French and Indian War and the Revolutionary War. His influence was especially manifest during stirring patriotic victories and hairbreadth escapes from the enemy. Convinced that his life had been spared for some larger purpose, Washington later expressed gratitude to Providence, "which has directed my steps and shielded me in the various changes and chances through which I have passed from my youth to the present moment."[18] Throughout his life he descried signs of heavenly approbation and seemed to know that he operated under the overarching guidance of a benign Providence.

Many of Washington's eminent contemporaries, ranging from Marshall to Madison, regarded him as "a sincere believer in the Christian faith, and a truly devout man," as Marshall attested.[19] Some of Washington's religious style probably reflected an Enlightenment discomfort with religious dogma, but it also reflected his low-key personal style. He was sober and temperate in all things, distrusted zealotry, and would never have talked of hellfire or damnation. He would have shunned anything, such as communion, that might flaunt his religiosity. He never wanted to make a spectacle of his faith or trade on it as a politician. Simply as a matter of personal style, he would have refrained from the emotional language associated with evangelical Christianity. This cooler, more austere religious manner was commonplace among well-heeled Anglicans in eighteenth-century Virginia.

Washington's pastor at Pohick Church before the war confirmed that he "never knew so constant an attendant at church as Washington."[20] His early biographer Jared Sparks recorded this comment from Washington's nephew George W. Lewis: "Mr. Lewis said he had accidentally witnessed [Washington's] private devotions in his library both morning and evening; that on those occasions he had seen him in a kneeling position with a Bible open before him and that he believed such to have been his daily practice."[21] General Robert Porterfield recalled that when he delivered an urgent message to Washington during the Revolutionary War, he "found him on his knees, engaged in his morning's devotions." When he mentioned this to Washington's aide Alexander Hamilton, the latter "replied that such was his constant habit."[22] Washington's adopted granddaughter saw his self-effacing religiosity as consistent with a hatred of pretension: "He was not one of those who act or pray 'That they may be seen of men.'"[23] Numerous people left vignettes testifying to Washington's simple faith. On the other hand, he lacked a speculative bent and was never one to ponder the fine points of theology.

One thing that hasn't aroused dispute is the exemplary nature of Washington's religious tolerance. He shuddered at the notion of exploiting religion for partisan purposes or showing favoritism for certain denominations. As president, when writing to Jewish, Baptist, Presbyterian, and other congregations—he officially saluted twenty-two major religious groups—he issued eloquent statements on religious tolerance. He was so devoid of spiritual bias that his tolerance even embraced atheism. When he needed to hire a carpenter and a bricklayer at Mount Vernon, he stated that "if they are good workmen," they could be "Mahometans, Jews, or Christian of any sect, or they may be atheists."[24] He took pleasure in dropping by Sunday services of other denominations. In Bishop White's words, "If there was no Episcopal Church in the town in which he happened to be, he would attend the services of any other denomination with equal cheerfulness."[25]

Washington loathed religious fanaticism, and on that subject he sounded like a true student of the Enlightenment. "We have abundant reason to rejoice that, in this land, the light of truth and reason has triumphed over the power of bigotry and superstition," President Washington wrote to one Baltimore church.[26] "Religious controversies are always productive of more acrimony and irreconcilable hatreds than those which spring from any other cause."[27] A convinced supporter of the separation of church and state, Washington declared that "no man's sentiments are more opposed to *any kind* of restraint upon religious principles than mine are."[28]

However ecumenical in his approach to religion, Washington never doubted its signal importance in a republic, regarding it as the basis of morality and the foundation of any well-ordered polity. "Of all the dispositions and habits which lead to political prosperity, religion and morality are indispensable supports," he declared in his farewell address.[29] For Washington, morality was so central to Christianity's message that "no man who is profligate in his morals or a bad member of the civil community can possibly be a true Christian."[30]

That Washington believed in the need for good works as well as faith can be seen in his extensive charity. George and Martha Washington never turned away beggars at their doorstep. "Let the hospitality of the house with respect to the poor be kept up," Washington informed his estate manager after being named commander of the Continental Army. "Let no one go hungry away . . . provided it does not encourage them in idleness."[31] The Washingtons tried to practice anonymous charity even when it would have been politically expedient to advertise it loudly. Washington's secretary, Tobias Lear, recorded hundreds of individuals, churches, and other charities that, unbeknownst to the public, benefited from presidential largesse. Even leftovers from the executive mansion were transferred to a prison for needy inmates. Washington had particular sympathy for those imprisoned for debt and gave generously to an organization—later called the Humane Society of the City of New York—that was formed to assist them. He took a special interest in the care and education of orphaned and indigent children and turned into a major benefactor of the Alexandria Academy, established for that purpose.

Washington's generosity toward friends, neighbors, and relatives could be quite breathtaking. With typical munificence, he paid for the education of several children of his friend Dr. Craik. In 1768, when his friend William Ramsay encountered financial difficulties, Washington remembered that he had expressed a wish to send his son to the College of New Jersey (later Princeton). He therefore volunteered to donate twenty-five pounds per annum to educating the young man there. In making the offer, Washington told Ramsay, "No other return is expected or wished for . . . than that you will accept it with the same freedom and goodwill with which it is made and that you may not even consider it in the light of an obligation or mention it as such, for be assured that from me it will never be known."[32] The biographer Douglas Southall Freeman calls this lovely comment "the most generous sentence" that ever flowed from Washington's pen.[33] On countless occasions Washington served as an executor for friends and family members, with many such commitments costing him years of backbreaking legal work. It should also be noted that Washington was community-minded long before he entered national politics. Like his forebears, he held multiple public offices as a young man, becoming a justice of Fairfax County and a trustee of Alexandria in the 1760s.

George Washington always seemed in quiet revolt against the licentious Virginia culture of his upbringing. Many fellow planters, addicted to pleasure, thrived on a constant round of parties, dances, horse races, cockfights, boat races, and card playing. Washington was a far more driven and disciplined man than most of his neighbors, and his hardworking existence stood in stark contrast to their indolent ways. He was guided by a code of conduct that was crystal clear to him and that he frequently enunciated to young relatives. A man with a powerful conscience, he always feared that he was being watched from afar and made sure his conduct could stand up to the most severe critical standards.

Washington was moralistic about several vices ubiquitous in Tidewater Virginia: excessive drinking (he enjoyed drinking in moderation), gambling, smoking, and profanity. It is revealing that this famous Virginian later considered sending his adopted grandson to Harvard rather than to a Virginia college, because "the greater attention of the people [there] generally to morals and a more regular course of life [makes them] less prone to dissipation and debauchery than they are at the colleges south of it."[34] One of his duties as a Truro Parish churchwarden was to dispatch to the county court those guilty of gambling, drinking, profanity, breaking the Sabbath, and "certain other offences against decency and morality."[35] It would have suited Washington's moralistic nature to pack off these offenders to condign punishment. The control of disruptive urges, for himself and others, always formed a central theme of his life.

Later on Washington developed a strong aversion to gambling, but it was likely the vice that most tempted his proper, upstanding nature. He had grown up in a raffish world where men gambled constantly at cards and billiards in smoky taverns and bet on races and cockfights. "Gambling is amazingly prevalent in Williamsburg," one northern visitor exclaimed.[36] Right before his marriage, Washington ordered from London a mahogany card table, two dozen packs of playing cards, and two sets of counters for quadrille, a popular card game. He enjoyed playing loo and whist for money and recorded small sums won and lost at cards and billiards, down to the last pence. His papers contain a fascinating list showing his card-playing expenses for 1772–74, revealing frequent indulgence. In Williamsburg, in the single month of May 1772, he gambled a dozen times, winning four times and losing eight. The following month he played six times and lost on five occasions—perhaps why his subsequent entries grew more infrequent. Washington even gambled once during the First Continental Congress in Philadelphia, walking away with seven pounds.

One wonders whether this detailed list simply reflected Washington's compulsive record keeping or whether it was a way to monitor a perceived moral failing. In 1783 he wrote to his nephew Bushrod and inveighed against gambling as one of many snares that trip up unsuspecting youths, his florid language suggesting that he knew about gambling from personal experience or close observation. "It is the child of avarice, the brother of inequity, and father of mischief. It has been the ruin of many worthy families, the loss of many a man's honor, and the cause of suicide. To all those who enter the list, it is equally fascinating. The successful gamester pushes his good fortune till it is overtaken by a reverse. The losing gamester, in hopes of retrieving past misfortunes, goes on from bad to worse."[37]

Washington had a far better record in controlling other urges. After a period in which he smoked his own tobacco in long-stemmed clay pipes, he seems to have forsworn the habit altogether. His swearing was so infrequent that people commented on it when it happened. Even though he took several glasses of wine with dinner, this was considered acceptable in an age of immoderate alcohol consumption. He once complained that Williamsburg's social life was a continual round of dinners and that "it was not possible for a man to retire sober."[38] After the Revolutionary War, he told one visitor with evident relief that Virginians were "less given to intoxication; . . . it is no longer fashionable for a man to force his guests to drink and to make it an honor to send them home drunk."[39]

Whether hiring overseers or appointing army officers, Washington insisted upon sobriety and saw no greater sign of weakness than a man's inability to control his drinking. Alcoholism was a chronic problem that he had to combat among the hired help at Mount Vernon. On one occasion he capitulated to the drinking of a talented gardener whose sprees he agreed to tolerate so long as the man confined them to certain holidays. In his employment contract, Washington stated that he would be given "four dollars at Christmas with which to be drunk four days and four nights; two dollars at Easter, to effect the same purpose; two dollars at Whitsuntide to be drunk for two days; a dram in the morning and a drink of grog at dinner at noon."[40] It was typical of Washington's thoroughness to pin down such an agreement in writing.

CHAPTER THIRTEEN

A World of His Own

IN 1763 the end of the French and Indian War appeared to foreshadow a halcyon season of peace and prosperity for the colonies, but the troubled aftermath sowed the seeds of conflict twelve years later. The national debt of Great Britain, inflated by military spending, had swollen to a stupendous 130 million pounds, with annual interest payments of 4.5 million pounds engrossing more than half the national budget. To shift this tax burden to its North American subjects, the British government introduced a stamp tax and other hated measures that ignited an insurrection in the colonies. At the same time, having banished the French from Canada, the war eliminated the colonists' need for imperial protection to the north.

The Crown's postwar policy caused colonists to feel penalized by a victory to which they had contributed. It outlawed the printing of paper money by the colonies—London merchants fretted over their losses from such depreciated paper—making currency scarce in Virginia. George Washington, suddenly unable to collect money from strapped debtors, predicted that the ban on colonial money might "set the whole country in flames."[1] Washington's first stirrings of anti-British fervor had arisen from his failure to receive a royal commission, but they were now joined by disenchantment over pocketbook issues. Great Britain was simply bad for local business, a fact that would soon foster the historical anomaly of a revolution inaugurated by affluent, conservative leaders. As potentates of vast estates, lords of every acre they saw, George Washington and other planters didn't care to truckle to a distant, unseen power.

Perhaps the most incendiary colonial resentment related to land policy, the wartime victory having liberated the acquisitive urges of speculators. In May 1763

Washington joined nine other investors in a plan to drain the Great Dismal Swamp in southeastern Virginia and turn it into lucrative farmland. United in a syndicate, Adventurers for Draining the Dismal Swamp, these speculators hoped to bypass royal regulations that restricted grants of Crown lands to one thousand acres per individual. To circumvent this limit, they manufactured 138 bogus names when they submitted their land petition in Williamsburg. Washington, with a fertile mind for development, envisioned that the ditch employed to drain the swamp could also serve as a canal leading to Norfolk, a farsighted plan finally realized in 1828. Like every economic activity in Virginia, the Dismal Swamp project relied on slave labor, and Washington contributed six slaves.

The natural vitality of the Virginia economy, combined with dynamic population growth, ensured unstoppable westward expansion. On September 9, 1763, Washington and nineteen other entrepreneurs banded together to launch the Mississippi Land Company, which hoped to claim 2.5 million acres of land in the Ohio Valley. This gargantuan chunk of real estate would encompass sections of what later became Ohio, Indiana, Illinois, Kentucky, and Tennessee. The shortsighted British preferred to save the fur trade with the Indians and, by a royal proclamation on October 7, 1763, banned settlers from regions west of the Allegheny Mountains. The Crown rationalized this policy by saying it was easier to defend subjects in seaport cities, but in a colony obsessed with real estate speculation, it was a catastrophic blunder to confine settlers to the eastern seaboard. The end of the war had no sooner disclosed tempting glimpses of riches than colonial masters in London snatched them away. Fearful that his western bonanza might evaporate, Washington condemned the move. "I can never look upon that Proclamation in any other light than as a temporary expedient to quiet the minds of the Indians," he said.[2] For Washington, the infamous decree was doubly damaging because it interfered with the bounty claims of veterans from the Virginia Regiment. To nobody's surprise, settlers from Germany, Ireland, and elsewhere continued to spill into the Ohio Valley in a resistless tide.

As early as May 1764, reports reached Virginia that Parliament was hatching a tax to force colonists to defray wartime costs and pay for future protection. This violated a long-standing tradition of reserving taxing powers to colonial legislatures. Convinced that they were heavily taxed already, a committee of burgesses protested to the king that December, issuing an appeal that grounded their opposition in hallowed English liberties. They pleaded for protection "in the enjoyment of their ancient and inestimable right of being governed by such laws respecting their internal polity and taxation as are derived from their own consent."[3] Deaf to these earnest pleas, Parliament in 1765 enacted the Stamp Act, which taxed legal documents, newspapers, almanacs, and even playing cards.

The response was immediate and full-throated in its militance. In the House of Burgesses, a young rabble-rouser, Patrick Henry, rose amid the dark wooden benches and brandished fiery resolutions. "Resolved," he announced, "that the taxation of the people by themselves or by persons chosen by themselves to represent them . . . is the distinguishing characteristic of British freedom."[4] For a young law student standing in the rear of the hushed chamber, these words sounded with a thrilling resonance. "He appeared to me to speak as Homer wrote," Thomas Jefferson remembered.[5] For some staid burgesses, Henry's remarks seemed excessively inflammatory. "Tarquin and Caesar each had his Brutus," Henry roared in response to them, "Charles the First his Cromwell, and George the Third—" He was interrupted by cries of "treason" from Washington's longtime patron, Speaker Robinson, who was enthroned in his lofty chair. Legend asserts, although many scholars now dispute, that Henry retorted, "If *this* be treason, make the most of it."[6]

In all likelihood, Washington had returned to Mount Vernon by the time these electrifying words shook the chamber. He was about to set out for Williamsburg in late July 1765 when he learned that Governor Fauquier, alarmed that Massachusetts legislators had invited the burgesses to send a delegation to New York to protest the Stamp Act, had summarily terminated the session. Of this decision, Washington surmised, "I am convinced . . . that the Governor had no inclination to meet an Assembly at this juncture."[7] For Fauquier, this Stamp Act Congress represented a blatant act of sedition, and he had no intention of allowing burgesses to participate. After he dissolved the assembly and held new elections, Washington used the opportunity to switch his seat from Frederick County to Fairfax County, closer to home. Until this point, Washington had mostly striven to please his royal masters in London, and he still had little patience with radicals who wanted to seize and incinerate the stamps, especially when a Williamsburg mob set upon his colleague George Mercer and burned him in effigy after he returned from England holding the despised post of stamp collector for the colony.

Nevertheless, angry feelings festered inside George Washington, and they erupted that September in a caustic letter to Robert Cary that showed how longstanding personal grievances were being transmuted into burning political causes. For the first eight paragraphs, Washington roundly chastised his London factors for the inferior prices his tobacco fetched and the shoddy, overpriced goods he had to swallow in return. When he turned to the Stamp Act, he wrote with almost gleeful vengeance. Distancing himself from "the speculative part of the colonists," who regarded "this unconstitutional method of taxation as a direful attack upon their liberties," he made it plain that he disagreed with their methods, not their opinions.[8] In threatening terms, he said the eyes of the colonists were beginning to open as they realized they could boycott British luxury goods by devising domestic substitutes, and he forecast that courts would be shut down, since England had starved the colonists of currency with which to pay the stamp tax. With courts closed, he hardly needed to add, British creditors would be unable to collect from their American debtors.

The young man who had worked so hard to ingratiate himself with his superiors in the British Army was suddenly breathing fire. Washington was always reluctant to sign on to any cause, because when he did so, his commitment was total. Just as he predicted, some colonial courts were shut down by the Stamp Act, leaving British creditors enraged. Washington wasn't the only one who found the Stamp Act a piece of self-destructive folly. In the House of Commons, Benjamin Franklin was asked how British soldiers sent to enforce the new taxes would be received. "They will not find a rebellion," he replied curtly. "They may indeed make one."[9] When the Stamp Act was repealed the following year, Washington told his London agent bluntly that if Parliament had remained mired in this error, the consequences "would have been more direful than is generally apprehended both to the mother country and her colonies."[10] The repeal had no lasting effect in the colonies, since it coincided with passage of the Declaratory Act, which denied that the emboldened colonies possessed any exclusive right to tax themselves.

Whatever rage Washington felt toward his London factors was contained by their extensive credit and his inability to check his expenditures. Planters needed funds to tide them over until crops were harvested and sold abroad. From the early 1760s till the time of his death, people imagined that George Washington was infinitely more prosperous than he was because they had no conception of his crippling debt. When Robert Stewart asked to borrow four hundred pounds in 1763, Washington declined and volunteered to show him a copy of his accounts at Robert Cary. "I doubt not but you will be surprised at the badness of their condition," he wrote in embarrassment.[11] Washington was not alone: Virginia gazettes were then chock-full of advertisements of large indebted estates for sale.

The following year Washington was mortified to receive a sharply worded reprimand from Robert Cary that he owed eighteen hundred pounds, coupled with a warning of a 5 percent interest charge on unpaid debt. Money was the one area where Washington tended to dodge personal responsibility and blame force majeure. Reacting with outrage to the letter, he protested that bad weather had caused him to fall into arrears. "For it was a misfortune that seasons and chance shou[l]d prevent my making even tolerable crops in this part of the country for three years successively and it was a misfortune likewise when they were made that I shou[l]d get little or nothing for them."[12] He also objected to the accusatory tone of Cary's letter.[13] Nonetheless, having voiced his anger, Washington took the hint and shaved his debt in half by 1770.

It is striking how moody and snappish Washington could be about money. This man who was generally so polite and courteous tended to shed all tact in business matters, the one dimension of his career unimproved by the passage of time. He adopted a blistering style whenever he thought someone had cheated him. Some of this anger reflected continuing financial travails, and some the troubling legacy of his insecure, fatherless childhood. For a man who loved control as much as Washington, it must have been trying to depend upon far-off brokers in London, known to him only by name.

The reliance upon foreign vendors fostered constant tension. To fill Washington's orders for goods, Robert Cary and Company drew upon a network of forty London shops. An invoice from April 1763 shows a small army of suppliers to Mount Vernon that included a linen merchant, woolen merchant, grocer, spice maker, shot maker (gunshot), pipe maker, pickler, rope maker, porter (beverage supplier), apothecary, toolmaker, haberdasher, cheesemonger, stationer, milliner, hosier, tin maker, plate maker, iron maker, wine merchant, turner (potter), and shoemaker.[14] However much Washington emphasized, for political reasons, the potential self-sufficiency of the colonies, he could never curtail his taste for luxury goods from London. With a superb eye for fashion, he was the first American to scrap white stoneware dishes, and in 1769 he ordered 250 pieces of the tony new cream-colored earthenware produced by Josiah Wedgwood. Not satisfied with bone or wooden handles for flatware, he purchased cutlery with silver handles, his griffin crest emblazoned on every implement. Everything from his gold-headed cane to his bookplates to his horse harnesses bore this proud crest.

The perils of transatlantic shopping grew apparent when Washington ordered a new four-horse coach in 1768. With his slavish regard for London style, he suggested gingerly that the coach be painted green "unless any other color more in vogue and equally lasting is entitled to precedency. In that case, I would be governed by fashion."[15] Washington sketched other desired features of this princely vehicle, including a sumptuous blue or green Moroccan leather lining and light gilding around the side panels to spotlight his coat of arms. Washington must have had a premonition that this coach, which cost three hundred pounds, would be flawed, for he warned that it should be "made of the best seasoned wood and by a celebrated workman."[16] As Washington suspected, the coach turned into an expensive fiasco. Instead of seasoned wood, Washington protested two years later, "it was made of wood so exceedingly green that the panels slip[pe]d out of the moldings before it was two months in use."[17] It says something about the predicament of Virginia planters that, despite his countless complaints about their service, Washington still handed over his business to Robert Cary and Company.

As a highly analytical, self-critical businessman, Washington decided to do something about his ruinous dependence on tobacco, which brought little money, depleted the soil, and furthered his reliance on London. In 1765 he began paring back on tobacco and the next year abandoned it altogether in favor of wheat, Indian corn, and other grains. With his experimental bent, Washington tested hemp, flax, and sixty different crops. His wheat, in particular, began to flourish and became his main cash crop, which he could sell locally in Alexandria. Tobacco had been demanding to grow, and as he phased it out, he started to derive more real pleasure from agriculture, which became his chief source of recreation. Free of labor-intensive tobacco farming, he was also able to transfer more of the workload to others. In 1765 he hired his distant cousin, twenty-eight-year-old Lund Washington, to manage the estate, and he treated the able Lund as a friend as well as an employee, socializing and even foxhunting with him.

Once Washington diversified his crops, he began to preside over something more akin to a small village than a mere plantation. He was a fantastically creative businessman and Mount Vernon evolved into a miniature polity, a self-contained economic universe. "When I reached his place, I thought I was entering a rather large village, but later was told that all of it belonged to him," said an impressed visitor.[18] Just as Washington agitated for autonomous colonies, he established a similar ideal for his personal domain, as his economic interests fused with his budding political awareness. In the late 1760s he began laying out roads to unite the five far-flung farms of Mount Vernon and eventually brought three thousand of their eight thousand acres under cultivation. The sheer scope of Mount Vernon's business operations, with the accompanying need to feed and clothe a sizable number of slaves and servants, endowed Washington with extensive managerial experience that later assisted him with the Continental Army. His zeal for businesses beyond agriculture also gave him an expansive economic vision that would predispose him to support the audacious manufacturing schemes of Alexander Hamilton.

In 1771 Washington started to supplement his farming income with proceeds from a gristmill he built at his Dogue Run farm. Housed in a three-story stone mill set astride a stream, this successful operation packed cornmeal and refined flour into big barrels and small casks for export to England, the West Indies, and even Portugal. To enhance profits further, Washington ground the corn and wheat of neighboring farmers. He also launched a weaving operation that produced home-spun clothing for slaves and made textiles for general sale. Similarly Washington took the blacksmith shop at Mount Vernon and began marketing its services to neighbors.

Posterity doesn't associate George Washington with fishing, but the pristine Potomac River had a plentiful supply of fish from which to forge a thriving enterprise. As Washington informed a British friend, the Potomac was "one of the finest rivers in the world—a river well stock[ed] with various kinds of fish at all seasons of the year and in the spring with shad, herring, bass, carp, sturgeon, and in great abundance."[19] Visitors to Mount Vernon shared his fascination with the teeming schools of fish, which created a churning turbulence in the river. "I have seen for several hours together in a summer's evening, hundreds, perhaps I might say thousands of sturgeon, at a great height from the water at the same instant, so that the quantity in the river must have been inconceivably great," proclaimed one Frenchman.[20] Washington was often astounded by the rich harvests of fish pulled up in his bulging seines. "The whitefish ran plentifully at my seine landing, having catched ab[ou]t 300 at one haul," he reported in his diary.[21] This number paled beside the stupendous herring runs caught each spring as they swam to upstream spawning grounds. "They fish for them in April," said one Polish visitor. "They have caught as many as 100 thousand of them with a single draw of the net."[22] By 1772 Mount Vernon's fishery netted almost a million herring per year.

At first the fishing operation supplied food for Mount Vernon's slaves, but Washington soon spied the potential profit and began to have the fish salted and packed in barrels for export to the West Indies. To facilitate this trade, he assembled a small fleet of boats, including a whaleboat and a schooner. Much of his yield he sold to Carlyle & Adam in Alexandria, and a single ledger entry for May 1771 shows that he delivered 679,200 herring and 7,760 shad at one shot. Even with his fishery, Washington felt hampered by senseless imperial policies. For instance, the finest salt for curing fish came from Lisbon, but England's mercantilist policies forced him to import inferior salt from Liverpool. He constantly felt snarled in a tangled web of perverse economic regulations drawn up by London bureaucrats.

As Washington switched from tobacco to other crops, the move had profound repercussions for his slaves. Since tobacco was more labor intensive than wheat or corn, its elimination led to a surplus of field hands. For the rest of his life, Washington grappled with the dilemma of having too many slaves, whose numbers only increased through normal population growth. At the same time he increasingly trained his slaves to perform a multitude of skilled tasks, producing a workforce of artisans proficient in diverse crafts. One Scottish visitor observed that Washington "has everything within himself—carpenters, bricklayers, brewers, blacksmiths, bakers, etc. etc.—and even has a well-assorted store for the use of his family and servants."[23] The skills possessed by his enslaved craftsmen were extremely impressive. According to Washington's editors, one slave named Isaac "constructed carts, wheels, plows, harrows, rakes, wheelbarrows, and other implements," while another slave, Tom Davis, was a "skilled bricklayer, who also harvested grain, painted exteriors, hung wallpaper, cut grass, and worked at Washington's fishery."[24]

To instruct his slaves, Washington imported indentured servants from Europe, many of them former convicts, who labored for a period of years, and their employment contracts obligated them to teach their trade to slaves they supervised. So pervasive were these arrangements that a full quarter of Mount Vernon's slaves qualified as skilled workers, and Washington farmed them out to other planters for extra income. While indentured servants weren't subject to the same punishing regimen as slaves, they felt their bondage strongly, and many ran away before their term expired. Just as he did with runaway slaves, Washington advertised for their return, and his notices show a minute knowledge of these hired hands. When William Orre escaped in 1774, Washington described him as "a well-made man about 5 foot 10 inches high and about 24 years of age. He was born in Scotland and talks that dialect pretty much. He is of a red complexion and very full-faced, with short, sandy-colored hair and very remarkable thumbs, they being both crooked."[25]

WHEN WASHINGTON ATTENDED the House of Burgesses in the spring of 1767, the furor over the Stamp Act had temporarily subsided. During this sleepy, uneventful session, Washington received one of the two surviving letters written to him by Martha. It shows her as a warm and affectionate if uneducated wife. The note reads in its entirety: "My Dearest: It was with very great pleasure I see in your letter th[at] you got safely down we are all very well at this time but it still [is] rainney and wett I am sorry you will not be at home soon as I expe[ct]ed you I had reather my sister would not come up so soon, as May wou[ld] be [a] much plasenter time than April we wrote to you las[t] post as I have nothing new to tell you I must conclude my self your most Affcetionate Martha Washington."[26]

Having failed to learn its lesson with the Stamp Act, Great Britain again provoked colonial discontent in 1767 with the Townshend Acts, which placed duties on paint, glass, paper, and tea and buttressed the power of royal officials by freeing them from reliance on colonial assemblies for money. Hardening its stance toward the restive colonists, the Crown dispatched the HMS *Romney* to Boston, where radicals had a chance in May 1768 to ponder the political message carried by its fifty guns. In September British warships disgorged two regiments of redcoats, who marched through town to the beat of fife and drums and then pitched tents on the Common in a show of strength designed to intimidate local protesters.

Of late Washington's attendance in Williamsburg had been haphazard, and he missed the debate in the burgesses that included vehement denunciations of the Townshend duties. The legislators cloaked their plea to the king in obsequious language, appealing to his "fatherly goodness and protection," but the royal heart remained unmoved.[27] Reflecting their tough position, officials in London sent to Virginia a new governor, Lord Botetourt, a peer of the realm with secret instructions to dissolve the Virginia assembly if it persisted in willful opposition to imperial wisdom. For all their ire over the Townshend duties, the burgesses still couldn't resist the allure of an honest-to-goodness British aristocrat, and on November 2, 1768, Washington and fellow burgesses flocked to a festive welcoming dinner for the royal governor.

One can argue plausibly that the events of the winter of 1768–69 converted George Washington from a rich, disaffected planter into a rabid militant against British policies. Had he died before that winter, he would have left no real record of distinction, aside from youthful bravery in the French and Indian War. That winter changed everything, and he began to evolve into the George Washington known to history. Moving beyond the disputes over self-advancement that had preoccupied his younger, insecure self, he suddenly seemed a larger figure in the nascent struggle against British injustice. All his seething frustration in seeking a royal commission during the war; all his vocal disaffection with Robert Cary and Company; all his dismay over British policies that handicapped him as a planter and real estate speculator—these enduring complaints now crystallized into splendid wrath against the Crown.

That winter Parliament grew so disgruntled over colonial protests against its tax policy that it was proposed (though never executed) that the ringleaders be shipped to England and tried for treason under an old statute dating from Henry VIII's reign. As word of this proposal spread, so did protest against the mother country. In early April Washington received a packet from Dr. David Ross of Bladensburg, Maryland, containing news of associations being set up in Philadelphia and Annapolis to boycott nonessential British imports as long as Parliament persisted in foisting unfair taxes on the colonies. The packet included plans for a comparable Virginia association, drawn up by a nameless writer. Washington sent it to his friend and neighbor George Mason, who turned out to be the author. A tall, bookish man trained in the law, Mason was more scholarly and less sociable than Washington. He inhabited a Georgian mansion called Gunston Hall, just south of Belvoir, which was in turn just south of Mount Vernon.

On April 5, 1769, Washington sent Mason a remarkable letter that gave both his private and his public reasons for supporting a boycott of British goods. Doubtless thinking of his own plight, he said a boycott would break the onerous cycle of debt that trapped many colonists, purging their extravagant spending. Before this the average colonial debtor was too weak to break this habit, "for how can I, says he, who have lived in such and such a manner, change my method? . . . besides, such an alteration in the system of my living will create suspicions of a decay in my fortune and such a thought the world must not harbor."[28] Washington provided here a key insight into the psychology of debt: fear that any attempt at a more frugal existence would disclose the truth about a person's actual wealth.

In the letter, Washington made clear that his opposition to arbitrary taxation had much to do with setting a precedent against further mischief. Just as the British assumed the right to taxation, so "they may attempt at least to restrain our manufactories, especially those of a public nature."[29] Striking a militant tone, Washington suggested that he had moved beyond petitions and now preferred direct action, although not yet arms. He suddenly found a clear, spirited voice of protest, one that spoke of abstract rights instead of just personal advancement or economic necessity. "At a time when our lordly masters in Great Britain will be satisfied with nothing less than the deprivation of American freedom, it seems highly necessary that something shou[l]d be done to avert the stroke and maintain the liberty which we have derived from our ancestors." In considering the best means to effect this, he balked at spelling out the treasonous word *arms*. "That no man shou[l]d scruple or hesitate a moment to use a—ms in defense of so valuable a blessing . . . is clearly my opinion. Yet a—ms, I wou[l]d beg leave to add, should be the last resource."[30] Noting the futility of sending more fawning petitions to the king, he said the only recourse was to starve British trade and manufactures.

In many ways, Washington's letter to Mason foretells the success of the American Revolution: he tried to be law-abiding, endorsed incremental change, and favored violence only if all else failed. Unlike the French Revolution, the American Revolution started with a series of measured protests by men schooled in self-government, a long, exhaustive search for a diplomatic solution, before moving toward open rebellion. Later on, nothing incensed Washington more than the notion that the colonists had proved unreasonable during the run-up to war.

In the following weeks, Washington discussed with Mason his proposal for a nonimportation association for Virginia. Then on April 30 Washington headed to Williamsburg to present this plan to the burgesses. Until this point he had been a minor, often absentee, legislator, too taciturn and aloof to emerge as a major political force. One observer characterized him as "too bashful and timid for an orator," while another described him as "a modest man, but sensible, and speaks little—in action cool, like a bishop at his prayers."[31] Now fired up with a newfound sense of leadership, Washington served on three standing committees, signifying an abrupt elevation in Virginia politics. In opening the new session of the burgesses in early May, Lord Botetourt reminded them of his royal auspices by riding to the capitol in a handsome coach behind a brilliant team of white horses. Held amid the uproar over the Townshend Acts, this spring session promised to be tumultuous and featured a surprising number of new members, including the lanky Virginian from Albemarle County, twenty-six-year-old Thomas Jefferson.

On May 16, with Washington present, the burgesses approved the sweeping Virginia Resolves, which contended that only they had the right to tax Virginians. They also insisted upon the right to petition the Crown for grievances and restrict trials for treason and other crimes to the colony itself. The next day, having heard enough seditious proposals from these upstart Virginians, Lord Botetourt had the sergeant at arms interrupt their session and summon them to a brief meeting in the council chamber, where he delivered an imperious message. "Mr. Speaker and Gentlemen of the House of Burgesses," he began, "I have heard of your resolves and augur ill of their effect. You have made it my duty to dissolve you and you are dissolved accordingly."[32]

This bald declaration shocked the assembled worthies into recognizing how little authority they wielded. They weren't the ultimate source of power, which was doled out sparingly at the whim of the Crown. Once Lord Botetourt issued his decree, Washington and many other burgesses adjourned to the Apollo Room of the Raleigh Tavern to ponder "their distressed situation."[33] In this highly emotional gathering, Washington introduced the boycott scheme over which he and Mason had labored. The dissident members formed a committee, including Washington, that accepted the plan for a nonimportation association. The next morning the burgesses reconvened in the Apollo Room and affixed their signatures to the plan to boycott any British goods subject to taxes in America. For good measure, they threw in a lengthy list of untaxed goods to shun. This Virginia Association would remain in force until the Townshend Acts were repealed. Caught up in the giddy spirit of the moment, Washington purchased *Letters from a Farmer in Pennsylvania to the Inhabitants of the British Colonies,* an influential dissident pamphlet written by a wealthy Philadelphia lawyer, John Dickinson.

During this early period of discontent, Washington and his fellow burgesses danced a strange minuet with Lord Botetourt, alternating defiance with reconciliation. The day after signing the nonimportation agreement, Washington mentioned in his diary: "Dined again at Mrs. Dawson's and went to the Queens birth night at the palace."[34] A proud, imposing building, the governor's palace boasted marble floors and stacks of muskets mounted on black walnut walls; its ballroom glistened with portraits of the king and queen. That Washington and other burgesses would celebrate the queen's birthday still seemed quite natural to them. As the *Virginia Gazette* commented, "The Governor gave a splendid ball and entertainment at the palace to a very numerous and polite company of ladies and gentlemen."[35] Nothing better illustrates the schizoid world of these unsettled legislators than the way they gravitated to the governor's genteel ball despite the political passions smoldering underneath. Even among the most hypercritical burgesses, there existed as yet no sense of an irrevocable split from England.

In late July Washington seemed to rejoice at the chance to inform Robert Cary and Company that he was "determined to adhere religiously" to the new boycott agreement. In submitting an invoice of goods he wanted, Washington apprised his agents that nothing should be sent to him that appeared on the list of products taxed by Parliament "as I have heartily enter[e]d into an association" bound to boycott such goods.[36] He welcomed the boycott as a chance to extend his far-reaching experiments in economic self-sufficiency at Mount Vernon. In the estimation of one observer, Washington "carried the scheme of manufacturing to a greater height than almost any man [in Virginia]."[37]

Washington remained a most unlikely revolutionary. When he was attending the burgesses that autumn, he, Martha, and her daughter, Patsy, traveled to Williamsburg in the glittering green coach, adorned with gilt-edged panels, that Washington had so painstakingly ordered from Robert Cary. The tone of this session was less confrontational than in the spring, and Lord Botetourt mollified members by supporting repeal of the Townshend duties, except for the fateful one on tea. His speech previewed a policy shift by the new administration, headed by Lord North, whose strategy was to undercut the dissidents by revoking the duties while retaining the one on tea to reaffirm parliamentary prerogative. This maneuver succeeded in cooling off the fervor of the Virginia Association, even after British grenadiers in early March 1770 fired on a disorderly crowd in Boston, killing five of them in what became known as the "Boston Massacre."

The many contradictions of Washington's world were on display in Williamsburg that spring. He attended the opening night of *The Beggar's Opera* and a luxurious ball to honor the king's birthday. Yet this same George Washington was dismayed that his fellow Virginians couldn't curb their appetite for imported goods. He was disappointed in June when a new nonimportation agreement relaxed many restrictions, allowing imports of barley and pork, pewter and gold, boots and saddles. Eminently realistic, already equipped with fine political instincts, Washington recognized that this watered-down agreement was "the best that the friends to the cause cou[l]d obtain here." At the same time he wished it were "ten times as strict" and frowned on it as "too much relaxed from the spirit with which a measure of this sort ought to be conducted."[38] Nevertheless that July Washington had no qualms about ordering from Robert Cary a pigskin saddle, gold jewelry, and other luxury items only recently proscribed.

GEORGE WASHINGTON BELIEVED FERVENTLY in the potential wealth of the western lands, a faith he touted in almost messianic tones. He had long maintained that the foremost Virginia estates were created "by taking up and purchasing at very low rates the rich back lands, which were thought nothing of in those days, but are now the most valuable lands we possess."[39] For Washington, land speculation was the ideal vehicle for amassing riches, a way to invest in his own future and that of the country, mingling idealism with profit. He continued to deplore the 1763 proclamation barring settlement beyond the Allegheny Mountains as both myopic and unworkable. When Charles Mason and Jeremiah Dixon completed their survey of the Pennsylvania-Maryland border, he foresaw that it would trigger a mad scramble for prime frontier acreage.

Washington didn't shrink from secrecy and even sharp dealings in real estate, as can be seen in his strenuous efforts to expand his western holdings in the late 1760s. Hoping to purchase up to two thousand acres, he turned to an old ally from the Forbes campaign, Captain William Crawford, who lived in the Ohio Country. Washington wanted to scout out forbidden lands beyond the so-called Proclamation Line and didn't think he could afford to wait, advising Crawford that anyone "who neglects the present opportunity of hunting out good lands and in some measure marking and distinguishing them for their own . . . will never regain it." Crawford agreed to search out large parcels in partnership with Washington, who urged him to "keep this whole matter a profound secret," lest other speculators discover their designs before they laid "a proper foundation for success."[40]

In late 1768 the British negotiated two treaties with the Indians that reopened the Ohio Country to settlers, ushering in frenzied competition among real estate speculators. At this point Washington renewed his clamor for 200,000 acres of bounty lands promised by Dinwiddie to veterans of the Fort Necessity campaign in 1754, a pledge he considered a sacred public trust. In the conciliatory mood temporarily existing in Williamsburg in late 1769, Washington prevailed upon Lord Botetourt to honor this commitment. The governor and council identified the confluence of the Ohio and Great Kanawha rivers as the site of these bounty lands. Washington proved a natural manager of this enterprise and undertook the necessary surveying work, but his situation was fraught with conflicts of interest, and the entire episode would be shadowed by accusations of sharp dealing from his former men. Washington summoned meetings of veterans and induced them to select William Crawford as surveyor of the bounty lands. Not only did Washington exploit his position to pin down prime real estate for himself, but he bought up rights surreptitiously from needy veterans to enlarge his holdings.

Washington also claimed land under a 1763 royal proclamation that promised land to veterans of the French and Indian War. He had his brother Charles buy up veterans' claims under his own name, even though Washington was their undisclosed owner; on another occasion, he effected such a purchase under Lund Washington's name. Washington also wanted to circumvent a regulation that limited land grants to officers who had remained with the Virginia Regiment until it dissolved in 1762. Since he had resigned before then, he had Charles buy up claims from those who had served until the end, instructing his brother to operate stealth-ily and "not let it be known that I have any concern therein."[41] When he purchased one property stretching more than forty miles along the Great Kanawha, he flouted a law prohibiting riverfront properties from being more than three times as long as they were deep, a way to prevent monopolies of choice riverine acreage. Most officers had a mile and a half of riverfront on their narrow properties, which then extended five miles back into the countryside. Even as Washington developed a wider political vision, he remained extremely aggressive in his real estate dealings. As the biographer James T. Flexner concluded: "In no other direction did Washing-ton demonstrate such acquisitiveness as in his quest for the ownership of land."[42] He was far from alone: hoarding cheap land was a universal madness in Virginia and the other colonies.

In early October 1770, accompanied by Dr. Craik, three slaves, and a packhorse, Washington began a tour of the Ohio Country to inspect properties for himself and his men. He had grown accustomed to having Billy Lee along on these long, rugged journeys, but the young mulatto slave fell ill and stayed behind. On this nine-week expedition, Washington felt an acute sense of urgency, since settlers were already flocking to the Ohio and Great Kanawha rivers, and he feared they might preempt the most productive soil. He also got wind of a huge scheme by English investors to obtain 2.5 million acres and inaugurate a new colony, Vandalia, whose borders might further curtail the bounty lands. When the British ministry approved this scheme, rebuffing a petition from Washington's Mississippi Land Company, he darkly decried London's "malignant disposition towards Americans," adding yet another grievance to his lengthening litany of complaints against Crown policies.[43]

During one leg of the journey, Washington was staying about four miles from present-day Pittsburgh when an Indian chief called the White Mingo and other chiefs of the Six Nations requested a meeting. The White Mingo bestowed upon Washington a ceremonial string of wampum, then stunned him with a vivid recol-lection dating back to the French and Indian conflict. Washington noted the gist of this speech in his diary: "that as I was a person who some of them remember to have seen when I was sent on an embassy to the French and most of them had heard of, they were come to bid me welcome to the country and to desire that the people of Virginia wou[l]d consider them as friends and brothers linked together in one chain."[44]

As he rode or paddled by canoe, Washington remained attentive to the commer-cial prospects of this sparsely populated region. In negotiating leases with western farmers, he retained timber and mineral rights and even visited a coal mine. "The coal seemed to be of the very best kind, burning freely and abundance of it," he remarked in his diary.[45] While he negotiated forest paths and mountain passes that he knew from the French and Indian War, he appraised these wild places with a cool business eye. Even though he bought two hundred acres of the Great Meadows in December 1770, he included no mention of its history in his diary. Of the site where hundreds had been brutally slaughtered under General Braddock, Washington merely observed that it wasn't level enough for agriculture. Not until 1772 did Washington and his veterans receive the land distributions they had long awaited. Washington was allotted more than twenty thousand acres on the Ohio and Great Kanawha rivers, augmented by another eleven thousand acres the following year, making him a major western landlord on the eve of the American Revolution.

As with all challenges to his integrity, Washington remained touchy on the subject of the bounty lands and whether he had taken unfair advantage of his men. Although he walked off with the finest properties, he also believed that he had devoted enormous time to surveying the area and that the whole operation hinged on his efforts. Suspicions about his conduct he thought unfair and baseless. When one officer, George Muse, accused him of shortchanging him of land, Washington didn't mince words: "As I am not accustomed to receive such from any man, nor would have taken the same language from you personally, without letting you feel some marks of my resentment, I would advise you to be cautious in writing me a second [letter] of the same tenor. For though I understand you were drunk when you did it, yet give me leave to tell you that drunkenness is no excuse for rudeness."[46] If Muse read the newspapers, Washington pointed out, he would have seen that he had been allotted the ten thousand acres he claimed, and he concluded by telling his former officer indignantly that he was sorry he had ever "engag[e]d in behalf of so ungrateful and dirty a fellow as you are."[47] While Washington was in the right here, the letter shows how his bottled-up anger could spew forth unexpectedly and why people intuited correctly that he had a terrible temper.

In his eagerness to unlock the riches of the heartland, Washington assigned a premier position to the busy river running by his home. If the Potomac could be improved by locks and other measures, he thought, it would emerge as the main thoroughfare for commerce with the interior, enhancing the value of his western holdings. In 1770 the attorney Thomas Johnson, who owned thousands of acres along the Potomac, tried to enlist Washington's aid for modest improvements along the river. A short, stocky man of unbounded energy and enthusiasm, he kindled in Washington a lasting enthusiasm for the project. Not to be outdone in Potomac boosterism, Washington espoused a far more ambitious plan that would connect the river with "a rising empire" in the western country.[48] Washington clearly foresaw the rich future of this wilderness expanse, if only it could be reached by water. Simple in theory but fiendishly complex in practice, his plan for Potomac commerce required not just endless locks but portages through the mountains of what is now West Virginia. This Potomac scheme would hypnotize his mind much as the vision of a mythical Northwest Passage once entranced transatlantic mariners. If the Potomac never became the grand commercial gateway he had envisioned, it was not for want of trying.

With considerable sophistication about business and politics that already belied his image as a mere planter, Washington told Johnson that they shouldn't just rely on legislative grants and the uncertain force of "motives of public spirit."[49] Better to rely on self-interest and blatantly appeal to "the monied gentry" who would be drawn by prospective profits.[50] To this end, Washington would devise a plan for a joint stock company that would receive charters from Virginia and Maryland and make the river navigable from Tidewater Virginia to the Ohio Country. It would pay back investors by charging tolls on river traffic. Washington himself steered a Potomac navigation bill through the House of Burgesses. Despite his insistence that the project would produce "amazing advantages" to both Virginia and Maryland, it foundered in the Maryland legislature because Baltimore businessmen feared it might divert trade from the Chesapeake Bay.[51] When the project stalled momentarily, it provided Washington with yet another early example of the need for intercolonial cooperation.

CHAPTER FOURTEEN

The Asiatic Prince

FOR SOMEONE of George Washington's enterprising nature, Martha Washington was the ideal spouse, with a work ethic to match his own. General Nathanael Greene once commented that Virginia ladies "appear to be brought up and educated with habits of industry and attention to domestic affairs," and Martha Washington certainly fit that description.[1]

Never the idle, pampered doyenne of Mount Vernon, she was involved in everything from distilling rose water to gathering ash for making soap. George Washington liked to say that "Virginia ladies pride themselves on the goodness of their bacon," and Martha derived special pleasure from the ham and bacon cured in their smokehouse.[2] Each day, after an hour dedicated to prayer and meditation, she supervised servants in cooking and cleaning and presided over her sewing circle of slaves, who produced up to twelve hundred yards of homespun cloth yearly. All the while, she retained a folksy, unpretentious style. It was said that even when she wore the same gown for a week, it somehow managed to remain spotless. A woman with a delicate constitution, Martha was often sick for weeks at a time with liver and stomach troubles, known as "bilious fever," but she never let illness slow her down in performing her domestic chores.

A gregarious person, Martha Washington wanted a home crowded with people. With her husband preoccupied by business and politics, she took charge of her two children and enjoyed the demands of motherhood, one visitor noting that "her happiness is in exact proportion to the number of objects upon which she can dispense her benefits."[3] She had special cause to worry about her daughter, Patsy. In Charles Willson Peale's watercolor of her at sixteen, Patsy is pretty and elegant, slight of build, her clear eyes sparkling with intelligence. The picture shows how lovingly the Washingtons spoiled her: her black hair is dressed with pearls, her dress edged with lace, and she wears costly garnet jewelry. Parental affection for Patsy was heightened by the fact that by age six she showed incipient signs of epilepsy. A sad irony of Martha Washington's life is that this fretful mother, chronically worried about her children's health, had a daughter with exactly the sort of terrifying illness she dreaded. In 1768 George and Martha were returning from Belvoir with twelve-year-old Patsy when she suffered her first full-scale seizure. As these ghastly convulsions occurred with greater regularity, Dr. William Rumney turned into a frequent visitor at Mount Vernon. He tried to halt the convulsions by bleeding and purging the girl, which only weakened her further. Although he prescribed a dozen different powders, including toxic mercury and the herb valerian, nothing appeared to alleviate the problem. As they watched the wrenching spectacle of this remorseless disease, George and Martha could only have experienced a paralyzing sense of helplessness.

Such is the nature of epilepsy that Martha would have been afraid to leave Patsy alone and would have made sure she was watched at all times. An epileptic child can drown while swimming or collapse into a seizure while descending a staircase. The convulsions can erupt at any time. In his diary for April 14, 1769, Washington told of the family setting out for a social visit when "Patcy being taken with a fit on the road by the mill, we turned back."[4] Since other children are often terrified when someone has a seizure, the disease would have isolated the adolescent girl. Even today, when it is treated with antiseizure medications, epilepsy is encrusted with baleful legends. In the eighteenth century, people commonly imagined that it signified diabolical possession or might even be contagious.

Given the rudimentary state of contemporary medicine, the Washingtons ended up mingling science with superstition in coping with the illness. In an exasperating quest for a cure, they took Patsy to the leading physicians in Williamsburg, including eight visits to Dr. John de Sequeyra, the scion of a prominent family of Sephardic Jews in London. (This visit is the only time we know for sure that George Washington had contact with a Jew before the Revolution.) The Washingtons also consulted the pompous and self-important Dr. John Johnson, who pumped Patsy full of everything from ether to barley water, to no avail. In all, the Washingtons consulted at least eight physicians in their search to relieve Patsy's symptoms.

Like many desperate parents, George and Martha Washington wound up in the hands of charlatans. In February 1769 a blacksmith named Joshua Evans came to Mount Vernon to forge an iron "cramp ring" for one of Patsy's fingers. Popular superstition contended that such rings, if accompanied by suitable mumbo jumbo, could banish epilepsy. That summer the Washingtons took Patsy to the mineral waters at Berkeley Springs, hoping for relief. The resort had become more fashionable since Washington and his brother Lawrence had first visited there and now offered everything from gambling to horse racing. In its springs, the women wore prudish, old-fashioned garments, with lead weights secreted in the hems to ensure that water didn't push up their gowns and indecently expose flesh. Writing from the spa, Washington informed a friend that Patsy was "troubled with a complaint" and "found little benefit as yet from the experiment" of taking the waters. "What a week or two more may do, we know not and therefore are inclined to put them to the test."[5] Washington never spelled out the nature of Patsy's "complaint," suggesting the stigma attached to discussing epilepsy openly.

The adolescent girl's fits grew more horrifying and frequent, sometimes striking twice a day. They recurred so often that Washington, in alarm, began to compile a record of them in the margin of his almanac calendars. During one frightful period from June 29 to September 22, 1770, Patsy fell to the floor in convulsions no fewer than twenty-six times. To compensate for her medical tribulations, Washington treated the girl to extra clothing and trinkets whenever possible. In Williamsburg that summer he bought her a pair of gold earrings and a tortoiseshell comb. By the following year, as shown by invoices to Robert Cary, he was ordering liquid laudanum, a powerful opiate that may well have been administered to Patsy.

In a poignant letter of July 1771, Washington disclosed that Martha didn't believe that her daughter would ever be cured or even survive into adulthood. Referring to her anxieties about her son, Jacky, Washington observed, "The unhappy situation of her daughter has in some degree fixed her eyes upon him as her only hope."[6] Washington harbored many reservations about Jacky, who was outwardly sweet and affectionate toward his mother and never less than respectful toward his stepfather. At bottom, however, he was a young wastrel who loved horse races, hunting, and outdoor pursuits far more than his studies. When Charles Willson Peale sketched a watercolor of him, he portrayed the eighteen-year-old Jacky dressed in a green coat with a red collar and a richly embroidered waistcoat. He had a round face with a small chin and slightly crossed eyes, a detail that subtly captured his restless, perhaps immature, nature.

Where Washington wrote about Patsy with unfeigned affection, with Jacky he always seemed to bite his tongue and resort to euphemisms. Something about Patsy's sweet simplicity he found irresistible, whereas Jacky's feckless nature was to him intolerable. To Washington fell the thankless task of being the family disciplinarian, and he had to tread delicately in criticizing Jacky for fear of antagonizing his indulgent mother. Lacking the full legitimacy of a biological father, he found himself in a predicament as he tried to reform Jacky's habits without running afoul of Martha.

Though he might be the master of Mount Vernon, George Washington was far less powerful in the tiny emotional domain of his nuclear family.

Having been denied an adequate education, Washington went to inordinate lengths to educate his stepchildren properly. Starting in 1761, he hired a young, self-effacing Scottish immigrant, Walter Magowan, to tutor the children at home, and they were soon introduced to the Greek Testament and Latin poets and other things George Washington never learned. Toward the end of 1767 Magowan surrendered the post and returned to England, hoping to be ordained as an Anglican minister. In seeking a new teacher for thirteen-year-old Jacky, Washington contacted the Reverend Jonathan Boucher, an Anglican clergyman who ran a small academy for wealthy boys in his home near Fredericksburg. In his introductory letter, Washington described Jacky as "a promising boy" who was "untainted in his morals and of innocent manners," but then he tipped his hand and confessed his "anxiety to make him fit for more useful purposes than a horse racer."[7] He was trying to be loyal to Jacky and frank at the same time, a tenuous balancing act he would perform for many years. A toadying character straight out of a Jane Austen novel, Boucher, with a tug of the forelock, answered in an unctuous manner: "Ever since I have heard of Mast[e]r Custis, I have wish[e]d to call him one of my little flock."[8] In short order, Washington rode off to Boucher's school with Jacky, Jacky's young slave Julius, and two horses.

At first Boucher expressed high hope for his young charge, and Washington placed an order in London for one hundred books, many in Latin. A transparently insincere fellow, Boucher laid on the flattery with a trowel, telling Washington what he thought he wanted to hear. His first letter described Jacky as a little angel, "a boy of so exceedingly mild and meek a temper" that Boucher worried he might be too artless, with "all the harmlessness of the dove" and none of "the wisdom of the serpent." Of this little paragon, he concluded, "I have not seen a youth that I think promises fairer to be a good and a useful man than John Custis."[9]

A year later, having discovered Jacky's profligate nature, Boucher whistled a different tune. "You will rem[embe]r my having complain[e]d of Jack's laziness, which, however, I now hope is not incurable," he wrote to Washington.[10] The reverend's dismay steadily deepened: "The chief failings of [Jacky's] character are that he is constitutionally somewhat too warm, indolent, and voluptuous." He trembled for the fate of the Custis fortune: "Sunk in unmanly sloth, [Jacky's] estate will [be] left to the managem[en]t of some worthless overseer and himself soon be entangled in some matrimonial adventure."[11] Cognizant of the exorbitant wealth he would inherit, Jacky saw little need to apply himself to studies, which couldn't help but distress his stepfather with his nagging work ethic.

In 1770 Jonathan Boucher became a rector in Annapolis, Maryland, and Jacky followed him there. Boucher's scathing strictures on Jacky's behavior came in private exchanges with Washington and probably weren't communicated to Martha. Always concerned with Jacky's health, she feared he would drown and urged Boucher not to let him swim too frequently. When Boucher devised an elaborate plan to chaperone Jacky on a grand European tour, Washington vetoed it as too expensive but probably suspected as well that Martha would never allow her son to travel for an extended period, especially on an ocean voyage.

In the end, Jacky became so uncontrollable that he started gallivanting about with friends after school and often spent the night elsewhere. Washington knew that Annapolis, with its horse races and theater, tempted his stepson with its many sinful haunts. "I would beg leave to request," Washington told Boucher, "that [Jacky] may not be suffered to sleep from under your own roof . . . nor allow him to be rambling about at nights in company with those who do not care how debauched and vicious his conduct may be."[12] No longer feeling obligated to flatter Master Custis, Boucher dropped all pretense. "I must confess to you," he replied, "I never did in my life know a youth so exceedingly indolent or so surprisingly voluptuous. One would suppose nature had intended him for some Asiatic prince."[13] When Boucher suggested that the best way to control Jacky was to send his two horses back to Mount Vernon, Martha furiously refused her permission.

In dealing with his stepson, Washington betrayed the exasperation of a hard-working man coping with a spoiled rich boy. Jacky was spurning the very education that Washington had so sorely missed. Having never learned French himself, Washington told Boucher to teach it to Jacky: "To be acquainted with the French tongue is become a part of polite education and, to a man who has an[y idea] of mixing in a large circle, absolutely necessary."[14] Jacky never learned French or Greek or mathematics, as he was supposed to do.

One reason that Washington monitored Jacky's education so narrowly was that he took seriously his role as guardian of the Custis estate. When he turned down Boucher's request for the grand tour, he explained that its costs would exceed Jacky's income, forcing him to draw down capital. This "might be deemed imprudent in me to allow without the sanction of the court, who are the constitutional guardians of orphans."[15] Jacky's estate consisted of four plantations in New Kent County, 15,000 acres of land, somewhere between 200 and 300 slaves, and nearly 10,000 pounds in financial securities. One wonders how Washington felt about this devil-may-care stepson whose immense wealth easily rivaled his own.

In early 1773 Washington decided that the time had come to ship Jacky off to college. For Martha, William and Mary would have been the most desirable place, given its proximity to Mount Vernon, but Washington found the atmosphere at the Virginia school too lax. He wanted to send Jacky to the College of New Jersey

(Princeton), but Boucher steered him instead to King's College (predecessor to Columbia) in New York. Boucher argued that King's was located in "the most fashionable and polite place on the continent," and that he counted its president, Dr. Myles Cooper, as a personal friend.[16] It is worth noting that Washington, taking a dim view of the moral climate in Virginia, wanted to educate his stepson in the North.

Once Washington decided in favor of King's, Jacky introduced a fresh complication into the picture. This sexually precocious youth had spent considerable time wooing the opposite sex. "Jack has a propensity to the sex," Boucher warned Washington, "which I am at a loss how to judge of, much more how to describe."[17] It was only a matter of time before Jacky became seriously involved with a young woman. In December 1771, when Jonathan Boucher moved again, this time to Prince George's County, Maryland, he took along three students. One was Jacky and another was Charles Calvert, son of the wealthy Benedict Calvert of Mount Airy. Jacky courted Eleanor (Nelly) Calvert, Charles's beautiful, dark-eyed sister, and by early 1773 had proposed to her. All this happened without the Washingtons' knowledge. Shocked by the news, they tried, at a bare minimum, to slow things down. On April 3, 1773, Washington wrote an artful letter to Benedict Calvert, stating that he had heard of Nelly's "amiable qualifications" and that "an alliance" with the Calverts would please him and Martha. He then went on to cite Jacky's "youth, inexperience, and unripened education" as "insuperable obstacles ... to the completion of the marriage."[18] Washington suggested that the marriage be deferred for two or three years until Jacky completed his education. In the letter, he distanced himself from Jacky and discreetly registered his disapproval without openly disavowing him. Benedict Calvert agreed that Jacky should spend two years at King's College before marrying his daughter.

FOR WASHINGTON, the other troubling family situation of these years involved his perennial attempt to please his mother, who refused to be satisfied. Mary Ball Washington had taken no apparent pride in her son's service in the French and Indian War, and when he resigned from the Virginia Regiment, she commented that there had been "no end to my trouble while George was in the army, but he has now given it up."[19] If he felt no real affection for his mother, he was first and last a dutiful son and showed integrity in caring for this self-centered woman. Frequently stopping off to see her in Fredericksburg, he made a point of giving her money. He extended many loans to her, even though she always reneged on repayment. In an account book for January 1772, noting that he had been lending his mother money since 1756, Washington offered the acidulous comment, "I suppose she never expected to pay."[20]

For decades, Mary Ball Washington had lived frugally at Ferry Farm, the ample spread fronting the Rappahannock that George had inherited from his father and that he had let her use freely all these years. For a long time she had delighted in her independence, riding about in an open chaise and supervising the slaves. Now about sixty-three, she was no longer able to superintend the run-down place, and in 1772 George encouraged her to move into Fredericksburg. To make a final provision for her, he spent 275 pounds for a charming white frame house on a one-acre lot at the corner of Charles and Lewis streets in Fredericksburg. He added a wide, deep porch with a slanting roof that overlooked the garden. The house was ideally situated for Mary: a brick footpath led straight to the imposing mansion of her daughter Betty and Fielding Lewis, who had eleven hundred acres and 125 slaves. Washington's brothers Charles, a Spotsylvania County justice, and Samuel, a plantation owner, also owned nearby houses. Although Mary Ball Washington spent the last seventeen years of her life in the Charles Street house and never paid a penny in rent, she never acknowledged George's generosity, as best we know.

Washington personally surveyed Ferry Farm in 1771 in preparation for selling it. He also agreed to take charge of a four-hundred-acre farm, Little Falls, that Mary owned two miles downriver and had inherited from her father. Washington was supposed to profit from Mary's ten slaves and livestock and pay her thirty pounds rent yearly in exchange, a deal approved by his brother Charles and brother-in-law Fielding Lewis. Because there was no mutual trust between mother and son, when Washington paid Mary the rent, he often did so in the presence of his sister Betty, then recorded in his ledger that the latter had witnessed the transaction.

One small incident from the early years of the Revolutionary War shows just how steely a woman Mary Washington was. She had reclaimed from Mount Vernon a slave woman named Silla. Lund Washington notified George of the heartrending scene that occurred when he informed Silla's partner, Jack (probably a slave cooper), that Silla was being sent down to Fredericksburg. "He cries and begs, saying he had rather be hang[e]d than separated," Lund reported. A week later Lund reiterated that "Jack and Silla are much distressed about parting."[21] George Washington respected slave marriages and refused to separate couples. Nevertheless Mary Washington evidently persisted in her demand and broke up the couple for her own convenience.

ON THE EVENING OF MAY 18, 1772, Jacky Custis returned to Mount Vernon with an unusual companion in tow, a thirty-one-year-old painter named Charles Willson Peale who lived in Annapolis and toted an introductory letter from the Reverend Jonathan Boucher. The handsome young stranger had relinquished a career as a saddle maker to specialize in portraits of affluent families. Peale was destined to have three wives and sixteen children and emerge as a towering figure in early American life, excelling as a painter, a writer, a soldier, an inventor, a silversmith, a taxidermist, a dentist, and the founder of a Philadelphia museum. He had studied painting in London under the foremost American expatriate artist, Benjamin West, and the Potomac gentry already prized his pictures. Nudged by Martha, George Washington, age forty, agreed to endure his first portrait. Though he never warmed to artistic scrutiny, he had enough vanity in his psychological makeup to want a picture of himself.

Even though more than thirteen years had passed since Washington resigned his military commission, he still prided himself on a military identity, and people often greeted him as Colonel Washington. The brouhaha over the Stamp Act and the Townshend duties also raised the distant prospect of a recourse to arms. So as the industrious Peale settled in at Mount Vernon, Washington donned a uniform—a blue coat trimmed with scarlet and a scarlet waistcoat—that called forth memories of the French and Indian War.

Never comfortable with self-exposure, Washington was alternately restive and sleepy in posing for Peale, as he described whimsically to Boucher. He seemed to sense what a baffling, enigmatic subject he was. "Inclination having yielded to importunity, I am now, contrary to all expectation, under the hands of Mr Peale, but in so grave, so sullen, a mood—and now and then under the influence of Morpheus, when some critical strokes are making—that I fancy the skill of this gentleman's pencil will be put to it in describing to the world what manner of man I am."[22]

This serene painting has a storybook quality. Instead of presenting Washington as a prosperous planter, it offers a nostalgic backward glimpse to the Washington of the 1750s. With one yellow-gloved hand thrust into his waistcoat, a musket slung behind him, and a golden sash hung diagonally across his chest, Washington gazes poetically into the distance. His face is smooth and innocent, his blue eyes clear, and he might be listening to bird whistles in the tree above him rather than live bullets. His facial features are mobile and animated, not yet etched with the strong character engraved there by the Revolutionary War. The picturesque scene pretends to capture Washington being summoned to battle, with an Order of March protruding from his fob pocket. Washington was so fond of the painting, which captured him in his prime, that it hung in the Mount Vernon parlor for the rest of his life. It seems to foretell his eagerness to resume his military career.

The artist spent a week at Mount Vernon and painted miniatures of Martha, Jacky, and Patsy along with the three-quarter-length portrait of George Washington. The picture of Martha was done at Jacky's request, and one wonders whether he made a point of demonstrating his love for his mother or perhaps implicitly rebuked his stepfather for not having included her in pictures by this visiting artist. It must be said that the picture of Martha Washington, in a mauve dress and pearls, is not especially flattering. Her face is cold and humorless, the tight lips primly disapproving. Nevertheless this was probably the miniature of Martha that her grandson later meant when he said that George Washington always "wore around his neck the miniature portrait of his wife. This he had worn through all the vicissitudes of his eventful career . . . to the last days at Mount Vernon."[23]

IN MAY 1773, hoping to put a safe distance between Jacky and his intended bride, Washington accompanied him to New York City and enrolled him in King's College. This sociable trip exposed Washington to personalities who were to be prominent in the coming conflict. It was almost the last moment when Washington could still mingle easily with people of differing ideologies. In Philadelphia he dined with Governor Richard Penn and in Burlington, New Jersey, with Governor William Franklin, Benjamin Franklin's illegitimate son and soon to be ostracized as a notorious Tory. At Basking Ridge, New Jersey, he stayed at the opulent estate of Lord Stirling, whose extravagant ways had already landed him in debt; before too long, Stirling would emerge as one of Washington's favorite generals. In New York he met with James DeLancey, shortly to command a Loyalist cavalry, and attended a dinner in honor of an old colleague from the Braddock campaign, Lieutenant General Thomas Gage, now commander of British forces in North America. It is amusing to think of George Washington drinking toasts to this future bugbear of the patriot cause. Washington also attended a performance of *Hamlet,* staged in a red theater building on John Street.

The president of King's College, the Reverend Myles Cooper, welcomed Jacky Custis and his personal slave Joe to the school. An accomplished scholar and poet, versed in classical tongues, Cooper had strengthened the college by adding new professors and a medical school and expanding the library. He had also turned the school into a hotbed of Tory sentiment as the colonies became polarized by the controversial taxes imposed by London. The school stood on the Hudson River, one block west of the common, where radicals congregated to spout anti-British venom. Myles Cooper, with no patience for such critics, branded the radical Sons of Liberty the "sons of licentiousness, faction, and confusion."[24]

There is no suggestion that Washington had any qualms about depositing Jacky in a school known for its Tory views. He must have alerted Cooper candidly to Jacky's wanton history, because he told the president that, if Jacky spent too freely, he hoped Cooper would "by your friendly admonitions . . . check the progress of it."[25] College life was shot through with class differences, and Jacky basked in his privileged station. Thanks to his wealth, the cosseted boy enjoyed social equality with his professors, who seemed to know his status and cater to it. Instead of socializing with other students, Jacky boasted of dining with President Cooper and his tutors. "I believe I may say without vanity that I am look[e]d upon in a particular light" by the faculty, Jacky told his mother. "There is as much distinction made between me and the other students as can be expected."[26] He also bragged that he and Joe had their own suite of rooms, with a large sitting room and two small bedrooms. At times Jacky wrote about King's College as if it were a swank resort staffed with servile employees hired to wait upon him, assuring his mother that "there has nothing been omitted by my good friend Doctor Cooper which was necessary to my contentment in this place."[27] After Washington returned to Mount Vernon, Jacky promised that he would prove a credit to his family. The young man's cozy relationship with the faculty suggested that things wouldn't turn out exactly as Washington had planned.

The concern over Jacky paled into insignificance, however, beside mounting trepidation over Patsy's medical condition. Charles Willson Peale remembered the palpable atmosphere of fear at Mount Vernon, writing that "we used to walk together to enjoy the evening breeze" and "danced to give exercise to Miss Custis . . . who did not enjoy good health. She was subject to fits and Mrs. Washington never suffered her to be a minute out of her sight."[28] Washington's diaries for early 1773 are rife with emergency visits by Dr. Rumney. During one particularly distressing time in late January, the doctor camped out at Mount Vernon for almost a full week. Then on Saturday, June 19, 1773, Patsy Custis died a sudden, painless death, leading her stepfather to make a terse entry in his diary: "At home all day. About five o'clock poor Patcy Custis died suddenly."

The next day, a shaken Washington wrote a note eloquent in its brevity to his brother-in-law Burwell Bassett:

> Dear Sir: It is an easier matter to conceive than to describe the distress of this family, especially that of the unhappy parent of our dear Patcy Custis, when I inform you that yesterday remov[e]d the sweet, innocent girl into a more happy and peaceful abode than any she has met with in the afflicted path she hitherto has trod. She rose from dinner about four o'clock in better health and spirits than she appear[e]d to have been in for some time. Soon after which she was seized with one of her usual fits and expir[e]d in it in less than two minutes without uttering a word, a groan, or scarce a sigh. This sudden and unexpected blow, I scarce need add, has almost reduced my poor wife to the lowest ebb of misery, which is increas[e]d by the absence of her son (whom I have just fixed at the College in New York).[29]

After five years of torment, Patsy had gently slipped away. It was unusual for a person with epilepsy to die so peacefully, suggesting that Patsy may have had a heart problem or some other condition associated with her epilepsy.

A private man who never flaunted his deep emotions, George Washington nonetheless gave way to a tremendous outpouring of grief. One observer remembered him kneeling by Patsy's bed as he "solemnly recited the prayers for the dying, while tears rolled down his cheeks and his voice was often broken by sobs."[30] In a week of sweltering heat, the heartbroken Washingtons decided it was wise to bury Patsy on the family property the next day. The coffin, draped in black, was buried in the brick vault down the hill from the house on the Potomac side. Martha assumed a black mourning cape for a full year. Her husband knew that, between her daughter's death and her son's absence, she was unspeakably bereft, and he canceled a western trip to stay near her.

When Patsy died, Jacky's fiancée, Nelly Calvert, was staying with the Washingtons, and her presence proved providential, for she stepped into the huge emotional void left by Patsy's death, becoming like a second daughter. She lingered at Mount Vernon for a week, fostering a lasting intimacy with Martha. Jacky wrote a tender condolence note to his mother, telling her to "remember you are a Christian" and saying of his lost sister that her situation was "more to be envied than pitied, for if we mortals can distinguish between those who are deserving of grace and those who are not, I am confident she enjoys that bliss prepar[e]d only for the good and virtuous."[31]

Patsy's death had a profound impact on the finances of her stepfather, who had been unable to shake his indebtedness to Robert Cary. Through skillful management, Patsy's estate had appreciated to sixteen thousand pounds, and half this amount went to Jacky and half to Washington by way of his wife. Later in the year Washington instructed Robert Cary to take the inheritance and discharge his large debt. Once again, as with his father and his brother Lawrence, Washington had profited enormously from a death that caused him grievous sorrow.

Beyond their obvious sadness, it is hard to overstate the impact that Patsy's death would have on George and Martha Washington in the coming years. The sudden financial windfall, by relieving pressure on Washington, allowed him the luxury of participating in the American Revolution without financial worries. In fact, it enabled him to take part on the gentlemanly terms that suited him, as he dispensed with a salary. The effect on Martha was no less consequential. She would spend about half the war in her husband's company, which would have been impossible if Patsy were alive. The sickly girl could never have managed the long coach journeys, or the continual tensions of a military camp, or being left alone. Patsy Custis's death, paradoxically, set up George and Martha Washington for their shining moment in history.

The inheritance also allowed Washington to launch the second major transformation of Mount Vernon, and he ordered sixty thousand bricks and nearly fifteen thousand shingles for this ambitious effort. In 1773 the main house was still a plain, nondescript building, small and unadorned and not particularly attractive. Now Washington decided to double the mansion's size, adding those trademark features—a cupola, the pediment over the west entrance, the spacious piazza on the river side—that we associate with it today. Never a professional architect, Washington admitted that he was "a person who avows his ignorance of architectural principles and who has no other guide but his eye to direct his choice."[32] Because he added rooms and wings as needed, the house lacked the elegance of a preconceived design and was marred by some clumsy touches. The facade wasn't quite symmetrical, and the pediment sat awkwardly on the window tops—errors the more refined Jefferson would have avoided. Nevertheless the house would gain undeniable grace and beauty, and the large colonnaded porch would stand out as a landmark in southern architecture. The piazza, with its spectacular view of the Potomac and wooded hills beyond, turned into Washington's favorite haunt, the place that Abigail Adams hailed as Mount Vernon's "greatest adornment."[33]

The renovation reflected the split in Washington's life between his deep desire for privacy and his growing need to entertain people and assume a grand public role. On the south side of the house, he would add a downstairs library and an upstairs bedroom, sealed off from the rest of the house to fend off intruders. On the north side, he would add an imposing two-story room, later called the Banquet Hall, with a magnificent Palladian window—a space in which Washington could receive luminaries with a dignity befitting his station. The renovation also introduced the curved arcades that gracefully attach the mansion visually to the smaller buildings flanking it. Many of these changes would be completed while Washington was with the Continental Army, but while he remained, he oversaw the work with typically fastidious attention to detail. "I am very much engaged in raising one of the additions of my house, which I think (perhaps it is fancy) goes on better whilst I am present than in my absence from the workmen," he wrote.[34]

Everything at the Mansion House Farm—the serpentine walks, the beautiful gardens, the undulating meadows—reflected Washington's taste. It is noteworthy that, as tensions mounted with Great Britain, his conception of Mount Vernon grew more regal. In its British style, the house reflected his love of the country against which he was about to rebel, suggesting that his hostility to the mother country was a case of thwarted love. "Examples of English taste are everywhere at Mount Vernon," write the historians Robert F. Dalzell, Jr., and Lee Baldwin Dalzell. "The taste in question also bears the indelible stamp of that most English of institutions—the aristocratic country house."[35]

Patsy Custis's untimely death meant that Martha Washington would now derive her emotional sustenance from the unpredictable Jacky Custis alone. Myles Cooper continued to ply Washington with favorable reports about his young charge, as had Jonathan Boucher before him. In September 1773 he informed Washington that Jacky's "assiduity hath been equal to his rectitude of principle and it is hoped his improvements in learning have not been inferior to either."[36] By December Cooper couldn't keep up these fake progress reports with a straight face and told Washington that he had yielded to Jacky's wish to quit college and marry. As a military man, Washington knew when he faced a losing battle. Having Jacky's "own inclination, the desire of his mother, and the acquiescence of almost all his relatives to encounter," Washington told Cooper, "I did not care, as he is the last of the family, to push my opposition too far and therefore have submitted to a kind of necessity."[37] One can again feel Washington's painful frustration in bowing to Martha's wishes when it came to her incorrigible son.

On February 3, 1774, Jacky Custis, nineteen, wed Nelly Calvert, sixteen, in Mount Airy, Maryland, the home of the Calvert clan. Only half a year had passed since Patsy's death, and one wonders what Martha Washington thought about the timing of this rushed marriage. She didn't think it proper to attend the wedding in mourning dress, so her husband carried a congratulatory letter from her to the newlyweds. Jacky had married into a prominent family, the Catholic proprietors of Maryland, who had issued a famous act of religious toleration in 1649. At the same time the family had its own salacious past to titillate Jacky's imagination. His new father-in-law, Benedict Calvert, was the illegitimate offspring of Charles Calvert, the fifth Lord Baltimore, and lived in a huge mansion graced with Van Dyke portraits of his ancestors. Whatever Jacky's flaws, Nelly Calvert seemed to be a universally popular young woman. Boucher said rhapsodically that she was "the most amiable young woman I have almost ever known . . . She is all that the fondest parent can wish for a darling child."[38]

During their first year of marriage, Jacky and Nelly divided their time between Mount Airy and Mount Vernon, despite the lonely Martha's wish that they move permanently to Mount Vernon. That May, George and Martha took them to an unusual boat race on the Rappahannock River. As the family unfolded twenty blankets and a picnic barbecue on the riverbank—Washington brought forty-eight bottles of claret to spread good cheer—they watched a macabre sporting event. Two boats, each manned by five or six muscular slaves, raced out to an anchored boat and back, while spectators cheered and placed bets onshore. It was an exceedingly strange vignette: the man who would be fighting for American liberty exactly one year later was being entertained by teams of strong, athletic slaves.

CHAPTER FIFTEEN

A Shock of Electricity

AFTER THE REVOCATION of all the Townshend duties, except the one on tea, the political world of Williamsburg had reverted temporarily to some semblance of normality. In October 1771 Washington was reelected as a Fairfax County burgess. To safeguard his seat, he paid four pounds to tavern keeper John Lomax to feed a hearty supper to voters; twelve shillings to a Harry Piper, so that his slave Charles could fiddle up a storm for them; and another pound for good measure to a Mr. Young, who sated the hungry electorate with free cakes.

In early 1773 Washington still operated in a world of flagrant contradictions. He stanchly backed measures criticizing Parliament and the North ministry, while also socializing with the royal governor, John Murray, Earl of Dunmore, a redheaded Scot with a large nose and fiery gaze who took office in 1771 with no inkling of just how stormy his tenure would be. In March 1773 Washington supported the burgesses' decision to form a Committee of Correspondence to harmonize defensive measures with other colonies and to "propose a meeting of deputies from every colony at some central place," as Jefferson was to recall.[1] Still slightly detached from the fray, Washington didn't serve on the committee and continued to straddle two worlds. Dining with Lord Dunmore and still ravenous for land, Washington badgered him for another five thousand acres in the Ohio Country under the royal proclamation of 1763, the one designed to reward French and Indian War veterans.

There matters stood on December 16, 1773, when a patriotic band, masquerading as Mohawk Indians, heaved 342 chests of tea into Massachusetts Bay. Such was the instinctive respect for private property in the colonies that even Boston firebrand Samuel Adams boasted that the tea party had occurred "without the least injury to the vessels or any other property."² The tea tax wasn't as punitive as is commonly supposed—the cost of tea to the colonists actually declined—but it threatened local merchants by eliminating smugglers and colonial middlemen, entrenching the East India Company's monopoly. It also perpetuated the hated practice of taxation without representation.

When the news from Boston reached Mount Vernon around New Year's Day, Washington deplored the methods of the tea party, even if he loathed the tax on tea. It was the next step in a fast-unfolding drama that would fully radicalize him. The administration of the bluff, portly Lord North had decided that Boston should pay for the destroyed tea and that Parliament should assert its supremacy, cracking down on harebrained schemes of independence now beginning to ferment in the colonies. In March Parliament passed the Boston Port Bill, shutting down the port of Boston until the townspeople reimbursed the East India Company for its lost tea. Along with other draconian measures that subverted the Massachusetts charter and clamped military rule on Boston, the harsh new laws were known as the Coercive Acts or "Intolerable Acts." Such ham-handed reprisals forged new unity among the colonists. Similarly, the tea party convinced many British sympathizers that colonial protesters had become a violent rabble who had to pay a steep price for their inexcusable crimes. General Thomas Gage counseled his superiors in London that the colonists would "be lions whilst we are lambs, but if we take the resolute part, they will be very meek."³

Washington was in Williamsburg when the thunderclap of the Boston Port Bill burst over the colony. He also learned that three thousand redcoats had landed in Boston, fortifying Gage's position. During the French and Indian War, Gage had written warmly to Washington, "It gave me great pleasure to hear from a person of whom the world has justly so good an opinion and for whom I have so great an esteem."⁴ Such fraternal sentiments between imperial warriors now belonged to a vanished world. Washington blasted military rule in Boston as "unexampled testimony of the most despotic system of tyranny that ever was practiced in a free gov[ernmen]t."⁵ He and his fellow burgesses enlisted the Lord on their side, declaring that June 1, the day of the port's closure, should be observed "as a day of fasting, humiliation, and prayer."⁶ In what was fast becoming a ritual, Dunmore dissolved the House of Burgesses. That very morning Washington had breakfasted with the governor at his farm outside Williamsburg. It was now plain that the rights of the burgesses dangled by a slender thread that could be severed at will by the golden shears wielded by the all-powerful royal governor.

The next day Washington and other militant burgesses moved to their familiar resort, the Raleigh Tavern, where they poured forth scorn for the Boston Port Bill, ratified a boycott of tea, and endorsed an annual congress with other colonies to protect their collective rights. They reached the critical conclusion that an assault on one colony was an assault on all. In this crazily illogical world, Washington and other burgesses threw a ball that evening to welcome the governor's wife. Quite obviously this was no typical revolt of the poor or dispossessed, but a fissure at the pinnacle of the social structure, involving men long accustomed to rule. Washington was one of twenty-five burgesses still lingering in Williamsburg in late May when a letter arrived from Samuel Adams, beseeching the Virginians to discontinue trade with England. The legislators decided to cease all imports and reconvene on August 1.

Land was never far from George Washington's thoughts, and he smarted at new British policies that curtailed speculative activities. The Quebec Act transferred the Great Lakes and territory north of the Ohio River to Catholic Quebec, restricting the acreage available to Virginians. Still more jarring was a ruling from London that land grants to French and Indian War veterans under the 1763 proclamation would be limited to British regulars, discriminating against colonial officers and reopening an ancient wound for Washington. "I conceive the services of a provincial officer as worthy of reward as a regular one and [it] can only be withheld from him with injustice," he observed with contempt.[7] As we have seen, the ambitious Washington took these slights personally, and they now tipped him over the edge into open revolt.

To gauge opinion before the August meeting of the burgesses, Washington chaired a gathering of his Alexandria constituents on July 5. Their response to the Boston turmoil was both swift and decisive: they agreed to send 273 pounds sterling, 38 barrels of flour, and 150 bushels of wheat to "the industrious poor of the town of *Boston* . . . who by a late cruel act of Parliament are deprived of their daily labor and bread."[8] Having dissolved the burgesses, Governor Dunmore ordered new elections, and Washington engaged in the bread and circuses of a fresh campaign on July 17, a gaudy spectacle at odds with the high-minded rhetoric in the air. One observer related how Washington and his ally, Major Charles Broadwater, gave Alexandria voters "a hogshead of toddy," or punch, followed by a ball that evening that was punctilious in its choice of beverages: "Coffee and chocolate, but no tea. This herb is in disgrace amongst them at present."[9] Washington and Broadwater were swept into office.

On Sunday, July 17, Colonel George Mason arrived at Mount Vernon for an overnight stay, and he and Washington refined a list of twenty-four resolutions that he had brought. The next day the resolutions were presented to their Fairfax County committee and, with Washington in the chair, adopted with minor changes. These Fairfax Resolves, as they became known, reflected the views of the "Country Party" of landed British gentry, who had protested what they saw as the corruption

of Britain's constitution by venal politicians during Robert Walpole's ministry earlier in the century. The resolves argued that people should obey only laws enacted
by their chosen representatives or else "the government must degenerate either into
an absolute and despotic monarchy or a tyrannical aristocracy." Another resolution
stated that "taxation and representation are in their nature inseparable." Still another called for an intercolonial congress to guarantee a common defense. Perhaps
the most surprising resolution passed under Washington's watchful eye was a plea
to suspend the importation of slaves into Virginia, along with a fervent wish "to
see an entire stop forever put to such a wicked, cruel, and unnatural trade."[10] It was
the first time Washington had publicly registered his disgust with the system that
formed the basis of his fortune. Because of surplus slaves in Virginia, the resolution
wasn't quite as courageous as it appeared and caused no immediate change in behavior at Mount Vernon. When the Fairfax County citizenry met at the Alexandria
Court House on July 18, in what Washington described as a mood of "hurry and
bustle," they adopted the Fairfax Resolves and named Washington head of a twenty-
five-member committee to chart future policy responses.[11]

With the Fairfax Resolves, Washington emerged as a significant political leader
a full year before being named to head the Continental Army. No fence-sitter, this
conservative planter was a true militant. When the *Boston Gazette* printed the Fairfax Resolves, Washington's renown reverberated through the colonies for the first
time since the French and Indian War. During this period he allowed his heated
opinions to bubble up and boil over as his pronouncements grew more vehement.
Later on he had to muzzle his public views for the sake of continental harmony, but
during the summer of 1774 he had no qualms about expressing open militance. He
scoffed at the notion that the forthcoming congress should submit more petitions
to the king when so many had failed: "Shall we, after this, whine and cry for relief?"[12] His slumbering conscience was now fully awakened. All the petty indignities
that he had endured at British hands exploded in revolutionary rage as his personal
pique was sublimated into something much grander. As the historian Joseph Ellis
notes, George Mason probably helped Washington "to develop a more expansive
vocabulary to express his thoughts and feelings, but the thoughts, and even more so
the feelings, had been brewing inside him for more than twenty years."[13]

NOT SURPRISINGLY the acrimonious quarrel with the Crown strained Washington's relations with the family that had long embodied for him the British Empire,
the Fairfaxes. In August 1773, shortly after Patsy's death, George William and Sally
Fairfax had sailed to England to pursue a complex inheritance suit in chancery
in London. George and Martha Washington were the last people to see them off,

waving farewell at the dock. By this point Sally Fairfax had entered into a period of chronic health problems, including a brush with smallpox. As it turned out, she and her husband never returned to Virginia or set eyes on the Washingtons again. Despite the manifold demands on his time, Washington agreed to oversee the Fairfax affairs in Virginia and got a power of attorney to do so—an act of friendship that lasted until he took command of the Continental Army. The Fairfaxes must have known that their farewell might be irrevocable because they gave Washington the authority to auction off Belvoir's furniture. It is hard to imagine that the commotion shaking the colonies played no part in their decision to decamp to England, but George William claimed to be an ardent friend of the patriotic cause and denied any political motivation behind their trip.

During the summer of 1774 Washington unburdened his thoughts freely to the Fairfaxes. Black with gloom, he wrote despondently to George William that the Crown was failing to protect Virginia from "cruel and bloodthirsty" Indians in the backcountry, while simultaneously "endeavoring by every piece of art and despotism to fix the shackles of slavery upon us."[14] He made clear that the "cause of Boston . . . now is and ever will be consider[e]d as the cause of America . . . and that we shall not suffer ourselves to be sacrificed by piecemeal, though God only knows what is to become of us."[15] Further souring his mood was that a bitter winter frost had given way to an equally bitter drought. In short, Washington concluded, "since the first settlem[en]t of this colony the minds of people in it never were more disturbed, or our situation so critical, as at present."[16]

Washington went on corresponding with George William as if communicating with a kindred spirit. Far different was his tense standoff with his longtime friend Bryan Fairfax, the half brother of George William and a former lieutenant in Washington's Virginia Regiment. Bryan Fairfax was a grave, austere fellow. In June 1774, when Washington had tried to coax his old foxhunting companion into running with him for the House of Burgesses, it became clear that a political gulf yawned between them. On July 4 Washington sent Bryan a letter that was neither soft-spoken nor conciliatory. Instead of ducking politics out of respect for their friendship, Washington gave an unusually forthright statement of his beliefs. As if the scales had fallen from his eyes, he embraced a conspiratorial view of British intentions. The Crown's policies weren't just fumbling or misguided but were part of a settled design to rob the colonists of their ancient liberties. "Does it not appear, as clear as the sun in its meridian brightness, that there is a regular, systematic plan formed to fix the right and practice of taxation upon us? . . . Ought we not then to put our virtue and fortitude to the severest test?"[17] George Washington passed here some personal Rubicon. Remarkably, in this fierce letter he argued that the colonists should refrain from purchasing British imports, but not renege on paying debts owed to British creditors, "for I think, whilst we are accusing others of injustice, we should be just ourselves."[18] It was this steadfast sense of fairness, even at the most feverish political moments, that set George Washington apart.

When Bryan Fairfax sent Washington a lengthy reply, defending petitions as the only legitimate means of protest, the hot-blooded Washington didn't mince words. On July 20 he sent Bryan a truculent letter that recounted the many colonial petitions spurned by Parliament, which had violated both the "law of nature and our constitution . . . I think the Parliament of Great Britain hath no more right to put their hands into my pocket without my consent than I have to put my hands in yours for money."[19] Instead of more petitions, Washington endorsed the non-importation scheme, "for I am convinc[e]d, as much as I am of my existence, that there is no relief for us but in their distress; and I think, at least I hope, that there is public virtue enough left among us to deny ourselves everything but the bare necessaries of life to accomplish this end."[20] Washington said he would mistrust his own judgment if he didn't recoil "at the thought of submitting to measures which I think subversive of everything that I ought to hold dear and valuable."[21] Washington's vision abruptly seemed richer and broader, his words now throbbing with passion. His letters to Bryan Fairfax make clear that, even though he didn't originate political ideas, he was a quick study who soaked them up rapidly, as he was coached by George Mason and other colonial leaders. His sudden eloquence is striking, as his ideas were forged in the crucible of powerful emotions. In a final blast at Fairfax late that summer, Washington wrote that "an innate spirit of freedom first told me that the measures which [the] administration hath for sometime been, and now are, most violently pursuing are repugnant to every principle of natural justice, whilst much abler heads than my own hath fully convinced me that it is not only repugnant to natural right, but subversive of the laws and constitution of Great Britain itself."[22]

By this point George Washington knew that a clash with the mother country was almost inevitable. For that reason, the auction of Belvoir's effects in August and December must have carried heavy symbolic overtones for him. For reasons of pride, status, and undoubtedly nostalgia, George Washington bought more than half of the Fairfax furniture, everything from window curtains to candlesticks to a bust of Shakespeare. He indulged his old penchant for mahogany, the expensive wood that signified wealth in the colonies. It must have been a melancholy task for Washington to see Belvoir's furnishings dismantled, ending the aristocratic world that had shaped his early dreams.

As the old world emptied out, a new one was being born that August in Williamsburg, where the rebel burgesses, trained in self-government, reconstituted themselves as the Virginia Convention. "We never before had so full a meeting . . .

as on the present occasion," Washington exulted, as more than one hundred delegates attended.[23] Within a week, the delegates had thrashed out a plan aligned with the Fairfax Resolves, thrusting Washington into the forefront of the action. They agreed to set up an association that would ban imports beginning in November and, if Great Britain still refused to redress their grievances, tobacco exports after August 1775. They also issued a stinging indictment of the arbitrary behavior in Boston of Washington's old colleague General Gage.

On Friday, August 5, 1774, George Washington's life changed forever when he was elected one of seven Virginia delegates to the general congress that would meet in Philadelphia, to be known as the First Continental Congress. When these statesmen were selected, Jefferson said, a "shock of electricity" flew through the air.[24] The vote underscored the dramatic elevation of Washington's standing: he trailed Speaker Peyton Randolph by only a few votes and received nine votes more than the superlative orator Patrick Henry. Before leaving Williamsburg, Washington obtained a copy of Jefferson's pamphlet *A Summary View of the Rights of British America,* which took dead aim at the notion that the colonies existed to benefit the mother country. Jefferson ended with a dire warning for George III: "Kings are the servants, not the proprietors of the people. Open your breast, Sire, to liberal and expanded thought. Let not the name of George the Third be a blot in the page of history."[25]

ON AUGUST 30, 1774, two influential burgesses, Patrick Henry and Edmund Pendleton, spent the night at Mount Vernon before departing with Washington and his manservant, Billy Lee, for the First Continental Congress. They left on a sultry, windless morning, and Martha Washington, infused with martial spirit, saw them off like a good, self-sacrificing matron from antiquity. Edmund Pendleton left an indelible portrait of Martha's unwavering commitment: "She seemed ready to make any sacrifice and was cheerful, though I know she felt anxious. She talked like a Spartan mother to her son on going to battle. 'I hope you will stand firm—I know George will,' she said. The dear little woman was busy from morning until night with domestic duties, but she gave us much time in conversation and affording us entertainment. When we set off in the morning, she stood in the door and cheered us with the good words, 'God be with you gentlemen.'"[26] It was a courageous show on the part of a woman who had already buried a husband and three children, the last of whom had died little more than a year before.

The three travelers rode into Philadelphia on September 4. The next morning they repaired to the City Tavern, where delegates decided to hold their meetings in Carpenters' Hall. The choice of the jowly Peyton Randolph to chair the Congress furnished Washington with a potent ally. He'd had business as well as political dealings with Randolph, having loaned him 250 pounds a few years earlier, and Randolph had been one of four people assigned to monitor Washington's handling of the Custis estate for the General Court.

The taciturn Washington, at forty-two, found himself in an assembly of splendid talkers who knew how to pontificate on every subject. John Adams left this slightly mocking commentary on the verbose gathering: "Every man in it is a great man—an orator, a critic, a statesman, and therefore every man upon every question must show his oratory, his criticism, and his political abilities."[27] Relegated to a secondary role, the modest, retiring Washington wasn't appointed to either of the two new committees: one on colonial rights, the other on trade policy with Great Britain. Nonetheless, in this conclave of talkative egomaniacs, Washington's understated style had an inevitable appeal. Amid gifted talkers, he was a masterful listener who characterized his role as that of "an attentive observer and witness."[28] It was slowly becoming clear that, in a fractious, boisterous gathering, a calm figure of sound judgment such as Washington could inspire confidence and serve as a unifying figure.

Amid much overheated rhetoric, Washington spoke hard, plain truths. Silas Deane of Connecticut reported home that the stony-faced George Washington had a "hard countenance" and was "a tolerable speaker . . . who speaks very modestly in a cool but determined style and accent."[29] A Virginian praised Washington as "a man noted as well for his good sense as his bravery."[30] From Washington's recent letters to Bryan Fairfax, we know that he could serve up impassioned language, so that his reticence in Philadelphia reflected not simply a circumspect personality but a fine-tuned political instinct. On the surface, Washington may have been cool and phlegmatic, but he was fiery underneath, blasting the British as "diabolic contrivers."[31]

The specter of military action preoccupied delegates who sized up Washington as a prospective commander in chief. There was an esprit de corps about Washington and his self-assured Virginians. According to John Adams, the Virginians "were the most spirited" people in the hall, and one Pennsylvanian said that, in comparison, "the Bostonians are mere milksops."[32] The delegates swapped tales of Washington's youthful exploits in the French and Indian War, with Silas Deane writing excitedly home that Washington "was in the first actions in 1753 and 1754 on the Ohio and in 1755 was with Braddock and was the means of saving the remains of that unfortunate army."[33] In an inspired mood, Dr. Solomon Drowne of Rhode Island composed a martial tribute in verse to Washington: "With manly gait / His faithful steel suspended by his side, / Pass'd W-shi-gt-n along, Virginia's hero." People buttonholed him and pressed him to accept the army command, if offered. While hoping to avert bloodshed, Washington warned one correspondent that "more blood will be spilt on this occasion (if the ministry are determined to push matters to extremity) than history has ever yet furnished instances of in the annals of North America."[34]

Increasingly a seasoned politician, gifted with a light touch, Colonel Washington seemed to know that self-promotion would only backfire among delegates who, by the nature of their revolt, possessed heightened fears of power-hungry leaders. The last thing they wanted was a general who pushed himself forward too overtly. As stories about Washington swirled around the Congress, he let them do the talking. Thomas Lynch of South Carolina told John Adams that Washington "had made the most eloquent speech at the Virginia Convention that ever was made. Says he, 'I will raise 1000 men, subsist them at my own expense, and march myself at their head for the relief of Boston.'"[35] That the rumor mill churned out such a thrilling (and likely apocryphal) tale about Washington foreshadowed the verdict of the following spring.

Washington worked the First Continental Congress like a mature candidate. He turned ecumenical in his churchgoing habits, attending services at Presbyterian, Quaker, Roman Catholic, and a pair of Anglican churches. With the weather consistently fine and clear, he socialized assiduously in the evenings, dining out in thirty-one private homes in two months and scarcely ever sticking to his lodgings. He became a habitué of something called the Governor's Club, summarized by one visitor as "a select number of gentlemen that meet every night at a certain tavern, where they pass away a few hours in the pleasures of conversation and a cheerful glass."[36] With his compulsion to record his everyday life, Washington asked Lund Washington to send on his diary, disguised for safekeeping as a letter. "It will be found, I presume, on my writing table," he wrote. "Put it under a good strong paper cover, sealed up as a letter."[37]

Washington showed a knack for expanding his network of acquaintances, meeting with "Farmer" John Dickinson and befriending two young Philadelphians— merchant Thomas Mifflin and lawyer Joseph Reed—who later served as his aides. Along with John Adams, Washington received a memorable guided tour of the Pennsylvania Hospital from Dr. William Shippen, Jr. The finest hospital in the colonies, it still had a vaguely medieval air, as Adams noted: "We saw in the lower rooms underground the cells of the lunatics . . . some furious, some merry, some melancholy."[38] An inveterate shopper, Washington also took time to buy a cloak for his mother and a pocketbook for his wife. This conservative revolutionary decided that Billy Lee should dress a little more fashionably for the historic occasion and plunked down fifteen shillings for new shoes for his slave.

The First Continental Congress balked at the still-radical idea of independence, and George Washington expressed the predominant mood when he declared flatly,

"I am well satisfied, as I can be of my existence, that no such thing is desired by any thinking man in all North America; on the contrary, that it is the ardent wish of the warmest advocates for liberty that peace and tranquillity, upon constitutional grounds, may be restored and the horrors of civil discord prevented."[39] The delegates clung to the pleasing fiction that a benevolent George III was being undermined by treacherous ministers, and they implored the king as their "loving father" to rouse himself and rescue his colonial subjects. Going beyond mere words, they set up a Continental Association (hence the name Continental Congress) that would block imports sooner, and exports later, from and to Great Britain. To police this agreement, delegates called for creation of local enforcement committees, which could spawn militias if necessary. They also vowed to "wholly discontinue the slave trade" and "discourage every species of extravagance and dissipation, especially all horse-racing, and all kinds of gaming, cock-fightings, exhibitions of shows, plays, and other expensive diversions and entertainments."[40] This emphasis on moral reformation could only have assisted the likelihood that the clean-living Washington would become commander in chief. An exceptionally conscientious delegate, he was one of only two Virginia delegates still in Philadelphia when the First Continental Congress adjourned on October 26, 1774.

On October 30 George Washington was back at Mount Vernon, where the most urgent matter claiming his attention was the sale of property owned by his business partner George Mercer, then in woeful financial straits. Several weeks later Washington conducted a sale of property, including ninety slaves, from Mercer's plantation at Bull Run Mountains. "The Negroes, horses, and stock have all sold exceeding high," Washington reported after the auction.[41] It shows the schizophrenic nature of Washington's world that he was auctioning off slaves in the immediate aftermath of the First Continental Congress, which had endorsed an end to importing slaves. Ditto for Washington's action in February 1775, when he paid fifty-two pounds "for value of a Negro boy Tom," whom he sent off to his western lands.[42]

While Washington was in Philadelphia, one hundred neighbors in Fairfax County, under the tutelage of George Mason, had organized themselves into a voluntary militia—probably the first in the colony—electing Washington their commander. Borrowing the colors of the English Whig party, the Fairfax Independent Company wore blue uniforms with buff facings and white stockings. Their military gear was a curious hybrid of European and American traditions: they carried bayonets and cartridge boxes for muskets right along with tomahawks. Washington knew of the unit's formation while he was still in Philadelphia, for they had asked him to order drums, fifes, and halberds. To that he added his own personal order for a silk sash, gorgets, epaulettes, and a copy of Thomas Webb's *A Military Treatise on the Appointments of the Army*. Across Virginia, Washington rejoiced, men were "forming themselves into independent companies, choosing their officers, arming, equipping, and training for the worst event."[43] As groups of militia sprang up, they clamored for Washington as their commander. Now ubiquitous in the cause, he accepted the field command of four independent companies: in Prince William, Fauquier, Richmond, and Spotsylvania counties. It is striking how forthright Washington had become. In January the *Virginia Gazette* thanked the aspiring hero in a quatrain: "In spite of Gage's flaming sword / And Carleton's Canadian troop / Brave Washington shall give the word, / And we'll make them howl and whoop."[44]

During the winter of 1774–75 Washington and Mason did everything they could to strengthen the Fairfax militia, even advancing it money for ammunition. In order to be reimbursed, they and other local leaders decided to levy a three-shilling poll tax on Fairfax County citizens "for the common benefit, protection and defense of the inhabitants."[45] The residents had little choice but to pay this "voluntary" tax: the local sheriff, among others, would collect the money, and laggards would be stigmatized on a special list. The poll tax was a highly coercive measure. Even amid the hubbub of revolutionary activity, Washington remained rather testy about money, accusing Mason of collecting money from those prepared to pay and leaving him "to scuffle as he could with the rest." Mason grew incensed at the notion that he wasn't going to share all proceeds equally: "It cannot but give me concern that I should be thought capable of such disingenuous conduct."[46] As chairman of the Fairfax County Committee, Washington expanded defensive preparations by urging residents to form sixty-eight-man companies and study military science. The joint efforts of Washington and Mason helped to convert Fairfax County into a rabid center of resistance to British rule.

In late December 1774 the arrogant, irascible Charles Lee arrived for a six-day visit to Mount Vernon. He was a painfully thin man with a small head set on a spindly body. Born in England, Lee had served as a major in the French and Indian War, then fought as a mercenary in various European wars before sailing back to America in 1773. Haughty, imperious, and overflowing with opinions, Lee seldom had a kind word for anyone's military talents except his own. Versed in Greek and Latin, worldly and well traveled, he had a razor-sharp wit and must have made Washington feel a bit insular in comparison. This eccentric and notably slovenly man was always trailed by his beloved dogs. "When I can be convinced that men are as worthy objects as dogs," he once explained, "I shall transfer my benevolence to them."[47] It was widely thought that the ambitious Lee had set his sights on the job of commander in chief, but he disclaimed any such intention. "To think myself qualified for the most important charge that ever was committed to mortal man is the last stage of presumption" was how he put it in a letter to Edmund Burke.[48]

In March 1775 Washington was summoned to Richmond to attend the Second Virginia Convention, held at Henrico Parish Church, an Anglican house of worship. This meeting ratified the resolutions of the First Continental Congress and applauded the work of the seven Virginia delegates. Patrick Henry argued that British troops intended to enslave the colonies, and he set pulses racing with his flaming response: "Is life so dear, or peace so sweet, as to be purchased at the price of chains and slavery? Forbid it, Almighty God! I know not what course others may take, but as for me, give me liberty or give me death!"[49] Buoyed by these words, the convention agreed that Virginia should be placed in "a posture of defense."[50] Along with Henry, Washington was named to a committee that recommended raising volunteer companies in every county; he served on another that was instructed to "prepare a plan for the encouragement of arts and manufactures in this colony."[51] Such was Washington's new preeminence that when the gathering chose seven members to attend the Second Continental Congress, Washington was the second one named, ahead of Patrick Henry and superseded only by Peyton Randolph. The vote was overwhelming, as he received 106 of 108 votes cast. On the same day, as if struck by a sudden premonition of what was about to happen in Philadelphia, Washington wrote to his brother Jack that "it is my full intention to devote my life and fortune in the cause we are engaged in."[52]

It is astonishing that Washington, having long brooded over money as he built up his fortune, should now be willing to hazard all on this highly speculative rebellion. The death of Patsy Custis had briefly afforded some financial relief, but the anxiety over money had quickly returned. A few weeks earlier, when his brother Jack asked to borrow two hundred pounds, George had turned him down cold, saying "I would gladly borrow that sum myself for a few months, so exceedingly difficult do I find it, under the present scarcity of cash, to collect enough to answer this emergency and at the same time comply with my other engagements."[53]

Although George Washington scarcely needed further reasons to detest British rule, Lord Dunmore inflicted one last blow. Back at Mount Vernon, Washington heard a distressing report that Dunmore planned to annul the land patents that Washington had received under the 1754 proclamation. Seizing upon a technicality, the royal governor claimed that Washington's surveyor, William Crawford, was improperly qualified. When Washington asked for clarification, Dunmore confirmed the worst, stating that "the surveyor who surveyed those lands did not qualify agreeable to the act of assembly directing the duty and qualification of surveyors."[54] This appalling decision, if upheld, would strip Washington of 23,000 acres of land. He told Dunmore that he found the decision "incredible," citing the enormous time and expense consumed by the nullified surveys.[55] Washington didn't buckle under pressure from Dunmore. As Douglas Southall Freeman notes, "If Washington suspected blackmail or reprisal, it did not deter him from a single act of military preparation or from the utterance of a word he would have spoken in aid of the colonial cause."[56]

That April it momentarily seemed as if an early chapter of the Revolutionary War would be written in Virginia. Lord Dunmore feared that one of the new militia companies might grab gunpowder stored in a Williamsburg magazine. To forestall this possibility, he had marines who were attached to the armed British schooner *Magdalen* empty fifteen barrels of gunpowder from the magazine, load them on a wagon, and abscond to a man-of-war anchored off Norfolk. To universal disbelief, Dunmore contended that he had removed the gunpowder to deal with a slave revolt and vowed to bring it back if needed to defend the colony. When enraged patriots threatened to invade the governor's palace, George Washington counseled caution and advised the five independent companies under his command not to march on Williamsburg. The young James Madison, twenty-four, condemned Washington and his ilk for having "discovered a pusillanimity little comporting with their professions or the name of Virginian" and blamed the fact that their "property will be exposed in case of civil war."[57] As a military man, Washington knew how indomitable the British military machine was and how quixotic a full-scale revolution would be. As he later said of America's chances in the spring of 1775, "It was known that . . . the expense in comparison with our circumstances as colonists must be enormous, the struggle protracted, dubious, and severe. It was known that the resources of Britain were, in a manner, inexhaustible, that her fleets covered the ocean, and that her troops had harvested laurels in every quarter of the globe . . . Money, the nerve of war, was wanting." But the colonists had something much more precious: "the unconquerable resolution of our citizens, the conscious rectitude of our cause, and a confident trust that we should not be forsaken by heaven."[58]

PART THREE

The General

George Washington at Princeton,
painted by Charles Willson Peale in 1779.

CHAPTER SIXTEEN

The Glorious Cause

BEFORE SETTING OUT for the Second Continental Congress, Samuel Adams and John Hancock decided to spend a quiet weekend in hiding in Lexington, Massachusetts. On April 14, 1775, General Gage received instructions from London to arrest these ringleaders of the insurgency, and he planned to seize a powder magazine in nearby Concord as well. Patriotic forces were tipped off to this raid, whereupon Paul Revere galloped off to alert Adams and Hancock. When overwhelming British forces descended on Lexington Green on April 19, they were confronted by a small but doughty band of volunteers. The historic shots were fired, killing eight Americans and wounding ten more before the British, having lost only one horse, moved on to Concord. When the redcoats marched back to Boston, however, they were suddenly engulfed on all sides by armed farmers, known as Minute Men, who shot with deadly accuracy, shielded by trees, buildings, and fences. By the time the frantic British troops had scrambled back to town, 273 had been killed or wounded versus only 95 colonials. As John Adams proclaimed with self-evident truth, "The battle of Lexington on the 19th of April changed the instruments of warfare from the pen to the sword."[1]

George Washington was sobered and dismayed by the shocking news; there was nothing bloodthirsty in his nature. As he lamented to George William Fairfax, "Unhappy it is . . . to reflect that a brother's sword has been sheathed in a brother's breast and that the once happy and peaceful plains of America are either to be drenched with blood or inhabited by slaves."[2] He fathomed the full import of what had happened. As he had already regretted to a friend a year earlier, he wished "the dispute had been left to posterity to determine, but the crisis is arrived, when we must assert our rights or submit to every imposition that can be heaped upon us."[3]

As the colonies submitted to a frenzy of military preparation, young men everywhere grabbed muskets and formed militias. Like others committed to the cause, Washington brushed up on warfare and dipped into military volumes. For all his frontier experience, he was still a neophyte when it came to large-scale conflict. In the weeks before he left for the Second Continental Congress, the early leadership of the Continental Army began to coalesce on his doorstep, as if power were already shifting toward him. Charles Lee came for dinner, as did another, unrelated Lee named Henry—later celebrated as Light-Horse Harry Lee—who was nineteen and had graduated from Princeton the previous fall, specializing in Latin. Another military figure spending the night at Mount Vernon was Horatio Gates, a British officer who had been wounded during the Braddock campaign. He was a ruddy, thickset man, with a large, aquiline nose and long hair flowing over his shoulders from a receding hairline. After rising to the rank of major in England, he had returned to Virginia and bought a plantation in the Shenandoah Valley. As Washington was to discover, Gates had more than a trace of egotism and duplicity in his nature.

On May 4, 1775, George Washington climbed into his chariot, which was guided by a coachman and a postilion (an elegant conveyance for the future leader of a revolutionary army), and sped north. He was probably joined by his friend Richard Henry Lee, a talented orator and fellow burgess. In his diary Washington recorded drily, "Set out for the Congress at Phila." and described the spring weather as "very warm indeed, with but little wind and clear."[4] Had he foreseen the many tempestuous years that would elapse before he again set eyes on his cherished estate, he might have gazed back longingly. En route to Baltimore, Washington and Lee encountered other coaches hastening to the same destination, a swelling column of southern delegates that included Peyton Randolph, Edmund Pendleton, and Benjamin Harrison of Virginia and Joseph Hewes and Richard Caswell of North Carolina. Previewing things to come, Baltimore's citizens asked Washington to review four volunteer companies on the town common. The southern delegates must have already felt a palpable crescendo of excitement as they approached Philadelphia, for six miles outside of town they were greeted by a throng of five hundred people on horseback—officers, town dignitaries, and curiosity seekers—who had ridden out as a welcoming party. Two miles from town they were embraced by a lively patriotic band and a spirited honor guard of foot and rifle companies, so that they streamed into Philadelphia enfolded in an extemporaneous parade. On the same day John Hancock, Samuel Adams, and John Adams rolled in from the north.

Held in the immediate aftermath of Lexington and Concord and favored with fine spring weather, the Second Continental Congress was supercharged with an atmosphere of high drama that made the first seem somnolent in comparison. Many delegates were already in a warlike mood. On May 9 a Loyalist named Samuel Curwen stayed up till midnight talking with Washington, whom he found "a fine figure and of most easy and agreeable address," and they discussed ways to block British ships from coming up the Delaware River to occupy Philadelphia. As he recorded sadly in his journal, he found a determined Washington, in no mood to bend to the British: "I could not perceive the least disposition to accommodate matters or even risk."[5]

For this Congress the delegates met in a lofty ground-floor chamber of the red-brick State House, surmounted by a high steeple, today known as Independence Hall. In this gracious neoclassical setting, the president's chair was flanked by fluted pilasters, and the doors were topped by pediments. Whereas the First Congress had dwelled on diplomatic niceties, this one turned briskly to matters of war. Meeting in secret sessions, delegates heard reports that Great Britain had rebuffed conciliatory overtures from the earlier Congress and that more British troops were crossing the Atlantic. They also learned that Massachusetts was prepared to raise 13,600 soldiers, and that New Hampshire, Rhode Island, and Connecticut would contribute troops in the same proportion; already patriotic militias and volunteers from across New England had congregated on the Cambridge Common outside Boston. There was no talk as yet of a commander in chief, for the simple reason that the Congress still regarded itself as representing a collection of colonies, not a sovereign nation.

In this civilian conclave, Washington stood out for his martial air and naturally majestic aura. As if to signal his availability for military duty and with an instinctive sense of theater, he came clad in the blue and buff uniform of the Fairfax militia, sewn by Andrew Judge, an indentured servant at Mount Vernon. More than a militant statement, it was an inspiring sign of southern solidarity with New England soldiers. People were transfixed by Washington's lean, virile presence. "Colonel Washington appears at Congress in his uniform," wrote John Adams, "and by his great experience and abilities in military matters is of much service to us."[6] Washington had the inestimable advantage of fully looking the part of a military leader. As Benjamin Rush stated, "He has so much martial dignity in his deportment that you would distinguish him to be a general and a soldier from among ten thousand people. There is not a king in Europe that would not look like a valet de chambre by his side."[7]

Clearly, for these rank amateurs in warfare, Washington's military résumé was neither sketchy nor irrelevant—and he was suddenly deemed the fountainhead of wisdom. A marginal figure at the earlier Congress, Washington was drafted onto nine committees and inserted into every cranny of decision making. Some of

Washington's committees dealt with purely military questions, such as how to defend New York, while others reflected his broad range of knowledge, such as how to print a new American currency. Each day he dined at the City Tavern with eight other delegates, helping to expand his circle of admirers.

The Congress still lacked a consensus about declaring independence from Great Britain, favoring a purely defensive posture instead of initiating hostilities. The delegates were both thrilled and flustered by news that colonial troops, spearheaded by Ethan Allen and Benedict Arnold, had overrun a British garrison at Fort Ticonderoga on Lake Champlain in upstate New York, producing a huge windfall of cannon and military stores. An ambivalent Congress vowed to return the fort to Great Britain after "the restoration of the former harmony" that the Congress "so ardently wished for."[8] The northern colonies protested, regarding the fort as a necessary bulwark against a British invasion from Canada. As evidenced by his uniform, Washington was dubious about reconciliation, but he continued, at least for the record, to support measures to resolve the conflict amicably. Chances for a happy outcome dimmed on May 25 when the frigate *Cerberus,* bearing thirty-two guns, arrived in Boston Harbor, and three major generals in the British Army—John Burgoyne, Henry Clinton, and William Howe—stepped ashore. Washington clung to the wistful hope that Parliament, not the king, was to blame for these measures, telling George William Fairfax on May 31 that "we do not, nor cannot yet prevail upon ourselves to call them the king's troops."[9]

On May 24 Peyton Randolph had to return to the Virginia assembly and was replaced as president by John Hancock of Massachusetts. When the Congress agreed in early June to buy gunpowder "for the Continental Army," the ragtag forces facing the British in Boston were still composed exclusively of New England militias.[10] Then on June 14 the Congress gave the conflict a more sweeping complexion by authorizing ten companies from Pennsylvania, Maryland, and Virginia to march north and reinforce those regional troops. There arose a sudden need for a commander to direct the disparate units and meld them into an effective fighting force. The senior figure in Cambridge was then Artemas Ward, a storekeeper from Shrewsbury, Massachusetts, whom Charles Lee ridiculed as "a fat old gentleman who had been a popular churchwarden."[11] While not everybody was so dismissive of the Harvard-educated Ward, few beyond New England considered him the ideal man to shoulder the burden of the patriotic cause.

Since Virginia was the most populous colony, it seemed logical that the perfect commander would hail from that state. Rich and ambitious John Hancock hoped to use the Congress presidency as his springboard to the top military job, but even some fellow New Englanders believed that, for the sake of political unity, a Virginian made eminently good sense. Both John and Samuel Adams regarded Washington's appointment as the political linchpin needed to bind the colonies together. Many southerners feared that the New Englanders were a rash, obstinate people, prone to extremism, and worried that an army led by a New England general might someday turn despotic and conquer the South. The appointment of George Washington would soothe such fears and form a perfect political compromise between North and South.

John Adams enjoyed the curious distinction of being Washington's most important advocate at the Congress and one of his more severe detractors in later years. Rather small and paunchy, with a sharp mind and an argumentative personality, Adams was a farsighted prophet of independence, the curmudgeon who spoke uncomfortable truths. He later worried that when the history of the American Revolution was written, he would be consigned to the role of spear carrier, while George Washington and Ben Franklin would be glorified as the real protagonists of the drama. No less driven than Adams, Washington kept his ambition in check behind a modest, laconic personality, whereas Adams's ambition often seemed irrepressible.

In 1807 John Adams would write a scathingly funny letter in which he listed the "ten talents" that had propelled George Washington to fame in June 1775. The first four dealt with physical attributes—"a handsome face," "tall stature," "an elegant form," and "graceful attitudes and movements"—traits that the short, rotund Adams decidedly lacked.[12] Two others concerned Washington's extraordinary self-possession: "He possessed the gift of silence" and "He had great self-command."[13] Since Adams was neither guarded nor silent, he would have been especially sensitive to these traits. He also saw that Washington exerted more power by withholding opinions than by expressing them. Still another advantage was that Washington was a Virginian, and "Virginian geese are all swans."[14] It also helped that Washington was wealthy—almost everyone at the Congress was mesmerized by his willingness to hazard his money in the cause: "There is nothing . . . to which mankind bow down with more reverence than to great fortune."[15] The ideology of the day claimed that property rendered a man more independent, which presumably made Washington immune to British bribery.

When comparing Washington with other rivals for the top position—especially Horatio Gates and Charles Lee—one sees that he had superior presence, infinitely better judgment, more political cunning, and unmatched gravitas. With nothing arrogant or bombastic in his nature, he had the perfect temperament for leadership. He was also born in North America, which was considered essential. Endowed with an enormous sense of responsibility, he inspired trust and confidence. A man of the happy medium, conciliatory by nature, he lent a reassuring conservatism to the Revolution. Smoothly methodical and solidly reliable, he seemed not to make mistakes. "He is a complete gentleman," Thomas Cushing, a Massachusetts delegate, wrote about Washington. "He is sensible, amiable, virtuous, modest, and brave."[16] The delegates favored Washington as much for the absence of conspicuous weaknesses as for his manifest strengths. Eliphalet Dyer of Connecticut captured Washington's steady presence: "He seems discreet and virtuous, no harum-scarum, ranting, swearing fellow, but sober, steady, and calm."[17] The hallmark of Washington's career was that he didn't seek power but let it come to him. "I did not solicit the command," he later said, "but accepted it after much entreaty."[18] No less important for a man who would have to answer to the Congress, he was a veteran politician with sixteen years of experience as a burgess, ensuring that he would subordinate himself to civilian control. Things seldom happened accidentally to George Washington, but he managed them with such consummate skill that they often *seemed* to happen accidentally. By 1775 he had a fine sense of power—how to gain it, how to keep it, how to wield it.

On June 14 the Congress officially took charge of the troops in Boston, giving birth to the Continental Army and creating an urgent need for a commander in chief. By this point the delegates were so impressed by the self-effacing Washington that his appointment was virtually a fait accompli. As a Virginia delegate wrote that day: "Col. *Washington* has been pressed to take the supreme command of the American troops encamped at Roxbury and I believe will accept the appointment, though with much reluctance, he being deeply impressed with the importance of that honorable trust and diffident of his own (superior) abilities."[19] The only serious competitor was Hancock, who had little military experience and was hobbled by gout. When John Adams rose to speak and alluded to Washington, the latter jumped up from his seat near the door and with "his usual modesty darted into the library room," recalled Adams.[20] Expecting Adams to nominate *him,* Hancock watched with smug satisfaction until Adams named Washington instead—at which point the smile fled from his face. "Mortification and resentment were expressed as forcibly as his face could exhibit them," Adams said. " . . . Mr. Hancock never loved me so well after this event as he had done before."[21] That Washington handled the moment with such tact, even as Hancock gave proof of patent egotism, only made his circumspect manner the more appealing.

The delegates deferred the final vote until the next day, when they passed a resolution "that a general be appointed to command all the continental forces raised, or to be raised, for the defense of American liberty."[22] In the ensuing debate, the only credible argument leveled against Washington was that the New England troops deserved one of their own. But with both John and Sam Adams placing his name in nomination, Washington was the tailor-made compromise candidate. "In the meantime," recollected John Adams, "pains were taken out of doors to obtain a unanimity and the voices were generally so clearly in favor of Washington that the dissenting members were persuaded to withdraw their opposition."[23] Washington was nominated by Thomas Johnson of Maryland and elected unanimously, initiating a long string of unanimous victories in his career.

Washington didn't learn of his appointment until the Congress had adjourned for the day, and suddenly he encountered delegates who saluted him as "General." In a twinkling, his world had changed forever. He was feted by delegates at a midday dinner, with Thomas Jefferson, thirty-two, and Benjamin Franklin, sixty-nine, lifting glasses in a postprandial toast to "the Commander in Chief of the American armies." Washington, deeply moved, sat there abashed. As Benjamin Rush remembered, Washington "rose from his seat and with some confusion thanked the company for the honor they did him. The whole company instantly rose and drank the toast standing. This scene, so unexpected, was a solemn one. A silence followed it, as if every heart was penetrated with the awful but great events which were to follow the use of the sword of liberty which had just been put into General Washington's hands by the unanimous voice of his country."[24] True to form, Washington devoted the evening to a committee impaneled to draw up army regulations. In his diary on that epochal day, Washington wrote simply: "Dined at Burns's in the field. Spent the even[in]g on a committee."[25] Even in the privacy of his diary, Washington feared any show of unseemly ambition.

On Friday morning, June 16, John Hancock officially announced that George Washington had been chosen "General and Commander in Chief of the army of the United Colonies."[26] Washington stood humbly at his seat during his reply. There was to be no chest-thumping from the new commander; this wasn't the Man on Horseback that every good republican dreaded. "Mr President," he said, "tho[ugh] I am truly sensible of the high honor done me in this appointment, yet I feel great distress from a consciousness that my abilities and military experience may not be equal to the extensive and important trust. However, as the congress desire it, I will enter upon the momentous duty and exert every power I possess in their service and for the support of the glorious cause." Washington's speech was rife with disclaimers; he had long ago perfected the technique of lowering expectations. "But, lest some unlucky event should happen, unfavorable to my reputation," he went on, "I beg it may be remember[e]d by every Gent[lema]n in the room that I this day declare, with the utmost sincerity, I do not think myself equal to the command I [am] honoured with." Then he made the proudly aristocratic gesture he had already practiced during the Braddock campaign—he waived the proposed salary of five hundred dollars a month: "As to pay, sir, I beg leave to assure the Congress that as no pecuniary consideration could have tempted me to have accepted this arduous employment at the expense of my domestic ease and happi[ness], I do not wish to make any profit from it. I will keep an exact account of my expenses; those I doubt not they will discharge and that is all I desire."[27]

Washington wanted to show that his motives were spotless, that he was a true gentleman and could be trusted with great power, and the delegates applauded his generosity. As John Adams declared, "There is something charming to me in the conduct of Washington. A gentleman of one of the first fortunes upon the continent, leaving his delicious retirement, his family and friends, sacrificing his ease and hazarding all in the cause of his country."[28] James T. Flexner dismisses the apparent generosity behind Washington's renunciation of a salary: "Financially, the distinction proved to be only a bookkeeping one, as he received in expenses what he would have received in salary."[29] But Washington's gesture captured people's imaginations and confirmed that this revolution was something new under the sun. Even the London newspapers were thunderstruck, one writing that Washington "is to attend to the hazardous duty allotted him from principle only. A most noble example and worthy of imitation in Great Britain."[30]

While some of Washington's humility can be traced to political calculation, it also reflected his frank admission that he lacked the requisite experience to take on the British Empire. It was both a gratifying and a terrifying moment for a man who was such a bundle of confidence and insecurity. Preoccupied, as always, with his sense of personal honor—his calling card as a gentleman—he feared disgrace as well as failure. When he ran into Patrick Henry after his appointment, an emotional Washington seemed full of foreboding. "Remember, Mr. Henry, what I now tell you: from the day I enter upon the command of the American armies, I date my fall, and the ruin of my reputation."[31] Henry said that Washington's eyes were full of tears— one of many times when, under stress, he betrayed his underlying emotions.

In accepting this appointment, Washington was haunted by the uncertain fate of his wife, who would be left alone and might become the target of British raids. In the wake of Patsy's death and Jacky's wedding, Martha Washington was already in a lonely, vulnerable state of mind. To be deprived now of her husband might knock the emotional props from under her. For three days Washington couldn't bring himself to write to her. Then on June 18 he sat down with trepidation to inform her of his extraordinary appointment:

> My Dearest, I am now set down to write to you on a subject which fills me with inexpressible concern and this concern is greatly aggravated and increased when I reflect on the uneasiness I know it will give you . . . You may believe me . . . when I assure you in the most solemn manner that, so far from seeking this appointment, I have used every endeavor in my power to avoid it, not only from my unwillingness

to part with you and the family, but from a consciousness of its being a trust too great for my capacity . . . it has been a kind of destiny that has thrown me upon this service . . . it was utterly out of my power to refuse this appointment without exposing my character to such censures as would have reflected dishonor upon myself and given pain to my friends.[32]

The editors of Washington's papers note that twenty years earlier Washington had marshaled almost identical arguments in writing to his mother, invoking force majeure in justifying his participation in the French and Indian War. But in this letter, even as he told Martha to summon her fortitude, his protective emotions surged to the fore. "I shall feel no pain from the toil or the danger of the campaign," he told her. "My unhappiness will flow from the uneasiness I know you will feel at being left alone."[33] He wondered whether she might feel safer in Alexandria or staying with close friends. It must have been sobering to Martha, who had already lost one husband, to learn that Washington had asked Edmund Pendleton to draft a new will for him.

For many years Martha's attachment to her son had been problematic for George Washington, but he now found solace in the thought that Jacky might care for her. On June 19 he informed Jacky of his appointment and told him that "my great concern upon this occasion is the thoughts of leaving your mother under the uneasiness which I know this affair will throw her into." He asked Jacky if he and his bride Nelly could stay full time at Mount Vernon, "when I think it absolutely necessary for the peace and satisfaction of your mother."[34] That same day Washington wrote to his brother-in-law, Burwell Bassett, and inquired whether he and Martha's sister, Anna Maria, could visit Mount Vernon or take Martha into their home. Although he had assured Martha that he would "return safe to you in the fall," he now told Bassett, much more candidly, that "I have no expectations of returning till winter and feel great uneasiness at [Martha's] lonesome situation."[35] Washington noted that he had exchanged his Mount Vernon coach for his riding horses as he traded peacetime paraphernalia for wartime matériel. Again he expressed his inadequacy for the job. "I can answer but for three things: a firm belief in the justice of our cause; close attention in the prosecution of it; and the strictest integrity. If these cannot supply the places of ability and experience, the cause will suffer."[36]

BEFORE LEAVING FOR BOSTON, Washington gathered the stage props for his command performance as top general. He bought five horses and a handsome four-wheeled open carriage, called a phaeton, the first charges to his expense account. He collected five books on military strategy. To spruce up his military apparel, he covered his black leather pistol holders with rich fabric, enhancing their beauty. In all likelihood, he employed the same red and white colors for this upholstery as he used for the servants' livery at Mount Vernon. Washington also ordered a new uniform, having decided to retain for the Continental Army the colors of the Fairfax Independent Company. For his tailor, he outlined a uniform consisting of "a blue coat with yellow buttons and gold epaulettes (each having three silver stars) . . . in winter, buff vest and breeches; in summer, a white vest and breeches of nankeen."[37]

When Washington was named commander in chief, he found himself in an anomalous situation: he was the only person officially on the rolls of the Continental Army; technically, he had been chosen to march at the head of a nonexistent army to fight an undeclared war. Nevertheless he began to assemble the top-flight team of personal aides he would refer to as his military "family." During the war Washington would develop intimate attachments to several dashing young men of intelligence and sensibility. En route to Boston, he was escorted by Joseph Reed of Philadelphia, a Trenton native educated at Princeton and trained in law at the Middle Temple in London. Smart, courteous, and charming, Reed had a long face with blue eyes and a kindly expression. John Adams praised him as "very sensible," "amiable," and "tender."[38] As a member of Washington's military escort to Boston, Reed fell under the general's spell and couldn't resist his insistence that he stay on as his secretary. As Reed remembered, Washington had "expressed himself to me in such terms that I thought myself bound by every tie of duty and honor to comply with his request to help him through the sea of difficulties."[39] For his first aide-de-camp, Washington chose another young Philadelphian, Thomas Mifflin, a radical member of the Congress with a broad, handsome face, "a sprightly and spirited speaker" with a reputation for being temperamental.[40] In opting for two young Philadelphians from prominent families, Washington showed partiality for members of his own class and a willingness to surround himself with young men more highly educated than he was.

The generals that the Congress picked to support Washington reflected the same calculus of geographic diversity that had shaped Washington's own appointment. Bowing to political realities, it chose the burly Artemas Ward of Massachusetts as the first major general; Ward would never warm to Washington and resented being upstaged by him. He was followed by Horatio Gates, named adjutant general with the rank of brigadier. Washington admired Gates, lauded his superior knowledge of military affairs, and personally recommended him for the high post, but he would shortly revise this opinion. "I discovered very early in the war symptoms of coldness and constraint in General Gates' behavior to me," he later observed. "These increased as he rose into greater consequence."[41] The next major general picked by

Congress was Charles Lee. He too had been recommended by Washington, who again would live to rue the choice. Washington credited Lee as "the first officer in military knowledge and experience we have in the whole army," but he also saw that he was "rather fickle and violent, I fear, in his temper."[42] Another major general was the patrician Philip Schuyler, a wealthy landlord with extensive holdings along the Hudson River. A member of the Anglo-Dutch aristocracy of New York, he had a bulbous red nose, a raspy voice, and a frosty attitude toward his social inferiors. Finally there was the colorful, rough-hewn farmer from Connecticut, the deep-chested Israel Putnam, who had won the endearing nickname "Old Put." Scarred, weather-beaten, and poorly educated, he was popular among his soldiers. It was said of the suspicious Putnam that he always slept with one eye open. At Bunker Hill he had supposedly uttered the famous words, "Don't fire, boys, until you see the whites of their eyes."[43] Silas Deane said with admiration that Putnam was "totally unfit for everything" except fighting.[44]

Washington's final hours in Philadelphia were long and frantic ones. When, on June 20, he sent a farewell note to officers of the five Virginia militias he had commanded, he sounded as if he tottered a bit under the stress. "I have launched into a wide and extensive field too boundless for my abilities and far, very far beyond my experience," he wrote tensely.[45] Before setting out for Boston on June 23, he dashed off a quick, reassuring missive to Martha, reminding her that "I retain an unalterable affection for you, which neither time nor distance can change."[46]

Washington received a festive send-off from the Philadelphia populace. Accompanied by Charles Lee and Philip Schuyler, he was ready to mount his horse when Thomas Mifflin sprinted out, bent down, and held out the stirrup for him—a small courtesy that drew a vast ovation from the crowd. John Adams recorded a genteel detail: many congressmen showed up with servants and carriages to bid farewell to the revolutionary warrior. Washington brought along his versatile manservant, Billy Lee, who would enter fully into the fervent emotions of the struggle; as a garrulous old veteran in later years, he would talk as if he had been a full-fledged member of the Continental Army, not a slave forcibly drafted into service. Nevertheless Lee and another slave named John wore not the blue and buff of the Continental Army but the red and white Washington livery. When John Trumbull later painted Lee, he depicted him as dark-skinned and round-cheeked in an exotic red turban. A skillful horseman, Lee remained at Washington's side throughout the war, a powerful symbol of the limitations of this fight for liberty. During the war, in a striking mark of their personal relationship, Washington would personally order clothing for Lee.

As he rode north, Washington ventured into terra incognita. With little talent for impromptu speeches, he was ill equipped for his sudden celebrity. Nonetheless, upon encountering large throngs in New York City, he displayed a touch of pure showmanship, wearing a plume in his hat and a bright purple sash. In a city violently torn between Loyalists and patriots, Washington's hosts worried that he might encounter the royal governor, William Tryon, who had returned from a trip to England that same day. To avoid this clash, Washington crossed the Hudson at Hoboken and arrived at four P.M. near present-day Canal Street, then well north of the town. Met by a military band, nine companies of militia, and a delegation from the New York Provincial Congress, Washington got a vivid glimpse of the cheering masses who counted on him for deliverance. The entire town, it seemed, had emptied out to receive him, and a local newspaper said that "a greater number of the principal inhabitants" had appeared than on any previous occasion.[47] Washington was whisked to the country estate of Leonard Lispenard. In a sign of the fluid political situation, some people who had welcomed Washington then met Governor Tryon when he landed at eight o'clock that evening, causing Loyalist Thomas Jones to bellow, "What a farce! What cursed hypocrisy!"[48] In another strange sign of this transitional period, Washington drank in the huzzahs of the multitudes while the *Asia,* a sixty-four-gun British warship, lay at anchor off the Battery, not far from where he was.

At the Lispenard mansion, Washington received an urgent dispatch from Boston. Although the sealed communiqué was addressed to John Hancock, Washington thought it prudent to open it in case it contained timely news. His instinct was correct: the dispatch reported that on June 17 more than two thousand British troops, led by General William Howe, had stormed fortified patriot positions on Breed's Hill, forcing an American retreat. (The battle was incorrectly labeled Bunker Hill.) Intent upon inflicting maximum terror on supposedly amateurish Americans, the British had incinerated the buildings of Charlestown, leaving the obliterated town a smoking ruin. Bunker Hill proved a Pyrrhic victory, for the British registered more than a thousand casualties. Americans had shown not only pluck and grit but excellent marksmanship as they picked off British officers; firing at officers was then considered a shocking breach of military etiquette. The Americans suffered 450 casualties, including the death of Major General Joseph Warren. Even while it dented British confidence, the Battle of Bunker Hill stirred patriotic spirits, exposing the first chinks in the British fighting machine and suggesting, wrongly, that green American militia troops could outfight British professionals. As the British reeled, a stunned General Howe admitted, "The success is too dearly bought."[49] Washington recognized that the British had been chastened—"a few more such victories woul[d] put an end to their army," he wryly told his brother Sam—but he insisted that the battle was a missed opportunity.[50] If the men had "been properly conducted," he concluded, "the regulars would have met with a shameful defeat."[51] At the same time, he would spend the first year or two of the war referring back to Bunker Hill and hoping to recapitulate the terrific beating inflicted on the startled British.

Though Washington yearned to be off to Boston, members of the New York Provincial Congress wanted to address him, and political decorum dictated that he linger. It was the start of the interminable ceremonies that would be the bane of his public life. Already tired from formalities and sacrificing precious time, he instructed his assistants to be ready to leave the instant the meeting ended. Washington sounded a conciliatory theme to the provincial congress, promising to apply his efforts to the restoration "of peace and harmony between the mother [country and the] colonies."[52] He minted a beautiful phrase that must have resonated deeply among his listeners: "When we assumed the soldier, we did not lay aside the citizen."[53] The citizen-soldier passed this first test of his political skills with flying colors. Gifted with perfect pitch, he knew how to talk the language of peace even as he girded for war.

As Washington and his party pushed northward, his mind was occupied with the situation awaiting him in Boston. A decade later he admitted that he wasn't sufficiently "at ease" to observe closely the countryside through which he passed.[54] He felt beleaguered by the social duties thrust upon him as he passed through an unending succession of towns and endured ritual greetings from their leading citizens. He was already swamped with letters from provincial legislators, who began to address him as "His Excellency"—a rather regal locution for a revolutionary leader. George Washington was already becoming more than a mere man: he was the face and form of an amorphous cause. As Garry Wills has noted, "Before there was a nation—before there was any symbol of that nation (a flag, a Constitution, a national seal)—there was Washington."[55] Knowing that people wished to see him astride a horse, Washington would step down from his carriage and mount a horse before entering a town, turning it into a theatrical performance.[56]

On Sunday, July 2, Washington arrived at Cambridge, Massachusetts, to assume control of the Continental Army, which had laid siege to Boston and the many redcoats bottled up inside the town. People in New England took the Sabbath seriously, and Washington respected religious observance, so on this historic day the stately Virginian made a quiet, unobtrusive entrance into the camp. The fledgling troops that had lined up on the parade ground to be inspected were dismissed when a steady daylong rain spoiled the reception, but Washington and Lee did meet with the officers' corps that evening. The rain screened any clear view of the British troops in the distance. Nevertheless, in taking up his duties, George Washington had crossed the threshold into a new life.

CHAPTER SEVENTEEN

Magnificent Bluff

ALTHOUGH GEORGE WASHINGTON had never attended college and regretted his lack of education, he moved into the Harvard Square home of college president Samuel Langdon, who retreated to a single room. Politicians and officers soon descended on Washington en masse, including the two New England generals Artemas Ward and Israel Putnam. By mid-July Washington had transferred to grander quarters on Brattle Street, occupying the three-story Georgian mansion of John Vassall, a rich Tory who had fled behind British lines in besieged Boston. The Vassalls had owned a slave family that remained in the house, and when Washington toured his new headquarters, he found a slave boy, Darby Vassall, swinging on the front gate. In a friendly manner, Washington expressed interest in taking him into his service, but Darby, imbued with the spirit of liberty, asked what his pay would be. At that interjection, Washington evidently lost interest. "General Washington was no gentleman," Darby later said, "to expect a boy to work without wages."[1]

By the time Washington and Charles Lee reviewed troops on the parade ground on July 3, the overcast skies had cleared and an effervescent mood filled the air. Twenty-one drummers and as many fife players treated the new generals to a full musical accompaniment as they inspected the New England soldiers. While some had muskets, many others toted primitive weapons, including tomahawks and knives lashed to poles. Despite these handicaps, Washington hoped the patriots could muster eighteen thousand men—at least, if one included the sick and absent—and enjoy a numerical superiority over British forces of no more than twelve thousand.

As Washington and Lee toured lengthy defensive fortifications being thrown up pell-mell to deter a British attack, they viewed the eerie reality of two armies, separated by scarcely more than a mile, enjoying panoramic, unobstructed views of each other. It was easy to make out British sentinels pacing on Bunker Hill. With some amazement, Washington told Richard Henry Lee that the British and Americans were "almost near enough to converse."[2] To Washington, it seemed that both sides had settled into an uneasy standoff.

On July 4 the Congress formally incorporated the state militias into the Continental Army, enabling Washington to issue general orders that would sound the signature themes of his tenure. This George Washington differed from the callow, sometimes grasping young colonel who had governed the Virginia Regiment and was narrowly absorbed in his career. From the outset, his official voice pulsated with high ideals. He tried to dissolve state differences into a new national identity, telling his men that the troops being raised from various colonies were "now the troops of the United Provinces of North America and it is hoped that all distinctions of colonies will be laid aside."[3]

Always buffed and polished, with an elegant sword strapped to his side and silver spurs on his boots, Washington roamed all over the camp. "His Excellency was on horseback, in company with several other military gentlemen," Dr. James Thacher wrote. "It was not difficult to distinguish him from the others; his personal appearance is truly noble and majestic."[4] A local diarist, Ezekiel Price, picked up reports on July 5 that "General Washington had visited the camps, and the soldiers were much pleased with him."[5] As at Mount Vernon, Washington rose at sunup to ride about the camp, lifting sagging spirits with his presence. Suddenly rejuvenated troops were happily digging trenches at four in the morning. "There is great overturning in the camp as to order and regularity," said an impressed chaplain. "New lords, new laws."[6] A beefy former bookseller from Boston named Henry Knox stood in awe of Washington's panache: "General Washington fills his place with vast ease and dignity and dispenses happiness around him."[7] An enthusiastic friend reported to John Adams that Washington "has in a manner inspired officers and soldiers with a taste for discipline and they go into it readily, as they all venerate and love the general."[8] His Excellency also left the ladies agog. "You had prepared me to entertain a favorable opinion of George Washington," Abigail Adams chided her husband, "but I thought the half was not told me. Dignity with ease and complacency, the gentleman and soldier, look agreeably blended in him."[9]

For all the favorable assessments, Washington, as a newcomer from Virginia, confronted pervasive Yankee suspicions, and he, in turn, was inwardly revolted by the alien world he surveyed daily in Cambridge. With little tolerance for error and scant patience for disorder, he was surrounded by an unruly, vociferous mass of men who didn't take well to orders. At this point, he never dreamed that these shabby men would someday show prodigious courage or that he would grow to love them. Soon he squawked to his brother Sam that he had "found a numerous army of provincials under very little command, discipline, or order."[10] Two months later, a shrill note entering his letter, he protested to John Hancock that "licentiousness and every kind of disorder triumphantly reign."[11] Two people seemed to coexist inside George Washington's breast. One was the political militant who mouthed republican slogans; this Washington thought his troops would fight better if motivated by patriotic ideals. The other, schooled in the British military system, believed devoutly in top-down discipline and rank as necessary to a well-run army. This Washington was also the Virginia planter who felt little in common with the scruffy plebeians around him.

Washington expressed dismay that many New England militias elected their own officers, choosing farmers, artisans, or storekeepers. It bothered him that egalitarian officers fraternized with their men, joined them in line for food, and even gave them shaves. In disbelief, he wrote to one Virginian that the Massachusetts officers "are *nearly* of the same kidney with the privates."[12] To Patrick Henry, Washington worried aloud about "the soldier and officer being too nearly on a level. Discipline and subordination add life and vigor to military movements."[13] In part, Washington had an old-fashioned faith in military hierarchy as likely to produce the most efficient army. He often evinced a partiality for wellborn officers, as if he wanted to transfer the hierarchy of civilian life intact into the army. As he once observed about choosing officers, "The first rule . . . is to determine whether the candidate is truly a gentleman, whether he has a genuine sense of honor and a reputation to risk."[14] At one point, while arguing for better pay for officers, Washington warned John Hancock that only such a move would "induce gentlemen and men of character to engage and till the bulk of your officers are composed of such persons . . . you have little to expect of them."[15] However much Washington theoretically preferred having his social peers as fellow officers, however, he would compile an outstanding record of advancing officers who lacked such pedigrees.

During his first month in Cambridge, to differentiate the army's upper echelons, Washington ordered field officers to sport red or pink cockades in their hats, captains yellow or buff, and subordinate officers green. It upset Washington when sentinels stopped generals because they didn't recognize them. He decreed a light blue sash for himself, a pink one for major and brigadier generals, and a green one for his aides-de-camp. It says much about Washington's evolution during the war that he emphasized these distinctions much less as the war progressed. "His uniform is exactly like that of his soldiers," a French officer noted four years later. "Formerly, on solemn occasions, that is to say on days of battle, he wore a large blue sash, but he has given up that unrepublican distinction."[16]

Even as he introduced distinctions between officers and their men, he struggled to obliterate differences among the states to forge a national army. When he arrived in Cambridge, there was no army as such, only a mosaic of New England militias, wearing a medley of homemade hats, shoes, and other clothing. A fervent nationalist, Washington wanted to eliminate regiments based on geography at a time when militias were identified with states—a visionary suggestion that was promptly rejected. As he later wrote, "In the early stages of this war, I used every means in my power to destroy all kind of state distinctions and labored to have every part and parcel of the army considered as continental."[17] Because of a shortage of wool, once imported from Great Britain, Washington planned to issue ten thousand linen hunting shirts, such as those used in the French and Indian War, creating a makeshift national uniform. But there wasn't enough tow cloth, and he had to settle for the motley array of costumes worn by state militias. Washington also argued futilely that the Congress should appoint officers instead of provisional governments. This proposal was vetoed since it clashed with republican ideology, which romanticized militias as superior to standing armies, a dilemma that was to bedevil him throughout the war.

Nobody would have found the camp's vile sanitary conditions more repellent than did the fastidious Washington. The open latrines emitted a potent stench, and it was a challenge to coax soldiers into using them. One orderly book complained that they left "excrement about the fields perniciously."[18] Having experienced firsthand the epidemics that can decimate armies, Washington urged officers to keep their men clean, tend their latrines, and forbid fishing in freshwater ponds, "as there may be danger of introducing the smallpox into the army."[19] Washington must also have recoiled at the queer collection of improvised tents. Of these outlandish dwellings, the Reverend William Emerson said, "Some are made of boards, some of sailcloth, and some partly of one and partly of the other. Others are made of stone and turf and others again of birch and other brush . . . others are curiously wrought with doors and windows done with wreaths . . . in the manner of a basket."[20] The troops lacked running water, and their filthy, tattered appearance excited disgust among onlookers, causing Loyalist Benjamin Thompson to say that Washington's army was "the most wretchedly clothed, and as dirty a set of mortals as ever disgraced the name of a soldier."[21] Some men were half naked, their clothing having been slashed at Bunker Hill. Small wonder that Washington groaned that his life was "one continued round of *annoyance* and *fatigue*."[22]

Maintaining unity among the men proved a perpetual struggle. In late July the New England troops were startled by the arrival of a rustic contingent of Virginia riflemen, led by Captain Daniel Morgan, who had trudged six hundred miles to join the fray. The rifles they carried were longer than muskets and could be fired with far more accuracy, but they took longer to load in combat. Army cook

Israel Trask remembered how soldiers from Marblehead, Massachusetts, outfitted in round jackets and fishermen's trousers, derided the Virginians with their fringed linen shirts, leggings, and tomahawks. Months later, on a snowy day, as the Virginians toured Harvard College, the Marblehead soldiers began to taunt and toss snowballs at them. Before too long, said Trask,

a fierce struggle commenced with biting and gouging on the one part, and knockdown on the other part with as much apparent fury as the most deadly enemy could create. Reinforced by their friends, in less than five minutes, more than a thousand combatants were on the field, struggling for the mastery. At this juncture General Washington made his appearance, whether by accident or design I never knew. I only saw him and his colored servant [Billy Lee], both mounted. With the spring of a deer, he leaped from his saddle, threw the reins of his bridle into the hands of his servant, and rushed into the thickest of the melee, with an iron grip seized two tall, brawny, athletic, savage-looking riflemen by the throat, keeping them at arm's length, alternately shaking and talking to them. In this position the eye of the belligerents caught sight of the general. Its effect on them was instantaneous flight at the top of their speed in all directions from the scene of the conflict. Less than fifteen minutes time had elapsed from the commencement of the row before the general and his two criminals were the only occupants of the field of action. Here bloodshed, imprisonment, trials by court-martial were happily prevented and hostile feelings between the different corps of the army extinguished by the physical and mental energies timely exerted by one individual.[23]

One notes how swiftly the fearless Washington displayed derring-do. In dealing with troublemakers, he meted out harsh punishments, including having them ride the wooden horse, an ordeal in which the offender sat on the sharp wooden rail of a sawhorse, his hands bound behind his back and heavy weights anchored to his feet to heighten the pain. One also notes in the anecdote the conspicuous presence of Billy Lee, who remained steadfastly at Washington's side throughout the Revolution.

As Washington examined his army with care, he was dismayed to find no more than 14,500 men fit for service—far fewer than the 20,000 fighting Yankees he had expected to find. This, the first of many unpleasant surprises, meant that he had to be an expert bluffer, pretending to a military strength he didn't possess. In confidence, he told James Warren, president of the Massachusetts Provincial Congress, "Your own prudence will suggest the necessity of secrecy on this subject, as we have the utmost reason to think the enemy suppose our numbers much greater than they are—an error which is not [in] our interest to remove."[24]

If Washington had taken away one lesson from the French and Indian War, it was the need for a compact defense. It therefore irked him that he had to maintain a vast defensive perimeter of breastworks and trenches stretching for eight or nine miles. On the other hand, he feared the psychological blow if he retreated from fortifications so laboriously constructed. He also had to contend with a grave gunpowder shortage. At first he was told that he had 308 barrels of powder, only to learn from Brigadier General John Sullivan that the actual number was 36, a risible nine rounds per man. When he conveyed this stunning news to Washington, Sullivan recalled, the general "did not utter a word for half an hour."[25] Washington realized how easily his army could be wiped out and was slightly mystified why the British didn't attack. He looked increasingly frazzled and careworn. "I pity our good general," wrote one observer, "who has a greater burden on his shoulders and more difficulties to struggle with than I think should fall to the share of so good a man."[26]

Washington was thrust into a terrible dilemma: he couldn't defend his own performance without citing the deficiencies of men, munitions, and supplies, but that would alert the enemy to his weaknesses. He had to swallow his doubts and appear the picture of confidence, making him more tight-lipped in his public pronouncements, if more vehement in private. An accomplished actor, he learned to exploit liberally the "gift of silence" that John Adams cited as one of his cardinal strengths. For the rest of his life, Washington remained the prisoner of roles that forced him into secrecy and evasion, accentuating an already reticent personality. His reserve was further reinforced by a view of military leadership that frowned on camaraderie. Abigail Adams made the insightful comment that Washington "has a dignity which forbids familiarity, mixed with an easy affability which creates love and reverence."[27] Washington's officers admired him, but with the slightest touch of fear. "The dignity of his presence," wrote Timothy Pickering, "large and manly, increased by steady, firm, and grave countenance and an unusual share of reserve, forbidding all familiarity, excited no little reverence in his presence."[28] Washington's public role threw up an invisible barrier that prevented true intimacy with all but a select handful of friends and family members.

HAVING HAD FIRSTHAND EXPERIENCE with smallpox, Washington was farsighted in his efforts to stem its spread among the troops through inoculation. By the time he arrived in Cambridge, General Ward had established a smallpox hospital in a secluded spot west of town and ordered daily inspections of his men for symptoms. "We shall continue the utmost vigilance against this most dangerous enemy," Washington vowed to Hancock, and he diligently quarantined soldiers who exhibited the first signs of the disease.[29]

In the fall of 1775, when smallpox surfaced in British-occupied Boston, Washington grew alarmed that it might be spread to his own men. "The smallpox is in every part of Boston," he informed Joseph Reed in mid-December. "The soldiers there who have never had it are, we are told, under inoculation . . . If we escape the smallpox in this camp and the country round about, it will be miraculous."[30] When General Howe herded 300 destitute Bostonians, riddled with disease, onto boats and dumped them near American lines, Washington feared that they carried smallpox; he sent them humanitarian provisions while carefully insulating them from his troops. After a second wave of 150 sickly Bostonians was expelled, Washington grew convinced that Howe had stooped to using smallpox as a "weapon of defense" against his army.[31] By January 1777 he ordered Dr. William Shippen to inoculate every soldier who had never had the disease. "Necessity not only authorizes but seems to require the measure," he wrote, "for should the disorder infect the army in the natural way and rage with its usual virulence, we should have more to dread from it than the sword of the enemy."[32] This enlightened decision was as important as any military measure Washington adopted during the war.

Meanwhile, in early August 1775, Washington grappled with the grave problem of a gunpowder shortage. To protect his troops, he circulated the fiction that he possessed eighteen hundred barrels of powder—an early American case of a successful disinformation campaign. In giving the go-ahead to a Rhode Island plan to send ships to the Caribbean in order to seize powder stored in Bermuda, he noted that "enterprises which appear chimerical" often succeed because they are unexpected.[33] This statement offers a key insight into Washington's military thinking—his belief that wildly audacious moves sometimes work because they seem too preposterous for the enemy to credit. As it turned out, General Gage had already removed the Bermuda gunpowder as a precaution.

Washington considered his army's lack of gunpowder such a "profound secret" that, in early August, he would divulge it in person only to the speaker of the Massachusetts House of Representatives, not trusting the entire legislature with the news.[34] Secrecy and deception were fast becoming essential aspects of his repertoire. Contributing to the depletion of gunpowder was the antic behavior of the trigger-happy Virginia riflemen, who loved to fire their weapons at random, exhausting the whole camp with the commotion. Without disclosing the real reason for his concern, Washington issued this general order: "It is with indignation and shame the general observes that, notwithstanding the repeated orders which have been given to prevent the firing of guns in and about camp . . . it is daily and hourly practiced."[35] It was a magnificent bluff: Washington made it sound as if he were irate only at insubordination, not at the waste of precious ammunition.

That August George Washington conducted a revealing exchange of letters with

General Gage. Upon hearing that the British had taken American officers captured at Bunker Hill and clapped them into jails with common criminals, Washington flew into a rage. He was furious that American prisoners were being mistreated and that officers were being mingled with other prisoners. He protested that Gage had shown "no consideration . . . for those of the most respectable rank when languishing with wounds and sickness." In demanding better treatment, Washington appealed to "the rights of humanity and claims of rank" and threatened to retaliate against British captives.[36] Two days later Gage sent Washington a reply reeking of condescension. He recognized no rank among American prisoners, he conceded, "for I acknowledge no rank that is not derived from the king." Then he pompously lectured the rebel chieftain: "Be temperate in political disquisition, give free operation to truth, and punish those who deceive and misrepresent and [then] not only the effects, but the causes of this unhappy conflict will be removed."[37]

The next day Washington, rising above pettiness, allowed British officers in captivity to walk about freely after they swore they wouldn't try to escape. When he replied to Gage, he no longer hedged his words with a British superior. Now he could openly and indignantly defy the highest British officer and ventilate a lifetime of frustration. He started out by saying that British prisoners were being "treated with a tenderness due to fellow citizens and brethren." Then he delivered his own stern lecture to Gage: "You affect, Sir, to despise all rank not derived from the same source with your own. I cannot conceive any more honorable than that which flows from the uncorrupted choice of a brave and free people—the purest source and original fountain of all power . . . I shall now, Sir, close my correspondence with you, perhaps forever. If your officers who are our prisoners receive a treatment from me different from what I wish[e]d to show them, they and you will remember the occasion of it."[38] This eloquent letter, brimful of passion, reflected both sides of George Washington. He appealed to the rights due to officers in an army, traditionally an aristocratic class among the British. At the same time, he issued a clarion appeal to natural rights as the source of all power, giving a ringing affirmation of American principles.

Beneath the high-flown rhetoric, Washington's private views were far more sober. During that troubled summer he wrestled with his ambivalence about the scruffy army he led. He wasn't by nature or background an egalitarian person, and to Virginia confidants he poured forth his chagrin. To Richard Henry Lee, he bemoaned that it was impossible to get these New England soldiers to be heedless of danger "till the bayonet is pushed at their breasts" and blamed "an unaccountable kind of stupidity in the lower class of these people."[39] He was no more charitable toward their officers, telling cousin Lund, "I daresay the men would fight very well (if properly officered), although they are an exceeding dirty and nasty people."[40] Washington frowned upon these Puritan descendants as greedy, sanctimonious hypocrites, telling Joseph Reed that "there is no nation under the sun (that I ever came across) pay greater adoration to money than they do."[41]

For Washington, thoughts of Mount Vernon offered solace from wartime scenes in New England and became his favorite form of mental refreshment. Perhaps admitting that his absence from Virginia might be prolonged, he gave the faithful Lund a generous raise to manage the estate in his absence. Throughout the war Washington remained exceedingly attentive to doings at home, penning hundreds of lengthy letters to Lund, typically one a week. He retained a staggering amount of detailed information about Mount Vernon inside his compartmentalized mind and seemed able to visualize every square foot of the estate—every hedge, every fence, every pond, every meadow. Often exacting in his demands, he supervised the planting of crops, the purchase of land, and the moves and countermoves of lawsuits as if he had never left the plantation. Forever daydreaming about the future, he was determined to persist with renovations to his mansion started the year before. Writing as if he might return that winter, he told Lund to "quicken" the introduction of a new chimneypiece, "as I could wish to have that end of the house completely finished before I return. I wish you had done the end of the new kitchen next the garden as also the old kitchen with rusticated boards."[42] Clearly Washington found psychological balm in these pleasing fantasies of a renovated Mount Vernon awaiting him when the war ended.

Continuing to fret about Martha, the commander in chief was beset by sporadic fears that Lord Dunmore might abduct her. Then he dismissed such actions as unworthy of a gentleman. "I can hardly think that Lord Dunmore can act so low and unmanly a part as to think of seizing Mrs. Washington by way of revenge upon me," he told Lund Washington in late August.[43] Should Lund believe it necessary, however, he advised him to move both Martha and his personal papers to safety in Alexandria.

Even as he privately berated the New Englanders, Washington enjoyed a special wartime camaraderie with two who stood out amid the dearth of able officers. Nathanael Greene of Rhode Island was one of the first brigadier generals picked by Congress; having turned thirty-three that summer, he was the youngest general in the Continental Army. Tall and solidly built with striking blue eyes, full lips, and a long straight nose, Greene had been reared in a pious Quaker household by a prosperous father who owned an iron forge, a sawmill, and other businesses. Discouraged from reading anything except the Bible, he had received little schooling and missed a college education as much as Washington. "I lament the want of a liberal education," he once wrote. "I feel the mist [of] ignorance to surround me."[44] To compensate for this failing, he became adept at self-improvement and devoured authors both ancient and modern, including Pope, Locke, Sterne, and Jonathan Swift.

After his father died in 1770, Greene inherited his business but was shadowed by mishaps. Two years later one of the forges burned, and the following year he was barred from Quaker meetings, possibly because he patronized alehouses. In 1774 Greene married the exceptionally pretty Catharine "Caty" Littlefield, who was a dozen years younger and a preeminent belle of the Revolutionary era. As relations with Great Britain soured that year, Greene struggled to become that walking contradiction, "a fighting Quaker," poring over military histories purchased in Henry Knox's Boston bookstore. At that point his knowledge of war derived entirely from reading. Greene was an improbable candidate for military honors: handicapped by asthma, he walked with a limp, possibly from an early accident. When he joined a Rhode Island militia, he was heartbroken to be rejected as an officer because his men thought his limp detracted from their military appearance. "I confess it is my misfortune to limp a little," he wrote, "but I did not conceive it to be so great."[45]

Nevertheless, within a year, by dint of dawn-to-dusk work habits, Greene emerged as general of the Rhode Island Army of Observation, leading to his promotion by the Continental Congress. Washington must have felt an instinctive sympathy for this young man restrained by handicaps and with a pretty and pregnant young wife. He also would have admired what Greene had done with the Rhode Island troops in Cambridge—they lived in "proper tents . . . and looked like the regular camp of the enemy," according to the Reverend William Emerson.[46]

Nathanael Greene had other qualities that recommended him to the commander in chief. Like Washington, he despised profanity, gambling, and excessive drinking among his men. Like Washington, he was temperamental, hypersensitive to criticism, and chary of his reputation, and he craved recognition. As he slept in dusty blankets, tormented by asthma throughout the war, he had a plucky dedication to his work and proved a battlefield general firmly in the Washington mold, exposing himself fearlessly to enemy fire. Years later Washington described Greene as "a man of abilities, bravery and coolness. He has a comprehensive knowledge of our affairs and is a man of fortitude and resources."[47] Henry Knox paid tribute to his friend by saying that he "came to us the rawest, the most untutored being I ever met with" but within a year "was equal in military knowledge to any general officer in the army and very superior to most of them."[48] This tactful man, with his tremendous political intuitions, wound up as George Washington's favorite general. When Washington was later asked who should replace him in case of an accident, he replied unhesitatingly, "General Greene."[49]

Washington's other favorite officer was the warm, ebullient Henry Knox, who weighed almost three hundred pounds and was promoted to colonel of the Continental artillery that December. Like many overweight people, Knox walked in a slightly odd, pigeon-toed fashion, with his legs bowed outward and his paunch, big as a cannonball, bulging under his vest. Still, he dressed smartly and moved with an erect military carriage, cutting a fine figure despite his weight. From a shotgun accident while hunting in 1773, he had lost two fingers of his left hand, which he disguised by wrapping it in a handkerchief. Knox was genial and outgoing, savored food and drink, and enjoyed instant rapport with people. Good-humored and rubicund, with a ready laugh, he relished telling funny stories in his resonant voice while his blue eyes twinkled with merriment. There was something exceptionally winning about Henry Knox, and one French admirer concluded, "It is impossible to know [him] without esteeming him, or to see [him] without loving him."[50] For those who looked deeply, however, Henry Knox carried a private melancholy beneath all the hearty bonhomie.

Born near Boston Harbor, Knox was the son of a failed shipmaster who deserted the family when Henry was nine, forcing him to drop out of Boston Latin Grammar School to support his mother and younger brother. He clerked in a Boston bookstore and took advantage of every spare moment to read, preferring military history and engineering. In 1771 the twenty-one-year-old Knox opened his own shop, the New London Book Store, which offered a "large and very elegant assortment" of imported works, as Knox claimed in an ad.[51] He soaked up military knowledge from the British officers who frequented the shop. All the while he was becoming a convinced patriot. In the last advertisement he placed in the *Boston Gazette,* he announced the sale of an anti-British tract, "The Farmer Refuted," an anonymous work written by a King's College student in New York named Alexander Hamilton.

Knox's wife, Lucy Flucker, the daughter of a highborn Tory, was a bright, socially ambitious woman who excelled at chess and loved to gamble at cards. She had a girth to match her husband's. Abigail Adams reported, "Her size is enormous; I am frightened when I look at her."[52] Perhaps because of her weight and high regard for fashion, Lucy Knox became something of a laughingstock in the Continental Army. Dr. Manasseh Cutler, an army chaplain, made Lucy sound like a ridiculous caricature out of Dickens, with her hair piled "up at least a foot high, much in the form of a churn bottom upward, and topped off with a wire skeleton in the same form, covered with black gauze, which hangs in streamers down her back. Her hair behind is a large braid confined in a monstrous crooked comb."[53] The tall, outrageous hairstyle was actually the modish *pouf* newly popularized by Marie-Antoinette.

Knox first met Washington and Lee on July 16, when they rode out to Roxbury to appraise the breastworks Knox had helped to engineer. "When they viewed the works," Knox told Lucy, "they expressed the greatest pleasure and surprise at their situation and apparent utility, to say nothing of the plan, which did not escape their praise."[54] Before long, Washington and Knox formed a bond of fraternal trust. Washington liked Knox's imagination, candor, and enterprise and the way he shot cannon with his own hands. In artillery matters Washington trusted Knox's judgment implicitly. In turn, Henry Knox rewarded Washington with unconditional devotion and delighted in calling him "Your Excellency," which some saw as a little too fawning. Even later on, amid widespread grumbling about Washington's military missteps, the loyal Knox never breathed a syllable of criticism. After the war Knox thanked Washington and expressed his "affection and gratitude to you for the innumerable instances of your kindness and attention to me."[55] In the ultimate tribute to Knox, Washington later told John Adams, "I can say with truth, there is no man in the United States with whom I have been in habits of greater intimacy; no one whom I have loved more sincerely; nor any for whom I have had a greater friendship."[56]

It says much about Washington's leadership style that he searched outside the ranks of professional soldiers and gave scope to talented newcomers—a meritocratic bent that clashed with his aristocratic background and grew more pronounced with time. With Greene and Knox, he encouraged two aspiring young men who bore psychological scars from their childhood. He boosted their courage and made them believe in themselves. This effort, of course, was driven by necessity: Washington had to deal with a chronic shortage of good generals, something Knox himself recognized in 1776 when he wrote that "there is a radical evil in our army—the lack of officers . . . the bulk of the officers of the army are a parcel of ignorant, stupid men, who might make tolerable soldiers, but are bad officers."[57] In the end, the generals who succeeded in the Continental Army weren't grizzled veterans, such as Horatio Gates and Charles Lee, but young, homegrown officers who were quite daring and stayed loyal to George Washington.

CHAPTER EIGHTEEN

Land of Freedom

FOR SOMEONE of George Washington's vigorous nature, nothing disturbed him more than the charge that he had proved timid when he possessed the high ground of Prospect Hill, Cambridge, and Roxbury, with General Gage's troops pinned down below inside Boston. "The commencement of [Washington's] command was the commencement of inactivity," wrote Thomas Paine after he later turned into a waspish critic of Washington's leadership. "If we may judge from the resistance at Concord and afterwards at Bunker Hill, there was a spirit of enterprise at that time, which the presence of Mr. Washington chilled into cold defense."[1]

The reality was that during the siege of Boston George Washington was restless and all too eager to pounce. Fond of crisp decisions, he wanted to be done with this devilish stalemate and return to Mount Vernon. As he insisted to brother John, "The inactive state we lie in is exceedingly disagreeable."[2] The caution for which he was legendary struggled against a strong, nearly reckless streak in his nature. As the British lobbed bombs futilely over the American camp—one soldier said "sometimes from two to six at a time could be seen in the air overhead, looking like moving stars in the heavens"—Washington felt powerless to retaliate.[3] "It would not be prudent in me to attempt a measure which would necessarily bring on a consumption of all the ammunition we have, thereby leaving the army at the mercy of the enemy," he explained to Richard Henry Lee. So dire was the gunpowder shortage that spears were distributed to save ammunition, and Washington concluded that he couldn't afford the big, bold action he desired: "I know by not doing it that I shall stand in a very unfavorable light in the opinion of those who expect much and will find little done . . . [S]uch, however, is the fate of all those who are obliged to act the part I do."[4]

Washington frequently had Billy Lee remove his mahogany and brass spyglass from its handsome leather case so he could engage in surveillance of his adversary. He discerned signs of a British desperation at least equal to his own. The enemy was hollowing out much of Boston, stripping wooden houses for firewood and removing combustible materials that might erupt in flames should the patriots attack. Washington received a much clearer picture of both British and American fortifications when the young John Trumbull crept through high grass on his belly to sketch some maps. The son of Connecticut's governor, the Harvard-educated Trumbull had exceptional talent as an artist despite a childhood injury that deprived him of sight in one eye, and he was destined to become the chief visual chronicler of the American Revolution. Enthralled by his accurate maps, Washington enlisted Trumbull as an aide-de-camp.

Fearing the onset of the New England winter, with an army short of both clothing and blankets, Washington hoped to strike a telling blow in the autumn. It would be expensive to build winter barracks for so many men, and he would have to chop down a forest of firewood to keep them warm. A minor mutiny among Pennsylvania riflemen on September 10 only fed Washington's sense of urgency. As Connecticut and Rhode Island enlistments expired with the new year, he feared a total dissolution of his army. "The paymaster has not a single dollar in hand," he told John Hancock, predicting that without money "the army must absolutely break up."[5] He gnashed his teeth over inexperienced militia soldiers, "dragged from the tender scenes of domestic life" and "unaccustomed to the din of arms," and doubted they could stand up to British regulars, the best trained and equipped army in the world.[6]

From the beginning, Washington heeded a congressional directive that all major military engagements should be approved by a council of war. This committee structure gave a conservative bias to his plans, curbing his more daring impulses. At a war council on September 11, 1775, he presented a dramatic plan for an amphibious assault across Back Bay in flat-bottomed boats, telling the eight generals present that, with the element of surprise, such a plan "did not appear impractical, though hazardous."[7] It was roundly defeated by generals who worried that any delay might expose men to a massacre in an outgoing tide. Washington could be persuasive, able to bend men to his will. He "has so happy a faculty of appearing to accommodate and yet carrying his point, that if he was really not one of the best-intentioned men in the world, he might be a very dangerous one," observed Abigail Adams.[8] But the vocal New England generals had no qualms about overruling Washington, and he abided, however grudgingly, by their decision. Before long Washington was to say that, had he anticipated the unending difficulties ahead, "all the generals upon earth should not have convinced me of the propriety of delaying an attack upon Boston."[9]

Despite his own hard-charging nature, Washington realized that, in view of the fragility of his army, it was sometimes better to miss a major opportunity than barge into a costly error. He once lectured the Marquis de Lafayette, "*No rational person* will condemn you for *not fighting* with the odds against [you] and while so much is depending on it, but all will censure a rash step if it is not attended with success."[10] The general strategy would develop into a war of attrition, with the major emphasis on preserving the Continental Army and stalling until it was in suitable condition to fight. To John Adams, Washington later summarized the dilatory strategy as one of "time, caution, and worrying the enemy until we could be better provided with arms and other means and had better disciplined troops to carry it on."[11] Washington was often likened to the Roman general Fabius, who held Hannibal at bay through a prudent strategy of dodging encounters that played to the enemy's strength. Nevertheless this commonly cited analogy can easily be over-stated, for Washington nursed fantasies throughout the war about fighting a grand climactic battle that would end the conflict with a single stroke.

In October Washington entertained a delegation of three congressmen, headed by Benjamin Franklin, who came to ponder military plans. Washington deplored the reliance on ephemeral New England volunteers. Hoping to graduate to a de-pendable professional army, he requested a new force of twenty thousand men, with enlistments lasting at least one year, a plan ratified by the politicians in Phila-delphia. He sensed his visitors' eagerness for a tremendous victory before the em-battled British Army could be relieved by fresh troops in the spring. That October, after King George III declared the upstart colonies to be in a state of open rebellion, the Crown replaced General Thomas Gage—ridiculed as "Blundering Tom" by his men—with the formidable Major General William Howe.[12] Washington knew that all hope for reconciliation with Great Britain had now been snuffed out. Prompted by his visitors, he convened a second war council on October 18, 1775, and informed his generals that he had received "an intimation from the Congress that an attack upon Boston, if practicable, was much desired."[13] Of the eight generals, only Na-thanael Greene showed enthusiasm for an attack and then only if ten thousand troops could be safely landed in Boston.

That the British were prepared to unleash patent terror to smash patriotic confi-dence became self-evident on October 24, when word reached camp that four Brit-ish vessels had arrived at Falmouth, Massachusetts; after warning the inhabitants to evacuate, they had incinerated more than three hundred houses. Profoundly shaken, Washington told General Schuyler that the perpetrators had acted "with every cir-cumstance of cruelty and barbarity which revenge and malice would suggest."[14] For Washington, who saw the Revolution as an old-fashioned struggle between good and evil, the Falmouth conflagration was further "proof of the diabolical designs" of the leadership in London.[15]

Responding to the Falmouth atrocities, the General Court of Massachusetts enacted legislation permitting American privateers to patrol the coast. With the war having idled much of the New England merchant fleet, Washington obtained congressional approval to arm several vessels as privateers that could keep one-third of the value of any British ships captured. Before long six such ships, dubbed "George Washington's Navy," prowled the eastern seaboard, marking the birth of the U.S. Navy.[16] Afraid they might operate like lawless pirate ships, Washington demanded impeccable behavior from these privateers. "Whatever prisoners you may take, you are to take with kindness and humanity as far as is consistent with your own safety," he exhorted the captain of the first schooner fitted out.[17] Washington's spirits were buoyed in late November by the capture of the British brig *Nancy,* carrying a small bonanza of weaponry, including two thousand small arms, which Washington celebrated as an "instance of divine favor."[18] In an action that bespoke exceptional trust in twenty-five-year-old Henry Knox, Washington gave him vast discretionary power to rove through upstate New York and procure any artillery he could find at Fort Ticonderoga or elsewhere and haul it back to Massachusetts.

Often dismayed by his men, Washington never tired in his efforts at moral improvement. Not just a citizen-soldier, he was a citizen-statesman who wanted his troops to uphold high standards of conduct. He wished them to be more than superb soldiers: they should set an example for patriots everywhere. In general orders to his troops, he articulated their ideals and scolded their vices almost daily. Even in the chaos of war, amid the squalor of an army camp, George Washington evinced unflagging belief in civilized conduct.

With the possible exception of gambling, no moral failing made Washington more apoplectic than alcohol abuse. Just as he had faulted Mount Vernon employees for excessive drinking, he grew vigilant about bibulous generals. In a "Memorandum on General Officers" that he later drew up as president, he recorded the demerits of each general and in almost every case commented on his drinking habits. He faulted one as "rather addicted to ease and pleasure—and no enemy it is said to the bottle," while another "by report is addicted to drinking."[19] The chief dilemma in curbing alcohol consumption was that strong drink fortified the spirits of troops. As Washington told John Hancock, the "benefits arising from moderate use of liquor have been experienced in all armies and are not to be disputed."[20] It was hard to keep drinking within bounds, however, especially when tavern keepers rushed to slake the thirst of idle men. Washington meted out dozens of lashes to those found guilty of drunkenness and began regulating purveyors of liquor.

As part of his campaign for personal improvement, Washington encouraged his men to attend divine service, being careful to project an ecumenical spirit. When troops were about to celebrate Pope's Day in early November—the colonial equivalent of Guy Fawkes Day—Washington learned of plans to burn the pope in effigy. Hoping to draw French Catholics in Canada to the patriotic side, he chastised his men for being "so void of common sense as not to see the impropriety of such a step at this juncture."[21] Early on Washington recognized that both armies competed for the loyalty of a wavering civilian population, and he held his men accountable for behavior on and off the battlefield, admonishing them that robbing local gardens would be "punished without mercy."[22] He approved a sentence for one man "to receive thirty-nine lashes upon his bare back" merely for stealing a cheese.[23] During the summer heat he allowed men to go swimming, then was horrified to learn they were "running naked upon the [Cambridge] Bridge, whilst passengers and even ladies of the first fashion in the neighborhood are passing over it."[24] In such general orders, one hears echoes of the decorous planter from Virginia, especially when it pertained to elegant members of the opposite sex.

In the fall of 1775 Washington banked enormous hope on an invasion of Canada led by General Richard Montgomery and Colonel Benedict Arnold. Washington feared that, if Canada remained in British hands, it would always represent a potential threat on the northern border. As Arnold led an expeditionary force through the Maine wilderness, it was slowed by heavy rains, swollen streams, and fierce rapids. Starving troops devoured soap and candles and gnawed on boiled moccasins. After braving inhospitable wilds, the detachment reached the walled city of Quebec in early December for a rendezvous with General Montgomery. Arnold's feat astonished Washington, who expressed jubilation over the "enterprising and persevering spirit" of the redoubtable colonel.[25] As he informed General Schuyler, "The merit of this gentleman is certainly great and I heartily wish that fortune may distinguish him as one of her favorites."[26] Washington was so supremely confident that Montgomery and Arnold would prevail at Quebec that he even asked them to forward blankets, clothing, and other military stores captured in the conquered city.

Even as Washington sent this request, Schuyler sat down to write a somber message, announcing General Montgomery's death in a shattering defeat at Quebec. "I wish I had no occasion to send my dear general this melancholy account," wrote Schuyler.[27] Moreover a musket ball had torn a jagged slash below Arnold's knee, the first of two major leg injuries that scarred him with a permanent limp. The Quebec catastrophe was a severe setback for Washington, whose first strategic plan had misfired. The defeat also confirmed his worst fears that inexperienced troops would lose their nerve and flee in panic. For Washington, the disaster underscored the danger of relying on men with short enlistments; had Montgomery not labored under that restriction, he believed, he might have continued a blockade of Quebec and averted disaster. Arnold's bravery, meanwhile, fostered an image, later hard to eradicate, of an officer who was dedicated root and branch to the cause and who acted courageously on his own initiative.

IN THE EARLY YEARS OF THE REVOLUTION, George Washington endured a Sisyphean nightmare of whipping raw recruits into shape, only to see them melt away when their one-year enlistments expired. Officers were reduced to drill sergeants training soldiers in rudimentary warfare, then lost them once they learned to fight. For Washington, the failure to create a permanent army early in the war was the original sin from which the patriots almost never recovered. Of the pernicious effect of short-term enlistments, he later wrote, "It may easily be shown that all the misfortunes we have met with in the military line are to be attributed to this cause."[28] Washington faced the grim prospect that on January 1, 1776, the bulk of his army would simply vanish.

Forced to deal with human nature as it was, Washington didn't rely on revolutionary fervor alone to win the war: he knew he had to cater to economic self-interest as well. This aim was complicated by the fact that some states offered higher bounties for enlistment in their militias. The soldiers exploited this system by dropping out of one unit, then popping up in another to collect a new bounty, a ruse so pervasive that Washington said disputes about it could have engrossed all his time.[29] Instead of raising bounties to attract new recruits, Washington would have preferred a draft, but it ran afoul of republican resistance to anything resembling a standing army.

By late November, as snow blanketed the American camp, Washington's spirits drooped along with the temperature. He felt himself sinking in a quicksand from which he might never escape. "No man, I believe, ever had a greater choice of difficulties and less means to extricate himself from them," he confided to his brother Jack.[30] By the end of November, a paltry 3,500 men had agreed to stay with the dwindling army. In a confidential letter to Joseph Reed, Washington succumbed to black despair, railing against the mercenary spirit of the New Englanders as they haggled for more money, better clothes, and more furloughs before reenlisting. The vehemence of his anguish belies the image of a cool, unemotional Washington. "Could I have foreseen what I have and am like to experience," he told Reed, "no consideration upon earth should have induced me to accept this command," he said with a touch of melodrama.[31]

As he mulled over various schemes to strengthen his frail army, Washington wrestled with the vexed question of whether to accept blacks into the Continental

Army, not as an instrument of social policy but as a matter of stark military necessity. Many people were struck, not always favorably, by the prevalence of black soldiers in Cambridge. Captain Alexander Graydon of Pennsylvania sniffed that the "number of Negroes . . . had a disagreeable, degrading effect."[32] In contrast, General John Thomas of Massachusetts told John Adams, "We have some Negroes, but I look upon them in general [as] equally serviceable with other men . . . many of them have proved themselves brave."[33]

During the summer Washington pretty much dismissed blacks as riffraff, halting the enlistment of "any deserter from the ministerial army, nor any stroller, negro, or vagabond."[34] For a large southern slaveholder, the idea of arming blacks stirred up uncomfortable fantasies of slave revolts. But Washington had to reckon with the tolerance of his New England men, who had accepted blacks as stouthearted comrades at Lexington and Concord and Bunker Hill. A black man, Peter Salem, had fought so heroically at Bunker Hill that he had been brought to Washington's attention. Nonetheless at an October war council, Washington and his generals voted unanimously "to reject all slaves and by a great majority to reject Negroes altogether."[35] A month later Washington made this exclusionary policy explicit: "Neither Negroes, boys unable to bear arms, nor old men unfit to endure the fatigues of the campaign are to be enlisted."[36] By lumping healthy black soldiers with boys and old men, Washington insinuated that they were inferior and could be counted on only as a last resort.

On November 7 Lord Dunmore announced that slaves or indentured servants who had fled from their rebel masters could join his Royal Ethiopian Regiment and win their freedom. Eight hundred slaves soon flocked to his banner and were clad in British uniforms with the motto "Liberty to Slaves" stitched across them.[37] For the first wave of escapees, such liberty proved deceptive: many died of smallpox on ships cruising Virginia's rivers. In early December Lund Washington informed the commander in chief of the "dreaded proclamation" and conjectured that, while white indentured servants at Mount Vernon might be tempted to escape, he didn't worry about the slaves. Washington already loathed Lord Dunmore, having recently observed that if "one of our bullets a[i]med for him, the world would be happily rid of a monster."[38] Outraged by his slave proclamation, he warned Richard Henry Lee that if "that man is not crushed before spring, he will become the most formidable enemy America has."[39] In an odd twist of self-serving logic, Washington branded Dunmore an "arch traitor to the rights of humanity."[40]

Whatever his personal trepidation as a slave owner, Washington knew he couldn't afford to cast off able-bodied men, even if they happened to be black. The Revolution forced him to contemplate thoughts that would have seemed unthinkable a year earlier. Even as he fumed about Lord Dunmore, in late December 1775 he dashed off a letter to John Hancock stating that "it has been represented to me that the free Negroes who have served in this army are very much dissatisfied at being discarded. As it is to be apprehended that they may seek employ in the ministerial army, I have presumed to depart from the resolution respecting them and have given licence for their being enlisted."[41] Two weeks later the Congress ratified this extraordinary decision and allowed free blacks to reenlist. Plainly Washington had acted under duress. He urgently needed more men before enlistments expired at year's end and feared that black soldiers might defect to the British. At the same time, he was forced to recognize the competence of black soldiers. Whatever his motivations, it was a watershed moment in American history, opening the way for approximately five thousand blacks to serve in the Continental Army, making it the most integrated American fighting force before the Vietnam War. At various times, blacks would make up anywhere from 6 to 12 percent of Washington's army.[42] Already the Revolutionary War was proving a laboratory for new ideas that operated outside the confines of the slavery system. Everyone felt the new force of liberty in whose name the colonists fought and recognized the flagrant contradiction of slavery. It was fitting that 1775 witnessed the formation of the first antislavery society in Philadelphia.

ON CHRISTMAS DAY 1775 Cambridge was gripped by freezing temperatures and covered with a foot of snow, only deepening Washington's gloom. So frigid was the weather that sentries had to be replaced hourly. With trees leveled in every direction for firewood, the Continental Army inhabited a bleak, denuded landscape. As soldiers left for home in droves, not enough remained to man the redoubts, leaving glaring gaps in the defensive lines. Washington took the high road in calling for reenlistments, but General Charles Lee couldn't govern his temper. As one soldier recorded in his diary, "We was ordered to form a hollow square and General Lee came in and the first words was, 'Men I do not know what to call you; [you] are the worst of all creatures,' and [he] flung and cursed and swore at us."[43] By contrast, Washington appealed to the New Englanders' honor, saying that "should any accident happen to them before the new army gets greater strength, they not only fix eternal disgrace upon themselves as soldiers, but inevitable ruin perhaps upon their country and families."[44]

As the year ended, only 9,650 men had signed up for the new army, less than half the number envisioned by Congress and scarcely a resounding affirmation of the patriotic spirit. Still, Washington struck an upbeat tone in his New Year's Day message, noting the official start of a genuine Continental Army: "This day giving commencement to the new army, which in every point of view is entirely continental . . . His Excellency hopes that the importance of the great cause we are engaged in will be deeply impressed upon every man's mind."[45] To start the new year with a fresh slate, Washington pardoned all offenders from the old army. In truth, it was an anxious interval for the commander in chief, who again hid his weakness. As one army was dismissed and another assembled in its place, the British could see thousands of soldiers leaving and might be tempted to take advantage of the situation. As he waited with bated breath, Washington told Hancock confidentially, "It is not in the pages of history perhaps to furnish a case like ours; to maintain a post within musket shot of the enemy for six months together, without [powder] and at the same time to disband one army and recruit another within that distance of twenty odd British regiments."[46]

In mid-January Washington complained that his army had no money, no powder, no cache of arms, no engineers, not even a tent for his own use in a field campaign. He sounded a note of sleepless despair, reminiscent of Shakespeare's Henry IV, saying that he experienced "many an uneasy hour when all around me are wrapped in sleep."[47] A man who hated failure, Washington again mused about whether he had erred in accepting the top command: "I have often thought how much happier I should have been if, instead of accepting of a command under such circumstances, I had taken my musket upon my shoulder and entered the ranks or . . . had retir[e]d to the back country and lived in a wigwam."[48] The British were feeling cocky about their prospects. At Faneuil Hall in Boston that January, enemy officers roared with delight at a farce entitled The Blockade, supposedly written by General John Burgoyne, which mocked Washington as a bumbling general in a big floppy wig, flailing about with a rusty sword.

At midday on January 1, 1776, the atmosphere of the conflict abruptly lurched toward total war when Lord Dunmore torched Norfolk, Virginia. The fleet under his command pounded the town with cannonballs for seven hours, and the blackened ruins smoked for days. "Thus was destroyed," wrote John Marshall, "the most populous and flourishing town in Virginia."[49] This conflagration banished any lingering traces of Anglophilia that Washington retained. He hoped the Norfolk holocaust would unite the country "against a nation which seems to be lost to every sense of virtue and those feelings which distinguish a civilized people from the most barbarous savages."[50]

The conflict sharpened further on January 10, 1776, with the publication of Thomas Paine's Common Sense, a landmark pamphlet that galvanized the colonies to seek outright independence. The thirty-eight-year-old Paine was a brilliant if abrasive personality who had arrived in Philadelphia two years before after a checkered career as a corset maker and shopkeeper in England. While many colonists clung to the fairy tale of George III as a benign father figure in thrall to a wicked ministry, Paine bluntly demolished these illusions, dubbing the king "the

Royal Brute of Great Britain."[51] Within three months Paine's astonishing work had sold 150,000 copies in a country of only three million people. Beyond its quotable prose, *Common Sense* benefited from perfect timing. It appeared just as Americans digested news of the Norfolk horror as well as George III's October speech to Parliament in which he denounced the rebels as traitors and threatened to send foreign mercenaries to vanquish them. The historian Bernard Bailyn has noted that "one had to be a fool or a fanatic in early January 1776 to advocate American independence," but Paine's work—"slapdash as it is, rambling as it is, crude as it is"— produced that magical effect.[52]

Common Sense was just the fillip needed by a demoralized Continental Army. In a letter to Washington, General Charles Lee pronounced the pamphlet "a masterly, irresistible performance" and said he had become a complete convert to independence.[53] From Virginia, Fielding Lewis, Washington's brother-in-law, informed him that talk of independence was rapidly gaining ground and that "most of those who have read the pamphlet *Common Sense* say it's unanswerable."[54] Although ignorant at first of the author's identity, Washington instantly grasped the work's significance. "A few more of such flaming arguments as were exhibited at Falmouth and Norfolk," he told Joseph Reed, "added to the sound doctrine and unanswerable reasoning contain[e]d (in the pamphlet) *Common Sense,* will not leave numbers at a loss to decide upon the propriety of a separation."[55] Once his identity became known, Paine endeared himself to the troops by donating proceeds from his pamphlet to purchase woolen mittens for them. Within a year he was traveling as an aide-de-camp to Nathanael Greene and formed a close relationship with Washington. Even after the war Washington remained solicitous about Paine's impoverished state, inquiring of James Madison, "Can nothing be done in our assembly for poor Paine? Must the merits and services of *Common Sense* continue to glide down the stream of time, unrewarded by this country?"[56]

WHILE GEORGE WASHINGTON TRIED GALLANTLY to hold his army together that winter, Martha was displaying her own brand of valor. Starting in June 1775, both Washingtons were borne on a powerful tide that would whirl them along for the rest of their lives. Unlike her husband, Martha wasn't naturally courageous, but she was a determined woman who could will herself to rise to the occasion. To aid her husband, she conquered whatever fears or anxieties might have kept her from his side. For more than eight years of war, she would exhibit the fierce loyalty of a Spartan wife, a trial that she endured from a combination of wifely duty and outright patriotism.

Despite fears that Lord Dunmore might abduct her from Mount Vernon, Martha had refused to move to the small town house that the Washingtons owned in Alexandria. Washington dwelled on this possibility in so many letters that it got Martha's attention, and she escaped to visit Jacky and Nelly in Maryland or stayed with her sister Anna Maria in New Kent County. Washington worried incessantly about her. "I could wish that my friends would endeavor to make the heavy and lonesome hours of my wife pass of[f] as smoothly as possible, for her situation gives me many a painful moment," he confessed to brother Samuel that fall.[57] Although he wrote weekly letters to Martha, many were opened en route by "scoundrel postmasters," as he styled them, and others never arrived at all.[58] Such postal lapses, besides isolating Martha, would have made Washington more guarded in communicating his thoughts.

In mid-October Washington concluded that he wouldn't be able to return to Mount Vernon that winter and invited Martha to join him in Cambridge. He knew that the biting chill of a New England fall would make the trip perilous and extremely uncomfortable, telling brother Jack, "I have laid a state of the difficulties . . . which must attend the journey before her and left it to her own choice."[59] With her nerves stretched taut, Martha kept postponing the trip, even though delay only increased the likelihood of heavy snow. If not born for heroics, Martha always heeded the summons of duty when her husband called.

At last, on November 16, 1775, the diminutive Martha Washington piled into her carriage and left Mount Vernon, accompanied by Jacky and Nelly, nephew George W. Lewis, and Elizabeth Gates, wife of General Horatio Gates. She traveled luxuriously, her clothing packed in elegant leather trunks studded with brass nails. She brought along five household slaves tricked out in the livery of Mount Vernon. On this arduous northward journey, Martha discovered her sudden elevation in the world and that she had left obscurity behind forever; henceforth fame would be her constant companion. When she reached Philadelphia, she was greeted by a military escort and was mystified by the fuss made over her. She had passed through the city, she observed in amazement, "in as great pomp as if I had been a very great somebody."[60] The church bells pealed when she reached Newark, and at Elizabethtown a light horse cavalry trotted beside her, providing an honorary escort. Nevertheless, for a woman who dreaded water, the constant ferry crossings must have been an ordeal, and to bump along six hundred miles of rutted roads in frigid weather must have tested even the faithful Martha. She expressed her stoic credo thus: "I am still determined to be cheerful and to be happy in whatever situation I may be."[61]

Historians often note that Martha Washington spent each winter of the war with her husband, leaving before fighting resumed in the spring, but this bland statement doesn't quite capture the scope of her sacrifice. Mount Vernon curator Mary Thompson has computed that Martha spent between 52 and 54 months with her husband in a war that would drag on for 103 months; in other words, she spent about half the war with the Continental Army.[62] At a minimum she stayed two or three months each winter, but some stays lengthened to seven, eight, or even nine months, until she jokingly referred to herself as "the great perambulator."[63] Because Washington couldn't afford to abandon his army, Martha's willingness to join him was of inestimable value. Due to his delicate position in the war, he had to keep his emotions bottled up. He couldn't afford to show weakness or indecision and needed a wife to whom he could reveal his frustrations.

The secretive Washington also had an acute need for male confidants to whom he could unbosom himself completely. He had enjoyed "unbounded confidence" in his closest aide, Joseph Reed, before the latter went off to Philadelphia in late October to attend his law practice and didn't return to Cambridge.[64] Distraught, Washington deemed Reed's services "too important to be lost" and tried to coax him into returning.[65] Chained to his desk with correspondence, Washington saw himself turning willy-nilly into a bureaucrat. He needed a surrogate who was not only a good scribe but could intuit the responses he himself would write. "At present my time is so much taken up at my desk that I am obliged to neglect many other essential parts of my duty," he pleaded to Reed. "It is absolutely necessary therefore for me to have persons that can think for me as well as execute orders."[66] Not until the advent of Alexander Hamilton and other proficient aides was Washington finally liberated from his clerical labors.

On December 11, 1775, Martha Washington arrived in Cambridge, not having seen her husband since May. To bedraggled soldiers in the wintry camp, her appearance in the glamorous coach with a slave retinue must have seemed unreal and resplendent. Lady Washington, as she was known in an incongruously aristocratic touch, was still comparatively young at forty-four. Yet when Charles Willson Peale painted her the following year, he noted something matronly in the face, plus a seriousness in her direct, unaffected gaze. When she joined her husband at the imposing Vassall mansion, she was thrust into a busy, working atmosphere. Here Washington mapped strategy, held war councils, and conducted his voluminous correspondence with Congress. Washington's aides also slept in the house, with several crammed into a single room, while the general commandeered one drawing room as his office. He soon pressed Jacky Custis into service as a messenger. A dozen servants, several of them slaves, waited on officers, and the staff even included a tailor and a French cook. Among the household staff was a free black woman, Margaret Thomas, who worked as a seamstress and entered into a love affair with Billy Lee. Possibly because of this, Thomas seemed to irritate Washington, who wished that he would "see her no more," but he retained her on the payroll, possibly for Billy, who came to consider himself married to her.[67]

In this crowded house, George and Martha Washington would have found privacy hard to come by. Washington made a bid for conjugal privacy by ordering a curtained four-poster bed before his wife's arrival. Despite these concessions to gentility, nothing could mask the stark reality of a military camp. By the end of December, as the British continued firing shells from Boston, Martha had trouble coping with the tension. If the men were inured to these intrusions, they were awful new realities to her. "I confess I shudder every time I hear the sound of a gun," she wrote to her friend Elizabeth Ramsay. ". . . To me that never see anything of war, the preparations are very terrible indeed. But I endeavor to keep my fears to myself as well as I can."[68] Since Washington had segregated his military from his home life, this was Martha's first exposure to war, and she showed real gumption in facing down her fears. The image of her as a small, grandmotherly woman overlooks the fortitude that made her a natural mate for Washington.

Observers noted the companionable relationship between George and Martha Washington. As Nathanael Greene informed his wife, "Mrs. Washington is excessive fond of the General and he of her . . . They are happy in each other."[69] Mercy Warren saw how Martha's gentle affability could "soften the hours of private life or . . . sweeten the cares of the hero and smooth the rugged pains of war."[70] Washington seemed more relaxed in Martha's presence, and they loved to share a humorous moment. One day eighteen-year-old Joseph White went to receive orders from Washington. He had adopted the fictitious rank of an officer, and Washington immediately detected the imposture. "Pray, sir, what officer are you?" he asked. The young man claimed to be an assistant adjutant in the artillery regiment. "Indeed," responded Washington, "you are very young to do that duty." "I told him I was young," White recalled, "but was growing older every day." He said that Washington had "turned his face to his wife and both smiled."[71]

Long a wealthy woman, Martha adapted to the austere camp life and looked askance on lavish consumption. Soon after her arrival, she was invited to a fancy dress ball at a local tavern, which local radicals protested as inappropriate in wartime. Four representatives met with her and requested that she boycott the event. One recalled that Martha reacted with "great politeness" and sent her "best compliments" to the protesters, assuring them "that their sentiments on this occasion were perfectly agreeable unto her own."[72] The ball was canceled on the spot. While Martha Washington could have ducked the issue, saying she would consult her husband, she showed confidence in her judgment and ingratiated herself to the men. At first Washington balked at Martha's suggestion that they celebrate their Twelfth Night anniversary, but he finally submitted and allowed a gala celebration to be held. Before long Martha took out her needles and was knitting stockings for the soldiers.

Since Washington had a good deal of entertaining to do, Martha oversaw the social side of headquarters. For morning visits, she offered oranges and wine to guests and heartier fare for midafternoon meals. At these gatherings, Washington experienced relief from his burdensome labors and enjoyed his favorite Madeira wine combined with the camaraderie of several pretty young women. A particular favorite was the fetching Caty Greene, wife of Nathanael. Washington's fondness for the young brunette was only enhanced that February when she gave birth to a boy christened George Washington Greene. A woman of stunning good looks, the sociable Caty was coy and high-spirited. Henry Knox dismissed her as superficial, but Washington didn't seem to care. Even as local gossips whispered about her flirting with the commander in chief, he seemed enchanted by her company and teased her good-naturedly about her "Quaker-preacher" husband.[73] Inasmuch as Martha was fond of the younger woman, Caty could hardly have enjoyed an illicit romance with the general.

It is testimony to Martha's social versatility that she won over women who were far more intellectual than she. Mercy Otis Warren, a prolific bluestocking who wrote poems, plays, and histories, called on Martha, and they immediately became fast friends. As Warren reported to Abigail Adams, "I took a ride to Cambridge and waited on Mrs. Washington at 11 o'clock, where I was receiv[e]d with that politeness and respect shown in a first interview among the well bred and with the ease and cordiality of friendship of a much earlier date."[74] Washington knew the shortcomings of Martha's education, and when she corresponded with intellectual women such as Mercy Warren, he or a secretary would draft her replies. There's no evidence that Martha objected to this practice and may even have felt that it spared her embarrassment.

During the long Cambridge winter, the Washingtons perceived the mythical stature that the hopeful populace was foisting upon them. A man named Levi Allen wrote to Washington, hailing him as "our political father," and in 1778 an almanac described him as the "father of his country."[75] A couple called the Andersons named their twins George and Martha, while three ships were christened for the general's wife. A town in western Massachusetts renamed itself Washington. In January 1776 Washington set eyes on a fictitious engraving of himself, printed in London, by an artist who falsely claimed to have based it on an actual sitting with him. With wry amusement, Washington noted drily that the artist had created "a very formidable figure of the Commander in Chief, giving him a sufficient portion of terror in his countenance."[76]

By far the most sparkling tribute came from the pen of a young woman, Phillis Wheatley, who resided in Boston and honored Washington with a flattering ode mailed to him in late October 1775. In polished couplets reminiscent of Alexander Pope, she burnished Washington's image: "Proceed, great chief, with virtue on thy side, / Thy ev'ry action let the goddess guide. / A crown, a mansion, and a throne that shine, / With gold unfading, Washington! Be thine." The youthful poetess lauded America as "the land of freedom's heaven-defended race!" which was the more remarkable given that Phillis Wheatley was a twenty-two-year-old slave.[77] Seized in Africa at age seven or eight, she had been sold to John Wheatley, a Boston tailor, as a personal slave for his wife. The Wheatleys recognized the girl's gifted nature, schooled her in Scriptures and ancient classics, and allowed her to live with the family. In 1773 she published in London a collection of verse, *Poems on Various Subjects, Religious and Moral.* The frontispiece showed an arresting picture of Wheatley in which her personality leaps out. She looks smart and self-assured, with her chin supported by her fingers and her quill poised above the page as she stares coolly into the distance. The volume made her the most celebrated black person in America.

Not until mid-December did Wheatley's poem come to Washington's attention, and he didn't find time to reply until late February. His cordial, respectful letter is little short of astonishing for a large Virginia slave owner replying to a young woman in bondage. This was the same Washington who had recently reviled Lord Dunmore as diabolical for promising freedom to defecting slaves. Washington started his note by saying that he should have replied sooner. "But a variety of important occurrences, continually interposing to distract the mind and withdraw the attention, I hope will apologize for the delay and plead my excuse for the seeming, but not real, neglect. I thank you most sincerely for your polite notice of me in the elegant lines you enclosed. And however undeserving I may be of such encomium and panegyric, the style and manner exhibit a striking proof of your great poetical talents."[78] He concluded with an invitation: "If you should ever come to Cambridge or near headquarters, I shall be happy to see a person so favour[e]d by the Muses and to whom nature has been so liberal and beneficent in her dispensations. I am with great respect your obed[ien]t humble servant."[79] This is the sort of exquisite letter that, once upon a time, Washington might have reserved for the eyes of a duchess. Few incidents in the early days of the war suggest how powerfully Revolutionary ideals were transforming George Washington as his reaction to Phillis Wheatley.

Washington considered publishing the poem, but feared it might be misinterpreted as a mark of vanity. Also the poem, with its imagery of crowns and thrones, had some uncomfortable overtones. Nevertheless Washington appears to have received Phillis Wheatley at his Cambridge headquarters in March with a "very courteous reception," and through Joseph Reed, the poem found its way into print in April.[80] It didn't seem to bother Washington that Wheatley was a slave, and it evidently didn't bother Wheatley that Washington was a substantial slave owner. Certainly there were Mount Vernon slaves whom Washington knew intimately and some to whom he spoke in a friendly manner, such as Billy Lee, but he had never met any black person on such terms of social equality. That Washington appreciated Wheatley's poetry and received her warmly showed his great potential for growth. Once again he had displayed a striking capacity to adapt to new circumstances, even though he still had an immense distance to travel on the slavery issue.

CHAPTER NINETEEN

The Heights

THE REPUBLICAN IDEOLOGY that Washington absorbed from his avid reading of Revolutionary pamphlets never fit easily with his patrician reflexes as a Virginia planter. Perhaps few actions he took during the war exhibited his inconsistent nature in such bold relief as his creation of a personal guard during the dispiriting Cambridge winter. In part, the decision arose from legitimate concerns for his safety. "To guard against assassination, which I neither expect nor dread, is impossible," Washington later wrote, but he knew that kidnapping attempts were always a possibility, especially since he himself would hatch a couple of failed schemes to kidnap British generals.[1]

His order to forge a personal guard or Life Guard, as it was commonly called, also sprang from a desire to be surrounded by a crack team of disciplined professionals who would accompany him whenever he rode out to review the troops. Protective of his historical reputation, Washington committed the care of his personal papers to this guard. Having such an elite corps at the beck and call of the chief general was a throwback to the glittering world of European armies.

In general orders for March 11, 1776, Washington instructed the commanding officer of each regiment to pluck out four men apiece for his guard. His description of what he wanted shows how much stock he placed in appearance. The men should be "from five feet eight inches high to five feet ten inches; handsomely and well made; and as there is nothing in his [i.e., Washington's] eyes more desirable than cleanliness in a soldier, he desires that particular attention may be made in the choice of such men as are neat and spruce."[2] This precision was strange indeed at a time when Washington feared his army might crumble into dust.

A year later Washington issued new instructions that tightened requirements for the unit. Now he wanted his bandbox men to "look well and be nearly of a size." He narrowed the height range—"I desire that none of the men may exceed in stature 5 feet 10 inches, nor fall short of 5 feet 9 inches"—and said they should be "sober, young, active, and well made."[3] Although Washington allowed class preferences to trump ideology, he didn't want it to get around and enforced secrecy on the officers: "I am satisfied there can be no absolute security for the fidelity of this class of people, but yet I think it most likely to be found in those who have family connections in the country. You will therefore send me none but natives and men of some property, if you have them. I must insist that in making this choice you give no intimation of my preference of natives as I do not want to create any invidious distinction between them and the foreigners."[4] It should be said that Washington had noticed that a disproportionate number of foreign-born troops defected to the British side to pocket lucrative bounties.

Washington decked out his handpicked men in blue and buff uniforms, their round hats sprouting blue and white feathers and ornamented with bearskin strips. Nervous about the expense, he again demanded secrecy, noting that these costs created an "expense which I would not wish should go forth."[5] His painstaking regard for appearances wasn't limited to his Life Guard. That January he told his troops that "nothing adds more to the appearance of a man than dress" and that he hoped "each regiment will contend for the most soldierlike appearance."[6] Even in the waning days of the war, he was preoccupied by an absence of hats, for the lack "of which the beauty and uniformity of the other articles will be in a great measure lost . . . and the troops can never make a military appearance."[7] He ordered officers to lend hats an attractive image "by cutting, cocking, or adding such other decorations as they think proper."[8] Washington's perfectionism about looks extended down to his horses. His most famous steed, Old Nelson, a chestnut horse with a white face, earned the distinction of being the first "nicked" horse in America—that is, the root of his tail was incised so that he carried it with a high flourish. Washington was well aware of the towering impression he made on horseback.

ON JANUARY 14, 1776, Washington informed John Hancock that the state of American arms was "truly alarming."[9] His prayers for more firepower were soon answered. Three days later, beaming with good news, Henry Knox lumbered into camp after a two-month absence. He reported the imminent arrival of heavy weapons carted three hundred miles from Fort Ticonderoga. Incredibly, Knox had taken almost sixty mortars and cannon, weighing about 120,000 pounds, and mounted them on forty-two giant sleds. Through thickening December snow, teams of oxen had hauled this ponderous artillery up and down mountain passes, across frozen rivers, and down village lanes as spectators gaped in wonder. The entire grand procession seemed quasi-miraculous, and Henry Knox became the hero of the hour, executing one of the war's legendary feats. In an instant, the entire conflict was transformed, for Washington could now contemplate offensive action against British troops bottled up in Boston.

The arrival of the big Ticonderoga guns was providential. Washington remained dangerously short of gunpowder and firearms, and two thousand men lacked muskets or ammunition. Things had come to such a desperate pass that Benjamin Franklin suggested to General Charles Lee that the troops be furnished with bows and arrows. "Those were good weapons," Franklin admonished him, "not wisely laid aside."[10] So perilous was the plight of his troops that Washington confessed to Joseph Reed, "I have been oblig[e]d to use art to conceal it from my own officers."[11] He had succeeded so brilliantly in pretending to be securely armed that his main supporters overestimated his strength and expected more zeal in dislodging the British. As Washington observed, "The means used to conceal my weakness from the enemy conceals it also from our friends and adds to their wonder."[12]

One missing prerequisite for an offensive operation was a blast of cold air to freeze the waterway between the Continental Army and the British troops, allowing an invasion of Boston without employing boats. When the temperature plummeted to near zero in late January, forming an icy crust on the water, Washington monitored it carefully. On February 13, at Lechmere Point, he determined that the ice had sufficiently thickened to freeze the channel all the way to Boston. Hence on February 16 he convened a war council to present a plan for "a bold and resolute assault upon the troops in Boston."[13] His skeptical generals unanimously voted it down, finding the plan flawed because they were short of gunpowder and couldn't soften up the British beforehand with heavy bombardments. They also believed that Washington had overstated the size of American forces and underrated British strength.

With reluctance, Washington accepted their verdict and said tartly to Joseph Reed that they had waited all year for the bay to freeze, but now that it had, "the enterprise was thought too dangerous!" At the same time, he admitted that his "irksome" situation had perhaps led him to advocate a rash action that might have miscarried.[14] There was nothing despotic in Washington's nature, making him the ideal leader of a republican revolution, but he still had to learn when to trust his instincts and overrule his generals. It was both Washington's glory and his curse that he was so sensitive to public opinion, so jealous of his image, and so willing to listen to others.

The veto of his generals steered the discussion to a second plan that turned into one of the war's inspired maneuvers. The high ground of Dorchester Heights, which loomed over Boston from the south, could be used to defeat the British if it was fortified. This strategic bluff, more than one hundred feet high, had remained unarmed for several reasons. Spies in Boston reported General Howe's solemn vow to "sally forth" and snuff out the rebellion if the Americans attempted to occupy it.[15] And thorny logistical questions remained. How could fortifications be built on ice-encrusted ground? How could the Americans move the Ticonderoga guns up to the lofty ridge within full view and range of enemy guns?

The ingenious solution was to haul the guns into position under cover of darkness during a single night. Noise from the operation would be muffled by firing steady salvos from Roxbury, Cobble Hill, and Lechmere Point and by wrapping wagon wheels with straw to deaden their sound. To obstruct the vision of British troops, the patriots would throw up intervening screens of hay bales. Washington and his generals hit upon the clever expedient of prefabricating the fortifications elsewhere, making it necessary only to transport them to the heights. By now a champion bluffer, Washington also had earth-filled barrels lined up before the parapets, giving a deceptive show of strength. These convenient props could also come thunderously crashing down on any British troops foolhardy enough to storm the hillside.

By late February, Washington was persuaded that the contemplated operation would lure the British into an engagement on terms favorable to the Americans. One lesson he had learned from the French and Indian War was that fear was contagious in battle, especially among inexperienced troops. Without disclosing the exact nature of the impending operation, he warned his soldiers bluntly that "if any man in action shall presume to skulk, hide himself, or retreat from the enemy without the orders of his commanding officer, he will be *instantly shot down* as an example of cowardice."[16]

At midnight on March 2 the patriots began firing diversionary volleys at the British, who replied with earsplitting cannon fire—sounds of war loud enough to startle Abigail Adams from her sleep in nearby Braintree. These cacophonous exchanges persisted through the next night. On the night of March 4, Washington recalled, the moon was "shining in its full luster," as the weather cooperated with the unfolding operation. "A finer [night] for working could not have been taken out of the whole 365," wrote the Reverend William Gordon. "It was hazy below [the Heights] so that our people could not be seen, though it was a bright moonlight night above on the hills."[17] Washington directed operations on horseback, his familiar form visible in silhouette to his men. Under the tutelage of Henry Knox, the American artillery strafed Boston in a ferocious cannonade. "Our shells raked the houses and the cries of the poor women and children frequently reached our ears," wrote Lieutenant Samuel Blachley Webb.[18]

Hidden by the roar and flash of cannon, General John Thomas supervised three thousand soldiers and oxen-led wagons as they dragged the big guns, weighty barrels, and preassembled ramparts up the steep slope. The unforgiving ground was covered with ice two feet thick, packed hard as rock. At sunrise on March 5 the British saw that something wondrous had happened overnight: Dorchester Heights had been converted into a full-fledged fortress, making the British occupation of Boston seem untenable. Not a single American soldier had been lost in the operation. Legend maintains that, upon beholding the massed American guns, an incredulous General Howe exclaimed, "My God, these fellows have done more work in one night than I could make my army do in three months."[19] On this anniversary of the Boston Massacre, Washington strode among his men, shouting at them to "remember it is the fifth of March, and avenge the death of your brethren," and the men roared back their assent.[20] As in the French and Indian War, Washington was no remote leader but an active, rousing presence. "His Excellency General Washington is present animating and encouraging the soldiers," wrote Dr. James Thacher, "and they in return manifest their joy, and express a warm desire for the approach of the enemy."[21]

The second phase of Washington's strategy called for Generals Putnam, Sullivan, and Greene to speed across the Charles River with four thousand men and pummel Boston if Howe's troops could be drawn out into a bloody engagement at Dorchester Heights. The British seemed about to wade into this cleverly laid trap. Despite skepticism among some officers, General Howe elected to throw more than two thousand troops against the heights, and legions of bystanders scurried eagerly across the surrounding hills to await the grand battle scene. Washington was convinced that, if he could flush the British from Boston, they could be bombarded by lethal fire.

John Trumbull remembered Washington making one last meticulous survey of his defenses, only to be frustrated by an unforeseen shift in the weather: "Soon after his visit, the rain, which had already commenced, increased to a violent storm and [a] heavy gale of wind, which deranged all the enemy's plan of debarkation, driving the ships foul of each other."[22] Girded for battle, Washington was woefully disappointed and told General Lee that the storm was "the most fortunate circumstance for them and unfortunate for us that could have happen[e]d. As we had everything so well prepared for their reception . . . I am confident we should have given a very good account of them."[23] Some chroniclers have interpreted the raging tempest as an accidental blessing that safeguarded American troops set to cross a mile of open water, only to encounter well-entrenched redcoats in Boston. "Had the storm not intervened," wrote James T. Flexner, " . . . the troops Washington had intended to land in Boston could never have regained their boats. They would have been trapped. They would either have had to annihilate the British or be themselves entirely defeated."[24] The one certainty is that the storm averted an engagement that might have been decisive for one side or the other.

The upshot of the successful arming of Dorchester Heights was a British decision to evacuate Boston, albeit with British forces largely unmolested. Some historians have argued that Howe planned to leave anyhow and that this fresh threat merely accelerated the timetable and afforded a convenient cover story. For Washington, it marked a triumphant finale. On the night of March 9 Howe unleashed a deafening cannonade against Dorchester Heights, firing seven hundred cannonballs, a move that barely camouflaged frantic movements inside Boston to abandon the town. As Washington monitored developments, the town deteriorated into a scene of tumultuous disorder; British troops pitched disabled cannon and produce barrels into the harbor so they wouldn't fall into patriot hands. Debris bobbed in the water everywhere or lay heaped upon the shore. Crowds of desperate Loyalists surged onto overloaded ships in a chaotic spectacle. The sense of shock was palpable among these refugees, prompting some to dive to death in the chilly waters. As Washington wrote to his brother Jack, "One or two have done what a great many ought to have done long ago—committed suicide. By all accounts, there never existed a more miserable set of beings than these wretched creatures now are, taught to believe that the power of Great Britain was superior to all opposition."[25] On Sunday, March 17, with the distant din of patriot cheers ringing in their ears, nine thousand quick-stepping redcoats and numerous Loyalists boarded an armada of 120 ships stretching nine miles out to sea and left Boston forever. "Surely it is the Lord's doings and it is marvelous in our eyes," wrote Abigail Adams.[26]

In a measure of Washington's growing maturity, he indulged in no public bragging, even if he gloated in the privacy of print. Priding himself on staying coolheaded, he didn't give way to jubilation, especially since it took ten days for the British ships to sail away. One of his hallmarks as a commander was unremitting vigilance, and he worried that British soldiers would slip ashore in disguise or even launch a surprise attack. On the alert for medical problems, Washington made sure that the first five hundred men who entered Boston were immune to smallpox. Instead of basking in the limelight, he permitted General Artemas Ward to lead the victorious vanguard into the city. When Washington himself entered on March 18, he did so unobtrusively, almost invisible to the elated multitudes, and studied the town with professional curiosity. It had suffered extensive damage, with buildings razed, churches gutted, supply depots emptied, and windows smashed, but Washington said the town was "not in so bad a state as I expected to find it."[27] He must have thanked the Lord for the freakish storm, since he found the British defenses "amazingly strong . . . almost impregnable, every avenue fortified."[28] He toured the

Beacon Hill home of John Hancock and found the furniture in decent shape, with family oil portraits still on the walls. In their haste to leave, the British had discarded a huge trove of supplies, including 30 cannon, 3,000 blankets, 5,000 bushels of wheat, and 35,000 planks of wood.

In general, Washington handled his maiden victory with aplomb. When he informed Hancock of the British evacuation, he had the tact to congratulate not himself but Hancock and "the honorable Congress."[29] Instead of condoning the plunder that accompanies victory, Washington threatened to punish offenders severely. He set an orderly tone and deferred to civilian authorities, demanding that suspected Tories still in Boston be guarded by his men until the Massachusetts legislature ruled on their future. "If any officer or soldier shall presume to strike, imprison, or otherwise ill-treat any of the inhabitants, they may depend on being punished with the utmost severity," he announced.[30] In a beautiful symbolic act, he returned a horse given to him after learning that it had been swiped from a departed Tory who had been "an avow[e]d enemy to the American cause."[31] Once again, by opposing vindictive actions, Washington shaped the tone and character of the American army.

Only in private letters did Washington allow himself to crow a little. As he told brother Jack, "No man perhaps since the first institution of armies ever commanded one under more difficult circumstances than I have done . . . I have been here months together with what will scarce be believed: not thirty rounds of musket cartridges a man." With so little ammunition, he had defeated "two and twenty regiments, the flower of the British army, when our strength have been little, if any, superior to theirs and at last have beat them in a shameful and precipitate manner out of a place the strongest by nature on this continent . . . strengthened and fortified in the best manner and at an enormous expense."[32] The modest boasting masked the fact that Washington would have preferred a bloody and decisive encounter to the self-protective British decision to sail away and fight another day.

For his feat, Washington was lionized as never before and exalted into a historic personage, collecting heaps of honors. By bestowing upon him an honorary degree, Harvard supplied the long-standing defect in his education. In a tribute drafted by John Jay, Hancock assured Washington that history would record that "under your direction an undisciplined band of husbandmen in the course of a few months became soldiers."[33] Showing steady progress in egalitarian sentiments, Washington conceded that his men had started out as a "band of undisciplined husbandmen," but that it was "to their bravery and attention to their duty that I am indebted for that success which procured for me the only reward I wish to receive, the affection and esteem of my countrymen."[34] This was a notable step forward for a man who had so recently wrinkled his nose at the filthy, money-grubbing New England troops. The

Massachusetts politician Josiah Quincy assured Washington that his name would be "handed down to posterity with the illustrious character of being the savior of your country."[35] Such effusive praise reflected the patriots' need for a certified hero as a rallying point as much as Washington's skill in expelling the British. Canonizing Washington was a way to unite a country that still existed only in embryonic form. Curtailing any show of vanity, Washington reacted with studied modesty and stole a line from Joseph Addison's *Cato,* telling Quincy, "To obtain the applause of deserving men is a heartfelt satisfaction; to merit them is my highest wish."[36]

As a way of celebrating Boston's liberation, Congress struck its first medal, showing Washington and his generals atop Dorchester Heights. It also commissioned a portrait by Charles Willson Peale in which Washington displays none of the swagger of a triumphant general. The look in his eyes is sad, anxious, even slightly unfocused, as if his thoughts had already turned to his upcoming troubles in New York. His shoulders appear narrow, and his body widens down to a small but visible paunch. It was way too soon for a full-fledged cry of triumph, Peale seemed to suggest, and events would prove him absolutely right.

EVEN BEFORE THE BRITISH SAILED for Nova Scotia, Washington had guessed correctly that they would end up in New York, whose numerous waterways would play to the strength of the world's mightiest navy. With the redcoats gone, he apprised Congress, he would "immediately repair to New York with the remainder of the army."[37] He knew that if the British controlled the Hudson River, they would effectively control the all-important corridor between Canada and New York City, bisecting the northern and southern colonies. New York was also a stronghold of fervent Tories, noted Washington, filled with disaffected people "who only wait a favorable opportunity and support to declare themselves openly."[38] Hoping to head off this prospect, he started the journey southward on April 4, accompanied by his new personal guard, moving as rapidly as the many ceremonial dinners allowed. He didn't yield to the euphoria that infected many compatriots and grimly prepared for the impending campaign, knowing that the patriots hadn't yet experienced the full brunt of British power. The Crown needed to crush this uprising conclusively and establish colonial supremacy, lest it endanger the structure of its entire empire. It couldn't afford to be humiliated by a ragged band of upstarts.

Having preceded Washington to New York, General Lee reacted with perplexity to the task of defending a city crisscrossed by waterways. Sleepless with worry and incapacitated by gout—he was carried into the city on a stretcher—Lee began to defend New York from naval assault by installing artillery at Governors Island in the upper bay, Red Hook in Brooklyn, and Paulus Hook (later Jersey City) on the

Hudson's western shore. The same qualities that made New York a majestic seaport turned it into a military nightmare for defenders. There was hardly a spit of land that couldn't be surrounded and thoroughly shelled by British ships. "What to do with the city, I own, puzzles me," a stumped Lee wrote to Washington. "It is so encircled with deep, navigable water that whoever commands the sea must command the town."[39] In hindsight, the city was certainly doomed, but Washington considered it "a post of infinite importance" that would be politically demoralizing to surrender without a fight.[40]

By the time Washington arrived on April 13, Lee had been posted to Charleston, South Carolina, leaving Israel Putnam in command. A mood of foreboding gripped the city, causing many inhabitants to flee. Washington set to work at his headquarters on lower Broadway, right beside the Battery. A despised symbol of royalty, an equestrian statue of George III, stood outside his door on Bowling Green. When Martha arrived four days later, she and her husband occupied a mansion north of the city that had been vacated by Abraham Mortier, the former deputy paymaster general of British forces in America. With its wide verandas and splendid views of the Hudson River, the house stood in bucolic Lispenard's Meadows, at what is now the intersection of Varick and Charlton streets.

Because British troops had been accused of abusing Boston's citizens when they were billeted there, Washington took pains to prevent such misbehavior by soldiers lodged in Manhattan houses. He comprehended the war's political dimension and swore that soldiers would have to answer for "any wood being cut upon the floors or any water or filth thrown out of the windows."[41] To win the allegiance of local farmers, he warned his men against trampling crops in their fields. More difficult to supervise were men frequenting the Holy Ground, the notorious red-light district near the Hudson River where up to five hundred prostitutes congregated nightly on land owned by Trinity Church. Venereal disease raced through several regiments, threatening to thin their ranks before the enemy arrived. As William Tudor of Boston wrote home, "Every brutal gratification can be so easily indulged in this place that the army will be debauched here in a month more than in twelve at Cambridge."[42]

Over the winter Washington had wondered whether his plenary authority over troops in Cambridge extended to operations in New York. Showing exemplary modesty with Congress, he had consulted John Adams, who proclaimed unequivocally that "your commission constitutes you commander of all the forces . . . and you are vested with full power and authority to act as you shall think for the good and welfare of the service."[43] This seminal moment wiped away any doubt that Washington wielded continental power and oversaw a national army. Where another man might have grown giddy, the new power sobered him. "We expect a very bloody summer of it at New York and Canada," he told brother Jack in late May, "as it is there I expect the grand efforts of the enemy will be aim[e]d, and I am sorry that we are not, either in men or arms, prepared for it."[44]

Having visited New York only twice before, Washington needed to familiarize himself with this new terrain. The harried general complained of being holed up in his office with endless paperwork when he wanted to be out in the field. He faced the herculean task of shoring up a chain of posts stretching across lower Manhattan to Brooklyn. Building on Lee's plans, he projected the construction of a pair of twin forts, to be known as Fort Washington and Fort Lee, on rocky high ground farther up the Hudson, outposts designed to prevent the British from turning the river into a thoroughfare to Canada. Washington knew that in New York the odds were badly stacked against him. To ward off attacks by sea, he sealed off the end of every street with a barricade and sank offshore obstructions to British ships. By early June the Continental Army had 121 cannon in Manhattan, on the New Jersey shore, on Governors Island, and in Brooklyn, all ready to bombard the British fleet.

Though satisfied with his progress, Washington was dismayed to learn in May that King George III had hired seventeen thousand German mercenaries to fight in North America. This news confirmed that the conflict would be resolved only through a long, bloody war. Soon to be a master at espionage, Washington wondered whether he could infiltrate patriotic Germans among the Hessians to stir up disaffection and spur desertions.

In late May he rode to Philadelphia to consult with Congress about military strategy, trailed by unfounded rumors that he intended to resign. The round of talks made clear that the patriots would contest every square inch of New York, however impossible that seemed. Philadelphia was ablaze with talk about declaring independence from Great Britain, but Washington, as a military man, withheld public comment. In private, however, he was more militant than ever and scoffed at congressmen who were "still feeding themselves upon the dainty food of reconciliation."[45] Prodded by Washington, Congress decided to offer ten-dollar bounties to attract new soldiers and also set up a Board of War, headed by John Adams, to improve recruiting and supply distribution.

By this point it was self-evident that Martha Washington would spend extended periods with her husband and might be exposed to smallpox. Washington could not advocate inoculation if his own wife shrank from it. After the liberation of Boston, Martha had refrained from entering the city to celebrate with officers' wives who enjoyed immunity to the disease. She had vowed to be inoculated against smallpox, but Washington remembered how anxious she was when Jacky was inoculated in 1771; he doubted she would now make good on her pledge. Nevertheless, when they reached Philadelphia, Martha conquered her fears and submitted to the procedure. She came down with a fever and developed only a dozen pustules (none on her face), spending several weeks in quarantine. On June 10 Jacky Custis, in Maryland with his wife, wrote an appreciative note to Washington about his mother's successful recovery. He used the occasion to express gratitude for everything his legal guardian had done, thanking him for the "parental care which on all occasions you have shown me. It pleased the Almighty to deprive me at a very early period of life of my father, but I cannot sufficiently adore His goodness in sending me so good a guardian as you Sir. Few have experienc[e]d such care and attention from real parents as I have done. He best deserves the name of father who acts the part of one."[46] It was an eloquent, well-deserved tribute for the often-thankless care that Washington had given to his stepson.

WITH MANY LOYALISTS scattered across the city, a more pervasive fear of espionage existed in New York than in Boston, where the patriots and British had been widely separated. With thousands of troops cooped up in southern Manhattan in a tense atmosphere, a vigorous hunt was launched in early June for Tories who allegedly supplied British warships off Sandy Hook and spied on patriots. On June 17 the New York Provincial Congress received a shocking report from a Loyalist named Isaac Ketchum, who was arrested on counterfeiting charges. While held at City Hall, Ketchum fingered two members of Washington's personal guard, Thomas Hickey and Michael Lynch, also detained on counterfeiting charges, as being in league with the British to sabotage the Continental Army as it defended New York. In their wild boasting, the two men had contended that when British warships anchored in the harbor, William Tryon, the royal governor, would distribute royal pardons to defectors. Lynch and Hickey also referred darkly to "riflemen on Staten Island" and "Cape Cod men" who were supposed confederates in the plot.

As the probe widened, investigators learned that a gunsmith named Gilbert Forbes was assigned to pay off turncoats to the British side and that Forbes was being supplied with money by David Mathews, New York's mayor. Once alerted to this allegation, Washington moved swiftly and had Mathews arrested at one o'clock in the morning at his Flatbush home. Under questioning, Mathews admitted that Governor Tryon had "put a bundle of paper money into his hands" and asked him to convey it to Forbes to purchase rifles and muskets. Only after the war did Mathews add the sensational disclosure that "he had formed a plan for the taking Mr. Washington and his guard prisoners."[47] Mathews named Thomas Hickey, a swarthy, brazen fellow, as a henchman in the plot. Washington believed that the conspiracy originated with Tryon, who had employed Mathews as his cat's-paw. A dozen arrests occurred as rumors ran through town that the commander in chief had refused to eat a plate of poisoned peas that had subsequently killed some chickens.

News of the plot unleashed a wave of fierce reprisals against New York Tories; some of them were tarred and feathered, and others were subjected to the torture of "riding the rail." Once the angry atmosphere cooled down and Hickey's court-martial began, the plot took on more modest proportions. The conspirators had planned to spike patriot guns when the British fleet arrived, in return for pardons and bonuses. One witness testified that seven hundred patriots had promised to defect. In his testimony, he made a claim that must have unnerved Washington: no fewer than eight members of Washington's personal guard formed part of the plot. Hickey showed no remorse, was found guilty of sedition and mutiny, and was singled out for hanging. Not taking any chances, Washington deployed 140 men to guard him and other prisoners at City Hall.

The entire conspiracy had the unintended effect of rallying support for Washington, whose life had been in jeopardy. But he didn't want to exaggerate the plot, which might have been demoralizing. In reporting it to John Hancock, he said it had been concocted by the guilty parties "for aiding the King's troops upon their arrival. No regular plan seems to have been digested, but several persons have been enlisted and sworn to join them."[48] He also believed that 200 to 250 Loyalist conspirators were hiding in the Long Island woods and swamps; he had boats patrol the Narrows at night to intercept anyone trying to flee to British-controlled Staten Island.

Mayor Mathews and several others were packed off to Connecticut to serve jail time—a lenient sentence for a treasonous plot—and either escaped or were let go without a trial. Washington decided to make an example of Hickey and ordered every brigade to witness his hanging at eleven A.M. on June 28, 1776. The gallows were erected in a field near the Bowery, and twenty thousand spectators—virtually the entire New York population—turned out to watch. Hickey waived his right to a chaplain, calling them "cutthroats," and managed to hold back tears until the hangmen actually looped the noose around his neck.[49]

In his general orders for the day, Washington drew a rather bizarre lesson from Hickey's fate. He hoped the punishment would "be a warning to every soldier in the army" to avoid sedition, mutiny, and other crimes "disgraceful to the character of a soldier and pernicious to his country, whose pay he receives and bread he eats."[50] The next sentence gave a strange twist to the whole affair. "And in order to avoid those crimes, the most certain method is to keep out of the temptation of them and particularly to avoid lewd women who, by the dying confession of this poor criminal, first led him into practices which ended in an untimely and ignominious death."[51] This coda, with its sternly puritanical lesson, shows that Washington may have been more worried about health hazards posed by the Holy Ground than by treasonous plots.

CHAPTER TWENTY

All London Afloat

BY THE SUMMER OF 1776 the British were convinced that they would make quick work of the rebel forces and took comfort in a superior, complacent tone. Braggadocio—always a poor substitute for analysis—grew fashionable in official circles in London. At the start of the year, Lord Rawdon assured the Earl of Huntingdon that "we shall soon have done with these scoundrels, for one only dirties one's fingers by meddling with them. I do not imagine they can possibly last out beyond this campaign."[1] Lord Sandwich, First Lord of the Admiralty, reacted contemptuously to the notion that the sheer number of colonists could overpower royal forces. "Suppose the colonies do abound in men, what does that signify? They are raw, undisciplined, cowardly men."[2] George Germain, secretary for the American colonies, cherished the hope that all that was needed was a "decisive blow."[3] What was required was a show of force so huge and terrifying that the deluded colonists would tremble at the assembled might of the British Empire.

While Great Britain did have a respectable army, it paled beside those of France, Austria, and Prussia. It was the Royal Navy that was peerless in Europe, and New York Harbor was a big enough basin to absorb this giant fleet. Awaiting these ships, Washington had his men strain every nerve to detect their arrival, even sleeping with their arms and "ready to turn out at a minute's notice."[4] On June 29 patriotic sentries stationed on Staten Island signaled to Washington that forty British ships, the first installment of the fleet, had been spotted off Sandy Hook and would soon glide majestically through the Narrows. The news touched off hysterical activity in Manhattan. Writing in rapid, telegraphic style, Henry Knox informed his brother:

"The city in an uproar, the alarm guns firing, the troops repairing to their posts, and everything in the height of bustle."[5]

Washington had decided to make a costly (and in the end, mistaken) gamble of trying to hold New York. In fairness, it must be said that Congress had assigned a high priority to retaining the city. A day earlier Washington had issued an urgent summons to Massachusetts and Connecticut to dispatch militia posthaste to the city, and he now accelerated preparations for an imminent British attack, having his men pile up sandbags everywhere. Faced with incessant work, the tireless Washington noted that he was "employed from the hour of my rising till I retire to bed again."[6] Prompted by fear, a tremendous exodus of women and children left New York, crossing paths with an influx of militia. "On the one hand," wrote the Reverend Ewald Shewkirk, "everyone that could was packing up and getting away; and on the other hand country soldiers from the neighboring places came in from all sides."[7] Reflecting the parlous state of things, Washington exiled Martha to the comparative safety of Philadelphia. To make their separation tolerable, she asked Charles Willson Peale to execute a miniature watercolor of her husband clad in his blue uniform and gold epaulettes.

Until reinforcements arrived, Washington was woefully shorthanded. He had fewer than 9,000 men, with 2,000 too sick to enter combat. Meanwhile, he steeled himself for the advent of 17,000 German mercenaries who would form part of a gigantic expeditionary force—the largest of the eighteenth century—that might total 30,000 soldiers. When this first wave of ships grew visible from Manhattan, an armada of 110 warships and transport boats, the sight was impressive, almost dreamlike, to behold. "I could not believe my eyes," Private Daniel McCurtin wrote after peering at the panoply of British power. "Keeping my eyes fixed at the very spot, judge you of my surprise when, in about ten minutes, the whole bay was full of shipping . . . I declare that I thought all London was afloat."[8]

These were the same ships that had evacuated Boston in March and marked time in Halifax before sailing south to New York. Fortunately for Washington, this advance guard under Major General William Howe, his former nemesis from the siege, decided not to force the issue. Some British ships dropped anchor off Gravesend, Long Island, and newly arrived British soldiers camped on Staten Island, but no offensive action materialized. General Howe was biding his time until the bulk of the fleet, sailing from England under the command of his brother Richard, Admiral Viscount Howe, joined him in New York.

In general orders for July 2, Washington tried to rouse his untried men with impassioned words. He had a genius for exalting the mission of his army and enabling the men to see themselves, not as lowly grunts, but as actors on the stage of history. "The time is now near at hand which must probably determine whether Americans are to be free men or slaves . . . The fate of unborn millions will now depend, under God, on the courage . . . of this army."[9] That same morning an alarming incident occurred when five British men-of-war passed through the Narrows and seemed on course to attack patriot forts. Confronting this threat, the Continental Army reacted with notable esprit de corps. Colonel Samuel Blachley Webb wrote in his diary that "never did I see men more cheerful. They seem to wish the enemies' approach."[10] Despite his uneasiness, Washington was encouraged by this spirited response, telling Hancock that "if the enemy make an attack, they will meet with a repulse as . . . an agreeable spirit and willingness for action seem to animate . . . the whole of our troops."[11] In the end the British ships approached no closer, and Washington concluded that General Howe had deferred action until his brother's arrival. Thus far Washington had commanded the Continental Army for an entire year without engaging in a single battle, but he knew he would shortly experience his first decisive test.

AN UNWAVERING ADVOCATE of independence, Washington thought his compatriots would eventually come to share his belief. "My countrymen, I know, from their form of government and steady attachment heretofore to royalty, will come reluctantly into the idea of independency," he wrote that spring. "But time and persecution brings many wonderful things to pass."[12] In May, to his delight, the Virginia Convention in Williamsburg favored independence, and his neighbor at Gunston Hall, George Mason, drew up an eloquent Declaration of Rights that featured the lines "That all men are born equally free and independent, and have certain inherent natural rights . . . among which are the enjoyment of life and liberty, with the means of acquiring and possessing property, and pursuing and obtaining happiness and safety."[13] Thomas Jefferson would prune and shape these words to famous effect. Still another Virginian, Richard Henry Lee, introduced a congressional resolution on June 7 declaring "that these United Colonies are, and of right ought to be, free and independent states."[14] On July 2 Congress approved Lee's resolution, then spent the next two days haggling over the precise wording of the Declaration of Independence. The final text was approved on July 4. Congress had two hundred broadsides printed up and disseminated throughout the colonies.

On July 6 Hancock sent Washington a copy and asked him to have it read aloud to his army. The Declaration made the rebels' treason official and reminded them of the unspeakable punishments the British government meted out for this offense. Only recently a British judge had handed down this grisly sentence to Irish revolutionaries: "You are to be drawn on hurdles to the place of execution, where you are to be hanged by the neck, but not until you are dead, for while you are still living your bodies are to be taken down, your bowels torn out and burned before your faces, your heads then cut off, and your bodies divided each into four quarters."[15] The British proved more lenient to captured American officers, but Washington knew that treason was a capital crime and that he had passed the point of no return. Employing a vivid metaphor, he later said that he and his colleagues had fought "with halters about their necks."[16] In the event of defeat, Washington knew, he would be hanged as the chief culprit; he decided that he would "neither ask for nor expect any favor from his most gracious Majesty."[17] He contrived a plan to flee, if necessary, to lands he owned in the Ohio Country, telling Burwell Bassett that "in the worst event, they will serve for an asylum."[18]

On July 8 Washington held in his hands a broadside of the Declaration of Independence for the first time and ordered his troops to gather on the common at six P.M. the next evening to hear it read aloud. In general orders for July 9, he previewed its contents by noting that Congress had declared "the United Colonies of North America" to be "free and independent states."[19] Lest this sound abstract, he underscored the practical significance for the average soldier, pointing out that each was "now in the service of a state possessed of sufficient power to reward his merit and advance him to the highest honors of a free country."[20] Among other things, Congress could now coin money and devise other lucrative incentives.

The troops rejoiced upon hearing the document. "The Declaration was read at the head of each brigade," wrote Samuel Blachley Webb, "and was received with three huzzas by the troops."[21] Washington was gratified by the "hearty assent" of his men and their "warmest approbation" of independence.[22] News of the Declaration elicited snide rebukes from the British side, one officer saying that it served to highlight "the villainy and the madness of these deluded people."[23]

Reading of the document led to such uproarious enthusiasm that soldiers sprinted down Broadway afterward and committed an act of vandalism: they toppled the equestrian statue of George III at Bowling Green, decapitating it, then parading the head around town to the lilting beat of fifes and drums. The patriots made excellent use of the four thousand pounds of gilded lead in the statue, which were melted down to make 42,088 musket bullets. Washington was appalled by the disorder. Ever the strict parent, he told his men that while he understood their high spirits, their behavior had "so much the appearance of riot and want of order in the army" that he disapproved their actions and urged that in future they should be left to the "proper authority."[24] His reproach might have sounded priggish, but Washington wanted this revolution to be an orderly one, with due respect for property, and he refused to abide even the desecration of the king's statue. He sounded rejuvenated by the Declaration, writing defiantly to Hancock on July 10 that should the

British mount an attack, "they will have to wade through much blood and slaughter before they can carry any part of our works."[25]

Such bravado proved premature. On the afternoon of July 12, propelled by a stiff breeze and a powerful tide, five British ships—the forty-gun *Phoenix* and the twenty-gun *Rose,* along with a schooner and two tenders—sailed toward the Battery. In their first test, American defenses failed miserably. Only half the artillerists manned their guns, and hundreds of gaping soldiers stood onshore transfixed by the enemy ships, as if attending a sporting regatta. It was an ominous sign for the still-amateurish Continental Army. Six patriots were killed in an artillery company under Captain Alexander Hamilton when their cannon exploded, possibly from defective training or from mishandling by intoxicated gunners.

Unscathed by steady fire from the Manhattan and New Jersey shores, the *Phoenix* and the *Rose* streamed up the Hudson River and pounded the urban population of New York with a terrifying two-hour cannonade that shrouded the city in smoke and panicked its occupants. The episode demonstrated the vulnerability to British warships of a town encircled by water. Attuned to the psychology of war, Washington saw with dismay that his soldiers were unnerved by the plight of overwrought civilians. Since his own early combat experience had been in frontier locations, this urban chaos was something altogether new for him. "When the men-of-war passed up the river," Washington observed, "the shrieks and cries" of the women and children were "truly distressing and I fear will have an unhappy effect on the ears and minds of our young and inexperienced soldiery."[26] Afterward Washington tried to clear the city of remaining civilians to avoid a repetition of the episode. He was especially indignant at soldiers who had stood hypnotized by British ships bombarding the town. The next day Washington chastised them unsparingly: "Such unsoldierly conduct must grieve every good officer and give the enemy a mean opinion of the army . . . a weak curiosity at such a time makes a man look mean and contemptible."[27] Just as Washington feared, the British ships' foray in the Hudson severed communications between New York and Albany and the strategically located upstate lakes.

Washington had gotten his first unforgettable taste of British sea power. Because of their speed and mobility, enemy ships could disappear, then surface anywhere, and they would keep him in suspense for the next seven years. As he would complain, "The amazing advantage the enemy derive from their ships and the command of the water keeps us in a state of constant perplexity."[28] On the evening of the *Phoenix* and *Rose* episode, Washington and his officers noticed that the appearance of a new ship, the *Eagle,* triggered delirious cheers from British soldiers aboard ships and encamped on Staten Island, and they deduced correctly that Admiral Richard Howe had arrived.

The Howe brothers, whose grandfather had been elevated to the peerage by King William III, boasted a blue-blooded pedigree that the young George Washington might have envied. Educated at Eton, befriended by King George III, they had become moderate Whig members of Parliament. Tall, well built, and graceful, the pleasure-loving General William Howe, forty-seven, had bold eyebrows, full lips, and a dusky complexion. He had fought bravely at Quebec in the French and Indian War and exposed himself to danger at Bunker Hill. He indulged the vices common to his class, especially gambling and whoring, and saw no reason why the American war should dampen his escapades. He took as his North American mistress the fetching Boston-born Elizabeth Lloyd Loring and made her husband, Joshua Loring, Jr., a commissary of prisoners. This opportunistic husband, content to be cuckolded, played the bawd for his wife, who became notorious as "the Sultana of the British army."[29] As one Loyalist writer said cynically, "Joshua had no objections. He fingered the cash, the general enjoyed madam."[30] Admiral Richard Howe, fifty, less of a bon vivant than his younger brother, had earned the nickname "Black Dick," which referred to both his complexion and to his downcast nature. He was a somber man, thin-faced and tight-lipped, with a cool, somewhat forbidding gaze. So marked was his reticence that Horace Walpole described him as "silent as a rock."[31] For all that, he was a superb seaman, renowned for his courage, fighting spirit, and ethical standards.

As convinced believers in the British Empire and sympathetic to colonial grievances, the Howe brothers didn't want to crush the patriots in a total war of annihilation. Still hopeful that their misguided American cousins could be restored to their senses, they came to North America bearing both peace and a sword. In the coming campaign, they would plot strategy with political as well as military considerations in mind.

On July 14, in their capacity as peace commissioners, the Howe brothers sent Lieutenant Philip Brown with a message for Washington. Backed by the intimidating presence of the British fleet, Richard Howe requested, in polite terms, a parley: "The situation in which you are placed and the acknowledged liberality of your sentiments, induce me very much to wish for an opportunity to converse with you on the subject of the commission with which I have the honor to be charged."[32] Washington tended to be skeptical of peace overtures as ruses used to "distract, divide, and create as much confusion as possible," as he characterized them in the spring when he first heard that Britain might send commissioners.[33]

Lieutenant Brown's boat was intercepted between Governors Island and Staten Island by three American boats, whose crews demanded to know his business. When Brown said that he had a letter for Washington, the Americans instructed him to stay put while they sought instructions onshore. The three American officers who came out to handle the situation—Henry Knox, Joseph Reed, and Samuel Blachley Webb—had been well coached by Washington. They told Brown that they refused to touch the letter until he told them to whom it was addressed. When Brown retorted that it was addressed to "George Washington Esq., etc. etc.," they said no such person existed and they couldn't receive it. Somewhat mystified, Brown asked to whom it should be addressed, and his interlocutors replied that "all the world knew who Gen[era]l Washington was since the transactions of last summer."[34] Brown tried to strike a conciliatory tone. "I am sure Lord Howe will lament exceedingly this affair, as the letter is quite of a civil nature and not a military one."[35] Thus ended the initial standoff.

Washington knew that this exchange involved much more than the fine points of decorum. He was now the de facto head of state of a newly minted country, and his treatment reflected the perceived legitimacy of his authority. "I would not upon any occasion sacrifice essentials to punctilio," Washington explained to Hancock, "but in this instance . . . I deemed it a duty to my country . . . to insist upon that respect which in any other than a public view I would willingly have waived."[36] Lord Howe's secretary, Ambrose Serle, grew hopping mad at Washington's rebuff. "So high is the vanity and the insolence of these men! . . . There now seems no alternative but war and bloodshed, which must lay at the door of these unhappy people."[37]

Washington suspected that the British would renew their entreaty, and on July 16 he spurned another letter addressed to "George Washington, Esq." Serle again gnashed his teeth, remarking that the letter "was refused for the same idle and insolent reasons as were given before."[38] His remark shows the condescending attitude of at least some British commanders toward Washington. Referring to him as if he were still a youthful subaltern in the French and Indian War, Serle sneered that "it seems to be beneath a little paltry colonel of militia at the head of banditti or rebels to treat with the representative of his lawful sovereign because 'tis impossible for him to give all the titles which the poor creature requires."[39] Washington planned to teach the British a lesson. They finally sent him a letter on July 17, addressed to "His Excellency, General Washington," with a request that he meet with Lieutenant Colonel James Paterson, the smooth-talking adjutant general of General William Howe. Believing that protocol had been satisfied, Washington agreed to meet with the British officer on July 20. He chose as his venue Henry Knox's headquarters at 1 Broadway, near the water; if a spot deeper inside the city had been chosen, he would have needed to blindfold Paterson, and he didn't care to demean him in that manner.

At noon on July 20 a barge arrived at the Battery with Colonel Paterson. Washington wanted to impress upon the British emissary that, as commander in chief of a sovereign nation, he should be treated with all due dignity. His personal guard lined up in crisp formation at the entrance, and Washington appeared in full battlefield regalia, leading Knox to tell his wife that the general was "very handsomely dressed and made a most elegant appearance."[40] The stagecraft had the desired effect upon Paterson, who "appeared awestruck, as if he was before something supernatural," wrote Knox. "Indeed, I don't wonder at it. He was before a great man indeed."[41] Paterson groveled considerably and prefaced every sentence with "May it please your Excellency" or "If your Excellency so pleases."[42] Washington exacted revenge for previous indignities. When Paterson laid on the table the original letter from Richard Howe, addressed to "George Washington Esq. etc. etc.," Washington wouldn't pick it up and balked at the et ceteras. Paterson explained that the et ceteras implied everything that might follow. To which Washington retorted, "It does so—and anything!"[43] He was suavely implacable before Paterson's studied servility.

At this point Paterson launched into a prepared speech about how the goodness and benevolence of the king had induced him to send the Howe brothers to reach an accommodation with the unhappy colonists, this meeting being the first step. Washington denied that he was vested with powers to negotiate a settlement. Then he showed what a deft diplomat he could be. According to Joseph Reed's memo, he argued that the Howe brothers had only the power "to grant pardons; that those who had committed no fault wanted no pardon; that we were only defending what we deemed our indisputable rights."[44] Paterson acknowledged that this opened a wide field for discussion. Washington remained polite, treating him with impeccable courtesy and even inviting him "to partake of a small collation" before he returned to his ship.[45] He was always careful to separate the personal from the political, the man from the mission. If the British had hoped to mollify Washington, their diplomatic overture failed. The same day that he received Colonel Paterson, Washington wrote to Colonel Adam Stephen and decried "the vile machinations of still viler ministerial agents."[46] Two days later he dismissed the peace efforts of the Howe brothers as a mere propaganda exercise calculated expressly "to deceive and unguard, not only the good people of our own country, but those of the English nation that were averse to the proceedings of the king and ministry."[47] Once Washington had set his sights on independence, his vision was unblinking, and his consistency proved one of his most compelling qualities.

By late July Washington's men were laboring in a parched city under a blazing sky. "From breakfast to dinner I am boiling in a sun hot enough to roast an egg," Knox groused to his wife. "Indeed, my dear Lucy, I never suffered so much from fatigue in my life."[48] It was precisely the atmosphere in which disease festered, and dysentery, typhoid fever, malaria, and smallpox infected the troops, disabling up to a third of them. "The vile water here sickens us all," wrote Philip Fithian, a Presbyterian chaplain attached to the New Jersey militia. "I am very sick."[49] Illness was so prevalent that some regiments couldn't field a single healthy officer. The men often relieved themselves in open ditches, until Nathanael Greene warned that "the stench arising from such places will soon breed a pestilence in the camp."[50] Responding to Greene's request, Washington allowed the regiments to switch more of their diet from meat to fresh vegetables to combat scurvy. The troops also lacked uniforms, and Washington advised them to wear hunting shirts so the British would think they faced an army of skilled backwoods marksmen. To remedy the weapons shortage, Greene handed out three hundred spears. All in all, the Continental Army was a bizarre, mongrel corps that flouted the rules of conventional warfare. It was a far more peculiar army than the British troops had ever faced, leading Ambrose Serle to belittle them: "Their army is the strangest that was ever collected: old men of 60, boys of 14, and blacks of all ages, and ragged for the most part, compose the motley crew."[51]

Chronically short of generals, Washington counted the bluff Israel Putnam as his only major general in New York. In response to Washington's pleas, Congress added William Heath, Joseph Spencer, John Sullivan, and Nathanael Greene as major generals. Of this group, Washington banked his highest hopes on Greene, appointing him commander of American forces on Long Island—a striking affirmation of trust in a man with only one year of army experience. Plagued by ill health, Greene had succumbed to jaundice earlier in the year. "I am as yellow as saffron, my appetite all gone, and my flesh too," he told his brother Jacob. "I am so weak that I can scarcely walk across the room." Now, in mid-August, as the Continental Army braced for battle, Greene reported to Washington that he was struggling with a "raging fever" and could scarcely sit up in bed.[52] It was a catastrophic development for Washington, who evacuated Greene to a house north of the city and replaced him with John Sullivan. A fiery, egotistical lawyer from New Hampshire, the son of Irish indentured servants, Sullivan had wild, unruly hair and a confrontational personality. Washington took a balanced view of Sullivan, crediting him with being "spirited and zealously attached to the Cause" but suffering from a "tincture of vanity" and an unhealthy "desire of being popular."[53] William Alexander, better known as Lord Stirling, who had been in charge of New York's fortifications, was appointed to take over Sullivan's division. Before the war Washington had tried to help the rich, free-spending Stirling with his crippling debts. A convivial man, excessively fond of drink, Stirling would distinguish himself as a brave soldier and a steadfast supporter of Washington.

With the patriots feeling beleaguered as never before, the question of military strategy preoccupied Washington and his officers. The armchair generals of the Continental Army, averaging only two years of military experience, had suddenly become real generals. Pessimism was rampant. With a sinking feeling, Henry Knox told his brother that the Continental Army was "not sufficiently numerous to resist the formidable attacks which will probably be made."[54] Joseph Reed espoused a cautious strategy, "a war of posts," which he defined thus: "prolong, procrastinate, avoid any general action, or indeed any action, unless we have great advantages."[55] Under this strategy, the patriots would fortify a few strong, impregnable positions and invite the British to attack at their peril. Charles Lee wanted to fragment the army into nimble mobile units that could swoop down and harass the enemy as opportunities arose. Washington was slowly being forced to adopt a cautious strategy of trying to survive as best he could and attacking only when unusual chances emerged. The aim was to keep the Continental Army intact and wear down Britain through a prolonged war of attrition, hoping all the while to attract European allies who might deal a devastating blow to the enemy.

The British, for their part, *did* have to win a military victory; a stalemate would be an expensive and humiliating defeat. They rejected a blockade of American ports as too daunting even for the Royal Navy. One faction favored the blatant application of terror to scare the colonists into submission—but that strategy, tried in Falmouth and Norfolk, had backfired and unified the Americans. The Howe brothers opted for a more subtle, complex agenda than their massive military presence implied, including a concerted attempt to regain the allegiance of the rebels and to mobilize Loyalists. They wanted to establish a British citadel in New York that would serve as a base of operations to sustain hit-and-run raids against Atlantic seaports, enabling their army to move more swiftly than the land-bound Continental Army. Most of all, they wanted to dominate the Hudson River and shut off New England from the other states.

Even as Washington awaited the British onslaught, his overburdened mind turned where it always did for comfort: to Mount Vernon, his mental sanctuary. That August, in his spare moments, he fantasized about the groves of trees that would brighten up each end of his mansion. Only recently he had heard from Jacky Custis that British men-of-war had sailed up the Potomac and burned houses to the ground, but Washington's mind preferred to dwell on sylvan visions of home. He could see the grounds clearly in his mind, down to the last bush. "There is no doubt but that the honey locust, if you could procure seed enough and that seed would come up, will make . . . a very good hedge," he wrote to Lund Washington. "So will the haw or thorn . . . but cedar or any kind of evergreen would look better. However, if one thing will not do, we must try another, as no time ought to be lost in rearing of hedges, not only for ornament but use."[56] A few days later this escapist vision would be blotted out by the bloodshed in Brooklyn.

Disaster

BY MID-AUGUST fresh contingents of British ships had converged on New York, rounding out an expeditionary force of 32,000 troops, including 8,000 Hessian mercenaries, and revealing the magnitude of the threat to the Continental Army. Making a major statement about the peril of the American revolt, the Crown had enlisted seventy warships, a full half of the Royal Navy, to deliver an overwhelming blow against the Americans. It decided to gamble all on a military solution to a conflict that was, at bottom, one of principle and that depended ultimately on recovering the lost trust of the former colonists.

A subdued Washington knew the stage was set for a major confrontation. "An attack is now therefore to be expected," he wrote, "which will probably decide the fate of America."[1] His army of only 10,500 men, 3,000 of them ailing, was sadly outnumbered and outgunned. Even though he tried to put on a brave face, he approached the impending confrontation with dread. "When I compare" the British Army "with that which we have to oppose them, I cannot help feeling very anxious apprehensions," he confided to Brigadier General William Livingston.[2] As more militiamen streamed into New York, Washington's army expanded to 23,000 soldiers, but many were callow youths grabbed from shops and farms who would soon confront a highly professional military force. Washington's pronouncements acquired a darker tinge, as if he intuited the many deaths that lay ahead. "We must resolve to conquer or die," he intoned in general orders. "With this resolution and the blessing of heaven, victory and success certainly will attend us."[3]

The night of August 21, almost the eve of battle, witnessed an electrical storm of such portentous grandeur that it might have been conjured up by Shakespeare.

Major Abner Benedict, posted on the elevated portion of Long Island known as Brooklyn Heights, which towered over the East River and housed the main American fortification, left this graphic description of the celestial pyrotechnics whizzing through the sky: "In a few minutes the entire heavens became black as ink, and from horizon to horizon the whole empyrean was ablaze with lightning . . . The lightning fell in masses and sheets of fire to earth, and seemed to strike incessantly and on every side."[4]

The Howe brothers postponed an invasion to give the Hessian troops a week to recuperate from their transatlantic journey and to see if their feeble peace overtures bore fruit. Baffled by the delay, Washington found "something exceedingly mysterious in the conduct" of these brothers, who spouted catchphrases of peace amid a huge military buildup.[5] The paramount question was whether the enemy would land on Manhattan or on Long Island, prompting Washington to hedge his bets by dividing his forces. This strategy, if seemingly prudent, ran the grave risk of having British ships storm up the East River, snapping links between the army's two wings. To avert this possibility, Washington sank wrecks in the channels of Upper New York Bay—one could see masts of submerged ships poking up from the water— and seeded the East River with spiked obstacles to thwart vessels.

As storm clouds dispersed the next morning, British light infantry and grenadiers began trickling ashore at Gravesend Bay, at the southwestern corner of Long Island. By day's end, 15,000 redcoats had established a solid beachhead in the kind of well-drilled maneuver at which European armies excelled. This main invading force would soon number 22,000 soldiers, but Washington, deceived by faulty intelligence, estimated it in the neighborhood of 8,000 or 9,000 men. The miscalculation led him to misconstrue the landing as a diversion from the main event in Manhattan—"a feint upon Long island to draw our forces into that quarter."[6] He was further led astray when British forces came to a dead halt at Flatbush, three miles from American lines. Retaining the majority of his men in Manhattan, Washington transferred ten battalions to Brooklyn, bringing total troop strength there to a paltry 6,000 men. In retrospect, it is hard to see how Washington's strategic vision could have been so clouded as ninety British ships conducted a grand-scale movement in the Narrows.

On August 23, after touring his Long Island defenses with General Sullivan, Washington decided to deploy 3,000 men farther south in a wooded, hilly area called the Heights of Guana (or Gowanus Heights), which ran roughly east-west and could cut off any northward thrusts by the enemy. With his men about to clash with superior forces, Washington suggested that courage could outweigh sheer numbers and implored them to show "what a few brave men, contending in their own land and in the best of causes, can do against base hirelings and mercenaries."[7]

Just in case noble principles didn't work, Washington reiterated that any cowards who fled would be shot. His own jitters became palpable when he promoted Israel Putnam over Sullivan, a panicky rotation of generals that exposed the flimsy command structure of the Continental Army. So murky was the situation that nobody quite knew how many American soldiers were based on Long Island. George Washington, age forty-four, was betraying his inexperience in guiding such a large army.

When a favorable wind arose, Washington imagined that the British would squeeze the Americans with a pincerlike movement, with British soldiers on Long Island swarming up toward Brooklyn Heights while British ships moved en masse toward southern Manhattan. On August 25 he again scrutinized the Long Island troops and was enraged by what he saw—something more like a crazy carnival atmosphere than a tidy military camp. Men roamed around higgledy-piggledy and fired muskets at random. Frustrated, he gave a tongue-lashing to Israel Putnam: "The distinction between a well regulated army and a mob is the good order and discipline of the first, and the licentious and disorderly behavior of the latter."[8] In his writings, Old Put seemed scarcely literate, once telling "his Excelancy ginrol Washenton" that he had asked "each ginrol ofesor [each general officer]" to transmit to him his "opinon in riteng [opinion in writing]."[9] Putnam's shaky command of English highlighted the difficulties Washington encountered in forming a competent officer corps.

On August 26, after visiting the Heights of Guana, Washington still didn't grasp the full scope of the threat. Though he surveyed the British troops through his spyglass and observed a sea of white tents stretching nearly five miles down to Gravesend Bay, he still kept more than half his men in Manhattan. Only when British ships retreated back down the Narrows did the uncomfortable truth dawn on him. As he informed Hancock, the enemy "mean to land the main body of their army on Long Island and to make their grand push there."[10] Incredibly, with the vast British expeditionary force set to pounce, Washington took time out to write to Lund Washington about selling a flour shipment in Hispaniola. He rambled on about chimney repairs and additions to the northern wing of the Mount Vernon mansion. Such incongruous thoughts confirm that Washington found a release from overwhelming pressure by daydreaming about his estate, his battlefield sedative. He confessed to Lund that being the top general was a joyless existence: "If I did not think our struggle just . . . sure I am that no pecuniary satisfaction upon earth can compensate the loss of all my domestic happiness and requite me for the load of business which constantly presses upon and deprives me of every enjoyment."[11]

The British had devised an ingenious battle plan that envisioned a fantastic triple assault against American forces on Long Island. In the first prong, Scottish major general James Grant would lead his Highlanders up the Gowanus Road in a diversionary maneuver along the west coast of Brooklyn. In the second prong, Lieutenant General Leopold Philipp, Freiherr von Heister, would march his Hessians through Flatbush, then swerve northward through central Brooklyn to the Heights of Guana. The pièce de résistance, however, would be the third movement farther east. Generals Howe, Henry Clinton, and Charles Cornwallis would sweep around to the right and make a huge looping movement up through Flatlands. Once past Sullivan's and Stirling's men, they intended to make a bold sweep west along the Jamaica Pass, punching through a flagrant gap in the American defenses—a shocking oversight by Washington and his generals. With these defenses breached, the wide flanking movement would carry them straight to Brooklyn Heights and bring them behind Sullivan's men, catching them in a lethal trap.

During the night of August 26 Washington was shaken from his sleep in Manhattan by news of General Grant's move up the Gowanus Road. This clever British stratagem seemed to confirm Washington's preconception that the enemy would favor this shore road, enabling the Royal Navy to provide cover. When Washington awoke again at sunrise, the British further fed his delusion by sending five warships, assisted by opportune winds and tides, toward the East River. Had the ships reached their destination, it might have been catastrophic for the American army, cutting it in half and threatening Brooklyn Heights from the rear. Luckily, the wind shifted direction, forcing the ships back down the harbor. At that point Washington and Joseph Reed took a small launch across the East River, joining Israel Putnam and four thousand Americans hunkered down inside the fort atop the Brooklyn bluff. Washington ordered more regiments to cross to Long Island as the center of gravity shifted irrevocably from Manhattan.

Riding among his troops, Washington transmitted conflicting messages. In the (possibly romanticized) memories of an old soldier, the commander issued blazing rhetoric: "Quit yourselves like men, like soldiers, for all that is worth living for is at stake!"[12] He mingled this admonition with unalloyed threats: "If I see any man turn his back today, I will shoot him through. I have two pistols loaded. But I will not ask any man to go further than I do. I will fight as long as I have a leg or an arm."[13] Unlike other battles, where Washington rode at the head of his troops, at Brooklyn Heights he hung back in the rear, surveying the fighting to the south through his telescope.

South of Gowanus Creek, the rotund, bibulous Lord Stirling led 1,600 men in fierce combat. With exceptional valor, the American troops fought for four hours until they were overwhelmed by more than 7,000 British and Hessian soldiers. In an unequal contest with a larger enemy force, the First Maryland Regiment under Colonel William Smallwood, experiencing battle for the first time, obstinately refused to surrender a small hill that ensured an escape path for Stirling's men. Though they saved many retreating Americans, their casualties were frightful: of 400 men sent into the fray, only 144 survived. "Good God!" Washington reportedly said, wringing his hands as he watched this action. "What brave fellows I must this day lose!"[14]

General Sullivan dealt with an equally hellish situation as his 3,500 men tried to prevent any British advance beyond the densely wooded Heights of Guana. The Americans were stretched perilously thin along a defensive line that extended for miles. An enormous number of Hessian soldiers suddenly scrambled up the slope toward them. When Sullivan tried to retreat, he discovered that British soldiers had encircled his men amid ferocious blasts of gunfire. Thousands of terrified Americans, lacking bayonets to defend themselves, tried to straggle back toward Brooklyn Heights across a blood-drenched plain. The Hessians, reacting with slashing brutality, bayoneted many men to death and impaled some captives against trees. Of this outright butchery, one British officer commented: "We were greatly shocked by the massacres made by the Hessians and Highlanders after victory was decided."[15] This was the American bloodbath the British had long envisioned, in which colonial yokels were properly vanquished by their betters. Facing an orgy of retribution, American prisoners were turned into slave labor. "As long as we had no horses," said one Hessian, "the prisoners were harnessed in front of the cannon."[16]

The main reason for this slaughter was the success of the eastern flanking movement along the Jamaica Pass. Marching silently by night, Howe, Clinton, and Cornwallis led ten thousand men in a column two miles long through the gaping hole in patriot defenses. So egregious was the security lapse that the British encountered only five mounted militia officers at the pass, allowing them to sneak up behind the unsuspecting Stirling and Sullivan. The American death toll for the Battle of Brooklyn (or Battle of Long Island) was grim: three hundred killed and another thousand taken prisoner, including, temporarily, Generals Stirling and Sullivan. For Washington, it had been an unmitigated disaster. As Douglas Southall Freeman concluded, "The American Commander-in-Chief had appeared to be a tyro, a bungler as well as a beginner, in comparison with the English General."[17] John Adams summed up the case succinctly: "In general, our generals have been out-generalled."[18] During this agonizing day, the commander in chief had been reduced to a helpless spectator of the carnage.

If George Washington stared into the abyss at any single moment of the war, it must have been as he contemplated the vast British force arrayed below him, poised to shatter his army forever. Luckily, General Howe didn't press his advantage and withdrew his men from cannon range, even though his troops scented blood and "it required repeated orders to prevail on them to desist."[19] Howe feared that the casualties would have been too high to justify a charge against the American fortress. As he explained, if the troops had "been permitted to go on, it is my opinion they would have carried the redoubt, but . . . I would not risk the loss that might have been sustained in the assault."[20]

The Howe brothers imagined that they could now deliver the coup de grâce to Washington by slipping warships behind him in the East River, catching him in a vise between royal sailors and soldiers. Once again the weather rescued Washington. On August 28 a chill drizzle descended steadily on Brooklyn, soaking already-soggy ground. Since many American soldiers lacked tents, they had difficulty keeping clothes and munitions dry. The next day grew even darker and wetter as Washington, riding among his men and peering through the mist, saw that British troops had inched forward overnight, digging trenches to within six hundred yards of his outermost position. His army was being slowly, insidiously, trapped by the enemy. He found his men sick, bedraggled, and badly demoralized, "dispirited by their incessant duty and watching."[21] The men assigned to trench duty stood waist-deep in pools of water—a sight that surely reminded Washington of Fort Necessity—and the mood was scarcely relieved by the incessant roar of British cannon pummeling American positions.

From a military standpoint, Washington stood in an untenable position, and not only because ships might entrap him from behind. If Howe now lurched toward a thinly guarded Manhattan, Washington would not be able to save the troops there. He had to do something daring. On August 29, at four P.M., he ordered his generals to attend a war council at a Brooklyn Heights house called Four Chimneys with a superlative vista of New York Harbor. They voted unanimously to take advantage of the lull in fighting to withdraw from Brooklyn to Manhattan. After days of dithering, with his back to the wall, Washington was now crisply decisive. Though one-fourth of his men were sick, he wanted to evacuate the entire American army of 9,500 men across the East River that night, winding up the operation by dawn. He was willing to wager everything on this operation, perhaps because he had no other choice. Leaving nothing to chance, he decided that his troops would be kept ignorant and told only that they were changing positions.

In a prodigious effort, operating on his last reserves of energy, Washington pushed himself past the point of exhaustion and personally led the evacuation. He would later claim that, for forty-eight hours, he scarcely dismounted from his horse or shut his weary eyes. He now trusted his intuitions, as if a powerful survival instinct simplified everything. Earlier in the day he had perpetrated an excellent hoax to prepare for the operation. On the pretense of bringing over fresh troops from New Jersey, he had instructed General Heath to collect boats of every description that he could find. Now, right after dark, the Continental Army lined up to begin its silent retreat across the water. Washington himself, an indomitable presence, presided at the ferry landing. At first the crossing was impeded by rough winds, and only rowboats could be used, their oars covered with cloth to mute sounds. Then winds rose from the southeast, and sailboats could be used as the river turned smooth as glass. In another piece of deceptive theater, Washington kept campfires going in Brooklyn Heights to conceal the evacuation. He maintained such strict secrecy that only general officers knew the scope of the undertaking. Since nobody could speak, the soldiers moved like ghostly sleepwalkers in a pantomime. "We were strictly enjoined not to speak, or even cough," wrote Private Joseph Plumb Martin.[22] Although Washington tried to remove all possible supplies, the wheels of the heaviest cannon got stuck in thick mud, and this ordnance had to be discarded.

Even at its narrowest point (close to the current Brooklyn Bridge), the East River was a mile wide and notorious for treacherous currents. The Continental Army was exceedingly fortunate to enjoy the services of Colonel John Glover, a ship captain from Marblehead, who led a regiment of seamen, including several free blacks, from the Massachusetts fishing ports. A small, brawny man with a broad, square face and wild red hair, Glover had been a fiery political radical. The uniforms his men wore evoked sailors' costumes: blue coats, white caps, and canvas breeches treated to make them waterproof. As they ferried soldiers across the river, these mariners piloted assorted small craft against brisk winds under a moonless sky. Some of them crossed a dozen times that night. The boats, often dangerously overloaded, sat only inches above the waterline. Amazingly enough, as these shadowy shapes glided through the night, the dozing British Army had no idea of this hectic activity.

For George Washington, patrolling the shore on horseback, it was a night of appalling tension. The one real blunder revealed the almost insupportable pressure he endured. He had assigned Colonel Edward Hand to defend the Brooklyn Heights ramparts until the last moment. General Mifflin gave Hand premature orders to come forward with his men to the ferry stop, and Washington was horrified to encounter them on the darkened road. At that moment, when Mifflin galloped up, Washington exploded in wrath. "Good God! General Mifflin, I am afraid you have ruined us!" he hissed in the dark. He labeled Mifflin's order a "dreadful mistake," said there was still "much confusion at the ferry," and told Hand to return at once to the bluff.[23]

As the sun rose on the morning of August 30, some American troops still lingered on the Brooklyn shore, including Washington, who swore he would cross on the last boat. Then with uncanny good fortune, a heavy fog rolled across the Brooklyn shore, screening evacuees from the stirring British. The fog lay so thick that one could "scarcely discern a man at six yards' distance," said Major Benjamin Tallmadge.[24] In this tumultuous final phase, a surplus of desperate men barged onto one boat and wouldn't budge until a furious Washington held aloft a huge stone and threatened to "sink [the boat] to hell" unless the men got out at once.[25] They promptly obeyed. True to his word, Washington boarded the last boat in the nick of time: he could hear the British firing as it pushed into the water. The enemy had awakened, aghast, to discover that more than nine thousand men had traversed the East River. Not a single American died in this virtually flawless operation.

There was no time to exult over this extraordinary feat. Although it was a defensive action, it had saved the American cause in spectacular fashion. The new nation could easily have been buried on that Brooklyn shore. Still, it was impossible to forget that Washington and his generals had bungled the defense of New York by an elementary failure to guard the Jamaica Pass. An exhausted Washington did not inform Congress of what had happened until a day later, after he had gotten some overdue sleep. In writing to Hancock, with becoming modesty, he did not boast about the nocturnal retreat from Long Island, but neither did he accept blame for the lost battle. Riding his favorite hobbyhorse, he blamed the absence of a professional army and argued that nobody could have predicted where the British would come ashore, forcing him to defend a vast expanse. He was especially eager to lambast the militia, saying they were deserting in droves; whole regiments had scampered away in fear. Fortunately for Washington, General Howe did not pursue his men right away and sent another peace overture to Congress on September 2, when he paroled General Sullivan as a prisoner of war. Washington scoffed at this diplomatic offering, noting caustically that "Lord Howe had nothing more to propose than that, if we would submit, His Majesty would consider whether we should be hung or not."[26]

Manhattan patriots were shocked at the pitiable state of the soldiers who washed up on their shores, as a defeatist mood enveloped the city. The Reverend Ewald Shewkirk wrote that "the sight of the scattered people up and down the streets was indeed moving. Many looked sickly, emaciated, cast down etc.; the wet clothes, tents . . . were lying about before the houses and in the streets to dry. In general, everything seemed to be in confusion."[27] Only two-thirds of the soldiers could take shelter in tents. In despair, some looted homes and even pillaged the mansion of Lord Stirling. Washington was so upset by this "plundering, marauding, and burning of houses" that he carried out a parade ground search of knapsacks.[28] Trying to calm his men, he rode along the East River and inspected his troops in full view of the enemy. The Hessian major Carl Leopold Baurmeister said that a Captain Krug of the artillery fired two shots at Washington and his retinue, "and he would have fired a third if their horses had not kept moving."[29] As in the French and Indian War, Washington seemed blessed with a supernatural immunity to bullets.

Later on Washington asserted that he had recommended burning New York; that he feared it would furnish the British with "warm and comfortable barracks" and would be a perfect haven for the Royal Navy; and that Congress had overruled him in a "capital error."[30] In fact, at Brooklyn Heights Washington assured the New York Provincial Congress that he did not intend to torch the town and deprive "many worthy citizens and their families" of their homes and businesses.[31] When he raised the issue in a letter to Hancock on September 2, he did so in a neutral manner; the next day Hancock conveyed the congressional verdict that "no damage should be done to the City of New York."[32] Unaware of how entrenched the British would soon become, the self-styled experts in Congress insisted that they had "no doubt of being able to recover" the city.[33]

At this point Nathanael Greene, having returned to service, urged Washington to burn and abandon a city teeming with Tories. The British, he feared, could isolate American troops in southern Manhattan as they had so effectively done in Brooklyn Heights. At a September 7 war council, Washington sided with a majority of generals who wanted to hold the town, lest its loss "dispirit the troops and enfeeble our cause."[34] The next day a chastened Washington informed Hancock of a compromise decision to keep five thousand men in the city, while removing the rest to points north on the island. The tone of this letter was diametrically opposed to the cocksure attitude Washington had exhibited after the Boston siege. Humbled by experience, Washington said that he and his generals had resolved to wage a defensive war, a policy from which he would only periodically deviate. "It has been even called a war of posts, that we should on all occasions avoid a general action or put anything to the risk unless compelled by a necessity into which we ought never to be drawn."[35] Never again, he swore, would he send young troops into "open ground against their superiors both in number and discipline."[36] This strategy was neither glamorous nor particularly congenial to Washington's personality, but it might prove sure and effective.[37] That Washington was able to adjust his strategic doctrine again showed his capacity for growth and his realistic nature.

On September 12, alarmed by British actions in the Harlem River, another war council revoked the earlier decision to defend New York. Two days later Washington transferred his headquarters to a graceful Palladian mansion set on a hilltop in the northern terrain of Harlem Heights. It was owned by Roger Morris, who had been Washington's successful rival for the hand of Mary "Polly" Philipse. Because many men remained behind, the British didn't realize that the Americans were relinquishing the city. While Putnam supervised American troops in lower Manhattan, some militiamen manned makeshift defenses in the center of the island. One of them, Joseph Plumb Martin, stationed at the cove of Kip's Bay on the East River (the East Thirties in modern-day Manhattan), ridiculed their defensive lines as "nothing more than a ditch dug along the bank of the river, with the dirt thrown out towards the water."[38] For some soldiers, their only weapons consisted of sharpened scythes fastened to poles, forming primitive spears.

During the night of September 14–15, five British ships dropped anchor in Kip's Bay, soon accompanied by eighty-four barges that had been secreted in Newtown Creek on Long Island, with four thousand British and Hessian troops on board. At eleven A.M. the warships' big guns swiveled toward Manhattan and began to thunder with a horrendous, sustained racket, blowing the American breastworks to smithereens. "So terrible and so incessant a roar of guns few even in the army and navy had ever heard before," wrote Ambrose Serle.[39] For the few hundred American hayseeds cowering onshore, the cannonade, lasting an hour, provoked a terrified flight. "I made a frog's leap for the ditch," wrote Joseph Plumb Martin, "and lay as still as I possibly could and began to consider which part of my carcass was to go first."[40]

Once the American defenses were demolished, British and Hessian troops waded ashore in neat rows, their bayonets flashing. As in the Battle of Brooklyn, the Hessians took no prisoners and oversaw mass executions, shooting in the head dozens of young Americans who tried to surrender; one Hessian decapitated an American prisoner and posted his head on a pike. These atrocities spread contagious fear among the American troops, but officers lost their nerve as well, abandoning their men. Joseph Plumb Martin bluntly parceled out blame: "I do not recollect of seeing a commissioned officer from the time I left the lines on the banks of the East River in the morning until I met . . . one in the evening."[41]

Four miles north, in the Dutch village of Harlem, George Washington heard "a most severe and heavy cannonade" and saw puffs of smoke rising from Kip's Bay. He traveled south as fast as he could. As usual, he plunged into the thick of the action, heedless of his own safety. Coming to a cornfield on Murray Hill, a half mile from Kip's Bay, he was shocked to encounter troops "retreating with the utmost precipitation and . . . flying in every direction and in the greatest confusion."[42] Faced with collapsed discipline, Washington flew into a rage. He was momentarily relieved by the appearance of Massachusetts militia and Connecticut Continentals and hollered at them to "take the wall" or "take the cornfield," motioning toward various spots. Then as sixty or seventy British grenadiers came up the hill, these terrified men also succumbed to panic and ran in confusion, dumping muskets, powder horns, tents, and knapsacks without firing a shot. William Smallwood claimed that Washington, Putnam, and Mifflin, appalled by the disorder, resorted to whipping fleeing men with their riding crops. Dr. James Thacher said that Washington "drew his sword and snapped his pistols" to check his men but still couldn't bring them to stand and shoot.[43] Washington's letters to John Hancock had hinted at mounting exasperation with his men, but now his frustration burst into the open. The man of consummate self-control surrendered to his emotions. Fuming, he flung his hat to the ground and shouted, "Are these the men with which I am to defend America?"[44] According to another account, he swore, "Good God! Have I got such troops as these?"[45] This display of Washington's wrath still could not stem the panic. As he told Hancock, "I used every means in my power to rally and get them into some order, but my attempts were fruitless and ineffectual."[46]

Colonel George Weedon says that Washington grew so distraught that "he struck several officers in their flight."[47] It is extraordinary to think of Washington flogging officers amid a battle—a measure of his impotent frustration and shattered nerves. Finally he was stranded alone on the battlefield with his aides, his troops having fled in fright. Most astonishingly, Washington on horseback stared frozen as fifty British soldiers started to dash toward him from eighty yards away. Seeing his strangely catatonic state, his aides rode up beside him, grabbed the reins of his horse, and hustled him out of danger. In this bizarre conduct, Nathanael Greene saw a suicidal impulse, contending that Washington was "so vexed at the infamous conduct of his troops that he sought death rather than life."[48] Weedon added the compelling detail that only with difficulty did Washington's colleagues "get him to quit the field, so great was his emotions."[49] It was a moment unlike any other in Washington's career, a fleeting emotional breakdown amid battle.

Once again General Howe tardily pursued the Americans, enabling Washington to evacuate almost all of his men safely to Harlem Heights. Nonetheless Howe had bagged a great prize, a city that would serve as a perfect British headquarters for the duration of the war. For all his valor, Washington had again been caught off guard and he smarted from the bitter defeat. He would spend the rest of the war trying to avenge the loss of New York and dreaming of its recapture. Moreover, the day had provided fresh proof of how skittish his men were, officers and infantry alike.

The next day Washington's spirits were lifted by a skirmish in the Harlem woods as a corps of rangers under Lieutenant Colonel Thomas Knowlton probed British positions. At one point, as these rangers retreated, the British soldiers taunted them, blowing a bugle with a sound used in foxhunting to signify the end of the chase. "I never felt such a sensation before," wrote Joseph Reed. "It seemed to crown our disgrace."[50] It was a clever, if cruel, way to jangle the nerves of the squire of Mount Vernon. Reed, who could be unfairly critical of Washington, claimed that the commander was still sunk in a terrible funk from the day before, his will paralyzed, and had to be "prevailed upon" to capitalize upon the situation.[51] In fact, Washington reacted to the British provocation with fighting spirit. His honor insulted, he sent into the fray Virginia riflemen and Knowlton's rangers, 1,800 men in all, who chased the British troops from the field in what became known as the Battle of Harlem Heights.

Although both sides counted about 150 casualties, Washington scored a small but timely victory that buoyed his downtrodden men, and his aide Tench Tilghman said that the American troops "gave a hurra[h] and left the field in good order."[52]

While congratulating his revived troops, Washington couldn't resist taking a swipe at their less glorious conduct at Kip's Bay: "The behavior of yesterday was such a contrast to that of some troops the day before as must show what may be done where officers and soldiers will exert themselves."[53] It was his way of stressing courage in warfare. Washington oscillated between severity and mercy toward his men. When a Connecticut soldier, Ebenezer Leffingwell, was found guilty of cowardice at Harlem Heights—he had fled and tried to shoot Joseph Reed, who tried to restrain him—Washington allowed the execution to proceed almost to the final moment. Leffingwell was already on his knees, waiting to die, when Washington decided that his army had gotten the message and pardoned him. Lest anyone misunderstand, Washington reiterated that soldiers who fled in battle "shall be instantly shot down, and all good officers are hereby authorized and required to see this done."[54] Dismayed by his officers' behavior, Washington scouted for new talent and was impressed by the proficiency of a young artillery captain named Alexander Hamilton as the latter superintended earthworks construction at Harlem Heights. Washington "entered into conversation with him, invited him to his tent, and received an impression of his military talent," wrote Hamilton's son.[55]

On the windy night of September 20, a mysterious fire started around midnight at the southern tip of Manhattan and burned until dawn, consuming most of the town between Broadway and the Hudson River. Trinity Church caught fire and collapsed in a thunderous crash. St. Paul's Chapel was spared only by the timely action of brave citizens on the roof, who smothered glowing embers blown there. Even at Harlem Heights, more than ten miles away, Washington saw the billowing smoke and huge showers of sparks, which surrounded the city with a luminous glow. "Providence, or some good honest fellow, has done more for us than we were disposed to do for ourselves," he responded.[56] The raging conflagration created pandemonium in the city. "The shrieks and cries of the women and children . . . made this one of the most tremendous and affecting scenes I ever beheld," said an eyewitness.[57] By the next morning the fire had destroyed five hundred houses, a good quarter of the town. In relating this incident to Lord Germain, William Tryon noted that no fire bells rang that night and that "many circumstances lead to conjecture that Mr. Washington was privy to this villainous act as he sent all the bells of the churches out of town under pretense of casting them into cannon."[58] The British never found convincing proof to corroborate their suspicion of patriotic involvement. However, they detained more than a hundred suspects, including Nathan Hale, who was hanged as a spy the next day.

On a sleepless night after the Battle of Harlem Heights, Washington renewed his pleas to John Hancock for long-term enlistments, saying that the unceasing turnover of men, reliance on unseasoned militia, and lack of discipline kept his mind "constantly upon the stretch."[59] Without decent pay for officers and men alike, nothing could be accomplished. Everything remained in scandalously short supply—tents, kettles, blankets, clothing. When visited by a congressional delegation, Washington snapped that he "never had officers, except in a few instances, worth the bread they eat."[60] No less than Washington, Henry Knox believed that only a standing army could defeat the British and that the current army had become "a receptacle for ragamuffins."[61] Prodded by Washington, Congress agreed to give twenty dollars and one hundred acres of land to anyone who signed up for the duration of the war. For Washington, the benefit was partly nullified by a decision to continue to allow state politicians to appoint officers for their own regiments, wresting power from his hands and making officers of men "not fit to be shoeblacks."[62]

As September ended, George Washington—stubborn, angry, indignant, and sleep deprived—was steeped in misery. His worst nightmare had materialized: he was doomed to fail because he hadn't been given adequate means to succeed. He needed a confidant, and Lund Washington remained the recipient of choice for his jeremiads: "In short, such is my situation, that if I were to wish the bitterest curse to an enemy on this side of the grave, I should put him in my stead with my feelings . . . In confidence I tell you that I never was in such an unhappy, divided state since I was born."[63] Mount Vernon again offered sustenance for his weary mind, and he pictured the new room under construction there. "The chimney in the new room should be exactly in the middle of it, the doors and everything else to be exactly answerable and uniform," he advised Lund. "In short, I would have the whole executed in a masterly manner."[64]

CHAPTER TWENTY-TWO

An Indecisive Mind

On the morning of October 12 General Howe applied renewed pressure on the Continental Army as 150 British ships sailed up the East River, slipping through pea-soup fog, and deposited four thousand men on the boggy turf of Throg's Neck, a peninsula on the Westchester shore. This marshy spot lay due east of Harlem Heights, and Washington again brooded that the wily British might entrap his embattled army as part of "their former scheme of getting to our rear."[1] While the intervening ground had numerous stone fences to deflect British advances, Washington couldn't take any chances. In this dismal season of defeats, he marched his endangered men eighteen miles north to the village of White Plains. He would long recall the hardships suffered by sick soldiers forced to limp along or be carried, so critical was the wagon shortage. The least fortunate were discharged as unfit for service and left behind as common vagrants to beg by the wayside on the road home. The plight of these pauperized soldiers, marooned on country lanes, only compounded the difficulties of recruitment.

On this northward march, the battle-weary soldiers found comfort in gallows humor. Joseph Plumb Martin told of a sojourn on Valentine's Hill, "where we continued some days, keeping up the old system of starving." When the soldiers resumed their march toward White Plains, they left behind a weighty iron kettle. "I told my messmates that I *could not* carry our kettle any further. They said they *would* not carry it any further. Of what use was it? They had nothing to cook and did not want anything to cook with."[2] Behind the macabre humor lay the somber reality of starving men having to swipe food from farmers' fields to survive. Deprived of tents and blankets, soldiers burrowed beneath heaps of autumn leaves to stay warm on cool nights.

Around this time, Washington welcomed back General Charles Lee, who had acquired something of a halo after defeating a British expedition to South Carolina. Lee had prevailed upon Congress to compensate him for time lost to civilian pursuits, awarding him $30,000. In private, Lee repaid their generosity by reviling them as "cattle" and urging Washington to flout their orders.[3] Lee's popularity in Congress only stoked his vanity and encouraged the delusion that he was being groomed as Washington's successor. Blind to this conceited rival, Washington renamed one of the twin forts on the Hudson—the one on the Jersey shore, opposite Fort Washington—Fort Lee.

Once at White Plains, the Continental Army found shelter on elevated ground above the Bronx River. The best it could manage for breastworks was to uproot cornstalks from local fields, then pile them high with freshly turned earth stuffed in between. On the morning of October 28 Washington surveyed Chatterton's Hill, a steeply wooded bluff, threaded by streams and ravines that tumbled down to the river below. Belatedly recognizing its strategic importance, Washington decided to fortify it. While he was on this plateau, a breathless messenger raced up to him. "The British are on the camp, sir!" he reported to Washington, who at once told his generals, "Gentlemen, we have now other business than reconnoitering."[4] He assigned sixteen hundred men under General Alexander McDougall, entrenched behind stone walls, to hold the hill.

The Americans soon faced thirteen thousand British and Hessian soldiers who must have looked brilliantly invincible in autumn sunlight as they stepped forward in smart columns. As General Heath recalled, "The sun shone bright, their arms glittered, and perhaps troops never were shown to more advantage." Amid this impressive display of force, British artillery fire began to darken the fine, crisp air. In the evocative words of a Pennsylvania soldier: "The air groaned with streams of cannon and musket shot; the hills smoked and echoed terribly with the bursting of shells; the fences and walls were knocked down and torn to pieces, and men's legs, arms, and bodies mangled with cannon and grape shot all around us."[5]

The bloodiest combat unfolded at Chatterton's Hill. In the first wave of attacks, Captain Alexander Hamilton, positioned with two fieldpieces on a rocky ledge, sprayed the invading forces with deadly fire, driving them back. After regrouping, the British grenadiers and Hessian soldiers forded the Bronx River and bravely clambered up the wooded slope under a thick hail of bullets. Their artillery set fire to autumn leaves, creating a thick canopy of smoke. As they rushed through burning grass, the Hessians hoisted their cartridge boxes above their heads so as not to blow themselves up. In the end, enemy soldiers succeeded in dislodging the American forces as the militia lost heart and ran. Their fright was understandable as cannonballs flew thick and fast. One Connecticut soldier recalled how a cannonball "first took the head of Smith, a stout heavy man and dash[e]d it open, then it took off Chilson's arm, which was amputated . . . it then took Taylor across the bowels, it then struck Serg[ean]t Garret of our company on the hip [and] took off the point of the hip bone . . . What a sight that was to see within a distance of six rods those men with their legs and arms and guns and packs all in a heap."[6]

For all that, the British and the Hessians suffered 276 casualties, or twice as many as the Americans. Once again General Howe dawdled after victory and bungled a major opportunity. In later testimony before Parliament, he traced his sluggish behavior to an aversion to unnecessary combat losses but also cited unnamed "political reasons"—perhaps his preference for a negotiated solution rather than outright conquest of the Continental Army.

Both sides continued to place a premium on commanding the Hudson River. The twin American outposts of Fort Washington and Fort Lee, combined with obstructions sunk in the river, were supposed to bar British ships. This assumption represented a triumph of hope over experience. On October 9, with Washington on hand to witness it, the British tested American defenses by sending three warships up the river. While American guns blasted away from both shores, killing nine British sailors, the ships coasted by largely intact, their movement unimpeded by submarine obstacles and a boom flung across the river. "To our surprise and mortification," Washington told Hancock, the ships passed "without receiving any apparent damage from our forts, though they kept up a heavy fire from both sides."[7] Nonetheless Congress refused to end reliance on this porous barrier and demanded that the river defenses be reinforced.

Of the two Hudson River stockades, Fort Washington was the more impressive, a huge pentagonal earthwork straddling the highest spot on Manhattan Island. Its defenses meandered across a rocky bluff stretching from present-day 181st to 186th streets. The fort had several significant defects. Without an internal water source, it had to rely on the Hudson River hundreds of feet below. Built on solid rock, it scarcely possessed any topsoil from which to dig trenches, and it lacked such rudimentary amenities as a powder magazine, palisades, or barracks. Its guns, permanently trained on the Hudson River, couldn't pivot to deal with land-based threats. Worst of all, it held only twelve hundred men and could not shelter the three thousand patriot soldiers who might need to seek asylum there. Most soldiers had to be posted outside the defensive perimeter, defeating the very idea of a fortress.

On November 5 three British ships again mocked the defenses of the two Hudson forts, passing by unharmed. Three days later Washington wrote to Nathanael Greene, who was in charge of the forts, and questioned the wisdom of retaining Fort Washington: "If we cannot prevent vessels passing up . . . what valuable purpose can it answer to attempt to hold a post from which the expected benefit cannot be had? I am therefore inclined to think it will not be prudent to hazard the men and stores at Mount Washington, but, as you are on the spot, leave it to you to give such orders as to evacuating Mount Washington as you judge best."[8] The letter bespoke tremendous confidence in Greene, at a time when a skeptical Washington should have been more autocratic; he should never have delegated such a crucial decision to an inexperienced general. One suspects that, in losing New York City, his self-confidence had suffered serious damage and that he had temporarily lost the internal fortitude to obey his instincts.

Oblivious to imminent danger, Greene regarded Fort Washington as an impregnable stronghold and thought it would be bloody folly for the British to attempt to take it. Should the worst happen, he reasoned, he could easily transfer troops to Fort Lee. Misled by these baseless assumptions, he ignored Washington's advice to empty Fort Washington of its rich store of supplies. Unknown to American commanders, a deserter named William Demont had defected to the British on November 2 and not only delivered a blueprint of Fort Washington but reported "great dissensions" and low morale in the rebel army.[9]

Washington worried that his army might simply melt into nothingness. The men were shivering with cold, ravenous for food, and prey to one malady after another. With many enlistments set to expire in late November, Washington forbade officers from "discharging any officer or soldier or giving any permission to leave the camp on any pretense whatsoever," as if he wanted to bolt his troops in place.[10] So many soldiers were giving up that one Washington aide described the roads as thick with ragged men "returning to their homes in the most scandalous and infamous manner."[11] While wishful thinkers in the Continental Army thought Howe might retreat into winter quarters in New York, Washington knew he might besiege Fort Washington. More likely, he believed Howe would race across New Jersey and try to pounce on Philadelphia. From his letters, it is clear that Washington was preoccupied with this imagined British threat, reflected in the fact that he himself took command of two thousand men in New Jersey. He left Greene in charge of Forts Washington and Lee; had General William Heath guard the Hudson Highlands with several thousand men; and assigned Charles Lee to protect the approach to New England with seven thousand men.

On the evening of November 13 Washington held a rendezvous with General Greene at his Fort Lee headquarters. Far from taking Washington's hint to downgrade Fort Washington, Greene had pursued the opposite tack, pouring in more troops and supplies. A chorus of staff officers, led by Joseph Reed, pleaded with Washington to countermand these orders. Reed left a striking image of a befuddled Washington who "hesitated more than I ever knew him on any other occasion and more than I thought the public service permitted."[12] In hindsight, Washington admitted to a secret "warfare in my mind" that led him to bow to Greene's faulty judgment, even though it was "repugnant to my own judgment."[13] He continued to misread signs of a British buildup aimed at Fort Washington, telling Hancock that "it seems to be generally believed on all hands that the investing [i.e., siege] of Fort Washington is one object" the British have in view. "But that can employ but a small part of their force."[14]

That General William Howe had unfinished business in New York grew plain on November 15 when he sent his trusted aide Colonel James Paterson to hand an ultimatum to Colonel Robert Magaw, the superior officer at Fort Washington. The British offered a frightening choice: either relinquish the fort within two hours or brace for its destruction. Washington had underestimated the British forces that would be mobilized to this task: Howe dedicated thirteen thousand men to the operation. With three thousand men at his command, the unbending Magaw vowed that he was "determined to defend this post to the very last extremity."[15] This wasn't the war's last instance of misplaced bravado. Washington learned of this ultimatum while in Hackensack, New Jersey, and he instantly spurred his horse to Fort Lee, arriving at sundown. Nathanael Greene and Israel Putnam had crossed to Fort Washington, and Washington jumped into a boat to follow them. He encountered them in the darkness in midstream, as they were being rowed back to the Jersey shore. Messrs. Greene and Putnam reassured an agitated Washington that the men at Fort Washington were "in high spirits and would make a good defense."[16] The three men then spent the night at Fort Lee.

The next morning refuted the generals' soothing words. Along with Greene, Putnam, and Brigadier General Hugh Mercer, Washington was boarding a rowboat to go to Fort Washington when they heard an uproar on the far bank: the British had launched a many-sided assault against the fort, the cannon thunder amplified by the rocky cliffs of the Hudson. Notwithstanding the danger, Washington and his generals sped across the river, landed on the opposite shore, and mounted to Harlem Heights, downriver from the besieged fort. They proceeded to the Roger Morris house, a mile south of Fort Washington, whose elevation enabled them to survey patriot defenses. There they stood, said Greene, "in a very awkward situation," watching the enemy advance, but they "saw nothing amiss" and derived a false sense of comfort.[17] American shells pulverized the Hessian lines, littering the battlefield with hundreds of enemy casualties. As one Hessian recalled: "They lay battered and in part shattered; dead on the earth in their own blood; some whimpering, looked at us, pleading that . . . we would ease their suffering and unbearable pain."[18] It attested to Washington's dauntless courage that he wished to stay with his exposed men, but his companions convinced him that he stood in extreme danger. After insisting that the three generals accompany him, Washington was rowed back across the Hudson out of harm's way. He made a hairbreadth escape: the British arrived at the Roger Morris house a scant fifteen minutes later.

From the rocky terrain of Fort Lee, Washington watched the disaster unfolding across the water. General Howe unleashed the full terror of his arsenal on Fort Washington, and by one P.M. almost all of the terrified American soldiers were squeezed inside the cramped fortress, now turned into a veritable death trap. The enemy then went on a rampage, bayoneting to death any American troops they could capture. As he stood high on the Jersey Palisades and watched through his telescope, George Washington gave way to strong emotions. As Washington Irving, who claimed to have heard the story from eyewitnesses, later wrote, the defeat "was said so completely to have overcome him that he wept with the tenderness of a child."[19]

An hour later the Hessian general, Baron Wilhelm von Knyphausen, called for the surrender of the doomed fort. By four P.M., 2,837 soldiers, including 230 officers, emptied out and marched down a gauntlet of Hessian soldiers, who kicked and punched them. Even some of the victors found the procession of shabby, unkempt men a heartrending sight. "A great many of them were lads under fifteen and old men, and few had the appearance of soldiers," wrote Lieutenant Frederick Mackenzie, who said that many colleagues guffawed at this sad mimicry of a professional army.[20] The American captives were dispatched to the grisly confinement of British prison ships in New York Harbor.

There was no way of putting a face-saving construction on this searing loss: it was a defeat without redeeming features. As David McCullough has summarized the debacle, "In a disastrous campaign for New York in which Washington's army had suffered one humiliating, costly reverse after another, this, the surrender of Fort Washington on Saturday, November 16, was the most devastating blow of all, an utter catastrophe."[21] The outcome could only have deepened Washington's nightmarish sense of helplessness. Just as he fretted about expiring enlistments, he had losses of almost three thousand men killed or captured. At the same time, a huge cache of valuable muskets and cannon had fallen into British hands.

The demise of Fort Washington could have scuttled the career of the distraught Nathanael Greene. As he told Knox the next day, "Never did I need the consoling voice of a friend more than now . . . This is a most terrible event; its consequences are justly to be dreaded."[22] It is a remarkable commentary on Washington's admiration for him that he didn't scapegoat Greene or drum him out of the ranks. Washington was honest enough to point out that his advice to Greene to evacuate the fort had been "discretionary" and took a portion of the blame on himself.[23] On the other hand, he had granted this discretion because Greene was on the scene and presumably better placed to form a judgment. Washington couldn't account for his own failure to reverse Greene's decision once he had reviewed the situation firsthand. Drawing on a thin pool of talented officers, Washington was forced by circumstance to tolerate a high rate of failure among his generals. A master politician in the making, he had a knack for spotting and rewarding faithful subordinates who repaid his trust with absolute devotion. He seemed to know implicitly that no loyalty surpassed that of a man forgiven for his faults who vowed never to make them again.

By contrast, General Charles Lee tried to capitalize upon Washington's tremendous stumble at Fort Washington. He claimed that, enraged upon hearing the news, he tore out a patch of his hair. "The ingenious maneuver of Fort Washington has unhinged the goodly fabric we have been building," he wrote to General Horatio Gates. "There never was so damned a stroke. *Entre nous,* a certain great man is damnably deficient."[24] He tried to undermine Washington further by informing Congressman Benjamin Rush that "I foresaw, predicted, all that has happened . . . had I the powers I could do you much good . . . but I am sure you will never give any man the necessary powers."[25] To Washington himself, Lee wrote more tactfully. "Oh, General, why would you be over-persuaded by men of inferior judgment to your own?"[26]

Even more bad news hung in the offing. On the morning of November 20 word reached Washington in Hackensack that thousands of enemy soldiers, camouflaged by a dark, rainy night, had crossed the Hudson River in a daring raid, landing six miles above Fort Lee. They had nimbly scaled the Palisades, a solid wall of rock and dense greenery, and now marched toward Fort Lee in great numbers. After the fall of Fort Washington, Fort Lee had shed its strategic importance, since it was impossible to thwart British ships from only one side of the Hudson. Having seen the importance of reacting quickly to threats, Washington raced on horseback to Fort Lee, covering six miles in forty-five minutes. Once at the fort, he ordered an immediate evacuation of its two thousand men, sacrificing the bulk of supplies on hand—two hundred cannon, hundreds of tents, and thousands of barrels of flour. The retreating Americans made it across the single bridge spanning the Hackensack River before it could be sabotaged by the enemy. The British cavalry under Charles Cornwallis chose not to chase them. General Howe again wanted to intimidate the rebels rather than to destroy them, and he overrode the judgment of Henry Clinton, who wanted to outflank the insurgents and smother them for good. The Crown seemed to side with Howe, decorating him as a Knight of the Bath, and henceforth he was called Sir William Howe.

For Washington, it came as yet another in a never-ending series of setbacks, a cascading series of colossal defeats. Finding it hard to resist total despair, he wrote, "I am wearied almost to death with the retrograde motion of things."[27] Yet despite the calamities at Forts Washington and Lee, the British had done Washington an inadvertent favor. They had shown him the futility of trying to defend heavily fortified positions along the seaboard and forced him out into the countryside, where he had mobility and where the British Army, deprived of the Royal Navy, operated at a disadvantage. For political reasons, Washington hadn't been able to countermand the congressional decision to defend New York City and the Hudson River, but now that he had done so and suffered predictable defeats, he would have more freedom to pick and choose his targets. With his drastically diminished army and depleted supplies, it was no longer a question of standing and confronting the British with their vastly superior troops and firepower.

WASHINGTON AND HIS BEDRAGGLED TROOPS began a dreary retreat across the flat, open terrain of New Jersey, their recent humiliation fresh in their memories. The British gloated over their string of stunning victories, the young Lord Rawdon boasting that the American army "is broken all to pieces, and the spirit of their leaders . . . is also broken." His smug verdict: "It is well nigh over with them."[28] The retreating army wore a defeated look as they shuffled slowly through villages. "They marched two abreast," said one inhabitant, "looked ragged, some without a shoe to their feet, and most of them wrapped in their blankets."[29] Washington's sole concern was saving his army. He knew that his men were "very much broken and dispirited," and with many enlistments ending December 1, he anticipated a catastrophic erosion of soldiers.[30] On that date, as Washington feared, 2,000 militia from New Jersey and Maryland drifted away, leaving him with only about 3,800 men in a state crawling with Tories. Around the same time Lord Howe issued a proclamation offering pardons to those who swore allegiance to the king, and thousands of discouraged Americans took up the offer.

During the retreat Washington rode in the perilous rear position, supervising the destruction of bridges to stall the enemy. "I saw him . . . at the head of a small band, or rather in its rear, for he was always near the enemy, and his countenance and manner made an impression on me which I can never efface," wrote James Monroe, then an eighteen-year-old lieutenant. "A deportment so firm, so dignified, but yet so modest and composed, I have never seen in any other person."[31] Thomas Paine also praised the New Jersey retreat as one of Washington's finest hours of quiet courage. "There is a natural firmness in some minds which cannot be unlocked by trifles, but which, when unlocked, discovers a cabinet of fortitude," he wrote, saying that God had endowed Washington "with uninterrupted health and given him a mind that can even flourish upon care."[32] One of the few bright spots occurred at the Raritan River near New Brunswick. On the afternoon of December 1, British soldiers appeared and threatened to cut off American troops as they crossed the river. Once again Captain Alexander Hamilton and his artillery company provided steady cover to the retreating men, while an admiring Washington observed his future aide and treasury secretary from the riverbank.

Washington's career had few moments of misplaced trust, but one occurred during this lonely, vulnerable time. He had confided to Joseph Reed that he needed someone with whom he could "live in unbounded confidence" and Reed himself had appeared to be that privileged person.[33] In June Reed was named adjutant general in order to retain him in Washington's service. Unfortunately, Reed harbored growing doubts about Washington's ability—doubts only strengthened by his boss's failure to override Nathanael Greene at Fort Washington. Reed decided to voice those doubts to Charles Lee, a man of atrocious judgment who was never circumspect in covering his tracks.

On November 21 Washington sent an urgent, confidential letter to Lee, exhorting him to bring his brigades from New York to help defend New Jersey, a task beyond the scanty powers of his own shrinking force. He was particularly worried that Howe might try to grab Philadelphia. In sending this letter, Joseph Reed had the temerity to slip into the dispatch satchel a secret note of his own to Lee. This blunt message suggested that Washington's personal staff had lost faith in him and viewed him as a vacillating leader. "I do not mean to flatter nor praise you at the expense of any other," wrote Reed, "but I confess I do think that it is entirely owing to you that this army and the liberties of America . . . are not totally cut off." He then delivered a damaging assessment of Washington: "Oh! General—an indecisive mind is one of the greatest misfortunes that can befall an army." In an act of outright treachery against Washington, Reed suggested to Lee that "as soon as the season will admit, I think yourself and some others should go to Congress and form the plan of the new army."[34]

At the end of November, Washington was busily at work in New Brunswick when he tore open a sealed letter that Charles Lee had sent to Reed, who was then conferring in Burlington with Governor William Livingston of New Jersey. The letter shocked him on two accounts. The impertinent Lee revealed that he was disobeying Washington's order to bring his army to New Jersey and instead was sending two thousand men assigned to General Heath, then protecting the Hudson Highlands. In one line Lee echoed Reed's secret letter, stating that he agreed with Reed about "that fatal indecision of mind which in war is a much greater disqualification than stupidity or even want of personal courage; accident may put a decisive blunder in the right, but eternal defeat and miscarriage must attend the man of the best parts if cursed with indecision."[35] Washington realized that Lee was quoting Reed.

On November 30 Washington, deeply injured, penned a note to Joseph Reed that was a masterpiece of subtle accusation. He included a copy of Lee's letter and wrote:

> Dear Sir: The enclosed was put into my hands by an express from the White Plains. Having no idea of its being a private letter, much less suspecting the tendency of the correspondence, I opened it, as I had done all other letters to you . . . upon the business of your office . . . This, as it is the truth, must be my excuse for seeing the contents of a letter which neither inclination *or* intention would have prompted me to. I thank you for the trouble and fatigue you have undergone in your journey to Burlington and sincerely wish that your labors may be crowned with the desired success. My best respects to Mrs. Reed.[36]

Washington knew perfectly how to wield silence as a weapon. The letter was conspicuous for what it omitted, not for what it said, allowing Reed to imagine Washington's wrath rather than experience it, leaving him in a torment of uncertainty. The refusal to berate Reed only shamed him more. By not fulminating against Reed, Washington concealed what he knew about his machinations with Lee, a cunning device he employed many times in his career. And his response showed how highly he regarded the gentlemanly code of honor. Before anything else, he wanted to account for having opened and read the letter, lest it seem a wanton violation of privacy. It was a mark of Washington's psychological subtlety that he sent a note of apology to a man who owed *him* an apology. Finally, by alluding to Reed's taxing journey and sending regards to Mrs. Reed, Washington stressed that he wouldn't stoop to anger in the face of provocation.

Upon receiving the letter, Reed tendered his resignation to Congress, but Washington got him to revoke it. Washington did not ask for a direct response to his letter; nor did he request a talk. Instead he resumed a civil, if guarded, relationship with Reed. The two exchanged many letters without referring to the episode, as Washington waited for the younger man to broach the subject. On March 8, 1777, Reed finally referred to the incident and told Washington that he had tried futilely to retrieve his original letter to Charles Lee. Disingenuously, he said there was nothing in the letter "inconsistent with that respect and affection which I have and ever shall bear to your person and character."[37] Reed made further efforts to repair the relationship, but Washington didn't bury the hatchet until June 11, 1777, when he sent Reed a conciliatory letter. He wasn't a man who rushed to forgive, but he didn't hold grudges either. He told Reed that it wasn't the criticism of his behavior that had stung him so much as the devious method: "True it is I felt myself hurt by a certain letter, which appear[e]d at that time to be the echo of one from you . . . I was hurt, not because I thought my judgment wrong[e]d by the expressions contained in it, but because the same sentiments were not communicated immediately to myself." Washington signed the letter "Your obedient and affectionate" George Washington.[38]

Washington never revealed to Lee his knowledge of the secret correspondence, and Lee's behavior toward Washington grew ever more imperious. Headquartered in Peekskill, New York, he admitted to Washington in late November that he had ignored his orders to proceed to New Jersey: "I cou[l]d wish you wou[l]d bind me as little as possible . . . from a persuasion that detach[e]d generals cannot have too great latitude."[39] Instead of sternly reprimanding Lee, Washington entreated him to bring his five thousand men to New Jersey, but Lee kept ignoring his requests in an infuriatingly cavalier manner. Washington at last had no choice but to lead his dwindling army across the Delaware River into Pennsylvania. He also began a low-key campaign to discredit Lee in the eyes of Congress—his political style always hinged on fine gradations—telling John Hancock in early December, "I have not heard a word from General Lee since the 26th last month, which surprises me not a little, as I have dispatched daily expresses to him desiring to know when I might look for him."[40] At last Lee and his men crossed the Hudson and began moving south through New Jersey, albeit at a glacial speed.

On the morning of December 13, General Charles Lee received a well-merited rebuke to his overweening vanity. He had spent the night at an inn near Basking Ridge, New Jersey, enjoying the company of a woman of easy virtue. In an elementary error, he chose a spot for this tryst three miles from the safety of his army. Colonel William Harcourt, a British cavalry officer heading a team of seventy British dragoons, learned of Lee's whereabouts from local Tories and surrounded the inn. Lee had just composed his acerbic letter about Washington to General Gates when he spied British horsemen outside the window and gasped, "For God's sake, what shall I do?"[41] The widow who owned the inn tried to conceal Lee above a fireplace as bullets ripped through the windows. After twenty-two-year-old Banastre Tarleton, later known for bloodthirsty tactics in the South, threatened to burn down the inn, Lee surrendered in slippers and a filthy shirt to the derisory cheers of his captors and a mocking trumpet blast. To make his degradation complete, the British didn't allow him to don a coat or a hat in the wintry weather. After all of his abrasive lectures to Washington, Charles Lee hadn't known how to protect himself, and his embarrassing capture proved the punch line of a grim joke. He would spend sixteen months in British captivity.

Whatever his misgivings about Charles Lee, Washington had no time for schadenfreude and could only regret the loss of an experienced general. It angered him that the capture was "the effect of folly and imprudence," as he privately told his brother Samuel, but he was in no mood for settling old scores.[42] Perhaps one side of him was relieved at the removal of a long-standing irritant. "I feel much for his misfortune," Washington wrote to a Massachusetts legislator, "and am sensible that in his captivity, our country has lost a warm friend and an able officer."[43] One again marvels at Washington's perfect pitch. He may sometimes have been indecisive as a military leader, as Joseph Reed had alleged, but he always displayed consummate skills as a politician.

CHAPTER TWENTY-THREE

The Crossing

WASHINGTON WAS NOT SURPRISED that thousands of New Jersey residents rushed to take the loyalty oath offered by the British and scrapped the cause of independence as a foolish pipe dream. Expecting a hefty influx of New Jersey militia, he had entertained hopes of making a brave stand against the British at Hackensack or New Brunswick. "But in this I was cruelly disappointed," he informed Connecticut governor Jonathan Trumbull. "The inhabitants of this state, either from fear or disaffection, almost to a man, refused to turn out."[1] He was down to a beleaguered rump army, a raggedy band of a few thousand men. During the trek across New Jersey, they had worn out their shoes and crafted makeshift footwear by slaughtering cattle, skinning their hides, and wrapping crude sections around their bare feet.

It took five days for the disheveled, footsore Americans to cross the Delaware River into Pennsylvania near Trenton, a rearguard action designed to protect nearby Philadelphia. Eager to conduct his army to safety, Washington kindled large bonfires onshore, so that boats could ply the waters through the night; he later recalled this anxious time as one of "trembling for the fate of America."[2] His heart sank as he watched his men, supposed saviors of the country, acting like "a destructive, expensive, disorderly mob."[3] One observant spectator of the crossing was Charles Willson Peale, who had painted a younger and happier Washington and now served with the Pennsylvania militia. Studying this "grand but dreadful" sight, Peale noted the hazardous drudgery of ferrying horses and heavy artillery across the water.[4] He characterized the spectacle as "the most hellish scene I ever beheld" and left an unforgettable anecdote to illustrate the sorry state of the begrimed troops. As Continental soldiers filed past him, "a man staggered out of line and came toward me.

He had lost all his clothes. He was in an old dirty blanket jacket, his beard long and his face full of sores . . . which so disfigured him that he was not known by me on first sight. Only when he spoke did I recognize my brother James."[5]

Acting with dispatch, Washington had his men scour the Delaware for sixty miles and commandeer or destroy any boats that might tumble into British hands. For future use, he had all sturdy boats secreted in nearby creeks or sheltered by islands in the river, laying special stress on the Durham boats, bargelike craft, some sixty feet in length, that ordinarily carried iron ore and other freight. These black boats, outfitted with two masts and sails, could be steered in inclement weather by huge eighteen-foot oars or pushed along by long poles —a feature that would make them a godsend on a snowy night a few weeks later. Washington also posted guards along the river to bar the passage not just of British soldiers but of any Pennsylvanians who might smuggle vital information to the enemy.

On December 8 General Howe and his army arrived in Trenton and exchanged fire with American troops on the Delaware. With twelve thousand men, Howe was tempted to snatch Philadelphia but, in true aristocratic style, he preferred to make a gentlemanly retreat for the winter to the softer haunts of New York City. To fortify Trenton, he left three Hessian regiments under Colonel Johann Gottlieb Rall. Howe was feeling, with good reason, that the tide had turned decisively in his favor, the British having reasserted their sway over three former colonies: New York, New Jersey, and Rhode Island. Panic had gripped Philadelphia, prompting many townspeople to padlock their homes and flee. On December 13 Congress abandoned the now-indefensible city and decamped to Baltimore.

To Washington's credit, instead of simply dwelling on the misery of his situation, he spied a possible opportunity in British complacency. A cold snap in mid-December fostered fears that the Delaware might freeze over, inviting the British to cross and attack. To forestall any prospect of Howe snatching Philadelphia and as a tonic to his dejected compatriots, Washington began to think creatively. He was now endowed with the clarity of despair, which unleashed his more aggressive instincts and opened his mind to unorthodox tactics. On December 14 he predicted to Governor Trumbull that a "lucky blow" against the British would "most certainly rouse the spirits of the people, which are quite sunk by our misfortunes."[6] He was awakening from the mental torpor that had shadowed his footsteps since the Long Island disaster. With fresh plans stirring in his brain, he ordered Horatio Gates to bring his regiments, now encamped in northern New Jersey, across the Delaware.

So many enlistments were set to elapse by year's end that it set an effective deadline for offensive action. Washington believed that British units, scattered along the New Jersey side of the Delaware, were "hovering" like vultures, waiting to swoop down after New Year's Day. Unless every nerve was "strained to recruit the new army with all possible expedition," Washington warned his brother Samuel, "I think the game is pretty near up."[7] He was more concerned by the accelerating decay of patriotic support than by Howe's overwhelming military strength. Adding further pressure for quick attention-getting action was the extreme disarray of American finances. "We are all of opinion, my dear General," Joseph Reed told him, "that something must be attempted to revive our expiring credit, give our cause some degree of reputation, and prevent a total depreciation of the continental money."[8]

Sensitive to public opinion, Washington knew that he had to act fast and he often seemed abstracted. "I saw him in that gloomy period," recalled one officer, "dined with him and attentively marked his aspect; always grave and thoughtful, he appeared at that time pensive and solemn in the extreme."[9] By December 22 Washington's army had been bolstered by regiments that had previously marched under Charles Lee and Horatio Gates, as well as some new militia units, boosting its strength to more than 7,600 men. Because of short enlistments, Washington had ten days to strike a mortal blow against the British; otherwise his troops would vanish into the woods. When Trenton residents reported to the Hessians rumors of an impending rebel attack, the foreign soldiers seemed incredulous. "We did not have any idea of such a thing," said one Hessian, "and thought the rebels were unable to do so."[10]

A timely spur to patriot spirits was the publication of a soul-stirring manifesto by Thomas Paine, who had been amazed by the Continental soldiers' pluck during their dreary hundred-mile march across New Jersey. To honor the thirteen states, he published thirteen essays in a collection entitled *The Crisis*. Scratched out by candlelight and campfire, these essays appeared in pamphlet form on December 23, and Washington had them read aloud to small clusters of men up and down the Delaware. The shivering listeners surely glowed with pride at the words: "These are the times that try men's souls. The summer soldier and the sunshine patriot will, in this crisis, shrink from the service of their country; but he that stands it now deserves the love and thanks of man and woman."[11] Washington had befriended the radical firebrand during the Jersey retreat, and Paine now celebrated his stoic fortitude: "Voltaire has remarked that King William never appeared to full advantage but in difficulties and in action; the same remark may be made on General Washington, for the character fits him."[12]

Washington and his generals decided to cross the Delaware on the night of Christmas Day and pounce upon the Hessian garrison in Trenton an hour before daylight as they slept off their holiday revels, gambling everything on one final roll of the dice. "For heaven's sake, keep this to yourself," Washington told Joseph Reed on December 23, "as the discovery of it may prove fatal to us . . . dire necessity will— nay must—justify any [attempt]."[13] His men had braved hunger, fatigue, sickness, and defeat from personal loyalty to him. On December 24 Colonel William Tudor explained to his fiancée in Boston why he stayed with the motley crew gathered on the Delaware: "I cannot desert a man . . . who has deserted everything to defend his country, and whose chief misfortune . . . is that a large part of it wants [i.e., lacks] spirit to defend itself."[14] Crossing the Delaware, Washington knew, would produce either storied success or utter calamity, and he seemed ready to pay the price. Dr. Benjamin Rush encountered Washington during the tense evening before the operation. "While I was talking to him," Rush recalled, "I observed him to play with his pen and ink upon several small pieces of paper. One of them by accident fell upon the floor near my feet. I was struck with the inscription upon it. It was 'Victory or Death.' "[15] Rush had glimpsed the password of the secret operation, which summed up its desperate all-or-nothing quality.

ON THE FRIGID CHRISTMAS EVE OF 1776 Washington convened a dinner meeting of officers at the home of Samuel Merrick to plot their moves for the following night. In a group of inspired talkers, Washington was the peerless listener and had developed excellent working relations with his generals. After the five-day ordeal of crossing the Delaware into Pennsylvania, skeptics questioned whether the entire army could be rowed across in a single night. The tightly structured plans left little margin for error or slippage in the schedule. Reassurance came from Colonel John Glover, the maritime wizard behind the East River retreat, who reassured the gathering "not to be troubled about that, as his boys could manage it."[16] The grand strategy, orchestrated in minute detail, envisioned the main force of 2,400 men, along with Henry Knox and his artillery, crossing the Delaware at McConkey's Ferry, nine miles above Trenton. Once across the river, this force would split into two columns: one marching under General Sullivan along a road hugging the river, and the second farther inland, along the higher Pennington Road, to be guided by Washington and Greene. These two columns would, in theory, rendezvous outside Trenton. Meanwhile, farther downstream, 700 militia led by General James Ewing would cross the river directly at Trenton, while 1,500 troops would cross at Bristol under Colonel John Cadwalader. Some historians have faulted Washington for the baffling intricacy of this nocturnal operation, but as it turned out, it gave him four separate chances to reach the Hessians at Trenton. Washington enjoyed the unified support of his generals, except for Horatio Gates, who showed his true colors by feigning sickness. While pleading that he was too sick to participate, he rode off to Congress to try to undermine Washington's plan, a transparent betrayal that Washington regarded with contempt.

CHRISTMAS DAY 1776 dawned cold but sunny, then grew overcast by late afternoon as the soldiers, ignorant of their destination, began to file toward the river. They paced more slowly than Washington had reckoned, their bare feet tracing bloody streaks in the snow. Delays threatened the demanding timetable for the crossing, which had to commence right after sundown. Once the men got across the Delaware, they needed to tramp nine miles to Trenton in pitch darkness and arrive by five A.M. Everything hinged on secrecy and faultless precision, and in his general orders Washington demanded "profound silence" during the operation, warning that no soldier was "to quit his ranks on the pain of death."[17]

At sundown light rain began to fall. In advance of his men, Washington crossed the river and staked out a place on the Jersey shore, the dangerous side of the river, a vulnerable patch if news of the raid leaked out. With the future of the country riding on his shoulders, the Virginia planter displayed an indomitable tenacity. Quite simply, if the raid backfired, the war was likely over and he would be captured and killed. Washington, gathering up his courage, responded brilliantly to the challenge. Legend depicts him shrouded in a cloak against the biting wind, sitting perched on an empty beehive, barking orders at Henry Knox, who relayed his words to the boatmen. Knox's resonant voice bellowed throughout the night, and Major James Wilkinson credited his "stentorian lungs" as essential to the operation.[18]

As always, Washington was the tutelary presence, never asking his men to take risks he didn't share. As chunks of ice traveled swiftly down the Delaware, the question arose whether it was possible to negotiate tricky currents under such dreadful conditions. "Who will lead us?" Washington asked, and John Glover and his stouthearted fishermen, aided by Philadelphia stevedores and local boatmen, promised to rise to the occasion. As was often the case, Washington attained his greatest nobility at times of crisis. "His Excellency George Washington never appeared to so much advantage as in the hour of distress," wrote Greene.[19]

The night was darkened by a moon sheathed in clouds. As 2,400 men boarded the Durham boats to begin their 800-foot journey across the river, they were tightly wedged in: 40 standing men were sometimes squeezed into a single craft. The task of transporting skittish horses and eighteen field guns—nearly 400 tons of cumbersome artillery—on the Delaware ferries was a prodigious undertaking. The elements delivered a bone-chilling mixture of rain, sleet, and wind that soaked everything. Around eleven P.M., as a grim northeaster began to churn up the waters, snow and hail pelted men exposed in the boats—"a perfect hurricane," in the words of fifer John Greenwood.[20] Since most of the soldiers couldn't swim, they must have experienced sheer terror at the thought of their boats capsizing. Along the shores, the river froze into such thick crusts that Washington said the "greatest fatigue" came from "breaking a passage" through them.[21] The storm significantly retarded

troop movements and heightened fears of arriving at Trenton after daybreak, jeopardizing the entire plan. But it also had the collateral advantage of muting sounds
from the river and blinding the enemy to the army's advance. Despite the delays,
Washington made the momentous decision to proceed with the perilous mission,
which had taken on its own irresistible logic. As he later wrote, "I well knew we
could not reach it [Trenton] before day was fairly broke, but as I was certain there
was no making a retreat without being discovered, and harassed on repassing the
river, I determined to push on at all events."[22] It was brilliant daring, combined with
a large measure of outright desperation.

Even though the army was supposed to scoot across by midnight, the last boat
didn't cross the river until three A.M. Not a single soldier died. On the Jersey shore,
Washington remained a study in quiet resolve and concentrated force. Not until
four A.M. was the assembled army ready to initiate its nine-mile march to Trenton.
Washington didn't know that the other two sections of his invading force, slated to
traverse the river downstream at Trenton and Bristol, had been canceled due to an
inability to pierce icy masses in the river. Colonel Cadwalader, who couldn't get his
artillery across, simply assumed that Washington had also aborted his plans on this
miserable night.

As the long column finally got under way in New Jersey, the road winding
through the woods was steep and treacherous, slippery to man and beast alike. The
slanting snow, sleet, and hail drove straight into the faces of men plunging forward in nearly total darkness. At least two exhausted soldiers tumbled into roadside
snowdrifts and froze to death. At a place called Jacob's Creek, the soldiers had to
execute the risky maneuver of rolling artillery across a deep chasm. On horseback,
Washington was directing their movements when the hind legs of his horse buckled
and began to skid down the ice-covered slope. His men then saw the greatest horseman of his age perform an equestrian tour de force. Twining his fingers through the
horse's mane, Washington yanked its large head upright with all his might. At the
same time, he rocked and shifted his weight backward in his saddle until the horse
regained its equilibrium. The amazing feat happened in the blink of an eye, then the
artillery movement continued.

It proved an agonizing ride for Washington. His army was only halfway to
Trenton when the first sunlight wanly colored the sky at six A.M. One soldier remembered Washington speaking "in a deep and solemn voice," cautioning his men,
"Soldiers, keep by your officers. For God's sake, keep by your officers."[23] Taking food
and drink on horseback in the thin dawn light, Washington held an impromptu
conference with his generals and they decided to proceed with their original plan,
splitting the column and heading on to Trenton by both high and low roads. With
his congenital penchant for punctuality, Washington pulled out his timepiece and

asked the generals to set their watches by it. Taking the upper Pennington Road with Greene, Washington chose the more arduous route. As the parallel detachments plodded on through a new wave of sleet and swirling snow, a messenger from Sullivan informed Washington that his men's sodden weapons were now useless. "Tell the general to use the bayonet," Washington said.[24] He then galloped along the lines, trying to speed the march's tempo in the brightening morning light. "Press on," he urged the men. "Press on, boys!"[25]

At around seven-thirty A.M., the operation was nearly derailed by a preposterous blunder committed by an old Washington colleague. General Adam Stephen had fought with Washington in Braddock's campaign and vied with him for a seat in the House of Burgesses. The day before the Delaware crossing, he had dispatched a company of Virginians to scout enemy positions in Trenton. Now, as he neared the town, Washington was shocked to meet these fifty Virginians and learn that they had exchanged fire with Hessian sentries, raising the appalling specter that the Hessians had been alerted to the Continental Army's advent. Under questioning, Captain George Wallis told Washington they had acted under instructions from Stephen. Washington summarily hauled the latter into his presence. "You, sir!" Washington scolded him. "You, sir, may have ruined all my plans by having put them on their guard."[26] Those present were amazed by the vivid show of temper, but Washington soon regained his self-mastery and told the Virginians to fall in with his column.

The mythology of the Battle of Trenton portrays the Hessian mercenaries as slumbering in a drunken stupor after imbibing late-night Christmas cheer. In fact, Colonel Johann Gottlieb Rall had kept his men on high alert, and they felt frazzled and exhausted from constant drills and patrols. Quite shrewdly, Washington had worn them down by irregular raids and small skirmishes in the surrounding countryside. If the Hessians were caught off guard that morning, it was only because they thought the forbidding weather would preclude an attack. These tough, brawny hirelings, with a reputation for ferocity, inspired healthy fear among the Americans. But handicapped by their patronizing view of the Americans, they couldn't conceive of something of quite the scale and daring that Washington attempted. "I must concede that on the whole we had a poor opinion of the rebels, who previously had never successfully opposed us," said Lieutenant Jakob Piel.[27] Having received multiple warnings of the surprise attack, Rall was so certain of the superiority of his men that he dismissed these reports with blithe bravado: "Let them come."[28]

As Washington approached Trenton, he was astounded by the valor of his men, who had marched all night and were still eager to attack. Though a snowy tempest still whirled around them, the squalls now blew at their backs as they raced forward at a brisk pace. Intent on exploiting the element of surprise, Washington wanted his men to startle the Hessians. Emerging from the Trenton woods shortly after eight A.M., he divided his wing of the army into three columns and spearheaded the middle column himself, trotting forward in an exposed position. As his men surged ahead, he reported to Hancock, they "seemed to vie with the other in pressing forward."[29] Washington heard artillery blasts exploding on the River Road, confirming that the two American wings had coordinated their arrival.

Trenton consisted of a hundred or so houses, long since deserted by their occupants. Knox's cannon began to fire with pinpoint accuracy down the two main streets, King and Queen, with Alexander Hamilton again in the thick of the fray. "The hurry, fright, and confusion of the enemy was [not] unlike that which will be when the last trump shall sound," said Knox, who forced the German gunners to abandon their weapons and scatter to the southern end of town.[30]

Colonel Rall mobilized a group of men in an apple orchard, then tried to steer a charge toward Washington. Responding to this move, Washington adroitly positioned his men on high ground nearby. As John Greenwood recalled, "General Washington, on horseback and alone, came up to our major and said, 'March on, my brave fellows, after me!' and rode off."[31] Washington's quick-witted action stopped the Hessian advance in its tracks. Colonel Rall, who was riddled with bullets, "reeled in the saddle" before being rescued from his horse and carried to a church. Washington conversed with the dying Rall and ordered that all Hessian prisoners be treated honorably. When he learned from Major James Wilkinson of the surrender of the last regiment, he beamed with quiet pleasure. "Major Wilkinson," he replied, shaking his hand, "this is a glorious day for our country."[32] Since he had crafted the strategy and led his men to glory, the stunning victory belonged to Washington lock, stock, and barrel.

The American triumph was accomplished in less than an hour. "It may be doubted," wrote George Trevelyan, "whether so small a number of men ever employed so short a space of time with greater and more lasting effects upon the history of the world."[33] The battle toll was a bloody one for the Hessians: 22 killed, 84 wounded, and nearly 900 captured (500 escaped to safety) versus only 2 American deaths in combat plus another 4 or 5 from exposure to cold. A huge bonanza of muskets, bayonets, cannon, and swords fell into American hands. The patriots also took possession of forty hogsheads of rum. Trying to enforce sobriety, Washington ordered the rum spilled on the ground, but many men, unable to resist the comfort of warming liquor, grew wildly intoxicated. The patriotic myth about Trenton inverts the reality: it wasn't the Hessians who were inebriated before the battle, but the patriots afterward.

Mindful of the frigid weather and the wobbly state of the drunken troops, Washington and his officers decided to hasten back to the Pennsylvania side of the Delaware, an operation complicated by the need to shepherd Hessian prisoners as well. The proud but weather-beaten army had endured a sixty-hour marathon of frostbite, disease, and exhaustion and needed rest. In his general orders for December 27, Washington thanked his men with unstinting fervor, banishing all traces of the snobbery he once felt toward them: "The General, with the utmost sincerity and affection, thanks the officers and soldiers for their spirited and gallant behavior at Trenton yesterday."[34] The army had harvested a trove of Hessian trophies, ranging from guns to horses, and Washington had the cash value of these spoils distributed proportionally among his soldiers. Even though some had gotten roaring drunk at Trenton, Washington relaxed his usual practice and had more rum ladled out to his thirsty men.

In truth, Washington had little time to rejoice after this bravura performance. Now headquartered in the "old yellow house" of widow Hannah Harris, he convened a war council on December 27 at which the generals digested a startling piece of news: that morning, Colonel Cadwalader had belatedly crossed the Delaware with eighteen hundred militiamen, hoping to mount a second New Jersey offensive. The generals grappled with a tough predicament. They voiced doubts about recrossing the Delaware and tempting fate again, but they were loath to strand Cadwalader and wanted to prove that the first crossing hadn't been a fluke. A consensus slowly took shape to strike again at Trenton. "It was a remarkable and very instructive success for Washington's maturing style of quiet, consultative leadership," notes David Hackett Fischer.[35] The Trenton victory had wrought a wondrous transformation; the deliberations of Washington and his generals were now informed by a newfound confidence.

On December 28, amid thickening snow flurries, Washington ordered militia units in northern New Jersey to stymie the enemy and "harass their flanks and rear."[36] Then on December 29 he set in motion the enormous gamble ratified by his generals, sending his men back across to Trenton. This second crossing, even more ambitious than the first, encompassed eight crossing points and twice as many cannon. A fresh sheet of ice impeded the boats and retarded the operation. Washington himself didn't cross the Delaware until December 30, when he stationed his men on a secure slope behind Assunpink Creek, a narrow, fast-moving creek at the southern end of Trenton. This entrenched position posed more formidable risks than the swift hit-and-run raid launched on Christmas Night.

The first Delaware crossing had afforded graphic proof of the advantages of speed and flexibility in improvising military operations. With many enlistments about to expire, General Greene had lobbied Congress to give Washington additional powers while "reserving to yourself the right of confirming or repealing the measures."[37] Greene insisted that Washington would never abuse a wide-ranging new grant of authority. "There never was a man that might be more safely trusted," he asserted.[38] On December 27 a once-carping, meddlesome Congress granted extraordinary powers to Washington for six months, allowing him to muster new troops by paying bounties, to commandeer provisions, and even to arrest vendors who didn't accept Continental currency. These powers, breathtaking in scope, aroused fears of a despot in the making—fears that Washington quickly laid to rest. He understood that liberties should be affirmed even as they were being temporarily abridged, and he planned to set aside emergency powers the instant they were no longer needed. As he informed Congress, "I shall constantly bear in mind that, as the sword was the last resort for the preservation of our liberties, so it ought to be the first thing laid aside when those liberties are firmly established."[39] In this manner, Washington strengthened civilian authority over the military.

The immediate task at hand was to persuade men to linger whose enlistments expired on New Year's Day. By bringing his soldiers to Trenton, Washington made it more difficult for them to decamp, and he mustered all his hortatory powers to retain them. On December 30 he had a recalcitrant New England regiment lined up before him. Sitting erect on his horse, he made an impassioned appeal, asking them to extend their service by six weeks and offering them a ten-dollar bounty. As one sergeant recalled, Washington "told us our services were greatly needed and that we could do more for our country than we ever could at any future date and in the most affectionate manner entreated us to stay."[40] The word that leaps out here is *affectionate*. Here was George Washington, patriarch of Mount Vernon, addressing farmers, shoemakers, weavers, and carpenters as intimate comrades-in-arms. A year earlier this hypercritical man had frowned on these soldiers as an unsavory rabble; now he lavished them with praise. When Jacky Custis told him of squawking in Virginia about New England troops, Washington took umbrage: "I do not believe that any of the states produce better men, or persons capable of making better soldiers."[41] Though he still believed in hierarchical distinctions, especially between officers and their men, the war was molding him into a far more egalitarian figure.

When drums rumbled out a roll call for volunteers, nobody at first stepped forward. One vocal soldier piped up and spoke of their shared sacrifices, how much they had dreamed of heading home. Pulling up his horse, Washington wheeled about and rode along the entire line of men. With his reserved manner and austere code of conduct, he didn't frequently voice his feelings, only making it more impressive when he did so. "My brave fellows," he said, "you have done all I asked you to do and more than could be reasonably expected. But your country is at stake, your wives, your houses, and all that you hold dear . . . If you will consent to stay one month longer, you will render that service to the cause of liberty and to your country which you probably can never do under any other circumstances."[42]

As the drums resumed beating, the soldiers huddled and conferred among themselves. One was overheard to say, "I will remain if you will," while another told his fellows that "we cannot go home under such circumstances."[43] A small knot of men stepped forward grudgingly, prompting several more to do so; finally all two hundred joined in. For Washington, the war had become a constant game of high-stakes improvisation, played out under extreme duress. For these two hundred men, the extra six weeks entailed no small commitment: half would perish from combat wounds or illness. The same scene was soon reenacted with other regiments as Washington, showing dramatic flair and plainspoken eloquence, held on to more than three thousand men. In another inspired gesture, he told subordinates that the men who agreed to stay didn't need to be formally enrolled but would be trusted to make good on their verbal pledges. He was treating them not as commoners, but as tried-and-true gentlemen.

To ferret out enemy intentions, Washington sent a cavalry patrol to reconnoiter around Princeton. Several captured British dragoons revealed that the British had amassed eight thousand men at Princeton and were girding themselves under General Cornwallis to attack Washington at Trenton. As this second Battle of Trenton loomed, the humiliated Hessians were in an especially vengeful mood, and their leader, Colonel von Donop, decreed a bloodthirsty policy of taking no prisoners.

Toward sundown at Trenton on January 2, 1777, Washington spotted the vanguard of Cornwallis, who had brought an army of 5,500 men. Washington arrayed his men on the slope behind Assunpink Creek in three horizontal bands, covering the entire hillside. As Hessian troops hurtled down King and Queen streets, American snipers fired at them. An advance force of Continental soldiers waded back across the rain-swollen creek while others fell back across the stone bridge. When it looked momentarily as if the retreating Americans would be hacked to death by Hessian bayonets, Washington swung into action. Sitting astride his horse at the far end of the bridge, he mobilized his men. Evidently he not only looked but *felt* like a godlike image of solidity; soldiers who bumped against him couldn't shake his granite poise. Private John Howland left this evocative portrait:

> The noble horse of Gen. Washington stood with his breast pressed close against the end of the west rail of the bridge, and the firm, composed, and majestic countenance of the general inspired confidence and assurance in a moment so important and critical. In this passage across the bridge, it was my fortune to be next [to] the west rail, and arriving at the end of the bridge rail, I was pressed against the shoulder of the general's horse and in contact with the general's boot. The horse stood as firm as the rider and seemed to understand that he was not to quit his post and station.[44]

This preternatural composure, coming in the heat of battle, made Washington a living presence to his men.

The British made three courageous attempts to take the bridge, and each time American artillery repulsed them, strewing many cadavers in their wake. "The bridge looked red as blood," wrote Sergeant Joseph White, "with their killed and wounded and red coats."[45] Several hundred British and Hessian soldiers died in vain attempts to storm the American positions. Nevertheless, the patriots were heavily outnumbered by Cornwallis's army and had no clear escape strategy. In the dying light of a winter day, Cornwallis and his officers conferred about whether to postpone the main attack. "If Washington is the general I take him to be," Sir William Erskine said, "he will not be found in the morning." An overly confident Cornwallis disputed this assertion. "We've got the old fox safe now," he supposedly said. "We'll go over and bag him in the morning."[46]

Washington worried that his men might be encircled by the superior British force—they were cooped up like a flock of chickens, in Henry Knox's colorful phrase—and knew that any retreat across a Delaware River chock-full of ice floes could be costly. Convening his generals on this frosty night, he stated that the loss of the corps he commanded "might be fatal to the country," and, under these circumstances, he asked for advice.[47] Once again a single misstep could be devastating. The war council decided to have the army slip away during the night, much as it had disappeared across the East River. Still better, it would convert a defensive move into an offensive measure, circling around the left flank of Cornwallis's army and heading north along unfrequented back roads to confront the British at Princeton. Washington again hid a political strategy behind his military strategy. "One thing I was sure of," he remarked afterward, was "that it would avoid the appearance of a retreat, which was of consequence."[48] This supremely risky strategy meant penetrating deep into enemy territory and possibly being entrapped. Nevertheless, Washington and his generals, who now operated with exceptional cohesion, embraced the course unanimously.

To camouflage the nighttime retreat, which would start after midnight, Washington reprised the same repertoire of tricks he had applied on Long Island. The wheels of the artillery were wrapped in rags to deaden sounds. Campfires were kept burning to foster the illusion of an army settled in for the night. Loud noises were broadcast with entrenching tools, as if the Americans were digging in for violent reprisals the next day. Again the troops were kept unaware of their destination. In fact, Washington stole away with such artful stealth, wrote one officer, that "the rear guard and many of his own sentinels never missed him."[49] In marching twelve miles through the night toward Princeton, Washington pushed his long-suffering men almost beyond human endurance. It was a long, harrowing march down dark country lanes congealed with ice. The weary men, wrapped in a numb trance, some barely awake, padded against stinging winds; many fell asleep standing up whenever the column halted.

The troops arrived at the college town later than scheduled, shortly after an exceptionally clear, beautiful dawn that James Wilkinson remembered as "bright, serene, and extremely cold, with a hoarfrost that bespangled every object."[50] The men rapidly repaired a bridge over Stony Brook, south of town, before the army divided into two groups: Sullivan's division veered northeast while Greene's moved due north. The first spirited fighting erupted unexpectedly. Lieutenant Colonel Charles Mawhood was about to rush two British regiments to Trenton to aid Cornwallis when, to his infinite surprise, he encountered American forces under General Hugh Mercer in a broad, rolling meadow. "I believe they were as much astonished as if an army had dropped perpendicularly upon them," declared Knox.[51] Mawhood ordered a ferocious bayonet charge that staggered Mercer's men. Mercer himself was knocked off his horse and given a merciless drubbing as he lay on the ground. In capturing the dapper, handsome Mercer—a physician from Fredericksburg and a friend of Washington's—the British imagined they had taken the commander in chief himself. "Call for quarters, you damned rebel," they taunted him. To which Mercer retorted, "I am no rebel," and slashed at them with his sword. [52] The British mauled him repeatedly with their bayonets, carving seven gashes, until he lay near death. For Washington, it was a disturbing preview of the fate awaiting him if ever he were captured.

The Battle of Princeton gave Washington another chance to show that he was the army's chief warrior in the antique sense. The eighteenth-century battlefield was a compact space, its cramped contours defined by the short range of muskets and bayonet charges, giving generals a chance to inspire by their immediate presence. When Mercer's men began to retreat, harried by redcoats flashing bayonets, General Greene directed Pennsylvania militia into the fray, only to have them collide with Mercer's fleeing men amid "a shower of grapeshot."[53] The American panic was stemmed by Washington himself, who suddenly circled into view and exhorted his rattled men to stand and fight. "Parade with us, my brave fellows!" he exclaimed, waving his hat. "There is but a handful of the enemy, and we will have them directly."[54] According to his aide-de-camp Colonel John Fitzgerald, Washington rallied the men with an act of unbelievable bravery: he reined in his horse, faced the enemy directly, and simply froze. Yet again the intrepid Washington acted as if he were protected by an invisible aura.

With the British entrenched beyond a hillside fence, Washington lengthened and strengthened the patriot line, instructing his men not to fire until told to do so. He exhibited exceptional sangfroid as he rode along the line. Then he personally led the charge up the hill, halting only when they had pushed within thirty yards of their adversaries. As he issued the command to fire, Washington, on his white charger, was such a conspicuous target that Fitzgerald clapped his hat over his eyes because he couldn't bear to see him shot. When the fusillade of bullets ended and the enemy scattered, Fitzgerald finally peeked and saw Washington, untouched, sitting proudly atop his horse, wreathed by eddying smoke. "Thank God, your Excellency is safe!" Fitzgerald said to him, almost weeping with relief. Washington, unfazed, took his hand fondly. "Away, my dear colonel, and bring up the troops. The day is our own!"[55] Fitzgerald wasn't the only one bowled over by Washington's coolness. "I shall never forget what I felt . . . when I saw him brave all the dangers of the field and his important life hanging as it were by a single hair with a thousand deaths flying around him," wrote a young Philadelphia officer. "Believe me, I thought not of myself."[56]

Washington spurred his horse after the retreating enemy, for once giving way to pure exhilaration. Perhaps repaying the old insult from the Battle of Harlem Heights, he shouted to his men, "It's a fine fox chase, my boys!"[57] Whatever joy he felt, however, was tempered by the horrifying spectacle of a snowy battlefield stained with American blood. One officer lay "rolling and writhing in his blood, unconscious of anything around him."[58] An adolescent lieutenant had a bullet hole in his chest and a skull smashed in by a bayonet. And so on.

In the battle's concluding chapter, two hundred British troops sought asylum in the principal college building, Nassau Hall. According to legend, Alexander Hamilton deployed his artillery against the building and decapitated a portrait of King George II with a cannonball. By the time a white flag of surrender popped from a window, the victorious Americans had inflicted more than five hundred casualties and taken between two hundred and three hundred prisoners; only about three dozen Americans were killed in the one-sided battle. To Washington's dismay, his soldiers, avid for booty, ransacked Nassau Hall and dragged out food, clothing, furniture, and even paintings. They also fleeced uniforms from British corpses on the battlefield. To stop this plunder, Washington had the field cordoned off by sentries. He also accompanied two wounded redcoats to private homes, where American surgeons treated them and performed amputations. In his humane treatment of prisoners, Washington wanted to make a major statement, telling one officer that British captives should "have no reason to complain of our copying the brutal example of the British army in their treatment of our unfortunate brethren."[59]

The consecutive victories at Trenton and Princeton resurrected American spirits, especially since the Continental Army had scored an undisputed victory over British regulars. The psychology of the war was dramatically reversed, with the once-dominant British presence in New Jersey "reduced to the compass of a very few miles," in Washington's view.[60] By rolling back British gains, he undercut the Crown's new strategy of securing territory and handing out pardons. Nathanael Greene estimated that the Americans had killed or captured up to three thousand enemy soldiers in a two-week stretch. Although Washington wanted to proceed to New Brunswick and raid a major storehouse of British supplies, his men hadn't slept for two days, and he didn't believe he could press them further.

The back-to-back victories had also changed the calculus of the war. Henceforth the British would have to conquer the colonists, not simply cow them into submission. The Americans, having bounced back from near despair, now showed an irrepressible esprit de corps. "A few days ago, they had given up the cause for lost," scoffed the Loyalist Nicholas Cresswell. "Their late successes have turned the scale and now they are all liberty mad again."[61] "Four weeks ago, we expected to end the war with the capture of Philadelphia," said the Hessian captain Johann Ewald, "and now we had to render Washington the honor of thinking about our defense."[62]

The consecutive battles exalted George Washington to a new pinnacle of renown. He had taken the demoralized men who shuffled wearily across New Jersey and shaped them into valiant heroes. Through the many newspaper accounts, these events passed directly into American legend. "Had he lived in the days of idolatry," said a rhapsodic piece in the *Pennsylvania Journal,* Washington would have "been worshiped as a god."[63] The battle's repercussions were worldwide, overturning the presumption that amateur volunteers could never defeat a well-trained European army. Even Frederick the Great added his congratulations: "The achievements of Washington and his little band of compatriots between the 25th of December and the 4th of January, a space of 10 days, were the most brilliant of any recorded in the annals of military achievements."[64]

For all the many virtues he had shown in his life, nothing quite foreshadowed the wisdom, courage, fortitude, and resolution that George Washington had just exhibited. Adversity had brought his best traits to the surface and even ennobled him. Sensing it, Abigail Adams told her friend Mercy Otis Warren, "I am apt to think that our later misfortunes have called out the hidden excellencies of our commander-in-chief." She quoted a line from the English poet Edward Young: "'Affliction is the good man's shining time.'"[65] One consistent thread from his earlier life had prefigured these events: Washington's tenacity of purpose, his singular ability to stalk a goal with all the resources at his disposal.

Another stalwart admirer of Washington was Charles Willson Peale. In 1779 the Supreme Executive Council of Philadelphia commissioned him to execute a full-length portrait of Washington to commemorate his Princeton triumph. Washington sat for the portrait over a two-week period, and the result was an inspiring work of easy, graceful lines. A debonair Washington stands with Nassau Hall in the background and a Hessian standard unfurled at his feet. His blue jacket with gold epaulettes opens to reveal a pale blue sash curving across his paunch. He holds one arm akimbo, the other resting on the barrel of a cannon. At the height of his power,

Washington stands tall and imposing in high black boots with gold-colored spurs; the left foot is elegantly drawn back, resting on its toes. The portrait breathes a manly swagger, an air of high-flown accomplishment. All traces of provincial tentativeness and uncertainty have disappeared from Washington's personality. This was the magnetic Washington that so enthralled his contemporaries, not the stiff, craggy figure made familiar to later generations by Gilbert Stuart.

Washington didn't pause to savor his victory at Princeton. Once Cornwallis awoke and discovered the American ruse, he rushed toward Princeton at a maddening, helter-skelter pace "in a most infernal sweat, running, puffing and blowing and swearing at being so outwitted," laughed Henry Knox.[66] The British arrived an hour after the Continental Army had deserted the town. Washington put his dazed, depleted men through the paces of another fifteen-mile march north to Somerset Court House. They arrived there after sundown and, exhausted, instantly fell asleep on any available bed of straw they could find.

The Busy Scenes of a Camp

FOR ALL THE ILLUSTRIOUS FEATS that Washington's soldiers performed at Trenton and Princeton, they were weary from their epic labors, and the euphoria of their victory was short-lived. The heroism of the patriot army, though quite real, would prove sporadic throughout the war, so that Washington's own constancy became necessary to sustain the Revolution. Notwithstanding the bounties they had pocketed, men kept vanishing into the woods every day, and Washington griped that he headed an army that was "here today, gone tomorrow, without assigning a reason or even apprising you of it."[1] To flesh out sixteen new regiments, he had to offer twenty-dollar bounties, one hundred acres of land, and a new suit of clothes to anyone older than seventeen but younger than fifty.

Washington remained frustrated with congressional reluctance to confer on him the power to appoint his own general officers. Some of the political resistance sprang from fear of arbitrary power, but it also testified to envy festering below the hero worship, a petulant undercurrent that would persist for the rest of Washington's career. Speaking of Washington, John Adams lectured his congressional colleagues not "to idolize an image which their own hands have molten." Adams thought Washington already had too much power: "It becomes us to attend early to the restraining [of] our army."[2]

After Princeton, an exhausted Washington took his shrunken army into winter headquarters in Morristown, New Jersey, instead of retreating back into Pennsylvania. This inspired decision enabled him to harass British supply lines and to expel the enemy from many parts of New Jersey. Nonetheless the decision carried grave risks. Washington was now perilously short of men, and as he admitted years later, the British could easily have vanquished this thinly guarded camp, "if they had only thought proper to march against us."[3] A small incident shows that he didn't wish to jinx his recent run of victories through any precipitate action. On January 8 he thanked the Pennsylvania Council of Safety for "your notice of the eclipse of the sun which is to happen tomorrow. This event, without a previous knowledge, might affect the minds of the soldiery."[4] In an age alive to portents, Washington feared that his soldiers might interpret a solar eclipse as a sign of providential displeasure.

Twenty-five miles west of New York City, ringed by protective hills, Morristown was rich in farms that could feed famished troops and provide a snug winter retreat. For his headquarters, Washington chose a building on the village green that once served as a tavern. He enjoyed a frugal life, compared to the sumptuous balls that General Howe was throwing for his officers in Manhattan. Once the hubbub of battle subsided, Washington longed for Martha's company and was starved for news of home. For months he had discontinued correspondence with friends and family in Virginia, "finding it incompatible with my public business," as he told Robert Morris. "A letter or two from my family are regularly sent by the post, but very irregularly received, which is rather mortifying, as it deprives me of the consolation of hearing from home on domestic matters."[5] With his emotional life still rooted in Mount Vernon and the war now threatening to drag on interminably, he contended that nobody "suffers more by an absence from home than myself."[6] Martha, unable to travel across a snowbound landscape, wouldn't arrive until nearly spring.

The commander in chief had no respite from the crisis atmosphere that had shadowed him for months. Conditions were so appalling in patriot hospitals that one doctor remembered having seen "from four to five patients die on the same straw before it was changed."[7] When smallpox appeared in his camp, Washington feared a calamity and hastily informed Hancock that he planned to inoculate all his troops. He also asked Dr. William Shippen to inoculate recruits passing through Philadelphia en route to his army, an enlightened action that helped stave off an epidemic.

Washington's tenure as commander in chief featured relatively few battles, often fought after extended intervals of relative calm, underscoring the importance of winning the allegiance of a population that vacillated between fealty to the Crown and patriotic indignation. The fair treatment of civilians formed an essential part of the war effort. Washington had a sure grasp of the principles of this republican revolution, asserting that "the spirit and willingness of the people must in a great measure take [the] place of coercion."[8] No British general could compete with him in this contest for popular opinion. With one eye fixed on the civilian populace, Washington showed punctilious respect for private property and was especially perturbed when American troops sacked houses under the pretext that the owners were Tories. His overriding goal was to contrast his own humane behavior with the predatory ways of the enemy.

Nothing expressed Washington's outrage over the abuse of civilians more powerfully than an October 1778 incident involving his personal guard. John Herring, a member of that guard, was sent to get supplies for Washington's table and was furnished with a horse and pass. When rebuffed at the home of a Tory named Prince Howland, he spied some costly objects he coveted and dispatched three others from Washington's guard—John Herrick, Moses Walton, and a fifer named Elias Brown—to procure them. The three men broke into Howland's house and looted silver spoons, silver dollars, and clothing, then repeated the performance at the home of one John Hoag. In protesting the incident, Howland described the three vandals as having worn the round hats adorned with bearskin strips that distinguished Washington's guard. Washington endorsed the death sentences handed down by a court-martial to Herring, Brown, and Walton, along with one hundred lashes for Herrick. "His Excellency the Commander in Chief approves these sentences," read the general orders. "Shocked at the frequent, horrible villainies of this nature committed by the troops of late, he is determined to make examples which will deter the boldest and most harden[e]d offenders."[9] While Walton and Brown escaped before execution, John Herring was duly hung, and John Herrick received his one hundred lashes.

The opinions of New Jersey's citizens became of paramount importance after the Trenton and Princeton victories removed the aura of protection that had sustained Loyalist families. A militant to his fingertips, Washington cherished no love for Tories, whom he portrayed as diabolical and branded "abominable pests of society."[10] He now promulgated an order that those who had sworn loyalty to England should swear allegiance to the United States. For those who demurred, Washington granted (in a lovely rhetorical ploy) "full liberty" to defect to the other side.[11] He devised an exquisitely civilized policy: Loyalists would be conducted to British lines with their personal possessions but would have the option of leaving behind their wives and children. Such Solomon-like solutions made George Washington the country's first chief executive a dozen years before he was officially elected to the post.

During the winter of 1776–77 the British sent out foraging parties from New York to raid the New Jersey countryside, and Washington directed the militia to "harass their troops to death" in what became a conflict of "daily skirmishes."[12] This small-scale warfare whittled away British power as the militia gathered horses, cattle, and sheep to feed the American army. Thomas Jones, a Loyalist judge in New York, wrote that not "a stick of wood, a spear of grass or a kernel of corn could the troops in New Jersey procure without fighting for it."[13] Congressmen constantly requested that Washington defend their districts but refused to appropriate money to do so. These amateur experts, he thought, had no idea of the handicaps under which he toiled. "In a word," he seethed, "when they are at a distance, they think it is but to say, 'Presto! Begone' and everything is done."[14] It took tremendous strength to parry requests from politicians whose support he desperately needed.

During the long Morristown winter, Washington made notable advances in organizing a spy network under his personal supervision. This operation had enjoyed a top priority from the moment he arrived in Cambridge in 1775. With his natural reticence and sphinxlike personality, Washington was a natural student of espionage. At first his spy operation was haphazard in nature, cohering into a true system only by 1779. To guarantee secrecy, he never hinted in letters at the identity of spies. Instead he assigned them names or numbers or employed vague locutions, such as "the person you mentioned."[15] He favored having the minimum number of people involved in any spy ring, and the diagram of the network existed in his mind alone. After 1779 he frequently had spies communicate via invisible ink, developed by John James's brother James, who was a doctor and an amateur chemist. This ink was usually applied to blank pages of books or interlined in family letters. "It is in my power, I believe, to procure a liquid which nothing but a counter liquor (rubbed over the paper afterwards) can make legible" was how he described its workings.[16] Secret notes were typically pressed between leather bindings and pasteboard covers of transported books.

To spy on New York—"the fountain of all intelligence," Washington anointed it—was his principal objective, and he soon had the town covered with informers. He preferred people who could gather intelligence in the course of their everyday affairs, and his mind proved inventive in its choices.[17] With some spies Washington even offered personal coaching, telling one to "mix with and put on the airs of a Tory to cover his real character and avoid suspicion."[18] With an insatiable appetite for intelligence, he entreated Presbyterian minister Alexander McWhorter, the chaplain of an artillery brigade, to press convicted spies for information, while offering them theological comfort before they were hung.

Right before the Princeton battle, Washington informed Philadelphia financier Robert Morris that "we have the greatest occasion at present for hard money to pay a certain set of people who are of particular use to us . . . Silver would be most convenient."[19] Washington considered Morris, a huge man with a ruddy complexion and a genial personality, the financier with the best mercantile knowledge and connections in North America. He often tapped Morris for money because he needed to bypass Congress, which couldn't be trusted to keep secrets. When Morris first approached a rich Quaker in Philadelphia for funds, the man balked, saying he was "opposed to fighting of any sort."[20] Morris overcame the man's religious scruples and sent Washington two canvas bags bulging with glittering coins, including Spanish silver dollars, French half crowns, and English crowns, an incident Washington always remembered. That he was allowed to supervise an espionage budget, without accounting to Congress, bespeaks the extraordinary trust placed in the commander in chief. Periodically he asked Congress for sums of gold for spies and kept the money bags with his personal belongings for safekeeping. He practiced the entire range of espionage tactics, including double agents and disinformation. In March 1777, for example, he passed along a litany of false information to Elisha Boudinot, who was supposed to relay it to a spy "to deceive the enemy."[21]

The circumspect Washington showed real artistry as a spymaster. This wasn't surprising, since he had repeatedly engaged in bluffs to fool the enemy. In April 1777 he alerted Joseph Reed that an unnamed man, recently arrested, had served as an American spy. He was such a valuable agent that Washington passed along orders that his allegiance should be reinforced by a "handsome present in money" and that he should then be released in such a way as "to give it the appearance of an accidental escape from confinement."[22] Washington's instructions sounded knowing: "Great care must be taken so to conduct the scheme as to make the escape appear natural and real. There must be neither too much facility, nor too much refinement, for doing too little, or overacting the part, would alike beget a suspicion."[23] In using spies as double agents to spread disinformation, Washington again seemed very expert: "It is best to keep them in a way of knowing as little of our true circumstances as possible and, in order that they may really deceive the enemy in their reports, to endeavour in the first place to deceive them."[24] On one occasion that winter, when an officer requested permission to arrest a spy, Washington shrewdly suggested that he woo the spy with a dinner invitation, then leave nearby, as if by sheer negligence, a sheet pegging the Continental Army's strength at a grossly exaggerated number. It was one of many ways that Washington misled the enemy to conceal his own weakness.

Washington devoted far more time to the onerous task of drafting letters than to leading men into battle. Running an embryonic government, he protested to Congress that he and his aides "are confined from morn till eve, hearing and answering the applications and letters of one and another," leaving him with "no hours for recreation."[25] He groaned at the huge stacks of correspondence and felt besieged by supplicants for various favors. At times the enormous quantity of paperwork must have seemed more daunting than British arms. When brother Samuel asked for a portrait of him, he pleaded a lack of time to sit for a painter: "If ever you get a picture of mine, taken from the life, it must be when I am remov[e]d from the busy scenes of a camp."[26] At times, he appeared overwhelmed by bureaucratic demands, with the "business of so many different departments centering with me and by me to be handed on to Congress for their information, added to the intercourse I am obliged to keep up with the adjacent states."[27]

Washington had trained himself to write pithy, meaty letters, with little frivolity or small talk. The letters were always clear, sometimes elegant, often forceful. Even Jefferson, a fluent wordsmith, praised Washington's correspondence, saying that "he wrote readily, rather diffusely, in an easy and correct style."[28] Because aides drafted most of Washington's superlative wartime letters, some historians have denied him credit. But Washington oversaw their work, first giving them the gist of messages, then editing drafts until they met his exacting standards. His aides became fine mimics of their boss, and their letters echo one another's because they were well schooled in Washington's style. He wanted letters so immaculate that he had them rewritten several times if they contained even small erasures.

Washington worked in close proximity with aides, who typically slept under the same roof. These scribes labored in a single room, bent over small wooden tables, while the commander kept a small office to the side. As at Mount Vernon, Washington adhered to an unvarying daily routine. Arriving fully dressed, he breakfasted with his aides and parceled out letters to be answered, along with his preferred responses. He then reviewed his troops on horseback and expected to find the letters in finished form by the time of his noonday return.

The best camaraderie that Washington enjoyed came in the convivial company of his young aides during midafternoon dinners. Up to thirty people attended these affairs, many sitting on walnut camp stools. As much as possible, Washington converted these repasts into little oases of elegant society, a reminder of civilized life at Mount Vernon. The company dined on damask tablecloths and used sparkling silver flatware bearing Washington's griffin crest, while drinking wine from silver cups. One aide sat beside Washington and helped to serve the food and drinks. These meals could last for hours, with a bountiful table covered by heavy, succulent foods. One amazed French visitor recalled that "the meal was in the English fashion, consisting of eight or ten large [serving] dishes of meat and poultry, with vegetables of several sorts, followed by a second course of pastry, comprised under the two denominations of 'pies' and 'puddings.'"[29] There followed abundant platters of apples and nuts. Washington liked to crack nuts as he talked, a habit that he later blamed for his long history of dental trouble.

At these dinners Washington seemed at his most unbuttoned. If he wasn't skilled at repartee, he was quite sociable and had no trouble making conversation, enjoying the company of his bright young disciples. A later visitor to Mount Vernon captured Washington's contradictory personality: "Before strangers, he is generally very reserved and seldom says a word." On the other hand, "the general with a few glasses of champagne got quite merry and being with his intimate friends laughed and talked a good deal."[30]

In early 1777 a large turnover occurred in Washington's military family as his first batch of aides gave way to a flock of new faces. Nathanael Greene briefly replaced Joseph Reed, who had resigned and was somewhat estranged from Washington. After the Fort Washington disaster, Greene was thrilled to be rehabilitated, even if it meant being temporarily demoted to clerical work. "I am exceedingly happy in the full confidence of His Excellency General Washington, and I found [that confidence] to increase every hour, the more [difficult] and distressing our affairs grew," Greene told his wife.[31] Washington demanded self-sacrifice from aides, who had to follow his schedule uncomplainingly. If he slept in the open air before a battle, so did they. "When I joined His Excellency's suite," wrote James McHenry, "I gave up soft beds, undisturbed repose, and the habits of ease and indulgence . . . for a single blanket, the hard floor or the softer sod of the fields, early rising, and almost perpetual duty."[32]

Washington's choices for his military family were permeated by an aristocratic ethos that could be hard to square with the republican spirit. He perpetuated the patrician ethos first encountered on General Braddock's staff; indeed, his use of the term "family" was borrowed from British practice. Of twenty-two aides-de-camp and military secretaries that he appointed during the first two years of the conflict, more than half came from Virginia and Maryland, many of them smart young men from his own social class. Robert Hanson Harrison of Virginia and Tench Tilghman of Maryland fit the bill perfectly, while Caleb Gibbs took the role of the token New Englander.

Washington was adept at identifying young talent. He wanted eager young men who worked well together, pitched in with alacrity, and showed esprit de corps. His own personality forbade backslapping familiarity or easy joviality. Beneath his reserve, however, he had an excellent capacity for reading people and adapting his personality to them. As before the war, he remained wary in relationships and lowered his emotional barriers only slowly, but he was trusting once colleagues earned his confidence. Washington's young aides satisfied a need for affection that men his own age, with whom he felt far more competitive, could scarcely have done.

Debilitated by never-ending bags of mail, Washington said he needed someone who could "comprehend at one view the diversity of matter which comes before me."[33] On March 1, 1777, that person appeared in the shape of Alexander Hamilton, the twenty-two-year-old boy wonder and artillery captain whose pyrotechnics at White Plains and the Raritan River had so impressed Washington. In the short, slim, and ingenious Hamilton, Washington encountered an ambition that could well have reminded him of his younger self.

Unlike the often affluent aides in Washington's family, Hamilton was an illegitimate young man who had been born on Nevis and spent his adolescence on St. Croix. Five years earlier he had been an impoverished clerk in a Caribbean trading house. Thanks to a subscription taken up by wealthy local merchants who spotted his potential, he was sent to school in North America. Starting in Elizabethtown, New Jersey, and then at King's College in New York, he displayed the same knack as the young Washington for capturing the confidence of influential older men. Possessed of an aristocratic savoir faire that belied his background, Hamilton turned himself, with uncommon speed, from an outcast of the islands into a Revolutionary insider. His perfectionist nature rivaled Washington's own. He toted about a sack of books, including *Plutarch's Lives,* to improve himself and made extensive notations in the empty pages of a pay book. Still, noticeable differences between the two men introduced tensions. Hamilton was more cerebral than Washington and less tolerant of human foibles, racing through life at a frenetic pace. Where Washington could usually subdue his strong emotions, Hamilton was often impetuous, with highly fallible judgment. For all his charm, he was much too proud and headstrong to be a surrogate son to George Washington or anyone else.

Hamilton rapidly became Washington's most gifted scribe and his "principal and most confidential aide," often attending war councils and enjoying a comprehensive view of the conflict.[34] One officer claimed that Hamilton "thought as well as wrote for Washington."[35] Hamilton revered Washington's courage, patriotism, and integrity and never doubted that he was the indispensable figure in the war effort. Nevertheless, no man is a hero to his valet, and Hamilton left some candidly critical views of Washington. He regarded Washington as a general of only modest ability and quickly sensed the powerful emotions bottled up inside his overwrought boss, whom he often found snappish and difficult.[36]

By this point in the war, Washington's leadership style was crystal clear. He never insulated himself from contrary opinions, having told Joseph Reed early in the war to keep him posted on even unfriendly scuttlebutt. "I can bear to hear of imputed or real errors," he wrote. "The man who wishes to stand well in the opinion of others must do this, because he is thereby enabled to correct his faults or remove the prejudices which are imbib[e]d against him."[37] Washington made excellent use of war councils to weigh all sides of an issue. Never a man of lightning-fast intuitions or sudden epiphanies, he usually groped his way to firm and accurate conclusions. Equipped with keen powers of judgment rather than originality, he was at his best when reacting to options presented by others. Once he made up his mind, it was difficult to dislodge him from his opinion, so thoroughly had he plumbed things through to the bottom.

Even as he fought the British, Washington deemed their army the proper model to emulate. As late as 1780 he made passing reference to "the British Army, from whence most of our rules and customs are derived, and in which long experience and improvement has brought their system as near perfection as in any other service."[38] As in choosing aides, Washington believed that well-bred people made the best officers, advising Patrick Henry that the most reliable way to select a candidate was to find someone with "a just pretension to the character of a gentleman, a proper sense of honor, and some reputation to lose."[39] As in the French and Indian War, he warned officers to avoid excessive familiarity with their inferiors. "Be easy and condescending in your deportment to your officers," he instructed a Virginia commander, "but not too familiar, lest you subject yourself to a want of that respect which is necessary to support a proper command."[40] He required noncommissioned officers to wear swords "as a mark of distinction and to enable them the better to maintain the authority due to their stations."[41] At the same time he pleaded with officers to lead by example and share their men's hardships, saying "it ought to be the pride of an officer to share the fatigue as well as danger to which his men are exposed."[42] That he championed Knox and Hamilton shows how the exigencies of the war forced him to search beyond his own social stratum and democratize the army almost in spite of himself.

During that Morristown winter Washington stressed the importance of clean clothing and sanitary quarters and a nutritious diet with vegetables and salads. He issued blanket prohibitions against playing cards and dice. While he couldn't ban alcohol outright—the daily rations of rum were bottled courage—he tried to have soldiers drink it in diluted form and avoid "the vile practice of swallowing the whole ration of liquor at a single draft."[43] Washington valued well-played music in army life and assigned a band to each brigade. At one point he chided a fife and drum corps for playing badly and insisted that they practice more regularly; a year later, after the drummers took this admonition to an extreme, Washington restricted their practice to one hour in the morning, a second in the afternoon. He was also irked by the improvisations of some drummers and, amid the misery of Valley Forge, took the trouble to issue this broadside to wayward drummers: "The use of drums are as signals to the army and, if every drummer is allowed to beat at his pleasure, the intention is entirely destroy[e]d, as it will be impossible to distinguish whether they are beating for their own pleasure or for a signal to the troops."[44]

In crusading for moral reformation among his men, Washington feared that profane language would undermine discipline. He winced when soldiers swore in his presence. As the general orders said of Washington, "His feelings are continually wounded by the oaths and imprecations of the soldiers whenever he is in hearing of them."[45] He was also apt to invoke the aid of religion. During the summer of 1776 the Continental Congress granted him permission to attach chaplains to each regiment, and he encouraged attendance at divine services by rotating his own presence among them. "The blessings and protection of Heaven are at all times necessary, but especially so in times of public distress and danger," he assured his men, hoping "that every officer and man will endeavor so to live and act as becomes a Christian soldier defending the dearest rights and liberties of his country."[46] This was one of the rare times Washington referred to Christianity rather than Providence. In fact, he favored having chaplains chosen by local military units so no denominational character could be imposed from above.

Washington construed favorable events in the war as reflections of Providence, transforming him from an actor in a human drama into a tool of heavenly purpose. This expressed his religious faith but also satisfied certain political needs. While it lifted from his shoulders the credit for victories, it also didn't burden him unduly with the crushing weight of defeat. He didn't have to feel as if the entire fate of the nation rested with him. For someone afraid of showing vanity, he could also avoid boasting by invoking the signal role of Providence, enabling him to discuss victories with seeming humility. Unquestionably Washington believed that Providence watched out for the United States of America *and* for him. Early in the war he told his brother Samuel that he had "a perfect reliance upon that Providence which heretofore has befriended and smiled upon me."[47] It's worth noting that Washington didn't see humans as passive actors and believed that God helped those who helped themselves: "Providence has done much for us in this contest," he said later in the war, "but we must do something for ourselves, if we expect to go triumphantly through with it."[48]

As a man laden with many secrets who unburdened himself to only a small circle of confidants, Washington had to hide moments of despondency from the army, giving few people access to his private grief. In the spring of 1777 a secondhand report reached Lord Howe's ears that a maid in Washington's employ "frequently caught him in tears about the house and [said] that, when he is alone, he appears constantly dejected and unhappy."[49] Washington weathered the winter's stern rigors, only to buckle beneath a ten-day illness in early March that left him so weakened that he dealt only with essential business. His army of Continental soldiers had thinned to a paltry 2,500 men. It must have been a huge relief to him when Martha arrived in camp in mid-March. She had long since bowed to her fate as faithful helpmeet, the person who could cater to his emotional needs and create an entertaining social life. It helped that she had struck up a warm rapport with his military family.

Martha set about to get her husband to relax and enjoy the convivial society of several ladies. She organized cordial dinners, pleasant jaunts on horseback, and other lighthearted escapes. Everyone watched the commander in chief visibly brighten in her presence, confirming that theirs was a happy marriage. A young French aristocrat shortly to arrive at camp, the Marquis de Lafayette, viewed Martha as "a modest and respectable person, who loves her husband madly."[50] A sharp-eyed newcomer to the scene, Martha Daingerfield Bland, wife of a Virginia colonel, corroborated the "perfect felicity" between the Washingtons.[51] Mrs. Bland enjoyed the outings on horseback, which gave her a chance to ogle the personable young aides—"all polite sociable gentlemen," as she informed her sister-in-law Fanny. She seemed especially attracted to Hamilton, describing him as "a sensible, genteel, polite young fellow, a West Indian."[52] Most of all she was positively smitten with Washington: "Now let me speak of *our* noble and agreeable commander (for he commands both sexes), one by his excellent skill in military matters, the other by his ability, politeness, and attention."[53] Washington had a teasing, flirtatious nature, she hinted; with attractive young women, there was nothing dour about him. At riding parties, she wrote, "General Washington throws off the Hero and takes on the chatty, agreeable companion. He can be downright impudent sometimes— such impudence, Fanny, as you and I like."[54]

Whenever possible, Washington enlisted the support of women in the war, especially in donating clothing, bandages, or other supplies. When Sarah Bache, Benjamin Franklin's daughter, sent such a gift on behalf of patriotic women, Washington replied gallantly that "the value of the donation will be greatly enhanced by a consideration of the hands by which it was made and presented."[55] Often, when he addressed women during the war, a gracious note leavened his careworn prose. Quite different were his stormy relations with the hundreds of women who tagged after the army. Some "camp followers" were undoubtedly prostitutes, but many more were wives and friends of soldiers who washed, sewed, and baked in exchange for daily rations. Washington objected that they bogged down the speedy movement of his army, and it especially irked him when women were given critically short spaces in wagons. As he complained early in the conflict, "The multitude of women . . . especially those who are pregnant, or have children, are a clog upon every movement."[56] In the end Washington threw up his hands in despair and concluded that he couldn't exile these women without sacrificing their husbands and lovers, "some of the oldest and best soldiers in the service."[57]

During the summer of 1777 Washington invited into his retinue a prepossessing young aide who brought dash and brilliance to the task. John Laurens, twenty-two, was the son of Henry Laurens, who would succeed John Hancock as president of the Continental Congress and was one of South Carolina's largest slave owners.

The younger Laurens had a classy European education—schooling in Geneva, legal study in London—and enhanced both the intellect and the reforming spirit of Washington's staff. In later describing Laurens, Washington issued the sterling appraisal that "no man possessed more of the amor patria—in a word, he had not a fault that I ever could discover, unless intrepidity bordering upon rashness could come under that denomination, and to this he was excited by the purest motives."[58] As with Hamilton, Tilghman, and several others, Washington showed a special affinity for ambitious young aides who looked trim in uniform or astride a horse and possessed great charm and intelligence.

Because Washington was childless and drew close to several aides, many biographers have been tempted to turn them into surrogate sons, but the only one who closely matched this description was the Marquis de Lafayette, who eagerly embraced the role. The young French nobleman was tall and slim, with a pale, oval face and thin, reddish-brown hair that receded sharply at the temples. His nose was long and slightly upturned, his mouth short but full-lipped. Like the young Washington, Lafayette had an extraordinary knack for endearing himself to older men, and he looked up to them admiringly.

Washington's fondness for Lafayette's boyish zest probably expressed some suppressed craving for paternal intimacy. So many things about the younger man—his florid language, his poetic effusions, his transparent ambitions, his well-meaning if clumsy manner—seemed the antithesis of himself. Lafayette was pure-hearted and high-spirited, with an impetuous streak of grandiosity. Where Washington was guarded about his pursuit of fame, Lafayette, Jefferson saw, was always "panting for glory" with an almost "canine appetite for popularity and fame."[59] Abigail Adams found him too assertive: "He is dangerously amiable, polite, affable, insinuating, pleasing, hospitable, indefatigable, and ambitious."[60] Indeed, despite a certain shyness, Lafayette showed a courtier's love of compliments, was a master of flattery, and liked to hug people in the French manner. Perhaps Washington doted on the young man because he dared to express emotions that he himself stifled, thawing his frosty reserve and opening an outlet for his suppressed emotions. Lafayette seemed to transport Washington back to his own youth, before he was stooped under the weight of responsibility, reminding him of love, passion, and chivalry.

Lafayette fell readily into the deferential, filial role. Unlike the arrogant French officers who flocked to America for self-serving reasons, Lafayette was actuated by true idealism. Though lacking battlefield experience, he was a fast study, showed courage under fire, and had an imaginative mind for military schemes. If he seemed slightly ridiculous at first, he turned into an intrepid warrior and a general of considerable finesse. Once again Washington showed an excellent eye for talent. By the end of the war, he delivered this encomium to Lafayette: "He possesses uncommon military talents, is of a quick and sound judgment, persevering and enterprising without rashness, and besides these, he is of a very conciliating temper and perfectly sober . . . qualities that rarely combine in the same person."[61]

Born into an illustrious family in 1757, Lafayette bore a baptismal name of stupefying grandeur: Marie-Joseph-Paul-Yves-Roch-Gilbert du Motier de La Fayette. "I was baptized like a Spaniard," he wrote, "with the name of every conceivable saint who might offer me more protection in battle."[62] When he was only two, his father was cut down by a British cannon. This untimely loss and his upbringing on a vast estate in central France bred dreams of military honor: "I remember nothing of my childhood more than my fervor for tales of glory and my plans to travel the world in quest of fame."[63] When he was twelve, his mother died, leaving the orphan with a huge inheritance and relatives sprinkled throughout the French aristocracy. He attended an exclusive riding school at Versailles, socializing with the king's grandsons and mingling with grandees. At age sixteen, he married fourteen-year-old Adrienne de Noailles, thereby attaching himself to one of France's noblest families; the marriage contract was signed by King Louis XV himself. Lafayette joined a Masonic military lodge and captained the Noailles Dragoons. He and his young bride became habitués of the masked balls and banquets hosted by Louis XVI and his foreign bride, Marie-Antoinette. Finding Versailles pretentious and decadent, Lafayette was convinced that he lacked the social talents to thrive there as a courtier: "My awkward manner made it impossible for me to bend to the graces of the court or to the charms of a supper in the capital."[64] So gauche was he that when he once danced with Marie-Antoinette, the queen threw back her head and laughed at him outright.

Perhaps Lafayette was searching for some escape when he attended a dinner in 1775 and heard rousing tales of the American independence movement: "When I first heard of [the colonists'] quarrel, my heart was enlisted, and I thought only of joining my colors to those of the revolutionaries."[65] He was then in a military camp at Metz, and Adrienne was pregnant with their first child, but he began to plot a path to North America. In April 1777 Lafayette, only nineteen, took charge of a cargo boat named *La Victoire,* stocked it with food and munitions, and secretly set sail in defiance of a royal order. The beau monde of Paris was electrified by this quixotic deed, and Voltaire knelt before Adrienne in homage to her husband. On the voyage, between bouts of seasickness, Lafayette brushed up on his English and studied military strategy. Already intoxicated with revolutionary rhetoric, he wrote to his wife, "The happiness of America is intimately connected with the happiness of all mankind."[66]

In June Lafayette landed in South Carolina and viewed this new land through rose-colored glasses. "What charms me here is that all the citizens are brothers," he told his wife. "In America there are no paupers, or even the sort of people we call peasants."[67] Armed with a letter from Benjamin Franklin, the starry-eyed young nobleman went straight to Philadelphia and met John Hancock. In his letter Franklin recommended that the well-connected Lafayette be coddled and shielded from danger, expressing hope that "his bravery and ardent desire to distinguish himself will be a little restrained by . . . prudence, so as not to permit his being hazarded much but on some important occasion."[68] Lafayette was so young that his friends wanted to send him money via Washington, who would then dole it out like an allowance. Heeding Franklin's advice, Congress found a way both to flatter and to constrain Lafayette: he would enjoy the rank of major general, with the caveat that the title was strictly honorary.

Washington first met Lafayette at the City Tavern in Philadelphia on the evening of July 31, 1777. On the spot the young man, already decked out in a major general's sash, was awestruck. "Although [Washington] was surrounded by officers and citizens," Lafayette wrote home, "the majesty of his figure and his height were unmistakable."[69] Aware of Lafayette's diplomatic value, Washington befriended the young man and invited him to tour Delaware River fortifications with him the next day. Despite immediate cordiality between the two, an unspoken tension lurked as well. Lafayette didn't accept that his rank was merely for show and asked for two aides and command of a division, thereby presenting Washington with an excruciating dilemma. "If Congress meant that this rank should be unaccompanied by command," Washington complained to one congressman, "I wish it had been sufficiently explained to him."[70] He decided to invite the young Frenchman into his military family as an honorary aide.

Notwithstanding his fervent devotion to the cause, Lafayette sensed that Washington didn't trust him. "This thought was an obsession," he recalled almost fifty years later, "and it made me very unhappy."[71] Fortunately, the young man possessed a superb sense of Washington's psychology and behaved in a becomingly modest fashion. A week after their first meeting, Washington asked him to review the Continental Army with him, which Lafayette described as "eleven thousand men, poorly armed and even more poorly clothed."[72] Watching these threadbare men, Washington confessed to Lafayette that "we should be embarrassed to show ourselves to an officer who has just left the French army."[73] Lafayette's response was inspired: "It is not to teach but to learn that I come hither."[74] Such modesty won Washington's affection, and he grew closer to this young French acolyte. Nothing pleased Washington more than unconditional loyalty, and Lafayette served it up in abundance. The marquis told his wife that the general, "surrounded by flatterers or secret enemies," had found in him "a sincere friend, in whose bosom he may always confide his most secret thoughts, and who will always speak the truth."[75]

Lafayette's modesty was especially beguiling considering that many French officers preened and jockeyed for positions. It had become fashionable in Paris for bumptious young officers and prodigal sons to seek commissions from American diplomats Benjamin Franklin and Silas Deane. "The noise of every coach now that enters my court terrifies me," Franklin admitted. "I am afraid to accept an invitation to dine abroad, being almost sure of meeting with some officer or officer's friend."[76] Unlike with Lafayette, these cynical officers were motivated less by idealism than by pure vanity. America simply represented a handy battlefield for winning honors. Washington bristled at the parade of pretentious French officers who strutted into his presence, demanding high appointments. He didn't speak French and delegated correspondence in that language to the bilingual Hamilton, whose mother came from a French Huguenot family, and to John Laurens, who had studied in Geneva. Swamped by foreign officers, Washington complained to John Hancock that they were "coming in swarms from old France and the islands . . . Their ignorance of our language and their inability to recruit men are insurmountable obstacles to their being ingrafted into our Continental battalions."[77] He pleaded with Franklin to stanch the flow of military frauds and pretenders. "Our corps being already formed and fully officered," he wrote, "every new arrival is only a source of embarrassment to congress and myself and of disappointment and chagrin to the gentlemen who come over."[78] Compared with the persistent French officers who clamored noisily for commissions, the Marquis de Lafayette seemed the soul of humility.

CHAPTER TWENTY-FIVE

Darkness Visible

FROM THE LATE SPRING through early summer of 1777, George Washington anxiously tracked British movements in New York, attempting to divine their hidden meaning. General Howe commanded an army double or treble the size of his own, keeping him in an agony of suspense. Would the British general suddenly lunge north to hook up with General Burgoyne, who was then marching south from Canada? Or would he head for Philadelphia by sea or land to exploit the propaganda triumph of expelling the Continental Congress from the city?

To guard against any action along the Hudson River, Washington kept forces in the Hudson Highlands; to protect Philadelphia, he kept another portion of his army stationed at Middlebrook, New Jersey, ready to rebuff thrusts into the state. As usual, Howe proved diabolically clever at deception, making several feints into New Jersey. When he had tried to draw the Americans camped in Morristown into open combat, Washington had refused to rise to the bait. "We have such contradictory accounts from different quarters," a confounded Washington reflected, "that I find it impossible to form any satisfactory judgment of the real motions and intentions of the enemy."[1] Reports that Howe was recruiting pilots acquainted with the Delaware River strengthened Washington's hunch that the British planned to invade Philadelphia by water. Howe's reconnaissance of American defenses on the Delaware would persuade him to try a novel approach to the city.

During this period, as he drilled his men, Washington had to sacrifice the comforts of his winter camp. At Middlebrook he slept for five weeks in one of his official tents, or "sleeping marquees." At one point he led his troops to a "very difficult and rugged gorge" called the Clove in the Hudson Highlands, where he found only a tumbledown log cabin for shelter. He occupied the sole bed, while aides dozed on the floor around him. "We had plenty of sepawn [boiled cornmeal] and milk and all were contented," said Timothy Pickering.[2]

While at the Clove, Washington was blindsided by shocking news: Fort Ticonderoga, in upstate New York, had fallen. In an ignominious defeat, the American garrison had surrendered without a shot. Simply staggered, Washington spluttered to General Schuyler that it was "an event of chagrin and surprise not apprehended, nor within the compass of my reasoning."[3] Washington feared that Ticonderoga's downfall was merely the prelude to a British attempt to slice the country in half along the Hudson River; Howe would move up the river from New York to rendezvous with Burgoyne. Then on July 23 Howe's New York–based fleet—the biggest armada ever to cruise North American waters—set sail from Sandy Hook, its mysterious movements keeping Washington suspended "in a state of constant perplexity."[4] Guessing correctly that Howe was bound for Philadelphia, Washington began deploying his men southward. After breakfast on July 31, a messenger came to him with fresh tidings: the British fleet of 228 ships had surfaced off the capes of the Delaware River. By occupying Philadelphia, Howe hoped to tap latent Tory sentiment in the mid-Atlantic states and break American morale.

In his maddening way, Howe then disappeared again with his fleet, unnerving Washington anew. "I confess the conduct of the enemy is distressing beyond measure and past our comprehension," he said.[5] His army wilted in oppressive heat during exhausting marches intended to counter British moves. In late August the wily Howe showed up in the Chesapeake Bay with an unorthodox strategy for taking Philadelphia. Instead of trying to capture it from the river, he planned to land his troops at Head of Elk, in the northern bay, then march north to Philadelphia. Frankly flummoxed, Washington surmised that Howe "must mean to reach Philadelphia by that route, though to be sure it is a very strange one."[6] The truth was that Howe aimed to lure his foe into a major confrontation. Washington now professed eagerness for such an engagement: "One bold stroke will free the land from rapine, devastations and burnings, and female innocence from brutal lust and violence."[7]

As he rushed to defend Philadelphia, Washington decided to march his men through the city before their looming encounter with British forces. A showman by nature, he wanted to advertise the size and élan of the Continental Army, and he choreographed their movements down to the last details. For this grand spectacle, each soldier was to wear a green sprig, a symbol of victory, affixed to his hat or hair. This stage-managed political march was designed, according to Washington, to "have some influence on the minds of the disaffected" in Philadelphia and on "those who are dupes" to the "artifices and opinions" of the British—in other words, Tories.[8]

On August 24, 1777, George Washington marched his army, twelve thousand strong, through Philadelphia, first down Front Street, then up Chestnut Street. Mounted on a white horse, he presented a shining figure at the head of the procession, with Lafayette riding at his side and Alexander Hamilton and John Laurens close behind. The tide of soldiers poured on for two hours, the men trooping twelve deep "with a lively smart step," said one observer, to the nimble beat of a fife and drum corps in each brigade.[9] A stickler for rhythm, Washington warned his soldiers to mind the beat, "without *dancing* along or totally disregarding the music, as too often has been the case."[10] Anyone who abandoned the parade route faced a stiff penalty of thirty-nine lashes. With every window and rooftop crammed with gaping spectators, the soldiers received a rousing reception from the exultant crowds. Although Washington tried to offer a sanitized version of his drab army, the half-clad soldiers fell short of the spic-and-span panache that John Adams wanted. "Our soldiers have not yet quite the air of soldiers," he protested. "They don't step exactly in time. They don't hold up their heads quite erect, nor turn out their toes exactly as they ought."[11] The rest of the crowd, however, seemed thrilled by the survival of this scrappy army against the world's foremost military machine.

As Howe moved toward Philadelphia, Washington decided to cut off his approach at a place called Brandywine Creek, a difficult stream to negotiate. He informed his men that the upcoming battle might be decisive. Should the British be defeated, he proclaimed, "they are utterly undone—the war is at an end. Now then is the time for our most strenuous exertions."[12] Not trusting to patriotism alone, he reminded his men that fleeing soldiers would "be instantly shot down as a just punishment to themselves and for examples to others."[13] Rediscovering the virtue of alcohol in battle, Washington issued an extra gill of rum (five fluid ounces) to each man on September 9 to fortify wavering courage.

A landscape of plunging ravines and forested hills, Brandywine Creek presented a natural line of defense southwest of Philadelphia. Washington concentrated the bulk of his forces on wooded high ground behind Chadds Ford, on the east side of the creek, where the major road crossed. Relying on flawed intelligence, he posted detachments the length of the creek, stretching up to what he thought was the northernmost crossing.

On the night of September 10, a spy informed Howe of the existence of two fords still farther north—a flagrant breach in American defenses that had gone unnoticed, in a manner reminiscent of the Battle of Brooklyn. Howe decided that he and Cornwallis, with 8,200 men, would secretly execute a bold sweeping movement to the north. They would then turn east, cross these newly discovered fords, circle back to the south, and sneak up behind the right flank of Washington's army. All the while, an advance column of 5,000 troops under Baron Wilhelm von Knyphausen would smash straight east into Washington's army at Chadds Ford, distracting the

Americans and duping them into thinking this was the main enemy offensive. While Washington's military instincts told him that Howe might steal up behind his right flank, he didn't assign a high enough priority to investigating this possibility and delegated a crucial scouting mission to General John Sullivan and Colonel Theodorick Bland. Unaccountably, the Americans proved ignorant of their own home turf, while Howe operated with faultless information.

In the predawn light of September 11, 1777, General Howe launched his maneuver. In the early morning, Knyphausen's units clashed, as planned, with the main American force at Chadds Ford. Washington presided over the troops there and, as usual, showed no qualms about exposing himself to enemy fire, even when it beheaded an artilleryman nearby. The story is told that the chivalrous Major Patrick Ferguson actually had Washington in his sights and could easily have killed him— he didn't know who it was—but refused to fire on a man with his back turned. Washington was pleased when Brigadier General William Maxwell rode up and boasted that his marksmen had killed or wounded three hundred British soldiers.[14] With Lafayette at his side, Washington rode the length of the line to the sound of cheering men, but he was blind to the true shape of the emerging battlefield.

Aware that he saw only a fraction of the British Army, Washington was tormented by a nagging question: What had happened to the bulk of the enemy's forces? Around noon Lieutenant Colonel James Ross of Pennsylvania informed him that, on a reconnaissance expedition, he had clashed with five thousand British troops on the west side of Brandywine Creek, along the Great Valley Road; he thought these troops had been led by General Howe himself. Washington didn't fathom the full meaning of this news, though he did, as a precaution, shift troops under Adam Stephen and Lord Stirling to bolster General Sullivan's men at Birmingham Hill, a position to his right that was well placed to resist any sudden flanking move from the upper forks.

On the spot, as his original battle plan unraveled, Washington sorted through a blizzard of contradictory information. Charles Cotesworth Pinckney of South Carolina remembered his patent frustration: "I heard him bitterly lament that Coll Bland had not sent him any information at all and that the accounts he had received from others were of a very contradictory nature."[15] Amid sharp clashes at Chadds Ford, General Sullivan relayed a report from Major Joseph Spear saying that he, too, had been at the Great Valley Road but found not a trace of Howe's army. Tricked by Howe many times, Washington feared that his nemesis was about to deceive him again. Indeed, he drew the wrong conclusion from Spear's report: he imagined that Howe had turned south and was doubling back to Chadds Ford. But in fact Howe was heading north in a long, looping movement; around noon his soldiers and horses, veiled by thick fog, waded across the northern crossing at Jeffries Ford, of whose existence Washington was unaware. As they splashed through waist-high water, the British and Hessians were flabbergasted to encounter no American resistance. By one-fifteen P.M. Washington had received reports of two British brigades moving upon Birmingham Hill from the north and abruptly realized that Howe had outwitted him. He spurred his horse toward the hill as fast as it would fly, but he still didn't comprehend that the two brigades were merely the advance guard of Howe's vast army.

Around four P.M., to the resounding beat of drums, British and German troops barreled forward in three sharply drawn columns, undeterred by a torrent of American canister and grapeshot. Piercing a wide hole in American lines, they engineered a deadly attack, firing muskets and charging in bayonet attacks. Tree branches snapped, leaves fluttered down, and gun smoke enveloped the battlefield. Soon the ground was thickly littered with dead bodies, mostly American, and some patriot divisions turned tail and ran. To complete a pincer movement against the Americans, Knyphausen and his men blasted their way across Brandywine Creek, diving at the Americans in a fierce bayonet attack that left the water dyed red with blood. The American private Elisha Stevens recorded the horror of "cannons roaring, muskets cracking, drums beating, bombs flying all round," not to mention the groans of dying men.[16] At five P.M. Washington dictated a message to Congress: "At half after four o'clock, the enemy attacked General Sullivan at the ford next above this and the action has been very violent ever since. It still continues. A very severe cannonade has begun here, too, and I suppose we shall have a very hot evening."[17] Washington had been completely deceived by Howe. "A contrariety of intelligence, in a critical and important point, contributed greatly, if it did not entirely bring on the misfortunes of that day," he later wrote.[18]

Three routed American divisions fell back "in the most broken and confused manner," according to Nathanael Greene, who managed to fight a noble rearguard action with his division. During the American retreat Lafayette showed his usual valor, jumping into the fray to rally his men. Shot in the left calf, he didn't grasp the severity of the wound until his boot was soaked with blood and he had to be lifted off the battlefield. Possibly with some exaggeration, he claimed years later that Washington told the surgeon, "Take care of him as if he were my son, for I love him the same."[19] If true, this was an extraordinary statement, given how briefly Washington had known Lafayette. It would confirm that the young French nobleman had touched him in some special way, and it again speaks to Washington's unseen emotional depths. He was always impressed by Lafayette's bravery, his eagerness to return to service. "When [Washington] learned I wanted to rejoin the army too soon," Lafayette told his wife, "he wrote the warmest of letters, urging me to concentrate on getting well first."[20]

With the sound of muskets still reverberating in their ears, the overpowered Americans streamed east toward Chester in an unruly flight. Lafayette recalled the confused swarm of carts, cannon, and other military paraphernalia that the soldiers managed to salvage. These battlefield refugees, who straggled into the American camp throughout the night, left behind so many hundreds of bleeding compatriots at Brandywine Creek that Howe asked Washington to send doctors to care for them. All told, the Americans lost about 200 killed, 500 wounded, and 400 captured versus only 90 killed and 500 wounded for the triumphant British.

Toward midnight, in a private home in Chester, Washington informed Congress of the shattering defeat. After asking Timothy Pickering to draft a note, he found the message so dispiriting that he said some "words of encouragement" were needed.[21] If this was self-serving, it also reflected Washington's firm belief that he had to uphold American morale at all costs. The management of defeat had become an essential aspect of his repertoire. Rather desperately, he tried to give a positive gloss to the terrible thrashing his men had taken, grossly understating American losses. His letter to John Hancock began, "Sir: I am sorry to inform you that in this day's engagement, we have been obliged to leave the enemy masters of the field."[22] It continued: "Our loss of men is not, I am persuaded, very considerable; I believe much less than the enemy's . . . Notwithstanding the misfortune of the day, I am happy to find the troops in good spirits; and I hope another time, we shall compensate for the losses now sustained."[23] This sounded, after the bloody disaster, like sheer fantasy, but the troops *had* fought in a spirited manner; the defeat resulted from the failed performance of the leaders, not the lethargy of the rank and file. Two weeks after the battle Washington still maintained that "the enemy's loss was considerable and much superior to ours."[24]

It had been an ignoble defeat for Washington, who had failed to heed clues that might have unlocked the key to Howe's strategy. The commander in chief had frequently seemed marginal to the battle. As Pickering said, Washington had behaved more like "a passive spectator than the commanding general."[25] Fighting on home territory near Philadelphia, he should have been able to master the terrain instead of relying on crude maps and erring scouts. The carnage and chaos of Brandywine only reinforced an image of Washington as dithering and indecisive.

Thomas Jefferson traced Washington's strengths and weaknesses as a general to a persistent mental trait. He prepared thoroughly for battles and did extremely well if everything went according to plan. "But if deranged during the course of the action," Jefferson noted, "if any member of his plan was dislocated by sudden circumstances, he was slow in readjustment."[26] With a mind neither quick nor nimble, Washington lacked the gift of spontaneity and found it difficult to improvise on the spot. Baron Johann de Kalb, who came to America with Lafayette, echoed Jefferson's critique when he said of Washington after the Brandywine defeat, "He is the most amiable, obliging, and civil man but, as a general, he is too slow, even indolent, much too weak, and is not without his portion of vanity and presumption."[27] Even Washington's faithful ally Nathanael Greene confided to Pickering that he found Washington indecisive. "For my part," he boasted, "I decide in a moment."[28] Washington's inestimable strength, whether as a general, a planter, or a politician, was prolonged deliberation and slow, mature decisions, but these were luxuries seldom permitted in the heat and confusion of battle.

Somewhat unfairly, congressional opinion found General Sullivan culpable for passing along bad information to Washington. The latter had the good grace to acquit Sullivan of any blame, but he didn't admit failure readily. Dr. Benjamin Rush left an acidulous portrait of Washington's compliant general staff after Brandywine. He saw the commander as a passive figure manipulated by Greene, Knox, and Hamilton and portrayed his generals as a rogues' gallery of incompetent buffoons: "The first [Greene] a sycophant to the general, speculative without enterprise. The second [Sullivan] weak, vain, without dignity, fond of scribbling, in the field a madman. The third [Stirling] a proud, vain, lazy, ignorant drunkard. The fourth [Stephen] a sordid, boasting, cowardly sot."[29] His description of the "undisciplined and ragged" American camp was scarcely more flattering, a scene of "bad bread, no order, universal disgust."[30] It was true that Washington surrounded himself with loyal men, but he never walled himself off from contrary opinion or tried to force his views on his generals.

After the Brandywine disaster, Washington marched his battered army north across the Schuylkill River to Pennypacker's Mill. No longer could he guarantee the safety of the American capital. He sent Alexander Hamilton and Henry Lee scurrying off on an urgent mission to burn flour mills on the Schuylkill before they were captured by the British. On the night of September 18, Hamilton alerted Hancock that the British might enter the city by daybreak, triggering a panicky exodus of congressmen in the night. Thomas Paine remembered Philadelphia's moonlit streets thronged by so many people that the town resembled high noon on market day. "Congress was chased like a covey of partridges from Philadelphia to Trenton, from Trenton to Lancaster," recalled John Adams, who was especially upset by the emergency move and disenchanted with the man he had once championed to lead the Continental Army.[31] In his diary he scribbled, "Oh, Heaven! Grant us one great soul! . . . One active, masterly capacity would bring order out of this confusion and save this country."[32]

The British didn't claim possession of the capital for another week, giving Washington a chance to gather vital supplies. Invoking emergency powers, he sent Hamilton into the city, assisted by one hundred men, to requisition supplies. Many soldiers had shed blankets and clothing, and one thousand were barefoot; with the weather turning colder, these items rated high on the list of goods Hamilton demanded from residents during two frantic days of activity. Always skittish about employing autocratic powers in a war fought for liberty, Washington had Hamilton issue receipts to residents, in the hope they would someday be reimbursed. This highly effective operation yielded forty rounds of ammunition per soldier.

Around this time Washington received another sickening piece of news. On the night of September 20–21 British infantry had crept through the woods near Paoli and massacred American troops led by General Anthony Wayne. To ensure surprise, the British did not load their muskets but rushed forward with fixed bayonets and pitilessly slashed their sleeping victims, killing or wounding three hundred Americans. Even the British soldiers seemed appalled by the blood-smeared corpses, one saying it was "more expressive of horror than all the thunder of the artillery . . . on the day of action."[33] To worsen matters, hungry American soldiers went marauding through the countryside, terrorizing inhabitants. Tired of marching in drenching rains, they sought shelter wherever they could find it. When the Reverend Henry Muhlenberg had to bury a child at his church near Valley Forge, he found Washington's men defiling it. An outraged Muhlenberg said that "several had placed the objects of their gluttony on the altar. In short, I saw, in miniature, the abomination of desolation in the temple."[34] If such desecration was the antithesis of the orderly behavior Washington craved, it was hard to maintain morale with meager pay and a dearth of military victories.

On September 26 the well-fed British Army entered Philadelphia and scored the propaganda victory of controlling America's capital and main metropolis. While frightened citizens applauded the soldiers, as they had their American counterparts a month earlier, the crowd consisted mostly of women and children, many men having fled. By this point Washington knew he was engaged in a war of attrition and that holding towns was less important in this mobile style of warfare. As he informed Henry Laurens, "The possession of our towns, while we have an army in the field, will avail [the British] little . . . It is our arms, not defenseless towns, they have to subdue."[35]

ALTHOUGH CORNWALLIS HAD TAKEN a detachment of British and Hessian soldiers into Philadelphia, General Howe retained the main body of his army at Germantown, a village just six miles northwest of the city, hard by the Schuylkill River. He expressly placed it there as a bulwark between Washington's army and the capital. Eager for a victory after so much wretched news, and with 8,000 Continentals and 3,000 militia at his disposal, Washington reckoned that he could stage a surprise raid on Howe's force of 9,000 men, an idea that grew on him when he learned that Howe had diverted two regiments to attack a small American fort on the Delaware.

At a war council on October 3, Washington told his receptive generals that Howe's maneuver made it an auspicious moment for an operation. Forever attuned to the psychological state of his men, he knew this might be the last chance for a victory before winter. Only something dramatic could revive his countrymen's flagging spirits. As he told his generals, "It was time to remind the English that an American army still existed."[36] Once again Washington's aggressive instincts forced him into an action both courageous and foolhardy, one that belied his cautious image as the American Fabius. As Joseph Ellis has written of Washington's conflicting urges, "The strategic decision to make the survival of the Continental Army the highest priority, the realization that he must fight a protracted defensive war, remained at odds with his own more decisive temperament."[37]

As usual, Howe had shrewdly chosen his army camp at Germantown, a place crisscrossed by creeks, ravines, and gorges. The town's main street, the Germantown Road, was lined for two miles with snug, stone houses, many protected by fences and hedges that could retard an American advance. Doubtless remembering his nocturnal raid across the Delaware, Washington devised another convoluted plan for a forced nighttime march. On October 3 four widely spaced but roughly parallel columns would start moving southeast at nightfall and would converge on Germantown by dawn. Along with General Sullivan, Washington would spearhead a column of 3,000 men charging down the Germantown Road. To the northeast, Greene would lead 5,000 men along a parallel path, the Lime Kiln Road, while still farther north General William Smallwood and another 1,000 militia would venture along a winding old Indian path called the Old York Road. To the south, General John Armstrong would guide 2,000 Pennsylvania militia along the Schuylkill. If all went according to plan, Washington's central column would swoop down on the unsuspecting British, while Greene's column swung around and pinioned their helpless army against the Schuylkill River.

As his troops gathered at dusk on October 3, Washington took several precautions that suggested a premonition of problems to come. Because the Continental Army lacked a common uniform, he had his men insert shining white papers in their hats so they wouldn't accidentally shoot each other. Short on supplies, one New Jersey regiment donned "redcoats" captured from British troops, awakening understandable fears of men's being killed by friendly fire. The fifteen-mile march overnight would be further complicated by a rolling fog that sealed off the four columns from one another. As had happened during the Delaware crossing, the operation ran hours behind schedule, and the element of surprise was sacrificed when a Loyalist warned the British of approaching Americans.

Washington's column was still stalled north of town when daylight streaked the sky. Up ahead, at an area known as Mount Airy, he could hear brisk musketry fire. Everything was so obscured by morning fog that he could only conjecture what was happening. Mindful that his men bore just forty rounds apiece, he instructed Pickering, "I am afraid General Sullivan is throwing away his ammunition. Ride forward and tell him to preserve it."[38] The fighting at Mount Airy took a savage turn as Americans tried to avenge the unspeakable massacre at Paoli, shouting "Have at the bloodhounds! Revenge Wayne's affair!"[39] After heavy casualties on both sides, the British regiment finally retreated. When Washington reached the outskirts of Germantown, he beheld a surreal sight: the British had torched the fields of buckwheat so that billowing smoke mingled with fog made the dawn "infinitely dark," as he remembered.[40] It was a hellish scene, with visibility restricted to thirty yards. For once the fog of war was more than metaphorical. One American officer remembered that "the smoke of the fire of cannon and musketry, the smoke of several fields of stubble, hay and other combustibles . . . made such a midnight darkness that [a] great part of the time there was no discovering friend from foe."[41] When Washington saw discarded British tents and cannon lying alongside the road, he concluded that the first phase of his operation was succeeding.

As he and his men advanced down the Germantown Road, they were startled by a withering shower of musket balls. Through the mist, they perceived that the fire emanated from the windows of a three-story country house owned by Benjamin Chew, which had been commandeered by one hundred British soldiers. Perched on high ground, the stone house was made of locally quarried schist, starred with mica; classical statuary dotted the grounds. The British had turned the Georgian house into an impregnable fortress by bolting and barricading the door, shuttering the many windows, and training their weapons on the Americans. For a moment, it seemed the entire patriotic effort might founder on this single stubborn obstacle. Washington summoned an impromptu conference of officers on horseback. Most favored cordoning off the Chew house and pushing on, leaving a single regiment in the rear to subdue it. Then Henry Knox, speaking with resonant authority, cited the military doctrine that, in hostile country, one never left a fortified castle in the rear. This sounded like the sage voice of experience, and Washington made a snap judgment to side with this minority view. It would prove a costly error.

Under orders from Washington, Lieutenant Colonel William Smith, carrying a white flag, approached the house with a demand for surrender. The British holed up inside instantly shot and killed the colonel. At this point Washington assigned three regiments to the thankless task of vanquishing the stout house. Knox ringed it with four cannon and pummeled it at oblique angles, but the stone walls seemed impervious. The prolonged attempt to take the Chew house held up part of Washington's column for half an hour and gave Howe's men a chance to regroup. Small squads of Americans kept darting toward the house, only to be pelted by British fire until the grounds were "strewn with a prodigious number of rebel dead," said a British officer.[42] Those who tried to clamber through the windows were pierced with bayonets. One Hessian officer, viewing this slaughterhouse the next day, "counted seventy-five dead Americans, some of whom lay stretched in the doorways, under the tables and chairs, and under the windows . . . The rooms of the house were riddled by cannonballs, and looked like a slaughter house because of the blood splattered around."[43] Three American regiments managed to kill a risible four British soldiers. In a scathing judgment of this misstep, General Anthony Wayne later wrote, "A *windmill* attack was made upon a house into which six light companies had thrown themselves to avoid our bayonets. Our troops were deceived by this attack, thinking it something formidable. They fell back to assist . . . confusion ensued and we ran away from the arms of victory open to receive us."[44]

Belatedly, Washington heeded his dissenting officers and told his army to move on, leaving a small detachment behind. Cool as ever, shielded only by a pack of aides, Washington again exposed himself to danger on his conspicuous white horse. "With great concern I saw our brave commander-in-chief exposing himself to the hottest fire of the enemy," recalled Sullivan, and "regard to my country obliged me to ride to him and beg him to retire."[45] Washington briefly withdrew to the rear, only to ride forward again. At first he imagined he was hearing the sound of British soldiers retreating, with the enemy falling back "in the utmost confusion."[46] He was so sanguine of victory that he nearly ordered his men to march to Philadelphia. Washington remained unalterably convinced that, until bad weather reversed the situation, the British had been on the brink of withdrawing from the battlefield.

Unfortunately, the strange conditions had played havoc with his overly intricate plan. Enveloped in fog and drifting smoke, the four columns found it hard to coordinate their actions. As so often with Washington's strategies, the many interlocking parts were hard to harmonize. American soldiers began firing at one another in the fog, precipitating a headlong retreat. False reports flew about of an enemy force in the rear, causing patriots to flee a phantom enemy. Washington ordered Major Benjamin Tallmadge to block these stampeding foot soldiers by lining up a row of horses across the road, only to have the infantry run around or crawl desperately beneath them. Washington shouted at his men, even struck at them with his sword, as he had done at Kip's Bay—to no effect. At the same time Greene's men to the north were falling back in disorderly fashion. The whole battle lasted less than three hours.

By nine P.M. the American troops had regathered at Pennypacker's Mill, twenty miles away. By all accounts, they weren't bowed or crestfallen. "They appeared to me to be only sensible of a disappointment, not a defeat, and to be more displeased at their retreating from Germantown than anxious to get to their rendezvous," said Thomas Paine.[47] But the final tally of battle—150 Americans killed, 520 wounded, and 400 captured versus 70 British killed, 450 wounded, and 15 captured—decidedly favored the British. "In a word," Washington told his brother Jack, "it was a bloody day. Would to heaven I could add that it had been a more fortunate one for us."[48]

In a letter Howe complained of the torching of flour mills and the suffering of law-abiding citizens; on October 6 Washington replied in a sternly worded reproach. He noted the "wanton and unnecessary depredations" committed by Howe's own army and the annihilation of Charlestown.[49] On that same day, in a magnificently gallant gesture, he sent Howe a two-line letter about a dog found roaming the Germantown battlefield. It said in full: "General Washington's compliments to General Howe. He does himself the pleasure to return [to] him a dog, which accidentally fell into his hands, and by the inscription on the collar appears to belong to General Howe."[50] How could the British portray such a man as a wild-eyed revolutionary?

Although Germantown ended in defeat, Washington had shown extraordinary audacity. With grudging admiration, Howe conceded that he didn't think "the enemy would have dared to approach after so recent a defeat as that at Brandywine."[51] The French foreign minister, the Count de Vergennes, who was pondering an alliance with America, claimed that "nothing struck him so much" as the Battle of Germantown.[52] He was impressed that Washington, stuck with raw recruits, had fought two consecutive battles against highly seasoned troops. In writing about the battle, Washington stressed how bravely his men had fought and how narrowly victory had eluded them. "Unfortunately, the day was overcast by a dark and heavy fog," he told one correspondent, "which prevented our columns from discovering each other's movement . . . Had it not been for this circumstance, I am fully persuaded the enemy would have sustained a total defeat."[53] In narrating events to Hancock, he disguised the fact that twice as many Americans as British had been killed. "Upon the whole," he wrote, "it may be said the day was rather unfortunate than injurious. We sustained no material loss of men . . . and our troops, who are not in the least dispirited by it, have gained what all young troops gain by being in actions."[54] Of these assertions, the last came closest to the mark: the battle was the sort of defeat that supplies a fillip to the confidence of the losing side. Now, Washington averred, his men knew they could "confuse and rout even the flower of the British army with the greatest ease."[55] Congress seemed to agree with this generous assessment and not only commended Washington for bravery but forged a medal in his honor. After the humiliating flight of Congress from Philadelphia, the Battle of Germantown had proved that the patriotic cause, if ailing, was far from moribund.

Rapping a Demigod over the Knuckles

TWO WEEKS AFTER the Battle of Germantown, George Washington digested the bittersweet news that General Horatio Gates had trounced General John Burgoyne at Saratoga, capturing his army of five thousand men. Just when Washington ached for a victory, his rival achieved a stunning conquest. A victory so incontestable made Gates the natural darling of Washington's critics. Washington knew that appearances would count heavily against him and that in the afterglow of Saratoga Gates's reputation would be gilded and his own recent defeats darkened. An anonymous pamphlet called *The Thoughts of a Freeman* made the rounds of Congress, indicting Washington's leadership with the damning remark that "the people of America have been guilty of idolatry in making a man their God."[1]

For all the adulation of Washington, a vocal, persistent minority of naysayers took issue with his leadership. As assorted voices of discontent echoed in Congress, these discussions were cloaked in secrecy. Writing to John Adams, Dr. Benjamin Rush voiced what others privately thought. Gates, he said, had planned his campaign with "wisdom and executed [it] with vigor and bravery," making a telling contrast with the hapless Washington, who had been "outgeneralled and twice beaten."[2] He extolled Gates's army as "a well-regulated family" while deriding Washington's as "an unformed mob."[3] The disgruntled Adams was relieved to see Gates victorious. "If it had been [Washington]," he said, "idolatry and adulation would have been unbounded, so excessive as to endanger our liberties."[4]

With excellent antennae for rivals, Washington knew that Gates represented a competitive threat to his leadership. In August Congress had arbitrated a feud between Philip Schuyler and Gates for control of the army's northern department.

Washington always felt warm friendship toward Schuyler, the undisputed favorite of the New Yorkers. But the bearish Gates, who often dispensed with etiquette, appealed to the rough, egalitarian instincts of the New Englanders, and his ambition only grew with success. In tactless letters, he accused Washington of everything from trying to monopolize "every tent upon the continent" to waylaying uniforms meant for his own regiments.[5]

In midsummer Schuyler had been blamed for the Ticonderoga debacle. In early August Congress had asked Washington to choose the next head of the army's northern department, and with commendable restraint, he declined. He didn't care to stir up a hornet's nest by meddling in the decision and sought to emphasize civilian control of the military. After all, it was Washington's reflexive restraint in seeking power that had enabled him to exercise so much of it. In this case, however, his neutrality paved the way for Congress to elect Gates. By ceding this power to Congress, Washington allowed his scheming rival to nourish the fantasy that he held an equal and independent command and was beholden only to Congress.

Washington performed another signal service for Gates that summer. Alarmed by Burgoyne's steady progress south from Canada, Washington grew convinced that only an "active, spirited officer" could stop him, and he recommended that General Benedict Arnold assist Gates: "He is active, judicious, and brave, and an officer in whom the militia will repose great confidence."[6] Washington also steered Daniel Morgan and five hundred sharpshooters to Gates. Many assigned the true credit for Saratoga to the impetuous Arnold, who had fought "inspired by the fury of a demon," one eyewitness said, suffering a severe gash in one leg from a musket ball.[7] Despite Arnold's contribution, Gates grew puffed up with his own power after the victory. If "old England is not by this taught a lesson of humility," he told his wife, "then she is an obstinate old slut."[8]

On October 15 Washington announced to his troops Gates's early victory at Saratoga, the Battle of Bemis Heights. His general orders suggest that he felt self-conscious about a possible comparison with his own performance. While he hailed "the troops under the command of General Gates," he also pointedly expressed hope that his own troops would prove "at least equal to their northern brethren in brave and intrepid exertions."[9] In a gesture pregnant with ominous implications, Gates didn't notify Washington directly of his victory. Instead, to underscore his autonomous command, he dispatched his flamboyant young aide, Colonel James Wilkinson, to apprise Congress. On October 18 Washington was informed of Burgoyne's surrender by a brief message from Governor George Clinton of New York. Charles Willson Peale was painting Washington's portrait when the news came. "Ah," Washington said tonelessly, reading the dispatch with an impassive face as he sat on the edge of a bed. "Burgoyne is defeated."[10] The unflappable Washington then continued with the session as if nothing had happened. It was a classic performance: he exercised the greatest self-control when roiled by the most unruly emotions. In public he tried hard to smile, but his private letters show he was saddened as well as gladdened by the news. "Let every face brighten and every heart expand with grateful joy and praise to the supreme disposer of all events," he told his troops, and detonated thirteen cannon to celebrate the victory.[11]

All the while Washington quietly steamed that Gates hadn't yet written to him. On October 24, when writing to John Hancock about a shortage of shoes and blankets, he confessed, "I am, and have been, waiting with the most anxious impatience for a confirmation of Gen[era]l Burgoyne's surrender. I have received no further intelligence respecting it."[12] Characteristically, he saved the most explosive lines until the end, trying to pass them off as an afterthought. Also characteristically, he waited nearly a week to complain and didn't mention Gates by name, as if he didn't want to tip his hand. In reply, Hancock, then stepping down as president of Congress, told Washington, "I have not as yet heard a word from Gen[era]l Gates . . . and his army. Should the agreeable news reach" him before he left town, he promised, he would forward it to Washington.[13] It was a bizarre situation: after one week, the outgoing president of the Continental Congress and the commander in chief still hadn't heard from Horatio Gates about the war's single most important development. When Washington received the articles of capitulation, signed by Burgoyne, they came via Israel Putnam. "As I have not rec[eive]d a single line from Gen[era]l Gates, I do not know what steps he is taking with the army under his command and therefore cannot advise what is most proper to be done in your quarter," Washington told Putnam, betraying considerable pent-up frustration.[14] Two days later he expressed to Richard Henry Lee his bitterness about Gates's snub and said that, for a time, he actually began to doubt that the Saratoga victory had taken place.

During this period Washington was camped at a farmhouse in Whitemarsh, Pennsylvania, a place so cramped that his aides slept on the floor before the fireplace and shared one tin plate. On November 2 Gates at last deigned to send him a short note, saying he was returning Colonel Morgan and his band of marksmen. Clearly, Gates had heard through the grapevine that Washington was agitated about not having heard from him and disposed of the matter in a cavalier line: "I am confident Your Excellency has long ago received all the good news from this quarter."[15] Never one to react on the spot, Washington bided his time to take his revenge upon Horatio Gates.

If he was elated by Burgoyne's capture, Washington also believed that many circumstances had favored Gates. The mid-Atlantic states, where Washington operated, was rife with Tories, while thousands of militiamen in upstate New York had harassed Burgoyne as his doomed soldiers struggled down the Hudson Valley.

"How different our case!" Washington complained, noting "the disaffection of [a] great part of the inhabitants of this state [and] the languor of others."[16] Washington had also never faced an enemy in Burgoyne's vulnerable situation of being dangerously cut off from supply lines. General Howe had never ranged far from his base in New York or other seaboard ports where he could fall back on British naval superiority, depriving Washington of a chance to strike a lethal blow. Still licking his wounds, Washington told Patrick Henry that he had been forced to defend Philadelphia "with less numbers than composed the army of my antagonist," even though popular opinion had wrongly attributed to him twice as many men.[17] Even Martha Washington heaved a weary sigh at the rank injustice of it all. Although she expressed "unspeakable pleasure" at Burgoyne's surrender, she added, "Would bountiful providence aim a like stroke at Gen[era]l Howe, the measure of my happiness would be complete."[18]

The Saratoga victory had a powerful resonance in European courts. Horace Walpole said that George III "fell into agonies" when he absorbed the terrible news.[19] Among the opposition party in Parliament, the defeat hardened resistance to approving more money and troops for a costly, faraway war. The repercussions were no less momentous in France. When Jonathan Loring Austin, fresh from America, rode up to Benjamin Franklin in Paris in early December, the elderly statesman gazed up at the young man on horseback and asked, "Sir, is Philadelphia taken?" "Yes, sir," replied Austin. Crestfallen, Franklin started to lumber off with a heavy heart. "But, sir, I have greater news than that," Austin shouted after him. "General Burgoyne *and his whole army are prisoners of war!*"[20] An ecstatic Franklin used this unexpected news as his most potent argument in luring France into the war on the American side.

Since Washington believed there was a significant numerical imbalance between his forces in Pennsylvania and those of Gates in upstate New York, he sent Alexander Hamilton streaking off toward Albany to request—and if necessary, demand—that Gates direct a portion of his troops southward to bolster Washington's army. Washington needed these troops to shore up forts along the Delaware, which might now be easy prey for Howe's army. He also reasoned that, with Burgoyne subdued, Gates required fewer troops. Hamilton's mission was a delicate one: these were heady days for the vainglorious Gates, who might well suspect that Washington was simply trying to steal his thunder, the better to vie with him for control of the Continental Army. Washington's choice of Hamilton as his emissary was astounding testimony to his faith in the young West Indian. Hamilton would have to ride at a breakneck pace, covering three hundred miles to Albany in five days, and he would need all the wit, toughness, and self-assurance at his disposal to stand up to Gates. It may have pleased Washington to tweak Gates's vanity by sending a twenty-two-year-old aide-de-camp to lay down the law to him.

On October 30 Washington handed Hamilton his marching orders, which stipulated that he should inform Gates of "the absolute necessity that there is for his detaching a very considerable part of the army at present under his command to the reinforcement of this."[21] When Hamilton arrived in Albany, Gates was predictably outraged to have to bargain with the youthful aide. That Hamilton regarded Gates as craven and inept didn't help matters. In a letter drafted but never sent to Washington, Gates fumed, "Although it is customary and even absolutely necessary to direct implicit obedience to be paid to the verbal orders of aides-de-camp in action . . . yet I believe it is never practiced to delegate that dictatorial power to one aide-camp sent to an army 300 miles distant."[22] Gates, in a cantankerous mood, insisted to Hamilton that he needed all his troops in case Sir Henry Clinton moved up the Hudson River. He seemed emboldened by his newly won renown. To Washington, Hamilton reported, "I found insuperable inconveniences in acting diametrically opposite to the opinion of a gentleman whose successes have raised him to the highest importance."[23] In a masterly performance, however, and after much wrangling, Hamilton extracted two brigades from the reluctant Gates.

The juxtaposition of Gates's victory and Washington's defeats crystallized congressional discontent with the latter's leadership. The rush of battles turned Congress into an assembly of would-be generals, determined to run the war by resolutions. There had always been sotto voce grumbling about Washington's military ability, but now serious questions arose as to whether he was up to the job. Henry Laurens told his son John that the assembly buzzed with detractors saying that "our army is under no regulations or discipline" and that Washington had failed to stem desertions or adequately provision his men.[24] Lafayette warned Washington of "stupid men" in Congress "who, without knowing a single word about war, undertake to judge you, to make ridiculous comparisons; they are infatuated with Gates."[25]

The discontent crested in October when Washington got wind of the rumored promotion to major general of Brigadier Thomas Conway. An engraving of Conway shows a man with a cool, haughty air. His small chin, tightly pursed lips, and alert eyes give him a petulant expression. Born in Ireland, he had been an officer in the French Army but, unlike Lafayette, was a self-aggrandizing fortune hunter. For him, the Continental Army was a convenient rung to grasp in clambering up the military hierarchy in France. Nathanael Greene saw him as "a man of much intrigue and little judgment" who joined the Continental Army to cash in on the fight.[26] "I freely own to you it was partly with a view of obtaining sooner the rank of brigadier in the French army that I have joined" the American army, Conway conceded to another officer that January.[27] An excellent judge of men, Washington recoiled from this self-promoting braggart and may also have learned that the sharp-tongued Irishman had denigrated him after Brandywine. "No man was more a gentleman than General Washington or appeared to more advantage at his table . . . but as to his talents for the command of an army, they were miserable indeed" was Conway's verdict.[28] Some of those skeptical of Washington's ability gravitated to Conway. "He seems to possess [General] Lee's knowledge and experience without any of his oddities and vices," Dr. Benjamin Rush declared. "He is, moreover, the idol of the whole army."[29]

Washington was incensed to learn about Conway's impending promotion, especially since he would be jumped over twenty more senior brigadiers. He had been dismayed by Conway's behavior at Germantown, accusing him of deserting his men, and now he departed from his usual practice of staying aloof from congressional deliberations. He wrote to Richard Henry Lee that Conway's promotion would "be as unfortunate a measure as ever was adopted."[30] Washington seldom spoke so brusquely, but there was more. "General Conway's merit then as an officer, and his importance in this army, exists more in his own imagination than in reality. For it is a maxim with him to leave no service of his untold."[31] Most shocking of all, Washington seemed ready to tender his own resignation. "To sum up the whole, I have been a slave to the service . . . but it will be impossible for me to be of any further service, if such insuperable difficulties are thrown in my way."[32] Washington was showing how adroit he could be at infighting, how skillful in suppressing lurking challenges to his supremacy. In many ways, he was more sure-footed in contesting political than military threats. He knew that power held in reserve—power deployed firmly but reluctantly—was always the most effective form. On October 20 Richard Henry Lee assured Washington that Conway would never be bumped up to major general, but Lee, a secret critic of Washington himself, disclosed something else disturbing: Congress intended to overhaul the Board of War, switching it from a legislative committee to an executive agency, staffed by general officers who would supervise the military. This news came as a revelation to Washington, who could only regard it as a powerful rebuke.

Amid an atmosphere of rampant suspicion, Washington received fresh proof that enemies in high places conspired against him. As mentioned, Gates had assigned his young aide James Wilkinson to carry the news of Saratoga to Congress. Later described by Washington as "lively, sensible, pompous, and ambitious," Wilkinson had a bombastic addiction to storytelling.[33] En route to Congress, this indiscreet young man paused in Reading, Pennsylvania, where he met with an aide to Lord Stirling and regaled him with stories of Gates's savage comments about Washington's actions at Brandywine Creek. He also showed him an inflammatory line that General Conway had written to General Gates, indicting Washington's leadership. "Heaven has been determined to save your country," Conway wrote, "or a weak general and bad councillors would have ruined it."[34] Lord Stirling, loyal to

Washington, passed along this offensive comment to him, remarking that "such wicked duplicity of conduct I shall always think it my duty to detect."[35] Washington was stunned to see the remark, which suggested blatant collusion between the two generals to blacken his name.

In meeting the threat, Washington reverted to his favorite technique, earlier used with Joseph Reed: sending an incriminating document to its author without comment. He would betray as little as possible of what he knew so as to let the guilty party incriminate himself. In sending Conway the line, Washington later said, he intended to convey "that I was not unapprised of his intriguing disposition."[36] Conway countered with a cagey note, telling Washington that he was "willing that my original letter to General Gates should be handed to you. This, I trust, will convince you of my way of thinking."[37] Of course, he didn't specify what his way of thinking was. On November 16, while avoiding any mention of their feud, Conway sent Washington a curt announcement: "The hopes and appearance of a French war, along with some other reasons, have induc[e]d me to send my resignation to Congress."[38] Since the resignation wasn't accepted, internecine warfare between the two men persisted.

When Washington confronted Gates about the letter, the latter described himself as "inexpressibly distressed" by the news, said he kept his papers closely guarded, and wondered about the identity of "the villain that has played me this treacherous trick."[39] Later on he contended the offending paragraph was a forgery. It didn't seem to occur to him that his own careless aide had caused the leak. Turning the tables on Washington, Gates even came up with a far-fetched accusation: that Alexander Hamilton, during his recent diplomatic mission, had purloined the papers from his files. "Those letters have been stealingly copied," Gates told Washington, turning himself into the injured party. "Crimes of that magnitude ought not to remain unpunished."[40] To Gates's mortification, Washington revealed that the culprit was Gates's own personal aide, the talkative James Wilkinson.

A principal instigator in the move to replace Washington was his former aide Thomas Mifflin, now a general. A portrait of Mifflin shows a man full of personality and high spirits who was very direct in manner. Even though Washington had befriended him and named him one of his initial aides, the handsome, eloquent Mifflin harbored a secret animosity toward his patron. Washington learned of his treachery with consternation. "I have never seen any stroke of ill fortune affect the general in the manner that this dirty underhand dealing has done," his aide Tench Tilghman wrote.[41] Washington had already developed doubts about Mifflin, whom he thought had exploited his job as quartermaster general for personal profit, and he later wrote about him with biting sarcasm as an opportunistic, fair-weather friend.

Although he had known and liked Conway in France, Lafayette had concluded that he was a menace to his mentor. In late November Lafayette warned Washington that certain elements in Congress "are infatuated with Gates . . . and believe that attacking is the only thing necessary to conquer."[42] Lafayette didn't exaggerate. Whatever inhibitions had existed about defaming Washington's name had now disappeared. "Thousands of lives and millions of property are yearly sacrificed to the insufficiency of our Commander-in-Chief," Pennsylvania attorney general Jonathan Dickinson Sergeant wrote to Massachusetts congressman James Lovell. "Two battles he has lost for us by two such blunders as might have disgraced a soldier of three months standing."[43] Benjamin Rush and Richard Henry Lee lent open or covert support to the attacks on Washington, while John Adams, for all his dyspeptic squawking, retained residual admiration for the commander in chief and never went so far as to try to oust him.

In late November Congress reorganized the Board of War, and Richard Henry Lee saw to it that Mifflin was named to it. Mifflin then confirmed Washington's worst fears by securing the appointment of Horatio Gates as its president. Gates would retain his rank as major general and gain a supervisory role over Washington. Leaving little doubt that he wanted Gates to usurp Washington's authority, Congressman Lovell told him, "We want you in different places . . . We want you most near Germantown."[44] Congress dealt out further punishment to Washington. When he protested that his men were famished, Congress passed a snide resolution, chastising him for excessive "delicacy in exerting military authority" to requisition goods from local citizens.[45] As Lovell gloated to Samuel Adams, the resolution "was meant to rap a demi-G[od] over the knuckles."[46]

A still heavier blow lay in the offing. On December 13 the Board of War created an inspection system to curb desertions, ensure efficient use of public property, and institute army drills. It named none other than Thomas Conway as inspector general and, directly flouting Washington's plea, boosted his rank to major general. Not only was Conway vested with sweeping powers, he would be exempt from Washington's immediate supervision. It was hard to imagine a more calculated insult against the commander in chief. Washington didn't learn of the decision until two weeks later, when Conway materialized at Valley Forge to announce his appointment. Although we don't know his exact words, Washington was always articulate when forced to break silence on a painful subject. To Conway's consternation, he received him with what he later called "ceremonious civility," an icy correctness that people found very unsettling. Not mincing words, he told Conway that his appointment would outrage more senior brigadiers in the army and that Conway couldn't inspect anything until he had explicit instructions from Congress. Conway protested that he was "coolly received" at Valley Forge and complained to Washington of being greeted in such a manner "as I never met with before from any general during the course of thirty years in a very respectable army."[47] Washington dug in his heels in self-defense: "That I did not receive him in the language of a warm and cordial friend, I readily confess the charge," he told Henry Laurens, who was now president of Congress. "I did not, nor shall I ever, till I am capable of the arts of dissimulation."[48]

Conway had never really responded to Washington about the notorious note written to Gates. Amid his frigid reception at Valley Forge, he sent Washington an insolent letter that flaunted his true colors. "I understand that your aversion to me is owing to the letter I wrote to General Gates," Conway began. He then said that subalterns in European armies freely gave their opinions of their generals, "but I never heard that the least notice was taken of these letters. Must such an odious and tyrannical inquisition begin in this country?" In conclusion, Conway said that "since you cannot bear the sight of me in your camp, I am very ready to go wherever Congress thinks proper and even to France."[49] The normally self-contained Washington was so infuriated by Conway's conduct that John Laurens thought that in private life Washington might have contemplated a duel. "It is such an affront," young Laurens told his father, "as Conway would never have dared to offer if the general's situation had not assured him of the impossibility of its being revenged in a private way."[50] Laurens was mistaken in one thing: Washington considered dueling an outmoded form of chivalry. In the end the Board of War desisted from trying to impose Conway on Washington, and he was assigned to join General McDougall in New York.

The various efforts of Gates, Conway, Mifflin, et al. to discredit and even depose Washington have been known to history as the Conway Cabal. *Cabal* is much too strong a word for this loosely organized network of foes. In later years Washington confirmed that he thought an "attempt was made by a party in Congress to supplant me in that command," and he sketched out its contours thus: "It appeared, in general, that General Gates was to be exalted on the ruin of my reputation and influence . . . General Mifflin, it is commonly supposed, bore the second part in the cabal, and General Conway, I know, was a very active and malignant partisan. But I have good reasons to believe that their machinations have recoiled most sensibly upon themselves."[51] The episode showed that, whatever Washington's demerits as a military man, he was a consummate political infighter. With command of his tongue and temper, he had the supreme temperament for leadership compared to his scheming rivals. It was perhaps less his military skills than his character that eclipsed all competitors. Washington was dignified, circumspect, and upright, whereas his enemies seemed petty and skulking. However thin-skinned he was, he never doubted the need for legitimate criticism and contested only the devious methods of opponents. Calling criticism of error "the prerogative of freemen," he still deplored such a "secret, insidious attempt . . . to wound my reputation!"[52] For the rest of the war, he didn't allow these things to cloud his judgment, never told tales indiscreetly, and confined his opinions of intramural feuding to a small circle of trusted intimates, lest such infighting demoralize his army.

At moments Washington viewed the controversy with philosophic resignation and wondered whether he should return to Mount Vernon. After receiving a confidential warning from the Reverend William Gordon that a faction was plotting to install Charles Lee in his stead, Washington replied ruefully: "So soon then as the public gets dissatisfied with my services, or a person is found better qualified to answer her expectation, I shall quit the helm with as much satisfaction and retire to a private station with as much content as ever the wearied pilgrim felt upon his safe arrival in the Holy Land."[53] He didn't need to worry. The so-called Conway Cabal taught people that Washington was tough and crafty in defending his terrain and that they tangled with him at their peril. Henceforth anyone who underestimated George Washington lived to regret the error. His skillful treatment of the "cabal" silenced his harshest critics, leaving him in unquestioned command of the Continental Army. The end of this war among Washington's generals augured well for the larger war against the British.

It should be said that the need to solidify Washington's position and humble his enemies had a political logic. With the possible exception of the Continental Congress, the Continental Army was the purest expression of the new, still inchoate country, a working laboratory for melding together citizen-soldiers from various states and creating a composite American identity. Washington personified that army and was therefore the main unifying figure in the war. John Adams regarded this as the main reason why people tolerated his defeats and overlooked his errors. To Dr. Benjamin Rush, he later pontificated: "There was a time when northern, middle, and southern statesmen . . . expressly agreed to blow the trumpet of panegyric in concert to cover and dissemble all faults and errors; to represent every defeat as a victory and every retreat as an advancement to make that character [Washington] popular and fashionable with all parties in all places and with all persons, as a center of union, as the central stone in the geometrical arch. There you have the revelation of the whole mystery."[54]

In the last analysis, Washington's triumph over the troublesome Gates, Mifflin, and Conway was total. For unity's sake, he was unfailingly polite to Gates: "I made a point of treating Gen[era]l Gates with all the attention and cordiality in my power, as well from a sincere desire of harmony as from an unwillingness to give any cause of triumph to our enemies."[55] Gates's defects as a general would become glaring in time. Thomas Mifflin resigned as quartermaster general amid charges of mis-

322

management. The most complete triumph came over Thomas Conway, who plied Congress with so many abusive letters and threatened to resign so often that delegates were finally pleased to accept his resignation in April 1778. Conway refused to muzzle his criticism of Washington, however, which led him in July into a duel with John Cadwalader, a stalwart Washington defender. Cadwalader shot Conway in the mouth and neck and is supposed to have boasted as he stared down at his bleeding foe, "I have stopped the damned rascal's lying anyway."[56] With incredible resilience, Conway recuperated from these wounds and sent Washington a chastened note before he returned to France. "I find myself just able to hold the pen during a few minutes," the convalescent soldier wrote, "and take this opportunity of expressing my sincere grief for having done, written, or said anything disagreeable to Your Excellency. My career will soon be over. Therefore justice and truth prompt me to declare my last sentiments. You are, in my eyes, the great and the good man. May you long enjoy the love, veneration, and esteem of these states whose liberties you have asserted by your virtues."[57]

$\mathcal{A}$ Dreary Kind of Place

IN DECEMBER 1777 General William Howe eased into comfortable winter quarters in Philadelphia. For British officers in the eighteenth century, warfare remained a seasonal business, and they saw no reason to sacrifice unduly as cold winds blew. "Assemblies, concerts, comedies, clubs, and the like make us forget that there is any war, save that it is a capital joke," wrote a Hessian captain, reflecting the overly confident attitude that prevailed among British and Hessian officers after the Brandywine and Germantown victories.[1]

George Washington struggled with the baffling question of where to house his vagabond, threadbare army during the frigid months ahead. The specter of a harsh winter was alarming: four thousand men lacked a single blanket. If Washington withdrew farther into Pennsylvania's interior, his army might be secure, but the area already teemed with patriotic refugees from Philadelphia. Such a move would also allow Howe's men to scavenge the countryside outside Philadelphia and batten freely off local farms. Further complicating his decision was that he had to ensure the safety of two homeless legislatures, now stranded in exile: the Continental Congress in York and the Pennsylvania legislature in Lancaster. "I assure you, sir," he told Henry Laurens, as he puzzled over the conundrum, "no circumstance in the course of the present contest, or in my whole life, has employed more of my reflection . . . than in what manner . . . to dispose of the army during the winter."[2]

Washington opted for a spot that was fated to become hallowed ground: Valley Forge, a windswept plateau, twenty miles northwest of Philadelphia, that he would depict as "a dreary kind of place and uncomfortably provided."[3] With its open, rolling fields and woods, the encampment stood a day's march from Howe's army and was therefore safe from surprise raids. In theory, it sounded like a promising place. Its high ridges would afford excellent defensive positions; its nearby woods would supply plentiful timber for fuel and construction; abundant local agriculture would nourish his army; and the nearby Schuylkill River and Valley Creek would provide pure water. What should have been an ideal resting place became instead a scene of harrowing misery.

Even before Washington arrived there, the Pennsylvania legislature had the cheek to criticize him for taking his men into winter camp, as if he were retiring into plush quarters. "I can assure those gentlemen," Washington wrote testily, "that it is a much easier and less distressing thing to draw remonstrances in a comfortable room by a good fireside than to occupy a cold bleak hill and sleep under frost and snow without clothes or blankets. However, although they seem to have little feeling for the naked, distressed soldiers, I feel superabundantly for them and from my soul pity those miseries which it is neither in my power to relieve or prevent."[4] This was a new voice for Washington, reflecting a profound solidarity with his men that went beyond Revolutionary ideology and arose from the special camaraderie of shared suffering.

Already on the icy road to Valley Forge, Washington had spotted streaks of blood from his barefoot men, portending things to come. He slept in the upstairs chamber of a compact, two-story stone mill house built by Isaac Potts, whose iron forges lent the place its name. The commander in chief worked in a modest downstairs room with a fireplace. So meticulous was Washington in his respect for private property that he rented the quarters instead of seizing them. The premises were so cramped that one observer recalled Washington's family as "exceedingly pinched for room."[5] Many aides slept jammed together on the floor downstairs. To provide extra space, Washington added an adjoining log cabin for meals.

With the treasury bankrupt, Washington experienced a grim foreboding that this winter would mandate stringency far beyond anything yet endured. In general orders for December 17, he suggested that the impending winter might call for preternatural strength and vowed to "share in the hardship and partake of every inconvenience" with his men.[6] Whatever his failings as a general, Washington's moral strength held the shaky army together. His position transcended that of a mere general, having taken on a paternal dimension. "The people of America look up to you as their father," Henry Knox told him, "and into your hands they entrust their all, fully confident of every exertion on your part for their security and happiness."[7]

The first order of business, Washington knew, was to erect warm, dry huts. To set an example, he slept in a tent as the camp succumbed to a building craze; regiments broken into squads of twelve soldiers chopped wood and made huts for themselves. Cleverly, Washington injected a competitive element into the operation: he would pay twelve dollars to the squad that completed the first hut and a hundred dollars to anyone who devised a way to roof these structures without consuming scarce wood. As the men hewed their houses with dull ax blades, they nonetheless seemed cheerful and hardy. "I was there when the army first began to build huts," wrote Thomas Paine. "They appeared to me like a family of beavers: everyone busy, some carrying logs, others mud, and the rest fastening them together."[8] Within a month a makeshift village, more than two thousand log cabins in all, materialized from the havoc.

Forming parallel avenues, the huts were small, dark, and claustrophobic; a dozen men could be squashed into spaces measuring fourteen by sixteen feet, with only six and a half feet of headroom. Narrow bunks, stacked in triple rows, stood on either side of the door. Many soldiers draped tents over their huts to keep at bay the sharp wintry blasts. While officers had the luxury of wooden floors, ordinary soldiers slept on dank earth. As more trees were felled for shelter and firewood, the campgrounds grew foul and slippery with mud. Dead horses and their entrails lay decomposing everywhere, emitting a putrid stench into the winter air.

For all its esprit de corps, the Continental Army was soon reduced to a ghastly state, its soldiers resembling a horde of unkempt beggars. Men dined on food called "fire cakes," crude concoctions of flour and water that were cooked on hot stones. Some days they couldn't scrape together any food at all. Dr. Albigence Waldo of Connecticut limned the horror:

> Poor food—hard lodging—cold weather—fatigue—nasty clothes—nasty cookery— vomit half my time—smoke out of my senses—the devil's in it—I can't endure it . . . There comes a bowl of beef soup—full of burnt leaves and dirt, sickish enough to make a Hector spew . . . There comes a soldier, his bare feet are seen through his worn-out shoes, his legs nearly naked from the tattered remains of an only pair of stockings; his breeches not sufficient to cover his nakedness; his shirt hanging in strings; his hair disheveled; his face meager; his whole appearance pictures a person forsaken and discouraged.[9]

The universal misery didn't spare officers, who suffered along with their men. One Frenchman strolling through camp caught glimpses of soldiers who "were using as cloaks and overcoats woollen blankets similar to those worn by the patients in our French hospitals. I realized a little later that those were officers and generals."[10] Some desperate soldiers tore canvas strips from tents to cobble together primitive shirts or shoes. The misery reached straight into Washington's headquarters. "I cannot get as much cloth as will make clothes for my servants," Washington wrote, "notwithstanding that one of them that attends my person and table is indecently and most shamefully naked."[11] One wonders whether this referred to the trusted Billy Lee. Exacerbating the clothing shortage was a dearth of wagons. To cart supplies around camp, men were harnessed to carriages like draft animals, saddled with yokes. Hoping to ameliorate the situation, Congress, at Washington's behest, soon appointed Nathanael Greene as the new quartermaster general, an office that had been negligently administered by Thomas Mifflin. At first Greene resisted the appointment, grumbling that "nobody ever heard of a quartermaster in history," but he submitted to his fate and brilliantly helped the Continental Army avoid starvation as he redeemed his own reputation.[12]

Part of Washington's inspirational power at Valley Forge came from his steady presence, as he projected leadership in nonverbal ways that are hard for posterity to re-create. Even contemporaries found it difficult to convey the essence of his calm grandeur. "I cannot describe the impression that the first sight of that great man made upon me," said one Frenchman. "I could not keep my eyes from that imposing countenance: grave yet not severe; affable without familiarity. Its predominant expression was calm dignity, through which you could trace the strong feelings of the patriot and discern the father as well as the commander of his soldiers."[13]

One of the most durable images of Washington at Valley Forge is likely invented. After his death Parson Mason Weems, who fabricated the canard about the cherry tree, told of Washington praying in a snowy glade. A well-known image of Washington, done by Paul Weber and entitled *George Washington in Prayer at Valley Forge,* depicts Washington praying on his knees, his left hand over his heart and his open right hand at his side, pointing to the earth. Washington's upturned face catches a shaft of celestial light. The image seems designed to meld religion and politics by converting the uniformed Washington into a humble suppliant of the Lord. The reason to doubt the story's veracity is not Washington's lack of faith but the typically private nature of his devotions. He would never have prayed so ostentatiously outdoors, where soldiers could have stumbled upon him.

While Washington was somewhat insulated from the camp's noisome squalor in the Potts house, the despondent men ventilated their grievances. As he strode past the huts, he heard them grumbling inside, "No bread, no soldier!"[14] On better days, they would burst into a patriotic tune called "War and Washington."[15] At one point a knot of protesters descended on his office in what must have seemed a mutinous act. Washington undoubtedly bristled at their disruptive presence. Nonetheless, when the men said they had come to make sure Washington understood their suffering, he reacted sympathetically. This man of patrician tastes had learned to value ordinary soldiers. "Naked and starving as they are," he wrote, "we cannot enough admire the incomparable patience and fidelity of the soldiery."[16]

That the Continental Army did not disintegrate or revolt en masse at Valley

Forge is simply astonishing. When Dr. Benjamin Rush toured the camp, General Sullivan lectured him, "Sir, this is not an army—it is a mob."[17] It shows the confidence that Washington produced in his men that they stuck by him in this forlorn place. Nor did he achieve popularity by coddling anyone, for he inflicted severe floggings on men caught stealing food. "The culprit being securely lashed to a tree or post receives on his naked back the number of lashes assigned to him by a whip formed of several small knotted cords, which sometimes cut through his skin at every stroke," wrote Dr. James Thacher, who described how men survived this ordeal by biting on lead bullets—the origin of the term "biting the bullet."[18] Governed by a powerful moral code and determined to maintain some semblance of military discipline amid woeful conditions, Washington perpetuated his ban on cards, dice, and other forms of gambling.

Perhaps most frightful at Valley Forge were the rampant diseases that leveled 30 percent of the men at any given time. Many underwent amputations as their legs and feet turned black from frostbite. Owing to pervasive malnutrition, filthy conditions, and exposure to cold, scourges such as typhus, typhoid fever, pneumonia, dysentery, and scurvy grew commonplace. Dr. Benjamin Rush deplored the army hospitals, located outside the camp, as gruesome sties, overcrowded with inmates "shivering with cold upon the floors without a blanket to cover them, calling for fire, for water, for suitable food, and for medicines—and calling in vain."[19] By winter's end, two thousand men had perished at Valley Forge, mostly from disease and many of them in the warm spring months. "Happily, the real condition of Washington was not well understood by Sir William Howe," wrote John Marshall, "and the characteristic attention of that officer [i.e., Washington] to the lives and comfort of his troops saved the American army."[20]

On December 23, with the situation deteriorating daily, Washington rushed an urgent message to Henry Laurens, warning that the Continental Army would "starve, dissolve, or disperse" without more food. To illustrate, he related a frightening anecdote of an incident the day before when he had ordered his soldiers to pounce on British soldiers scouring the countryside for forage. The operation was scuttled because his men were too enervated from lack of food to carry out the mission. Washington testified that there was "not a single hoof of any kind to slaughter and not more than 25 bar[re]ls of flour!" He made the astonishing prediction that "three or four days [of] bad weather would prove our destruction."[21] In heartbreaking fashion, he evoked an army devoid of soap; men with one shirt, half a shirt, or no shirt at all; nearly three thousand unfit for duty for lack of shoes; and men who passed sleepless nights, crouched by the fire, for want of blankets.

Ever since the war started, Washington had saved his laments for Congress, even though much of the real power resided with the states. But he was reluctant to appeal to the states, lest he seem to circumvent Congress or violate military subordination to civilian control. Now, in desperation, he began to issue circulars to the states, which gave him license to rail against the rickety political structure that hampered his army. That November Congress had completed drafting the Articles of Confederation, creating a loose confederacy of states with a notably weak central government. Dreading the hobgoblin of concentrated power, states shrank from levying taxes and introducing other measures to aid the federal war effort. Washington was dismayed that the states now shipped off their mediocrities to Congress while more able men stayed home "framing constitutions, providing laws, and filling [state] offices."[22] A leitmotif of his wartime letters was that the shortsighted states would come to ruin without an effective central government. Increasingly Washington took a scathing view of lax congressional leadership.

The Christmas dinner at Valley Forge was an austere one for Washington and his military family, who shared a frugal collation of mutton, potatoes, cabbage, and crusts of bread, accompanied by water. The liquor shortage produced the worst grumbling among the officers. Sometime around the Battle of Brandywine, Washington had lost his baggage, with its complement of plates, dishes, and kitchen utensils, and he now made do with a single spoon. He experienced no self-pity, however, so woebegone was the comparative plight of his men. On the last day of the year, he compressed the suffering of Valley Forge into a single piercing cry: "Our sick naked, our well naked, our unfortunate men in captivity naked!"[23]

What made Valley Forge so bitterly disenchanting for Washington was that selfishness among the citizenry seemed to outweigh patriotic fervor. In choosing winter quarters at Valley Forge, he had surmised, correctly, that the surrounding countryside possessed ample food supplies. What he hadn't reckoned on was that local farmers would sell their produce to British troops in Philadelphia rather than to shivering patriots. Some of this behavior could be attributed to blatant greed and profiteering. But prices also soared as the Continental currency depreciated and an inflationary psychology took hold. Holding a debased currency, the patriots simply couldn't compete with the British, who paid in solid pounds sterling. "We must take the passions of men as nature has given them," Washington wrote resignedly. "... I do not mean to exclude altogether the idea of patriotism ... But I will venture to assert that a great and lasting war can never be supported on this principle alone."[24] Washington presented a rare case of a revolutionary leader who, instead of being blinded by political fervor, recognized that fallible human beings couldn't always live up to the high standards he set for them. Though often embittered by the mercenary behavior of his countrymen, he tried to accept human nature as it was. He believed that many Americans had expected a speedy end to the conflict and, when the first flush of patriotism faded, were governed by self-interest. In 1778 there were far more political fence-sitters than in the giddy days after Lexington and Concord.

By late January Washington was so enraged about farmers engaging in contraband trade with the enemy that he issued orders "to make an example of some guilty one, that the rest may be sensible of a like fate, should they persist."[25] Many farmers tried to bypass restrictions by having women and children drive food-laden wagons to Philadelphia, hoping American sentries wouldn't stop them. Nothing short of the death penalty, Washington insisted, would terminate this reprehensible practice. Finally, he saw no choice but to sabotage American mills turning out supplies for the enemy and sent teams of soldiers to break off the spindles and spikes of their water wheels. With a beef shortage looming, he had Nathanael Greene and almost a thousand men fan out across the countryside and confiscate all cattle and sheep fit for slaughter. As word of the operation spread, farmers hid their livestock in woods and swamps. Despite such draconian measures, Washington warned that his army still stared at starvation: "For some days past, there has been little less than a famine in camp. A part of the army has been a week without any kind of flesh and the rest three or four days."[26]

At Valley Forge, Washington composed numerous screeds against American greed that make uncomfortable reading for those who regard that winter as a purely heroic time. Seeing the decay of public virtue everywhere, he berated speculators, monopolists, and war profiteers. "Is the paltry consideration of a little dirty pelf to individuals to be placed in competition with the essential rights and liberties of the present generation and of millions yet unborn?" he asked James Warren. " . . . And shall we at last become the victims of our own abominable lust of gain? Forbid it heaven!"[27] Washington himself could be a hard-driving businessmen, yet he found the rapacity of many vendors unconscionable. As he told George Mason, he thought it the intent of "the speculators—various tribes of money makers— and stock jobbers of all denominations to continue the war for their own private emolument, without considering that their avarice and thirst for gain must plunge everything . . . in one common ruin."[28]

Besieged by critics, heartsick at the shabby state of his troops, and angry at congressional neglect and the supine behavior of the states, Washington refused to abandon his army and again deferred a visit to Mount Vernon. Martha did not arrive at Valley Forge until early February. Right before Christmas she had suffered the grievous loss of her younger sister and best friend, Anna Maria Bassett. Death had been omnipresent for Martha, who had now lost a husband, a father, five siblings, and three of her four children. Whether her second husband would survive this interminable war remained an open question. A touching condolence note to her brother-in-law, Burwell Bassett, shows that her mind was darkly tinged with thoughts of mortality. Anna "has, I hope, made a happy exchange and only gone a little before us," she said of her sister. "The time draws near when I hope we shall meet, never more to part . . . I must [own] to you that she was the greatest favorite I had in the world."[29] She pleaded with Burwell to send his ten-year-old daughter Fanny to Mount Vernon. "If you will let her come to live with me, I will, with the greatest pleasure, take her and be a parent and mother to her as long as I live."[30] Bassett complied, and Fanny came to occupy a special place in Martha's affections.

While wishing to join her husband at Valley Forge, Martha was temporarily detained at Mount Vernon by the birth of her second grandchild to Jacky's wife on New Year's Eve 1777. Though Washington understood the reason for her delay, he pined for her presence. The long winter journey on bumpy, frozen roads must have taxed Martha to the utmost. When she arrived at Valley Forge, the soldiers cheered her, but she was taken aback by her husband's humble quarters, somber mood, and frayed nerves. "The General is well but much worn with fatigue and anxiety," she confided to a friend. "I never knew him to be so anxious as now."[31]

That Martha Washington was made of stern stuff soon grew evident as she pitched in with good-natured energy. One observer left this touching vignette of her at work:

> I never in my life knew a woman so busy from early morning until late at night as was Lady Washington, providing comforts for the sick soldiers. Every day, excepting Sunday, the wives of the officers in camp, and sometimes other women, were invited . . . to assist her in knitting socks, patching garments, and making shirts for the poor soldiers when material could be procured. Every fair day she might be seen, with basket in hand and with a single attendant, going among the keenest and most needy sufferers and giving all the comforts to them in her power.[32]

Her selfless, devoted style reminded one admiring Frenchman "of the Roman matrons of whom I had read so much and I thought that she well deserved to be the companion and friend of the greatest man of the age."[33] By and large Martha Washington wasn't overtly political, yet she shared her husband's firm commitment to the cause, writing to Mercy Warren, "I hope and trust that all the states will make a vigorous push early this spring . . . and thereby putting a stop to British cruelties."[34]

The wives of several generals stayed at Valley Forge that winter—including the flirtatious Caty Greene, the amusing but increasingly obese Lucy Knox, and the elegant Lady Stirling, accompanied by her fashionable daughter, Lady Kitty—and tried to lighten the dismal mood. Washington was especially beguiled by Lady Kitty, who requested a lock of his hair. These women dispensed with dancing and card playing as inappropriate to such mournful times and settled for quiet musical evenings where people took turns singing; tea and coffee replaced more potent beverages. That February, on Washington's forty-sixth birthday, a little levity was allowed as he was entertained by a fife and drum corps.

To relieve residual gloom several months later, Washington allowed junior officers to stage his favorite play, *Cato,* before a "very numerous and splendid audience."[35] Written by Joseph Addison, this classic tale told of a Roman statesman, Cato the Younger, who had defied the imperial sway of Julius Caesar and committed suicide rather than submit to tyranny. No longer able to ransack British history for heroes, many patriots turned to classical history for inspiration. Ancient Rome in its republican phase provided uplifting examples, while its decline and fall into despotism offset them with cautionary tales. Washington identified with the stern code of honor and duty in ancient Rome, taking Cato as a personal model. He had seen the play performed several times in Williamsburg and he frequently quoted it. One of his stock phrases—"Thy steady temper . . . can look on guilt, rebellion, [and] fraud . . . in the calm lights of mild philosophy"—was plucked from the play.[36] Other treasured epigrams included " 'Tis not in mortals to command success / But we'll do more . . . we'll deserve it," a commentary on the fickle power of fate and how we must acquit ourselves nobly despite it, and "When vice prevails and impious men bear sway, / The post of honour is a private station."[37] The rhetoric of *Cato* saturated the American Revolution. Two of its most famous lines, one from Nathan Hale, the other from Patrick Henry, derived from the play: "What pity is it / That we can die but once to serve our country" and "It is not now a time to talk of aught / But chains or conquest, liberty or death."[38]

During this Valley Forge winter Washington conquered his initial misgivings about Lafayette and embraced him as his most intimate protégé. In late November, in Gloucester, New Jersey, Lafayette spearheaded a party of four hundred men in a surprise raid on a Hessian detachment, leading to twenty enemy deaths versus only one American casualty. Washington admired the Frenchman's swashbuckling courage. No longer just another foreign nobleman to be tolerated, Lafayette was rewarded with command of a division. He knew he had attained a unique place in Washington's heart. "I see him more intimately than any other man," he boasted to his father-in-law. ". . . His warm friendship for me . . . put[s] me in a position to share everything he has to do, all the problems he has to solve, and all the obstacles he has to overcome."[39]

Washington found irresistible this young Frenchman who saw him in such Olympian terms, but Lafayette was also canny and hardworking and constantly honed his military skills: "I read, I study, I examine, I listen, I reflect . . . I do not talk too much—to avoid saying foolish things—nor risk acting in a foolhardy way."[40] Lafayette opened an emotional spout deep inside the formal Washington. Although he seldom showed such favoritism, Washington made no effort to mask his fond-ness for Lafayette. He did not fear the young French nobleman as a future rival and was convinced of his ardent idealism. When Lafayette and his wife had a son, they decided to name him Georges Louis Gilbert Washington du Motier, Marquis de Lafayette—for short, George Washington Lafayette. Lafayette vowed that the next child would be christened Virginia, prompting Franklin to quip that Lafayette had twelve more states to go.[41]

THE CONTINENTAL ARMY'S RISE from the ashes of Valley Forge owed much to a newcomer, Friedrich Wilhelm Ludolf Gerhard Augustin, Baron von Steuben, a soldier who liked to decorate himself with sonorous names. While Steuben could legitimately claim wartime experience, having served as a Prussian captain during the Seven Years' War and on the military staff of Frederick the Great, the *baron* title was bogus. When, in the summer of 1777, Franklin and Deane in Paris sent him to America, they embellished his credentials to make him more acceptable to Washington; on the spot, the unemployed captain was puffed up to the rank of a lieutenant general. He agreed to waive a salary temporarily and serve only for expenses. In late February 1778 the self-styled baron with the fleshy nose, jowly face, and uncertain command of English (he resorted to French to make himself understood) showed up at Valley Forge, where his bemedaled figure made a huge impression. "He seemed to me a perfect personification of Mars," said one private. "The trappings of his horse, the enormous holsters of his pistols, his large size, and strikingly martial aspect, all seemed to favor the idea."[42]

As he strode about the camp, trailed by his greyhound, Steuben was taken aback by the misery everywhere: "The men were literally naked . . . The officers who had coats had them in every color and make. I saw officers . . . mounting guard in a sort of dressing gown made of an old blanket or woollen bedcover."[43] Well versed in military practice, Steuben writhed at the unsanitary conditions; horse carcasses rot-ted near men preparing food, and sick men mingled with the healthy. He instituted many necessary reforms, such as having latrines dug at least three hundred feet away from huts, then promptly filled and abandoned after four days of use.

Steuben's advent came at an auspicious time. After the widespread fatalities at Valley Forge and the tremendous attrition among officers, Washington was ner-vous as he contemplated a resumption of fighting in the spring. Two hundred to three hundred officers had resigned since the summer. Washington needed a tough drillmaster like Steuben to instill discipline and ready his army for combat. Unlike the British, whose units moved in brisk, marching steps, the Continental Army had no uniform methods. Washington had long admired an army manual written by

Frederick the Great, *Instructions to His Generals,* which may have predisposed him to value Steuben's advice. Schooled in European courts, Steuben stooped to sometimes unctuous flattery with Washington, telling him that "your Excellency is the only person under whom (after having served under the King of Prussia) I could wish to pursue an art to which I have wholly given up myself."[44]

As he introduced professionalism into this motley army, the mercurial Prussian performed wonders. Washington started out by assigning one hundred men to him to be trained for his headquarters guard; he accomplished it so expertly that Washington soon sent him more. Steuben taught the men new skills, including how to wield bayonets. "The American soldier, never having used this arm, had no faith in it," recalled Steuben, "and never used it but to roast his beefsteak."[45] All day long he drilled men on the broad, open parade ground at the center of the encampment, teaching them to march and wheel in formation, to switch from line to column and back to line. All the while he tossed off a storm of profanities in French, English, and German and galloped about in "whirlwinds of passion."[46] Steuben was foul-mouthed and colorful, and the men were charmed by their strangely flamboyant new drillmaster.

With editorial assistance from John Laurens and Alexander Hamilton, Steuben began to compile his famous "blue book," an instruction manual for drills and marches that gave new precision to the infantry. This booklet was so well done that it remained in use until the Civil War. Thrilled with his ersatz baron, Washington hailed him as a "gentleman of high military rank, profound knowledge, and great experience in his profession."[47] In another letter, he allowed his personal affection to peep through. "I regard and esteem the baron as an assiduous, intelligent, and experienced officer."[48] Washington always felt special gratitude to Steuben for helping to rescue the army that winter. When he later drafted a brief evaluation of him, he described him thus: "Sensible, sober, and brave; well acquainted with tactics and with the arrangement and discipline of an army. High in his ideas of subordination, impetuous in his temper, ambitious, and a foreigner."[49]

That winter the projected shortage of soldiers led Washington to introduce another significant change in policy. In January 1778 Brigadier General James Mitchell Varnum of Rhode Island asked the unthinkable of the Virginia planter: the right to augment his state's forces by recruiting black troops. "It is imagined that a battalion of Negroes can be easily raised there," he assured Washington.[50] Washington knew this was an incendiary idea for many southerners. Nevertheless, desperate to recruit more manpower, he gave his stamp of approval, telling Rhode Island's governor "that you will give the officers employed in this business all the assistance in your power."[51] The state promised to free any slaves willing to join an all-black battalion that soon numbered 130 men. Massachusetts followed Rhode Island's lead in enlisting black soldiers, and in Connecticut, slave masters were exempt from military service if they sent slaves in their stead. That August a census listed 755 blacks as part of the Continental Army, or nearly 5 percent of the total force. Later in the war Baron Ludwig von Closen, attached to the French Army, said of Washington's men, "A quarter of them were Negroes, merry, confident, and sturdy." This estimate sounds grossly exaggerated. Closer to the mark was the Frenchman's unstinting praise for these self-confident black soldiers, saying they made up three-quarters of a Rhode Island regiment, "and that regiment is the most neatly dressed, the best under arms, and the most precise in its maneuvers."[52]

Even as the American Revolution broadened George Washington, he had to reconcile his changed outlook with his private decisions as a slave owner. It seems more than coincidental that, in the aftermath of approving the black Rhode Island battalion, he signaled to Lund Washington a momentous shift at Mount Vernon: henceforth he wouldn't sell slaves against their will. Until this point Lund preferred selling slaves at public auctions to fetch the highest price. But in early April, upon learning of the new policy, Lund reported back to Washington that two slaves put up for sale had balked at leaving, binding his hands. One slave, Phillis, "was so alarmed at the thoughts of being sold that the [prospective purchaser] cou[l]d not get her to utter a word of English, therefore he believed she cou[l]d not speak." Lund drew the moral quite starkly for Washington, saying that "unless I was to make a public sale of those Negroes and to pay no regard to their being willing or not, I see no probability of sell[in]g them."[53] On August 15 Washington transmitted a still more revolutionary statement to Lund. While discussing possible land purchases in the Northern Neck, he referred to his slaves and made the astounding parenthetical statement "(of whom I every day long more and more to get clear of)."[54] Still, he would not figure out how to banish slavery from Mount Vernon until the end of his life.

AS THE WEATHER WARMED and spring beckoned, Washington decided to honor his men for their hardy resilience during their long winter trial. He issued resounding paeans to the freed slaves and former indentured servants, farmers and shopkeepers, who made up his army: "The recent instance of uncomplaining patience during the scarcity of provisions in camp is a fresh proof that they possess in an eminent degree the spirit of soldiers and the magnanimity of patriots." His soldiers had won the "admiration of the world, the love of their country, and the gratitude of posterity!"[55] To show he meant business, Washington issued a gill of rum or whiskey to every man. The food situation started to improve in mid-February, and in March Washington looked forward to putting twelve thousand well-trained men in the field, even though three thousand were still disabled by smallpox and other diseases.

No matter how much Baron von Steuben sharpened the army's skills, it seemed unlikely ever to defeat the enemy without a foreign ally to neutralize British sea power. Washington had long doubted that anything other than covert aid would come from France, which had secretly supplied arms to America through a fictitious trading company. He could never decide whether French aid was a rope with which to hang the British or a leash to restrain the Americans. Significantly those Americans, such as Washington and Hamilton, who had direct contact with French officers retained the deepest skepticism about their motives. To guarantee the flow of munitions from France, Washington had tolerated the pretensions of a steady stream of French officers. Lafayette was the person best positioned to promote this strategic alliance. At a critical moment during the so-called Conway Cabal, the marquis had reminded Congress that George Washington personified America for the Court of Versailles and couldn't be replaced without doing grave damage to the sub-rosa French alliance.

Even as the Continental Army huddled by fires at Valley Forge, Benjamin Franklin pulled off a magnificent diplomatic feat in the opulent ministries of Paris. On February 6 France recognized American independence through a pair of treaties: the first granting French goods most-favored-nation status in America, and the second committing the French to a military alliance. In the splendid halls of Versailles, Franklin was now addressed not as the representative of thirteen colonies but as an emissary of the United States. In getting a monarchy to bestow its blessings upon an upstart republic, he had won a staggering achievement.

In late April Washington received unofficial word of the French alliance and fully realized its vast significance. At the news, Lafayette gave Washington—the man nobody touched—a double-barreled French kiss on both cheeks. Washington was exultant as tears of joy welled up in his eyes. "I believe no event was ever received with a more heartfelt joy," he informed Congress.[56] For Washington, the French treaties gave proof that heaven had indeed smiled upon the United States. As he told his troops, in orotund prose, "It having pleased the Almighty ruler of the Universe propitiously to defend the cause of the United American States and finally, by raising us up a powerful friend among the princes of the earth, to establish our liberty and independence upon lasting foundations, it becomes us to set apart a day for gratefully acknowledging the divine goodness."[57]

On May 6, with his fondness for pageantry, George Washington staged a celebration of the French treaties, beginning with mustering brigades at nine A.M. The treaties were solemnly read aloud, followed by the firing of thirteen cannon. The infantry then fired their muskets in sequence, a *feu de joie* that swept the double rows of soldiers, who chanted with gusto, "Long Live the King of France."[58] French officers were embraced everywhere. Steuben showed off the crack precision of his men, who strutted smartly before a beaming Washington. As a reward, Steuben was appointed inspector general with the rank of major general. "Through it all," John Laurens told his father, Washington "wore a countenance of uncommon delight."[59] This was more than a celebration of the French treaties; it was a day of thanksgiving for surviving the horrid winter. In a dreamlike transformation, the officers now partook of a bountiful alfresco dinner. "Fifteen hundred persons sat down to the tables, which were spread in the open air," said General Johann de Kalb. "Wine, meats, and liquors abounded, and happiness and contentment were impressed on every countenance."[60] Washington even played cricket with younger officers. When he rode off contentedly at five o'clock, his men clapped their hands, cheered "Long live George Washington!" and twirled a thousand hats in the air.[61] Washington and his aides kept stopping and looking back, sending huzzahs in return.

It was Washington's nature to ponder the darker side of things, and that night he sent out special patrols to guard the camp, lest the enemy try to exploit the festivities, as Washington had done with the Hessians on Christmas Night in 1776. The sudden turn of events both emboldened him and made him cautious. Although he thought the French alliance would tip the scales and that things were now "verging fast to a favorable issue," he fretted that this bonanza might breed overconfidence.[62] In the short run, although it yielded no immediate benefits, the French alliance was an immense tonic to American spirits. Not until midsummer would France be officially at war with England, and in the meantime the Continental Army fended as best it could against a newly alarmed British Empire.

The Long Retreat

THE FIRST CASUALTY the French alliance claimed was General William Howe, who informed his troops that spring of his imminent departure for England after a winter of fun and revelry in Philadelphia. He was replaced by General Henry Clinton, who at first glance scarcely projected a heroic image. A lonely widower, Clinton was a short man with a low, balding brow and dark eyebrows; in one image, his hooked nose and large jaw looked much too massive for his tiny face. The entire effect might have been unappealing, were it not for the kindly, intelligent expression in his eyes. If he could be rash, quarrelsome, and hypersensitive, Clinton also had a long and distinguished military record, including early service in a New York militia and a stint in the Coldstream Guards. For his valorous leadership at New York in 1776, he was decorated as a Knight of the Bath. Six months earlier George Washington had expressed contempt for Clinton when he referred to his "diabolical designs" in a letter to a Virginia friend.[1]

France's entry into the war would precipitate a radical shift in British strategy. Both empires controlled lucrative islands in the West Indies, whose vast sugar and cotton slave plantations had yielded considerable profits. When Clinton was ordered that spring to divert eight thousand men, or a third of his army, to reinforce the West Indies and Florida, he concluded that staying in Philadelphia was untenable and decided to evacuate his troops across New Jersey to New York City. The British still dreamed of a mass Loyalist uprising that would turn the war decisively in their favor, but many Americans who fraternized with the enemy merely sought lucrative business. Those Loyalists in Philadelphia who had curried favor with the British were thrown into a panic by their decision to quit the city and made bootless attempts to travel north with the army. By failing to safeguard these turncoats, the British committed a major propaganda blunder. "No man," said one royal official, "can be expected to declare for us when he cannot be assured a fortnight's protection."[2] With excellent political judgment, Washington opposed a plan to levy punitive taxes on rich Tory sympathizers when the patriots regained the town. "A measure of this sort . . . would not only be inconsistent with sound policy," he reflected, "but would be looked upon as an arbitrary stretch of military power."[3] He named Benedict Arnold commandant of the reclaimed city.

Often mystified by British intentions, Washington had accurate intelligence in mid-May that the British would leave Philadelphia and repair to their more secure base in New York. He did not know whether Clinton would return by land across New Jersey or by sea. With three thousand men still sick, and short of supplies, Washington doubted he could capitalize on a land retreat. Ironically in view of what was to happen, he envisioned a lightning march of quick-stepping British soldiers across New Jersey, led by "the flower of their army, unencumbered with baggage," and did not think he could harass such fleet-footed units.[4]

In April Washington had been rejoined by General Charles Lee, who was released in a prisoner exchange after sixteen months of captivity in New York. As queer a fish as ever, the imprisoned Lee had written to Washington that he should forward his beloved dogs, "as I never stood in greater need of their company than at present."[5] His opinion of Washington's military talents had hardly improved with incarceration. When Elias Boudinot, commissary general of prisoners, visited Lee that January, the latter launched into a diatribe about "the impossibility of our troops, under such an ignorant Commander in Chief, ever withstanding British grenadiers and light infantry," as Boudinot recorded in his journal.[6] Attempting to woo the capricious Lee to their side, the British had pampered him with choice food and wine and a warm bed "into which he tumbled jovially mellow every night."[7] The strategy produced the desired effect. It was later learned that Lee may have sketched out for General Howe a comprehensive plan on how to crush patriotic resistance and end the war.

Washington knew none of this that April, when he amicably greeted Lee on horseback, with all the honors due to his second in command, on a road outside Valley Forge. The two rode companionably into camp together, flanked by troops exhibiting the precision marching drilled into them by Steuben. Lee immediately exhibited bizarre behavior. When he awoke the next morning, "he looked as dirty as if he had been in the street all night," said Boudinot, staggered that Lee had brought along "a miserable dirty hussy with him from Philadelphia and had actually taken her into his room by a back door and she had slept with him that night."[8]

Lee was guilty of more than bad manners. Far from giving Washington credit for saving the army at Valley Forge, he snickered in private that Washington was "not fit to command a sergeant's guard," that the army was "in a worse situation than he had expected," and that Washington couldn't do without him, since he surrounded himself with toadying officers.[9] But Lee was careful to conceal this venom from Washington himself: in a sympathetic note in mid-June, he apologized obsequiously to Washington for intruding on his time as it "must necessarily be taken up by more and a greater variety of business than perhaps ever was impos[ed] on the shoulders of any one mortal."[10] With his usual certitude, Lee believed that the superior British forces would not retreat to New York but would lurch west and try to engage the Americans near Lancaster, Pennsylvania.

On June 16 Washington received a clue that the British stood on the verge of leaving Philadelphia: peace commissioners sent by George III to Philadelphia had asked for the immediate return of their clothing from the laundry. Two days later ten thousand British and Hessian troops began shuffling across New Jersey toward New York, slowed by a baggage train of fifteen hundred wagons that stretched for twelve miles. Coincidentally, Washington had recently lectured his men on the hazards of getting bogged down with bulky, overloaded baggage: "An army by means of it is rendered unwieldy and incapable of acting with that ease and celerity which are essential . . . to its own security."[11]

Washington summoned a war council to consider whether to pounce on the retreating army. Most of his generals, after the previous fall's defeats and the traumatic winter, urged extreme caution. The usually daring Henry Knox warned that "it would be the most criminal madness to hazard a general action at this time," while Charles Lee passionately opposed any action.[12] Despite the overall air of skepticism, some of Washington's generals wanted to engage the British aggressively; the impetuous Anthony Wayne declared his desire of "*Burgoyning* Clinton."[13] On June 18, as soon as he received definite word that the British were leaving Philadelphia, Washington sent six brigades in pursuit of them. The last remnants of the Continental Army crossed the Delaware River into New Jersey on June 22.

Two days later, at Hopewell, Washington again weighed the conflicting views of his generals. In sweltering, rainy weather, the British Army had turned east toward Sandy Hook and trudged across gravelly, uncertain terrain at a rate of only six miles per day, making them a tempting target. Their woollen uniforms and cumbersome gear turned their march into a torturous ordeal. Some soldiers dropped dead from sunstroke, and the British ranks were badly thinned by desertions. For once the Continental Army, twelve thousand strong, enjoyed a numerical advantage. At a war council on June 24 Charles Lee reiterated his view that it was in the patriots' interest to have the British evacuate Philadelphia and that they should, to this end, construct "a bridge of gold" to New York and let the British cross it.[14] Once again the generals opposed a major engagement and favored a more circumscribed operation in which fifteen hundred men under Brigadier General Charles Scott would harass the British Army. Such caution led Alexander Hamilton to comment tartly that the timid conclave "would have done honor to the most honorable society of midwives."[15] Greene, Wayne, Lafayette, and Steuben knew the country clamored for strong action. "People expect something from us and our strength demands it," Greene advised in a letter. "I am by no means for rash measures, but we must preserve our reputation."[16] Lafayette, who privately ridiculed the war council "as a school of logic," urged Washington to defy its meek counsel.[17] Washington, with growing confidence in his own judgment, overruled the majority of generals and decided to undertake a more assertive operation against the British, led by an advance contingent of four thousand men.

On June 25 he learned that British troops were approaching the tiny crossroads village of Monmouth Court House (now Freehold) and deputized Charles Lee to lead the offensive. When Lee balked at the assignment as beneath his lofty dignity, fit only for a "young volunteering general," Washington handed the job to Lafayette, who would command the vanguard force to harry the British rear.[18] "The young Frenchman, in raptures with his command and burning to distinguish himself, moves toward the enemy who are in motion," the aide James McHenry wrote in his diary.[19] Suddenly afraid that Lafayette would steal his glory, Lee informed Washington that he had reconsidered. "They say that a corps consisting of six thousand men, the greater part chosen, is undoubtedly the most honorable command next to the Commander in Chief; that my ceding it wou[l]d of course have an odd appearance," he wrote with considerable understatement. "I must entreat therefore . . . that, if this detachment does march, that I may have the command of it."[20] If he did not get the command, Lee asserted, he would be disgraced, which meant he might have to resign.

Whatever Washington thought of Lee's attempts to gratify his own self-importance, he couldn't afford a feud with his second in command on the eve of battle, even if Lee had shown little sympathy for the planned attack. On the other hand, he didn't wish to disappoint Lafayette. So he crafted a nice compromise, adding one thousand men to the operation and placing Lafayette under Lee's nominal command. As James McHenry wrote, "To prevent disunion, Lee is detached with 2 brigades to join the Marquis and as senior officer to the command. His detachment consists of 5,000 men, four-fifths of whom were picked for this service."[21]

On June 27, as the British reached the vicinity of Monmouth Court House, the advance American forces pulled to within six miles of the tail end of their column. Meeting with his generals, Washington ordered Lee to attack the British column the next morning, as soon as it sprang into motion. He himself would hang in the rear with six thousand men, prepared to move forward with the main body of the army.

In retrospect, Washington conceded too much latitude to Lee, and the open-ended nature of the battle plans would breed fatal confusion the following day.

Many romantic yarns have been spun about the eve of the Battle of Monmouth. One describes the Reverend David Griffith, a chaplain in the Continental Army, going to Washington and warning him that General Lee planned to make him seem inept the next day so as to nab the top army spot for himself. Another tale claims that several generals approached Washington's friend Dr. James Craik and asked him to appeal to Washington to safeguard his own person in the coming conflict instead of exposing himself to danger. This advice, if given, ran counter to Washington's active conception of leadership on the battlefield. It is also said that Charles Lee, overtaken by a case of nerves, paced through a sleepless night before the battle. As for Washington, he is said to have shown a touching solidarity with his men, akin to Shakespeare's Henry V before the Battle of Agincourt, sleeping under a tree amid his army.

Around dawn Washington learned that the British Army had risen early and was already marching toward Sandy Hook. He sent orders for General Lee "to move on and attack them unless there should be very powerful reasons to the contrary," and started toward Monmouth Court House with his men.[22] Washington recommended that Lee's men jettison their packs and blankets to accelerate their speed. Unfamiliar with the local topography, Lee found himself penetrating terra incognita, a problem that had troubled the Continental Army in previous contests. On this morning of brutal weather, the temperature would zoom close to one hundred degrees, and many men stripped off their shirts and rode bare-chested. Joseph Plumb Martin opined that "the mouth of a heated oven seemed to me to be but a trifle hotter than this ploughed field; it was almost impossible to breathe."[23] At eleven A.M. Washington, accompanied by troops under Stirling and Greene, wrote to Henry Laurens that several men had already expired from the heat.

Toward noon, as his main force advanced toward Monmouth Court House, Washington couldn't see what was happening up ahead and assumed that all was going according to plan. In reality, Lee had made only a confused, halfhearted attack against Clinton and Cornwallis who, anticipating a possible attack, had concentrated their finest soldiers in the rear. They turned the tables, gathered six thousand men, and chased back the outnumbered Americans, who fell back in terror. Washington's first inkling of disaster came when a farmer told him that American troops were retreating. Having received no report from Lee himself, Washington was at first incredulous. Then a frightened young fifer who was hustled into his presence assured him that "the Continental troops that had been advanced were retreating." Washington was shocked. Fearful that a false report might trigger chaos, Washington categorically warned the boy that "if he mentioned a thing of the sort, he would have him whipped."[24]

Taking no chances, Washington spurred his horse toward the front. He had not gone fifty yards when he encountered several soldiers who corroborated that the entire advance force was now staggering back in confused retreat. Soon Washington saw increasing numbers of men, dazed and exhausted from the stifling heat, tumbling toward him. He told aides that he was "exceedingly alarmed" and could not figure out why Lee had not notified him of this retreat.[25] Then Washington looked up and saw the culprit himself riding toward him: General Lee, trailed by his dogs. "What is the meaning of this, sir?" Washington demanded truculently. "I desire to know the meaning of this disorder and confusion!"[26] According to some witnesses, it was one of those singular moments when Washington showed undisguised wrath. Indignant, Lee stared blankly at him and spluttered in amazement. "Sir? Sir?" he asked, offended by Washington's tone.[27]

In his self-serving view of events, Lee believed that he had performed a prodigious feat, rescuing his overmatched army from danger and organizing an orderly retreat. "The American troops would not stand the British bayonets," he insisted to Washington. "You damned poltroon," Washington rejoined, "you never tried them!"[28] Always reluctant to resort to profanities, the chaste Washington cursed at Lee "till the leaves shook on the tree," recalled General Scott. "Charming! Delightful! Never have I enjoyed such swearing before or since."[29] Lafayette said it was the only time he ever heard Washington swear. "I confess I was disconcerted, astonished, and confounded by the words and the manner in which His Excellency accosted me," Lee recalled. He said Washington's tone was "so novel and unexpected from a man whose discretion, humanity, and decorum" he admired that its effect was much stronger than the words themselves.[30] Lee, babbling incoherently, tried to explain to Washington that he found himself facing the British on an open plain, making his men easy prey for British cavalry. Washington brusquely dismissed Lee's reminder that he had opposed the attack in the first place: "All this may be very true, sir, but you ought not to have undertaken it unless you intended to go through with it!"[31] In retrospect, Washington had trusted too much to an erratic general who had supported the mission only reluctantly, and he now banished him to the rear. Lafayette later said of Washington's encounter with Lee that "no one had ever before seen Washington so terribly excited; his whole appearance was fearful."[32] This was the temperamental side of Washington that he ordinarily kept well under wraps.

Washington now moved toward the front and learned that the brunt of the enemy forces would arrive in fifteen minutes. As Tench Tilghman recalled, Washington "seemed at a loss, as he was on a piece of ground entirely strange to him."[33] The battlefield was an idyllic spot of steeply rolling farmland, split down the middle by deep ravines and creeks. Though spontaneity was never his strong suit, Washington reacted with undisputed flair and sure intuition. Fired up with anger as well as courage, he instructed Anthony Wayne to hold the enemy at bay with two nearby regiments while he rallied the confused rout of men. Commanding as always on horseback, he succeeded in stemming the panic through pure will. When he asked the men if they would fight, they loudly responded with three lusty cheers—a novel occurrence in Washington's experience, suggesting the deep affection he inspired after the shared sacrifice at Valley Forge. His cool presence emboldened his men to resist the approaching British bayonets and cavalry charges. All the while American artillery shelled the British from a nearby ridge. Lafayette stood in awe of Washington's feat: "His presence stopped the retreat . . . His graceful bearing on horseback, his calm and deportment which still retained a trace of displeasure . . . were all calculated to inspire the highest degree of enthusiasm . . . I thought then as now that I had never beheld so superb a man."[34] Sometimes critical of Washington's military talents, Hamilton ratified Lafayette's laudatory appraisal: "I never saw the general to so much advantage. His coolness and firmness were admirable . . . [He] directed the whole with the skill of a master workman."[35] Stirling and Greene particularly distinguished themselves during the action, although Washington reserved his highest praise for Brigadier General Anthony Wayne, "whose good conduct and bravery thro[ugh] the whole action deserves particular commendation."[36]

The bloody battle that afternoon was a fierce seesaw struggle that took many casualties on both sides. For two hours in blazing heat, British and Continentals exchanged cannon fire. As in previous battles, Washington experienced narrow escapes. While he was deep in conversation with one officer, a cannonball exploded at his horse's feet, flinging dirt in his face; Washington kept talking as if nothing had happened. He was everywhere on horseback, forming defensive lines, urging on his men, and giving them the chance to display the marching skills acquired at Valley Forge under Steuben. Lines of patriot soldiers fired muskets with discipline not seen before. Several times the well-trained Americans withstood vigorous charges by British regulars. Earlier in the day Washington had ridden a white charger, a gift from Governor Livingston of New Jersey. As the battlefield turned into a furnace, this beautiful horse suddenly dropped dead from the heat. At that point Billy Lee trotted up with a chestnut mare, which Washington rode for the duration.

In this marathon, daylong battle, the fighting ground on until six in the afternoon. Though tempted to pursue the British, Washington bowed to the exhausted state of his men and decided to wait until morning to storm enemy positions. Clinton pulled his men back half a mile, beyond the range of American artillery. To keep his weary troops ready, Washington had them sleep on their arms in the field, ready to resume their offensive at daybreak. They inhabited a battlefield strewn with blood-spattered bodies. That night Washington draped his cloak on the ground beneath a sheltering tree, and he and Lafayette sat up chatting about Charles Lee's insubordination before falling asleep side by side. They could see campfires burning on the British side, unaware that it was a ruse used by Clinton to camouflage the British Army stealing off at midnight. At daybreak Washington awoke and realized that the British had quietly drifted away, headed for New York. He had been tricked by the same gimmick that he himself had employed at Brooklyn and at Trenton. With his men spent from battle, Washington knew it was pointless to trail after the fleeing British.

Both sides claimed victory after the battle, and the best casualty estimates show something close to a draw: 362 killed, wounded, or missing Americans, versus British casualties that ranged anywhere from 380 to 500. After the drubbing at Brandywine Creek and Germantown, Washington may be forgiven for crowing about Monmouth as a "glorious and happy day."[37] Having weathered the horrendous winter at Valley Forge, American soldiers, with new élan, had proved themselves the equal of the best British professionals. In general orders for June 29, Washington trumpeted the battle as an unadulterated triumph: "The Commander in Chief congratulates the army on the victory obtained over the arms of his Britannic Majesty yesterday and thanks most sincerely the gallant officers and men who distinguished themselves upon the occasion."[38] Washington's joy at the outcome owed much to the fact that he had rescued the army from a disaster in the making.

As always, however, Washington disclaimed credit and directed attention to a higher power. He ordered his men to put on decent clothes so that "we may publicly unite in thanksgiving to the supreme disposer of human events for the victory which was obtained on Sunday over the flower of the British troops."[39] The Battle of Monmouth added luster to Washington's reputation as someone who could outwit danger. Writing on behalf of Congress, Henry Laurens predicted that Washington's name would be "revered by posterity" and alluded to his miraculous escapes from harm: "Our acknowledgments are especially due to Heaven for the preservation of Your Excellency's person, necessarily exposed for the salvation of America to the most imminent danger in the late action."[40]

Washington's role at Monmouth stands out with special vividness because it was the last such major battle in the North during the war. Henceforth the British high command would shift its focus to the South, where it hoped to exploit widespread Loyalist sentiment. This move would thrust Washington into the odd situation of often being an idle spectator of distant fighting in the South. Not until Yorktown, more than three years later, would he again be directly exposed to the hurly-burly of a full-scale battle. The Battle of Monmouth clarified that Washington did not need to save towns but only to preserve the Continental Army and keep alive the sacred flame of rebellion. As he told Laurens, the British were now well aware "that the possession of our towns, while we have an army in the field, will avail them little.

It involves *us* in difficulty, but does not by any means insure *them* conquest."[41] A war of attrition, however deficient in heroic glamour, still seemed the most certain path to victory.

Before Monmouth, George Washington had been unusually tolerant of the antic, impertinent behavior and self-congratulatory rhetoric of Charles Lee, but that patience had now expired. Retaining his elevated opinion of his own military genius, Lee blustered indiscreetly that he had been on the brink of rallying his men when Washington showed up and ruined everything. "By all that's sacred," he exclaimed, "General Washington had scarcely any more to do in [the battle] than to strip the dead!"[42] To top things off, Lee said that Washington had "sent me out of the field when the victory was assured! Such is my recompense for having sacrificed my friends, my connections, and perhaps my fortune."[43]

Charles Lee did not realize that he had crossed a line with Washington, and that anyone who offended his dignity paid a terrible price. He saw himself as the victim and, for two days after the battle, awaited an apology from Washington. Then he sent him an insolent letter in which he blamed "dirty earwigs" for poisoning Washington's mind against him: "I must conclude that nothing but the misinformation of some very stupid, or misrepresentation of some very wicked person cou[l]d have occasioned your making use of so very singular expressions as you did on my coming up to the ground where you had taken post. They implied that I was guilty either of disobedience of orders, or want of conduct, or want of courage." The presumptuous Lee then added that "the success of the day was entirely owing" to his maneuvers.[44] This intemperate communication sealed Charles Lee's fate.

With officers who crossed him, Washington tended to exhibit infinite patience and overlook many faults, but when a day of reckoning came, he unleashed the full force of his slow-burning fury at their accumulated slights. As with many overly controlled people, Washington's anger festered, only to burst out belatedly. He now returned a blistering reply in which he branded Lee's letter "highly improper" and said his own angry words at Monmouth were "dictated by duty and warranted by the occasion." He accused Lee of "a breach of orders and of misbehavior" in not attacking the enemy "as you had been directed and making an unnecessary, disorderly, and shameful retreat."[45] When he received this rebuke, Lee said, "I was more than confounded. I was thrown into a stupor. My whole faculties were, for a time, benumbed. I read and read it over a dozen times."[46] To clear his name, Lee demanded a court-martial, and Washington called his bluff, promptly sending Adjutant General Alexander Scammell to arrest him and bring him up on charges.

Lee was charged with disobeying orders, permitting a disorderly retreat, and disrespecting the commander in chief. A court-martial, presided over by twelve officers, took testimony for six weeks, found Lee guilty, and suspended him from the army for twelve months. The verdict effectively ended his military career. With exemplary restraint, Washington did not comment on the decision until Congress certified it. As Congress procrastinated for four months, word of the verdict leaked out. Intent on fairness, Washington wrote in confidence to his brother Jack, "This delay is a manifest injustice either to the Gener[a]l himself or the public; for if he is guilty of the charges, punishment ought to follow; if he is innocent, 'tis cruel to keep him under the harrow."[47] Charles Lee proclaimed to anyone who would listen that he had been subjected to an "inquisition" worthy of Mazarin or Cardinal Richelieu.[48] The inept Lee may not have been guilty of all the charges directed against him, but neither had he covered himself with glory at Monmouth.

Washington had not heard the last from Charles Lee. In early December Lee published a vindication of his conduct, contending that Washington had failed to give him definite orders at Monmouth Court House. If Washington chafed at the accusation, it wasn't his style to engage in public feuding. At the same time he worried that, if he didn't refute Lee's charges, it might seem "a tacit acknowledgment of the justice of his assertions," as Washington told Joseph Reed. He confessed that he had always found Lee's temperament "too versatile and violent to attract my admiration. And that I have escaped the venom of his tongue and pen so long is more to be wondered at than applauded."[49]

Even though Congress confirmed the court-martial verdict and suspended Lee in December 1778, Washington still worried that Lee's charges had sullied his honor. In late December John Laurens, with Alexander Hamilton acting as his second, challenged Lee to a duel. "I am informed that in contempt of decency and truth you have publicly abused General Washington in the grossest terms," Laurens informed Lee. "The relation in which I stand to him forbids me to pass such conduct unnoticed."[50] At the duel Laurens wounded Lee in the side, but the latter survived. Whether the duel had Washington's tacit approval remains unclear. Unlike many military men, Washington opposed dueling and had advised Lafayette against fighting a duel that year, chiding him gently that "the generous spirit of chivalry, exploded by the rest of the world, finds a refuge, my dear friend, in the sensibility of your nation *only*."[51] On the other hand, it is hard to imagine that Laurens and Hamilton would have defied the explicit wishes of Washington, who had felt gagged in responding to Lee's libelous comments.

From the retirement of his farm in Virginia, Charles Lee, as irascible as ever, continued to wage a campaign of vituperation against Washington. In 1780 he sent to Congress a letter whose tone was so obnoxious that he was cashiered for good from the armed forces. Before his death in 1782, Lee requested that he be buried somewhere other than a churchyard, stating that "since I have resided in this country, I have kept so much bad company while living, that I do not choose to continue it when dead."[52]

Pests of Society

EVEN AS THE CONTINENTAL ARMY FOUGHT in the gritty heat of Monmouth Court House, then filed wearily toward the Hudson River, blessed relief seemed to arrive when a French fleet dropped anchor off Delaware Bay on July 8, 1778. This majestic armada of twelve enormous ships of the line and four frigates, bearing four thousand soldiers, ended Britain's undisputed dominance in sea power in the war. A few weeks earlier French and British ships had exchanged fire in the English Channel, dragging France irrevocably into the hostilities. Henceforth the Revolutionary War would gradually evolve into a global conflict, with theaters of battle extending from the West Indies to the Indian Ocean.

The French fleet was headed by a forty-eight-year-old French nobleman and vice admiral with a long, flowery name: Count Jean-Baptiste-Charles-Henri-Hector d'Estaing. D'Estaing had his own reasons for joining the fight, having clashed with the British in the East Indies and been captured by them twice. With his army background, he had never entirely gained the trust of skeptical naval officers, who sometimes reflexively addressed him as "General."[1] He had won the high-prestige American assignment less from naval prowess than from his intimacy with the royal family. The day he arrived off the Chesapeake, d'Estaing sent Washington a rather rapturous letter of introduction: "The talents and great actions of General Washington have insured him in the eyes of all Europe the title, truly sublime, of deliverer of America."[2]

It proved a bittersweet moment for Washington, who imagined that, if the French fleet had shown up weeks earlier, it might have delivered a mortal blow to the British Army in Philadelphia; had that happened, Sir Henry Clinton might have "shared (at least) the fate of Burgoyne."³ Destiny had robbed George Washington of a spectacular chance to eclipse Horatio Gates. Whatever his regrets, Washington dispatched his faithful aide John Laurens to coordinate plans with the admiral and reverted to his fond daydream of recapturing New York. From his camp in White Plains, he mused how the war had now come full circle, giving him an unexpected chance to redeem past errors: "It is not a little pleasing, nor less wonderful to contemplate, that after two years' maneuvering and undergoing the strangest vicissitudes that perhaps ever attended any one contest since the creation, both armies are brought back to the very point they set out from."⁴ Momentarily it appeared that d'Estaing might pull off a quick miracle. With his fleet anchored off Sandy Hook, the prospect arose that he could trap the Royal Navy in New York Bay. Then it was discovered that the harbor channel was too shallow for the deep draft of his huge ships, and Washington believed yet another exquisite chance to shorten the war had been fumbled.

The inaugural effort at cooperation with the French squadron ended up riddled with acrimony. The new allies decided to demolish the British garrison at Newport, Rhode Island, through a joint effort of the American army under Major General John Sullivan and the French fleet under d'Estaing. The swarthy Sullivan was a competent but notoriously cantankerous officer. A year earlier Washington had felt duty-bound to challenge his pretensions. "No other officer of rank in the whole army has so often conceived himself neglected, slighted, and ill-treated as you have done," Washington warned him, "and none, I am sure, has had less cause than yourself to entertain such ideas."⁵ The brawny Irishman hardly seemed the ideal person to coordinate a military mission with a highborn French count.

When an untimely storm and the appearance of a British fleet interfered with the Newport assault, d'Estaing decided to scuttle it and take refuge in Boston. For Washington, this was yet the third time that a stupendous opportunity had been bungled. "If the garrison of that place (consisting of 6,000 men) had been captured . . . it would have given the finishing blow to British pretensions of sovereignty of this country," Washington asserted to his brother Jack.⁶ Fuming, Sullivan swore that the French had left his men dangerously stranded in Rhode Island. On August 22 he and Nathanael Greene sent an explosive letter to d'Estaing, accusing him of craven betrayal. However much Washington might have sympathized with their critique, he didn't believe he could afford to spar with his French allies, so he tried to hush up the letter and sent the politic Greene to mend fences with d'Estaing. He also pleaded with Sullivan to restore cordial relations and avoid festering mistrust: "First impressions, you know, are generally longest remembered, and will serve to fix in a great degree our national character among the French."⁷

With d'Estaing, Washington swallowed his pride and flattered the Frenchman's pride unashamedly. "It is in the trying circumstances to which your Excellency has been exposed that the virtues of a great mind are displayed in their brightest luster," he wrote, claiming that the unforeseen storm had stolen a major prize from the admiral.[8] As part of the effort to repair frayed relations, John Hancock hosted a gleaming banquet at his Beacon Hill mansion in Boston, where the count was presented with a portrait of Washington. "I never saw a man so glad at possessing his sweetheart's picture, as the admiral was to receive yours," Lafayette reported from the scene.[9]

For Washington, the French alliance never flowed smoothly. The bulk of France's fleet remained based in the Caribbean, which hindered joint operations, and the alliance with a mighty power placed Washington in an uncomfortably subservient position. By now he was accustomed to command, and a junior partnership didn't suit his strong-willed nature. He admired French military know-how, but as an outwardly cool and reticent personality, he had limited patience with French histrionics. That summer he described the French as "a people old in war, very strict in military etiquette, and apt to take fire where others scarcely seem warmed."[10] Whenever he wrote to Count d'Estaing, his language seemed to grow more stilted, as if he were trying to ape French diplomatic language, and it never sounded quite natural. Somewhere inside Washington there still lurked the insecure provincial, trying to impress these snobbish Europeans.

Compared to their American counterparts, the French, in their handsome white uniforms, looked positively foppish, right down to their high-heeled shoes. On the eve of one operation with the French, Washington ordered his field officers to fix upon a uniform look for regimental clothing, explaining that "it has a very odd appearance, especially to foreigners, to see the same corps of officers each differing from the other in fashion of the facings, sleeves, and pockets, of their coats."[11] The French condescended to American soldiers, especially the militia. "I have never seen a more laughable spectacle," said one French officer. "All the tailors and apothecaries in the country must have been called out . . . They were mounted on bad nags and looked like a flock of ducks in cross belts."[12]

The Franco-American partnership soon gave way to reciprocal disillusionment. The French had imagined that Washington commanded an army double the size of the one they found, while Washington had hoped for more than four thousand French troops. His skepticism about French motives would harden into a cornerstone of his foreign policy. His fellow citizens, he thought, were too ready to glorify France, which had entered the war to damage Britain, not to aid the Americans. "Men are very apt to run into extremes," he warned Henry Laurens. "Hatred to England may carry some into an excess of confidence in France, especially when motives of gratitude are thrown into the scale."[13] John Adams summed up the situation memorably when he said that the French foreign minister kept "his hand under our chin to prevent us from drowning, but not to lift our heads out of water."[14] In yet another sign of his growing political acumen, Washington generalized this perception into an enduring truth of foreign policy, noting that "it is a maxim founded on the universal experience of mankind that no nation is to be trusted farther than it is bound by its interest."[15] For Washington, the Continental Army was a practical school in which he received an accelerated course in statecraft, completing the education started by the first tax controversies in Virginia. One suspects that his dinner table talk with well-educated officers and aides, ranging over a vast spectrum of political, military, and financial topics, made Washington well versed in many issues, belying the notion that he was a narrow, uncomprehending leader.

The question of French motives acquired more than academic interest when Lafayette advocated an invasion of Canada. For all his affection for his youthful protégé, Washington retained an admirable skepticism about his motives. "As the Marquis clothed his proposition when he spoke of it to me, it would seem to originate wholly with himself," Washington warned Henry Laurens, "but it is far from impossible that it had its birth in the cabinet of France and was put into this artful dress to give it the readier currency."[16] If the French were embraced as liberators in Quebec, Washington feared, they might be tempted to reclaim Canadian territory relinquished at the time of the French and Indian War.

At first, Washington hesitated to voice opinions to Congress that went beyond his military bailiwick. Then in early November he sent Laurens a persuasive letter that laid out his misgivings about a northern operation. Any such invasion would introduce "a large body of French troops into Canada" and put them "in possession of the capital of that province, attached to them by all the ties of blood, habits, manners, religion, and former connection of government."[17] Once entrenched in Quebec, France would be well placed to control the United States, which was "the natural and most formidable rival of every maritime power in Europe."[18] Of this eloquent statement of realpolitik, Edmund Morgan has commented that it "remains one of the more striking examples of the quick perception of political realities that lay behind Washington's understanding of power."[19]

Perhaps corroborating Washington's worst fears, Lafayette went to Philadelphia without seeking his approval and lobbied Congress for a Canadian invasion. To Washington's dismay, some members endorsed the proposal with unthinking enthusiasm. When Lafayette traveled up the Hudson Valley to confer with Washington, the Frenchman fell ill with a high fever at Fishkill, New York, sixteen miles from the Continental Army camp. When it looked as if Lafayette might die, Washington was on such tenterhooks, according to Lafayette's later florid account, that he rode over every day to "inquire after his friend, but fearing to agitate him, he only conversed with the physician and returned home with tearful eyes and a heart oppressed with grief."[20] By late November Lafayette had sufficiently recovered to leave for Boston, hoping to catch a ship back to France for a quick visit and "present myself before the king and know in what manner he judges proper to employ my services."[21]

THAT FALL THE ATMOSPHERE grew thick with rumors that the British might evacuate New York, but even though a large number of British ships sailed south to destinations unknown in November, Sir Henry Clinton remained fixed in the city. As for winter quarters, Washington decided to house the main body of his troops at Middlebrook, New Jersey, west of Staten Island, in countryside much prettier than Valley Forge. Washington shared the home of the Philadelphia merchant John Wallace, who lived on the Raritan River, four miles west of Bound Brook. His extended absence from Mount Vernon preyed on his mind, for it began to look as if he might be trapped in some form of permanent exile. "I am beginning to throw the troops into cantonments for their winter quarters," he told brother Jack, "giving up all idea this fourth winter of seeing my home and friends, as I shall have full employment during the winter to prepare for the campaign that follows it."[22]

While the Continental Army was better clothed than at Valley Forge, it hadn't solved all the problems of the previous winter, thanks to congressional ineptitude. By now, Washington had become habituated to a draining atmosphere of a perpetual, slow-motion crisis. "Our affairs are in a more distressed, ruinous, and deplorable condition than they have been in since the commencement of the war," Washington insisted to Benjamin Harrison.[23] He had learned a valuable lesson at Valley Forge, where he had made the mistake of concentrating his men in one compact group. This time he scattered his troops across a broad area, extending north to the Hudson Valley and as far off as Connecticut, a strategic dispersal that facilitated the hunt for forage and supplies. He also ordered the application of more sanitary methods in the camp, forbidding earthen floors in huts and requiring that they be roofed with boards, slabs, or shingles.

On December 23 Washington took a brief respite from his incessant labors and traveled to Philadelphia to confer with Congress about the prospective Canadian invasion. Perhaps in preparation for this trip, he ordered new clothing for Billy Lee—two coats, two waistcoats, and a pair of breeches—that would do credit to both slave and master in the city's tony salons. Washington had already asked Martha to meet him in Philadelphia and she had eagerly awaited him there since late November. They would celebrate their twentieth wedding anniversary in the city that January. The *Pennsylvania Packet* noted with gratitude that this sojourn was "the only relief" Washington had "enjoyed from service since he first entered into it," yet the trip would prove anything but a vacation. Staying at the Chestnut Street home of Henry Laurens, Washington got a view of civilian life that would revolt him with an indelible vision of private greed and profligacy. Like soldiers throughout history, he was jarred by the contrast between the austerity of the army and the riches being earned on the home front through lucrative war contracts.

Ever since Valley Forge, Washington had lamented the profiteering that deprived his men of critically needed supplies, and he remained contemptuous of those who rigged and monopolized markets, branding them "the pests of society and the greatest enemies we have to the happiness of America," as he erupted in one fire-breathing letter. "I would to God that one of the most atrocious of each state was hung in gibbets upon a gallows five times as high as the one prepared by Haman."[24] Because of hoarding and price manipulation, among other reasons, the mismanaged currency had lost 90 percent of its value in recent months. As he contemplated these problems, Washington was also distraught over popular disunity and wished that the nation could move beyond factional disputes, telling Joseph Reed that "happy, happy, thrice happy the country if such was the government of it, but, alas! we are not to expect that the path is to be strewed w[i]t[h] flowers."[25]

Broadening his critique of the political situation, Washington traced the source of the nation's problems to the very structure of the Articles of Confederation. Deprived of taxing power, Congress had to rely on requests to the states. Instead of dealing with such structural defects, the legislature had deteriorated into partisan backbiting. "Party disputes and personal quarrels are the great business of the day," he wrote, while the "great and accumulated debt, ruined finances, depreciated money, and want of credit" were "postponed from day to day, from week to week, as if our affairs wore the most promising aspect."[26] One can see here the seeds of Washington's later version of federalism, shaped by the fear that the public would become so wedded to local government that the national government would be left weak and ineffective in consequence.

Washington trod a fine line in dealing with Congress, finding himself in an inherently contradictory position. He had far more power than any congressman and felt it his duty to make his opinions known. On the other hand, ideology required the military leader to submit to the wishes of Congress and acknowledge civilian control. The situation demanded exquisite tact from Washington, who could exploit his fame only up to a certain point. This balancing act explains why he felt both very powerful and, at moments, completely impotent during the war. In Philadelphia he met Conrad-Alexandre Gérard, the first French minister to the United States, who found him "cold, prudent, and reserved," but nonetheless detected the essence of his greatness. "It is certain that if General Washington were ambitious and scheming, it would have been entirely in his power to make a revolution, but

nothing on the part of the general or the army has justified the shadow of a suspicion," he informed Versailles. "The general sets forth constantly this principle, that
one must be a citizen first and an officer afterwards."[27]

As he tried to straighten out the nation's affairs, Washington developed a fine
rapport with the new president of Congress, John Jay, whom he had known since
the First Continental Congress. Despite their best efforts, Washington and Nathanael Greene found their serious work obstructed by an unceasing round of parties. To fulfill his duties, Greene said, he "was obliged to rise early and go to bed late
to complete them. In the morning, a round of visiting came on. Then you had to
prepare for dinner after which the evening balls would engage your time until one
or two in the morning."[28] The toast of the town, sought by every hostess, Washington was shocked at the decadent civilian life that contrasted with the hardscrabble
world of his men. He stared in outraged wonder at the stately carriages rolling by,
the opulent parties unfolding around him. It infuriated him that people feasted as
his men suffered. "Speculation, peculation, and an insatiable thirst for riches seem
to have got the better of every other consideration and almost of every order of
men," he wrote.[29] As Greene aptly noted, the city's luxurious life gave Washington
"infinitely more pain than pleasure."[30] He began to feel vaguely guilty about lingering in Philadelphia while his men still wallowed in poverty. By now he had developed something close to a mystic bond with his men and placed great store on his
presence among them. "Were I to give in to private conveniency and amusement,"
he told Joseph Reed, "I should not be able to resist the invitation of my friends to
make Phila[delphia] (instead of a squeezed up room or two) my quarters for the
winter, but the affairs of the army require my constant attention and presence."[31]

When Washington returned to Middlebrook in February 1779, after a six-week
stay in Philadelphia, he and Martha tried to brighten up the winter camp. Since the
tin plates at meals had grown rusty, Washington ordered a set of china for the table
along with six genteel candlesticks. The fare was less spartan than at Valley Forge,
and the Washingtons entertained in modest style. As the surgeon James Thacher
said of one dinner, "The table was elegantly furnished and the provisions ample,
but not abounding in superfluities . . . In conversation, His Excellency's expressive
countenance is peculiarly interesting and pleasing; a placid smile is frequently observed on his lips, but a loud laugh, it is said, seldom, if ever, escapes him. He is
polite and attentive to each individual at table and retires after the compliments of
a few glasses."[32] Thacher assessed Martha with an approving eye: "Mrs. Washington
combines in an uncommon degree great dignity of manner with the most pleasing
affability, but possesses no striking marks of beauty."[33]

Washington remained a man of unusual physical stamina who was still strong,
manly, and youthful, while Martha had aged more quickly. One telling difference

was that while George still loved to dance, especially with lovely young women, Martha had renounced the practice. In November Washington had expressly asked Nathanael Greene to have his young wife, Caty, come to the winter camp, and she duly arrived with her little boy, George Washington Greene. At a dance in February to celebrate the first anniversary of the French alliance, Washington danced first with the obese Lucy Knox. Having done his social duty, he then indulged in an experience that recalled happier times: he danced all evening with Caty Greene. "His Excellency and Mrs. Greene danced upwards of three hours without once sitting down," Nathanael Greene wrote. "Upon the whole we had a pretty good frisk."[34] Perhaps it was the aftereffect of the social whirl of Philadelphia, but Washington now seemed more attentive to women. "It is needless to premise that my table is large enough to hold the ladies; of this they had ocular proof yesterday," he told one correspondent, echoing a famous line from *Othello*. Henry Knox also arranged a splendid fireworks show for the celebration and boasted of the fashionable spectators who sat on a specially erected stage. "We had about seventy ladies, all of the first *ton* [French for breeding or manners] in the state, and between three and four hundred gentlemen."[35]

As at Valley Forge, Washington wondered whether he could retain his restive officers, who had grown disenchanted as they saw civilians pocketing huge wartime profits while they lacked money to tide over their struggling families. "The large fortunes acquired by numbers out of the army affords a contrast that gives poignancy to every inconvenience from remaining in it," Washington warned Congress.[36] To stem the wholesale defection of ordinary soldiers, he offered land, clothing, and bounties of up to two hundred dollars to keep his fragile army together.

Amid these fears of a shrinking force, Washington's twenty-four-year-old aide John Laurens hatched an audacious plan to raise a black regiment of three thousand slaves from South Carolina and Georgia, who would win their freedom at the close of the contest. Laurens had been emboldened by the success in recruiting black soldiers from Rhode Island. At Valley Forge Washington had lent Laurens qualified support, telling him that "blacks in the southern parts of the continent offer a resource to us that should not be neglected."[37] Yielding to his son's wishes, Henry Laurens had canvassed congressional support for a scheme that would allow blacks to fight in exchange for emancipation, but he returned a somber assessment: "I will undertake to say there is not a man in America of your opinion."[38] The idealistic John Laurens tabled the idea for a year, then revived it at Middlebrook.

Handsome, smart, and dashing, John Laurens was no ordinary advocate for emancipation. His father had traded slaves on an immense scale, importing between seven thousand and eight thousand captive souls from Africa. The younger Laurens had long meditated on ways to free these slaves and expunge the family taint, telling his father a year earlier, "I have long deplored the wretched state of these men."[39] No idle dreamer, John Laurens was prepared to free his family's slaves as part of his program, which he saw as the prelude to general emancipation. In the aftermath of the overwhelming British victory at Savannah, Georgia, in late December 1778, John Laurens warned that South Carolina urgently needed a black force to avert "impending calamity."[40] On March 16 Henry Laurens wrote to Washington and accentuated the strategic utility of the concept, asserting that if the patriots had three thousand armed blacks in the Carolinas, "I should have no doubt of success in driving the British out of Georgia."[41]

By this point, with a heavy influx of black soldiers from New England, the Continental Army had become a highly integrated force. But Washington knew that it was one thing to train and equip blacks from the northern states and quite another those from the South. He must have wondered whether such an action might someday sound the death knell for slavery at Mount Vernon. Like many southern slaveholders who were uncomfortable with slavery in principle, Washington hoped the institution would wither away on some foggy, distant day. By contrast, the Laurens plan was radical and immediate, with incalculable consequences. Washington found Laurens's motives both "laudable" and "important," but he had pointed reservations about his plan.[42]

On March 20 Washington sent Henry Laurens a letter that threw away a major historic opportunity. Although surrounded by staunch abolitionists such as Laurens, Hamilton, and Lafayette, he couldn't break loose from the system that formed the basis of his fortune. With his darkest fears as a planter trumping his hopes, he cast doubt on prospects for the Laurens plan and advanced the dubious argument that, if Americans armed their slaves, the British would simply retaliate in kind— an odd statement, since Lord Dunmore had already raised American hackles with his Ethiopian Regiment. Then Washington broached a still more deeply rooted fear: that a black regiment in South Carolina might foment dangerous thoughts of freedom among slaves everywhere. As slaves saw their black brethren marching off in arms, it might "render slavery more irksome to those who remain in it." Trying to wriggle free of this topic, which he obviously found exceedingly unpleasant, Washington ended on a disingenuous note. "But as this is a subject that has never employed much of my thoughts, these are no more than the first crude ideas that have struck me upon the occasion."[43]

Overcoming doubts from southern delegates, Congress approved a resolution on March 29 that might have paved the way for abolishing southern slavery: "That it be recommended to the states of South Carolina and Georgia, if they shall think the same expedient, to take measures immediately for raising three thousand able-bodied negroes."[44] The resolution proposed that masters would be compensated at a rate of $1,000 per slave, while armed slaves would be liberated at the conclusion of the war. Because John Laurens was a member of the South Carolina legislature, Washington allowed him to head home and argue his case in person. But that assembly, dominated by slaveholders, was scandalized by the Laurens plan and rejected it resoundingly, despite the security it might have afforded against a British invasion. In a postmortem, Washington told Laurens, "I must confess that I am not at all astonished at the failure of your plan. That spirit of freedom, which at the commencement of this contest would have gladly sacrificed everything to the attainment of its object, has long since subsided and every selfish passion has taken its place."[45]

What Washington couldn't acknowledge was that he himself had been lukewarm about the plan for self-interested reasons. Whatever his reservations about slavery, he never showed courage on the issue in public statements, restricting his doubts to private letters. Even before the war Washington had felt burdened by slavery, not so much on moral grounds, but as a bad economic system that saddled him with high fixed costs from a large, sullen, and inefficient labor force. Washington prided himself on being a progressive, up-to-date farmer and thought that human bondage mired him in an antiquated system. Two months before being chosen as commander in chief, he made a revealing comment about notices for the sale of indebted estates that appeared daily in Virginia gazettes. Without "close application," he said, Virginia estates were forever doomed to lapse into debt "as Negroes must be clothed and fed [and] taxes paid . . . whether anything is made or not."[46]

Even as he brooded about the Laurens proposal, Washington contemplated a drastic plan to sell all his slaves and invest the proceeds in interest-bearing loan office certificates to help finance the war effort. Perhaps this made him reluctant to press a plan that involved emancipating blacks. On February 24, 1779, Washington sent a chilling letter to Lund Washington in which he pondered aloud a liquidation scenario. If America lost the war, he noted, "it would be a matter of very little consequence to me whether my property is in Negroes or loan office certificates, as I shall neither ask for, nor expect, any favor from his most gracious Majesty . . . the only points therefore for me to consider are . . . whether it would be most to my interest, in case of a fortunate determination of the present contest, to have negroes and the crops they will make, or the sum they will now fetch and the interest of the money."[47] Clearly slaves were just another form of salable property for Washington, and the only question was what price they fetched or what profit they yielded compared to other assets. While he had scruples about breaking up slaves' families, he evidently had none about selling them, provided they stayed together.

The dilemma of what to do with his slaves would hound Washington for the rest of his life. Virginia still lacked a free labor force, and, at bottom, he probably could not figure out how to farm in the absence of slaves. So however much he admired the economies of the New England and mid-Atlantic states in which he spent the war, he did not see how he could re-create that freer world at home.

CHAPTER THIRTY

The Storm Thickens

IN FRAMING POLICY toward Native Americans, George Washington spoke in many conflicting voices. As an inveterate speculator in western lands and a military man with firsthand knowledge of Indian raids on frontier outposts, he was capable of railing against Indians as savages who committed barbaric acts. In a less-than-enlightened letter of 1773, he told George William Fairfax that the colonists had "a cruel and bloodthirsty enemy upon our backs, the Indians . . . with whom a general war is inevitable."[1] Yet this same man could sound sage and statesmanlike in urging his countrymen to treat the Indians fairly and coexist with them in peace. He always advocated buying Indian lands "in preference to attempting to drive them by force of arms out of their country."[2] Frequently he manifested horror at the avarice of real estate speculators and the wanton depredations of settlers against Native American communities. His tone, however, varied subtly with the audience and the situation.

The American Revolution did not give Washington the option of developing a broad-minded Indian policy, especially when dealing with the Six Nations of the Iroquois Confederacy. These proud warriors felt more endangered by American westward expansion than by British policy, which had banned settlements beyond the Alleghenies, starting with the 1763 proclamation that had so infuriated the young Washington. The Six Nations weren't uniformly pro-British—the Oneidas sided with the Americans—but such fine distinctions often got overlooked in the heat of battle.

Of special concern to Washington was the capable Mohawk chieftain Joseph Brant, who had plotted with the British to attack American settlements in the Mohawk Valley of upstate New York. In November 1778 Brant took three hundred Seneca Indians, united them with two Tory companies under Major Walter Butler, and ravaged an American settlement at Cherry Valley, New York: they set fire to the village and killed more than thirty settlers. The attack generated hair-raising stories of atrocities, some credible tales of scalpings, others far-fetched claims of cannibalism. The assault produced such outrage that Washington had no choice but to take decisive action. "It is in the highest degree distressing to have our frontier so continually harassed by this collection of banditti under Brant and Butler," he told General Edward Hand, warning of retaliatory measures.[3]

At various junctures Washington extended diplomatic overtures to the Indians. As early as January 1776 he had presided over a parley of Indian sachems. John Adams was then visiting the camp, and Washington, with a droll flight of fancy, introduced him as belonging to the "Grand Council Fire at Philadelphia."[4] During the Middlebrook winter of 1778–79, Washington invited Native American chieftains to tour the camp and witness the size of his army. James Thacher wrote how his brigade was "paraded for the purpose of being reviewed by General Washington and a number of Indian chiefs . . . His Excellency, with his usual dignity, [was] followed by his mulatto servant Bill, riding a beautiful gray steed."[5] The French alliance helped Washington to woo Indian tribes that were erstwhile French supporters. Nonetheless most tribes made the rational, if ultimately calamitous, decision that they had to protect their homelands and that the best way to do so was by supporting Great Britain, which they thought more likely to win the war.

By March 1779 Washington had steeled himself to act ruthlessly against the Six Nations and resort to cold-blooded warfare against civilians as well as warriors. His aim, he told Horatio Gates, was to "chastise and intimidate" these foes and "cut off their settlements, destroy their next year's crops, and do them every other mischief of which time and circumstances will permit."[6] Even when Cayuga Indians sent out peace feelers in early May, Washington dismissed them as mere tactical ploys. "A disposition to peace in these people can only be ascribed to an apprehension of danger," he told Congress, "and would last no longer than till it was over and an opportunity offered to resume their hostility with safety and success."[7]

Fearful of further Indian defections to the British, Washington entertained six Delaware Indian chieftains on May 12. He thought that, as long-standing Iroquois enemies, they might be drawn squarely into the American camp. His speech to them began bluntly: "Brothers, I am a warrior. My words are few and plain, but I will make good what I say. 'Tis my business to destroy all the enemies of these states and to protect their friends."[8] He scorned the British as a "boasting people" who didn't deliver on promises and contrasted them with the trustworthy French: "Now the Great King of France is become our good brother and ally. He has taken up the hatchet with us and we have sworn never to bury it till we have punished the English."[9] The speech, likely drafted by an aide, included Washington's most explicit reference to Jesus: "You do well to wish to learn our arts and ways of life and, above all, the religion of Jesus Christ. These will make you a greater and happier people than you are."[10]

From the safe distance of a carriage, Martha Washington monitored the curious proceedings, escorted by a gawking Lucy Knox and Caty Greene. As one might expect from a genteel Virginia lady, Martha was taken aback by the Indians and their seemingly outlandish regalia. "The General and Billy [Lee], followed by a lot of mounted savages, rode along the line," she told her daughter-in-law. "Some of the Indians were fairly fine looking, but most of them appeared worse than Falstaff's gang. And such horses and trappings! The General says it was done to keep the Indians friendly toward us. They appeared like cutthroats all." The editor of Martha Washington's papers notes that this "letter, if authentic, has undergone editing."[11]

Such diplomacy didn't forestall the punitive measures Washington initiated against Indian settlements three weeks later. Clearly in a vengeful mood after attacks on American civilians, he contemplated a drastic removal of the Six Nations from their traditional hunting grounds and farms. He ordered General Sullivan and about four thousand soldiers to march to the Finger Lakes in upstate New York and the Susquehanna Valley in Pennsylvania and undertake "the total destruction and devastation" of Iroquois settlements, grabbing women and children as hostages for bargaining purposes.[12] The Indians must have been forewarned, for Sullivan's men often swooped down on deserted villages, which didn't stop the Americans from reducing forty towns to ashes and incinerating 160,000 bushels of crops. As Sullivan laid down this trail of devastation, Washington recounted to Lafayette in jubilant terms how Sullivan had "completed the entire destruction of the whole country of the Six Nations, except so much of it as is inhabited by the Oneidas, who have always lived in amity with us."[13]

Although Washington admitted that Indian families were fleeing in terror, he rationalized these harsh measures as fit punishment for assorted cruelties practiced by the Indians on "our unhappy, frontier settlers, who (men, women, and children) have been deliberately murdered in a manner shocking to humanity."[14] This wasn't the last word on Indian policy from Washington, who still hoped to develop friendly relations with even hostile tribes. "To compel a people to remain in a state of desperation and keep them at enmity with us . . . is playing with the whole game against us," he told Philip Schuyler.[15] Nonetheless the cumulative devastation wrought against Indian tribes during the war crippled their power and disrupted their communities, causing incalculable harm and making them vulnerable to forced resettlement policies later inflicted upon them by several American presidents.

"WASHINGTON WAS NEVER VERY GOOD AT WAITING," writes the historian Edward G. Lengel, "but that is how he spent the years between 1778 and 1781."[16] The year 1779 was perhaps the war's most sluggish, characterized by minor skirmishes in lieu of major battles. Although Washington busied himself with espionage, the Continental Army mostly settled into an indolent mode. Aside from the Indian offensive, Congress was bent upon conserving money, forcing Washington into an unwanted defensive posture as he awaited the return of the unaccountable Count d'Estaing. He found it extremely dispiriting to be suspended again in a limbo of inaction as the war dragged on interminably.

In May the major locus of fighting switched back to the Hudson River, as Sir Henry Clinton overran two American forts at Stony Point and Verplanck's Point. This placed the enemy twelve miles south of the American fortress at West Point and made it seem as if the British might at last attain their strategic will-o'-the-wisp—cutting off New England from the rest of the country. Washington hastily relocated his base of operations to New Windsor, New York, overlooking the Hudson, where he could interdict British movements on the water. Afraid that its loss would be catastrophic, he assigned top strategic priority to West Point. For his summer headquarters, he chose the commodious West Point dwelling of a well-known New York merchant named John Moore.

Washington doubted that he could ever dislodge the British from their new entrenched positions, but he had a general who warmed to the task: Anthony Wayne, a fighter by nature as much as by training. Born in Chester County, Pennsylvania, he had been educated by his uncle, Gilbert Wayne, who found the wayward boy's mind inflamed by dreams of battle. "He has already distracted the brains of two-thirds of the boys under my charge by rehearsals of battles, sieges, etc.," Gilbert Wayne sighed. "During noon, in place of the usual games of amusement, he has the boys employed in throwing up redoubts, skirmishing, etc."[17] A surveyor and a tanner before the war, then a member of Pennsylvania's assembly, Wayne had gained Washington's admiration for his bravery at Brandywine Creek, Germantown, and Monmouth Court House. He fought with often-bloodthirsty glee, shouting to his men, "I believe that [a] sanguine God is rather thirsty for human gore!"[18] This rabble-rousing style earned him the nickname of "Mad Anthony" Wayne.

Bluff and familiar, Wayne was a great favorite among his men. Washington's coolly reserved style of leadership was so antithetical to Wayne's that he admired this impetuous officer with reservations. Washington found Wayne, for all his courage, imprudent and cursed by erratic judgment. As president, Washington would render this mixed appraisal of him: "More active and enterprising than judicious and cautious . . . Open to flattery, vain, easily imposed upon, and is liable to be drawn into scrapes. Too indulgent . . . to his officers and men. Whether sober, or a little addicted to the bottle, I know not."[19] On the other hand, Washington knew that Wayne was an effective missile if fired with accuracy. While crediting Wayne's bravery, Thomas Jefferson contended that he was the sort of obstinate man who might "run his head against a wall where success was both impossible and useless."[20]

Washington chose Wayne to lead a picked force of 1,350 infantry to mount a surprise raid against the new British outpost at Stony Point. The commander sketched out a plan to scale the 150-foot-high cliff overhanging the river, prompting Wayne, according to legend, to boast, "I'll storm hell, sir, if you'll make the plans!"[21] To which Washington retorted drily, "Better try Stony Point first, general."[22] On the night of July 15 Wayne and his men approached the promontory with fixed bayonets, so as not to alert the British. When Wayne's head was grazed by a musket ball, he cried out, "Carry me into the fort and let me die at the head of my column."[23] True to form, he pushed up the bluff and overran the fort, slaying sixty-three British soldiers and taking five hundred prisoners, in a virtuoso performance. He sent a courier to Washington to announce the victory, writing with customary spirit, "Dear General, The fort and garrison with Colonel Johnston are ours. Our officers and men behaved like men who are determined to be free. Yours most sincerely, Ant[hon]y Wayne." Never loath to credit his officers, Washington trumpeted Wayne's virtues to Congress: "He improved upon the plan recommended by me and executed it in a manner that does signal honor to his judgment and to his bravery."[24] The victory stopped the enemy's northward advance up the Hudson Valley at a time when a gunpowder shortage had virtually ruled out large-scale American operations.

Washington gradually resigned himself to a lull in the fighting. Baffled by the movements of his French allies, he concluded that America needed another European power if it ever hoped to match British superiority at sea. In late September that wish was fulfilled when he received news that Spain had entered the war against England. "The declaration of Spain in favor of France has given universal joy to every Whig," Washington wrote to Lafayette, "while the poor Tory droops like a withering flower under a declining sun."[25] It turned out that Spain was more interested in harassing the British monarchy than in fostering American independence, which might threaten Spanish territories in North America. Before long a subdued Washington realized that no sudden windfalls would result from Spanish intervention. "We ought not to deceive ourselves," he wrote the following spring. "The maritime resources of Great Britain are more substantial and real than those of France and Spain united."[26] For this reason Washington was overjoyed by news that autumn that John Paul Jones had armed an old French ship, christened it the

Bonhomme Richard in homage to Ben Franklin, and defeated the British ship *Serapis* off the English coast. In the throes of battle, Jones thundered his immortal line, "I have not yet begun to fight."[27]

Aside from Stony Point and an intrepid raid led by Major Henry Lee against a feeble British garrison installed at Paulus Hook, on the west bank of the Hudson, the summer was uneventful, leaving Washington with time to savor society. With food plentiful, he could lay out ample spreads for visitors. Touches of whimsy and flashes of wit resurfaced in his letters. In mid-August Washington extended a dinner invitation to Dr. John Cochran that signaled a fleeting return to normality:

> Since our arrival at this happy spot, we have had a ham (sometimes a shoulder) or bacon to grace the head of the table; a piece of roast beef adorns the foot; and a small dish of greens or beans (almost imperceptible) decorates the center. When the cook has a mind to cut a figure . . . we have two beefsteak pies or dishes of crabs in addition, one on each side [of] the center dish . . . Of late, he has had the surprising luck to discover that apples will make pies. And it's a question if, amidst the violence of his efforts, we do not get one of apples instead of having both of beef. If the ladies can put up with such entertainment and will submit to partake of it on plates, once tin, but now iron . . . I shall be happy to see them.[28]

On September 12 the French minister, the Chevalier de La Luzerne, and his highly observant secretary, François Barbé-Marbois, met with Washington at Fishkill, New York. Barbé-Marbois jotted down valuable vignettes of an unbuttoned Washington, who personally squired them by boat to his headquarters and showed that he was adept at navigation. "The general held the tiller," recalled Barbé-Marbois, "and during a little squall which required skill and practice proved to us that this work was no less known to him than are other bits of useful knowledge."[29] Greatly taken with Washington, the secretary found him becomingly modest, gracious, and urbane: "He is fifty years old, well built, rather thin. He carries himself freely and with a sort of military grace. He is masculine looking, without his features being less gentle on that account. I have never seen anyone who was more naturally and spontaneously polite."[30]

Accustomed to imperious officers, Barbé-Marbois was charmed by Washington's more democratic manner, which, contrary to the behavior of most generals, had grown more pronounced as the war progressed. The Frenchman noted Washington's cordial relations with his aides: "I have seen him for some time in the midst of his staff and he has always appeared even-tempered, tranquil, and orderly in his occupations and serious in his conversation. He asks few questions, listens attentively, and answers in a low tone and with few words. He is serious in business."[31] In another sharp departure from European formality, Washington engaged in sports with subordinates and "sometimes throws and catches a ball for whole hours with his aides-de-camp."[32] Aware of the impression he made, Washington knew that he needed to exhibit sterling republican simplicity to the French as proof of American virtue. "It was not my intention to depart from that plain and simple manner of living which accords with the real interest and policy of men struggling under every difficulty for the attainment of the most inestimable blessing of life—*Liberty*," Washington wrote to Lafayette. "The Chevalier was polite enough to approve my principle and condescended to appear pleased with our spartan living."[33]

With his flair for political stagecraft, Washington set up his dining marquee—an oval tent with a dark green ceiling—on the Hudson shore, so close to the river that the tide periodically tugged at pins holding the tent erect. Ever the attentive host, he had musicians play a medley of French and American martial tunes. Barbé-Marbois saw that Washington displayed quiet dignity in dealing with people and in social settings allowed himself a "restricted gaiety."[34] "He is reverent without bigotry and abhors swearing, which he punishes with the greatest severity," he reported.[35] At meals the self-effacing Washington allowed his young aides to propose toasts. "All the generals and the higher officers were there," Barbé-Marbois remembered. "It was interesting to see this meeting of these warriors, each of them a patriot renowned for some exploit."[36] To add extra luster to the toasts, Washington fired cannon to celebrate the health of Louis XVI and Marie-Antoinette.

At one point Washington asked Barbé-Marbois if he had seen Lafayette in France, and the secretary answered in the affirmative, saying Lafayette had spoken of Washington with the "tenderest veneration." Barbé-Marbois recounted how Lafayette's American exploits had elicited praise from the king. "Washington blushed like a fond father whose child is being praised," Barbé-Marbois wrote in his diary. "Tears fell from his eyes, he clasped my hand, and could hardly utter the words: 'I do not know a nobler, finer soul, and I love him as my own son.' "[37] It was yet another extraordinary proof of the powerful feelings surging beneath the seemingly placid surface of the commander in chief.

Two weeks later Washington wrote a voluminous letter to Lafayette in which this outwardly stolid man allowed sentimental emotions to gush freely to the surface. His "first impressions of esteem and attachment" for Lafayette, he said, had ripened into "perfect love and gratitude." Politely declining Lafayette's invitation to visit France, he noted that he was unacquainted with French, was too old to learn it, and would seem "extremely awkward, insipid, and uncouth, . . . especially with the *Ladies*," if he spoke through interpreters.[38] On the other hand, he pressed Lafayette and his wife to visit Mount Vernon after the war and see "my rural cottage, where homely fare and a cordial reception shall be substituted for delicacies and costly living."[39] Exactly how Washington transformed a slave plantation into a quaint "rural cottage" remains a mystery.

In the letter, Washington presented a lighthearted but vivid picture of his own ardent nature as a young man, as if Lafayette brought out some buried romanticism in him. Washington asked Lafayette to tell the marchioness

> that I have a heart susceptible of the tenderest passion and that it is already so strongly impressed with the most favorable ideas of her that she must be cautious of putting love's torch to it, as you must be in fanning the flame. But, here again, methinks I hear you say, I am not apprehensive of danger. My wife is young, you are growing old, and the Atlantic is between you. All this is true, but know, my good friend, that no distance can keep *anxious* lovers long asunder, and that the wonders of former ages may be revived in this.[40]

He ended on a somber note: "But, alas! will you not remark that amidst all the wonders recorded in holy writ no instance can be produced where a young woman from *real inclination* has preferred an old man."[41] Clearly Washington, forty-seven, was lapsing into the wistful mood of an older man nostalgic for his passionate youth. Whether he was thinking of Martha Washington or Sally Fairfax when he wrote this confessional letter, we do not know. At the end, as if amazed at how he had rambled on, he remarked, "When I look back to the length of this letter, I am so much astonished and frightened at it myself that I have not the courage to give it a careful reading for the purpose of correction."[42]

Though French diplomats were impressed with Washington, he remained in the dark about the plans of the Count d'Estaing. He heard stray rumors about his fleet's return to northern waters and stationed Major Henry Lee on the New Jersey shore to greet it, but he could not verify the information. The day after the state dinner with the French, Washington wrote to d'Estaing that the British had beefed up their strength in New York to fifteen thousand men. Reviving his favorite fantasy, he wondered aloud whether the count planned to attack New York. Reduced to an almost servile status, Washington had to beg for scraps of information about French plans. "I have taken the liberty to throw out these hints for your Excellency's information," Washington wrote gingerly, "and permit me to entreat that you will favor me as soon as possible with an account of your Excellency's intentions."[43] Washington yearned to hurl the weight of his army against the British in New York or Rhode Island, and he seeded New York City with spies to ascertain the strength of the British garrison— all to no avail, as he felt increasingly powerless vis-à-vis his French allies.

In late September Washington learned that d'Estaing's fleet had appeared off the Georgia coast. When another month passed without information, Washington vented his frustration to Jacky Custis, complaining of his fickle French ally that "we begin to fear that some great convulsion in the earth has caused a chasm between this and that state that cannot be passed."[44] Then Washington learned that d'Estaing and General Benjamin Lincoln had launched a disastrous foray to recapture Savannah. They had stormed British fortifications and suffered more than eight hundred American and French casualties, leaving behind a "plain strewed with mangled bodies."[45] Amid the general carnage, d'Estaing suffered wounds in the arm and leg before retreating with his fleet to the West Indies. As far as Washington was concerned, this unfortunate performance rounded out a misbegotten year of botched battles, missed chances, and enforced idleness.

Resigned to the seasonal end of combat in the northern states, Washington took the bulk of his army into the safe haven of a winter cantonment in Morristown, New Jersey. Confronted by early snow and hail, the soldiers chopped down two thousand acres of timber and roughed out a city of nearly a thousand log cabins. Washington—and a month later, Martha—took up residence in the handsome mansion of Mrs. Theodosia Ford, a substantial three-story house with shutters and dormer windows that must have seemed palatial compared to the compact Potts house at Valley Forge. Unfortunately the unbending Mrs. Ford refused to yield two of four downstairs rooms, forcing the Washingtons to share the floor with her. The kitchen, in particular, was a scene of pure bedlam. "I have been at my present quarters since the first day of December," an irritable Washington wrote to Nathanael Greene in January, "and have not a kitchen to cook a dinner in." His retinue of eighteen servants "and all Mrs. Ford's are crowded together in her kitchen and scarce one of them able to speak for the colds they have caught."[46] To accommodate his aides, Washington completed a couple of rooms upstairs and constructed an adjoining log cabin for daytime duties.

Washington braced for a winter that, for sheer misery, threatened to rival the trials of Valley Forge. As early as October, there wasn't a single pair of shoes in army depots, and the situation was equally lamentable for shirts, overalls, and blankets. Since the Continental currency now fetched only three cents to the dollar, Congress stopped printing money and appealed to the states to pay their own troops. As the latter issued their own paper currency, prices soared even further. Washington captured graphically the ruinous hyperinflation when he told John Jay that "a wagon load of money will scarcely purchase a wagon load of provisions."[47] To Gouverneur Morris, he protested, "A rat, in the shape of a horse, is not to be bought at this time for less than £200."[48] He took seriously intelligence reports that the British in Philadelphia had purloined reams of the paper used to print currency and planned to crush the rebellion by swamping the country with counterfeit money.

Washington faced double jeopardy from the debased currency. Besides placing goods beyond the budget of his quartermasters, it was whittling away his personal fortune. Like many rich planters, Washington had large loans outstanding in Virginia that were being repaid in debased currency. As he complained to his brother-in-law, "I am now receiving a shilling in the pound in discharge of bonds which ought to have been paid me and would have been realized before I left Virginia, but for my indulgence to the debtors."[49] Washington estimated that personal losses occasioned by his absence from home had swollen to ten thousand pounds. Further embittering him was the selfish behavior of Jacky Custis, who stalled in settling debts to him so he could repay in cheaper currency. Washington, finally losing his temper, scolded his stepson: "You might as well attempt to pay me in old newspapers and almanacs, with which I can purchase nothing."[50] For political reasons, Washington accepted payment for land in Continental currency, so he wouldn't be seen as questioning American credit, but by the summer of 1779 he could no longer afford these massive losses and discontinued the practice.

The previous winter Washington had been sufficiently confident of his troops to risk a six-week stay in Philadelphia, but he now felt compelled to stick close to his restive men, "to stem a torrent which seems ready to overwhelm us."[51] Reports from New York told of mutinous sentiments brewing among the militia for want of food, and Washington feared the contagion might spread to New Jersey. If Sir Henry Clinton invaded Morristown, the Continental Army would be easy prey. Clinton "is not ignorant of the smallness of our numbers," Washington alerted New Jersey governor Livingston. "He cannot be insensible of the evils he would bring upon us by dislodging us from our winter quarters."[52] In mid-December he informed Congress that his army had gone for days without bread, making its prospects "infinitely worse than they have been at any period of the war and . . . unless some expedient can be instantly adopted, a dissolution of the army for want of subsistence is unavoidable."[53] For Washington, it was one crisis too many, straining already taut nerves. Worried that his army would simply disintegrate, he shed his stoic composure, and people began to gossip about his sulky moods. Nathanael Greene told Jeremiah Wadsworth, the commissary general, that Washington was in a "state [of] distress" and was blaming "everybody, both innocent and guilty."[54]

As in previous winters, Washington was appalled by the lack of patriotism displayed by private citizens. He did not want to imitate British precedent and force nearby residents to house officers, but voluntary offers were not forthcoming. He reprimanded men who plundered food or livestock from local farms and warned his soldiers that "a night scarcely passes without gangs of soldiers going out of camp and committing every species of robbery, depredation, and the grossest personal insults. This conduct is intolerable and a disgrace to the army."[55] On the other hand, he privately confessed that he felt powerless to stop this marauding.

Then on January 2, 1780, thick snow began to descend on Morristown, accompanied by fierce winds, and continued steadily for four days. It was a blizzard of such historic proportions, said James Thacher, that "no man could endure its violence many minutes without danger of his life."[56] Four feet of snow blanketed the winter camp and drifted to six feet in many places, sealing off the army from incoming supplies and compounding the misery of men shivering in their bunks. Before the winter was through, the Morristown encampment would be pounded by a record twenty-eight snowfalls. It would qualify as one of the most frigid winters on record, so severe that New York Bay crusted over with ice thick enough for the British to wheel cannon across it. Because the ice formed land bridges, Washington meditated a surprise attack on the British garrison at Staten Island. The plan was for 2,500 men under Lord Stirling to cross over from New Jersey, destroy British supplies, and carry off sheep and cattle. Washington, who must have dreamed of reliving the Delaware crossing on Christmas Night 1776, grew so enamored of this plan that he worried the cold snap would end, thawing the ice. The plan was shelved when the British picked up intelligence about it, eliminating the element of surprise. Washington promptly confiscated the caps and mittens issued to men who were to conduct the raid. The British were cooking up their own surprises. In February a British raiding party of three hundred men on horseback crept up stealthily on Morristown in an apparent plot to kidnap Washington. When they couldn't traverse the deep snow, they turned back and abandoned the plan.

As a howling blizzard swirled around the Ford mansion, Washington filed a dreary report with Congress: "Many of the [men] have been four or five days without meat entirely and short of bread and none but on very scanty supplies."[57] Horror stories abounded of ill-clad men gnawing tree bark or cooking shoes or dining on pet dogs. Washington said his men were eating every kind of horse food but hay. As at Valley Forge, they were starving in the midst of fertile farming country, adding an extra dimension of tragic gloom to their suffering. As Greene lamented, "A country overflowing with plenty are now suffering an army, employed for the defense of everything that is dear and valuable, to perish for want of food."[58] Even forced requisitions didn't alleviate the abominable situation. As late as April 12 Washington bewailed the perilous scarcity of food: "We have not at this day one ounce of meat, fresh or salt, in the magazine," and he didn't know of any carts loaded with meat rolling toward Morristown.[59] Further aggravating matters was the fact that his army hadn't been paid in months. Alexander Hamilton, never one to shy away from strong opinions, probably spoke for many soldiers when he wrote, "We begin to hate the country for its neglect of us."[60] The winter wasn't a complete loss for Hamilton, who met and fell in love with his future wife, Elizabeth Schuyler, the daughter of General Schuyler. The young woman never forgot Martha Washington's kindness: "She was quite short: a plump little woman with dark brown eyes, her hair a little frosty, and very plainly dressed for such a grand lady as I considered her . . . She was always my ideal of a true woman."[61]

The war continued to serve as Washington's political schoolroom. Once again a harrowing winter forced him to think analytically about the nation's ills. On both the civilian and the military side of the conflict, he condemned slipshod, amateurish methods. America needed professional soldiers instead of men on short enlistments, just as it needed congressmen who stayed in office long enough to gain experience. Most of all Americans had to conquer their excessive attachment to state sovereignty. "Certain I am," Washington told Joseph Jones, a delegate from Virginia, "that unless Congress speaks in a more decisive tone, unless they are vested with powers by the several states competent to the great purposes of war . . . our cause is lost."[62] "I see one head gradually changing into thirteen," he confessed to Jones. "I see one army branching into thirteen and, instead of looking up to Congress as the supreme controlling power of the United States, [they] are considering themselves as dependent on their respective states."[63]

Washington viewed the restoration of American credit as the country's foremost political need, and he supported loans and heavy taxation to attain it. While fighting Great Britain, he pondered the source of its military power and found the answer in public credit, which gave the enemy inexhaustible resources. "In modern wars," he told Joseph Reed, "the longest purse must chiefly determine the event," and he feared that England, with a well-funded debt, would triumph over America with its chaotic finances and depleted coffers. "Though the [British] government is deeply in debt and of course poor, the nation is rich and their riches afford a fund which will not be easily exhausted. Besides, their system of public credit is such that it is capable of greater exertions than that of any other nation."[64] This letter prefigures the Hamiltonian program that would distinguish Washington's economic policy as president. It took courage for Washington, instead of simply demonizing Great Britain, to study the secrets of its strength. Throughout the war, he believed that an American victory would have been a foregone conclusion if the country had enjoyed a strong Congress, a sound currency, stable finances, and an enduring army. Not surprisingly, many other officers in the Continental Army became committed nationalists and adherents of a robust central government. One virtue of a war that dragged on for so many years was that it gave the patriots a long gestation period in which to work out the rudiments of a federal government, financial mechanisms, diplomatic alliances, and other elements of a modern nation-state.

The hardship of the Morristown winter persisted well into the spring. On May 25 two mutinous regiments of the Connecticut Line, defying Washington's orders, burst from their huts at dusk, flashing weapons, and declared they would either return home or confront local farmers to "gain subsistence at the point of the bayo-net."[65] These men, not having been paid in five months, saw no relief in sight. The officers calmed them down without further incident, but they were no less dis-traught than their men. Instead of feeling resentful toward his rebellious troops, Washington directed his anger at apathetic citizens who permitted this deplorable state. "The men have borne their distress with a firmness and patience never ex-ceeded . . . but there are certain bounds beyond which it is impossible for human nature to go," Washington warned Congress.[66]

In coping with this high-pressure situation, Washington receded deeper into himself, as if afraid to voice his true feelings aloud, lest it demoralize his men. "The great man is confounded at his situation," Greene reported to Joseph Reed, "but appears to be reserved and silent."[67] Martha Washington, who stayed in Morris-town until June, told her brother-in-law that "the poor General was so unhappy that it distressed me exceedingly."[68] At times Washington pretended to a deeper philosophic serenity than he could honestly claim. "The prospect, my dear Baron, is gloomy and the storm thickens," he told Steuben, then went on to say, "I have been so inured to difficulties in the course of this contest that I have learned to look on them with more tranquillity than formerly."[69] In a revealing letter to Robert Mor-ris that May, Washington noted, with restrained jollity, that in the absence of wine, he had been forced to substitute grog made from New England rum and drink it from a wooden bowl. Then he made a comment that suggested how his wartime experience had dampened his general experience of things. When his "public duty" ended, he told Morris, "I may be incapable of . . . social enjoyments."[70]

What lifted Washington from the worst depths of dejection was the extraordi-nary heroism of his army, which had been reduced to eight thousand men, one-third still unfit for duty. Looking back upon the ghastly conditions of that winter, he found the army's survival almost beyond belief. To brother Jack, he expressed amazement: "that an army reduced almost to nothing (by the expiration of short enlistments) should sometimes be five or six days together without bread, then as many without meat, and once or twice two or three without either; that the same army should have had numbers of men in it with scarcely clothes enough to cover their nakedness and a full fourth of it without even the shadow of a blanket, severe as the winter was, and that men under these circumstances were held together, is hardly within the bounds of credibility, but is nevertheless true."[71]

The Traitor

IN THE SPRING OF 1780 Washington's most immediate concern was the uncertain fate of the threatened American garrison in Charleston, South Carolina. Sir Henry Clinton and Lord Cornwallis had set sail with a large flotilla from New York and besieged Charleston as the main theater of war shifted irreversibly to the South. The American force was commanded by Major General Benjamin Lincoln, a husky former farmer from Massachusetts. Lincoln was popular and widely respected, and Washington credited him with being "an active, spirited, sensible man."[1] The commander in chief remained a far-off observer of the Charleston deadlock, however, since Congress and the Board of War had deprived him of jurisdiction over the southern department, and he didn't care to quarrel with this blatantly political decision.

Queasily aware of what the loss of a major seaport would mean, Washington prophesied that the fall of Charleston would probably "involve the most calamitous consequences to the whole state of South Carolina, and even perhaps beyond it."[2] At the very least it would expose the Carolinas to merciless British raids. By massing his men in the coastal city, Lincoln had left the interior pretty much defenseless. "It is putting much to the hazard," Washington confided to Steuben. "I have the greatest reliance on General Lincoln's prudence, but I cannot forbear dreading the event."[3] Washington's dread was not misplaced. On May 12, 1780, Charleston capitulated to the British, and 2,571 Continental soldiers, 343 artillery pieces, and almost 6,000 muskets fell into enemy hands. Under the arcane rituals of eighteenth-century warfare, defeated forces were typically allowed to surrender with dignity and march out with their colors flying proudly. To shame the Americans, the British forbade them this customary honor, forcing them to lay down their arms in humiliated silence. The defeated soldiers then faced the unpleasant choice of either becoming prisoners of war or returning home with a solemn vow to refrain from further fighting, reverting to loyal British subjects.

As he reflected on this devastating blow, Washington sounded alternately bitter and philosophical. He believed the British had expertly timed their campaign to exploit his army's weakness at Morristown and knew this resounding victory would "give spirit to our enemies."[4] He also suspected the British would use Charleston as a springboard to launch incursions into the Carolinas and Virginia. True to his prediction, Clinton, while steering a large portion of his forces back to New York, left Cornwallis with a sizable force to terrorize the South. At the same time Washington wondered whether the British had now stretched themselves too thin, forcing them to pay a steep price in blood and treasure to maintain this faraway outpost.

With the American treasury empty, Washington could not contemplate a potent offensive campaign without French largesse. That winter the French had decided to send an enormous expeditionary force to America, commanded by Jean-Baptiste Donatien de Vimeur, the Count de Rochambeau. It was the first time the French had supplemented a fleet with a massive army. France had elevated the illustrious Rochambeau to the lofty rank of lieutenant general but, in a diplomatic concession to American sensibilities, agreed that he would be placed, at least nominally, under Washington's orders. The French fleet under the Chevalier de Ternay would also be subject to Washington's control, yet after his frustrations with the mercurial d'Estaing, Washington entertained no illusions about exercising any real influence.

The person assigned to herald this impending force was a natural choice for the job. In early March Lafayette set sail for America, ready to resume his post as a major general and act as intermediary between Washington and Rochambeau. As soon as he disembarked in Massachusetts in late April, Lafayette, never bashful about his starring role in the American drama, rushed off a typically histrionic letter to Washington that throbbed with boyish excitement: "Here I am, my dear general, and in the midst of the joy I feel in finding myself again one of your loving soldiers . . . I have affairs of the utmost importance which I should at first communicate to you alone."[5] Washington grew emotional as he read the message. Then on May 10 the beaming author himself strode into his presence, and the two men eagerly clasped each other. Recounting this sentimental reunion, Lafayette wrote that Washington's "eyes filled with tears of joy . . . a certain proof of a truly paternal love."[6] Washington lost no time in lobbying Lafayette for a Franco-American invasion of New York, which would possess the collateral advantage of lessening British pressure on the southern states.

Uplifted by the splendid news from France, Washington pressed Congress for an expanded army of at least twenty thousand Continental troops to cooperate with their ally. As a matter of both pride and policy, Washington didn't want the stylish French soldiers to patronize his men in their tattered clothing, and he appealed to Congress to rectify the matter. His army had come to a standstill, lacking money and supplies. "For the troops to be without clothing at any time is highly injurious to the service and distressing to our feelings. But the want will be more peculiarly mortifying when they come to act with those of our allies."[7] In early July, with the arrival of the French fleet imminent, Washington was chagrined by the states' failure to muster new troops or even keep him posted on their plans. He again blamed the bugaboo of a permanent military force—the "fatal jealousy . . . of a standing army"—for the shocking failure to buttress his army.[8] "One half the year is spent in getting troops into the field," Washington complained to his brother Samuel, "the other half is lost in discharging them from their limited service."[9]

When the French fleet arrived in Newport on July 10, it proved almost anticlimactic. Only five thousand soldiers, it turned out, had made the crossing, and a significant fraction were unfit for service. No sooner did Washington learn of the French dropping anchor than he received dreadful tidings from New York: Rear Admiral Thomas Graves had arrived in the harbor with a British fleet of comparable size. Washington dispatched Lafayette to confer with Rochambeau and Ternay, introducing him to the French officers as "a friend from whom I conceal nothing . . . I entreat you to receive whatever he shall tell you as coming from me."[10] In assigning Lafayette as his go-between, Washington committed a terrible gaffe that betrayed his provinciality. However blue-blooded Lafayette was in social terms, he had been only a captain in the French reserve and was much too low in the military hierarchy to parley with a French lieutenant general with decades of service. Still worse, Lafayette had tried to wangle the very assignment Rochambeau now held. Undeterred, Lafayette poured out flattery so liberally that Rochambeau pleaded with him to stop: "I embrace you, my dear Marquis, most heartily, and don't make me any more compliments, I beg of you."[11]

Although Washington had resurrected his plan to besiege New York, Lafayette could not budge Rochambeau and Ternay from their resolve to wait for more French troops before setting their men in motion. The French balked at relying on their American allies. Rochambeau was secretly appalled at the minute size of Washington's army and the bankruptcy of American credit. "Send us troops, ships, and money," he wrote home, "but do not depend on these people nor upon their means; they have neither money nor credit; their means of resistance are only momentary and called forth when they are attacked in their own homes."[12] Privately he mocked Washington's plan to attack New York as absurd, given the beggarly state of American finances, and blamed Lafayette for abetting Washington's unrealistic fantasies. The French general would be two-faced in his relationship with Washington, pretending to credit his ideas, then doing exactly as he pleased. For political reasons, both sides subscribed to the polite fiction that Washington was in charge, but another year elapsed before the alliance with France bore fruit in a major joint military operation.

IN THE WAKE of the aborted "Conway Cabal," George Washington had remained unfailingly polite to Horatio Gates, even though he thought the latter still intrigued against him. But his courtesy failed to mollify his implacable foe. In spring 1779 Gates protested to John Jay that Washington deliberately kept him in the dark, which led Washington, in turn, to pen an acerbic note to Jay, relating how he had sent Gates no fewer than forty letters in the last seven months of 1778. "I think it will be acknowledged," observed Washington tartly, "that the correspondence was frequent enough during that period."[13] Far from snubbing him, Washington noted, "I made a point of treating Gen[era]l Gates with all the attention and cordiality in my power, as well from a sincere desire of harmony as from an unwillingness to give any cause of triumph to our enemies."[14]

After the British captured Charleston, Gates was appointed to command the southern department of the army, and Washington refrained from comment so as not to be accused of meddling from personal pique. If Washington quietly rooted for Gates's comeuppance, the British delivered it in shattering form near Camden, South Carolina, on August 16, 1780. Gates deployed a force of nearly four thousand men, considerably bigger than the force marshaled by Cornwallis, but many were callow militia. Determined British troops smashed through the American lines and sent men flying in terror. Only the detachment under General Johann de Kalb tried to withstand the frenzied onslaught. The British cavalry under Colonel Banastre Tarleton—nicknamed "Bloody Tarleton" and "The Butcher" for his take-no-prisoners approach—slashed at Kalb's helpless men, while Kalb himself was bludgeoned to death with bayonets and rifle butts. Educated at Oxford, from a wealthy family, the young Tarleton was a beefy, redheaded man who was brash and cocky about his exploits on and off the battlefield. "Tarleton boasts of having butchered more men and lain with more women than anybody else in the army," Horace Walpole reported.[15] Having lost two fingers in battle, he delighted in waving his truncated hand and shouting, "These gave I for King and country!"[16] At Camden, Tarleton's men did their deadly work so efficiently that nine hundred Americans were slain and a thousand taken prisoner.

The debacle knocked Gates off his perch, especially after the terror-stricken general scampered away on horseback and raced 180 miles before mustering the equanimity to report to Congress. Washington, who had an unerring knack for letting his enemies dig their own graves, was tight-lipped about the defeat. Still, his loyal aides heaped scorn on the discredited Gates, who became the laughingstock of Washington's staff. "Was there ever an instance of a general running away, as Gates has done, from his whole army?" Alexander Hamilton whooped with glee. "One hundred and eighty miles in three days and a half. It does admirable credit to the activity of a man at his time of life."[17] With the American defeat, Georgia and the Carolinas fell under British sway, making Virginia more vulnerable to invasion. For the moment, Lord Cornwallis looked invincible. Drawing the moral for Congress, Washington sidestepped Gates's cowardice to concentrate on the militia's amateurish performance. "*No militia* will ever acquire the habits necessary to resist a regular force . . . The firmness requisite for the real business of fighting is only to be attained by a constant course of discipline and service."[18]

After the Camden battle, Congress relieved a chastened Gates of his command and launched an inquest into his ignominious behavior. Gates had been the last serious rival left to Washington, whose supremacy now stood unchallenged. Gates's downfall paved the way for the return to power of General Nathanael Greene, who yearned to get back to the battlefield. He had labored successfully at the thankless job of quartermaster general and was fully rehabilitated from the disgrace of Fort Washington. Washington praised Greene for introducing both "method and system" to army supplies and reposed more confidence in him than in any other general.[19] Despite Washington's patronage, however, Greene could be an anxious, insecure man, very sensitive to slights. After the Battle of Brandywine, he had licked his wounds when Washington didn't single out for praise his division, which had included a Virginia brigade under General Weedon. "You, sir, are considered my favorite officer," Washington told him candidly. "Weedon's brigade, like myself, are Virginians. Should I applaud them for their achievement under your command, I shall be charged with partiality."[20]

Greene often experienced Washington as a difficult, caviling boss, which was hard for him as he needed periodic hand-holding and reassurance. In 1778 Greene wrote a self-pitying letter to Washington that almost begged for praise: "As I came into the Quartermaster's department with reluctance, so I shall leave it with pleasure. Your influence brought me in and the want of your approbation will induce me to go out."[21] However brusque he could be to his colleagues, Washington was also finely responsive to their psychological needs. He replied to Greene's letter: "But let me beseech you, my dear Sir, not to harbor any distrusts of my friendship or conceive that I mean to wound the feelings of a person whom I greatly esteem and regard."[22]

In removing Gates from his command, Congress certified Washington's consolidation of power by ceding to him the choice of a successor. Always sure-handed in dealing with Congress, he decided to "nominate" Nathanael Greene for the southern command instead of choosing him outright, and Congress confirmed this superb choice on October 14, 1780. The story is sometimes told that Greene initially rejected the demanding post. "Knox is the man for this difficult undertaking," he told Washington. "All obstacles vanish before him. His resources are infinite." "True," Washington retorted slyly, "and therefore I cannot part with him."[23]

Owing to the huge British presence in New York, Washington didn't think he could spare many men for the southern campaign. In giving Greene instructions, he revealed his own remoteness from the southern theater: "Uninformed as I am of the enemy's force in that quarter, of our own, or of the resources which it will be in your power to command . . . I can give you no particular instructions, but must leave you to govern yourself entirely."[24] When Caty Greene expressed concern about her husband being sent south, Washington made the magnanimous offer to serve as her post office and relay messages to her husband. "If you will entrust your letters to my care," he told her, "they shall have the same attention paid to them as my own."[25]

As THE END OF SUMMER APPROACHED, it seemed more than a little peculiar that Washington still hadn't set eyes on the Count de Rochambeau and the Chevalier de Ternay. The simple truth was that he feared the American army might fall apart in his absence and was too embarrassed by its frightful shape to chance an encounter with the French. Aside from more men, he estimated that he needed five thousand muskets and two hundred tons of gunpowder to field a viable force. When Lafayette informed him of Rochambeau's express wish to meet him, Washington owned up to the problem: "With respect to the Count's desire of a personal interview with me, you are sensible, my dear Marquis, that there is nothing I should more ardently desire than to meet him. But you are also sensible that my presence here is essential to keep our preparations in activity, or even going on at all."[26] It was an extraordinary commentary on his army's enfeebled state. In late August the bread shortage grew so alarming that he faced the severe dilemma of whether to dismiss the militia because he couldn't feed them or accept new recruits and let them "come forward to starve."[27] In early September, in order to conserve food, he sent home four hundred militiamen.

In mid-September 1780, accompanied by Lafayette, Hamilton, Knox, and an entourage of twenty-two horsemen, Washington set out for his long overdue rendezvous with Rochambeau and Ternay. The spot chosen for the parley, Hartford, Connecticut, stood equidistant between the two armies. Washington dealt with the French from a weakened position: he had only ten thousand soldiers in his army, half the number he wanted, and the total would be halved on January 1 as enlistments expired. He thought it essential that Americans, not Frenchmen, should have credit for winning the American Revolution: "The generosity of our allies has a claim to all our confidence and all our gratitude, but it is neither for the honor of America, nor for the interest of the common cause, to leave the work entirely to them."[28] En route to Hartford, Washington and his retinue paused near West Point so that he could lunch with its commandant, Benedict Arnold. Pleased with Arnold but apprehensive about the state of West Point's defenses, Washington promised to stop by on his return trip and tour the fortifications.

As Washington approached Hartford, then a humble village consisting of a single road along the Connecticut River, French cannon thundered thirteen times and local citizens broke forth in ecstatic cheers. With Lafayette acting as translator, Washington and Rochambeau had their first chance to size each other up. Rochambeau looked the part of a rough-hewn soldier who had put in thirty-seven years in the army. Short and thickset, he had a scar above one eye and shuffled about with a mild limp from an old war wound. Whatever his reservations about Washington's military plans, he was tactful, even affable, at this first meeting, but too temperamental to keep his moods in check for long. Claude Blanchard, his chief quartermaster, claimed that Rochambeau distrusted everyone and saw himself "surrounded by rogues and idiots. This character, combined with manners far from courteous, makes him disagreeable to everybody."[29]

Perhaps because they had to humor a crotchety boss, Rochambeau's staff were instantly charmed by Washington. Blanchard professed to be "enchanted" with the American general, who exhibited "an easy and noble bearing, extensive and correct views, [and] the art of making himself beloved."[30] Washington suited the idealized expectations of the world-weary French as to how a New World liberator should behave. "We had been impatient to see the hero of liberty," said the Count de Dumas. "His dignified address, his simplicity of manners, and mild gravity surpassed our expectation and won every heart."[31] Count Axel von Fersen found Washington "handsome and majestic" but was perceptive enough to discern trouble behind the placid countenance. "A shade of sadness overshadows his countenance, which is not unbecoming and gives him an interesting air."[32] It is perhaps surprising that more French officers didn't pick up the anxiety that beset Washington that summer.

As Washington and Rochambeau commenced their talks, it quickly grew apparent that the likelihood of a combined military operation that year was remote. Even though Rochambeau paid lip service to Washington's eternal plan to regain New York, he insisted on first having clear naval superiority and awaiting reinforcements from France. On their second day, the two men drew up an appeal for additional men, money, and ships from France. Although Washington and Rochambeau established instant rapport, their meeting yielded no immediate tangible results.

Rochambeau's affirmation of Washington's preeminence in the partnership didn't mislead the American general for a second. As Washington admitted ruefully to Lafayette, "My command of the French troops stands upon a very limited scale."[33]

At the close of the meeting, the Count de Dumas rode with Washington to a nearby town and beheld the worshipful feelings of the populace toward Washington.

> We arrived there at night; the whole of the population had assembled from the suburbs, we were surrounded by a crowd of children carrying torches, reiterating the acclamations of the citizens; all were eager to approach the person of him whom they called their father, and pressed so closely around us that they hindered us from proceeding. General Washington was much affected, stopped for a few moments, and, pressing my hands, said, "We may be beaten by the English; it is the chance of war; but behold an army which they can never conquer."[34]

If Washington had hoped that French and Spanish support would tip the balance of the war, the inconclusive meeting with Rochambeau left him despondent. French naval superiority hadn't yet materialized, and Washington had grown weary of this interminable conflict with its American lethargy and congressional ineptitude. Writing to John Cadwalader, he noted plaintively how the year began with a "favorable complexion" and seemed pregnant with wonderful events, but such optimism had been exposed as a delusion. The Continental Army had no money, no munitions, and soon would have no men. "I hoped," he wrote, "but hoped in vain, that a prospect was displaying which w[oul]d enable me to fix a period to my military pursuits and restore me to domestic life . . . but alas! these prospects, flattering as they were, have prov[e]d delusory and I see nothing before us but accumulating distress."[35] Since the Battle of Monmouth, Washington had soldiered on for more than two years without a major battle, and Lafayette told him of impatience at Versailles with his supposed passivity. Washington replied that this inactivity was involuntary: "It is impossible, my dear Marquis, to desire more ardently than I do to terminate the campaign by some happy stroke, but we must consult our means rather than our wishes."[36]

IF WASHINGTON THOUGHT his upcoming meeting at West Point with Benedict Arnold would revive his drooping spirits, he was proved wrong. In many ways, Arnold had been a battlefield commander after his own heart, a fearless daredevil who liked to race about the field on horseback, spurring on his men. Even George Germain lauded Arnold as "the most enterprising and dangerous" of the American generals.[37] Like Washington, he had many horses shot from under him and "exposed himself to a fault," as one soldier said.[38] In an officer corps with the usual quota of shirkers, braggarts, and mediocrities, Washington valued Arnold's derring-do and keen taste for combat, and he treated this touchy man with untiring respect. In fact, Arnold was one of the few generals who seemed not to arouse Washington's competitive urges or suspicions.

Impetuous and overbearing, Benedict Arnold was a short man with a powerful, compact body. His penetrating eyes, aquiline nose, dusky complexion, and thick, unruly hair lent him a dashing but restless air. Growing up in a well-to-do Connecticut family, he had been a bright, mischievous boy with an incurably alcoholic father. His father's drinking led to bankruptcy when Benedict was fourteen, a traumatic event that overshadowed his childhood. The boy was apprenticed to a relative who worked as a pharmacist, and then his mother died when he was eighteen. The deep shame and poverty of his childhood produced an energetic, headstrong young man who was obsessed with status and money. After opening a pharmacy in New Haven, Arnold diversified into trading, became a sea captain, and engaged in lucrative mercantile activities. Commercial success did not cool his temperament. He was pugnacious, often resorted to duels, and was litigious when libeled. In the early stages of the Revolution, he drifted into radical politics, starting as a captain in the Connecticut militia, then rising through the ranks.

Arnold's early wartime exploits made him a legendary figure. After leading the impossible trek through the Maine woods in the failed mission against Quebec, he constructed a fleet on Lake Champlain and bade defiance to a superior British force. Most notably, he turned in such a fabled performance at Saratoga that General Burgoyne gave Arnold, not Gates, the laurels for the American victory. When Arnold took a musket ball in the leg at Saratoga, the doctors wanted to amputate the maimed limb, but he scoffed at this as "damned nonsense" and refused to muddle on as a single-legged cripple.[39] This left him with one leg two inches shorter than the other, giving him a pronounced limp and forcing him to rely on crutches for a prolonged period. If Arnold was a blustery character who browbeat subordinates, his heroism and war wounds encouraged people to make allowances for him.

The quarrelsome Arnold never forgot the slight he suffered in February 1777 when Congress passed him over in naming five new major generals, all brigadiers junior to him. Even after Washington helped him to become a major general, Arnold still chafed over having lost seniority to these five men, and his bitterness curdled into settled malice. He wasn't about to be placated by anyone. When he visited Washington at Valley Forge, his injured leg, in which slivers of shattered bone were embedded, was in such dreadful shape that two soldiers had to prop him up. Washington sympathized with Arnold's plight, naming him military commandant of Philadelphia after the British evacuated in June 1778. During his time in Philadelphia, Arnold set up a fine household and courted the rich, fetching eighteen-year-old Peggy Shippen, who was half his age, and they wed the following year. Peggy was trailed by rumors of having fraternized with British officers during their occupation of Philadelphia. For his part, Arnold was shadowed by allegations that he had exploited his position as commandant to enrich himself. To clear his name, Arnold demanded a court-martial, which found him guilty of two relatively minor counts of misconduct, then let him off with a mild reprimand.

The whole episode lengthened Arnold's extensive litany of grievances and convinced him that a conspiracy existed against him. As he told Washington, "Having made every sacrifice of fortune and blood and become a cripple in the service of my country, I little expected to meet the ungrateful returns I have received from my countrymen."[40] He believed that Washington, during the court-martial, had withheld the unconditional support he merited, by maintaining a studious neutrality. Afterward, Washington pledged to Arnold that he would give him "opportunities of regaining the esteem of your country."[41] Unbeknownst to Washington, Arnold had by now established contact with Major John André, adjutant general of the British Army, and was prepared to assist Sir Henry Clinton in a secret plan to seize West Point. Peggy Arnold, having befriended André during the British occupation, was a full-fledged confederate of the plot. Heavily in debt, the mercenary Arnold brokered a rich deal for his treachery, charging the British six thousand pounds sterling and a commission in the British Army for delivering West Point into their hands.

In June 1780 West Point took on added importance. Washington feared that Clinton might return from Charleston with a hundred vessels and aim a deadly blow at the fortress. His worries were only compounded in July when Admiral Marriot Arbuthnot appeared in New York Harbor with sixty or seventy more ships. Washington swore he would do everything in his power to shore up West Point and other defensive posts along the Hudson River. At about this time Arnold rode up to Washington on the bluff at Stony Point and asked if he had "thought of anything for him." When Washington offered him a "post of honor," commanding the "light troops," Arnold blushed and grew flustered. "His countenance changed and he appeared to be quite fallen," Washington remembered, "and instead of thanking me or expressing any pleasure at the appointment, never opened his mouth."[42] When Washington met Arnold at his headquarters, his limp was unaccountably accentuated. Arnold had already impressed upon Washington's aide Tench Tilghman that he could no longer ride horses for long or undertake active commands and indicated his desire for the sedentary post at West Point. "It then appeared somewhat strange to me that a man of Arnold's known activity and enterprise should be desirous of taking so inactive a part," Washington later reflected. "I, however, thought no more of the matter."[43] Submitting to Arnold's importunate wishes, Washington announced on August 3, 1780, that "Major General Arnold will take command of the garrison at West Point."[44]

That September, not realizing that Arnold was in league with the enemy, Washington enjoined him to improve West Point's defenses. Arnold pretended to embark on a whirl of improvements at the fortress, while continually weakening them. He made it seem as if hundreds of men were hard at work when mere dozens were enlisted. When Washington alerted Arnold that he would pass through the Hudson Valley on the way to Hartford—"I want to make my journey a secret," Washington stressed—Arnold relayed this letter to his British accomplices, listing places Washington would spend the night.[45] Had the letter not been delayed, Washington might well have been taken by the British.

While Washington was returning from Hartford, Major André, traveling under the pseudonym of John Anderson, slipped behind American lines to collect intelligence from Arnold, who handed him papers outlining West Point's troop strength and artillery, along with the minutes of a September 6 war council sent to him by Washington. André tucked these tightly folded papers into his boot for safekeeping. Arnold also gave him a letter designed to smooth his way past sentries, which read: "Permit Mr. John Anderson to pass the guards to the White Plains, or below, if he choose. He being on public business by my direction."[46] While returning to the British man-of-war *Vulture,* anchored in the Hudson, André was detained in Westchester County on September 23 by three American militiamen, who stripped him and unearthed the explosive documents. In vain, he tried to bribe his way to freedom. That André was elegantly dressed in mufti, outfitted in a purple coat trimmed with gold lace and a beaver hat, became damning evidence in the trial against him. Unaware of the significance of the documents found on him, Lieutenant Colonel John Jameson conveyed them to Washington with the following note: "Inclos[e]d you'll receive a parcel of papers taken from a certain John Anderson, who has a pass signed by General Arnold." André had asked to retain the papers, Jameson continued, but "I thought it more proper your Excellency should see them."[47]

Two days later, not yet having seen this letter, Washington awoke at dawn in Fishkill, New York, and set off with a long train of aides (including Lafayette) and guards to breakfast with Benedict and Peggy Arnold. The couple occupied a roomy mansion on the east bank of the Hudson River, the former residence of Washington's friend Beverley Robinson, who had raised a Loyalist regiment. En route to the house, which stood two miles below West Point, Washington made a detour to inspect several defensive positions along the river, occasioning banter from his young aides. Lafayette reproached Washington playfully, saying how the young men awaited their breakfast with the ravishing Peggy Arnold. Washington knew the coquettish charm she exerted over his men—he had known her for many years—and said gaily to his aides, "Ah, I know you young men are all in love with Mrs. Arnold . . . You may go and take your breakfast with her and tell her not to wait for me."[48] Two aides, Samuel Shaw and James McHenry, went ahead with the message that the large party of guests had been delayed but would shortly arrive for breakfast.

For Washington, it was a surreal day of curious absences, missed hints, and odd anomalies that he did not piece together into a picture of outright treason. That he found nothing suspicious in Arnold's behavior for so many hours showed his implicit trust in him. When Washington dismounted at the Robinson house at ten-thirty A.M., one of Arnold's aides, Major David Franks, explained that his boss had been summoned to West Point on an urgent call and that Peggy Arnold lay abed upstairs. After a more solitary breakfast than anticipated, Washington boarded an awning-shaded barge, which ferried him across the Hudson to West Point, where he expected to be saluted by his host. But Arnold did not show up, and everyone professed ignorance of his whereabouts. The mystery only deepened as Washington scrutinized West Point's defenses and was shocked by their decrepit state, which showed none of the strenuous attention promised by Arnold. "The impropriety of his conduct, when he knew I was to be there, struck me very forcibly," Washington later said. "I had not the least idea of the real cause."[49]

Late in the afternoon a puzzled Washington was rowed back to the Robinson house. There was still no sign of Benedict, and Peggy Arnold remained incommunicado upstairs. As Washington rested in his room before dinner, Hamilton tapped on his door and laid before him a sheaf of papers, including the letter from Colonel Jameson. To his inexpressible horror, Washington set eyes on the war council minutes he had sent to Arnold, along with confidential information about West Point. Washington was thunderstruck. "Arnold has betrayed us!" he exclaimed. "Whom can we trust now?"[50] As he gave way to strong feelings, he struggled to get a grip on his emotions. From his reaction it is clear that he was innocent enough, or trusting enough, to find Arnold's treachery almost inconceivable. The supreme betrayal had come not from Horatio Gates or Charles Lee or others long suspected of disloyalty, but from a man whom he had trusted, admired, and assisted. Despite a healthy dose of cynicism about most people, Washington had missed all the warning signs with Benedict Arnold.

At this point Washington learned of an episode that made sense of his enigmatic day. At breakfast that morning Arnold had been given some papers, had grown agitated, said goodbye to his wife, left the house abruptly, and disappeared. The papers had alerted him to André's arrest, prompting him to flee down the Hudson to the safety of the *Vulture*. Although Washington sent Hamilton and McHenry in hot pursuit, Arnold had long since hopped on board a barge and found asylum with his British masters.

It was Arnold's aide, Lieutenant Colonel Richard Varick, who notified Washington of the delirious behavior of Peggy Arnold upstairs. He had found her roaming the halls in a state of partial undress and coaxed her back into bed, where she insisted that "there was a hot iron on her head and no one but General Washington could take it off."[51] In a drawing of Peggy Arnold done by John André, she looks cool-eyed and cunning, with just a hint of a smirk, her tall beehive hairdo towering above a small, pretty face. When Washington went upstairs to calm her, he found her hugging her baby to her breast, her abundant blond curls tumbling across her face and her dressing gown thrown open for easy viewing. She didn't seem to recognize Washington. "There is General Washington," Varick urged her gently, but she assured him he was wrong. "No, that is not General Washington! That is the man who was a-going to assist Colonel Varick in killing my child."[52] Peggy Arnold seemed too wildly distracted to participate in anything so methodical as a plot. "General Arnold will never return," she informed her gullible male audience. "He is gone forever, *there, there, there.*" She motioned toward the ceiling. "The spirits have carried him up there. They have put hot irons in his head."[53]

In cahoots with her husband, Peggy Arnold played her mad scene to perfection. Blinded by chivalry, Washington, Hamilton, and Lafayette were duped by her lunatic ravings, if not aroused by her immodest getup. They assumed that Arnold had confessed his guilt to her before fleeing and that she was still reeling from the shock. Lafayette wrote tenderly about Peggy Arnold, "whose face and whose youthfulness make her so interesting."[54] Hamilton proved especially susceptible to her wiles. "It was the most affecting scene I ever was witness to," he wrote to Elizabeth Schuyler. For a considerable time Peggy Arnold had "entirely lost her senses . . . One moment she raved, another she melted into tears. Sometimes she pressed her infant to her bosom and lamented its fate, occasioned by the imprudence of its father, in a manner that would have pierced insensibility itself."[55] In dealing with Arnold's wife, Washington and Hamilton left something to be desired as psychologists. The sudden onset of her madness and her exaggerated theatrics should have aroused their incredulity. "Mrs. Arnold is sick and General Arnold is away," Washington told the assembled officers when he went downstairs. "We must therefore take our dinner without them."[56]

Washington had no idea whether other conspirators were still at large. With impressive self-control, he sat through the four P.M. dinner without disclosing what had happened. For security reasons, he sealed off the house and did not permit anyone to enter or exit. Stunned by events, he proved slow to take precautionary steps. Hamilton, showing more initiative, took it upon himself to order a Connecticut regiment to bolster West Point. In the early evening Washington issued rapid-fire bulletins to tighten security there in case Clinton tried to exploit the confusion with a preemptive strike. Amid a mood of tense expectation, he directed troops toward

West Point and served notice that the Continental Army might be deployed on a moment's notice. He also informed Arnold's two chief aides, Franks and Varick, that he had no reason to suspect their complicity with Arnold but felt duty-bound to place them under arrest, a decision the two understood. The next day Washington announced the terrible revelation to his men: "Treason of the blackest dye was yesterday discovered!"[57] As in many major moments in the war, he traced exposure of the conspiracy to divine intervention: "In no instance since the commencement of the war has the interposition of providence appeared more conspicuous than in the rescue of the post and garrison of West Point from Arnold's villainous perfidy."[58]

Washington soon received a pair of letters from the perfidious Arnold himself. In the first, written to Washington, Arnold blamed American ingratitude for his actions and presented himself as a patriot of a higher order than Washington. He had the gall to ask the commander to forward his clothes and baggage, as if he had hastily absconded from a busy inn. The request was a commentary on Arnold's vulgar mind, but the punctilious Washington honored it. Arnold also tried to exculpate his young wife of any wrongdoing. "She is as good and as innocent as an angel and is incapable of doing wrong," he insisted.[59]

The second letter was addressed to Peggy Arnold, and Washington did not dare tamper with a sealed letter from a gentleman to his lady. Instead, he sent it upstairs, unopened, along with a soothing reassurance to Peggy that her husband was unharmed. It is hard to say whether this chivalric behavior was foolhardy or sublime. It shows that, for all the atrocities Washington had witnessed, he still believed that well-bred people inhabited a genteel world, governed by incontrovertible rules. The next morning Peggy Arnold, miraculously recovered from her madness, expressed fear that "the resentment of her country will fall upon her who is only unfortunate."[60] Still convinced of her innocence, Washington asked whether she wanted to be reunited with her husband in New York or with her father in Philadelphia. Playing the wronged patriot to the hilt, she declared her wish to join her father, and Washington drafted a special order guaranteeing her safe conduct. "It would be exceedingly painful to General Washington if she were not treated with the greatest kindness," Lafayette explained to the Chevalier de La Luzerne.[61] All the male actors had played their parts perfectly in the tragedy of Peggy Arnold, unaware that the performance was actually a farce.

AT THIRTY, Major John André was handsome, cultivated, and charming. Educated in Switzerland and something of a poet—during the occupation of Philadelphia, he had perused Benjamin Franklin's library and engaged in amateur theatricals—he was also a proficient artist, skilled at drawing quick sketches of people. In an oval portrait of André, he stares out with a powdered wig and gold epaulettes and the soft, unformed face of a boy. In the eighteenth century soldiers often identified with their social peers on the other side of the conflict because they subscribed to the same code of class honor. André's youth and gallantry touched the imagination of Washington's officers. Hamilton visited André several times at the tavern in Tappan, New York, where he was held captive and left breathless with admiration. "To an excellent understanding, well improved by education and travel, [André] united a peculiar elegance of mind and manners and the advantage of a pleasing person," he attested.[62]

The case of Major André became a cause célèbre because of his aristocratic manner and his controversial claim that he hadn't really functioned as a spy. Nobody disputed that he had been caught with concealed papers from the turncoat Arnold. The spying allegation arose because he had crossed into American lines, donned civilian clothes, and assumed a nom de guerre. André countered that he had come ashore in uniform and met Arnold in neutral territory, but the latter had then lured him into American territory. While making his way back to the *Vulture,* he had had no choice but to shed his uniform and adopt a fake name. André asserted less his innocence than his honorable conduct, telling Washington that he wished to clear himself "from an imputation of having assumed a mean character for treacherous purposes or self-interest."[63] The practical significance of this esoteric dispute was that spies were treated like common criminals and hung from the gallows, whereas a British officer in uniform caught communicating with an American spy would be shot by a firing squad in a manner befitting a gentleman.

Although Washington understood the appeal of Major André's personality, he also knew that the plot to take West Point, had it succeeded, could have been catastrophic, and this toughened him against lenient treatment of the prisoner. He instructed André's captors that he did not deserve the indulgences accorded to prisoners of war and should "be most closely and narrowly watched."[64] Intent upon seeing justice swiftly enacted, Washington impaneled a board of fourteen generals to hear André's case in a village church in Tappan. André answered their questions with such honesty and candor that his captors were moved. "I can remember no instance where my affections were so fully absorbed in any man," said Major Benjamin Tallmadge.[65] It was one of those singular moments in wartime when class solidarity overtook ideology.

Washington received a plea for mercy from an unlikely source. Benedict Arnold had the cheek to threaten Washington that, should he execute the adjutant, Arnold would "retaliate on such unhappy persons of your army as may fall within my power . . . I call heaven and earth to witness that your Excellency will be justly answerable for the torrent of blood that may be spilt in consequence."[66] Arnold thereby rubbed salt into an open wound. "There are no terms that can describe the baseness of his heart," Washington said of Arnold.[67]

The board of officers returned a guilty verdict against André and ruled that he should die as a spy—that is, by hanging. André pleaded with Washington to allow him to be shot by a firing squad. Refusing to capitulate under duress, Washington decided that André's offense was so grave that he had to make an example of him, even if it offended the sensibilities of many officers. André was sentenced to hang in full view of soldiers drawn from various quarters of the army. The decision rankled Hamilton in particular, who already chafed at Washington's exacting treatment of him. "The death of André could not have been dispensed with," Hamilton later told Knox, "but it must still be viewed at a distance as an act of *rigid justice*."[68] Trying to avert a hanging, Washington sounded out the British on a swap of André for Benedict Arnold, but the enemy declined the offer.

At noon on October 2, 1780, John André marched to the gallows. As he neared the spot, he bowed his head to those who had befriended him and showed a serene acceptance that startled everyone. "Such fortitude I never was witness of . . . To see a man go out of time without fear, but all the time smiling, is a matter I could not conceive of," marveled the army surgeon John Hart.[69] When André reached the hangman, whose face was blackened with grease, he asked if he had to die in this manner and was told it was unavoidable. "I am reconciled to my fate," he replied, "but not to the mode."[70] People heard him whisper to himself that "it will be but a momentary pang."[71] Leaping upon the cart from which his body was to be released, André took the rope from the hangman and tightened it around his own neck, then drew a handkerchief from his pocket and blinded his own eyes. When told that the time had come and asked if he had any final words, he replied, "Nothing but to request you will witness to the world that I die like a brave man."[72] His body hung slackly from the gibbet for nearly half an hour before being cut down. André's noble conduct only enhanced the misgivings of those who thought he should have been shot. It seemed hard on Washington's part to refuse the request of a man sentenced to death. Lafayette wrote to his wife that André had "conducted himself in such a frank, noble, and honorable way that, during the three days we imprisoned him, I was foolish enough to develop a real liking for him. In strongly voting to sentence him to the gallows, I could not help [but] regret what happened to him."[73]

Washington boycotted the execution. He had no special animus toward André and shared the respect felt by his men. "André has met his fate and with that fortitude which was to be expected from an accomplished man and gallant officer," he wrote to John Laurens.[74] Clearly he didn't relish hanging André, yet he also believed he had to mete out punishment for a heinous crime that might have given the American cause "a deadly wound, if not a fatal stab."[75] For Washington, who never shrank from doing the right thing, however hard or unpopular, it was a lonely moment of leadership. Even as a young officer in the French and Indian War, his justice had often seemed stern and inflexible. As he told Rochambeau, the circumstances of André's capture necessitated the hanging and "policy required a sacrifice, but as he was more unfortunate than criminal in the affair, and as there was much in his character to [excite] interest, while we yielded to the necessity of rigor, we could not but lament it."[76]

By contrast, Washington's desire for revenge against the villainous Arnold, whom he saw as "lost to all sense of honor and shame," intensified in the coming months.[77] He backed a scheme concocted by Major Henry Lee to abduct Arnold from New York City. On the night of October 20–21 a sergeant in Lee's cavalry, John Champe, pretended to desert from the American army and convinced Sir Henry Clinton that he was disaffected from the patriot cause. He then accosted Benedict Arnold in the street and struck up an acquaintance. The idea was for Champe and an American agent from New Jersey named Baldwin to grab Arnold as he strolled in his garden one night and row him across the Hudson, making it seem as if they were struggling with a drunken soldier. Washington endorsed the plan with the proviso that Arnold be brought to him alive. "No circumstance whatever shall obtain my consent to his being put to death," Washington informed Lee. "The idea which would accompany such an event would be that ruffians had been hired to assassinate him. My aim is to make a public example of him."[78] For their trouble, Champe was promised a promotion and Baldwin one hundred guineas, five hundred acres of land, and three slaves.

Champe and Baldwin were set to execute their plan in December, when Arnold was sent to Virginia, a state largely untouched by the war thus far, with a fleet of forty-two ships and seventeen hundred soldiers. Despite a warning from Washington, Virginia governor Thomas Jefferson procrastinated in summoning the state militia, and Arnold swept into the state capital at Richmond, burning supply depots and buildings. The scheme to abduct Arnold had been foiled, but Washington remained grimly implacable in his resolve to capture the blackguard. In February 1781 he sent Lafayette to Virginia with twelve hundred troops to pursue Arnold and toughened the terms for dealing with him. Should Arnold "fall into your hands," he ordered Lafayette, "you will execute [him] in the most summary way."[79] Washington never did capture Arnold. In the spring Arnold wrote to George Germain and suggested a neat way of seducing Washington to the British side. "A title offered to General Washington might not prove unacceptable," he wrote.[80] In the end, Arnold proved no better at reading George Washington's character than Washington had been at penetrating his disguise.

CHAPTER THIRTY-TWO

Mutiny

AFTER THE DRAMA of Benedict Arnold's treachery, Washington returned to the mundane issues that had long bedeviled his army, especially the abysmal food shortages and barren warehouses that failed to supply winter outfits. His desperate men started to swarm across the countryside, engaging in "every species of robbery and plunder," Washington reported.[1] Earlier in the fall he had grown so distressed over his men ransacking citizens' homes that he had sentenced to death one David Hall, who stole money and silver plates from a local resident. He assembled fifty men from every brigade to watch the execution and ponder its significance. For all his dismay over such misbehavior, however, Washington was far more livid with the venal farmers who illegally sold "fresh meats and flour of the country" to the British Army, which feasted on ample supplies in New York.[2]

In late November 1780 Washington sent his army into winter quarters, assigning the bulk of them to West Point, while he lodged in a cramped Dutch farmhouse overlooking the Hudson River at New Windsor, New York. Depressed by this "dreary station," he had to requisition supplies from nearby residents to set his meager table and pleaded with Congress for emergency funds.[3] "We have neither money nor credit," he wrote, "adequate to the purchase of a few boards for doors to our log huts . . . It would be well for the troops if, like chameleons, they could live upon air, or, like the bear, suck their paws for sustenance during the rigor of the approaching season."[4] Things grew so grim that Washington's own horses were starving for want of forage.

Perhaps it was the aborted plan to kidnap Benedict Arnold that planted the idea in Washington's mind of attempting a daring abduction of Sir Henry Clinton. On

Christmas Night he gave the go-ahead to Lieutenant Colonel David Humphreys to row down the Hudson to New York with a small band of men, their oars muffled to avert detection. The nature of the top secret mission was disclosed only to participants, right before they shoved off. "I prefer a small number to a large one," Washington said, "because it is more manageable in the night and less liable to confusion."[5] The party was supposed to land at Clinton's house on the Hudson, disarm the guards, pinion Clinton, then hurry back up the Hudson with their high-ranking prize. In the event, a brisk wind sprang up and blew the boats into the bay, scuttling the operation.

On New Year's Day 1781 Washington's worst nightmares were realized when thirteen hundred troops from the Pennsylvania Line, encamped near Morristown, mutinied and killed several officers. Much inflamed by rum, these men aired a host of legitimate grievances: insufficient food, clothing, and pay. After grabbing every musket in sight and six cannon, they angrily stormed off toward Philadelphia, where they intended to intimidate Congress into providing relief. The insurgents stressed that they acted under duress—"We are not Arnolds" was a favorite battle cry—but they could no longer stomach the inhumane treatment inflicted on them by politicians. Among other things, they could not tolerate that newly enlisted men were being paid cash bounties while they had received no pay in more than a year.

The ranking officer on the scene was the valiant but hot-blooded Anthony Wayne. Washington encouraged him to stick close to his men as they marched and not brake their movement until they crossed the Delaware into Pennsylvania. Washington experienced an overriding fear of massive desertion or even full-blown defection to the British—Sir Henry Clinton sent emissaries to entice them into exactly such treachery—and he thought it would help to stem such flight if the river stood *behind* the mutineers. Because his officers warned of smoldering discontent among the New Windsor troops, Washington feared abandoning them and tried to screen them from inflammatory news of the mutiny. Taking personal charge of the situation, he also worried about a loss of face if he ordered mutineers to desist and they ignored him. Bypassing Congress, Washington wrote directly to the states and demanded more provisions along with three months' pay for the troops. Sympathetic to their complaints, if aggrieved by their methods, he spluttered in wrath that "it is in vain to think an army can be kept together much longer under such a variety of sufferings as ours has experienced."[6]

The Pennsylvania Line stopped at Princeton and Trenton and never reached Philadelphia. To squash the uprising, Wayne drew on New Jersey soldiers and summoned additional militia. He negotiated a settlement with the mutineers under which half would be discharged and another half furloughed until April. The soldiers would receive certificates to compensate them for their depreciated currency and would be issued extra clothing. Although Washington accepted the expediency of this bargain, he hated negotiating with disobedient soldiers. Wayne also decided, with Washington's blessing, to make an example of the ringleaders. He called out twelve refractory members of the revolt and lined them up in a farmer's field before firing squads made up of their fellow soldiers. One fifer described this brutal scene: "The distance that the platoons stood from [the condemned men] at the time they fired could not have been more than ten feet. So near did they stand that the handkerchiefs covering the eyes of some of them were set on fire . . . The fence and even the heads of rye for some distance within the field were covered with the blood and brains."[7] When one firing squad victim lay bleeding but still alive, Wayne ordered a soldier to bayonet him to death. The soldier balked, saying he couldn't kill his comrade. With that, Wayne drew his pistol and said he would kill the man on the spot if he didn't obey orders. The hapless soldier then stepped forward and plunged his bayonet into the writhing man. To ensure that the bloody message of these deaths lingered, Wayne ordered the entire Pennsylvania Line to circle around the dead soldiers.

Anthony Wayne had no qualms about his action and wrote proudly to Washington that "a liberal dose of niter [gunpowder] had done the trick."[8] Washington, who could be extremely tough when necessary, didn't second-guess Wayne's reprisals. Months later he told Wayne, "Sudden and exemplary punishments were certainly necessary upon the new appearance of that daring and mutinous spirit which convulsed the line last winter."[9] Washington had long believed that mutinies, if not stamped out vigorously, would only multiply.

No sooner was the Pennsylvania mutiny suppressed than the contagion spread to the New Jersey Line in Pompton. As two hundred mutinous troops, giddy with liquor, headed for the state capital at Trenton, Washington decided he had had enough. He refused to negotiate with the rebels, demanded unconditional submission, and vowed to execute several of the leaders. To quell the uprising, he ordered five hundred or six hundred troops under Major General Robert Howe to march from West Point toward New Jersey. He also tried to impress upon the loyal troops "how dangerous to civil liberty the precedent is of armed soldiers dictating terms to their country."[10] Sending troops was a high-stakes gamble, since Washington didn't know whether they would fire upon rowdy fellow soldiers, "but I thought it indispensable to bring the matter to an issue and risk all extremities," he told Congress.[11] On January 27 General Howe surrounded the mutineers, snuffed out the revolt, and made an example of several instigators. He lined up a firing squad composed of a dozen mutineers and ordered them to execute two mutinous sergeants. Three of the executioners were told to shoot at the head and three at the heart, while the other six stood ready to finish off victims that lay squirming on the ground. Once again Washington feared he would squander his authority if men disobeyed him, and he kept his distance from the scene at Ringwood, New Jersey. Once he heard that the New Jersey men had surrendered and repented, he took up their crusade to lobby politicians for better pay, food, and housing.

A critical element of the relief effort lay in soliciting fresh money from France. In December Congress drafted John Laurens as a special envoy to France, where it hoped he would team up with Benjamin Franklin to wrest a huge loan from the court at Versailles. Laurens, with Thomas Paine acting as his secretary, was to fire up French enthusiasm through compelling eyewitness accounts of the war. Because of Washington's renown in France, Congress also hoped that a certified member of his military family would receive an effusive welcome. For three days Washington huddled with Laurens and Paine to forge a strategy. "We are at the end of our tether," Washington told them, "and now or never our deliverance must come."[12] He deemed a foreign loan essential, since America had only a tiny moneyed elite and Congress had mismanaged its finances. If he had to keep confiscating produce from farmers, Washington feared that supporters would find the Continental Army's methods "burdensome and oppressive," defeating the idea of a fight for liberty.[13]

Even as Washington jockeyed to keep his northern army from unraveling, the prospects for victory brightened in the South. On January 17 Brigadier General Daniel Morgan pulled off a spectacular victory at Cowpens, South Carolina, routing a veteran army under the notorious Tarleton. For once, it was the Americans who spread terror by sprinting forward with fixed bayonets. The tally of casualties decisively favored the Americans: more than 300 British soldiers were killed or wounded versus a mere 70 Americans; 500 able-bodied enemy soldiers were captured along with 800 muskets. Sir Henry Clinton later identified the Cowpens disaster as "the first link of a chain of events that followed each other in regular succession until they at last ended in the total loss of America."[14] Washington celebrated the "decisive and glorious victory" and insisted it would have a dramatic effect on the southern campaign.

INEVITABLY, the private appraisal of Washington by his close subordinates was less glowing than their public eulogies. He was too much of a perfectionist to enjoy an easy rapport with his aides, and his discontent sometimes festered before erupting unexpectedly. By dint of the superlative letters he had drafted and his military acumen, Alexander Hamilton had risen to become Washington's de facto chief of staff. When Congress decided to create three new positions—ministers of war, finance, and foreign affairs—Hamilton's name was bandied about as a prospective "superintendent of finance." Before Robert Morris accepted the post, General

Sullivan asked Washington to comment on Hamilton's financial abilities, and the commander seemed taken aback: "How far Colo. Hamilton, of whom you ask my opinion as a financier, has turned his thoughts to that particular study, I am unable to ans[we]r, because I never entered upon a discussion on this point with him. But this I can venture to advance from a thorough knowledge of him, that there are few men to be found of his age who has a more general knowledge than he possesses and none whose soul is more firmly engaged in the cause or who exceeds him in probity and sterling virtue."[15]

Although Hamilton subscribed to Washington's values and principles—which was why he could mimic him so expertly in letters—he expressed misgivings about his personality. Hamilton had taken a long and searching look at George Washington. Working in daily contact with a man burdened by multiple cares, Hamilton inevitably was exposed to Washington's bad-tempered side. A stoic figure who strove to be perfectly composed in public, Washington needed to blow off steam in private, and the proud, sensitive young Hamilton grew weary of dealing with his boss's varying moods.

Like many talented subordinates, Hamilton nurtured a rich fantasy life and could easily have imagined himself in Washington's place. He found a desk job, even such a prestigious one, too lowly and monotonous for his tastes and dreamed of battlefield glory, repeatedly requesting a field command. But he wielded such a skillful pen that Washington was reluctant to dispense with it and turned him down. In December 1780 he also scotched Hamilton's chance of becoming adjutant general, which would have jumped him over several officers of superior rank and thereby created endless trouble.

On December 14, 1780, Hamilton married Elizabeth Schuyler, which catapulted the young West Indian into a more rarefied social sphere. The orphaned young man must have felt buoyed by a sense of security altogether new in his experience. That January he resolved that "if there should ever happen [to be] a breach" with Washington, instead of settling their differences, he would "never to consent to an accommodation."[16] In other words, Hamilton would not provoke a break, but he was fully prepared to exploit one. The timing couldn't have been worse for Washington, who felt beleaguered after two mutinies in New Jersey.

Because Washington was obsessed with punctuality, it probably wasn't coincidental that his rift with Hamilton came when his aide kept him waiting. On the night of February 15, 1781, Washington and Hamilton frantically labored till midnight, preparing paperwork for a meeting with French officers in Newport. The next day Hamilton was going downstairs in the New Windsor farmhouse when he passed Washington coming upstairs. Washington told Hamilton that he wished to see him. Hamilton figured that Washington would wait in his office, so he paused

Lawrence Washington. George Washington revered his older half brother, who set a pattern of military service that George faithfully followed.

Lieutenant Governor Robert Dinwiddie. Though he was an early champion of Washington during the French and Indian War, the two men clashed before the end of Dinwiddie's tenure as colonial governor of Virginia.

Sarah "Sally" Cary Fairfax, the enchanting woman who captivated Washington's imagination in his early adulthood and perhaps in the years beyond. This rather romanticized painting, done in the early twentieth century, is based on a photograph of an original but now vanished portrait of her.

George William Fairfax. Washington's longtime friend chose either to accept or to overlook Washington's fascination with his wife.

On a visit to Mount Vernon in 1772, Charles Willson Peale sketched these delicate miniatures of Washington's family.

Martha Dandridge Custis Washington. Though never a radiant beauty, Martha Washington provided the ideal social setting and emotional support for her husband's career.

John Parke "Jacky" Custis. Washington grew frustrated with the incurable indolence of his wayward stepson, who died shortly after the Yorktown campaign.

Martha Parke "Patsy" Custis. Washington harbored tender feelings for his stepdaughter, who was afflicted with epilepsy from an early age.

General Charles Lee. This caricature of the vain, eccentric general, a rival to Washington, pokes fun at his love of dogs and spindly body. Lee's misconduct at Monmouth effectively terminated his career.

Puffed up to heroic proportions after his victory at Saratoga, General Horatio Gates failed to dislodge Washington as commander in chief and was later disgraced during the battle of Camden.

FACING PAGE: When John Trumbull painted this dashing portrait of Washington in 1780, he inserted at right William Lee, the slave who served the general devotedly throughout the Revolutionary War.

The warm, ebullient Henry Knox served with distinction as Washington's artillery chief during the war but had a checkered success as secretary of war during his presidency.

Nathanael Greene. Always touted as Washington's favorite general, Greene met an untimely death after the war, robbing Washington of an influential political ally.

POEMS

ON

VARIOUS SUBJECTS,

RELIGIOUS AND MORAL.

BY

PHILLIS WHEATLEY,

NEGRO SERVANT to Mr. JOHN WHEATLEY,
of BOSTON, in NEW ENGLAND.

LONDON:
Printed for A. BELL, Bookseller, Aldgate; and sold by
Messrs. COX and BERRY, King-Street, BOSTON.
MDCCLXXIII.

Published according to Act of Parliament, Sept.ʳ 1.1773 by Archᵈ Bell.
Bookseller Nᵒ 8 near the Saracens Head Aldgate.

ABOVE: Phillis Wheatley. Washington's appreciative response to the ode written about him by this Boston slave signaled an early advance in his views on slavery.

RIGHT: Brilliant, crusty, and opinionated, John Adams evolved from an early booster of Washington into an envious detractor in later years.

Sir Henry Clinton, one of the many distinguished British commanders whom George Washington managed to send down to defeat.

Charles Cornwallis, first Marquess Cornwallis. Although associated with the stunning defeat of British forces at Yorktown, Cornwallis was an aggressive commander who inspired a healthy fear among American generals.

Benedict Arnold. A staunch admirer of Arnold's derring-do throughout the war, Washington was staggered by the exposure of his massive treachery.

Peggy Shippen Arnold. Feigning temporary madness when her husband's treason was revealed, she managed to hoodwink Washington, Hamilton, and Lafayette into believing her innocent of the scheme.

Fired by sparkling intelligence and unstoppable ambition, Alexander Hamilton flourished as a wartime aide to Washington and later as treasury secretary because the two men agreed on so many policy issues.

"Baron" von Steuben. Colorful, flamboyant, and profane, Steuben performed wonders as the drillmaster at Valley Forge, introducing a new professionalism and forging discipline in the Continental Army.

FACING PAGE: George Washington portrayed in the aftermath of his Yorktown victory. The Marquis de Lafayette stands between Washington and his beloved aide-de-camp Tench Tilghman, who grasps the articles of capitulation.

The chief political opponents of Washington's presidency.

At first a trusted adviser to Washington and his peerless tutor on the Constitution, James Madison emerged unexpectedly as his most formidable adversary in Congress.

While Washington's secretary of state, Thomas Jefferson teamed up with Madison, in a sometimes covert partnership, to contest the policies of the administration, inaugurating a major political party in the process.

An ardent admirer of Washington early in the Revolutionary War, Thomas Paine later turned into a scathing critic.

As the editor of an opposition paper, Philip Freneau heaped so many aspersions on Washington that the exasperated president denounced him as a "rascal."

Elizabeth Willing Powel, a married woman of exceptional intelligence and literary flair, was Washington's most intimate female friend and confidante during his presidency.

This image of Martha Washington captures both her sweetness and her sadness in later years.

Frances "Fanny" Bassett, a niece of Martha Washington's, came to live at Mount Vernon in early adolescence and, with her winning personality, ended up as a much-loved surrogate daughter.

The WASHINGTON FAMILY. / La FAMILLE de WASHINGTON.

ABOVE: *The Washington Family.* This classic portrait of George and Martha Washington includes the two Custis grandchildren they reared: George Washington Parke Custis, left, and Eleanor Parke Custis, right. The slave depicted at right may have been William Lee or Christopher Sheels.

LEFT: This painting of an aging President Washington shows just how haggard and careworn he appeared during his contentious second term.

briefly to hand a letter to Tench Tilghman and conversed with Lafayette, then turned around and headed back upstairs. He found Washington glowering at the top of the stairs. "Colonel Hamilton," Washington said testily, "you have kept me waiting at the head of the stairs these ten minutes. I must tell you, sir, you treat me with disrespect." "I am not conscious of it, sir," Hamilton retorted, "but since you have thought it necessary to tell me so, we part." "Very well, sir," Washington replied, "if it be your choice."[17] Hamilton estimated that two minutes had elapsed. Under ordinary circumstances, the two men would have quickly repaired the damage, but Hamilton elected to push things past the breaking point.

While Washington could be gruff, he knew when he crossed a line and was quick to extend apologies. He hated friction with people and avoided personal confrontations whenever possible. Now he showed exemplary patience with the brashly capable Hamilton. Instead of pulling rank and waiting for the young man to make amends, Washington responded with a magnanimous gesture. An hour later he sent Tench Tilghman to offer apologies and requested "a candid conversation to heal a difference which could not have happened but in a moment of passion."[18] Hamilton was having none of it. As he told his father-in-law, "I requested Mr. Tilghman to tell him that I had taken my resolution in a manner not to be revoked; that as a conversation could serve no other purpose than to produce explanations mutually disagreeable, though I certainly would not refuse an interview if he desired it, yet I should be happy [if] he would permit me to decline it."[19] Doubtless shocked by his aide's intransigence, Washington regretfully acquiesced in Hamilton's decision to leave his staff.

Since Philip Schuyler was a friend of Washington, Hamilton knew he owed his father-in-law an explanatory letter. He conjured up a moody, irritable boss and said he had found that Washington "was neither remarkable for delicacy nor good temper."[20] He made the startling statement that he had rebuffed Washington's attempts at social intimacy. "For three years past," Hamilton wrote, "I have felt no friendship for him and have professed none. The truth is our own dispositions are the opposites of each other and the pride of my temper would not suffer me to profess what I did not feel. Indeed, when advances of this kind" were made, Hamilton responded in a way that showed "I wished to stand rather upon a footing of m[ilitary confidence than] of private attachment."[21] Hamilton also portrayed Washington as somewhat vain and insulated from criticism, a man "to whom all the world is offering incense."[22] If Washington promised him better treatment and succeeded in inducing him to return to work, Hamilton predicted, "his self-love would never forgive me for what it would regard as a humiliation."[23] Evidently the young Alexander Hamilton intended to teach George Washington a lesson. As he boasted to James McHenry, Washington "shall, for once at least, repent his ill-humor."[24]

Hamilton agreed to stay on temporarily as Washington sought a replacement.

For a brief interval even Martha Washington was pressed into secretarial service, drawing up a fair copy of at least one letter for her husband. Hamilton had suggested to Washington that they keep their altercation secret for the sake of the war effort. Washington agreed and was then startled to discover that Hamilton had babbled about the episode to several friends, giving his version of events. To Lafayette, Washington expressed astonishment: "Why this injunction on me while he was communicating it himself is a little extraordinary! But I complied and religiously fulfilled it."[25] Perhaps because he spied facets of his younger self in Hamilton, Washington was forgiving toward him, even when he tested his patience. He may even have felt some secret guilt for not having rewarded Hamilton with the field command he coveted. Whatever the tensions of their relationship, Washington never shed his admiration for Hamilton's outstanding abilities.

In April, having left Washington's family, Hamilton began to badger his ex-boss for a field command, and Washington reacted with perplexity. "I am convinced that no officer can with justice dispute your merit and abilities," he assured Hamilton, but he didn't see how he could promote him without offending more senior officers.[26] He feared that Hamilton would interpret his decision as belated punishment for their rift: "My principal concern arises from an apprehension that you will impute my refusal of your request to other motives than those I have expressed."[27] Once again Washington had responded to their difficulties in a classy and dignified manner.

Eventually rumors circulated about the temporary estrangement between the two men. Years later John Adams recalled the episode thus: Hamilton "quitted the army for a long time, as I have heard, in a pet and a miff with Washington."[28] On another occasion, Adams wrote, "those who trumpeted Washington in the highest strains at some times spoke of him at others in the strongest terms of contempt . . . Hamilton, [Timothy] Pickering, and many others have been known to indulge themselves in very contemptuous expressions, but very unjustly and ungratefully."[29] In the spring of 1783 Hamilton opened up in private to James Madison about Washington's occasionally querulous personality. As Madison recorded in his journal, "Mr. Hamilton said that he knew General Washington intimately and perfectly. That his extreme reserve, mixed sometimes with a degree of asperity of temper, both of which were said to have increased of late, had contributed to the decline of his popularity."[30] At the same time Hamilton regarded Washington as a man of unimpeachable integrity who would "never yield to any dishonorable or disloyal plans."[31]

Whatever his reservations, Hamilton had hitched his fortunes to Washington's career and refrained from public criticism of him. He knew that Washington alone had held the army together since its creation. Most important, the two men were shaped by the same wartime experiences and shared basic concerns about the country's political structure, especially the shortcomings of the Articles of Confederation and the need for a powerful central government that would bind the states into a solid union, restore American credit, and create a more permanent army. As an immigrant, Hamilton bore no loyalty to a particular state, which perhaps made it easier for him to adopt a continental perspective congenial to Washington's. Their congruent political values lashed Washington and Hamilton together into a potent political partnership that would last until the end of Washington's life.

Part of Washington's attachment to Hamilton sprang from his persistent concern for his personal papers, which he saw as guaranteeing his posthumous fame and preserving his record from distortion by posterity. The way Washington fussed over these documents confirms that he knew he was a historic personage and reflected his awareness that his personal saga was inextricably entwined with that of the new nation. As early as August 1776, while bracing for Howe's assault on New York, he had shown solicitude for his papers, sending a box of them to Philadelphia for safekeeping. The following year he had a chest with strong hinges constructed to hold them. After Hamilton left his employ in April 1781, Washington asked Congress to hire secretaries to make copies of his wartime correspondence. "Unless a set of writers are employed for the sole purpose of recording them," he explained, "it will not be in my power to accomplish this necessary work and equally impracticable perhaps to preserve from injury and loss such valuable papers."[32] Instead of the rough originals, Washington wanted clerks who wrote "a fair hand" to produce a magnificent set of bound papers.[33]

Lieutenant Colonel Richard Varick, the former aide to Benedict Arnold, was appointed to head the editorial team and at various times hired six different clerks to assist him. With his customary attention to detail, Washington told Varick that he wanted "a similarity and beauty in the whole execution" with "all the writing . . . to be upon black lines equidistant. All the books to have the same margin and to be indexed in so clear and intelligent a manner that there may be no difficulty in the references."[34] It was astounding that, in the midst of war, Washington would issue such precise guidelines. It was no less astounding that he elicited an appropriation for the project, even as he complained about the poor pay and provisions granted to his army. For more than two years, Varick and his clerks beavered away at the gigantic effort in Poughkeepsie, New York. They worked eight-hour days and filled up twenty-eight volumes with correspondence. Washington hoped this written record would stand as a polished monument to his wartime achievement—the perfect strategy for a man who shrank from overt self-promotion.

ONE AMERICAN WHO ALMOST NEVER acknowledged Washington's wartime heroism was his mother, who left behind scarcely a single memorable sentence about her son's outsize success. With more to brag about than any other mother in American history, she took no evident pride in her son's accomplishments. As early as 1807 one Washington biographer wrote that Mary was "so far from being partial to the American revolution that she frequently regretted the side her son had taken in the contest between her king and her country."[35] The best one can say about Mary Washington is that she did not exploit her son's renown for her own benefit. Instead, she leveled a steady stream of criticism at him, the gist being that he had abandoned her. "She had always been resentful of anything he had done that was not in her service," wrote James T. Flexner, "and she had talked so against George's activities that she was believed by many to be a Tory. Her perpetual complaint was of neglect."[36] For a son as dutiful as George Washington, this was a strange accusation and only made him more distant from his mother. He seems not to have sent her a single letter during the entire war, prompting Douglas Southall Freeman to comment that the "strangest mystery of Washington's life" was "his lack of affection for his mother."[37] Observers noted a similarity between mother and son. When Baron Ludwig von Closen, an aide to Rochambeau, visited Mary Washington, he left this impression: "The afternoon I passed with Mrs. Washington and her sister, both ladies no less venerable in their way than the General was in his."[38]

Before the Revolution, as noted earlier, Washington had set up his mother with a house and garden in Fredericksburg and instructed Lund Washington to attend to her financial needs in his absence. He agreed to pay rent to her based on the proceeds from the slaves and farmland she still owned. This mismanaged property had never yielded even half the money he agreed to pay her, so that the "rent" constituted a large outright subsidy. He had even sold off slaves to pay the exorbitant property taxes. During the war Washington had never received a single complaint about Lund's treatment of his mother and must have assumed she was perfectly content. In fact, Mary was far from content as she struggled with poor health, wartime food shortages, and the grave illness of her son-in-law and next-door neighbor, Fielding Lewis. Yet Washington heard nothing from her directly about these problems and learned about them only in an embarrassing fashion.

After consulting with the French at Newport in February 1781, Washington returned to New Windsor to discover one of the most bizarre letters of his career. Benjamin Harrison, speaker of the Virginia assembly, informed Washington, with some trepidation, that his mother had instigated a movement in the legislature to provide her with an emergency pension: "Some Gent[leme]n of the last assembly proposed to apply to that body for assistance to your mother, who, they said, was in great want, owing to the heavy taxes she was oblig[e]d to pay. I took a liberty to put a stop to this, supposing you would be displeased at such an application. I make no doubt but the assembly would readily grant the request and it now only rests with you to say whether it shall be made or not."[39] Perhaps afraid of infuriating or insulting Washington, Harrison had stalled in writing the letter. Clearly Mary had made no effort to forewarn her son of her petition. She had now progressed from quaint or eccentric to dangerously erratic.

From Washington's abashed response, one can tell that he had not heard about the matter before or communicated with his mother in years. He was mortified by the insinuation that he was an unfeeling son and that his mother had consequently thrown herself upon the charity of the state. The charge of neglect was substantially the same one Mary had trotted out since he first rode off to the French and Indian War. Now, amid his manifold wartime duties, Washington sat down and recounted for Harrison his tortured history with his mother, telling how he had set her up in Fredericksburg before the war and instructed Lund to take care of her. He seemed baffled and hurt by her charges: "Whence her distresses can arise, therefore, I know not, never having received any complaint . . . Confident I am that she has not a child that would not divide the last sixpence to relieve her from *real* distress. This she has been repeatedly assured of by me. And all of us, I am certain, would feel much hurt at having our mother a pensioner while we had the means of supporting her. But, in fact, she has an ample income of her own."[40] Washington asked the assembly to desist from taking any action.

CHAPTER THIRTY-THREE

Plundering Scoundrels

As THE WAR WANED in the northern states, it waxed ever hotter in the South. The British, stymied in their goal of galvanizing southern Loyalists, nonetheless continued to fight aggressively. Lord Cornwallis ached to avenge the humiliation Banastre Tarleton suffered at Cowpens in January. For three weeks Nathanael Greene's ragtag army led him on a long wild-goose chase; then, on March 15, 1781, Cornwallis spotted his chance, as his men approached a phalanx of local militia that Greene had lined up south of Guilford Court House in North Carolina. After firing one volley, the North Carolina men dispersed, as Greene had ordered, but the Continental soldiers stubbornly held their ground in fierce combat until Greene signaled a belated retreat. "I never saw such fighting since God made me," declared a thunderstruck Cornwallis, who had a horse shot from under him in the carnage.[1] Desperate for victory and in defiance of his officers, Cornwallis ordered his men to fire grapeshot amid hand-to-hand combat, causing British marksmen inadvertently to slay British soldiers.

Technically a British victory, the battle cost Cornwallis dearly: 532 dead and wounded soldiers, more than a quarter of his force. As Charles James Fox pointed out in Parliament, "Another such victory would ruin the British Army."[2] Nathanael Greene concurred: "They had the splendor, we the advantage."[3] Cornwallis decided to move his bruised and exhausted troops into Virginia to link up with Benedict Arnold. He was being worn down by the wily, resourceful Greene, who came into his own during the campaign. Washington understood that Greene, despite the defeat, had acquitted himself nobly. "Although the honors of the field did not fall to your lot," Washington told him, "I am convinced you deserved them."[4]

With the war intensifying in Virginia, the piecemeal transfer of men to the

South hollowed out Washington's army. As British forces pushed deep into the Virginia heartland, they gladly laid waste to the estates of Revolutionary leaders, and Washington knew that Mount Vernon might be next. In January and again in April, Brigadier General Benedict Arnold led his British and Tory troops along the James River in a rampage of unbridled destruction, burning homesteads and tobacco warehouses. Britain's naval strength operated to advantage in a state well watered by rivers. After activating the militia, Governor Thomas Jefferson appealed to Washington to move southward, saying his presence "would restore [the] full confidence of salvation."[5] For Washington, who longed to be home, this message was hard to hear. "Nobody, I persuade myself, can doubt my inclination to be immediately employed in the defense of that country where all my property and connections are," he replied.[6] Nonetheless he cited "powerful objections" to leaving his army or marching them hundreds of miles south.[7] He had already diverted a large number of men to Virginia under Lafayette, but he didn't wish to join him when there was a chance of collaborating with the French to take New York, which Washington still envisioned as the climactic battle of the Revolution.

Intermittently Washington lapsed into passing reveries about his old life at Mount Vernon. Early on he had written home frequently and at length, the mental connection with his estate still unbroken. Now, he told a correspondent, he had "long been a stranger" to such "private indulgences."[8] Nevertheless he still deluged Lund Washington with minute questions about a place he hadn't set eyes on for six years. "How many lambs have you had this spring?" he asked in March 1781. "How many colts are you like to have?" He inquired about the progress of the covered walkways connecting the main house to the outlying buildings. "Are you going to repair the pavement of the piazza?" he wished to know.[9]

These nostalgic recollections of Mount Vernon were shattered weeks later when a British sloop, the *Savage,* dropped anchor in the Potomac near the plantation. Captain Thomas Graves had burned homes on the Maryland side to soften up his victims on the Virginia bank. Then he sent ashore a party to Mount Vernon to demand a large store of food and offered asylum to any slaves; seventeen of Washington's slaves—fourteen men and three women—fled to the ship's freedom, embarrassing the leader of the American Revolution. Lund Washington knew that his boss wanted him to resist any cooperation with the British, and at first he balked at their demands. Then he went aboard the *Savage,* bearing provisions as a peace offering. After this conference he consented to send sheep, hogs, and other supplies to save Mount Vernon and possibly to recover the departed slaves. Maybe Lund wondered whether Washington, at bottom, was prepared to sacrifice his majestic estate. An indignant Lafayette warned Washington of the unfortunate precedent Lund had set: "This being done by the gentleman who, in some measure, represents you at your house will certainly have a bad effect and contrasts with spirited answers from some neighbors that had their houses burnt accordingly."[10]

As Lafayette expected, Washington reacted with unalloyed horror when he learned that Lund had boarded the *Savage* to negotiate with the enemy, and he promptly administered a grave rebuke to his steward for his decision to "commune with a parcel of plundering scoundrels,"[11] as he dubbed them. "It would have been a less painful circumstance to me to have heard that, in consequence of your non-compliance with their request, they had burnt my house and laid the plantation in ruins."[12] Washington showed his classic stoicism here, his uncompromising refusal to beg or bow to anyone. Since Lund was his proxy, he felt personally humiliated by the incident. In a fatalistic mood, he concluded that, unless the French brought a superior naval force to Virginia, "I have as little doubt of its ending in the loss of all my Negroes and in the destruction of my houses. But I am prepared for the event."[13] He ordered Lund to remove at once any valuables from the estate. Martha Washington was then laid up with recurrent liver trouble, abdominal pain, and jaundice. So traumatized was her husband by the *Savage* incident that when the widow of a British Army paymaster sent Martha a parcel of citrus fruits as a get-well present— the Washingtons had stayed at her New York home in 1776—he brusquely returned it as an unacceptable gift from the enemy.

Sinking into a morose mood in the early spring of 1781, Washington again believed that the Continental Army was disintegrating before his eyes, that he had been doomed to lead a phantom army. So many enlistments had expired during the winter that it was at times difficult even to garrison West Point. His idle troops had languished since November, and "instead of having the prospect of a glorious offensive campaign before us," he lamented, "we have a bewildered and gloomy defensive one."[14] As Greene and Lafayette won honors in the South, he was reduced to a helpless bystander, upstaged by his own disciples.

Washington dispatched Major General William Heath to raise supplies from the northern states and predicted his army would starve or disband without them. In May his hungry army was down to a one-day ration of meat. Even when states scraped up supplies, Washington couldn't pay the teamsters to transport them. It was all too familiar and wearisome to Washington, who began to think he would never see the end of the conflict. As he confided to General John Armstrong, he didn't doubt the outcome of the war, believing that "divine government" favored the patriots, "but the period for its accomplishm[en]t may be too far distant for a person of my years, whose morning and evening hours and every moment (unoccupied by business) pants for retirement."[15]

THROUGH THE COMBINED EFFORTS of Benjamin Franklin and John Laurens in Paris that winter, the French agreed to an indispensable loan and a munificent gift of six million livres to purchase arms and supplies. For all that, the French foreign minister, Vergennes, was reluctant to commit more French troops. In the early going, he had fancied that the French would score a rapid victory; now, as things dragged on, he shrank from an open-ended involvement. All along Washington and Lafayette had stressed the vital importance of sea power, and Vergennes decided the French would mount one last naval effort. In the spring he notified Lafayette that a French squadron would cruise off America's coast during the year: "M. Le Comte de Grasse, who commands our fleet in the Antilles, has been ordered to send part of his fleet to the coast of North America sometime before next winter or to detach a portion of it to sweep the coast and cooperate in any undertaking which may be projected by the French and American generals."[16] On May 8 the Count de Barras, the newly assigned French naval commander, arrived with the invigorating news that 26 ships of the line, 8 frigates, and 150 transports had sailed from Brest in late March, bound for the West Indies.

On May 21 Washington met in Wethersfield, Connecticut, with Rochambeau, who confirmed that an enormous French fleet under Admiral de Grasse was on its way. During the winter Washington had worked out in detail the plan that had long bewitched his mind: a siege of New York, with the Americans attacking Manhattan and the French Brooklyn. He cited the comforting statistic that Sir Henry Clinton, in sending detachments south, had cut his New York force in half. An operation against New York, he argued vigorously, would force Clinton to withdraw more troops from the South. Washington also had legitimate logistical concerns about the difficulties of marching his army to Virginia and its environs. He wasn't opposed to a southern operation per se, but his unswerving passion for retaking New York was patent. "General Washington, during this conference, had scarcely another object in view but an expedition against the island of New York," Rochambeau wrote.[17]

Rochambeau had to play a delicate game of deception with Washington. Although he didn't want to stifle Washington's enthusiasm or rebuff him outright, he tried to steer the conversation toward a joint operation in the South, where they might rendezvous with the French fleet and surprise Cornwallis. Even as Rochambeau humored Washington and initialed a document saying that New York held top priority, he secretly relayed word to de Grasse that he should think about sailing to Chesapeake Bay instead of to New York. In the coming weeks Rochambeau pretended to lend credence to Washington's plans, while focusing his real attention on quite a different strategy.

Why did Washington botch this major strategic call? Aside from settling old scores, he may well have believed that his army would enjoy a paramount role in a

New York siege, compared to an auxiliary role in any southern battle. Or perhaps he honestly believed that it was easier to concentrate American and French forces in the North and that a long march southward in summer heat would sacrifice large numbers of soldiers through sickness and desertion. Having prodded the northern states to aid his army in any Franco-American campaign, he doubtless feared that their enthusiasm might cool with any southern strategy. Since he believed that his army's existence depended on the outcome of Heath's diplomatic mission to the states, this counted as no minor factor in his thinking at the moment.

While both Washington and Rochambeau labored to fashion a harmonious facade of Franco-American amity, perceptive observers detected subtle tensions. Their interpreter at Wethersfield, the Chevalier de Chastellux, a man of many parts—soldier, philosopher, member of the French Academy, intimate of Voltaire—was well placed to study their complex interaction. A handsome fellow with watchful eyes, he was gathering material for a book about the United States and was immensely taken with the forty-nine-year-old Washington, applauding him as "the greatest and the best of men."[18] He was chagrined by the treatment Washington received from his French counterpart. Rochambeau, he claimed, handled the Virginian with "all the ungraciousness and all the unpleasantness possible," and he worried that Washington would be left with "a sad and disagreeable feeling in his heart."[19] Washington secretly carried this grief but exposed it to no one outside a small circle of advisers.

When Chastellux arrived that winter, Washington was instantly charmed by this friend of Lafayette, whom he praised as a gentleman of "merit, knowledge, and agreeable manners."[20] At his first meals with Washington, Chastellux was struck by how Washington was "always free and always agreeable" with his officers, unlike the rigidly formal Europeans.[21] When he couldn't offer the Frenchman a separate bedroom for lack of space, Washington apologized, "but always with a noble politeness, which was neither embarrassing nor excessive."[22] For Chastellux, Washington seemed a man of the happy medium: "brave without temerity, laborious without ambition, generous without prodigality, noble without pride, virtuous without severity."[23] He captured well how Washington was at once amiable and yet a shade aloof: "He has not the imposing pomp of a *Maréchal de France* who gives *the order* . . . The goodness and benevolence which characterize him are evident in all that surrounds him, but the confidence he calls forth never occasions improper familiarity."[24] Most impressive was Washington's implicit submission to the people's representatives: "This is the seventh year that he has commanded the army and he has obeyed Congress: more need not be said."[25] Later on, Chastellux left a fine epitaph for Washington when he said that "at the end of a long civil war, he had nothing with which he could reproach himself."[26]

That Washington found it frustrating to be junior partner in the French alliance was confirmed when he returned to New Windsor after meeting with Rochambeau. At Wethersfield, Washington had advised Rochambeau to relocate the French fleet from Newport to Boston. Then the Duke de Lauzun arrived with a message that a French council of war had opted to keep it in Newport. This was a direct slap at Washington, who was "in such a rage," the duke said, that he didn't reply for three days. He had to accept that the French were his superiors, notwithstanding their public claims that he supervised the two armies. When Washington finally replied, he said he took "the liberty still to recommend" that the fleet be moved to Boston.[27] The French seemed to acquiesce, for on May 31 he recorded in his journal that Admiral de Barras "would sail with the first fair wind for Boston."[28]

On June 10 Rochambeau informed Washington that the Count de Grasse would bring his fleet north that summer to coordinate an attack with the French and American armies. Washington reiterated his hope that de Grasse would sail to New York. In reply, Rochambeau continued to string Washington along, contending that de Grasse had been informed "that your Excellency preferred that he should make his first appearance at New York . . . that I submitted, as I ought, my opinion to yours."[29] In reality, Rochambeau alerted de Grasse to his private preference for heading first to the Chesapeake Bay.

In the early years of the war Virginia had been spared bloodshed, but in June 1781 fighting raged there with blazing ferocity. Lord Cornwallis had joined forces with Benedict Arnold, and despite able defensive maneuvers by Lafayette, the two men spread terror through the state. "Accounts from Virginia are exceedingly alarming," Washington told Rochambeau, reporting that the enemy was marching through the state "almost without control."[30] Still bent on taking New York, Washington pleaded that an attack there would be the best way to siphon off British troops from Virginia. In mid-June he wrote again with a new twist—if they had clear naval superiority, he would contemplate targets other than New York: "I wish you to explain this matter to the *Count de Grasse*, as, if I understand you, you have in your communication to him, confined our views to *New York* alone."[31] Clearly Washington had been fooled as to what Rochambeau had whispered in the admiral's ear.

With the benefit of hindsight, Washington's preoccupation with New York seems a colossal mistake, just as Rochambeau's emphasis on Cornwallis and Virginia seems prescient. As a rule, Washington did not tamper with history and implicitly trusted the record. In this case, however, he later tried to rewrite history by suggesting that his tenacious concentration on New York was a mere feint to mislead the British in Virginia, while maintaining the political allegiance of the eastern and mid-Atlantic states. Responding to a query from Noah Webster in 1788, Washington defended his behavior with unusual vehemence, as if the inquiry had touched a raw nerve. He alleged that his preparations against New York were in-

404 ❧ THE GENERAL

tended "to misguide and bewilder Sir Henry Clinton in regard to the real object [i.e., the Chesapeake] by fictitious communications as well as by making a deceptive provision of ovens, forage and boats in his neighborhood . . . Nor were less pains taken to deceive our own army."[32] He went so far as to say that "it never was in contemplation to attack New York."[33] But in confidential correspondence with Rochambeau he pushed for no Chesapeake operation, and the record shows that he had repeatedly favored a strike against New York. Only on the very eve of the Yorktown campaign did he undertake the deceptive maneuvers described to Webster.

In general, Washington lived up to his vaunted reputation for honesty, but it was awkward for him to admit that he had, at least initially, opposed a campaign that served as the brilliant capstone of his military career. He wanted to portray himself as the visionary architect of the Yorktown victory, not as a general misguidedly concentrating upon New York while his French allies masterminded the decisive blow. Washington made it difficult for people to catch his lie because he alleged that he had tried to deceive his own side as well as the enemy; hence any communication could be construed as part of the master bluff. When Washington's letter to Noah Webster was published in the *American Museum* in 1791, Timothy Pickering, the former adjutant general and quartermaster general of the Continental Army, shook his head sadly. "It will hurt [Washington's] moral character," he wrote to Dr. Benjamin Rush. "He has been generally thought to be honest and I own I thought his morals were good, but that letter is false and I know it to be so."[34]

Whatever his shortcomings as a military strategist, the French understood that Washington's greatness as a general lay in his prolonged sustenance of his makeshift army. He had done something unprecedented by cobbling together a creditable fighting force from the poor, the young, the black, and the downtrodden, and he had done it in the face of unprecedented political obstacles. In early July the French and American armies camped close together near Dobbs Ferry, on the east bank of the Hudson, giving the French officers a chance to study the Continental Army and marvel at what Washington had wrought. It was a heterogeneous, mongrel army such as no European had ever before witnessed. "I admire the American troops tremendously!" said Baron von Closen. "It is incredible that soldiers composed of men of every age, even of children of fifteen, of whites and blacks, almost naked, unpaid, and rather poorly fed, can march so well and withstand fire so steadfastly." He gave all credit to "the calm and calculated measures of General Washington, in whom I daily discover some new and eminent qualities."[35]

Von Closen's amazement was shared by his colleague the Count de Clermont-Crèvecoeur. As the latter roamed about the American army camp, he was stunned "by its destitution: the men were without uniforms and covered with rags; most of them were barefoot. They were of all sizes down to children who could not have

been over fourteen. There were many negroes, mulattoes, etc. Only their artil-
lerymen were wearing uniforms."[36] Such tributes are the more noteworthy in that
Washington was ashamed of the slovenly state of his army, which only heightened
the admiration of the flabbergasted French.

Predictably, French officers carped at the quality of American food. On the
other hand, they couldn't fault the quantity, except the way it all seemed thrown indiscriminately on one plate: "The table was served in the American style and pretty
abundantly: vegetables, roast beef, lamb, chickens, salad dressed with nothing but
vinegar, green peas, puddings and some pie, a kind of tart . . . all this being put
upon the table at the same time. They gave us on the same plate beef, green peas,
lamb & etc."[37] One wonders how Washington squared this groaning table with his
constant pleas to Congress about food shortages. The French stared in amazement
at all the beer and rum consumed and the interminable toasts with raised glasses
of wine. They found Washington in an expansive mood at these dinners, convivial
and relaxed—the Count de Ségur spoke of his "unaffected cheerfulness"—and he
lingered long into the night after the evening meals.[38]

On July 18 Washington and Rochambeau wandered along the Hudson at the north
end of Manhattan, surveying enemy positions. So many years had elapsed since 1776
that land denuded of its thick vegetation early in the war had started to grow back.
"The island is totally stripped of trees and wood of every kind," Washington wrote,
"but low bushes (apparently as high as a man's waist) appear in places which were
covered with wood in the year 1776."[39] He knew that de Grasse's arrival off the coast
was imminent, though he didn't know whether it would be off Sandy Hook, New
Jersey, or the Virginia capes. Meeting with Rochambeau the next day, Washington
reprised his idée fixe: that if de Grasse's fleet could navigate its way into New York
Harbor, then "I am of opinion that the enterprise against New York and its dependen-
cies should be our primary object."[40] In his journal Washington confessed that the
Massachusetts governor hadn't responded to his plea for more men and that he was
petrified that, after de Grasse's arrival, it would be found "that I had neither men nor
means adequate" for a military operation.[41] Even as he knew he might be on the brink
of a major triumph, he was also distraught at the impotence of his position vis-à-vis
his French allies. When he wrote to the Count de Grasse on July 21, he ducked the essential question of exactly how many men he had. "The French force consists of about
4,400 men," he told the French admiral. "The American is at this time but *small,* but
expected to be *considerably augmented.* In this, however, we may be disappointed."[42]
Contrary to his later statement, Washington told de Grasse that he hoped there would
be no need to go to Virginia, "as I flatter myself the glory of destroying the British
squadron at New York is reserved for the king's fleet under your command."[43]

CHAPTER THIRTY-FOUR

The World Turned Upside Down

IN EARLY AUGUST 1781 George Washington began to surrender his dream of taking New York and avenging its early loss. Ironically, his own inadvertent action helped bring about this change. Sir Henry Clinton intercepted a letter in which Washington named New York as his main strategic objective, prompting the British to strengthen their forces there and rendering Virginia more vulnerable. "It seems reduced almost to a certainty that the enemy will reinforce New York with part of their troops from Virginia," Washington notified Robert Morris on August 2.[1] Turning his attention to Virginia, Washington asked Morris if he could amass a fleet of thirty double-decker transport vessels to ferry the Continental Army southward. Even though Washington reversed course the next day and dangled before the Count de Barras the shimmering prospect of New York Harbor "open and defenseless" for the taking, his mind was preoccupied for the first time by the logistics of a southern move.[2]

If Washington muddled along in something of a strategic dither, his heroic stature remained unimpaired among ordinary citizens, who thanked him for keeping alive the embers of rebellion. On August 4 Abbé Robin, a chaplain with Rochambeau's army, witnessed the adulation firsthand at the allied camp at Philipsburg, New York: "Through all the land, [Washington] appears like a benevolent god; old men, women, children—they all flock eagerly to catch a glimpse of him when he travels and congratulate themselves because they have seen him."[3] He noted Washington's gift for inspired leadership, his capacity to make men vie for his favor. Washington "knew how to impress upon his soldiers an absolute subordination, to make them eager to deserve his praise, to make them fear even his silence."[4]

On August 14, while still distracted by reports of a large British fleet arriving in New York, Washington absorbed dramatic news from the Count de Barras in Newport: Admiral de Grasse had sailed from St. Domingue with a mighty fleet of up to twenty-nine ships of the line and 3,200 troops. If all unfolded according to plan, the fleet would show up off Chesapeake Bay by September 3. Stunned, Washington retired forever his ambition to conquer New York. In his journal he acknowledged the "apparent disinclination" of his French partners to tackle New York and noted the feeble response from state governors to his despairing pleas for more troops. He decided to discard "all idea of attacking New York," the fulcrum upon which his strategic calculations had hinged for years.[5]

De Barras told Washington that de Grasse would need to sail back to the Caribbean by mid-October, leaving only a brief interval for a joint operation against Cornwallis. This gave Washington and Rochambeau three weeks to transport two cumbersome armies 450 miles to Chesapeake Bay while de Barras and eight ships of the line and four frigates sailed south from Newport. After a desultory war that had shuffled along for years, Washington, Rochambeau, and de Barras now engaged in a headlong rush to reach Virginia. But orchestrating the movements of three armies and two navies over a vast portion of the eastern seaboard was to prove a fiendishly intricate maneuver.

Two days later Washington learned something from Lafayette that, in its way, was no less momentous than the startling news about de Grasse. Cornwallis had retreated to the eastern tip of the Virginia peninsula that jutted into Chesapeake Bay, dividing the York and James rivers. On high, open ground at a place called Yorktown, he and his men were furiously shoveling trenches and throwing up earthworks. As it turned out, Cornwallis had barged into a trap that Washington had spotted years earlier when Brigadier General Thomas Nelson wanted to station troops at Yorktown to track British ships. Washington had pointed out to Nelson that his troops "by being upon a narrow neck of land would be in danger of being cut off. The enemy might very easily throw up a few ships into York and James's river . . . and land a body of men there, who by throwing up a few redoubts, would intercept their retreat and oblige them to surrender at [their] discretion."[6] The letter uncannily foreshadowed the events of 1781.

As his army hurried south, Washington launched diversionary measures to dupe the enemy into thinking that New York remained his objective. He pitched a small city of tents on the west bank of the Hudson with wagons bustling in and out of this imaginary camp. American boats worked the nearby waters, laying down pontoons, as if readying an amphibious assault. To deceive the enemy, Washington needed to deceive his own men, who thought they were embarked for Staten Island. Instead they found themselves marching inland toward Trenton and then crossed paths with the French at Princeton, where Washington enjoyed a gratifying encounter with French officers. As he strode past their tent, he saw maps unfurled of Boston, Trenton, and Princeton: the officers were re-creating his victorious battles. One observer caught his reaction: "Despite his modesty . . . [Washington] seemed pleased to find thus assembled all the successful and pleasant events of the war."[7] The group repaired to a tavern to share Madeira and punch. One wonders whether the French made a fuss over Washington's early triumphs to soothe his wounded vanity and draw the sting from his disappointment over abandoning New York.

To march his men through New Jersey without betraying his intentions to the enemy, Washington contrived ingenious stratagems. He broke his army into three parallel columns and brought them forward at staggered intervals. The troops had no inkling of their true destination until they reached Trenton, where heavy guns were loaded on boats to carry them down the Delaware River to near Christiana, Delaware. From there it would be a twelve-mile march to Head of Elk, at the northern end of Chesapeake Bay. The original plan envisioned troops sailing with them, but Washington couldn't rustle up the requisite vessels, so he and Rochambeau made a hugely daring decision to have the men traverse the immense distance to Maryland on foot.

The southern landscape was unknown territory for Washington's men, who braced for sweltering heat and disease. Fearful of a mutiny, Washington implored Robert Morris to come up with a month's pay to pacify the men: "The service [in Virginia] they are going upon is disagreeable to the northern regiments, but I make no doubt that a douceur [bribe] of a little hard money would put them in proper temper."[8] Perhaps to garner popular support, Washington marched his army through Philadelphia, and cheering ladies jammed every window as a column two miles long filed through sunstruck streets. "The general officers and their aides, in rich military uniform, mounted on noble steeds, elegantly caparisoned, were followed by their servants and baggage," noted James Thacher.[9] The common soldiers, lean, sunburned, and spent from their march, padded along wearily to fifes and drums. At night the entire capital was illuminated in honor of Washington, who was thronged by crowds of admirers.

Washington's stay in Philadelphia was fraught with worry. He was on edge, having heard nothing from de Grasse or de Barras since they sailed from their respective positions. "If you get anything new from any quarter," he entreated Lafayette, "send it, I pray you, *on the spur of speed,* for I am almost all impatience and anxiety."[10] It was highly unorthodox for Washington to confess to such jitters. On the morning of September 5, after riding out of Philadelphia, he was overtaken at Chester by a messenger bearing phenomenal news: the Count de Grasse had shown up in Chesapeake Bay with a full panoply of military and naval power: 28 ships of the line, 4 frigates, and 3,500 troops. Washington shortly learned that de Grasse had engaged the Royal Navy under Admiral Thomas Graves off the Virginia capes, sending the British squadron scurrying back to New York and leaving the French in undisputed control of Chesapeake Bay. Between Lafayette's small army on the land side and de Grasse's massive fleet at sea, Cornwallis was bottled up near the end of the Yorktown peninsula.

As Rochambeau and his generals glided down the Delaware, they beheld something that overturned their preconceptions of a staid Washington. He stood on the riverbank in delirious elation, signaling gleefully with a hat in one hand and a handkerchief in the other. From across the water they heard him shouting "De Grasse."[11] "I caught sight of General Washington," wrote Rochambeau, "waving his hat at me with demonstrative gestures of the greatest joy."[12] Once the French commander came ashore, the two men hugged with a mighty embrace. One French officer, Guillaume de Deux-Ponts, was amazed by Washington's ebullience. Before, he had been convinced of Washington's "natural coldness," but now he had to reckon with the "pure joy" shown by the American: "He put aside his character as arbiter of North America and contented himself for the moment with that of a citizen, happy at the good fortune of his country. A child, whose every wish had been gratified, would not have experienced a sensation more lively."[13] The Duke de Lauzun agreed: "I never saw a man so thoroughly and openly delighted."[14] Washington's boyish exuberance testified to the years of suppressed anxiety from which he was now beginning to feel emancipated.

Perhaps restoring his spirits, too, was knowledge that, for the first time in six years, he would soon set eyes on Mount Vernon. He spent a long day in Baltimore, trying to get more transports to ferry his men and enduring the ceremonial occasions he loathed. Then early the next morning he set out on horseback with a single aide, David Humphreys, and streaked across sixty miles of Virginia countryside in a day. The last time Washington had set eyes on Mount Vernon was May 4, 1775, when he departed for the Second Continental Congress, little realizing how his life would be turned topsy-turvy. To experience Mount Vernon anew after his long, itinerant military life must have been a heady sensation. The household was now enlivened by newcomers, especially the four children of Jacky and Nelly Custis, whom he had never seen; the baby boy had been christened George Washington Parke Custis. Humphreys, a young man of literary aspirations, versified the slaves' reaction to Washington's return: "Return'd from war, I saw them round him press / And all their speechless glee by artless signs express."[15] One wonders whether this homecoming was staged by slaves eager to parade their fidelity; the "speechless glee" doesn't jibe with the discontent of the seventeen slaves who had raced to freedom aboard the British sloop *Savage*.

Within twenty-four hours Washington's and Rochambeau's entourages had arrived at Mount Vernon, ready to chart the Yorktown siege. For these battle-tested veterans, the mansion was a refreshing oasis. It was a tribute to Martha Washington's talents that she could entertain in style amid wartime conditions. Colonel Jonathan Trumbull, Jr., complimented the gracious and well-appointed reception lavished upon the visitors. "A numerous family now present," he wrote in his diary. "All accommodated. An elegant seat and situation: great appearance of opulence and real exhibitions of hospitality and princely entertainment."[16]

The French officers appraised Mount Vernon and its hostess with considerable curiosity. After the frippery of the French court, Martha Washington struck them as the pattern of republican austerity. "Mrs. Washington is . . . small and fat, her appearance is respectable," wrote Claude Blanchard. "She was dressed very plainly and her manners were simple in all respects."[17] In surveying the estate, Blanchard detected the tarnished glory inflicted by neglect. "As to the house, it is a country residence, the handsomest that I have yet seen in America . . . There are in the places around many huts for the negroes, of whom the general owns a large number . . . The environs of his house are not fertile and the trees that we see there do not appear to be large. Even the garden is barren."[18] Baron von Closen found the house's relative modesty suitable for America's hero: "The spacious and well-contrived mansion house at Mount Vernon was elegantly furnished, though there was no remarkable luxury to be seen anywhere; and, indeed, any ostentatious pomp would not have agreed with the simple manner of the owner."[19]

Washington must have been distressed by the creeping signs of decay everywhere. Whatever the war's outcome, he would be left a poorer man, which weighed heavily on his mind. That June, in a letter to William Crawford, the steward of his western lands, he broke down and confided his concern about his wealth withering away as the war progressed: "My whole time is . . . so much engrossed by the public duties of my station that I have totally neglected all my private concerns, which are declining every day, and may possibly end in capital losses, if not absolute ruin, before I am at liberty to look after them."[20]

Among the pleasures of his return was the chance to see the mansion's new north wing and the stylish dining room where he would entertain state visitors. It was likely here that he held a dinner for his guests on the night of September 12 before departing for Williamsburg the next morning. Jacky Custis prevailed upon his stepfather to take him along as a personal aide, a belated stint of service that must have awakened mixed feelings in Washington.

Arriving in Williamsburg late on the afternoon of September 14, Washington settled into the two-story brick home of George Wythe, a signer of the Declaration of Independence and Thomas Jefferson's old law professor. Washington moved about the town in a casual, unobtrusive fashion. "He approached without any pomp or parade, attended only by a few horsemen and his own servants," observed St. George Tucker, a well-to-do young Virginia lawyer and militia colonel.[21] Although Washington eschewed the swagger of power, his self-effacing presence sent an electric jolt through the ranks of soldiers.

As Tucker discovered, Washington had a retentive mind for detail and a politician's knack for remembering names: "To my great surprise, he recognized my features and spoke to me immediately by name."[22] The young man also witnessed the fervent reunion between Washington and Lafayette, conjuring it up in a letter to his wife the next day. The marquis "caught the General round his body, hugged him as close as it was possible, and absolutely kissed him from ear to ear once or twice . . . with as much ardor as ever an absent lover kissed his mistress on his return."[23] Washington also remained accessible to ordinary soldiers. "He stands in the door, takes every man by the hand," twenty-year-old Ebenezer Denny of Pennsylvania wrote home, still atremble with excitement. "The officers all pass in, receiving his hand and shake. This is the first time I had seen the general."[24]

That evening Washington was entertained with an elegant supper and the overture from a French opera. The next morning he informed de Grasse of his wish to confer with him. The French admiral had already issued a rather huffy letter to him, questioning the dilatory pace of the Continental Army. "The season is approaching when, against my will, I shall be obliged to forsake the allies for whom I have done my very best and more than could be expected," he wrote reprovingly.[25] It was easy for the French admiral to quibble. The soldiers marching south from Head of Elk to Annapolis faced an exhausting trek through an inhospitable landscape that one soldier depicted as "abominable, cut by deep ravines and many small rivers, which the soldiers were obliged to ford after removing their shoes and stockings." The next day they negotiated a riverbed "so rocky that the horses risked breaking their legs. All the way across we were in water up to our waists, and the horses up to their knees."[26] At Annapolis the soldiers could finally sail the rest of the way down the Chesapeake to the James River.

On September 17 the Count de Grasse sent a boat to convey Washington, Rochambeau, and their aides to his flagship, the *Ville de Paris,* riding at anchor off Cape Henry. Not since his Barbados trip as a teenager had Washington spent so much time afloat. It was noon the next day before the generals reached the French armada and gazed at the grand spectacle of thirty-two giant ships spanning the horizon. Reputed to be the world's biggest warship, the towering *Ville de Paris*— a gift from the city of Paris to the king—bristled with 110 guns and 1,300 men. Varnished to a high gloss, it was given an extra coat of French glamour by flowers and plants festooning the quarterdeck. Admiral de Grasse turned out to be a good-looking man of imposing height and girth. "The admiral is a remarkable man for size, appearance, and plainness of address," noted Jonathan Trumbull, Jr.[27] A scion of an aristocratic family, de Grasse had naval experience dating back to the War of Jenkins' Ear in 1740, when he had fought against Lawrence Washington. At six foot two, de Grasse was slightly taller than Washington, whom he embraced with gusto, kissing him on both cheeks and exclaiming, *"Mon cher petit général!"*[28] Never comfortable with physical affection, Washington was less amused than Knox and his officers, who roared with unrestricted laughter.

Despite the formal dinner and other marks of courtesy that de Grasse had arranged, the talks did not go smoothly. He set a deadline of no later than November 1 for his time in Virginia, and Washington hoped the Yorktown siege would fit into this abbreviated timetable. He gave de Grasse a mixed grade, calling him a "gallant officer" while also bemoaning his "impetuosity."[29] Mostly Washington felt powerless in dealing with the arrogant admiral. When their talks ended, de Grasse devised an elaborate sunset send-off for Washington, with crewmen on all the ships scrambling up into the riggings and firing muskets in the sequence known as a *feu de joie.*

For three days Washington's departing boat was buffeted by gusts, and he didn't return to Williamsburg until September 22. By then, the last remnants of the Continental Army had tramped in from their marathon journey. No sooner was Washington back than he received an unpleasant surprise. Admiral Graves had returned with his fleet to New York, where he hoped to be reinforced; to avert this, de Grasse contemplated a move north to cut off any British movements by sea. Writing to de Grasse, Washington communicated his "painful anxiety" at any action that might compromise the Yorktown siege. "The enterprise against York[town] under the protection of your ships is as certain as any military operation can be rendered by a decisive superiority of strength and means," he pleaded.[30] Washington by now had gotten religion about the Yorktown mission, and de Grasse decided to cancel the voyage to New York. Nevertheless, in a mildly irritated tone, he told Washington, "Your Excellency may be very sure that I have, so to speak, more at heart than yourself that the expedition to York may terminate agreeably to our desires."[31]

On September 28 Washington and his army began the twelve-mile march to Yorktown through scenery he depicted as "beautiful, fertile country."[32] The day was so sultry that at least two men perished from the heat. That night Washington slept safely behind the lines in a wooded glade under "the small spreading branches of a tree," with a spring running nearby.[33] The next day he pitched a couple of tents, including a large dining marquee that would enable him to entertain up to forty guests at a time during the siege.

Cornwallis and his troops were holed up on the bluff of Yorktown village, which was set above the broad, gleaming expanse of the York River, with the town of Gloucester lying directly across the water. This bucolic spot was more salubrious than the low-lying swamps nearby. Most British troops stayed behind the main fortifications, but Cornwallis had expanded the defensive perimeter with ten low earthen redoubts that projected into the sandy battlefield. From the outset it was an uneven contest, for Cornwallis had almost 9,000 troops versus nearly 19,000 French and Americans. Seeing his precarious situation, Cornwallis counted on Sir Henry Clinton to redeem his pledge and relieve him with thousands of fresh troops. "This place is in no state of defense," Cornwallis warned on September 17. "If you cannot relieve me very soon, you must be prepared to hear the worst."[34] Failing to heed the urgent warning, Clinton procrastinated, in one of the foremost blunders of the war.

As British soldiers peered from behind their earthworks, they could see French troops and artillery to their right and American to their left. The Frenchmen looked almost fashionably garbed compared with their impoverished American counterparts. As Anthony Wayne said of the troops who came with de Grasse, they made "a very fine soldierly appearance, they being all very tall men, their uniform is white coats turned up with blue, their underclothes are white."[35]

The Battle of Yorktown proceeded like a textbook European siege. The patriots were poorly tutored in this military science in which the veteran French engineers excelled, relegating Washington again to a secondary position. On October 1 Washington and Rochambeau scouted ground for the first of several parallel trenches that would edge progressively closer to the enemy. Each morning the two men reviewed the progress, but Washington deferred to French expertise about sieges, putting the French general in command. As Rochambeau wrote, "I must render the Americans the justice to say that they conducted themselves with that zeal, courage, and emulation, with which they were never backward," although they were "totally ignorant of the operations of a siege."[36]

The British camp showed early signs of extreme distress. On October 2, while scouring the York River through his spyglass, St. George Tucker noticed dozens of dead horses bobbing in the water. Having run short of forage, the British had shot the animals and dumped them in the river, crowding the water with four hundred carcasses. A fetid and lasting stench hung over the town as dead animals rotted in the tidal flats. Two days later two British deserters drifted into the allied camp and retailed horror stories of widespread disease among Cornwallis's men—two thousand were already laid up in the hospital.

On the night of October 5, laboring in darkness and secrecy, the allies began to carve out a trench two miles long. By the next morning they had thrown up sufficient dirt to form earthworks in front of it, enabling them to work while shielded from British fire. Washington toured the nocturnal site, wrapped in a cloak, without revealing his identity. During the clear, unseasonably mild autumn days, the British raked the allied lines with almost continuous fire, making it risky to move about. They threw everything imaginable at the allies: a thick hail of musket fire, cannonballs, grapeshot, shells, and bombs. Washington again showed preternatural calm in braving shots and never deviated from his fearless stand. It was futile for people to insist that he protect himself. One day a cannonball landed near him, tossing a huge cloud of sand in the sky, which filtered down on Chaplain Israel Evans. He removed his hat, examined it, and said to Washington, "See here, general!" "Mr. Evans," Washington replied, "you had better carry that [ball] home and show it to your wife and children."[37] Washington bore the stress gracefully, and Jacky Custis wrote home that "the general, tho[ugh] in constant fatigue, looks very well."[38]

When the first parallel was completed on October 9, the French, in a gesture of respect, allowed Washington to ignite the first gun aimed at the British, which scored a memorable shot. "I could hear the ball strike from house to house," recalled Philip Van Cortlandt of New York, "and I was afterwards informed that it went through the one where many of the officers were at dinner, and over the tables, discomposing the dishes and either killed or wounded the one at the head of the table."[39] While American gunners lacked pinpoint accuracy, they wreaked terrible devastation on the enemy. "One could not avoid the horribly many cannonballs, either inside or outside the city," said one of Cornwallis's soldiers. ". . . Many men were badly injured and mortally wounded by the fragments of bombs . . . [so that] their arms and legs [were] severed or themselves struck dead."[40]

A standard siege inched forward in a slow, creeping motion, with each trench nearer the enemy. On October 12 a second trench was begun only three hundred yards from enemy lines, and once again miners and sappers worked diligently through the night, astounding the British the next morning with their overnight progress and doubtless inducing a claustrophobic feeling. Day and night the cannon fire was deadly, cacophonous, and incessant. Cornwallis issued a cri de coeur to Sir Henry Clinton, asking him to send a fleet and asserting that "nothing but a direct move to York River—which includes a successful naval action—*can save me.*" He concluded bleakly that "we cannot hope to make a long resistance."[41]

As the second parallel neared completion, the next priority became seizing two outlying British defenses, redoubts nine and ten, which blocked any further advance. In a spirit of Franco-American harmony, Washington assigned one redoubt to the French, the other to Americans under Lafayette. Since the siege had been the handiwork of gunners and engineers, affording little opportunity for swashbuckling heroism, a spirited competition arose to lead the charges. At first Lafayette drafted his personal aide, the Chevalier de Gimat, but this seemed unsporting to

American soldiers, especially the determined Alexander Hamilton. After wearing down Washington with petitions for a field position, he had been rewarded with command of a New York light infantry battalion. Now Hamilton, claiming seniority over Gimat, applied his persuasive powers to win the assignment of leading four hundred men against redoubt ten. That Washington acceded to his wishes shows not only his respect for Hamilton's ability but his willingness to rise above personal pettiness to patch up a quarrel.

John Adams later insisted that Hamilton had blackmailed Washington into granting him the assignment. "You inquire what passed between Washington and Hamilton at Yorktown?" wrote Adams (who wasn't there) to Benjamin Rush. "Washington had ordered . . . another officer to take the command of the attack upon the redoubt. Hamilton flew into a violent passion and demanded the command of the party for himself and declared if he had it not, he would expose General Washington's conduct in a pamphlet."[42] The idea that Washington would have been cowed by a crude threat shows little understanding of the man. Such patent blackmail would have cost Hamilton his relationship with Washington forever.

At dusk on October 14 Washington delivered a pep talk to Hamilton's men, urging them to "act the part of firm and brave soldiers" in storming the redoubt.[43] "I thought then that His Excellency's knees rather shook," said Captain Stephen Olney, "but I have since doubted whether it was not mine."[44] The artillery pounded the two redoubts to weaken them for the assault. Then, as night fell, with shells illuminating the sky, Hamilton and his party rose from their trenches and sprinted across the open field. To ensure speed and surprise, they had orders not to shoot their muskets but only to employ fixed bayonets. Standing on elevated ground, Washington watched the dramatic scene with Generals Lincoln and Knox. "Sir, you are too much exposed here," urged Washington's aide David Cobb, Jr. "Had you not better step a little back?" "Colonel Cobb," Washington said coolly, "if you are afraid, you have liberty to step back."[45]

When they reached the redoubt, the sappers had to leap a moat and contend with an abatis—felled trees sharpened to lethal points—which they slashed with axes to form an opening. The French operation against redoubt number nine suffered high casualties, while Hamilton's group sustained minimal losses. Among the heroes of the charge was the largely black First Rhode Island Regiment. "The bravery exhibited by the attacking troops was emulous and praiseworthy," Washington recorded in his journal. "Few cases have exhibited stronger proofs of intrepidity, coolness, and firmness than were shown upon this occasion."[46] By capturing the two redoubts, the allies could now install short-range howitzers that fired ricochet projectiles, which bounced along the ground toward their target, then killed and maimed with ghoulish efficiency.

The situation looked pretty desperate for Cornwallis. In a portrait painted by Thomas Gainsborough two years later, the highborn earl has a well-fed, sagging face and heavy-lidded eyes; his expression is downcast, as if Yorktown still threw a shadow. Short and stout, he had been educated at Eton and Cambridge, served as aide-de-camp to George III, and compiled a commendable record during the French and Indian War. Mostly amiable, he was also prone to temperamental fits. As a Whig member of Parliament, he had questioned government policy in North America but had fought no less fiercely for all that and proved popular among his men. American generals retained a healthy respect for his fighting spirit. "Lord Cornwallis's abilities are to me more frightening than his superiority of forces," Lafayette wrote to Knox that August. "I even have a great opinion of him. Our papers call him a madman, but was ever any advantage taken of him where he commanded in person? To speak plain English, I am devilish afraid of him!"[47]

Cornwallis's grave situation was aggravated by intramural squabbling with Clinton. The two men had whined and bickered all year: Cornwallis complained to Clinton that he was being kept "totally in the dark as to the intended operations of the summer."[48] Clinton, in turn, distrusted Cornwallis, believing that he had by-passed his own authority to communicate directly with London. Aggravating matters was Clinton's insistence that the French and Americans might swoop down on New York and that he couldn't spare men for Virginia.

As Cornwallis awaited reinforcements from New York, rumors circulated that the trapped commander had "built a kind of grotto . . . where he lives underground."[49] Scooping out space from a hillside, Cornwallis formed his own private bunker. By October 15 he despaired of any relief from Clinton and sent a message that the situation was so "precarious that I cannot recommend that the fleet and army should run great risk in endeavoring to save us."[50] That same day the firing of shells from both sides reached such a feverish pitch of intensity that they sketched patterns of hideous beauty in the sky. "They are clearly visible in the form of a black ball in the day," wrote James Thacher, "but in the night, they appear like fiery meteors with blazing tails, most beautifully brilliant."[51]

More than one hundred allied cannon terrorized the town with punishing consistency. One Hessian wrote that "the bombs and cannonballs hit many inhabitants and negroes of the city and marines, sailors, and soldiers."[52] In desperation Cornwallis took former slaves who had defected to British lines and contracted smallpox and pushed them toward the allied lines in a version of germ warfare. One American soldier reported "herds of Negroes" who had been "turned adrift" by Cornwallis for this grisly purpose.[53] Jacky Custis, scanning the defecting blacks for runaway slaves from Mount Vernon, found none. "I have seen numbers [of blacks] lying dead in the woods," he informed his mother, "and many so exhausted they cannot walk."[54]

On the night of October 16 the allies crept so close to the British line that Cornwallis made a frantic effort to evacuate his army across the river to Gloucester. Banastre Tarleton, who was stationed there, sent over sixteen craft for the crossing. The first boat didn't depart from Yorktown until almost eleven P.M., but a substantial number of men made it across the river. Cornwallis scribbled a note to Washington, asking for mercy toward the sick and wounded left behind. Then shortly before midnight a violent storm drove the boats downriver, terminating the operation and forcing Cornwallis to recall his men from Gloucester the next morning. He had exhausted his last option. Surrender was now the only course left open to him.

At ten A.M. on October 17, 1781—the fourth anniversary of Burgoyne's surrender at Saratoga—a British officer appeared before the ramparts, flapping a white flag and bearing a missive from Cornwallis. The battlefield, pulverized by bombs, fell silent. An American escort rushed to the British officer, bandaged his eyes, and shepherded him behind allied lines. Then a messenger on horseback transmitted the all-important letter to Washington, who opened it and read: "Sir, I propose a cessation of hostilities for twenty-four hours and that two officers may be appointed by each side to meet at Mr. Moore's house to settle terms for the surrender of the posts of York and Gloucester. I have the honor to be, &c, Cornwallis."[55] Never one to gloat, Washington remarked only that the message came "at an earlier period than my most sanguine hopes had induced me to expect."[56]

Washington sent Cornwallis a terse, businesslike note. "My Lord: I have had the honor of receiving your Lordship's letter of this date. An ardent desire to spare the further effusion of blood will readily incline me to such terms for the surrender of your posts and garrisons of York and Gloucester as are admissible. I wish previously to the meeting of commissioners that your Lordship's proposals in writing may be sent to the American lines, for which purpose a suspension of hostilities during two hours from the delivery of this letter will be granted. I have the honor etc."[57] Cornwallis's return proposals conformed closely enough to Washington's wishes that hostilities were suspended for the night as an eerie calm settled over Yorktown. "A solemn stillness prevailed," St. George Tucker wrote. "The night was remarkably clear and the sky decorated with ten thousand stars. Numberless meteors gleaming through the atmosphere."[58] The next day soldiers waded across a hellish battlefield paved with cadavers, one recalling that "all over the place and wherever you look [there were] corpses lying about that had not been buried."[59] The majority of the bodies, he noted, were black, reflecting their importance on both sides of the conflict. Some of these black corpses likely belonged to runaway slaves who had sought asylum with Cornwallis, only to be stricken during the siege with smallpox or "camp fever"—likely typhus, a disease spread by lice and fleas in overcrowded camps.

In negotiations between the commissioners, a major sticking point involved Cornwallis's request that his men be allowed to save face and surrender with full military honors. John Laurens and Lafayette objected that, when Charleston fell, Sir Henry Clinton had denied the Americans that consolation. Even though this would deepen the dishonor of the British Army, Washington informed Cornwallis, "The same honors will be granted to the surrendering army as were granted to the garrison of Charleston."[60]

In the shadow of a redoubt near the river, the articles of surrender were signed at eleven A.M. on October 19. At two P.M. the French and American troops lined up on opposite sides of a lane stretching a half mile long. Baron von Closen noted the contrast between the "splendor" of the French soldiers, with their dress swords and polished boots, and the Americans "clad in small jackets of white cloth, dirty and ragged, and a number of them . . . almost barefoot."[61] Led by drummers beating a somber march, thousands of defeated British and Hessian soldiers trudged heavily between the allied columns, their colors tightly folded. As they ran this gauntlet, they had to pass by every allied soldier. Legend claims that British fifes and drums played "The World Turned Upside Down." In another reminder of allied revenge for Charleston, General Benjamin Lincoln, who had been refused the honors of war there, led the procession. Even at the end the British evinced a petty, spiteful attitude toward the Americans, gazing only at the French soldiers until Lafayette prodded the band to strike up "Yankee Doodle," forcing the conquered army to acknowledge the hated Americans. At the end of the line, the British soldiers emerged into an open field, where they tossed their weapons contemptuously onto a stockpile, trying to smash them. Then they filed back past the double column of victors. The entire wonder of the American Revolution was visible for all to see. It wasn't the well-dressed French Army who were the true victors of the day, but the weather-beaten, half-clad American troops.

Washington and Rochambeau waited patiently on horseback at the end of the line. For the occasion, Washington had chosen his favorite steed, Nelson. In yet another snub to the Americans, Cornwallis deemed it beneath his dignity to attend the ceremony and, delivering the lame excuse that he was indisposed, sent Brigadier General Charles O'Hara in his place. When O'Hara rode up to Rochambeau and proffered Cornwallis's sword, the French general motioned toward Washington as the proper recipient. Washington had no intention of accepting the sword from Cornwallis's deputy and, with his usual phlegm, asked O'Hara if he would be good enough to hand it to his American counterpart, General Lincoln. The British behavior at Yorktown, so graceless and uncouth, was the last time Americans had to suffer such condescension.

Washington in victory was the picture of humility. In reporting to Congress, he deflected attention from himself: "The unremitting ardor which actuated every officer and soldier in the combined army on this occasion has principally led to this important event."[62] It was Washington's decisive moment, but he had long since perfected the role of bashful hero. "In performing my part towards its accomplishment," he said, "I consider myself to have done only my duty and in the execution of that, I ever feel myself happy."[63] That evening, taking the high road, he threw a dinner for the French, British, and American general officers. Although Cornwallis was invited, he pleaded poor health and sent the sociable O'Hara in his stead. Commissary Claude Blanchard picked up the resentment of the Americans as the British and French officers fraternized on cordial terms. These officers shared an identity as Europeans, aristocrats, and members of the same professional military caste. Such camaraderie could only have strengthened Washington's view that French involvement in the Revolution had been motivated less by ideological sympathy than by realpolitik. On the other hand, he knew that the Yorktown victory had depended upon the French skill at sieges, backed up by French naval supremacy. From an emotional standpoint, Yorktown couldn't have been an entirely satisfying climax for Washington, who had been consigned to a somewhat secondary role.

The next day Cornwallis made a courtesy call on Washington, and the two established a rapport based on mutual respect. They toured the Yorktown defenses on horseback to oversee the demolition of defenses that had been erected with meticulous care. The Yorktown victory netted more than eight thousand prisoners, who would be ordinary prisoners of war; their officers would be allowed to return to Europe or New York or any other port that Britain controlled. Washington dealt leniently with Tory sympathizers who had found sanctuary with Cornwallis and faced patriotic reprisals. He didn't want to give them a formal reprieve, but neither did he wish to condone vigilante actions against them. He solved the dilemma with a subtle compromise: he allowed the British to send a ship to New York, which the Tories could clamber aboard as an escape route.

Yorktown struck a stirring blow for American liberty with one exception: those slaves who had flocked to the British side to win their freedom were now restored to the thrall of their owners. Washington retrieved two young house slaves—twenty-year-old Lucy and eighteen-year-old Esther—who had been among the seventeen who had escaped aboard the British sloop *Savage* six months earlier, thinking their freedom assured. He was determined to recover the remaining fifteen slaves he had lost.

In retrospect, the Yorktown victory dealt a mortal blow to British aspirations in America. When Lord North, the portly prime minister, digested the news at 10 Downing Street, he went wild with despair. "O God!" he repeated, pacing the floor. "It is all over!"[64] The unreconstructed King George III refused to accept this reality and wanted to throw even more resources into prosecuting a hopeless conflict. The victory encouraged a skeptical world to believe in American independence, and the Dutch would grant diplomatic recognition in the spring. It isn't clear whether Washington grasped the full import of the victory. He praised the battle as "an interesting event that may be productive of much good if properly improved, but if it should be the means of relaxation and sink us into supineness and [false] security, it had better not have happened."[65] As reports drifted back from London that the British had conceded the war was hopeless, Washington remained cautious, since the enemy's presence in North America was still formidable. Throughout the conflict he had resisted wishful thinking, and now dreaded that the Yorktown victory might waylay people into premature complacency. Along with Lafayette, he went out to the *Ville de Paris* to see if he could parlay the great triumph into joint action against Charleston, South Carolina, or Wilmington, North Carolina, but de Grasse declined any follow-up operation.

Washington was sufficiently vexed by the Frenchman's fitful cooperation that he decided to send Lafayette to France to agitate for a more durable naval presence. "A constant naval superiority would terminate the war speedily," Washington told Lafayette in mid-November. "Without it, I do not know that it will ever be terminated honorably."[66] Washington also hoped for more French generosity in the form of a large loan or grant. "Adieu, my dear general," Lafayette wrote from Boston before his departure. "I know your heart so well that I am sure that no distance can alter your attachment to me. With the same candor, I assure you that my love, my respect, my gratitude for you are above expression."[67]

A coda to the Yorktown campaign must have mortified Lord Cornwallis. On October 17, the day of the surrender, General Clinton and his fleet of six thousand troops began their departure from New York, hoping to rescue him. When they arrived off Chesapeake Bay a week later, they encountered three people in a small craft who apprised them of the calamity that had occurred. Having no desire to do battle with thirty-three French ships still lingering off the Virginia coast, they turned around and went back to New York. The French admiral stayed in the area long enough to protect the Continental Army as it gathered its supplies and set sail up the bay, then headed for the long trip back to its familiar northern haunts.

The presence at Yorktown of Jacky Custis as a volunteer aide to Washington has sparked a certain cynicism among historians. Before then Jacky had contributed only modestly to the war effort, serving for two years as a delegate in the Virginia assembly, where he showed a grandiosity that sometimes vexed his stepfather. He had also invested with Washington in a privateer that prowled the Atlantic in quest of British merchant ships. Yet he had never placed his life in jeopardy, leading to snickers that he went to Yorktown to bask in a major victory without having paid his dues. If it irked Washington to see the raffish Jacky mingling with brave, hard-bitten men who had sacrificed years to the cause, he never admitted it openly.

Amid the unsanitary conditions at Yorktown, Jacky Custis contracted camp fever. Since the condition often proved fatal, Jacky expressed a last wish to witness Cornwallis's surrender and was lifted to a high spot atop a redoubt, giving him a panoramic glimpse of the ceremonies. Then he was carted thirty miles to Eltham in New Kent County, the estate of his uncle, Burwell Bassett. Martha Washington and Jacky's wife, Eleanor (Nelly) Calvert Curtis, were summoned to attend him. Preoccupied with the aftermath of victory, Washington couldn't extricate himself from Yorktown until November 5, when, alerted to Jacky's perilous condition, he hastened to Eltham. By the time he arrived, he learned that the doctors' ministrations had failed and that Jacky Custis was dying. The young man expired a few hours later, three weeks before his twenty-seventh birthday.

For a disconsolate Martha Washington, it was an indescribably sad moment. Having already lost three children, she had doted on Jacky, and Washington alluded to her "deep and solemn distress."[68] By some accounts, Washington had a profound emotional response to Jacky's death, clasping his bereaved widow to his bosom and proclaiming that henceforth he regarded Jacky's two youngest children as his own. One French observer described Washington as "uncommonly affected" by the death and said his friends "perceived some change in his equanimity of temper subsequent to that event."[69] In a less sentimental vein, biographer James T. Flexner wrote bluntly that Washington expressed "no personal grief."[70] If Washington reacted deeply to the death, it is not surprising, for it meant that he would have no chance to improve his strained relationship with his stepson. It was also a sobering reminder that, after years of war, he might not return to the happy home life he had pictured.

After spending a week at Eltham and attending to Jacky's funeral, Washington escorted Martha and Nelly back to Mount Vernon, where they dealt with the fate of the three small girls and baby boy who had lost their father. The Washingtons decided to adopt informally the two youngest children, Eleanor Parke Custis, then two years old and like her mother called Nelly, and George Washington Parke Custis, seven months old. Such informal adoptions were commonplace in the eighteenth century, when life expectancy was shorter and children often lost parents. A gay, whimsical child, Nelly would turn into a vivacious, dark-haired little girl, while the baby boy, nicknamed Washy or Tub, had blond hair and blue eyes and inherited both his father's charm and his wayward nature. With his solemn sense of responsibility, Washington took seriously his duties toward the children and wrote in his will that it had "always been my intention, since my expectation of having issue has ceased, to consider the grandchildren of my wife in the same light as I do my own relations."[71]

These two adopted children reciprocated the intense love they received and treated George and Martha more as adored parents than as grandparents. In later years, when she had to spend time with her biological mother, Nelly expressed her absolute devotion to her surrogate parents: "I have gone through the greatest trial I ever experienced—parting with my beloved grandmama ... Since my father's death, she has been ever more than a mother to me and the president the most affectionate of fathers. I love them more than anyone."[72] Two years later Jacky's widow, Nelly, married David Stuart of Alexandria, a physician trained in Edinburgh. They brought up the two eldest girls from the earlier marriage, Elizabeth Parke Custis and Martha Parke Custis, and added more children to the rich private lives of the Washingtons. Despite being a childless couple, George and Martha Washington had extensive experience in raising children and actually had much more of a family life, over a longer period, than most other married couples.

Jacky Custis left behind a murky legacy. Many years later his eldest daughter, Elizabeth, who was born a year after George Washington rode off to war, told how her father would hoist her on a table and force her to sing indecent songs that he had taught her in order to divert his inebriated friends. "I was animated to exert myself to give him delight," she wrote. "The servants in the passage would join their mirth and I, holding my head erect, would strut about the table to receive the praises of the company. My mother remonstrated in vain." Because he had been denied a son, Jacky told his guests that little Elizabeth "must make fun for him until he had."[73] It would be hard to imagine a stepson more alien to George Washington.

FOLLOWING YORKTOWN, Washington had to deal with another troubled dimension of his life: his prickly seventy-three-year-old mother. After Jacky's burial, he stopped by Fredericksburg to see her and learned that she had gone west on a trip to Frederick County with daughter Betty and ailing son-in-law Fielding Lewis. Mindful of her waspish comments about his financial neglect, Washington dropped off ten guineas before riding on to Mount Vernon. The poorly educated Mary sent him a thank-you letter in which she misspelled his name. This letter, full of self-pity, solicited more money: "My dear Georg I was truly unesy by Not being at hom when you went thru Fredriceksburg it was a onlucky thing for me now I am afraid I Never Shall have that pleasure agin I am soe very unwell this trip over the Mountins has almost kill'd me I gott the 2 five ginnes you was so kind to send me i am greatly obliged to you."[74] Now that George had bought her a house in Fredericksburg, she wanted one beyond the western mountains—"some little hous of my one if it is only twelve foot squar." In a postscript, she asked to be remembered to Martha, then crossed out the words "I would have wrote to her but my reason has jis left me."[75] The world might be buzzing excitedly about Yorktown, but Mary Washington resolutely refused to congratulate her son or even mention the event. "When others congratulated her and were enthusiastic in [George's praise]," wrote Washington Irving, "she listened in silence and would temperately reply that he had been a good son, and she believed he had done his duty as a man."[76] Neither did she extend condolences or refer to Jacky's death. Mary Washington had always been a peevish, egocentric woman, but one suspects that some mild form of dementia may have set in by this point. The failure to mention Jacky Custis's death suggests a lapse in short-term memory, and her allusion to her reason having "left" her indicates an awareness of impaired mental faculties.

When Washington attended a ball in Fredericksburg to honor the French and American officers who had fought valiantly at Yorktown, Mary was told that His Excellency was coming for the occasion. "His Excellency!" she snapped. "What nonsense!"[77] As during the French and Indian War, Mary seemed to regard her son's long years of military service as a trick perpetrated to deprive her of his attention. Rumors of her Loyalist sympathies continued to make the rounds, and one French officer, the Count de Clermont-Crèvecoeur, was "amazed to be told that this lady, who must be over seventy, is one of the most rabid Tories."[78]

George squired his aged mother to the Fredericksburg ball, the only occasion when we know for sure that the two appeared in public together. Perhaps George wanted to squelch rumors that he had abandoned his mother. Mary didn't stay long at the dance. At nine o'clock she announced that "it was time for the old people to be at home" and left on her son's arm.[79] The ball was noteworthy as one of the last times that George Washington danced away the evening, displaying the graceful virility for which he was known. Before the decade was over, his body would become stiffer, his face worn and impassive, and history would forget the lithe, magnetic younger man who had led the Revolution.

Man of Moderation

FOR ALL WASHINGTON'S SKEPTICISM that the war had ended, his behavior that autumn and winter reflected an altered reality. He lingered at Mount Vernon for several weeks, consoling Martha and enjoying some much-needed rest. The man who had shuddered at the thought of prolonged separation from his restive army spent four leisurely winter months in Philadelphia, nestled in a town house on Third Street. From the moment he descended on the capital, Washington was lionized at every turn. Two artistic residents, Charles Willson Peale and Alexander Quesnay, unrolled giant transparent paintings of him in windows that, when lit from the back, projected his glowing vision into the night, showing laurel wreaths crowning his brow and an antique spear grasped in his hand as he crushed a British crown underfoot. The theater offered no surcease from his own omnipresent image. Washington attended a performance of *The Temple of Minerva,* perhaps the first serious American opera, only to hear the chorus thunder from the stage, "He comes, he comes, with conquest crowned. / Hail Columbia's warlike son! / Hail the glorious Washington!"[1]

Washington was the honored guest at every gathering and admitted sheepishly to the Chevalier de Chastellux that his time was "divided between parties of pleasure and parties of business. The first, nearly of a sameness at all times and places in this infant country, is easily conceived . . . The second was only diversified by perplexities and could afford no entertainment."[2] Taking time to lobby the states, he urged them not to disband their regiments and asked Congress to renew its focus on pay and provisions to stifle any mutinous stirrings among his men.

Washington also received a valuable education in finance from Robert Morris, who had raised money for the Continental cause on his own credit. Because the states had refused to collect their quota of taxes, Morris couldn't service the sizable debt raised to finance the war. He warned that creditors "who trusted us in the hour of distress are defrauded" and that it was pure "madness" to "expect that foreigners will trust a government which has no credit with its own citizens."[3] To end Congress's servile reliance on the states for money, Morris proposed that it have the right to collect customs duties, and the fight for this "impost"—the first form of federal taxation—became a rallying cry for proponents of an energetic central government.

After George and Martha Washington had enjoyed their fill of Philadelphia politics and society, they took up residence in late March on the Hudson River in their new headquarters in the town of Newburgh. They occupied a two-story stone farmhouse with a pitched roof and twin chimneys, which sat high atop a bare bluff on the Hudson at a dreamy bend in the river. The heart of the house was the parlor, which Washington turned into his dining room, an eccentric space claiming the odd distinction of having seven doors and one window.

While there, Washington approved one of the war's most adventurous schemes: a plot to kidnap Prince William Henry, son of King George III, along with the British admiral Robert Digby, both now resident in New York. Washington worried that all the talk of peace would sap America's will and act as a "fresh opiate to increase that stupor" into which the states had fallen, giving them an excuse to renege on taxes and fail to complete their battalions.[4] The kidnapping of Prince William Henry might serve to dishearten George III. As we have seen, Washington had long been beguiled by kidnapping plans, having first approved one for Benedict Arnold, then another for Sir Henry Clinton, and the plan for Prince William Henry followed a similar script. On a dark, rainy night, a squad of thirty-six men, dressed up as sailors, would board four whaleboats on the Jersey shore of the Hudson and row across to Manhattan. They would disable British sentinels, then grab the prince and admiral in their riverfront quarters. With his penchant for espionage, Washington was minutely involved in mapping out the operation.

On March 28, 1782, Washington sent a sober set of instructions to Colonel Matthias Ogden, the operation commander, setting the tone for the abduction. His overriding concern was that the abducted dignitaries be treated respectfully, not manhandled like ruffians. "I am fully persuaded," he wrote, "that it is unnecessary to caution you against offering insult or indignity to the persons of the prince or admiral . . . but it may not be amiss to press the propriety of a proper line of conduct upon the party you command."[5] Washington knew that any abuse by the captors could translate into a propaganda victory for the British, yet in demanding gentlemanly treatment of the prisoners, he also betrayed some residual respect for royalty and rank. The plan was never carried out, and Washington was enraged at Ogden for snatching away his chance for a surprise victory. Many years later the U.S. minister to Great Britain showed Prince William Henry, now King William IV, Washington's March 28 letter to Ogden. "I am obliged to General Washington for his humanity," the king replied, "but I'm damned glad I did not give him an opportunity of exercising it towards me."[6]

Despite Washington's skepticism about British intentions, it was hard to discount the extraordinary upheaval that occurred in London in early 1782 when antiwar sentiment engulfed British politics and toppled Lord North's ministry. In a spiteful mood, King George III reflected that it might be better if he lost America, since "knavery seems to be so much the striking feature of its inhabitants that it may not be in the end an evil that they become aliens to this kingdom."[7] That spring the Crown recalled Sir Henry Clinton and replaced him with the commander of Canada, Sir Guy Carleton, a move that threw into relief Washington's own amazing longevity as commander in chief. When Carleton tested Washington's position with peace overtures, the latter dismissed them as more examples of British trickery.

For Washington, 1782 was taken up with matters possessing more symbolic than military meaning. The most vexing involved the treatment of prisoners, and none caused more controversy than the case of Captain Joshua Huddy, a member of the New Jersey militia. In April 1782 the British had captured Huddy at Toms River and handed him over to a civilian Tory group, the Associated Loyalists, who placed him in the custody of Captain Richard Lippincott. In a brutal act of reprisal, Lippincott decided to punish Huddy for the death of a Loyalist partisan named Philip White, who had been captured and executed by American militiamen after he killed one of his captors. Huddy was strung up from a tree with a note fastened to his chest that read "Up Goes Huddy for Philip White," along with threats of further retribution.[8] Going through the motions of justice, Sir Henry Clinton subjected Captain Lippincott to a court-martial, which exonerated him on the ground that he had merely obeyed orders. This caused a furor on the American side because those orders had emanated from none other than William Franklin, the estranged Loyalist son of Benjamin Franklin.

Aghast that the perpetrator of such a "horrid deed" was freed, Washington ordered Brigadier General Moses Hazen to choose by lot a British officer to be executed in retaliation for Captain Huddy. Palpably torn by this decision, Washington instructed Hazen that "every possible tenderness that is consistent with the security . . . should be shown to the person whose unfortunate lot it may be to suffer."[9] The person selected at random to die powerfully enlisted his captors' sympathy. Captain Charles Asgill of the First British Regiment of Foot was only nineteen and of distinguished parentage; his father, a former lord mayor of London, had been a Whig sympathetic to American grievances. Making the decision still more agonizing was that Asgill had been captured at Yorktown, where Washington had guaranteed the safety of prisoners in the articles of capitulation. A conflicted Washington admitted that Captain Asgill was a young man "of humor and sentiment" and that his plight engendered the "keenest anguish."[10]

The projected execution blossomed into a cause célèbre as protests flooded in to Washington from abroad. Congress approved the execution, and public opinion overwhelmingly favored it. The brouhaha reawakened memories of the Major André affair and enlisted some of the same partisans. Evidently, some coolness still existed between Hamilton and Washington, for Hamilton protested the execution via Henry Knox rather than directly to Washington. Of the scheduled hanging, Hamilton insisted that "a sacrifice of this kind is entirely repugnant to the genius of the age we live in and is without example in modern history . . . It is a deliberate sacrifice of the innocent for the guilty and must be condemned."[11]

Still haunted by André's execution, Washington didn't care to execute another sensitive young British officer and protested to one general that "while my duty calls me to make this decisive determination, humanity dictates a fear for the unfortunate offering and inclines me to say that I most devoutly wish his life may be saved . . . but it must be effected by the British commander-in-chief."[12] Interestingly enough, the unsentimental Benjamin Franklin favored a tough, uncompromising stand. "If the English refuse to deliver up or punish this murderer," he wrote, "it is saying that they choose to preserve him rather than Captain Asgill."[13] Aware that he might be the target of patriotic reprisals, William Franklin fled to London.

In the end Washington handled the matter shrewdly and temporized instead of rushing to judgment. In an unexpected development, Lady Asgill pleaded her son's case so eloquently at the court of Versailles that the king had his foreign minister request mercy for Captain Asgill. That November Congress obliged France by passing a resolution that granted clemency to the young British captain. It was a neat solution to a ticklish dilemma: Captain Asgill would be released at the behest of Louis XVI and Marie-Antoinette. Undoubtedly with enormous relief, Washington issued a pass that would take Captain Asgill to New York, thus ending the affair. He had dealt with it the way he would with many controversies during his presidency: by letting them simmer instead of bringing them to a premature boil.

The French partnership, however useful most of the time, was awkward at others, requiring Washington to pay homage to the French monarchy even as Americans fought against King George III. In the spring of 1782, when Louis XVI had a male heir, Washington was duty-bound to celebrate "the auspicious birth of a dauphin" and hope divine providence would "shed its choicest blessings upon the King of France and his royal consorts and favor them with a long, happy, and glorious reign."[14] Having fought for independence, Americans still had no idea what sort of government would emerge in the aftermath of a successful war. Thus far the new nation had no real executive branch, just a few departments; no independent judiciary; and only an ineffectual Congress. For most Americans, the idea of royalty was still anathema. On the other hand, at least a few Americans feared chaos and touted monarchy as a possible way to fill the dangerous vacuum of executive power.

On May 22, 1782, Colonel Lewis Nicola of the Continental Army had the effrontery to suggest to Washington that he reign as America's first monarch. He sent him a seven-page diatribe, citing "the weakness of republics" and the Continental Army's privations at the hands of a feckless Congress, then conjured up a benevolent monarchy with Washington seated splendidly on the throne. "Some people have so connected the ideas of tyranny and monarchy as to find it very difficult to separate them . . . but if all other things are once adjusted, I believe strong arguments might be produced for admitting the title of king."[15]

While he had roundly berated congressional ineptitude, Washington had never entertained the idea of a monarchy and was left to wonder whether Nicola was the instrument of a covert army faction that favored a king. His reply, sent the same day, fairly breathed with horror. What makes the letter so impressive is its finality—this serpent must be killed in the egg: "Be assured, sir, no occurrence in the course of the war has given me more painful sensations than your information of there being such ideas existing in the army as you have expressed and [that] I must view with abhorrence and reprehend with severity."[16] He didn't dare tell a soul about Nicola's letter, he said, lest it contaminate men's minds: "I am much at a loss to conceive what part of my conduct could have given encouragement to an address which to me seems big with the greatest mischiefs that can befall my country. If I am not deceived in the knowledge of myself, you could not have found a person to whom your schemes are more disagreeable . . . Let me conjure you then, if you have any regard for your country, concern for yourself or posterity, or respect for me, to banish these thoughts from your mind."[17] Washington set such store by this momentous letter that, for the only time in the war, he demanded proof from his aides that his response was sealed and posted. Stunned, Nicola stammered out three replies in as many days, offering apologies for broaching the taboo subject.

During the summer of 1782 Washington showed his willingness to accept recognition of a more democratic sort when the newly incorporated Washington College was named in his honor in Chestertown, Maryland. Washington seldom allowed the use of his name, suggesting that he was flattered by this distinction. "I am much indebted for the honor conferred on me by giving my name to the college at Chester," he wrote to the Reverend William Smith, the school's first president, a Scottish

Anglican clergyman. Washington donated fifty guineas to the school—promptly used to purchase optical instruments—and also served on its board.[18] Always regretting his own lack of a college education, Washington had surrounded himself with college-educated men, and his patronage of Washington College was perhaps a final way of wiping away that ancient stigma. In 1789 he received an honorary degree from the school.

At times during this uneventful year, Washington sent halfhearted letters to Rochambeau, proposing operations against New York or Charleston—suggestions that came to naught. Suspecting a British ploy, Washington scoffed at rumors of a negotiated peace in the offing and grew especially vigilant after Admiral Rodney defeated de Grasse in the Caribbean in April, sending London into a delirium of joy. Even when official word came in August from the British command in New York that peace talks had been opened in Paris, Washington still couldn't conquer his ingrained suspicion. "That the King will push the war as long as the nation will find men or money admits not of a doubt in my mind," he said flatly.[19] A thoroughgoing skeptic in foreign policy, Washington denigrated the British as devoid of idealism and driven only by pride and self-interest. Before setting aside arms, he wanted nothing less than "an absolute, unequivocal admission of American independence," he told Thomas Paine.[20] After all these years of war, Washington was still a hot-blooded militant and railed against "the persevering obstinacy of the king, the wickedness of his ministry and the haughty pride" of the British nation.[21] Such moral fervor had sustained him during the prolonged conflict.

Afraid that his army might relax its guard prematurely, he kept drilling troops on the parade ground, demanded that his men look sharp, and barked out a steady stream of instructions: "The commander in chief recommends to the officers to pay particular attention to the carriage of their men either upon parade or marching . . . Nothing contributes so much to the appearance of a soldier, or so plainly indicates discipline, as an erect carriage, firm step, and steady countenance."[22] He indicated his displeasure that soldiers didn't "step boldly and freely, but short and with bent knees."[23] Not only did he want his men to look bright and snappy, but he wanted them housed in style, insisting that "*regularity, convenience,* and even some degree of *elegance* should be attended to in the construction of their huts."[24]

To maintain the fighting spirit of his army, Washington introduced a decoration that came to be known as the "Purple Heart." In cases of "unusual gallantry" or "extraordinary fidelity and essential service," soldiers would receive a purple heart-shaped cloth, to be worn over the left breast.[25] Since it was to be conferred on noncommissioned officers and ordinary soldiers, the decoration supplied further proof of Washington's growing egalitarian spirit during the war. (After a lapse in its use, the Purple Heart was revived by presidential order in 1932, and anyone in the

U.S. Army became eligible for it.) At the time when Washington inaugurated the honor, fighting had largely ceased, and only isolated deaths remained in the war. One of the last victims was his sparkling young aide John Laurens, who had hoped to raise black troops in the South. "Poor Laurens is no more," Washington wrote glumly to Lafayette that October. "He fell in a trifling skirmish in South Carolina, attempting to prevent the enemy from plundering the country of rice."[26]

Washington didn't know that on November 30, 1782, a preliminary peace treaty had been signed in Paris and that the American side had won everything it could have wished, including recognition of independence and broad borders stretching north to the Great Lakes and west to the Mississippi. Washington got a glimmer of the truth in mid-December when the British general Alexander Leslie and his troops sailed from Charleston, South Carolina; a few hours later Nathanael Greene entered the city, bringing the southern war to a close. Washington congratulated Greene "on the glorious end you have put to hostilities in the southern states."[27] Whenever Washington lauded Greene, his praise never contained even a twinge of envy, only unmistakable pride. In marking the conclusion of southern combat, he paid lavish tribute to Greene, stating that "this happy change has been wrought, almost solely, by the personal abilities of Major Gen[era]l Greene."[28] This rosey outcome justified the faith Washington had shown early in the war, when Greene had blundered at Fort Washington and another commander might have lost all confidence in him.

What should have been a joyous moment for Washington turned into a troubled one. The national treasury had again run empty, the states having failed to make their requisite payments. As another icy winter loomed, Washington sensed deep discontent roiling his troops. Suddenly reluctant to leave them alone in Newburgh, he relinquished his cherished hope of returning to Mount Vernon. At first he even declined to ask Martha to make her annual pilgrimage to the camp, although he relented and she arrived in December. "The temper of the army is much soured," he told one congressman in mid-November, "and has become more irritable than at any period since the commencement of the war."[29] Girding himself for disturbances, he vowed to stick close to his men and "try like a careful physician to prevent if possible the disorders getting to an incurable height."[30]

Sitting in his snowbound Newburgh quarters, Washington wouldn't hear about the provisional peace treaty until February. In the meantime, he knew the time "will pass heavily on in this dreary mansion in which we are fast locked by frost and snow."[31] Affected by the frigid weather and isolation of Newburgh, Washington sounded a somber note in his letters. He wrote to General Heath, "Without amusements or avocations, I am spending another winter (I hope it will be the last that I shall be kept from returning to domestic life) among these rugged and dreary mountains."[32]

The army's sullen discontent revolved around the same stale complaints that had beset Washington throughout the war. As he recounted them to Major General John Armstrong, "The army, as usual, are without pay and a great part of the soldiery without shirts. And tho[ugh] the patience of them is equally threadbare, the states seem perfectly indifferent to their cries."[33] The soldiers were so famished that when local vendors peddled produce at their huts, they often plundered these simple country folk. Once again Washington couldn't locate forage for his starving horses, complaining at Christmas that they "have been four days without a handful of hay and three of the same without a mouthful of grain."[34] The upshot of this outrageous situation was that officers canceled business that could be conducted only on horseback and found it impossible to confer with Washington at headquarters.

Dissatisfaction in the ranks was only sharpened by talk of demobilizing the army, which was rattled by the possible outbreak of peace. As long as soldiers remained together, they shared a common sense of purpose; once sent home, they would contrast their own impecunious state with that of the well-fed civilian population. As Washington explained to General Benjamin Lincoln, they were "about to be turned into the world, soured by penury and what they call the ingratitude of the public, involved in debts, without one farthing of money to carry them home."[35] What made the disaffection most disturbing was that it stemmed from the officers, who subsisted on such meager rations that, even when entertaining French officers, they could offer little more than "stinking whiskey" and "a bit of beef without vegetables."[36] Many doubted they would receive years of back pay owed to them or that Congress would redeem its 1780 pledge to provide veterans with half pay for life. Washington wondered darkly what would happen if the officers who had suppressed previous mutinies turned mutinous themselves.

As he dealt with this discontent, Washington again had to deal with his disgruntled mother. Mary Washington had written to apprise him that the overseer at her Little Falls Quarter farm was pocketing all the profits for himself, and this made George no less upset than his mother. As he told brother Jack, he had maintained this place for her with "no earthly inducement to meddle with it, but to comply with her wish and to free her from care," but he hadn't received a penny in return. He protested that it was "too much while I am suffering in every other way (and hardly able to keep my own estate from sale), to be saddled with all the expense of hers and not be able to derive the smallest return from it."[37] This parenthetical statement—that he could hardly keep Mount Vernon safe from sale again—reveals the dreadful toll that his neglected business interests had taken on his personal fortune.

After asking Jack to stop by Little Falls to replace the overseer, Washington mentioned that he had heard nothing further of their mother's petition for a pension from the Virginia assembly. But it turned out that Mary was still up to her old antics and broadcasting her financial grievances to anyone who cared to listen. As Washing-

ton worried anew that she would blacken his reputation, his repressed anger toward
her, long tamped down, spilled out. He told his brother that he had learned "from
very good authority that she is upon all occasions and in all companies complaining
of the hardness of the times, of her wants and distresses; and if not in direct terms,
at least by strong innuendoes, inviting favors which not only makes *her* appear in an
unfavorable point of view, but *those* also who are connected with her."[38] As someone
who jealously guarded his reputation, Washington was crestfallen by Mary's unending torrent of abuse, and he dispatched Jack on a private mission to visit her and
"inquire into her real wants and see what is necessary to make her comfortable."[39]
As always, Washington was ready to pay what she needed, but he demanded that she
halt the character assassination: "I wish you to represent to her in delicate terms the
impropriety of her complaints and acceptance of favors, even where they are voluntarily offered, from any but relations."[40] As always, the headstrong mother and son
were locked in a fierce contest of wills in which both sides refused to yield an inch.

Around this time Washington discovered that his vision had grown slightly
blurry and that it cleared when he borrowed spectacles from his colleagues. He had
become older and wearier during this long war, and the eyestrain caused by reading
his copious correspondence had been enormous. He ordered a pair of handsome
silver-framed reading glasses from David Rittenhouse of Philadelphia, a renowned
astronomer and optical expert. Washington sampled the lenses of various people,
then asked Rittenhouse to duplicate the ones that worked best. By mid-February he
had the new reading glasses in hand but had to keep tilting them at different angles
until his eyes adjusted to the novel experience. "At present, I find some difficulty in
coming at the proper focus," he informed Rittenhouse, "but when I do obtain it,
they magnify properly and show those objects very distinctly which at first appear
like a mist, blended together and confused."[41] Little did Rittenhouse know, as he
fashioned these spectacles, that they would soon serve as a key prop in one of the
most emotionally charged scenes in American history.

IN EARLY JANUARY, amid rumors of mass resignations, a three-man delegation
of officers went to Philadelphia to lay before Congress a petition that catalogued
their pent-up grievances: "We have borne all that men can bear—our property is
expended—our private resources are at an end."[42] This delegation met with two
dynamic young members of Congress: James Madison of Virginia, a member since
1780, and Alexander Hamilton of New York, who had joined Congress a little more
than a month earlier. However alarmed by the prospect of an officer mutiny, Hamilton believed it might represent a handy lever with which to budge a lethargic Congress from inaction, leading to expanded federal powers.

On February 13 Hamilton wrote to Washington in a candid tone that presupposed that a profound understanding still existed between them. He talked of the critical state of American finances and suggested that the officer revolt could be helpful: "The claims of the army, urged with moderation but with firmness, may operate on those weak minds which are influenced by their apprehensions rather than their judgment . . . But the difficulty will be to keep a *complaining* and *suffering* army within the bounds of moderation."[43] In suggesting that Washington exploit the situation to influence Congress, Hamilton toyed with combustible chemicals. He also tried to awaken anxiety in Washington by telling him that officers were whispering that he didn't stand up for their rights with sufficient zeal. "The falsehood of this opinion no one can be better acquainted with than myself," Hamilton emphasized, "but it is not the less mischievous for being false."[44]

On March 4 Washington sent Hamilton a thoughtful response and disclosed grave premonitions about the crisis. "It has been the subject of many contemplative hours," he told Hamilton. "The sufferings of a complaining army, on one hand, and the inability of Congress and tardiness of the states on the other, are the forebodings of evil."[45] He voiced concern at America's financial plight and told of his periodic frustration at being excluded from congressional decisions. If Congress didn't receive enlarged powers, he maintained, revolutionary blood would have been spilled in vain. After spelling out areas of agreement with Hamilton, however, Washington said he refused to deviate from the "steady line of conduct" he had pursued and insisted that the "sensible and discerning" officers would listen to reason. He also asserted that any attempt to exploit officer discontent might only "excite jealousy and bring on its concomitants."[46] It was a noble letter: Washington refused to pander to any political agenda, even one he agreed with, and he would never encroach upon the civilian prerogatives of Congress. In a later letter Washington was even blunter with Hamilton, warning him that soldiers weren't "mere puppets" and that the army was "a dangerous instrument to play with."[47]

The officers continued to believe that Philadelphia politicians remained deaf to their pleas, and Washington had no inkling that they would soon resort to more muscular measures. In his general orders for March 10, he dwelt on a mundane topic, the need for uniform haircuts among the troops. Then he learned of an anonymous paper percolating through the camp, summoning officers to a mass meeting the next day to air their grievances—a brazen affront to Washington's authority and, to his mind, little short of outright mutiny. Then a second paper made the rounds, further stoking a sense of injustice. Its anonymous author was, in all likelihood, John Armstrong, Jr., an aide-de-camp to Horatio Gates, who mocked the peaceful petitions drawn up by the officers and warned that, come peace, they might "grow old in poverty, wretchedness, and contempt."[48] Before being stripped of their weapons by an armistice, they should now take direct action: "Change the milk and water style of your last memorial—assume a bolder tone . . . And suspect the man who would advise to more moderation and longer forbearance."[49] The man of moderation was, of course, George Washington. When handed a copy of this manifesto, he conceded its literary power, later saying that "in point of composition, in elegance and force of expression" it had "rarely been equaled in the English language."[50] That only made it the more threatening, for it aroused the prospect of a military putsch.

Washington banned the outlaw meeting. In announcing the measure, he subtly tried to shame the officers by saying that their good sense would lead them to "pay very little attention to such an irregular invitation."[51] Instead of negating their grievances, he tried to champion and divert them into orderly channels and called his own meeting at noon on March 15. Suspicious of how quickly events had moved, Washington voiced his fears to Hamilton the next day. A nameless gentleman— Colonel Walter Stewart—had come to the Newburgh camp, he said, and told the officers that public creditors would support their mutiny as a way to guarantee repayment of their loans. Stewart further suggested that certain congressmen supported the mutiny as a way of prodding delinquent states into paying promised taxes to the central government. There is no overt sense in this letter of Washington accusing Hamilton of orchestrating the plot from Philadelphia. Rather, he exhorted him to take timely action to redress the officers' complaints, contending that many were so short of funds that they might be clapped into debtors' prisons upon release from the army. The failure to take appropriate measures, Washington forewarned, would plunge the country "into a gulf of civil horror from which there might be no receding."[52]

In calling his meeting, Washington waited a few days to allow cooler heads to prevail. For its venue, he chose the same place as that proposed for the subversive gathering, a new building nicknamed the Temple of Virtue, a cavernous wooden structure completed a month earlier for Sunday services, dances, and Masonic meetings. Although this meeting proceeded under Washington's auspices, he was not expected to attend, heightening the dramatic effect when he slipped through a side door into the packed hall. It was one of the infrequent occasions when his self-control crumbled and an observer described him as "sensibly agitated."[53]

It was the first and only time Washington ever confronted a hostile assembly of his own officers. Mounting the podium, he drew out his prepared remarks, written on nine long sheets covered with exclamation points and dashes for pauses, revealing the strong sense of cadence he gave to his speeches. He began by chastising the officers for improper conduct in calling an irregular meeting and disputed that Congress was indifferent to their plight, stressing the need for making dispassionate decisions. Then, with considerable agility, he cast aside the stern tone and stressed his personal bond with his fellow officers, speaking as a man as well as a general and building rhetorical force through repetition:

> If my conduct heretofore has not evinced to you that I have been a faithful friend to the army, my declaration of it at this time w[oul]d be equally unavailing and improper. But as I was among the first who embarked in the cause of our common country. As I have never left your side one moment, but when called from you on public duty. As I have been the constant companion and witness of your distresses and not among the last to feel and acknowledge your merits . . . it can *scarcely be supposed* at this late stage of the war that I am indifferent to [your] interests.[54]

Instead of elevating himself above his men, Washington portrayed himself as their friend and peer.

Having softened them up with personal history, he delivered an impassioned appeal to their deep-seated patriotism. The idea floated by the anonymous pamphleteer that they should take up arms against their country "has something so shocking in it that humanity revolts at the idea. My God! What can this writer have in view by recommending such measures? Can he be a friend to the army? Can he be a friend to this country? Rather, is he not an insidious foe? Some emissary, perhaps, from New York, plotting the ruin of both by sowing the seeds of discord and separation between the civil and military powers of the continent?"[55]

He pleaded with them to oppose any man "who wickedly attempts to open the floodgates of civil discord and deluge our rising empire in blood."[56] Give Congress a chance to address your grievances, he implored the officers, saying he would do everything in his power to help them. Then, in ringing tones, he said that if they trusted Congress to take action, "you will, by the dignity of your conduct, afford occasion for posterity to say, when speaking of the glorious example you have exhibited to mankind, 'Had this day been wanting, the world had never seen the last stage of perfection to which human nature is capable of attaining.'"[57]

It was an exemplary performance from a man uncomfortable with public speaking. He had castigated his officers but also lifted them to a higher plane, reawakening a sense of their exalted role in the Revolution and reminding them that illegal action would tarnish that grand legacy. For all his eloquence, Washington achieved his greatest impact with a small symbolic gesture. To reassure the men of congressional good faith, he read aloud a letter from Congressman Joseph Jones of Virginia and tripped over the first few sentences because he couldn't discern the words. Then he pulled out his new spectacles, shocking his fellow officers: they had never seen him wearing glasses. "Gentlemen, you must pardon me," he said. "I have grown gray in your service and now find myself growing blind."[58] These poignant words exerted a powerful influence. Washington at fifty-one was much older and more haggard than the young planter who had taken charge of the Continental Army in 1775. The disarming gesture of putting on the glasses moved the officers to tears as they recalled the legendary sacrifices he had made for his country. When he left the hall moments later, the threatened mutiny had ended, and his victory was complete. The officers approved a unanimous resolution stating they "reciprocated [Washington's] affectionate expressions with the greatest sincerity of which the human heart is capable."[59] Luckily, Congress delivered on Washington's promise and, instead of half pay for life, granted the officers payment equal to five years of full pay. The threat of a military takeover had been averted by Washington's succinct but brilliant, well-timed oratory.

Making good on his pledges, Washington wrote impassioned letters to Congress on behalf of the officers' finances. In one to Joseph Jones, he said that Congress shouldn't rely on him again to "dispel other clouds, if any should arise, from the causes of the last."[60] Perhaps he sensed that a deity couldn't step down from the clouds more than once without dispelling his mystique. He had tamed his mutinous officers and established congressional supremacy in the nick of time. A few days later he received word that a preliminary peace treaty had been signed in Paris. In mid-April Congress ratified the treaty, leading to a formal cessation of hostilities eight years after the first shots rang out in Lexington and Concord.

The man who had pulled off the exemplary feat of humbling the most powerful military on earth had not been corrupted by fame. Though quietly elated and relieved, he was neither intoxicated by power nor puffed up with a sense of his own genius. On April 15 a Jamaican visitor dined with Washington at his Newburgh headquarters and was amazed at the simplicity of the scene: "The dinner was good, but everything was quite plain. We all sat on camp stools ... Mrs. W[ashington] was as plain, easy, and affable as [the general] was and one would have thought from the familiarity which prevailed here that he saw a respectable private gentleman dining at the head of his own family."[61] Washington shunned the conqueror's bravado. "In his dress he was perfectly plain—an old blue coat faced with buff, waistcoat and britches ... seemingly of the same age and without any lace upon them composed his dress," the visitor wrote. "His shirt had no ruffles at the wrists, but [was] of very fine linen ... His hair is a little gray and combed smoothly back from the forehead and in a small queue—no curls and but very little powder to it. Such is the man, but his character I cannot presume to describe—it is held in the highest veneration over the whole continent."[62]

CHAPTER THIRTY-SIX

Closing the Drama with Applause

BY THE SPRING OF 1783 George Washington had visibly aged, as evidenced by his gray hair and failing eyesight. "He was fine-looking until three years ago," an aide to Rochambeau had reported a year earlier, adding that "those who have been constantly with him since that time say that he seems to have grown old fast."[1] It could only have saddened a man of his athletic vitality to feel his powers begin to ebb. One great blow to Washington's sense of well-being was the steady deterioration of his teeth. While in the eyes of posterity his dental problems rank among his best-known attributes, he did everything he could to screen the trouble from contemporaries. An air of extreme secrecy shrouded his dealings with dentists, as if he were dabbling in a dark, shameful art. Perhaps he sensed that nothing could subvert his heroic image more unalterably than derisory sniggers about his teeth.

As early as the French and Indian War, Washington had had a tooth pulled, and thereafter his papers are replete with allusions to dental tribulations. From one London apothecary, he ordered "sponge" toothbrushes and bottles of tincture designed to soothe toothaches. A typical complaint in his diaries reads: "indisposed with an aching tooth and swelled and inflamed gums."[2] By 1773 he found it agonizing to chew meals. His customary solution was to pull troublesome teeth, and, while sitting in the House of Burgesses, he kept busy a Williamsburg dentist, Dr. John Baker. When he painted Washington in 1779, the observant Charles Willson Peale spotted an indentation just below Washington's left cheekbone, the by-product of an abscessed tooth.

By 1781 Washington had partial dentures made with a bone and ivory framework, secured to natural teeth and held together by a primitive mesh of wires. Before marching south to Yorktown, he wrote with some urgency to Dr. Baker, asking for "a pair of pincers to fasten the wire of my teeth" and also "one of your scrapers, as my teeth stand in need of cleaning."[3] At this point Washington had a small arsenal of devices to keep his aching mouth in working order. In a secret, locked drawer of his desk at Mount Vernon, he preserved a pair of pulled teeth and not long before the Newburgh mutiny asked Lund to wrap them up carefully and send them along. His objective was to have Dr. Baker insert them into a partial bridge; the dentist was to send him plaster of paris or some other powder to create a model of his mouth. When this letter was intercepted by the British, it occasioned some sadistic merriment while leaving poor Washington in considerable distress. The episode could only have strengthened his self-consciousness about his dental problems.

As it turned out, deliverance lay at hand in the person of an eminent French dentist, Dr. Jean-Pierre Le Mayeur, who had worked in occupied New York, treating Sir Henry Clinton and other British generals. One day a British officer made a cutting remark about the French alliance with America, and the dentist rushed indignantly to his country's defense, ending the honeymoon with the British. Having established his patriotic credentials, Dr. Le Mayeur passed over to the American side, where his reputation preceded him. Washington was eager to consult the Frenchman, "of whose skill much has been said," but he wanted the matter treated with utmost discretion, telling his intermediary categorically that "I would not wish that this matter should be made a parade of."[4] Thorough in all things, Washington demanded "a private investigation of this man's character and knowledge of his profession" before he opened up his mouth to his ministrations.[5]

In June 1783, when Washington consulted the urbane Le Mayeur in confidence at Newburgh, he handled their relationship as furtively as if he were meeting a master spy. (He seemed mystified by the spelling of the Frenchman's name, calling him La Moyuer at one point, as if he dared not check the spelling with a potentially indiscreet third party.) Evidently, the dentist agreed to craft a pair of partial dentures. Washington responded with an elliptical letter that resorted to euphemisms, never mentioning such explosive words as *dental* or *dentures* in case unfriendly eyes stumbled upon it. "The valise arrived safe, as did the three articles which accompanied your card," Washington wrote cryptically. ". . . The small matters [his teeth?] which were expected from Virginia are not yet received, and it is to be feared will never be found."[6]

Always a tough, leery customer, Washington was skeptical about claims made for transplanted teeth. The following year, when Le Mayeur performed a successful transplant upon Richard Varick, it made a convert of Washington. According to Mary Thompson, Washington bought nine teeth in 1784 from certain nameless "Negroes" for thirteen shillings apiece.[7] Whether he wanted the teeth implanted directly in his mouth or incorporated into dentures, we cannot say. However ghoulish this trade sounds to modern readers, it was then standard practice for rich people to purchase teeth from the poor. In his advertisements, Dr. Le Mayeur offered to buy teeth from willing vendors and bid "three guineas for good front teeth from anyone but slaves."[8] This suggests a stigma among white people about having slaves' teeth. We can deduce that Washington's dental transplant miscarried, since by the time of his presidential inauguration in 1789, he had only a single working tooth remaining.

ON APRIL 18, 1783, Washington announced the cessation of hostilities between America and Great Britain and seemed to pinch himself with wonder as he evoked "the almost infinite variety of scenes thro[ugh] which we have passed with a mixture of pleasure, astonishment, and gratitude."[9] The normally prudent Washington, throwing caution to the winds, rhapsodized about America's future, saying of the patriotic soldiers who had wrested freedom from Great Britain that "happy, thrice happy shall they be pronounced hereafter . . . in erecting this stupendous *fabric of freedom and empire* on the broad basis of independence . . . and establishing an asylum for the poor and oppressed of all nations and religions."[10] As always when casting events in grandiose historical terms, he fell back on a theatrical metaphor: "Nothing now remains but for the actors of this mighty scene to preserve a perfect, unvarying consistency of character through the very last act" and then "close the drama with applause."[11] Washington ordered his quartermaster general to gather up discharges so he could begin sending soldiers home. In a wonderful tribute to his men, he personally signed thousands of these documents. His hand surely ached from this gesture, which spoke volumes about the affection and empathy he had developed for them.

Unwilling to abandon his command until the final peace treaty was signed and the British had evacuated New York, Washington still had no firm plans to return to Virginia. He had to cope with nettlesome racial issues, as the armistice reopened questions about the status of former slaves. When a slaveholder named Jonathan Hobby tried to recapture a runaway slave serving in the Third Massachusetts Regiment, Washington shunted the matter to a board of inquiry, which ruled that the soldier in question hadn't yet served out his term. Refusing to release the black soldier, Washington dodged the deeper issue of whether a slave master could reclaim a fugitive slave in the Continental Army. Hardly an abolitionist, Washington fielded messages from incensed southern slaveholders inquiring about the fate of slaves who had dashed to freedom behind British lines. Washington seemed caught off guard. "Although I have several servants in like predicament with yours," he told one Virginia slaveholder, "I have not yet made any attempt for their recovery."[12]

During the war, encouraged by the idealistic camaraderie of Laurens, Hamilton, and Lafayette, Washington may have entertained occasional thoughts of abolishing slavery. Now the war's imminent end turned the question of runaway slaves into an urgent practical matter. Deeply ambivalent, he straddled both sides of the issue. That April, when Governor Benjamin Harrison of Virginia sent him a list of his slaves who had defected to the British side, Washington forwarded it to a Daniel Parker, who was deputized to recapture them. Washington feigned a cavalier indifference toward the fate of his own slaves who had found refuge aboard the *Savage*. "I scarce ever bestowed a thought on them," he assured Harrison. "They have so many doors through which they can escape from New York that scarce anything but an inclination to return or voluntarily surrender of themselves will restore many to their former masters."[13] Did Washington, after eight years of fighting for freedom, feel vaguely guilty about reclaiming fugitive slaves? Did that clash with the way he had presented himself as a potential abolitionist in wartime discussions with his devoted young aides? When he contacted Parker in late April, Washington expressed skepticism that his own fugitive slaves would be found, while leaving no doubt he yearned for their recapture: "If by chance you should come at the knowledge of any of them, I will be much obliged by your securing them, so that I may obtain them again."[14]

By now Washington had opened a civilized correspondence with Sir Guy Carleton about enforcing the peace treaty. No vengeance was apparent in Washington's letters, only a humane spirit of wishing to retire any residual bitterness. This goodwill was soon threatened by the fate of three thousand escaped slaves in New York, many eking out a desperate existence as they squatted in camps of makeshift huts roofed with sailcloth. The city swarmed with slave catchers hired by southern masters to nab runaway slaves before they left aboard British ships. Even though one article of the peace treaty stipulated that Americans would be allowed to reclaim their slaves, Carleton balked at relinquishing these black refugees, claiming they had won their freedom when they reached British lines. To buttress this ruling, he issued three thousand certificates to protect the former slaves, making it a crime for anyone to abduct them.

Under mounting pressure from southern slave masters, Washington arranged a meeting with Carleton in early May at his own temporary headquarters on the Hudson River at Tappan, New York. Although they also discussed prisoner exchanges and evacuating British posts, slavery formed the crux of the meeting. Washington conducted himself with impeccable ceremony, greeting Carleton's frigate *Perseverance* by the river, then proceeding with him by carriage up to a quaint little gabled house with beamed ceilings. Though suffering from a slight fever, Carleton sat tall and ramrod-straight, a man of inflexible integrity. In their talks, Washington's demeanor was gravely cordial, and one of Carleton's aides said that he "delivered himself without animation, with great slowness, and a low tone of voice."[15]

Refusing to shrink from his unpleasant task, Washington said he intended to take possession "of all negroes and other property of the inhabitants of these states" being held by the British.[16] When Carleton retorted that he had just evacuated six thousand people from New York to Nova Scotia, many of them black, Washington bridled at this apparent violation of the treaty. "Already embarked!" he exclaimed.[17] One internal British memo portrayed Washington as demanding the slaves' return "with all the grossness and ferocity of a captain of banditti."[18] Although Washington didn't know it at the time, four of his slaves were among those being protected by the British. A former slave named Henry Washington had escaped from Mount Vernon in 1776 and would ultimately wind up in Sierra Leone, where he would apply agricultural techniques learned from George Washington. Of the seventeen slaves who found refuge on the *Savage* in 1781, Washington regained two of the women at Yorktown and at least six of the men in Philadelphia.

Seizing the moral high ground, the honorable Carleton insisted that the British would not renege on wartime promises to free slaves who had joined their ranks and stated with memorable certitude that "the national honor . . . must be kept with all colors."[19] Returning the former slaves "would be delivering them up, some possibly to execution and others to severe punishment, which in his opinion would be a dishonorable violation of the public faith pledged to the Negroes in the proclamations."[20]

Although they didn't say so openly, the British feared that some ex-slaves would commit suicide rather than return to bondage. Trepidation was rampant in the community of ex-slaves at the thought of returning to their masters. "This dreadful rumor filled us all with inexpressible anguish and terror," said a young black carpenter named Boston King, "especially when we saw our old masters coming from Virginia, North Carolina, and other parts and seizing upon their slaves in the streets of New York or even dragging them out of their beds."[21] Carleton claimed that the British had pledged not to *carry off* slaves but never promised to *restore* them to owners. He left open the possibility of compensating the owners of slaves who had fled after hostilities ended and claimed to be keeping a register of former slaves for this purpose. Washington insisted that slaves would give false names and make detection impossible. Both sides agreed to name commissioners to arbitrate the issue and check passengers boarding ships in New York, although Washington doubted that former slaves would ever be reclaimed. Whatever his displeasure, he conducted himself like a gentleman. "Washington pulled out his watch, and, observing that it was near dinner time, offered wine and bitters," recalled Carleton's aide. "We all walked out and soon after were called to [a] plentiful repast under a tent."[22] In the aftermath of the meeting, the British refused to water down Carleton's noble stand, and King George III indicated "his royal approbation" in "the fullest and most ample manner."[23] Before long the American commissioners in New York City found that they could only watch former slaves boarding ships and lacked any power to detain them.

AS WASHINGTON CONTEMPLATED the postwar world and wondered how to make America happy, free, and powerful, he was uniquely well positioned to affect the outcome. Adams, Jay, and Franklin were off on diplomatic assignment in Europe, while Hamilton and Madison were too junior to assume leadership roles. Washington had eliminated or outlived his military rivals, leaving his stature unequaled. Since the Continental Army had suffered most from the defective Articles of Confederation, Washington was a natural proponent of national unity and worried about anarchy and bloodshed erupting in the war's aftermath. He saw that the states, to protect themselves against European interference, needed to band together in a more effective union and that Congress required an independent revenue source to service wartime debt.

The prospect of peace posed exceptional challenges for Washington. Throughout the war, he had scrupulously respected congressional supremacy and restricted expressing his political opinions to private correspondence. By serving as a blank slate onto which Americans could project their values, he had been able to unify the country and enhance his own power. Now, as he returned to the status of a private citizen, those inhibitions were lifted, and he did not know how far to go in articulating his views openly. His instincts were the antithesis of a demagogue's: he feared his own influence and agonized over exerting too much power. On March 31 he broached this dilemma to Hamilton, noting that his private letters "teemed" with opinions about political reforms, "but how far any further essay by me might be productive of the wished for end, or appear to arrogate more than belongs to me, depends so much upon popular opinion and the temper and disposition of [the] people that it is not easy to decide."[24] A major unresolved issue was whether he should cast off the burdens of public life and return to private citizenship. Writing to Lafayette, he sounded as if he meant to retire permanently to Mount Vernon. Echoing *Hamlet,* he stated that henceforth "my mind shall be unbent and I will endeavor to glide down the stream of life 'till I come to that abyss from whence no traveler is permitted to return."[25]

In early June the sphinx issued a lengthy valedictory statement about the problems facing the newborn country. In this "Circular to State Governments," Washington emerged emphatically from behind his pose of military neutrality and advised the citizenry in an almost fatherly tone. This enduring document, also known as "Washington's Legacy," codified his views no less memorably than his later farewell address. Reprinted in newspapers and later excerpted in countless school textbooks, it gained a wide readership. So that the circular wouldn't smack of political ambition, Washington started out by reassuring readers that he was about to retire from public life and "pass the remainder of life in a state of undisturbed repose."[26] This pledge gave him license to publish his views: by denying any political ambition, he could dispel charges of self-interest. Striking an oracular note, he envisioned a vibrant future for America: "The citizens of America, placed in the most enviable condition, as the sole lords and proprietors of a vast tract of continent, comprehending all the various soils and climates of the world and abounding with all the necessaries and conveniences of life, are now . . . acknowledged to be possessed of absolute freedom and independency." Heaven had vouchsafed to Americans "a fairer opportunity for political happiness than any other nation has ever been favored with."[27] Locating events in the wider sweep of history, he saw the American Revolution as favored by the Age of Enlightenment: "The foundation of our empire was not laid in the gloomy age of ignorance and superstition, but at an epocha when the rights of mankind were better understood and more clearly defined than at any former period."[28]

It would have been easy for Washington to dwell on wartime accomplishments and bask in the sweet glow of victory. Instead, he pushed the agenda to the challenges ahead, offering alternate visions of glory and ruin. Americans had to choose whether they would be "respectable and prosperous or contemptible and miserable as a nation."[29] Worried that a weak confederacy would tempt European powers to play off one state against another, he called for "an indissoluble union of the states under one federal head."[30] The war had scrubbed quixotic notions from his mind. At a time when many Americans, influenced by Whig ideology, equated centralized power with tyranny, Washington argued that only a supreme central power could safeguard liberty. However tempting it might be to repudiate the enormous government debt, he asserted the need to "render complete justice to all the public creditors."[31] Instead of recommending a professional army for the country, as he might have wished, Washington, making a concession to the bête noire of a "standing army," opted for a halfway measure: uniform standards for state militias.

In closing, Washington referred to the character of Jesus, "the Divine author of our blessed religion."[32] It was a fitting ending: despite his paean to the Enlightenment, the entire circular had the pastoral tone of a spiritual father advising his flock rather than a bluff, manly soldier making a dignified farewell. The ending rose to the fervor of a benediction: "I now make it my earnest prayer that God would have you, and the state over which you preside, in his holy protection; that he would incline the hearts of the citizens to cultivate a spirit of subordination and obedience to government; to entertain a brotherly affection and love for one another, for their fellow citizens of the United States at large, and particularly for their brethren who have served in the field."[33]

With the war drawing to a close, Henry Knox spearheaded the formation of a fraternal order of army officers called the Society of the Cincinnati. Its aims seemed laudable enough: to succor the families of needy officers, to preserve the union and liberties for which they had fought, and to maintain a social network among the officers. Its very name paid homage to George Washington: Lucius Quinctius Cincinnatus was a Roman consul who had rescued Rome in war, then relinquished power. Little dreaming how controversial the organization would become, Washington agreed to serve as president and was duly elected on June 19, 1783. Something of an honorary president, he was fuzzy about his actual duties and asked Knox that September to tell him "in *precise terms* what is expected from the President of the Cincinnati previous to the general meeting in May next. As I never was present at any of your meetings and have never seen the proceedings of the last, I may, for want of information . . . neglect some essential duty."[34] What Washington didn't foresee was that the hereditary character of the society—eldest sons could inherit the memberships of deceased fathers—would engender fears that the society was fomenting an embryonic American aristocracy.

Perhaps nothing signaled the war's end so dramatically as the sudden resumption of correspondence between Washington and his friend George William Fairfax, Sally's husband, who had repeatedly sent Washington letters during the war only to have them confiscated by the British government. One letter that made it through in early July 1783 told how influential figures in England, who had once shunned Fairfax as pro-American, now pestered him for letters of introduction to the American general. On July 10 Washington sent an affectionate reply, calling upon the Fairfaxes to return to Virginia and become his neighbors once again: "Your house at Belvoir, I am sorry to add, is no more, but mine (which is enlarged since you saw it) is most sincerely and heartily at your service till you could rebuild it."[35] It says much about Washington's nostalgia for prewar life at Mount Vernon that he wished to re-create the status quo ante in this fashion. He reported to Fairfax that Martha had been in poor health, suffering from chronic liver and abdominal problems. All in all, it was clear that any romance between George Washington and Sally Fairfax had receded into ancient history and that he thought it safe to summon back that ghost from his past.

In the interlude before the signing of the final peace treaty, Washington toted up his expenses from eight years in the army. The deal he had struck with Congress back in 1775 stipulated that he would forgo a salary but would be compensated for food, travel, entertaining, equipment, and other incidental expenses. Congress still owed him money, starting with the uniform he had purchased for his original journey to Cambridge back in 1775. At first he wavered about including Martha's annual travel expenses to the American camp, then decided to list them, since he would otherwise have incurred the expense of round trips to Mount Vernon himself. In his final tally, Washington submitted a bill for 8,422 pounds for household expenses and another 1,982 pounds paid out of pocket for "secret intelligence."[36] Since Congress trusted Washington wholeheartedly, he received every penny he listed. He had kept scrupulous records of his spending, recorded in account books in his own handwriting, and was baffled when the total fell far short of his expectations. "Through hurry, I suppose, and the perplexity of business (for I know not how else to account for the deficiency)," he had "omitted to charge" many items.[37]

Another major project consuming Washington's time was the preservation of his wartime papers. Early in the war he had had aides cart his personal annals from campsite to campsite, conserving them like sacred relics. Even before the war ended, he had received queries from historians who wished to examine this archive, and he hoped it would someday preserve his future fame. That June, to transport his papers safely to Mount Vernon, he ordered six strong trunks, covered with hide and "well clasped and with good locks," each one bearing a brass or copper plate with his name and the year on it. In August Richard Varick delivered to Washington the twenty-eight volumes of correspondence that his team had transcribed over two years. "I am fully convinced," Washington told Varick, "that neither the present age or posterity will consider the time and labor which have been employed in accomplishing it unprofitably spent."[38] Afraid of sending the bundled papers by sea, Washington took inordinate pains to organize a wagon train laden with this precious cargo, which he sent to Virginia accompanied by a full military escort. Those transported papers, he knew, would prove the final bulwark of his historical reputation.

In the summer of 1783, as he awaited news of the definitive peace treaty, Washington found himself trapped in a strange limbo. About two-thirds of his army had been sent home, enabling him to indulge thoughts of relaxation for the first time in eight years. Having always wanted to visit upstate New York, he now seized the chance. Traveling by horseback and canoe, he covered 750 miles in a little more than two weeks, showing he was still a hardy specimen. It was a measure of Washington's self-assurance that he wanted to visit the Saratoga battlefield, the scene of Horatio Gates's signal triumph. Reverting to prewar form, Washington even engaged in some land speculation along the Mohawk River. Back at camp, Washington and his officers had so much extra time on their hands that they took turns stepping on a scale and recording their weight. For all the austerity of war, they weren't a terribly lean bunch: Washington weighed 209 pounds, Henry Knox a robust 280 pounds, and eight of eleven officers tipped the scale at more than 200 pounds.

In late August Congress summoned Washington to its temporary home in Princeton, New Jersey. The legislature had temporarily been banished there after mutinous troops from Lancaster, Pennsylvania, brandishing weapons, had stormed into Philadelphia and demanded back pay. Washington briefly postponed the trip to Princeton because Martha was "exceedingly unwell" and he didn't wish to leave her behind.[39] When they finally made the journey, they resided at a farmhouse in Rocky Hill, a few miles outside Princeton, where Washington planned to stay until the definitive peace treaty arrived.

This restful time for Washington peeled away layers of tension built up during the stressful war years. One day he threw a dinner for Congress in a grand trophy of the war, a capacious tent captured from the British, and his guests delighted in his newfound calm. "The general's front is uncommonly open and pleasant," said David Howell of Rhode Island. "The contracted, pensive phiz [face], betokening deep thought and much care . . . is done away, and a pleasant smile and sparkling vivacity of wit and humor succeeds."[40] This dinner afforded rare vignettes of Washington succumbing to a merry mood. When the president of Congress regretted that Robert Morris had his hands full, Washington retorted, "I wish he had his pockets full."[41]

Congress needed to discuss with Washington military arrangements for the postwar period. Doubtless with Yorktown in mind, when only the French possessed the requisite skills for a siege, he endorsed the creation of a military academy to train engineers as well as artillery officers. Following up on his "Circular to State Governments," he outlined plans for a "national militia" made up of individual state units guided by consistent national standards. And worried that the United States would be vulnerable if it disarmed too quickly, he favored a peacetime army of 2,631 men. Most of all, he approved the creation of a navy that could repel European intruders. Washington also sounded out Henry Knox on whether Knox might take the post of secretary at war, showing that, despite his professions of retreating from public life, Washington was still prepared to intervene directly in the country's future affairs.

During his stay at Rocky Hill, Washington learned that Thomas Paine was in the neighborhood and invited him for a chat with a gracious note. Paine was a difficult man, even something of a malcontent, and although Congress had offered him a job as official historian of the American Revolution, he preferred to chide it for "continued neglect" of his services.[42] Congress decided that individual states should reward him instead, and Washington agreed to lobby friends in the Virginia legislature on his behalf. "That his *Common Sense* and many of his *Crisis* [essays] were well timed and had a happy effect upon the public mind, none, I believe . . . will deny," Washington wrote. "Does not common justice then point to some compensation?"[43] Although Paine eventually received a large honorarium from Congress and ample property from New York, he continued to nurse grievances about his treatment and would later lash out at his erstwhile hero.

Cincinnatus

THE PEACE NEGOTIATIONS IN PARIS were hampered by an array of baffling issues, not the least of which was the contentious question of fishing rights off the Newfoundland coast. As John Adams recalled wearily, the sessions droned on in "a constant scuffle morning, noon, and night about cod and haddock on the Grand Bank, deerskins on the Ohio, and pine trees at Penobscot, and what were worse than all the [Loyalist] refugees."[1] Although the final treaty was signed on September 3, 1783, the news was delayed for two months by transatlantic travel, and Washington didn't find out indisputably that the war had ceased until November 1. To his horror, Congress promptly adjourned without making adequate provision for the peacetime army or overdue pay for his long-suffering men.

A virtuoso of farewell messages, Washington disseminated from Rocky Hill his "Farewell Address to the Armies of the United States." It was his fondest wish that the same process that had welded men from various states into the Continental Army would now form a model for the country: "Who that was not a witness could imagine that the most violent local prejudices would cease so soon and that men who came from the different parts of the continent . . . would instantly become but one patriotic band of brothers."[2] In this affectionate valedictory, Washington reminisced about the high drama and dreamlike events of the war, telling his men that what they had experienced together "was little short of a standing miracle" and that such events had "seldom if ever before taken place on the stage of human action, nor can they probably ever happen again."[3]

After forwarding his baggage to Mount Vernon, Washington rejoined his remaining troops on the Hudson one last time. Martha Washington, who had a special capacity to enter into whatever captivated her husband, had grown to love the men as much as he did. By the end of the war, the woman who in 1775 had shuddered in fright at cannon blasts was enchanted by the sight of well-drilled units and thrilled to the lilt of fifes and drums. One postwar visitor to Mount Vernon, a young Scot named Robert Hunter, heard an earful from Martha Washington about the Continental Army's crisp efficiency: "It's astonishing with what raptures Mrs. Washington spoke about the discipline of the army, the excellent order they were in, superior to any troops, she said, upon the face of the earth towards the close of the war."[4] She never forgot the "heavenly sight" of the troops in those closing weeks. "Almost every soldier shed tears at parting with the general, when the army was disbanded," she told Hunter, calling it "a most melancholy sight."[5]

That fall the mood in the camp was hardly all sweetness and light, as Washington had to contend with residual bitterness among his officers. When Robert Morris couldn't muster one month's pay for departing officers, they grew surly again. Washington made a pitch to Morris for more money, even though federal coffers were depleted. Morris promised to do what he could while admitting that "the goodwill is all which I have in my power . . . I am constantly involved in scenes of distress . . . and there is not any money in the treasury."[6] So furious were the officers over the absence of promised pay that they canceled a climactic dinner intended as a parting tribute to their commander in chief. Washington ended the war still smarting under the humiliation that he had had to beg for money for his men.

Although Washington was geared up to enter New York City in triumph the moment the British departed, they kept postponing the promised day. On November 20, having moved down the Hudson River to the Harlem River, just north of the city, he waited in the wings amid mounting suspense. To ensure the safety of American spies in the city, Washington sent Benjamin Tallmadge on ahead to protect them against any reprisals as their identities became known. He received reports of "universal consternation" among departing Tories in New York, who were frantic to get aboard ships before the remnants of the Continental Army marched into town. Washington described these distraught refugees as "little better than a medley of confused, enraged, and dejected people. Some are swearing, and some crying, while the greater part of them are almost speechless."[7]

On the cold morning of November 25, 1783, Washington and a small contingent of eight hundred men tarried at a barrier north of the city, awaiting word of the British departure. The day was so overcast and blustery that British ships in the harbor kept deferring their sailing. In one last vindictive gesture, the British greased the flagpole at Fort George in lower Manhattan, causing a delay before the American flag could be hoisted in its place. Then the cannon sounded thirteen times, signaling that Washington, astride his fine gray horse, could lead the cavalcade down the

Boston Post Road into the city. Always sensitive to political symbolism, he rode beside Governor George Clinton of New York to show his deference to civilian authority and was also accompanied by the Westchester Light Dragoons, a surefire local crowd-pleaser. It was a boisterously elated procession of citizens and soldiers that trooped into the liberated city, marching eight abreast, along streets lined with wildly cheering citizens.

For one woman in the crowd, the contrast between the splendidly uniformed British troops who had just left and the unkempt American troops in homespun dress who now straggled in conveyed a telling message:

> We had been accustomed for a long time to military display in all the finish and finery of garrison life; the troops just leaving us were as if equipped for show, and, with their scarlet uniforms and burnished arms, made a brilliant display. The troops that marched in, on the contrary, were ill-clad and weatherbeaten and made a forlorn appearance. But then they were *our* troops, and as I looked at them and thought upon all they had done and suffered for us, my heart and my eyes were full and I admired and gloried in them the more, because they were weatherbeaten and forlorn.[8]

For seven years, the British had flattered themselves that only they could maintain order in this raucous city. In a self-congratulatory spirit, they had insisted that anarchy would descend without them. But when one British officer returned briefly from his ship to retrieve some forgotten personal items, he was struck dumb by the law-abiding crowds. "This is a strange scene indeed!" he commented. "Here, in this city, we have had an army for more than seven years, and yet could not keep the peace of it . . . Now [that] we are gone, everything is in quietness and safety. The Americans are a curious, original people. They know how to govern themselves, but nobody else can govern them."[9]

Casting his eyes beyond the jubilant onlookers, Washington could discern a desolate city of empty lots, burned-out buildings, and churches despoiled of pews to house British troops. Animals roamed the streets freely. The British surrendered only five hundred American prisoners at the end, which attested both to the large number already freed in exchanges and the appalling number who died in captivity. Most had been kept aboard British prison ships anchored in the East River, where they languished in infernal conditions. Stuffed in airless spaces belowdecks, they had been wedged together in vermin-infested holds slick with human excrement and forced to eat worm-infested rations or devour their own body lice. Typhus, dysentery, and scurvy were common scourges. For years afterward the bones of dead prisoners washed up on East River shores. The American Revolution was never a bloodless affair, as is sometimes imagined. Of 200,000 Americans who served in the war, about 25,000 died, or approximately 1 percent of the population, making it the bloodiest American war except for the Civil War.

During eight hectic days in New York, Washington's calendar was crowded with dinners, receptions, and fireworks galore. Suddenly an avid consumer again, he went shopping for teapots, coffee urns, and other silverware for entertaining guests at Mount Vernon. Earlier that fall, when inquiring of his nephew Bushrod about silverware purchases, he had asked "whether French plate is fashionable and much used in genteel houses in France and England," showing that the great American liberator was still enslaved to European styles. On Saturday night, November 29, a rare earthquake struck New York—three quick tremors rumbled through town after midnight—and people started from their sleep, darting into the streets for safety. Asleep at the former Queen's Head Tavern, a three-story brick building at the corner of Broad and Pearl streets better known to history as Fraunces Tavern, Washington scarcely stirred: a man accustomed to the alarums of war wasn't about to be unsettled by the earth's minor trembles.

On December 1 Sir Guy Carleton wrote to Washington that, if wind and weather permitted, he hoped to remove the last of his troops from Long and Staten islands and depart by December 4. Washington sent back such an exceedingly polite note that he might have been saying goodbye to an affable weekend guest at Mount Vernon: "I have received your favor [i.e., letter] of yesterday's date, announcing the time of your departure, and sincerely wish that your Excellency, with the troops under your orders, may have a safe and pleasant passage."[10]

When it came time for Washington to bid farewell to his officers, Fraunces Tavern seemed the ideal spot. The innkeeper, Samuel Fraunces, was a West Indian called Black Sam; his nickname probably refers to a swarthy complexion rather than African parentage. An excellent cook and a Freemason, Fraunces was partial to wigs and fancy clothing and had a rather aristocratic air. A secret friend to the American cause during the war, he had helped to relieve the agony of American prisoners held in New York and also worked to thwart a plot to assassinate Washington. Congress would later repay him handsomely by housing government offices in Fraunces Tavern. Well aware of his heroism, Washington wrote to Fraunces warmly that summer and thanked him for his "constant friendship and attention to the cause of our country."[11]

Shortly before noon on December 4, Washington assembled his men in the long banquet room on the second floor of Fraunces Tavern. One tends to picture Washington on this occasion surrounded by a full complement of officers, but those on hand represented the sturdy, resilient band who had held out until the very end. Only three major generals—Knox, Steuben, and McDougall—and one brigadier general attended; a handful of lesser officers rounded out the crowd of thirty or forty. When Washington strode into their midst in his familiar blue and buff uniform, they all rose in respect. He invited them to heap their plates with cold buffet meats but was too overwrought to have much appetite himself. Amid what one officer described as "breathless silence," glasses were handed around and filled with wine.[12] Raising his glass with a shaking hand, Washington began to speak, his voice breaking with emotion: "With a heart filled with love and gratitude, I now take leave of you. I most devoutly wish that your latter days may be as prosperous and happy as your former ones have been glorious and honorable."[13]

The officers, moved, lifted their glasses and drank in silence. Tears welled up in Washington's eyes, as if he suddenly relived eight emotional years of sacrifice with these battle-tested men and was pained at the thought of parting from them. "I cannot come to each of you," he said tenderly, "but shall feel obliged if each of you will come and take me by the hand."[14] The moment was legendary, not for any feat of oratory, but for the simple heartfelt emotion palpable in Washington's words.

The first officer to step forward was Henry Knox, a mere bookseller before Washington had drawn him from obscurity and boosted him to chief of artillery. Famous for his self-control and his reluctance to let people touch him, Washington not only shook hands with Knox but hugged and kissed him in silence while tears streamed down their faces. Then Steuben, the fake baron whom Washington had allowed to train troops at Valley Forge, stepped forward and was similarly embraced. All the officers were "suffused in tears" as they surged forward for a final farewell kiss from Washington. As Benjamin Tallmadge wrote, "Such a scene of sorrow and weeping I had never before witnessed . . . *The simple thought* . . . that we should see his face no more in this world seemed to me utterly insupportable."[15] The moment captured many of Washington's finest qualities: his innate dignity and laconic eloquence, his frank affection behind the impassive front, his instinctive command of the theatrical gesture. He had a magisterial way of directing the major scenes in his life. One senses that, as he struggled with deep feelings, he feared that he would surrender control of his emotions if he said any more. No moment in his life showcased his gift of silence to better effect.

After all the junior officers had come forward to be clasped, Washington walked across the room, lifted his arm in a stately gesture of farewell, and left without looking back. The spell was hypnotic and the officers shuffled out "in mournful silence," according to Tallmadge.[16] When Washington arrived at the Whitehall wharf to board the ferry that would take him to New Jersey, a large crowd of citizens had gathered for an emotional goodbye. Washington raised his three-cornered hat, and his officers and the throng waved their hats in response. Then he stepped into the boat, and twenty-two oarsmen swung into motion, rowing him across the water until he vanished from sight.

Washington's destination was the State House in Annapolis, Maryland, where an itinerant Congress had taken up residence after leaving Princeton (hoping that with its theaters, balls, and other amusements, Annapolis might entice absentee delegates to attend sessions). Once he resigned his commission as commander in chief, Washington planned to return to Mount Vernon, vowing to Martha that he would join her for Christmas dinner. Having slept in 280 houses during the war, he must have had a special craving for the banal comforts of home. It took him four days to reach Philadelphia, and even as he mused about returning to private life, the trip showed how profoundly his life had changed. He had surrendered all right to privacy. Wherever he went, he was draped with honors and became a captive of the invariable crowds. A stream of letters trailed him, entreating his aid in securing employment or other favors. All the while he had the burden of having to act like a model citizen and was allowed no normal moods or imperfections.

The extraordinary hero worship Washington inspired can be vividly seen in the correspondence of Gerard Vogels, a Dutch businessman in Philadelphia. Writing to his wife of the commander's arrival in Philadelphia, Vogels made it sound as if the Messiah had stepped down from the heavens: "I saw the greatest man who has ever appeared on the surface of this earth. His Excellency arrived at 6 o'clock escorted by light cavalry . . . We all waved our hats three times over our heads. Then came the excellent Hero himself, riding an uncommonly beautiful horse . . . I don't know if, in our delight at seeing the Hero, we were more surprised by his simple but grand air or by the kindness of the greatest and best of heroes."[17]

Happily or not, Washington seemed resigned to being a form of public property. "His Excellency promises to walk daily through the town to give the grateful Americans the pleasure of seeing him," Vogels informed his wife. "Then he says farewell to all honors and the world's turmoil to live quietly in retirement on his estate."[18] At receptions Washington must have wondered whether he was the honored guest or a prisoner. All the turgid toasts in his praise drew forth from him equally stilted replies, as he took refuge in safe platitudes. Evidently there were limits to how much reverence the Hero could endure. He had always seemed uncomfortable with compliments. He left one concert as the chorus was about to sing a hymn in his honor, set to music by Handel. Vogels, who was in the audience, commented afterward, "Evidently His Excellency is above hearing his praise sung and retires before the just acclamations of his people."[19] He noted how Washington's presence acted as an aphrodisiac on the panting ladies: "It was amusing to see how, in a place so crowded with the fair sex, everybody had eyes only for this Hero. Indeed, we only now and then stole a glance at our girls. His Excellency drew everyone's attention."[20]

Before Washington arrived, the Pennsylvania assembly had ordered construction of a triumphal wooden arch in the classical style; suspended in the center was an enormous transparency of Cincinnatus, returning to his plow, his brow crowned with laurels. In case anyone was dim-witted enough to miss the allusion, the legislature said the "countenance of Cincinnatus is [to be] a striking resemblance of General Washington."[21] The portrait commission went to Charles Willson Peale, and Washington more or less good-humoredly submitted to a session under his studio skylight. Washington left a whimsical image of his cooperation, telling one correspondent that "no dray moves more readily to the thill than I do to the painter's chair"—that is, no workhorse was more readily harnessed to the shafts of a wagon than himself.[22] Peale exchanged letters about Washington with Benjamin West, the great expatriate painter in London, who had risen to become court history painter to George III. One day the king asked West whether Washington would be head of the army or head of state when the war ended. When West replied that Washington's sole ambition was to return to his estate, the thunderstruck king declared, "If he does that, he will be the greatest man in the world."[23]

Before Peale had finished the portrait, Washington decided to quit town; he left Philadelphia on December 15 with a diminished retinue. As he slowly shed the trappings of power, he retained only two aides, David Humphreys and Benjamin Walker, and a team of slaves. For a short stretch of the journey, one of his companions was John Dickinson, Pennsylvania's chief executive, who anticipated a problem that was to harry Washington in his postwar incarnation. Washington had negotiated neither a pension nor an expense account to entertain the hordes poised to descend upon Mount Vernon. Dickinson had privately warned Congress that "the admiration and esteem of the world may make [Washington's] life in a very considerable degree public, as numbers will be desirous of seeing the great and good man . . . His very services to his country may therefore subject him to improper expenses unless he permits her gratitude to interpose."[24] Congress failed to take action, and it would prove a serious omission in the coming years as the pilgrims to Mount Vernon imposed gigantic expenses.

On December 19 Washington approached the outskirts of Annapolis and was greeted by a delegation of dignitaries that included Horatio Gates. Both men must have been struck by the totality of Washington's triumph and Gates's demotion. Accompanied to George Mann's Tavern, Washington arrived to thirteen blasts of cannon fire, a cliché of which Washington surely tired. The next day he submitted a letter to Thomas Mifflin, his former aide and disloyal critic during the Conway affair and now president of Congress, asking whether he should submit his resignation in writing or in a public ceremony. Washington wanted to do everything in his power to dramatize his humility before civilian power. Congress decided that, after being feted with a magnificent dinner on December 22, he would return his commission before that body at noon the next day.

Several hundred people attended the celebratory dinner, which exuded a mood of uproarious good spirits. "The number of cheerful voices, with the clangor of knives and forks, made a din of a very extraordinary nature and most delightful influence," James Tilton wrote.[25] After suffering through the obligatory thirteen toasts, Washington made a toast with a pertinent point: "Competent powers to Congress for general purposes."[26] The toast suggested that Washington's mind still fretted over the inadequate Articles of Confederation and that his postwar retirement might be short-lived. The message, in many ways, foretold the rest of his political life. After the dinner Washington attended a brilliantly lit ball, dancing first with twenty-two-year-old Martha Rolle Maccubin, a prominent local belle. With women fawning all over him—the fashionable style dictated thirteen curls tumbling down the neck—Washington never left the dance floor and must have grown slightly giddy from the adulation. "The general danced every set, that the ladies might have the pleasure of dancing with him, or, as it has since been handsomely expressed, *get a touch of him,*" reported Tilton.[27]

The next morning Washington squeezed in a last personal letter to Baron von Steuben. Among other things, he reassured Steuben that the country would reward his inestimable service during the war. The quiet fervor of this letter says something about the enduring tie uniting the two men. "I wish to make use of this last moment of my public life to signify in the strongest terms my entire approbation of your conduct," Washington wrote. ". . . This is the last letter I shall ever write while I continue in the service of my country. The hour of my resignation is fixed at twelve this day; after which I shall become a private citizen on the banks of the Potomac, where I shall be glad to embrace you and to testify [to] the great esteem and consideration" in which he held him.[28]

Washington's resignation was a minutely prepared affair, designed to show a doubting world that this new republic would not degenerate into disorder. Shortly before noon he arrived at the State House, wearing his familiar uniform for the last time. He was greeted by Charles Thomson, the secretary of Congress, who led him to a seat on the dais, where he was flanked by David Humphreys and Benjamin Walker. In the audience was a sparse contingent of legislators, only twenty representatives, who sat with their hats on. This was no sign of disrespect but an antimonarchical gesture: in European kingdoms, commoners always stood in the presence of royalty and doffed their hats. Then the doors opened, and the leading Maryland politicians and town gentry poured into the hall, with men crowding into seats downstairs and bright-eyed ladies packing the galleries. Everyone pressed into the hall to sneak a peek at this historic transaction.

As the audience sat in rapt silence, Thomas Mifflin rose. "Sir," he intoned, "the United States in Congress assembled are prepared to receive your communications."[29] Following a precise script, Washington rose and bowed to the congressmen, who removed their hats out of respect and then returned them. As Washington spoke, he held the speech in his right hand, which began to shake so violently that he had to steady it with his left.

In a voice hoarse with emotion, he recalled his feelings of inadequacy when first appointed commander in chief and stated that he had been sustained only "by a confidence in the rectitude of our cause, the support of the supreme power of the union, and the patronage of heaven."[30] He paid tribute to the men who had served with him and gently urged Congress to take care of them, reminding them of the troops sent home unpaid. It was at this point that he had to grasp the speech with two trembling hands. When he recommended "our dearest country to the protection of Almighty God," said James McHenry, Washington's voice "faltered and sank and the whole house felt his agitations."[31] After a pause he regained his composure and closed on a poetic note, hinting at his permanent withdrawal: "Having now finished the work assigned me, I retire from the great theater of action; and bidding an affectionate farewell to this august body under whose orders I have so long acted, I here offer my commission and take my leave of all the employments of public life."[32] Then, drawing the original parchment commission from his coat, he handed it to Thomas Mifflin along with a folded copy of his speech. The emotional impact was overpowering. "The General was so much affected himself that everybody felt for him," commented a woman named Mary Ridout, who said that "many tears were shed."[33]

In dignified fashion, Thomas Mifflin gave a prepared response that had been drafted by Thomas Jefferson, then a delegate from Virginia, who was also swept up in the Washington worship and fully understood the unprecedented nature of Washington's surrender of power. As Jefferson later wrote to Washington, "The moderation and virtue of a single character . . . probably prevented this revolution from being closed, as most others have been, by a subversion of that liberty it was intended to establish."[34] In the speech, Mifflin cited the peerless way Washington had "conducted the great military conflict with wisdom and fortitude, invariably regarding the rights of the civil powers."[35]

After Mifflin's speech, there came more formal bowing, and Washington prepared to leave. He shook hands and bade farewell individually to each member of Congress, thus ending his years of military service. Before the speech he had packed his bags and checked out of George Mann's Tavern, so that his horse and attendants awaited him at the State House door, enabling him to make a quick escape. He mounted his horse and rode off in a hush. "It was a solemn and affecting spectacle, such a one as history does not present," said McHenry. "The spectators all wept and there was hardly a member of Congress who did not drop tears."[36] A small delegation escorted Washington to the nearby South River ferry. Then he was finally alone on horseback with his two aides and servants, heading for Mount Vernon.

The figure hurrying back to his long-forgotten past had just accomplished something more extraordinary than any military feat during the war. At war's end, he stood alone at the pinnacle of power, but he never became drunk with that influence, as had so many generals before him, and treated his commission as a public trust to be returned as soon as possible to the people's representatives. Throughout history victorious generals had sought to parlay their fame into political power, whereas Washington had only a craving for privacy. Instead of glorying in his might, he feared its terrible weight and potential misuse. He had long lived in the shadow of the historical analogy to the Roman patriot Cincinnatus, and now, with his resignation at Annapolis, that analogy was complete. When John Trumbull later painted a series of portraits for the U.S. Capitol, he chose Washington's resignation at Annapolis as one of the crowning moments of the founding era and the highest proof of Washington's virtue. At the time of the resignation, Trumbull was in London and recorded European wonderment at the news, saying that it "excites the astonishment and admiration of this part of the world."[37]

Washington had served as commander in chief for eight and a half years, the equivalent of two presidential terms. His military triumphs had been neither frequent nor epic in scale. He had lost more battles than he had won, had botched several through strategic blunders, and had won at Yorktown only with the indispensable aid of the French Army and fleet. But he was a different kind of general fighting a different kind of war, and his military prowess cannot be judged by the usual scorecard of battles won and lost. His fortitude in keeping the impoverished Continental Army intact was a major historic accomplishment. It always stood on the brink of dissolution, and Washington was the one figure who kept it together, the spiritual and managerial genius of the whole enterprise: he had been resilient in the face of every setback, courageous in the face of every danger. He was that rare general who was great between battles and not just during them. The constant turnover of his army meant that he continually had to start from scratch in training his men. He had to blend troops from different states into a functioning national force, despite deep ideological fears of a standing army. And before the French alliance, he had lacked the sea power that was all-important in defeating the British.

Seldom in history has a general been handicapped by such constantly crippling conditions. There was scarcely a time during the war when Washington didn't grapple with a crisis that threatened to disband the army and abort the Revolution. The extraordinary, wearisome, nerve-racking frustration he put up with for nearly nine years is hard to express. He repeatedly had to exhort Congress and the thirteen states to remedy desperate shortages of men, shoes, shirts, blankets, and gunpowder. This meant dealing with selfish, apathetic states and bureaucratic incompetence in Congress. He labored under a terrible strain that would have destroyed a lesser man. Ennobled by adversity and leading by example, he had been dismayed and depressed but never defeated. The cheerless atmosphere at Valley Forge was much more the rule than the exception during the war. Few people with any choice in the matter would have persisted in this impossible, self-sacrificing situation for so long. Washington's job as commander in chief was as much a political as a military task, and he performed it brilliantly, functioning as de facto president of the country. His stewardship of the army had been a masterly exercise in nation building. In defining the culture of the Continental Army, he had helped to mold the very character of the country, preventing the Revolution from taking a bloodthirsty or despotic turn. In the end, he had managed to foil the best professional generals that a chastened Great Britain could throw at him. As Benjamin Franklin told an English friend after the war, "An American planter was chosen by us to command our troops and continued during the whole war. This man sent home to you, one after another, five of your best generals, baffled, their heads bare of laurels, disgraced even in the opinion of their employers."[38]

PART FOUR

The Statesman

Bust of George Washington by Jean-Antoine Houdon,
sculpted in 1785.

American Celebrity

WITH PERFECT TIMING, George Washington made it home to the loving embrace of his family on Christmas Eve. His return to Mount Vernon made him acutely aware of the enormous distance he had traveled since he left for the Second Continental Congress in May 1775. In writing to Lafayette, he noted time's steady passage, observing that he had "entered these doors an older man by nine years than when I left them."[1] He indeed cut a very different figure from the tentative, uncertain arriviste of the prewar years. Secure in himself and his place in history, he little resembled that edgily combative young man who never missed a chance for self-advancement. That bumptious, sharp-elbowed character would emerge again sporadically in business dealings but would now coexist uneasily with a far more mature self.

A heavy snowfall soon cast a hush over Mount Vernon—it was a winter of historic coldness—so that Washington discovered himself "fast locked up in frost and snow" and sequestered at home by icy gusts and impassable roads.[2] Only his wartime trophies, including the banners of captured flags that decorated the downstairs walls, evoked his extraordinary exploits. This isolation must have been sweetly congenial to Washington after the toilsome years of battle and the attendant lack of privacy. Ever the dutiful if exasperated son, he planned to visit his mother, but bad weather intervened, forcing him to defer the trip and enabling him to savor an unaccustomed solitude.

As he gazed back over the hazardous odyssey he had survived, he wondered at his own unaccountable preservation, telling Henry Knox, "I feel now, however, as I conceive a wearied traveler must do who, after treading many a painful step, with a heavy burden on his shoulders, is eased of the latter, having reached the goal . . . and from his housetop is looking back and tracing with a grateful eye the meanders by which he escaped the quicksands and mires which lay in his way and into which none but the all-powerful guide and great disposer of human events could have prevented his falling."[3] This hardheaded, practical man increasingly struck a reflective tone, experience having forced him to ponder the world more deeply.

Long burdened by wartime correspondence, Washington took a vacation from letter writing for several blissful days. It took a while to break his military habit of waking early and revolving in his overcrowded mind the day's manifold duties. He kept realizing, with a start, that he "was no longer a public man or had anything to do with public transactions."[4] On December 28 he composed his first letter from home, proclaiming to New York governor George Clinton, "I am now a private citizen on the banks of the Potomac . . . I feel myself eased of a load of public care. I hope to spend the remainder of my days in cultivating the affections of good men and in the practice of the domestic virtues."[5] These early postwar letters emit an elegiac whiff, as if Washington thought his best days now lay behind him, and he dwelt inordinately on his own mortality. Sounding more like a sage than an aging warrior, he portrayed himself, in Old Testament language, as sitting "under the shadow of my own vine and my own fig tree, free from the bustle of a camp," as he told Lafayette. "Envious of none, I am determined to be pleased with all, and this, my dear friend, being the order for my march, I will move gently down the stream of life until I sleep with my fathers."[6]

For more than a month Washington postponed the trip to his mother due to inclement weather. When he at last set out for Fredericksburg in February 1784, he allotted a full week to his sojourn, which soon became enlarged into a state visit. The *Virginia Gazette* hailed his arrival in town "on a visit to his ancient and amiable parent."[7] Washington could not avoid a public dinner and elegant ball in his honor, capped by a twenty-one-gun salute from local artillery. As best we can tell, Mary Washington skipped these festivities, but her son voiced the obligatory pieties to town dignitaries, touting Fredericksburg as "the place of my growing infancy" and expressing pleasure at "the honorable mention which is made of my revered mother, by whose maternal hand (early deprived of a father) I was led to manhood."[8]

Try though he might, Washington couldn't completely extricate his thoughts from politics and feared that the still immature country would blunder into errors before arriving at true wisdom. As he affirmed, "all things will come right at last. But, like a young heir come a little prematurely to a large inheritance, we shall wanton and run riot until we have brought our reputation to the brink of ruin." Only when a crisis materialized would the country be "*compelled* perhaps to do what prudence and common policy pointed out as plain as any problem in Euclid in the first instance."[9] This statement tallied with Washington's often expressed view that citizens had to feel before they saw—that is, they couldn't react to abstract problems, only to tangible ones. The long fight against British tyranny, paradoxically, only strengthened his view that the foremost political danger came not from an overly powerful central government but from an enfeebled one—"a half-starved, limping government that appears to be always moving upon crutches and tottering at every step."[10]

The snowbound house was enlivened by young people. The Washingtons ran something akin to a small orphanage, and the general must have fled sometimes from the rambunctious shouts of skylarking children to the silence of his study. As we recall, after Jacky's death, George and Martha had taken in his two youngest children, Nelly, now four, and Washy, now two. Although the situation was never formalized, Washington referred to them as his "adopted" children. Martha seemed to transfer her affections intact from Patsy and Jacky to Nelly and Washy, including her propensity to spoil the boy and anguish over his health. "My pretty little dear boy complains of a pain in his stomach," Martha wrote in one letter. ". . . I cannot say but it makes me miserable if ever he complains, let the cause be ever so trifling . . . I hope the almighty will spare him to me."[11] She couldn't conceive of a happy home devoid of children. "My little family are all with me," she exulted to a friend, declaring that, without them, "I almost despair of ever enjoying happiness."[12]

This second set of children seemed far happier than the epileptic Patsy and the feckless Jacky, and family life at Mount Vernon was less troubled than before. When Robert Edge Pine painted the children, he captured their contrasting natures. A sprightly girl, clever and sociable, Nelly stares out boldly, even impudently, at the viewer. Washy has a soft mop of well-brushed hair that falls over his forehead, and he seems gentle, almost feminine, his thoughts trailing far away. When Washington hired tutors for them, he sounded far more tolerant and relaxed than he had been with Jacky and Patsy, saying their education would "be mere amusement, because it is not my wish that the children should be confined."[13] Though much loved, Washington was sometimes a grandly remote figure to these two stepchildren. "He was a silent thoughtful man," Nelly said years later. "He spoke little generally, never of himself. I never heard him relate a single act of his life during the war."[14]

The Washingtons agreed to provide guidance or financial support for an amazing assortment of nieces and nephews. As noted earlier, after her sister, Anna Maria Dandridge Bassett, died early in the war, Martha pledged to raise her charming daughter Frances, or "Fanny," who was now a teenager and had moved permanently to Mount Vernon. In a Robert Edge Pine portrait, Fanny has pretty features, big deep-set eyes, a rosebud mouth, and long wavy hair that falls across her shoulder and slightly exposed bosom. Martha adored Fanny and let her function as an assistant plantation hostess. "She is a child to me," she later wrote, "and I am very lonesome when she is absent."[15] Washington also delighted in Fanny's "easy and quiet temper."[16] In fact, the girl with her cheerful, winning personality was universally popular. "There was something so pleasing in her appearance and manner that even a stranger could not see her without being interested in her welfare" was one visitor's impression.[17]

The bulging household incorporated other young relatives. George Augustine Washington, the son of Washington's hard-drinking brother Charles, had been an aide to Lafayette during the war and was already plagued by a lingering bout of tuberculosis that would only worsen with the years. Washington was also saddled temporarily with three children from his late brother Samuel, who had been married five times and died heavily in debt. "In God's name," Washington had wondered to brother Jack earlier in the year, "how did my broth[e]r Sam[ue]l contrive to get himself so enormously in debt?"[18] Samuel's three children by his fourth marriage—Harriot, Lawrence Augustine, and George Steptoe Washington—ranged in age from eight to eleven and had been left indigent. All three presented special challenges. Harriot, an awkward, slovenly young girl, found herself trapped in a household of manic perfectionists. Starting in 1784 and for the next eight years, Washington footed the bill to educate her two brothers at a Georgetown academy, but they were wild and uncontrollable and a constant trial to Washington, who was extremely generous with young relatives but quite exacting if they failed to measure up to his high standards.

By war's end, Martha Washington was round and matronly in face and form, a fact recorded by one visitor: "Mrs. Washington is an elegant figure for a person of her years . . . She is rather fleshy, of good complexion, has a large, portly double chin, and an open and engaging countenance."[19] Although her hair was now gray, she still had smooth, unlined skin, and her eyes were warm and bright. She was fond of wearing sheer fabrics in light pastel colors that comfortably fit her full figure. By her own description, Martha was never either sick or well but hovered somewhere in between. Perhaps because she was short, she believed in a proud, erect posture and bought stiff collars for Nelly to encourage her upright carriage. The travel-weary Martha was slow to admit that her marital life had now changed forever: her husband could surrender his commission but not his fame. Later on, in a wistful mood, she would recollect to Mercy Warren that when her husband returned from the war that Christmas, she had little thought "that any circumstance could possibly happen to call the general into public life again" and that she "anticipated that from that moment they should have grown old together in solitude and tranquillity. This, my dear madam, was the first and fondest wish of my heart."[20] Whatever ambitions she might have harbored for her husband's career had long since been gratified, and she never dreamed that the curtain would soon rise again on a vast and thrilling new pageant in their lives.

Whatever the strains of returning to private life, the period between the war and his presidency was a halcyon time for Washington, who laid aside the gigantic labors of nation building. Those who had seen him amid the tumult of war were struck by his happy metamorphosis back into a private citizen. Although he fondly invoked the "rural amusements" of his country cottage, such pastoral imagery didn't quite square with the desperate economic plight he faced upon his homecoming.[21] As he devoted every morning to business matters, the scenes of bucolic harmony he had envisioned while in uniform faded from the hard collision with reality. For nine years Mount Vernon had suffered terrible neglect, thinning his fortune. "I made no money from my estate during the nine years I was absent from it and brought none home with me," he told his nephew Fielding Lewis, Jr.[22] Great Britain exacted a high price from American farmers after the war by shutting West Indian markets that had once been open to the colonists. To further his economic woes, Washington's debtors paid him in depreciated wartime currency, making it difficult for him to satisfy his own creditors. While France yearned to welcome the American hero, Washington told Lafayette that his straitened circumstances precluded an Atlantic crossing and might "put it forever out of my power to gratify this wish."[23]

If Washington thought he could repair his affairs quickly, he was soon disabused, and more than a year after returning to Mount Vernon, he told Henry Knox despondently that his business affairs "can no longer be neglected without involving my ruin."[24] He had frequently reassured his estate steward, Lund Washington, of his confidence in leaving his wartime business in his hands. Nevertheless, as the war drew to a close, he berated Lund for failing to provide adequate financial statements and accused him of keeping him ignorant since Valley Forge. From brother Jack, Washington learned that his frontier tenants had fallen years behind in their rent, and he pleaded with Lund to travel west and collect the overdue money, accusing him of "an unconquerable aversion to going from home."[25] Unknown to Washington as he issued these intemperate charges, Lund had forgone his steward's salary since the Valley Forge period. When he discovered it, Washington was mortified but had no immediate way of making up the shortfall.

In 1785, beset by growing financial troubles, Washington began to edge Lund aside and took over daily supervision of the five farms—Muddy Hole, Dogue Run, River, Union, and Mansion House—that constituted Mount Vernon, which had burgeoned to seven thousand acres. Now in his early fifties, Washington no longer had time to stay on top of his far-flung operations. When Lund stepped down as manager after twenty-one years, he was replaced by Washington's nephew-in-residence, the sickly George Augustine Washington. Although Washington lacked the time to make the daily rounds, he didn't wish to relinquish all control of plantation life and instituted a detailed system of weekly reports from each farm. As he told the departing Lund, "I am resolved that an account of the stock and every occurrence that happens in the course of the week shall be minutely detailed to me every Saturday."[26] There never seemed to be enough detail to satisfy his insatiable appetite for information.

Even as his finances suffered from his long enforced absence, Washington needed to keep up a show of prosperity and entertain the stream of visitors, friends and strangers alike, who descended upon the shrine of Mount Vernon. He was never able to enjoy fully the respite from national duty that he had so richly earned. He didn't cultivate adulation so much as endure it and played the fifty-two-year-old smiling public man. Toward the war's end he had begun bracing for the rigors of receiving visitors on a lavish scale. After the British evacuation of New York, he tried to hire a cook who could whip up a proper dinner for thirty guests at a time. Reverting to the man of fashion, he asked Lafayette to send him French silver salvers that could hold up to twelve glasses; where possible, he still attempted to boycott British goods. He retained his old aristocratic habits, having his arms engraved on new silverware, and he didn't see any contradiction between such behavior and the war he had just waged against British nobility.

In eighteenth-century Virginia, where roadside taverns were sparse and travelers could easily be stranded in transit, feeding and lodging travelers who showed up unannounced at one's doorstep were considered necessary marks of hospitality. The polite Washington was victimized by this tradition as veterans and curiosity seekers descended on his home in massive numbers. Much of the mystique later attached to the White House first crystallized around Mount Vernon, which became a sort of proto–presidential mansion. Except for Ben Franklin in Paris, Washington was the first American celebrity, and he only partially succeeded at shielding himself from supplicants. Strangers arrived intent upon seeing Washington, who had to figure out ways to bar their prying eyes. He often greeted people at the door, only to hand them off to slaves, then disappeared into his study or rode off to his farms. "Even friends who make a point of visiting him are left much to themselves, indeed scarcely see him from breakfast to dinner, unless he engages them in a ride, which is very agreeable to him," said a visitor named Elizabeth Ambler Carrington.[27] Sometimes, like a dutiful innkeeper, Washington showed up in the room of a sick guest, proffering a hot cup of tea and showing his basic decency.

He never resolved the problem of the tremendous expenses he incurred in taking care of visitors. Not only did guests devour his food, but their horses freely ate his forage. "My situation is very little understood by most people," he explained in later life. "Whatever may be my property, the income of it is inadequate to my expenses. Not from any wish or desire I have to live extravagantly, but from *unavoid-able* necessity proceeding from the public walks of life in which I have been and the acquaintances made thereby, which fill my house continually with company."[28] At a typical dinner, half the people might be guests. "There is not one single officer on the whole continent who will forsake the pleasure of spending a few days with his General," said Philip Mazzei, Jefferson's Florentine-born friend. ". . . The result is that his house is continuously filled with strangers who bring with them an even larger number of servants and horses. As there is no village in the vicinity and no inn within reach, the General has to take charge of everything."[29]

As legions of hopeful tourists made a pilgrimage to this mecca, George and Martha Washington struggled to retain some modicum of privacy. Sometimes they behaved like inmates held hostage by an overflowing wave of visitors, condemned to make small talk with complete strangers. One of the sadder lines in Washington's copious papers occurs in his diary entry for June 30, 1785, where he notes that he "dined with only Mrs. Washington, which I believe is the first instance of it since my retirement from public life."[30] One can almost hear the sigh of relief. Washington admitted to Franklin that "retirement from the public walks of life has not been so productive of the leisure and ease as might have been expected."[31] Benjamin Franklin scarcely needed a lesson. "Celebrity may for a while flatter one's vanity," he wrote, "but its effects are troublesome."[32]

The nation wouldn't let Washington enjoy the ease of a private citizen, and he had to learn to manage his celebrity. One unspoken trick he used to deter unwanted visitors was to post inadequate signs indicating the way to his house, erecting a natural barrier against intruders. The nine-mile ride between Alexandria and Mount Vernon confounded travelers, forcing them to traverse bogs, thick woods, and winding trails; the visitor files at Mount Vernon abound with comic tales of travelers getting hopelessly lost in this trackless maze. Although Washington weeded out guests by asking for letters of introduction, he was too civil to turn people away even if they lacked referrals. When a French officer showed up for dinner without papers, Washington confessed in his diary that "I was at a loss how to receive or treat him." Then he added: "He stayed [for] dinner and the evening."[33] One stranger who arrived in Washington's absence was astounded by his courteous treatment: "Immediately on our arrival, every care was taken of our horses, beds were prepared, and an excellent supper provided for us."[34]

The visitors' accounts during these years give many candid glimpses of Washington. Their impressions vary dramatically, suggesting that he reacted quite differently to people—so much so that, at times, he scarcely seemed the same person. He could be merry and convivial or, if he didn't care for the guests, silent and morose. This mutable personality, reflecting his shifting levels of trust in his listeners, has made it hard for historians to form a coherent sense of his personality. Seldom quotable in person, Washington could never be surprised into confessional statements. But if few visitors came away with treasured table talk, he made his presence powerfully felt.

A young Scottish visitor, Robert Hunter, left this portrait of Washington's venerable appearance: "The General is about six foot high, perfectly straight and well made, rather inclined to be lusty. His eyes are full and blue and seem to express an air of gravity."[35] He picked up Washington's fastidious regard for appearance. When they first met, the general "was neatly dressed in a plain blue coat, white cashmere waistcoat, and black breeches and boots, as he came from his farm."[36] Washington left him briefly with Martha and Fanny, shed his work clothes, then reappeared in more fashionable garb, "with his hair neatly powdered, a clean shirt on, a new plain drab coat, white waistcoat, and white silk stockings."[37] Hunter conjured up a Washington who seemed relaxed after the great labors of war, a man still healthy and vital who could be elegant in the drawing room and energetic in the field. He noted that Washington was talkative with intimates, but that, cherishing his privacy, he was far more guarded and laconic with people he distrusted.

Hunter recorded the clockwork regularity of Washington's days as the latter followed a farmer's routine of going to bed at nine, then rising with the sun. Mornings he devoted to the masses of mail that swamped him. "It's astonishing the packets of letters that daily come for him from all parts of the world," noted Hunter.[38] With evident pride, Washington showed him the vast archive of wartime letters he had transcribed for posterity: "There are thirty large folio volumes of them upstairs, as big as common ledgers, all neatly copied."[39] Hunter discovered that his study, with a thousand books shelved behind glass, was the inner sanctum to which he denied admittance to strangers. As Washington gave him a tour of his extensive fields and gardens, Hunter reported that his "greatest pride is now to be thought the first farmer in America."[40] Far from being an aloof boss, Washington often dismounted from his horse to work alongside slaves and indentured servants, especially to ensure that construction matched his specifications: "It's astonishing with what niceness he directs everything in the building way, condescending even to measure the things himself, that all may be perfectly uniform."[41]

While Washington opened up in Hunter's company, he clammed up with others. If he didn't like someone, he would be correct but never warm. As one European visitor observed, "There seemed to me to skulk somewhat of a repulsive coldness, not congenial with my mind, under a courteous demeanor."[42] One Dutchman also came away disgusted: "I could never be on familiar terms with the General—a man so cold, so cautious, so obsequious."[43] It did not occur to these tourists that Washington felt burdened by uninvited visitors gaping at him, particularly since he wasn't a backslapping soul who feigned friendship with total strangers. His modesty disappointed those who expected him to narrate the wartime drama especially for them. "He announces a profound discretion and a great diffidence in himself," said the French journalist Brissot de Warville. ". . . His modesty is astonishing to a Frenchman; he speaks of the American war and of his victories as of things in which he had no direction."[44] Of course, the many volumes of letters upstairs underscored Washington's sense of his own overwhelming importance in the war, but he preferred to let his deeds speak for themselves.

Sharp-eyed visitors noted how Martha Washington, in her cheerful, self-effacing way, facilitated social interactions, making her husband's life easier. "As to his lady, she appears to me to be a plain, good woman, very much resembling the character of Lady Bountiful," wrote Captain John Enys. She "is very cheerful and seems most happy when contributing towards the happiness of others."[45] Neither plain nor showy, she occupied a congenial middle ground. As a Rhode Island merchant noted, "Mrs. Washington is an elegant figure for a person of her years . . . She was dressed in a plain black satin gown with long sleeves" and a gauzy black cap with black bows. "All very neat, but not gaudy."[46] One snobbish female visitor professed shock at the doyenne's unpretentious appearance. She and a friend had "dressed ourselves in our most elegant ruffles and silks and were introduced to her ladyship. And don't you think, we found her *knitting and with* a specked [checked] apron on!"[47]

Among the major tourist attractions at Mount Vernon was Washington's stable of Thoroughbred horses, especially those he rode during the war, who had earned a rest. Early in the war his steed of choice had been Blueskin, so named for its bluish-gray skin. In 1785 Washington gave the horse to a lady friend, Elizabeth French Dulany, adding an affectionate note of apology: "Marks of antiquity have supplied the place of those beauties with which this horse abounded—in his better days."[48] Even more renowned was his chestnut Nelson, who had served at Yorktown and withstood gunfire better than any other horse. After the war, Old Nelson was exempt from all work and able to graze to his heart's content. "They have heard the roaring of many a cannon in their time," one appreciative visitor said of these two horses. ". . . The General makes no manner of use of them now; he keeps them in a nice stable, where they feed away at their ease for their past services."[49]

For the most part, Washington stuck close to home after his years of military exile and resigned from the vestry of Truro Parish, a position he'd held for twenty-two years. Some scholars have attributed this to political motives. In the immediate aftermath of the war, Anglican vestrymen still had to vow obedience to the "doctrine and discipline of the Church of England," which had George III at its head.[50] Obviously George Washington couldn't submit to such a public pledge without provoking a brouhaha. During the next few years, as the Anglican Church distanced itself from its British roots and evolved into the Protestant Episcopal Church, Washington's church attendance still remained intermittent. One explanation has been that a minister once chided Washington for failing to take communion, preaching that great men needed to set an example for the community. Perhaps taking umbrage, Washington continued to attend the church but avoided Sundays when communion was offered. One also wonders whether Washington didn't feel an unseemly sense of being on public display at church, his presence attracting large crowds and adding to the already weighty burden of his celebrity.

After the war Washington was a far more voracious reader than generally recognized. Though hardly a Renaissance man on a par with Jefferson and Franklin, he pursued a broad range of interests throughout his life. Long an attentive reader of agricultural treatises and other books of practical knowledge, he also read the important literature of his time, and his library included volumes of Alexander Pope, Jonathan Swift, John Milton, and Oliver Goldsmith, as well as Dr. Johnson's famous dictionary. In the spring of 1783, from his Newburgh headquarters, he had ordered books advertised for sale in a gazette, and one is impressed by the substantial works on the purchase list. For his eclectic postwar reading he had lined up Voltaire's *Letters to Several of His Friends,* John Locke's *An Essay Concerning Human Understanding,* and Gibbon's *The History of the Decline and Fall of the Roman Empire.* Showing a decided biographical bent, he ordered lives of Charles XII of Sweden, Louis XV of France, and Peter the Great of Russia. Apparently still hoping to make a trip to France, he ordered a French dictionary and grammar, although he showed little aptitude for foreign languages and made no discernible headway.

Though not notable for scintillating repartee, Washington enjoyed the society of writers and never felt intellectually threatened by their company. In May 1785 the lexicographer Noah Webster spent a day at Mount Vernon, angling to get Washington to support a copyright law in Virginia. In all likelihood, he furnished Washington with a copy of his *Sketches of American Policy,* which made the case for a strong central government. A surprising wheeler-dealer, Webster attempted to cut a deal with Washington: he would tutor Nelly and Washy gratis in exchange for unrestricted access to Washington's papers. Scenting a bad bargain, Washington spurned the offer.

For ten days in June he entertained a well-known British historian, Catharine Macaulay Graham, and her younger husband. Taken with his visitor, he told Henry Knox that a "visit from a lady so celebrated in the literary world could not but be very flattering to me."[51] A woman with a very long, pale face, sharply accentuated by a very long, pale nose, she was an expert in English and Roman history. A radical Whig and a distinguished friend to American liberty, she entered into serious political talks with Washington. "It gave me pleasure to find that her sentim[en] ts respecting the inadequacy of the powers of Congress . . . coincided with my own," Washington told Richard Henry Lee.[52] Perhaps Washington was also subtly screening a potential biographer for himself, for he confessed to his diary: "Placed my military records into the hands of Mrs. Macaulay Graham for her perusal and amusem[en]t."[53] Dr. Samuel Johnson memorably satirized the female historian as a high-minded hypocrite, once asking her to show her faith in her egalitarian beliefs by inviting her footman to dine at her table. She never forgave Johnson for the taunt.

Washington's desire to socialize with literary personalities likely arose from his belief that writers crowned those who won fame and ended up in history's pantheon. In 1788, when he steered Lafayette to the American poet Joel Barlow, then resident in France, Washington described Barlow as "one of those bards who hold the keys of the gate by which patriots, sages, and heroes are admitted to immortality. Such are your ancient bards who are both the priest and doorkeepers to the temple of fame. And these, my dear Marquis, are no vulgar functions."[54] Washington went on to say that military heroes, far from being passive, could groom their own advocates: "In some instances . . . heroes have made poets, and poets heroes. Alexander the Great is said to have been enraptured with the poems of Homer and to have lamented that he had not a rival muse to celebrate his actions."[55] The passage shows Washington's underlying hunger for posthumous glory and how calculating he could be in gaining it. He ended the letter by lauding the golden ages of arms and arts under Louis XIV and Queen Anne and by expressing the hope that America would not be found "inferior to the rest of the world in the performance of our poets and painters."[56]

For all of Washington's professions of modesty, the thought of his high destined niche in history was never far from his mind. Few historical figures have so lovingly tended their image. As we have seen, he had issued detailed instructions for preserving his wartime papers. When the wagon train loaded with these bulky papers set out for Mount Vernon in November 1783, he fussed over their transport, telling the lieutenant entrusted with the mission that he shouldn't cross the Susquehanna or the Potomac by ferry if the winds were too high or any other dangers arose. As if the wagons were encrusted with precious jewels, he delivered this warning: "The wagons should never be without a sentinel over them; always locked and the keys in your possession."[57] He experienced vast relief when the papers showed up safely at his home.

No sooner had these documents arrived than a would-be biographer, John Bowie, and a would-be historian of the Revolution, Dr. William Gordon, emerged from the woodwork. In an extraordinary tribute, Congress had given Washington access to its secret papers on the same terms as its members, enhancing the value of his cooperation to future historians. To maintain the tradition of military submission to civilian authority, Washington decided not to open his papers until Congress did likewise with its archives. Washington wasn't reluctant to disclose the historical record; he just thought it might seem conceited and presumptuous to do so first and that a congressional decision would make it seem less self-aggrandizing. Of the two projects, Washington was more troubled by the biography, fearing his cooperation might smack of vanity. "I will frankly declare to you . . . that any memoirs of my life, distinct and unconnected with the general history of the war, would rather hurt my feelings than tickle my pride whilst I lived," he told Dr. James Craik. "I had rather glide gently down the stream of life, leaving it to posterity to think and say what they please of me, than by an act of mine to have vanity or ostentation imputed to me."[58]

Washington looked favorably upon William Gordon's history, as long as Congress first gave him license to open up his papers. A dissenting minister from Roxbury, Massachusetts, Dr. Gordon had been a staunch supporter of the independence movement. When Congress gave Washington its approval to unseal his papers, the indefatigable Gordon spent more than two weeks at Mount Vernon in June 1784, reading himself blind all day, pausing only for meals. In a letter to Horatio Gates written soon afterward, he summarized the scope of Washington's extraordinary literary repository: "thirty and three volumes of copied letters of the General's, besides three volume of private, seven volumes of general orders, and bundles upon bundles of letters to the General."[59] When Gordon's multivolume history appeared in 1788, Washington bought two sets for himself and urged friends to buy it.

Despite the years of work devoted to conserving his papers, Washington thought they had not yet attained an acceptable state and planned to dedicate the winter of 1784–85 to rescuing them from "a mere mass of confusion."[60] To his dismay, he never had time to tidy the letters or "transact any business of my own in the way of acco[un]ts . . . during the whole course of the winter or, in a word, since my retirement from public life."[61] He remained the prisoner of a clamorous procession of visitors. Even more time-consuming were the reams of mail that arrived daily, badgering him for recommendations, referrals, and answers to war-related queries. Feeding this flood tide of correspondence was a well-meant congressional decision to exempt from postage all mail to and from Washington. Someone else of Washington's Olympian stature might have simply ignored unsolicited letters, but with his innate courtesy, he replied dutifully to all of them, even at the expense of his business. Duty had long since become a deadly compulsion that he was helpless to conquer, however much it exhausted him. During the war his large staff of quick-witted young aides had handled his correspondence; and now he complained that "not in the eight years I served the public have I been *obliged* to write so much *myself* as I have done since my retirement" from military service.[62]

Unable to escape fame even in his own home, Washington felt confined to his desk, and his health suffered for lack of sufficient exercise. "I already begin to feel the effect," he told Henry Knox. "Heavy and painful oppressions of the head and other disagreeable sensations often trouble me."[63] A physician, possibly James Craik, advised him that the worrisome head symptoms resulted from excessive paperwork and that he had to stop. The solution grew crystal-clear to Washington: "I am determined therefore to employ some person who shall ease me of the drudgery of this business."[64] In July 1785, he hired a young man, William Shaw, as his factotum to draft letters, organize his papers, and even tutor Nelly and Washy. But Shaw had a habit of gallivanting about whenever Washington needed him and lasted only thirteen months.

Far happier was Washington's association with Lieutenant Colonel David Humphreys, who had served as his aide late in the war. A Yale graduate and former Connecticut schoolmaster, he was a husky young man in his mid-thirties with a dense thatch of wavy hair, a soft, jowly face, and an engaging gleam in his eyes. Washington doted on Humphreys to the point that John Trumbull said, with only a touch of mockery, that he was the "belov'd of Washington."[65] Humphreys had turned in such a stellar performance at Yorktown that Washington honored him with a special distinction: he had carried the twenty-four captured British flags to Congress and was presented, in turn, with a commemorative sword. An able writer, Humphreys drafted many of Washington's remarks at the stultifying round of receptions that followed the evacuation of New York.

After the war Humphreys worked in Paris with Jefferson and helped to negotiate commercial treaties. In July 1785 Washington acceded to Humphreys's request to write a biography of him. In laying out the conditions of employment, which would include arranging his papers, Washington smothered the younger man with attention, promising to provide him with oral reminiscences and access to his archives: "And I can with great truth add that my house would not only be at your service during the period of your preparing this work, but . . . I should be exceedingly happy if you would make it your home. You might have an apartment to yourself in which you could command your own time. You would be considered and treated as one of the family."[66] By now Washington had guaranteed that objectivity would be impossible for Humphreys, embraced as he was by the American god. In a telling comment, Washington told his prospective Boswell that he would have undertaken his own memoir but lacked the time and was also "conscious of a defective education and want of capacity to fit me for such an undertaking."[67] It is striking that

Washington's earlier insecurity still resided beneath his confident air. One visitor picked up an interesting verbal tic of Washington's that may reflect a lack of education, the way he tripped over words: "The general converses with great deliberation and with ease, except in pronouncing some few words: in which he has a hesitancy of speech."[68] Such pauses may also have owed something to Washington's slippery dentures.

Starting in the summer of 1786, Humphreys came to Mount Vernon to compile research for his book. His admiring but incomplete narrative of Washington's life proved less important than the four-thousand-word marginal commentary penned by Washington on portions dealing with the French and Indian War. At some point after returning to Mount Vernon, Washington had assistants transcribe his letters from that period, and in another instance of old insecurities rearing their head, he corrected his youthful spelling and grammar and polished awkward passages. Addicted as always to self-control, he opposed inadvertent revelations of self.

During his Mount Vernon stays, Humphreys was a charming, amiable companion of the family. With a deep passion for poetry, he was wont to burst into recitations on the spur of the moment. He became the roving poet of the plantation, spouting verses *en plein air* when he quit work for the day. As happened with Lafayette, Humphreys brought out a youthful idealism in Washington, even a buried utopian streak. The man who had headed an army for more than eight years told Humphreys, in biblical cadences, that he longed to see the curse of war ended: "My first wish is to see this plague to mankind banished from the earth and the sons and daughters of this world employed in more pleasing and innocent amusements." He also wanted America to function as the promised land for the world's downtrodden: "Rather than quarrel about territory, let the poor, the needy, and oppressed of the earth . . . resort to the fertile plains of our western country, to the second land of promise, and there dwell in peace, fulfilling the first and great commandment."[69]

Slowly, Washington assembled a cadre of bright, capable young men—the peacetime equivalent of his military family—to assist him with the mounting stacks of paperwork. In January 1786 General Benjamin Lincoln recommended as a private secretary twenty-three-year-old Tobias Lear of New Hampshire, a Harvard graduate who read French and was a fluent letter writer. In reply, Washington explained that such an assistant would also tutor Washy and "will sit at my table—will live as I live—will mix with the company which resort to the Ho[use]."[70] Despite his unstinting admiration for Washington, Lear expressed one reservation about working at Mount Vernon: he abhorred slavery. Only when Washington declared his ultimate intention to free his slaves and said they would meanwhile be better off under his tutelage than anywhere else did Lear relent. The personal and professional relationship with Lear lasted much longer than that with the self-absorbed David Humphreys. Lear became yet another of the surrogate sons who supplied the absence of biological children for George and Martha Washington. The feeling was reciprocated, as can be seen in Lear's praise of Martha Washington as "everything that is benevolent and good. I honor her as a second mother and receive from her all those attentions which I should look for from her who bore me."[71]

CHAPTER THIRTY-NINE

Gentleman Farmer

GEORGE WASHINGTON might resign his commission—might spurn an impertinent suggestion that he be anointed king—but he refused to renounce a princely style in his private life, as if his highest social ambition after the war were to return to Virginia and resurrect the privileged world he had left behind. He had, in many ways, been transformed by the war, but he had not yet realized how profoundly the democratic message of the American Revolution would filter down to the masses and even, in the fullness of time, threaten slavery itself. He clung to the tastes of a British country squire while making few concessions to a more egalitarian ethos. Strange as it may sound, Mount Vernon after the war did not evolve in notable ways that reflected American independence, except for greater efforts at agricultural modernity.

Many improvements that Washington had first projected in the early 1770s came to fruition only after the long hiatus of the war. Where visitors had once approached Mount Vernon by a straight path, they now rode along a symmetrical pair of serpentine drives that tantalized them with flickering glimpses of the distant mansion. At the end, right before they alighted, their carriages ran over rough gravel and curved around a bowling green and a small circular courtyard. Unable to tell a lie, Washington admitted in his diary that he had "cut down the two cherry trees in the courtyard."[1] The house was now attached to the outlying buildings by graceful covered walkways that, instead of shutting out nature, disclosed distant vistas of natural beauty. All in all, Mount Vernon contained fourteen or fifteen separate buildings, giving newcomers the impression that they had rolled into a small, bustling rural village.

The most imposing expansion of the house was the soaring chamber at the north end, dubbed the New Room or Banquet Hall. The splendid stage set for many social and political gatherings, it was the closest approximation Washington could obtain to a state dining room. Executed in a grander and more refined style than anything else in the house—it made the rest seem fairly humdrum by comparison—the room rose two stories high, its height emphasized by a tall Palladian window. At the time, green and blue were the most expensive imported pigments, prompting a status-conscious Washington to opt for bright green wallpaper, which gave the room a cheerful buoyancy by day but must have lent guests a lurid sheen at candlelit dinners. Washington ordered gilded borders that endowed the green walls with "a rich and handsome look."[2]

When he mentioned to Samuel Vaughan of Philadelphia that the room lacked a chimneypiece, the English-born merchant spontaneously sent one of Italian marble, flanked by fluted columns and topped by pastoral imagery—farm animals, plows, contented peasants—evocative of Cincinnatus. This exquisite ornament, shipped in ten bulky cases, made Washington blush with embarrassment. Always dealing with an unresolved tension between his aristocratic tastes and republican ideology, he confessed to discomfort about the chimneypiece. "I greatly fear it is too elegant and costly for my room and republican style of living," he told Vaughan's son.[3] In the end, Washington overcame his doubts and held on to the piece. Clearly preparing to entertain sumptuously, he ordered seventy yards of red and white livery lace to outfit slaves tending guests.

In these early postwar years, Mount Vernon acquired the architectural touches that became its trademark and marked its owner's new self-assurance. Most striking was the two-story piazza fronting the Potomac, supported by eight square wooden pillars and with an English flagstone walkway. Porches were relatively new in America, and this one transcended anything Washington might have seen, underscoring his architectural daring. The stately piazza, with expansive views of the Potomac, lent itself to hospitality. The porch also signaled to river traffic coming around the bend—one visitor remembered an "amazing number of sloops . . . constantly sailing up and down the river"—the elevated standing of the plantation's owner.[4] "The view down the river is extensive and most charming," said Samuel Powel of Philadelphia, who called Mount Vernon "the most charming seat I have seen in America."[5] Washington paid a penalty in indoor comfort for his magnificent piazza, since the projecting roof plunged the rooms on that side into perpetual shadow. On the other hand, he had Windsor chairs and light portable tables brought onto the piazza in warm weather, which allowed guests to enjoy alfresco dining, cooled by river breezes and serenaded by parrots.

Adding grandeur to the west side was an octagonal cupola, surmounted by a weathervane, figured as the Dove of Peace, with a green olive branch in its black beak. It was a powerful statement from the former commander in chief, a silent prayer for peace. The gracious quality of Mount Vernon in the 1780s surely owed something to Washington's desire for a restful atmosphere after the backbreaking years of combat.

The man who won American independence nonetheless remained in thrall to British fashion. When he told Samuel Vaughan of his desire to redo the New Room in stucco, he added an anxious aside, as if seeking urgent confirmation—"which, if I understood you right, is the present taste in England."[6] On the slope between the piazza and the river, Washington laid out a deer park in the English style, with a mixed herd of English and American deer—an innovation that forced him to reduce hunting nearby, since foxhounds might have scared them away. He also tried to follow the English fashion of planting "live fences" or hedgerows instead of standard wooden fences. Along the sinuous drives, he laid out a formal English landscape, fragrant with groves, shrubs, and extensive pleasure gardens that invited strollers to enter and wander. His garrulous German gardener told anyone who cared to listen that he had served as gardener to the kings of Prussia and of England. Forming the ornamental centerpiece of the gardens was a handsome brick greenhouse with seven tall, narrow windows that spanned almost the entire wall. An uncommon structure in rural Virginia, this enclosure enabled Washington to grow palm trees and semitropical plants as well as lemons, limes, and oranges. In the surrounding meadows he selected trees with a discerning artistic eye, and in the springtime the estate was radiant with the bloom of peach, cherry, apple, apricot, lilac, and dogwood blossoms.

All this display impressed visitors, often wrongly, with the magnitude of the owner's wealth. When one English merchant toured Mount Vernon in 1785, he stumbled into this understandable error: Washington's "gardens and pleasure grounds . . . were very extensive . . . He is allowed to be one of the best informed as well as successful planters in America."[7] Washington was indeed well informed, but his success was more problematic. The merchant would have been shocked to hear Washington grumble that year that "to be plain, my coffers are not overflowing with money."[8] Unable to curtail his free-handed spending and with his crops faring poorly, he started out 1786 with a paltry eighty-six pounds in cash.

Although Washington delegated authority to managers and overseers, he never really developed a right-hand man or someone equivalent to him in power. Even after George Augustine Washington succeeded Lund, Washington kept a tight-fisted grip on operations, monitoring them through weekly reports, a process so rigorous that some detected a military mentality at work. Senator William Maclay later wrote of Mount Vernon as regimented to the point of madness: "It is under different overseers. Who may be styled generals . . . The Friday of every week is appointed for the overseers, or we will say brigadier generals, to make up their returns. Not a day's work but is noted what, by whom, and where done; not a cow calves or ewe drops her lamb but is registered . . . Thus the etiquette and arrangement of an army is preserved on his farm."[9]

To repair his damaged finances, Washington set out for his western holdings in September 1784, hoping to retrieve lost rents. He was accompanied by Dr. Craik and his son, his nephew Bushrod Washington, and three slaves. He had never ceased to be a prophet of the pristine Ohio Country, declaring during the Revolution that there was "no finer country in the known world than is encircled by the Ohio, Mississippi, and Great Lakes."[10] On the basis of prewar patents, Washington claimed thirty thousand western acres, with survey rights to an additional ten thousand. On an abstract level, Washington portrayed the western lands as a new American Eden, telling the Reverend John Witherspoon, a Presbyterian minister and president of the College of New Jersey, that "it would give me pleasure to see these lands seated by particular societies or religious sectaries with their pastors."[11] When it came to his actual behavior as a landlord, however, Washington never ascended to these giddy rhetorical heights and could sound like a downright skinflint.

The early postwar years witnessed a mad and often lawless scramble for western lands, and many settlers had little regard for eastern landlords who claimed their property. Throughout the Revolution Washington received reports of squatters occupying his land while legitimate tenants fell behind on payments. At first, inclining toward leniency, he said that those squatters who improved the land should be allowed to stay at reasonable rents. Giving them the benefit of the doubt, he said they might have inadvertently settled the land without realizing it was his. By the summer of 1784, however, he had lost all patience. Western rents had become his main source of revenue, and he decided to take matters into his own hands by personally dunning recalcitrant tenants. Less than a year after laying down his commission at Annapolis, the American Cincinnatus, badly strapped for cash, was reduced to a bill collector.

For this rugged journey across the Appalachian Mountains, Washington loaded up the horses with a large tent, camp utensils, a boat, medicine, and hooks and lines for fishing. He retraced the footsteps of earlier journeys into the western country, a landscape rife with youthful memories, including the march with Braddock's army. Still a fearless traveler, he didn't shrink from roughing it—at one campsite he slept under nothing but his cloak in a torrential downpour—but his diaries contain more references to fatigue than in earlier years as well as to rain running in rivulets down the trails.

A man of strongly fixed enthusiasms, Washington was also bent on reviving his long-standing but stalled project of improving the Potomac River navigation. He was still bedazzled by the vision of a watery gateway to the Ohio Valley that ran right by his home. When he arrived at Berkeley Springs, he came under the sway of a gifted inventor endowed with glib patter, James Rumsey, who had devised a mechanical boat that could churn upstream against the current. Always open to innovation, Washington was beguiled by Rumsey's craft. Spying a way to promote Potomac traffic, he did more than pay lip service to this device: he issued a written endorsement for Rumsey, vouching that he had actually seen his ungainly invention move upstream against the current.

When Washington stopped at his property at Great Meadows, scene of the Fort Necessity debacle, he made no reference in his diary to its bloody history. As before the war, he scrutinized the western frontier with the coolly appraising eyes of a landlord. He seemed exclusively concerned with the meadow's commercial value, commenting that it would make "a very good stand for a tavern. Much hay may be cut here when the ground is laid down in grass and the upland, east of the meadow, is good for grain."[12] Unsentimental about property, he ordered his local agent to rent the tract "for the most you can get for the term of ten years."[13]

In this wilderness area, Washington's fame counted for little and even exposed him to heightened danger. Protecting it as their rightful territory, Indians had engaged in violent confrontations with settlers on the northwest side of the Ohio River. Congress had banned settlers from this region, but speculators were still drawn by visions of colossal land grabs. "Men in these times talk with as much facility of fifty, a hundred, and even 500,000 acres as a gentleman formerly would do of 1,000 acres," noted Washington, who sounded sympathetic to Indian grievances.[14] Upon hearing stories of murdered settlers, he canceled a scheduled trip down the Ohio. "Had you proceeded on your tour down the river," one adviser told him, "I believe it would have been attended with the most dreadful consequences." The Indians had seized General James Wilkinson under the mistaken impression that he was Washington, and only with "much difficulty of persuasion and gifts" had he escaped.[15] To Washington's consternation, the violent clashes with Indians prevented him from visiting his extensive bounty lands on the Ohio and Great Kanawha rivers—lots measured not in feet but in miles—which were being brazenly offered for sale by speculators as far away as Europe.

On September 14 Washington had his first encounter with the families that had allegedly invaded his property Millers Run (not far from today's Canonsburg, Pennsylvania, southwest of Pittsburgh). While Washington's deputy, William Crawford, had surveyed the property as early as 1771, squatters contended that they had come upon an empty tract and occupied it before the patent was granted. If Washington expected special deference in these remote mountain hollows, he quickly learned otherwise. On the frontier, he did not enjoy the veneration he did back east, a rowdy new democratic culture having taken root.

As he bargained with poor, defiant settlers, members of a dissenting Presbyterian sect, Washington sounded a different note from his rhapsodic speech to John Witherspoon about seeding the West with religious sects or from his grandiloquent boast to Lafayette that Congress had "opened the fertile plains of the Ohio to the poor, the needy, and the oppressed of the earth."[16] After his first meeting with the Reed family, Washington noted sarcastically their effort "to discover all the flaws they could in my deed and to establish a fair and upright intention in themselves."[17] At their next meeting the tone turned even more confrontational. To settle the controversy, the Reeds offered to buy the land but balked at the steep price quoted by Washington. The standoff ended acrimoniously; the family decided to sue him, and Washington threatened to evict them. Reed family legend contended that a tetchy Washington responded "with dignity and some warmth, asserting that they had been forewarned by his agent, and the nature of his claim fully made known; that there could be no doubt of its validity, and rising from his seat and holding a red silk handkerchief by one corner, he said, 'Gentlemen, I will have this land just as surely as I now have this handkerchief.'"[18] The lawsuit wound bitterly through the courts for two years before Washington emerged victorious. Conciliatory in victory, he permitted the squatters to lease the property instead of evicting them.

By October 4 Washington had completed his 680-mile trip, which proved his last visit to the Ohio Country. While the dispiriting journey had failed to satisfy his economic objectives, it sharpened his views of policies needed to develop the region. He saw how fickle were the loyalties of the western settlers and how easily they might be lured someday by a designing foreign power. Since Spain had obstructed American commerce on the Mississippi River, Washington thought the United States could cement its grip on these inhabitants by offering them navigable waterways to the eastern seaboard, preferably through Virginia, creating "a smooth way for the produce of that country to pass to our markets before the trade may get into another channel."[19] He believed that "commercial connections, of all others, are most difficult to dissolve," which foreshadowed his faith as president in enduring commercial rather than political ties with other countries.[20] He also feared that thirteen squabbling states would be powerless to act in a timely fashion as the world was being swiftly reshaped on the western frontier.

FAR MORE GRATIFYING TO WASHINGTON than bullying hardscrabble farmers was his attempt to modernize postwar agriculture at Mount Vernon. He found farming congenial to his temperament and talked about it with undisguised relish, but he sometimes sounded more like a yeoman farmer, toiling by the sweat of his brow, than the master of a vast slave plantation. In 1788 he wrote that "the life of a husbandman, of all others, is the most delectable . . . To see plants rise from the earth and flourish by the superior skill and bounty of the laborer fills a contemplative mind with ideas which are more easy to be conceived than expressed."[21] Many dinner guests noted that Washington's flagging attention perked up whenever agriculture was discussed. Farming was a safe topic for him, deflecting conversation from political controversy, but it also ranked as a genuine passion. "Indeed, I am told that he feels more animation and throws off more of his natural phlegm when conversing on that topic than on any other," a young British diplomat later noted.[22]

Washington liked to affect a patrician tone about farming, as if it were merely an amusing pastime, but his livelihood depended upon it. His fascination with scientific agriculture was spurred initially by an urgent practical need: to figure out what to do with soil depleted by tobacco cultivation. He believed devoutly that American agriculture had to change and looked toward England as the model to emulate. "It may not in this place be amiss to observe to you that I still decline the growth of tobacco," he wrote to George William Fairfax in 1785, "and to add that it is my intention to raise as little Indian corn as may be. In a word, that I am desirous of entering upon a compleat course of husbandry as practiced in the best farming counties of England."[23] A curious boast coming from George Washington. With a genuine yearning for agricultural reform, he experimented with different seeds, grafted fruit trees, tested grapes for a homegrown Virginia wine, and collected cuttings from friends. Not to be outdone by Jefferson, he also devised a new agricultural plow that could seed and harrow fields at the same time. This was the golden age of amateur gentlemen scientists, and when Washington wanted to learn whether spermaceti candles or tallow candles were cheaper, he set up an experiment, recorded how long it took each type to burn, then computed that spermaceti candles were more than twice as expensive as tallow.

During the 1780s, with agricultural prices depressed, Washington found it hard to make any headway as a farmer. In November 1785 he told George William Fairfax that he never viewed his plantations "without seeing something which makes me regret having [continued] so long in the ruinous mode of farming which we are in."[24] The following year, perplexed by what to do, he launched an important correspondence with a renowned English agronomist, Arthur Young, who sent him his four-volume *Annals of Agriculture*. Candid about his own inadequacies as a farmer, Washington asked for advice about more than just the ruinous practices and backward farm implements at Mount Vernon. Rather, he saw the agricultural system of the whole country as bogged down in outdated methods and was especially critical of Virginia planters who exhausted their soil with endless rounds of tobacco, Indian corn, and wheat. Deciding to conserve his soil through crop rotation, Washington ordered a variety of new seeds from Young—including cabbage, turnips, rye, and hop clover—and under Young's tutelage eventually planted sixty different crops at Mount Vernon. A severe drought and a boll weevil infestation drastically cut his wheat yield in 1787. Nonetheless, determined to rotate his crops, he had by 1789 planted wheat, barley, oats, rye, clover, timothy, buckwheat, Indian corn, pumpkins, potatoes, turnips, peas, and flax. As president, he lent the prestige of his office to espousing a national board of agriculture that could diffuse scientific information to farmers.

In 1788 Washington commenced work on a two-story brick and timber barn, a hundred feet long, which would be "the largest and most convenient one in this country," as he bragged.[25] This massive construction project taxed the resources of Mount Vernon, where all 40,000 bricks were made; more than 35,000 board feet of pine planks and 100,000 juniper shingles were bought ready-made. Washington intended to store his grain and other crops in this commodious structure. "The barn is so well planned that a man can fill the racks with hay or potatoes easily and without any danger," noted Brissot de Warville, who appreciated the novelty of both barn and barnyard, which "were innovations in Virginia, where they have no barns and do not store fodder for cattle."[26] Starting in 1792, Washington also erected a specialized sixteen-sided barn for threshing wheat. As horses circled around the barn at a trot, trampling the wheat, the grain fell cleanly between gaps in the wooden floorboards to a granary on the lower level.

Always musing about the future of American agriculture, Washington introduced ingenious innovations at a merchant gristmill that he had first installed at his Dogue Run farm in the early 1770s. He recruited a Delaware inventor, Oliver Evans, who had figured out a way to automate all the mill elements through gears and conveyor belts. Powered by a sixteen-foot waterwheel, the mill hoisted the grain by buckets, ground it, then spread the high-quality flour to cool before it was poured into barrels for export. The sheer variety of business activities at Mount Vernon would make President Washington as receptive to the manufacturing visions of an Alexander Hamilton as to the agrarian dreams of a Thomas Jefferson.

Perhaps nothing better illustrated Washington's pioneering farm work than his development of the American mule, a hardy animal representing a cross between a male donkey (also called a jack) and a female horse. Mules were less fragile than horses but more docile than donkeys and cheap to maintain. Before Washington championed these creatures, they had hardly existed in the country. He started breeding them when he received a gray jack from the king of Spain called Royal Gift and a black jack called Knight of Malta from Lafayette. Royal Gift was big and lumbering but lacking in animal spark, whereas Knight of Malta was small but lusty. Washington cunningly bred the two animals and ended up with a jack known as Compound that merged the size of Royal Gift with the feisty nature of Knight of Malta. After some early difficulties, the resulting donkeys settled down and performed their duties, producing fifty-seven mules at Mount Vernon by century's end and enabling Washington to realize his hope to "secure a race of extraordinary goodness that will stock the country."[27] In addition to his better-known title of Father of His Country, Washington is also revered in certain circles as the Father of the American Mule.

CHAPTER FORTY

Devil's Bargain

FOR ALL THE TALK of agricultural modernity at Mount Vernon, there was something unreal about the entire topic for a plantation economy premised on that most antiquated and repressive of systems: slavery. As the most glaring negation of the American Revolution's ideals, slavery was bound to ignite controversy after the war. All the talk of liberty clashed with the reality of widespread bondage. Slavery posed the supreme challenge to the ideas that Washington had imbibed during the war and tested the pronouncements about peace and understanding that permeated his postwar correspondence. For the Marquis de Lafayette, the notion that an independent America would tolerate slavery was more than a contradiction in terms: it was anathema to everything he believed. As he told British abolitionist Thomas Clarkson, "I would never have drawn my sword in the cause of America if I could have conceived that thereby I was founding a land of slavery."[1] So profoundly in earnest was Lafayette that Clarkson called him "as uncompromising an enemy of the slave trade and slavery as any man I ever knew."[2]

As early as February 5, 1783, Lafayette made it overwhelmingly clear in a letter to Washington that his idol couldn't evade this touchy subject: "Permit me to propose a plan to you which might become greatly beneficial to the black part of mankind. Let us unite in purchasing a small estate where we may try the experiment to free the Negroes and use them only as tenants."[3] As he pointed out, Washington's sterling reputation could make this revolutionary act "general practice" in the United States.[4] As impulsive as Washington was cautious, Lafayette gloried in his iconoclasm. "If it be a wild scheme," he maintained, "I had rather be mad that way than to be thought wise on the other tack."[5] Lafayette's abolitionism may have been influenced by his wartime association with James Armistead, a slave who served under him in Virginia and operated as a valuable spy, infiltrating the British lines under the guise of being an escaped slave.

When Washington received Lafayette's letter, the war was winding down and he was dwelling on his impaired finances. His economic well-being depended on slavery, so that whatever his theoretical sympathy with Lafayette's idea, he could not have been thrilled by the timing. Not wanting to disillusion his worshipful protégé, he replied the way a fond father might write to an ardent but impractical son: "The scheme, my dear Marq[ui]s, which you propose as a precedent to encourage the emancipation of the black people of this country . . . is a striking evidence of the benevolence of your heart. I shall be happy to join you in so laudable a work, but will defer going into detail of the business till I have the pleasure of seeing you."[6] This was Washington's canny way of crediting Lafayette's noble project while also sidestepping any specific commitment to it.

At his home in Paris, Lafayette flaunted his ties to the American Revolution, posting a portrait of Washington and American flags on the walls. His infatuation did not cool with time. He seemed to live in an eternal, high-flown rapture with Washington and wrote to him in language that was almost ecstatic. In one letter he labeled Washington "the savior of his country, the benefactor of mankind, the protecting angel of liberty, the pride of America, and the admiration of the two hemispheres"—all in a single sentence.[7] After the war Washington was powerfully tempted to go to Paris, especially when a French nobleman assured him that King Louis XVI and Marie-Antoinette had "expressed their desire to be acquainted with the circumstances of a life which has so much contributed to the liberty of your country."[8] Washington felt the full force of this royal favor, which he labeled "one of the most flattering incidents" of his life.[9] When Lafayette pleaded with him to visit France, Washington had to rule it out because of his financial plight and because Martha was "too far advanced in life and is too much immersed in the care of her little progeny to cross the Atlantic." Writing like a pious hermit instead of a world-renowned general, Washington urged Lafayette and his wife to travel to Mount Vernon "and call my cottage your home . . . You will see the plain manner in which we live and meet the rustic civility. And you shall taste the simplicity of rural life."[10]

Nothing could stop Lafayette's triumphant return to America. While projecting a trip there in the spring of 1783, he wrote to Washington in a typical burst of enthusiasm, "Happy, ten times happy will I be in embracing my dear general, my father, my best friend."[11] Not until the following March did Lafayette assure Washington that, before the summer was out, "you will see a vessel coming up [the] Potomac, and out of that vessel will your friend jump with a panting heart and all the feelings of perfect happiness."[12] Washington responded with gratitude to the buckets of Gallic charm that Lafayette poured over his head at every turn.

Upon arriving at Mount Vernon in August 1784, Lafayette was delighted to find a group portrait of himself and his family in an honored place in the parlor. He bore a cherished gift from Paris, a Masonic apron that Adrienne had embroidered for the general. Lafayette was instantly entranced by Nelly and Washy. "The general has adopted them and loves them deeply," he told his wife. "It was quite funny when I arrived to see the curious looks on those two small faces who had heard nothing but talk of me the entire day and wanted to see if I looked like my portrait."[13]

Finding Washington busy but relaxed, Lafayette delighted in his company and treasured their dinner conversations, when they swapped wartime anecdotes. Washington guided him around the grounds and quizzed him about European flowers that might flourish there. All the while the vexed question of slavery hung heavily in the air. Earlier in the summer, during William Gordon's two-week stay, Washington had admitted to a desire to be rid of his slaves and mentioned Lafayette's abolitionist plans. "I should rejoice beyond measure could your joint counsels and influence produce it," Gordon responded, "and thereby give the finishing stroke and the last polish to your political characters."[14] Unfortunately, we don't know the specifics of the conversation between Washington and Lafayette about slavery. When Lafayette encountered James Madison, the former said he was now gripped by three obsessions: the French-American alliance, the unity of the thirteen states, and "the manumission of the slaves."[15] Madison, a large slave owner, wrote to Jefferson, another large slave owner, that Lafayette's position on slavery "does him real honor, as it is a proof of his humanity."[16] After the Revolution it was unquestionably fashionable to utter such high-minded sentiments, but talk was cheap and direct action was quite another matter.

While in Richmond, Lafayette had a consequential encounter with James Armistead, the handsome, round-faced slave who had gallantly assisted him during the war. To help him sue for his freedom, Lafayette furnished him with an affidavit that testified to his valor: "His intelligence from the enemy's camp were industriously collected and most faithfully delivered."[17] Not only did Armistead win his freedom and a pension from the legislature (which also compensated his master), but he changed his name in gratitude to James Armistead Lafayette.

Since Lafayette was slated to return to France in December, Washington, in a loving gesture, volunteered to escort him to his ship in New York—the first time he had ventured out of state since the war. When they reached Annapolis, however, the two men found themselves trapped in such a tedious round of receptions that Washington dreaded the ovations yet to come in Philadelphia and New York. So one day in early December, Washington and Lafayette gave each other an affectionate farewell hug and climbed into their respective carriages. Afterward, in an affecting letter that showed his powerful, if often suppressed, need for intimacy and how he equated Lafayette with his own lost youth, Washington told Lafayette of his turbulent emotions at their parting:

> In the moment of our separation upon the road, as I traveled and every hour since, I felt all that love, respect, and attachment for you with which length of years, close connection, and your merits have inspired me. I often asked myself, as our carriages distended, whether that was the last sight I ever should have of you? And tho[ugh] I wished to say no, my fears answered yes. I called to mind the days of my youth and found they had long since fled to return no more; that I was now descending the hill I had been 52 years climbing; and that tho[ugh] I was blessed with a good constitution, I was of a short-lived family and might soon expect to be entombed in the dreary mansions of my father's. These things darkened the shades and gave a gloom to the picture, consequently to my prospects of seeing you again. But I will not repine—I have had my day.[18]

One of Washington's premonitions in these melancholy musings proved correct: he never set eyes on Lafayette again.

Back in France, Lafayette showered Washington with gifts, including seven hounds sent in the custody of John Quincy Adams. He also sent along French pheasants and nightingales, which Washington had never seen before. All the while, Lafayette perfected his manumission scheme and acted on it the next year with breathtaking speed. He bought a large sugar plantation in Cayenne (French Guiana), on the South American coast, which came with nearly seventy slaves. He promptly began to educate and emancipate them, paying wages to those old enough to work, providing schooling for the children, and banning the sale of human beings. To make this scheme self-perpetuating, Lafayette instructed his agent to keep on adding more lands and freeing more slaves.

In congratulating him, Washington displayed enormous admiration while again shrinking from any firm commitment to a comparable project: "The benevolence of your heart, my dear Marquis, is so conspicuous upon all occasions that I never wonder at any fresh proofs of it. But your late purchase of an estate in the colony of Cayenne, with a view of emancipating the slaves on it, is a generous and noble proof of your humanity. Would to God a like spirit would diffuse itself generally into the minds of the people of this country, but I despair of seeing it."[19] To set the slaves "afloat" abruptly, he feared, would "be productive of much inconvenience and mischief, but by degrees it certainly might, and assuredly ought to be effected and that, too, by legislative authority."[20]

The news of Lafayette's feat came as Washington was being prodded to take a public stand on abolishing slavery. Before the war it had required an act of the royal governor and his council to free a slave. Then in 1782 a new law gave masters permission to free their own slaves, and hundreds manumitted at least a few. Influenced by the Revolution, antislavery societies sprang up across Virginia. In 1785 the Virginia legislature debated whether freed slaves should be permitted to stay in the state—something that might give their enslaved brethren seditious ideas—and abolitionist petitions were introduced. Washington became the target of a subtle but persistent campaign by abolitionists to enlist him in their cause. When Elkanah Watson visited Mount Vernon in January 1785, he bore books on emancipation written by British abolitionist Granville Sharpe, founder of the African colony of Sierra Leone. And then there were people such as Robert Pleasants, a Virginia Quaker who liberated seventy-eight of his slaves and proclaimed that Washington's failure to follow suit would leave an everlasting stain on his reputation.

That May, Thomas Coke and Francis Asbury, two eminent Methodist ministers, brought to Mount Vernon an emancipation petition that they planned to introduce in the Virginia legislature. Although Washington refrained from signing it, he voiced "his opinion against slavery," Asbury recorded in his diary, and promised to write a letter supporting the measure if it ever came to a vote.[21] This typified Washington's ambivalent approach to slavery in the 1780s: he privately made no secret of his disdain for the institution, but neither did he have the courage to broadcast his views or act on them publicly. After endorsing abolition, he shunted direct action onto other shoulders. Amid a blistering debate, the Coke-Asbury petition failed in the Virginia House of Delegates that November, with Madison reporting to Washington, "A motion was made to throw it under the table, which was treated with as much indignation on one side, as the petition itself was on the other."[22] Such fierce emotions must have given pause to Washington, if he harbored any unspoken thoughts about a future return to the political arena.

Washington's quandary over slavery was thrown into high relief by a visit on April 9, 1786, from a local slave owner, Philip Dalby, who had recently traveled to Philadelphia with his slave, a mulatto waiter named Frank. After Frank was spirited away by a team of Quaker abolitionists, Dalby filed suit in the Pennsylvania assembly and, to drum up support, placed a shrill ad in the Alexandria newspaper, warning planters about the "insidious" work of Philadelphia Quakers.[23] Incensed over the incident, Washington dashed off a strongly worded letter to his Philadelphia friend Robert Morris that expressed no sympathy for the Quakers, decrying instead their "acts of tyranny and oppression."[24] Unless these practices ceased, he warned, "none of those whose *misfortune* it is to have slaves as attendants will visit the city if they can possibly avoid it, because by so doing they hazard their property or they must be at the expense . . . of providing servants of another description for the trip."[25] This wasn't the only time Washington talked of slavery as a curse visited *on* him rather than a system of privilege enforced *by* him.

At this point in the letter, Washington suddenly remembered that he opposed slavery and had to justify his righteous indignation about the Quaker actions: "I hope it will not be conceived from these observations that it is my wish to hold the unhappy people who are the subject of this letter in slavery. I can only say that there is not a man living who wishes more sincerely than I do to see a plan adopted for the abolition of it [slavery], but there is only one proper and effectual mode by which it can be accomplished, and that by legislative authority. And this, as far as my suffrage will go, shall never be wanting."[26] Of course, Washington lacked a vote in the state legislature and took refuge in a position that was largely symbolic. The idea that abolition could be deferred to some future date when it would be carried out by cleanly incremental legislative steps was a common fantasy among the founders, since it shifted the burden onto later generations. It was especially attractive to Washington, the country's foremost apostle of unity, who knew that slavery was potentially the country's most divisive issue.

Historians often quote a September 1786 letter from Washington to John Francis Mercer as signaling a major forward stride in his thinking on slavery: "I never mean (unless some particular circumstance should compel me to it) to possess another slave by purchase, it being among my first wishes to see some plan adopted by the legislature by which slavery in this country may be abolished by slow, sure, and imperceptible degrees."[27] But this noble statement then took a harsh turn. Washington mentioned being hard pressed by two debts—to retire one of which, "if there is no other resource, I must sell land or Negroes to discharge."[28] In other words, in a pinch, Washington would trade slaves to settle debts. Clearly, the abolition of slavery would have exacted too steep an economic price for Washington to contemplate serious action. A month later Washington made a comment that narrowed the scope of his possible action: "It is well known that the expensive mansion in which I am, as it were, involuntarily compelled to live will admit of no diminution of my income."[29] In other words, for all his rhetorical objections to slavery, Washington found it impossible to wean himself away from the income it produced. Habituated to profligate spending and a baronial lifestyle, he was in no position to act forcefully on his principled opposition to slavery until the very end of his life.

It has long been debated whether Washington's growing aversion to slavery resulted from moral scruples or from a sense that slavery was a bad economic bargain, in which masters paid more for slaves' upkeep than they reaped in profit from their labor. The latter problem weighed on him in the mid-1780s, when the failure of his corn crop, the principal food for his slaves, slashed the profitability of his operations. Though he probably never read it, Washington would have agreed with Adam Smith's theory in *The Wealth of Nations* (1776) that slavery was a backward system because workers lacked economic incentives to improve performance. Slavery grew especially inefficient for Washington after he switched from labor-intensive tobacco cultivation to grain production, leaving him with surplus hands. In February 1786 he sat down in his study to tote up the number of slaves at his five farms and came up with a figure of 216. He must have been alarmed to discover that the number of slave children had risen to a startling 92, or nearly half the slaves, a figure that guaranteed that his slave population would burgeon from natural increase.

Whenever Washington discussed slavery with other planters, the inefficiency of the system dominated discussion, whereas with Lafayette, Washington sounded as if he were motivated purely by humanitarian concerns. Writing to Mercer in late 1786, he indicated that he felt burdened by more slaves than he could profitably employ: "For this species of property, I have no predilection nor any urgent call, being already overstocked with some kind of it."[30] He haggled with Mercer over settling money owed to him and expressed his willingness to take six male slaves in exchange for three hundred pounds of debt. Mercer evidently declined, because Washington replied, "I am perfectly satisfied with your determination respecting the Negroes. The money will be infinitely more agreeable to me than property of that sort."[31] Writing to Henry Lee, Jr., on February 4, 1787, Washington again announced that he was "in a great degree principled against increasing my number of slaves"; then in the next breath, he told Lee to buy him a slave, a bricklayer, whose sale was advertised in the newspaper.[32] Washington declared he would drop the deal if the slave had a family and refused to be separated. In 1788 Washington accepted another thirty-three slaves at Mount Vernon in settlement of a debt related to the estate of Martha's brother Bartholomew Dandridge.

In charting Washington's conflicting statements about slavery after the Revolution, one begins to sense that he had developed a split personality on the issue. On the one hand, his views still reflected his acquisitive prewar personality that had few, if any, ethical qualms about slavery. His business behavior had always been his least attractive side, showing the imprint of early hardship. On the other hand, another part of his personality reflected the countless years of conversations with Lafayette, Laurens, Hamilton, and other young aides inflamed by Revolutionary ideals, when he was headquartered in the North and uprooted from the southern plantation culture. With a politician's instinct, Washington spoke to different people in different voices. When addressing other Virginia planters, he spoke in the cold, hard voice of practicality, whereas when dealing with Revolutionary comrades, he blossomed into an altruist.

Nothing better illustrated his humanitarian views on slavery than a famous

statement he made to David Humphreys, the young New England poet who resided at Mount Vernon while working on his authorized biography. At some point
in 1788 or early 1789, Washington made an eloquent, if self-serving, statement—
Humphreys may have prettied it up—expressing qualms about slavery and the paternalistic compromises he had forged over the issue: "The unfortunate condition
of the persons whose labor in part I employed has been the only unavoidable subject of regret. To make the adults among them as easy and as comfortable in their
circumstances as their actual state of ignorance and improvidence would admit,
and to lay a foundation to prepare the rising generation for a destiny different from
that in which they were born, afforded some satisfaction to my mind and could
not, I hoped, be displeasing to the justice of the Creator."[33] The passage makes plain
that guilt tugged at Washington's mind as he struggled to square slavery with his
religious beliefs. The question remains: Did he really make life for the adult slaves
"as easy and as comfortable" as possible and prepare the slave children for a different destiny?

Whether from genuine concern or from patent self-interest, Washington prided
himself on his treatment of his slaves: "It has always been my aim to feed and clothe
[the slaves] well and be careful of them in sickness."[34] While we have no proof that
Washington wished to educate his slaves, we do know that Lund Washington's wife,
Elizabeth, a devout woman, taught slaves to read and distributed Bibles among
them—an activity that would have been considered taboo on many plantations.
There is no proof that Washington took sexual advantage of his slaves, although
one French visitor noted that many house servants were mulattoes, "some of whom
have kinky hair still but skin as light as ours."[35]

In recent years a controversy has raged as to whether Washington might have
fathered a mulatto slave named West Ford, who was born in the immediate aftermath of the Revolutionary War and bore a vague resemblance to the Washington
clan. The controversy first surfaced in 1940 but gained a new lease on life in 1998,
when DNA tests strongly pointed to Thomas Jefferson as having had children with
his slave Sally Hemings. This dramatic discovery lent fresh credence to the oral history of mixed-race families that claimed direct descent from America's slaveholding
founders.

The son of a slave named Venus, West Ford was owned by Washington's brother
Jack and his wife, Hannah, and grew up on their plantation, Bushfield, in Westmoreland County. When Hannah died around 1801, she singled out West Ford as
the only slave to receive his freedom when he reached twenty-one. Ford's privileged
status was further confirmed when Jack and Hannah's son Bushrod, who would
inherit Mount Vernon, gave him 160 acres adjoining the estate. Beyond such undeniable evidence of partiality, legend passed down through two branches of Ford

descendants that Venus had identified George Washington as the little boy's father and that he had attended church with Washington and even gone hunting and riding with him.

While historians have learned not to repudiate such stories with knee-jerk rigidity, George Washington's paternity of West Ford seems highly doubtful. The notion that he might have met and impregnated Venus during a trip that her mistress, Hannah, made to Mount Vernon seems unlikely. (Washington didn't visit Bushfield during the years in question.) Where the Sally Hemings affair was exposed during Jefferson's lifetime and her son Madison later published a memoir about it, the West Ford story slumbered suspiciously for a century and a half. With Mount Vernon invaded by visitors after the Revolutionary War, Washington constantly regretted his lack of privacy, and he would not likely have gambled his vaunted, hard-earned reputation by sleeping with a visiting slave. There is also the problem that Washington was likely sterile, although the problem with having children may have come from Martha. Perhaps the most compelling evidence against Washington being West Ford's father is that, in this abundantly documented life, not a single contemporary ever alluded to his having this mulatto child around him. Nor is there a single reference to Venus or West Ford in his voluminous papers. By contrast, one notes how frequently the ubiquitous Billy Lee pops up in Washington's papers or in contemporary accounts. Had the decorous Washington fathered West Ford, he most certainly would not have flaunted this lapse by taking him to church or riding to hounds with him. It is also hard to believe that Washington's malicious political enemies during his presidency would not have dredged up this damaging episode to discredit him. The most likely explanation of West Ford's singular status is that he was sired by Jack Washington or one of his three sons, Bushrod, Corbin, or William Augustine.

Washington's most commendable side was the respect he accorded to slave marriages, which enjoyed no standing under Virginia law. In April 1787, needing a bricklayer, he bought a slave named Neptune from a John Lawson. When Neptune showed up at Mount Vernon, Washington was dismayed to learn that he was distraught at being separated from his wife. Washington at once informed Lawson that he was "unwilling to hurt the feelings of anyone. I shall therefore, if agreeable to you, keep him a while to see if I can reconcile him to the separation (seeing her now and then), in which case I will purchase him; if not, I will send him back."[36] Taking matters into his own hands, Neptune escaped from Mount Vernon and returned to Lawson's plantation and a reunion with his wife. Interestingly enough, Neptune wasn't punished for this misbehavior and agreed to a compromise whereby he was hired out to Washington on a monthly basis.

The most striking case of Washington's respect for the inner life of slaves was his constant solicitude for Billy Lee, whom he endowed with the fancy title "Valet de Chambre" after the war.[37] Lee may be the dark-skinned slave standing off in the shadows of Edward Savage's famous painting *The Washington Family*, completed during the 1790s. In the group portrait, Washington sits at a table with Martha, unfurling a map of the new federal city of Washington, while Nelly and Washy stand beside them. Off to the right, the nameless slave is a dignified presence in a gray jacket with one hand thrust into a red waistcoat, his black hair falling straight over his collar. If Lee is the slave depicted, it would certainly attest to his special place in the Washington household.

During the war Lee had entered into a romantic liaison with Margaret Thomas, a free black or mulatto cook on Washington's staff, and they considered themselves married. Six months after returning to Mount Vernon, Lee sank into a funk because of his separation from Thomas, who resided in Philadelphia. Under prodding from Lee, Washington agreed to reunite them. The all-powerful Washington didn't care for Thomas but submitted to the pleas of the one slave he found it hard to deny. Contacting his Philadelphia friend Clement Biddle, he laid out the situation, explaining that Margaret Thomas had been "in an infirm state of health for some time and I had conceived that the connection between them had ceased, but I am mistaken. They are both applying to me to get her here, and tho[ugh] I never wished to see her more, yet I cannot refuse his request (if it can be complied with on reasonable terms) as he has lived with me so long and followed my fortunes through the war with fidelity."[38] Washington asked Biddle to track down Thomas, then living with a free black couple, Isaac and Hannah Sills, who also worked as cooks in Philadelphia. Biddle was instructed to pay Thomas's passage to Virginia by coach or ship. We don't know what happened to Margaret Thomas, and no evidence exists that she ever made it to Mount Vernon. Without question, a free black or mulatto woman would have dreaded traveling alone to a slave state such as Virginia, even under the auspices of George Washington. At the very least, as a Mount Vernon cook, she would have been forced to live and work with slaves, while retaining the rights of a free person—hardly a comfortable situation for all involved. One wonders exactly how Washington planned to negotiate this delicate situation. Did he expect Billy Lee to continue as a slave while married to a resident cook and free woman? And how would the other Mount Vernon slaves have reacted to the subversive presence of a free woman of color, wedded to Washington's favorite slave?

What we do know is that, by the standards of master-slave relationships, Washington remained uncommonly attentive toward Billy Lee. In April 1785 he was surveying land with Lee, who was carrying one of the chains when he slipped and broke his knee, an injury so severe that Washington had to order a sled to transport him home. Three years later Lee tripped again and broke the second knee, turning him into a cripple. We know that Lee had an alcohol problem, but we don't know whether it was the cause or an effect of these injuries. When two broken knees left Lee incapacitated, Washington converted him into a cobbler and sometime overseer of other slaves. In later years the outgoing Lee was reputedly a loquacious storyteller as he greeted veterans and exhibited his affection for Washington. Despite his servitude, he reminisced nostalgically about the war, even wearing a cocked hat to emphasize his earlier service. Of course, it is impossible to know, as Lee rambled on, what obscure hurts he concealed at being denied the status of a full-fledged soldier.

One also wonders to what extent Washington's attachment to Lee influenced his later determination to emancipate his slaves. His proximity to a single slave during many years of war must have made it harder for him to believe that slaves were inferior beings and that their bondage could be justified. Lee was not only an expert hunter and horseman but also an energetic raconteur with a vibrant personality and rich emotional life that shines through in the smattering of stories about him. On the other hand, there's no sense that Washington confided in Lee or treated him as anything like a peer.

While Washington was never sadistic or abusive toward slaves, he could be a demanding boss with minimal patience for error. When English farmer Richard Parkinson visited Virginia in 1798, he picked up scuttlebutt from local planters that Washington "treated [his slaves] with more severity than any other man."[39] Washington's temperamental outbursts likely stemmed in part from his unrelenting money problems. He also suffered from a conceptual blind spot about slavery, tending to regard it as a fair economic exchange: he clothed and fed his workers, and "in return, I expect such labor as they ought to render."[40] He could never seem to understand why his slaves might regard this tacit bargain as preposterous. Any slaves who shirked work, he believed, were cheating him, and he wouldn't stand for it. In 1785 he conducted a frosty exchange with a slave whose arm was injured and in a sling. Washington didn't see why the man couldn't work. Grasping a rake in one hand and thrusting the other in his pocket, he proceeded to demonstrate one-handed raking. "See how I do it," Washington said. "I have one hand in my pocket and with the other I work. If you can use your hand to eat, why can't you use it to work?"[41] Similarly, Washington expected pregnant women and elderly slaves to work, albeit at less strenuous jobs closer to home.

So intent was Washington on extracting the full measure of work from slaves that he could be shockingly oblivious to their hardships. Perhaps the most agonizing work at Mount Vernon involved reclaiming swamps. Even in the iciest weather Washington didn't relax his grip or halt this grueling outdoor labor. In January and February 1788 eastern Virginia suffered through a winter so frigid that the Potomac froze for five weeks and Mount Vernon lay "locked fast by ice," as Washington told Henry Knox.[42] As the temperature dipped to ten degrees, Washington often found it too cold to attend meetings away from home. Nevertheless, his hands spent more than a week taking ice from the frozen river and packing it into the icehouse.

During this deep freeze Washington refused to cancel any slave activities, and the heavy-duty field work went on unabated. On January 3 he noted that the thermometer stood at twenty-five degrees as he made the chilly rounds of his plantations. Nevertheless everyone was outdoors working. At Dogue Run, he wrote, "the women began to hoe the swamp they had grubbed in order to prepare it for sowing in the spring with grain and grass seeds." At Muddy Hole, "the women, after having threshed out the peas, went about the fencing." And at another farm, "the women were taking up and thinning the trees in the swamp, which they had before grubbed."[43] It is hard to imagine more brutal manual labor than women pulling up tree stumps in icy swamps in record-setting cold, but Washington seems not to have found this inhuman scene objectionable and in no way diminished the work. On February 5 the notably rugged Washington informed Knox that "the air of this day is amongst the keenest I ever recollect to have felt."[44] When he made the circuit of his farms the next morning, he introduced an unusual notation: "Rid out, but finding the cold disagreeable, I returned."[45] Despite this fierce cold, with nine inches of snow covering the ground, Washington kept everyone busy in the fields and noted approvingly in his diary, "Hands of all the places (except the men) working in the new ground" at the mansion house.[46] It was as if Washington feared that even the slightest concession would lead to a raft of others, so he insisted on getting the daily quota of work from his slaves.

Like all other plantation owners, Washington had become so accustomed to slavery that the bizarre began to seem normal. He had always kept a strict separation between his social and professional lives and for a long time went foxhunting and toured his farms on separate days. Then on January 4, 1786, he began to mix these two incompatible tasks, riding to hounds and visiting field hands at the same time. "After breakfast, I rid by the places where my Muddy Hole and Ferry people were clearing," he wrote in his diary. "Thence to the [grist] mill and Dogue Run plantations and, having the hounds with me, in passing from the latter toward Muddy Hole plantation, I found a fox, which, after dragging him some distance and running him hard for near an hour, was killed by the cross road in front of the house."[47] Thereafter he routinely combined foxhunting with tours of the outlying slave plantations. One can only imagine what thoughts passed through the minds of field hands who wearily lifted their heads from stoop labor, only to see the jolly master and his friends careering past them in the wintry landscape behind a pack of foxhunting hounds.

The Ruins of the Past

WHEN WASHINGTON CONSENTED IN 1783 to serve as first president of the Order of the Cincinnati, he imagined himself signing on to a fraternal organization that was charitable in intent and incontrovertibly good. So convinced was he of its virtue that he did not agonize over becoming president the way he mulled over comparable decisions in his life. Though not a founder of the group, he felt a fraternal camaraderie with his fellow officers and cottoned to the idea of perpetuating their comradeship. He even offered a five-hundred-dollar gift to invigorate the Cincinnati. Distracted by other matters, he didn't heed at first the rancorous debates brewing over the organization's character. "I was conscious that my own proceedings on that subject were immaculate," he later declared a shade defensively.[1] As shown by the slavery issue, Washington didn't wish to be ensnared in political controversy or do anything that might mar his hard-won image as the incarnation of national unity.

But the formation of a hereditary society, with membership inherited through eldest sons, awakened the hostility toward aristocracy bred by the Revolution. Blasted as elitist, the society raised the dread specter of a military caste that might dominate American political life. That Washington lacked a male heir spared him no criticism. After all, the society's very name paid tribute to his ineffable mystique. In hunting down monarchical plots, the new nation displayed an active, often paranoid imagination. In later years Jefferson stated that it had "always been believed" that some army officers, especially Steuben and Knox, had offered a crown to Washington and started the Cincinnati only when he rejected it, hoping the hereditary order would "be engrafted into the future frame of government and placing Washington still at the head."[2] There was no evidence whatsoever that Steuben and Knox ever contemplated such an offer.

When Benjamin Franklin's daughter transmitted to him press reports about the new society, he replied that he could understand the Chinese practice of honoring one's parents, who after all had achieved something. To honor descendants, however, merely from the accident of biology, was "not only groundless and absurd but often hurtful to that posterity." Any sort of hereditary society, he declared, would stand "in direct opposition to the solemnly declared sense" of the new country.[3] John Adams also went on the warpath against the Cincinnati, damning the group as "the deepest piece of cunning yet attempted . . . the first step taken to deface the beauty of our temple of liberty."[4]

No sooner had Washington announced the first national meeting, to be held in Philadelphia in May 1784, than he was taken aback by angry rumbles about the hereditary requirement, an early inkling of the boisterous democratic tendencies that would reshape the country and challenge the preeminence of the former officer corps. Henry Knox, the society's first secretary general, summed up this dissent for Washington: "The idea is that it has been created by a foreign influence in order to change our forms of government."[5] Even Lafayette in Paris, heading the French chapter, wound up embroiled in conflict: "Most of the Americans here are indecently violent against our association . . . [John] Jay, [John] Adams, and all the others warmly blame the army."[6] For Washington, it was a painful contretemps: his first public act since the war had backfired, and it engulfed him in a flaming controversy. Since the group's power derived largely from its identification with Washington, he lacked the option of staying aloof and remaining deaf to this rising storm of criticism.

Always jealous of his reputation for republican purity, Washington hated to have his integrity questioned. To defuse the controversy, he was eager to eliminate the group's more odious features. As he told Jonathan Trumbull, Jr., "If we cannot convince the people that their fears are ill-founded, we should (at least in a degree) yield to them and not suffer that which was intended for the best of purposes to produce a bad one which will be the consequence of divisions."[7] As was his wont, he responded to criticism by soliciting disparate opinions. He turned to Jefferson, who predictably faulted the group for relying on "preeminence by birth" and also worried that some future president of the Cincinnati might "adopt a more mistaken road to glory."[8]

By the time of the Philadelphia meeting, Washington was eager to respond to criticism swirling around the group. Some of it he thought maliciously exaggerated "by designing men to work their own purposes upon terrified imaginations," but he acknowledged the genuine kernel of discontent.[9] In his inaugural speech, he stated categorically that the Society of the Cincinnati must mend its ways. In notes prepared for the speech, he listed his reform agenda: "Strike out every word, sentence, and clause which has a political tendency. Discontinue the hereditary part in all its connections . . . Admit no more honorary members into the society. Reject subscriptions or donations from every person who is not a citizen of the United States."[10] Delivering this blunt message, the ordinarily circumspect Washington was fiery and outspoken. As one of those present, Winthrop Sargent, observed, "In a very long speech, and with much warmth and agitation, he expressed himself on all the parts of the institution deemed exceptionable and reiterated his determination to vacate his place in the society, if it could not be accommodated to the feeling and pleasure of the several states."[11]

Washington's performance in Philadelphia showed that he could be a forceful orator who spoke at length and with passion if he wanted to. That he often failed to do so was because he preferred to keep his own counsel and reveal only a tiny portion of his thoughts, keeping his options open. He knew his power before a crowd of people, as shown during the Newburgh uprising, and could turn on the spigot of his oratory at will. The speech also showed Washington's awareness of his unique political standing—and his willingness to exploit it by threatening to resign if objectionable traits of the Cincinnati were not removed. His emotional comments also suggest extreme irritation at being dragged into the unwelcome glare of public controversy. The methodical Washington didn't like to be taken by surprise. The French engineer Pierre-Charles L'Enfant had designed for the society an insignia with a bald eagle, hung from a pale blue and white ribbon. When French officers gave Washington this medal, adorned with diamonds and emeralds, he secreted it in a drawer and never wore it for fear of being branded a pseudoroyalist.

Although he agreed to serve a three-year term as president, he later said that it was "much against my inclination," a way to salve any wounded feelings among his fellow officers.[12] His success in purging the society of its disputed features was only partial. He wanted the group to discard national meetings and limit assemblies to state chapters, which, among other things, would lower his own high-profile connection with it. Openly opposing him, delegates voted to retain the general gatherings, and several state chapters refused to accept the alterations adopted at the national meeting, leaving the hereditary feature intact. If Washington had shown political agility in tackling the group's problems and juggling conflicting demands, he had also seen that he couldn't determine the final outcome and was reluctant to be party to something beyond his control.

Having quieted the uproar temporarily, Washington knew that "the jealousies of the people are rather asleep than removed on this occasion."[13] Had it not been for his deep sense of solidarity with American and French officers and a respect for the group's laudable work for widows and orphans, Washington probably would have severed his ties with the Cincinnati and proposed its abolition. The intransigence of state societies in contesting reforms only hardened his resolve to insulate himself from them. He devised a compromise whereby he remained a figurehead and signed official forms, while keeping a self-protective distance, planning all the while to step down as president before the next general meeting in 1787.

A far happier association was with the Masons. Whatever conspiracy theories later circulated about the group, the brotherhood provoked no suspicions in late-eighteenth-century America, and Washington seldom missed a chance to salute their lodges. The group's soaring language, universal optimism, and good fellowship appealed to him. When he was sent Masonic ornaments late in the war, he recast the struggle in Masonic imagery, saying that all praise was due "to the *Grand Architect* of the Universe, who did not see fit to suffer his superstructures and justice to be subjected to the ambition of the princes of this world."[14] In June 1784 he was inducted into the Alexandria lodge as an honorary member, which gave him dual membership there and in the Fredericksburg lodge. Later elevated to master of the Alexandria lodge, he earned the distinction of being the only Mason to hold this post while simultaneously serving as president of the United States. Where he had kept a wary attitude toward the Cincinnati, he proudly embraced Masonic rituals. When an elderly resident of Alexandria, William Ramsay, was buried in 1785, Washington noted in his diary that he had not only attended the funeral but "walked in procession as a free mason, Mr. Ramsay in his lifetime being one and now buried with the ceremonies and honors due to one."[15]

In 1785 Washington formed an institutional tie that led him ineluctably back into national politics. His western trip the previous autumn had rekindled his fervent faith in the Potomac River as the gateway to America's interior. After the trip he lobbied Virginia governor Benjamin Harrison to form a company that would make the Potomac, with its stony obstructions, waterfalls, and rapids, navigable to the headwaters of the Ohio. Completing the linkage would require additional canals, locks, and portages. However partial he was to the Potomac, Washington also held out the possibility of extending the James River. He pressed Madison and others in the Virginia House of Delegates to champion the navigation project, then took up the same cause with Maryland legislators in Annapolis. Since Virginia and Maryland shared rights to the Potomac, any project required the joint approval of both states. "It is now near 12 at night," an exhausted Washington wrote to Madison from Annapolis on December 28, "and I am writing with an aching head, having been constantly employed in this business since the 22nd without assistance from my colleagues."[16] Madison was agog at Washington's stamina. "The earnestness with which he espouses the undertaking is hardly to be described," he remarked to

Jefferson, "and shows that a mind like his, capable of grand views . . . cannot bear a vacancy."[17]

Washington's advocacy of the Potomac project united a private motivation (to enhance the wealth of western landowners such as himself) with a political motivation (to bind western settlers to the United States and forge a national identity). He was disturbed by ongoing clashes between settlers and Indians but thought it fruitless to try to stem the restless droves of immigrants pushing ever farther westward. Although the government couldn't halt this tide, it could guide it into constructive channels. "The spirit of emigration is great," he told Richard Henry Lee. "People have got impatient and tho[ugh] you cannot stop the road, it is yet in your power to mark the way."[18]

Washington became something of a monomaniac about the Potomac River project, and more than one Mount Vernon visitor was trapped in the talons of this obsession. When Elkanah Watson stayed there in January 1785, he described the inland navigation scheme as Washington's "constant and favorite theme."[19] Waving away questions about the Revolutionary War and dwelling compulsively on the river project, Washington computed the distances from Tidewater Virginia to spots in the interior. "Hearing little else for two days from the persuasive tongue of the great man," wrote Watson, "I confess completely infected me with the canal mania."[20]

In early January 1785 Virginia and Maryland decided to survey the two potential waterways to the Ohio Country and incorporated a pair of private companies, the Potomac River Company and the James River Company, to extend those rivers into the interior. To finance this extensive work, the legislatures would allow entrepreneurs to charge tolls on the waterways. Imagining that the companies would be quite lucrative, Washington had no qualms about businessmen booking large profits as long as their work served the public weal and provided a model for future government action.

While Washington rejoiced over his legislative victories, the state of Virginia threw him into a profound dilemma by deeding him a gift of fifty shares of Potomac River Company stock and one hundred shares of James River Company stock to recognize his services to the state. Having sacrificed a salary throughout the war, Washington was not about to accept payment now; nor did he want to seem vain or offend his fellow Virginians by brusquely dismissing their kind gesture. He admitted to Governor Harrison that "no circumstance has happened to me since I left the walks of public life, which has so much embarrassed me." If he spurned the gift, he feared, people would think "an ostentatious display of disinterestedness or public virtue was the source of the refusal." On the other hand, he wanted to remain free to articulate his views without arousing suspicions that "sinister motives had the smallest influence in the suggestion."[21] He valued his reputation for integrity, calling it "the principal thing which is laudable in my conduct."[22] Noting that such "gratuitous gifts are made in other countries," Washington wanted to establish a new benchmark for the behavior of public figures in America and eliminate petty or venal motives.[23]

Perplexed, Washington sent a flurry of letters to confidants, asking how to handle the unwanted gift. Beleaguered by money problems at Mount Vernon, he nevertheless tried to project the cavalier image of an affluent planter who had far more money than he needed. Throughout his life he cherished the pose of noblesse oblige in public service, even if he could scarcely afford it. Referring to his lack of children, he told Henry Knox airily, "I have nobody to provide for and I have enough to support me through life in the plain and easy style in which I mean to spend the remainder of my days."[24] In fact, Washington had insufficient money to support himself, his wards, and his slaves, and his style of life was scarcely plain and easy. He came up with an enlightened solution: he would hold the gift shares in trust for public education, possibly for the creation of "two charity schools, one on each river for the education and support of the children of the poor and indigent," especially those who had lost fathers in the war.[25] The final disposition of the money was deferred for many years.

To iron out differences between Virginia and Maryland over Potomac navigation, Washington presided over an interstate conference at Mount Vernon in 1785. He was also elected president of the Potomac River Company, for which he tirelessly proselytized. In early August he climbed into a canoe and undertook the first of his periodic inspection tours of the Potomac, investigating submerged obstacles at Seneca Falls and Shenandoah Falls by personally shooting the rapids. He was also involved in hiring a European superintendent and dozens of indentured servants to build the canals and locks. Soon teams of slaves went to work, their heads shaved to make it more difficult for them to escape without detection. Washington's ambition was huge: the lock canal constructed around Great Falls alone would rank as the biggest civil engineering project in eighteenth-century America. To carve open the interior, the Virginia legislature authorized the building of the Chesapeake and Ohio Canal, which would connect the Potomac and Ohio rivers, and the Kanawha Canal, linking the James with the Great Kanawha River in western Virginia. Both projects took decades to reach fruition.

A determined man, George Washington reveled in having overcome great skepticism to establish the Potomac River Company. When Robert Hunter visited Mount Vernon in November, he noticed that his host engaged in uncharacteristic gloating: "The general sent the bottle about pretty freely after dinner and gave 'Success to the navigation of the Potomac' for his toast, which he has very much [at] heart, and when finished will, I suppose, be the first river in the world . . . He is quite pleased at the idea of the Baltimore merchants laughing at him and saying it was a ridiculous plan and would never succeed."[26]

The plan to extend navigation of the Potomac influenced American history in ways that far transcended the narrow matter of commercial navigation. It created a set of practical problems that could be solved only by cooperation between Virginia and Maryland, setting a pattern for a seminal interstate conference at Annapolis in September 1786 and indeed the Constitutional Convention itself in 1787. Coordinating the efforts of two states confirmed Washington's continental perspective and sense of the irreparable harm that could be done by squabbling among states unconstrained by an effective national government. When Edward Savage painted *The Washington Family,* he shrewdly made the Potomac River, wending its way west in the background, a central element of the composition. Washington continued to tout the Potomac as "the great avenue into the western country . . . which promises to afford a capacious asylum for the poor and persecuted of the earth."[27] The Potomac River Company never lived up to these grandiose expectations: in the nineteenth century it went bankrupt, having penetrated no farther than Cumberland in the foothills of the Allegheny Mountains. But its real value in American politics had long since been realized.

FOR ALL THE HOPEFULNESS of his postwar life, Washington retained wistful recollections about his prewar existence, especially his relationship with George William and Sally Fairfax. Wartime duties had precluded him from acting as caretaker of Belvoir, and he was alarmed to hear rumors as early as 1778 that the estate was "verging fast to destruction."[28] Before the war the Fairfaxes had returned to England to follow a suit in Chancery, which involved a sizable estate left to George William by a relative; the case degenerated into a ghastly, never-ending Dickensian donnybrook. George William told Washington in August 1778 that the case was "as far from a conclusion as ever, owing to the villainy of my solicitor."[29] Lacking the income expected from the suit's resolution and deprived of any money from Virginia, the hitherto rich couple had to retrench drastically. They were both broken in health and had bought a small cottage near Bath so they could take the spa waters. There a chastened General John Burgoyne, after his Saratoga defeat, sought out the couple and hand-delivered a personal letter from General George Washington.

During the last year of the war, Belvoir had been severely damaged by fire, but for more than a year Washington could neither find the time nor muster the nerve to visit it. Then in late January 1785 he made a midwinter visit and grew awash in nostalgia. On February 27 he sent a heartfelt letter to George William in which he described the ravages visited upon their beloved Belvoir:

I took a ride there the other day to visit the ruins—and ruins indeed they are. The dwelling house and the two brick buildings in front underwent the ravages of the fire; the walls of which are very much injured. The other houses are sinking under the depredation of time and inattention and I believe are now scarcely worth repairing. In a word, the whole are, or very soon will be, a heap of ruin. When I viewed them—when I considered that the happiest moments of my life had been spent there—when I could not trace a room in the house (now all rubbish) that did not bring to my mind the recollection of pleasing scenes, I was obliged to fly from them and came home with painful sensations and sorrowing for the contrast.[30]

Whenever he gazed longingly toward Belvoir, he admitted, he wished that George William and Sally Fairfax would return to America and rebuild their residence while staying at Mount Vernon. He added that Martha joined him in this fervent wish.

This letter is remarkable in two ways. Washington states that the happiest moments of his life were spent not with his wife but with George William and Sally Fairfax, although one suspects he really had Sally in mind. Does the letter suggest that George William knew of the romantic liaison between his wife and Washington? Or does it tell us that their relationship was more an affectionate friendship than an adulterous affair, enabling Washington to refer to it with complete safety? Perhaps it confirms that Washington's fondness for Sally Fairfax had been a youthful dalliance that everyone now recognized as such. We will never know the full truth of this tantalizing but finally murky story. The letter is also notable in showing us how incurably sentimental Washington was beneath the surface—he could experience an eruption of memories so overpowering that he had to flee the scene.

In reply, George William Fairfax talked of the picturesque valley of dairy farms in which he and Sally lived and asserted they were too old to contemplate a return to America. Sally had pored over Washington's letter with great care, and his description of the ride to Belvoir had provoked an equally strong response in her. "Your pathetic description of the ruin of Belvoir House produced many tears and sighs from the former mistress of it," wrote George William—doubtless what Washington yearned to hear.[31] Sally volunteered to send Washington seeds for trees and shrubs for Mount Vernon, and he reacted with typical gallantry, reassuring George William that "while my attentions are bestowed on the nurture of [the seeds], it would, if anything was necessary to do it, remind me of the happy moments I have spent in conversations on this and other subjects with that lady at Belvoir."[32] So Washington again openly alluded to his special relationship with Sally Fairfax without fearing repercussions. After years of precarious health, George William Fairfax died on April 3, 1787. By that point the Constitutional Convention was looming, and Washington, sidetracked by political business, declined to act as American executor of his friend's estate.

The themes of love and marriage were often on Washington's mind after the war. Before it ended, Lund Washington had sounded him out on the prospective marriage of Jacky Custis's widow, Eleanor Calvert Custis, to Dr. David Stuart. Washington customarily refrained from giving advice in such situations because if he supported it, he might push a couple into an unwanted marriage, but if he opposed it, the young couple would blithely ignore him anyway. Nevertheless he went on to say that if Eleanor asked him, he would counsel her thus: "I wish you would make a prudent choice, to do which many considerations are necessary: such as the family and connections of the man, his fortune (which is not the *most* essential in my eye), the line of conduct he has observed, and disposition and frame of his mind. You should consider what prospect there is of his proving kind and affectionate to you; just, generous, and attentive to your children; and how far his connections will be agreeable to you."[33] Rather glaringly absent from this eminently reasonable list is romance—perhaps the sole ingredient lacking in Washington's otherwise happy, satisfying match with Martha. At the same time, he knew that genuine friendship formed the foundation of a marriage, and this, at the very least, he had found in abundance with his wife.

Martha viewed marriage in a similarly pragmatic light. When her niece Fanny contemplated marriage to George Augustine Washington, Martha tried to coach her in sizing up marital prospects. She recommended that Fanny look at a man's character and worldly prospects—whether he was honest, upright, hardworking, and likely to be a good provider. She didn't mention looks or charm or compatibility or any of the other romantic prerequisites that might preoccupy a modern woman.

When Fanny and George Augustine decided to get married, the Washingtons were jubilant about the match of these two young favorites. Before the October 1785 wedding, Washington paid for his nephew to spend time in the West Indies in an attempt to repair his health. Although the Washingtons invited the young couple to share the Mount Vernon mansion with them, the suggestion came loaded with one big caveat. As Washington told Lund, the young couple had been urged to "make this house their home till the squalling and trouble of children might become disagreeable."[34] By this point, the Washingtons had probably had their fill of the responsibility of caring for children.

Just as Washington's postwar years were touched with many intimations of mortality, so Martha had many somber occasions to reflect on life's brevity. In April 1785 an express messenger arrived at Mount Vernon bearing a double dose of dreadful news for her: her mother, seventy-five-year-old Frances Dandridge, and her last surviving brother, forty-eight-year-old Judge Bartholomew Dandridge, had died within nine days of each other. These deaths lengthened the already-long list of family losses Martha had endured, starting with the demise of her first husband and all four of her children. The death of her younger brother meant that, among her seven siblings, only her youngest sister, Betsy, was still alive. Like the Washingtons, the Dandridge clan seemed doomed to suffer untimely deaths.

The following year George Washington suffered two tremendous blows. He had always delighted in the bright young men in his military family, often finding it easier to befriend these protégés than his peers, and he had felt special warmth for Lieutenant Colonel Tench Tilghman, who handled his business matters in Baltimore. "I have often repeated to you that there are few men in the world to whom I am more sincerely attached by inclination than I am to you," Washington had assured him.[35] Genial and unassuming, Tilghman had entered fully into Washington's confidence, and the latter was grief-stricken when the younger man died at age forty-one in April 1786. In a mighty tribute, Washington told Jefferson that his former aide had "as fair a reputation as ever belonged to a human character," and he speculated that he mourned the death more keenly than anyone outside of Tilghman's own family.[36]

Perhaps more consequential for America's future was the demise of General Nathanael Greene at forty-three. Just as Washington and Greene had seen eye to eye on war-related matters, so they had viewed the country's postwar turmoil with similar apprehension. Like Washington, Greene had developed a federal perspective and feared that the total autonomy of the states would culminate in feuding and anarchy. As he warned Washington, "Many people secretly wish that every state should be completely independent and that, as soon as our public debts are liquidated, that Congress should be no more—a plan that would be as fatal to our interest at home as ruinous to it abroad."[37] Unfortunately, Greene's personal finances were in no less disorderly a state than those of the country at large: he had accumulated such heavy debts guaranteeing contracts for the southern army that it gave him "much pain and preyed heavily upon my spirits."[38] He also revealed to Washington in August 1784 that for two months he had experienced a "dangerous and disagree[able] pain" in his chest, which sounds like heart disease.[39] In June 1786, while at his estate near Savannah, Georgia, he was seized at the table with a "violent pain in his eye and head," followed by his death a few days later.[40]

Washington mourned Greene's death for many months. Beyond personal grief, he knew that the country had lost a man cut out for bigger things. He had counted on Greene as a political ally and kindred spirit and said he regretted "the death of this valuable character, especially at this crisis, when the political machine seems pregnant with the most awful events."[41] It seems likely that, had Greene lived, Washington would have chosen him as the first secretary of war in preference to Henry Knox. Greene died in such dire economic straits that Washington volunteered to pay for the education of his son, George Washington Greene. It was yet another example of Washington's extraordinary generosity in caring for the offspring of friends and family, whatever his own financial stringency.

CHAPTER FORTY-TWO

A Masterly Hand

FOR A MAN WHO EMPHASIZED HIS DISCOMFORT when posing for artists, George Washington dedicated an extraordinary amount of time to having his likeness preserved for posterity. As shown by his constant attention to his papers, he guarded his fame with vigilance. Sensitive to charges of self-promotion—charges that seemed to ring in his ears alone—he preferred sitting for artists when he could cite a plausible political excuse for doing so. Such was the case in the late summer of 1783, when Congress commissioned an equestrian statue of him and gave the prestigious assignment to artist Joseph Wright, who had the perfect pedigree to appease Washington's strict conscience. His mother, Patience Wright, a Quaker sculptor from Philadelphia, specialized in waxwork portraits. While mother and son were based in wartime London, she had patented a unique form of espionage by relaying secret messages to Benjamin Franklin and American politicians at home through messages sealed inside her waxed heads.

After studying with Benjamin West in London, Joseph Wright returned to America and received the coveted commission for the Washington statue. He began with an oil portrait of the general that many deemed "a better likeness of me than any other painter has done," Washington conceded.[1] Washington was then residing at Rocky Hill, outside Princeton, giving him time for this diversion. Protective of his image and afraid of appearing pretentious, Washington rebuffed Wright's request that he don a Roman toga. As a result, the painting is plain and powerfully realistic, showing a uniformed but unadorned Washington who eschews the standard props of power. Wright caught the weighty toll that the war years had exacted on Washington, whose face is long, gaunt, and devoid of animation; his eyes lack sparkle or luster. The nose is thick and straight and blunter than in earlier portraits. As Washington commented justly about Wright's style, "His forte seems to be in giving the distinguishing characteristics with more boldness than delicacy."[2] The painting also pinpointed an important quirk of Washington's face: the lazy right eye that slid off into the corner while the left eye stared straight ahead.

To prepare for the equestrian statue, Wright crafted a life mask of Washington's face with plaster of paris. Cooperating with artists brought out a certain drollery in Washington, and work on the mask led to a charming comic vignette with Martha Washington. As Washington recalled, the artist "oiled my features over, and, placing me flat upon my back upon a cot, proceeded to daub my face with the plaster. Whilst [I was] in this ludicrous attitude, Mrs. Washington entered the room, and, seeing my face thus overspread with the plaster, involuntarily exclaimed [in alarm]. Her cry excited in me a disposition to smile, which gave my mouth a slight twist . . . that is now observable in the bust which Wright afterward made."[3] Although Wright constructed the preparatory bust, he never completed the equestrian statue.

Another eminent artist with a special claim to Washington's time was Robert Edge Pine, who had lived near George William and Sally Fairfax in Bath, England. A vocal supporter of American independence, Pine had consulted the Fairfaxes about a controversial print Pine executed showing the "oppressions and calamities of America" and portraying Washington as the country's heroic liberator, as George William informed Washington.[4] It was a courageous action for an artist with a wife and six daughters and earned him "so many enemies in this selfish nation that he is compelled to go to America to seek bread in his profession."[5] There was no way Washington could reject an artist who kept alive the link with George William and Sally Fairfax.

On April 28, 1785, Pine arrived at Mount Vernon, intending to paint Washington for a grand sequence of works about the American Revolution. Earlier in his life, Washington said, he had been as restive "as a colt is of the saddle" when sitting for artists, but he was now amused at how docile he had become. "I am so hackneyed to the touches of the painter's pencil that I am now altogether at their beck and sit like Patience on a monument whilst they are delineating the lines of my face."[6] Pine spent three weeks at Mount Vernon and must have ingratiated himself with the entire family, for Washington agreed to additional portraits of Martha, all four of her grandchildren, and Fanny Bassett.

The most elaborate effort to capture Washington's image was the brilliant, painstaking work of an illustrious French sculptor. In June 1784 the Virginia legislature decided to commission a statue of Washington "of the finest marble and best workmanship" to grace the rotunda of the new state capitol in Richmond.[7]

Governor Harrison turned to Jefferson and Franklin in Paris to identify the "most masterly hand" for the job.[8] Assuming that a European sculptor would simply work from a painting, Harrison had Charles Willson Peale forward a full-length portrait of Washington. This simplistic conception of the job scarcely anticipated the complex demands of the formidable genius recruited by Jefferson and Franklin: Jean-Antoine Houdon, who was famous for his naturalistic style. The premier sculptor at European courts, he asked for a colossal fee, but Jefferson bargained him down to a thousand guineas.

Jefferson and Franklin artfully persuaded Washington to work with the French sculptor, Jefferson saying that Houdon was "the first statuary in the world" and had excitedly agreed to the assignment. In case Washington didn't comprehend the high honor involved, Jefferson mentioned that Houdon was currently finishing a statue of Louis XVI and had crafted a celebrated bust of Voltaire. Knowing that Houdon worked with fanatic intensity, Jefferson thought he should prepare Washington for the sculptor's exhausting demands. Houdon was, Jefferson wrote, "so enthusiastically fond of being the executor of this work that he offers to go himself to America for the purpose of forming your bust from the life, leaving all his business here in the meantime. He thinks that being three weeks with you would suffice to make his model of plaster, with which he will return here, and the work will employ him three years."[9] With two transatlantic crossings ahead of him and a projected absence from Paris of six months, Houdon insisted that Jefferson take out an insurance policy on his life for that time.

Cognizant of Washington's highly organized existence, Jefferson took a huge risk when he told Washington that, if Franklin concurred in selecting Houdon, "we shall send him over [at once], not having time to ask your permission and await your answer."[10] Fortunately, Houdon's sailing was delayed for several months due to illness. To ensure that Washington didn't back out, Jefferson informed him that Houdon had turned down an assignment from Catherine the Great of Russia to sculpt Washington, "which he considers as promising the brightest chapter of his history."[11] In a follow-up letter, Franklin said that, since the Europeans despaired of ever coaxing Washington across the ocean, they needed an excellent bust by Houdon to supply his place.

The only way that Washington could feel comfortable with such royal attention was to remind everyone that he was a purely passive recipient of the honor. Writing to Houdon, he stressed that, although the commission was "not of my seeking, I feel the most agreeable and grateful sensations."[12] On Sunday night, October 2, 1785, Houdon made a dramatic entrance at Mount Vernon, pulling up to the dock at eleven P.M. Washington was already in bed when the household was roused by the famous Frenchman, three young assistants, and an interpreter. In his diary, Washington pointedly noted that Houdon had come from nearby Alexandria, implying that he could easily have waited until morning instead of pouncing upon him at night. Anyone who knew Washington's rigid daily schedule and stern sense of decorum would have avoided this faux pas. A room was hastily prepared for these newcomers babbling in an exotic tongue.

The conscientious Houdon had brought along calipers and, when he got to work, proceeded to make meticulous measurements of Washington's body. He also asked if he could shadow Washington on his daily rounds and study his face and movements in social interactions. During the next two weeks he even attended a funeral with Washington and took part in the wedding of George Augustine Washington and Fanny Bassett. It reveals a good deal about Houdon's genius that the most expressive moment for him came when Washington flared up indignantly as he haggled over a pair of horses; always a tough bargainer, Washington thought the other trader was asking too much. During this sudden flash of anger, Houdon thought he spied the inner steel in Washington's nature.

Methodical in his own habits, Washington was naturally fascinated by the systematic effort that Houdon poured into each step of the artistic process. On October 6 the Frenchman began working on a terra-cotta bust that was likely a preliminary step in creating the full-length sculpture. The bust may have been dried in a Mount Vernon oven ordinarily reserved for baking. Houdon gave it as a gift to Washington, who treasured it in his private study for the rest of his life. Many people credited it as being the best likeness of him ever done. To the extent possible, Houdon dispensed with artistic conventions and pared down the bust to essential truths about Washington, making him life-size and lifelike. The sculpted face is strong and commanding, and the skin smooth, without the crags time later carved into the cheeks. As Washington turns his head, his shrewdly appraising eyes seem to scan the far horizon. Washington's expression is forceful, his determination evident in his narrow gaze, matched by the muscular strength of his shoulders. Because his hair isn't fluffed out at the sides, the bust accentuates the hard, lean strength of his face. Houdon captured both the aggressive and the cautious sides of Washington, held in perfect equipoise.

On October 10 Houdon moved on to preparing the plaster of paris for the life mask. Washington was so riveted by this procedure that he made an extended diary entry about it, describing how Houdon sifted the plaster until it obtained the consistency of thick cream, then mixed it with water and beat the combination with an iron spoon. The sculptor himself covered Washington's face with wet plaster in the few minutes before it began to harden and inserted a pair of quills in his nostrils for breathing. Nelly Custis never forgot her fright when she saw Washington laid out like a corpse in a morgue:

I was only six years old at the time and perhaps should not have retained any recollection of Houdon and his visit, had I not seen the General, as I supposed, dead and laid out on a table cover[e]d with a sheet. I was passing the white servants hall and saw, as I thought, the corpse of one I consider[e]d my father. I went in and found the general extended on his back on a large table, a sheet over him, except his face, on which Houdon was engaged in putting on plaster to form the cast. Quills were in the nostrils. I was very much alarmed until I was told that it was a bust, a likeness of the general, and would not injure him.[13]

The life mask repaid the effort applied to its preparation, and Houdon proudly called it "the most perfect reproduction of Washington's own face."[14] Showing Washington's face at rest, the mask's expression is gentle and pensive yet also powerful because of the strong cheekbones and musculature. Due to the loss of teeth on the left side, with the attendant bone decay, Washington's asymmetrical chin slants down obliquely to the right.

On October 17, as abruptly as they had appeared, Houdon and his assistants packed up their implements, marched down to the dock, and boarded Washington's barge for the short ride to Alexandria, where they caught a stagecoach bound for Philadelphia. Acknowledging Houdon's tremendous investment of time, Washington praised the French sculptor "for his trouble and risk of crossing the seas."[15] During the winter, Jefferson wrote to say that Houdon had arrived safely in Paris with the life mask, from which he would sculpt the standing statue for the Virginia capitol. Jefferson then posed an odd question: How would Washington like to be costumed in the sculpture? Once again Washington opted for modern dress in lieu of a Roman toga. The manner in which he expressed this to Jefferson betrayed his old provincial insecurity, as if he weren't sure he was entitled to an opinion in the artistic sphere and feared committing an error:

I have only to observe that not having a sufficient knowledge in the art of sculpture to oppose my judgment to the taste of connoisseurs, I do not desire to dictate in the matter. On the contrary, I shall be perfectly satisfied with whatever may be judged decent and proper. I should even scarcely have ventured to suggest that perhaps a servile adherence to the garb of antiquity might not be altogether so expedient as some little deviation in favor of the modern custom, if I had not learnt from Colo. Humphreys that this was a circumstance hinted in conversation by Mr [Benjamin] West to Houdon. This taste, which has been introduced in painting by West, I understand is received with applause and prevails extensively.[16]

Washington is quite knowing in his comment, although he advances it with a touching timidity.

No less a perfectionist than Washington, Houdon toiled for years over the Richmond statue, which wasn't set in the capitol rotunda until 1796. In the final version, Houdon played on the Cincinnatus theme of Washington returning to Mount Vernon and divesting himself of the instruments of war. Still dressed in uniform, his outer coat unbuttoned, Washington seems quietly self-possessed, his great labor finished. He has exchanged his sword for a walking stick in his right hand while his left arm rests on a column topped by his riding cape. He is tall and proud, erect and graceful, as he gazes into the bountiful future of his country. With true humility, Washington had asked to have the sculpture life-size instead of larger than life, and Houdon had heeded this noble request.

During that fall of 1785 Washington entertained another French visitor at Mount Vernon who was much less famous than Houdon but probably no less welcome. The dentist Jean-Pierre Le Mayeur had stayed in close touch with Washington ever since he visited the Continental Army's headquarters in 1783. During the summer of 1784 he spent enough time with the Washington family to become a close companion and endeared himself to Washy through the gift of a toy wooden horse. We know that Washington bought nine teeth that year from slaves for either implants or dentures in his own mouth. Wanting to stay in Le Mayeur's good graces, Washington promoted his career and furnished him with introductory letters to political luminaries in Virginia. Le Mayeur was such a frequent visitor at Mount Vernon, showing up three times in June 1786 alone, that he and Washington became fast friends. The dentist was a fancier of horseflesh, and Washington allowed him to drop off his mares to be serviced by his famous stallion Magnolio. For all the ingenuity Le Mayeur devoted to Washington's teeth, he couldn't seem to arrest the decay, and Washington continued to lose teeth. Martha Washington had previously had a cheerier history with her teeth, but by now she too had been fitted out with dentures in what must have become a new form of marital compatibility.

EVEN AS HOUDON WORKED ON HIS STATUE OF WASHINGTON, which reflected a hopeful stance toward America's future, the latter was heartsick at the country's disarray and feared that peace would undo the valiant work accomplished by the Continental Army. His complaints about the Articles of Confederation were consistent with those voiced during the war. The government had no real executive branch, just an endless multiplicity of committees. The few executive departments were adjuncts of a chaotic, ramshackle Congress, which Washington condemned as "wretchedly managed."[17] This legislative body required a quorum of nine states to do business; operated on a one-state, one-vote basis; and could pass major laws only with a unanimous vote. The United States wasn't a country but a confederation of thirteen autonomous states, loosely presided over by Congress. The states' blatant selfishness frustrated any effort to run a sound national government, which had no real enforcement powers over them. As Washington phrased it in a letter, "We are either a united people under one head . . . or we are thirteen independent sovereignties, eternally counteracting each other."[18] Americans now defined themselves as the antithesis of everything English, even if that acted to their detriment.

Thanks to congressional impotence, the government was unable to repay creditors who had financed the Revolution. The paper issued to them now traded at a tiny fraction of its face value, and Congress was powerless to redeem it. Still lacking an independent revenue source, Congress could request money from the states but not compel them to pay. Meanwhile America was fast becoming an irredeemably profligate nation. Despite his own checkered history with London creditors, Washington was adamant that Americans should pay their prewar debts to England, as stipulated in the peace treaty. The federal government also lacked the power to regulate trade among states or with foreign nations. Many states imposed duties on goods from neighboring states, and as Madison cynically interpreted it for Jefferson, "the predominant seaport states were fleecing their neighbors."[19] The resulting trade disputes led to scorching interstate battles. As England imposed restrictions on American trade in the West Indies, the federal government was helpless to retaliate. Without such power, Washington thought, the United States could never negotiate commercial treaties or bargain advantageously with other countries. If the states tried individually to regulate trade, he warned, "an abortion or a many-headed monster would be the issue."[20]

Washington also perceived a pressing need for American military power. Still hemmed in by hostile foreign nations in North America, the country had a federal army of fewer than a thousand men. England refused to surrender a string of forts that stretched in a broad arc from the St. Lawrence River to the Great Lakes and the Ohio Valley. Spain also figured as a threat. The peace treaty had granted the United States the territory between the Appalachian Mountains and the Mississippi. This produced friction with Spain, which shut the lower Mississippi River to American commerce, threatening the livelihood of restive western farmers. There was a more distant threat to peace: in 1785 Barbary pirates from northern Africa began preying on American merchant vessels, which no longer enjoyed the protection of the British Navy. "Would to Heaven we had a navy to reform those enemies to mankind or crush them into non-existence," Washington told Lafayette.[21] There was no way to create a sizable army or navy without shoring up federal power.

Perhaps most disturbing to Washington was the prospect that liberty would descend into anarchy. Some populist demagogue, he feared, might exploit the weakness of a feeble central government to establish a dictatorship. Where Jefferson and Madison dreaded a powerful national government as the primrose path to monarchy, Washington and Hamilton continued to view a strong central government as the best bulwark against that threat. "What astonishing changes a few years are capable of producing!" Washington exclaimed to John Jay in 1786. "I am told that even respectable characters speak of a monarchical form of government without horror."[22]

George Washington trusted the long-term wisdom of the American people, but his deep, abiding faith was often qualified in the short run by a pessimistic view. In 1786 he expressed this ambivalence to Madison: "No morn ever dawned more favorable than ours did—and no day was ever more clouded than the present!"[23] Washington was amazingly sensitive to America's unseen audience of European skeptics. Far from thumbing his nose at such doomsday prophets, he wanted to prove them wrong and earn their good opinion. In advocating enlarged powers for Congress, he said that it was "evident to me we never shall establish a national character, or be considered on a respectable footing by the powers of Europe," unless this was accomplished.[24] That Washington responded so keenly to European derision reveals, once again, residual traces of his old insularity. On some level he remained the country cousin, eager to vindicate his country's worth in the metropolitan hubs of Europe.

As someone who thought people should look to the educated, well-to-do members of the community for leadership, Washington had an instinctive sense of public service. From the time he returned to Mount Vernon after the war, his mind dwelled actively on political problems. He must have sensed he would be allowed only a brief interval of repose before being plunged back into the hurly-burly of politics. As political power reverted back to state capitals, he might have guessed that the nucleus of any future federal government would come from the general staff of the Continental Army, which had experienced so dramatically the perils of an ineffective government. His comforting fantasy of a serene Mount Vernon retirement began to fade. "Retired as I am from the world," he told Jay during the summer of 1786, "I frankly acknowledge I cannot feel myself an unconcerned spectator." Then he backed away from the implications of that statement: "Yet having happily assisted in bringing the ship into port and having been fairly discharged, it is not my business to embark again on a sea of troubles."[25]

At times Washington pretended that he was too remote from political affairs to know what Americans thought about key issues, telling Jefferson, "Indeed, I am too much secluded from the world to know with certainty what sensation the refusal of the British to deliver up the western posts has made on the public mind."[26] Such protestations of ignorance flew in the face of several factors: Washington entertained a large, heterogeneous group of visitors at Mount Vernon; he subscribed to many gazettes; and he conducted a rich correspondence with political intimates. As early as March 1786 he heard from Jay about a movement gathering force to revise the Articles of Confederation. While sympathetic, Washington told him that implementing those changes would require a crisis atmosphere: "That it is necessary to revise and amend the Articles of Confederation, I entertain *no* doubt. But what may be the consequences of such an attempt is doubtful. Yet, something must be done or the fabric must fall."[27] By that summer Washington sounded as if things had reached a critical impasse, and he described the country's state as "shameful and disgusting."[28] In mid-August he believed that a great turning point was at hand. "Your sentiments, that our affairs are drawing rapidly to a crisis, accord with my own," he assured Jay.[29]

One man shaping Washington's views was James Madison. On a Saturday evening in early September 1785, Madison had appeared at Mount Vernon and was quickly closeted in conversation with Washington, lingering through breakfast on Monday morning. A rigorous political theorist with a coolly skeptical intellect, the diminutive, bookish Madison was alarmed by the irresponsible behavior of the state legislatures. Though just thirty-four, he seemed prematurely aged, with thinning hair combed flat atop his head. His dark, intense eyes stared from a pale face with heavy eyebrows. Only five foot four and plagued by delicate health, he was abstemious in his habits. To some, he seemed an austere personality. The wife of one Virginia politician called him "a gloomy stiff creature," while another woman found him "mute, cold, and repulsive."[30] He was wont to croak and mumble, could scarcely be heard during speeches, and was painfully retiring at first meeting. Nevertheless, with his political allies and students of history, Madison could be an absorbing conversationalist. "He is peculiarly interesting in conversation, cheerful, gay, and full of anecdote . . . sprightly, varied, fertile in his topics, and felicitous in his descriptions and illustrations," wrote Jared Sparks, an early editor of Washington's papers.[31]

Appearances could be deceiving with James Madison. However professorial in manner, he was the largest slaveholder in Orange County, Virginia, and his fragile health masked a fanatic determination. Never a pushover in political debates, he plumbed every subject to the bottom and was invariably the best-prepared person in the room. To prepare for the revision of the Articles of Confederation, he plowed through an entire "literary cargo" of books that Jefferson forwarded from Paris.[32] For a young man, he possessed extensive legislative experience, first as an effective member of Congress and now as a member of the Virginia assembly. A skillful legislator, secretive and canny, he exerted his influence in mysteriously indirect ways. Political foes who underrated James Madison did so at their peril.

In September 1786, Madison attended a conference in Annapolis ostensibly devoted to interstate commerce. Here commissioners from five states discussed ways to resolve the trade disputes roiling the country. The Annapolis conference determined that the only way to cure trade disputes was to perform radical surgery on the Articles of Confederation. One of the commissioners, Alexander Hamilton, drafted a bold communiqué calling upon the thirteen states to send delegates to a convention in Philadelphia in May 1787 that would "render the constitution of the federal government adequate to the exigencies of the union."[33] Two days after the Annapolis meeting, Edmund Randolph, head of the Virginia delegation, arrived at Mount Vernon to brief Washington, who fully endorsed Hamilton's appeal. In late October Madison, accompanied by James Monroe, spent another three days at Mount Vernon and found common ground with Washington as they dissected the Articles of Confederation. Clearly Madison, Monroe, and Randolph were trying to cajole Washington from retirement and enlist him in the growing movement to reform the political structure. He was slowly being swept up in a swelling tide that he would find difficult to resist.

As Washington considered his future role, an outbreak of violence in rural Massachusetts sharpened the reform debate. If ever American history had a useful crisis, it occurred in western Massachusetts in the autumn of 1786. To retire a heavy debt load, the state had boosted land taxes and thereby provoked the wrath of farmers, many of whom lost their land in foreclosures. Led by Daniel Shays, a militia captain during the war, thousands of rebels, heaving pitchforks, swarmed into rural courthouses to menace judges and block foreclosures. Invoking the Revolution's militant spirit, many donned old uniforms from the Continental Army. When they threatened to march on the army arsenal in Springfield, Congress rushed Henry Knox to the scene to supervise defensive measures. Henry Lee sent Washington an alarming report about the rebels' plans to subvert state government, abolish debt, and redistribute property: "In one word, my dear General, we are all in dire apprehension that a beginning of anarchy, with all its calamities, has approached." Citizens appealed to Washington to go to Massachusetts, saying his steadying presence would "bring them back to peace and reconciliation."[34]

The events in Massachusetts struck the law-abiding Washington with horror, and the pitch of his letters instantly rose in intensity. "But for God's sake, tell me, what is the cause of all these commotions?" he asked David Humphreys. If there were legitimate grievances, why had they not been redressed? If it was merely a case of licentiousness, why didn't the government step in at once? "Commotions of this sort, like snowballs, gather strength as they roll, if there is no opposition in the way to divide and crumble them."[35] Once again Washington feared disgrace among Europeans, who would seize upon any lapse to validate their cynical view of America, and this became a leitmotif of his letters during the Massachusetts crisis: "I am really mortified beyond expression that, in the moment of our acknowledged independence, we should by our conduct verify the predictions of our transatlantic foe and render ourselves ridiculous and contemptible in the eyes of all Europe."[36] However much he wished to refute these skeptics, Washington had clearly internalized their doubts.

In late October Knox told Washington that the rebels paid little in taxes and had seized on that issue as a pretext to wage class warfare. He warned of the insidious spread of a radical leveling doctrine. "They feel at once their own poverty, compared with the opulent," he said, and want to convert private property into "the common property of all."[37] Overstating the menace, Knox conjured up a desperate army of twelve thousand to fifteen thousand young men prowling New England and challenging lawful government. If this movement spread, he thought, the country would be drawn into the horror of civil war. From New Haven, David Humphreys predicted that a civil war would flush Washington from retirement, forcing him to take sides: "In case of civil discord, I have already told you, it was seriously my opinion that you could not remain neuter and that you would be obliged, in self defence, to take part on one side or the other."[38]

For Washington, who cherished his retirement, this news must have been disturbing. Not surprisingly, Shays's Rebellion crystallized for him the need to overhaul the Articles of Confederation. "What stronger evidence can be given of the want of energy in our governments than these disorders?" he asked Madison. "If there exists not a power to check them, what security has a man of life, liberty, or property?"[39] What most troubled Washington was that people were flouting a political order for which they had recently risked their lives: "It is but the other day we were shedding our blood to obtain the constitutions under which we now live—constitutions of our own choice and framing—and now we are unsheathing the sword to overturn them!"[40]

The Massachusetts uprising terminated in a full-blown military confrontation. In late January Shays and his followers marched on the Springfield arsenal, intending to seize its stores of muskets and powder, when a Massachusetts militia fired point-blank into the crowd, killing several rebels. The next day General Benjamin Lincoln arrived with four thousand soldiers and dispersed the remnants of the dissident army, ending the protest. Even though Washington had supported the overwhelming show of force, once the insurrection was broken, he favored leniency for the culprits, showing how subtly he could parse the political demands of a complex situation. That Congress had abdicated its role in squashing the protest again exposed a dangerous vacuum of national power. Madison believed that Shays's Rebellion "contributed more to that uneasiness which produced the constitution and prepared the public mind for a general reform" than all the defects of the Articles of Confederation combined.[41] It made it almost certain that George Washington's days as a Virginia planter were numbered.

CHAPTER FORTY-THREE

A House on Fire

IN LATE 1786 George Washington's life was again thrown into turmoil when Madison informed him that the Virginia legislature planned to name him head of the state's seven-man delegation at the forthcoming convention in Philadelphia. Having made no effort to join the group, Washington was cast into a terrible state of indecision. "Never was my embarrassment or hesitation more extreme or distressing," he wrote.[1] Deep questioning was typical of Washington's political style. Holding himself aloof, he had learned to set a high price on his participation, yielding only with reluctance. Whenever his reputation was at stake, he studied every side of a decision, analyzing how his actions would be perceived. Having learned to accumulate power by withholding his assent, he understood the influence of his mystique and kept people in suspense.

Complicating his attendance in Philadelphia was that he had already declined to attend the triennial meeting of the Society of the Cincinnati, which by an extraordinary coincidence was also slated for May 1787 in Philadelphia. He had just sent out a mailing to members, explaining that he would neither attend nor stand for reelection as president. It irked him that many state chapters had voted down his proposed reforms, especially the one banning the hereditary provision. He had wanted to remain with the organization long enough to dispel any speculation that he had repudiated its principles. Now that the dissent had died down, he thought it an opportune moment to extricate himself. In declining the invitation, he also cited the press of private business and "the present imbecility of my health, occasioned by a violent attack of the fever and ague, succeeded by rheumatic pains (to which till of late I have been an entire stranger)."[2]

If Washington used his health problems as an excuse, he didn't conjure them from thin air. In late August 1786 he had contracted a "fever and ague" that lasted for two weeks. Since Dr. Craik prescribed the bark of the cinchona tree, a natural source of quinine, one suspects a recurrence of the malaria that had pestered him as a young soldier. Despite early illnesses, the younger Washington had been mostly a picture of ruddy health. Now as aches and pains invaded his body, he was losing his youthful grace, and he complained to Madison of feeling his rheumatic pains "very sensibly."[3] These pains became so debilitating that he couldn't "raise my hand to my head or turn myself in bed."[4] By April 1787, to counter this sharp pain, he had to immobilize his arm in a sling. He went from having a boundless sense of health to feeling his age abruptly—what he called "descending the hill"—and may have wondered whether he possessed the necessary fund of energy for the momentous political challenges ahead.[5] Washington may also have worried anew about his poor genetic endowment after his favorite brother, John Augustine, yet another short-lived Washington male, died suddenly in early January from what Washington called "a fit of gout in the head."[6]

On November 18 Washington explained to Madison that, having spurned the Cincinnati meeting, he couldn't attend the Constitutional Convention without being caught in an embarrassing lie, "giving offense to a very respectable and deserving part of the community—the late officers of the American Army."[7] Were it not for this dilemma, he said, he would certainly attend an event so vital to the national welfare. He wanted to be true to the principles of the Revolution, but he also wanted to be faithful to his colleagues, a sacred trust for him. In his 1783 circular letter to the states, he had solemnly pledged that he would not reenter politics, a public vow that the honorable Washington took seriously. The mythology that he could not tell a lie had some basis in fact. He may also have hesitated to attend the Constitutional Convention from a premonition that it would initiate a sequence of events that would pull him away indefinitely from Mount Vernon. After all, the last time he heeded his country's call in a crisis, it had embroiled him in more than eight years of war.

Refusing to let Washington off the hook, Madison argued that his presence in Philadelphia would enhance the convention's credibility and attract "select characters" from every state.[8] In reply, Washington laid out his deeply conflicted feelings about the Cincinnati. He reviewed the organization's history, telling how it had started as a charitable fund for widows and saying that he never dreamed it would give birth to "jealousies" and "dangers" that threatened republican principles.[9] Washington stood in an acute bind: he didn't wish to insult his fellow officers, but he also refused to support measures he deemed incompatible with republican principles. His response to the predicament shows how delicately he could weigh conflicting claims and cloak the real reason behind an apparent one.

Writing to Governor Edmund Randolph on December 21, Washington formally declined appointment to the convention, secretly hoping his Virginia associates would drop the matter. But when Madison learned of Washington's decision, he requested that he keep the door ajar "in case the gathering clouds should become so dark and menacing as to supersede every consideration but that of our national existence or safety."[10] All winter long, Washington rested in a curious limbo vis-à-vis the convention. "My name is in the delegation to this convention," he told Jay, "but it was put there contrary to my desire and remains there contrary to my request."[11]

Washington was frankly baffled and, in his time-honored executive style, canvassed friends about how to resolve his dilemma, enlisting Madison, Humphreys, Knox, and Jay. Each exchange disclosed another layer of doubt on his part. To Humphreys, Washington confessed his fear that the Constitutional Convention might fail, much as he had been haunted by fear of failure when named commander in chief in 1775. Failure "would be a disagreeable predicament for any of them [the delegates] to be in, but more particularly so for a person in my situation," he wrote.[12] Since he personified the country, he stood to lose the most from accusations of partisanship. On the other hand, this might be a last opportunity to salvage a deteriorating nation. Any failure, he said, could be construed "as an unequivocal proof that the states are not likely to agree in any general measure . . . and consequently that there is an end put to federal government."[13] In soliciting opinions, he again preferred to give a passive appearance to active decisions, making it seem that he was being reluctantly borne along by fate, friends, or historical necessity, when he was actually shaping as well as reacting to events. This technique allowed him to cast himself into the modest role of someone answering the summons of history. It also permitted him to wait until a consensus had emerged on his course of action. If Washington could never entirely resist the allure of fame, neither could he openly welcome it.

Not all of Washington's advisers thought he should attend. Humphreys reminded him of the potentially illegal nature of the gathering and, consequently, the huge reputational risk. "I concur fully in sentiment with you concerning the inexpediency of your attending the convention," he wrote.[14] Knox favored Washington's going but felt obliged to point out that the Philadelphia convention might be "an irregular assembly," even an illegal one, since it would operate outside the amendment process spelled out in the Articles of Confederation. It might even expose delegates to conspiracy charges. On the other hand, Washington's presence would draw New England states that had boycotted the Annapolis conference, converting it into a truly national gathering. To pique Washington's interest, Jay sent him a clairvoyant sketch of a new government divided into legislative, executive, and judicial branches. "Let Congress legislate," he told Washington. "Let others execute. Let others judge."[15] The letter foreshadowed the exact shape of the future government.

During February and March 1787 Washington alternated between passionate concern for saving the union and an insistence that he couldn't go to Philadelphia. He likened the confederacy to a "house on fire," saying that unless emergency measures were taken, the building would be "reduced to ashes"; but somebody else would apparently have to extinguish the blaze.[16] Washington's internal deliberations began to shift on February 21, when Congress approved a convention "for the sole and express purpose of revising the Articles of Confederation."[17] While the convention ended up exceeding this mandate, the decision momentarily retired the legality issue. With the country "approaching to some awful crisis," he told Knox, he began to fret about a public outcry if he *didn't* go to Philadelphia.[18] Suddenly he seemed to lean in the other direction. "A thought, however, has lately run through my mind, which is attended with embarrassment," he confided to Knox in early March. "It is, whether my non-attendance in this convention will not be considered as a dereliction to republicanism."[19]

Wisely, Washington had allowed the issue to percolate for months, encouraging the perception that he was following rather than leading events. On March 19 Knox sent him a letter that may have clinched his decision. He said that he took it for granted that Washington would be elected president of the convention. If the convention still faltered and produced only a "patchwork to the present defective confederation, your reputation would in a degree suffer." But if the convention forged a vigorous new federal government, "it would be a circumstance highly honorable to your fame . . . and doubly entitle you to the glorious republican epithet 'The Father of Your Country.'"[20] This was the perfect double-barreled appeal to Washington's vanity and patriotism. Because of the high caliber of the delegates selected, Knox wagered that the convention would spawn a superior new system, and "therefore the balance of my opinion preponderates greatly in favor of your attendance."[21]

In retrospect, it seems foreordained that Washington, with his unerring sense of duty, would go to Philadelphia. He was a casualty of his own greatness, which dictated a path in life from which he couldn't deviate. Had he turned down the call to duty, he would have felt something incomplete in his grand mission to found the country, but he patently had to convince himself and the world of his purely disinterested motives. Now he could proceed as if summoned from self-imposed retirement by popular acclaim.

On March 28 Washington wrote to Governor Randolph and submitted to his fate: he would indeed attend the convention. He made it clear that he was doing so involuntarily and only submitting to the entreaties of friends. In Washington's life, however, one commitment led ineluctably to the next, and he acknowledged that his attendance would have "a tendency to sweep me back into the tide of public affairs."[22] To solve his dilemma with the Cincinnati, he planned to go to Philadelphia a week early and address the group, so they would not attribute his attending the Constitutional Convention instead "to a disrespectful inattention to the Society."[23] Henry Knox was bowled over by Washington's decision. "Secure as he was in his fame," he wrote to Lafayette, "he has again committed it to the mercy of events. Nothing but the critical situation of his country would have induced him to so hazardous a conduct."[24] Having made his decision, Washington gave unstinting support to a convention that would do far more than just tinker with the Articles of Confederation: like Madison, he wanted root-and-branch reform. He told Knox that the convention should "probe the defects" of the Articles of Confederation "to the bottom," and he worried that some states might not send delegates or would hobble them with "cramped powers," fostering an impasse.[25] By this point, Washington was clearly primed for decisive action in Philadelphia.

BEFORE TAKING ON THE BURDEN OF AMERICA, Washington had to deal with a piece of unfinished family business: the chronic discontent of his mother. Mary Washington, with her flinty independence, was still stewing with grievances. Right before John Augustine died in early January, she had written to him to complain of an absence of corn at her four-hundred-acre farm in the Little Falls quarter of the Rappahannock River. "I never lived soe pore in my life," she insisted.[26] Had it not been for succor from a neighbor and her daughter, Betty, she contended, "I should be almost starvd, butt I am like an old almanack, quit out of date."[27] After Mary's wartime petition to the Virginia legislature, John Augustine, at George's behest, had taken charge of her mismanaged property. This letter about her supposed poverty shows that she did not restrict her whining to her famous son. She had mixed feelings about allowing others to govern her business. When her late son-in-law, Fielding Lewis, volunteered to take over her business affairs, Mary Washington had shot back, "Do you, Fielding, keep my books in order, for your eyesight is better than mine, but leave the executive management to me."[28]

News that Mary was again denigrating him drifted back to George, who wrote to her in mid-February and enclosed another fifteen guineas. In this stilted letter, Washington revealed that his relations with her had grown so frosty that the two hadn't even communicated after Jack's death. Indignant at his mother's accusation that he was being stingy, he poured out his grievances, explaining in brutal detail the miserable state of his finances:

> I have now demands upon me for more than 500£, three hundred and forty odd
> which is due for the tax of 1786; and I know not where, or when, I shall receive one
> shilling with which to pay. In the last two years, I made no crops. In the first I was

obliged to buy corn and this year have none to sell and my wheat is so bad that I cannot neither eat it myself nor sell it to others, and tobacco I make none. Those who owe me money cannot or will not pay it without [law]suits . . . whilst my expenses . . . for the absolute support of my family and the visitors who are constantly here are exceedingly high; higher indeed than I can support, without selling part of my estate, which I am disposed to do rather than run in debt . . . This is really and truly my situation.[29]

Washington went on to protest that, despite their business agreement, he had received not a penny from his mother's farm, even though he had paid 122 pounds in annual rent for her plantation and slaves; either Mary or her overseer had skimmed off the profits and forwarded nothing to him. Beyond that, he had given her more than 300 pounds in unpaid loans over a dozen years—all carefully documented in his ledgers. As a result of her accusations, he told her, "I am viewed as a delinquent and considered perhaps by the world as [an] unjust and undutiful son."[30] Once again Washington was preoccupied with a world that might sit in disapproving judgment upon him. To relieve his mother's distress, he suggested that she hire out her servants and live with one of her children. In fact, shortly before his death, John Augustine had volunteered to take her in.

Anticipating her next request, Washington said that she was welcome to live at Mount Vernon, but he warned her that "in truth it may be compared to a well-resorted tavern, as scarcely any strangers who are going from north to south, or from south to north, do not spend a day or two at it. This would, were you to be an inhabitant of it, oblige you to do one of 3 things, 1st to be always dressing to appear in company, 2d to come into [it] in a dishabille or 3d to be, as it were, a prisoner in your own chamber."[31] This image of Mount Vernon as a crowded, noisy inn, swarming with strangers, was not exactly an inviting one, and Mary never came to live there. The letter is conspicuously devoid of warmth or family affection: Washington and his mother were simply locked in an unhappy business relationship. Washington's reasons for dissuading his mother from living at Mount Vernon confirm that he perceived her as a coarse countrywoman who would be ill at ease in more polished society.

On March 7 Washington returned to Fredericksburg for what he imagined would be the "last act of personal duty"—that is, the last time he might see his aged mother.[32] Then in late April, as he prepared to leave for Philadelphia, he was summoned to Fredericksburg by news that both Mary, who was apparently suffering from breast cancer, and his sister, Betty, were gravely ill. Even though his arm now rested in a sling from rheumatic pain, Washington made the urgent trip to Fredericksburg, telling Henry Knox that he was "hastening to obey this melancholy call, after having just bid an eternal farewell to a much loved brother."[33] In correspondence, Washington always sounded like the conscientious son, telling Robert Morris that he had been called to Fredericksburg for "the last adieu to an honored parent and an affectionate sister."[34]

Although the trip proved a false alarm, Washington found his mother vastly changed, her illness having "reduced her to a skeleton, tho[ugh] she is somewhat amended."[35] Oddly, Washington had made no previous reference to her medical situation, which made her complaining far more comprehensible. Betty had improved as well and was now out of danger. One Fredericksburg resident was shocked by the transformation in Washington's own appearance: "Gen[era]l Washington has been here to see his mother, who has been ill . . . The Gen[era]l is much altered in his person, one arm swung with rheumatism."[36] After a few days Washington returned to Mount Vernon, but the trip must have formed a sobering backdrop to his journey to the Constitutional Convention.

On May 9, 1787, shortly after sunrise, George Washington set off for Philadelphia. While his rheumatic misery had abated, he was beset by other complaints, including a violent headache and an upset stomach—perhaps the somatic expression of his dread about the convention. Until this time Martha Washington had been the loyal, submissive wife in dealing with her husband's career. Now, as she saw George sentenced to life imprisonment in American politics, she began to rebel and decided to skip the Constitutional Convention. "Mrs. Washington is become too domestic, and too attentive to two little grandchildren to leave home," Washington explained to Robert Morris, "and I can assure you, sir, that it was not until after a long struggle [that] I could obtain my own consent to appear again in a public theater."[37] This was a more independent Martha than the one who had rushed off to her husband's winter camps despite her fears of travel and gunfire.

On Sunday, May 13, Washington arrived at Chester, Pennsylvania, and was escorted into Philadelphia by a long procession of dignitaries and a troop of light horse. Greeted by booming artillery and saluting officers, Washington must have been reminded of the worshipful attention he had generated during the war. Despite inclement weather, the sidewalks were densely packed with enthusiastic throngs. Noted the *Pennsylvania Packet,* "The joy of the people on the coming of this great and good man was shown by their acclamation and the ringing of bells."[38] Washington having shed his arm sling, the newspaper expressed joy in finding "our old and faithful commander in the full enjoyment of his health and fame." [39] Washington saw nothing incongruous about arriving in Philadelphia flanked by three of his slaves, Giles, Paris, and the durable Billy Lee; the fate of such slaves would form a contentious issue at the convention. Although James Madison hoped that the entire Virginia delegation would stay at the same lodging house, hard by the Pennsylvania

State House, Washington succumbed to the entreaties of Robert Morris and stayed with him and his wife, Mary.

Guided by a fine sense of decorum, Washington made his first courtesy call on the venerable Benjamin Franklin, whom he had not seen since 1776, and his elderly host broke open a cask of dark beer to receive him. Washington had long revered Franklin as a "wise, a great and virtuous man."[40] Throughout the war he had addressed the older man with exquisite respect, extending to him the title "Your Excellency" that the rest of the world also applied to him. After the war Franklin had tried to woo Washington into a joint tour of Europe, which would have made a sensation by uniting the two most famous Americans. Now, as president of the Executive Council of Pennsylvania, Franklin was Washington's only serious rival for the convention presidency. His medical situation, however, militated against his selection: he was tormented by gout and kidney stones, even though he tossed off witticisms about the latter. "You may judge that my disease is not grievous," he said, "since I am more afraid of the medicines than of the malady." [41]

The assembly of demigods got off to a rather sluggish start. Although the convention was supposed to begin on May 14, only the Virginia and Pennsylvania delegations arrived on time, forcing a delay. A punctual man, Washington was irritated by the absence of a quorum of seven states and groused to George Augustine that the deferrals were "highly vexatious to those who are idly and expensively spending their time here."[42] Throughout his time in Philadelphia, Washington plied George Augustine with detailed advice about Mount Vernon, just as he had with Lund Washington during the war. Two days after the convention opened, he asked his nephew if he had "tried both fresh and salt fish as a manure" and recommended that he plant buckwheat.[43] As a farmer, it frustrated him that Philadelphia was being drenched with rain while drought prevailed in Virginia.

The delay thrust Washington into a knotty predicament vis-à-vis the Society of the Cincinnati, for it suddenly gave him time to attend their meetings. Reluctant to become more deeply involved, he came up with a clever alternative. Instead of attending meetings, he dined on May 15 with twenty members of the society, thus preserving a self-protective distance. Because he didn't wish to affront old comrades, he accepted reelection as president on May 18, making clear that the actual duties would devolve on the vice president. That he steered clear of the Cincinnati was fine with the more diehard members, one saying, "I could almost wish for the absence of the illustrious chief, whose extreme prudence and circumspection . . . may cool our laudable and necessary ebullition with a few drops, if not a torrent, of cold water."[44]

While awaiting the convention's start, Washington hobnobbed with tony members of Philadelphia society, starting with Robert and Mary White Morris. Among his other hosts were the wealthy William Bingham and his beautiful wife, Anne Willing Bingham, whose splendid house on Third Street formed the centerpiece of Philadelphia society. There was nothing surprising in Washington's seeking out such rich company: their social milieu was the same as his at home. Very receptive, as always, to the ladies, he noted in his diary any feminine company he shared. He attended a charity event with Mary White Morris "and some other ladies" to hear a Mrs. O'Connell deliver a discourse on eloquence.[45] Later in the week he attended a wedding for the daughter of Benjamin Chew, whose stone house in Germantown had presented such a costly obstacle to the Continental Army. He evidently enjoyed it: "Drank tea there in a very large circle of ladies."[46] One wonders whether Washington enjoyed this brief vacation from Martha's company.

Washington renewed an important friendship, formed during the First Continental Congress, with the wealthy, laconic Samuel Powel, a former mayor of Philadelphia, and his sophisticated, entrancing wife, Elizabeth (or Eliza). The Powels inhabited a three-story rococo mansion on Third Street that was so tastefully opulent that the Chevalier de Chastellux had praised this "handsome house . . . adorned with fine prints and some very good copies of the best Italian paintings."[47] But during the First Continental Congress, the puritanical John Adams had recoiled from the "sinful feast" he attended there, which had everything that "could delight the eye or allure the taste."[48] George Washington had no such trouble with the regal atmosphere at the Powels' and was a frequent guest at their soirées.

An immensely charming, erudite, and witty woman, who wrote with literary flair and elegance, Elizabeth Willing Powel eclipsed her stolid husband and could have held her own in the spirited repartee of any European salon. The daughter as well as the wife of a mayor, this socially proficient and politically opinionated hostess loved to flirt with powerful men, and George Washington fell under her spell. A portrait by Matthew Pratt shows an extremely handsome older woman whose low-cut yellow dress and purple sash amply display her voluptuous figure. She looks calm and poised, with a penetrating eye and a slightly melancholy air after the death of her two sons. Elizabeth Powel provided virtually the only instance in his later years when Washington befriended a couple but was much closer with the wife. She revered Washington, whom she saw on a par with the loftiest heroes of antiquity. As with George William and Sally Fairfax, Washington was careful to stay on good terms with Samuel Powel and equally careful to include Martha Washington in the friendship. Nevertheless, his friendship with Elizabeth Powel was his only deep, direct one with a woman who qualified as an intellectual peer and treated him as such. In this relationship Washington escaped the narrow bounds of marriage, met Powel alone for teas, and corresponded with her. We have no evidence that their closeness ever progressed beyond that, but if George Washington ever contemplated romance with another woman, it surely must have been Elizabeth Powel.

One of Samuel Powel's hobbies was making silhouettes, and he got Washington to sit for one. It was a measure of Washington's regard for his image that he faulted the silhouette for a small wattle sagging from his chin and asked Powel to redo the portrait. The drooping chin was duly excised from the finished product.

For all his mixing in high society, Washington was an extremely hardworking delegate at the convention. At some point before it started, he took the ideas for constitutional reform presented to him by Jay, Knox, and Madison and boiled them down into a handy digest. Back in 1776 he had delivered a comment on Virginia's new constitution that shows how studiously he approached such work: "To form a new government requires infinite care and unbounded attention, for if the foundation is badly laid, the superstructure must be bad."[49]

Because the entire Virginia delegation arrived on time, its members developed a powerful early cohesion. Headed by Governor Edmund Randolph, the distinguished group included Madison and George Mason; the latter informed his son that the hardworking Virginians met "two or three hours every day in order to form a proper correspondence of sentiments."[50] Their deliberations yielded the so-called Virginia Plan, spearheaded by Madison, which proposed for a tripartite government and proportional representation in both houses of Congress. Madison and Washington, who favored a vigorous central government, carried the day against objections from Randolph and Mason, making their strongly nationalist views the official opening position of the Virginia delegation.

On a rainy Friday, May 25, the convention obtained its seven-state quorum and began to meet officially. It had been decided that Franklin would nominate Washington as president. When the ailing Franklin was grounded by heavy rain, he asked Robert Morris to nominate Washington in his stead. (When Franklin finally did arrive at the sessions, he had to be carried aloft in a sedan chair, hoisted by four convicts from the Walnut Street jail.) The delegates appreciated Franklin's magnanimous gesture, and Madison wrote that "the nomination came with particular grace from Pennsylvania, as Dr. Franklin alone could have been thought of as a competitor."[51] After being seconded by John Rutledge, Washington was unanimously elected the convention president, while Major William Jackson, who had been on General Lincoln's wartime staff, became its secretary.

After Washington was chosen, Morris and Rutledge accompanied him to a tall wooden chair in front, placed on an elevated platform and adorned with a rising sun on its carved back. Perhaps to conjure up the spirit of 1776 or remind delegates of his military garb at the Second Continental Congress, Washington appeared in his old uniform. He made a short acceptance speech, full of vintage touches, including confessions of inadequacy and a plea for understanding if he failed—pretty much the same speech he made after every major appointment in his life. As recorded by Madison, Washington "reminded them of the novelty of the scene of business in which he was to act, lamented his want of [better qualifications], and claimed the indulgence of the house towards the involuntary errors which his inexperience might occasion."[52]

The post of president raised Washington to a nonpartisan, nonspeaking role—ideal for his discreet nature. The Constitutional Convention was yet another situation where the need for national unity imposed a congenial silence upon him. It spared him the need to voice opinions or make speeches, enabling him to bridge divisions and restricting his lobbying to the social hours. He followed the debates closely and later said he "attentively heard and read every oral and printed information on both sides of the question that could be procured."[53] Occasionally he cast a vote, descending briefly from his Olympian perch, then resumed his high place. Most of the time he stood forth as a neutral arbiter and honest broker.

Although highly intelligent, Washington lacked a philosophical mind that could originate constitutional ideas. John Adams once observed that the founding generation had "been sent into life at a time when the greatest lawgivers of antiquity would have wished to live," but this particular brand of greatness eluded George Washington.[54] It is hard to picture him springing to his feet in debate or remonstrating over an issue. He was doubtless content to be consigned to the sidelines and contributed little during the debates. At the same time he lent the proceedings his tacit blessing, allowing others to act as architects of the new order. He embodied the public excluded from the secret proceedings, and his mere presence reassured Americans that the delegates were striving for the public good instead of hatching a secret cabal behind closed doors.

As convention president, Washington assumed a dignified and sometimes severe air. William Pierce of Georgia recounted how one day a delegate dropped a copy of some proposed resolutions. This paper was brought to Washington, who was appalled that someone had so carelessly threatened the secrecy of the deliberations. He promptly rose to chastise the delegates and, as always, had a knack for projecting suppressed wrath: "Gentlemen, I am sorry to find that some one member of this body has been so neglectful of the secrets of the convention as to drop in the State House a copy of their proceedings, which by accident was picked up and delivered to me this morning. I must entreat [the] gentlemen to be more careful, lest our transactions get into the newspapers and disturb the public repose by premature speculations." He tossed the paper onto the table before him. "I do not know whose paper it is, but there it is—let him who owns it take it."[55] Washington donned his hat and strode angrily from the room. Momentarily unable to find his own copy, Pierce crept to the rostrum with some trepidation and was relieved to see someone else's handwriting on the paper. In the end, nobody had the nerve to claim it and confront Washington. The vignette shows how Washington functioned as the conscience of the convention and could make this room full of dignitaries feel like guilty schoolboys, summoned to the headmaster's office for a reprimand.

Washington paid such strict heed to the convention's secrecy rule that, even in his diary, he refrained from recording developments, limiting himself to saying, "Attended convention as usual." Otherwise he drew a discreet veil across the proceedings, dwelling on his social activities. In correspondence, however, he drummed up support for the convention's work, telling Jefferson that the central government had virtually ceased to function and that "unless a remedy is soon applied, anarchy and confusion will inevitably ensue."[56]

A story told of Washington at Philadelphia that may be apocryphal highlights several truths about his relations with his colleagues. One evening some Continental Army veterans were discussing the general's aloofness and the way he communicated to people that he didn't like to be touched or treated familiarly. Gouverneur Morris, dismissing this as nonsense, said he could be as familiar with Washington as with anyone else. Alexander Hamilton proposed a wager: he would buy dinner for a dozen delegates if Morris strode up to Washington, gave him a friendly slap on the shoulder, and said, "My dear General, how happy I am to see you look so well."[57] Morris tried the experiment—and Washington turned and fixed him with an icy glare that made Morris regret his error.

The convention sessions, which ran from ten A.M. to four P.M. daily, left considerable time for delegates to tour the city. Wherever Washington went, he was treated as a head of state, and people flocked after him. "In 1775, we beheld him at the head of the armies of America, arresting the progress of British tyranny," intoned the *Pennsylvania Gazette*. "In the year 1787, we behold him at the head of a chosen band of patriots and heroes, arresting the progress of American anarchy."[58] When a local resident, Jacob Hiltzheimer, tried to sneak a peek at the hero at close range, he found him swallowed up in large crowds. "In the evening [of June 4]," he wrote, "my wife and I went to Market Street gate to see that great and good man, General Washington. We had a full view of him and Major [William] Jackson, who walked with him, but the number of people who followed him on all sides was astonishing."[59]

Perhaps hoping to flee the crowds, Washington rose early in the morning and took brisk rides with his slave and coachman Giles. Spotted all over Philadelphia with his slaves, Washington made sure they were suitably dressed for the national stage, especially Billy Lee. Two days after arriving, Washington went on a special shopping expedition to get soap powder, a puff, and a black silk handkerchief for

Lee; a month later he bought him two pairs of stockings and a pair of breeches. The chief consideration was surely that Lee should reflect credit on his master, but one wonders whether Washington felt any extra gratitude for the services Lee had rendered in the Continental Army. It would also be intriguing to know whether Lee, Paris, and Giles lingered outside the State House as Washington and the other delegates debated inside the meaning of freedom and the fate of slavery in America.

CHAPTER FORTY-FOUR

Rising Sun

FOR MOST OF THE CONVENTION, Washington sat in splendid isolation at the front. On May 29, when Edmund Randolph presented the Virginia Plan, the convention reverted to a committee of the whole, and Nathaniel Gorham temporarily supplanted Washington in the presidential chair. After June 19 Washington resumed his place in the high seat that previewed his future status in the federal government. In the early days in Philadelphia he was heartened by the seeming harmony among the delegates, telling George Augustine that "the sentiments of the different members seem to accord more than I expected they would, as far as we have yet gone."[1] The general contours of the system that Jay and Madison had sketched out for him—a tripartite government, with a bicameral legislature—enlisted general support. Nonetheless, sharp clashes soon emerged, especially on the explosive issue of representation. On June 6 James Madison spoke in favor of direct election to the House of Representatives, based on proportional representation—a position supported by the populous states—and conjured up a vision of a broad, pluralistic republic. In mid-June William Paterson of New Jersey, champion of the smaller states, countered with a plan that foresaw states represented equally in Congress. Though mute on the podium, Washington supported Madison's view.

Fueled by the apprehensions of smaller states, the amity celebrated by Washington in early June had crumbled by the end of the month. On June 30, the weather having grown sweltering, Gunning Bedford of Delaware delivered a hot-tempered tirade, aimed at the larger states, demonstrating just how bruising the discourse had become. "I do not, gentlemen, trust you," he told them. He even hinted at secession, saying apropos of the smaller states that "sooner than be ruined, there are foreign powers who will take us by the hand."[2] Washington and Madison gazed in dismay as their worst fears of disunion threatened to materialize before their eyes. In early July a disappointed Alexander Hamilton returned temporarily to New York on business and dropped a pessimistic note to Washington, saying how "seriously and deeply distressed" he was by the convention's divisive sniping: "I fear that we shall let slip the golden opportunity of rescuing the American empire from disunion, anarchy, and misery."[3] Hostile to new federal powers, the two other New York delegates, Robert Yates and John Lansing, Jr., left the convention by July 5, never to return.

Although he held his tongue during the debates, Washington was never a neutral party, and the interminable squabbling only reinforced his view that the country needed a potent central government to override the selfish ambitions of local politicians. The man associated with so many triumphs shuddered at the prospect of being associated with public failure. "I *almost* despair of seeing a favorable issue to . . . the convention and do therefore repent having had any agency in the business," he informed Hamilton on July 10, chastising "narrow-minded politicians . . . under the influence of local views."[4] In a gentle, almost fatherly way, he begged Hamilton, the prodigal son, to return to the fold. "I am sorry you went away," he said. "I wish you were back. The crisis is equally important and alarming and no opposition under such circumstances should discourage exertions till the signature is fixed."[5]

While the convention dragged on, Washington drank enormous quantities of tea at the City Tavern and the Indian Queen, two haunts frequented by delegates. In his social life, he exhibited expert political instincts and embraced a wide spectrum of citizens, as if he already saw the presidency looming dimly on the horizon. On one of his first Sundays, he attended a Roman Catholic mass and also dined with Mark Prager, Sr., a Jewish merchant. On several occasions he joined fraternal dinners hosted by the Irish American Sons of St. Patrick. In early June he yielded to the importunate General Mifflin and reviewed the infantry, cavalry, and artillery of Philadelphia, as if he were already more than merely president of the convention.

Washington's Philadelphia itineraries reflected his far-ranging interests. Surgeon Abraham Chovet gave him a private tour of his Anatomical Museum, with its ingenious displays of human figures. Washington also gratified his abiding love of theater by catching plays at the Southwark Theater, which lay beyond Philadelphia's borders because of a law banning theater performances in the city proper. He evinced continuing solicitude for artists, sitting for an engraving by Charles Willson Peale and a portrait by Robert Edge Pine, who needed to touch up work begun at Mount Vernon two years earlier. In his wanderings, he visited a gristmill on the Schuylkill River and exhausted the proprietor with questions. "This day, Gen. Washington, Gen. Mifflin and four others of the convention did us the honor of paying us a visit in order to see our vineyard and bee houses," said Peter Legaux, a French immigrant. "In this they found great delight, asked a number of questions, and testified their highest approbation with my manner of managing bees."[6] At Franklin's house, Washington revealed a sharp interest in mechanical inventions, marveling at a mangle used for pressing items after they were washed.

As always, Washington's silences were as eloquent at his pronouncements. In late July he accompanied Robert Morris on a trout-fishing expedition to a creek near Valley Forge, prompting him to ride over to his old army cantonment. In his diary, Washington mentioned having "visited all the works, which were in ruins, and the encampments in woods, where the ground had not been cultivated."[7] When he last saw Valley Forge, it had been cold and gloomy, bare of all foliage. Now it was a balmy place, lush with summer greenery. The sight undoubtedly stirred deep-seated memories in Washington, but his diary entry for that day is curiously reticent; even by Washingtonian standards, it is a gem of emotional evasion. After a one-sentence allusion to Valley Forge, he continued, "On my return back to Mrs. Moore's, observing some farmers at work and entering into conversation with them, I received the following information with respect to the mode of cultivating buckwheat and the application of the grain."[8] He then listed various ways to sow, plow, and harrow buckwheat, as if that were the day's major occurrence. On some level, Washington felt the powerful lure of the past yet could never articulate it. He proved only a touch more expansive after visiting the site of the Germantown battle, stating that he had "contemplated on the dangers which threatened the American Army at that place."[9] That was his total commentary. Active and forward-looking, Washington did not amble very often down memory lane, though some dinner guests at Mount Vernon recalled him reminiscing about the war.

In the absence of Martha's company, Washington continued to gravitate toward alluring female society. When he dined at a club composed of the city's leading gentlemen, he noted that they invited female family members on alternate Saturdays. Not surprisingly, Washington chose that day to attend, specifying, "This was the ladies day."[10] Several times he called upon Elizabeth Powel and dusted off a musty streak of gallantry. As he wrote to her on July 23, "Gen[era]l Washington presents his respectful compliments to Mrs. Powel and will do himself the honor of calling upon her at or before 5 o'clock (in his carriage) in hopes of the pleasure of conducting her to Lansdown this evening."[11] From the chivalrous tone of these messages, one senses that Washington could sometimes enjoy flirtatious banter. A week later, noting his trout-fishing trip to the Valley Forge area, he declined an invitation to escort Mrs. Powel to a performance of Sheridan's *School for Scandal:* "The Gen[era]l can but regret that matters have turned out so unluckily after waiting so long to receive a lesson in the School for Scandal."[12] Washington seldom allowed himself the liberty of jesting with a married lady in this manner. His lighthearted tone with Elizabeth Powel makes one wonder anew about the role of repressed sexuality in George Washington's life. We have no evidence that he ever talked to Martha in this coy manner, nor is it easy to imagine. For all the happiness of their marriage, Martha had become his life's standard prose while Elizabeth Powel, like Sally Fairfax, may have introduced some forbidden spice of poetry. It was as if, during his extended sojourn in Philadelphia, the footloose Washington permitted himself to explore sides of his personality that he kept firmly under wraps at home.

Not long after Washington wrote so gloomily to Hamilton, the Constitutional Convention experienced a spectacular breakthrough. In mid-July it was agreed that the small states would be represented equally in the Senate, while the House would have proportional representation based on population. For Washington and other Virginia delegates, it was a bitter pill to swallow, threatening to weaken the federal government critically. Nonetheless, an eminently pragmatic man, Washington accepted the need for painful compromises to form a union, assuring Henry Knox that the government being shaped by the delegates was "the best that can be obtained at the present moment, under such diversity of ideas as prevail."[13]

Perhaps the most uncomfortable debate hinged on the slavery issue. The abolitionist movement had made considerable headway in New England but was losing ground in the South after a brief flurry of postwar interest. Slavery was the most vexing topic at the convention. As Pierce Butler of South Carolina commented, "The security the southern states want is that their negroes may not be taken from them, which some gentlemen within or without doors have a very good mind to do."[14] Employing thinly disguised blackmail, some southern delegates vowed to quit the convention if anyone interfered with their peculiar institution. "The true question at present is whether the southern states shall, or shall not, be parties to the union," said John Rutledge of South Carolina.[15]

The delegates agreed that slavery wouldn't be mentioned by name in the Constitution, giving way to transparent euphemisms, such as "persons held to service or labor." Slaveholders won some substantial concessions. For the purposes of representation in the House of Representatives and the Electoral College, they would be able to count three-fifths of their slave population. This was no mean feat: slaves made up 40 percent of the population in Virginia, for instance, and 60 percent in South Carolina. The slave trade would also be shielded from any tampering for at least twenty years. Through a fugitive slave clause, masters would be able to reclaim runaway slaves in free states—a provision George Washington would liberally employ in future years. Referring to these hard-fought victories for the southern states, the abolitionist William Lloyd Garrison would later castigate the Constitution as "a covenant with death and an agreement with hell."[16]

Whatever his own nascent abolitionist views, George Washington wasn't about to make an open stand at the convention and joined other delegates in daydreaming that slavery would fade away at some nebulous future date. Isolated critics branded Washington a hypocrite for clinging to his slaves after a revolution fought in the name of freedom. At the Massachusetts convention that ratified the Constitution, one speaker deplored his status as a slaveholder. "Oh, Washington, what a name he has had! How he has immortalized himself!" he exclaimed, then remarked that Washington "holds those in slavery who have as good a right to be free as he has. He is still for self and, in my opinion, his character has sunk 50 percent."[17] A Massachusetts newspaper, echoing this charge, regretted that Washington had "wielded the sword in defense of American liberty yet at the same time, was, and is to this day, living upon the labors of several hundreds of miserable Africans as freeborn as himself."[18]

The debate over the executive branch was likewise steeped in controversy. Delegates had difficulty conceiving a mighty presidency that did not look suspiciously like a monarchy, and they trod gingerly in this treacherous territory. The idea of a separate executive branch with a president independent of the legislature and able to veto its laws was regarded as heretical in some quarters. Benjamin Franklin so distrusted executive power that he pushed for a small executive council instead of a president. In advancing this idea, he had the courtesy to note, with a figurative nod toward Washington, that the first president would likely be benevolent, but he feared despotic tendencies in his successors.

That the delegates overcame their dread of executive power and produced an energetic presidency can be traced directly to Washington's imperturbable presence. Pierce Butler doubted that the presidential powers would have been so great "had not many members cast their eyes toward General Washington as president and shaped their ideas of the powers to a president by their opinion of his virtue."[19] As convention president, Washington sat through extensive discussions of what was turning into his job description. There was a tacit assumption that, the office having been conceived with him in mind, Washington would serve as the first president. With his image before their eyes, the delegates were inevitably governed by their hopes instead of their fears. Still, with memories of the Revolution fresh, they reserved significant powers for Congress, endowing it, for instance, with the authority to declare war, thereby avoiding the British precedent of a monarch who retained this awesome power.

For all his inscrutable silence, Washington disclosed specific views several times during the convention. When Elbridge Gerry proposed a constitutional limit of three thousand men in any standing army, Washington supposedly remarked drily that "no foreign enemy should invade the United States, at any time, with more than three thousand troops."[20] At the end of the convention, he also took a decidedly democratic stand on the question of how many people each congressman should represent, opting for thirty thousand instead of forty thousand to ensure "security for the rights and interests of the people."[21] Blessed by Washington, the convention adopted this change unanimously, in a striking instance of his irresistible appeal. That Washington was an exponent of an energetic presidency was also evident when he voted for requiring a three-fourths majority in Congress to override a presidential veto. Despite Washington's backing, it was reduced to a two-thirds majority to forestall abuses of executive power.

Whatever pleasure he derived from being away from Mount Vernon had disappeared by September 9, when he wrote to George Augustine that the convention would likely wind up its deliberations within a week: "God grant I may not be disappointed in this expectation, as I am quite homesick."[22] The long hours and sedentary job must have proved an ordeal for him. A day earlier the convention had convened a committee on style, with Gouverneur Morris as its head, to give the Constitution its finished form. The foppish, peg-legged Morris was a delightful bon vivant with considerable verbal resources who relished Washington's "cool, steady temper."[23] Washington, in turn, enjoyed Morris's lively flow of quips, his "first-rate abilities," and his "lively and brilliant imagination."[24] It was Morris who drafted the great preamble to the Constitution that began with the memorable flourish "We the People." On September 12 delegates received printed copies of the final document, and as he led them through it, Washington personally inserted the changes that had been approved while the committee on style was hard at work.

Whatever his misgivings about individual provisions, Washington was no lukewarm supporter of the final document. As he later expressed it, the Constitution was "the result of a spirit of amity and mutual concession" and more coherent than anyone had a right to expect from so many discordant delegates with passionate opinions.[25] It struck him as "little short of a miracle," he told Lafayette, that "delegates from so many different states . . . should unite in forming a system of national government so little liable to well-founded objections."[26] In another letter he said, "It approached nearer to perfection than any government hitherto instituted among men."[27] Especially sensitive to allegations that the president was vested with excessive power, he stressed the numerous safeguards put in place, telling Lafayette that the new constitution "is provided with more checks and barriers against the introduction of tyranny . . . than any government" previously devised by mortals.[28] As president, Washington went so far as to say that the "invisible hand" of providence had been manifest in the enactment of the Constitution.[29]

In correspondence Washington admitted to imperfections in the new charter but trusted to the amendment process to refine it. The Constitutional Convention was no conclave of sages in Roman togas, handing down eternal truths engraved in marble, and he wondered how long the document would last. He parted company with Edmund Randolph, who refused to sign the Constitution unless it provided for a second convention to enact necessary amendments. For Washington, the beauty of the document was that it charted a path for its own evolution. Its very brevity and generality—it contained fewer than eight thousand words—meant it would be a constantly changing document, susceptible to shifting interpretations. It would be left to Washington and other founders to convert this succinct, deliberately vague statement into a working reality. He also knew that the American public needed to contribute its share; the Constitution "can only lay the foundation—the community at large must raise the edifice."[30] Benjamin Franklin shared this view. Legend claims that as he left the State House, Franklin bumped into Elizabeth Powel, who inquired about the form of government produced inside. "A republic, madam, if you can keep it," Franklin replied.[31] Powel later claimed that she had no recollection of the famous retort, but she did say that "the most respectable, influential members of the convention" had gathered at her house and that "the all important subject was frequently discussed" there.[32]

On Monday, September 17, 1787, the convention's last day, the delegates adopted the Constitution "unanimously," although there was poetic license in the use of the word. It had taken four long months to attain this historic agreement. After starting out with 55 delegates—all of them white and male, and many affluent—the convention had suffered a high rate of attrition, with only 42 present at the end; of those, 39 signed the document. Eleven states approved the Constitution; Alexander Hamilton signed individually as the sole remaining delegate from New York. Rhode Island had boycotted the convention altogether. To Madison, Washington explained how important "the appearance of unanimity" was in presenting the Constitution to Congress: "Not everyone has opportunities to peep behind the curtain, and as the multitude often judge from externals, the appearance of unanimity in that body, on this occas[io]n, will be of great importance."[33] It was a telling comment from a man who placed a premium on political stagecraft.

Of the three convention holdouts, two came from Virginia—Edmund Randolph and George Mason—and happened to be close friends of Washington; the third was Elbridge Gerry of Massachusetts. As heir apparent to the presidency, Washington undoubtedly took offense when Mason declared that the new government "would end either in monarchy or a tyrannical aristocracy" and complained that the Constitution "had been formed without the knowledge . . . of the people."[34] Their thirty-year friendship did not survive their heated split. "Col. Mason left

Philad[elphi]a in an exceeding ill humor," Madison afterward told Washington. "He returned to Virginia with a fixed disposition to prevent the adoption of the plan if possible. He considers the want of a Bill of Rights as a fatal objection."[35] The convention's secrecy rule deplored by Mason had stimulated candor but was immediately blasted by critics and engendered a thousand conspiracy theories. "I am sorry they began their deliberations by so abominable a precedent as that of tying up the tongues of their members," Jefferson complained to John Adams.[36] To guarantee confidentiality, William Jackson, the convention secretary, burned all loose scraps of paper and entrusted the official journals to George Washington's care—another act of tremendous faith in his integrity.

On the final day, Benjamin Franklin mentioned to some delegates that during the previous months he had often stared at the presidential chair in which Washington sat with its image of the sun: "I have often and often in the course of the session . . . looked at that [sun] behind the president without being able to tell whether it was rising or setting. But now at length I have the happiness to know that it is a rising and not a setting sun."[37] After Franklin dispensed this famous aperçu, the delegates adjourned to the City Tavern for one last round of drinks. In sending the Constitution to Congress, Washington wisely made an understated case for approval, noting the conciliatory spirit that had led to its passage: "That it will meet the full and entire approbation of every state is not perhaps to be expected . . . That it is liable to as few exceptions as could reasonably have been expected, we hope and believe."[38]

On September 18, accompanied by John Blair of Virginia, Washington boarded his newly varnished coach and set out for Mount Vernon. The two men traveled in high style, Washington having refurbished his vehicle in Philadelphia, outfitting it with glass panes, brass plates, stuffed cushions, and a new carpet. In his eagerness to return home, he was misled into an uncharacteristic error. Near the Head of Elk he had to ford a river swollen by torrential rains. Instead of waiting for the turbulent waters to subside, the overly eager Washington decided to take the carriage across an "old, rotten, and long disused" bridge, as he described it.[39] One of the two harnessed horses suddenly slid off the bridge and nearly dragged the other horse, along with the baggage-laden carriage, into the foaming waters. Only the prompt intervention of some nearby millers, who managed to disengage the first horse from its harness, prevented the total destruction of the carriage and Washington's belongings.

At sunset on September 22 Washington's coach pulled up before the mansion house at Mount Vernon. That he was ready to resume his everyday life is evident in his diary, where he jotted down his absence of "four months and 14 days."[40] The precision of detail suggests how onerous Washington considered the lost time, and he bewailed to a correspondent having "sacrificed every private consideration and personal enjoyment" to attend the convention.[41] What he discovered upon returning home confirmed his latent anxieties about his neglected business affairs. As he told Henry Knox, he "found Mrs. Washington and the family tolerably well, but the fruits of the earth almost entirely destroyed by one of the severest droughts (in this neighborhood) that ever was experienced. The crops generally below the mountains are injured, but not to the degree that mine and some of my neighbors' are here."[42] For Washington, this dispiriting discovery reenacted a now-familiar tale of making huge private sacrifices whenever he was forced to be away from home for public service.

Mounting the Seat

THE CONSTITUTION cherished by generations of Americans was fiercely controversial at first, producing heated polemics on both sides. So that its legitimacy would derive from the people, not the state governments, the framers required ratification by a special convention in each state; the document would be activated when nine states approved. By all accounts, Washington overflowed with enthusiasm for the new charter. When Richmond merchant Alexander Donald stayed at Mount Vernon in early October 1787, he was impressed by Washington's ebullient advocacy. "I never saw him so keen for anything in my life as he is for the adoption of a new form of government," Donald informed Jefferson.[1] The months in Philadelphia, however trying, had given Washington a needed respite from business worries and revived his faltering health. "He is in perfect good health," Donald wrote, "and looks almost as well as he did twenty years ago."[2]

Everybody recognized the signal importance of Washington's imprimatur on the new charter, reassuring a public skittish about such fundamental change. His cachet emboldened advocates (called federalists) even as it undermined critics (called antifederalists). "I have observed that your name [attached] to the new constitution has been of infinite service," Gouverneur Morris wrote. "Indeed, I am convinced that, if you had not attended the convention and the same paper had been handed out to the world, it would have met with a colder reception . . . As it is, should the idea prevail that you would not accept of the presidency, it would prove fatal in many parts."[3]

One Boston newspaper regretted that the combined prestige of Washington and Franklin in favor of the Constitution made "too strong an argument in the minds of many to suffer them to examine, like freemen, for themselves."⁴ Some antifed-eralists took refuge in hyperbole, portraying the Constitutional Convention as a baleful nest of conspirators—a charge given some resonance by the secret nature of the proceedings. "The evil genius of darkness presided at its birth; it came forth under the veil of mystery," wrote an opponent who styled himself "Centinel."⁵ That Washington and Franklin had mingled among those conspirators made it more difficult to defame the enterprise. To bypass this problem, "Centinel" depicted Washington as an unwitting tool of "aspiring despots" who were "prostituting the name of a Washington to cloak their designs upon your liberties."⁶ Washington dismissed such conspiracy theories as preposterous: "At my age and in my circumstances, what sinister object or personal emolument had I to seek after in this life?"⁷

After a pleasing October visit from Elizabeth and Samuel Powel, Washington had to cope with another frigid winter at Mount Vernon. Severed from the outside world by snow, he stayed in touch by mail with federalists in many states. Resigning himself to a common eighteenth-century practice, he assumed that his letters would be opened, telling Lafayette, "As to my sentiments with respect to the merits of the new constitution, I will disclose them without reserve (although by passing through the post offices they should become known to all the world) for, in truth, I have nothing to conceal on that subject."⁸

While preserving an air of Olympian detachment, Washington moved stealthily in the background of the ratification process, one of his chief worries being that the Constitution's detractors would prove more adept than its advocates. Although he admitted to defects in the charter, he tended to regard supporters as righteous and reasonable, opponents as wrongheaded and duplicitous. As a stalwart realist, he thought it dangerous to demand perfection from any human production and questioned "the propriety of preventing men from doing good, because there is a possibility of their doing evil."⁹ When Lieutenant John Enys stopped by Mount Vernon in February, Washington explained that he had followed doggedly the constitutional debates, consuming all the pertinent literature. "He said he had read with attention every publication," Enys wrote, "both for and against it, in order to see whether there could be any new objections, or that it could be placed in any other light than what it had been in the general convention, for which . . . he said he had sought in vain."¹⁰

New York quickly emerged as a major locus of dissent, and Madison, based there as a delegate in the waning days of the Confederation Congress, warned Washington of a powerful backlash gathering force: "The newspapers here begin to teem with vehement and virulent calumniations of the proposed gov[ernmen]t."¹¹ After leaving the convention in July, Hamilton had fired anonymous salvos in the New York press against Governor George Clinton, who felt threatened by centralized power. On September 20 the Clinton forces retaliated with vicious glee, accusing Hamilton of insinuating himself into Washington's good graces during the war. Said the nameless critic: "I have also known an upstart attorney palm himself upon a great and good man, for a youth of extraordinary genius and, under the shadow of such a patronage, make himself at once known and respected. But . . . he was at length found to be a superficial, self-conceited coxcomb and was of course turned off and disregarded by his patron."[12] This remark hatched an enduring mythology of a wily Hamilton tricking the dunderheaded Washington into supporting him.

Distraught over these accusations, the hypersensitive Hamilton appealed to Washington to rebut the notion that he had imposed himself upon the commander in chief and had then been dismissed by him: "This, I confess, hurts my feelings and, if it obtains credit, will require a contradiction."[13] By return mail, Washington laid both falsehoods to rest: "With respect to the first, I have no cause to believe that you took a single step to accomplish [it] or had the most distant [ide]a of receiving an appointment in my [fam]ily till you were invited thereto. And [with] respect to the second . . . your quitting [it was] altogether the effect of your own [choic]e."[14]

To combat vocal foes of the Constitution in New York, Hamilton published in late October the first essay of *The Federalist* under the pen name "Publius" and rushed a copy to Washington. Washington had told David Humphreys that the Constitution's acceptance would depend upon "the recommendation of it by good pens," and *The Federalist* must have seemed a case of answered prayers.[15] Indeed, the federalists possessed the preponderance of literary talent. "For the remaining numbers of Publius," Washington informed Hamilton, "I shall acknowledge myself obliged, as I am persuaded the subject will be well handled by the author."[16] The perceptive Washington saw that *The Federalist* transcended journalism and would take on classic status, telling Hamilton that "when the transient circumstances and fugitive performances which attended this crisis shall have disappeared, that work will merit the notice of posterity."[17]

In November, when Madison sent Washington the first seven installments of *The Federalist,* he admitted in confidence to being one of its unnamed authors and urged Washington to convey the essays to influential Virginians who might get them published. Without tipping his hand, Washington became a secret partner in the *Federalist* enterprise, transmitting the essays to David Stuart in Richmond. "Altho[ugh] I am acquainted with some of the writers who are concerned in this work," wrote Washington, playing things close to the vest, "I am not at liberty to disclose their names, nor would I have it known that they are sent by *me* to *you* for promulgation."[18] To maintain the flow of reprints in Virginia, Madison sent Washington packets of new *Federalist* essays and bound editions as they appeared. Curiously, Washington had not figured out that John Jay was the third member of the *Federalist* triumvirate. When a letter appeared in a Baltimore paper announcing that Jay had denounced the Constitution as "a wicked conspiracy," Madison had to reassure Washington that the letter was "an arrant forgery."[19] In March, Henry Knox finally let the cat out of the bag: "The publication signed *Publius* is attributed to the joint efforts of Mr. Jay, Mr. Madison and Colo. Hamilton."[20]

By mid-January 1788 the Constitution had been adopted by decisive margins in Pennsylvania, New Jersey, Delaware, Georgia, and Connecticut. These early victories were deceptive, however, for closely contested state conventions lay ahead. The most formidable opposition, Washington surmised, would be marshaled in New York and Virginia. As the biggest, richest, and most populous state, Virginia had to be the linchpin of any union. While he believed that most Virginians stood four-square behind the Constitution, Washington conceded the influential nature of its opponents, especially George Mason, Edmund Randolph, and Patrick Henry, who he feared would stoop to demagoguery. With these dissenting delegates, Washington engaged in low-key lobbying, telling Randolph that the new charter was "the best constitution that can be contained at this epoch and that this or a dissolution of the union . . . are the only alternatives before us."[21] In a sign of subtle disenchantment with Virginia, Washington observed that it was "a little strange that the men of large property in the south should be more afraid that the constitution should produce an aristocracy or a monarchy than the genuine democratical people of the east."[22] It is hard not to see a veiled criticism of southern slavery behind this comment.

As he awaited its convention, Washington knew that, if Virginia failed to join the union, he would be ineligible for the presidency. After the first five states voted for the Constitution, political wrangling intensified over the future leadership of the impending government. In Massachusetts, scheduled to hold the sixth ratifying convention, federalists tried to woo a wavering John Hancock by promising to support him for vice president if Washington ran for president. They also intimated that, if Virginia didn't ratify and Washington couldn't run for president, they would line up solidly behind Hancock for the top job.

By May, Massachusetts, Maryland, and South Carolina had also ratified the Constitution, bringing the total to eight states, one short of the magic number needed to enact it. This put additional pressure on the states that were about to hold their conventions. Washington followed the cascading victories with mounting excitement. "The plot thickens fast," he told Lafayette. "A few short weeks will determine the political fate of America for the present generation and probably produce no small influence on the happiness of society through a long succession of ages to come."[23]

In early June, as Washington visited his "aged and infirm mother" in Fredericksburg, national attention turned to the Virginia Ratifying Convention.[24] Though he was ailing and felt "extremely feeble," James Madison delivered astounding oratory on behalf of the new charter.[25] Washington's nephew Bushrod, awed by Madison's talents, reported to Mount Vernon that Madison had spoken "with such force of reasoning and a display of such irresistible truths that opposition seemed to have quitted the field."[26] In a pivotal shift, Governor Randolph capitulated and teamed up with the federalists from fear that Virginia would be ostracized if it didn't ratify. This argument gained additional currency when New Hampshire became the ninth state to ratify and ended all suspense about the Constitution's future. Still unaware of what had happened in New England, Virginia four days later approved the Constitution by a ten-vote margin. In late July New York became the eleventh state to sign on, leaving only Rhode Island and North Carolina beyond the pale of union. Not until June 28 did Washington receive news of the Virginia and New Hampshire victories. He must have known that these tidings would carry in their wake an insistent plea for him to become the first president. In backing the new charter, Washington had waged an enormous high-stakes campaign, and his prestige soared even higher with its enactment. "Be assured [Washington's] influence carried this government," declared James Monroe.[27]

The town of Alexandria blazed with lights in celebration of the Constitution as the news ricocheted up and down the Potomac by precisely timed discharges of cannon. When Washington rode to Alexandria for a festive dinner, he "was met some miles out of town by a party of gentlemen on horseback and escorted to the tavern, having been saluted on his way by the light infantry company in a respectful manner," he told Charles Cotesworth Pinckney.[28] On June 3 he welcomed the triumphant Madison back to Mount Vernon but found him worn down by the tremendous campaign he had conducted. With paternal delicacy, Washington advised the younger man "to take a little respite from business" and linger at Mount Vernon: "Moderate exercise and books occasionally, with the mind unbent, will be your best restoratives." He coaxed the harried Madison into staying for four days, during which time the two men remained in seclusion for many hours, discussing practical details of the upcoming government.

With the Constitution having squeaked by in Virginia, George Washington owed an incalculable debt to Madison for making his presidency possible. Some Virginia foes of the new charter reacted graciously in defeat. By shifting ground, Edmund Randolph had redeemed his political future, later telling Washington that "the constitution would never have been adopted, but from a knowledge that you had once sanctified it and an expectation that you would execute it."[29] Quite different was the obstinacy of George Mason, which provoked a caustic aside from Washington: "Pride on the one hand and want of manly candor on the other will not, I am certain, let him acknowledge an error in his opinions . . . though conviction should flash on his mind as strongly as a ray of light."[30] What bothered Washington was less Mason's opposition than his bullheaded rigidity. Of Mason's followers, he said, "They are in the habit of thinking that everything he says and does is right and (if capable) they will not judge for themselves."[31] As later became clear, George Washington refused to appoint anyone to the new government who had been overtly hostile to the Constitution that brought it into being.

Once the Constitution was adopted, Washington could not evade the question of whether he would serve as president. He stood in a league of his own, his stature inimitable. Like other founders, he regarded any open interest in power as unbecoming to a gentleman. As a result, he preferred to be drawn reluctantly from private life by the irresistible summons of public service. He eschewed the word *president,* as if merely saying it might connote an unsavory desire on his part. As with attending the Constitutional Convention, he again worried that people would think he had yielded to the allure of worldly pomp and had cynically broken his pledge not to return to public life. His usual besetting fears of failure also reemerged. Years later, chatting confidentially with Madison, Washington recalled that "he had from the beginning found himself deficient in many of the essential qualifications [for president], owing to his inexperience in the forms of public business, his unfitness to judge of legal questions and questions arising out of the constitution."[32] Once again he was preoccupied with presumed taunts and criticisms, the inner voice of his own unspoken fears.

For both political and psychological reasons, Washington needed to undergo a protracted period of indecision about the presidency. Part of him felt genuinely burdened by public life, especially since he experienced "the increasing infirmities of nature," as he told Lafayette.[33] He was torn, as always, by unacknowledged ambition mingled with self-doubt. During his October visit to Mount Vernon, Alexander Donald felt that Washington's pro forma denial of interest in the presidency masked his true feelings. "As the eyes of all America are turned towards this truly great and good man for the first president, I took the liberty of sounding him upon it," Donald told Jefferson. "He appears to be greatly against going into public life again, pleads in excuse for himself his love of retirement and his advanced age. But, notwithstanding of these, I am fully of opinion he may be induced to appear once more on the public stage of life."[34]

Having been lionized for renouncing power at the war's end, Washington found it hard to concede normal human ambition. In the *Columbian Magazine* of November 1787, a poet calling himself "Cinna" wrote rapturous verses that cast him in superhuman terms. Evoking the universal fraud and avarice of a corrupt age, "Cinna" held forth Washington as the rare exception, the man "Whom boundless

trust ne'er tempted to betray, / Nor power impelled to arbitrary sway."[35] Such idolatry made it difficult for Washington to be truthful about his feelings. He also had to
reckon with heightened paranoia after the convention, a widespread apprehension
that the new president might transform himself into a king. The only way he could
proceed, it seemed, was to show extreme reluctance to become president, then be
swept along by others.

As his name was bruited about for president, Washington was caught in an excruciating predicament. Merely to broach the topic, even in strict confidence with
friends, might seem to betray some secret craving on his part. As he later confessed
to Hamilton, he dared not seek advice: "For situated as I am, I could hardly bring the
question into the slightest discussion, or ask an opinion, even in the most confidential manner, without betraying, in my judgment, some impropriety of conduct."[36]
For this reason he must have been grateful to friends who talked to him forthrightly
about the presidency. A month after Washington left Philadelphia, Gouverneur
Morris told him that among the "thirteen horses now about to be coupled together,
there are some of every race and character. They will listen to your voice and submit
to your control. You therefore must, I say, *must* mount this seat."[37] From abroad,
Lafayette cheerfully added his voice to the chorus: "I beg you, my dear general, do
not refuse the responsibility of the presidency during the first few years. You alone
can make this political machine operate successfully."[38] This was a powerful argument for Washington, who had gone to Philadelphia feeling that the war would be
incomplete without a new Constitution; now, he knew, the Constitution would be
incomplete without an effective new government.

Perhaps the most subtly persuasive pleas emanated from Hamilton, who could
easily picture himself holding a significant place in a Washington administration.
He stalked Washington for the presidency with all the cunning at his disposal, piling up every good, unselfish reason for running. In mid-August 1788 he wrote to
Washington and introduced the forbidden subject but never used the word *president*. He presented the first presidency as the logical, nay inevitable, sequel to the
Constitutional Convention for Washington: "You will permit me to say that it is
indispensable you should lend yourself to [the new government's] first operations.
It is to little purpose to have *introduced* a system, if the weightiest influence is not
given to its firm *establishment* in the outset."[39] Washington had to undergo this
ritual of spurning the proffered crown. "On the delicate subject with which you
conclude your letter, I can say nothing," Washington replied. "For you know me
well enough, my good Sir, to be persuaded that I am not guilty of affectation when I
tell you, it is my great and sole desire to live and die, in peace and retirement, on my
own farm . . . while you and some others who are acquainted with my heart would
acquit, the world and posterity might probably *accuse* me of *inconsistency* and *am-*

bition."[40] So among those whose opinion Washington considered was posterity. He portrayed himself as paralyzed by indecision and referred to the "dreaded dilemma of being forced to accept or refuse" the presidency.[41] Whenever he mused about the problem, he told Hamilton, he "felt a kind of gloom upon my mind."[42]

As their exchanges continued, Hamilton upped the stakes, telling Washington he had no choice but to assume the presidency. Now older and more self-confident than the wartime aide-de-camp, Hamilton addressed Washington as a peer. The success of the new government was hardly self-evident, and only Washington, he argued, could put the new Constitution to a fair test. If the first government failed, "the framers of it will have to encounter the disrepute of having brought about a revolution in government, without substituting anything that was worthy of the effort."[43] Hamilton contended that Washington's refusal to become president would "throw everything into confusion."[44] This was what Washington yearned to hear: that overwhelming necessity demanded that he make the supreme sacrifice and serve as president.

Washington believed that the new government needed a fair trial and an auspicious start. He always credited the power of first impressions and now imagined that "the first transactions of a nation, like those of an individual upon his first entrance into life, make the deepest impression."[45] With Madison, he employed a powerful metaphor: "To be shipwrecked in sight of the port would be the severest of all possible aggravations to our misery."[46]

Beyond the image projected by the first government, also important was the fact that the first president, in conjunction with Congress, would shape its institutional structure. In Madison's words, the first two years would "produce all the great arrangements under the new system and . . . may fix its tone for a long time to come."[47] Washington knew this, but the prospect of such crushing responsibilities only intensified his dilemma. Having sat through the Constitutional Convention, he knew the sketchy nature of Article II, which dealt with the presidency: "I should consider myself as entering upon an unexplored field, enveloped on every side with clouds and darkness."[48] He also knew the presidency would convert him into a partisan figure, threatening his chaste reputation as the personification of America. In this vein, the *Federal Gazette* of Philadelphia worried that his wartime reputation would be blotted as he shifted from the "fields of military glory" into "the thorn-covered paths of political administration."[49]

The public clamor for Washington to become president arose from his heroism, his disinterested patriotism, and his willingness to surrender his wartime command. Another, if minor, factor was his apparent sterility and lack of children, which made it seem that he had been divinely preserved in an immaculate state to become the Father of His Country. In March 1788, in listing the arguments for elect-

ing Washington, the *Massachusetts Centinel* included this one: "As having no son—
and therefore not exposing us to the danger of an hereditary successor."[50] This was
a plausible fear at a time when monarchs routinely made dynastic marriages and
when people worried that European powers would subvert the new republican government. John Adams expressed to Jefferson his relief that Washington would be
a childless president: "If General Washington had a daughter, I firmly believe she
would be demanded in marriage by one of the royal families of France or England,
perhaps by both; or, if he had a son, he would be invited to come a courting to Europe."[51] To sway Washington to run, Gouverneur Morris slyly alluded to his childless state: "You will become the father to more than three millions of children."[52]

Assailed by doubts, Washington decided to serve only if convinced that "very disagreeable consequences" would result from his refusal.[53] As the election drew near, he
made it plain that accepting the presidency would be his life's most painful decision.
"Be assured, my dear sir," he told Lafayette, "I shall assume the task with the most
unfeigned reluctance and with a real diffidence, for which I shall probably receive no
credit from the world."[54] One way Washington reconciled himself to the job was to
regard it as a temporary post that he would occupy only until the new government
was established on a firm footing. In early October 1788 he confided to Hamilton
that, if he became president, it would be with the hope "that at a convenient and
an early period my services might be dispensed with and that I might be permitted
once more to retire."[55] In fact, Washington later admitted to Jefferson that he had
not planned to serve out a single term as president and had been "made to believe
that in 2 years all would be well in motion and he might retire."[56] It seems safe to say
that Washington never dreamed he would serve out even one full term as president,
much less two. Had he realized that his decision would entangle him in eight more
years of arduous service, he likely would never have agreed to be president.

The thing that, at a stroke, ended Washington's vacillation was the timetable set
up by Congress for the election: presidential electors would be chosen in January
1789 and then vote in February. With his rather formal personality, Washington was
lucky that he didn't need to engage in electioneering, for he lacked the requisite
skills for such campaigning. Had he been forced to make speeches or debate on the
stump, he would not have fared very well. Tailor-made for this transitional moment
between the patrician style of the colonial past and the rowdy populism of the Jack-
sonian era, Washington could remain incommunicado as the electors voted.

In late January he was heartened by signs of a resounding victory for federalists
in the first congressional elections, showing broad-gauged support for the Constitution. "I cannot help flattering myself [that] the new Congress on account of
the . . . various talents of its members will not be inferior to any assembly in the
world," he told Lafayette.[57] This would only have enhanced the presidency's attrac-

tions for Washington. If his election was predictable, it wasn't foreordained that he would win unanimously. In mid-January Henry Lee foresaw that even antifederalist electors would feel obliged to vote for Washington. Casting their votes on February 4, 1789, they vindicated Lee's prediction: all 69 electors voted for Washington, making him the only president in American history to win unanimously.

Lee also forecast with accuracy that the vote for vice president would be far more competitive. Under electoral rules then in force, each elector cast two ballots, the victor becoming president and the runner-up vice president. About the vice president, Washington remained studiously neutral, saying only that he would probably come from the powerful state of Massachusetts—which boiled down to a competition between John Adams and John Hancock. By early January Washington had heard that Adams was the likely choice, and he let it be known that he was "entirely satisfied with the arrangement for filling the second office," especially since it would forestall the election of an antifederalist.[58]

In retrospect, it seems certain that Washington would have outstripped Adams, but some were concerned that Adams might be popular enough in the northern states to edge out Washington as president. An unscrupulous campaign by antifederalists might sabotage Washington's candidacy by withholding votes for him. To prevent such a fiasco, Hamilton suggested privately to a few electors that they withhold votes from Adams to ensure Washington's victory. As it turned out, Hamilton's fears were grossly exaggerated: Washington's 69 votes far outpaced the 34 cast for Adams and 9 for John Jay. Vain and thin-skinned, Adams felt demeaned by receiving only half as many votes as Washington. Hamilton had not attempted to undercut Adams so much as to protect the presidency for Washington. Nonetheless, when Adams later learned of this covert campaign, he was outraged and faulted Hamilton for unconscionable duplicity, poisoning relations between the two men.

Supposed to assemble on March 4, the new Congress could not put together a quorum for another month. The reason for the delay spoke poorly for the country: the delegates had been hampered by the "extreme badness of the roads," Henry Knox informed Washington.[59] Confronted by many problems, the country could ill afford this anxious interregnum. It was a discouraging start, making America look like the backward nation of rude bumpkins derided by British Tories. Washington's election remained unofficial until the new Congress mustered a quorum in early April. Since a landslide victory for him was widely assumed, Washington would have been entitled to travel to New York for the opening of Congress. But detained by a punctilious regard for form, he refused to budge until Congress officially counted the votes on April 6. Things had proceeded much as Washington had wished: instead of seeming to clutch at power, he had let it descend slowly upon his shoulders, as if deposited there by the gentle hand of fate.

Just as Washington had renounced his salary as commander in chief of the Continental Army, so he tried to waive his presidential salary, but Congress insisted adamantly that he accept it. It proved a handsome $25,000 per annum compared to $5,000 for the vice president and $3,500 for the secretaries of state and treasury. Washington's desire to forgo a salary blended his past and present selves: he wanted to display his customary noblesse oblige and advertise his freedom from financial care, while also acting as the ideal public servant, devoid of mercenary motives. It was his way of emphasizing that he was less a professional politician than a gentleman graciously donating his time. In truth, Washington could not afford such magnanimity, and as he prepared for the presidency, he struggled to straighten out his disordered finances. He breathed not a word of his financial troubles to his political associates, who never knew of the handicaps he overcame.

From an economic standpoint, the period after Washington's return to Mount Vernon in December 1783 had been complicated by numerous setbacks. The persistent failure of his corn and wheat crops, thanks in part to a severe chinch bug infestation, had slashed his income drastically. The elements conspired against him again when the drought of the summer of 1787 gave way to the chilly winter of 1787–88. All the while Washington's expenses ballooned from entertaining guests and renovating Mount Vernon's buildings. In a painful comedown, he had been forced repeatedly to dun delinquent debtors. Short of cash, he suffered the indignity of having to press an indebted widow for money from her husband's estate, a task so ghoulish he felt obliged to apologize: "I beg leave to add that it is from the real want of [money] I make such frequent and pressing applications."[60]

On the eve of the Constitutional Convention, Washington had thrown up his hands in despair, confessing to Lund Washington that he could not balance his books: "My estate for the last 11 years have not been able to make both ends meet . . . I mention this for no other purpose than to show that, however willing, I am not able to pay debts unless I could sell land—which I have publicly advertised, without finding bidders."[61] As the convention proceeded, Washington, at his wit's end, told George Augustine that he knew no more "than the man in the moon where I am to get money to pay my taxes"—a shocking admission for a man universally touted as the first president.[62] The failure of his corn crop obligated him to buy eight hundred barrels of corn to feed his army of slaves. Preoccupied with money, Washington hoped the ratification of the Constitution would reverse the country's real estate deflation and alleviate his plight. The day before the Constitution was signed, Washington notified his land agent in western Pennsylvania that he now expected higher prices for his property: "I cannot consent to take two dollars an acre for the land in Washington County. If the government of this country gets well toned and property perfectly secured, I have no doubt of obtaining the price I have fixed on the land, and that in a short time."[63] This turned out to be wishful thinking. Forced to eliminate debt by selling land, he put up for sale a staggering 32,373 acres in the Ohio Country.

As the ratifying conventions progressed, Washington felt a direct financial stake in their outcome, hoping the Constitution would restore American credit. He told one business colleague that the loss of his corn crop and his inability to recoup money from debtors had "caused more perplexity and given me more uneasiness than I ever experienced before from the want of money."[64] Trapped in this predicament, he looked for salvation to the government paper he owned. These promissory notes, used to finance the Revolution, had shed most of their value because of collapsing confidence in the Confederation Congress. Washington had kept these notes, he said, "without having an idea that they would depreciate as they were drawn for interest . . . The injustice of this measure is too obvious and too glaring to pass unobserved."[65] Washington understood firsthand the need for Alexander Hamilton's fiscal program as treasury secretary.

In the spring of 1788 Washington's contemporaries would have been shocked to know that his western taxes for 1785, 1786, and 1787 stood in arrears and that he had posted his lands there for sale to pay them off. Hardly wishing to be a scofflaw at this juncture, Washington tried to pay his taxes promptly with tobacco notes and IOUs that he had received early in the Revolution for supplying articles to the Fairfax County militia. When he learned that Greenbrier County, where the property was located, would not accept such forms of payment, he was enraged. The Father of His Country was being treated with barefaced contempt for financial stresses arising from his wartime sacrifice. "I have been called upon for taxes and threatened at the same time with a sale of the land after June, if the money is not paid before, by the sheriff of Greenbrier County," he wrote. "As I have been suffering loss after loss for near[ly] ten years, while I was in the public service and have scarcely had time to breathe since . . . this procedure seems to me to be a little hasty."[66] In another sign of his eroding financial position, on three occasions he rebuffed the sheriff of Fairfax County when he came around to collect taxes due on Mount Vernon.

By June Washington had paid his outstanding taxes but still seemed cursed by biblical extremes of weather that descended on him with unnerving regularity. "The rains have been so frequent and abundant on *my* plantations that I am, in a manner, drowned," he complained to David Stuart. "What will become of *my* corn is not easy, at this moment to decide. I am working it ankle deep in water and mud."[67] All of Washington's hopes of becoming a model scientific farmer had been scuttled by bad weather.

As Virginia and New York ratified the Constitution during the summer of 1788, Washington's plight had only worsened. That August he told Dr. Craik that "with much truth, I can say I never felt the want of money so sensibly since I was a boy of 15 years old, as I have done for the last 12 months, and probably shall do for 12 months more to come."[68] In other words, Washington foresaw that, if he served as president, he would assume the job amid a full-blown financial crisis. The subsequent year must have been a strange interlude: his name was being bandied about for president as he struggled desperately with his debt load. The day after Christmas 1788 he informed his business agent that "I have never before felt the want of cash so severely as at present."[69] Finally, in early March 1789, after the Electoral College unanimously chose him as president, he took an unprecedented step to salvage his finances. He had suffered a treble blow: another year of poor crops, a continuing inability to collect debts except through long, tedious lawsuits, and the failure to sell land at decent prices. At this nadir of his business life, he sought a loan from a Captain Richard Conway of Alexandria. As he told Conway, "I am inclined to do what I never expected to be reduced to the necessity of doing—that is, to borrow money upon interest. Five hundred pounds would enable me to discharge what I owe in Alexandria . . . and to leave the state (if it shall not be permitted me to remain at home in retirement) without doing this, would be exceedingly disagreeable to me."[70]

No sooner had Washington received the five hundred pounds from Conway at 6 percent interest than he had to request another hundred pounds two days later for "the expenses of my journey to New York, if I go thither."[71] It was an extraordinary admission: Washington needed money to attend his own inauguration as president. Even though he was shortly to receive a presidential salary, he would have to defray the expenses of the executive mansion, imposing yet another gargantuan tax upon his shrinking wealth. One can only imagine Washington's humiliation in cadging money on the eve of his presidency. It would have been especially tough on the tender pride of a man who liked to emit an air of comfortable prosperity. That his second request for money apparently failed could only have aggravated matters.

On March 31, 1789, Washington drew up instructions for George Augustine Washington to guide his supervision of Mount Vernon in his absence. Washington had implicit faith in his nephew's integrity and entrusted him with a general power of attorney. For the next eight years, however distracted he was by his country's affairs, Washington would demand weekly reports down to the minute particulars of wind and weather, and he would send long weekly responses.

Washington's money anxiety had often expressed itself in a sharp tone toward subordinates at Mount Vernon. His financial troubles now added to his recurring frustration with personnel. As his funds dwindled in 1785, he had turned his wrath against his miller. "My miller (William Roberts) is now become such an intolerable sot, and when drunk so great a madman," he complained, "that, however unwilling I am to part with an old servant (for he has been with me 15 years) I cannot with propriety or common justice to myself bear with him any longer."[72] With little confidence in his employees and a deeply rooted reluctance to delegate authority, Washington could not have relished the thought of being absent from Mount Vernon again during his presidency.

A scalding letter that he wrote to his head carpenter, Thomas Green, on March 31, 1789—little more than two weeks before his departure for his inauguration— shows how insecure he felt about leaving his money-losing estate. Always on guard against alcohol abuse, which he branded "the ruin of half the workmen in this country," Washington was exasperated by Green's intractable drinking problem. He warned him that if George Augustine found him unfaithful to his engagements, "either from the love of liquor [or] from a disposition to be running about—or from proneness to idle[ness] when at your work," his nephew had full power "to discard you immediately and to remove your family from their present abode."[73] Not content to leave it at that, Washington grew hotter under the collar, reminding Green that drinking left "a body debilitated, renders him unfit . . . from the execution of [work]. An aching head and trembling limbs, which are the inevitable effects of drinking, disincline the hands from work. Hence begins sloth and that listlessness, which end in idleness." Washington warned him sternly that for the same wages he paid him, he could hire "the best workmen in this country."[74] It was a curiously graceless letter for a man about to ascend to the highest office in the land. Clearly George Washington worried dreadfully about money and whether Mount Vernon would lapse back into the dilapidated state he had found it in more than five years earlier. Now he also had to wonder whether his depleted wealth would support the enhanced celebrity he was about to enjoy as first president of the United States.

PART FIVE

The President

President George Washington,
painted by Gilbert Stuart, 1795–1796.

The Place of Execution

THE CONGRESSIONAL DELAY in certifying Washington's election as president only allowed more time for doubts to fester as he faced the herculean task ahead. He savored his wait as a welcome "reprieve," he told Henry Knox, adding that his "movements to the chair of government will be accompanied with feelings not unlike those of a culprit who is going to the place of his execution."[1] His "peaceful abode" at Mount Vernon, his fears that he lacked the requisite skills for the presidency, the "ocean of difficulties" facing the country—all gave him pause on the eve of his historic journey to New York.[2] In a letter to Edward Rutledge, he made it seem as if the presidency were little short of a death sentence and that, in accepting it, he had given up "all expectations of private happiness in this world."[3] In many ways, the presidency had already come to Mount Vernon as Washington was besieged by obsequious letters from office seekers. "Scarcely a day passes in which applications of one kind or another do not arrive," he told a correspondent.[4] To simplify his life and set a high standard for future presidents, Washington refused to favor friends or relations in making appointments.

The day after Congress counted the electoral votes, declaring Washington the first president, it dispatched Charles Thomson, the secretary of Congress, to bear the official announcement to Mount Vernon. The legislators had chosen a fine emissary. A well-rounded figure, known for his work in astronomy and mathematics, the Irish-born Thomson was a tall, austere man of inborn dignity with a narrow face and keenly penetrating eyes. He couldn't have relished the trip to Virginia, which was "much impeded by tempestuous weather, bad roads, and the many large rivers I had to cross."[5] Yet he rejoiced that the new president would be Washington, whom he revered as singled out by providence to be "the savior and father" of the country.[6] Having known Thomson since the Continental Congress, Washington esteemed him as a faithful public servant and exemplary patriot.

Around noon on April 14, 1789, Washington flung open the door at Mount Vernon and greeted his visitor with a cordial embrace. Once in the privacy of the mansion, he and Thomson conducted a stiff verbal minuet, each man reading from a prepared text. Thomson began by declaring, "I am honored with the commands of the Senate to wait upon your Excellency with the information of your being elected to the office of the President of the United States of America" by a unanimous vote.[7] He read aloud a letter from Senator John Langdon of New Hampshire, the president pro tempore: "Suffer me, sir, to indulge the hope that so auspicious a mark of public confidence will meet your approbation and be considered as a sure pledge of the affection and support you are to expect from a free and enlightened people."[8] There was something deferential, even slightly servile, in Langdon's tone, as if he feared that Washington might renege on his pledge and refuse to take the job. Thus was greatness once again thrust upon George Washington.

Any student of Washington's life might have predicted that he would acknowledge his election in a short, self-effacing speech, loaded with disclaimers. "While I realize the arduous nature of the task which is conferred on me and feel my inability to perform it," he replied to Thomson, "I wish there may not be reason for regretting the choice. All I can promise is only that which can be accomplished by an honest zeal."[9] This sentiment of modesty jibed so perfectly with Washington's private letters that it could not have been feigned: he wondered whether he was fit for the post, so unlike anything he had ever done. The hopes for republican government, he knew, rested in his hands. As commander in chief, he been able to wrap himself in a self-protective silence, but the presidency would leave him with no place to hide and would expose him to public censure as nothing before.

Because the vote counting had been long delayed, Washington felt the crush of upcoming public business and decided to set out promptly for New York on April 16, accompanied in his elegant carriage by Thomson and David Humphreys. His diary entry conveys a sense of foreboding: "About ten o'clock, I bade adieu to Mount Vernon, to private life, and to domestic felicity and, with a mind oppressed with more anxious and painful sensations than I have words to express, set out for New York . . . with the best dispositions to render service to my country in obedience to its call, but with less hope of answering its expectations."[10] He sounded like someone marching off, head bowed, to the gallows. Waving goodbye was Martha, who wouldn't join him until mid-May. She watched her husband of thirty years depart with a mixture of bittersweet sensations, wondering "when or whether he will ever come home again." She had long doubted the wisdom of this final act in his public life. "I think it was much too late for him to go into public life again," she told her nephew, "but it was not to be avoided. Our family will be deranged as I must soon follow him."[11]

Determined to travel rapidly, Washington and his entourage set out each day at sunrise and put in a full day on the road. Along the way he hoped to keep ceremonial distractions to a minimum, but he was soon disabused: eight exhausting days of festivities lay ahead. He had traveled only ten miles north to Alexandria when the townspeople waylaid him with a dinner, lengthened by the mandatory thirteen toasts. Adept at farewells, Washington was succinctly eloquent in response: "Unutterable sensations must then be left to more expressive silence, while, from an aching heart, I bid you all, my affectionate friends and kind neighbors, farewell."[12]

Before long, Washington saw that his journey would form the republican equivalent of the procession to a royal coronation. As if already a seasoned politician, he left a trail of political promises in his wake. While in Wilmington, he addressed the Delaware Society for Promoting Domestic Manufacturers and imparted a hopeful message: "The promotion of domestic manufactures will, in my conception, be among the first consequences which may naturally be expected to flow from an energetic government."[13] Arriving in Philadelphia, he was met by local dignitaries and asked to mount a white horse for his entry into town. When he crossed a bridge over the Schuylkill, it was wreathed with laurels and evergreens, and a cherubic boy, aided by a mechanical device, lowered a laurel crown over his head. Recurrent cries of "Long Live George Washington" confirmed what James McHenry had already told him before he left Mount Vernon: "You are now a king under a different name."[14]

As Washington entered Philadelphia, he found himself, willy-nilly, at the head of a full-scale parade. Twenty thousand people lined the streets, their eyes fixed on him in wonder. "His Excellency rode in front of the procession, on horseback, politely bowing to the spectators who filled the doors and windows by which he passed," reported the *Federal Gazette,* noting that church bells rang as Washington proceeded to his old haunt, the City Tavern.[15] After the bare-knuckled fight over the Constitution, the newspaper editorialized, Washington had brought the country together: "What a pleasing reflection to every patriotic mind, thus to see our citizens again united in their reliance on this great man who is, a second time, called upon to be the savior of his country!"[16] By the next morning Washington had grown tired of the jubilation. When the light horse cavalry showed up to accompany him to Trenton, they discovered he had sneaked out of the city an hour earlier "to avoid even the appearance of pomp or vain parade," reported one newspaper.[17]

As Washington approached the bridge over Assunpink Creek in Trenton, the spot where he had stood off the British and Hessians, he saw that the townsfolk had erected a magnificent floral arch in his honor and emblazoned it with the words "December 26, 1776" and the proclamation "The Defenders of the Mothers will also Defend the Daughters."[18] As he rode closer, thirteen young girls, robed in spotless white, walked forward with flower-filled baskets, scattering petals at his feet. Astride his horse, tears standing in his eyes, he returned a deep bow and noted the "astonishing contrast between his former and actual situation at the same spot."[19] With that, three rows of women—young girls, unmarried ladies, and married ones—burst into a fervent ode on how he had saved fair virgins and matrons alike. Beneath his public composure, the adulation only crystallized Washington's self-doubt. "I greatly apprehend that my countrymen will expect too much from me," he wrote to Rutledge. "I fear, if the issue of public measures should not correspond with their sanguine expectations, they will turn the extravagant . . . praises which they are heaping upon me at this moment into equally extravagant . . . censures."[20] There was no way, it seemed, that he could lower expectations or escape public reverence.

As Washington approached New York City, a parallel journey from Mount Vernon was in progress that, in many ways, was no less fascinating. Billy Lee, the slave and manservant with whom he had shared so many exploits, longed to join Washington for the inauguration. Once a physical specimen perhaps as imposing as his master, Lee had by now fractured both knees, but he still wanted to make the journey and serve in the presidential household, where he would have to climb three flights of stairs. Dubious that Lee could do it, Washington tried to dissuade him from coming. Nevertheless he always found it difficult to resist Lee's pleas and finally consented that he should travel to the inauguration with Tobias Lear.

When Lear and Lee reached Philadelphia around April 19, Lee's inflamed knees made it impossible for him to soldier on. Lear contacted Clement Biddle and asked if he could minister to Lee until the slave was ready to complete his journey. "Will appears to be in too bad a state to travel at present," Lear wrote. "I shall therefore leave him and will be much obliged to you if you will send him on to New York as soon as he can bear the journey without injury, which I expect will be in two or three days. I shall pay his expenses . . . He dresses his knee himself and therefore will stand in no need of a doctor, unless it should grow worse."[21] In a remarkable act of faith in Lee's fidelity as a slave, Lear left him in Philadelphia while he proceeded to New York. For more than a month, Biddle gave Lee excellent care, calling in two doctors to treat his knee. He even had a steel brace manufactured at "heavy expense" that enabled him to walk, though with difficulty.[22] The care lavished on Billy Lee again confirms that Washington treated him in a singular way among his slaves and dealt with him as a man whose pride and feelings had to be taken into account. From his behavior, it is clear that Washington felt the need to reason with Lee, as if he were an employee, instead of simply bossing him about as a slave. Of course, Lee's exceptional treatment only pointed up the powerless state of other slaves.

Although Lee missed the inauguration, he still yearned for a job in the presidential household. A few days after Washington was inaugurated, Lear wrote to Biddle and tried again to discourage Lee from coming to New York, pointing out that "he cannot possibly be of any service here" and expressing the hope that he would catch the "first vessel that sails for Alex[andri]a" after he recuperated.[23] Lee remained obdurate. Submitting to the slave's wish, Lear instructed Biddle that, if Lee was "still anxious to come on here, the president would gratify him, altho[ugh] he will be troublesome. He has been an old and faithful serv[an]t. This is enough for the president to gratify him in every reasonable wish."[24] On June 22 Lear informed Biddle that "Billy arrived here safe and well."[25] Again, Lear spared no expense with Lee, who was brought by coach from the ferry stop to the presidential mansion. To dress him up for his new duties, Lear went out and got him suitable stockings. Unwilling to spurn Lee's demand for a place in the executive residence, Washington allowed him to work there, probably as a butler, during his first term, even though Lee had, by some accounts, become difficult and temperamental.

BY NOW SATED WITH ADULATION, Washington preserved a faint hope that he would be allowed to make an inconspicuous entry into New York. He had pleaded with Governor George Clinton to spare him further hoopla: "I can assure you, with the utmost sincerity, that no reception can be so congenial to my feelings as a quiet entry devoid of ceremony."[26] But he was fooling himself if he imagined he might slip unobtrusively into the temporary capital. Never reconciled to the demands of his celebrity, Washington still fantasized that he could shuck that inescapable burden. When he arrived at Elizabethtown on April 23, an impressive phalanx of three senators, five congressmen, and three state officials awaited him. He must have intuited, with a sinking sensation, that this welcome would eclipse even the frenzied receptions in Philadelphia and Trenton. Moored to the wharf was a special presidential barge, glistening with fresh paint, constructed in his honor and equipped with an awning of red curtains in the rear to shelter him from the elements. To nobody's surprise, the craft was steered by thirteen oarsmen in spanking white uniforms.

As the barge drifted into the Hudson River, Washington made out a Manhattan shoreline already "crowded with a vast concourse of citizens, waiting with exulting anxiety his arrival," a local newspaper said.[27] Many ships anchored in the harbor were garlanded with flags and banners. If Washington gazed back at the receding Jersey shore, he would have seen that his craft led a huge flotilla of boats, including one bearing the portly figure of Henry Knox. Some boats carried musicians and female vocalists on deck, serenading Washington across the waters. "The voices of the ladies were superior to the flutes that played with the stroke of the oars in Cleopatra's silken-corded barge," was the imaginative verdict of the *New York Packet*.[28] These wafted melodies, enhanced by repeated cannon roar and thunderous acclaim from crowds onshore, again oppressed Washington with their implicit message of high expectations. As he confided to his diary, the intermingled sounds "filled my mind with sensations as painful (considering the reverse of this scene, which may be the case after all my labors to do good) as they are pleasing."[29] To guard himself against later disappointment, he seemed not to allow himself the smallest iota of pleasure.

When the presidential barge landed at the foot of Wall Street, Governor Clinton, Mayor James Duane, James Madison, and other luminaries welcomed him to the city. The officer of a special military escort stepped forward briskly and told Washington that he awaited his orders. Washington again labored to cool the celebratory mood. "As to the present arrangement," he replied, "I shall proceed as is directed. But after this is over, I hope you will give yourself no further trouble, as the affection of my fellow-citizens is all the guard I want."[30] Nobody seemed to take the hint seriously.

The streets were solidly thronged with well-wishers, and it took Washington a half hour to arrive at his new residence at 3 Cherry Street, tucked away in the northeastern corner of the city, a block from the East River, near the present-day Brooklyn Bridge. One week earlier the building's owner, Samuel Osgood, had agreed to lease it to Congress as the temporary presidential residence. The descriptions of Washington's demeanor en route to the house confirm that he finally surrendered to the general high spirits, especially when he viewed the legions of adoring women. As Elias Boudinot told his wife, Washington "frequently bowed to the multitude and took off his hat to the ladies at the windows, who waved their handkerchiefs and threw flowers before him and shed tears of joy and congratulation. The whole city was one scene of triumphal rejoicing."[31]

America's second-largest city, with a population of about thirty thousand, New York was a small, provincial town compared to European capitals. Lavishly appointed carriages sped through streets heaped with horse droppings and rubbish. Rich and robust, New York already had a raucous commercial spirit that grated on squeamish sensibilities. "New York is less citified than Philadelphia," said a French visitor, "but the bustle of trade is far greater."[32] Before the war John Adams, passing through town, huffed that "with all the opulence and splendor of this city, there is very little good breeding to be found. There is no modesty. No attention to one another. They talk very loud, very fast, and all together."[33] Although Vice President Adams had arrived before Washington, the town did not endear itself to him on this trip either. Congress had failed to locate a residence for the new vice president, who lodged with John Jay for several weeks.

New York had not yet recovered fully from the dislocations of the war. First Americans and then Britons had uprooted trees and fences for firewood, leaving weed-strewn lots in their path. In the aftermath of the British occupation, said Mayor Duane, New York resembled a place that "had been inhabited by savages or wild beasts."[34] The great conflagration that consumed a quarter of the city in 1776 had left behind blocks of rubble and skeletal houses, some of them yet to be razed. Like many ports, New York catered to a rough, brawling population of sailors and traders and boasted more than four hundred taverns. One French visitor in the 1790s expressed surprise that the city had "whole sections given over to streetwalkers for the plying of their profession" and that it was filled with "houses of debauchery."[35] With its wealthy merchants and brawny laborers, the city already presented a picture of vivid extremes.

THOUGH THE CONSTITUTION SAID NOTHING about an inaugural address, Washington, in an innovative spirit, contemplated such a speech as early as January 1789 and asked a "gentleman under his roof"—David Humphreys—to draft one.[36] Washington had always been economical with words, but the collaboration with Humphreys produced a wordy document, seventy-three pages long, which survives only in tantalizing snippets. In this curious speech, Washington spent a ridiculous amount of time defending his decision to become president, as if he stood accused of some heinous crime. He denied that he had accepted the presidency to enrich himself, even though nobody had accused him of greed: "In the first place, if I have formerly served the community without a wish for pecuniary compensation, it can hardly be suspected that I am at present influenced by avaricious schemes."[37] Addressing a topical concern, he disavowed any desire to found a dynasty, pleading his childless state. Closer in tone to future inaugural speeches was his ringing expression of faith in the American people. He devised a perfect formulation of popular sovereignty, writing that the Constitution had brought forth "a government of the people: that is to say, a government in which all power is derived from, and at stated periods reverts to, them—and that, in its operation . . . is purely a government of laws made and executed by the fair substitutes of the people alone."[38] Showing an Enlightenment spirit, he generalized the American Revolution into a movement blazing a path toward the universal triumph of freedom: "I rejoice in a belief that intellectual light will spring up in the dark corners of the earth; that freedom of inquiry will produce liberality of conduct; that mankind will reverse the absurd position that *the many* were made for *the few;* and that they will not continue slaves in one part of the globe, when they can become freemen in another."[39]

This ponderous speech never saw the light of day. Washington sent a copy to James Madison, who wisely vetoed it on two counts: it was much too long, and its lengthy legislative proposals would be interpreted as executive meddling with the legislature. Instead, Madison helped Washington draft a far more compact speech that avoided the tortured introspection of its predecessor. A whirlwind of energy, Madison would seem omnipresent in the early days of Washington's administration. He drafted not only the inaugural address but also the official response by Congress and then Washington's response to Congress, completing the circle. This service established Madison, despite his major role in the House, as a preeminent adviser and confidant to the new president. Oddly enough, he was not troubled that his advisory relationship to Washington might be construed as violating the separation of powers.

Washington knew that everything he did at the swearing-in would establish a tone for the future. "As the first of everything in *our situation* will serve to establish a precedent," he reminded Madison, "it is devoutly wished on my part that these precedents may be fixed on true principles."[40] He would shape indelibly the institution of the presidency. Although he had earned his reputation in battle, he made a critical decision not to wear a uniform at the inauguration or beyond, banishing fears of a military coup. Instead, he would stand there aglitter with patriotic symbols. To spur American manufactures, he would wear a double-breasted brown suit made from broadcloth woven at the Woolen Manufactory of Hartford, Connecticut.[41] The suit had gilt buttons with an eagle insignia on them; to complete his outfit, he would wear white hosiery, silver shoe buckles, and yellow gloves. Washington already sensed that Americans would emulate their presidents. "I hope it will not be a great while before it will be unfashionable for a gentleman to appear in any other dress," he told Lafayette, referring to his American attire. "Indeed, we have already been too long subject to British prejudices."[42] To burnish his image further on inauguration day, Washington powdered his hair and wore a dress sword on his hip, sheathed in a steel scabbard.

The inauguration took place at the building at Wall and Nassau streets that had long served as New York's City Hall. It came richly laden with historical associations, having hosted John Peter Zenger's trial in 1735, the Stamp Act Congress of 1765, and the Confederation Congress from 1785 to 1788. Starting in September 1788, the French engineer Pierre-Charles L'Enfant had remodeled it into Federal Hall, a suitable home for Congress. L'Enfant introduced a covered arcade at street level and a balcony surmounted by a triangular pediment on the second story. As the people's chamber, the House of Representatives was accessible to the public, situated in a high-ceilinged octagonal room on the ground floor, while the Senate met in a second-floor room, buffering it from popular pressure. From this room Washington would emerge onto the balcony to take the oath of office. In many ways, the first inauguration was a hasty, slapdash affair. As with all theatrical spectacles, rushed preparations and frantic work on the new building continued until a few days before the event. Nervous anticipation spread through the city as to whether the two hundred workmen would complete the project on time. Only a few days before the inauguration, an eagle was hoisted onto the pediment, completing the building. The final effect was stately: a white building with a blue and white cupola topped by a weathervane.

A little after noon on April 30, 1789, following a morning filled with clanging church bells and prayers, a contingent of troops on horseback, accompanied by carriages loaded with legislators, stopped at Washington's Cherry Street residence. Escorted by David Humphreys and Tobias Lear, the president-elect stepped into his appointed carriage, which was trailed by foreign dignitaries and crowds of joyous citizens. The procession wound slowly through the narrow Manhattan streets, emerging two hundred yards from Federal Hall. After alighting from his carriage, Washington strode through a double line of soldiers to the building and mounted to the Senate chamber, where members of Congress awaited him expectantly. As he entered, Washington bowed to both houses of the legislature—his invariable mark of respect—then occupied an imposing chair up front. A profound hush settled on the room. Vice President Adams rose for an official greeting, then informed Washington that the epochal moment had arrived: "Sir, the Senate and House of Representatives are ready to attend you to take the oath required by the constitution." "I am ready to proceed," Washington replied.[43]

As he stepped through the door onto the balcony, a spontaneous roar surged from the multitude tightly squeezed into Wall and Broad streets and covering every roof in sight. This open-air ceremony would confirm the sovereignty of the citizens gathered below. Washington's demeanor was stately, modest, and deeply affecting: he clapped one hand to his heart and bowed several times to the crowd. Surveying the serried ranks of people, one observer said they were jammed so closely together that "it seemed one might literally walk on the heads of the people."[44] Thanks to his simple dignity, integrity, and unrivaled sacrifices for his country, Washington's conquest of the people was complete. A member of the crowd, the Count de Moustier, the French minister, noted the solemn trust between Washington and the citizens who stood packed below him with uplifted faces. As he reported to his government, never had "sovereign reigned more completely in the hearts of his subjects than did Washington in those of his fellow citizens . . . He has the soul, look, and figure of a hero united in him."[45] One young woman in the crowd echoed this when she remarked, "I never saw a human being that looked so great and noble as he does."[46] Only Congressman Fisher Ames of Massachusetts noted that "time has made havoc" upon Washington's face, which already looked haggard and careworn.[47]

The sole constitutional requirement for the swearing-in was that the president take the oath of office. That morning a congressional committee decided to add solemnity by having Washington place his hand on a Bible during the oath, leading to a frantic, last-minute scramble to find one. A Masonic lodge came to the rescue by providing a thick Bible, bound in deep brown leather and set on a crimson velvet cushion. By the time Washington appeared on the portico, the Bible rested on a table draped in red.

The crowd grew silent as New York chancellor Robert R. Livingston administered the oath to Washington, who was visibly moved. As he finished the oath, he bent forward, seized the Bible, and brought it to his lips. Washington felt this moment from the bottom of his soul: one observer noted the "devout fervency" with which he "took the oath and the reverential manner in which he bowed down and kissed the Bible."[48] Legend has it that he added "So help me God," though this line was first reported sixty-five years later. Whether or not Washington actually said it, very few people would have heard him anyway, since his voice was soft and breathy. For the crowd below, the oath of office was enacted as a kind of dumbshow. Livingston had to lift his voice and inform the crowd, "It is done." He then intoned: "Long Live George Washington, President of the United States."[49] The spectators responded with huzzas and chants of "God bless our Washington! Long live our beloved President!"[50] They celebrated in the only way they knew, as if greeting a new monarch with the customary cry of "Long Live the King!"

When the balcony ceremony was concluded, Washington returned to the Senate chamber to deliver his inaugural address. In an important piece of symbolism, Congress rose as he entered, then sat down after Washington bowed in response. In England, the House of Commons stood during the king's speeches, so that the seated Congress immediately established a sturdy equality between the legislative and executive branches.

As Washington began his speech, he seemed flustered and thrust his left hand into his pocket while turning the pages with a trembling right hand. His weak voice was barely audible. Fisher Ames evoked him thus: "His aspect grave, almost to sadness; his modesty, actually shaking; his voice deep, a little tremulous, and so low as to call for close attention."[51] Those present attributed Washington's low voice and fumbling hands to anxiety. "This great man was agitated and embarrassed more than ever he was by the leveled cannon or pointed musket," said Senator William Maclay in sniggering tones. "He trembled and several times could scarce make out to read, though it must be supposed he had often read it before."[52] Washington's agitation might have arisen from a developing neurological disorder or might simply have been a bad case of nerves. The new president had long been famous for his physical grace, but the sole gesture he used for emphasis in his speech seemed clumsy—"a flourish with his right hand," said Maclay, "which left rather an un-gainly impression."[53] For the next few years Maclay would be a close, unsparing observer of the new president's quirks and tics.

In the first line of his inaugural address, Washington expressed anxiety about his fitness for the presidency, saying that "no event could have filled me with greater anxieties" than the news brought to him by Charles Thomson.[54] He had grown despondent, he said candidly, as he considered his own "inferior endowments from nature" and his lack of practice in civil government.[55] He drew comfort, however, from the fact that the "Almighty Being" had overseen America's birth: "No peo-ple can be bound to acknowledge and adore the invisible hand, which conducts the affairs of men, more than the people of the United States."[56] Perhaps referring obliquely to the fact that he suddenly seemed older, he called Mount Vernon "a retreat which was rendered every day more necessary, as well as more dear to me, by the addition of habit to inclination and of frequent interruptions in my health to the gradual waste committed on it by time."[57] In the earlier inaugural address drafted with David Humphreys, Washington had included a disclaimer about his health, telling how he had "prematurely grown old in the service of my country."[58]

Setting the pattern for future inaugural speeches, Washington did not delve into minute policy matters but outlined the big themes that would govern his adminis-tration, the foremost being the triumph of national unity over "local prejudices or attachments" that might subvert the country or even tear it apart.[59] National policy needed to be rooted in private morality, which relied on the "eternal rules of order and right" ordained by heaven itself.[60] On the other hand, Washington refrained from endorsing any particular form of religion. Knowing how much was riding on this attempt at republican government, he said that "the sacred fire of liberty, and the destiny of the republican model of government, are justly considered as *deeply,* perhaps as *finally* staked, on the experiment entrusted to the hands of the American people."[61]

After this speech, Washington led a broad procession of delegates up Broadway, along streets flanked by armed militia, to an Episcopal prayer service at St. Paul's Chapel, where he was given his own canopied pew. After these devotions ended, Washington had his first chance to relax until the evening festivities. That night lower Manhattan was converted into a shimmering fairyland of lights. From the residences of Chancellor Livingston and General Knox, Washington observed the fireworks at Bowling Green, a pyrotechnic display that flashed in the sky for two hours. Washing-ton's image was displayed in transparencies hung in many windows, throwing glow-ing images into the night. Such a celebration, ironically, would have been familiar to Washington from the days when new royal governors arrived in Williamsburg and were greeted by bonfires, fireworks, and illuminations in every window.

All of New York was astir with the evening festivities, and Washington had trouble returning to Cherry Street with Tobias Lear and David Humphreys. "We returned home at ten on foot," wrote Lear, "the throng of people being so great as not to permit a carriage to pass through it."[62] The comment shows how closely people pressed against Washington in the thickly peopled streets. By the time he went to bed, he had initiated many enduring customs for presidential inaugurations, including the procession to the swearing-in venue, taking the oath of office *en plein air,* delivering an inaugural speech, and holding a gigantic celebration that evening. Because Martha was still absent, the inaugural ball was deferred until May.

The odyssey of George Washington from insecure young colonel in the French and Indian War, through his tenure as commander in chief of the Continental Army, and now to president of the new government, must have seemed an almost dreamlike progression to him. Perhaps nothing underlined this improbable turn of events more than the extraordinary fact that while Washington had debated whether to become president that winter, on the other side of the ocean King George III had descended into madness. In late January Samuel Powel conveyed this startling piece of news to Washington: "I do not recollect any topic which, at present, occupies the conversation of men so much as the insanity of the king of Great Britain. I am told . . . that Dr. Franklin's observation upon hearing the report was that he had long been of opinion that the King of Great Britain was insane, tho[ugh] it had not been declared to the world till now."[63]

There was nothing vindictive in Washington's nature, no itching for retribution, and he reacted with sympathy to news of the king's malady. "Be the cause of the British king's insanity what it may," he told Powel, "his situation . . . merits commiseration."[64] The strangely contrasting fates of the two Georges grew stranger still in late February, when Gouverneur Morris reported from Paris an unlikely development in the king's madness. "By the bye," he wrote to Washington, "in the melancholy situation to which the poor King of England has been reduced, there were, I am told, in relation to you, some whimsical circumstances." In a deranged fit, wrote Morris, the king had "conceived himself to be no less a personage than George Washington at the head of the American Army. This shows that you have done something or other which sticks most terribly in his stomach."[65] The delusion proved fleeting. On April 23, 1789, exactly one week before George Washington was sworn in to cheering crowds, George III recovered so miraculously from his delusional state that a thanksgiving service was conducted at St. Paul's Cathedral in London. It is hypothesized by some that he had suffered from a rare hereditary disorder called porphyria, a condition not properly diagnosed until the twentieth century. Restored to his senses, he had to contemplate the sobering reality that the upstart George Washington, who had once scrounged for advancement in his royal army, now served as president of an independent American republic.

Martha Washington wasn't thrilled at being first lady and, like her husband, talked about the presidency as an indescribable calamity that had befallen her. She professed a lack of interest in politics, having told her niece Fanny the previous year that "we have not a single article of news but politic[s], which I do not concern myself about."[66] Whether she was really so blasé about politics, or merely preferred not to express her opinions, is unclear. The tone of her letters grew wistful as she thought about New York. She and her husband had already sacrificed more than eight years to the war, and after so much hardship Mount Vernon had seemed like their long-deserved sanctuary. Now Washington's presidency would likely eliminate any chance for a private final phase of their lives. Martha couldn't have found it easy to be married to a man who was also married to the nation, but she understood his reasoning in becoming president, telling Mercy Otis Warren that she could not blame him "for having acted according to his ideas of duty in obeying the voice of his country."[67]

Martha Washington never defied her husband openly, but when forced to do anything against her will, she could be quietly willful. She would pout and sulk and drag her feet in silence. In one letter Washington said that he wanted to be "well fixed at New York" before he sent for her, but one suspects that Martha's delay reflected her disinclination to leave Virginia.[68] A few days after his inauguration, Washington wrote with some urgency to George Augustine, asking him to hasten Martha's departure, "for we are extremely desirous of seeing her here."[69] This suggests that her delay had lasted longer than expected. By that point, Washington knew that she would miss the ceremonial ball planned for May 7 at the Assembly Rooms on Broadway. Evidently Martha's presence had been anticipated, for a special elevated sofa had been created that would enable the president and first lady to preside in state over the celebration.

On May 14 Washington's nephew, nineteen-year-old Robert Lewis, arrived at Mount Vernon to escort his aunt to New York and discovered with amazement that "everything appeared to be in confusion."[70] Martha was still supervising the packing in an unusually chaotic scene for this well-organized woman. Finally on May 16, with one wagon heaped with nothing but baggage, she piled into her coach with her two grandchildren, Nelly and Washy, accompanied by a retinue of six slaves. As a crowd of slaves clustered around the departing group, emotions ran high. "The servants of the house and a number of the field Negroes made their appearance to take leave of their mistress," Robert Lewis recorded in his journal. "Numbers of these poor wretches seemed greatly *agitated, much affected.* My aunt equally so."[71] The slaves' tears were surely genuine, but one wonders whether they were shed for the six friends and family members being forcibly relocated to New York; perhaps the remaining slaves feared mistreatment at the hands of overseers in the Washingtons' absence. Martha decided to take two personal slaves, Molly (or Moll) and a sixteen-year-old mulatto girl named Ona (or Oney) Judge, who had become her favorite. Two other slaves, Austin and Christopher Sheels, would act as waiters in New York, while Giles and Paris, who had accompanied Washington to the Constitutional Convention, would reprise their roles as coachmen.

The Martha Washington who set out for New York was a more matronly woman than the doughty wife who showed up regularly at the Continental Army camp each winter. Like her husband, she now wore spectacles on occasion. Ever dutiful, she did her best to live up to her new station on the national scene. With political instincts to rival her husband's, she had ordered green and brown wool from Hartford to make riding costumes for herself and was lauded in the press for being "clothed in the manufacture of our country."[72]

En route to New York, Martha had no better luck than her husband in escaping the hordes who competed to greet her. Nevertheless, as she got her first taste of being first lady—the term was not adopted until later administrations—she experienced a rising sense of excitement. Upon reaching the outskirts of Philadelphia, she was hailed by the state's chief executive, and a cavalry honor guard conducted her into town. On May 27 the new president took time out from his duties to receive his wife at Elizabethtown, where she got the same tumultuous reception bestowed on him a month earlier. As Martha wrote appreciatively to Fanny, the welcoming committee had come "with the fine barge you have seen so much said of in the papers, with the same oarsmen that carried the P[resident] to New York."[73] Little Washy Custis was flabbergasted by the boat ride and by the grand parade that swept up the entire party the moment the big, burly governor of New York, George Clinton, received them on the Manhattan side. Meanwhile sister Nelly spent hours at the window on Cherry Street, transfixed by the fancy carriages passing down below.

No sooner had she arrived in the capital than Martha learned that she would be a prop in an elaborate piece of political theater. One day after her arrival, she had to host a dinner for congressional leaders, and the day after that, all of New York society seemed to cram into the Cherry Street mansion for her first reception—a function for which she had not been consulted. She was plunged into a giddy whirl of activity. "I have not had one half hour to myself since the day of my arrival," she told Fanny in early June.[74] She narrated this abrupt transformation with a note of quiet wonder: the woman who had been dubious about this new life sounded positively breathless with amazement. She had been taken in hand by a professional hairdresser, a novel experience for her. "My hair is set and dressed every day and I have put on white muslin habits for the summer," she wrote home in early June. "You would, I fear, think me a good deal in the fashion if you could but see me."[75]

The town was enchanted with Martha Washington, whose conviviality offset her husband's reserve. She won over the toughest critic: the wife of the vice president, who found her the perfect republican counterpart of her husband. "I took the earliest opportunity . . . to go and pay my respects to Mrs. Washington," Abigail Adams informed her sister. "She received me with great ease and politeness. She is plain in her dress, but that plainness is the best of every article . . . Her hair is white, her teeth beautiful, her person rather short than otherwise."[76] The favorable impression grew upon second viewing: "Mrs. Washington is one of those unassuming characters which create love and esteem. A most becoming pleasantness sits upon her countenance and an unaffected deportment which renders her the object of veneration and respect."[77]

A pragmatic woman, Martha Washington resigned herself to the duties of a presidential wife, but a distinct touch of discontent lingered. She was quietly rebellious, chafing at her restricted freedom. In late October she unburdened herself to Fanny: "I live a very dull life here and know nothing that passes in the town. I never go to the public place. Indeed, I think I am more like a state prisoner than anything else." She complained of "certain bounds set for me which I must not depart from. And as I cannot do as I like, I am obstinate and stay at home a great deal."[78] Obviously there were limits to her acquiescence, and she adopted an increasingly satiric tone when talking about the fashionable people of New York. When she sent Fanny a watch, she described it as "of the newest fashion, if that has any influence on your taste." Then she added tartly: "It will last as long as the fashion—and by that time you can get another of a fashionable kind."[79]

At year's end Martha Washington aired her frustrations to Mercy Otis Warren, pointing out that her grandchildren and Virginia family constituted the major source of her happiness: "I shall hardly be able to find any substitute that would indemnify me for the loss of a part of such endearing society."[80] She knew other women would gladly swap places with her: "With respect to myself, I sometimes think the arrangement is not quite as it ought to have been—that I, who had much rather be at home, should occupy a place with which a great many younger and gayer women would be prodigiously pleased."[81] But she would not rail against her destiny: "I am still determined to be cheerful and to be happy in whatever situation I may be, for I have also learned from experience that the greater part of our happiness or misery depends upon our dispositions and not upon our circumstances."[82] To the end of her life, Martha Washington would speak forlornly of the presidential years as her "lost days."[83]

CHAPTER FORTY-SEVEN

Acting the Presidency

WHEN GEORGE WASHINGTON BECAME PRESIDENT, the executive departments had not yet been formed or their chieftains installed, so he placed unusual reliance on his personal secretaries, whom he dubbed "the gentlemen of the household."[1] He put a premium on efficiency, good manners, discretion, and graceful writing. The staff mainstay was Harvard-educated Tobias Lear, the agreeable young man brought up from Mount Vernon. In these early days Lear was a man for all seasons: dashing off private letters for Washington, cranking out dinner invitations, tending files, tutoring grandchildren, accompanying Washington on afternoon strolls or Martha on shopping sprees. So trusted was Lear that he kept the household accounts, and Washington turned to him for petty cash. His loyalty had no limits. "I have never found a single thing that could lessen my respect for him," Lear remarked of Washington. "A complete knowledge of his honesty, uprightness, and candor in all his private transactions has sometimes led me to think him more than a man."[2] When Lear married Polly Long in April 1790—Martha called her "a pretty, sprightly woman"—the Washingtons invited the young couple to share their household, enriching their lives with an extended family as they had done at Mount Vernon.[3]

For a second secretary, Washington retained David Humphreys, with his agile pen. Now seasoned by diplomatic experience in Paris with Jefferson, Humphreys advised Washington on questions of etiquette and was anointed chamberlain, or master of ceremonies, for the administration. The third team member was Major William Jackson, an orphan from South Carolina who had won high marks as secretary of the Constitutional Convention, having taken notes of the deliberations while preserving their secrecy—a man of discretion after Washington's own heart.

The closest that Washington came to a security guard, Jackson remained a protective presence at his side, whether he was out walking, riding, or performing official duties. Rounding out the group were Thomas Nelson, Jr., son of the late Virginia governor, and Washington's young nephew Robert Lewis, who had escorted his aunt Martha to New York.

Among members of Congress, James Madison stood in a class by himself in his advisory capacity to Washington. When he ran for Congress, Madison had consulted Washington about how to campaign without descending to crass electioneering. It is not surprising that Washington leaned on Madison early in his presidency, since nobody possessed a more nuanced grasp of the Constitution. In 1789 Congress had to shape both the executive and the judicial branches, which would act to enhance Madison's prestige. Gradually, as the three branches of government assumed more separate characters and political differences between the two men surfaced, Madison shed his advisory role.

By the time Washington was sworn in, the federal government had already been set in motion; the first order of business was to generate money to guarantee the new government's survival. Three weeks before the inauguration, Madison introduced in the House a schedule of duties on imported goods to provide revenues. Nothing better proclaimed the new government's autonomy: the impotent Confederation Congress had never commanded an independent revenue stream.

Washington's first days in office were dominated by seemingly trivial symbolic issues that spoke to larger questions about the character of the new government. "Many things which appear of little importance in themselves . . . at the beginning may have great and durable consequences, from their having been established at the commencement of a new general government," Washington instructed Vice President Adams.[4] Every action, he knew, would be subjected to exhaustive scrutiny: "My political conduct . . . must be exceedingly circumspect and proof against just criticism, for the eyes of Argus [the hundred-eyed monster in Greek mythology] are upon me and no slip will pass unnoticed."[5] Washington had long felt those searching eyes trained upon him and would try hard as president to be a paragon.

Of the various government posts, it was the presidency that had the potential to slip into monarchy and subvert republican government, so every decision made about it aroused a firestorm of controversy. For many Americans, presidential etiquette seemed like the back door through which aristocratic corruption might infiltrate the system. On April 23 the Senate appointed a committee to devise suitable titles for addressing the president. Vice President Adams favored highfalutin ones. "A royal, or at least a princely, title, will be found indispensably necessary to maintain the reputation, authority, and dignity of the president," he insisted.[6] The final Senate recommendation was absurdly pretentious: "His Highness, the President of the United States of America, and Protector of their Liberties."[7] Sensitive to criticism that high-flown titles were reminiscent of monarchy, Washington gladly accepted the simpler form adopted by the House: "The President of the United States." An approving Madison later noted that Washington had been irritated by efforts to "bedizen him with a superb but spurious title."[8] The controversy served notice on Washington that such matters had powerful resonance as the new republic tried to find dignified forms that didn't smack of European decadence. "Nothing could equal the ferment and disquietude occasioned by the proposition respecting titles," David Stuart wrote from Virginia. "As it is believed to have originated from Mr. Adams and [Richard Henry] Lee, they are not only unpopular to an extreme, but highly odious."[9]

For Washington, the etiquette issue was also related to how he would preserve his privacy and sanity as president. From the time he occupied the Cherry Street mansion, he found himself hounded by legislators, office seekers, veterans, and well-wishers. Before long, he felt himself under siege, unable to accomplish any work. After making inquiries, he learned that presidents of the Confederation Congress had been "considered in no better light than as a maitre d'hotel . . . for their table was considered as a public one."[10] As in everything else, Washington operated in uncharted waters. "I was unable to attend to any business whatsoever," he told Stuart, "for gentlemen, consulting their own convenience rather than mine, were calling from the time I rose from breakfast—often before—until I sat down to dinner."[11] With his days cluttered with ceremonial visits, Washington complained, "I had no leisure to read or answer the dispatches which were pouring in from all quarters."[12] As he tried to barricade himself from strangers, he wondered how he could avoid the extremes of either rebuffing visitors in a "mimickry of royalty" or becoming so secluded that he would shut out important communications. In short, how to find the "discriminating medium"?[13]

As he had always done, Washington solicited written opinions from several advisers, including Adams, Madison, Hamilton, Jay, and Robert R. Livingston, from which he would distill his preferred policy. The hallmark of his administration would be an openness to conflicting ideas. In wartime Washington had urged officers to find a happy medium between being too close to and too remote from their men. Now, in remarkably similar language, he told Madison that he wanted to avoid the "charge of superciliousness" if he held himself too aloof, as well as the diminished presidential dignity that might arise from "too free an intercourse and too much familiarity."[14] In many ways, Washington's solution borrowed from two worlds, adapting kingly traditions to a republican ethos. Presidential conduct would be true to revolutionary principles but imbued with the forms of polite society that Washington had known his entire life.

To strike a proper balance, Hamilton suggested that Washington hold weekly levees—the term was borrowed from royal receptions—in which visitors could chat with him. The president would enter, remain half an hour, make small talk with guests, then disappear. A man of congenial formality, who kept an impenetrable zone of privacy around himself, Washington did not enjoy socializing with strangers, so Hamilton's scenario held an obvious appeal. The latter also suggested dinners with small groups of legislators, especially senators who shared with the president constitutional responsibilities, such as concluding foreign treaties and approving major appointments. "This makes them, in a degree, his constitutional counselors," Hamilton noted.[15] He also recommended that Washington refuse invitations to dine elsewhere, lest it impair presidential authority. Washington sympathized with any proposal that curtailed his social obligations. "I have no relish for formal and ceremonious engagements," he explained to James McHenry, "and only give in to them when they cannot be avoided."[16]

To handle the stampede of people wishing to see him, Washington decided to hold his levees every Tuesday afternoon at three P.M. The newspapers let it be known that, on other days, visits would "not be agreeable" to the president.[17] Guests would need introductions from suitable personages. Ordinarily Washington's secretaries would assist them from their carriages, but the president was capable of performing this courtesy when ladies and old comrades came calling. When the widows of Nathanael Greene and Richard Montgomery appeared, for instance, Washington went outside to help them down from their carriages.

The president was a punctual man, and, precisely at three, the folding doors of his dining room were flung open to guests; at three-fifteen, they were shut to further visitors. By the time guests arrived, Washington had struck a stately pose by the fireplace, encased in rigid protocol. The room was largely empty, most of the furniture having been cleared to make space. Since Washington's hearing was failing, David Humphreys announced him and his visitors in a raised voice. At the first levee Humphreys announced Washington in such a loud, pompous voice that, according to Madison, Washington shot him a reproachful look.

In a well-directed sequence, visitors came in and bowed to Washington, who then bowed in return before they took their place in a standing circle. With an excellent memory for names, Washington seldom required a second introduction. In a manner that reminded some of European kings, Washington never shook hands, holding on to a sword or a hat to avoid direct contact with people. Slowly he made the round of standing visitors, chatting briefly with each, then resuming his original position by the fireplace. Then the guests, moving like so many marionettes, came up to him one by one, bowed, and went their way. The reception concluded promptly at the stroke of four. Like a stage actor leaving nothing to chance, Washington reproduced this ritual exactly each week. Small wonder that John Adams said that if Washington "was not the greatest president, he was the best actor of the presidency we have ever had."[18]

One guest, describing the president's magnificent presence, recalled

> the tall manly figure of Washington clad in black velvet; his hair in full dress, powdered and gathered behind in a large silk bag; yellow gloves on his hands; holding a cocked hat with a cockade in it, and the edges adorned with a black feather about an inch deep. He wore knee and shoe buckles; and a long sword, with a finely wrought and polished steel hilt, which appeared at the left hip; the coat worn over the sword, so that the hilt, and the part below the folds of the coat behind, were in view. The scabbard was white polished leather.[19]

From the description, one can see how meticulously Washington fashioned the image that he broadcast to the world. Walter Buchanan, a New York physician, left a revealing tale of a visit to the Cherry Street mansion during the president's first Fourth of July in office. When told that a small delegation from the Society of the Cincinnati had appeared on his doorstep, Washington disappeared upstairs, donned his black velvet suit and dress sword, then invited the veterans in for cakes and wine. "On their departure," noted Buchanan, "the general again retired and came down to dinner in his usual costume of pepper-and-salt colored clothes."[20]

The Tuesday-afternoon levees, wooden and boring, were excruciating affairs, unrelieved by spontaneity. Washington's heroic stature, an essential part of his strength, was turned into a plaster cast that imprisoned him. During these scripted functions, people found it impossible to engage in substantive discussions with him, and perhaps that was the point. The taciturn Washington could see people without worrying that they would solicit him for jobs or pump him for political opinions. In searching for the happy medium between "much state" and "too great familiarity," Washington largely succeeded in finding it.[21] Despite the benign look in his eye, he managed to preserve a certain official distance. "He is polite with dignity," Abigail Adams attested that spring, "affable without formality, distant without haughtiness, grave without austerity, modest, wise, and good."[22]

Since Washington's Tuesday levees were limited to men, he and Martha decided that she would entertain female visitors every Friday evening from seven to ten, serving tea, coffee, ice cream, and lemonade. The plump little Martha, seated on a sofa as guests entered, enjoyed sampling the desserts. She dressed well but avoided jewelry as inappropriate for the new republic and was addressed by the democratic nomenclature of "Mrs. Washington." Never a sparkling talker, she was invariably a capable one, falling easily into conversation with people and making even complete strangers feel welcome. Usually seated at her right elbow was Abigail Adams, who noted how Washington chided anyone who violated protocol: "The president never fails of seeing that [the seat] is relinquished for me, and having removed ladies several times, they have now learnt to rise and give it to me."[23]

Dispensing with hat and sword, Washington made a minor concession to informality by wearing a brown coat on Friday evenings. More relaxed than at his own levees, he circulated and chatted amiably with guests, displaying "a grace, dignity, and ease that leaves Royal George far behind him," Abigail Adams reported.[24] Washington delighted in the company of pretty women, who found his appeal only heightened by the presidency. "The young ladies used to throng around him and engage him in conversation," said one visitor. "There were some of the well-remembered *belles* of that day, who imagined themselves to be favorites with him. As these were the only opportunities which they had of conversing with him, they were disposed to use them."[25] Another observer noted that Washington seemed less austere at his wife's teas, where he "talks more familiarly with those he knows and sometimes with the ladies."[26] Washington never engaged in flirtatious looks, but he unquestionably paid special attention to women in attendance. "The company this evening was thin, especially of ladies," he complained in his diary after one Friday soirée.[27] Because the Washingtons rose early, Martha often terminated the gatherings before the allotted ten o'clock deadline, saying that she and the president had to go to bed.

Even as the Washingtons sought an optimal balance between presidential splendor and republican austerity, an opposition press emerged that accused them of trying to foist a monarchy on the country. For anyone who had seen the opulence of Versailles or Windsor Castle, such accusations would have seemed wildly overblown. But every revolution breeds fears of counterrevolution, and worries about a reversion to monarchism were perhaps predictable after a war against royal absolutism. Each morning as he read the gazettes, Washington was stung by commentary on his receptions. Berating his dinners, the *Daily Advertiser* warned readers that "in a few years we shall have all the paraphernalia yet wanting to give the superb finish to the grandeur of our AMERICAN COURT! The purity of republican principle seems to be daily losing ground . . . We are on the eve of another revolution."[28] Even Martha's rather wholesome Friday-night gatherings were depicted darkly in some quarters as "court-like levees" and "queenly drawing rooms."[29] When Washington's birthday was celebrated in February 1790 as a national holiday, purists disparaged it as yet another showy monarchical exercise.

Among the leading critics of Washingtonian excess was William Maclay, the caustic senator from Pennsylvania with a thin, bony face. The son of Scotch-Irish Presbyterian immigrants, Maclay had a pronounced populist streak that predisposed him to spot signs of incipient monarchy. In June 1789 he recorded his private fears that fancy people around town had seduced the president: "Indeed, I entertain not a doubt but many people are aiming, with all their force, to establish a splendid court with all the pomp of majesty. Alas, poor Washington, if you are taken in this snare, how will the gold become dim?"[30]

In copious diary entries, written with the satirical eye of a gadfly, Maclay left vivid impressions of President Washington in social situations during his first term. An eager purveyor of gossip, Maclay was scarcely objective, taking a mordant, often jaundiced, view of people. Sometimes his tattle was downright mean-spirited, as when Robert Morris's wife told him of a presidential dinner at which she bit into a dessert only to find it full of rancid cream. When informed of it, the president "changed his plate immediately. But, she added with a titter, Mrs. Washington ate a whole heap of it."[31] His observations could be laced with patent envy: "No Virginian can talk on any subject but the perfections of Gen[era]l Washington."[32]

Nonetheless, Maclay left some priceless glimpses into the social world of George and Martha Washington, whom he satirized as boors and bumpkins, overshadowed by more elegant couples they were trying to impress. He reported Washington's misery in social settings, picking up little fidgety habits that showed him enduring these occasions rather than enjoying them. He did not realize how much Washington hated dealing with so many strangers. In trying to impart dignity to presidential protocol, Washington sometimes became frozen in this studied role, eliminating the levity and conversational flow that enlivened at least some dinners at Mount Vernon or with his military family during the war.

Every other Thursday the Washingtons held an official dinner at four P.M. The president, seeking geographic diversity, often tried to balance northern and southern legislators on his guest list. If guests were even five minutes late by the hall clock, they found the president and his company already seated. Washington would then explain curtly that the cook was governed by the clock and not by the company. In his diary, Maclay described a dinner on August 27, 1789, in which George and Martha Washington sat in the middle of the table, facing each other, while Tobias Lear and Robert Lewis sat on either end. John Adams, John Jay, and George Clinton were among the assembled guests. Maclay described a table bursting with a rich assortment of dishes—roasted fish, boiled meat, bacon, and poultry for the main course, followed by ice cream, jellies, pies, puddings, and melons for dessert. Washington usually downed a pint of beer and two or three glasses of wine, and his demeanor grew livelier once he had consumed them.

Maclay painted a deadly portrait of Washington at one dinner as a veteran bore, devoid of conversation except platitudes, and very jittery: "The president kept a fork in his hand when the cloth was taken away—I thought for the purpose of picking nuts. He ate no nuts, but played with the fork, striking on the edge of the table with it."[33] Washington could neither relax nor converse spontaneously, leading Maclay to conclude that "it was the most solemn dinner ever I ate at . . . The ladies sat a good while and the bottles passed about, but there was a dead silence almost."[34]

On March 4, 1790, Maclay wrote an account of another stifling dinner and again portrayed a consistently somber Washington: "The president seemed to bear in his countenance a settled aspect of melancholy. No cheering ray of convivial sunshine broke thro[ugh] the cloudy gloom of settled seriousness. At every interval of eating or drinking, he played on the table with a fork or knife, like a drumstick."[35] Sitting at Washington's right side, John Adams fared no better at the hands of Maclay, who derided the vice president as "mantling his visage with the most unmeaning simper that ever dimpled the face of folly."[36] Senator Samuel Johnston of North Carolina, who attended the same dinner, was entranced by it: "I have just left the president's, where I had the pleasure of dining with almost every member of the Senate. We had some excellent champagne and after it, I had the honor of drinking coffee with his lady, a most amiable woman. If I live much longer, I believe that I shall at last be reconciled to the company of old women for her sake."[37]

Two months later, finding Washington in better spirits, Maclay provided a possible clue to the awkward silences of earlier gatherings: "Went to dine with the president, agreeable to invitation. He seemed more in good humor than ever I saw him, tho[ugh] he was so deaf that I believe he heard little of the conversation."[38] That Washington's hearing had deteriorated—not surprising after eight years of roaring cannon—may explain the gruesome conversational gaps that Maclay so freely mocked. Deafness can be an isolating experience, especially for a president. People would naturally have waited for him to respond to statements before proceeding with the conversation; to conceal his deafness, a self-conscious Washington may well have feigned hearing what they said and sat there in silence. It was yet another sign of the aging process that had transformed the once dashing, athletic Washington.

On January 20, 1791, Maclay, a lame duck senator, attended a last dinner with the president. Though Maclay had developed into a sharp political opponent, the president still treated him with instinctive decorum, not the royal hauteur of his imaginings. Maclay took a final measure of the man, and his description shows how dramatically time had altered Washington: "Let me take a review of him as he really is. In stature about six feet, with an unexceptionable make, but lax appearance. His frame would seem to want filling up. His motions rather slow than lively, tho[ugh] he showed no signs of having suffered either by gout or rheumatism. His complexion pale, nay, almost cadaverous. His voice hollow and indistinct owing, as I believe, to artificial teeth before in his upper jaw."[39]

Washington had clearly undergone a startling change. Described as "lusty" by Robert Hunter in 1785, he was now slow and shuffling. Instead of being ruddy with buoyant health, he was gaunt and "cadaverous." Where earlier observers had commented on his well-padded muscles, Washington's frame now wanted "filling up." And the voice was again described as thin and whispery. An unaccustomed stiffness had overtaken his movements, he knew. When one Virginian criticized his clumsy bows at receptions, he said they were "the best I was master of" and remarked plaintively to David Stuart, "Would it not have been better to have thrown the veil of charity over them, ascribing their stiffness to the effects of age . . . than to pride and dignity of office, which, God knows, has no charms for me?"[40]

According to Jefferson, Washington told him that "nobody disliked more the ceremonies of his office and he had not the least taste or gratification in the execution of its function; that he was happy at home alone."[41] Suffering from the stultifying etiquette imposed by his office, he later railed against those who had prescribed such formality. He was especially upset that, having tried to strike a balance between pomp and austerity, he had been roundly criticized and misunderstood. As Jefferson wrote after a 1793 conversation, Washington "expressed the extreme wretchedness of his existence while in office and went lengthily into the late attacks on him for levees etc., and explained to me how he had been led into them by the persons he consulted at New York and that, if he could but know what the sense of the public was, he would most cheerfully conform to it."[42]

Washington found it hard to live frugally, and the chief steward he hired to supervise the kitchen made economy that much more difficult. Sam Fraunces had formerly owned the tavern at which Washington had enacted his lachrymose farewell to his officers at the war's end.[43] In the mid-1780s Fraunces had run into serious debt and even appealed to Washington for financial aid. By the time Washington hired him to manage his household, Fraunces had opened another tavern on Cortlandt Street.

A shrewd operator with a flamboyant manner, Fraunces seemed ubiquitous at Washington's dinner parties, "resplendently dressed in wig and small-clothes," according to one historian.[44] A skillful cook, he knew how to dress a table, supervise waiters, prepare desserts, and bring forth a sumptuous meal. Somewhat to Washington's chagrin, Fraunces preened himself on the "bountiful and elegant" dinners he presented.[45] Tobias Lear stared agog at the heaps of lobster, oysters, and other dishes, saying Fraunces "tossed up such a number of fine dishes that we are distracted in our choice when we sit down to table and obliged to hold a long consultation upon the subject, before we can determine what to attack."[46] In time Washington began to reprimand his steward for unconscionable extravagance. However fond he was of lavish living, he minded his pennies and personally reviewed household bills.

Unfortunately, the feisty Fraunces wasn't one to be deterred, not even by a sitting president. "Well he may discharge me," Frances declared. "He may kill me if he will, but while he is President of the United States and I have the honor to be his steward, his establishment shall be supplied with the very best of everything that the whole country can afford."[47] Washington's attempts to rein in Fraunces led to a running battle that raged until Fraunces quit in February 1790. To show there were no hard feelings, Washington bestowed on him a last bonus for his tavern.

Even before Washington occupied 3 Cherry Street, he had grumbled about the cost of renovating it. The handsome three-story building had a high stoop, balusters along the roof, and seven fireplaces inside. It stood on a boisterous thoroughfare crawling with traffic. The day before Washington arrived, Sally Robinson, niece of owner Samuel Osgood, inspected the premises and found "every room furnished in the most elegant manner," she told a friend. "The best of furniture in every room and the greatest quantity of plate and china I ever saw. The whole of the first and second stories [are] papered and the floors covered with the richest kinds of Turkey and Wilton carpets ... There is scarcely anything talked about now but General Washington and the Palace."[48] For all the fuss made over the house, it did not work well for the Washingtons. It had to house thirty people and was sufficiently cramped that three secretaries—Humphreys, Nelson, and Lewis—slept in a single room on the third floor. Humphreys, then writing a play, reportedly strode the hall after dark in his nightshirt, loudly declaiming verse from the epilogue. The house was located at an inconvenient spot near the East River, distant from the tony seats of government and society situated on Broadway.

The impresario of entertaining, Washington took personal charge of selecting the ornaments that defined the grandeur of his dining room. Far from shunting off decorating on his wife or subordinates, he trusted his detailed knowledge of the decorative arts. To create a tea service, he melted down some old silver and had the finished products engraved with his griffin crest. When he asked Gouverneur Morris, then resident in Europe, to purchase wine coolers for dinners, he showed a characteristic concern with orderly appearance. To keep the wine cool, the bottles would be placed in silver wire baskets partly immersed in ice. Washington issued precise instructions for their manufacture so that "whether full or empty, the bottles will always stand upright and never be at variance with each other." [49] With an educated eye for furnishings that might lend brilliance to state dinners, he also had Morris ship him decorative mirrors for the tabletop, so that silverware and candlesticks would emit shimmering reflections. As if part of his job were refining American taste, Washington oversaw the purchase of many objets d'art, including porcelain figures, silver spoons, and a china set embellished with the eagle of the Society of the Cincinnati.

No small part of the splendor of Washington's establishment was his household contingent of twenty servants, seven of them slaves. All the servants, white and black, were buffed to a high gloss. A few slaves were bedecked in the same costumes as the white servants: a white livery with red trim on the cuffs and collars. Cocked hats, gloves, and well-polished shoes completed the glossy outfit. To posterity, it seems shocking that Washington imported slaves into the presidential mansion, but Jefferson would bring a dozen slaves from Monticello to the White House; the tradition of having slaves in the presidential household unfortunately lasted until the death in 1850 of Zachary Taylor, the last of the slaveholding presidents.

Washington extended the grandeur of his presidency to morning horseback rides. He kept a dozen horses in New York and made a daily a tour of his stables. Aware of how impressive he looked atop a white mount, he once instructed a friend to buy him a horse, specifying that he "would prefer a *perfect* white."[50] In the early days of his presidency, he rode a pair of spotless white parade horses, Prescott and Jackson. Perhaps he had a subliminal memory of Lord Botetourt riding to the palace in colonial Williamsburg behind a coach with shining white horses. So taken was Washington with his unblemished chargers that he had grooms rub them with white paste at night, bundle them in cloths, then bed them down on fresh straw. In the morning the hardened white paste gleamed, its paleness accentuated by black polish applied to the horses' hooves. For command performances, the animals' mouths were rinsed and their teeth scrubbed. In another fancy touch, Washington set his saddles in leopard skins edged with gold braiding.

On a fine spring day New York residents might glimpse the president and first lady out for a ride in their ornate, varnished coach, drawn by six well-matched bay horses. With four postilions attired in leather breeches and glazed leather hats, the coach made an exquisite impression as it rolled through the crowded streets. "When he travels," a British diplomat later observed, "it is in a very kingly style."[51] Sometimes the Washingtons stared out the window and at other times drew the Venetian blinds or black leather curtains for privacy. In 1790 Washington adorned the coach with allegorical scenes of the four seasons, executed on the outside panels, affixing his personal crest to four small quarter panels.

Occasionally in the early afternoon, Washington descended from Mount Olympus and ambled through the city streets, where he greeted citizens in a more egalitarian manner. On one such promenade, he encountered in a shop six-year-old Washington Irving, attended by a Scottish maid. "Please your honor," said the maid, pushing the little boy forward, "here's a bairn [child] was named after you."[52] Washington patted the head of the little boy fated to be his future biographer. That Washington walked the streets and made himself accessible to ordinary people carried important political overtones. As David Stuart reported from Virginia, "It has given

me much pleasure to hear every part of your conduct spoke[n] of with high approbation, and particularly your dispensing with ceremony occasionally and walking
the streets, while [John] Adams is never seen but in his carriage and six."[53]

Another place Washington encountered New Yorkers was at his presidential
pew at St. Paul's Chapel, where he often appeared on Sunday mornings. He devoted
Sunday afternoons to writing lengthy communications to George Augustine Washington about Mount Vernon matters, ranging from crop rotation to mule breeding.
On Sunday evenings he read aloud sermons or passages from Scriptures and continued to say grace at meals. An integral component of his religiosity was his charitable largesse to the indigent and others in need. When destitute veterans flocked to
his door, Washington frequently dispensed alms to them. He gave scores of charitable contributions, preferring anonymity, though he sometimes made exceptions
on public holidays to set an example for the citizenry. After he designated Thursday,
November 26, 1789, as the first Thanksgiving Day, for example, he contributed beer
and food to those jailed for debt.

Washington lost no time becoming a regular visitor to the John Street Theater.
A simple red wooden building, large and bare as a barn, it had its own presidential
box, emblazoned with the arms of the United States. When the theater manager told
Washington that he usually started plays at seven P.M. but would gladly delay them
until his arrival, Washington set him straight, saying he would always be punctual
and that the audience would never have to wait. Washington invariably appeared
at seven on the dot. The instant he did, the orchestra struck up "The President's
March," later known as "Hail, Columbia," and the audience erupted with robust
cheers. Since Washington's presence was typically announced in advance, the performances usually drew veterans who doffed their caps and waved up to him.

At the time theatergoing was still considered a bit racy. When Washington invited
John and Sarah Jay to join him in his box, he said he would understand if they declined
from "any reluctance to visiting the theater."[54] The Jays accepted with pleasure. That
George Washington was a habitué of risqué plays indicates he was hardly a prude. The
first play he saw, on May 11, 1789, was his all-time satirical favorite, Richard Sheridan's
The School for Scandal. His box was large enough to accommodate several guests, and
he invited along Senator Maclay. Even the curmudgeonly Maclay was thrilled by the
experience and regretted not having brought his children: "Long might one of them
[have] live[d] to boast of their having been seated in the same box with the first character in the world."[55] That box was often packed with government dignitaries and leading personalities. On the evening of November 24, 1789, the Washingtons were joined
by Abigail Adams, Alexander and Elizabeth Hamilton, Philip Schuyler, and Catharine
"Caty" Greene, the general's widow. Such evenings constituted a perfect form of entertainment for the man who acted the presidency better than anybody else.

The Cares of Office

FOR A MAN OF SUCH PRODIGIOUS STRENGTH, Washington had been pestered by recurrent medical problems, and his presidency proved no exception. He had weathered more than eight years of war partly because as a planter he was accustomed to a rugged outdoor life. As president, he found it hard to adapt to a sedentary job in an urban setting, which may have weakened his health. In mid-June 1789 he ran a fever as a fast-growing tumor appeared on his left thigh. The area grew so tender and inflamed that it became excruciating for him to sit. Four years earlier Washington had watched his Mount Vernon overseer, John Alton, "reduced to a mere skeleton" from a fatal abscess on his thigh, and he must have been alarmed when he developed a comparable symptom.[1]

The president summoned Dr. Samuel Bard, a prominent New York physician, who diagnosed the condition as the cutaneous form of anthrax. Petrified that Washington would expire, Bard refused to leave his bedside for several days. The situation must have shocked everyone around Washington: no sooner had the federal government been formed than its president lay in mortal peril. In all likelihood, Washington had a carbuncle or soft tissue infection. As might be expected, he was the picture of stoic courage. "I am not afraid to die and therefore can bear the worst," he told Bard evenly. "Whether tonight, or twenty years hence, makes no difference. I know that I am in the hands of a good Providence."[2] The public knew something was wrong, if only because Tobias Lear had servants cordon off Cherry Street, stopping traffic. The household staff also sprinkled straw outside the mansion to deaden passing footsteps. Still, the public had no notion of the gravity of the president's illness.

On June 17, when Dr. Bard operated on Washington's thigh, he brought along his father, Dr. John Bard, to supervise the proceedings. The elder Bard, a veteran surgeon, felt too old to undertake the procedure himself. Surgery was then a hellish ordeal, as the patient gritted his teeth and endured excruciating pain. While the younger Dr. Bard split open the abscess, his father exhorted him to persevere: "Cut away—deeper—deeper still! Don't be afraid. You see how well he bears it!"[3] Tobias Lear claimed that the tumor was "very large and the incision on opening it deep."[4] In all likelihood, the younger Bard excised the mass of infected tissue and scraped away any pus or dead tissue, all of which would have been enormously painful for Washington, who remained unfailingly courteous. As Samuel Bard assured his daughter, "It will give you pleasure to be told that nothing can exceed the kindness and attention I receive from him."[5]

For weeks afterward, as Washington lay bedridden, some friends thought he might never recover his legendary strength. "I have now the pleasure to inform you that my health is restored," Washington apprised James McHenry on July 3, "but a feebleness still hangs upon me, and I am yet much incommoded by the incision which was made in a very large and painful tumor on the protuberance of my thigh."[6] In extreme discomfort, unable to walk or sit, he reclined on his right side for six weeks and couldn't even draft a letter. When Abigail Adams visited, she found him, with becoming presidential dignity, stretched out on the sofa and praised this "singular example of modesty and diffidence."[7]

The interior of Washington's coach was reconfigured so he could lie down, although he had to be lifted and deposited gently inside by four servants. For an hour each day, he made salutary tours of the town with Martha. On July 4, 1789, Baron von Steuben and Alexander Hamilton—now, respectively, president and vice president of the New York Society of the Cincinnati—trooped to 3 Cherry Street to pay their respects before Hamilton delivered a eulogy to Nathanael Greene at St. Paul's Chapel. In a moving homage to Greene's memory, Washington, despite his discomfort, dressed up in full regimentals to greet his visitors at the door—an unusual instance of Washington donning a military costume during his presidency. To the limited extent possible, he kept up appearances and tried to convey an aura of calm.

By early September, Washington reassured Dr. James Craik that the inflammation had dwindled to "the size of a barleycorn" and that he expected it would shortly disappear altogether.[8] Martha Washington was hugely relieved, although a visitor noticed that when she discussed her husband's health, "a tear of apprehension for futurity was in her eye."[9] Except with intimates, Washington was discreet about discussing his malady. Dr. Craik and other friends urged him to launch a brisk regimen of outdoor exercise to offset his staid indoor life. Washington conceded that his job might have contributed to his ailment and might even kill him, but he was resigned to the sacrifice. Echoing Shakespeare, he said, "The want of regular exercise, with the cares of office, will, I have no doubt, hasten my departure for that country from whence no traveler returns."[10] Nevertheless, his official duties, he maintained, would remain "the primary consideration in every transaction of my life, be the consequences what they may."[11]

Washington took to heart his friends' advice to do more exercise, which was one reason he made a trip to New England that fall. Upon his return, he and Martha, along with Nelly and Washy, began extended coach rides around Manhattan, often cruising a fourteen-mile loop that took them to the scenic northern reaches of the island. Even in the winter, Washington supplemented these excursions with strolls around the Battery. Sometimes he mixed in a smattering of politics, as happened in January when he went horseback riding with Senator Samuel Johnston of North Carolina and William Cushing, an associate justice of the Supreme Court—a perfect equestrian union of all three branches of government.

WASHINGTON'S ILLNESS coincided with the final stages of Mary Ball Washington's protracted struggle with breast cancer. Showing belated maternal warmth, Mary had her daughter, Betty, write to the new president, apropos of his convalescence, that she "wishes to hear from you; *she will not believe you are well till she has it from under your own hand.*"[12] Mary had always been a hardy woman and, even as she aged, retained "full enjoyment of her mental faculties," according to her famous son.[13] Clinging to her independence, she still made daily visits to her farm in an open carriage, until illness rendered that impossible. When he visited his redoubtable mother in early March 1789, Washington knew he might never see her again and that it would be "the last act of *personal* duty I may . . . ever have it in my power to pay my mother."[14] It is significant that he employed the word *duty,* since affection had never formed part of the picture. Whatever she may have said privately, Mary Washington took no more public pride in his being president than she had in his command of the Continental Army. But it's hard to imagine that on his last visit to his mother, Washington was unmoved by the sight of a dying parent, cruelly disfigured by disease, or that he felt no residual gratitude toward her. Whatever her glaring flaws, Mary Washington had worked hard to raise him in the absence of a father.

By mid-August Mary Ball Washington had drifted into a coma; she finally passed away on August 25, 1789, at eighty-one. On September 1 Washington was hosting a dinner party, with Steuben keeping the table in uproarious merriment, when the laughter was abruptly silenced by a message announcing her death. Despite his reservations about his mother, Washington was much too decorous to dispense with the proper forms of mourning. Always correct in his conduct toward his mother, he ordered black cockades and ribbons for his household staff, while government members wore black crape on their arms; black ribbons and necklaces became de rigueur for ladies. Official New York went into mourning for a woman whom they had never seen and who had shown scant interest in the new government. The formal levees were canceled for three weeks. Soon the capital resumed its normal social rhythm, but Washington wore badges of mourning for at least five months. In what seems like shocking neglect, however, he failed to erect a tombstone on his mother's grave. "The grave of Washington's mother is marked by no visible object, not even a mound of earth, nor is the precise spot of its locality known," noted an astonished Jared Sparks during an 1827 visit to Fredericksburg. ". . . For a long time a single cedar tree was the only guide to the place; near this tree tradition has fixed the grave of Washington's mother, but there is no stone to point out the place."[15] No special memorial arose at Mary Washington's graveside until three decades after George Washington's death.

Washington spoke no eulogies, told no fond anecdotes of the hard, sometimes shrewish mother who had served as the lifelong whetstone of his anger; he took refuge instead in empty generalities. Whether responding to an unspoken accusation from Betty Lewis that he had been derelict in his filial duties, or feeling guilty that his sister had borne the burden of caring for their infirm mother, Washington sent her a detailed accounting of his financial generosity to their mother:

> She has had a great deal of money from me at times, as can be made [to] appear by my books and the accounts of Mr. L[und] Washington during my absence. And over and above this [she] has not only had all that was ever made from the plantation, but got her provisions and everything else she thought proper from thence. In short, to the best of my recollection, I have never in my life received a copper from the estate and have paid many hundred pounds (first and last) to her in cash. However, I want no retribution. I conceived it to be a duty whenever she asked for money and I had it to furnish her.[16]

In her will, Mary Washington named George as executor, a responsibility he couldn't have relished as president. She left him a bed, curtains, a blue and white quilt, and a dressing mirror—items he identified as "mementoes of parental affection," but he never took possession of them and left them for his sister's use.[17] Entitled to a one-fifth portion of his mother's estate, he received two slaves, which meant that Mary Ball Washington had owned as many as ten slaves, certifying that she had scarcely been destitute. The auction of Mary's belongings that October also suggested that, for all her complaints, the elderly widow had accumulated considerable property. Among the auction items cited in a newspaper advertisement were "stocks of horses, cattle, sheep and hogs, plantation utensils of every kind, carts, hay, and fodder."[18] In fact, Mary had amassed such substantial landholdings that George alone inherited four hundred acres of valuable pine land; he gave it to Robert Lewis, Betty's son. All of this property had been owned by a woman who saw fit to petition the Virginia legislature for a private pension during the war because of her son's alleged neglect.

THE MENACING GROWTH ON HIS THIGH and his mother's death slowed Washington down only slightly as he forged the office of the presidency, which immediately involved him in a thicket of constitutional issues. Could the Supreme Court give advisory opinions to the legislative and executive branches? Would the executive branch supervise American foreign policy, subject to congressional approval, or vice versa? Numberless questions about the basic nature of the federal government would be decided during Washington's presidency, often in the throes of heated controversy. Although Washington had not been an architect of the system of checks and balances or separation of powers, he gave sharp definition to them by helping to draw the boundaries of the three branches of government in a series of critical test cases.

A central component of the Whig orthodoxy that had spurred the American Revolution was the supremacy of the legislative branch, viewed as a curb to the executive. By design, the framers of the Constitution devoted Article I to a lengthy description of legislative powers, giving Congress the ability to help shape the other two branches. Left deliberately vague was the office of the presidency, allowing its first occupant to fill in the blanks. The earnest Washington tried to adhere to the letter of the Constitution and hoped to enjoy harmonious relations with Congress. But he soon realized that the Constitution was less a precise blueprint for action than a set of general guidelines whose many ambiguities required practical clarification. If bemused by some congressional practices, he tried not to trespass on legislative prerogatives. For instance, he privately opposed the Senate's closed-door policy, but he kept a discreet silence in public. For its part, Congress groped to define its relationship to the president. In June 1789 some congressmen wanted Washington to have to gain senatorial approval to fire as well as hire executive officers—the Constitution was silent on the subject; the House duly approved that crippling encroachment on executive authority. When the Senate vote ended in a tie, Vice President Adams cast the deciding vote to defeat the measure, thereby permitting the president to exert true leadership over his cabinet and, for better or worse, preventing the emergence of a parliamentary democracy.

The first formal clash between Washington and Congress arose on August 5, 1789, when the Senate rejected Washington's nomination of Benjamin Fishbourn as collector of the Port of Savannah. Though still ailing, Washington made his way to Federal Hall and mounted to the second-floor Senate chamber, decorated on its ceiling with thirteen stars and suns. Washington's unexpected entrance stunned the legislators. Undoubtedly feeling a bit befuddled, Vice President Adams rose from his canopied chair of crimson velvet and offered it to Washington, who then proceeded to upbraid the twenty-two members of the Senate, demanding to know why they had spurned his appointee. "The president showed [a] great want of temper . . . when one of his nominations was rejected," said Senator Ralph Izard of South Carolina.[19] It was an unusual public display of emotion by Washington.

After a long, awkward silence, Senator James Gunn of Georgia, whose state included Savannah, rose and from "personal respect for the personal character of Gen[era]l Washington" explained his opposition to Fishbourn.[20] At the same time he wanted it understood that the Senate felt no obligation to explain its reasoning to the president. The episode marked the start of "senatorial courtesy," whereby senators reserved the right to block nominations in their home states. Despite Gunn's respectful treatment, Washington went off in a great huff, and Tobias Lear said that as soon as he returned from the Senate, he "expressed his very great regret for having gone there."[21]

This skirmish turned out to be trifling compared to the conflict over Indian policy some weeks later. The episode began in mid-June, when Henry Knox, secretary of war, wrote a well-meaning letter to Washington, fleshing out a farsighted approach to Indian affairs. Noting the bloody battles between Indians and American settlers on the frontier, Knox declared that the Indians, as rightful owners of the land, should not be deprived of it by violence or coercion. Rather, he advocated paying them for their land and concentrating them in a system of federally protected enclaves. Knox wanted to initiate this policy by negotiating a treaty with Alexander McGillivray, chief of the Creek Nation, whose hunting grounds extended over parts of modern-day Georgia, Florida, Alabama, and Mississippi. The corrupt Georgia legislature was ready to make a mockery of any enlightened policy toward the Indians by selling to speculators millions of acres claimed by the Creeks and other southern tribes.

In early August Knox informed Washington that he had worked out a treaty with the Creeks, including several secret articles. Among other things, Knox wanted the executive branch to dominate Indian affairs as a way of bolstering presidential authority. As part of the treaty process, Washington planned to send a three-man commission to broker peace between Georgia and the Creeks, but when Knox drew up instructions for this parley, Washington thought he needed to consult the Senate about them. This time, instead of pouncing unexpectedly, he gave ample warning of his visit. He interpreted the "advice and consent" requirement of the Constitution to include such direct meetings with the Senate, but the ensuing contretemps changed the course of American history. When Washington arrived on August 22, he again occupied Adams's seat, with Knox seated to his left. They delivered a copy of the treaty papers to Adams, who tried to read them aloud but was drowned out by traffic below. "I could tell it was something about Indians," grumbled William Maclay, "but was not master of one sentence of it."[22] When the windows were shut, Adams read aloud the seven articles of the treaty, to be followed by a yea or nay vote on each. After he read the first one, Robert Morris stood and said he hadn't been able to hear anything above the racket, forcing Adams to reread the whole treaty. He then recited the first article again, followed by an uncomfortable silence.

Some in the Senate believed that Washington wanted them merely to rubber-stamp treaties and appointments instead of exercising independent judgment. When Maclay requested a reading of the supporting treaties between the southern Indians and three southern states, Washington fixed him with an icy glare. "I cast an eye at the president of the United States," Maclay wrote. "I saw he wore an aspect of stern displeasure."[23] Robert Morris moved that the papers brought by Washington be referred to a committee. When Maclay defended the propriety of this motion, Washington's expression grew even more forbidding, and he hotly contested the idea of committing anything to a committee. "'This defeats every purpose of my coming here' were the first words that he said," Maclay wrote in his diary. "He then went on that he had brought his Secretary at War with him to give every necessary information."[24] Washington refused to yield on the committee proposal, although he agreed to postpone the matter. In Maclay's version of events, Washington, having shown flashes of temper, withdrew with "a discontented air" and a sense of "sullen dignity."[25]

A couple of days later Washington returned to the Senate, which approved the three commissioners to negotiate with the Creeks. It proved his farewell appearance in the Senate chamber. In a decision pregnant with lasting consequences, Washington decided that he would henceforth communicate with that body on paper rather than in person and trim "advice and consent" to the word *consent*. For instance, when Washington appointed David Humphreys as a diplomat to the Court of Portugal in February 1791, Maclay noted that the choice was sent to the Senate as a fait accompli: "The president sends first and asks for our advice and consent after."[26]

This decision may have done more to define the presidency and the conduct of American foreign policy than an entire bookshelf of Supreme Court decisions on the separation of powers. Where the Constitution had been sketchy about presidential powers in foreign affairs, Washington made the chief executive the principal actor, enabling him to initiate treaties and nominate appointees without first huddling with the Senate. It was an instinctive reaction from a man who had grown accustomed to command during the war. If a touch imperious, it was a far more realistic approach to foreign policy than constant collaboration and horse-trading between the president and Senate. For one thing, the presidency was continuously in session, unlike Congress, and it was much easier for one man to take decisive action, especially in an emergency. Washington's decision also widened the distance between president and Senate, enabling the latter to function as an independent, critical voice in foreign policy rather than as a subordinate advisory panel.

An enduring mystery of Washington's presidency is why he relegated John Adams to a minor role. A Washington biographer is struck by the paucity of letters exchanged between the two men; Adams was clearly excluded from the inner circle of advisers. Partly this was a structural phenomenon. Under the Constitution, the vice president served as president of the Senate, thus overlapping two branches of governments. Nowadays we tend to think of the vice president as the president's agent in the legislature, but Adams saw the vice president as a creature of that branch. He stated bluntly, "The office I hold is totally detached from the executive authority and confined to the legislative."[27] On another occasion he insisted that the Constitution had created "two great offices," with one officer "placed at the head of the executive, the other at the head of the legislature."[28] As Washington tried to protect the presidency from senatorial intrusion, Adams was bound to suffer a demotion in the process.

Washington also had a long memory for wartime critics and knew that in the Congress Adams had sometimes been a vocal opponent of his performance. The Virginian demanded loyalty from those around him, and Adams had forfeited that trust during the war, never to regain it completely. An envious man, Adams was secretly exasperated by Washington's unprecedented success. Always brooding about history's judgment, he dreaded that Washington and Franklin would dwarf him in the textbooks. As he memorably told Dr. Benjamin Rush, the crux of the story would be "that Dr. Franklin's electrical rod smote the earth and out sprung General Washington. That Franklin electrified him with his rod and thenceforward these two conducted all the policy, negotiations, legislatures, and war."[29] Adams went so far as to say privately that Washington's waiving of his salary as commander in chief and retiring after the war had been egotistical acts: "In wiser and more virtuous times, he would not have [done] that, for that is an ambition."[30] There was also a profound temperamental gulf between Washington and Adams. Both were stubborn, gritty men with courageous devotion to American liberty, but Washington was far more restrained and self-effacing. It also couldn't have helped relations between the two men that Adams was an age peer and political rival to Washington, who preferred drawing on the talents of younger men, such as Madison and Hamilton. Of his time as vice president, John Adams would render a glum assessment: "My country has, in its wisdom, contrived for me the most insignificant office that ever the invention of a man contrived or his imagination conceived."[31]

Rays of Genius

THROUGHOUT 1789 George Washington was oppressed by the need to make appointments to the new government. With nearly a thousand posts to fill—the federal government was quite unlike the states in its preponderance of appointed posts—the president was inundated with several times as many applications. Among the tidal wave of letters flooding in were those from wounded veterans and women who had sacrificed husbands or sons in the war. William Maclay noted the unending crush of aspiring officeholders who besieged the hapless president: "Men of pride, ambition, talents all press forward to exhibit their abilities on the theater of the general government."[1] At its inception, the executive branch was extraordinarily small—Washington initially oversaw a larger staff of slaves and servants at Mount Vernon than he did as president of the United States—but the new government quickly overshadowed his estate in size.

In dealing with office seekers, Washington became hypersensitive to pressure, which usually backfired. As Jefferson once observed of him, "To overdo a thing with him is to undo it."[2] Washington believed that forming an honest, efficient civil service was a critical test for the young republic. A model president in making appointments, he never cut deals or exploited patronage and ruled out "blood or friendship" in picking people.[3] The criteria he valued most were merit, seniority, loyalty to the Constitution, and wartime service, as well as an equitable distribution of jobs among the states. By sticking to a policy of "utmost impartiality" with appointees, he sought to strengthen the government's legitimacy.[4] "If injudicious or unpopular measures should be taken . . . with regard to appointments," he told nephew Bushrod, "the government itself would be in the utmost danger of being utterly subverted."[5] He turned down Bushrod's own request for a job as U.S. attorney in Virginia, preferring to hire older and more seasoned lawyers.

Washington fretted over the design of the new government, which was still formless. From the Confederation Congress, he had inherited four departments—Foreign Affairs, War, Post Office, and the Board of Treasury—that would report to Congress until new departments were created; meanwhile they kept Washington up to date with reports. Only lightly did the Constitution sketch in the contours of the executive branch, giving Washington freedom to maneuver. In the summer of 1789 Congress created in rapid succession the Department of Foreign Affairs (soon renamed the State Department), the War Department, and then the Treasury Department in September. Assigned to lower rungs were the offices of the attorney general, who would advise the president on constitutional matters, and the postmaster general, who would preside over post offices and postal roads. That these departments belonged to the executive, not to the legislative branch, as under the Articles of Confederation, signaled a major shift in the American polity.

While the Constitution talked about executive departments, it made no reference to a cabinet, stipulating only that the president could request "the opinion, in writing" of department heads.[6] Once again constitutional brevity presented an opportunity for Washington. At first he drew on the model of his wartime councils, requesting opinions from department heads, but this differed from the true cohesion of a cabinet that met to thrash out policy. As Alexander Hamilton, the first treasury secretary, later told a British minister, "We have no cabinet and the heads of departments meet on very particular occasions only."[7] Thomas Jefferson, the first secretary of state, would dub Washington "the hub of the wheel," with the department heads arrayed like brilliant spokes around him.[8]

In choosing those heads, Washington surrounded himself with a small but decidedly stellar group. With his own renown secure, he had no fear that subordinates would upstage him and never wanted subservient courtiers whom he could overshadow. Aware of his defective education, he felt secure in having the best minds at his disposal. He excelled as a leader precisely because he was able to choose and orchestrate bright, strong personalities. As Gouverneur Morris observed, Washington knew "how best to use the rays" given off by the sparkling geniuses at his command.[9] As the first president, Washington assembled a group of luminaries without equal in American history; his first cabinet more than made up in intellectual firepower what it lacked in numbers.

The one holdover from a previous executive department was Henry Knox, who was confirmed as secretary of war in early September. Washington retained his old wartime affection for Knox and used the word *love* to describe his feelings for his rotund friend. A few years earlier Washington had told Knox that he should "be assured that, to correspond with those I love is among my highest gratifications, and I persuade myself you will not doubt my sincerity when I assure you, I place you among the foremost of this class."[10] Expert at fending off political pressure, Washington established a rule that nobody could discuss political appointments with him unless he first brought up the topic. Frustrated by this rule, Roger Sherman of Connecticut asked Hamilton if he would champion a certain appointment with the president. "No, I dare not do it," Hamilton replied. "I know General Washington too well. But I can tell you where your only hope lies. Go to General Knox. They say Washington talks to him as a man does with his wife."[11] With his hearty appetite and ebullient personality, Henry Knox stood forth as an immense social presence in the new administration. Maclay aptly referred to him as "a Bacchanalian figure."[12]

On most political issues, Washington saw eye to eye with Knox, who had labored hard for the new Constitution. But Knox was destined to be the least capable of the three department heads. He worked diligently, gave Washington unquestioning loyalty, and promptly responded to requests, but he was not an original policy thinker and was relatively passive compared to the assertive Hamilton and the quietly tenacious Jefferson. He also worked in an area where Washington himself was highly competent. The War Department further suffered from the popular bugaboo about a standing army, which meant that Knox started out with 840 federal troops and never supervised a force larger than 5,000 men.

For the all-important Treasury post, Washington turned to the war's preeminent financier: Robert Morris. En route to the inauguration, Washington had broached the subject with him in Philadelphia. Pleading business reasons, Morris declined the invitation and recommended Hamilton in his stead. James Madison also touted Hamilton as the person "best qualified for that species of business," although he later came to rue his sponsorship.[13]

Even before the inauguration, Washington had received anonymous warnings about Hamilton, previewing things to come. A poison-pen artist who styled himself "H.Z." warned the president-elect to "beware of the artful designs and machinations of your late aide-de-camp, Alexander Hamilton, who, like Judas Iscariot, would, for the gratification of his boundless ambition, betray his lord and master."[14] (Even Madison said later that Hamilton "spoke disparagingly of Washington's talents" after the war.[15]) Hamilton was also trailed by accurate rumors that at the Constitutional Convention he had advocated a president who would serve for life on good behavior, planting the notion that he was a closet monarchist. Nevertheless Washington was convinced of Hamilton's talents and integrity and selected him for the Treasury post, for which he was easily confirmed in early September. Whatever their wartime differences—and Hamilton was much too headstrong to admire anyone uncritically—the two men had worked together closely and productively during the first two phases of the American experiment, the Revolutionary War and the Constitutional Convention. Now they would collaborate on the critical third phase: the formation of the first federal government.

Although Washington seemed unaware of it, Hamilton had been training for the Treasury post throughout the war, boning up on subjects as diverse as foreign exchange and central banks. Like Washington, Knox, and other Continental Army officers, Hamilton had perceived an urgent need for an active central government, and he grasped the reins of power with a sure-handed gusto that set the tenor for the administration. He headed a Treasury Department that, with thirty-nine employees, instantly surpassed the rest of the government in size. Of particular importance, he presided over an army of customs inspectors whose import duties served as the government's main revenue source.

In Hamilton, Washington found a cabinet secretary of tireless virtuosity who would function as his unofficial prime minister. Taunted as an aspiring upstart by his enemies, Hamilton did not hide his intellectual lights under a bushel. At a time when politicians were supposed to be self-effacing, Hamilton was openly ambitious and, in many respects, the antithesis of his mentor. Where Washington had no compulsion to shine in company, Hamilton, who was charming, urbane, and debonair, wanted to be the most brilliant figure in every group, and he usually was. A prolific writer of letters, essays, and pamphlets, he was a systematic thinker who knew how to translate principles into workable policies. Hamilton saw the advantage of setting a brisk tempo to the administration and pushing through quickly an ambitious legislative package. Setting a pattern for future administrations, he wanted to capitalize on the short-lived goodwill granted to a new president. However sophisticated Washington was as a businessman, he found public finance an esoteric subject and had to rely on Hamilton's expertise, whereas he could question Knox on war matters or Jefferson on foreign affairs from personal experience.

Nothing drew the contrast between Hamilton and Jefferson so graphically as the speed with which the former accepted the Treasury post versus the latter's reluctance to become secretary of state. At first Washington had favored John Jay for the State Department, but when Jay preferred the chief justice spot, Washington opted for Jefferson. Although he had seen little of Jefferson in recent years, he cherished fond memories of him from the House of Burgesses, where he had "early imbibed the highest opinion" of him.[16] Since Jefferson was crossing the ocean that September, returning temporarily from his ministerial post in Paris, Washington could not consult him before picking him. Only two months later, when Jefferson arrived in Norfolk, Virginia, did he learn of Washington's decision. As a sympathetic spectator of the budding French Revolution, Jefferson would have preferred to return to

France and therefore reacted with extreme ambivalence to the cabinet offer. Still, he had the good grace to tell Washington that, if he took the job, "my chief comfort will be to work under your eye, my only shelter the authority of your name and the wisdom of measures to be dictated by you."[17] In late January 1790 Jefferson, still vacillating, had to be cajoled by both Washington and Madison into accepting the post. Washington pushed him gently. "I know of no person who, in my judgment, could better execute the duties of it than yourself," he reassured him.[18] Not until February did Jefferson formally accept the post, and he arrived in New York only in late March. In pointed contrast, Hamilton had bustled into office with irrepressible energy and immediately launched a far-reaching series of programs.

One wonders whether Jefferson's hesitation reflected an equivocal attitude toward the new federal government itself, since he had been, at best, a lukewarm supporter of the Constitution. At first he had preferred tinkering with the Articles of Confederation and favored only "three or four new articles to be added to the good, old, and venerable fabric."[19] He was especially chagrined by the absence of a bill of rights and the "perpetual re-eligibility" of the president, which he feared would make the job "an office for life first and then hereditary."[20] Jefferson also retained a congenital distrust of politics, which he personally found a form of sweet torture, the source of both exquisite pain and deep satisfaction. He especially hated bureaucracy, whereas Hamilton had no such qualms.

On Sunday, March 21, 1790, Washington spent the morning in prayer at St. Paul's Chapel before setting eyes on his new secretary of state at one P.M. The next day the two were locked in policy discussions for more than an hour. Jefferson was tall and lean, with reddish hair, hazel eyes, and a fair complexion. Jefferson, who was slightly taller than Washington but long-limbed and loose-jointed, and his new boss would have stared each other straight in the eye, both towering over Hamilton. A reserved man whose tight lips bespoke a secretive personality, Jefferson had calm eyes that seemed to comprehend everything. Shrinking from open confrontations, he often resorted to indirect, sometimes devious methods of dealing with disagreements. He could show a courtly charm in conversation and was especially seductive in small groups of like-minded listeners, where he became a captivating talker and natural leader. At the same time his mild manner belied his fierce convictions and relentless desire to have his views prevail. The idealism of his writings and his almost utopian faith in the people did not quite prepare his foes for his taste for political intrigue.

Washington relied upon younger men during his presidency, much as he had during the war. Jefferson was a decade and Hamilton more than two decades younger. Whatever their later differences, Jefferson started out by venerating Washington; he had once identified Washington, along with Benjamin Franklin and David Rittenhouse, as one of three geniuses America had spawned. "In war we have produced a

Washington, whose memory will be adored while liberty shall have votaries, whose name shall triumph over time."[21] He adorned Monticello with a painting of Washington and a plaster bust of him by Houdon. Jefferson always revered Washington's prudence, integrity, patriotism, and determination. "He was, indeed, in every sense of the words, a wise, a good, and a great man," he stated in later years.[22] Jefferson claimed that his dealings with President Washington were always amicable and productive. "In the four years of my continuance in the office of secretary of state," he was to say, "our intercourse was daily, confidential, and cordial."[23]

Nevertheless, as the years progressed, Jefferson's judgment of Washington grew far more critical. He viewed the president as a tough, unbending man: "George Washington is a hard master, very severe, a hard husband, a hard father, a hard governor."[24] Nor did he see Washington as especially deep or learned: "His time was employed in action chiefly, reading little, and that only in agriculture and English history."[25] He also found Washington leery of other people: "He was naturally distrustful of men and inclined to gloomy apprehensions."[26]

If profound foreign policy differences emerged between Washington and Jefferson, some of this can be ascribed to contrasting outlooks. At least on paper, Jefferson was quixotic and idealistic, even if he could be ruthless in practice. Washington was a hardheaded realist who took the world as it came. Jefferson would be far more hostile than Washington toward the British and far more sympathetic to the unfolding French Revolution. While Washington grew increasingly apprehensive about the violent events in Paris, Jefferson viewed them with philosophical serenity, lecturing Lafayette that one couldn't travel "from despotism to liberty in a featherbed."[27] Unlike Washington, Jefferson regarded the French Revolution as the proud and inevitable sequel to the American Revolution.

From the outset Jefferson was dismayed by the political atmosphere in New York. In his cultivated taste for fine wines, rare books, and costly furnishings, he was very much a Virginia aristocrat. One British diplomat noted his regal ways: "When he travels, it is in a very *kingly* style . . . I am informed that his secretaries are not admitted into his carriage but stand with their horses' bridles in their hands, till he is seated, and then mount and ride before his carriage."[28] Nonetheless Jefferson was extremely vigilant about the possible advent of a pseudo-aristocracy in America. His years spent witnessing the extravagant court of Versailles had only confirmed his detestation of monarchy. As he made the rounds of New York dinner parties, he was appalled to hear people voice their preference for "kingly over republican government."[29] Only Washington, he thought, could check this fatal drift toward royal government, although he finally harbored doubts as to whether he would do so. It also upset Jefferson that Hamilton seemed to be poaching on his turf, a problem partly of Washington's own making. With departmental lines still blurry,

Washington invited all department heads to submit opinions on matters concerning only one of them, producing sharp collisions and intramural rivalries. On the other hand, this method gave the president a full spectrum of opinion, saving his administration from monolithic uniformity.

The first attorney general, Edmund Randolph, thirty-six, was a handsome young man descended from one of Virginia's blue-ribbon families and well known to Washington. The son of a Tory father who had fled to England, he had graduated from William and Mary and studied law. He had even handled legal matters for Washington, who had chosen him partly because of his "habits of intimacy with him."[30] As Virginia governor, Randolph had led the state delegation to the Constitutional Convention but balked at signing the resulting document, only to switch positions during the Virginia Ratifying Convention, where he proved "a very able and elegant speaker," according to Bushrod Washington.[31] As a cabinet member, Randolph chafed at his subordinate position. The attorney general oversaw no department, causing him to gripe about his "mongrel" status.[32] So little was expected of the first attorney general that he was encouraged to take outside clients to supplement his modest $1,500 salary. Jefferson faulted Randolph as a weak, wavering man, calling him "the poorest chameleon I ever saw, having no color of his own and reflecting that nearest him."[33]

The Constitution was especially vague about the judiciary, which left a good deal to congressional discretion. The document did not specify the number of Supreme Court justices, so the Judiciary Act of 1789 set them at six; it also established thirteen district courts and three circuit courts. To balance federal and state power, each circuit court blended two Supreme Court justices, riding the circuit, with a district court judge selected from the particular state in which the trial was held. For Supreme Court justices, the need to "ride circuit" twice yearly was the most onerous part of their job, a lonesome task that could consume weeks or months. In the absence of federal courthouses, circuit courts met in government buildings or roadside taverns. Having to travel backcountry roads and sleep in squalid inns further detracted from judicial prestige. Such was the misery of riding circuit that several of Washington's judicial selections declined for that reason, prompting a high turnover in the Supreme Court's early years. In early April 1790 Washington inquired whether the justices had any problems to report, and in September they returned a lengthy list of objections. They were especially upset with having to ride circuit, noting that it created an untenable legal situation, since they might have to rule as Supreme Court justices on appeals of cases they had tried in those very courts.

In no area did Washington exert more painstaking effort than in selecting judges, for he regarded the judicial branch as "that department which must be considered as the keystone of our political fabric," as he told Jay in October 1789.[34] Once the

Judiciary Act passed in late September 1789, he nominated Jay as chief justice along with five associate judges from five different states, establishing regional diversity as an important criterion in such appointments. In stark contrast to the acrimonious hearings in later American history, the six justices breezed through the Senate confirmation process in forty-eight hours, their selection sparking little debate. Also without apparent protest, Washington named a large batch of district judges, U.S. attorneys, and marshals. In all, George Washington would appoint a record eleven justices to the Supreme Court.

As secretary of foreign affairs under the Articles of Confederation, John Jay kept warm the seat at the State Department until Jefferson arrived in New York. Washington felt palpable affection for Jay, confiding to him late in the war, "I entertain the friendly sentiments toward you, which I have ever experienced since our first acquaintance."[35] In sending along his commission as chief justice, Washington appended an enthusiastic note: "It is with singular pleasure that I address you as Chief Justice of the Supreme Court of the United States."[36] Prematurely balding, John Jay was a lean man with a pale, ascetic face, an aquiline nose, a melancholy air, and a wary look in his piercing, intelligent eyes. He had not handled a legal case in more than a decade and his skills had grown rusty, but Washington wanted a well-known national figure whose reputation transcended legal expertise. While Washington widened the distance between the presidency and the Senate, he at first narrowed it between the presidency and the Supreme Court, soliciting Jay's viewpoint on an eclectic array of issues ranging from the national debt, Indian affairs, and the census to counterfeit coins, postal roads, and inspection of beef exports.

On February 1, 1790, the Supreme Court held its inaugural meeting in the Merchants Exchange on Broad Street, with four justices present; its first session lasted only ten days. When Associate Justice William Cushing arrived in a British-style judicial wig, he was jeered in the streets and had to return to his residence for a more pedestrian wig. In the beginning, the Court lacked the majesty it would later attain and often seemed like an institution in search of a mission. Because of the newness of the federal judiciary, appeals had yet to percolate up from lower courts, resulting in little work at first. The Court's early procedures now seem quaintly antiquated. Instead of issuing written opinions, justices handed them down verbally from the bench without an official reporter to record decisions.

WASHINGTON'S ACCOMPLISHMENTS as president were no less groundbreaking than his deeds in the Continental Army. It is a grave error to think of George Washington as a noble figurehead presiding over a group of prima donnas who performed the real work of government. As a former commander in chief, he was accustomed to a chain of command and delegating important duties, but he was also accustomed to having the final say. As president, he enjoyed unparalleled power without being autocratic. He set out less to implement a revolutionary agenda than to construct a sturdy, well-run government, and in the process he performed many revolutionary acts.

Starting from scratch, Washington introduced procedures that made his government a model of smooth efficiency. Based on the fleeting mention in the Constitution that he could request written opinions from department heads, he created an impressive flow of paperwork. Jefferson noted that he would forward them letters he received that fell within their bailiwick, then asked to peruse their replies. They would gather up daily bundles of papers for his approval. Although this briefly delayed replies, Jefferson explained, "it produced [for] us in return the benefit of his sanction for every act we did."[37] This paper flow also meant that Washington was "always in accurate possession of all facts and proceedings in every part of the Union and . . . formed a central point for the different branches; preserved a unity of object and action among them," and enabled him to assume personal responsibility for all decisions.[38] Besides giving him a spacious view of the executive branch, this practice also kept his cabinet members on a tight leash. Jefferson noted that, however open-minded Washington was in asking for opinions, he took umbrage when offered unsolicited advice—the technique of someone who wanted to set the agenda and remain in control.

Among his department heads, Washington encouraged the free, creative interplay of ideas, setting a cordial tone of collegiality. He prized efficiency and close attention to detail and insisted that everybody make duplicate or even triplicate copies of letters, demanding clarity in everything. Once he upbraided an American diplomat in Europe by saying, "I will complain not only of your not writing, but of your writing so illegibly that I am half a day deciphering one page and then guess at much of it."[39] He wanted to be able to sit at leisure and compare conflicting arguments. Through his tolerant attitude, he created a protective canopy under which subordinates could argue freely, but once decisions were made, he wanted the administration to speak with one voice. Understanding the intellectual isolation of the presidency, he made sure that people didn't simply flatter him. He told Henry Lee, "A frank communication of the truth . . . respecting the public mind would be ever received as the highest testimony of respect and attachment."[40] Washington grew as a leader because he engaged in searching self-criticism. "I can bear to hear of imputed or real errors," he once wrote. "The man who wishes to stand well in the opinion of others must do this, because he is thereby enabled to correct his faults or remove prejudices which are imbibed against him."[41] The one thing Washington could not abide was when people published criticisms of him without first giving him a chance to respond privately.

As in other walks of life, Washington exhibited to a clockwork order in his daily routine and employed his time economically. There is poetic justice in the fact that when the capital shifted to Philadelphia, he often stopped at his watchmaker on his daily constitutionals. One British diplomat observed of Washington that "his time is regularly divided into certain portions and the business allotted to any one portion strictly adhered to."[42] When he settled upon weekly levees, Tobias Lear noted that they would allow "a sufficient time for dispatching the business of the office" and give "dignity to the president by not obliging him to expose himself every day to impertinent and curious intruders."[43]

Many people observed that President Washington spoke slowly and took time to make decisions, letting plans ripen before enacting them. Politics gave him more time to deliberate than did warfare, and he made fewer mistakes as president than as a general on the battlefield. To Catharine Macaulay Graham, he summed up his executive style: "Much was to be done by *prudence*, much by *conciliation*, much by *firmness*."[44] Hamilton concurred that the president "consulted much, pondered much; resolved slowly, resolved surely."[45] By delaying decisions, he made sure that his better judgment prevailed over his temper. At the same time, once decisions were made, they "were seldom, if ever, to be shaken," wrote John Marshall.[46] Jefferson agreed, saying that Washington's mind was "slow in operation, being little aided by invention or imagination, but sure in conclusion."[47] Once a decision was made, Washington seldom retreated unless fresh evidence radically altered his view. "Perhaps the strongest feature in his character was prudence," Jefferson wrote, "never acting until every circumstance, every consideration, was maturely weighed; refraining if he saw a doubt but, when once decided, going through with his purpose whatever obstacles opposed."[48] Jefferson did not rank Washington as a first-rate intellect on the order of a Newton, Bacon, or Locke, but he admitted that "no judgment was ever sounder."[49] Well aware of his own executive style, Washington once instructed a cabinet member "to deliberate maturely, but to execute promptly and vigorously."[50]

Washington was a perceptive man who, behind his polite facade, was unmatched at taking the measure of people. People did not always realize how observant he was. "His eyes retire inward . . . and have nothing of fire or animation or openness in their expression," said Edward Thornton, a young British diplomat, who added that Washington "possesses the two great requisites of a statesman, the faculty of concealing his own sentiments, and of discovering those of other men."[51] Washington once advised his adopted grandson that "where there is no occasion for expressing an opinion, it is best to be silent, for there is nothing more certain than that it is at all times more easy to make enemies than friends."[52] Washington's seemingly veiled eyes were penetrating, and Gouverneur Morris credited him with a cool, unblinking perspicacity: "He beheld not only the affairs that were passing around, but those also in which he was personally engaged, with the coolness of an unconcerned spectator."[53]

A taciturn man, Washington never issued opinions promiscuously. A disciplined politician, he never had to retract things uttered in a thoughtless moment. "Never be agitated by *more than* a decent *warmth* and offer your sentiments with modest diffidence," he told his nephew Bushrod, noting that "opinions thus given are listened to with more attention than when delivered in a dictatorial style."[54] He worried about committing an error more than missing a brilliant stroke. Washington also hated boasting. Bishop William White of Pennsylvania observed, "It has occasionally occurred to me when in his company, that if a stranger to his person were present, he would never have known from anything said by the president that he was conscious of having distinguished himself in the eyes of the world."[55]

For all his many admirable traits, Washington was never a warm, cozy, or folksy figure. As a man of moderation, he delivered praise sparingly and feared that excess familiarity with subordinates might weaken their performance. He kept people slightly off balance, guessing and vying for his favor. He managed relations with colleagues through subtle hints and gestures, and they learned to decipher his subliminal messages with accuracy. He had powerful ways of communicating his likes and dislikes, through subtle gradations of tone. With strangers or acquaintances, he addressed letters to "Sir." As he warmed up, he wrote to them as "Dear Sir," and when he grew very close, they were favored with "My Dear Sir." He was no less artful in closing letters. If he went from signing "Humble Obedient Servant" to "Affectionate Obedient Servant," the recipient had made a major leap forward in his emotions. Washington expressed displeasure with people less often with open rebukes than with the silent treatment, a sudden chill in the air, and a reversion to curt, businesslike communications.

Another politician would have been intoxicated by the idolatry Washington received. But through it all he maintained a striking personal stability and never let hero worship go to his head. The country was probably lucky that he was somewhat wearied by all the attention. There was cunning in Washington's nature but no low scheming. He never reneged on promises and was seldom duplicitous or underhanded. He respected the public, did not provoke people needlessly, and vowed at the time of his inauguration "that no man shou[ld] ever charge me *justly* with deception," as he told James McHenry.[56] When asked for advice on how to navigate "the dark and thorny path of politics," he said he could "only repeat what I have formerly told my countrymen in a very serious manner 'that honesty will be found, on every experiment, the best policy.'"[57] The charge of elitism against Washington can easily be overstated, for he immensely respected public opinion. When Madison later compared Washington and Adams as presidents, he contrasted their sensitivity to the public mood. Washington, he said, was always "scrutinizing into the public opinion and ready to follow where he could not lead it," while Adams was "insulting it by the most adverse sentiments and pursuits."[58]

Perhaps no president has tried so persistently to set an example of good conduct. He grew agitated whenever people gave him gifts, lest it be thought he was accepting bribes. When David Humphreys sent him elegant shoe buckles, he protested: "Presents . . . to me are of all things the most painful; but when I am so well satisfied of the motives which dictated yours, my scruples are removed."[59] It would have been easy for him to turn into a demagogue. Instead he tried hard to float high above all partisan considerations. In September 1792 he grew incensed at reports that he had supported the candidacy of John Francis Mercer for a Virginia congressional seat. Washington sent Mercer an indignant letter, pointing out that his interference in congressional elections would be "highly improper, as the people ought to be entirely at liberty to choose whom they pleased to represent them in Congress."[60] In such incidents Washington showed that he was forever on guard against the abuse of his presidential powers.

When Washington was sworn into office, North Carolina and Rhode Island had not yet embraced the Constitution and stood apart from the new Union. A major stumbling block was the absence of a bill of rights attached to the Constitution. At the time of the Constitutional Convention, Washington deemed a bill of rights superfluous on the grounds that American citizens would retain all rights that they did not expressly renounce in the document. During the ratifying conventions, he worried that opponents would seek to subvert the new political system by "attempting premature amendments."[61] When David Humphreys drafted Washington's original inaugural speech, Washington still worried that agitation for a bill of rights was a political ruse being exploited by antifederalist forces. One surviving fragment of the undelivered speech says: "I will barely suggest whether it would not be the part of prudent men to observe [the Constitution] fully in movement before they undertook to make such alterations as might prevent a fair experiment of its effects?"[62]

A critical convert to adopting a bill of rights was James Madison, who had initially opposed the idea. While running for Congress in a strongly antifederalist district in Virginia, he had been forced to emphasize his commitment to such amendments. As he informed Washington in January 1789, "It has been very industriously inculcated that I am dogmatically attached to the constitution in every clause, syllable, and letter, and therefore not a single amendment will be promoted by my vote, either from conviction or a spirit of accommodation."[63] In retrospect, it seems ironic that Madison should have been accused of irremediable hostility toward the amendments that came to be so gloriously associated with his name. He became convinced that a bill of rights was necessary to shore up support for the Constitution among hostile and wavering elements alike.

In defending the Constitution, Washington had often invoked its amendment powers to appease critics. After the inauguration, Madison showed him a dozen amendments he had drafted; after being whittled down to ten, they were to achieve renown as the Bill of Rights. Encountering heavy resistance in the new Congress, Madison asked Washington for a show of support for the amendments and elicited from him an all-important letter in late May 1789. While some of the proposed amendments, Washington wrote, "are importantly necessary," others were needed "to quiet the fears of some respectable characters and well meaning men. Upon the whole, therefore . . . they have my wishes for a favorable reception in both houses."[64] This letter helped to break the logjam in Congress. "Without Washington's help," writes Stuart Leibiger, "Madison's crusade for what has become a constitutional cornerstone would have been hopeless."[65] Washington's involvement was all the more notable in that he normally hesitated to meddle in the legislative process.

By September 1789, under Madison's guidance, Congress had approved the amendments and ordered Washington to send copies to the eleven state governors, as well as to the chief executives of North Carolina and Rhode Island. Even though the amendments were not approved by the states and formally adopted until December 15, 1791, North Carolina entered the Union in November 1789 and Rhode Island in May 1790, completing the reunification of the original thirteen states. In mid-October 1789 Washington wrote to Gouverneur Morris in a well-merited spirit of triumph, "It may not, however, be unpleasing to you to hear . . . that the national government is organized, and, as far as my information goes, to the satisfaction of all parties—that opposition to it is either no more, or hides its head."[66]

CHAPTER FIFTY

The Traveling Presidency

IN THE EARLIEST DAYS OF HIS ADMINISTRATION, Washington decided to visit every state in the Union and permit people to view him firsthand. His impulse was profoundly republican: he wanted to monitor public opinion. As a southern president, he thought it politic to tour the northern states first. After consulting with Hamilton, Knox, and Jay, he mapped out a monthlong tour of New England, once Congress had recessed in late September 1789. He wanted to educate himself about the "principal character and internal circumstances" of each section of the country and meet "well-informed persons, who might give him useful informations and advices on political subjects."[1] He was especially eager to discover whether citizens had embraced their new experiment in republican government. This all formed part of his concerted effort to break out of the airtight bubble that can seal any fledgling president in a suffocating vacuum.

Washington had other cogent reasons for making the trip. To refute stories about his supposedly regal style, he decided to travel with only Tobias Lear, David Humphreys, and William Jackson, in addition to six servants. Since he was traveling to Massachusetts, Washington thought it proper to invite along Vice President Adams, who committed a major faux pas by snubbing his invitation. The trip would also enable Washington, after his recent prolonged illness, to indulge in fresh air, exercise, and relaxation. To rebuild his shattered health, he now rode for two hours each morning and strolled for an hour in the late afternoon, but he still led a confined existence in New York and must have eagerly anticipated the freedom of the open road.

When he set out in mid-October, the business of government did not grind to a halt. Congress had instructed Alexander Hamilton to draw up a report on public debt and to devise an all-encompassing plan to fund it. It was a huge and punishing task—Congress wanted it in hand when it reconvened in early January—but Hamilton, a dynamo who thrived on hard work, gloried in his ability to produce outstanding results on short notice. Prior to leaving New York, Washington also signed a proclamation for the first Thanksgiving on November 26, declaring that "Almighty God" should be thanked for the abundant blessings bestowed on the American people, including victory in the war against England, creation of the Constitution, establishment of the new government, and the "tranquillity, union, and plenty" that the country now enjoyed.[2]

To execute a sweeping tour of the northern states, Washington knew, he would encounter many problems that had bothered him before. He had no flair for impromptu public speaking or small talk and could not divert audiences with a casual joke or anecdote. "In public, when called on for a sudden opinion, he was unready, short, and embarrassed," Jefferson recalled, noting that Washington "had neither copiousness of ideas, nor fluency of words."[3] He also had to worry about a more humiliating possibility: his dentures popping out unexpectedly. Opening his mouth relaxed the pressure on the curved metal springs connecting the upper and lower dentures, which might cause them to slip out. That Washington risked such embarrassment in order to make direct contact with the people shows his self-sacrificing nature. Perhaps afraid he would be held captive to the hospitality of various families and eager to salvage some privacy, he laid down a rule that he would not stay in private residences during the trip.

By now Washington well understood the machinery of fame. Usually he rode through the countryside in an open carriage, attended by servants in livery and jockey caps. Behind him a baggage wagon rumbled along, and one of his slaves, either Paris or Giles, supervised his white charger in the rear. As they entered a town, Washington would dismount from his carriage, mount the white steed, then enter with magnificent solemnity. He clung to the hope that he might avoid fanfare and enter cities unobtrusively, and at his first stop in New Haven, Connecticut, he deliberately bypassed the welcoming committee. "By taking the lower road," he admitted in his diary, "we missed a committee of the assembly who had been appointed to wait upon and escort me into town."[4] Typically, as word leaked out about his imminent arrival, a volunteer cavalry corps rushed to greet him before he could outwit them. Doomed to his own celebrity, he tried to submit with the best possible grace.

Aside from scouting places for future canals, roads, and other internal improvements, Washington kept a weather eye out for innovations in manufacturing and agriculture. The country already stood in the early throes of the Industrial Revolution, and unlike Jefferson, Washington did not recoil from the mills that had begun to dot the landscape. He stopped by the Hartford Woolen Manufactory and examined its textile business. While he did not find their broadcloths to be first-rate, he ordered a suit for himself and material for breeches for his servants. Engaging in a bit of amateur sociology, he observed the greater income equality of the northern states. Soon after crossing into Massachusetts, he wrote, "There is a great equality in the people of this state. Few or no opulent men and no poor—great similitude in their buildings . . . The farms . . . are small, not averaging more than 100 acres."[5] His comment provides yet another example of Washington's growing appreciation of the northern states and his shedding of a purely Virginia identity.

Boston loomed as the first major city on the itinerary; plans for a full-dress military parade as he entered the city only stoked Washington's anxiety. A committee of Boston dignitaries traveled to meet him in Spencer, west of Worcester, and, just as he feared, they presented their celebratory plans. Not for the last time during the trip, Washington fell on his sword: "Finding this ceremony was not to be avoided, though I had made every effort to do it, I named the hour of ten to pass the militia of the above county at Cambridge and the hour of 12 for my entrance into Boston."[6]

Boston had never properly thanked Washington for its liberation from the British, and it now intended to seize the opportunity. Knowing this would be a tribute to his wartime prowess, Washington departed from his usual practice and decked himself out in his Continental Army uniform, topped by rich gold epaulettes. If he had been resistant at first to the adulation of the Boston populace, he entered wholly into the spirit of the occasion. The morning of his arrival was cold and overcast, and his cavalcade was halted at Cambridge by a dispute as to whether state or local authorities would receive him. The president grew irritated with the maddening delay. "Is there no other avenue into the town?" he demanded.[7] The stern reproof had an immediate effect: he would be greeted by municipal officials.

As he entered Boston, church bells chimed, and a French fleet in the harbor erupted with bursts of artillery fire. In a symbolic gesture, cannon roared from Dorchester Heights, recalling the triumph Washington had engineered there during the Boston siege. People crammed the streets, bent on seeing him as he trotted by on his white steed. "He did not bow to the spectators as he passed," said one observer, "but sat on his horse with a calm, dignified air."[8] At the State House he passed beneath an enormous arch emblazoned with the words "To the man who unites all hearts," surmounted by a laurel wreath with the inscription "Boston relieved March 17th. 1776."[9] When Washington appeared on a balcony of the building and set eyes on the vast multitude below, there arose a tremendous roar. George Washington was always more emotional than people realized, and by the time he emerged from the State House and heard a choir crooning an ode to him, he could no longer contain himself, giving way to tears. One startled eyewitness described how "every muscle of his face appeared agitated, and he was frequently observed to pass . . . his handkerchief across his eyes."[10]

Washington's visit to Boston embroiled him in a delicate diplomatic impasse with Governor John Hancock, who invited him to stay in his richly decorated Beacon Hill home. Hancock was something of a strutting peacock, wearing fancy clothes and riding about in a radiant coach. In replying to this invitation, Washington explained his decision to stay in prearranged lodgings, although he accepted an invitation to dine informally with Hancock. Always scrupulously attentive to form, Washington assumed that Hancock would obey protocol and call on him at his lodgings before he went to this dinner. Pleading gout, Hancock failed to do so. To Hancock's emissaries, Washington expressed his displeasure. He knew that Hancock was trying to establish that he outranked the president in Massachusetts. Behind the dispute over etiquette lay an unspoken struggle between state and federal power. "I informed them in explicit terms that I should not see the Gov[erno]r unless it was at my own lodgings," Washington wrote in his diary.[11] Perhaps he remembered Hancock's peevish reaction when Washington had been appointed commander in chief instead of him. Hancock quickly got the message. Writing grandly about himself in the third person, he told Washington that "the Governor will do himself the honor to pay his respects in half an hour. This would have been done much sooner had his health in any degree permitted."[12] To flaunt his martyrdom, Hancock wrapped himself up in red flannel bandages and had his servants carry him into Washington's lodging.

By this point Washington had come down with a cold and an eye inflammation. Even before he left New York, he had received reports of an "epidemical cold" gripping the New England states.[13] On the day he entered Boston, so many local citizens were wheezing with heavy coughs and chest colds that the illness was dubbed "the President's Cough" or "Washington's influenza."[14] Now it seemed that Washington himself had succumbed. Nonetheless he toured the Harvard College library and museum and went aboard the flagship of the French fleet, receiving maritime honors accorded only to kings. Bemused, he noted, "The officers took off their shoes and the crew all appeared with their legs bared."[15] Still the heartthrob of American females, Washington agreed to a request from the ladies at an elegant dinner to sit for a portrait that would grace Faneuil Hall. The smitten ladies, all aflutter, explained that "his benign countenance made such an impression on their hearts as they wish to recognize in his portrait in future."[16] From this portrait, copies were made that would hang in many Boston households.

On his trip Washington followed his ecumenical practice of praying in churches of various denominations, including Episcopal, Presbyterian, and Congregational. In Boston he attended a concert in King's Chapel (Stone Chapel), where a young

Danish artist named Christian Güllager, seated in a pew behind the pulpit, drew a rapid, unauthorized sketch of him. A week later, in Portsmouth, New Hampshire, Washington granted Güllager a two-and-a-half-hour sitting that produced a remarkably fresh and candid portrait of Washington that was perhaps influenced by the painter's first glimpse of him in Boston. Leaning back in his chair, Washington seems to turn and suddenly catch the artist's eye. His face is broad and open, his torso massive and powerful in a dark coat, and his aura commanding.

On October 28, as he toured the Boston Sailcloth Manufactory, Washington's attention was distracted from the wonders of American manufactures by the wonders of American women. One observer spied Washington's frisson of delight, saying that he "made himself merry on this occasion, telling the overseer he believed he collected the prettiest girls in Boston."[17] When feted that evening, Washington was again encircled by adoring women and recorded happily in his diary that "there were upwards of 100 ladies. Their appearance was elegant and many of them were very handsome."[18] So began a habit of counting the fashionable women as he basked in their attention. "He is much more open and free in his behavior . . . in the company of ladies . . . than when solely with men," someone later noticed.[19] Washington can be forgiven his wandering eye, for others noted the way pretty women gathered around him. One observer wrote that while Washington sat in state on a crimson velvet settee, "the ladies were very handsomely dressed and every one strove here, as everywhere else, who should pay the most respect."[20] It says much about Washington's declining health that this once-celebrated dancer seemed not to take the floor at these functions. According to Elizabeth Schuyler Hamilton, after the war, Washington "would always choose a partner and walk through the figures correctly, but he never danced. His favorite was the minuet, a graceful dance, suited to his dignity and gravity."[21]

After leaving Boston, Washington proceeded north along the coast, accompanied by four hundred cavalry, as the towns grew much less glamorous. In the fishing port of Marblehead, no fashionable women swooned over his presence. "The houses are old," Washington wrote, "the streets dirty, and the common people not very clean."[22] Washington seemed to grow heartily tired of all the festive barges, honor guards, thirteen-gun salutes, and commemorative arches thrown in his path. In Salem one citizen saw how oppressed Washington was by all the pomp: "His appearance as he passed thro[ugh] Court Street in Salem was far from gay or making anyone else so. He looked oppressed by the attention that was paid him, and as he cast his eye around, I thought it seemed to sink at the notice he attracted. When he had got to the Court House and had patiently listened to the ditty they sung at him and heard the shouts of the multitudes, he bowed very low and, as if he could bear no more, turned hastily around and went into the house."[23]

Desperate for some relief in Portsmouth, New Hampshire, Washington went deep-sea fishing with some local fishermen. The outing turned into a fiasco: he caught not a single fish, and when one local fisherman hooked a cod, he handed the rod to the disappointed president so he could reel it in. Doubtless feeling a little foolish, Washington gave the man a silver dollar. He was much happier attending a sumptuous dinner in Portsmouth, where he resumed his head count of the ladies and showed himself a connoisseur of female coiffure. At this assembly, he wrote, "there were about 75 well dressed and many of them very handsome ladies. Among whom (as was also the case at the Salem and Boston assemblies) were a greater proportion with much blacker hair than are usually seen in the southern states."[24]

As he circled back to New York, Washington stopped at Lexington and "viewed the spot on which the first blood was spilt in the dispute with Great Britain on the 19th of April 1775."[25] After treading this hallowed ground, Washington proceeded south along crooked back roads to Waltham. Incredible as it seems, the presidential party had to ask directions of bystanders, who often gave Washington misleading information to the point that he complained of "blind and ignorant" advice.[26] In his diary, he sounded the universal lament of travelers, grousing about room reservations that suddenly vanished, forcing the party to move on to another town for the night, or the atrocious entertainment at many taverns. The trip had been a colossal undertaking for Washington, especially after his recent malady. In the space of a month, he had toured or passed through almost sixty cities and villages. The journey had been an undisputed triumph, however, consolidating Washington's popularity and giving citizens a sense of belonging to a single nation. For all its rigors, the journey had also revived Washington's health. John Trumbull said he returned to the capital "all fragrant with the odor of incense."[27] With what must have been indescribable relief, he arrived back at his Cherry Street mansion at three P.M. on November 13, 1789, "where I found Mrs. Washington and the rest of the family all well."[28] There would be no rest for the weary: having reappeared on a Friday, he had to mingle with visitors at Martha's weekly reception that evening.

ANOTHER EFFECTIVE WAY that Washington transmitted his image to the country and sought national unity was by sitting for portrait artists, an activity for which he set aside a huge amount of time. In early October he devoted two hours to an Irish artist, John Ramage, who daubed a miniature on ivory of him at Martha's behest. Ramage depicted a notably dour Washington dressed in a uniform adorned by the badge of the Society of the Cincinnati. In this unflattering portrait, Washington's nose looks too long and too hooked, his chin too sharp, and his expression morose, perhaps reflecting his fatigue before the northern trip reinvigorated him.

Around the same time, Washington posed for the Marquise de Bréhan, who was variously described as either the sister or the sister-in-law of the Count de Moustier, the French minister, with whom she lived in a scandalous liaison. A friend of Jefferson, the marquise had imagined that she was coming to an American Arcadia and been sorely disappointed. The count, a bright but tactless eccentric, dressed in the red-heeled shoes of French nobility and wore earrings. Both the count and the marquise were frowned upon by most New Yorkers, who had small tolerance for European decadence. "Appearances . . . have created and diffused an opinion that an improper connection subsists between [Moustier] and the marchioness," Jay informed Jefferson. "You can easily conceive the influence of such an opinion on the minds and feelings of such a people as ours."[29] One local resident ridiculed the pair thus: the count was "distant, haughty, penurious, and entirely governed by the caprices of a little singular, whimsical, hysterical old woman, whose delight is in playing with a negro child and caressing a monkey."[30] Perhaps reluctant to offend the French minister, Washington flouted convention and allowed himself to be painted by the marquise, who completed a cameo miniature of Washington in neoclassical style, his head bound by a laurel wreath. In this profile, Washington has the massive head and thick neck of a Roman emperor, a clear brow, a straight nose, and a steady, godlike gaze as he stares straight ahead.

Another portrait done around this time was a direct outgrowth of Washington's northern trip. After giving him a tour of Philosophical Hall, with its display of scientific instruments, Harvard College president Joseph Willard asked Washington if the university could have a portrait of him, and he agreed to sit for Edward Savage. In late December and early January, Washington generously granted three sessions to Savage, who portrayed him in uniform with the badge of the Society of the Cincinnati pinned to his left lapel. That Washington twice wore the badge for portraits early in his presidency shows his desire to reassert his solidarity with the group despite his rocky relationship with it. Savage's finished portrait shows a calm, powerful, but stolid Washington with a spreading paunch. There is no fire in the eyes or expression in the face—so unlike his smiling, expressive wartime portraits—again hinting at the extreme physical changes he underwent in his later years.

During this period Washington dedicated the most time to portraits by his former aide John Trumbull, perhaps because the artist situated him in historical settings. Washington wrote admiringly of Trumbull's "masterly execution" and "capacious mind" and showed toward him none of the petulance or impatience he did toward Gilbert Stuart.[31] In 1790 alone Washington granted Trumbull a dozen sessions and even went riding with him, so the painter could study him on horseback. While training with Benjamin West in London in the early 1780s, Trumbull had been imprisoned as a secret American agent, which could only have endeared him to Washington. Trumbull now did a towering portrait of Washington for New

York's City Hall, with British ships evacuating New York in 1783 in the background, as well as portraits celebrating the Battles of Trenton and Princeton. The Trenton picture showed Washington in all his earlier magnificence, standing trim, and erect, one gloved hand clasping his sword, his chin lifted in an elegant pose. For the Princeton portrait, Trumbull presented Washington on the eve of battle. "I told the President my object," he later wrote; "he entered into it warmly, and, as the work advanced, we talked of the scene, its dangers, its almost desperation. He looked the scene again and I happily transferred to the canvas the lofty expression of his animated countenance, the high resolve to conquer or to perish."[32]

Despite his presidential cares, Washington remained a devoted family man and doted on nobody more than Nelly. She was such a bright, vivacious girl that Martha described the ten-year-old in 1789 as "a wild little creature" with boundless curiosity.[33] She had a sharp eye for people's foibles and later on loved to poke fun at the many young beaux who courted her. As she got older, she liked to sprinkle her letters playfully with French and Italian expressions.

Even as a girl, Nelly was smart and cultivated, if a trifle too dreamy for her grandparents. The Washingtons never penalized her because she was a girl, and they sent her to a boarding school in New York as a day student. They also made sure she acquired the necessary artistic graces. She studied painting with William Dunlap and turned out beautiful still lifes, often floral arrangements set against a black backdrop. Later on, in Philadelphia, a dancing master named James Robardet taught Nelly and Washy the fashionable steps required for polite society. Because she was so creative, the Washingtons also bought Nelly an English guitar and a harpsichord and gave her lessons with the Austrian composer Alexander Reinagle. In the musical realm, Martha was a martinet, forcing Nelly to practice the harpsichord for hours on end until tears sprang to her eyes. "The poor girl would play and cry, and cry and play, for long hours under the immediate eye of her grandmother, a rigid disciplinarian in all things," said her brother.[34] Nelly also told of how, against her grandmother's warning, she wandered alone by moonlight in the Mount Vernon woods. When she came home, "the General was walking up and down with his hands behind him, as was his wont," said Nelly, while Martha, "seated in her great armchair . . . opened a severe reproof."[35] Elsewhere Martha Washington is portrayed as overly indulgent with her grandchildren. After spending a day with the family in October 1789, Abigail Adams wrote that "Mrs. Washington is a most friendly, good lady, always pleasant and easy, dotingly fond of her grandchildren, to whom she is quite the grandmamma."[36] Several years later Nelly wrote to Washington of how she looked up to him "with grateful affection as a parent to myself and family."[37] Part of Nelly's appeal for Washington was her lightness of being, which relieved the gloom that sometimes cloaked the careworn president.

According to Washy, Nelly observed how Washington's grave presence inhibited children at play and that even grown-up relatives "feared to speak or laugh before him . . . not from his severity" but from "awe and respect . . . When he entered a room where we were all mirth and in high conversation, all were instantly mute."[38] When this happened, Washington would "retire, quite provoked and disappointed."[39] It is a powerful commentary on the way in which fame estranged Washington from the casual pleasures of everyday life, making it hard for him to get the social solace he needed. Yet here, too, there are contrary views. His nephew Howell Lewis wrote that when Washington was "in a lively mood, so full of pleasantry, so agreeable to all . . . I could hardly realize that he was the same Washington whose dignity awed all who approached him."[40] And in his memoirs, Washy reported how his sister charmed the president, stating that "the grave dignity which he usually wore did not prevent his keen enjoyment of a joke and that no one laughed more heartily than he did when she herself, a gay, laughing girl, gave one of her saucy descriptions of any scene in which she had taken part or any one of the merry pranks she then often played."[41]

While Washington doted on Nelly, Martha took special pleasure in spoiling Washy. When he was away from home, Martha grew anxious, as she had with Jacky. On one occasion when Washy was gone and failed to write, Washington reminded him "how apt your grandmama is to suspect that you are sick, or some accident has happened to you, when you omit this."[42] Exasperated with the boy's laxity, Washington criticized him in the terms he had once reserved for Washy's father. In New York, Washington hired a private tutor to work with Washy, who made temporary progress in Latin but was hopeless in math and other subjects. In general, he was an indifferent and easily distracted pupil. Washington constantly coached Washy and advised him to mend his ways. The boy would make all the right noises, then completely ignore his advice, leading to tooth-gnashing frustration for Washington.

Like his father, Washy knew that he would inherit the Custis fortune, which made him lazy and unfocused. George was again afraid to cross Martha on the loaded subject of the children and the Custis money. In a fascinating letter written in 1791, Tobias Lear talked about this uneasy standoff between the Washingtons: "I clearly see that [Washy] is in the high road to ruin . . . The president sees it with pain, but, as he considers that Mrs. W's happiness is bound up in the boy, he is unwilling to take such measures as might reclaim him, knowing that any rigidity towards him would perhaps be productive of serious effects on her."[43] This was one area where the most powerful man in the country tread cautiously. Where Washington did succeed was in introducing the two children to the theater. The boy was sufficiently imbued with the love of acting that he played Cassius in a performance of *Julius Caesar*, enacted at the presidential mansion, and later made an effort to become a playwright—a literary urge that resulted in a flowery memoir of his grandfather.

From the outset of the administration, the Washingtons did their best to cope with the inconveniences of the Cherry Street house. Though roomy by ordinary standards, it could not accommodate enough people for large formal dinners and receptions. In the fall of 1789, when Washington heard that the Count de Moustier was being recalled to France, he jumped at the chance to occupy his house at 39–41 Broadway, on the west side of the street south of Trinity Church (erected two years earlier by merchant Alexander Macomb). This second presidential mansion was four stories high, featured two high-ceilinged drawing rooms, and was much more stately than its predecessor. When one New Yorker toured the house and its two neighbors under construction in 1787, he was thrilled by their imposing dimensions, saying that "they are by far the grandest buildings I ever saw and are said to excel any on the continent."[44]

On February 23, 1790, the Washingtons moved from their old cramped quarters to this airy, commodious new residence. Where they could seat only fourteen people at state dinners before, they now had room for more than two dozen. In the rear of the house, glass doors opened onto a balcony with unobstructed views of the Hudson River. Washington also built a stable nearby with handsome planked floors and twelve stalls for horses. With his eye for furnishings, he bought from Moustier everything from a dozen damask armchairs to huge gilt mirrors to a bidet. Eager to augment presidential dignity, he bought more than three hundred pieces of gilt-edged porcelain for dinner parties. Green was the omnipresent color of the house, which had green silk furniture and a green carpet spotted with white flowers. Washington's love of greenery was further reflected in his purchase of ninety-three glass flowerpots scattered throughout the residence. It is curious that America's first president chose a residence so thoroughly saturated with a French sensibility.

This executive mansion never had the dark, smoky atmosphere that we associate with an age of candlelight dinners. Attuned to the spirit of technical innovation, Washington bought fourteen lamps of a new variety patented by Aimé Argand, a Swiss chemist. They used whale oil and burned with a cleaner, brighter light than anything used before, chasing away evening shadows and affording up to twelve times the illumination of candlepower. Washington mounted these lamps in the drawing rooms, hallway, entries, and stairwells, banishing shadows from the residence. As he wrote excitedly, "These lamps, it is said, consume their own smoke, do no injury to furniture, give more light, and are cheaper than candles."[45] In this manner, Washington initiated America's insatiable appetite for oil, provided theatrical lighting to burnish the splendid statecraft that he practiced, and introduced a welcome touch of modernity.

The State of the President

A LITTLE AFTER NOON ON JANUARY 8, 1790, George Washington climbed into his cream-colored coach and rode off to Federal Hall behind a team of four snow-white horses. In its sparsely worded style, the Constitution mandated that the president, from time to time, should give Congress information about the state of the Union, but it was Washington who turned this amorphous injunction into a formal speech before both houses of Congress, establishing another precedent. Trailing him in his entourage were the chief justice and members of his cabinet, leading to yet another tradition: that the State of the Union speech (then called the annual address) would feature leading figures from all three branches of government.

Everything about the new government still had an improvised feel, and Washington's advent occasioned some last-minute scurrying in the Senate chamber. Maclay referred to "nothing but bustle about the Senate Chamber in hauling chairs and removing tables" for his arrival.[1] Once at Broad and Wall, Washington entered the hall—on later occasions, constables held back the crowd with long white rods—and mounted to the second-floor hall. Everyone clung nervously to protocol, and the president went through an awkward comedy of manners with the legislators. When he entered, they rose; when he was seated, they sat. Still dressed in shades of mourning for his mother, he was garbed in a suit of midnight blue, verging on black, that he had brought back from the Hartford factory.

In a hopeful speech, Washington anticipated Hamilton's financial program by endorsing the need to establish public credit and promote manufacturing, agriculture, and commerce. He sounded a theme already resonant in his wartime letters: the need to ensure a strong national defense: "To be prepared for war is one of the most effectual means of preserving peace."[2] He also advocated the advancement of science, literature, and learning through the formation of a national university. The speech was composed in the didactic style of a wise parent, patiently lecturing his children, that characterized Washington's public pronouncements and defined his political rhetoric. When it ended, the legislators stood, Washington bowed, and then he descended to the street. William Maclay did not fault Washington's speaking style, but ever watchful for monarchical tendencies, he carped that Washington had fallen into "the British mode of business" by asking department heads to lay certain documents before Congress.[3]

When Washington delivered his speech, he had little sense that a furor was about to erupt over Hamilton's funding system or that American politics would become fractious and nasty. Even before Hamilton took office, Congress had enacted legislation to create a string of lighthouses, beacons, and buoys along the eastern seaboard for the customs service, placing Hamilton in charge of a vast public works project. He also had enormous patronage powers, as he named customs inspectors and other revenue officials. During the colonial era, the evasion of customs duties had become a time-honored practice, and Hamilton had to seek Washington's approval for constructing ten boats called revenue cutters to police the waterways and intercept smugglers, giving birth to what later became the Coast Guard. For political harmony, Washington and Hamilton distributed the construction work and skipper jobs to different parts of the country, but for a nation already wary of bureaucracy, the program represented a significant, and for some ominous, expansion of government power.

As the office handling money matters, the Treasury Department was bound to be a flash point for controversy. When Congress debated its shape in 1789, republican purists wanted it headed by a three-member board as a safeguard against concentrated power. When a single secretary was chosen instead, Congress tried to hem in his power by requiring that, unlike the other cabinet secretaries, he should file periodic reports directly with them. Instead of subordinating Hamilton to the legislature, however, this approach enmeshed him in its workings. The treasury secretary's aggressive style guaranteed that the executive branch, not Congress, would oversee economic policy. As with foreign policy, executive primacy in economic matters ran counter to the view of many framers who had hoped that Congress would enjoy policy-making centrality, but this development promised greater efficiency and consistency than would otherwise have been the case.

On January 14, 1790, Hamilton delivered the *Report on Public Credit* that Congress had requested in the fall. With his nimble mind and encyclopedic store of knowledge, Hamilton served up a magnum opus that eclipsed anything the legislators had envisioned. No evidence exists that Hamilton consulted Washington before he completed it. Since the president was not well schooled in the arcana of public finance, Jefferson thought he had been hoodwinked: "Unversed in financial projects and calculations and budgets, his approbation of them was bottomed on confidence in the man [Hamilton]."[4] Jefferson's insinuation that Washington was a helpless dupe of Hamilton is highly misleading. Dating back to their wartime frustrations with Congress, Washington and Hamilton had shared a common worldview and an expansive faith in executive power. They had seen firsthand how Britain's well-funded public debt had enabled it to prosecute the war with seemingly limitless resources. Late in the war Washington had blasted the fanciful notion that "the war can be carried on without money, or that money can be borrowed without permanent funds to pay the interest of it."[5]

The federal government had fallen woefully in arrears in paying off the enormous debt—$54 million in national and $25 million in state obligations—amassed to fight the Revolutionary War. It would have been tempting for the young nation to repudiate this burden, but as a matter of policy and morality, Washington and Hamilton thought nations should honor their debts if they aspired to full membership in the community of nations. "With respect to the payment of British debts," Washington had written before becoming president, "I would fain hope . . . that the good sense of this country will never suffer a violation of a public treaty, nor pass acts of injustice to individuals. Honesty in states, as well as in individuals, will ever be found the soundest policy."[6] If Washington gave Hamilton something close to carte blanche on fiscal matters, it was because they essentially agreed on the steps needed to tame America's staggering debt. But he had also set up a policy-making apparatus in which major decisions had to cross his desk for approval, so he was confident that he could control the sometimes-brash Hamilton.

Hamilton's audacious report argued that, to restore fiscal sanity, the government did not have to retire the debt at once. All it had to do was devise a mechanism to convince people that, by setting aside revenues at predictable intervals, it would faithfully retire it in future years. Such a well-funded debt, Hamilton argued, would be a "national blessing" inasmuch as it would provide investment capital and an elastic national currency.[7] The report foresaw a medley of taxes, from import duties to excise taxes on distilled spirits, to pay off existing debt and to service a new foreign loan. With its new taxes and its funded debt, Hamilton's program was bound to dredge up unwelcome memories of the British ministry.

In his report, Hamilton championed several controversial measures. Some original holders of the wartime promissory notes, including many Continental Army veterans, had sold them after the war at a tiny fraction of their face value, believing that they would never be repaid in full. Hamilton planned to redeem them at face value and wanted current holders of the paper, even if they were speculators, to reap the rewards of the steep price appreciation that would follow enactment of his program. Only by doing this, he thought, could he establish the principle that owners of securities were entitled to all future profits and losses. Without such a policy, the United States could never establish thriving securities markets. Hamilton was also persuaded that, since the debt had been raised to finance a national war, the federal government should assume responsibility for the states' debts as well. Such an act of "assumption" would have extraordinarily potent political effects, for holders of state debt would transfer their loyalty to the new central government, binding the country together. It would also reinforce the federal government's claim to future tax revenues in any controversies with the states. Peerless in crafting policies embedded with a secret political agenda, Hamilton knew how to dovetail one program with another in a way that made them all difficult to undo.

Until the publication of Hamilton's report, James Madison had been Washington's most confidential adviser. That began to erode on February 11, 1790, when Madison rose in the House and, in a surprising volte-face, denounced the idea that speculators should benefit from Hamilton's program. It was a stunning shot across the bow of the administration. Madison favored a policy of so-called discrimination—that original holders of the debt, mostly former soldiers, should share in the windfall as the price of government paper soared. Many Americans found it hard to see speculators rewarded instead of veterans, and Madison's speech tapped a powerful vein of discontent. Speculation in government debt, Madison affirmed, was "wrong, radically and morally and politically wrong."[8] As a Virginia congressman and budding advocate of states' rights, Madison was moving away from the continental perspective that had united him with Hamilton when they co-authored *The Federalist*. For Madison, the funded debt and the expanding ranks of Treasury employees were far too reminiscent of the British model. Feeling betrayed by Madison, Hamilton argued that his former comrade's discrimination proposal was simply unworkable. To track down the original holders of securities and parcel out their shares of the profits would be a bureaucratic nightmare. He also considered speculation to be an inescapable, if unsavory, aspect of functioning financial markets.

As the hero of the old soldiers, Washington confronted a ticklish dilemma, and Madison later attested that the president's mind was "strongly exercised" by the debate.[9] On the one hand, Washington sympathized with veterans who had unloaded their IOUs to "unfeeling, avaricious speculators."[10] At the same time, he had warned his men at the end of the war not to part with these certificates, telling them bluntly in general orders in May 1783: "The General thinks it necessary to caution the soldiers against the foolish practice . . . of disposing of their notes and securities of pay at a very great discount, when it is evident the speculators on those securities must hereafter obtain the full payment of their nominal value."[11] Washington's words had been prophetic. Because Congress had ordered Hamilton's report, Washington did not want to overstep his bounds by lobbying for it, and he remained cagey in discussing it. To David Stuart, he wrote circumspectly, "Mr Madison, on the question of discrimination, was actuated, I am persuaded, by the purest motives and most heartfelt conviction. But the subject was delicate and perhaps had better not have been stirred."[12]

While Washington introduced no ringing opinion during the debate, his silence was tantamount to approval of the Hamiltonian system. At this point he was still a sacred figure in American politics, making Hamilton a convenient lightning rod for protests. It was also expedient for Washington to allow Hamilton to engage in the rough-and-tumble of political bargaining, while he himself held fast to the ceremonial trappings of the presidency. Taken aback by Madison's defection and the vehement schism provoked by the public credit report, Washington was especially disheartened that the country had split along geographic lines, placing him at odds with the South. He wrote privately that if the northern states moved "in a solid phalanx" and the southern states were "less tenacious of their interest," then the latter had only themselves to blame.[13]

The debate over the Hamiltonian program opened a rift between Washington and his Virginia associates that only widened through the years. Reflecting their bias in favor of landed wealth and against paper assets, members of the chronically indebted gentry recoiled in horror at the northern financial revolution ushered in by Hamilton. The tobacco market had fallen into a deep slump, making these pinched Virginia planters ripe for tirades against northern speculators, who seemed to profit from easy winnings. Also, Virginia had already paid much of its debt and therefore opposed a federal takeover of state debt, which would reward irresponsible states that had repudiated their loans. Things went so far that in some Virginia circles Washington was regarded as almost a traitor to his class. When David Stuart reported that spring on extreme hostility in Virginia toward the new government, Washington grew distressed. "Your description of the public mind in Virginia gives me pain," he replied. "It seems to be more irritable, sour, and discontented than . . . it is in any other state in the Union."[14] On February 22 Madison's proposal to discriminate in favor of original holders of government debt was roundly defeated in the House, 36–13. In a preview of problems to come for Washington, 9 of the 13 negative votes came from his home state of Virginia.

THE DISCONTENT OF SOUTHERN PLANTERS was further inflamed in February 1790 when Quakers, clad in black hats and coats, filed a pair of explosive petitions with Congress. One proposed an immediate halt to the slave trade, while the other urged the unthinkable: the gradual abolition of slavery itself. Because they did not believe that God discriminated between blacks and whites, many Quakers had freed their own slaves and even, in some cases, compensated them for past injustice. Washington had torn feelings about the Quakers. The previous October he had sent an address to the Society of Quakers, full of high praise, asserting that "there is no denomination among us who are more exemplary and useful citizens."[15] At the same time the Quakers, as pacifists, had tended to shun wartime duty.

On the slavery question, Washington reacted with extreme caution. Although he had voiced support for emancipation in private letters, to do so publicly, as he tried to forge a still precarious national unity, would have been a huge and controversial leap. The timing of the Quaker petitions could not have been more troublesome. To David Stuart, he worried that the petitions "will certainly tend to promote" southern suspicions, then added: "It gives particular umbrage that the Quakers should be so busy in this business."[16] Washington and other founders who opposed slavery, at least in theory, thought they had conveniently sidestepped the issue at the Constitutional Convention by stipulating that the slave trade was safe until 1808. But because Benjamin Franklin, as president of the Pennsylvania Abolition Society, had signed one of the Quaker petitions, they could not be summarily dismissed. James Jackson of Georgia warned grimly of civil war if the petitions passed, claiming that "the people of the southern states will resist one tyranny as soon as another."[17] Responding to planter panic, James Madison led congressional opposition to any interference with slavery, unfurling the banner of states' rights. Although Hamilton had cofounded the New York Manumission Society, he, like Washington, remained silent on the issue, hoping to push through the controversial funding program. In fact, virtually all of the founders, despite their dislike of slavery, enlisted in this conspiracy of silence, taking the convenient path of deferring action to a later generation.

Washington tended to conceal his inmost thoughts about slavery, revealing them only to intimates who shared his opposition. He knew of the virulence of Virginia's reaction to the Quaker petitions, especially when Stuart told him that the mere talk of emancipation had alarmed planters and lowered the price of slaves, with many "sold for the merest trifle."[18] In replying to Stuart, Washington seemed to have no sympathy with the petitions, which he dismissed as doomed. On the morning of March 16 he met with Warner Mifflin, a leading Quaker abolitionist, and deemed the conversation important enough to record in his diary. Mifflin had decried the "injustice and impolicy of keeping these people in a state of slavery with declarations, however, that he did not wish for more than a gradual abolition, or to see any infraction of the Constitution to effect it." Washington listened attentively to Mifflin, then employed his famous gift of silence: "To these I replied that, as it was a matter which might come before me for official decision, I was not inclined to express any sentim[en]ts on the merits of the question before this should happen."[19]

The Quaker memorials ended up stillborn in Congress. In late March, under Madison's leadership, legislators quietly tabled the proposals by deciding they lacked jurisdiction to interfere with the slave trade prior to 1808. "The memorial of the Quakers (and a very mal-apropos one it was) has at length been put to sleep" and will not "awake before the year 1808," Washington informed Stuart.[20] His failure to use the presidency as a bully pulpit to air his opposition to slavery remains a blemish on his record. He continued to fall back on the self-serving fantasy that slavery would fade away in future years. The public had no idea how much he wrestled inwardly with the issue. His final comments to Stuart on the Quaker petitions are complacent in tone, designed to conceal his conflicted feelings: "The introductions of the [Quaker] memorial respecting slavery was, to be sure, not only an ill-judged piece of business, but occasioned a great waste of time."[21]

In April, shortly after his noble defeat over the slavery issue, Benjamin Franklin died. He was the only American whose stature remotely compared to that of Washington. During his final weeks Franklin had insisted that liberty should extend "without distinction of color to all descriptions of people."[22] In his will Franklin paid a typically ingenious compliment to Washington: "My fine crabtree walking stick, with a gold head curiously wrought in the form of the cap of liberty, I give to my friend, and the friend of mankind, General Washington. If it were a scepter, he has merited it and would become it."[23] After the Senate voted down a motion to wear mourning for Franklin, Jefferson turned to Washington for an appropriate tribute: "I proposed to General Washington that the executive department should wear mourning. He declined it because he said he would not know where to draw the line if he once began that ceremony."[24] One wonders whether, after the Quaker petitions, Washington had more than presidential etiquette in mind in the decision. The country was curiously devoid of public eulogies to Franklin; the National Assembly in Paris outdid Congress in its tributes, as the Count de Mirabeau paid eloquent homage to "the genius who liberated America and poured upon Europe torrents of light."[25]

Washington very nearly followed Franklin to his grave. On Sunday, April 4, he reported in his diary: "At home all day—unwell."[26] Two days later he sat for a second portrait by Edward Savage, commissioned by Vice President John Adams. Unlike the earlier Savage portrait done for Harvard, which showed a man of magisterial calm, this one presented a far more troubled man, the left side of his face dipped in shadow. With a double chin protruding over his jabot and a prominent bag drooping under his right eye, he has a deeply unsettled look. People gossiped that a mysterious fever had gripped the president. "I do not know the exact state of GW's health for a day or two last," Pennsylvania congressman George Clymer wrote on April 11, "but it is observed here with a great deal of anxiety that his general health seems to be declining. For some time past, he has been subject to a slow fever."[27] Georgia congressman Abraham Baldwin agreed. "Our great and good man has been unwell again this spring," he told a friend. "I never saw him more emaciated."[28] From April 20 through 24, in a concerted effort to rescue his health, Washington toured Long Island, traveling as far east as Brookhaven on the south shore before heading up to Setauket on the north shore, then circling back to Manhattan. Upon his return, everybody said Washington looked more robust; Robert Morris reassured his wife that the president had "regained his looks, his appetite, and his health."[29] The improvement did not last. By this point a severe influenza epidemic was proliferating in the city. James Madison had contracted it, and Washington imprudently asked him to stop by his house on April 27, which may have infected him with the influenza as well. On May 7 William Maclay informed Dr. Benjamin Rush that the president had "nearly lost his hearing" from the illness, which must have been a heavy blow for Washington.[30]

On Sunday, May 9, Washington noted: "Indisposed with a bad cold and at home all day writing letters on private business."[31] The next day he was confined to bed. By this time Madison, having rebounded from his illness, said that the president suffered from "peripneumony, united probably with the influenza," and others mentioned pleurisy as well.[32] This suggests that he suffered from a combination of labored breathing, sharp pains in his side, harsh coughing, and blood in his spittle. Whatever the original disease, it deepened into pneumonia. In addition to hearing loss, eyewitnesses mentioned that Washington's eyes were rheumy and that he seemed prematurely aged. He was far from alone in a city seized by widespread illness. By mid-May the influenza had exploded in such epidemic proportions that Richard Henry Lee described Manhattan as "a perfect hospital—few are well and many very sick."[33]

As fears mounted about whether the president would survive, three eminent doctors were consulted: Dr. Samuel Bard, Dr. John McKnight, and Dr. John Charlton. As Washington's condition worsened, they decided on May 12 to summon Dr. John Jones, a surgeon from Philadelphia, who had been the personal physician to Ben Franklin. So as not to alert the public to Washington's true condition, the presidential aides tried to sneak Dr. Jones in under conditions of extraordinary secrecy. "The doctor's prudence will suggest the propriety of setting out as privately as possible," Major William Jackson told Clement Biddle of Philadelphia. "Perhaps it may be well to assign a personal reason for visiting New York, or going into the country."[34]

The street in front of Washington's residence was again cleared of traffic and carpeted with straw to mute sounds. With such precautions, rumors inevitably circulated about Washington's perilous condition. "Called to see the president," William Maclay wrote on May 15. "Every eye full of tears. His life despaired of."[35] With Washington coughing up blood and running a high fever, Dr. McKnight hinted to Maclay that there was little hope of recovery and that death might be imminent. Beset by hiccups, Washington made strange gurgling noises that were interpreted as a death rattle. What one observer described as "a universal gloom" overspread a country long accustomed to Washington's steady presence.[36]

On May 16, against all expectations and after the team of physicians had pronounced the case hopeless, the president rallied and underwent a startling improvement. At four in the afternoon he broke into a tremendous sweat, his coughing abated, and he spoke more clearly than he had in days. In a tone of joy and mild disbelief, Jefferson told his daughter that "from a total despair, we are now in good hopes of him."[37] On May 18 the president's condition surfaced in a press that had preserved discreet silence. "The President of the United States has been exceedingly indisposed for several days past," the *New-York Journal* informed readers, "but we are rejoiced at the authentic information of his being much relieved the last evening."[38] For the next two weeks, although a convalescent Washington could not perform presidential duties, he was now clearly on the mend. In early June he assured Lafayette that he was well out of danger and had rebounded "except in point of strength."[39]

Throughout the ordeal, Martha Washington supervised the sickroom and behaved with stoic equanimity. To Mercy Otis Warren, she admitted that the tremendous display of public sympathy had been "very affecting" to her. Her self-possessed husband, she said, had gone through the crisis with typical composure: "He seemed less concerned himself as to the event than perhaps almost any other person in ye United States. Happily, he is now perfectly recovered."[40] From the time he was a young man, Washington had faced death with uncommon fortitude, and this time proved no exception. By May 20 his fever had ebbed, and two days later Richard Henry Lee found him sitting up in a chair. Helped by his naturally hardy nature, the president made rapid strides. "The President is again on his legs," Philip Schuyler reported the next day. "He was yesterday able to traverse his room a dozen times."[41] A couple of days later he was even out riding. On May 27 Jefferson declared an official end to the crisis when he stated that Washington was "well enough to resume business."[42] The country had narrowly averted catastrophe, for John Adams, whatever his merits, would never have been the unifying figure needed to launch the constitutional experiment. Still, Washington remained in a weakened state, so drained of energy that he did not resume his diary until June 24.

As in the crisis of Washington's infected thigh a year earlier, the federal government had been poorly prepared for this serious lapse in the president's health. With Tobias Lear out of town, Major William Jackson effectively ran the presidential office. No official procedure for deputizing someone during a presidential illness existed, and Washington may have been reluctant to grant precedence to any cabinet officer. As he lobbied for his financial program, the high-flying Hamilton functioned as de facto head of state. In later unpublished comments about this anxious time, Hamilton said that Jefferson viewed him then for the first time as "a formidable rival in the competition for the presidential chair at a future period." While others brooded about the president's fate, Hamilton alleged, the situation "only excited the ambitious ardor of the secretary [of state] to remove out of his way every dangerous opponent. That melancholy circumstance suggested to him the probability of an approaching vacancy in the presidential chair and that he would attract the public attention as the successor to it, were the more popular Secretary of the Treasury out of the way."[43] Hamilton offered no proof to back up his assertion, and Jefferson likely would have made the same claim about Hamilton. Before too long the mutual suspicions simmering between the two men would burst into open warfare.

The president having withstood two grave illnesses, the capital was rife with copious opinions as to how best to preserve his precious health. A chorus of friends and physicians alike urged him to dedicate more time to exercise and lessen the strain of public business. Even in mid-June Washington could not quite get rid of the remnants of his chest pains, coughing, and shortness of breath and acknowledged the dreadful toll that dinners, meetings, and receptions had taken on his constitution. "Within the last twelve months," he told David Stuart, "I have undergone more and severer sickness than thirty preceding years afflicted me with, put it altogether."[44] The next bout of illness, he predicted, would "put me to sleep with my fathers."[45] By nature a conscientious, hardworking man, Washington confessed to Lafayette that he could not stop doing all the things necessary "to accomplish whatever I have undertaken (though reluctantly) to the best of my abilities."[46]

Washington heeded the doctors' stark warning that he should get more outdoor activity. On June 6 he accompanied Jefferson and Hamilton on a fishing trip off Sandy Hook. It was a fine spring day, and the newspapers hoped the president felt reinvigorated by the sea air. "We are told he has had excellent sport," one paper commented, "having himself caught a great number of sea bass and blackfish."[47] After resuming his diary, Washington jotted down many instances of riding in his coach or on horseback as he tried to pry himself away from his sedentary life. For health reasons, Washington also contemplated the purchase of a farm outside Philadelphia, which never happened.

Washington's back-to-back illnesses in 1789 and 1790 contributed to the sudden aging of a man who had long been associated with graceful virility. The two episodes would have greatly deepened his sense that he was sacrificing his life for his country and that he would likely have little or no retirement beyond the presidency. Washington had grown more haggard during these medical emergencies. Fanny Bassett Washington wrote the following year, "The president looks better than I expected to see him, but still there be traces in his countenance of his two last severe illnesses, which I fear will never wear off."[48] The crises also left Martha Washington in a reflective, despondent mood. She told Mercy Otis Warren, "But for the ties of affection which attract me so strongly to my near connection and worthy friends, I should feel myself indeed much weaned from all enjoyments of this transitory life."[49]

Capital Matters

AFTER MOST OF THE STATES had ratified the Constitution by the summer of 1788, James Madison had broached to George Washington a topic that engaged both their emotional loyalties and their financial interests: the location of the future capital. Aware that New York and Philadelphia would emerge as serious candidates, Madison hoped the banks of the Potomac River might ultimately house the federal government. As flourishing population growth on the western frontier enhanced the prospects for a southern capital, Madison believed that time was on the South's side. Washington's red-hot enthusiasm for the Potomac had scarcely cooled, and he still embraced the river as the ideal portal to the interior and hence the optimal site for the capital. The Potomac was the natural "center of the union," he had explained to Arthur Young. "It is between the extremes of heat and cold . . . and must from its extensive course through a rich and populous country become in time the grand emporium of North America."[1]

Since it would exert far-reaching influence, the choice of venue for the capital was fraught with controversy. Most obviously, it would mean a commercial windfall for nearby property owners; Madison and Henry Lee scooped up land along the Potomac to profit from any future capital. The political leanings of the surrounding region would affect legislators isolated from constituents back home. Jefferson and other agrarians also wanted a capital remote from the noxious impact of large cities and northern manufacturing. Finally, many southern legislators preferred a southern city where they could transport their slaves without being harassed by abolitionists. So vexed was the capital question that Madison almost despaired of a satisfactory solution. "The business of the seat of government is become a labyrinth for which the votes printed furnish no clue," he lamented in June 1790.[2]

The deadlock over the issue coincided with a stalemate over Hamilton's plan to have the federal government assume state debts. Washington noted that the two debates had ensnared Congress in ceaseless rancor, telling David Stuart that June that "the questions of assumption, residence, and other matters have been agitated with warmth and intemperance, with prolixity and threats."[3] Washington's fantasy of nonpartisan civility in politics was being rapidly eroded by growing polarization along north-south lines. Still recuperating from illness, he found it easy to stay aloof from the debates on assumption and the capital, but he clearly supported Hamilton's objectives, echoing his treasury secretary's belief that the "cause in which the expenses of the war was incurred was a common cause" and should be borne by the federal government.[4] It was also universally known that he favored a Potomac capital. "It is in fact the interest of the President of the United States that pushes the Potomac," William Maclay protested in his diary. "He by means of Jefferson, Madison . . . and others urges this business."[5]

In early June 1790 the House enacted Hamilton's funding bill but omitted his contentious plan to assume state debt. Maclay, among others, spied a political agenda lodged deep in the proposal, which would give the federal government a "pretext for seizing every resource of government and subject of taxation in the Union."[6] Madison was enraged that states that had mostly paid their debts— Virginia, Maryland, and Georgia—would subsidize profligate states that had not. Complicating matters was the incipient feud between Hamilton and Jefferson. Now detecting signs of monarchy sprouting everywhere, Jefferson associated a funded debt with the British Empire and, despite his presence in the cabinet, secretly joined forces with Madison against Hamilton. He was chagrined by Hamilton's decision to reward speculators in government debt, whom he saw as "fraudulent purchasers of this paper . . . filched from the poor and ignorant."[7]

The twin debates over assumption and the capital grew so venomous that it seemed the Union might dissolve in acrimony. It was against this backdrop that, on June 19, Jefferson ran into Hamilton before Washington's residence on Broadway. Usually Hamilton cut a dapper figure, but Jefferson found him strangely transformed by the hubbub surrounding him. "His look was somber, haggard, and dejected . . . Even his dress uncouth and neglected," Jefferson wrote.[8] For half an hour the two men paced before Washington's door as Hamilton expatiated on the dangerous disunity in Congress, the urgent need for cabinet solidarity, and the malaise threatening the new government. The upshot was that, the next day, Jefferson hosted a dinner for Hamilton and Madison at his lodgings at 57 Maiden Lane. During this famous meal, in an apartment adorned with engravings of Washington, a grand deal was brokered. Jefferson and Madison agreed to aid passage of the assumption bill, while Hamilton promised to lobby the Pennsylvania delegation to endorse Philadelphia as the temporary capital and the Potomac as its final destination. For Hamilton, who favored New York as the capital, it was a bitter pill to swallow, but he viewed the assumption of state debt as the crux of federal power. Only belatedly did Jefferson, a states' rights advocate, realize his colossal strategic error, grumbling to Washington that he had been royally "duped by Hamilton" and saying that "of all the errors of my political life, this has occasioned me the deepest regret."[9] He believed that Hamilton, to consolidate federal power and promote a northern financial cabal, wanted to make the federal debt so gigantic that it would never be extinguished.

In July Congress approved the Residence Act, naming Philadelphia as the temporary capital for ten years, followed by a permanent move to a ten-mile-square federal district on the Potomac by December 1, 1800. There is no firm evidence that Washington was consulted about the dinner deal hatched by Hamilton, Jefferson, and Madison. Nevertheless everybody knew that he had large landholdings along the river, was involved in its improvement, and would benefit immensely from the decision. In his diary, Maclay fumed that Washington stood behind the dinner deal: "The President of the U.S. has (in my opinion) had great influence in this business."[10] He saw Washington as a tool manipulated by the dexterous Hamilton, saying that "the president has become in the hands of Hamilton the dishclout [dishcloth] of every dirty speculation, as his name goes to wipe away blame and silence all murmuring."[11]

The Residence Act had not selected the precise spot on the Potomac for the capital, merely specifying a sixty-five-mile stretch of the river and granting Washington the power to choose the site. He would officially supervise the federal district, appointing and overseeing three commissioners charged with surveying and constructing the new city, and he was to exert an incalculable influence on its development. In a proclamation that January that shocked nobody, he announced the choice of a site just north of Mount Vernon. There was muted grumbling about Washington's conflict of interest here. Long after Washington died, John Adams stated baldly that Washington had profited "from the federal city, by which he raised the value of his property and that of his family a thousand percent at an expense to the public of more than his whole fortune."[12] Washington was also accused of high-handed behavior in arrogating the right to pick the spot instead of yielding to his three commissioners. Maclay seemed overwrought: "I really am surprised at the conduct of the president . . . To take on him to fix the spot by his own authority, when he might have placed the three commissioners in the post of responsibility, was a thoughtless act."[13] The controversy shattered some magic spell that had spared Washington from criticism, and people no longer felt muzzled about challenging him directly.

Whatever his bias in choosing a southern capital, Washington still took to heart his position as president of all Americans. So long as Rhode Island had refused to ratify the Constitution, it had been ostracized as a renegade state, and Washington had boycotted it during his northern tour. As soon as the state joined the Union in May 1790, however, Washington was eager to remedy that omission. A few days after Congress adjourned on August 12, Washington set out for Rhode Island, accompanied by Jefferson and New York governor George Clinton, sailing out through Long Island Sound. The first stop was Newport, where a Jewish merchant and fellow Mason, Moses Seixas, greeted the president on behalf of Congregation Yeshuat Israel, assuring him that the Lord had "shielded your head in the day of battle" and protected him as "chief magistrate in these states."[14] As if seeking words of reassurance, Seixas noted that the Jewish congregation had formerly been deprived of "the invaluable rights of free citizens."[15] This elicited from Washington a letter to the Hebrew Congregation that ranks as his most beautifully enduring statement on religious toleration, showing that he had no notion of foisting a Christian state on the nation:

> All possess alike liberty of conscience and immunities of citizenship. It is now no more that toleration is spoken of, as if it was by the indulgence of one class of people that another enjoyed the exercise of their inherent natural rights. For happily the government of the United States, which gives to bigotry no sanction, to persecution no assistance, requires only that they who live under its protection should demean themselves as good citizens . . . May the children of the stock of Abraham, who dwell in this land, continue to merit and enjoy the goodwill of the other inhabitants.[16]

Three months earlier Washington had shown similarly affectionate respect for the Jews in writing to a congregation in Savannah, Georgia. With deft artistry, he identified both American Christians and ancient Jews as recipients of God's mercy in their days of bondage: "May the same wonder-working deity, who long since delivering the Hebrews from their Egyptian oppressors, planted them in the Promised Land—whose providential agency has lately been conspicuous in establishing these United States as an independent nation—still continue to water them with the dews of heaven."[17] As patriarch of the nation, Washington naturally fell into biblical phraseology that encompassed elevated language from both the Old and New Testaments.

The next day, having arrived in Providence in time for a private dinner, Washington was on the verge of turning in for the night when he was informed that students had lit up the windows of Rhode Island College (later Brown University) in his honor. As one host recalled of Washington's exceedingly courteous response, the students said they "would be highly flattered at the president's going to see it, which he politely agreed to do, though he never goes out at night and it then rained a little and was a disagreeable night. We now made a nocturnal procession to the college, which indeed was worth seeing, being very splendidly illuminated."[18] The next day was unseasonably raw and cold, but Washington still had bountiful energy to see the city. He walked for hours, toured the college, inspected a merchant ship in drydock, drank wine and punch, and sat patiently through numberless speeches before a town hall dinner.

On August 22 he returned to New York for what would prove a brief final interval for the temporary capital. Under the Residence Act, the government was set to transfer to Philadelphia by early December, yet the exodus had begun in earnest in midsummer once Congress concluded its work on August 12. Washington craved the tranquillity of Mount Vernon, where he could rest and recover fully from his recent illness, and decided to make an extended stay there before the transition to Philadelphia.

When he left New York on August 30, 1790, Washington again indulged the impossible daydream of avoiding any pageantry to mark his official farewell. At dawn he gathered his wife, two grandchildren, two aides, four servants, and four slaves for a last glimpse of the Broadway house, when he suddenly heard the strains of a band outside striking up a tune called "Washington's March." A glum Washington saw no surcease from the cloying adulation. Outside Governor Clinton, Chief Justice Jay, and a mass of excited citizens had shown up to tender their last respects and send him off on a barge, climaxed by a thirteen-gun salute from the Battery.

As the boat drifted off into the Hudson River, Washington stood erect in the stern, then swung around toward the Manhattan shore and waved his hat in farewell, provoking a responsive roar from the spectators. When the barge had floated halfway across the Hudson, he picked up the sprightly peal of trumpets from the Jersey shore at Paulus Hook (now Jersey City), where Governor Richard Howell and the cavalry waited to escort him on the first leg of his journey. As he traversed the route south from Newark to Trenton, across which a ragged Continental Army had retreated in defeat in 1776, Washington was cheered at every hamlet along the way.

When he reached Philadelphia, Washington beheld the new capital in the grip of unabashed Washington mania. Ascending his white charger, he trailed the cavalry as it sliced an opening through pedestrian-packed streets. At the City Tavern his burly, outgoing friend Robert Morris awaited him with an outstretched hand. The city of Philadelphia had rented Morris's house at 190 High Street (later Market Street) near the corner of Sixth as the new presidential mansion. Surrounded by stately brick walls that afforded privacy both to the building and to a well-shaded garden, the house was a substantial, four-story brick structure with tall, handsome windows. During his short stay Washington traipsed through its rooms and cast a discerning, but also critical, glance at its appointments. "It is, I believe, the best *single house* in the city," Washington told Tobias Lear, who lingered in Manhattan with Billy Lee. "Yet, without additions, it is inadequate to the *commodious* accommodation of my family."[19] Although Washington and his entourage headed toward Mount Vernon on September 6, the president, with his strong visual powers and grasp of detail, never stopped dwelling on the decoration of the house. Throughout the fall he peppered Tobias Lear with nine long letters, spelling out the changes he wanted, right down to the color of the curtains, once the Morrises had vacated the premises and relocated to another house down the block.

In corresponding with Lear, Washington was intent on turning the house into a showpiece for visiting dignitaries. On the first floor, which would have two reception rooms, he had the south wall demolished and installed bow windows to afford visitors a view of the clock tower atop Independence Hall. This room, with its curved windows, is thought by some historians to have been the prototype of the Oval Office that would later grace the White House. Lear tried frantically to ready the house for the Washingtons, carting in fifty-eight loads of new furniture. Because so many Philadelphia buildings were being renovated at once for the new government, a drastic labor shortage made it difficult to hire workers, even at extortionate wages. "House rent has risen here to an exorbitant pitch and many other things are following very fast," Lear complained.[20]

The return to Mount Vernon, instead of offering a respite, only reminded Washington of the parlous state of his personal finances. In July he had corresponded with Clement Biddle about buying a farm the latter owned outside Philadelphia, hoping to trade it for some properties he owned in western Pennsylvania. The president admitted he was flat broke. "I shall candidly declare that to pay money is out of the question with me—I have *none* and would not, if it was to be had, run in debt to borrow."[21]

Planning to bring a full complement of servants to Philadelphia, Washington scribbled detailed notes about their distribution in their sleeping quarters. Before returning north in late November, he also wanted to ensure that his slaves were suitably attired. Capable of paying microscopic attention to their clothing—his account books brim with notations for shirts, stockings, hats, ruffles, and other fancy articles he bought for his slaves—he advised Lear on the fashionable hats he wanted for Giles and Paris, his coachman and postilion, and for Hercules, whom he was bringing along as the new household chef. "Upon examining the caps of Giles and Paris," he wrote, "I find they (especially Paris's) are much worn and will be unfit to appear in with decency after the journey from hence is performed. I therefore request that you will have two handsome ones made, with fuller and richer tassels at top than the old ones have."[22] There is something sad about George Washington's decking out his slaves in this gaily elegant clothing as part of the presidential retinue.

The journey to Philadelphia left Washington in high dudgeon because of what he condemned as "the most infamous roads" and the chronic drunkenness of his coachman, Arthur Dunn, who was banished from the coach and consigned to the baggage wagon, which he twice overturned. When he arrived in Philadelphia, expecting to find a tidy residence, Washington was aghast at the incomplete state of the presidential mansion. Even the main dining room and his private study needed further work. The contrite Lear could only plead a dearth of workmen. As a presidential headquarters, the house left much to be desired, with Washington's public office on the third floor obligating visitors to ascend two steep flights to reach him. The chaos and clutter in the house could only have exasperated Washington, who had to deliver his annual message to Congress in a week. Even though he had emerged as a vocal critic of Hamilton's policies, Madison retained enough of the president's ear that he assisted in drafting the speech.

The new Congress convened in the State House on Chestnut Street that had hosted the Continental Congress in 1775 and witnessed the Declaration of Independence in 1776. To provide comfortable seating, the House of Representatives had ordered sixty-five armchairs, upholstered in black leather, while the Senate, not to be outdone, had twenty-seven seats richly done up in "red Morocco," all beautifully adorned with brass tacks.[23] On December 8, dressed in black velvet, Washington delivered his speech to Congress in such a soft, breathy voice that Vice President Adams had to repeat it to legislators after he left. Aside from bitter wrangling over Hamilton's program, this moment was a peaceful interlude in American politics. Commerce had flourished under Washington's aegis, and he offered an optimistic assessment of the country. At the beginning of his talk, he pointed to the appreciation of American debt as a direct consequence of Hamilton's program: "The progress of public credit is witnessed by a considerable rise of American stock abroad as well as at home."[24] Government paper had tripled in value since the new government started. At the same time, Washington reacted to charges that Hamilton favored perpetual government debt and invited opposing legislators to reduce it by selling western lands. The way Washington defended his controversial treasury secretary, while subtly leaving the door ajar to a modification of his programs, was a fine example of his finesse in managing to be both forceful and conciliatory at once.

When the House asked Hamilton that December for further measures to strengthen public credit, he proposed an excise tax on whiskey and other domestically distilled spirits. For many western communities, this was a radical and incendiary measure. Not only did many farmers have an unquenchable thirst for homemade brew, but they often found it economical to convert grain into whiskey and sell it in this portable form. As with his program to assume state debt, Hamilton admitted to Washington that the whiskey tax was a way to strengthen the federal government by laying "hold of so valuable a resource of revenue before it was generally preoccupied by the state governments."[25]

The excise tax kindled fierce debate in Congress as well as widespread doubt that it could be enforced in western communities that had flouted previous efforts to tax their moonshine. Anticipating resistance, Hamilton drew up a plan for a small army of inspectors and tax collectors, breeding fears of a vast new bureaucracy applying draconian measures. Among the predictable skeptics was William Maclay. On the day the excise tax passed the Senate, he scoffed that it would be unenforceable in the rambunctious precincts of western Pennsylvania. "War and bloodshed is the most likely consequence of all this," he predicted accurately. "Congress may go home. Mr. Hamilton is all powerful and fails in nothing which he attempts."[26] While bracing for a probable backlash against the tax, Hamilton maintained that the government needed more revenues and insisted that opponents would deem other possible taxes, such as one on land, still more odious. Washington and Hamilton had the thankless task of implementing the first tax systems in a country with a deeply ingrained suspicion of all taxes.

BEFORE THE CAPITAL MOVED to Philadelphia, Washington had no trouble incorporating his suite of seven slaves into the presidential household. Martha also traveled about in a coach with a personal escort of slaves, as Colonel Thomas Rodney observed when he went riding in Manhattan with her and Polly Lear: "Just before them [were] a mulatto girl behind the carriage and a Negro manservant on horseback behind."[27] Washington must have sensed that the government's switch to Philadelphia would complicate matters with his slaves, for Pennsylvania had been the first state to undertake the gradual abolition of slavery, in 1780. Philadelphia, in particular, had a large community of free blacks and a robust abolitionist movement. In bringing his slaves north, Washington violated his long-standing policy of not breaking up slave families. In late October, when Tobias Lear described how the slaves would be housed in sleeping quarters in Philadelphia, he admitted as much: "None of the men will have their wives in the family."[28] It was decided to lodge some slaves, including Billy Lee, in the four garret rooms; some in the former smokehouse; and some in an outlying building called the Servants Hall. The composition of Washington's team of slaves also underwent significant changes. In

New York he had chafed at the tasteless cooking and unsanitary habits of his cook, Rachel Lewis. As he contemplated the move to Philadelphia, Washington decided to fire her, informing Lear that "the dirty figures of Mrs. Lewis and her daughter will not be a pleasant sight in view ... of the principal entertaining rooms in our new habitation."[29]

Instead, Washington brought his favorite chef from Mount Vernon, the able Hercules, also known as Uncle Harkless, who teamed up with Samuel Fraunces to keep an immaculately clean, bustling kitchen. Handsome and muscular, Hercules was a dandyish figure who moved about Philadelphia with considerable freedom, attending theater and other entertainments. By dint of talent and hard work, he forced Washington to treat him as more than just a slave and got permission to sell scraps from the presidential kitchen, pocketing the proceeds. He also got the president to bring his adolescent son Richmond to Philadelphia to serve as his scullion. Washington seemed miffed by the request, confiding sarcastically to Lear that the idle boy hadn't gotten the appointment "from his appearance or merits," but he obviously felt that he could not turn Hercules down.[30] In much the same way, Washington sometimes obliged Billy Lee against his better judgment. Left behind at Mount Vernon was Richmond's mother, a seamstress known as Lame Alice.

Also setting out for Philadelphia in the fall of 1790 was the adolescent slave Christopher Sheels, who would eventually replace Billy Lee as Washington's body servant. A third-generation Mount Vernon slave, the fifteen-year-old Sheels was separated from his mother, Alice, a spinner, and his grandmother Doll, a cook. The mulatto slave Austin, separated from his wife at Mount Vernon, arrived in Philadelphia by stagecoach along with Hercules. Martha also brought along her two dower slaves, Moll and the teenage Ona Judge, for her personal entourage. As the person who dressed Martha's hair and laid out her clothes, Ona Judge held a special place in the presidential household.

In early April 1791 Attorney General Edmund Randolph delivered a startling piece of news to the Washingtons. Under the 1780 Pennsylvania statute, any adult slaves resident in the state for six consecutive months were automatically free. Three of Randolph's own slaves had served notice that they planned to claim their freedom. Bizarrely, the attorney general of the United States urged the president and first lady to evade this local law. Coaching them how to do so, he noted that once slaves were taken out of Pennsylvania and then brought back, the clock was reset, and another six months needed to elapse before they could demand their freedom. At first Washington imagined, wrongly, that federal officials in the capital were exempt from the law. Still, he fretted to Tobias Lear that people in "the practice of *enticing* slaves" might not make such fine distinctions.[31] With paternalistic certitude, he doubted that, even if any of his slaves opted for freedom, they would be "benefitted by the change, yet the idea of freedom might be too great a temptation for them to resist."[32] Washington was especially alarmed about this prospect, since all of his slaves in Philadelphia, except Hercules and Paris, were dower slaves, meaning that Washington would have to reimburse the Custis estate if they fled his household.

Not taking any chances, Washington decided to shuttle his slaves back to Mount Vernon for brief stays before their six-month time limits expired. As minors, Christopher Sheels, Richmond, and Ona Judge were all debarred from seeking their freedom. To keep the adult slaves in bondage, Washington resorted to various ruses so they would not know why they were being sent home temporarily. As he said bluntly, "I wish to have it accomplished under pretext that may deceive both them [i.e., the slaves] and the public."[33] This was a rare instance of George Washington scheming, and Martha Washington and Tobias Lear connived right along with him. In April Martha sent Austin back to Mount Vernon under the pretext of honoring a promise that he could return periodically to see his wife. In writing to Fanny about the visit, Martha showed how coolly she could lie, saying that Austin's stay at Mount Vernon "will be short, indeed. I could but illy spare him at this time, but to fulfill my promise to his wife."[34] That spring, when Martha took a short excursion to Trenton, she deliberately took two slaves across state lines. In a similarly duplicitous vein, Washington advised her to return to Mount Vernon in May, then summon Hercules home to cook for her. So top secret were these machinations that Washington advised Tobias Lear, "I request that these sentiments and this advice may be known to none but *yourself & Mrs. Washington*."[35]

Such devious tactics ran counter to Washington's professed abhorrence of slavery, not to mention his storied honesty. Even more startling was the acquiescence of Tobias Lear, the young idealist who had balked at working for Washington because the latter owned slaves. In the midst of corresponding with Washington over foiling the Pennsylvania law, Lear suddenly remembered that he and Washington were supposed to be long-term opponents of slavery, and he wrote guiltily to the president: "You will permit me now, Sir . . . to declare that no consideration should induce me to take these steps to prolong the slavery of a human being had I not the fullest confidence that they will, at some future period, be liberated and the strongest conviction that their situation with you is far preferable to what they would probably obtain in a state of freedom."[36] This strange declaration shows that Washington had already told a few confidants of his intention to free his slaves someday, while saying that, in the interim, the slaves were somehow better off than if they were emancipated.

Washington and Lear wondered whether the slaves knew of the Pennsylvania law that lay behind these subterfuges. They were especially curious about Hercules, who had been told he would be sent by stagecoach to Mount Vernon in June. Since he would arrive a little ahead of the president, Tobias Lear informed him that "being at home before [Washington's] arrival, he will have it in his power to see his friends."[37] When somebody in the presidential household evidently tipped off Hercules to the true reason for his return, he was outraged, but not for the obvious reason. As Lear wrote privately to Washington, Hercules "was mortified to the last degree to think that a suspicion could be entertained of his fidelity or attachment to you. And so much did the poor fellow's feelings appear to be touched that it left no doubt of his sincerity."[38] As we shall see, Hercules was an extremely shrewd man who knew how to feign loyalty and play his master to perfection. To reaffirm her faith in Hercules, Martha Washington told him that he could stay in Philadelphia past the six-month expiration point before returning to Virginia. Hercules took her up on the offer, stayed past the deadline, then dutifully returned to Mount Vernon. Perhaps to make the return more tolerable, Tobias Lear bought Hercules two new shirts for the trip.

All this collusion occurred against a backdrop of unusual turmoil on the slavery issue. Even as Washington and Lear conspired to keep slaves in bondage, Lafayette rose in the National Assembly and demanded the extension of full civil rights to free blacks in the French colonies. In August 1791, inspired by the French Revolution, slaves in the French colony of St. Domingue (later Haiti) began a bloody rebellion that raged for a dozen years. Many slave owners fled to American seaboard cities, where they stoked dread among American masters that their slaves, too, would stage a bloody insurrection. In 1792 the House of Commons in London enacted its first ban on the slave trade, further fueling fears among slave owners that abolitionism might spread.

Faced with such ferment, Washington struggled to find a stand on slavery that reconciled his economic interests with his private principles. As president, he insisted that the British compensate Americans for slaves spirited away during the Revolution. Politically, his weakest backing lay in the southern states, which were alarmed by Hamilton's financial system, and this disaffection made it difficult, if not impossible, for him to take a courageous public stand against slavery. All the while he remained the symbol of American liberty, so that abolitionists yearned to claim his aegis for their cause. One antislavery society was named "The Washington Society for the Relief of Free Negroes, and Others, Unlawfully Held in Bondage."[39] The same George and Martha Washington who circumvented the Pennsylvania law also donated money in May 1792 to a slave who approached them with a list of "respectable" people assisting him to obtain his freedom.[40] The same George Washington reacted with dismay when the South Carolina legislature refused to renew a two-year ban, enacted in 1791, on importing slaves. The president, of course, had been pleased two years earlier when Congress buried the Quaker proposal for banning the slave trade.

Washington's moral confusion over slavery was also apparent in his directives to stewards at Mount Vernon. Despite the enormous demands of the presidency, he continued to exercise close scrutiny of his overseers through elaborate weekly letters. Even as his mind was consumed with affairs of state, he forgot nothing about Mount Vernon. After an unusually large number of slaves died during the winter of 1790–91, possibly from influenza, Washington wrote fervently to his estate manager, Anthony Whitting, about the timely care of sick slaves. Saying the subject was "foremost in my thoughts," he instructed Whitting to "be particularly attentive to my Negroes in their sickness and to order every overseer *positively* to be so likewise."[41] Washington saw himself as a benevolent master who deplored cruelties practiced elsewhere. To Arthur Young, he made the revealing (if questionable) point that farmers who had only two or three slaves lived not much differently from their slaves. He went on to say that "far otherwise is the case with those who are owned in great numbers by the wealthy, who are not always as kind . . . as they ought to be."[42]

Still, Washington remained a tough master. Slavery depended on exerting a sizable degree of terror to cow slaves into submission. Before the war Washington had shipped two difficult slaves to the West Indies, where life expectancy was short in the tropical climate. In March 1793, when Whitting told Washington about a refractory slave named Ben, Washington replied that, if he persisted in his misbehavior, Whitting should warn Ben that "I will ship him off as I did Waggoner Jack for the West Indies, where he will have no opportunity to play such pranks."[43] While Washington ordinarily did not allow slaves to be whipped, he sometimes condoned it if all else failed. Such was the case in January 1793 with a slave named Charlotte, whom Martha had found "indolent" and "idle."[44] "Your treatment of Charlotte was very proper," Washington advised Whitting, "and if she, or any other of the servants, will not do their duty by fair means or are impertinent, correction (as the only alternative) must be administered."[45] It is unnerving to find the president of the United States writing such cold-blooded sentences.

In the army, in his cabinet, and on his plantation, Washington demanded high performance and had little patience with sluggards and loafers. But in the army and the presidency, Washington fought in a noble cause, whereas that same diligence was repugnant when applied to the loathsome system of slavery. The president never lightened up on his tough demands. "Keep everyone in their places and to their duty," he lectured Whitting, warning that slaves tended to slack off and test overseers "to see how far they durst go."[46] If slaves were crippled, he still demanded their participation. Of his slave Doll, who was apparently lame, he told Whitting that she "must be taught to knit and *made* to do a sufficient day's work of it. Otherwise, (if suffered to be idle) many more will walk in her steps. Lame Peter, if nobody else will, must teach her and she must be brought to the house for that purpose."[47] When Billy Lee returned to Mount Vernon, Washington assigned him to be the overseer of the house slaves. At the same time he made clear to Whitting that those slaves must "be kept *steadily* to work at that place under Will, or some other, if he cannot keep them to their business."[48] When two slaves died, Washington tossed off this heartless remark: "The death of Paris is a loss, that of Jupiter the reverse."[49] And when grooming a young slave named Cyrus as a house servant, Washington directed his estate manager to take "a strong horn comb and direct [Cyrus] to keep his head well combed that the hair or wool may grow long."[50]

Washington felt beleaguered by his slaves, who never delivered the crisp efficiency he expected. During his presidency he ordered a time-and-motion study of the productivity of Mount Vernon's female slaves while they sewed. Not surprisingly, he found that the slaves produced nine shirts weekly when Martha was there but only six when she was gone. Only a measure of coercion could force slaves to produce anything efficiently, since they had no economic incentive to do so. "There are few Negroes who will work unless there be a constant eye on them," Washington warned one overseer, and he believed that he could never slacken pressure if the slaves were to produce a decent return on his investment.[51] Unable to curb rampant thievery at Mount Vernon, Washington was convinced that slaves were stealing him blind. He continued to chastise overseers for "frolicking at the expense of my business," when they should have spent more time "watching the barns, visiting the negro quarters at unexpected hours, waylaying the roads, or contriving some device by which the receivers of stolen goods might be entrapped."[52] At the same time, Washington ordered his overseers to feed the slaves well, since he didn't wish to "lie under the imputation of starving my negroes and thereby driving them to the necessity of thieving to supply the deficiency."[53] George Washington desperately wanted to think well of himself and believed he was merciful toward the slaves even as the inherent cruelty of the system repeatedly forced him into behavior that questioned that belief.

Southern Exposure

NOT THE LEAST OF WASHINGTON'S TROUBLES in relocating to Philadelphia was that he left behind in New York a consequential figure in his life, his dentist John Greenwood, who had replaced his earlier friend and dentist, Jean-Pierre Le Mayeur. By the time he was sworn in as president, Washington was down to a single tooth, a lonely lower left bicuspid, which bore the entire brunt of a complete set of dentures. These large, ungainly contraptions forced Washington's lower lip to thrust so far forward that George Washington Parke Custis called it his outstanding facial feature in the 1790s. Tooth decay was, of course, a universal malady in the eighteenth century. Even Martha Washington, who had once boasted a beautiful set of teeth, had dentures by her husband's second term, if not before, and constantly badgered her grandchildren to use toothbrushes and cleansing powders. George's problems, however, were so severe to as to be incapacitating and affected his life in numberless ways.

A miniature portrait of John Greenwood shows an elegantly clad man in a scarlet velvet coat and white jabot, his graying hair combed straight back from a broad forehead. Having fought in the Revolutionary War and studied dentistry with Paul Revere, he had an excellent patriotic pedigree and crafted several sets of dentures for President Washington. The dentures that Greenwood fashioned during Washington's first year as president used natural teeth, inserted into a framework of hippopotamus ivory and anchored on Washington's one surviving tooth. Some dental historians have argued that these dentures were forged from walrus or elephant ivory; the one thing they were *not* made from is the wood so powerfully entrenched in popular mythology. That historical error arose from the gradual staining of hairline fractures in the ivory that made it resemble a wood grain. Curved gold springs in the back of the mouth attached the upper and lower dentures. As mentioned earlier, these springs made public speaking a nightmare, especially when Washington was enunciating sibilant sounds. The dentures also limited him to a diet of soft foods, chewed carefully with the front teeth, and would certainly have limited his outbursts of unrestrained laughter at the dinner table.

With their wiring, pins, and rough edges, such dentures rubbed painfully against the gums, forcing dentists to prescribe soothing ointments or opiate-based powders to alleviate discomfort. With or without the dentures, Washington had to endure constant misery. He spent Sunday, January 17, 1790, at home in excruciating tooth pain, writing in his diary the next day, "Still indisposed with an aching tooth and swelled and inflamed gum."[1] Later in the year Tobias Lear bought laudanum for Washington's household account, which was likely used to relieve the tortured presidential mouth. Washington could also have derived opiates from poppies grown at Mount Vernon.

One of Greenwood's attractions for Washington must have been his steadfast discretion, for Washington demanded absolute secrecy and could not afford a blabbermouth dentist. After he moved to Philadelphia, he and Greenwood swapped letters in cloak-and-dagger style; Washington entrusted dental letters to secret intermediaries, afraid to commit them to the mails. Writing to Greenwood in February 1791 about some needed adjustments of his dentures, Washington maintained the tone of hugger-mugger. "Your letter of the 6th and the box which accompanied it came safe to hand," he wrote enigmatically. "The contents of the latter were perfectly agreeable to me and will . . . answer the end proposed very well."[2] Greenwood confessed to Washington that there were limits to what he could accomplish via long distance, noting that "it is difficult to do these things without being on the spot," and he promised to travel to Philadelphia to make needed alterations.[3]

During his two terms Washington chomped his way through several pairs of dentures, and his letters to Greenwood explain why they so often wore out. Bars holding the teeth together were either too wide on the side or too long in the front, leading Washington to complain that they "bulge my lips out in such a manner as to make them appear considerably swelled."[4] To relieve this discomfort, he often filed down the dentures but ended up loosening the teeth in the process. So embarrassed was he by the way the dentures distorted his facial appearance that he pleaded with Greenwood to refrain from anything that "will in the *least* degree force the lips out more than [they] *now* do, as it does this too much already."[5] In the portrait of Washington done by Christian Güllager in 1789, Washington's lower lip juts out rather grotesquely. Apparently the president undertook some amateur dentistry of his own, telling Greenwood to send a foot of spiral spring and two feet of gold wire that he could shape himself.

Washington must have been very fond of Greenwood, for when his last tooth was pulled in 1796, he allowed Greenwood to retain this valuable souvenir, which the dentist inserted into a little glass locket on his watch fob. Without this tooth to serve as an anchor, keeping new dentures in place became an ordeal. Washington never overcame his dental tribulations and as late as December 1798 still protested that his new set "shoots beyond the gums" and "forces the lip out just under the nose."[6] Usually tightfisted, he gave Greenwood carte blanche to spend whatever it took to solve the problem. "I am willing and ready to pay whatever you may charge me," he wrote in some despair.[7]

If Washington was self-conscious about smiling in later years, it may also have been because his dentures grew discolored. When he sent Greenwood a pair of dentures for repair in December 1798, the dentist noted that they had turned "very black," either because Washington had soaked them in port wine or because he drank too much of it. Greenwood gave Washington a terse lesson in denture care: "I advise you to either take them out after dinner and put them in clean water and put in another set or clean them with a brush and some chalk scraped fine."[8] For someone who took inordinate pride in his appearance, the highly visible dentures must have been mortifying, especially since public speaking and socializing were constant, obligatory duties for a president.

AT THE TIME Philadelphia became the temporary capital, it ranked, with 45,000 inhabitants, as America's largest city, overshadowing New York and Boston in size and sophistication. Its spacious brick abodes and broad thoroughfares, illumined by streetlamps at night, gave the city an orderly air, matched by a rich cultural life of theaters and newspapers. Among its intellectual ornaments were the American Philosophical Society and the Library Company, both founded under the aegis of Ben Franklin. Having profited from wartime trade, the town's wealthy merchants set the social tone—one French visitor said, "The rich alone take precedence over the common people"—and much of its political life centered on their brilliant affairs.[9] The social demands placed on George and Martha Washington grew apace as rounds of extravagant parties enlivened the new capital. One resident stood amazed at the sheer number of sumptuous gatherings. "You have never seen anything like the frenzy which has seized upon the inhabitants here," he informed a friend. "They have been half mad ever since the city became the seat of government."[10] Notwithstanding the city's Quaker heritage, its social life was quite racy and luxurious, with heavy gambling at many parties. The straitlaced Abigail Adams was scandalized by the daringly low-cut dresses exhibited by women at soirées: "The style of dress . . . is really an outrage upon all decency . . . Most [ladies] wear their clothes scant upon the body and too full upon the bosom for my fancy."[11] Even French émigré aristocrats were struck by all the finery, one marveling that the "women of Philadelphia wore hats and caps almost as varied as those of Paris and bestowed immense expense in dressing their heads."[12]

Martha Washington felt emancipated by Philadelphia's freer ways. In New York she had been inhibited by protocol, whereas in the new capital she was emboldened to pay visits on friends. She kept up her Friday-evening receptions, which came to be ridiculed as the Republican Court, even though Martha, the most unaffected of first ladies, frequently prepared tea and coffee for visitors herself. Of one crowded Friday reception, Abigail Adams wrote, "The room became full before I left it, and the circle very brilliant," and she commented on the "constellation of beauties" present.[13] She judged the president more unbuttoned in this new environment. "On Thursday last, I dined with the president in company with the ministers and ladies of the court," she reported to her daughter. "He was more than usually social . . . He asked affectionately after you and the children and at table picked the sugarplums from a cake and requested me to take them for Master John."[14]

Washington regained the vigor lost during his two illnesses and strode about town with Tobias Lear and William Jackson tagging behind him. He often presented a romantic image; the corner of his blue cape was flung back over his shoulder to reveal a scarlet lining, giving him the gallant bearing of a stage character. One Philadelphian remembered watching the Washingtons emerge from their High Street doorway and enter their majestic coach, hitched to a team of six bay horses. When the mansion door opened, Washington stepped out "in a suit of dark silk velvet of the old cut, silver or steel hilted small sword at left side, hair full powdered, black silk hose and bag, accompanied by Lady Washington, also in full dress, [who] appeared standing upon the marble steps—presenting her his hand, he led her down to the coach with that ease and grace peculiar to him in everything and . . . with the attentive assiduity of an ardent, youthful lover."[15]

For all the loose talk of a Republican Court, those who had actually haunted the royal courts of Europe were utterly disarmed by the quaint simplicity of the executive residence. When the French writer Chateaubriand stopped in Philadelphia, he was startled by the absence of pretension, and his description is a salutary corrective to contemporary critics who saw Washington as aping European royalty:

> A small house, just like the adjacent houses, was the palace of the President of the United States; no guard, not even a footman. I knocked; a young maid servant opened the door. I asked her whether the general was at home; she answered that he was. I added that I had a letter for him. The girl asked for my name; it is not an easy one to pronounce in English and she could not repeat it. She then said gently: "Walk

in, Sir. *Entrez, Monsieur,*" and she walked ahead of me through one of these narrow
passageways which form the vestibule of English houses. Finally she showed me into
a parlor and bade me wait for the general.[16]

One wonders whether Chateaubriand also noticed that a hairdressing shop stood
next door to the presidential "palace."

The president hobnobbed with the city's commercial elite, especially the two
wealthy couples he had befriended during earlier stays in Philadelphia: William and
Anne Willing Bingham and Samuel and Elizabeth Willing Powel. Washington was
chivalrous with both wives. When he sent Anne Bingham a watercolor version of
the portrait of him by the Marquise de Bréhan, he appended this stylish note: "In
presenting the enclosed (with compliments to Mrs. Bingham), the President fulfills
a promise. Not for the representation—not for the value—but as the production of a
fair hand, the offering is made and the acceptan[ce] of it requested."[17] With Elizabeth
Powel, Washington continued to permit himself social liberties that he took with no
other woman. In an age when subtle social signals counted a great deal, Washington
boldly signed his letters to her, "With the greatest respect and affection"—extremely
unusual for Washington.[18] She, in turn, addressed her letters to "My dear Sir" and
signed them, "Your sincere affectionate friend."[19] We know from Washington's letters
that he met with Elizabeth Powel many times but often failed to note their meetings
in his diaries. At the very least he was beguiled by this social and political confidante.
On the other hand, Powel was also a good friend of Martha, and George consulted
her before buying gifts for his wife. In a sign that the Washingtons were slightly awed
by this rich bluestocking, George would draft letters for Martha to send to Eliza
Powel, and Martha would then rewrite them in her own hand.

On Sundays the president attended church and afterward was enveloped by
throngs of admirers. One observer recalled him leaving Old Christ Church, wrapped
in his blue cloak, with organ music bellowing behind him. Instead of touching
people, he nodded to the hushed crowd that instinctively parted before him, so that
there was something vaguely ecclesiastical about his presence: "His noble height
and commanding air . . . his patient demeanor in the crowd . . . his gentle bend-
ings of the neck, to the right and to the left, parentally, and expressive of delighted
feelings on his part; these, with the appearance of the awed and charmed and silent
crowd of spectators, gently falling back on each side, as he approached, unequivocally announced to the gazing stranger . . . *behold the man!*"[20]

Even as president, Washington's interests were wider, his curiosity more far-
ranging, than is commonly supposed. Confident in his own taste, he personally
selected the paintings that adorned the presidential mansion—"fancy pieces of my
own choosing," he called them.[21] He had an occasional sense of fun that belied his

grave air. In April 1793 he led a party of eight to see the first American circus, staged by an English equestrian acrobat, John Bill Ricketts, who had set up a Philadelphia riding school. And he remained a keen theatergoer, absorbing a steady diet of history plays, farces, and satires. He patronized the South Street Theater so frequently that he had his own private box, complete with cushioned seats and plush red drapery. With a soldier stationed at each stage door and four distributed in the gallery, Washington probably enjoyed better security than did Lincoln the night of his assassination at Ford's Theater.

However bowed down by presidential tasks, Washington always found time for family and for the many waifs and wards who sheltered under his roof. Harriot Washington, the daughter of his deceased brother Samuel, had lived at Mount Vernon since 1785. A wayward girl, slovenly and lazy, she clashed with Fanny Bassett Washington. Nonetheless, Washington still hoped to make a lady out of Harriot and in the fall of 1790 tried to install her at a proper boarding school in Philadelphia. Harriot stayed at Mount Vernon until 1792, when she moved to Fredericksburg and lived with Washington's sister, Betty, before marrying Andrew Parks in 1795. When Harriot committed the faux pas of not consulting Washington about the marriage, the paterfamilias was miffed. When he belatedly congratulated her, he hinted that she would have to subdue her headstrong nature and that success in marriage would depend upon her subordinating her views to her husband's.

In the fall of 1790 he brought to Philadelphia Harriot's two unruly brothers, George Steptoe and Lawrence Augustine, who entered the College of Philadelphia (afterward the University of Pennsylvania). The status-conscious president wrote the boys long-winded letters about being clean and presentable and shying away from bad company—suggesting that his ungovernable nephews did neither. Although he footed the bill for their education, he did not invite them to stay in the presidential mansion, either from a shortage of space or because the mischievous boys lacked proper decorum. In writing to Betty, he revealed how financially strapped he felt in caring for Samuel's three children: "I shall continue to do for [Harriot] what I have already done for seven years past and that is to furnish her with such reasonable and proper necessaries as she may stand in need of, notwithstanding I have had both her brothers upon my hands, and I have been obliged to pay several hundred pounds out of my own pocket for their boards, schooling, clothing etc."[22] Washington's family munificence was all the more commendable in view of his financial difficulties. The two brothers must have matured in Philadelphia and outgrown their youthful indiscretions, for Washington later rewarded them handsomely in his will.

.   .   .

On December 14, 1790, Alexander Hamilton issued another electrifying state paper, this time on the need to charter the first central bank in American history. Capitalized at $10 million, the Bank of the United States would blend public and private ownership; the government would take a 20 percent stake and private investors the remaining 80 percent. This versatile institution would lend money to the government, issue notes that could serve as a national currency, and act as a repository for tax payments. The bank was patterned after the Bank of England—Hamilton kept its charter on his desk as he wrote—and coming on the heels of his report on public credit and excise taxes, it unsettled opponents with the insidious specter of a British-style executive branch.

Five weeks later the bank bill passed the Senate with deceptive ease, prompting Madison to marshal stiff opposition in the House. Once again the southern states feared that Hamilton's system would consolidate northern financial hegemony over agrarian southern interests. Madison responded boldly to the views of his dismayed constituents. Where he had articulated a broad view of federal power as coauthor of *The Federalist,* he now balked at what he deemed a dangerous extension of that power. In the Constitution he could find no specific license for a central bank—in his evocative phrase, the bank bill "was condemned by the silence of the Constitution."[23] In defiance of his determined efforts, the bill passed the House on February 8 by a margin of 39 to 20. In an omen of future strife, the vote again divided sharply along geographic lines: the northern states were almost solidly for the bank, and the southern states were largely lined up against it. To skittish southerners, the treasury secretary seemed triumphant and unstoppable in his quest for centralized power, rolling out programs in rapid succession, each one meshing with the next in a seamless system of interlocking parts.

Madison urged Washington, who was still undecided on the measure, to snuff out the bank with a veto. Washington's slow, deliberate handling of this matter proved a model of the way he resolved complex disputes. First he impartially canvassed his cabinet officers to assemble the widest spectrum of opinion, making sure that, whatever he did, he could answer all critics. He kept his cabinet in suspense, forcing them to vie for his approval through the strength of their arguments. At the same time, one senses that he already tilted toward signing the bill, for he subtly stacked the deck in favor of approval by first asking Edmund Randolph and Thomas Jefferson for their views, which he then relayed to Hamilton. This gave Hamilton an edge, since he could see his predecessors' objections and register the last word on the subject.

Attorney General Randolph submitted an unimpressive memorandum that branded the bank as unconstitutional. Succinct but more trenchant was Jefferson's brief memorandum arguing for "strict construction" of the Constitution. For Jefferson, state-sponsored monopolies and central banks were oppressive tools of executive power associated with British royalty. He scorned Hamilton's bank as the symbol of a Yankee world of commerce that would subvert his fond vision of America as a rural Eden. In the last analysis, the debate hinged on the interpretation of three words in Article I, Section 8, of the Constitution—that Congress had all powers "necessary and proper" to carry into law its enumerated responsibilities. Taking a cramped view of this clause, Jefferson contended that it limited Congress to legislation that was strictly *necessary* to its assigned duties, not merely convenient or useful. Though not queried for an opinion, John Adams was also steaming about the bank. "This system of banks begotten, hatched, and brooded by . . . Hamilton and Washington, I have always considered as a system of national injustice," he spluttered years later, calling it a "sacrifice of public and private interest to a few aristocratical friends and favorites."[24]

Though he had sat through every session of the Constitutional Convention, Washington did not pretend to any expertise in constitutional nuances—he once wrote that he had "had as little to do with lawyers as any man of my age"—and engaged in much hand-wringing over the bank bill.[25] He would be forced to issue a black-and-white opinion that would alienate some, gratify others, and irrevocably shape the future government. He called in Madison, supremely well versed in the Constitution, for a series of quiet, confidential talks. "The constitutionality of the national bank was a question on which his mind was greatly perplexed," Madison would recall, noting that Washington was already biased in favor of a national bank and "a liberal construction of the national powers."[26] On the other hand, Washington was shaken by the uncompromising verdicts from Randolph and Jefferson and asked Madison, as a precaution, to draft a veto message for the bank bill.

When Washington turned to Hamilton, he made plain that, unless he could vanquish the arguments of Randolph and Jefferson, he planned to veto the bank bill, telling him that he wished to "be fully possessed of the arguments *for* and *against* the measure before I express any opinion of my own."[27] By this point Washington knew the vigor of Hamilton's mind and his extraordinary knack for legal argument. In little more than a week, Hamilton, in a superhuman burst of energy, produced more than thirteen thousand words that buried his opponents beneath an avalanche of arguments. His exegesis of the "necessary and proper" clause not only made way for a central bank but would enable the federal government to respond to emergencies throughout American history. Hamilton interpreted the "necessary and proper" clause to mean that "every power vested in a government is in its nature sovereign and includes, by force of the term, a right to employ all the means requisite and fairly applicable to the ends of such power."[28] In other words, the Constitution gave the federal government not only the powers explicitly enumerated but also a series of unstated or "implied powers" indispensable to attain those ends.

Washington had ten days to sign or veto the bank bill and stalled in making up his mind. Perhaps by design, Hamilton delivered, and Washington accepted, the argument in favor of the bill right before that deadline expired, leaving no time for an appeal inside the cabinet. When Washington signed the bill on February 25, 1791, it was a courageous act, for he defied the legal acumen of Madison, Jefferson, and Randolph. Unlike his fellow planters, who tended to regard banks and stock exchanges as sinister devices, Washington grasped the need for these instruments of modern finance. It was also a decisive moment legally for Washington, who had felt more bound than Hamilton by the literal words of the Constitution. With this stroke, he endorsed an expansive view of the presidency and made the Constitution a living, open-ended document. The importance of his decision is hard to over- state, for had Washington rigidly adhered to the letter of the Constitution, the fed- eral government might have been stillborn. Chief Justice John Marshall later seized upon the doctrine of "implied powers" and incorporated it into seminal Supreme Court cases that upheld the power of the federal government.

In approving the bank bill, Washington again championed Hamilton as an agent of modernity, a man who represented the thriving commerce of the seaport cities rather than the Virginia gentry from which he himself had emerged. Wash- ington agreed with Hamilton's defense of the bank, not simply from its superlative reasoning but because the two men subscribed to a common view of economic na- tionalism. Contrary to his critics, who thought him a credulous tool of Hamilton, Washington was a proud and knowing sponsor of the Hamiltonian program.[29] That July he insisted to David Humphreys, "Our public credit stands on that ground which, three years ago, it would have been considered as a species of madness to have foretold."[30]

THE UPROAR OVER THE HAMILTONIAN SYSTEM made it all the more im- perative that Washington undertake a tour of the southern states, much as he had done with New England. At the time when the Quaker petitions to abolish the slave trade had awakened southern fears of northern interference, David Stuart had warned Washington, "It is represented that the northern phalanx is so firmly united as to bear down all opposition, while Virginia is unsupported."[31] The region also feared that the northeastern states would pay less heed to frontier communi- ties, which were mostly peopled with settlers from the southern states. Faced with reported discontent, Washington wanted to see for himself whether the South was really so disenchanted with his programs. Also, as the country grew—by the spring of 1792, Congress had approved the admission of Kentucky and Vermont as new states—Washington wanted to maintain a sense of national cohesion amid pell-mell expansion.

The southern tour was a hugely ambitious adventure. Washington would once again have to hazard nonstop socializing. As Tobias Lear noted, he found these occasions "fatiguing and often times painful," sticking him with a dreadful conflict. "He wishes not to exclude himself from the sight or conversation of his fellow citizens, but their eagerness to show their affection frequently imposes a heavy tax upon him."[32] The projected itinerary of 1,816 miles was an enormous distance to traverse by horse and carriage. At a time of poor roads, Washington would have to withstand dust, mud, and assorted indignities. And in an era of primitive communications, he would be absent from Philadelphia for three months, making it hard to settle major policy disputes. Washington had never gone farther south than the northern part of North Carolina, and the Carolina and Georgia roads were terra incognita. Leaving nothing to chance, he consulted southern congressmen and even a Supreme Court justice about precise distances en route, which he referred to as his "line of march."[33] The whole trip was plotted out like a military campaign, with each day mapped out in advance, complete with arrival and departure times and the name of each inn.

On March 20, 1791, Washington departed from Philadelphia in his carriage with a train of servants. A big, rough-hewn Hessian named John Fagan drove the coach, with James Hurley as the postilion. Major William Jackson, presidential porter John Mauld, and valet William Osborne trotted alongside on horseback. Washington's slave Giles drove the baggage wagon with two horses, while his other slave in the rear, Paris, rode the white parade horse, Prescott, that Washington would ride into towns. In a playful touch, Washington included his greyhound, which he had named Cornwallis. In New York and Philadelphia, Giles and Paris had served as coachman and postilion, and their demotion to the back of the presidential procession may have been designed to placate southern sensibilities. It may also have reflected Washington's displeasure with the two men. By the end of the tour, Washington would drop Paris from his presidential household, describing him as "lazy, self-willed, and impudent," while Giles developed an injury that made it impossible for him to ride a horse.[34]

Washington's diaries for the early stages of his southern trip sometimes read like a disaster chronicle. The succession of horrors started with the sail down Severn River in Maryland. Washington had borrowed a large boat manned by an incompetent crew, and in the course of a dark, stormy night, with "constant lightning and tremendous thunder," the boat ran aground twice. The befuddled crew had no notion where they were. All the while the president lay curled up in a bunk belowdecks, so cramped he could not fully stretch out. The nightmare ended with the boat's arrival at Annapolis, where Washington was installed in the familiar comfort of George Mann's Tavern.

At this point Washington paused for an important piece of public business: he officiated at a meeting of property owners in Georgetown and Carrollsburg who were competing to have government buildings for the new federal district erected on their land. In a pleasant surprise to the two warring groups, Washington informed them that the ten-mile-square district would encompass land in both their domains. In his usual tactful style, he urged the landowner groups to cooperate rather than compete and also pored over a survey of the new federal district prepared by Andrew Ellicott, as well as preliminary plans drawn up by Pierre-Charles L'Enfant, the French engineer tapped to design the federal city.

Washington gave himself a week's respite at Mount Vernon and made the daily rounds of his five farms for the first time since the previous fall. On April 7, with the horses "well refreshed and in good spirits," his entourage resumed the journey, and as they boarded the Colchester ferry, Washington hoped things would go smoothly. During this crossing he decided to keep the four horses harnessed to his coach. But one horse got skittish and dashed off the side of the boat, pulling the other startled horses with it. Fortunately the boat had drifted close enough to shallow water that the horses could be saved and the coach prevented from plunging in.

As the presidential cavalcade approached Fredericksburg on April 8, the towns-folk were taken aback to see Washington—he had concealed his arrival to avoid any fuss. One paper noted that the citizens, "not being apprised of his approach, were disappointed in the opportunity of evincing their respect . . . by meeting him previous to his arrival."[35] After a festive welcome in Richmond, Washington proceeded to Petersburg, where several thousand people greeted him and threw up clouds of dust that irritated his throat. To avoid a repetition of this problem, Washington let it be known that he would leave town at eight the next morning, "but I did it a little after five," he confessed in his diary, perhaps with a guilty thrill, "by which means I avoided the inconveniences" of the dust.[36]

When he spent the night at Emporia, Virginia, in Greensville County, the rain had settled the dust hanging in the air. The next morning the rain resumed, but the president decided he would rather brave the elements than the admiring crowds: "Although raining moderately . . . I continued my journey, induced to it by the crowds which were coming into a general muster at the Courthouse of Greensville, who would, I presumed, soon have made the [house] I was in too noisy to be agreeable."[37] When the dust-choked roads turned muddy, Washington wrote that "my passage was through water."[38]

As the presidential cavalcade rattled along bumpy roads down the eastern seaboard, the slapstick comedy persisted. In Craven County, North Carolina, Washington stayed with a Colonel John Allen in the belief that his house was a roadside tavern. When the error was discovered, Washington concluded that "it was too late to rectify the mistake."[39] He then pushed on to New Bern, where the townsfolk threw him a public dinner, and he resumed his favorite pastime of counting the female attendees. These visits were elaborately prepared; the local citizenry presented welcoming addresses to Washington, who delivered replies composed by Major Jackson. Benjamin Franklin's grandson, Benjamin Franklin Bache, blasted this innocuous protocol in his Philadelphia newspaper, finding incriminating evidence of royalist tendencies: "We find by the southern papers that the president on his journey is still perfumed with the incense of *addresses*. However highly we may consider the character of the chief magistrate of the union, yet we cannot but think the fashionable mode of expressing our attachment to the defender of the liberty of his country favors too much of monarchy to be used by republicans."[40]

Bache would have been appalled by the acclaim Washington received in Wilmington, North Carolina, where he mounted his white horse and threaded his way through town amid a fanfare of trumpets and "an astonishing concourse of people." Ladies waved to him from windows and balconies, while ships in the harbor ran up streaming colors. He counted sixty-two ladies at the Wilmington ball; one newspaper observed that the president "appeared to be equally surprised and delighted at the very large and brilliant assembly of ladies whom admiration and respect for him had collected together."[41] In Georgetown, South Carolina, fifty ladies hosted him at a tea party. Here and elsewhere on his tour, Washington made a point of addressing local Freemasons, telling General Mordecai Gist, the grand master in South Carolina, "Your sentiments on the establishment and exercise of our equal government are worthy of an association whose principles lead to purity of morals and are beneficial of action . . . I shall be happy on every occasion to evince my regard for the fraternity."[42]

Perhaps the most elegant reception Washington received came in Charleston, where twelve formally dressed ship captains, manning a barge with twelve oars, ferried him into town. About forty boats brimming with gentlemen and ladies bobbed around him, while others freighted with musicians sailed alongside to serenade him. One floating chorus sang, "He comes! he comes! The hero comes. / Sound, sound your trumpets, beat your drums."[43] As Washington walked the streets, he submitted to hero worship such as no other American president has perhaps ever experienced. One observer said the crowds "look up to him as the savior of the country, all respect him as the founder of our states and cherish him as a father who would come to see for himself if his children are happy."[44] In the afternoon he was visited by "a great number of the most respectable ladies of Charleston," but they paled beside the female contingent that evening.[45] In his diary, Washington wrote that he had gone "to a concert at the exchange at w[hi]ch there were at least 400 lad[ie]s—the number and appearances of w[hi]ch exceeded anything of the kind I had ever seen."[46] To further his delight, the women wore bandeaux upon which his image had been sketched or that were stamped with the words "Long life to the President" or "Welcome to the hero" in golden letters.[47]

The southern tour turned into a marathon as the cavalcade crossed the Georgia pine barrens. The "abominably sandy and heavy" roads wore down the horses, including Prescott.[48] The journey was a heroic labor for Washington, who had to deal with the hazards of the road coupled with the tiring social demands. From Georgia, he wrote to Tobias Lear that he was so busy in each town that it "scarcely allowed me a moment I could call my own."[49] He pushed on to Augusta, where the local newspaper stated that the presidential ball was attended by "the largest number of ladies ever collected at this place."[50] The presidential connoisseur estimated the female turnout at between "60 and 70 well dressed ladies."[51] While there, Washington also engaged in more serious business, meeting with Governor Edward Telfair and handing him dispatches for the Spanish governor of East Florida, warning him to stop providing a safe haven for runaway American slaves.

In late May Washington began the journey northward and used the opportunity to tour scenes from the Revolutionary War that he had watched from afar, including Camden and Guilford Court House. He exhibited mounting irritation with the attention bestowed on him—only between towns did he have some modicum of privacy. To his annoyance, the North Carolina governor sent an escort for him. "On my approach to this place [Guilford]," he wrote, "I was met by a party of light horse, which I prevailed on the governor to dismiss and to countermand his orders for others to attend me through the state."[52]

In undertaking this lengthy trip, Washington had wanted to learn the state of public opinion directly rather than by hearsay. Most of all, he hoped to ascertain whether the South was as discontented as legend claimed. In his diary, he professed pleasure with what he saw, convinced that the people "appeared to be happy, contented and satisfied with the gen[era]l government under which they were placed. Where the case was otherwise, it was not difficult to trace the cause to some demagogue or speculating character."[53] Contrary to reports that the South would resist the whiskey tax, Washington found general approval for it. In writing to Catharine Macaulay Graham, he cited the "prosperity and tranquillity under the new government" and added that "while you in Europe are troubled with war and rumors of war, everyone here may sit under his own vine and none to molest or make him afraid."[54] Clearly Washington's picture of the southern mood was overly rosy; perhaps local politicians didn't care to deliver upsetting news to a heroic president on a jubilant tour. Within a year the country would be hopelessly divided over Washington's policies, and the primary locus of discontent would be centered in the southern states.

On June 11 the presidential caravan arrived at Mount Vernon, giving Washington two weeks of rest before he returned to Philadelphia. After a rocky start, the tour had unfolded with miraculous precision, and Washington was relieved that it had proceeded without "any interruption by sickness, bad weather, or any untoward accident."[55] In a major logistical feat, he had arrived at each town on the exact date set on his itinerary. The three-month trip had also been a tonic to his health. Escaping from his office and filling his lungs with fresh air, he had put on weight and wiped away the gaunt look of the previous year. Not only had his health improved, but he told one correspondent that "my happiness has certainly been promoted by the excursion."[56] The trip ended in a fitting spirit on July 6, when he rode into Philadelphia to the sound of cannon and the ringing of church bells and set eyes on Martha for the first time in nearly four months.

No sooner had Washington returned than a tumor reappeared on his thigh, in exactly the spot as the one excised in June 1789. It threw the government into a state of general gloom. "The president is indisposed with the same blind tumor, and in the same place, which he had the year before last in New York," Jefferson alerted Madison. Although it seemed not as bad as the earlier tumor, Jefferson said that Washington was "obliged to lie constantly on his side and has at times a little fever."[57] The protuberance was lanced, and pus and other matter cleaned out, and within a month Washington declared that he was fully recovered. Still, this was the third time that he had been leveled by an ailment as president, and it must have made him wonder about the wisdom of continuing in office.

Running into Extremes

EARLY IN HIS ADMINISTRATION, George Washington had figured out that for foreign policy advice he would have to rely on his cabinet rather than the Senate, but the cabinet members were no less split in the foreign policy realm than they were on pressing domestic issues. The most divisive topic was whether the United States should lean toward France or Great Britain. Even after waging war against Britain for more than eight years, Washington took a coldly realistic view of the strategic need for cordial relations with London. The federal government depended upon customs duties as its principal revenue source and could scarcely afford to antagonize its major trading partner. After the war, as American trade with England swiftly rebounded, Washington had observed, "Our trade in all points of view is as essential to G[reat] B[ritain] as hers is to us."[1] In the postwar period, American merchants had bristled at the exclusion of their ships from the British West Indies. Scarcely a raging Anglophile, Washington had a long list of other grievances against the English—their refusal to make restitution for runaway slaves, their unwillingness to evacuate western posts, their reluctance to send a minister to the United States—but he never allowed those complaints to stymie his earnest efforts to improve relations with the Crown.

In the autumn of 1789 Washington decided to post the witty Gouverneur Morris to England as an unofficial envoy to iron out problems between the two governments. Jefferson feared that America would import Britain's monarchical ways along with its products and strongly favored warmer relations with France, whose revolution he monitored with enthusiasm. Where Hamilton and Jay supported Morris's appointment, Jefferson staunchly opposed it, viewing Morris as a "high-flying monarchy man" and overly friendly to England.[2] He later faulted the fun-loving Morris for prejudicing Washington's mind against the French Revolution.

Because Jefferson did not take office until March 1790, Hamilton was able to poach on territory usually reserved for the secretary of state and attempted to strengthen ties with Great Britain, with whom the United States still lacked formal diplomatic relations. In October 1789 he conducted a secret meeting with a British diplomat, Major George Beckwith, assuring him, "I have always preferred a connection with you to that of any other country. *We think in English* and have a similarity of prejudices and predilections."[3] Washington likewise believed that the common laws, language, and customs of America and England made them natural allies, and he fully concurred with Hamilton's desire to negotiate a commercial treaty between the two countries. By the summer of 1790 Morris's talks in London began to bear fruit. After a meeting with Beckwith, Hamilton relayed to Washington the startling news that Sir Guy Carleton, now the governor general of Canada, "had reason to believe that the Cabinet of Great Britain entertained a disposition not only towards a friendly intercourse but towards an alliance with the United States."[4] Jefferson scoffed at such views emanating from an unofficial emissary.

Accepting the need for creative diplomacy, Washington sought to profit from the back channel established by Hamilton with Beckwith. That summer the specter of war between England and Spain arose after their military confrontation at Nootka Sound on Vancouver Island in western Canada. Not ready to choose sides, Washington noted in his diary the instructions he had given Hamilton, saying that "the Secretary of the Treasury was to extract as much as he could from Major Beckwith and report it to me without committing . . . the Government of the U[nited] States."[5] In subsequent meetings with Beckwith, Hamilton warned the British diplomat that while Washington was "perfectly dispassionate" toward a commercial treaty with England, Secretary of State Jefferson "may possibly frustrate the whole."[6]

In September 1791 the overtures made by Hamilton, with Washington's approval, resulted in a major breakthrough in Anglo-American relations, as George III named George Hammond as the first British minister to America. When Hammond and his secretary, Edward Thornton, arrived that autumn, they immediately sensed the amicable disposition of the treasury secretary and the implacable hostility of the secretary of state. Writing home, Thornton evoked Jefferson's "strong hatred" of the British and his "decided and rancorous malevolence to the British name."[7] Not surprisingly, Hammond and Thornton gravitated to the pro-British circle clustered around Hamilton.

America's fervent attachment to France arose from gratitude for its indispensable help during the Revolutionary War, and no country saluted its revolution with more fraternal warmth. In a variety of ways, the French Revolution had been spawned by its American predecessor, which had bred dreams of liberty among French aristocrats who fought in the war, then tried to enshrine its principles at home. The most visible standard-bearer of these hopes was the Marquis de Lafayette, who told Washington from Paris that the "ideas of liberty have been, since the American Revolution, spreading very fast."[8] As Jefferson stated proudly, the French had been "awakened by our revolution . . . Our proceedings have been viewed as a model for them on every occasion."[9] As early as 1780 Washington had predicted that France, to pay for its American adventure, would face a huge deficit and resort to ruinous taxes that "the people of France are not in a condition to endure for any duration."[10] Those taxes and other hardships had provoked immense discontent, leading King Louis XVI to convene a special advisory assembly called the Estates-General in May 1789, which mingled commoners with the clergy and nobility.

Always a perceptive student of politics, George Washington, from the first stirrings of the French Revolution, was astonishingly prophetic about its course. He regarded Louis XVI as a good-hearted but fallible king who would make a clumsy, self-destructive effort to foil revolutionary impulses. "Liberty, when it begins to take root, is a plant of rapid growth," Washington remarked to Madison in 1788. "The checks [the king] endeavors to give it . . . will, more than probably, kindle a flame which may not easily be extinguished, tho[ugh] for a while it may be smothered by the armies at his command."[11] With his sure instincts, Washington intuited that the French Revolution might veer off into fanaticism and warned Lafayette "against running into extremes and prejudicing your cause."[12] On the other hand, he also thought that if the king managed change properly, a constitutional monarchy might ensue. Paradoxically, Jefferson, an eyewitness to the revolution's outbreak, seemed blind to its violent potential. In August 1788 he blithely reported to James Monroe from France, "I think it probable this country will, within two or three years, be in the enjoyment of a tolerably free constitution and that without its having cost them a drop of blood."[13] Perhaps because of his association with enlightened Parisian intellectuals, Jefferson missed the bloodthirsty spirit of the French Revolution, its lust for gore and its gratuitous butchering of innocent victims.

The early days of the French Revolution, so giddily triumphant, produced general rejoicing among Americans. In the spring and summer of 1789 they applauded the creation of the National Assembly and the Declaration of the Rights of Man and Citizen, written by Lafayette with assistance from Jefferson. The Bastille's downfall, however, displayed the bloody predilections of the Parisian mobs, who decapitated the prison governor and sported his head on a pike. Such grisly details seemed lost upon many Americans cheering the event. The day after the Bastille was stormed, Lafayette, who hoped for a "fusion between the royalty and the people," was named head of the National Guard of Paris, further encouraging Americans to believe that their revolution had engendered a fitting sequel in France.[14] In a masterful stroke, Lafayette sent Washington the ponderous old key to the Bastille gate plus a sketch of the infamous fortress. "Give me leave, my dear general, to present you with a picture of the Bastille just as it looked a few days after I had ordered its demolition, with the main key of that fortress of despotism," he wrote. "It is a tribute which I owe as a son to my adoptive father, as an aide-de-camp to my general, as a missionary of liberty to its patriarch."[15] Later on, the president hung the key inside a wall lantern at Mount Vernon, with the picture below it, spurring Chateaubriand's mordant comment, "If Washington had seen the 'victors of the Bastille' disporting themselves in the gutters of Paris, he would have felt less respect for his relic."[16]

While careful to support France in public, Washington succumbed to deep foreboding in private and predicted a cascading series of violent events. Like other Americans, he wanted to embrace the French Revolution, but he recoiled from its excessive zeal. In October 1789 he told Gouverneur Morris that while France "has gone triumphantly through the first paroxysm, it is not the last it has to encounter before matters are finally settled. In a word, the revolution is of too great magnitude to be effected in so short a space and with the loss of so little blood."[17] He feared both the frenzied mobs and the benighted aristocrats plotting to restore their privileges. Morris's letters from Paris had a profound impact on Washington, as Jefferson suspected, because they captured with a cool eye the demagogic logic of the revolution and the fanaticism fast taking hold.

Lafayette's tragedy in the French Revolution was that he tried to model himself after Washington and re-create his success in a situation that mocked his ambitions. In January 1790, calling himself Washington's "filial friend," Lafayette wrote to say how often he had wished for his mentor's "wise advices and friendly support!"[18] He was not oblivious to the revolution's defects, but he thought they would be mended in time and hoped for the French equivalent of a Constitutional Convention in ten years. There was a note of quiet apprehension in Lafayette's letters, a lonely whistling in the dark, as he recorded the wholesale destruction of the aristocracy, while hoping that liberty would somehow thrive in the resulting vacuum. Still wedded to replicating the American Revolution, he wrote in the slightly defensive tone of a man trying too hard to convince himself that all was well.

As news of Parisian atrocities reached American shores, Washington remained guardedly supportive of the French Revolution in public, confining his misgivings to a small circle of intimates. Writing to Rochambeau on August 10, 1790, he dismissed the horror stories printed in the London papers as reminiscent of British propaganda during the war: "Happily for you, we remembered how our own armies, after having been all slain to a man in the English newspapers, came to life again and even performed prodigies of valor against that very nation whose newspapers had so unmercifully destroyed them."[19] In truth, Washington lent considerable credence to British reports, as he confided to Lafayette: "I will avow the accounts we received through the English papers . . . caused our fears of a failure almost to exceed our expectations of success."[20]

When deputies in the National Assembly abolished aristocratic titles in June 1790, Lafayette surprised his fellow noblemen by supporting the measure, claiming it had "something of the American character."[21] Henceforth, the Marquis de Lafayette was known simply as Lafayette. Even as he curried favor with the masses, however, Lafayette worried that mob violence would supplant the rule of law, telling Washington in August 1790, "I have lately lost some of my favor with the mob and displeased the frantic lovers of licentiousness, as I am bent on establishing a legal subordination."[22] It was Lafayette's misfortune that the lower classes regarded him as too conservative while patricians jeered at him as too radical. Nothing better illustrates the distance between the American and French revolutions than the fact that Lafayette, who was so at home in the Continental Army, seemed tragically out of place in France, naïvely pursuing the chimera of a constitutional monarchy among political cutthroats on the Paris streets.

Among those trying to place the French Revolution squarely in the American grain, perhaps none was more influential than Thomas Paine. In 1791 he published *The Rights of Man* as a response to Edmund Burke's influential denunciation, *Reflections on the Revolution in France.* Burke had condemned the royal family's mistreatment and prophesied bloodshed to come. Paine, in contrast, portrayed events in France as reprising the spirit of 1776 and called for a written constitution, with an elected assembly and chief executive. Paine, who could be both arrogant and presumptuous, dedicated his polemic to Washington without first seeking his permission and published his screed in London on February 22, 1791—Washington's birthday. Drawing further parallels to the American Revolution, Paine informed Washington that he wanted to "make a cheap edition, just sufficient to bring in the price of the printing and paper, as I did by *Common Sense*."[23]

Thomas Jefferson helped to arrange for publication of *The Rights of Man* in Philadelphia, telling the printer that he was "extremely pleased to find it will be reprinted here and that something is at length to be publicly said against the political heresies which have sprung up among us."[24] Jefferson professed amazement when the printer used this letter as a preface to Paine's work. Since Jefferson's reference to "political heresies" was widely construed as a swipe at the supposed cryptomonarchism of John Adams's treatise *Discourses on Davila,* it created a brouhaha. The mortified Jefferson wrote a long, repentant letter to Washington, claiming that his letter had been used without permission and denying any intention to vilify the vice president. Washington's failure to acknowledge Jefferson's apology suggests his silent fury. Jefferson's own letters to Paine reflect his fear of highly placed monarchists in Washington's administration who were "preaching up and panting after an English constitution of king, lords, and commons and whose heads are itching for crowns, coronets, and mitres."[25]

Because of the controversy over Paine's work, Washington responded to his letter with a blandly evasive reply. He pleaded the pressing duties of office and his imminent return to Mount Vernon as reasons why he couldn't react in detail: "Let it suffice, therefore, at this time to say that I rejoice in the information of your personal prosperity and . . . that it is the first wish of my heart that the enlightened policy of the present age may diffuse to all men those blessings to which they are entitled and lay the foundation of happiness for future generations."[26] Washington had a matchless talent for skirting unwanted controversies.

In June 1791 King Louis XVI and the royal family fled Paris in disguise—the king dressed as a valet, the queen as the children's governess—only to be stopped and arrested by Lafayette's National Guard at Varennes, northeast of Paris. Although Lafayette duly informed the king and queen that the National Assembly had placed them under a full-time guard, he was nonetheless denounced as a traitor on the Paris streets, and Danton accused him of engineering the royal family's escape. The underground press in France went so far as to caricature Lafayette in pornographic poses with Marie-Antoinette. These events dimmed any hope for a constitutional monarchy. Jefferson delivered to Washington the stunning news from Paris. "I never saw him so much dejected by any event in my life," Jefferson reported of his reaction.[27] A crestfallen Lafayette was dismayed by the behavior of the royal couple, lamenting that Marie-Antoinette was "more concerned about looking beautiful in the face of danger than about staving it off."[28]

In September 1792 the monarchy would be abolished. Beset by terrible premonitions, Washington was extremely concerned about Lafayette's endangered position and, in a letter to him, identified a cardinal characteristic of the French Revolution that especially upset him: the urban mob. "The tumultuous populace of large cities are ever to be dreaded," he wrote. "Their indiscriminate violence prostrates for the time all public authority, and its consequences are sometimes extensive and terrible."[29] In October 1791 Lafayette resigned from the National Guard and retreated to the rural serenity of his home, the Château Chavaniac. He sent Washington a letter that breathed contentment, as if his troubles had suddenly evaporated. "After fifteen years of revolution, I am profiting from a new and agreeable life of calm in the mountains where I was born."[30] Given the turbulent events unfolding in Paris, this peaceful interlude was fated to be of short duration.

EVEN AS WASHINGTON worriedly tracked events in France, he had to deal with a brilliant, charming, but difficult Frenchman at home. Though historians often pin the label of military engineer or architect on Major Pierre-Charles L'Enfant, he had trained as a painter at the Royal Academy of Painting and Sculpture in Paris. At twenty-two, he joined the Continental Army with other French volunteers, forming part of the engineering corps, and sketched soldiers at Valley Forge. After the war he had turned New York's City Hall into Federal Hall, establishing his credentials as a talented architect. As early as September 1789 he proposed himself to Washington as designer of the new federal capital. A peerless judge of talent, Washington soon grasped L'Enfant's visionary powers, but their relationship was never smooth.

A portrait of L'Enfant shows a man with a coolly superior air. With an imagination shaped by the courts, palaces, and public works of Europe, L'Enfant would be hotheaded and autocratic in negotiating the intricacies of the new capital. Hypersensitive, with a touch of grandiosity, he was the perfect man to hatch a dream but not to implement it. It was characteristic of Washington that L'Enfant's hauteur did not deter him; the president had faith in his ability to control even the most intractable personalities and extract the best from them. His checkered relationship with L'Enfant was a classic encounter between a consummate pragmatist and an uncompromising dreamer.

In early 1791 Washington asked L'Enfant to review the grounds selected for the new capital and identify the most promising sites for the chief government buildings. Local proprietors had already granted the president sweeping powers to shape the city. "The President shall have the sole power of directing the Federal City to be laid off in what manner he pleases," they agreed. "He may retain any number of squares he may think proper for public improvements or other public uses."[31] On March 28, at the outset of his southern tour, Washington met with L'Enfant, who laid before him a rough pencil sketch of the new capital. He envisioned the seat of Congress on the brow of the highest wood, a steep spot called Jenkins Hill, which he praised as "a pedestal waiting for a superstructure."[32] This building would be the visual centerpiece of the city, with broad, diagonal thoroughfares radiating outward. Its centrality bore an unmistakable message about the primacy of the people's branch of government. Rejecting a simple grid for the capital as "tiresome and insipid," he argued that such a pattern made sense only for flat cities.[33] Not only would diagonal streets provide "contrast and variety," but they would serve as express lanes, shortening the distance between places.[34] Town squares would be situated where diagonal avenues crossed. The kernel of the future Washington, D.C., lay in that conception. Striking a note of buoyant optimism that appealed to the president, L'Enfant wanted the city to be able to grow in size and beauty as "the wealth of the nation will permit it to pursue, at any period, however remote."[35]

Aside from trimming the number of diagonal streets, Washington gave L'Enfant an unrestricted hand to pursue his plan. At the close of his southern tour, he rode across the federal district with L'Enfant and Andrew Ellicott to experience the elevations chosen for Congress and other public buildings. While he endorsed Jenkins Hill for Congress, he balked at a site chosen for the executive mansion and opted for higher ground farther west, thereby asserting executive power and giving it visual parity with the Capitol. In endorsing the spot for the future White House, L'Enfant cunningly played to Washington's interests by observing that it would possess an "extensive view down the Potomac, with a prospect of the whole harbor and town of Alexandria"—that is, it would face Mount Vernon.[36] The entire project gratified Washington's vanity on another level: people assumed that the new city would be named either Washington or Washingtonople. In September Washington learned that the commissioners had indeed decided, without fanfare, to call the city Washington and the surrounding district Columbia, giving birth to Washington, D.C. Washington would never have signed the original Residence Act had the capital then been called Washington—it would have seemed supremely vain—but now he was merely acceding to the will of the three bureaucrats he had appointed.

That October Washington sneaked in a monthlong stay at Mount Vernon before Congress reconvened. The health of his tubercular nephew and estate manager, George Augustine Washington, had deteriorated so sharply that he had gone to Berkeley Springs for rest. He was a likable young man who pleased many visitors; one praised his "gentle manner and interesting face" and another described him as a "handsome, genteel, attentive man."[37] By this point, however, he could scarcely ride a horse, much less manage an estate, and Washington named his secretary, Robert Lewis, as temporary manager of Mount Vernon. Lewis would eventually be succeeded by Anthony Whitting.

In the federal district L'Enfant, schooled in a European tradition where master builders ruled entire projects, refused to take direction from anyone. The first lots were auctioned off in Georgetown on October 17, with Jefferson and Madison in attendance; L'Enfant declined to show anyone his map, afraid that buyers would shun parcels in sections distant from the main government buildings. The most he deigned to share with bidders was a verbal description of the town layout. Washington had expected to be on hand for the three-day sale but was caught in an embarrassing error. In planning his return trip to Philadelphia, he knew that Congress would meet the fourth Friday of October, which he calculated as October 31. He was mortified to discover that he had miscalculated and that Congress would meet October 24. "I had no more idea of this than I had of its being doomsday," he told Tobias Lear.[38] Thrown for a loop, he departed hastily for Philadelphia to give his annual address to Congress and arrived in time to deliver an upbeat assessment of the state of the Union, noting "the happy effects of that revival of confidence, public as well as private, to which the Constitution and laws of the United States have so eminently contributed."[39] L'Enfant had been instructed to bring to Philadelphia a plan of the federal city, which Washington would submit to Congress with his annual message, but the mercurial Frenchman never delivered it.

In late October the three commissioners informed Washington that L'Enfant's high-handed refusal to turn over his plans had impeded the auction; scarcely more than thirty lots had been sold. Washington replied angrily that while he had suspected that L'Enfant might be obstinate in defending his plan, he had not thought he would go so far as to sabotage the sale. Clearly L'Enfant would make no concessions to attract real estate speculators and considered himself answerable only to the president. His feud with the commissioners festered. At one point, when L'Enfant demolished a building erected by a commissioner because it intruded on one of his grand avenues, the clash erupted into open warfare. Washington confidentially told Jefferson that he could tolerate the French prima donna up to a point, but "*he must know* there is a line beyond which he will not be suffered to go."[40] Much as he hated losing L'Enfant, Washington knew that, unless he reined him in tightly, he might lose his three commissioners. He had Jefferson draft a stern reprimand to the Frenchman, to be sent out under his own signature. "Having the beauty and harmony of your plan only in view," Washington wrote, "you pursue it as if every person and thing was *obliged* to yield to it, whereas the commissioners have many circumstances to attend to, some of which, perhaps, may be unknown to you."[41]

L'Enfant seriously misread Washington, who wanted harmony and cooperation among those involved in planning the new capital. In January 1792 the self-important L'Enfant submitted a lengthy memorandum to Washington, which was a barefaced attempt to push aside the commissioners and take sole control of the project. After proposing a one-million-dollar expenditure and a workforce of a thousand men, L'Enfant ended by saying, "It is necessary to place under the authority of one single director all those employed in the execution."[42] Washington grew apoplectic. "The conduct of Maj[o]r L'Enfant and those employed under him astonishes me beyond measure!" he told Jefferson, who drew up an ultimatum in which he asked L'Enfant point-blank whether he intended to subordinate himself to the commissioners.[43] Always eager to compromise, Washington sent Tobias Lear to patch things up with L'Enfant, but the latter blustered that he needed complete freedom from the commissioners. On February 27, 1792, bowing to the inevitable,

Jefferson terminated L'Enfant's services. Washington ended up feeling bitter toward L'Enfant for his imperious treatment of the commissioners. Nevertheless, the broad strokes of L'Enfant's design for Washington, D.C., left their imprint on the city. As John Adams concluded years later, "Washington, Jefferson, and L'Enfant were the triumvirate who planned the city, the capitol, and the prince's palace."[44]

Philadelphia's citizens were by no means resigned to their city being only a temporary capital and continued to throw up new government buildings, hoping to sway legislators to stay. When they tried constructing a new presidential residence, Washington saw their secret intent and insisted that his current house was perfectly satisfactory. Sensing an even split in public opinion about moving the capital to the Potomac, he divulged his fears to Jefferson: "The current in *this* city sets so strongly against the Federal City that I believe nothing that *can* be avoided will ever be accomplished in it."[45] Washington grew paranoid about the wily Philadelphians, even imagining that local printers stalled in producing engraved designs of the Potomac capital. Any delays, he feared, might doom the enterprise. He pressed for buildings in the District of Columbia that would foreshadow America's future might and rival the great cities of Europe. "The buildings, especially the Capitol, ought to be upon a scale far superior to anything in *this* country," he insisted to Jefferson. The house for the president should be both "chaste" and "capacious."[46] In time the city of Washington would come to justify the grandiose dimensions envisioned by both Washington and L'Enfant.

As EARLY AS THE FALL OF 1789, Washington emphasized to General Arthur St. Clair, first governor of the Northwest Territory, that he preferred a peace treaty with the hostile Indians of the Ohio Country to war. On the other hand, as long as those tribes, instigated by the British, pursued depredations on frontier communities, the government would be "constrained to punish them with severity."[47] During the summer of 1790 the Miami and Wabash tribes flouted peace overtures from the government and conducted fierce raids against American traffic on the Ohio and Wabash rivers. In response, Washington and Knox instructed St. Clair to summon the militia and destroy crops and villages of the offending Indians, hoping a show of strength would prod them into a negotiated peace. Selected to command the fifteen-hundred-man force, made up mostly of militia, was Brigadier General Josiah Harmar, a Revolutionary War veteran whose drinking habits caused concern in Philadelphia. Henry Knox scolded Harmar for being "too fond of the convivial glass" and pointed out that Washington was aware of this problem.[48]

At the end of that September, Harmar led his men on an expedition against the Wabash Indians northwest of the Ohio River. By mid-November, with the fate of the operation wrapped in mysterious silence, Washington girded for bad news and confessed to Knox his forebodings of a "disgraceful termination" to the expedition. Always moralistic about alcohol problems, he reserved harsh words for General Harmar. "I expected *little* from the moment I heard he was a *drunkard*," he told Knox.[49] Washington's worries about the expedition were prescient: Harmar's men suffered a stunning defeat at a Miami Indian village near the present-day city of Fort Wayne, Indiana. The dreadful performance of American troops—they killed two hundred Indians but suffered an equal number of casualties—only reinforced Washington and Knox's long-standing prejudice against militia. Nonetheless, a military court of inquiry vindicated Harmar, labeling his conduct "irreproachable."[50]

Washington always tried to be evenhanded in dealing with the Indians. He hoped that they would abandon their itinerant hunting life and adapt to fixed agricultural communities in the manner of Anglo-Saxon settlers. He never advocated outright confiscation of their land or the forcible removal of tribes, and he berated American settlers who abused Indians, admitting that he held out no hope for pacific relations with the Indians as long as "frontier settlers entertain the opinion that there is not the same crime (or indeed no crime at all) in killing an Indian as in killing a white man."[51] When addressing Seneca chiefs that December, he conceded provocations by American settlers: "The murders that have been committed upon some of your people by the bad white men, I sincerely lament and reprobate, and I earnestly hope that the real murderers will be secured and punished as they deserve."[52] Nevertheless Indians saw only a pattern of steady encroachment and unrelenting westward advancement by white settlers that threatened their traditional way of life. In the end, Washington's hope of "civilizing" the Indians by converting them to agriculture and Christianity was destined to fail.

It was only a matter of time before Washington and Knox got authority to raise a new regiment and mount a major reprisal against the Indians. Arthur St. Clair, elevated to a major general, was to lead fourteen hundred troops to the Miami village with an unsparing mandate: "Seek the enemy and endeavor by all possible means to strike them with great severity."[53] Born in Scotland, trained as a physician, St. Clair was a seasoned officer who had fought in the French and Indian War. Patriotic if a bit pompous, he had turned in a mixed record during the Revolutionary War but performed well enough that Washington valued him as a soldier in "high repute."[54] For his 1791 expedition, St. Clair led a threadbare, inexperienced army described by one officer as "badly clothed, badly paid, and badly fed."[55] As this force dragged brass field pieces through the wilderness, it was depleted by illness and desertion. St. Clair, suffering from agonizing gout, had to be borne aloft on a stretcher. The general grew peevish over lax discipline among his men and paused during the march to construct a gallows to punish insubordination.

On November 4, 1791, right before sunrise, St. Clair and his men were camped near the Miami village when up to fifteen hundred Indians pounced in a surprise attack. Hurling aside artillery and baggage, the Americans fled in a panic-stricken rout. All discipline broke down amid the general slaughter, and gruesome stories of butchery filtered back from the wilderness. As one soldier related, "I saw a Capt. Smith just after he was scalped, setting on his backside, his head smoking like a chimney."[56] The heart of General Richard Butler was supposedly sliced into pieces and distributed to the victorious tribes. In a ghoulish warning to stay off their land, the Indians stuffed the mouths of some victims with soil. St. Clair's troops suffered shocking casualties—900 out of 1,400 men—versus only 150 Indians.

According to an account based on an 1816 talk with Tobias Lear, the dreadful tidings arrived in Philadelphia on December 9, in the middle of one of Martha Washington's demure Friday-evening receptions. After knocking at the president's door, the courier informed Lear that he had dispatches to deliver directly to Washington. After being pulled from the reception, the president was closeted for a time with this unusual messenger and read St. Clair's description of "as warm and unfortunate an action as almost any that has been fought."[57] When he returned to the reception, he apologized to his guests but revealed nothing of the extraordinary news. Instead, he went dutifully through his social paces, conversing with each lady in attendance. With extraordinary self-control, Washington allowed nothing in his demeanor to hint at the pent-up rage churning inside him. When the guests were gone, Washington and Lear sat alone by the parlor fire, and Washington blew up in tremendous wrath, throwing up his hands in agitation, scarcely able to contain his emotions. The editors of the George Washington papers note that the story "contains some credible details" but also point out that by the date in question "unofficial reports of the defeat already were circulating in Philadelphia."[58] At a later cabinet meeting, Washington, reaching back to his early frontier experience, faulted St. Clair for failing to keep "his army in such a position always as to be able to display them in a line behind trees in the Ind[ia]n manner at any moment."[59]

In early January the first news reports of the disaster cast St. Clair in a heroic light. In February the tenor abruptly changed when Colonel William Darke published an anonymous diatribe against Washington for having dispatched a woefully infirm general, bedridden and propped up with pillows, into battle: "That the executive should commit the reputation of the government . . . to a man who, from the situation of his health, was under the necessity of traveling on a bier, seems to have been an oversight as unexpected as it has been severely censured. A general, enwrapped ten-fold in flannel robes, unable to walk alone, placed on his car, bolstered on all sides with pillows and medicines, and thus moving on to attack the most active enemy in the world was . . . a very tragicomical appearance indeed."[60]

Congressman William B. Grove labeled the St. Clair defeat "the most complete victory ever known in this country obtained by Indians."[61]

When Knox submitted a request to Congress for an expanded army and a new assault on the refractory Indians, several congressmen took advantage of it to condemn administration policy. One critic rebuked the administration for "preparing to squander away money by millions" and contended that nobody, "except those who are in the secrets of the Cabinet, knows for what reason the war has been thus carried on for three years."[62] In general, Washington did not dignify such criticisms with responses, but he asked Knox to draw up a document that could also be published as a broadside—a distinct departure showing a new sensitivity to public opinion. Knox's statement recounted the deaths of white frontier settlers and numerous peace overtures toward the Indians. But these measures having failed, he now argued for a new and larger army. In early February the House voted its approval of five new regiments, with almost a thousand men apiece. To allay fears of a standing army, the new units were to be disbanded once the Indian threat in the Northwest Territory subsided.

The wrangling between Congress and the administration over Indian warfare reached a crisis when legislators launched an investigation and asked Knox in late March for his correspondence relating to the ill-fated St. Clair campaign. Aware that revealing these papers might redefine the separation of powers, Washington assembled his cabinet and told them, according to Jefferson, that he wished their decision "should be rightly conducted" because it might "become a precedent."[63] The cabinet ruled that "the executive ought to communicate such papers as the public good would permit and ought to refuse those the disclosure of which would injure the public."[64] This equivocal decision left the question of executive privilege up in the air. In its final report, Congress vindicated St. Clair's management of the debacle, placing the onus squarely on Washington's administration by lambasting the logistical support the army had received.

Thus far Washington's Indian policy added up to a well-meaning failure: he had been able neither to negotiate peace nor to prevail in war. To restore the army's battered reputation, he appointed Anthony Wayne, the quondam hero of Stony Point, to lead the new augmented army in the Northwest Territory. The redoubtable Wayne instituted tough measures to instill discipline in the new army and shaved, branded, and whipped soldiers to sharpen their performance. While pleased with Wayne's rigor, Henry Knox introduced a caveat: "Uncommon punishment not sanctioned by law should be admitted with caution."[65] The creation of this new, more professional army only heightened the qualms of those who feared a standing army and exacerbated the growing political divisions in Philadelphia. Nonetheless, under Wayne's leadership, the army would reverse the disastrous direction that Indian warfare had taken during the unsuccessful Harmar and St. Clair campaigns.

A Tissue of Machinations

AS THE FIRST PRESIDENT, George Washington hoped to float above the political fray and avoid infighting, backbiting, and poisonous intrigue. He wanted to be an exemplary figure of national unity, surmounting partisan interests, and was therefore slow to spot the deep fissures yawning open in his administration. In June 1790 he told Lafayette, "By having Mr Jefferson at the head of the Department of State . . . Hamilton of the Treasury and Knox of that of War, I feel myself supported by able coadjutors, who harmonize together extremely well."[1] Washington always worked hard to appear impartial and to impress the electorate that he was president of *all* the people. This pose of immaculate purity was congenial to him, as he sought a happy medium in his behavior. Despite holding firm opinions, he was never an ideologue, and his policy positions did not come wrapped in tidy ideological packages. Rather, they developed in a slow, evolutionary manner, annealed in the heat of conflict.

Washington and other founders entertained the fanciful hope that America would be spared the bane of political parties, which they called "factions" and associated with parochial self-interest. The first president did not see that parties might someday clarify choices for the electorate, organize opinion, and enlist people in the political process; rather he feared that parties could blight a still fragile republic. He was hardly alone. "If I could not go to heaven but with a party," Jefferson opined, "I would not go there at all."[2] Yet the first factions arose from Jefferson's extreme displeasure with Hamilton's mounting influence. They were not political parties in the modern sense so much as clashing coteries of intellectual elites, who operated through letters and conversations instead of meetings, platforms, and conventions.

Nonetheless these groups solidified into parties during the decade and, notwith-standing the founders' fears, formed an enduring cornerstone of American demo-cratic politics.

Disturbed by the expansion of federal power under Hamilton's programs, Jef-ferson and Madison suspected a secret counterrevolution was at work, an incipient plot to install a monarchical government on the British model. Their defeat over the bank bill in late February 1791 convinced them that Hamilton had hopelessly bewitched the president. Hamilton's assertion of federal power also awakened fears that meddlesome northerners might interfere with southern slavery. As one Vir-ginian later said, "Tell me, if Congress can establish banks, make roads and canals, whether they cannot free all the slaves in the United States."[3]

Unlike the Anglophile Hamilton, Jefferson and Madison often seemed to want to make the American government everything that the British government was not. To denigrate his foes, Jefferson applied to them hyperbolic labels, including "mono-crats" and "Anglomen"—words with an evocative conspiratorial ring. As the French Revolution grew more sanguinary, Hamilton in turn demonized the Jeffersonians as involved in a worldwide Jacobin conspiracy emanating from Paris.

To organize opposition to the dangerous political backsliding that they per-ceived, Jefferson and Madison took a tour of New York and New England in May–June 1791. The cover story Jefferson supplied to Washington was that he needed a break "to get rid of a headache which is very troublesome, by giving more exercise to the body and less to the mind."[4] Jefferson and Madison supposedly planned to collect botanical specimens, but they actually intended to recruit political parti-sans, especially on Hamilton's home turf of New York. A courtly, charismatic leader, Jefferson was adept at fostering camaraderie among like-minded politicians. If more circumspect, Madison was no less crafty or committed to the cause. The long-standing friendship of these two men now deepened into a powerful political partnership.

It seems strange that the revolt against Washington's administration originated with a member of his own cabinet and a close confidant. When the president deliv-ered his annual message to Congress in October 1791, Madison chaired the House committee that drafted a response, and Washington asked him to draft his own reply to that document. At the time, no political protocol insisted that disgruntled cabinet members should resign from an administration with which they disagreed. Nor was there yet a tradition of a loyal opposition. Washington sometimes found it hard to differentiate between legitimate dissent and outright disloyalty. He tended to view criticism as something fomented by wily, demagogic people, manipulating an otherwise contented populace.

In an extreme act of duplicity, Madison and Jefferson installed a flaming critic of Washington right in the heart of his own government. They wanted to counter the views of John Fenno, editor of the pro-administration *Gazette of the United States,* which Jefferson accused of peddling "doctrines of monarchy, aristocracy, and the exclusion of the influence of the people."[5] To woo him to Philadelphia, Jefferson offered a job as State Department translator to the poet Philip Freneau, who knew only one language and was scarcely qualified. The suggestion came from Madison, a friend and former Princeton classmate of his. During the war Freneau had written a rhapsodic paean to Washington entitled "Cincinnatus." After being incarcerated in a loathsome British prison ship, he came to detest everything British and turned against President Washington and the Hamiltonian program with a vengeance. In late October 1791, after taking the State Department job, Freneau launched the *National Gazette,* which became the virulent organ of the Jeffersonian opposition. In its premier issue, it accused Hamilton of being the kingpin of a monarchist conspiracy and touted Jefferson as the "colossus of liberty."[6]

Before long the two factions took on revealing names. The Hamiltonian party called itself Federalists, implying that it alone supported the Constitution and national unity. It took a robust view of federal power and a strong executive branch, and it favored banks and manufacturing as well as agriculture. Elitist in its politics, it tended to doubt the wisdom of the common people, but it also included a large number of northerners opposed to slavery. The Jeffersonians called themselves Republicans to suggest that they alone could save the Constitution from monarchical encroachments. They believed in limited federal power, a dominant Congress, states' rights, and an agrarian nation free of the corrupting influence of banks, federal debt, and manufacturing. While led by slaveholders such as Jefferson and Madison, the Republicans credited the wisdom of the common people. Washington and Hamilton believed wholeheartedly in an energetic federal government, whereas Jefferson and Madison feared concentrated power.

By 1792 Washington's cabinet was split down the middle; Knox typically leaned toward Hamilton, and Randolph toward Jefferson. Washington never openly identified with the Federalists and steadfastly hewed to his nonpartisan self-image, though he sided more often with Hamilton and Knox. Jefferson never doubted Washington's integrity or patriotism and could hardly claim that the man who had resigned his commission at the end of the war and rejected pleas to become a king harbored royal ambitions. So he ended up explaining Washington's support for Hamilton's policies by suggesting that the treasury secretary, a cunning mastermind, had duped the credulous president into supporting programs he did not fully comprehend.

ON DECEMBER 5, 1791, Hamilton aroused the darkest fears of his opponents when he submitted to Congress another major state paper, the *Report on Manufactures*. At a time when the country was overwhelmingly agricultural, Hamilton devised a visionary blueprint of ways that the federal government, through selective bounties and import duties, could galvanize manufacturing. He and Washington recalled how reliance on foreign manufactures had crippled America in wartime; the report was driven partly by the desire for strategic self-sufficiency. As an adjunct to this report, Hamilton fostered the growth of an organization, the Society for Establishing Useful Manufactures (SEUM), to demonstrate the feasibility of American manufacturing. At the Great Falls of the Passaic River in New Jersey, the society planned to set up the town of Paterson as a model for American manufacturing.

Far from being Hamilton's willing dupe, Washington understood his programs thoroughly. Though he knew America would remain agricultural, he wanted to augment its manufacturing capacity. Starting with his inauguration, he had delighted in wearing clothes of American manufacture to stimulate the textile industry. At Mount Vernon he refused to drink porter or eat cheese that was not produced in America. In his discarded first inaugural address, he had endorsed government action to open canals, improve roads, and stimulate internal improvements. It was Washington who encouraged Hamilton to assist the growth of cotton and hemp through government bounties. Though a planter, Washington was receptive to labor-saving gadgetry, even if it meant using female and child labor. In January 1790 he viewed the operation of a new threshing machine and came away enthusiastic. "Women or boys of 12 or 14 years of age are fully adequate to the management of the mill or threshing machine," he wrote in his diary. "Upon the whole, it appears to be an easier, more expeditious, and much cleaner way of getting out grain than by the usual mode of threshing."[7] When he toured a Philadelphia cotton factory, one newspaper reported that the president "attentively viewed the machinery and saw the business performed in its different branches, which met with his warmest approbation."[8] Congress failed to act on Hamilton's manufacturing report. In Washington's view, it didn't "comport with the temper of the times," but he still availed himself of every opportunity to promote American manufacturing.[9]

The same day that Hamilton delivered his report to Congress, Madison unleashed an anonymous assault on the Washington administration, accusing it of laying the groundwork for a monarchy. He deplored the "increasing splendor and number of prerogatives" enjoyed by the executive branch, which might "strengthen the pretexts for an hereditary designation of the magistrate."[10] Hamilton, aware of the orchestrated nature of these salvos, wrote to Vice President Adams, "The plot thickens."[11]

Starting in the summer of 1791, the Jeffersonians followed with alarm the rampant speculation in government bonds and bank shares. On July 4, 1791, the Treasury had begun selling shares in the new Bank of the United States, and pent-up demand proved so explosive that the entire subscription sold out in one frantic hour. Swarms of investors invaded the Treasury building, mobbing the clerks. For Hamilton's supporters, it was dramatic proof of the trust that investors placed in the new institution. Now an unashamed bank booster, Washington exulted over this initial offering: "The astonishing rapidity with which the newly instituted bank was filled gives an unexampled proof (here) of the resources of our countrymen and their confidence in public measures."[12] Although the par value of bank stock was $400 per share, Hamilton, to make it affordable to small investors, allowed them to make $25 down payments; in exchange, they received certificates called scrip, which entitled them to purchase full shares in future installments.

In the next few weeks, as the price of scrip soared, it produced a speculative frenzy that was dubbed "scrippomania." Far from construing it as symptomatic of Hamilton's success, Madison was appalled by this "scramble for so much public plunder."[13] Equally aghast, Jefferson wondered aloud to Washington whether "such sums should have been withdrawn from . . . useful pursuits to be employed in gambling."[14] Hamilton erred in selling most scrip in Philadelphia, Boston, and New York, feeding southern fears of a northern hegemony. In August the price of scrip touched such dizzying heights that Senator Rufus King of New York reported that business had ground to a halt as people rushed to buy scrip, with "mechanics deserting their shops, shopkeepers sending their goods to auction, and not a few of our merchants neglecting the regular and profitable commerce of the city."[15] According to Dr. Benjamin Rush, the madness engulfed Philadelphia as well: "The city of Philadelphia for several days has exhibited the marks of a great gaming house."[16] By August 11 bank scrip had zoomed from the $25 offering price to $300, with government bonds also touching delirious new heights. When bankers drained credit from the market, speculators dumped their scrip, the bubble burst, and prices plummeted. Hamilton steadied the market by buying government securities, but Jefferson was convinced that scrip had already worked its evil influence. "The spirit of gaming, once it has seized a subject, is incurable," he wrote.[17]

The speculative fever abated temporarily, and Hamilton had to counter an organized effort to revive it. His friend William Duer, recently departed as assistant treasury secretary, had hatched a plan to corner the market in government bonds and bank shares and enlisted Alexander Macomb, a wealthy merchant, to join the effort. What made this situation so distressing for Hamilton was that he had just tapped Duer as governor of the SEUM, where Macomb was also a governor. The two men emerged as ringleaders of a speculative clique known as the Six Per Cent Club because they tried to manipulate the price of government bonds yielding 6 percent.

In early 1792 financial markets grew feverish as the creation of several new banks spurred a mania for bank shares. "Bancomania" surpassed even the "scrippomania" of the previous summer. Hamilton was staggered by the disorder: "These extravagant sallies of speculation do injury to the government and to the whole system of public credit by disgusting all sober citizens and giving a wild air to everything."[18] Far from seeing Hamilton as trying to restrain Duer, Jefferson believed they were in cahoots and warned Washington that the financial mania was not only "destructive of morality" but had "introduced its poison into the government itself."[19] The fight over financial policy was fast becoming a fight over the proper direction of the country; Washington was caught in the blazing crossfire between his brilliant treasury secretary and his equally brilliant secretary of state.

After bank shares attained giddy levels in January 1792, they began to slide, creating a crisis for Duer, who had borrowed scandalously large amounts from New York creditors. "Widows, orphans, merchants, mechanics, etc. are all concerned in the notes," Hamilton's friend Robert Troup informed him.[20] By March 9, with bank shares plunging, Duer stopped payment to creditors, with catastrophic repercussions. Two dozen financiers went bankrupt the next day, and Duer was packed off to debtors' prison, as much to protect him from angry mobs as to punish him. Feeling grimly vindicated, Jefferson gloated over the mayhem, writing that "the credit and fate of the nation seem to hang on the desperate throws and plunges of gambling scoundrels."[21] Hamilton again restored order to the market by purchasing government securities, but the damage to his reputation had been done, especially when it surfaced that William Duer had raided the SEUM coffers for speculative funds. In the *National Gazette* Freneau seized this chance to revile the Hamiltonian system, which he blamed for "scenes of speculation calculated to aggrandize the few and the wealthy, while oppressing the great body of the people."[22] In this situation, neutrality was not an option for Washington, who would be forced to choose sides between Hamilton and Jefferson.

ALTHOUGH WASHINGTON had originally planned to resign during his first term, many Americans could not imagine another president and automatically assumed he would stay in office indefinitely. Whatever their quibbles about his policies, citizens still honored his exalted character and place in history. As Lund Washington wrote from Virginia, "No person has an idea but that you must remain at the head of the government so long as you live."[23] It wasn't the first time Washington became the captive of a position from which he could not extricate himself. Once again, as the indispensable man in a crisis, he was held hostage to events. Further signs of aging were visible in the craggy face, the whitening hair, the slightly stooped gait.

On February 21, 1792, the eve of his sixtieth birthday, Philadelphians toasted him with an exuberant celebration, throwing a fancy ball in his honor and draping huge transparencies over buildings inscribed with the words "Vive Le Président." Amid the growing strife in American politics, the public was gripped by a pervasive fear that Washington might serve only one term. Tobias Lear articulated the widespread sentiment: "I fear more from the election of another president, whenever our present great and good one quits his political or natural career, than from any other event."[24] Protective of her husband and well aware of the grave medical problems that punctuated his first term, Martha Washington hoped he would decline a second.

In this increasingly dark, conspiratorial atmosphere, Washington received three malicious letters, warning him anonymously of the secret presidential ambitions of Jefferson and of Madison's treachery: "When you ask the opinion of the S[ecretary] of S[tate], he affects great humility and says he is not a judge of military matters. Behind your back, he reviles with the greatest asperity your military measures and ridicules the idea of employing any regular troops . . . His doctrines are strongly supported by his cunning little friend Madison."[25] In another letter, the poison-pen artist made sure Washington knew of the intrigue behind Freneau's hiring at the State Department: "I do not believe you know that the *National Gazette* was established under the immediate patronage of Mr. Jefferson and Mr. Madison, and that Mr. Freneau, the printer of it, is a clerk in the Secretary of State's office with a salary as interpreter."[26] The object of these men, the author averred, was to make Washington "odious" and "destroy Mr. Hamilton."[27]

At this point Washington sloughed off suspicions about Jefferson, as evidenced by two remarkable meetings they held in February 1792. At the first, Jefferson lobbied to make the postal service part of the State Department rather than Treasury, hoping that would choke the excessive growth of Hamilton's department. In passing, Jefferson mentioned that if Washington ever retired, he would too. This comment reverberated in Washington's mind overnight, and at breakfast the next morning, he launched into a frank discussion of his political future. He noted to Jefferson that he had agreed reluctantly to attend the Constitutional Convention and serve as first president. But now,

> were he to continue longer, it might give room to say that, having tasted the sweets of office, he could not do without them; that he really felt himself growing old, his bodily health less firm, his memory, always bad, becoming worse; and perhaps the other faculties of his mind showing a decay to others of which he was insensible himself; that this apprehension particularly oppressed him; that he found moreover his activity lessened, business therefore more irksome, and tranquillity and retirement become an irresistible passion. That however he felt himself obliged for these reasons

to retire from the government, yet he should consider it as unfortunate if that should bring on the retirement of the great officers of the government and that this might produce a shock on the public mind of dangerous consequence.[28]

This remarkable burst of candor, as recounted by Jefferson, showed that Washington still trusted the secretary of state. In a private memorandum on the talk, Jefferson disclosed that he himself was "heartily tired" of his job and stayed only from a sense that Hamilton would linger for several years.[29] Later Jefferson wrote how much he had hated doing battle with Hamilton in the cabinet, descending "daily into the arena like a gladiator to suffer martyrdom in every conflict."[30] When Washington made plain that he could not contemplate retirement because of "symptoms of dissatisfaction" toward the administration, Jefferson made bold to say that there was only a single source of discontent, the Treasury Department, and "that a system had there been contrived for deluging the states with paper money instead of gold and silver, for withdrawing our citizens from the pursuits of commerce, manufactures, buildings, and other branches of useful industry to occupy themselves and their capitals in a species of gambling."[31] Throwing caution to the wind, Jefferson said Hamilton had suborned congressmen who "feathered their nests with [government] paper" and therefore voted for his system.[32] Hamilton's *Report on Manufactures,* Jefferson claimed, would destroy any pretense of limited government and enable the government to undertake any measure it liked. Washington must have been shocked as he fathomed the depth of animosity between his two most talented lieutenants. At the same time Madison was slashing away anonymously at Hamilton in the *National Gazette,* inveighing against "a government operated by corrupt influence, substituting the motive of private interest in place of public duty."[33]

What made the rising tide of criticism more troublesome for Washington was that much of it originated from Virginia, where he was increasingly regarded as an apostate. Edward Thornton, secretary to the British minister, observed in April 1792 that Washington "has very few who are on terms of intimate and unreserved friendship" with him and "what is worse, he is less beloved in his own state than in any part of the United States."[34] Three years later Washington told Edmund Randolph that, if the Union were to break up into North and South, "he had made up his mind to remove and be of the northern."[35] That Washington now identified with northern finance, commerce, and even abolitionism would have major consequences for American history. Had he sided with Jefferson and Madison, it might have deepened irrevocably the cleavage between North and South and opened an unbridgeable chasm seventy years before the Civil War.

Washington was expert at keeping his woes to himself and not showing the stress of office. While he now knew the extent of Jefferson's antipathy toward Hamilton, he did not believe the wilder charges swirling around his secretary of state. When Eliza Powel sent him a pamphlet accusing Jefferson of pro-French policies, he replied that the writer should investigate the facts more closely. "Had he done this," wrote Washington, quoting Shakespeare's *The Tempest*, "he would . . . have found many of his charges as unsupported as the 'baseless fabric of a vision.'"[36]

Starting in November 1791 and running for more than a year, James Madison published eighteen essays excoriating the administration in the *National Gazette*. Nevertheless, on May 5, 1792, apparently unaware of his authorship, Washington unburdened himself to Madison about his political plans. The recent financial panic in New York had added to the uproar over the administration's policies. Washington said that he had already made known to Madison his intention to retire at the end of his first term and asked for Madison's opinion "on the *mode* and *time* most proper for making known that intention."[37] He further said that he had apprised Hamilton, Knox, and Jefferson and that all had argued strenuously against his retirement. Washington had the modesty to state that he was not "arrogantly presuming on his re-election in case he should not withdraw himself," though that was a foregone conclusion.[38] Madison buttressed the consensus that it would be perilous for Washington to withdraw and that he alone could reconcile the warring parties. Another four years under Washington, Madison maintained, would "give such a tone and firmness to the government as would secure it against danger" from enemies on either side.[39]

At this point Washington discarded his impenetrable reserve and poured out his inmost thoughts, humbly confessing to feelings of inadequacy and saying that he could not conceive of himself as necessary to the "successful administration of the government; that, on the contrary, he had from the beginning found himself deficient in many of the essential qualifications . . . that others more conversant in such matters would be better able to execute the trust; that he found himself also in the decline of life, his health becoming sensibly more infirm and perhaps his faculties also; that the fatigues and disagreeableness of his situation were, in fact, scarcely tolerable to him."[40]

That Washington dwelled on his inability to arbitrate constitutional disputes showed the heavy toll taken by the cabinet debate over the Bank of the United States. The president also complained of memory lapses, poor vision, and growing deafness—all socially confining conditions. Despite Washington's fears, his letters show no evidence of his mental powers' fading, and they were often amazingly vigorous. That Jefferson and Madison took such a decline seriously perhaps reflects their wish to portray Washington as softheaded and easily manipulated by Hamilton.

In chatting with Madison, Washington also deplored the press onslaught against his administration, little knowing that the man from whom he was seeking com-miseration was a secret author of some of those assaults. The episode showed Mad-ison's capacity for duplicity—that he could act as Washington's confidant even as he betrayed him. Although Jefferson and Madison wanted to elect a Republican vice president instead of John Adams, they had no desire to replace Washington, doubtless afraid that an unfettered Hamilton would succeed him.

As with all major decisions, Washington pondered long and hard whether to remain in office. On May 20 he told Madison that he had mulled over his argu-ments for a second term but remained unconvinced and wanted to end his days "in ease and tranquillity."[41] He also thought that stepping down and letting someone else serve as president would be "more congenial" with ideas of liberty.[42] Despite worries that it might be interpreted as a ploy to prod the American public to urge him to stay in office, Washington asked Madison to draft a valedictory address. He outlined the main themes, including the need for national unity and civility in pub-lic life. At this point Washington sounded pretty definite in his decision. Madison composed a farewell address, even though he told Washington that he hoped he would make "one more sacrifice . . . to the desire and interests of your country."[43] Even while drafting Washington's plea for unity and mutual respect, Madison was writing surreptitiously for the *National Gazette,* and that summer he and Jefferson took the precaution of exchanging letters in code.

As Federalists and Republicans envisioned life without Washington, both feared they would be left to the tender mercies of each other. About the only thing Hamil-ton and Jefferson agreed upon was the absolute need to keep Washington as presi-dent. On May 23 Jefferson urged Washington to remain in office and dropped his circumspection about Hamilton. In a full-throated diatribe, he warned that Ham-ilton's bank, funded debt, and excise taxes were intended "to prepare the way for a change from the present republican form of government to that of a monarchy, of which the English constitution is to be the model."[44] With the South filled with debtors and the North creditors, Jefferson feared the country would break apart along sectional lines. Jefferson underscored Washington's special status: "North and south will hang together if they have you to hang on."[45] If an honest Congress was elected in the fall, Jefferson predicted, Washington could step down in safety before completing his second term, knowing the government had been saved.

No less than Jefferson, Hamilton was convinced that the opposition party was engaged in a secret plot to subvert the government. In a furious letter to Edward Carrington of Virginia, he claimed to be certain of the following: "That Mr. Madi-son, cooperating with Mr. Jefferson, is at the head of a faction decidedly hostile to me and my administration and actuated by views, in my judgment, subversive of the principles of good government and dangerous to the union, peace and happiness of the country."[46] Despite the venomous split in his cabinet, Washington worked mightily to defuse the controversy and appease Hamilton and Jefferson. He was not intimidated by these men of exceptional intelligence. Neither Hamilton nor Jefferson liked being subordinate to anyone, and both must have found it hard to submit to Washington, which only made his feat of controlling them the more remarkable.

On June 20 Madison sent Washington a draft of the farewell address, which he suggested should be published in mid-September. "You will readily observe that in executing it, I have aimed at that plainness and modesty of language which you had in view."[47] From the letter's diffident tone, Washington would never have suspected Madison's brazen role in pounding his administration in the *National Gazette*. On July 4 Freneau published a front-page polemic listing the "rules for changing a limited republican government into an unlimited hereditary one," and he singled out Hamilton's policies as the surest way to accomplish it.[48] Rubbing salt into the wounds, Freneau had three copies of his paper delivered daily to Washington's doorstep.

On July 10 Washington sat down at Mount Vernon for another candid chat with Jefferson about whether he should remain as president. He clearly felt trapped in office. He pointed out that he had intended to serve only two years, then was induced to stay for a third because of the country's unsettled state; now he was again being told it was dangerous for him to depart. He grew indignant at Freneau's charge that he headed a monarchical party. While a few might wish for a monarchy "in the higher walks of life, particularly in the great cities . . . the main body of the people in the eastern states were steadily for republicanism as in the southern."[49] He protested the insinuation that he was a dim-witted tool in Hamilton's hands and took dead aim at those who flattered him while seeking to discredit him indirectly by attacking Hamilton. Jefferson recorded Washington as saying that "in condemning the administration of the gov[ern]ment, they condemned him, for if they thought there were measures pursued contrary to his sentiment, they must conceive him too careless to attend to them or too stupid to understand them."[50] In this statement, Washington exploded the myth that he was a puppet jerked about by an all-powerful Hamilton or a ceremonial caretaker of his own administration.

While at Mount Vernon, Washington absorbed southern grumbling about his policies. Meanwhile he asked Tobias Lear, then traveling in New England, to canvass sentiment there about whether he should serve a second term. Lear reported strong sentiment in favor of a second term in order to give the still-new federal government a fair chance to establish itself. The people said that "most of the important things hitherto done under this government . . . had not yet been long enough in operation to give satisfactory proof whether they are beneficial or not" and they would not have a fair experiment under any administration other than Washington's.[51] People were so convinced that Washington needed to remain in power, Lear asserted, "that no other person seems ever to have been contemplated for that office."[52] Attorney General Randolph also issued a dramatic plea for Washington to stay, saying that "The public deliberations need stability."[53]

On July 25 the feud between Hamilton and Jefferson acquired new ferocity when Hamilton, for the first time, published an anonymous essay rebuking Jefferson. Writing in Fenno's *Gazette of the United States*, he posed a simple question about Freneau and his State Department stipend: "Whether this salary is paid him for *translations* or for *publications*, the design of which is to vilify those to whom the voice of the people has committed the administration of our public affairs . . . ?"[54] The attack, one paragraph in length, showed that Hamilton had thrown down a gauntlet to Jefferson and was prepared to take his case to the public.

Washington would now have to stop the sparring between his two cabinet members; their feud was far more vitriolic than he had dreamed possible. On July 29, in a confidential letter, he told Hamilton that he had sought the views of people en route to Mount Vernon and at home and found that they viewed the country as "prosperous and happy" but were alarmed at certain policies and interpretations of the Constitution.[55] He enumerated twenty-one complaints that touched on Hamilton's policy initiatives, including accusations that he had created excessive public debt, imposed onerous excise taxes on the people, promoted financial speculation, and corrupted the legislature. Although Washington cited George Mason as the source of these complaints, the language was drawn verbatim from Jefferson, and Hamilton could scarcely have missed the allusion. One can only assume that Washington, sensitive to nuance, wanted Hamilton to hear echoes of Jefferson's phraseology. The most damning charge was the final one: that the real object of Hamilton's policies was "to prepare the way for a change from the present republican form of government to that of a monarchy, of which the British Constitution is to be the model."[56] Disquieted by the political backlash against his programs in the South, he asked Hamilton to respond to his letter as soon as possible.

Even before receiving Washington's complaints, Hamilton had implored him to soldier on as president for another year or two. The failure to do so, he stressed, would be "deplored as the greatest evil that could befall the country at the present juncture."[57] Reading Washington's psychology astutely, Hamilton emphasized the damage that would be done to Washington's character if he retired. By now Hamilton had declared all-out warfare against Jefferson and Madison. In the *Gazette of the United States* that August, he took off the velvet gloves and showed the clenched fist of steel, charging that the *National Gazette* had been set up as a vehicle to publicize

Jefferson's views and that Madison had been the intermediary for bringing Freneau to his State Department sinecure.

On August 18 the frustrated Hamilton sent Washington a fourteen-thousand-word letter, listing his own accomplishments in office and defending his policies. What troubled him was less the criticisms of specific programs than the character assassination practiced by his opponents: "I trust that I shall always be able to bear, as I ought, imputations of errors of judgment, but I acknowledge that I cannot be entirely patient under charges which impeach the integrity of my public motives or conduct. I feel that I merit them *in no degree* and expressions of indignation sometimes escape me in spite of every effort to suppress them."[58]

At this point Washington could no longer stand aside while Hamilton and Jefferson tore each other to ribbons. He warned Edmund Randolph that if press diatribes against his cabinet members continued, "it will be impossible . . . for any man living to manage the helm or to keep the machine together."[59] His vision of a unified government now seemed hopelessly utopian. In late August he exhorted Hamilton to end his bloody clash with Jefferson. Asking for civility, he hoped that "wounding suspicions and irritating charges" would give way to "mutual forbearances and temporizing yieldings *on all sides*. Without these, I do not see how . . . the union of the states can be much longer preserved."[60] Searching for common ground, Washington hinted that Hamilton and Jefferson had "the same *general* objects in view and the same upright intentions to prosecute them."[61] To underline his support for Hamilton, Washington invited him to Mount Vernon and ended by saying that Hamilton could rest assured of his "sincere and affectionate regard."[62] Aiming to be impartial, Washington also admonished Jefferson to end the squabbling, noting that attacks on his administration—attacks Jefferson himself had orchestrated—had "for a long time past filled me with painful sensations."[63]

On September 9 Hamilton wrote to Washington that he was the injured party to the dispute and that the day would soon come "when the public goodwill will require *substitutes* for the *differing members* of your administration."[64] For the first time, Hamilton singled out Jefferson as his adversary and accused him of starting the *National Gazette* to sabotage his fiscal program: "I *know* that I have been an object of uniform opposition from Mr. Jefferson from the first moment of his coming to the city of New York to enter upon his present office."[65] Although Hamilton and Jefferson were often on their best behavior when dealing with Washington, they were now like two rowdy, boisterous students, brawling in the schoolyard whenever the headmaster turned his back. Far from desisting in his broadsides against Jefferson, Hamilton, under the pen name "Catullus," commenced a new series of newspaper essays, disputing that the Federalists were plotting to abolish the republic. Turning the tables, Hamilton said it was the Republicans, led by Jefferson, who were engaged in a conspiracy to undermine the government. He even made veiled references to Jefferson's being a closet libertine, perhaps hinting at secret knowledge of his relations with his slave concubine, Sally Hemings.

The same day that Hamilton wrote to Washington to defend his conduct, Jefferson at Monticello did likewise. In an unusually long and heated letter, Jefferson charged that Hamilton had duped him into supporting his schemes and had trespassed on State Department matters by meeting with French and British ministers. He admitted hiring Freneau but made it seem as if Freneau had initiated the contact, and he swore that he had no influence over the *National Gazette*. This may have been technically true, since Jefferson turned to surrogates, especially Madison, for his political dirty work. The supreme populist of early American history then slandered Hamilton, the self-made immigrant, with the hauteur of a born aristocrat chastising a pushy upstart: "I will not suffer my retirement to be clouded by the slanders of a man whose history, from the moment at which history can stoop to notice him, is a tissue of machinations against the liberty of the country which has not only received and given him bread, but heaped its honors on his head."⁶⁶ Clearly, Washington's efforts to arbitrate a truce between his warring cabinet chieftains had failed, but he never wavered in his effort to terminate the intrigue.

As Washington wrestled with the problem of whether to remain as president, he was preoccupied by the fading health of his nephew George Augustine, who had grown so weak that summer that he was spitting up blood and could scarcely walk. By early August he was confined to his room at Mount Vernon, and Washington did not expect him to survive much longer. If he recovered his strength, he would probably require a quiet interlude in some milder climate. His illness returned Washington's thoughts to the management of Mount Vernon and made him eager to reassert control of his neglected business affairs.

On October 1, 1792, Washington, still at Mount Vernon, met with Jefferson before breakfast in yet another attempt to thrash out their differences. Still wavering about a second term, Washington cited his dislike of "the ceremonies of his office" and said his nephew's plight made his presence at Mount Vernon desirable.⁶⁷ For the first time Washington seemed to lean toward a second term, however, remarking that "if his aid was thought necessary to save the cause to which he had devoted his life principally, he would make the sacrifice of a longer continuance."⁶⁸ Jefferson stated that only Washington could rise above partisan wrangling and fortify the government. Washington confessed that, while he had been aware of political differences between Jefferson and Hamilton, "he had never suspected it had gone so far in producing a personal difference and he wished he could be the mediator to put an end to it."⁶⁹ In spite of everything, Washington wanted to retain Jefferson in the cabinet and maintain an ideological balance.

Until this point the discussion had been cordial. But now an exasperated Washington, fed up with conspiracy theories, squarely told Jefferson that "as to the idea of transforming this government into a monarchy, he did not believe there were ten men in the U.S. whose opinions were worth attention who entertained such a thought,"[70] as Jefferson noted his words. This was tough language, tantamount to branding Jefferson a crackpot, and unlike anything Washington ever said to Hamilton. The secretary of state replied with stiff dignity: "I told him there were many more than he imagined . . . I told him that tho[ugh] the people were sound, there was a numerous sect who had monarchy in contemplation, that the Sec[retar]y of the Treasury was one of these."[71] Here the two men encountered a fundamental difference that could not be bridged. When Jefferson again talked about Hamilton corrupting the legislature, with many in Congress owning government paper, Washington described the problem as unavoidable "unless we were to exclude particular descriptions of men, such as the holders of the funds, from all office."[72] The president saw the real test of the funding system as its effectiveness and "that for himself, he had seen our affairs desperate and our credit lost and that this was in a sudden and extraordinary degree raised to the highest pitch."[73]

At this point Jefferson must have realized that he had irrevocably lost the battle for George Washington's soul to Alexander Hamilton. In his memo on the talk, he simply wrote in defeat at this point, "I avoided going further into the subject."[74] After this meeting the obdurate Jefferson never unburdened himself so openly to Washington again, and a coolness entered their relationship. In his diary, Jefferson speculated that the president's mind was weakened by age and said that he showed "a willingness to let others act and even think for him."[75]

Back in Philadelphia in mid-October, Washington again tried to negotiate a truce between Hamilton and Jefferson. At moments he seemed genuinely baffled by their intransigence, as if he could not believe that men of goodwill could not work out their differences. Perhaps the decisive stroke in convincing Washington to run for a second term came after a meeting with Eliza Powel that November, in which Washington said he might resign. In a masterly seven-page follow-up letter, Powel, a confirmed Federalist, gave Washington the high-toned reasons he needed to stay in office, shrewdly playing on his anxious concern for his historic reputation. If he stepped down now, she wrote, his enemies would say that "ambition had been the moving spring of all your actions—that the enthusiasm of your country had gratified your darling passion to the extent of its ability and that, as they had nothing more to give, you would run no farther risk for them." She warned that the Jeffersonians would dissolve the Union: "I will venture to assert that, at this time, you are the only man in America that dares to do right on all public occasions."[76] Evidently she managed to convince Washington, who decided to stand for a second term.

CHAPTER FIFTY-SIX

Citizen Genet

ONCE HE DECIDED to serve a second term, George Washington was reelected by a unanimous 132 votes in the Electoral College. If one counted his selection as commander in chief, president of the Constitutional Convention, and president in his first term, he had compiled a string of four straight unanimous victories. Again inaction had been his most potent form of action, silence his most effective form of expression. Still, it was a subdued triumph for the overburdened president, who confessed to Henry Lee that he "would have experienced chagrin if my re-election had not been by a pretty respectable vote. But to say I feel pleasure from the prospect of *commencing* another tour of duty would be a departure from truth."[1]

On December 13, 1792, Washington conversed with Jefferson about buying porcelain in Germany to dress up the presidential table. He had inquired whether Samuel Shaw, the U.S. consul at Canton, could acquire china there, but Shaw told him that it would take at least two years to arrive. Washington emphasized to Jefferson that he would be gone from office by then, and Jefferson recognized the heavy-handed hint. "I think he asked the question about the manufactories in Germany," Jefferson concluded, "merely to have an indirect opportunity of telling me he meant to retire, and within the limits of two years."[2] Once again, if he thought he could cut short his captivity to public service, Washington was fooling himself, and people kept reminding him how much the Union needed him. "There is a prevailing idea in G[reat] B[ritain]," wrote one correspondent, "if not in other parts of Europe, that whenever you are removed, the federal union will be dissolved, the states will separate, and disorder succeed."[3]

With a presidential victory assured for Washington, the Jeffersonians tried to register their disaffection and covertly chip away at his power by ousting John Adams as vice president. Purely as a matter of propriety, Washington never openly endorsed Adams, who retained office with 77 votes against a stiff challenge from Governor George Clinton of New York, a firm Jeffersonian, who garnered 50 votes. Washington likewise worried that, if he got involved in congressional races, he might trespass on the separation of powers. This same reasoning made him reluctant to veto legislation, and he did not overrule a bill until April 1792. As their populist rhetoric led to significant inroads among farmers, shopkeepers, and artisans, Republican adherents gained a clear majority in the House of Representatives, guaranteeing a contentious second term for Washington.

A notable feature of that term would be an end to Washington's special exemption from direct criticism. That winter the new landscape was previewed when Freneau took direct shots at Washington in the *National Gazette,* accusing him of aping royalty in his presidential etiquette. He published a mock advertisement for a fawning poet laureate who would write obsequious birthday odes to the president. Even Washington's habit of not shaking hands received a sinister slant: "A certain *monarchical prettiness* must be highly extolled, such as *levees, drawing rooms, stately nods instead of shaking hands,* titles of office, seclusion from the people."[4] It would now be open season for sweeping attacks on Washington.

However trying he often found the press, Washington understood its importance in a democracy and voraciously devoured gazettes. Before becoming president, he had lauded newspapers and magazines as "easy vehicles of knowledge, more happily calculated than any other to preserve the liberty . . . and meliorate the morals of an enlightened and free people."[5] In his unused first inaugural address, he had gone so far as to advocate free postal service for periodicals. As press criticism mounted, however, Washington struggled to retain his faith in an independent press. In October 1792 he told Gouverneur Morris that he regretted that newspapers exaggerated political discontent in the country, but added that "this kind of representation is an evil w[hi]ch must be placed in opposition to the infinite benefits resulting from a free press."[6] A month later, in a more somber mood, he warned Jefferson that Freneau's invective would yield pernicious results: "These articles tend to produce a separation of the Union, the most dreadful of calamities; and whatever tends to produce anarchy, tends, of course, to produce a resort to monarchical government."[7]

To an unusual extent, early American politics was played out in print—one reason the founding generation of politicians was so literate. Publications were avowedly partisan and made no pretense of objectivity. It was a golden age for wielding words as rapier-sharp political weapons. The penchant for writing essays under Roman pseudonyms, designed to underscore the writer's republican virtues, lent a special savagery to journalism, freeing authors from any obligation to tone down their rhetoric.

For all his years in public service, Washington never developed a thick rind for the cut-and-thrust of politics, and Freneau's barbed comments stung him to the core. As Jefferson wrote after one talk with Washington that February, the president had bemoaned the "extreme wretchedness of his existence while in office and went lengthily into the late attacks on him for levees &c."[8] One wonders whether Washington was implicitly blaming Jefferson for Freneau's bruising critiques. Another newspaper tormenting the embattled president in his second term was the *General Advertiser*, later the *Aurora*, published by Benjamin Franklin Bache, whose scurrilous attacks on Washington earned him the nickname of "Lightning Rod, Jr."[9] Like Freneau, Bache made the modest presidential levees sound like lavish scenes of decadence from Versailles. Shameless in maligning Washington, Bache even accused him of incompetence during the Revolutionary War and, in the ultimate outrage, doubted that he had supported American independence. "I ask you, sir," he confronted Washington in an open letter, "to point out ONE SINGLE ACT which *unequivocally* proves you a FRIEND to the INDEPENDENCE OF AMERICA."[10] Washington dismissed Bache as an "agent or tool" of those out to destroy confidence in the government.[11]

A president who carefully tended his image found it hard to see it falsely defined by his enemies. And a man who prided himself on his honesty and integrity found it painful to stare down a rising tide of falsehoods, misrepresentations, and distortions about his record. His opponents struck where he was most sensitive—questioning his sense of honor and accusing him of base motives, when he had spent a lifetime defending himself against charges, both real and imaginary, of being motivated by thinly disguised ambition. Pilloried by an increasingly vituperative press, Washington did not respond publicly to criticism at first, having once said that "to persevere in one's duty and be silent is the best answer to calumny."[12] By the summer of 1793, however, he feared that falsehoods circulating in the press would take root and had to be rebutted aggressively. "The publications in Freneau's and Bache's papers are outrages on common decency," he complained to Henry Lee, noting that their allegations only grew more flagrant when treated with silence.[13]

The vendetta against Washington's administration took a bold new turn in January 1793, when Congressman William Branch Giles of Virginia launched an investigation of the Treasury Department and sought to oust Hamilton for official misconduct. Giles was an intimate of Jefferson, who secretly helped to draft the congressional resolutions condemning his fellow cabinet officer. Although Giles accused Hamilton of shuffling money dishonestly from one government account to another, the subsequent congressional investigation thoroughly vindicated the secretary. On March 1, 1793, all nine of Giles's resolutions against Hamilton were resoundingly defeated.

That winter, Washington's gloom deepened with the death of George Augustine Washington on February 5, leaving his widow, Fanny, with three small children. Penning a tender note to Fanny, the president invited her to live at Mount Vernon: "You can go no place where you will be more welcome, nor to any where you can live at less expense or trouble."[14] Though Fanny declined, the gesture typified Washington's exceptional generosity in family matters. Among his many duties, Washington became executor of his nephew's estate. As he brooded about the decaying state of his farms, he would never again have someone he trusted so totally with his affairs as George Augustine. The death also dealt a terrible blow at a moment when he worried about the future of his business. To David Humphreys, he confessed that "the love of retirement grows every day more and more powerful, and the death of my nephew . . . will, I apprehend, cause my private concerns to suffer very much."[15]

As Washington approached his second inaugural on March 4, the *National Gazette* stepped up attacks on what it derided as presidential pretension. The sneering Freneau served up heaps of abuse about Washington's birthday celebration—widely honored in Philadelphia—branding it a "monarchical farce" that exhibited "every species of *royal pomp and parade*."[16] This tirade may explain the extreme simplicity of Washington's second inauguration. With no precedent for swearing in an incumbent president, Washington asked his cabinet for guidance, and they suggested a public oath at noon in the Senate Chamber, administered by Associate Justice William Cushing, whose circuit encompassed Pennsylvania. The cabinet also advised that "the President go without form, attended by such gentlemen as he may choose, and return without form, except that he be preceded by the marshal."[17] Perhaps to advertise his lack of ostentation, Washington went alone in his carriage to Congress Hall, strode into the Senate Chamber with minimal fanfare, and delivered the shortest inaugural speech on record—a compact 135 words—in a ceremony intended as the antithesis of monarchical extravagance. As the *Pennsylvania Gazette* reported, after taking the oath, the president retired "as he had come, without pomp or ceremony. But on his departure from [Congress Hall], the people could no longer refrain [from] obeying the genuine dictates of their hearts, and they saluted him with three cheers."[18]

WASHINGTON'S SECOND TERM, a period of domestic strife, was dominated by the French Revolution and its profound reverberations in American politics. In March 1792, during a short-lived burst of optimism, Lafayette had reassured Washington that the anarchy in France was transitory: "Do not believe . . . my dear General, the exaggerated accounts you may receive, particularly from England."[19] That spring Austria and Prussia, bent upon snuffing out the revolutionary upstarts in Paris, invited England, Holland, and Russia to participate in an alliance of imperial states. Then in late April, France declared war against Austria and Prussia; they returned the favor by invading France a few months later. In the resulting atmosphere of fear and suspicion, the radical Jacobins declared a state of emergency. With formidable courage, Lafayette denounced the Jacobins to the National Assembly: "Organized like a separate empire in the city . . . this sect has formed a separate nation amidst the French people, usurping their powers and subjugating their representatives . . . I denounce them . . . They would overturn our laws."[20]

In August 1792, to Lafayette's horror, the Jacobins incited a popular insurrection that included the storming of the Tuileries in Paris and the butchery of the Swiss Guards defending the palace. The king was abruptly dethroned. Refusing to swear an oath of allegiance to the civil constitution, nearly 25,000 priests fled the country amid a horrifying wave of anticlerical violence. A month later Parisian mobs engineered the September Massacres, slaughtering more than fourteen hundred prisoners, many of them aristocrats or royalist priests. Ejected from his military command and charged with treason, Lafayette fled to Belgium. "What safety is there in a country where Robespierre is a sage, Danton is an honest man, and Marat a God?" he wondered.[21] Arrested by Austrian forces, he spent the next five years languishing in ghastly Prussian and Austrian prisons. With cruel irony, he was charged with having clapped the French king in irons and kept him in captivity. While claiming the rights of an honorary American citizen, Lafayette was confined in a small, filthy, vermin-infested cell.

On September 21 France abolished the monarchy and declared itself a republic. Two weeks later Madame Lafayette informed Washington of her husband's dreadful plight and thwarted plans to defect to America: "His wish was that I should go with all our family to join him in England, that we might go and establish ourselves together in America and there enjoy the consoling sight of virtue worthy of liberty."[22] She pleaded with Washington to dispatch an envoy who might reclaim her husband in the name of the United States. However distraught he was about Lafayette, Washington was entangled in a political predicament. He could not afford to antagonize the new French republic, and Lafayette's name was now anathema among the French revolutionaries. Gouverneur Morris, named minister to France in early 1792, warned Washington against undertaking any rash actions on Lafayette's behalf. "His enemies here are as virulent as ever," he cautioned.[23] For the moment, the only permissible response was personal charity. Drawing on his own money, Gouverneur Morris extended 100,000 livres to Lafayette's wife, while Washington deposited 2,300 guilders from his own funds into an Amsterdam account for her use. He assured Madame Lafayette that he wasn't indifferent to her husband's plight, "nor contenting myself with inactive wishes for his liberation. My affection to his nation and to himself are unabated."[24]

Developments in France only aggravated the growing discord in American politics. Regarding the French revolutionaries as kindred spirits, Republicans rejoiced at the downfall of the Bourbon dynasty, while Federalists, dreading popular anarchy, dwelled on the grisly massacres. The fate of France was more than an academic question after it promulgated its Edict of Fraternity, promising fraternal support to revolutionary states around the globe. Amid this revolutionary camaraderie, in August 1792 the French conferred honorary citizenship upon Washington, Hamilton, Madison, and Thomas Paine. For Jeffersonians, it fulfilled their fondest dream of a worldwide democratic revolution, while Federalists found the universal dream disturbing. Alexander Hamilton protested, "Every nation has a right to carve out its own happiness in its own way."[25] Among the imperial powers, the Edict of Fraternity generated widespread fear of subversion, sharpening tensions throughout Europe.

On January 21, 1793, the former King Louis XVI, who had helped win American independence, was decapitated before a crowd of twenty thousand people intoxicated with a lust for revenge. After stuffing the king's head between his legs, the executioner flung his remains into a rude cart piled with corpses, while bystanders dipped souvenirs into the royal blood pooled under the guillotine. Vendors soon hawked patches of the king's clothing and locks of bloodstained hair, in a spectacle of sadistic glee that shocked many people inside and outside France. On February 1 France declared war on Great Britain and Holland.

Thomas Jefferson seemed unfazed by the regicide and the large-scale massacres preceding it. After William Short wrote of horrifying beheadings in Paris, Jefferson saw little cause for alarm. "My own affections have been deeply wounded by some of the martyrs to this cause," he conceded, then added cold-bloodedly, "but rather than it should have failed, I would have seen half the earth desolated. Were there but an Adam and Eve left in every country, and left free, it would be better than it is now."[26] Persuaded that tales of French atrocities were propaganda exploited by Federalists, Jefferson became an apologist for the burgeoning horrors of the Jacobins. "I begin to consider them the true revolutionary spirit of the whole nation," he told Madison.[27] Madison also viewed the revolution through rose-colored spectacles. While Washington and Hamilton refused to acknowledge their election as honorary French citizens, Madison sent back a warmly fraternal response, extolling the "sublime truths and precious sentiments recorded in the revolution of France."[28]

Washington hoped to win respectability from foreign powers, but he also wanted to stay free of foreign entanglements so the young nation could prosper. He gave

Gouverneur Morris a succinct formulation of his credo: "My primary objects . . . have been to preserve the country in peace, if I can, and to be prepared for war, if I cannot."[29] In general, he favored economic rather than political involvement with the outside world. This neutrality policy was practical in that the United States was too small to exert significant leverage among the great powers and high-minded enough to shy away from European balance-of-power politics. Washington had no desire to exploit wrangling among foreign states, telling Morris that "this country is not guided by such narrow and mistaken policy as will lead it to wish the destruction of any nation under an idea that our importance will be increased in proportion as that of others is lessened."[30] As war convulsed Europe, Washington, a former war hero, might have been tempted to become a warlike president, but he wisely abjured the use of force at this first serious threat.

In early April, while vacationing at Mount Vernon, Washington received a letter from Hamilton in Philadelphia, announcing that England and France were at war. In forwarding instructions to Jefferson, Washington left no doubt of his desire for unconditional American neutrality: "War having actually commenced between France and Great Britain, it behooves the government of this country to use every means in its power to prevent the citizens thereof from embroiling us with either of those powers by endeavoring to maintain a strict neutrality."[31] As he rushed back to the capital, he asked Jefferson to draw up a document spelling out the terms of neutrality. Washington was especially concerned that American ships might be recruited as privateers to prey on British vessels, luring the country into war.

After the abortive attempt by Giles to expel him from office, Hamilton was not eager to defer to Jefferson and turned to Chief Justice Jay for advice on drafting a neutrality proclamation. Even though Jefferson complained bitterly about Hamilton's meddling in affairs of state, Washington did not always segregate foreign policy matters. Back in Philadelphia on April 18, he addressed thirteen questions on the crisis to all his department heads. The first two were the most urgent: Should the United States issue a declaration of neutrality, and should it receive a minister from the French republic? Ever alert to Hamilton's unseen influence, Jefferson noted that while the handwriting was Washington's, "the language was Hamilton's and the doubts his alone."[32]

At a cabinet meeting the next day, the thirteen questions spurred a brisk exchange between Jefferson and Hamilton. Sympathetic to the French Revolution, Jefferson opposed an immediate neutrality declaration, preferring to have England and France bid for American favor. Thunderstruck at the notion of auctioning American honor, Hamilton favored an immediate declaration. Their dispute hinged on fundamentally disparate views of what America owed France for her wartime assistance. Like many Americans, Jefferson thought the United States should embrace a longtime ally and honor the 1778 treaties with France, while Hamilton deemed them invalid because they had involved only a defensive alliance and had been signed by the now-beheaded Louis XVI. "Knox subscribed at once to H[amilton]'s opinion that we ought to declare the treaty void, acknowledging at the same time, like a fool as he is, that he knew nothing about it," an embittered Jefferson wrote.[33] Hamilton contended that France had aided the American Revolution only to undercut the British Empire. He won the debate about issuing a neutrality proclamation, and agreement to receive a minister from the French Republic was unanimous.

Drafted by Attorney General Randolph, the neutrality proclamation signed on April 22, 1793, was a monumental achievement for Washington's administration. This milestone of foreign policy, which refrained from employing the word *neutrality,* exhorted Americans to "pursue a conduct friendly and impartial toward the belligerent powers" and simultaneously warned them against "committing, aiding or abetting hostilities against any of the said powers" or carrying contraband articles.[34] Washington, a hardheaded realist, believed devoutly in neutrality and never doubted that nations are governed by their interests, not by their emotions.

This proud, courageous proclamation became a centerpiece of foreign policy for the next century, but it had no shortage of congressional critics. In a key assertion of executive power—denigrated by Republicans as a royal edict—Washington had bypassed the Senate, refusing to call it into session. Many in Congress reasoned that, if Congress had the power to declare war, it also had the power to declare neutrality. Many Americans had difficulty countenancing an end to the French alliance. Madison was especially disturbed by what he deemed a violation of congressional prerogatives, a betrayal of Franco-American ties, and capitulation to "the unpopular cause of Anglomany."[35] He feared that the president would abuse war-making powers: "The constitution supposes, what the history of all governments demonstrates, that the executive is the branch of power most interested in war, and most prone to use it," he wrote. "It has accordingly, with studied care, vested the question of war in the legislature."[36] Executive power in foreign affairs would grow steadily during the next two centuries, perhaps confirming the truth of Madison's warning.

As England and France studied the exact meaning of American neutrality, the proclamation prompted a significant constitutional debate. Writing under the pen names of "Pacificus" and "Helvidius," respectively, Hamilton and Madison sparred over its legality; Hamilton claimed executive branch primacy in foreign policy, while Madison made the case for the legislature. Unless he deliberately feigned ignorance, Washington had little inkling that the secretive Madison had led the charge against his neutrality policy. "The president is extremely anxious to know your sentiments on the proclamation," Jefferson confided to Madison in early August. "He has asked me several times. I tell him you are so absorbed in farming, that you write to me always about plows, rotations, etc."[37]

The political ramifications of the quarrel over the neutrality proclamation were no less far-reaching than the constitutional ones. The dispute over supporting England versus France further polarized an already divided country, and the Republicans sensed, with some satisfaction, that they could capitalize on a deep-seated attachment to France. "The war between France and England seems to be producing an effect not contemplated," Jefferson observed to Monroe in May in a tone of pleasant surprise. "All the old spirit of 1776 is rekindling."[38]

Bringing the controversy to full boil was the arrival in Charleston, South Carolina, on April 8 of the new French minister, Edmond-Charles Genet, who incarnated the new militance of French foreign policy following the king's deposition. French radicals had taken to hailing each other as *citoyen* and *citoyenne* ("citizen" and "citizeness") to supplant the bourgeois terminology of *monsieur* and *madame*, so the new minister became known as Citizen Genet. Gouverneur Morris had already predicted that Washington would find him insufferable and see in him "at the first blush, the manner and look of an upstart."[39] Only thirty years old, well versed in music and foreign languages, with a personality as flamboyant as his flaming red hair, Genet had already rendered diplomatic service in London and St. Petersburg. Dispensing with diplomatic niceties, he would take flagrant liberties and brazenly interfere in American politics.

The rabble-rousing diplomat lost no time in trying to nullify the neutrality proclamation. He set about converting American ships into privateers, manned by American and French sailors, hoping they would pounce on British merchant vessels and bring them into American ports as prizes of war. He also tried to recruit Americans to infiltrate Spanish and British possessions in Louisiana, Florida, and Canada and instigate uprisings. The dizzying acclaim that greeted Genet in Charleston foreshadowed his reception as he worked his way north to Philadelphia. More than a month elapsed before he presented his credentials to Washington; in the meantime he engaged in open politicking along the eastern seaboard, to the delight of Francophile citizens. But to the horror of Federalists, this brash, impetuous man, prone to grand pronouncements, drew huge throngs as he disseminated the messianic message of the French Revolution.

As Washington braced for his advent, he adopted a finely calibrated policy to suit both Hamilton and Jefferson. He would receive Genet, to please Jefferson, but without "too much warmth or cordiality," to satisfy Hamilton.[40] On May 16 Genet arrived in Philadelphia to an enthusiastic popular response. When he addressed a large crowd at the City Tavern, it reacted with hearty shouts and salutations. Slow to perceive Genet's folly or the way he overplayed his hand, Jefferson at first saw only another grand chapter of the democratic revolution unfolding. "He offers everything and asks nothing" was his early estimate of the ambassador.[41] When Jefferson presented Genet to Washington, the president received him at the executive mansion with the touch of coolness already decided upon.

The Frenchman's mere presence in Philadelphia opened floodgates of press criticism. Continuing its vendetta against the president, the *National Gazette* blasted Washington for toadying to England and showing base ingratitude toward France, complaining that the United States should not "view with cold indifference the struggles of those very friends to support their own liberties against an host of despots."[42] A few days later, in an open letter to Washington, the paper accused him of being isolated from the masses while surrounding himself with sycophants. "Let not the little buzz of the aristocratic few and their contemptible minions," read the letter, "of speculators, Tories, and British emissaries, be mistaken for the exalted and general voice of the American people. The spirit of 1776 is again roused."[43] It was an extraordinary declaration, for who embodied the spirit of 1776 more than General George Washington?

In early June Washington contracted a fever, and the press volleys fired against him only worsened his health. Beneath the tough surface, Washington was easily wounded. Having long bathed in adulation, he was unaccustomed to such blistering criticism. "Little lingering fevers have been hanging about him, and affected his looks most remarkably," Jefferson commented to Madison. He blamed the president's poor health on the press onslaught: "He is extremely affected by the attacks made . . . on him in the public papers. I think he feels these things more than any person I have ever met with. I am sincerely sorry to see them."[44] It was a strange remark to pass between the two men whose sponsorship had launched the *National Gazette*. Jefferson's self-described sympathy did not prevent him from presiding over further attacks against Washington, and he condemned the president as isolated, used to "unlimited applause," and unable to "brook contradiction or even advice offered unasked."[45]

The press slander could only have stiffened Washington's resolve to step down after two years, but the hubbub over relations with France kept deferring that day. As Gouverneur Morris wrote from France, "It will be time enough for you to have a successor when it shall please God to call you from this world's theater."[46] Oddly enough, both Hamilton and Jefferson also yearned to retire from the public stage. As he admitted to Madison, Jefferson felt worn down by the political backstabbing: "The motion of my blood no longer keeps time with the tumult of the world."[47] In February, when Washington asked him if he would serve as minister to France, Jefferson declined, citing his wish to retire to Monticello. In response, an irritable Washington grumbled that he himself had refused to retire.

One inescapable issue created by Genet was what to do about British ships brought into American ports as "prizes" captured by French privateers. In early May the French ship *Embuscade* docked in Philadelphia with two British merchant ships in tow. According to Jefferson, thousands of jubilant Philadelphians rent the air with "peals of exultation" when they set eyes on the captured vessels. Except for Jefferson, Washington and his cabinet members were appalled by Genet's action in outfitting privateers in American ports. On June 5 Jefferson warned Genet to desist from this practice and stop luring Americans into such service. Still intoxicated from the cheering crowds, the deluded Genet ignored the warning and turned one captured British merchant ship, the *Little Sarah,* into an armed French privateer christened *La Petite Démocrate.* The high-handed Frenchman then informed Jefferson that France had the right to outfit such ships in American ports. Echoing the Jeffersonian press, he dared to imply that Washington was "subservient to a Federalist party ... whose only aim is to establish Monocracy in this country."[48] Hamilton, bristling, termed this letter "the most offensive paper perhaps that ever was offered by a foreign minister to a friendly power with which he resided."[49] Citizen Genet, oblivious of his blunder, informed his superiors at home of his triumph over Washington: "Everything has succeeded beyond my hopes: the true Republicans triumph, but old Washington, *le vieux Washington,* a man very different from the character emblazoned in history, cannot forgive me for my successes and the eagerness with which the whole city rushed to my house, while a mere handful of English merchants rushed to congratulate him on his proclamation."[50]

The *National Gazette* parroted Genet's charges. In a July 4 column signed "A Citizen," the author noted that only three hundred people had come to applaud Washington's neutrality declaration while thousands cheered Genet in Charleston. Still more seriously, the author lectured Washington that, on this birthday of independence, he had relinquished his heroic standing from Revolutionary days: "There was a time when your *name* occupied an elevated position in the minds of your countrymen and your character was beloved by every genuine son of America ... But alas! What an astonishing revolution has a few years of peace produced in the sentiments of your countrymen?"[51]

As if he didn't have troubles enough, Washington had to make a sudden return to Mount Vernon to cope with the death of Anthony Whitting, who had replaced George Augustine as manager of Mount Vernon. The president, at his wit's end, complained that "my concerns at Mount Vernon are left as a body without a head."[52]

On July 8, while Washington was at Mount Vernon, the cabinet discussed what to do about *La Petite Démocrate,* anchored in the Delaware River. Hamilton and Knox wanted to fortify Mud Island, farther down the Delaware, to intercept the ship if it tried to sail—advice rejected by Jefferson. Two days later Jefferson took up the matter with Genet, who assured him that the renegade ship would stay put until Washington returned. Swollen with power, Genet also threatened, in a grave violation of diplomatic protocol, to appeal over Washington's head to the American people to overturn the neutrality policy. Washington was incensed over Genet's conduct, which brought to the surface his bottled-up rage against Jefferson. He flatly asked his secretary of state: "Is the minister of the French Republic to set the acts of this government at defiance—*with impunity* and then threaten the executive with an appeal to the people?"[53] Struggling with a fever, Jefferson relayed to Washington Genet's assurance that the ship would stay put until Washington determined its fate. Within a day or two Genet violated his promise as *La Petite Démocrate* slipped past Mud Island and fled out to sea, in a flagrant breach of American neutrality. The beleaguered president, weary of the tussle between the French and British ministers, told Henry Lee that since his return to Philadelphia "I have been more than ever overwhelmed with their complaints. In a word, the trouble they give is hardly to be described."[54]

In the absence of a Justice Department, Washington intermittently turned to Chief Justice Jay for legal advice. In July the cabinet sent Jay twenty-nine queries to clarify the meaning of neutrality and rule on American jurisdiction over the French seizure of ships in American waters. On August 8, replying on behalf of the Supreme Court, Jay declined to render an advisory opinion. The Constitution, he said, had set up three independent branches of government, and it would be improper for "judges of a court in the last resort" to issue an opinion that could be accepted or rejected by the president.[55] This decision set a major precedent, placing a protective barrier between the presidency and an independent judiciary and sharply defining lines that had hitherto been indistinct. In lieu of the Court's opinion, Washington's cabinet issued a set of rules governing the conduct of belligerents, prohibiting them from arming privateers or bringing prizes captured in American waters into American ports.

Genet's conduct stirred up a tempest in Philadelphia, and howling mobs of his supporters marched on the presidential mansion. "The town is one continuous scene of riot," the British consul reported. "French seamen range the streets night and day with cutlasses and commit the most daring outrages. Genet seems ready to raise the tricolor and proclaim himself proconsul."[56] This British hyperbole was corroborated by John Adams, years later, in a letter to Jefferson: "You certainly never felt the terrorism excited by Genet in 1793 when ten thousand people in the streets of Philadelphia, day after day, threatened to drag Washington out of his house and effect a revolution in the government or compel it to declare war in favor of the French Revolution and against England."[57]

Against this backdrop Washington convened a tense cabinet session on July 23 to discuss whether there was a way to demand Genet's recall without insulting France. Refusing to be swayed by the Frenchman's blackmail, he thought Genet's intemperate letters should be shown to the French. Hamilton seized on the occasion to float his theory that a "faction" wished to "overthrow" the government and that, to stop people from joining these "incendiaries," the administration should disclose the whole story of Genet's insolent conduct.[58] Of course, Hamilton knew that the chief instigator of that faction sat right there in the room: Thomas Jefferson. At this point even Jefferson concluded that Genet was "absolutely incorrigible" and was harming the Republican cause.[59] After repeated brushes with Genet, Jefferson described him in these caustic terms: "Hot-headed, all imagination, no judgment, passionate, disrespectful and even indecent toward the president."[60]

By this point the vicious cabinet infighting was tearing Washington apart. No sooner had he agreed to serve a second term than he regretted it. He was staggered by the rabid abuse spewed out by the Republican press. During his presidency, many newspapers had gone from being staid and neutral to being organs of party politics and propaganda. In May he asked Jefferson to dismiss Freneau from his State Department job after the editor made the nonsensical statement that Washington had issued the neutrality statement only after "Anglomen" had threatened to chop off his head. Jefferson resisted the presidential request. Then at a memorable cabinet meeting on August 2, Henry Knox brought a copy of a Freneau squib entitled "The Funeral Dirge of George Washington and James Wilson, King and Judges." Knox showed the president a savage satirical cartoon in which his head was being inserted in a guillotine, as if he were Louis XVI. It triggered a volcanic display of Washington's temper. The graphic scene was recorded by Jefferson:

> The President was much inflamed; got into one of those passions when he cannot command himself; ran on much on the personal abuse which has been bestowed on him; defied any man on earth to produce one single act of his since he had been in the government which was not done on the purest motives; [said] that he had never repented but once the having slipped the moment of resigning his office and that was every moment since; that *by God* he had rather be in his grave than in his present situation; that he had rather be on his farm than to be made *emperor of the world;* and yet they were charging him with wanting to be a king. That that *rascal Freneau* sent him three of his papers every day, as if he thought he would become the distributor of his paper; that he could see in this nothing but an impudent design to insult him. He ended in this high tone.[61]

So concerned was Henry Knox about Washington's nervous strain that he sat down three days later to compose a letter on the need for the president to pull himself together and project an aura of calm fortitude: "The prudent and sober part of the community regard, as in the case of a storm, the mind and countenance of the chief pilot. While he remains confident and composed, happiness is diffused around, but, when he doubts, then anxiety and fear have their full effect."[62] It was a measure of the trust between the two men that Knox could write such an unvarnished message to Washington.

For all the bitter strife in his cabinet, Washington valued the superior talents of Hamilton and Jefferson and was dismayed at the thought of losing them. On July 31 Jefferson submitted a letter announcing his intention to leave office at the end of September. A week later Washington stopped by Jefferson's country house and made a personal appeal for him to postpone his departure. The president referred to his own regret at having stayed in office, commenting "how much it was increased by seeing that he was to be deserted by those on whose aid he had counted."[63] Few men were better versed in foreign affairs or the intrigues of foreign courts than Jefferson, he said. In response, Jefferson alluded to his "excessive repugnance to public life" and how hard he found it to serve when "merchants connected closely with England" as well as speculators "bear me peculiar hatred."[64] Washington then tackled head-on the ubiquitous conspiracy theories. He credited the good intentions of the Republicans and said he understood that sincere people had fears of a monarchical party. But, he went on, "the constitution we have is an excellent one, if we can keep it where it is; that it was indeed supposed there was a party disposed to change it into a monarchical form, but that he could conscientiously declare there was not a man in the U.S. who would set his face more decidedly against it than himself."[65] Washington successfully cajoled Jefferson into staying stay in office a little longer.

Meanwhile Citizen Genet was not about to depart quietly. In mid-August, when John Jay and Rufus King revealed in a New York newspaper that Genet had threatened to make a direct appeal to the American people over the president's head, the country reacted with righteous indignation. Genet's intemperance ultimately proved a bonanza for the Federalists. In late August the cabinet agreed unanimously to demand his recall and give the French a full accounting of his behavior. As it happened, the Jacobins had already dispatched his successor, Jean-Antoine Fauchet, who had orders to send Genet home to stand trial for "crimes" against the revolution. Whatever his misgivings about Genet, Washington did not care to send him to his death and granted him asylum in the United States. The Frenchman married the daughter of Governor George Clinton and passed the remainder of his days in upstate New York.

The saga of Citizen Genet had an ongoing afterlife, since his visit spawned a new form of political club—the so-called Democratic-Republican Societies. Their organizers intended them to evoke the Sons of Liberty chapters, while apprehensive Federalists found them eerily reminiscent of the French Jacobin clubs. The first one was established in April 1793 in Philadelphia; ten more were formed before year's end, and at least two dozen more the next year. Washington always distinguished between legitimate criticism of government and an illegitimate, "diabolical" sort that sought to destroy confidence in public servants. Early on, he concluded that the new societies were of the illegitimate variety, spouting popular rhetoric while tearing down the fabric of government, "even at the expense of plunging this country in the horrors of a disastrous war."[66] He regarded them as tools of a French plot to destroy American neutrality and drag the country into war. While he acknowledged their right to protest, he was persuaded that the new societies constituted a menace because their permanence showed a settled hostility to the government.

Washington's views on dissent were colored by his political philosophy. Along with other Federalists, he thought that officials, once elected, should apply their superior judgment and experience to make decisions on behalf of the populace. As he enunciated this position: "My political creed therefore is, to be wise in the choice of delegates—support them like gentlemen, while they are our representatives—give them competent powers for all federal purposes—support them in the due exercise thereof—and, lastly, to compel them to close attendance in Congress during their delegation."[67] As an extension of this view, Washington believed that voters, having once elected representatives, should lend them support. He found it difficult to execute the philosophical leap that voters reserved the right to a continuing critique of their elected officials. The Republicans, by contrast, wanted representatives to be continually responsive to voters and receptive to political criticism.

Some historians have faulted Washington for being intolerant of dissent, but mitigating circumstances should be cited. The concept of republican government was new, and nobody knew exactly how much criticism it could withstand. From the close of the war, Americans had worried about foreign intrusion, especially attempts by European imperial powers to roll back the Revolution, and many members of the new Democratic-Republican Societies openly flaunted their admiration for the French Revolution. Also, many members of the opposition, most notably Jefferson, had opposed or felt highly ambivalent about the Constitution, and it was not unthinkable that they would repudiate it once in power. Washington did not see himself, as did many critics, as leader of the Federalist party, so the Republicans struck him as a harmful faction rather than simply the opposing party. Once again Washington was a transitional figure who bore many traces of the colonial past while slowly evolving into the representative of a more egalitarian age.

What is indisputable is that the Democratic-Republican Societies led to a much more raucous style of American politics. Instead of discussing politics politely at dinner tables or in smoky taverns, these groups were likely to take to the streets in mass rallies. These government critics also had fewer qualms about chastising their leaders. By the end of 1793 the diatribes against Washington no longer dwelled simply on his supposed imitation of the crowned heads of Europe. Now the opposition sought to debunk his entire life and tear to shreds the upright image he had so sedulously fostered. That December, the *New-York Journal* said that his early years had been marked by "gambling, reveling, horse racing and horse whipping," that he was "infamously niggardly" in business matters, and that despite his feigned religious devotion, he was a "most horrid swearer and blasphemer."[68] For George Washington, American politics had become a strange and disorienting new world.

CHAPTER FIFTY-SEVEN

Bring Out Your Dead

THE FORCE THAT COOLED, at least temporarily, the fervid agitation of the Democratic-Republican clubs was not political but medical: the yellow fever epidemic that lashed the capital during the summer of 1793. Later on John Adams was adamant that "nothing but the yellow fever ... could have saved the United States from a total revolution of government."[1] One of its first victims was a treasured figure in the presidential household, Polly Lear, the wife of Washington's secretary Tobias, who had assisted Martha with numerous household duties. Martha had converted her into another surrogate daughter, while George valued her as "an amiable and inoffensive little woman."[2] When Polly died on July 28, age twenty-three, Washington honored her with the sort of full-dress funeral that might have bid farewell to a cabinet officer. Deviating from his strict policy of never attending funerals, he led a procession that included Hamilton, Jefferson, Knox, and three Supreme Court justices as pallbearers. It was the one time that Washington attended a funeral as president. When Tobias Lear, after a seven-year association with Washington, resigned his post to make money in business, he was replaced by Martha's nephew Bartholomew Dandridge and George's nephew Howell Lewis. "In whatever place you may be, or in whatever walk of life you may move," Washington assured Lear, "my best wishes will attend you, for I am and always shall be your sincere friend."[3]

As August progressed, the yellow fever scourge spread from the wharves to the city's interior: victims ran high fevers, spewed black vomit, hemorrhaged blood from every orifice, and developed jaundice before they expired. By late August the sights and smells of death saturated the city, especially the groaning carts, stacked high with corpses, that trundled through the streets as their drivers intoned, "Bring out your dead."[4] To stem the fever, the authorities tried burning barrels of tar, which polluted the air with a potent, acrid stench. The epidemic was by then carrying away twenty victims daily. Emptied by spreading panic, most public office buildings shut down, and government employees decamped from the city. The Supreme Court sat for only two days before deciding to swell the general exodus.

Whether from instinctive courage or a stoic belief in death as something foreordained, George Washington again behaved as if endowed with supernatural immunity. He showed the same sangfroid as when bullets whizzed past him during the French and Indian War. He urged Martha to return with their grandchildren to Mount Vernon, but she refused to desert him. By early September yellow fever had taken a grim toll on government workers: six clerks died in the Treasury Department, seven in the customs service, and three in the Post Office. On September 6, upon learning that Hamilton had shown early symptoms of the fever, Washington rushed to him six bottles of wine, coupled with a sympathetic message. Treated by his childhood friend Dr. Edward Stevens, Hamilton survived the disease and then fled with his wife, Elizabeth, to the Schuyler mansion in Albany. Since Martha wouldn't abandon him, Washington opted to leave for Mount Vernon on September 10, departing in sufficient haste that he left behind his official papers. He and Martha invited Eliza Powel to escape with them to Virginia. Though deeply touched by the gesture, Powel decided that she could not abandon her husband, then the speaker of the Pennsylvania Senate, lest he get sick and require help. "The conflict between duty and inclination is a severe trial of my feelings," she told the Washingtons, "but, as I believe it is always best to adhere to the line of duty, I beg to decline the pleasure I proposed to myself in accompanying you to Virginia at this time."[5] Her caution was prophetic: three weeks later her husband joined the growing list of fatalities. Ironically, Eliza was off at her brother's farm at the time and experienced "a lasting source of affliction" for not having been present at her husband's bedside at the end.[6]

After urging him to safeguard the War Department clerks, Washington left Henry Knox in charge as acting president, with instructions to submit a weekly report on developments in the now-deserted capital. The doughty Knox was the last high-ranking official to depart. "All my efficient clerks have left me from apprehension," Knox reported in mid-September, noting that fatalities in the capital had zoomed to one hundred per day. "The streets are lonely to a melancholy degree. The merchants generally have fled . . . In fine, the stroke is as heavy as if an army of enemies had possessed the city without plundering it."[7] After Jefferson found only a single clerk toiling at the State Department, he decided it was high time to head for Virginia. By mid-October 3,500 Philadelphians, or one-tenth of the population, had succumbed to yellow fever, leaving the city, in Washington's words, "almost depopulated by removals and deaths."[8]

Eager to resume government operations and show that the republic could function even under extreme duress, Washington wanted to convene emergency sessions of Congress outside the capital, but he was unsure of their constitutionality. To his credit, he did not automatically assume autocratic powers in a crisis but tried to conform faithfully to the letter of the law. As alternate sites, he considered several nearby cities, among them Germantown, Wilmington, Trenton, Annapolis, and Reading. When he stopped at Mount Vernon, Jefferson, a strict constructionist, gave Washington his opinion that the government could lawfully assemble only in Philadelphia, even if Congress had to meet in an open field. Reluctant to be hamstrung by this restrictive view, Washington turned to the one person guaranteed to serve up a more liberal view of federal powers: Alexander Hamilton. In tapping his treasury secretary, Washington hinted broadly at his preferred outcome, telling him that "as none can take a more comprehensive view and . . . a less partial one on the subject than yourself . . . I pray you to dilate fully upon the several points here brought to your consideration."[9] Engaging in fancy semantic footwork, Hamilton cracked open the legal logjam by saying that Washington could *recommend* that the government meet elsewhere, although he couldn't *order* it. Hamilton favored Germantown, close to Philadelphia, as the optimal site, and it was duly chosen.

Washington decided to convene a cabinet meeting there in early November. On October 28 he packed and left Mount Vernon, teamed up with Jefferson in Baltimore, and arrived in Germantown on November 1. The small village was scarcely impervious to the troubles crippling the nearby capital, and hundreds of Philadelphia refugees milled about, fearful of venturing back to their homes. After renting the meager home of Isaac Franks, Washington had furniture carted out from Philadelphia. The sage of Monticello was reduced to sleeping in a bed tucked into the corner of a local tavern. As the weather cooled, the yellow fever epidemic in Philadelphia waned, although the city would still struggle for months to return to normal. In early December, amid lightly falling snow, Washington saddled his horse and returned to a place sadly transformed by disaster. "Black seems to be the general dress in the city," Martha noted. "Almost every family has lost some of their friends."[10] Out of respect for the dead, plays and dances were canceled, and as the town's foremost citizen, Washington took the lead in dispensing charity to widows and orphans left stranded by the epidemic.

Members of Congress were now rapidly flocking back to the capital, and as soon as Washington learned on December 2 that a quorum had been mustered, he decided to deliver his fifth annual address to Congress the next day, escorted for the last time by his first-term cabinet, the warring triumvirate of Jefferson, Hamilton, and Knox. As war raged in Europe, Washington felt the need to combat pacifist fantasies and insisted upon the need for sufficient "arms and military stores now in [our] magazine and arsenals."[11] As always, he touted military preparedness as the best way to prevent war and gently raised the question of whether militias were adequate to the country's defensive needs. He also defended his neutrality proclamation and explained the rationale behind the seeming betrayal of the historic French alliance. Beyond its policy particulars, the speech reaffirmed that the government had weathered the yellow fever epidemic and would now revert to some semblance of normality.

WHILE THE TEMPORARY CAPITAL suffered from the horrors of yellow fever, the permanent capital was beginning to emerge in all its splendor. That September Washington had been on hand in the federal city for the ceremonial laying of the cornerstone for the U.S. Capitol. Among his endless responsibilities, he was bogged down in administrative minutiae related to the new capital, having to approve personally, for example, the contract for a bridge over Rock Creek. The Residence Act of 1790 had stipulated that government buildings in the district should be ready by December 1800, and an impatient public clamored for visible signs of progress.

Disclaiming any special talent as an architect, Washington nonetheless endorsed a design for the new home of Congress sketched by Dr. William Thornton, a versatile doctor, inventor, and abolitionist. Thornton came up with a clever amalgam of classical architecture and modern American themes. Jefferson rejoiced in the building's style as "Athenian" and, to emphasize the parallel with antiquity, changed its name from the plain-sounding Congress House to the far more grandiose Capitol.[12] Washington was especially enamored of the dome, which he thought would lend "beauty and grandeur to the pile," its visual effect enhanced by a magnificent colonnade.[13] Washington's approval also helped the Irish architect James Hoban win the commission for the President's House, later known as the White House. "He has been engaged in some of the first buildings in Dublin," Washington wrote admiringly of Hoban, "appears a master workman, and has a great many hands of his own."[14] The White House cornerstone was laid on October 13, 1792. As in all matters pertaining to the capital, Washington wanted an elastic design that would accommodate future growth. "It was always my idea . . . that the building should be so arranged that only a part of it should be erected at present," he told the commissioners, "but upon such a plan as to make the part so erected an entire building, and to admit of an addition in future."[15] Curiously enough, the Supreme Court was then held in such low regard that it did not merit its own edifice and had to settle for a room in the Capitol.

Washington's strategy of building slowly and allowing for future expansion was an apt metaphor for his strategy for developing the entire country. An unintended metaphor perhaps cropped up in the composition of the downtrodden workforce laboring to complete the capital. Washington had favored importing indentured servants to do the building—he praised Germans for their steady work habits, Scots for their mechanical abilities—but there was no way that a southern capital could emerge without drawing heavily on slaves, given the local shortage of free labor. Hundreds of slaves pulled up stumps, leveled trees, made bricks, and scooped out trenches. Because Congress had authorized no money to acquire property and construct buildings, the project had to subsist on the proceeds of land auctions, and using slave labor helped cushion the budgetary stringency. By 1795 three hundred slaves were hard at work in the federal district, hurrying to finish public or private buildings.

On September 18, 1793, at Mount Vernon, Washington greeted a fife and drum corps from Alexandria and presided over a festive procession to install the cornerstone of the Capitol. After he crossed the Potomac, many Masons gathered to receive him, appareled in their order's ceremonial garb. The grand parade to the Capitol site proceeded under the auspices of Lodge No. 22 of Alexandria and the Grand Lodge of Maryland and its assorted chapters. Officiating as Grand Master, Washington donned the elaborately embroidered Masonic apron that, in happier times, had been a gift from Lafayette's wife. To the sharp reports of cannon, Washington stepped into a trench, hoisted a trowel, and spread cement on the cornerstone before pouring oil, corn, and wine over it as spectators offered up Masonic chants. Incorporated into this southeast corner of the Capitol was a silver plate engraved with the words "the year of Masonry 5793."[16] That Washington performed Masonic rituals at the new capital proved not that he was in thrall to a secret society but probably something more banal: that he believed that the "grand object of Masonry" was "to promote the happiness of the human race," and that nobody could possibly object to such an inarguable, community-minded goal.[17] After parading by the President's House, the gathering settled down to celebrate by dining on the barbecued remains of a five-hundred-pound ox.

With the town named after him, Washington was especially solicitous about the course of its building campaign and bought four lots there. At many points he prodded the three commissioners to speed up their work, insisting that they live in the federal district to expedite flagging construction. As he surveyed the muddy terrain, he worried that, should the project lag behind schedule, the southern states might well lose the capital to the avid boosters of Philadelphia. "The year 1800 is approaching with hasty strides," he warned. "So ought the public buildings to advance towards completion."[18] The pace of progress seemed so sluggish that James Madison began to despair that the capital would ever escape from the great "whirlpool of Philadelphia."[19] Whenever the project stagnated, Washington purchased more parcels to give things a timely fillip. He preferred selling individual lots to modest investors rather than multiple lots to large speculators, persuaded that the former would work harder to make long-term improvements. At every turn, Washington advanced his pet project for a national university in the new capital where students could attend congressional debates and absorb the basic principles of representative government. It had long disturbed Washington that American students attended universities abroad, where they might imbibe foreign ideas inimical to a republican polity.

ONCE WASHINGTON AGREED to serve a second term, the decision only fueled his apprehension about the state of his business affairs at Mount Vernon. There had been some improvements during his presidency, most notably the innovative, sixteen-sided threshing barn that Washington had designed. But in his absence, despite such scientific strides, Mount Vernon was overtaken by general decay, and his letters are replete with long-running complaints about dilapidated buildings, fences, hedges, barns, gates, and stables needing repair.

Having lost the services of George Augustine and Anthony Whitting, Mount Vernon lacked a guiding hand, and it was all Washington could do to keep the place running from afar. He never overcame his chronic financial anxieties, which only worsened with the distractions of his political career, and he remained a notably relentless, hard-driving boss. His incomparable success in life seemed not to soften his views or lighten his touch with employees, as if his economic insecurity were too deeply rooted ever to be extirpated. It never seemed to dawn on him to apply the same courtesy to his employees that he did to colleagues in Philadelphia, where he was such an exquisitely tactful politician. In December 1792 he badgered Anthony Whitting to keep a slave named Gunner hard at work, even though Gunner was probably around eighty-three years old. "It may be proper for Gunner to continue throwing up brick earth," the president wrote.[20] Despite his theoretical opposition to slavery, he cautioned his overseers against the "idleness and deceit" of slaves if not treated with a firm hand.[21]

Washington's business letters home have an unpleasantly caustic tone, as if he felt himself at the mercy of so many dunces and knaves. He was constantly on guard against inept overseers, whom he thought too lax in dealing with slaves. If overseers weren't up with the sun, he warned, slaves would sleep late, loaf, and cost him money. In essence, the overseers became slaves to the long hours of the slaves they supervised. In petulant weekly letters to the consumptive Whitting in 1792 and 1793, Washington scarcely ever offered an encouraging syllable. With painful consistency, he faulted Whitting's work, loaded him with advice, and seemed to accuse everyone of malingering.

In mid-March 1793, as Whitting was spitting up blood, Washington informed

Fanny Bassett Washington that the doctors had pronounced his tuberculosis "criti-cal and dangerous."[22] Whitting himself wrote pathetically to the president: "I am just now able to walk a little. Am very much reduced and very weak."[23] Nonetheless that spring, as he grappled with neutrality and Citizen Genet, Washington continu-ally lambasted Whitting and talked to him as if he were a fool or a child. When he thought Whitting did not respond adequately to his questions, he told him to take a slip of paper, jot down all the instructions, then cross off each item on the checklist as it was accomplished. At the time Whitting was so weak that he could scarcely mount a horse; a month later he lay in critical condition. Bedridden, barely able to speak, he nonetheless fretted about his failure to file weekly reports with Washing-ton. As Tobias Lear reported from the scene: "Mr. Whitting was much concerned at your not having received the reports of last week, but observed that he had directed [James] Butler [the Mansion House overseer] to take them, as he was unable to do it himself."[24] A few days later the estate manager was dead.

Preoccupied with political problems, Washington was thrown into turmoil by Whitting's death and promptly launched a search for a successor, looking for an honest, sober bachelor between the ages of thirty-five and forty-five. Only after Whitting's death did Washington learn to appreciate his virtues, telling one cor-respondent, "If I could get a man as well qualified for my purposes as the late Mr. Whitting . . . I sh[oul]d esteem myself very fortunate."[25] Even so, Washington con-tinued to defame Whitting, claiming that he "drank freely, kept bad company at my house and in Alexandria, and was a very debauched person."[26]

In late September, Washington hired William Pearce as the new estate manager and quickly trained him in his own exacting style, telling him how he liked every-thing in tip-top shape, humming smoothly along. As with Whitting, he told Pearce to keep a checklist of his instructions and review them often, "because I expect to have them complied with or reasons assigned for not doing it."[27]

By this point Washington was convinced that Mount Vernon was veering toward chaos and that he had to crack down on overseers and slaves alike. In the same lan-guage he had long used with his military and political associates, he coached Pearce on how to handle recalcitrant overseers: "To treat them civilly is no more than what all men are entitled to, but my advice to you is to keep them at a proper distance; for they will grow upon familiarity in proportion as you will sink in authority, if you do not."[28] He gave Pearce scathing character sketches of the five overseers, calling one "a sickly, slothful, and stupid fellow," and urging him to correct the abuses that had crept into the daily workings of Mount Vernon.[29] Ironically, the only one of the five overseers for whom he spared a kind word was the one black: "Davy at Muddy Hole carries on his business as well as the white overseers and with more quietness than any of them. With proper directions, he will do very well."[30]

Priding himself on being a progressive farmer, Washington was frustrated by his inability to introduce modern methods. When Henry Lee told him about a new threshing machine, Washington responded that "the utility of it among careless Negroes and ignorant overseers will depend *absolutely* upon the simplicity of the construction, for if there is anything complex in the machinery, it will be no longer in use than a mushroom is in existence."[31] His letters teem with regrets that his overseers refused to apply the crop-rotation system that had been his will-o'-the-wisp for many years.

Finally, on December 23, 1793, right before Christmas, Washington devoted a large portion of the day to writing five consecutive letters to his five overseers, blaming them for ruining his hopes for crop rotation and for the general decline of his business. In terms of pure, unadulterated rage, these five letters have no equal in Washington's papers: they suggest a daylong temper tantrum and show just how sharp-tongued and frustrated he could be. Their jeering tone is almost willfully cruel, as if Washington wanted to say things with brutal clarity and telegraph a tough new regimen. They show how exceedingly anxious he was about his financial position and the economic situation at Mount Vernon. They may also express some displaced anger from the violent attacks being made on him in the Jeffersonian press and by the Democratic-Republican Societies. Not mincing words, Washington wrote to overseer Hiland Crow that he had been

> so much disturbed at your insufferable neglect [of plowing] that it is with difficulty I have been restrained from ordering you instantly off the plantation. My whole place for next year is ruined by your conduct. And look ye, Mr. Crow, I have too good reasons to believe that your running about and entertaining company at home . . . is the cause of this now irremediable evil in the progress of my business . . . I am very willing and desirous to be your friend, but if your conduct does not merit it, you must abide the consequences from Y[ou]rs.[32]

Crow was a savage overseer in flogging slaves, Washington describing him to Pearce as "swayed more by passion than by judgment in all his corrections."[33]

Washington criticized overseer Henry McCoy for failing to plow after the late October rains, jeopardizing his spring oat crop: "How durst you disobey this order and, instead of bringing the whole force of your plows to this, you employ them now and then only, or one or two a week, as if it were for amusement, thereby doing everything which was in your power to derange my whole plan for the next year."[34] If McCoy remained inattentive to business, Washington threatened to banish him "at any season of the year without paying you a shilling . . . If I suffer by your neglect, you shall not benefit by the money of one who wishes to be your friend."[35]

Overseer William Stuart suffered a similar drubbing for his failure to plow as soon as the October rains had ceased.

Washington chastised overseer Thomas Green for failing to perform work at the Dogue Run barn. "I know full well," Washington told him, "that to speak to you is of no more avail than to speak to a bird that is flying over one's head; first, because you are lost to all sense of shame and to every feeling that ought to govern an honest man, who sets any store by his character; and, secondly, because you have no more command of the people over whom you are placed than I have over the beasts of the forests." If Green did not shape up, Washington threatened to "discharge you that mom[en]t and to dispossess your family of the house they are in, for I cannot, nor will not, submit to such infamous treatment as I meet with from you."[36]

After instructing overseer John Christian Ehlers on how to graft fruit and plant trees properly, Washington administered a stern lecture on the evils of alcohol: "I shall not close this letter without exhorting you to refrain from spirituous liquors. They will prove your ruin if you do not. Consider how little a drunken man differs from a beast; the latter is not endowed with reason, the former deprives himself of it; and when that is the case acts like a brute, annoying and disturbing everyone around him . . . Don't let this be your case." Then, punning harshly on Ehlers's middle name, Washington concluded, "Show yourself more of a man and a Christian than to yield to so intolerable a vice."[37]

The stress of managing Mount Vernon had finally become so draining for Washington that he wanted to free himself of the burden of supervising overseers and slaves. Since he contemplated stepping down as president in a year, his mind already dwelt on retirement, and he felt oppressed by a surplus of both slaves and white indentured servants. So he concocted an ambitious plan to rent out four of the Mount Vernon farms to four capable English farmers, retaining only the Mansion House farm for himself. In expounding this rental scheme to Tobias Lear, Washington admitted candidly that his motive was "that the remainder of my days may thereby be more tranquil and freer from cares; and that I may be enabled . . . to do as much good with it as the resource will admit. For although in the estimation of the world I possess a good and clear estate, yet, so unproductive is it, that I am oftentimes ashamed to refuse aids which I cannot afford, unless I was to sell part of it to answer the purpose."[38]

The cash-strapped Washington knew that the world reckoned him a much richer man than he really was. Mount Vernon's glorified facade of wealth and grandeur covered up an operation that was, at best, only marginally profitable. Running the estate forced Washington to keep up appearances and act with the openhanded largesse of an affluent planter. He still felt hounded by visitors stopping by Mount Vernon and partaking liberally of his food and drink. (In one letter, he expressed exasperation with Fanny for giving away dozens of bottles of expensive wine to voy-euristic travelers and listed only three classes of people who deserved those coveted bottles: close friends, foreign dignitaries, and members of Congress and other po-liticos.) Part of Washington's plan called for raising cash by selling more than thirty thousand acres of western land at a time when prices were appreciating sharply.

To help find suitable English farmers, Washington turned to the English agron-omist Arthur Young, summarizing for him the riches of the four farms in question, which then had 3,260 acres of arable land, 54 draft horses, 12 working mules, 317 head of black cattle, and hogs that "run pretty much at large in the woodland."[39] Washington had no qualms about touting the proximity of the farms to the federal capital rising nearby. "The federal city in the year 1800 will become the seat of the general government of the United States. It is increasing fast in buildings and ris-ing into consequence and will, I have no doubt . . . become the emporium of the United States."[40] Washington's rental plan gave him yet another economic incentive to accelerate the dilatory pace of construction of the new capital.

The most momentous aspect of the plan concerned the destiny of the 170 to 180 slaves confined on the four farms. It was Washington's fervent hope that the new owner would free the slaves and then rehire them "as he would do any other laborers which his necessity w[oul]d require him to employ."[41] Emancipating slaves was a startling innovation for any major Virginia planter to contemplate, especially if he was president of the United States. The scheme harked back to the plan that Lafayette had proposed for his experimental farm in French Guiana. In disclosing the idea to Lear, Washington explained that he had a motive "more powerful than all the rest, namely to liberate a certain species of property which I possess, very repugnantly to my own feelings, but which imperious necessity compels."[42]

From the timing of his decision, one suspects that Washington's disgust with slavery owed something to pure principle but also much to the pure fatigue of try-ing to wrest profits from an intractable workforce held in bondage. The realistic and idealistic sides of George Washington both conspired to rebel against the pecu-liar institution. Interestingly enough, when he mentioned possible obstacles to his plan, he talked of the difficulty of mingling white workers with black, but he never mentioned a far more glaring problem: a political backlash in the South against such a courageous move by the country's foremost citizen.

As always, Washington had manifold reasons for his actions, and his response to slavery was shaped by a complex blend of impulses. On November 23, 1794, he wrote a revealing letter to his nephew Alexander Spotswood that dealt with his views on slavery—a subject, Washington admitted, that "I do not like to even think, much less talk of."[43] Washington suggested that the main hindrance to emancipat-ing his slaves related to his fear of auctioning them off indiscriminately and breaking up families: "Were it not, then, that I am principled ag[ains]t selling Negroes, as you would cattle in the market, I would not, in twelve months from this date, be possessed of one as a slave."[44] He went on to say that he feared trouble might be brewing with the slave population and that a day of reckoning might soon be at hand: "I shall be happily mistaken if they are not found to be a very troublesome species of property 'ere many years pass over our heads."[45]

The anxious foreboding about slave revolts was immeasurably heightened by the massive slave revolt in the French colony of St. Domingue (modern-day Haiti), led by Toussaint Louverture starting in August 1791. This, the largest slave revolt in history, had led to thousands of deaths among rebel slaves and white masters, fomenting hysterical fears among American planters. When Charles Pinckney worried about the impact of these events on southern slaves, Washington shared his alarm: "I feel sincerely those sentiments of sympathy which you so properly express for the distresses of our suffering brethren [the slave owners] in that quarter and deplore their causes."[46] It seemed a terrifyingly vivid realization of the nightmares of slaveholders who feared the hatred that simmered deep inside their slaves. In response, Virginia enacted more stringent rules against slave gatherings as well as an "act against divulgers of false news."[47]

President Washington extended money and arms to the French government to combat the insurrection and also made a personal donation of $250 to relieve the affected white colonists. By July 1793 thousands of white refugees from St. Domingue had streamed into American ports, where they retailed hideous tales of rape and mass killings by enraged slaves. That month Thomas Jefferson wrote to James Monroe, saying that the situation of these fugitive planters "calls aloud for pity and charity. *Never was so deep a tragedy presented to the feelings of man* . . . I become daily more convinced that all the West India islands will remain in the hands of the people of color and a total expulsion of the whites sooner or later take place. It is high time we should foresee the bloody scenes which our children certainly and possibly ourselves (south of Potomac) will have to wade through and try to avert them."[48] In February 1794 France decided to free the slaves in its empire, partly to hold on to St. Domingue by appeasing the agitated black population. Washington's comments to Alexander Spotswood must be set against the backdrop of the slave revolt in St. Domingue and the conviction of many southern planters, reflected in Jefferson's comment, that it was only a matter of time before American slaves took matters into their own hands, rebelling in bloody wrath against their masters.

CHAPTER FIFTY-EIGHT

Hercules in the Field

THE WINTER OF 1793–94 was a cold and dreary one in Philadelphia; the Delaware River was so choked with ice floes that vessels could not navigate. After the yellow fever epidemic, the capital remained a ghostly place, with the usual diversions of theater and dancing still temporarily taboo. "We have been very dull here all winter," wrote Martha Washington, lapsing into the general funk. "There has been two assemblies and it is said that the players are to be here soon. If they come and open the new theater, I suppose it will make a very great change."[1]

On December 31, 1793, Thomas Jefferson resigned as secretary of state, thereby liberating himself from the intolerable company of Alexander Hamilton. For all their pronounced differences, Washington and Jefferson had experienced parallel frustrations with public service. Both men gave the impression of serving under duress, yearned to regain the domestic pleasures of their plantations, and disclaimed political ambition, however dubious that notion seemed to impartial observers. A worn-out Jefferson could not wait to return to the repose of Monticello, telling one correspondent in late November, "I hope to spend the remainder of my days in occupations infinitely more pleasing than those to which I have sacrificed 18 years of the prime of my life."[2] Since the political animosity toward him had spilled over into Federalist-dominated high society, he wished to retire "from the hated occupations of politics and sink into the bosom of my family, my farm, and my books."[3] In a parting shot as secretary of state, Jefferson proposed to Congress a series of trade restrictions designed to throttle commerce with Great Britain. In Hamilton's scornful opinion, Jefferson "threw this firebrand of discord" on congressional desks "and instantly decamped to Monticello."[4] Outwardly, Washington's parting with

Jefferson was amicable enough, and he sent him a civil farewell letter, but privately he felt that Jefferson had betrayed him by deserting him at a troubling moment in foreign affairs.

Jefferson's preferred self-image was that of a bookish, unworldly fellow, more at home with intellectual pursuits than in the hurly-burly of politics. Once back at Monticello, he presented himself as a monkish stranger to all political striving, as if it were a youthful folly he had outgrown. "The little spice of ambition, which I had in my younger days," he told Madison, "has long since evaporated . . . The question is forever closed to me."[5] To less friendly observers, however, the matter was far from closed. As early as 1792 Hamilton claimed to penetrate the secret workings of Jefferson's mind and discover it was worm-eaten with ambition: " 'Tis evident beyond a question, from every movement, that Mr. Jefferson aims with ardent desire at the presidential chair."[6] He interpreted Jefferson's withdrawal from the scene as a temporary maneuver until the time had ripened for his triumphant return. Similarly, John Adams dismissed gruffly Jefferson's pose of philosophical detachment, declaring upon the latter's exit from Philadelphia: "A good riddance of bad ware . . . He is as ambitious as Oliver Cromwell . . . His soul is poisoned with ambition."[7] For Adams, Jefferson's resignation was a calculated first step in a determined campaign for the presidency. "The whole anti-Federal party at that time considered this retirement as a sure and certain step towards the summit of the pyramid," he said in later life.[8] As he observed tartly, "Political plants grow in the shade."[9]

At first Jefferson professed sublime indifference to politics. "I live on my horse from morning to night," he declared to Henry Knox. "I rarely look into a book or take up a pen. I have proscribed newspapers."[10] In departing from office, Jefferson maintained that his political activity would henceforth be restricted to his hobbyhorse, "the shameless corruption of a portion" of Congress and "their implicit devotion to the treasury."[11] But when asked whether Washington was "governed by British influence," Jefferson supposedly replied, facetiously, that no danger existed so long as Washington "was influenced by the wise advisers or advice, which [he] at present had."[12] When Governor Henry Lee told him about this patent gibe that he was biased toward Britain and hoodwinked by Hamilton's malevolent influence, Washington reacted with fury. Jefferson could not honestly accuse him of such bias, he retorted, unless "he has set me down as one of the most deceitful and uncandid men living," because Jefferson had heard him "express very different sentiments with an energy that could not be mistaken by *anyone* present."[13] Two years later, hotly rejecting the accusation of being a "party man," Washington insisted to Jefferson that he had ruled against Hamilton in the cabinet as often as he had sided with him.[14]

After leaving office, Jefferson was demoted to a lower rung in Washington's ever-shifting hierarchy of relationships. Their correspondence, however friendly, centered on mundane matters, such as crops and seeds, and Washington never again sought him out for policy advice. He dropped the salutation "My dear Sir" in favor of the cooler "Dear Sir." Thus did the subtle Washington consign ex-colleagues to slow oblivion. If Washington suspected that Jefferson belonged to a cabal against him, Jefferson was no less insistent that "federal monarchists" had captured the president's ear in order to vilify him, Jefferson, as a "theorist, holding French principles of government, which would lead infallibly to licentiousness and anarchy."[15] For someone as cordial as Washington, the avoidance of meetings with an old friend underlined the true depth of his hostility toward Jefferson.

We are accustomed to viewing the founding era as endowed with an inexhaustible supply of superlatively able men available for public service. But once the most gifted public servants—Jefferson, Hamilton, Adams, Madison, and Jay—were already accounted for, Washington, like many later presidents, had a fiendishly hard time finding replacements for his sterling first-term cabinet and turned by default to comparative mediocrities. Moreover, some worthy figures weren't prepared to make the financial sacrifice that accompanied public office. To perpetuate some modicum of geographic and political diversity, Washington tapped Edmund Randolph as his new secretary of state and brought in a Federalist, William Bradford of the Pennsylvania Supreme Court, to replace him as attorney general. Nevertheless Randolph fell woefully short of Jefferson's intellectual standard and was viewed in Republican quarters as an unreliable partner. His shortcomings tilted the cabinet's power balance decisively toward Hamilton, giving a far more Federalist tint to Washington's second term. Both Hamilton and Knox had promised to stay on until the end of 1794; Hamilton's stature was only enhanced after a second House inquiry into his conduct granted him a full vindication in May 1794.

One of the first challenges for the new team was to figure out how to deal with the lawless North African, or "Barbary," states—Algiers, Tripoli, and Tunis—which plundered foreign vessels in the Mediterranean and enslaved their crews. Many European powers had grown resigned to paying "tribute"—a polite word for ransom money—to win the release of their crews. As American crews succumbed to these pirates and were threatened with forced conversion to Islam, Washington was offended by the need to pay bribes, especially after Algiers seized eleven American merchant ships and a hundred prisoners. Reluctantly, he authorized the payment of money to Algiers and even tried to negotiate a treaty of amity and commerce with the city-state, but he thought the time had come to back up American diplomacy with military might. In March 1794 Congress approved a proposal, backed by Washington and Knox, to build six frigates "adequate for the protection of the commerce of the U.S. against Algerian corsairs."[16] This action officially inaugurated the U.S.

Navy, although it would take four more years before a separate Navy Department was born. While the six frigates represented a landmark in Washington's plan to foster a professional military, he never neglected diplomacy and wrested treaties from both Morocco and Algiers.

Another foreign policy crisis arose from the swelling casualties spawned by the French Revolution and the concomitant European turmoil. Supported by his cabinet, Washington made a private overture to the king of Prussia, asking him to release Lafayette as a gesture of friendship toward America. Although Washington failed to win his freedom, the king eased the shockingly bad conditions of Lafayette's confinement and allowed him books, fresh air, and more appetizing food. The respite, alas, was brief. Lafayette was soon transferred to the Austrian authorities, who shut him up in a filthy, fly-infested cell in Olmütz, where he lay in chains and ragged clothing. After Lafayette's wife was arrested in France, Gouverneur Morris interceded on her behalf, leading Robespierre to spare her from the guillotine, but her mother, sister, and grandmother wound up as victims of the Terror.

In April 1793 the French government had established the Committee of Public Safety, giving it sweeping powers to arrest people for treason and try them under its jurisdiction; by September a Reign of Terror ensued that would claim as many as forty thousand lives.[17] As an eyewitness to the bloodletting, Gouverneur Morris provided Washington with a running commentary on the atrocities. "The Queen was executed the day before yesterday," he wrote of Marie-Antoinette that October. "Insulted during her trial and reviled in her last moments"—she had been taken through the streets of Paris in an open cart to the guillotine—"she behav'd with dignity throughout."[18] The perceptive Morris saw that the violence was no incidental by-product of the revolution but fundamental to its spirit. As he put it in lapidary prose, "In the groves [of the revolution], at every end of every vista, you see nothing but gallows."[19] An essential difference between the American and French revolutions was that the American version allowed a search for many truths, while French zealots tried to impose a single sacred truth that allowed no deviation.

By July 1794 the revolutionary tribunal in Paris accelerated the tempo of its trials and issued nine hundred death sentences per month.[20] Many victims of the Terror had been stalwart friends of the American Revolution. Pulled from his quarters in the middle of the night, Thomas Paine had been tossed into prison and stayed there for months. From Paris, James Monroe, who replaced Gouverneur Morris as American minister, informed Madison that Paine was loudly blaming Washington for his predicament: "He thinks the president winked at his imprisonment and wished he might die in gaol, and bears his resentment for it; also he is preparing an attack upon him of the most virulent kind."[21] Whatever displeasure Washington might have felt toward Paine, there is no evidence that he wanted him either abused or incarcerated.

Many Frenchmen who had admired or even participated in the American Revolution were casualties of its bloody Gallic sequel. After testifying in favor of Marie-Antoinette, the former Count d'Estaing was beheaded. The erstwhile Count de Rochambeau, locked up in the Conciergerie in Paris, was condemned to the guillotine and survived only because Robespierre fell from power as he was about to be decapitated. The massacre of French aristocrats widened the rift between Federalists, who feared that France would export anarchy, and Republicans, who cheered the radical spirit of events in Paris, whatever their unfortunate excesses.

At the same time that France was testing American patience, England, at war with France, was straining Anglo-American relations as never before. Starting in June 1793, the British government directed the Royal Navy to intercept neutral ships bearing foodstuffs destined for French ports and seize their cargo; five months later the policy was briefly expanded into a total blockade of the French West Indies. In short order, British warships stopped and seized 250 American ships, confiscating their wares. At the same time, to boost manpower in the depleted Royal Navy, captains grabbed British deserters aboard American ships—a practice known as "impressment"—accidentally tangling in their nets many innocent Americans. These high-handed maneuvers summoned up old memories of British arrogance and precipitated a political firestorm. Even Federalists waxed indignant that England was pursuing a counterproductive policy that would feed sympathy for France, foster a vengeful mood toward England, and threaten the neutrality proclamation.

Having authorized a new navy, Federalist leaders in Congress worked to marshal support for a 25,000-man army to deal with any foreign threats that materialized. They made plans to fortify harbors and, to combat the old bugaboo of a standing army, mobilize militiamen on short notice. For Republicans, such measures raised the specter of an oppressive military establishment that might be directed against homegrown dissidents. Those who deemed George Washington an uncritical admirer of Great Britain would have been surprised by the venomous letters he wrote that spring. In one, he mocked those "who affect to believe that Great Britain has no hostile intention towards this country" and insisted that its political conduct "has worn a very hostile appearance latterly."[22] He was convinced that Britain was inciting Indian nations against America and angling to alter the U.S.-Canadian border in Britain's favor.

The impression grew among Federalists that it would be wise to dispatch a special envoy to London to avert war, maintain trade, seek reparations for plundered ships, and settle outstanding disputes, including many lingering from the end of the war, such as Britain's failure to evacuate forts in the northwest. Among other things, Washington wanted to forestall any trade sanctions against England in the Congress. When Hamilton's name surfaced as the Federalists' first choice for the new envoy, Washington seriously considered it until Republicans protested that Hamilton, a patent Anglophile, would lack all credibility at home. Washington was swayed by this objection, especially after Hamilton removed himself from consideration and pushed forward Chief Justice Jay as an ideal substitute. To Republican eyes, the Anglophile Jay was hardly free of sin; indeed, Madison whispered in Washington's ear that Jay was a secret monarchist. But Washington proceeded with the appointment. The choice of Jay, less controversial than Hamilton, still caused an enormous uproar among government critics, and Madison affirmed that it was "the most powerful blow ever suffered by the popularity of the president."[23] For Washington, negotiation with England seemed the only alternative to outright war, and he stuck courageously by his decision to display Jay.

During his diplomatic mission Jay remained as chief justice, which struck some observers as unconstitutional. At the very least it softened the lines between the executive and judicial branches—lines that Jay himself had tried to sharpen. As Senator Aaron Burr argued, the decision created the prospect of the executive branch exercising a "mischievous and impolitic" influence over the judiciary.[24] Washington was agile in making appointments, and to make the choice of Jay more palatable, he shrewdly juggled political forces. To mollify Republicans, he recalled Gouverneur Morris from France, sending in his stead the Francophile senator James Monroe. Hamilton's influence had not been entirely neutralized, for when Jay sailed to England on May 12, 1794, applauded by a thousand bystanders on the New York docks, the instructions he carried bore Hamilton's imprint. Among other things, Jay would enjoy the leeway to negotiate a full-fledged commercial treaty, should the English prove amenable—something that was anathema to the Republicans. In his own instructions to Jay, Washington breathed fire against English intransigence. Of the British surrender of the frontier posts, he said: "I will undertake, without the gift of prophecy, to predict that it will be impossible to keep this country in a state of amity with G[reat] Britain long if the posts are not surrendered."[25] No one who saw Washington's correspondence could have imagined that he was a lackey of England or plotting to install a pro-British monarchy in America.

WASHINGTON'S LETTERS show that during his second term he was bruised and disillusioned by the scathing tone of the opposition. Increasingly deaf and embattled, he desperately needed rest at Mount Vernon, but the crush of public business allowed him only a brief stay there in June. While at home, as he was inspecting the canal and locks being built at the Little Falls of the Potomac, his horse lost its footing and nearly dashed him against the rocks. A masterful horseman, Washington nimbly pulled the animal away from danger with "violent exertions," but the effort so badly strained his back that afterward he could not even mount a horse.[26] Afraid his aching back could not withstand the long ride, he postponed his return to Philadelphia until July 3 and even then took the trip by easy stages. "I very much fear that it will be a troublesome complaint to him for some time," Martha worried of his back condition, "or perhaps as long as he lives he will feel it at times."[27] That July and August, to escape the sweltering heat of a Philadelphia summer, he and Martha took a house in Germantown.

People noticed that Washington seemed worn down by his cares. When English manufacturer Henry Wansey breakfasted with him, he found the president affable, obliging, and fit for a man of his age, but he detected "a certain anxiety visible in his countenance, with marks of extreme sensibility."[28] Still, he thought the president looked much younger than Martha: "She appears something older than the president, though I understand they were both born in the same year. [She was] short in stature, rather robust, very plain in her dress, wearing a very plain cap, with her gray hair closely turned up under it."[29]

Among the many burdens borne by Washington that summer was the fate of Anthony Wayne's expedition against Indians on the northwestern frontier. In January Wayne had informed Knox of his belief that his well-drilled army, the Legion of the United States, was capable of avenging St. Clair's ignominious defeat. The nation, in Wayne's opinion, had a "golden opportunity . . . for advancing and striking . . . those haughty savages . . . with the bayonet . . . and fire of the American Legion."[30] On August 20, in the Battle of Fallen Timbers, near present-day Toledo, Ohio, Wayne and a force of 3,500 soldiers delivered a stunning defeat to Indian tribes. The Americans went on an unbridled rampage, trampling Indian houses and crops over a vast territory. Nonetheless Washington sang Wayne's praises for having "damped the ardor of the savages and weakened their obstinacy in waging war against the United States."[31] The victory broke the back of Indian power in the region and ended British influence with the dominant tribes.

While Washington dealt remorselessly with Indians who menaced white settlers, he never surrendered hope of a humane rapprochement with them. Both Washington and Knox recognized that Indian depredations were understandable responses to the impingement of white communities on their traditional lands. Neither man engaged in bullying jingoism, and Knox even regretted that whites who murdered Indians were not dealt with as severely as Indians who did the same to whites. "It is [a] melancholy reflection," Knox wrote, "that our modes of population have been more destructive to the Indian natives than the conduct of the conquerors of Mexico and Peru. The evidence of this is the utter extirpation of nearly all the Indians in the most populous parts of the Union."[32] No less sympathetic to the Indians' plight, Washington noted despairingly that "the encroachments . . . made on their lands by our people" were "not to be restrained by any law now in being or likely to be enacted."³³

Washington's Indian policy was a tragedy of noble intentions that failed to fix a seemingly insoluble problem. He wanted to fashion a series of homelands that might guarantee the permanent safety of Indian tribes. In his last year in office, he issued his "Address to the Cherokee Nation," which attempted to define a way for Americans and Native Americans to coexist in harmony. He again advised the Indians to abandon traditional hunting and gathering and to imitate the civilization of white settlers by farming and ranching. He urged them to domesticate animals, to farm crops, and to encourage spinning and weaving among their women. He even offered Mount Vernon as a model: "Beloved Cherokees, what I have recommended to you, I am myself going to do. After a few moons are passed, I shall leave the great town and retire to my farm. There I shall attend to the means of increasing my cattle, sheep, and other useful animals; to the growing of corn, wheat, and other grain; and to the employing of women in spinning and weaving."³⁴ As was so often the case when slavery was involved, Washington did not see the absurdity of presenting himself, a large slave owner, as a shining example for the Indians to emulate.

If the speech was enlightened in its warm, friendly tone toward the Cherokees, it was unrealistic in asking them to abandon their culture and adopt that of their rivals. It was, in essence, telling the Indians that to survive they had to renounce their immemorial way of life—that is, cease to be Indians and become white men. At bottom lurked the unspoken threat that, if they flouted this advice, harm would follow. For all of Washington's good intentions, it proved impossible for the federal government to prod speculators and state governments into dealing fairly with the Indians, who continued to lose millions of acres from the rapacious practices of white men.

THE MAIN CRISIS that monopolized Washington's time in the summer of 1794 came not from troublesome Indians but from restive white settlers. From the time Congress imposed an excise tax on distilled spirits in 1791—an important component of Hamilton's plan to pare the federal deficit—Washington had expected resistance and vowed to exercise his legal powers "to check so daring and unwarrantable a spirit."³⁵ The new government, he believed, had to punish infractions and instill reverence for the law. If laws were "trampled upon with impunity," he warned, "and a minority . . . is to dictate to the majority, there is an end put at one stroke to republican government."³⁶ The chief locus of opposition to the whiskey tax arose in western Pennsylvania, where many farmers owned small stills and converted their grain into whiskey to make it more portable to seaboard markets. They were especially outraged by the investigative powers granted government inspectors, who could inspect barns and cellars at will. Compared to inhabitants of eastern cities, frontier settlers had a more tenuous allegiance to the federal government and tended to resent its intrusions more keenly, especially when it came to internal taxes such as the whiskey tax.

As opposition flared into violent discontent, the first target was Colonel John Neville, a revenue inspector who had seen service in the Continental Army. In mid-July 1794 Neville and U.S. Marshal David Lenox tried serving processes on farmers who had not registered their stills, as required by law. In retaliation, protesters attacked Neville's house, putting it to the torch, and also fired at Lenox. On August 1 the protests assumed a more ominous character when six thousand dissidents appeared in Braddock's Field outside Pittsburgh—the same place where Washington had shown such heroism four decades earlier. The mood of bravado and secession was symbolized by a flag with six stripes, representing the four counties in Pennsylvania and two in western Virginia that were in armed revolt over the whiskey tax. "Sodom had been burnt by fire from heaven," thundered one speaker. "This second Sodom [Pittsburgh] should be burned with fire from earth."[37] The protesters talked of seizing the federal garrison in Pittsburgh and pledged to force the resignation of anyone enforcing the whiskey tax. Fulfilling the worst Federalist fears, one dissident, taking inspiration from Robespierre, urged the creation of a committee of public safety and weeks later called for guillotines.

On August 2 Washington assembled his cabinet to ponder measures to counter the uprising. Reluctantly convinced that he had to crack down on those defying the whiskey tax, he urged Pennsylvania officials to take the lead, but they balked at military action. When Washington canvassed his cabinet, Hamilton and Knox wanted to call out the militia posthaste, while Randolph demurred, fearing force would embolden the protesters. Washington solicited an opinion from Justice James Wilson, who certified the president's authority to mobilize the militia. On August 7 Washington issued a proclamation calling up the militia and warned the western insurgents to "disperse and retire peaceably to their respective abodes" by September 1.[38] The same day, Knox alerted the governors of Pennsylvania, New Jersey, and Virginia to ready thirteen thousand militia to squash the rebellion. Washington exhausted all peaceful means before resorting to force and sent out a three-man commission, headed by Attorney General Bradford, to parley with the insurgents in western Pennsylvania.

The day after the proclamation, Knox received the president's reluctant permission to take a six-week leave of absence in Maine, where he had encountered business setbacks. All year Washington had brooded about whether Knox's financial plight would force him to resign. In 1790 Knox had bought two million acres in Maine with the notorious speculator William Duer, whose machinations had touched off financial panic in New York. Eager to become a country squire, Knox borrowed lavishly and constructed a baronial mansion. With its nineteen rooms and twenty-four fireplaces, the house ranked among New England's majestic private residences. Since Knox had been the soul of loyalty to Washington, it seems puzzling that he deserted him during the Whiskey Rebellion; the president must have wondered whether his protégé had lost his way amid his social aspirations. In a major step, Washington had Alexander Hamilton assume the additional duties of secretary of war until Knox returned. It was a tough moment for Hamilton, too, since his wife was going through a difficult pregnancy and one of his sons lay desperately ill.

When the three commissioners met with local residents in western Pennsylvania in mid-August, they encountered defiant vows to resist the whiskey tax "at all hazards."[39] Only the "physical strength of the nation," they told Washington, could guarantee compliance with the law.[40] Governor Henry Lee of Virginia was deputized to lead the army formed to put down the insurgents. In confidence, Washington sent him a vehement letter about the revolt, which he thought had been fomented by Genet and other "*artful* and *designing*" men who wished to destroy confidence in government. "I consider this insurrection as the first *formidable* fruit of the Democratic Societies."[41] He saw himself as the target of a whispering campaign conducted by his political opponents: "A part of the plan for creating discord is, I perceive, to make me say things of others, and others of me, w[hich] have no foundation in truth."[42] Washington's political views sometimes sounded as if they were plucked from a study of *Plutarch's Lives* or Shakespeare's Roman plays, in which shrewdly ambitious demagogues preyed upon credulous masses.

The evidence of unrest in western Pennsylvania mounted. A mob descended on Captain William Faulkner, who had allowed John Neville to establish an office in his home, threatening to tar and feather him and incinerate his house unless he stopped giving sanctuary to Neville. New reports suggested that the turmoil might be spreading to Maryland and other states. Eager to show governmental resolve in the face of disorder, Hamilton had long spoiled for a showdown with the instigators. "Moderation enough has been shown; 'tis time to assume a different tone," he had advised Washington.[43] Having hoped for a diplomatic settlement, Washington reluctantly agreed that a show of force had become necessary in western Pennsylvania.

Amid the crisis, Washington bowed to the wishes of his Alexandria lodge and sat for a portrait by William Joseph Williams that featured him in a Masonic outfit. After suffering through many portraits early in his presidency, Washington had decided to scale back drastically. He admitted to Henry Lee in 1792 that he had grown "so heartily tired of the attendance which . . . I have bestowed on these kind of people [artists] that it is now more than two years since I have resolved to sit no more for any of them . . . except in instances where it has been requested by public bodies or for a particular purpose . . . and could not without offense be refused."[44] He detested the crude engravings of him made from paintings, which were crassly peddled by vendors. The pastel portrait that Williams executed on September 18, 1794, shows a particularly dour, cranky Washington, with a tightly turned-down mouth. Posing in a black coat, he wears Masonic symbols on a blue sash that slants diagonally across his chest. His face is neither friendly nor heroic but looks like that of a bad-tempered relative, suggesting that the presidency was now a trial he endured only for the public good. Unsparing in its accuracy, the Williams portrait shows various blemishes on Washington's face—a scar that curves under the pouch of his left eye; a mole below his right earlobe; smallpox scars on both his nose and cheeks—ordinarily edited out of highly sanitized portraits.

On September 25 Washington issued a final warning to the whiskey rebels, who had dismissed his "overtures of forgiveness" and now constituted, in his view, "a treasonable opposition."[45] He viewed their actions as a grave test of the Constitution, raising the question of "whether a small proportion of the United States shall dictate to the whole Union."[46] Prepared to don his uniform to lead the fight, Washington told his tailor to make up an outfit patterned after the one he had worn during the war. He planned to travel as far west as Carlisle, Pennsylvania, where the Pennsylvania and New Jersey militia were encamped, before deciding whether to proceed farther west with the troops. Still recovering from his June back injury, Washington, accompanied by Hamilton, rode out of Philadelphia in a genteel carriage, rather than on horseback, as if they were going off on a peaceful jaunt in the autumn countryside. No longer accustomed to the alarums of war, Martha was all aflutter with fear. "The president . . . is to go himself tomorrow to Carlyle to meet the troops," she wrote Fanny. "God knows when he will return again. I shall be left quite alone with the children."[47]

In sallying forth to command the troops, Washington, sixty-two, became the first and only American president ever to supervise troops in a combat situation. It irked him that Knox had not returned as promised, then compounded his misdemeanor by not bothering to write to him. "Under the circumstances which exist to exceed your proposed time of absence so long is to be regretted," Washington wrote Knox in unusually pointed language. "But hearing nothing from you for a considerable time has given alarm, lest some untoward accident may have been the cause of it."[48] Knox's absence magnified the power of Hamilton, who believed in an overwhelming demonstration of military strength. "Whenever the government appears in arms," Hamilton proclaimed, "it ought to appear like a *Hercules* and inspire respect by the display of strength."[49] For Hamilton, an armed force of thirteen thousand soldiers was a suitable number to confront an estimated six thousand to seven thousand insurgents, but Republicans thought he was conjuring up a phantom revolt to establish an oppressive army. The Whiskey Rebellion, Madison insisted, was being exploited to "establish the principle that a standing army was necessary for *enforcing the laws*," while a skeptical Jefferson scoffed that an "insurrection was announced and proclaimed and armed against, but could never be found."[50]

Crowns and Coronets

AS HE ROLLED WESTWARD toward the army assembled at Carlisle, Washington's writing reverted to the factual almanac style of his travel diaries, as if he were a touring naturalist and not president of the United States: "The Susquehanna at this place abounds in the rockfish of 12 or 15 inches in length and a fish which they call salmon."[1] The president still had sufficient spunk and energy that, when his carriage forded the river, he drove it across himself. When he arrived at Carlisle, troops lined the roadway, eager to catch a glimpse of him, and Washington knew that, for this command performance, they wanted the charismatic military man on horseback, not the aging president ensconced in a carriage. A Captain Ford of the New Jersey militia thrilled to the sight of Washington: "As he passed our troop, he pulled off his hat, and in the most respectful manner, bowed to the officers and men and in this manner passed the line."[2] From Washington's dignified deportment, everyone recognized the solemnity of the occasion. A large, euphoric crowd had assembled in the town, and they were hushed into silence by his sudden appearance. When he reviewed the soldiers standing at attention in front of their tents, these men were also awed into "the greatest silence," according to Captain Ford.[3]

Experiencing "the bustle of a camp" for the first time in a decade, Washington kept a relatively low profile and was eager to accentuate the role of the state governors and their militias.[4] Eyewitnesses observed Hamilton briskly taking charge while Washington seemed a bit detached. One young messenger who deposited dispatches at headquarters said that Hamilton was clearly "the master spirit. The president remained aloof, conversing with the writer in relation to roads, distances, etc. Washington was grave, distant, and austere. Hamilton was kind, courteous, and frank."[5]

While Washington was at Carlisle, Henry Knox belatedly returned to Philadelphia. It must have dawned on him just how annoyed Washington was by his protracted absence, for he sent him a letter awash with "inexpressible regret that an extraordinary course of contrary winds" had delayed his return.[6] Knox volunteered to join Washington at Carlisle and must have been shocked by his curt reply: "It would have given me pleasure to have had you with me on my present tour and advantages might have resulted from it, if your return in time would have allowed it. It is now too late."[7] This was a remarkable message: the president was banishing the secretary of war from the largest military operation to unfold since the Revolutionary War. In addition to giving Knox a stinging rap on the knuckles, Washington must also have seen that Hamilton had assumed a commanding posture and would have yielded to Knox only with reluctance.

With general prosperity reigning in the country, Washington found something perverse in the discontent of the whiskey rebels, telling Carlisle residents that "instead of murmurs and tumults," America's condition called "for our warmest gratitude to heaven."[8] He faulted the insurgents for failing to recognize that the excise law was not a fiat, issued by an autocratic government, but a tax voted by their lawful representatives. To avert bloody confrontations, two representatives of the rebel farmers traveled to Carlisle to hold talks with Washington. Born in northern Ireland, Congressman William Findley was a solid foe of administration policies, and David Redick, also born in Ireland, was a former member of Pennsylvania's Supreme Executive Council. On their way to Carlisle, the two had received disturbing reports of an unruly federal army that could not wait to wreak havoc on the western rebels. Rough, shrewd men from the Pennsylvania backwoods, Findley and Redick were realists and let Washington know that frontier settlers were now prepared to pay the whiskey tax.

At two meetings Washington received them courteously enough and pledged to curb vengeful feelings in his army. "The president was very sensible of the inflammatory and ungovernable disposition that had discovered itself in the army before he arrived at Carlisle," Findley recollected, "and he had not only labored incessantly to remove that spirit and prevent its effects, but he was solicitous also to remove our fears."[9] Washington, who sensed that the two emissaries were frightened, believed that the insurgents were defiant only when the army remained distant. He warned that "unequivocal *proofs* of absolute submission" would be required to stop the army from marching deeper into the western country.[10] He also stated categorically that if the rebels fired at the troops, "there could be no answering for consequences in this case."[11] Viewing the Whiskey Rebellion as the handiwork of the Democratic-Republican Societies, bent on subverting government, he did not intend to relent too easily. Such was his outrage over the menacing and irresponsible behavior of these groups that it threatened his longtime friendship with James Madison. In a private letter to Secretary of State Randolph, Washington wrote, "I should be extremely sorry therefore if Mr. M——n *from any cause whatsoever* should get entangled with [the societies], or their politics."[12]

As he proceeded west toward Bedford, the president cast a discerning eye on the surrounding scenery, not as a future battlefield but as a site for future real estate transactions. "I shall summarily notice the kind of land and state of improvements along the road I have come," he vowed in his diary.[13] However conciliatory he was with Findley and Redick, he clung to the conviction that the incorrigible rebels would submit only under duress. When he heard reports of insurgents cowering as the army approached, he wrote cynically that "though submission is professed, their principles remain the same and ... nothing but coercion and example will reclaim and bring them to a due and unequivocal submission to the laws."[14]

Reaching Bedford, Washington rode in imposing style along the line of soldiers—his back troubles had miraculously eased—and the army reacted with palpable esteem for its commander in chief. As Washington passed, a Dr. Wellington noted in his diary, the men "were affected by the sight of their chief, for whom each individual seemed to show the affectionate regard that would have been [shown] to an honored parent ... Gen[era]l Washington ... passed along the line bowing in the most respectful and affectionate manner to the officers. He appeared pleased."[15] Washington must have been buoyed by his reception and the return to the rugged life of a field command, away from the sedentary urban duties of the presidency. Because the whole point of the expedition was to establish the sovereign principle of law and order in the new federal system, he warned his men that it would be "peculiarly unbecoming" to inflict wanton harm on the whiskey rebels and that civil magistrates, not military tribunals, should mete out punishment to them.[16] He huddled with Hamilton and Henry Lee to work out plans for two columns to push west toward Pittsburgh. On October 21, once the military arrangements were completed, he disappeared into his carriage and doubled back to Philadelphia through heavy rain, leaving Hamilton in charge and sending the Jeffersonian press into a frenzy. Benjamin Franklin Bache's *Aurora* flayed Hamilton as a military despot in the making, construing his current position as but "a first step towards a deep laid scheme, not for the promotion of the country's prosperity, but the advancement of his private interests."[17]

On October 28, after days of sliding along muddy roads, Washington rolled back into Philadelphia, right before Congress came into session. In his sixth annual address to Congress, on November 19, he defended his conduct in western Pennsylvania and singled out "certain self-created societies" as having egged on the protesters and assumed a permanently threatening character to government authority.[18] For those who missed the glaring reference, the Federalist Fisher Ames claimed that the Democratic-Republican Societies, inspired by the French Jacobin clubs, "were born in sin, the impure offspring of Genet," and produced "everywhere the echoes of factions in Congress."[19] Washington's rare display of public temper generated a mood of high drama; one Federalist congressman vouched that he had "felt a strange mixture of passions which I cannot describe. Tears started into my eyes, and it was with difficulty that I could suppress an involuntary effort to swear that I would support him."[20]

Washington's allusion to the new societies, which sounded sinister, produced deep reverberations in American politics. The Senate applauded his warning, but in the House James Madison denounced what he saw as the censure of legitimate political clubs. "If we advert to the nature of republican government," he said, "we shall find that the censorial power is in the people over the government, and not in the government over the people."[21] It was an astounding development: James Madison, the former confidant of Washington, was now openly condemning his mentor. So unwarranted did Madison consider Washington's criticism of the "self-created societies" that he privately told Jefferson that it was "perhaps the greatest error" of Washington's political life.[22] Madison descried a strategy to denigrate the societies by associating them with the Whiskey Rebellion, and then to denigrate congressional Republicans by associating them with the societies—all as part of an effort to boost the Federalist party. For Jefferson, Washington's speech was a patent attack on free speech, confirming a monarchical mentality that was "perfectly dazzled by the glittering of crowns and coronets."[23] For Madison and Jefferson, this was the pivotal moment when Washington surrendered any pretense of nonpartisanship and became the open leader of the Federalists.

As Washington anticipated, the display of military might in western Pennsylvania caused the uprising to wither. But it would stand as the biggest display of armed resistance to the federal government until the Civil War. Approximately 150 prisoners were taken into custody, and Washington showed commendable clemency in dealing with them. After two rebel leaders were tried and sentenced to death, Washington, drawing on this constitutional power for the first time, pardoned both men. Throughout the ordeal, he had shown consummate judgment, acting with firmness and moderation, trying diplomacy first but then, like a stern parent, preparing to dole out punishment. Given the giant scale of the protest and the governmental response, there had been remarkably few deaths. In a classic balancing act, he had conferred new luster on republican government, showing it could contain large-scale disorder without sacrificing constitutional niceties, and his popularity only grew in consequence.

The aftermath of the Whiskey Rebellion led to a dramatic shift in Washington's cabinet. If the episode augmented Republican fears about Hamilton's influence, the treasury secretary had a surprise in store for them. On December 1, the same day he returned to Philadelphia, he notified Washington that he planned to relinquish his Treasury post at the end of January, a decision possibly influenced by his wife's miscarriage in his absence. As the contrasting behavior of Hamilton and Knox during the Whiskey Rebellion made clear, Washington warmed to Hamilton because the latter never let him down, never disappointed him, and always delivered in an emergency. Washington had allowed no Republican diatribes against Hamilton to weaken his opinion of a supremely gifted, if sometimes flawed, public servant. Just how highly Washington rated Hamilton was shown in the letter he wrote in accepting his resignation, an encomium that embraced both his wartime and his government service: "In every relation which you have borne to me, I have found that my confidence in your talents, exertions, and integrity has been well placed. I the more freely render this testimony of my approbation, because I speak from opportunities of information w[hi]ch cannot deceive me and which furnish satisfactory proof of your title to public regard. My most earnest wishes for your happiness will attend you in your retirement."[24] To replace Hamilton, Washington elevated the comptroller of the treasury, Oliver Wolcott, Jr., the Connecticut lawyer who had earlier been the department's auditor.

Even as the Whiskey Rebellion deepened the bond between Washington and Hamilton, it appeared to dissolve the almost-twenty-year connection between Washington and Knox. Underscoring his displeasure with Knox, Washington sent him few letters that fall. In early December Knox told a friend that he contemplated stepping down at the end of the month, a decision only strengthened by another episode. On December 23 Senator Pierce Butler complained to Washington about abuses committed during the construction of the new U.S. frigates. In forwarding this letter to Knox, Washington was notably brusque, merely saying, "I request that strict inquiry may be instituted into the matter and a report thereupon made to me."[25] Knox knew how to read his chief's subtleties. On December 28 he submitted his resignation to Washington, beginning the letter with the frosty "Sir" instead of the customary "Dear Sir." In explaining his decision, Knox cited the claims of "a wife and a growing and numerous family of children" and tried to end on a personal note. "But in whatever situation I shall be, I shall recollect your confidence and kindness with all the fervor and purity of affection of which a grateful heart can be susceptible."[26]

Where Washington had accepted the resignations of Hamilton and even Jefferson with "Dear Sir" letters, he addressed Knox as "Sir." He made no effort to urge him to stay in office, and his letter, while correct, did not begin to capture the former warmth of their relationship: "I cannot suffer you, however, to close your public service without uniting, with the satisfaction which must arise in your own mind from a conscious rectitude, my most perfect persuasion that you have deserved well of your country. My personal knowledge of your exertions . . . justifies the sincere friendship which I have ever borne for you and which will accompany you in every situation of life."[27] One senses that Washington was trying to temper old gratitude with recent disenchantment. He had never made personal excuses for himself at times of crisis and apparently had little tolerance for Knox's doing so. It is hard to avoid the impression that Washington thought Knox had behaved negligently during the whiskey crisis, and Knox was never fully reinstated in his good graces.

For Knox's successor, Washington chose Timothy Pickering, a curmudgeonly character who, during his wartime stint as adjutant general, was critical of Washington. In 1791 the president had chosen him as postmaster general and also employed him periodically on diplomatic missions to the Indian nations. The choices of Wolcott and Pickering confirmed that Washington could not duplicate the quality of his first-term team and was moving toward a more overtly Federalist cabinet. After the flap over the Democratic-Republican Societies and his estrangement from Jefferson, Washington began to think that he deserved absolute loyalty from department heads and could no longer strive for political balance. The departures of Jefferson, Hamilton, and Knox only made Washington long more wistfully for the solace of Mount Vernon. In January 1795 he told Edmund Pendleton that "altho[ugh] I have no cause to complain of the want of health, I can religiously aver that no man was ever more tired of public life, or more devoutly wished for retirement, than I do."[28] Unfortunately, the cabinet turnover pushed the day of retirement ever further into a cloudy future.

CHAPTER SIXTY

Mad Dog

EVEN WITH THE BENEFIT OF HINDSIGHT, George Washington insisted that, in sending John Jay to England, he had selected the person best qualified to ensure peace. Because of long delays in transatlantic communications, Washington had no precise notion of the deal Jay was hammering out in London and warned his emissary that "many hot heads and impetuous spirits" wished him to speed up his work.[1] While not wanting to rush Jay, he reminded him, quoting his beloved Shakespeare, that "there is a 'tide in human affairs' that ought always to be watched" and that he should proceed with all possible haste.[2] By February 1795 reports made the rounds in Philadelphia that Jay had concluded a treaty and would shortly arrive on American shores.

On March 3, with Congress set to adjourn, Washington notified legislators that he would convene a special session on June 8 to debate the treaty, which would surely arrive in the interim. As it happened, four days later the document sat on his desk. Washington must have quietly gagged as he pored over its provisions, which seemed heavily slanted toward Great Britain. The treaty failed to stem the odious British practice of seizing American sailors on the high seas. Shockingly, it granted British imports most-favored-nation status, even though England did not reciprocate for American imports. Once the treaty was revealed, it would seem to many as if Jay had groveled before his British counterparts in a demeaning throwback to colonial times. The treaty would strike southerners as further damning proof that Washington was a traitor to his heritage, for Jay had failed to win compensation for American slaves carted off at the end of the war. For all that, the treaty had several redeeming features. England finally consented to evacuate the forts on the Great

Lakes; it opened the British West Indies to small American ships; and it agreed to compensate American merchants whose freight had been confiscated. And these concessions paled in comparison to the treaty's overriding achievement: it arrested the fatal drift toward war with England. On balance, despite misgivings, Washington thought the flawed treaty the best one feasible at the moment.

Fully aware of its explosive contents, Washington elected to shroud the treaty in "impenetrable secrecy," as Madison termed it, until Congress reconvened in June. By the time the Senate debated it, Jay had returned from England, having been elected in absentia governor of New York. (He would shortly resign as chief justice.) It was not an auspicious homecoming for Jay. The Senate had agreed to debate the treaty in secret, but Republicans gasped in horror as they perused its contents. Its fate seemed uncertain until the Federalists granted the Republicans a critical concession: they would oppose the notorious Article XII, which limited American trade in the British West Indies to ships under seventy tons. Strengthened by this compromise, the treaty effectively passed the Senate in late June by a 20-to-10 vote, the bare minimum needed under the Constitution's two-thirds rule. The next step would be for Washington to sign the treaty, which caused him an agony of indecision.

In early July, word came that the British had issued bellicose new orders to seize ships laden with food bound for France. Having crafted delicate compromises to steer the treaty through the Senate, Washington was appalled at British insensitivity and protested to resident minister George Hammond. Washington felt sufficiently jittery about signing the treaty that he privately asked Hamilton, now returned to legal practice in Manhattan, to aid him with a high-level crib sheet. Evidently Washington and Hamilton had not been in touch, since Washington admitted that he did not know how Hamilton had been occupied of late. "My wishes," Washington explained, "are to have the favorable and unfavorable side of *each* article stated and compared together, that I may see the bearing and tendency of them and, ultimately, on which side the balance is to be found."[3] That Washington turned to Hamilton for guidance reflects his lack of confidence in his newly installed cabinet and his continuing reliance on Hamilton as his economic tutor. When Hamilton was treasury secretary, Washington had had to keep him at arm's length, juggling him against Jefferson, but he had no such inhibitions with Hamilton out of office. Despite reservations about the Jay Treaty, Hamilton provided Washington with a generally laudatory fifty-three-page analysis, urging him to sign the highly imperfect document. Amazed at the breadth of this sparkling dissection, Washington in his reply sounded sheepish about having inadvertently taken up so much of Hamilton's time.

Before he put his signature on the treaty, Washington was preparing to publish it when the *Aurora* printed a précis on June 29 that left the public so aghast that Madison said the treaty "flew with an electric velocity to every part of the union."[4] On July 1 the paper issued the complete text, and an official version ran in the Federalist *Gazette of the United States*. The uproar was overwhelming, tagging Jay as the chief monster in the Republicans' bestiary. In the treaty, Republicans saw a blatant partiality for England and equally barefaced hostility toward France. Critics gave way to full-blown paranoid fantasies that Jay, in the pay of British gold, had suborned other politicians to introduce a monarchical cabal. Some protests bordered on the obscene, especially a bawdy poem in the Republican press about Jay's servility to the British king: "May it please your highness, I John Jay / Have traveled all this mighty way, / To inquire if you, good Lord, will please, / to suffer me while on my knees, / to show all others I surpass / In love, by kissing of your ————."[5] By the July Fourth celebrations, Jay had been burned in effigy in so many towns that he declared he could have traversed the entire country by the glare of his own flaming figure.

The targets of the protest went far beyond Jay. At a rally in New York, when Hamilton rose to defend the treaty, protesters hurled stones at him, while in Philadelphia a menacing mob descended on George Hammond's residence, smashed the windows, and "burned the treaty with huzzahs and acclamations."[6] Treaty opponents had no compunctions about besieging the presidential mansion, and John Adams remembered it "surrounded by an innumerable multitude from day to day, buzzing, demanding war against England, cursing Washington, and crying success to the French patriots and virtuous Republicans."[7] From across the country, inflammatory resolutions against the treaty piled up on Washington's desk, many of them too obnoxious to warrant replies. "No answer given. The address too rude to merit one," Washington scrawled atop a New Jersey petition, while he chided another from Virginia thus: "Tenor indecent. No answer returned." On still another from Kentucky, he scribbled: "The ignorance and indecency of these proceedings forbade an answer."[8] Though tepid in his enthusiasm for the treaty, Washington was not prepared to go to war with England and thought the treaty would prevent a harmful deterioration in Anglo-American trade.

In mid-July Washington left sultry Philadelphia for a breathing spell at Mount Vernon, enduring a debilitating six-day journey in "hot and disagreeable" weather.[9] If he hoped to escape the brouhaha over the Jay Treaty, he was disabused when Secretary of State Randolph reported on the spreading commotion and some preposterous accusations against Washington. One newspaper writer had charged that the president "insidiously aims to dissolve all connections between the United States and France and to substitute a monarchic for a republican ally."[10] Washington felt powerless to stop this sometimes-ludicrous barrage of falsehoods. Owing to "party disputes," he complained to Pickering, the "truth is so enveloped in mist and false representations that it is extremely difficult to know through what channel to seek it."[11] Washington was especially pleased when his ex–treasury secretary launched a lengthy series of essays under the signature of "Camillus," providing a detailed defense of the Jay Treaty. Washington gave way to gloomy musings about republican government, viewing his Republican opponents as full of passionate intensity—"always working, like bees, to distill their poison"—while government supporters were either cowed or spineless, trusting too much to the good sense of the people.[12]

Such was the hubbub over the treaty that at the end of July Washington debated whether to hurry back to Philadelphia to deal with its critics. "At present," he told Hamilton, "the cry against the treaty is like that against a mad dog and everyone, in a manner, seems engaged in running it down."[13] The Mount Vernon weather seemed emblematic of the political storm he faced: extremely violent rains destroyed crops and washed away bridges, impeding Washington's communications with his cabinet. Both Randolph and Pickering sent Washington urgent pleas to return, but Pickering inserted a cryptic reference that must have mystified the president. The secretary of war said that due to "a *special reason,* which can be communicated to you only in person, I entreat therefore that you will return with all convenient speed to the seat of government."[14] Even more startling was Pickering's admonition that Washington should refrain from making any important political decisions until he arrived in Philadelphia.

The "special reason" proved to be nothing less than suspicions that Secretary of State Edmund Randolph was engaged in treason. The maddeningly vague and ambiguous charges arose in a roundabout fashion. In late October the French minister, Jean-Antoine Fauchet, sent a secret dispatch to his superiors in France, summarizing conversations with Randolph about the Whiskey Rebellion. According to Fauchet, Randolph intimated that if France handed over thousands of dollars, he could induce certain Pennsylvania officials to resolve the whiskey dispute on terms beneficial to French interests. He also hinted that certain flour merchants, if relieved of their indebtedness to English creditors, could reveal that England had fomented the rebellion. Talking as if Randolph might have extorted a bribe, Fauchet wrote, "Thus, the consciences of the pretended patriots of America have already their scale of prices! . . . What will be the old age of this government, if it is thus early decrepit!"[15] When a British warship captured the French vessel carrying this message, Fauchet's letter was routed to London and then rerouted to George Hammond in Philadelphia, who was told to show it to "well disposed persons in America" when a convenient time arose.[16] That opportunity presented itself on July 28, 1795, when Hammond shared the incriminating letter with Treasury Secretary Wolcott, who brought it to the scandalized attention of Pickering. The latter then dashed off his mysterious missive to Washington. At the very least the Fauchet dispatch showed

Randolph voicing strong pro-Republican sentiments, disloyal to Washington's administration, and grossly exaggerating his influence over the president.

After returning to Philadelphia, Washington asked Pickering to come and speak with him, and coincidentally, the latter arrived while Washington was enjoying a convivial dinner with none other than Randolph. Picking up a glass of wine, Washington excused himself and ushered Pickering into an adjoining room. When the door was shut behind them, Washington asked, "What is the cause of your writing me such a letter?" Motioning toward the other room, Pickering blurted out his bald accusation: "That man is a traitor!" Washington listened in thunderstruck silence. When Pickering was through, Washington said calmly, "Let us return to the other room to prevent any suspicion of the cause of our withdrawing."[17] Washington did not immediately confront Randolph. The next morning the main topic of a cabinet meeting was whether Washington should sign the Jay Treaty, and he announced his intention to do so. Whether suspiciously or not, Randolph was the only cabinet officer who opposed it, having already introduced numerous objections to the document. In retrospect, he came to believe that the revelation of his supposed treachery had led Washington to overcome his earlier doubts and endorse the treaty.

For a full week Washington proceeded with business as usual, dropping no hints to Randolph of any mistrust he harbored. Washington, who never did anything lightly, tried to anticipate all the political repercussions of the affair. He examined thoroughly the question of whether the incriminating letter, or just damaging parts, should be published. "A part, without the whole, might be charged with unfairness," he advised Wolcott and Pickering. "The public would expect reasons for the sudden removal of so high an officer."[18] He knew Republicans would try to convert Randolph into a political martyr, sacrificed for his opposition to the Jay Treaty, and that the Fauchet letter would be dismissed as a transparent excuse for getting rid of him. On the evening of August 18, to forestall suspicions of what was afoot, Washington included Edmund Randolph among his dinner guests. Although he asked Randolph to arrive at his office at ten-thirty the next morning, he had Wolcott and Pickering come earlier to devise a strategy for dealing with him. They fell back on a standard technique of detective work: they would hand Randolph the Fauchet dispatch and closely watch his expression as he absorbed its contents. This would be "the best means of discovering his true situation" and figuring out his line of defense.[19]

When Randolph entered, Washington reacted in a formal manner, producing the dispatch from his pocket. "Mr. Randolph," he announced, "here is a letter which I desire you to read and make such explanations as you choose."[20] Although Randolph reddened, he kept his composure and scanned it in silence. Then he lifted his eyes and told Washington that the letter must have been intercepted. Washington nodded in confirmation. "I will explain what I know," said Randolph, who denied having solicited or received money from the French. He would be glad to commit his defense to paper, he asserted, if he could retain the letter. "Very well," Washington replied, "retain it."[21] At Washington's invitation, Pickering and Wolcott began to interrogate their colleague, a prosecutorial grilling that rattled Randolph.

At one point Washington asked Randolph to step outside while he, Pickering, and Wolcott remained closeted. As they appraised Randolph's behavior, they were all struck that he had remained so collected during their confrontation. Nevertheless, when Randolph returned, his composure had suddenly crumbled. When Washington asked how quickly he could come up with a written defense, Randolph grew indignant. "As soon as possible," he replied hotly, blustering that he "couldn't continue in the office one second after such treatment."[22] With that, he turned on his heels and left. Washington accepted his resignation, the first time a cabinet member had left involuntarily. The next day Washington informed Randolph that as long as he was trying to clear his name, Washington would keep an open mind and the matter would remain strictly confidential.

It was an uncertain time in the capital, with scattered reports of yellow fever flaring up again, a fear heightened by uncommon summer heat. The tactless, abrasive manner in which Randolph handled his defense strengthened Washington's conviction of his guilt. Randolph stalled in producing an explanation, leading Washington to speculate that his strategy was "to gain time, to puzzle, and to try if he cannot discover inconsistencies in the conduct of others relative to it."[23] In a move that Washington found unforgivable, Randolph published letters to him in the opposition press before sending them to him first. Characteristically, Washington worried that his own integrity might be impugned and gave Randolph permission to publish "*any* and *every* private and confidential letter I ever wrote you," as well as every word he ever uttered to him.[24] What most infuriated Washington was that Randolph upbraided him for being in league with the Federalist party. Washington reminded Randolph of the countless times he had heard him "lament from the bottom of my soul that differences of sentiments should have occasioned those heats which are disquieting a country otherwise the happiest in the world."[25] Randolph found Washington's tone so abhorrent that a week later, writing to Madison, he faulted the president for "profound hypocrisy" and having practiced "the injustice of an assassin" against him.[26]

On December 18 Randolph published a 103-page pamphlet called *A Vindication* that presented a fairly credible defense against the bribery charge but made offensive remarks about Washington, who was stung to the quick. As soon as he saw the pamphlet, Washington exclaimed in disgust, "He has written and published this," flinging it to the floor.[27] Washington felt deeply betrayed by Randolph. Out of friendship for his uncle, Peyton Randolph, Washington had aided the young man and pushed him forward, and this was his reward. In trying to figure out how to minimize political damage, Washington consulted Hamilton. Although Hamilton found it hard to muzzle his opinions in political disputes, he knew that silence was Washington's preferred method and that presidential dignity reinforced that need. "It appears to me that by you no notice can be or ought to be taken of the publication," he wrote back. "It contains its own antidote."[28] Indeed, even Republicans found the *Vindication*'s tone misguided; Jefferson confessed to Madison that while it exonerated Randolph of the bribery charges, "it does not give . . . high ideas of his wisdom or steadiness."[29] Washington thereafter referred to Randolph as a rascal or a villain.

Bereft of trustworthy advisers that summer, Washington turned to John Adams more than before and praised the diplomatic acumen of his son, John Quincy, the precocious young minister to Holland. Washington held the young man's talents in such high regard that he predicted that, before too long, John Quincy would be "found at the head of the Diplomatic Corps."[30] With Edmund Randolph's resignation, Washington began a long and dispiriting search for a successor. As with all appointments, he handled the correspondence himself without any apparent assistance from aides. A disillusioned Washington capitulated to the reality that he could no longer tolerate appointees "whose political tenets are adverse" to his own policies.[31] He had had enough with gross disloyalty from his cabinet. But he then suffered the indignity of having five candidates in succession turn down the secretary of state job—William Paterson, Thomas Johnson, Charles Cotesworth Pinckney, Patrick Henry, and Rufus King. Honorable in his dealings, Washington informed each candidate of the previous refusals. By the time he approached Patrick Henry, fourth on the list, he experienced mounting frustration: "I persuade myself, Sir, it has not escaped your observation that a crisis is approaching that must, if it cannot be arrested, soon decide whether order and good government shall be preserved or anarchy and confusion ensue."[32] After the fourth rebuff, Washington spilled out his woes to Hamilton, asking plaintively, "What am I to do for a Secretary of State?"[33] When Hamilton sounded out Rufus King for the post, the latter spurned the offer because of "the foul and venomous shafts of calumny" now directed at government officials.[34]

To fill the vacancy, Washington finally shifted the prickly Timothy Pickering from war to state. Instead of warming to this plum assignment, Pickering accepted it to spare Washington any further embarrassment. Devoted to Hamilton, Pickering adhered to that true-blue wing of the Federalists known as High Federalists. To plug the resulting vacancy at the War Department, Washington was again reduced to the unseemly position of peddling a cabinet post and was stymied three times before James McHenry accepted. A doctor by training, McHenry had served as a wartime aide to Washington, a member of the Confederation Congress, and a delegate to the Constitutional Convention. Fond of McHenry, Washington had sung his praises as a young man of "great integrity . . . an amiable temper, very obliging, and of polished manners."[35] Whatever his merits, McHenry's talents did not measure up to the post, as Washington soon learned. "I early discovered after he entered upon the duties of his office that his talents were unequal to great exertions or deep resources," Washington later admitted to Hamilton. "In truth, they were not unexpected for the fact is, it was a Hobson's choice."[36] With a second-string cabinet of Wolcott, Pickering, and McHenry, Washington had purged it of apostasy but had also exchanged creative ferment for mediocrity; the numerous rejections had given him little choice. With this cabinet overhaul, Republicans regarded the Federalist triumph as complete, and a forlorn Madison asked Jefferson rhetorically, "Through what official interstice can a ray of republican truths now penetrate to the P[resident]?"[37]

A few days after Washington's confrontation with Randolph, Attorney General William Bradford died, saddling Washington with yet another appointment. Eager to restore a geographic mix to his cabinet, he turned to John Marshall, the tall, handsome Virginian destined to stand out as the foremost legal mind of the age. "When future generations pursue the history of America," Washington once said, "they will find the name of Marshall on its sacred page as one of the brightest ornaments of the age in which he lived."[38] In approaching Marshall, Washington appealed to self-interest as well as loftier goals, noting that in Philadelphia Marshall could supplement his income with "a lucrative practice."[39] Marshall still declined. When Washington then considered Colonel Harry Innes for the job, he said that Innes's reputation for extreme laziness did not disqualify him, since "the office of attorney general of the U[nited] States does not require constant labor or attention."[40] Washington ended up choosing Charles Lee as attorney general (not to be confused with the wartime general with whom Washington feuded). Even though Washington had emphasized the job's part-time nature, Lee left Philadelphia so often that Washington warned him that "unpleasant remarks" were made about his continual absences as well as charges that he had made "a sinecure of the office."[41]

Even the choice of a new chief justice to replace John Jay became the source of endless wrangling. Neither busy nor prestigious, the Supreme Court did not yet attract top legal minds. Perhaps for that reason, Hamilton turned down Washington's invitation to become the new chief justice. Washington then proposed John Rutledge of South Carolina, who served briefly as chief justice through a recess appointment but whose nomination was ultimately defeated by partisan sniping in the Senate. Washington then named William Cushing of Massachusetts, already an associate justice on the Court. Cushing was confirmed by the Senate but considered himself too old and infirm for the job and surrendered it a week later. In the end Washington selected Oliver Ellsworth of Connecticut, who, as a senator, had been the main architect of the Judiciary Act of 1789, which shaped the federal court system. A former judge of the Connecticut Superior Court, Ellsworth was confirmed on March 4, 1796, and, to Washington's vast relief, remained in place past the end of his second term.

IN SEPTEMBER 1795, at an inopportune moment, Lafayette's adolescent son materialized in America, confronting Washington with an excruciating dilemma. Escorted by his tutor, Félix Frestel, George Washington Lafayette came armed with a letter to his godfather, hoping to involve the president more deeply in efforts to liberate his father. The once-dashing Lafayette père had grown gaunt and deathly pale from years in hellish dungeons, suffering from swollen limbs, oozing sores, and agonizing blisters. He was to remain persona non grata for the five-man Directory that governed France after the end of the Reign of Terror. However strongly he felt, Washington was reluctant to receive young Lafayette for fear of offending the French government, especially after the Jay Treaty furor. Beyond his official duty to safeguard American interests, Washington dreaded that any move might worsen the precarious plight of Lafayette's wife in France, and he was openly stumped about what to do. "On one side, I may be charged with countenancing those who have been denounced the enemies of France," Washington confided to Hamilton. "On the other, with *not* countenancing the son of a man who is dear to America."[42]

When Washington received a letter from Senator George Cabot, announcing young Lafayette's arrival in Boston, he reassured the boy that he would be like a *"father, friend, protector,* and *supporter"* to him privately but would have to remain steadfastly discreet in public. Many French émigrés having congregated in Philadelphia, Washington could not afford to invite young Lafayette to the capital, where he might be spotted on the streets, so he asked Cabot to enroll his godson temporarily at Harvard College, "the expense of which, as also of every other mean for his support, I will pay," Washington emphasized.[43] Anxious to gauge the political response to the boy's presence, Washington adopted a watchful posture. His fondness for Lafayette had not lessened one jot. "My friendship for his father," he insisted to Cabot, "so far from being diminished, has increased in the ratio of his misfortune."[44]

That fall young Lafayette traveled incognito to New York to visit Alexander Hamilton. Washington told the boy that Hamilton was "warmly attached" to his father because of their wartime camaraderie and that he could rely on his friendship.[45] Paralyzed by indecision, Washington took the extraordinary step of telling

Hamilton that he should converse with the boy about what to do. Washington was plainly tortured by his predicament. When young Lafayette failed to reply to his letter, Washington concluded glumly that he must be furious. "Have you seen or heard more of young Fayette since you last wrote to me on that subject?" Washington wrote dolefully to Hamilton. " . . . His case gives me pain and I do not know how to get relieved from it."[46] Washington's response shows both his ardent devotion to Lafayette and his rigorous self-discipline as a politician when U.S. interests were at stake.

In replying to Washington, Hamilton informed him that Lafayette junior was staying with him and would remain there through the spring; nevertheless he thought Washington should invite the boy to visit him. This advice threw Washington into a painful quandary. In response, he made a shrewd political move—for the first time in a long while, he consulted James Madison: "I wish to know what you think (considering my public character) I had best do to fulfill the obligations of friendship and my own wishes without involving consequences."[47] In this manner Washington not only previewed Republican reactions but also forced Republicans to share responsibility in the matter. Until mid-February Washington wrestled with the issue, then asked Hamilton to send the boy and his tutor to see him in Philadelphia, "without avowing or making a mystery of the object."[48] He stalled in the exact timing, however, suggesting that the two young Frenchmen should come in early April, when "the weather will be settled, the roads good, and the traveling pleasant."[49] In the meantime the boy's presence in America had a galvanizing effect on Washington, who sent word to the Austrians, via their London ambassador, that Lafayette's freedom was "an ardent wish of the people of the United States, in w[hi]ch I sincerely add mine."[50]

Once Washington received young Lafayette, he displayed boundless generosity toward him. Discarding earlier caution, he informed Madison that if circumstances permitted, he would take the boy "with his tutor into my family and, in the absence of his father, to superintend his education and morals."[51] The sight of the boy and the "visible distress" on his face deeply moved Washington.[52] After hearing his heartrending pleas on his father's behalf, Washington decided, strictly as a private person, to dispatch a handwritten letter to the Austrian emperor, requesting that Lafayette be released and allowed to come to America.

Washington delivered on his pledge to bring young Lafayette and his tutor into the household as long as Lafayette senior was imprisoned. Not surprisingly, Washington grew extremely fond of his young ward, whom he found "a modest, sensible, and deserving youth."[53] The boy was tall, kindly, and charming and delighted all who met him. Like his father before him, he made rapid strides in English, surpassing even his tutor. When architect Benjamin Latrobe stopped by Mount Vernon for dinner, he was very taken with young Lafayette's savoir faire: "His manners are easy and he has very little of the usual French air about him . . . and seemed to possess wit and fluency."[54] Latrobe noticed that the president doted on the youth: "A few jokes passed between the President and young Lafayette, whom he treats more as his child than as a guest."[55] The situation was further testimony to Washington's hidden emotional nature and his capacity to incorporate young people into his household as surrogate children. Young Lafayette and Félix Frestel remained with the Washingtons until October 1797, when word arrived that Lafayette had been freed after five years in prison. The two young men decided to sail back to Europe with all due speed. In a touching farewell, George Washington Lafayette wrote to his godfather how grateful he was for his efforts to rescue his real father and how happy he had been to form a temporary part of his family. Washington fully recip- rocated the feeling. When young Lafayette was reunited with his father, he handed him a letter from Washington, who said that young Lafayette was "highly deserving of such parents as you and your amiable Lady."[56] The boy's family were astonished at how much he had grown, not to mention his striking resemblance to his father. Instead of coming to America, however, the impoverished Lafayette and his no- madic family spent the next two years wandering across northern Europe, living in Hamburg, Holstein, and Holland.

The Colossus of the People

AMID THE TRAVAIL OVER THE JAY TREATY, Washington was able to claim a spectacular diplomatic breakthrough with Spain. Settlers in the western hinterland had long chafed at Spanish restrictions on shipping their produce down the Mississippi River. Frustrated with governmental inaction, Kentucky residents threatened to secede from the Union, prompting President Washington to post Thomas Pinckney to the Spanish court as envoy extraordinary. In October 1795, in the Treaty of San Lorenzo, Pinckney won the right for Americans to use the Mississippi freely and trade in the port of New Orleans. The treaty also gave the United States ironclad guarantees that the waterway defined the nation's western border, a signature achievement for a president whose spacious vision of America had always stressed westward expansion. The Spanish treaty coasted to victory.

In contrast, Washington continued to face a hue and cry over the Jay Treaty, which had been ratified by King George III but still lacked funding for major provisions. Having stood by helplessly as it cleared the Senate, House Republicans jumped at the chance to wreck the treaty through their budgetary powers. The boldest challenge arose from Edward Livingston of New York, who introduced a resolution demanding that Washington lay before Congress Jay's original instructions and subsequent correspondence about the treaty. When the resolution passed the Republican-dominated House in March 1796, it opened up a constitutional can of worms. Did the resolution represent legislative encroachment on the executive branch? Did it undermine powers granting the president and Senate the exclusive right to make foreign treaties? And could the president assert executive privilege to protect the confidentiality of such internal deliberations?

Washington smarted at what he deemed a dangerous threat to presidential prerogative. "From the first moment," he confessed to Hamilton, "and from the fullest conviction in my own mind, I had resolved to *resist the principle* w[hi]ch was evidently intended to be established by the call of the House of Representatives."[1] Characteristically, despite fierce misgivings, he dispassionately polled his cabinet members, who unanimously advised resistance to the House resolution. To buttress his arguments, Washington requested a brief from Hamilton, who supplied an ample memorandum on the wisdom of withholding treaty papers. Now nearing the end of his second term, Washington thanked Hamilton tenderly, as if wishing to acknowledge his many years of loyal service, saying that he wanted to "express again my sincere thanks for the pains you have been at to investigate the subject and to assure you, over and over, of the warmth of my friendship and . . . affectionate regard." He signed the letter "I am your affectionate . . ."[2] Such emotional flourishes were highly unusual in the often straitlaced correspondence of George Washington.

In defying House Republicans, Washington delivered a stern lecture on the legal issues involved, reminding lawmakers that the Constitution restricted treaty-making powers to the president and the Senate, confining deliberations to a handful of people to ensure secrecy. He had already shared the relevant papers with the Senate. He lectured the legislators, "To admit then a right in the House of Representatives to demand . . . all the papers respecting a negotiation with a foreign power would be to establish a dangerous precedent."[3] Only in case of impeachment was the president duty-bound to disclose such papers to the House. In private, Washington insisted that House Republicans tried "at *every* hazard to render the treaty-making power a nullity without their consent; nay worse, to make it an absolute absurdity."[4] He even expounded the Constitution to its chief architect, James Madison, whom he saw as reversing views he had expressed at Philadelphia in 1787. The debate had evolved into a colossal clash of personalities over a mighty principle. So bloody was the clash and so ferocious its rhetoric that Washington believed the public mind agitated "in a higher degree than it has been at any period since the Revolution."[5]

During this bruising dispute, House Republicans, for the first time, held a caucus, giving a new institutional reality to the party split between Jeffersonians and Hamiltonians. After Washington won the debate over the Jay Treaty papers, House Republicans launched a prolonged campaign to starve the treaty by refusing to appropriate money for it. For Republicans, the treaty controversy was a stalking horse for a deeper political aim, defined by John Beckley, clerk of the House and a key strategist, as opening the way for "a Republican president to succeed Mr. Washington."[6] At first Madison imagined that the Jay Treaty would be the Achilles' heel of the administration, but as the debate dragged on and it gained new adherents, an outflanked Madison admitted to Jefferson that "our majority has melted" thanks to the machinations of "Tories" and "monarchists."[7] Either from concern over the constitutional implications or because of a groundswell of treaty support from constituents, Republican congressmen slowly backed down and defected to Washington's side. John Adams took comfort that Madison, having staked so much on the outcome, was being ground down by the struggle: "Mr. Madison looks worried to death. Pale, withered, haggard."[8] Madison himself conceded that it was "the most worrying and vexatious" political battle of his career, and it was to prove a losing one.[9]

When it came down to a vote on April 30, 1796, the Federalists got the House to approve money for the Jay Treaty by a wafer-thin margin of 51 to 48. Madison, shocked by the outcome, thought of retiring to his plantation. The crisis that was supposed to strengthen the Republican cause had instead "left it in a very crippled condition," he informed Jefferson.[10] Washington, who believed that Madison and his followers had "brought the Constitution to the brink of a precipice," felt immense relief, intermingled with thinly veiled anger.[11] After this wounding debate, an indignant Washington cut off further contact with Madison and never again invited him to Mount Vernon. Many Federalists predicted, prematurely as it happened, that James Madison had ruined his career. William Cobbett, a Federalist gadfly, was among those who wrote an early obituary for him. "As a politician, he is no more. He is absolutely deceased, cold, stiff, and buried in oblivion for ever and ever."[12]

Jefferson's relationship with Washington also suffered from the momentous events of that spring. Where Jefferson had wanted Washington to stay on as president for a second term, he now dismissed him as the unwitting tool by which corrupt, elitist Federalists duped the common people. As he told Monroe, the Federalists "see nothing can support them but the colossus of the president's merits with the people, and the moment he retires, . . . his successor, if a monocrat, will be overborne by the republican sense of his constituents."[13] As far as Jefferson was concerned, Washington stood forth as an unmovable obstacle to reform. He preached patience to his followers: "Republicanism must lie on its oars, resign the vessel to its pilot," and wait for Washington to exit the scene.[14] Since Jefferson's political philosophy was based on faith in the common people, Washington's persisting popularity thrust him into the uncomfortable position of being at odds with the people's apparent choice.

Now convinced that the two-faced Jefferson had plotted against him in the shadows, Washington no longer labored under any illusions about him. His ire surfaced that summer when Jefferson wrote to deny being the source of confidential information published in the *Aurora*. He also disclaimed making malicious remarks about Washington, as reported by an unnamed person—apparently Henry

Lee. In responding on July 6, 1796, Washington dispensed with the fine points of diplomacy. As the dam burst, his stifled bitterness poured forth, and he confronted Jefferson more openly than ever before. Stating that he had previously had "no conception that parties" could go to such lengths, he claimed he had been vilified in "indecent terms as could scarcely be applied to a Nero, a notorious defaulter, or even to a common pick-pocket."[15] Even though he had done his utmost "to preserve this country from the horrors of a desolating war," he was still charged with "being the enemy of one nation [France] and subject to the influence of another [Great Britain]."[16] He noted that he had long defended Jefferson against charges of duplicity, invariably replying that he had "never discovered anything in the conduct of Mr. Jefferson to raise suspicions in my mind of his insincerity."[17] Now, he said starkly, "it would not be frank, candid, or friendly to conceal that your conduct has been represented as derogatory from that opinion *I* had conceived you entertained of me. That to your particular friends and connections you have described . . . me as a person under a dangerous influence; and that if I would listen *more* to some *other* opinions, all would be well."[18] Washington seldom resorted to such frankness or so pointedly dressed down an ex-colleague, confirming that their relationship now lay beyond redemption. He ended by saying that he had "already gone farther in the expression of my feelings than I intended" and changed the subject to more gentlemanly topics, such as clover, wheat, and peas.[19]

In the aftermath of the Jay Treaty, the diatribes against Washington reached a new pitch of savagery as his foes were emboldened to disparage his presidency and blacken his wartime reputation. In the *Aurora,* Benjamin Franklin Bache dredged up moldy British forgeries from the war, purporting to show that Washington had pocketed bribes from the enemy and was a double agent for the Crown. Washington was not the only family member crestfallen over these vicious attacks. The British minister's wife noted that Abigail Adams "has spirit enough to laugh at [Bache's] abuse of her husband, which poor Mrs. Washington could not."[20] Such was the bitter discord that many Republicans stopped drinking toasts to the president's health after dinner.

With the Jay Treaty, Washington had made good on his solemn oath to maintain peace and prosperity during his presidency. British evacuation of the northwestern posts triggered new settlements in the Ohio Country, including Cleveland, Dayton, and Youngstown. The skies darkened considerably on the diplomatic front, however, as rumors filtered back to Washington that the French government, incensed over the treaty, contemplated sending a fleet to American waters to seize ships bound for Great Britain. In time France would make good on the threats, launching the Quasi-War against the United States during the presidency of John Adams. Washington would privately castigate Republicans for instigating France, which was "endeavoring with all her arts to lead" the United States into war on her side.[21] To Hamilton, Washington issued a ringing manifesto of his foreign policy creed: "We will not be dictated to by the politics of any nation under heaven farther than treaties require of us . . . If we are to be told by a foreign power . . . what we *shall do,* and what we shall *not do,* we have independence yet to seek."[22]

Another casualty of the treaty fracas was Washington's relationship with James Monroe, who had fought with him at Trenton. "He has in every instance," Washington then declared, "maintained the reputation of a brave, active, and sensible officer."[23] In appointing Monroe as minister to France in 1794, Washington aimed to reduce tensions between Federalists and Republicans. As a protégé of Jefferson and Madison, however, Monroe threw aside any pretense of neutrality, showed blatant favoritism toward the French, and allowed himself to be embraced by leading French politicians. According to Washington, Monroe had also tried to pry loose advance details of the Jay Treaty to give the French an unauthorized preview and, instead of allaying French anger over the treaty, actively incited it. When Monroe published in the *Aurora* an anonymous piece critical of Washington, entitled "From a Gentleman in Paris to His Friend in the City," Washington quickly figured out its author. (Wolcott and Pickering had somehow obtained a copy of the original letter.) In July 1796 he recalled Monroe and replaced him with Charles Cotesworth Pinckney, leaving Monroe mortified at such treatment.[24]

Back in Philadelphia, still seething over his recall, Monroe published a 473-page indictment of Washington's handling of the incident called *A View of the Conduct of the Executive in the Foreign Affairs of the United States.* Jefferson, who coached Monroe on this diatribe, was delighted by the result. "Monroe's book is considered masterly by all those who are not opposed in principle, and it is deemed unanswerable," he informed Madison.[25] When Washington pored over the book, he not only snorted with rage but scrawled in its margins sixty-six pages of sardonic comments. These dense notes afford a rare glimpse of Washington in the grip of uncensored anger. Responding to one comment by Monroe, he scoffed, "Self importance appears here."[26] In another aside, he wrote, "Insanity in the extreme!"[27] Another time, he mocked Monroe's statement as "curious and laughable."[28] The gist of many of Washington's remarks was that French actions toward America had been motivated by self-interest, not ideological solidarity, and flouted American neutrality in seeking to enlist the United States in the war against England. The imbroglio with Monroe signaled the demise of yet another Washington friendship with a prominent Virginian, a list that now encompassed George Mason, James Madison, Thomas Jefferson, and Edmund Randolph.

Now that it was open season on Washington in the press, he took a pounding from yet another Revolutionary War hero. Thomas Paine believed that Washington had made no effort to free him after he was imprisoned in France as a British-born resident and a Girondin supporter who had opposed the execution of the king. Having advanced a dubious claim to American citizenship, he accused Washington of "*connivance* at my imprisonment."[29] He was finally released with help from Monroe, who then invited him to lodge in his residence. In October 1796 Paine published in the *Aurora* an open letter to Washington, accusing him of "a cold deliberate crime of the heart" in letting him rot in prison, and he also took dead aim at his command of the Continental Army.[30] "You slept away your time in the field till the finances of the country were completely exhausted," he fumed, "and you have but little share in the glory of the event."[31] Paine alleged that Horatio Gates and Nathanael Greene deserved true credit for the patriots' victory, abetted by French assistance: "Had it not been for the aid received from France in men, money, and ships, your cold and unmilitary conduct . . . would in all probability have lost America."[32]

Not content to denigrate Washington's military performance, Paine defamed him as an unfeeling man, lonely and isolated, who ruthlessly crushed anyone who crossed him. Among his associates, Paine contended, it was known that Washington "has no friendships; that he is incapable of forming any; [that] he can serve or desert a man or a cause with constitutional indifference."[33] Paine ended with the most vicious swipe of all: "As to you, sir, treacherous in private friendship (for so you have been to me, and that in the day of danger) and a hypocrite in public life, the world will be puzzled to decide whether you are an apostate or an impostor; whether you have abandoned good principles, or whether you ever had any."[34] This intemperate outburst cast more doubt on Paine's erratic judgment than on Washington's performance. In writing to Abigail, John Adams gave this verdict on Paine's letter: "He must have been insane to write so."[35]

FOR A TIME DURING HIS PRESIDENCY, Washington had shunned the tedium of sitting for portraits, but with the end now in sight, he was amenable to pictures that might immortalize his waning days. Since the Revolutionary War, he had been fond of Charles Willson Peale, the multifaceted artist who had opened an eccentric museum in Philadelphia, a cabinet of curiosities crammed with exotic specimens of natural history, coupled with a portrait gallery of wartime heroes. In 1795 the artist's son Rembrandt Peale, age seventeen, received a commission to paint the president. Doubtless rewarding a faithful ally by posing for his son, Washington agreed to three sessions with Rembrandt in Peale's Museum, with each sitting lasting three hours. The president stipulated a seven A.M. starting time, and on the appointed day young Rembrandt rose at dawn, trembling with anxiety. So nervously did the young man prepare for the sitting that he could scarcely mix his colors and decided to proceed only if his father sketched a portrait beside him, ensuring "that the sitting would not be unprofitable by affording a double chance for a likeness. This had the effect to calm my nerves, and I enjoyed the rare advantage of studying the desired countenance whilst in familiar conversation with my father."[36] At the second session, a third family member, James Peale, Charles's brother, daubed a miniature of Washington while two of Rembrandt's brothers, Raphaelle and Titian, knocked off sketches as well. Never before had Washington allowed two, much less five, artists to record his image at the same time.

Gilbert Stuart, who was then painting his iconographic images of Washington, happened to stroll by as Washington sat in thrall to the busy swarm of painting Peales: "I looked in to see how the old gentleman was getting on with the picture, and, to my astonishment, I found the general surrounded by the whole family." As Stuart walked away, he ran into Martha. "Madam," said Stuart, "the general's in a perilous situation." "How sir?" "He is beset, madam—no less than five upon him at once; one aims at his eye—another at his nose—another is busy with his hair—the mouth is attacked by a fourth; and the fifth has him by the button. In short, madam, there are five painters at him, and you who know how much he has suffered when only attended by one, can judge of the horrors of his situation."[37]

The two best-known portraits to emerge from these sessions tell a doleful tale of George Washington late in his second term. In the Charles Willson Peale version, a suddenly older Washington sits in a dark velvet coat, with an upturned collar and ruffled shirtfront. There is no sparkle in the immobile face, and his drooping eyelids make him appear sleepily inactive. A bag has formed under his left eye, which seems half shut, and the right eye does not open much wider. All in all the portrait depicts a weary, dispirited president, fatigued after long years in office and depleted by the battle royal over the Jay Treaty. The Rembrandt Peale portrait makes Washington seem a bit enfeebled and even more geriatric, his skin parched with age. As he stares worriedly ahead, the lips of his wrinkled mouth are tightly compressed with displeasure. Ironically, in his later years, Rembrandt Peale painted heroic portraits of Washington in his Continental Army uniform, nobly fired by youthful energy.

In many ways, it was unfortunate that Gilbert Stuart's lasting images of Washington date from this period, when the swagger and panache of his early days had faded. Embittered by partisan feuding and feeling burdened by public life, Washington had made massive sacrifices to his country, and the luster had fled from his eye. Although Stuart captured the ineffable grandeur of the man, who sometimes seemed to float in a timeless realm, his images gave posterity a far more dour and haggard Washington than the charismatic general known to contemporaries from earlier times. Stuart was cognizant of the distortions that time had visited upon

Washington. "When I painted him," he said, "he had just had a set of false teeth inserted, which accounts for the constrained expression so noticeable about the mouth and lower part of the face."[38] To help rectify such distortions, he turned to Houdon's bust and life mask, but Stuart's portraits still reflect the physiognomy of the mid-1790s.

Already in the 1780s Washington had tired of artistic conventions that cast politicians in Roman togas. Averse to idealizing his subjects, Gilbert Stuart dressed them in modern clothing and took a hard, cold look at them. So Stuart, for all the antics and fast talk that may have irritated Washington, was very much to his taste as a portrait painter. Only in the so-called Lansdowne portrait, where a visionary Washington stands with a fixed gaze and stiffly outstretched arm, does Stuart resort to the props of republican power, showing copies of *The Federalist* and the Constitution in bound form at his feet. Perhaps the memories of a healthier and happier husband predisposed Martha Washington to criticize Stuart's work. "There are several prints, medallions, and miniatures of the president in the house, none of which please Mrs. Washington," John Pintard wrote when he visited Mount Vernon in 1801. "She does not think Stuart's celebrated painting a true resemblance."[39] Stuart converted the Washington portraits into a thriving industry, stamping out copies for so many years that he laughingly referred to them as his hundred-dollar bills—that being the price he charged for each. His daughter Jane contended that he could crank out a copy in a couple of hours and sometimes finished two portraits in a single session.

As PATERFAMILIAS OF THE CLAN, the president loved to shower his young wards with sage advice, especially in affairs of the heart. Despite pressing political concerns, he enjoyed playing the didactic role of the grizzled adviser. George and Martha Washington were thrilled in 1795, when Fanny Washington, widowed by George Augustine's death, wed Tobias Lear, who had lost his wife, Polly, to yellow fever. To bind them more closely, the Washingtons bestowed upon the young couple a rent-free house and 360 acres at Mount Vernon. Since Fanny had three children from her previous marriage and Tobias Lear a little boy from his, the wedding seemed a fairy-tale solution for the grieving young couple. Then in March 1796 Lear informed the Washingtons that Fanny had fallen gravely ill, and they were stunned when she breathed her last. "Your former letters prepared us for the stroke," the Washingtons commiserated with Lear, "but it has fallen heavily notwithstanding."[40] For Martha Washington, who had been overjoyed by the marriage, touting Lear as "a worthy man . . . esteemed by everyone," it extended the dreadful pattern in her life of the untimely death of children, both real and substitute.[41]

Another young woman who preoccupied Washington's thoughts was Elizabeth

Parke Custis, Nelly's oldest sister, an attractive brunette raised by her mother and David Stuart. The girl so adored her stepgrandfather that she was once paralyzed by nerves when he descended for a visit. "The General said that, although he thought a young girl looked best when blushing," she recalled, "yet he was concerned to see me suffer so much."[42] When requesting a portrait from Washington, she professed herself indifferent to love: "It is my first wish to have it in my power to contemplate at all times the features of one who I so highly respect as the Father of his Country and look up to with grateful affection as a parent to myself and family."[43] While Washington obliged her with a miniature by Irish artist Walter Robertson, he teased her gently and inquired whether "emotions of a softer kind" did not move her heart.[44]

Elizabeth's desire to join the Washington household in Philadelphia in 1795 must have filled the older couple with misgivings. However devoted she was to them, she had a fiery temper and was cursed with what one aunt called "a violent and romantic disposition."[45] That same aunt regretted that in "her tastes and pastimes, she is more man than woman and regrets that she can't wear pants."[46] When she first came to Philadelphia, she was sulky and querulous and boycotted church and dances. Martha Washington, a confirmed believer in social duties, could not sympathize with such morbid brooding. Washington, however, enjoyed Elizabeth's company, and she accompanied him for sittings with Gilbert Stuart. One day, as Stuart painted, Elizabeth abruptly barged into the room and, folding her arms across her chest, cast an appraising look at his work. He was so struck by this self-assured pose that he painted her in exactly this manner, holding a straw hat embellished with a red ribbon. Her sidelong glance in the portrait is proud, spirited, and obstinate, as if she refused to budge from the viewer's glance. Elizabeth appeared indifferent to her own beauty, as if it were something too trivial to occupy her attention.

In 1796 an Englishman twice her age, Thomas Law, revealed his plans to marry her, a move that took the Washingtons by surprise, Elizabeth having concealed the courtship. After running up a fortune in India, Law had come to America to dabble in real estate and promptly bought five hundred lots in the new federal district. Even before Washington knew he would someday have a familial connection with Law, he had recoiled at the scale of these purchases. "Will it not be asked," he inquired, "why are speculators to pocket so much money?"[47] When Law apprised him of his intention to marry Elizabeth, Washington was quietly livid and must have known that he could not talk the stubborn Elizabeth out of the marriage. In replying to Law, he faulted him for the deceptive manner in which he had proceeded but did not protest the marriage outright: "No intimation of this event, from any quarter, having been communicated to us before, it may well be supposed that it was a matter of surprise. This being premised, I have only to add . . . my approbation, in which Mrs. Washington unites."[48]

It was a typically shrewd response from Washington, who offered qualified support to Law while privately gathering more information about him. He confronted Elizabeth gingerly, saying that she had "more honesty than disguise" in her nature and should disclose more details of her engagement: "This I have a right to expect in return for my blessing so promptly bestowed, after you had concealed the matter from me so long."[49] Wary of Law's motives, Washington wrote on the sly to Elizabeth's stepfather, David Stuart, suggesting a strong prenuptial agreement that would have Law "make a settlement upon her previous to marriage, of her own fortune, if no more."[50] When the couple married in Virginia the next month, the wedding was conducted in a studiously low-key style, devoid of dancing or festivities, as if the family had no wish to invest in premature celebration. The marriage proved a misalliance, and the couple separated in 1803.

Elizabeth's petulant nature threw into shining relief the sterling qualities of her vivacious sister Nelly, who was so varied in her interests, including horseback riding, singing, playing the harpsichord, studying French, and drawing. One smitten male visitor marveled that she "has more perfection of form of expression, of color, of softness, and of firmness of mind than I have ever seen before."[51] With keen wit she skewered her enraptured male admirers. When she heard false rumors that she was romantically involved with one young man, she admitted that he had pleasing manners but had "been told too often of his merit and accomplishments, and it has given him more affectation than is by any means agreeable."[52] She mocked another young man for his pseudoromantic babble about "*hearts, darts, hopes, fears, heart-aches*" and other terms related to the "*tender passion*."[53] With such merciless comments, Nelly murdered the hopes of many young suitors, and it seemed unlikely she would marry anytime soon.

Martha sometimes found Nelly a little unconventional for her tastes, but the president adored her. Far more trying was his relationship with George Washington Parke Custis, who recapitulated his father's history of academic apathy. He had grown into a handsome teenager, crowned with curly hair, a broad face, and large, attractive eyes. When Washy entered Princeton in the autumn of 1796—the president thought the school had "turned out better scholars" and "more estimable characters" than any other—the president didn't know whether he would adjust to the academic rigors or loaf his way through.[54] As with Jacky, Washington smothered the young man with advice, warning him against idle amusements, dissipated company, and hasty friendships. Trying to instill his own prudent habits, he told him to "select the most deserving only for your friendships, and, before this becomes intimate, weigh their dispositions and character *well*."[55] Washington's vague bromides about Washy becoming a scholar and a useful member of society seemed like so much wishful thinking.

Within six months of Washy's arrival at Princeton, Washington was confronted by disturbing reports from the boy's tutor. "From his infancy, I have discovered an almost unconquerable disposition to indolence," Washington informed the professor in words that echoed his chronic dismay with Jacky Custis.[56] Like Jacky, Washy apologized profusely for his misdemeanors and promised to reform. He assured Washington that "like the *prodigal son*," he would be "a sincere penitent," but such noble intentions lasted only as long as it took the ink to dry.[57] However good-natured and ingratiating in his letters, Washy was, at bottom, feckless and incorrigible. He would say all the right things, then do all the wrong things, and he lasted only a year at Princeton.

THE TWO-TERM PRESIDENCY had taxed Washington in many ways, not least in his personal finances. In March 1795, when his friend Charles Carter, Jr., approached him for a thousand-dollar loan, Washington, always touchy about borrowing, burst into a recitation of his financial stringency: "My friends entertain a very erroneous idea of my pecuniary resources . . . Such has been the management of my estate for many years past, especially since my absence from home, now six years, as barely to support itself."[58] He protested that his government allowance barely covered the extravagant costs of entertaining and that he had resorted to selling western lands to escape debt.

As he meditated on the end of his presidency, he mused about the prospect of "tranquillity with a *certain* income" and decided to pursue his earlier scheme of selling his western lands and leasing out the four Mount Vernon farms, while retreating to the fifth, the Mansion House, with Martha.[59] On February 1, 1796, he posted advertisements for the sale of thirteen tracts along three western rivers—the Ohio, Great Kanawha, and Little Miami—amounting to a whopping 36,000 acres. These ads were posted in Philadelphia papers and well-frequented taverns in western Pennsylvania. The properties dated from the distant period when the young Anglophile officer had received bounty lands for service in the French and Indian War and had cornered aggressively the rights of fellow soldiers. In undertaking these sales, Washington harbored a secret agenda, hoping to use the proceeds to help emancipate his slaves.

In recruiting able farmers to rent the four outlying farms, the Father of His Country had so little faith in American farmers that he placed anonymous ads not only in eastern newspapers but as far afield as England, Scotland, and Ireland. "My wish is to get associations of farmers from the old countries, who know how . . . to keep the land in an improving state rather than the slovenly ones of this [country], who think (generally) of nothing else but to work a field as long as it will bear anything," he told William Pearce, Mount Vernon's estate manager.[60] He now resolved to introduce the crop-rotation scheme that he had worked out on paper but that his hapless overseers had never been able to put into practice. Having long known that tobacco depleted the soil, he wanted to plant corn, wheat, clover, potatoes, and grass in a scientific sequence.

Conscious that he would someday free his slaves, Washington wanted to avoid doing anything that might interfere with that plan. His letters betray growing disgust with slavery, as when he told Pearce that "opulent" Virginians were made "imperious and dissipated from the habit of commanding slaves and living in a measure without control."[61] However benevolent his intentions were, he remained a largely absentee owner, able to exercise scant control over his overseers' harsh practices, as shown in one 1795 letter to Pearce: "I am sorry to find by your last reports that there has been two deaths in the [slave] family since I left Mount Vernon, and one of them a young fellow. I hope every necessary care and attention was afforded him. I expect little of this from McCoy, or indeed from most of his class, for they seem to consider a Negro much in the same light as they do the brute beasts on the farms, and often treat them as inhumanly."[62] Washington mentally divided his slaves into productive ones who warranted favor and those unable or unwilling to work. When Pearce distributed linen to slaves, Washington instructed him to provide the good stuff "to the grown people and the most deserving, whilst the more indifferent sort is served to the younger ones and worthless."[63]

Whatever his shortcomings as a master, Washington continued to refine his plan to free his slaves someday. So long as he was president, the subject was taboo; Washington told David Stuart that "reasons of a political, indeed of [an] imperious nature" forbade any such action.[64] He wrote these words during the brouhaha over the Jay Treaty, when southern planters were especially upset over his policies and he could not afford to antagonize them further. Starting in 1795, Washington's letters reflect a growing preoccupation with knowing who were his dower slaves, over whom he had no control, and those he owned outright and could free.

Washington's plans to lease the four farms and simplify his future life came to naught. Adding to his nagging economic uncertainty was the regretted departure of William Pearce due to an "increasing rheumatic affection."[65] For the demanding Washington, the seasoned Pearce had been a godsend, a man of reliable industry and integrity. In October 1796 Washington replaced him with James Anderson, a native of Scotland well trained in agriculture, who would take the operations at Mount Vernon in some unexpected directions. The switch, which came as the president contemplated retirement, could only have exacerbated his worries about the situation that awaited him at home.

CHAPTER SIXTY-TWO

The Master of Farewells

In 1796 George Washington was often in a somber, pessimistic mood. One visitor who encountered him on his sixty-fourth birthday that February said "he seemed considerably older. The innumerable vexations he has met with in his different public capacities have very sensibly impaired the vigor of his constitution and given him an aged appearance."[1] He had long fathomed the peculiar dynamics of fame, the way fickle crowds respond first with adulation and then scorn to any form of hero worship. From partisan quarters, he was experiencing the rude comeuppance he had long known hovered in the background. Patrick Henry was shocked at his slanderous treatment: "If he whose character as our *leader during the whole war* . . . is so roughly handled in his old age, what may be expected of men of the common standard?"[2]

Nothing required Washington to leave office—the Twenty-second Amendment, limiting a president to two terms, was not ratified until 1951—but he had always planned to remain as president only until the new Constitution had taken root, never dreaming it would take a full two terms to reach that point. Despondent over the Jay Treaty attacks, Washington had now firmly resolved to leave office. Most Federalists hoped he would stay in office indefinitely; John Jay exhorted him to "remain with us at least while the storm lasts and until you can retire like the sun in a calm, unclouded evening."[3] In reply, Washington alluded darkly to all the "trouble and perplexities" he had endured, aggravated by the infirmities of age, and said only a national emergency would postpone his retirement.[4]

Where Washington had asked Madison to draft a farewell address in 1792 and then stashed it in a drawer, he now turned to Hamilton as his preferred wordsmith for a valedictory message. On May 15 he sent the latter Madison's address, along with additions he himself had recently made to reflect the "considerable changes" wrought by the intervening years.[5] He dangled before Hamilton two options: either edit and update Madison's version or start afresh and "throw the *whole* into a different form."[6] It was not in Hamilton's headstrong nature to bow to another scribe, and while he would offer Washington a revised version of Madison's 1792 address, he also forged a magisterial new version of his own.

As always, Washington fretted over possible misinterpretations of his motives, speculating that people might whisper he was leaving office because of his "fallen popularity and despair of being re-elected." In his farewell statement, he wanted Hamilton to refer to the earlier farewell address as irrefutable proof that, far from hiding megalomaniacal ambitions, he had longed to return home. While the words of this second farewell belonged to Hamilton, Washington defined its overarching themes and lent it his distinctive sound. He wanted the message written in a plain, unadorned style, presenting a timeless quality and avoiding references to specific personalities and events that had given rise to many observations.

In the past, Washington had been the circumspect personality and Hamilton the hotheaded one. Now Hamilton became the man of impeccable judgment. Washington's additions to Madison's draft had been laced with bitterness, wallowing in partisan squabbles. He had scribbled ill-advised lines about newspapers that "teemed with all the invective that disappointment, ignorance of facts, and malicious falsehoods could invent to misrepresent my politics."[7] Noting his financial sacrifices, Washington had remarked petulantly that "if my country has derived no benefit from my services, my fortune, in a pecuniary point of view, has received no augmentation from my country."[8] Hamilton rescued Washington from such petty gripes and made the address coolly statesmanlike, the words of a self-assured man speaking to posterity. It was the lofty Washington, not the wounded man smarting with secret hurts, that Hamilton set out to capture.

Washington displayed tremendous anxiety about the timing of his farewell address. In late June, he told Hamilton that he regretted not having published it as soon as Congress adjourned. Its postponement until the fall might lead people to surmise "that I delayed it long enough to see that the current was turned against me before I declared my intention to decline."[9] Hamilton pointed out the wisdom of waiting until the fall in case a national emergency, especially a military clash with France, forced him to reconsider a third term. "If a storm gathers," Hamilton wondered, "how can you retreat?"[10] To avoid interfering with the fall elections, Washington set a deadline of no later than October for publishing his farewell address.

At Mount Vernon that summer, Washington still licked his wounds over the rabid commentary in the *Aurora*. "That Mr. Bache will continue his attacks on the government, there can be no doubt," he told Treasury Secretary Wolcott, "but that they will make no impression on the public mind is not so certain, for drops of water will impress (in time) the hardest marble."[11] Because of Washington's public silence about his future plans, the presidential campaign played out in the shadows. It was assumed that, if Washington retired, Vice President Adams would emerge as the Federalist candidate for president, with Thomas Pinckney as his running mate. Political propriety demanded that they await official word from Washington before engaging in overt campaigning. By July it was also apparent that the Republicans would run Jefferson for president, joined by Aaron Burr as vice president.

Hamilton toiled over the farewell address in deep secrecy. Instead of sending his reactions through the mail, Washington, who thought his letters were being opened, conveyed them to New York via personal couriers. When Washington received the two versions of the farewell address in early August, he immediately discarded Madison's revised draft and opted for Hamilton's new version. As a literary stylist, Hamilton's abiding sin had always been prolixity. Since the farewell address was meant to be read in newspapers, not delivered as a speech, Washington objected to its length and asked Hamilton to trim it down. "All the columns of a large gazette would scarcely, I conceive, contain the present draft," he protested.[12] Always honest and self-critical, Washington saw that Hamilton had purged the address of his own personal whining; he conceded that it was "more dignified on the whole and with less egotism" than the earlier version.[13]

Washington succeeded in keeping his farewell message a closely held secret. On the morning of September 16, 1796, Tobias Lear appeared unexpectedly at the office of David Claypoole, who published a Philadelphia newspaper. In mysterious fashion, he told Claypoole that the president wanted to see him and promptly whisked him off to the executive mansion, where he huddled alone with Washington in a drawing room. There Washington disclosed the dramatic news that he was leaving the presidency and wished his farewell address to appear in *Claypoole's American Daily Advertiser*. The two men agreed that the publisher would "usher it to the world and suffer it to work its way afterwards" on Monday, September 19.[14] That weekend Washington corrected the proofs himself, right down to the punctuation marks, and he graciously allowed Claypoole to retain the invaluable manuscript. Even though Washington had given him exclusive rights to the address, it was widely disseminated at lightning speed. That same afternoon three Philadelphia papers jumped to print it, followed by a New York newspaper the next day, so that Washington achieved something close to a synchronized, universal publication. The address also appeared in pamphlet form.

An old hand at farewells, Washington, by design, rolled out of Philadelphia in his coach and headed for Mount Vernon, just as local citizens began to consume his address. He wished the words to speak for themselves, without any elaboration on his part. Washington never identified the document as his "farewell address," a label pinned on it by others. It appeared under the rubric "To the PEOPLE of the UNITED STATES," and began with the words "Friends and Fellow Citizens."[15] It was the perfect touch, echoing the opening of the Constitution, "We the People of the United States." While Washington could have informed Congress of his resignation, he went instead to the source of all sovereignty, the people, just as the Constitutional Convention had bypassed state legislatures and asked the people to approve the document directly through ratifying conventions.

In the address, Washington started by mentioning the earlier farewell letter and his hope that he could have retired sooner. The "increasing weight of years" had now made withdrawal from office necessary.[16] After talking of the vicissitudes of his presidency, he evoked America's grand future, sounding the oracular strain he had patented.[17] In a paean to unity, he warned that national identity must trump local attachments: "The name of AMERICAN, which belongs to you, in your national capacity, must always exalt the just pride of patriotism, more than any appellation derived from local discriminations."[18] This continental perspective had informed his work ever since the Revolution. Washington stressed the need to safeguard western territories from foreign encroachments, and without mentioning the Whiskey Rebellion by name, he enunciated the need for law and order: "The very idea of the power and the right of the people to establish government presupposes the duty of every individual to obey the established government."[19] Instead of flattering the people, Washington challenged them to improve their performance as citizens. Most of all he appealed to Americans to cling to the Union, with the federal government as the true guarantor of liberty and independence. As Joseph Ellis has written, "In the Farewell Address, Washington reiterated his conviction that the centralizing impulses of the American Revolution were not violations but fulfillments of its original ethos."[20]

As the address proceeded, it grew increasingly evident that Washington and Hamilton directed their shafts at the Republicans in coded language. Their denunciations of "combinations and associations" that sought to counteract the constituted authorities recalled their earlier strictures against the Democratic-Republican Societies. While such groups "may now and then answer popular ends, they are likely, in the course of time and things, to become potent engines by which cunning, ambitious and unprincipled men will be enabled to subvert the power of the people."[21] It was still hard for Washington to conceive of parties that were not disloyal cabals against duly elected government. A party spirit exists in all types of government, Washington observed, "but in those of the popular form, it is seen in its greatest rankness and is truly their worst enemy."[22] For Washington, parties weren't so much expressions of popular politics as their negation, denying the true will of the people as expressed through their chosen representatives.

Although he said that debt should be used sparingly and paid down in times of peace, Washington endorsed the Hamiltonian program. He warned against an unreasonable aversion to taxes, without which the debt could not be retired—a jab at those Jeffersonians who loudly took issue with the funded debt, then opposed the whiskey tax and other measures designed to whittle it down. By asserting executive vigor, his disclaimers notwithstanding, the farewell address placed Washington decidedly in the Federalist camp.

The genius of the farewell address was that it could be read in strictly neutral terms or as disguised pokes at the Jeffersonians. This was especially true when Washington laid out his sweeping views on foreign policy, recycling many ideas advanced in promoting the Jay Treaty. Tacitly railing against Republican support for France, he expounded a foreign policy based on practical interests instead of political passions: "The nation which indulges towards another an habitual hatred, or an habitual fondness, is in some degree a slave."[23] Sympathy with a foreign nation for purely ideological reasons, he said, could lead America into "the quarrels and wars of the latter without adequate inducement or justification."[24] He clearly had Jefferson and Madison in mind as he took issue with "ambitious, corrupted or deluded citizens (who devote themselves to the favorite nation)" and "sacrifice the interests of their own country."[25] Restating his neutrality policy, he underlined the desirability of commercial rather than political ties with other nations: " 'Tis our true policy to steer clear of permanent alliances with any portion of the foreign world."[26] It was Jefferson, not Washington, who warned against "entangling alliances," although the concept was clearly present in Washington's message.

For all the swipes at the opposition, Hamilton infused a placid tone into the address, replacing the bitter scold with the caring father. At the end Washington sounded a little like Shakespeare's Prospero, stepping off the stage of history. Whatever errors he had committed, he hoped that "my country will never cease to view them with indulgence and that, after forty-five years of my life dedicated to its service, with an upright zeal, the faults of incompetent abilities will be consigned to oblivion, as myself must soon be to the mansions of rest."[27] It was fitting that Washington closed by conflating the end of his life with the termination of his public service.

In general, Americans applauded the farewell address. Washington had seen himself as rising above partisanship, but some Republicans detected the barbs aimed at their party, and the effect was perhaps more divisive than Washington hoped. One visiting Frenchman resented its "marked antipathy to France and a predilection for England," while an opposition paper characterized Washington's words as "the loathings of a sick mind."[28] There was no mourning for Washington's departure in the editorial office of the *Aurora,* which had this to say about his retirement: "Every heart in unison . . . ought to beat high with exultation that the name of Washington from this day ceases to give a currency to political iniquity and to legalized corruption."[29] Well aware of the anti-Republican subtext of the address, Madison voiced his displeasure to Monroe about Washington's "suspicion of all who are thought to sympathize with [the French] revolution and who support the policy of extending our commerce" with France.[30]

An active guessing game arose as to who had composed the farewell address, which remained a well-kept secret for many years. In 1805 Dr. Benjamin Rush inquired of John Adams, "Did you ever hear who wrote General W.'s farewell address to the citizens of the United States? Major [Pierce] Butler says it was Mr. Jay. It is a masterly performance."[31] Jay had reviewed Hamilton's draft and made suggestions but in no way qualified as a coauthor. Eager to boost Washington's standing, Hamilton and other intimates kept their lips tightly sealed on the question of authorship. One day as Hamilton and his wife ambled down Broadway in New York, they encountered an old soldier hawking copies of the address. Buying a copy, Hamilton said amusedly to his wife, "That man does not know he has asked me to purchase my own work."[32]

Just as Washington feared, some observers attributed his departure to his dread of a poor showing in the fall election. "He knew there was to be an opposition to him at the next election and he feared he should not come in unanimously," John Adams remarked years later. "Besides, my popularity was growing too splendid, and the millions of addresses to me from all quarters piqued his jealousy."[33] In a still more paranoid vein, Adams surmised that Washington had retired because a malign Hamilton wielded veto power over his appointees: "And this necessity was, in my opinion, the real cause of his retirement from office. For you may depend upon it, that retirement was not voluntary."[34] Somewhat more objectively, Adams noted how spent the sixty-four-year-old Washington was after his prodigious labors: "The times were critical, the labor fatiguing, many circumstances disgusting, and he felt weary and longed for retirement."[35] This was much closer to the portrait that emerges from Washington's own letters.

To less envious eyes, Washington's resignation represented another milestone in republican government. Just as he had proved at the end of the war that he did not lust for power, so his departure from the presidency elevated his moral standing in the world. One encomium came from an unexpected quarter. By giving up first military and now political power, he stood out as "the greatest character of the age," according to George III, who had belatedly learned to appreciate his erstwhile enemy.[36] Though it was not his main intention, Washington inaugurated a custom of presidents serving only two terms, a precedent honored until the time of Franklin Roosevelt. For opponents who had spent eight years harping on Washington's supposed monarchical obsessions, his decision to step down could only have left them in a dazed state of speechless confusion.

THE MOST FLAGRANT OMISSION in Washington's farewell statement was the subject most likely to subvert its unifying spirit: slavery. Whatever his private reservations about slavery, President Washington had acted in accordance with the wishes of southern slaveholders. In February 1793 he signed the Fugitive Slave Act, enabling masters to cross state lines to recapture runaway slaves. He remained zealous in tracking down his own fugitive slaves, although like Jefferson, he didn't care to call attention to such activities. When a slave named Paul ran away in March 1795, Washington, while approving measures to apprehend him, advised William Pearce that "I would not have my name appear in any advertisement, or other measure, leading to it."[37] He was especially worried about his name surfacing in northern papers. Even in Philadelphia, Washington monitored the status of runaway slaves at Mount Vernon. "I see by the last week's report that Caesar has been absent six days," he asked Pearce in early 1796. "Is he a runaway? If so, it is probable he will escape altogether, as he can read, if not write."[38]

Beyond moral scruples, Washington found slave ownership a political embarrassment. During his second term, the Aurora taunted him by declaring that, twenty years after independence, Washington still possessed "FIVE HUNDRED of the HUMAN SPECIES IN SLAVERY."[39] On another occasion it mocked him as a hypocritical emblem of liberty, arguing that it "must appear a little incongruous then that Liberty's Apostle should be seen with chains in his hands, holding men in bondage."[40] This was a dangerous game for Bache to play, since it could easily backfire on Jefferson and Madison, two sizable slaveholders who figured as his populist champions. In later correspondence with John Adams, Benjamin Rush served up this tidbit about Washington: "Mr. Jefferson told me he once saw [Washington] throw the Aurora hastily upon the floor with a 'damn' of the author, who had charged him with the crime of being a slaveholder."[41] Federalist polemicists also exploited the slavery issue to excoriate Republicans and their southern base. "Oh, happy Carolina! Happy, thrice Virginia!" wrote William Cobbett. "After having spent the day in singing hymns to the Goddess of Liberty, the virtuous Democrat [i.e., Republican] gets him home to his peaceful dwelling and sleeps with his *property* secure beneath his roof, yea, sometimes in his very *arms*."[42]

During their Philadelphia years, George and Martha Washington must have wondered how long their slaves imported from Mount Vernon would remain loyal. First there had been the flap over the local law that liberated slaves after six months of continuous residence. Slave masters often assumed that slaves brought north and exposed to free blacks were forever "tainted" by the experience; Washington subscribed to the view that otherwise happy, contented slaves could be "tampered with and seduced" by meddlesome northern abolitionists.[43] Even though Washington favored abolition in theory, he thought that as long as slavery existed, his slaves ought to cooperate in exchange for the food and shelter he provided.

Washington permitted his household slaves a modicum of freedom to roam the city, sample its pleasures, and even patronize the theater. Household accounts for June 1792 disclose expense money doled out for "Austin, Hercules & Oney to go to the play."[44] In the spring of 1793 two of Martha's maids were given money to attend "tumbling feats," followed by money to view a local circus. The two slaves most favored with such treats and held in highest esteem by the Washingtons were Ona (or Oney) Judge, Martha's maid, and Hercules, the master chef. One wonders whether their fleeting experiences of freedom in Philadelphia whetted their appetites for permanent freedom. Washington must have known that their contacts with the large community of free blacks in the capital could only strengthen their desire to throw off the yoke of slavery.

A young mulatto woman, light-skinned and freckled, Ona Judge was the daughter of Andrew Judge, an indentured servant at Mount Vernon, and a slave named Betty. She was Martha's personal maid and widely known as her pet. Each morning Ona brushed Martha's hair, laid out her clothing, and assisted her with household sewing. In the president's words, Ona Judge was "handy and useful to [Martha], being perfect mistress of her needle."[45] Naive about the true feelings of her slaves, Martha assumed that, because Ona enjoyed a relatively privileged status as her personal chambermaid, she would never rebel against her bondage. In 1796 Ona, then about twenty-two, realized that the Washingtons might soon return to Mount Vernon for good, eliminating any possibility of a flight to freedom. As if the young slave would be thrilled by the news, Martha mentioned to Ona one day that she planned to bequeath her to her granddaughter Elizabeth, who was notorious for her grim moods. Far from feeling flattered, Ona felt deep terror at the prospect, later saying with disdain that "she was determined not to be *her* slave."[46] Since "she did not want to be a slave always," she later recalled, "she supposed if she went back to Virginia, she would never have a chance to escape."[47]

As the Washingtons got ready for a return trip to Mount Vernon in May 1796, Ona Judge set in motion her scheme to escape. While servants boxed belongings for the trip, she used the preparations as camouflage to gather her things, and as the Washingtons dined one evening, she slipped out of the executive mansion and blended into the free black community. After lying low for a month, she sailed north aboard a ship called the *Nancy*, staffed by a large contingent of black sailors, and eventually wound up in Portsmouth, New Hampshire.

When the Washingtons discovered the escape, they were convinced that Judge would have fled only if she had been cajoled by a wily seducer. They flattered themselves into thinking that, as a supposedly contented slave, Judge would never have pined for freedom if some intriguing fellow had not planted the forbidden idea. They could not conceive of a slave being the agent of her own fate or running out of a simple hunger for liberty. They felt obliged to denigrate any man who helped her as an unscrupulous cad rather than someone who might have loved her and honestly wanted to assist her.

The protracted hunt for Ona Judge began when a young woman, Elizabeth Langdon, who had befriended Nelly Custis, spotted her in Portsmouth. When Langdon realized that Martha Washington was nowhere to be seen and that Judge had escaped, she asked Judge, "But why did you come away? How can Mrs. Washington do without you?" "Run away, misses," Judge replied. "Run away!" said Langdon. "And from such an excellent place! Why, what could induce you? You had a room to yourself and only light nice work to do and every indulgence." "Yes, I know, but I want to be free, misses; wanted to learn to read and write."[48] Ona Judge, who had stored up grievances that Martha Washington could little comprehend, afterward complained that she had "never received the least mental or moral instruction of any kind, while she remained in Washington's family."[49]

After Judge was spotted, Martha pressured her husband into wielding the powers of the federal government to recapture her. She felt miffed by Judge's flight and could never understand why blacks felt no gratitude toward lenient masters. As she once wrote to Fanny, "The blacks are so bad in their nature that they have not the least gratitude for the kindness that may be showed to them."[50] Since the Treasury Department ran the customs service and had officers in every major port, Washington wrote confidentially to Secretary Wolcott, asking for aid. He explained that Judge's escape had "been planned by someone who knew what he was about and had the means to defray the expense of it and to entice her off, for not the least suspicion was entertained of her going or having formed a connection with anyone who could induce her to such an act."[51] Abusing his presidential powers, Washington instructed Wolcott to have the Portsmouth customs collector kidnap Judge and send her back to Virginia: "To seize and put her onboard a vessel bound immediately to this place [Philadelphia] or to Alexandria, which I should like better, seems at first view to be the safest and least expensive [measure]."[52] Perhaps contributing to Washington's vigilance in hunting down Judge was that she was a dower slave, which meant that he would have to reimburse the Custis estate for her loss.

As with runaway slave ads, Washington struggled to confine knowledge of the situation to Virginia and keep it from carping northern abolitionists—hence his preference for whisking Judge off to Alexandria. Dreading publicity, he also convinced Martha that it would be unwise to post a fugitive slave notice. He apologized to Wolcott for the trouble he was giving him "on such a trifling occasion, but the ingratitude of the girl, who was brought up and treated more like a child than a servant (and Mrs. Washington's desire to recover her) ought not to escape with impunity if it can be avoided."[53] That the Washingtons faulted Judge for "ingratitude" and pretended that she was like a daughter again shows the moral blindness of even comparatively enlightened slave owners. Judge's flight belied whatever sedative fantasies the Washingtons might have had that slaves developed familial relations with their masters, transcending the indignity of bondage.

The Portsmouth customs collector, Joseph Whipple, tracked down Judge and, to lure her aboard a ship bound for Virginia, cooked up a bogus story about employing her to work for his family. Then something unaccountable happened: Whipple engaged in conversation with Judge and discovered that "she had not been decoyed away, as had been apprehended, but that a thirst for complete freedom . . . had been her only motive for absconding."[54] Remarkably, Judge said that she was prepared to return to servitude, but only if her emancipation were guaranteed at a later date. In Whipple's words, "she expressed great affection and reverence for her master and mistress and, without hesitation, declared her willingness to return and serve with fidelity during the lives of the president and his lady if she could be freed on their decease, should she outlive them; but that she should rather suffer death than return to slavery and [be] liable to be sold or given to any other persons."[55] Perhaps doubtful that any slave master could really be trusted, Judge's friends in Portsmouth persuaded her to rescind her offer to return to Mount Vernon.

When Washington heard about the bargaining, he dismissed such negotiations as "totally inadmissible."[56] He found himself tangled in the coils of a terrible contradiction: just as he meditated the emancipation of *all* his slaves, he was trying to return *one* of them to bondage. Abashed, he told Whipple that "however well disposed I might be to a gradual abolition, or even to an entire emancipation of that description of people (if the latter was in itself practicable at this moment), it would neither be political or just to reward *unfaithfulness* with a premature preference and thereby discontent beforehand the minds of all her fellow servants, who by their steady attachments are far more deserving than herself of favor."[57] In other words, Washington insisted that, as long as slavery existed, he must obey its cruel logic. He and Martha clung to the self-serving tale that Judge had "been seduced and enticed off by a Frenchman" who had roguishly sated his lust and then discarded her.[58] Unwilling to compromise, Washington demanded that Judge either return voluntarily and "be forgiven by her mistress" or be put "on board a vessel bound either to Alexandria or the Federal City," conveniently bypassing Philadelphia.[59] In a telling concession, Washington instructed Whipple to forget about capturing Judge if forcibly abducting her served to "excite a mob or riot."⁶⁰ Shortly to leave office, Washington wanted no incident that might tarnish his departure, especially since he feared that Judge might be pregnant, which would only augment public sympathy for her escape. The evocation of a possible mob or riot suggests how abolitionist sentiment had spread in the New England states, so that Washington defied it at his peril.

Ona Judge never returned to slavery or the South. In late December Joseph Whipple informed Washington that she would shortly get married, making a mockery of Washington's scenario of a cunning Frenchman who had duped and impregnated her. That January she married a "colored sailor" named John Staines, and about a year later they had a daughter, the first of three children, proving that Judge had not been pregnant at the time of her flight. Despite this news, Martha refused to let the matter drop. During the summer of 1799, when she learned that her nephew, Burwell Bassett, Jr., was traveling to Portsmouth, the news led to one last attempt to recapture Judge. While instructing Bassett to shy away from doing anything "unpleasant or troublesome," Washington told him that if Judge could be brought back by "easy . . . and proper means . . . it would be a pleasing circumstance to your aunt."⁶¹ Bassett located Judge, who was now a mother, and assured her that no punishment would occur if she returned. Apparently she had heard rumors that Bassett would seize her and her child by force, if necessary, and she would not be coaxed back into bondage. "I am free now and choose to remain so," she declared, settling the matter for good.⁶²

The other slave who shocked the Washingtons by his disappearance was Hercules, who was owned directly by the president. We recall that he had noisily protested his loyalty to Washington over the issue of the six-month slave law in Pennsylvania. Hercules oversaw a mixed staff of slaves and indentured servants who worked in a separate kitchen building, attached to the executive residence by an underground passage. Being top chef for the president carried high status, and the dandyish Hercules, who was partial to black silk waistcoats, coats with velvet collars, cocked hats, and gold-headed canes, relished his eminence around town. He also appreciated the money he made from selling kitchen leftovers, spending it on fancy clothes, watches, and shoe buckles. One Mount Vernon visitor got this report of the headstrong Hercules: "The cook who rejoiced in the name of *Hercules* was . . . something of a tyrant, as well as a capital cook."⁶³

The freedom that Hercules enjoyed in Philadelphia could only have made more oppressive the prospect of returning to Virginia, emboldening him to escape. Around the time that Washington left the presidency, Hercules suddenly disappeared. Although Washington made efforts to retrieve him, they were neither as systematic nor as prolonged as with Ona Judge. For one thing, he knew that Hercules had friends in the local black community who could hide him and that with his culinary skills he could easily make a living. George and Martha Washington did not seem to feel as personally betrayed by Hercules's flight as by Judge's, perhaps because he was an older and more independent personality who had nothing to gain by remaining a slave now that the presidency had ended.

In January 1798 Washington sent a pair of notes to Frederick Kitt, a household steward during his presidency, laying out secret plans for recapturing Hercules. As with Judge, Washington wanted to have Hercules hustled aboard a ship bound for Alexandria "with a strict charge to the master not to give him an opportunity of escaping."[64] Washington showed implicit respect for Hercules's shrewdness, warning Kitt that if he gets "the least hint of the design, he would elude all your vigilance."[65] Although Kitt made inquiries and verified Washington's hunch that Hercules had indeed lingered in Philadelphia, the ex-slave was never caught and succeeded in winning his freedom. He paid a hefty price for it. He left behind his son Richmond, who had been sent back to Mount Vernon for allegedly stealing money, possibly the prelude to a joint escape with his father. He also had to say goodbye to a six-year-old daughter at Mount Vernon. When a French visitor confronted the little girl as to whether she was upset at her father's action, she retorted, "Oh! Sir, I am very glad, because he is free now."[66]

After the Washingtons returned to Mount Vernon in March 1797, the kitchen was a hectic, demanding place that had to handle the sudden advent of unexpected guests. Hercules's flight threw the household into turmoil, and extensive inquiries were made to find a skilled cook to replace him. Martha wrote despondently to Eliza Powel, "The inconvenience I am put to since the loss of my cook is very great and rendered still more severe for want of a steward, who is acquainted with the management of such like matters."[67] Not a moment too soon, Washington found Eleanor Forbes, an English widow, to function as housekeeper and help supervise the kitchen. Washington told his nephew Bushrod that Martha had been "exceedingly fatigued and distressed for want of a good housekeeper."[68] For Washington, the search for a new slave cook ran into an insurmountable problem: it would force him to break his rule of not buying new slaves. "The running off of my cook has been a most inconvenient thing to this family," he told a relative, "and what renders it more disagreeable is that I had resolved never to become the master of another slave by *purchase;* but this resolution, I fear I must break."[69] Washington did not stop to savor the irony here: Hercules would have had to remain a slave in order for Washington to make good on his pledge to end his purchases of slaves. However, the Washingtons could find no slave who replicated what the talented Hercules had done for many years and so decided to make do with Mrs. Forbes.

Exiting the Stage

IN THE LAST YEAR of Washington's presidency, James Sharples executed portraits of the first couple in the profile format that was his trademark. The George Washington he sketched still stood out as a powerfully commanding presence, with a long, pointed nose and thick sideburns that curled down almost to the chin line. Washington applied pomade to the hair that bulged from both sides of his face, making it wavy and shiny, while he drew the remaining hair straight back in military style and tied it in a big black bow, as he had done since the French and Indian War. Judging by the Sharples portrait, the years had been less kind to Martha. Time had sharpened her chin and made her nose more aquiline, and her strangely shaped headgear only emphasized the irregularity of her face.

Washington worked up the energy for one final address to Congress. Donning his black velvet suit and strapping his dress sword to his hip, he strode into the House on December 7, 1796, and discovered the gallery packed "with the largest assemblage of citizens, ladies, and gentlemen ever collected on a similar occasion."[1] In his thirty-minute address, he crowed about Britain's evacuation of the northwestern forts and the liberation of American prisoners in Algiers. He also expounded on the need for a military academy, a vision later fulfilled at West Point, and issued a stirring plea for a national university in the new capital. Only in the final paragraph did Washington strike a private note, saying the present occasion aroused memories of "the period when the administration of the present form of government commenced."[2]

For the most part, the speech was well received, although the lone congressman from the new state of Tennessee, Andrew Jackson, who was enraged by the Jay

Treaty, refused to salute the departing chief or join in the congressional response applauding him. The *Aurora* enjoyed bidding good riddance to Washington. "If ever a nation has suffered from the improper influence of a man," it intoned, "the American nation has suffered from the influence of Washington."[3] Nor did many Republicans any longer feel the need to cloak their disenchantment with Washington. "The retirement of General Washington was a cause of sincere, open, and indecent rejoicing among the French party in the United States," one Federalist reported. "The real friends of this country . . . considered the loss of Washington's personal influence a public calamity."[4] A small anecdote speaks volumes about the lethal political atmosphere. After Washington published the farewell address, Federalists in the Virginia House of Delegates introduced a motion hailing "the virtue, patriotism, and wisdom of the President of the United States." In a deliberate snub, the Republicans lobbied to delete the word *wisdom* from the resolution, prompting John Marshall to lead the battle to retain the disputed noun. "Will it be believed that the word was retained by a very small majority?" he later said. "A very small majority in the legislature of Virginia acknowledged the wisdom of General Washington."[5]

As soon as the farewell address was published, the presidential campaign got under way in earnest. In many respects, Washington had made it difficult for the Federalists to emerge as a genuine national party. With his exalted stature, he never wanted to dirty his fingers with lowly organizational matters or countenance that detestable thing called a party; he wanted merely an association of like-minded gentlemen. His unassailable popularity also made it unnecessary for the Federalists to develop the broad-based popular leadership that Republicans had developed under the tutelage of Jefferson and Madison. The opposition had attained a powerful cohesion simply by sustained resistance to administration policies.

The 1796 election was the first contested presidential campaign in American history. With 71 electoral votes, Adams became the president, narrowly edging out Jefferson, with 68 votes. Since Jefferson nosed out Adams's "running mate," Thomas Pinckney, with 59 votes, he became vice president under rules governing the Electoral College at the time. At a presidential reception that December, Martha Washington, privy to rumors of Adams's victory, pressed his hand in congratulation and said how pleased Washington was. As a glowing Adams reported to Abigail, "John Adams never felt more serene in his life."[6] At first, the mixed ticket seemed to promise a less partisan era, and people cited the importance of the friendship of Adams and Jefferson, dating back to Revolutionary days. More presciently, Fisher Ames saw an impending collision between the new president and vice president: "Two presidents, like two suns in the meridian, would meet and jostle for four years, and then vice would be first."[7]

Thomas Jefferson believed that George Washington had led a charmed life, stealing credit from the more deserving while sticking them with his blunders. This envy was reflected in a comment he made to Madison that January: "[Washington] is fortunate to get off just as the bubble is bursting, leaving others to hold the bag. Yet, as his departure will mark the moment when the difficulties begin to work, you will see that they will be ascribed to the new administration and that he will have his usual good fortune of reaping credit from the good acts of others and leaving to them that of his errors."[8] Embittered by his dealings with Washington, Jefferson clearly thought that the first president had been terribly lucky and overrated. By 1814 Jefferson would arrive at a more balanced verdict on Washington: "On the whole, his character was, in its mass, perfect, in nothing bad, in few points indifferent; and it may truly be said, that never did nature and fortune combine more perfectly to make a man great."[9]

During a Philadelphia winter so frigid that residents skated on an ice-encrusted Delaware River, Washington ended up pioneering in one last area: how to behave as a lame duck president. Like later presidents, he endured an excruciating round of farewell parties, balls, dinners, and receptions. Though harassed by the final duties of public office, he seemed rejuvenated as the albatross was slowly lifted from his shoulders. Sick of party rancor, homesick for Mount Vernon, he craved a little privacy before he died. Martha too looked forward to the retirement that had always been her fond but forlorn dream.

Washington's last birthday in office, his sixty-fifth, was crammed with festivities, including an "elegant entertainment" at Ricketts' Amphitheater, followed by a dinner and ball "which for splendor, taste, and elegance was perhaps never excelled by any similar entertainment in the United States," judged Claypoole's newspaper.[10] The vast gathering of twelve hundred guests took place in the cavernous circus hall, floored over for dancing. Like the couple atop a wedding cake, George and Martha Washington sat on a raised couch beneath a canopy and periodically descended to mill about with guests. Washington indulged in one last bout of gallantry with the ladies when he rose to present his toast: "May the members thereof [the dancing assembly] and the *Fair* who honor it with their presence long continue the enjoyment of an amusement so innocent and agreeable."[11] Showing her esteem for the outgoing president, Elizabeth Powel emerged from extended mourning for her husband and appeared radiant in a black velvet dress. There was no question that George and Martha, overcome by emotion, felt that an epic saga was ending. "Mrs. Washington was moved even to tears with the mingled emotions of gratitude for such strong proofs of public regard and the new prospect of uninterrupted enjoyment of domestic life," a Judge Airedale reported to his wife. " . . . I never saw the president look better or in finer spirits, but his emotions were too powerful to be concealed. He could sometimes scarcely speak."[12]

On March 2, in one of his last acts in office, Washington wrote a condolence note to Henry Knox for his loss of three children. Perhaps moved by his old friend's pitiable plight, he sought to repair the unfortunate damage inflicted on their long friendship by the Whiskey Rebellion. When he returned to Mount Vernon, Washington planned to travel no more than twenty miles from home again, which would sever him forever from old friends. This led him to say to Knox, "I am not without my regrets at parting with (perhaps never more to meet) the few intimates whom I love, among these, be assured, you are one."[13]

The next day, his last in office, Washington toiled under fierce pressure to sign legislation dumped on his desk at the last minute. The Constitution gave the president ten days to sign bills, and Washington resented that legislators had allowed him "scarcely an hour to revolve the most important" ones, as he protested to Jonathan Trumbull. "But as the scene is closing with me, it is of little avail *now* to let it be with murmurs."[14] At the end he struck a note of serenity, a faith that the American experiment, if sometimes threatened, would prevail. While fearful of machinations, he told Trumbull, "I trust . . . that the good sense of our countrymen will guard the public weal against this and every other innovation and that, altho[ugh] we may be a little wrong now and then, we shall return to the right path with more avidity."[15] It was an accurate forecast of American history, both its tragic lapses and its miraculous redemptions.

On March 4, inauguration day, Washington did not even bother to mention the event in his diary, preferring to jot down the temperature. "Much such a day as yesterday in all respects. Mercury at 41," says the entry in its entirety.[16] Shortly before noon, dressed in a suit of solemn black, he marched alone to Congress Hall. As he approached the building and entered the House chamber, the cheers and applause of an immense multitude showered down on him. Jefferson next appeared in a blue frock coat and sauntered down the aisle in his loose-limbed style. President-elect Adams then disembarked from a splendid new coach operated by servants in livery. As he made his way into the chamber and up to the dais, he wore a pearl-colored suit with wrist ruffles and a powdered wig and toted a cockaded hat. Looking sleepless, harried, and a little overwhelmed, he glanced over at Washington, who seemed to be shedding his worldly cares. "A solemn scene it was indeed," Adams wrote, "and it was made affecting to me by the presence of the General, whose countenance was as serene and unclouded as the day. He seemed to me to enjoy a triumph over me. Methought I heard him say, 'Ay! I am fairly out and you fairly in! See which of us will be happiest!'"[17] From the outset, Adams confronted a tough assignment: any president who followed Washington was doomed to seem illegitimate for a time, a mere pretender to the throne.

After introducing Adams, Washington read a short farewell message, filling the

silent hall with an overwhelming sense of sadness. The country was losing someone who had been its constant patriarch from the beginning. Adams said that the
weeping in the galleries surpassed the sobbing of any audience at a tragic play. "But
whether it was from grief or joy," he wondered aloud to Abigail, "whether from the
loss of their beloved president or . . . from the novelty of the thing . . . I know not."[18]
A woman named Susan R. Echard captured the scene's emotional intensity: "Every
now and then there was a suppressed sob. I cannot describe Washington's appearance as I felt it—perfectly composed and self-possessed till the close of his address.
Then, when strong nervous sobs broke loose, when tears covered the faces, then the
great man was shaken. I never took my eyes from his face. Large drops came from
his eyes."[19] It was one last proof, if any were now needed, of just how emotional the
man of marble was beneath the surface. After taking the oath of office, administered by Chief Justice Oliver Ellsworth, President Adams talked of Washington as
someone who had "secured immortality with posterity."[20] Doubtless relieved that
he was no longer the protagonist of the American drama, Washington ended the
inauguration ceremony with an exquisite gesture: he insisted that President Adams
and Vice President Jefferson exit the chamber before him, a perfect symbol that
the nation's most powerful man had now reverted to the humble status of a private citizen.

Afterward Washington walked from the executive mansion to the Francis Hotel,
where President Adams was temporarily staying, and he became aware of a tremendous throng of people surging around him. "An immense company," said one
observer, had gone "as one man in total silence as escort all the way."[21] When Washington reached the hotel and turned around, the crowd saw that his face was again
washed with tears. "No man ever saw him so moved," said a second observer.[22] In a
very Washingtonian feat, he touched the crowd by simply staring at them in silence
before disappearing into the hotel.

Like Washington, Adams viewed himself as an incorruptible figure rising above
the bane of parties. And like Washington, his political enemies insisted on tagging
him as a Federalist. In this rancorous atmosphere, he was denied the political
honeymoon usually reserved for new presidents and felt stranded between two extremes. "All the Federalists seem to be afraid to approve anybody but Washington,"
he complained to Abigail. "The Jacobin papers damn with faint praise and undermine with misrepresentation and insinuation."[23]

There was no moratorium on criticism of the outgoing president; the *Aurora*
unleashed a frontal attack on Washington, condemning him for having "cankered
the principles of republicanism in an enlightened people."[24] In desperation, Benjamin Franklin Bache dredged up the earliest controversy that had shadowed Washington's life: the 1754 Jumonville incident in which, Bache charged, Washington had

"fired on a flag of truce; killed the officer in the act of reading a summons under the sanction of such a flag"; then "signed a capitulation in which the killing of that officer and his men was acknowledged as an act of *assassination*."[25] Responding to this abuse, the *Gazette of the United States* decried the "hellish pleasure" that Bache took in defaming Washington.[26] "That a man who was born in America and is part of the great family of the United States should thus basely aim his poisoned dagger at the FATHER OF HIS COUNTRY," scolded the *Gazette,* "is sorely to be lamented."[27]

Though Washington preferred having Adams rather than Jefferson as his successor, their relationship had never been close and was further marred by haggling over the presidential furnishings. John and Abigail Adams claimed to be appalled by the slovenly state of the executive mansion, and Abigail in particular derided the house as a pigsty, having "been the scene of the most scandalous drinking and disorder among the servants that I ever heard of."[28] Washington magnanimously offered the furnishings of two large drawing rooms at reduced prices and didn't "cull the best and offer him the rest."[29] The Adamses, however, would not touch the stuff, and in a fit of petty sniping, Adams groused that Washington had even tried to palm off two old horses on him for $2,000.

Rebuffed, Washington gave away many household items of historic value. He sold his private writing desk at cost to his dear friend Elizabeth Powel and, as a lagniappe, threw in a free pair of mirrors and lamps. A week later she sent him a teasing letter, claiming that she was shocked to unearth incriminating love letters stuffed in a drawer of the desk: "Suppose I should prove incontestably that you have without design put into my possession the love letters of a lady addressed to you under the most solemn sanction."[30] After more banter, she admitted that the letters in question were "a large bundle of letters from Mrs. Washington, bound up and labeled with your usual accuracy."[31] Washington's reply was exceptionally revealing about his marriage. After thanking Powel for handling the matter delicately, he said that he knew that no such illicit love letters existed and that even had the letters in question fallen into "more inquisitive hands, the correspondence would, I am persuaded, have been found to be more fraught with expressions of friendship than of *enamored* love." Anyone looking for "passion . . . of the *Romantic order,*" he contended, would have chosen to commit them to the flames.[32] The letter confirms that by this point Washington's relationship with Martha had settled into one of deep friendship, devoid of carnal desire or lusty romance.

On March 9 the former president gathered up his wife, who was nagged by a bad cold and a cough, the family dog, his granddaughter Nelly and her parrot, and George Washington Lafayette and his tutor and commenced the six-day journey to Mount Vernon. "On one side, I am called upon to remember the parrot, on the other to remember the dog," he related whimsically to Tobias Lear. "For my own part, I should not pine much if both were forgot."[33] Although the wagons were encumbered with heaps of bags, they represented only a tiny fraction of the mementos accumulated over many years, and it would take ninety-seven boxes, fourteen trunks, and forty-three casks to ship home the remaining belongings and souvenirs.

In those days of poor transportation, farewells left an especially melancholy aftertaste, since many friendships were ended irrevocably by sheer distance. "How many friends I have left behind," Martha Washington wrote wistfully to Lucy Knox. "They fill my memory with sweet thoughts. Shall I ever see them again? Not likely, unless they shall come to me here, for the twilight is gathering around our lives."[34] En route to Mount Vernon, Washington tried, as usual, to curtail the time devoted to townsfolk who wanted to smother him with adulation. Although enormous crowds received him in Baltimore, he contrived to skip festivities planned in Alexandria, expressing satisfaction that he "avoided in every instance, where [he] had any previous knowledge of the intention . . . all parades or escorts."[35] The one detour he surely savored was the ride by, to the thunderous welcome of a sixteen-gun salute, the new President's House under construction in Washington, D.C.

The presidential legacy he left behind in Philadelphia was a towering one. As Gordon Wood has observed, "The presidency is the powerful office it is in large part because of Washington's initial behavior."[36] Washington had forged the executive branch of the federal government, appointed outstanding department heads, and set a benchmark for fairness, efficiency, and integrity that future administrations would aspire to match. "A new government, constructed on free principles, is always weak and must stand in need of the props of a firm and good administration till time shall have rendered its authority venerable and fortified it by habits of obedience," Hamilton wrote.[37] Washington had endowed the country with exactly such a firm and good administration, guaranteeing the survival of the Constitution. He had taken the new national charter and converted it into a viable, elastic document. In a wide variety of areas, from inaugural addresses to presidential protocol to executive privilege, he had set a host of precedents that endured because of the high quality and honesty of his decisions.

Washington's catalog of accomplishments was simply breathtaking. He had restored American credit and assumed state debt; created a bank, a mint, a coast guard, a customs service, and a diplomatic corps; introduced the first accounting, tax, and budgetary procedures; maintained peace at home and abroad; inaugurated a navy, bolstered the army, and shored up coastal defenses and infrastructure; proved that the country could regulate commerce and negotiate binding treaties; protected frontier settlers, subdued Indian uprisings, and established law and order amid rebellion, scrupulously adhering all the while to the letter of the Constitution.

During his successful presidency, exports had soared, shipping had boomed, and state taxes had declined dramatically. Washington had also opened the Mississippi to commerce, negotiated treaties with the Barbary states, and forced the British to evacuate their northwestern forts. Most of all he had shown a disbelieving world that republican government could prosper without being spineless or disorderly or reverting to authoritarian rule. In surrendering the presidency after two terms and overseeing a smooth transition of power, Washington had demonstrated that the president was merely the servant of the people.

Whatever their mandarin style and elitist tendencies, the Federalists had an abiding faith in executive power and crafted the federal government with a clarity and conviction that would have been problematic for the Republicans, who preferred small government and legislative predominance. Washington had established the presidency instead of Congress as the driving force behind domestic and foreign policy and established sharp boundaries between those two branches of government. He was the perfect figure to reconcile Americans to a vigorous executive and to conquer deeply rooted fears that a president would behave in the tyrannical manner of a monarch. He also provided a conservative counterweight to some of the more unruly impulses of the American Revolution, ensuring incremental progress and averting the bloody excesses associated with the French Revolution.

Washington never achieved the national unity he desired and, by the end, presided over a deeply riven country. John Adams made a telling point when he later noted that Washington, an apostle of unity, "had unanimous votes as president, but the two houses of Congress and the great body of the people were more equally divided under him than they ever have been since."[38] This may have been unavoidable as the new government implemented the new Constitution, which provoked deep splits over its meaning and the country's future direction. But whatever his chagrin about the partisan strife, Washington never sought to suppress debate or clamp down on his shrill opponents in the press who had hounded him mercilessly. To his everlasting credit, he showed that the American political system could manage tensions without abridging civil liberties. His most flagrant failings remained those of the country as a whole—the inability to deal forthrightly with the injustice of slavery or to figure out an equitable solution in the ongoing clashes with Native Americans.

By the time Washington left office, the Union had expanded to include three new states—Vermont, Kentucky, and Tennessee—creating powerful new constituencies with outspoken needs. In this nascent democratic culture, the political tone was becoming brash and rude, sounding the death knell for the more sedate style of politics practiced by the formal Washington. Although he had securely laid the foundations of the federal government, he was still the product of his genteel Virginia past and accustomed to the rule of well-bred gentlemen such as himself. He would never have been fully at home with the brawling, roaring brand of democracy that came to dominate American politics in the era of Andrew Jackson. Nonetheless he had proved the ideal figure to lead the new nation from its colonial past into a more democratic future.

PART SIX

The Legend

Apotheosis of Washington, *by David Edwin,*
after Rembrandt Peale, engraved circa 1800.

Samson and Solomon

FOR AT LEAST A SHORT INTERVAL, the return to Mount Vernon was a heavenly sensation for the wandering Washington family, who experienced again some modicum of normality after their long exile in the nation's capital. "Since I left Philadelphia, everything has appeared to be a dream," Nelly Custis told a friend. "I can hardly realize my being *here* and that grandpapa is no longer in office."[1] As far as Nelly was concerned, the ex-president had been restored to his natural habitat: "Grandpapa is very well and has already turned farmer again."[2] Martha basked in newfound domestic joy. "I cannot tell you, my dear friend," she wrote to Lucy Knox, "how much I enjoy home after having been deprived of one so long, for our dwelling in New York and Philadelphia was not home, only a sojourning. The General and I feel like children just released from school."[3] Washington invoked his preferred pastoral image of domestic bliss: "I am once more seated under my own vine and fig tree and hope to spend the remainder of my days—which, in the ordinary course of things . . . cannot be many—in peaceful retirement."[4] Relieved to be at home, he spurned a wedding invitation from his nephew Lawrence Augustine Washington, explaining that "I think it not likely that either of us will ever be more than 25 miles from Mount Vernon again."[5]

If George Washington expected a belated season of repose, he was bound to be disappointed. Soon after he got home, he had to deal with the death of his sister, Betty Lewis, which filled him with "inexpressible concern."[6] Her death left George and his younger brother Charles as the last survivors of their generation of the Washington clan. Washington generously invited Betty's son Lawrence to live at Mount Vernon, but he also had an ulterior agenda, thinking his nephew might lift a social burden from his shoulders. "As both your aunt and I are in the decline of life and regular in our habits, especially in our hours of rising and going to bed," Washington told him, "I require some person . . . to ease me of the trouble of entertaining company, particularly of nights, as it is my inclination to retire . . . either to bed or to my study soon after candlelight."[7] When Lewis delayed joining his uncle, having to deal first with a runaway slave, Washington commiserated: "I wish from my soul that the legislature of this state could see the policy of a gradual abolition of slavery. It would prev[en]t much future mischief."[8]

As had happened in December 1783, Washington again encountered a decaying Mount Vernon that had never regained its antebellum efficiency. The buildings looked dilapidated, the furnishings shabby, the soil depleted. With his plantation, Washington seemed to suffer the curse of Sisyphus—he was forever away, forever falling behind, forever forced to rely on undependable help. "We are like the beginners of a new establishment, having everything in a manner to do," Washington told Elizabeth Powel after surveying the place. "Houses and everything to repair. Rooms to paint, paper, whitewash, etc. etc."[9] A constant parade of carpenters, masons, and painters trooped through the house, kicking up clouds of dust everywhere. So enormous were the repairs that Washington estimated they would cost almost "as much as if I had commenced an entire new establishment."[10]

Once again, with Roman fortitude, Washington endured an invasion of unwanted visitors. Far from being a rustic retreat, Mount Vernon became a way station for travelers eager to glimpse the retired national leader. On July 31, 1797, when he invited Tobias Lear to dinner, Washington made this startling comment: "Unless someone pops in unexpectedly, Mrs. Washington and myself will do what I believe has not been done within the last twenty years by us—that is, to set down to dinner by ourselves."[11] Although visitors said they had made the pilgrimage as a mark of respect, the ex-president expressed skepticism about their true motives: "Pray, would not the word curiosity answer as well? And how different this, from having a few social friends at a cheerful board?"[12]

Many visitors viewed Washington through the golden haze of fame, with no real awareness of his underlying strain, and gushed about his stately serenity. When Amariah Frost of Massachusetts stopped by, he was struck by the exemplary courtesies extended to visitors. After slaves brought rum to him and his companions, they sat down with the Washingtons for a succulent meal consisting of "a small roasted pig, boiled leg of lamb, beef, peas, lettuce, cucumbers, artichokes . . . puddings, tarts, etc."[13] Although Washington led discussions on current affairs, Martha was now also a repository of anecdotes about the historic events of the past quarter century. "The extensive knowledge she has gained in this general intercourse with persons from all parts of the world has made her a most interesting companion, and having a vastly retentive memory, she presents an entire history of half a century," said a female visitor.[14]

Fond of routine, Washington returned to his old daily schedule of rising at dawn, eating breakfast, then touring his five farms on horseback in a wide-brimmed hat with a hickory switch in hand. If slaves and overseers weren't hard at work when he arrived, Washington said only half humorously, he sent them "messages expressive of my sorrow for their indisposition."[15] The considerable demands of refurbishing Mount Vernon caused him to fall behind on correspondence and made sustained reading difficult. As he told Secretary of War McHenry, "I have not looked into a book since I came home, nor shall I be able to do it until I have discharged my workmen; probably not before the nights grow longer, when possibly I may be looking in [the] doomsday book."[16] For all that, Washington remained well informed and enjoyed reading newspapers aloud to company. Since he still complained about their bias, he asked Treasury Secretary Wolcott to send him the unvarnished truth about various issues.

One of Washington's cherished activities was arranging the huge trove of papers he had lugged back from Philadelphia. Before leaving office, he had instructed his secretaries to skim off documents needed by President Adams and ship the rest to Mount Vernon. He also had them forward a letterpress device so he could make copies of letters. One visitor was staggered by the sheer size of his Revolutionary War archives: "They consist of between 30 and 40 cases of papers, containing all the military expeditions, reports, journals, correspondence with Congress, with the generals, etc. What a wealth of material!"[17] As if envisaging the first presidential library, Washington planned to build a house at Mount Vernon dedicated to his records, a project that never came to fruition even though he ordered bookcases for it before his death.

Another labor of love was adding the finishing touches to the renovation of the main house. At the north end Washington completed the New Room, the stately dining room featuring a long table that seated ten people. From Philadelphia he carted home twenty-four mahogany dining chairs, enabling him to expand the number of people he entertained. Unfortunately, delays in completing the room had so weakened the underlying girders that "a company only moderately large would have sunk altogether into the cellar," Washington complained before undertaking expensive corrective work.[18] Outside the house, the kitchen garden, greenhouse, and serpentine walks along the lawn created a beautiful geometric area where elegant, well-dressed people could stroll through fragrant, refreshing spaces. After negotiating the bad roads and thick woods nearby, visitors found the mansion house a sudden oasis of order. "Good fences, clear grounds, and extensive cultivation strike the eye as something uncommon in this part of the world," noted architect Benjamin Latrobe.[19]

Spared the onus of public office, Washington permitted his mind to roam into the pathways of the past. In the spring of 1798, when he learned that Belvoir, the old Fairfax estate, was up for sale, he was flooded with memories about his youthful dalliance with Sally Fairfax. On some subterranean level, the entrancing memory of Sally, now a widow of nearly seventy, had stayed evergreen in his mind. In May 1798 he learned that Bryan Fairfax, Sally's brother-in-law, was traveling to England, and he handed him an elegiac letter to Sally, which mixed frank references to their amorous past with staple Washingtonian rhetoric about America's glorious future. Very often, he admitted to Sally, he cast a nostalgic glance toward Belvoir and wondered whether she would spend her final days near her Virginia relatives "rather than close the sublunary scene in a foreign country."[20] He acknowledged the many extraordinary events he had lived through, then abruptly declared that none of these events, "not all of them together, have been able to eradicate from my mind the recollection of those happy moments—the happiest of my life—which I have enjoyed in your company."[21] This unexpected line offered the ultimate romantic compliment: Washington had won a long war, founded a country, and created a new government, but such accomplishments paled beside the faded recollections of a youthful love affair. In its autumnal tone, the letter represented a farewell address of sorts. Having written it, he wanted to ensure that Sally did not misinterpret it as an invitation to revive their relationship. So the next day, using the same self-protective device he had employed with Elizabeth Powel, he drafted a letter to Sally under Martha's signature in which the latter said it was among her great regrets that she no longer had Sally as her "neighbor and companion."[22]

Washington's life was more weighted with care than he admitted to Sally. For all the beauty and scenic vistas of his estate, the financial pressure remained unrelenting. His elaborate plan for renting four of the Mount Vernon farms had faltered because he wanted to rent them all at once, which was impossible. In the spring of 1797 he compromised and offered them for rent individually. In hiring his new estate manager, James Anderson, Washington had hoped that this "honest, industrious, and judicious Scotchman" would alleviate his chronic financial woes, but Anderson struggled in vain to make Mount Vernon more productive.[23] He turned out to be too impulsive and improvident for Washington's fastidious taste, though he did introduce signal innovations. The enterprising Anderson devised the concept of taking grain grown at Mount Vernon and converting it into corn and rye whiskey at a commercial distillery on the estate. For Washington, always rabid on the subject of alcoholism, it was an ironic turn of events, to put it mildly. Although the distillery started modestly, by 1799 it had five gleaming copper stills and produced eleven thousand gallons yearly, so that it may have ranked as the largest whiskey producer in America. Nevertheless, when Anderson talked of quitting in 1798,

Washington chided him for having coaxed him into assuming "a very serious expense in erecting a distillery of which I had no knowledge . . . But do as you please in this matter. I never did, nor ever shall, wish to retain any person in my employ contrary to their inclination."[24]

Washington again found himself sliding into a slow-motion financial crisis. Just as he had been forced to borrow to attend his own inauguration in 1789, he had had to sell "two valuable tracts of land" in western Pennsylvania and land in Virginia's Great Dismal Swamp to make the journey home in 1797 and "lay in a few necessaries for my family."[25] In his presidency's waning days, he had been reduced to the indignity of personally dunning tenants in arrears on rent, threatening one with a lawsuit. Degraded to a bill collector, he had warned, "I w[oul]d fain avoid this appeal, but if I am obliged to resort to it, remember that it is brought upon you by your own default."[26] Upon returning to Mount Vernon, he scratched out testy notes to people, trying to settle their land disputes. When nephew Samuel Washington approached him for an emergency $1,000 loan, Washington grudgingly agreed, while lecturing him on the perils of borrowing and warning that "you are under the same mistake that many others are in supposing that I have money always at command."[27] To improve his financial situation, Washington started an economy campaign and froze the wages of overseers. He also began a gradual shift from agriculture to grazing, which curbed expenses and averted the need for more slave labor.

AFTER LEAVING OFFICE, Washington made a futile attempt to distance himself from politics. Because the post office lay nine miles away, he collected his mail only thrice weekly, so the bags when they arrived bulged with political letters, gazettes, and pamphlets. Inevitably, the irascible President Adams suffered from comparison with the tactful Washington. "There never was perhaps a greater contrast between two characters than between those of the present president and his predecessor," James Madison observed. "The one cool, considerate, and cautious, the other headlong and kindled into flame by every spark that lights on his passions."[28] For all his vast legislative experience, the temperamental Adams was a complete tyro as an executive. Much as Jefferson predicted, Adams immediately had to contend with multiple crises as France seized nearly three hundred neutral American vessels and the popular mood turned bellicose. It did not help matters that Vice President Jefferson, far from aiding the president, functioned as a staunch opponent.

With the country irrevocably divided into two hostile camps, Washington expected to have no further dealings with Jefferson, whose followers had so vilified him. Then an incident occurred that ensured that there would be no rapprochement between the two Virginians. Jefferson had befriended a Florentine named

Philip Mazzei, who sold wine in London before moving to Virginia, where he hoped to introduce vineyards. After Mazzei returned to Europe, he exchanged letters with Jefferson, who tended to express himself much more colorfully on paper than in person. In April 1796 Jefferson sent Mazzei a scathing letter about the Washington administration: "The aspect of our politics has wonderfully changed since you left us. In place of that noble love of liberty and republican government which carried us triumphantly thro[ugh] the war," a monarchical party had "sprung up whose avowed object is to draw over us the substance, as they have already done the forms, of the British government . . . It would give you a fever were I to name to you *the apostates* who have gone over to these heresies, men who were Samsons in the field and Solomons in the council, but who have had their head shaved by the harlot England."[29] Though Washington was not mentioned by name, he surely qualified as the Samson, if not the Solomon, in question.

In a notorious lapse of judgment, Mazzei printed this private letter in a Florentine newspaper. It was then translated and published in a French and then an English journal, finally cropping up in Noah Webster's *Minerva* in New York in May 1797. Pretty soon the letter appeared everywhere, and Thomas Jefferson was startled when he read it on May 9. Usually unflappable, he was completely nonplussed. "Think for me on this occasion," he pleaded with Madison, "and advise me what to do."[30] In private, Jefferson insisted that the translation had misrepresented his original communication and that the Samsons and Solomons referred to were the Society of the Cincinnati. As someone who liked to duck uncomfortable public clashes, Jefferson beat a hasty retreat into diplomatic silence. He told Madison that he could offer no public explanations of the letter because it would create "a personal difference between Gen[era]l Washington and myself" and entangle him "with all those with whom his character is still popular, that is to say, nine-tenths of the people of the U.S."[31] The letter gave the world a peek into a very different Thomas Jefferson: not the political savant but the crafty, partisan operative marked by unrelenting zeal. While Washington refused to dignify the episode with a response, it is widely believed that the Mazzei letter ended all further communication between him and Jefferson. "I never saw him afterwards or these malignant insinuations should have been dissipated before his just judgment, as mist before the sun," Jefferson later said.[32] Whatever the case, both Jefferson and Madison had disappeared from Washington's life with stunning finality. When Washington alluded to Jefferson in a letter the following year, he referred to him with patent disdain as "*that man*."[33]

Hamilton took an even greater pounding in the Republican press. Back in 1792 James Monroe and other Republican legislators had gotten wind of a possible scandal involving Hamilton, who had made secret payments to a man named James Reynolds. Monroe and two other legislators had then confronted the treasury secretary and demanded to know whether he had colluded with Reynolds to profit from surreptitious trading in government securities. While admitting to the payments, Hamilton explained that they represented hush money to cover up an affair with Reynolds's beautiful young wife, Maria. There the matter temporarily ended. Then in June 1797 James T. Callender, a scandal-mongering journalist in the Republican camp, published a pamphlet that accurately described the payments but mistakenly charged Hamilton with insider trading. To vindicate his integrity as a public official, Hamilton confessed to the adulterous affair in a ninety-five-page pamphlet; even his closest friends thought a delicately worded paragraph or two might have done the trick nicely.

Opinion differed among Federalists as to whether Hamilton's political career would survive these damaging revelations. "Hamilton is fallen for the present," David Cobb, a former aide to Washington, conceded to Henry Knox, "but if he fornicates with every female in the cities of New York and Philadelphia, he will rise again."[34] Many other Federalists and a gleeful majority of Republicans thought Hamilton's self-inflicted wound would prove mortal. Although Washington could easily have avoided the incident with polite silence, Hamilton had stood loyally by him through many crises, and he must have felt that the time had come to reciprocate.

Washington forwarded to Hamilton one of the silver-plated wine coolers that Gouverneur Morris had sent to him from Europe early in his presidency. The accompanying note was potent in its simplicity. "My dear Sir," it began. "Not for any intrinsic value the thing possesses, but as a token of my sincere regard and friendship for you and as a remembrancer of me, I pray you to accept a wine cooler for four bottles . . . I pray you to present my best wishes, in which Mrs. Washington joins me, to Mrs. Hamilton and the family, and that you would be persuaded that with every sentiment of the highest regard, I remain your sincere friend and affectionate h[onora]ble servant Go: Washington."[35] This succinct note is a marvelous example of Washington's social finesse. He expressed solidarity with Hamilton without ever mentioning the scandal or referring to Hamilton's misbehavior. Although Hamilton's career survived, albeit in a diminished state, he began a long, tragic descent. He had achieved his most stellar feats under Washington's benign auspices and seemed to lose his moral compass when he no longer operated under his direct guidance. For all his brilliance, Hamilton's judgment was as erratic as Washington's seemed unerring.

In terms of politics, Washington's life would have anything but a placid final stage. In a rather grisly joke, Philip Freneau kept sending him issues of his new publication, the *Time Piece,* until Washington, annoyed, asked to have it discontinued. In the privacy of Mount Vernon, he no longer felt muzzled in expressing scorching political opinions. He was appalled by the French Directory's treatment of three American commissioners sent to negotiate peace and by French depredations against American shipping. Fiercely opinionated, even strident, Washington was now avowedly partisan in private, fulminating against the Republicans as pawns of the French in their attempt to manipulate American politics. As he told Thomas Pinckney, time would show the difference between those "who are true Americans" and "those who are stimulating a foreign nation to unfriendly acts, repugnant to our rights and dignity."[36]

For Washington, the one bright spot in an otherwise dark political picture was the release from prison that September of Lafayette, with the expectation that he would proceed to Holland or even America. At once Lafayette lavished Washington with high-flown prose reminiscent of old times: "With what eagerness and pleasure I would hasten to fly to Mount Vernon, there to pour out all the sentiments of affection, respect and gratitude . . . to you."[37] Now plump and hearty, his ebullient self restored, Lafayette had a touching vision of landing in Chesapeake Bay, rushing to see Washington at Mount Vernon, and buying a farm nearby.

With tensions running high over French policy, Washington had to send his protégé deflating news that he would not be well received in America. To counter French moves, Congress had already authorized a military expansion and the construction of more frigates. Lafayette, as a Frenchman, would be snubbed by Federalists and/or embraced by Republicans, and either way the situation would prove untenable. However ardently Lafayette defended the French Directory as having peaceful intentions toward the United States, Washington was having none of it, replying heatedly that the United States would not "suffer any nation under the sun . . . to trample upon their rights with impunity."[38] With his wife still ailing, Lafayette deferred his trip to America, spending the winter in Denmark. He was a man marooned by history, a tragic figure freed from prison only to emerge into a world in which he could find no fitting place. No longer accepted in his own country, he could not flee to America either and had to content himself with rehashing anecdotes about the American Revolution.

Even without the persistent tensions with France, Washington's mood would have been morose. His crops had been damaged by drenching autumn rains; then a winter of unusual severity froze nearby creeks and left the Potomac congested with ice floes. If business was bad, politics was even worse. In Paris Talleyrand waited five months to meet with the three American commissioners and, when he did, complained about anti-French innuendos that, he claimed, had pervaded Washington's farewell address. For a long time the American public was kept ignorant about the fate of this diplomatic mission. "Are our commissioners guillotined," Washington wondered aloud to James McHenry, "or what else is the occasion of their silence?"[39]

In early March 1798 one of the commissioners, John Marshall, alerted Washington to the scandalous news that the French had tried to extort money from the American diplomats, in what would be billed as the XYZ Affair, named for the three nameless agents employed by Talleyrand to extract the payments.

When President Adams finally released dispatches from the envoys to France, the American public was outraged and none more so than Washington, who felt grimly vindicated. "What a scene of corruption and profligacy has these communications disclosed in the Directors of a people with whom the United States have endeavored to treat upon fair, just, and honorable ground!" he told one senator.[40] Federalists profited from the disastrous turn in Republicans' fortunes produced by the XYZ Affair. France claimed the right to seize and confiscate British cargo aboard American ships; Adams promptly pushed through measures to protect American shipping and strengthen coastal defenses. In late April he signed legislation creating the Navy Department and a month later approved a new army of more than ten thousand men, styled a provisional army to quiet fears of a standing army, which would be activated in the event of a French invasion. In July Congress authorized an additional force of twelve regiments to be organized at once. As the United States abrogated its former treaties with France, American naval vessels were permitted to open fire on any French ships threatening American merchant vessels. The Quasi-War—or what President Adams called "the half war with France"—was now officially under way.[41]

War fever gripped the country and, judging by Nelly Custis's letters, infected Mount Vernon itself. Insisting that Americans must "extirpate the *demons*"—the French—Nelly gave her friend some humorous advice on preparations: "You must procure a black dress, the *fashion* of it we will settle hereafter. We shall have black helmets of morocco leather, ornamented with black bugles, and an immense plume of black feathers."[42] Martha Washington also reacted in shrill tones to events in Paris, decrying the arrogance and deception of the French Directory.

Whether to his dread or secret relief, Washington felt a powerful tide tugging him back into politics. On May 19 Hamilton sent him a provocative letter saying that the Jeffersonians were conspiring with the French to subvert the Constitution and convert America into "a province of France."[43] Hamilton recommended that Washington tour the southern states, "under some pretense of health," to make speeches combating virulent pro-French feeling in the region.[44] "You ought also to be aware, my dear sir," Hamilton continued, pulling him into the political vortex, "that in the event of an open rupture with France, the public voice will again call you to command the armies of your country."[45] Cooling off Hamilton's overheated rhetoric, Washington replied that he could not make a tour for health reasons because his health had never been finer. He also foresaw no immediate threat of war or "formidable invasion" of America by France.[46] Still, if war came, Washington thought the public would prefer "a man more in his prime."[47] Then just as it looked as if Washington, aged sixty-six, might slam the door shut on his political career forever, he nudged it open a crack. In the event of war, he declared, "I should like, previously, to know who would be my coadjutors and whether you would be disposed to take an active part, if arms are to be resorted to."[48]

This statement—that Washington would sally forth only if accompanied by Hamilton—was to be pregnant with the most extraordinary consequences. For all his sentimental talk about vegetating under his vine and fig tree, Washington was still passionate about politics and incensed by French behavior. As he had told Lafayette with fervor, after having fought the British for American freedom, he could not "remain an unconcerned spectator" as France tried to obliterate that freedom.[49] As soon as Washington responded to his gambit, Hamilton quickly upped the stakes, telling Washington that if he served under him, he would expect to be "Inspector General with a command in the line."[50] Because Washington did not expect to take the field, the inspector general would function as acting commander, charged with safeguarding both Washington's reputation and national security. In short order, a deal had been struck that Alexander Hamilton would be second in command to Washington—an understanding that was to have fateful consequences for President Adams.

On June 13 Washington sat under the portico of Mount Vernon with Polish nobleman Julian Niemcewicz and talked politics. As they savored breezes coming off the Potomac, Washington upbraided the French government with such "passionate wrath" that Niemcewicz was taken aback.[51] The ex-president, protesting the plunder of American shipping and the unforgivable insults to American envoys, sounded warlike. "Submission is vile," Washington thundered, saying that rather than see "freedom and independence trodden under foot," he would "pour out the last drop of blood which is yet in my veins."[52] He expressed sympathy for Adams's truculent stance: "I, in his place, perhaps would be less vehement in expression, but I would prepare myself steadily and boldly in the same fashion."[53]

Washington mentioned that he and Adams had exchanged no letters since he had left office. Four days later he addressed a letter to the second president, inviting him to stay at Mount Vernon should he visit the federal district that summer. In a friendly tone, Washington lauded Adams's speeches, making one wonder whether he did not already have command of the new army in mind. Setting the stage for later problems, Adams replied with a frank admission of his inadequacy in military matters and said he was vacillating on whether to call out the "old generals or to appoint a young set" in forming an army.[54] "I must tap you sometimes for advice," Adams concluded. "We must have your name, if you . . . will permit us to use it. There will be more efficacy in it than in many an army."[55] This was tantamount to an offer to command the new army, but Adams showed little awareness of its impact upon someone as strong-willed as George Washington. Sure in his command of nuance, Washington informed Adams that he would gladly serve in case of "*actual* invasion by a formidable force."[56] Foreshadowing his preference for Hamilton as his chief deputy, Washington also urged Adams to appoint seasoned officers from the late war "without respect to grade."[57]

In early July President Adams officially named Washington head of the new army, with the rank of lieutenant general and commander in chief. Before making this decision, Adams did not bother to consult Washington, who was thunderstruck to learn from the newspapers of his appointment and unanimous Senate confirmation. For three days, starting on July 11, Washington conferred at Mount Vernon with Secretary of War McHenry, who brought his commission. Adams had decided to retain McHenry, Pickering, and Wolcott from Washington's second-term cabinet and would come to question the loyalty of these men who revered Washington and Hamilton and were often baffled by Adams's quirkily unpredictable behavior.

Adams had asked McHenry to sound out Washington on his preferred officers without realizing that Washington would regard his advice as binding. The ex-president voiced all the familiar fears that had accompanied his return to politics in 1787 and 1789—that people would whisper scornfully that he was breaking his public pledges to retire, that he was power-hungry, and so on. Washington himself marveled at his own willingness to return to service, telling John Trumbull that "this is an age of wonders, and I have once more consented to become an actor in the great drama."[58] Before long, applications for army appointments tumbled in upon him.

In taking the position, Washington reiterated his view that it would be unwise for him "to come forward before the emergency *becomes evident*."[59] For this reason, he thought it all-important to select his own general officers, who would shape up the army before he assumed direct command. He also decided to repeat his wartime precedent of waiving a salary and being reimbursed only for any expenses incurred.

Both McHenry and Secretary of State Pickering favored Hamilton as second in command. Unfortunately, as Pickering warned Washington in confidence, this choice was anathema to the president: "From the conversation that I and others have had with the president, there appears to us to be a disinclination to place Colo. Hamilton in what we think is his proper station, and that alone in which we suppose he will serve—the *second* to you—and the *chief in your absence*."[60] Here lay the dilemma in a nutshell: neither Hamilton nor Washington would serve without Hamilton being the main deputy, while Adams found this intolerable. It would prove excruciatingly difficult to break this impasse between the former and current presidents.

When McHenry returned to Philadelphia, he bore a slip of paper on which Washington had scrawled the names of the three men he wanted as his major generals: Hamilton, Charles Cotesworth Pinckney, and Henry Knox. He wanted them ranked in that order, even though Pinckney and Knox had outranked Hamilton in the war. In Washington's view, the old hierarchy of the Continental Army had vanished with its demise. In the meantime, while Pickering sang Hamilton's virtues to Adams, the president had others in mind for the number-two spot. When Adams rattled off his three favorite generals, Pickering pointedly caviled at each one: Daniel Morgan, for having "one foot in the grave"; Horatio Gates, for being "an old woman"; and Benjamin Lincoln, for being "always asleep."[61] Despite his avowed ignorance of military matters, John Adams stoutly maintained that these men were superior to his longtime nemesis, Hamilton. "Hamilton had great disadvantages," Adams later mused. "His origin was infamous; his place of birth and education were foreign countries; his fortune was poverty itself; the profligacy of his life—his fornications, adulteries, and his incests—were propagated far and wide."[62]

Washington made clear to Adams that his acceptance of the post had been premised on the condition that "I shall not be called into the field until the army is in a situation to require my presence."[63] Adams seemed flummoxed by the matter of Washington's deputy. On July 18 he sent to the Senate the three names Washington had submitted, hoping their order of priority would be reversed. "General Knox is legally entitled to rank next to General Washington," Adams told McHenry, "and no other arrangement will give satisfaction."[64] To worsen matters, Adams also insisted that Charles Cotesworth Pinckney "must rank before Hamilton," throwing everything into utter confusion.[65]

It may have been the stress of this situation that sent Washington into a medical tailspin. On August 18 he came down with an ague—chills and sweats—and succumbed a couple of days later to a fever so intense that he shed twenty pounds in short order. He was so weakened by illness that even writing letters proved a wearisome task. In late August McHenry warned Washington that Adams was hardening his stand about the ranking of the three generals.

Aside from Adams's opposition to Hamilton, the touchiest matter for Washington was the likely wounded feelings of Henry Knox (a major general), who had far outranked both Hamilton (a colonel) and Pinckney (a brigadier general) during the war. Since Washington felt national security was at stake, he was not about to allow past friendships to overrule his military judgment. However close they had been during the war, Knox had gravely disappointed Washington during the Whiskey Rebellion. With all the diplomacy at his command, Washington wrote to Knox and explained that Pinckney had to precede him because the latter was a southerner and any war with France would likely unfold in the South. Washington also thought the French might try to foment a slave uprising to conquer the region. What he didn't state openly was that he thought the Jeffersonians might form a fifth column in the South, aiding France and sowing dissension. Given the grave threat, he told Knox, "I would fain hope, as we are forming an army *anew*, which army . . . is to fight for everything that ought to be dear and sacred to free men, that former rank will be forgot."[66] Washington may have had sound military reasons for downgrading Knox, but if he thought Knox would accept this with good grace, he was a poor psychologist. When Knox received Washington's letter, he was in the throes of yet another financial crisis. His life had also been blighted by family tragedy; the ninth of his twelve children had recently died—one room of his house was dubbed "the dead room" because so many dead children had been laid out there—and he must have been in a highly vulnerable state.[67]

Knox's anguished reply made it manifestly clear how devastated he was by Washington's letter. He had broken open the letter with delight, he said, only to absorb its contents with astonishment. He stated that "for more than twenty years, I must have been acting under a perfect delusion. Conscious myself of entertaining for you a sincere, active, and invariable friendship, I easily believed it was reciprocal. Nay more, I flattered myself with your esteem and respect in a military point of view. But I find that others greatly my juniors in rank have been . . . preferred before me."[68] By not consulting him first, he implied, Washington had exposed him to public humiliation.

In self-defense, Washington professed surprise that Knox had reacted so strongly in the matter and denied any intent "to see you in a degraded point of view."[69] He contended that the Federalists had chosen Hamilton as his second in command and presented the selection as a fait accompli—an atypical case of Washington shading the truth. In an emotional mistake, he pleaded that Hamilton had a large family to support and needed special inducements to accept the military post—which could only have bruised Knox after losing so many children. It was a sad denouement to the warm, fruitful relationship between Washington and Knox. Nevertheless, behind the scenes, Washington scrambled to see if he could give Knox seniority over Pinckney, "if it would satisfy Knox."[70] All the while Knox remained adamant that the rules should "decide in favor of [the] former rank" that prevailed at the end of the Revolution.[71]

Amid this impasse, John Marshall and Bushrod Washington appeared at Mount Vernon for a three-day visit. Washington entreated both men to run for Congress from their Virginia districts, stressing the need to oust Republican incumbents during a national emergency and lamenting the "violent and outrageous" mood prevalent in the state.[72] In the past Washington had shied away from such blatantly partisan advice, but he was now almost bullheaded in supporting Federalist candidates, honestly believing that the Republicans were only pretending, for election reasons, to be ready to fight a French invasion.[73] He thought it would be necessary to ban them as officers in the new army because they would "divide and contaminate the army by artful and seditious discourses."[74]

Bending to his uncle's inexorable request, Bushrod Washington, a young man with a small, pale face and large, brooding eyes, consented to run. The handsome, intelligent Marshall, a man of iron willpower, balked at the idea. At the end of his stay, he rose early in the morning, hoping to slip away unobtrusively before Washington could renew his pressure. No stranger to early-morning escapes, Washington anticipated Marshall's flight and blocked his path on the piazza as Marshall moved toward the stables. In coaxing Marshall to stand for Congress, Washington pointed out that he himself had agreed "to surrender the sweets of retirement and again to enter the most arduous and perilous station which an individual could fill," Marshall recalled.[75] Unable to withstand such an appeal, Marshall agreed to become a candidate for Congress.

With his wide streak of envy, John Adams found it difficult to be president in the aftermath of Washington. By late August, he believed that the time had come to assert his presidential prerogative over his predecessor. He told McHenry that he would gladly resign the presidency to Washington, if he could, "but I never said I would hold the office and be responsible for its exercise, while he should execute it."[76] Suspecting intrigue between his cabinet members and Washington, Adams was determined to resist it. McHenry reported to Washington, "The president is determined to place Hamilton last and Knox first."[77] Pickering added what was already obvious: that Adams had "an extreme aversion to Colo. Hamilton—a personal resentment," and would never let him supersede Knox and Pinckney.[78] It was a unique moment in American history: a political stalemate between a current and former president. As if to spite his predecessor, Adams decided, without consulting Washington, to name his feckless son-in-law, Colonel William Smith, as a brigadier general. Washington grew enraged at the news. "What in the name of military prudence could have induced the appointment of [William Smith] as brigadier?" he tartly inquired of Timothy Pickering. "The latter never was celebrated for anything that ever came to my knowledge except the murder of Indians."[79] The Senate, agreeing with Washington, rejected Smith, but the incident further inflamed relations between Washington and Adams.

In high dudgeon, Washington sent Adams a stinging letter in which he did not bother to tone down his indignation. Intent upon showing who was still the more powerful figure, he reminded Adams that he had picked Washington to command the army "without any previous consultation of my sentiments."[80] If Adams had inquired first, he would have learned the conditions of his consent. Washington had stated plainly to McHenry that he would accept command only if he controlled his general staff. He reproached Adams for submitting the three names to the Senate in the order he suggested only to object to their ranking afterward: "But you have been pleased to order the last to be first, and the first to be last."[81] He also noted caustically that Adams had taken it upon himself to appoint his brigadier generals, including his own son-in-law.

Perhaps especially vexing to Adams was that Washington issued the most ringing endorsement of Hamilton he had ever uttered. He reviewed Hamilton's history as his "principal and most confidential aide" during the war and later as treasury secretary. "By some he is considered as an ambitious man and therefore a dangerous one," Washington wrote with genuine feeling. "That he is ambitious, I shall readily grant, but it is of that laudable kind which prompts a man to excel in whatever he takes in hand. He is enterprising, quick in his perceptions, and his judgment intuitively great: qualities essential to a great military character and therefore I repeat that his loss will be irreparable."[82] As for Knox, Washington said there was no man "for whom I have had a greater friendship. But esteem, love, and friendship can have no influence in my mind when . . . possibly our all is at stake."[83] Washington ended this brutally candid letter by asking Adams point-blank "whether your determination to reverse the order of the three major generals is final."[84]

Washington felt so strongly on the subject that he was prepared to publish his grievances if Adams didn't back down. The one flaw in his thinking was that he had assumed that McHenry had given Adams an honest account of their meeting at Mount Vernon, with the preconditions he had laid down for service. On the other hand, it was shockingly naive of Adams to imagine that he could woo George Washington as commander in chief, coax him from retirement, then dictate his general officers.

On October 9 President Adams sent Washington a conciliatory letter from his home in Quincy, Massachusetts. However furious he was inside, he wrote a nuanced message in which he was careful to affirm the president's right to determine officer ranks but also promised that he would not override Washington's judgment. Placated by this generosity, Washington emphasized to McHenry that he did not want knowledge of his confrontation with Adams to leak out, lest it injure the president. In replying to Adams, Washington, with consummate tact, made no mention of the controversy over the major generals and simply inquired after Abigail's failing health. George Washington was always the maestro of eloquent silences.

Still grieved by his festering feud with Henry Knox, Washington sent him a lovely personal note, describing the "sincere pleasure" he would derive from having Knox as one of his major generals. He asked him to "share in the glory of defending your country" and pleaded with him to "display a mind superior to embarrassing punctilios," such as disputes over rank.[85] Not to be appeased, Knox informed Washington that all his friends had warned him against accepting any demotion. It still rankled that Washington tried to minimize the significance of the dispute over rank, which "precludes decisively my having the satisfaction proposed of sharing your fate in the field. I will not detain you one moment longer than to say, in the presence of Almighty God, that there is not a creature upon the face of the globe who was, is, and will remain more your friend than H. Knox."[86] While Washington had been uncharacteristically clumsy in the whole affair, Knox ended their exchange on a particularly bleak, bitter note.

Notwithstanding his pledge to stir no more than twenty-five miles from Mount Vernon in retirement, Washington spent five weeks in Philadelphia in November and December, conferring with Hamilton and Charles Cotesworth Pinckney about the new army. He traveled to the capital in relative simplicity: four servants and six or seven horses. Starting with the usual festivities in Alexandria, he again underwent the trial of public adulation and entered Philadelphia to clanging church bells, streets lined with cavalry, and an ovation from thousands of spectators.

In working sessions on the army, Washington seemed something of a figurehead. The vigorous Hamilton exercised the true authority, having beavered away at the task from a small office in lower Manhattan. The generals labored five hours daily, and Washington found the job of selecting officers for twelve new regiments an onerous task "of infinite more difficulty than I had any conception of."[87] In appraising candidates, Washington's criteria had changed little from French and Indian days, and he was still glad to find "so many gentlemen of family, fortune, and high expectations."[88] Once again he stressed the need for handsome officer uniforms of blue and buff and took amazing pains to design his own uniform, including "a blue coat, with yellow buttons and gold epaulettes" and a white hat plume meant to add "a further distinction."[89] All the while Washington's enthusiasm for the new army quietly began to wane.

While in Philadelphia, Washington delighted in joining Elizabeth Willing Powel for a number of teas and breakfasts that he conspicuously failed to enter into his diaries. We know of these encounters only from notes they exchanged. That Washington made efforts to conceal these meetings again raises the question of whether he was perhaps more attracted to Eliza Powel than he cared to admit. At the very least, there was a special emotional and intellectual rapport between them. Although Powel was careful to buy gifts for Nelly Custis and Martha Washington, one wonders whether this was a ploy to mask her true feelings for Washington. On the eve of his departure, she sent him a letter that suggests the deep bond between them: "My heart is so sincerely afflicted and my ideas so confused that I can only express my predominant wish—that God may take you into his holy keeping and preserve you safe both in traveling and under all circumstances and that you may be happy here and hereafter."[90] Perhaps Eliza Powel simply had a premonition that she would never again set eyes on her dear friend. As if wishing to lessen expectations and protect himself from prying eyes, Washington sent a more formal reply: "For your kind and affectionate wishes, I feel a grateful sensibility and reciprocate them with all the cordiality you could wish, being my dear madam your most obed[ien]t and obliged h[onora]ble servant Go: Washington."[91]

Surely the most haunting reunion of Washington's stay in Philadelphia was with his bluff, genial companion Robert Morris. Once so rich and powerful that a creditor crowned him the "Hannibal" of finance, Morris had become overextended in buying millions of acres of land and could not pay taxes or interest on his loans. In desperation, the financial wizard of the American Revolution auctioned off the plate and furnishings of his opulent home—all in vain. "I can never do things in the small," he once said prophetically. "I must be either a man or a mouse."[92] Now Washington dined with Robert Morris in a milieu far distant from the sumptuous settings of past meetings: debtors' prison. When Morris saw Washington, he grasped his hand in silence, tears welling up in his eyes. Morris wasted away in prison for three years.

While in Philadelphia, Washington made time to dine with President Adams and attempted to mend fences, but Adams still reacted to Washington in a manner tinged with paranoia. He had come to feel that his cabinet officers were "puppets danced upon the wires of two jugglers behind the scene and these jugglers were Hamilton and Washington."[93] One day in February 1799 Senator Theodore Sedgwick, a convinced Federalist, happened to ask Adams whether Washington would carry the title of *General* in the new army. The mere question kindled an explosive retort from the president. "What, are you going to appoint him general over the president?" Adams sputtered, his voice throbbing. "I have not been so blind but I have seen a combined effect among those who call themselves the friends of government to annihilate the essential powers given by the president."[94] The relationship between the first and second presidents never improved.

CHAPTER SIXTY-FIVE

A Mind on the Stretch

BY 1798 the Federalist party had grown haughty by being too long in power. "When a party grows strong and feels its power, it becomes intoxicated, grows presumptuous and extravagant, and breaks to pieces," Johns Adams later wrote, having presided over just such a situation as president. As the political atmosphere became ever more combative, Federalist overreaching arrived at its apex with passage of the Alien and Sedition Acts, which tried to squelch criticism of war measures that President Adams and his congressional allies had undertaken during the undeclared Quasi-War with France. Among other things, these repressive measures endowed the government with broad powers to deport foreign-born residents deemed a threat to the peace; brand as enemy aliens any citizens of a country at war with America; and prosecute those who published "false, scandalous, or malicious" writings against the U.S. government or Congress, with the intent of bringing them "into contempt or disrepute."[1] This last act posed a special menace to civil liberties, since a largely Federalist judiciary would be pursuing Republican journalists.

The Alien and Sedition Acts reflected a prevalent Federalist assumption, shared by Washington, that American "Jacobins" colluded with France in treasonous fashion. While these acts were enacted on Adams's watch, Washington lent them his quiet sympathy. Writing to a relative, he at first declined to comment on them, then observed that resident aliens had entered the country "for the express purpose of poisoning the minds of our people," thereby estranging "their affections from the government of their choice" and "endeavoring to dissolve the Union."[2] On another occasion, he endorsed a Sedition Act prosecution of William Duane of the *Aurora*, who had accused the Adams administration of being corrupted by the British government. Given the sheer number of lies that he thought were being peddled in the service of propaganda, Washington's dismay was understandable. At the same time, his support for censorship is disappointing given his exemplary record as president in tolerating even irresponsible press tirades against his administration. Washington often seemed blind to the perils of the Alien and Sedition Acts, arguing that Republican criticism was just another partisan maneuver to discredit the government and "disturb the public mind with their unfounded and ill-favored forebodings."[3]

Even as many Federalists hankered for war with France, President Adams, with typically feisty resolution, decided in early 1799 to essay diplomacy, sending William Vans Murray to negotiate peace with France and causing howls of outrage in his own party. Although Washington thought Talleyrand was merely toying with Adams, he sensed a political shift in the air. With his sound instincts, he suspected the Murray mission would undercut public support for military preparations, tempering his enthusiasm for the new army. With Hamilton hell-bent on raising that army, Washington told him what he didn't want to hear: that the *political* moment for its creation had passed. Had it been mustered right after the XYZ uproar, he speculated, the timing would have been auspicious. But now "unless a material change takes place, our military theater affords but a gloomy prospect to those who are to perform the principal parts in the drama."[4] That spring, as Hamilton began recruiting for the new army in New England, he acknowledged to Washington that he had, at best, tepid support from President Adams. In the meantime he secretly meditated the use of the new army to suppress what he saw as traitorous Republican elements in the South. By May 1800 the new army would be disbanded, having long outlived its usefulness.

In his final year George Washington inhabited a world dramatically different from the more halcyon visions he had foreseen for the country. The storybook ending might call for an elderly Washington to bask in the serene glow of wisdom. Instead he took to the warpath against the Jeffersonians with a vengeance. The nonpartisan dream enunciated in the farewell address had expired as the last vestiges of political civility disappeared. With Washington now a rabid booster of Federalist candidates, he applauded the election to Congress that spring of Henry Lee and John Marshall. He had wanted his lean, pale nephew Bushrod to run for Congress, but instead Adams appointed him to the Supreme Court. Washington's letters reverberated with partisan rhetoric as he admonished Bushrod against "any relaxation on the part of the Federalists. We are sure there will be none on that of the Republicans, as they have very erroneously called themselves."[5]

One area where his foresight had been infallible was in the creation of the federal district. The Residence Act had mandated that the city and its public buildings should be ready for occupancy no later than December 1800, but the project had been plagued by excessive costs, recurrent delays, and inept management. Washington feared further mishaps would scuttle the whole plan. In his last months as president, he had ordered the commissioners to suspend work on the President's House to focus their energies on the Capitol, the city's premier symbol. "The public mind is in a state of doubt, if not in despair, of having the principal building in readiness for Congress," he told the commissioners.[6]

During the summer of 1797 he had toured the fledgling city and thrilled to the sight of its rising buildings. The President's House and one wing of the Capitol stood ready to receive their roofs, while an "elegant bridge" had been thrown across the Potomac.[7] Where construction of the new capital had appealed to Washington's imagination, President Adams groaned under the unwanted burden. "The whole of this business is new to me," he complained, telling one commissioner that he would not "make himself a slave to the Federal City; that he would do what his official duty required of him *and no more*."[8] Washington gladly stepped into the vacuum and even submitted his views on architectural details, as when he advised that the Senate chamber should feature Ionic columns. With a clear vision of how the city should function, he insisted that executive departments should be situated near the President's House to facilitate daily contact between department heads and the president.

As proof of his unswerving commitment to the city, Washington purchased lots in various locations to avoid accusations of favoritism toward any section. After hearing criticism that the neighborhood near the Capitol would lack housing for congressmen, he bought adjoining parcels on North Capitol Street, between B and C streets, and constructed a pair of attached three-story brick houses designed by Dr. William Thornton. Boasting that they stood upon "a larger scale than any in the vicinity of the Capitol," he said they would be capable of housing "between twenty and thirty boarders"—an excellent example of Washington's take-charge spirit.

Much as its backers had intended, the new capital was a southern city that would be hospitable to slavery, and it continued to owe its existence to slave labor. Noting the arduous work involved in draining swampland, one commissioner admitted that the project "could not have [been] done without slaves."[9] Five slave carpenters now labored over the President's House, and future presidents who lived there, starting with Jefferson, would enjoy the residence in undisturbed possession of their human property. When Julian Niemcewicz toured the Capitol in 1798, it pained him to see slaves hard at work: "I have seen them in large numbers, and I was very glad that these poor unfortunates earned eight to ten dollars per week. My joy was not long lived. I am told that they were not working for themselves; their masters hire them out and retain all the money for themselves. What humanity! What a country of liberty."[10] For many decades, Washington, D.C., would qualify as a work in progress. George Washington never lived to see John Adams occupy a still-unfinished, sparsely furnished President's House. As he had feared, congressmen complained about the incomplete Capitol and inadequate lodgings, and the huge Capitol dome was completed only during the Civil War. For a long time the Capitol and President's House stood out as splendid but incongruous fragments in a still barren landscape; only later would the city expand to fill the spacious contours of Washington's buoyant dream.

DESPITE HIS CHILDLESS STATE, Washington had enjoyed a happy, abundant family life, having first stepchildren and then stepgrandchildren while also serving as guardian for numerous family orphans at Mount Vernon. After his sister, Betty, died, he had brought her son Lawrence, a childless widower, to Mount Vernon to aid with surplus visitors. Like most males, Lawrence fell instantly in love with Nelly Custis, only this time she reciprocated the attention, producing yet another union of the Washington and Custis clans. So that Nelly could marry at age twenty, Washington made official his position as her legal guardian, enabling him to sign the marriage license. In a tribute to Nelly's love for her adoptive grandfather, the wedding was celebrated by candlelight at Mount Vernon on February 22, 1799, Washington's sixty-seventh birthday. Deferring to the bride's wishes, Washington appeared in his old blue and buff wartime uniform. Martha "let all the servants come in to see" the wedding, one slave recalled, and gave them "such good things to eat" as part of the celebration.[11] The newlyweds stayed on as Mount Vernon residents after Washington gave them the vast Dogue Run farm.

Washington's history with Nelly's brother, Washy, remained problematic. Despite Washington's constant exhortations and the boy's eternal pledges to reform, the latter dropped out of Princeton, and in 1798 Washington enrolled him in the smaller St. John's College in Annapolis. "Mr. Custis possesses competent talents to fit him for any studies," Washington promised the school's president, "but they are counteracted by an indolence of mind, which renders it difficult to draw them into action."[12] For Washington, who felt keen deprivation at having missed college, his grandson's apathy must have been frustrating. The boy was never less than affectionate or respectful to him, but like his father before him, he was simply incorrigible.

When young Washington posed the question of whether he should not drop out of St. John's as well, the former president threw up his hands in despair: "The question . . . really astonishes me! for it would seem as if *nothing* I could say to you made more than a *momentary* impression."[13] Bowing to the futility of pushing the boy any further, Washington had him tutored at Mount Vernon by Tobias Lear. When Washy then contemplated an inappropriate marriage, Washington tried to prevent it by getting him appointed to a cavalry troop. He ended up with a fatalistic attitude toward his trying adopted grandson as someone who meant well but suffered from a congenital inability to make good on his pledges.

A deeper source of discontent in Washington's last year was the continuing financial worries that preyed on his mind, reaching their nadir in the spring of 1799. Even when he rode off to Philadelphia in November 1798, cheered by the adulatory multitudes, he gnashed his teeth over his finances, bewailing that "nothing will answer my purposes like the money, of which I am in extreme want, and *must* obtain on disadvantageous terms."[14] Never able to economize, he confessed that "I find it no easy matter to keep my expenditures within the limits of my receipts."[15] Another drought during the summer of 1799 ruined his oat crop, threatened his corn, and left his meadows barren, only aggravating his long-standing woes.

With mounting desperation, he badgered people for overdue money and dished out tough lectures to deadbeats, telling one, in the tone of a surly bill collector, that "however you may have succeeded in imposing upon and deceiving others, you shall not practice the like game with me with impunity."[16] While horrified at sending people to debtors' prison, he believed that he had no choice but to summon sheriffs to collect the money. For the first time in his life, he took recourse to bank loans, renewed at sixty-day intervals and set at what he termed "ruinous" interest rates.[17] His sales of western lands for emergency infusions of money scarcely kept pace with his insatiable demands for cash.

Two incidents underlined the gravity of his economic predicament. In October 1799 he decided to sell the houses he had built in the new capital—a terribly public blow to his pride as well as harmful to the project's hard-won image. That fall he also declined two months' salary as commander in chief. In thanking Secretary of War McHenry, Washington was frank about his embarrassing predicament: "I shall not suffer false modesty to assert that my finances stand in no need of it."[18] He complained of applicants for army appointments who came "with their servants and horses . . . to aid in the consumption of my forage and what to me is more valuable—my time."[19] While public life forced Washington into expenditures beyond his control, during his entire adult life he had exhibited an inability to live within his means.

Hard as it was for him to admit, he could no longer supervise alone his far-flung operations, whose inspection had always formed part of his daily routine. In March 1798 he hired a clerk, Albin Rawlins, whose duties went beyond keeping accounts and drafting letters. Even though Washington still strode around in blue overalls and mud-spattered boots and was every bit the master of Mount Vernon, for the first time he alluded to difficulty in riding his horse. As he told a relative, he had hired Rawlins, in part, because he now found it "impracticable to use the exercise (on horseback) which my health, business, and inclination requires."[20]

Washington had never made Mount Vernon the thriving productive enterprise he wanted. In his last months, he kept saying that the "first wish" of his heart was to simplify and contract operations and live "exempt from cares."[21] To this end, he planned to rent out his mill, distillery, and fishery businesses and dispose of one of his farms. Three of the farms—River, Union, and Muddy Hole—he decided to manage himself, restoring their exhausted fields through the scientific crop rotation that had long tantalized his imagination. The simple truth was that he had spent too many years away from Mount Vernon ever to attain the modern, advanced plantation of his daydreams. Sadly, the date he set for the new dispensation that would free him from onerous managerial duties was New Year's Day 1800—a date he would not live to see.

BY 1799 George Washington must have realized that the only respite he would ever get from politics resided in a peaceful afterlife. That June Jonathan Trumbull, Jr., reminding him of the pending presidential election, expressed the hope that if Washington's name were brought forward, "you will not disappoint the hopes and desires of the wise and good ... by refusing to come forward once more to the relief ... of your injured country."[22] Trumbull spoke for many Federalists who worried that Adams was a weak candidate and were terrified that the Francophile Jefferson might emerge as the next president. In response, Washington talked like an unabashed Federalist, sarcastically deriding Republican sophistry: "Let that party set up a broomstick and call it a true son of liberty ... and it will command their votes in toto!"[23] His passionate words mocked the Jeffersonian myth that his mental powers were impaired, and he satirized the scuttlebutt that he had lapsed into "dotage and imbecility."[24] He declined Trumbull's request on political grounds, claiming that he could not draw a single new vote from the opposition. His personal reasons were far more cogent. Citing declining health, he said it would be "criminal therefore in me, although it should be the wish of my countrymen ... to accept an office under this conviction."[25] Dismayed that, since mid-March, President Adams had absented himself from the capital, staying at his home in Quincy, Washington said that Federalists were aggrieved at his behavior while Republicans "chuckle at and set it down as a favorable omen for themselves."[26] With his usual sense of courtesy, Washington thought it would be unbecoming for him to advise the president: "It has been suggested to me to make this communication, but I have declined it, conceiving that it would be better received from a private character—m[ore] in the habits of social intercourse and friendship."[27]

At the end of August Washington tossed cold water on Trumbull's entreaties a second time. He now sounded even more categorical that "no eye, no tongue, no thought may be turned towards me for the purpose alluded to therein."[28] If he ran, he would only be battered with charges of "inconsistency, concealed ambition, dotage."[29] Having experienced more than enough venom for one lifetime, he did not care to expose himself further: "A mind that has been constantly on the stretch since the year 1753, with but short intervals and little relaxation, requires rest and composure. And I believe that nothing short of a serious invasion of our country . . . will ever draw me from my present retirement."[30]

Thanks to the astute, if mercurial, diplomacy of John Adams, such an invasion never happened. When the president sent two envoys to France that October, without consulting his cabinet first, Washington was beset by serious doubts. "I was surprised at the *measure,* how much more so at the manner of it?" he told Hamilton. "This business seems to have been commenced in an evil hour and under unfavorable auspices."[31] But Washington proved wrong, and because of the administration's successful diplomacy in resolving differences with France, he never had to take the field with the new army.

On November 10, 1799, McHenry warned Washington of burgeoning Republican strength in the upcoming campaign. For many Federalists, it foreshadowed a threat to the Constitution and the still-fragile strength of the federal government. "I confess, I see more danger to the cause of order and good government at this moment than has at any time heretofore threatened the country," McHenry concluded.[32] If Republicans saw the Federalists as threatening republican government, the Federalists saw themselves as upright custodians of the constitutional order. Previously unaware of the opposition's strength, Washington claimed to be "stricken dumb" by McHenry's letter and replied that political trends seemed "to be moving by hasty strides to some awful crisis, but in what they will result that Being, who sees, foresees, and directs all things, alone can tell."[33] So only weeks before his death, Washington, for all his long-term faith in America's future, viewed its short-term prospects as fairly dismal.

On December 9 Gouverneur Morris added his voice to the Federalist chorus and made a last plea to lure Washington from retirement. The next president, he pointed out, would hold office in Washington, D.C. "Will you not, when the seat of government is in your neighborhood, enjoy more retirement as President of the United States than as General of the Army?"[34] Making a shrewd pitch, Morris reviewed the way that each time Washington had returned reluctantly to the public stage, he had been catapulted to higher levels of glory: "If General Washington had not become [a] member of the [constitutional] convention, he would have been considered only as the defender and not as the legislator of his country. And if the president of the convention had not become president of the United States, he would not have added the character of a statesman to those of a patriot and a hero."[35] This clever, eloquent appeal went unanswered.

CHAPTER SIXTY-SIX

Freedom

IT MAY SAY SOMETHING about the American blind spot toward slavery that some of the most affecting vignettes of slaves at Mount Vernon emanated from foreign visitors, while American visitors selectively edited them from the scene. In April 1797 Louis-Philippe, a young French aristocrat who would become the so-called citizen king of France, toured Mount Vernon and showed commendable curiosity about the slaves' condition. They were well aware, he learned, of abolitionist clubs in Alexandria and Georgetown and the violent slave uprising in St. Domingue, making them hopeful that "they would no longer be slaves in ten years."[1] No less fascinating was the Frenchman's observation that many house servants were mulattoes and that some looked strikingly white. Because Washington was often away from Mount Vernon and seemingly could not have children of his own, suspicion has never settled on him as having sired biracial children, except for the questionable case of West Ford mentioned earlier.

When Julian Niemcewicz visited Virginia in June 1798, he played billiards with Washington and enjoyed conversing with Martha, who "loves to talk and talks very well about times past."[2] He rated Washington as a relatively benevolent slave master: "G[enera]l Washington treats his slaves far more humanely than do his fellow citizens of Virginia. Most of these gentlemen give to their blacks only bread, water, and blows."[3] In some respects, Niemcewicz left an absurdly rosy picture of slave existence: "Either from habit, or from natural humor disposed to gaiety, I have never seen the blacks sad."[4] One recurring theme he overheard was far more accurate: that slavery was not only cruel but unprofitable. Estate manager James Anderson estimated that only one hundred of the more than three hundred slaves actually worked, while Washington hypothesized that, from a purely economic standpoint, his farms held twice as many slaves as needed. The growing number of slave children and elderly slaves meant more mouths to feed and fewer able-bodied hands. Dr. David Stuart, the husband of Jacky Custis's widow, flatly asserted that it simply did not pay to own slaves: "Their support costs a great deal; their work is worth little if they are not whipped; the [overseer] costs a great deal and steals into the bargain. We would all agree to free these people, but how to do it with such a great number?"[5]

As it happened, George Washington, closeted in his study, was devoting considerable time to answering this most insoluble of questions. He saw, with some clairvoyance, that slavery threatened the American union to which he had so nobly consecrated his life. "I can clearly foresee," he predicted to an English visitor, "that nothing but the rooting out of slavery can perpetuate the existence of our union, by consolidating it in a common bond of principle."[6] Beyond moral objections to slavery, he had wearied of its immense practical difficulties. In September 1798 he regretted that his slaves were "growing more and more insolent and difficult to govern," and he seemed to want to be free of the sheer unpleasantness of keeping so many human beings in bondage.[7]

Because of natural increase since 1786, the Mount Vernon slave population had soared from 216 to 317, of whom Washington owned outright 124, with 40 rented from a neighbor, Penelope Manley French. The remaining 153 dower slaves, who belonged to the Custis estate, would be inherited by her grandson after Martha died. Writing to Robert Lewis on August 17, 1799, Washington reflected on the baffling conundrum posed by the excess slaves: "To sell the overplus [of slaves] I cannot, because I am principled against this kind of traffic in the human species. To hire them out is almost as bad because . . . to disperse the families I have an aversion. What then is to be done? Something must or I shall be ruined."[8] He possessed "a thorough conviction that half the workers I keep on this estate would render me a greater *net* profit than I *now* derive from the whole."[9] That he owned fewer than half the slaves himself perhaps set the stage for the most courageous action of his career. If he emancipated his own slaves in his will, he would satisfy his conscience, set a sterling example for futurity, and still leave a viable plantation behind. In 1799 a convenient convergence of economic and moral factors enabled Washington to settle the issue that had so long gnawed at his mind.

George and Martha Washington had to perceive that their smartest slaves and those in highest standing were most likely to escape, Hercules and Ona Judge being prime recent examples. In early 1798 a slave called Caesar, in his late forties and able to read and write, ran away. Partial to black-and-white clothing, he had functioned as a self-appointed preacher among Mount Vernon's slaves. In a runaway slave notice inserted in the newspaper, Washington offered a reward for Caesar's arrest and attested that he had fled "without having received any correction, or threats of punishment, or, in short, without any cause whatever."[10] The escape formed part of a now-familiar pattern: seemingly docile slaves quietly bided their time, called no attention to themselves, then suddenly fled when the moment was propitious.

After Billy Lee was crippled, Washington had turned to a young slave, Christopher Sheels, as his body servant. After Washington stepped down as president, Sheels had been bitten by a rabid dog. Washington valued him so highly that he sent him back to Pennsylvania for treatment, informing the doctor there that "besides the call of humanity, I am particularly anxious for his cure, he being my own body servant."[11] When Sheels asked Washington for permission to marry a mulatto slave on another plantation, Washington blessed the match, even though it opened up fresh temptations for Sheels to escape. In September 1799 Washington discovered that Sheels indeed intended to flee with his bride aboard a ship. Although Washington must have reprimanded him, there is no evidence that he punished him. The incident surely made him question anew the wisdom of owning human beings who naturally yearned to be free, no matter how well treated. Over the previous four decades, at least forty-seven slaves belonging to George and Martha Washington had made a brave dash for freedom.[12]

Always a methodical, well-organized man, George Washington experienced the "greatest anxiety" about leaving his affairs in order after he died. No less than in life, he craved the world's posthumous approval and was eager "that no reproach may attach itself to me when I have taken my departure for the land of spirits."[13] In early July 1799 he summoned up the courage, in the seclusion of his study, to draft a remarkable new will. He did not use a lawyer and laboriously wrote out the twenty-nine pages in his own handwriting, disclosing his plans to nobody. In the text, he mentioned that "no professional character has been consulted," observed that it had taken many "leisure hours to digest" the document, and hoped it wouldn't "appear crude and incorrect"—an odd apology for an ex-president, harking back one last time to his insufficient education.[14] Everything was spelled out with painstaking precision, including an inventory that listed 51,000 acres of land.

In a comprehensive catalog of his slaves, Washington divided them by farms and jotted down their names and ages. These statistics offered dramatic proof that, without prompt remedial action, his slave population would burgeon. Of the 277 slaves he and Martha controlled, no fewer than 98 were under the age of twelve. The trickiest issue he faced was strikingly evident: 90 slaves were reported as married. Many of Washington's slaves had married Martha's dower slaves or else slaves at nearby plantations.

The portions of the will relating to the slaves stand out as written with special vigor. At the outset, Washington referred to Martha as "my dearly beloved wife" and gave her the use of his whole estate.[15] He made clear that he did not want to deprive her of income generated by the slaves as long as she lived: "Upon the decease [of] my wife, it is my will and desire th[at] all the slaves which I hold in [my] *own right* shall receive their free[dom]."[16] While he had "earnestly wished" to free them upon his own death, that would entail breaking up marriages between his own slaves and dower slaves, provoking "the most painful sensations, if not disagreeable consequences."[17] Of course, waiting to free the slaves he owned until Martha died only postponed the problem instead of solving it. (Martha could not free the dower slaves, who were committed to the Custis heirs.) Mindful of the young and elderly slaves who might have difficulty coping with sudden freedom, Washington made special provision that they "shall be comfortably clothed and fed by my heirs while they live."[18] At a time when black education was feared as a threat to white supremacy, Washington ordered that the young slaves, before being freed, should "be taught to read and write and to be brought up to some useful occupation."[19] He also provided a fund to care for slaves too sick or aged to enjoy the sudden fruits of freedom. Unlike Jefferson, Washington did not wish to banish free blacks from Virginia and made no mention of colonizing them elsewhere, as if he foresaw them becoming part of a racially mixed community. Nor did he express fear of racial intermingling once his slaves were emancipated. He must have had a premonition that Martha or other family members would water down or bypass these daring instructions, so he expressly said that they should be "religiously fulfilled" by the executors.[20]

Singled out for special treatment was Billy Lee, who had earned an honored place in the annals of Washington's life. Now incapacitated by his knee troubles, he worked as a shoemaker at the Mansion House farm. Washington directed that "my mulatto man William (calling himself William Lee) I give immediate freedom; or, if he should prefer it (on account of the accidents which have befallen him and which have rendered him incapable of walking or of any active employment) to remain in the situation he now is, shall be optional in him to do so. In either case, I allow him an annuity of thirty dollars during his natural life" beyond the food and clothing he already received. Washington gratefully acknowledged "his attachment to me and . . . his faithful services during the Revolutionary War."[21]

By freeing his slaves, Washington accomplished something more glorious than any battlefield victory as a general or legislative act as a president. He did what no other founding father dared to do, although all proclaimed a theoretical revulsion at slavery. He brought the American experience that much closer to the ideals of the American Revolution and brought his own behavior in line with his troubled conscience. On slave plantations, the death of a master usually unleashed a mood of terror as slaves contemplated being sold to other masters or possibly severed from their families. Now Washington reversed the usual situation, relieving the dread and making the death of the master and mistress an occasion for general rejoicing among the slaves—at least if one set aside the thorny complexities of the intermingling through marriage of Washington's slaves and Martha's dower slaves.

In another visionary section of the will, Washington left money to advance the founding of a university in the District of Columbia, possibly under government auspices, where students could observe government firsthand and shed their "local attachments and state prejudices."[22] This phrase was more than a mere restatement of Washington's nationalism: it spoke to the way his own life had transcended his parochial background. Back in 1785 Washington had been flustered and embarrassed when the state of Virginia granted him shares in the Potomac and James River companies, and he had accepted them only with the proviso that they would be dedicated to public uses. Now he pledged his fifty shares of the Potomac River Company to the new university in the capital and his hundred shares of the James River Company to Liberty Hall Academy in western Virginia, which later became Washington and Lee University. He also left twenty shares in the Bank of Alexandria for a school, associated with the Alexandria Academy, to educate orphaned and indigent children.

In a demonstration of his humility, Washington did not seek to preserve Mount Vernon as a monument to his career; rather he planned to dismantle the estate he had spent a lifetime assembling, dividing it among relatives after Martha's death. A thoroughgoing family man, he included more than fifty relatives in his will. His nephew Bushrod Washington would receive the coveted Mansion House and surrounding four thousand acres of farm. In part, Washington wished to repay a debt to Bushrod's father, who had managed Mount Vernon while he fought in the French and Indian War. Washington may also have believed that Bushrod, as a Supreme Court justice, needed a suitably high-toned place for entertaining dignitaries. He also demonstrated his faith in his nephew by leaving him a prized possession: the civil and military papers that he had tended with such assiduous care. Washington remarked that, once he realized he would not have children of his own, he had decided to consider Martha's grandchildren "as I do my own relations and to act a friendly part by them."[23] This was especially true of Nelly and Washy. That fall Lawrence and Nelly Lewis had already received the two-thousand-acre farm at Dogue Run, while George Washington Parke Custis got twelve hundred acres in Alexandria and an entire square that Washington owned in the new capital. The two orphaned sons of George Augustine Washington split another two-thousand-acre farm.

A story, likely apocryphal, is told that one morning that September Washington awoke from a disturbing dream, which he narrated to Martha. An angel had appeared to him in a sudden burst of light and stood whispering in Martha's ear. Martha then became pale and began to fade from sight altogether, leaving Washington feeling alone and desolate. According to lore, he interpreted this dream as a premonition of his own death and was oppressed for days by its lingering memory. Whatever the veracity of this story, it expressed a truth about the mortality-laden mood of the Washington household that fall. For nearly two months in September and October Martha tried to shake a fever that produced "uneasy and restless symptoms" and resulted in at least one midnight summons to Dr. Craik.[24] No less stoical than her husband and sharing his philosophy of minimal medication, she at first refused to take any remedy that might moderate the fever, but she recovered by late October.

On September 20, while she was sick, Washington absorbed the additional bad news that the last of his siblings, his younger brother Charles, had died. "I was the *first*, and am now the *last*, of my father's children by the second marriage who remain," he remarked. "When I shall be called upon to follow them is known only to the giver of life."[25] In late November Martha's younger sister Elizabeth Henley also died, meaning that she had outlived all seven of *her* siblings. George and Martha Washington must have felt that their remaining time was brief and that their accomplishments already belonged to history.

Homecoming

AFTER LEAVING THE PRESIDENCY, Washington had sworn a whimsical pledge to friends that he would not "quit the theater of *this* world before the year 1800," and it looked as if he might deliver on his half-humorous resolve to finish out the century.[1] When Elizabeth Carrington socialized with the Washingtons that fall, she found them in good spirits, with Martha looking "venerable, kind and plain."[2] Though increasingly deaf, the ex-president was in a convivial mood and happy to relive the glories of yesteryear, staying up past midnight to spin out wartime narratives. On December 9 he bade nephew Howell Lewis a memorable farewell at the door of Mount Vernon. "It was a bright, frosty morning," Howell recalled, "and . . . the clear, healthy flush of [Washington's] cheek and his sprightly manner brought the remark . . . that we had never seen the General look so well."[3]

Resigned to the close of his political career, Washington remarked in November that, with the ship of state now afloat, he was content to be "a passenger only" and would "trust to the mariners, whose duty it is to watch, to steer it into a safe port."[4] On December 12, he composed a last letter to Hamilton, applauding his plan for an American military academy. In a fitting finale to a patriotic life, he endorsed the concept wholeheartedly: "The establishment of an institution of this kind . . . has ever been considered by me as an object of primary importance to this country."[5] This was the last political letter that flowed from his prolific pen.

From his earliest days, Washington had led an outdoors life, trusting to his body's recuperative powers and suffering poor health early in his presidency when he became too sedentary. Perhaps, as one relative later reflected, he had relied too much on his health and "exposed himself without common caution to the heat in summer and cold in winter."[6] In late November, renewing his old surveying skills, he spent three days running property lines in northern Fairfax County. This heedless behavior—if such it was—might have proved his undoing. On the other hand, had he not spent his whole life defying fate, bullets, the British Empire, and the elements?

On Thursday, December 12, Washington brushed aside inclement weather to make a full five-hour tour of his farms on horseback. His diary entry told of the dreadful weather: "About 1 o'clock, it began to snow—soon after to hail and then turned to a settled, cold rain."[7] When he arrived home for the midday meal, his nape was slick with rain, his hair matted with snow. With customary courtesy, the sodden host did not wish to keep his guests waiting and sat down to eat without changing his damp clothes. The next day the snow fell even harder, piling up three inches deep on the ground. Despite a sore throat, Washington trudged down the hill toward the Potomac in the late afternoon light. Still determined to perfect Mount Vernon, he planned a gravel walk and fishpond by the river and now marked out trees that he wanted cut down to improve the landscape. In a final letter to James Anderson, he carped about the filthy cattle stalls at one farm: "Such a pen as I saw yesterday at Union Farm would, if the cattle were kept in it one week, destroy the whole of them."[8] It was apt that, in this valedictory letter, Washington came across as the same old exacting, hypercritical boss.

Although he experienced hoarseness and chest congestion that evening, Washington's mood was cheerful. He smarted at old political wounds from onetime allies. When he read aloud a newspaper story that James Madison had nominated James Monroe for Virginia governor, he allowed himself some acerbic comments. He spurned Lear's advice to take medicine. "You know I never take anything for a cold," he protested. "Let it go as it came."[9] Instead, he sat up late in his library before mounting the steps to his bedroom. Martha expressed dismay that he had not come upstairs earlier, but he said that he had done so as soon as he had finished his business. In the middle of the night, he awoke with a raw, inflamed throat. When he shook Martha awake, she grew alarmed by his labored breathing and wanted to fetch a servant, but he feared she might catch a chill on this cold night. Once again relying on his body's restorative powers, he had Martha wait until daybreak to call for help. When a slave named Caroline kindled a fire in the early morning, Martha asked her to scout out Tobias Lear, who found Washington breathing with difficulty and scarcely able "to utter a word intelligibly."[10] Christopher Sheels propped up his master in a chair by the fire as Lear sent a swift slave to Alexandria for Dr. Craik, the Scottish physician who had served Washington with such fervent devotion since the French and Indian War. Meanwhile, to soothe his flaming throat, Washington consumed a syrupy blend of molasses, vinegar, and butter, though he nearly choked when he tried to swallow it.

Washington's last day was spent in a lovely but simple setting, a plain bedroom prettily decorated with a table, armchair, and dressing table. As he faced death, Washington's indomitable poise was remarkable. With preternatural self-control, he had an overseer named George Rawlins bleed him before Dr. Craik arrived. When the overseer blanched, Washington gently but firmly pressed him. "Don't be afraid," he said, and once Rawlins had sliced into the skin, making the blood run freely, he added, "The orifice is not large enough."[11] Martha showed better medical judgment and pleaded for a halt to the bleeding, but Washington urged Rawlins on, saying "More, more!" until nearly a pint of blood had been drained.[12] A piece of moist flannel was wrapped around his throat while his feet were soaked in warm water.

As they awaited Dr. Craik, Martha summoned the eminent Dr. Gustavus Richard Brown of Port Tobacco. Dr. Craik, arriving first, perpetuated the medieval treatments already in use, emptying more blood and applying to the throat cantharides, a preparation made from dried beetles, to draw the inflammation to the surface. He also had Washington inhale steam from a teapot filled with vinegar and hot water. When Washington tilted back his head to gargle sage tea mixed with vinegar, he nearly suffocated. Alarmed, Dr. Craik summoned a third doctor, Elisha Cullen Dick, a young Mason from Alexandria, who had studied under Dr. Benjamin Rush. Upon entering, he joined Craik in siphoning off more blood, which "came very slow, was thick, and did not produce any symptoms of fainting," wrote Lear.[13] They also evacuated Washington's bowels with an enema. Joined at last by Dr. Brown, they took two more pints from Washington's depleted body. It has been estimated that Washington surrendered five pints of blood altogether, or about half of his body's total supply.[14] Dr. Dick recommended a still rare and highly experimental procedure—a tracheotomy that would have punched open a hole in Washington's trachea, easing his breathing—only to be overruled by Craik and Brown. "I shall never cease to regret that the operation was not performed," Dick said afterward, likening the three physicians to drowning men grasping at straws.[15] It is highly improbable, however, that Washington would have survived such a procedure, given his already weakened state.

As Tobias Lear sat by the bedside, grasping his mentor's hand, Washington issued some final instructions that reflect his preoccupation with both his posthumous fame and his solvency: "I believed from the first that the disorder would prove fatal. Do you arrange and record all my late military letters and papers. Arrange my accounts and settle my books . . . and let Mr. Rawlins finish recording my other letters, which he has begun."[16] When Lear remarked that he hoped the end wasn't near, Washington smiled calmly and said that he regarded his own demise "with perfect resignation."[17]

After Dick and Brown left the room, Craik lingered by his old friend. "Doctor, I die hard," Washington said, "but I am not afraid to go."[18] Convinced the end was imminent, he told Martha to go downstairs to his study and remove a pair of wills from his desk drawer. He then took the earlier will—likely the one he drew up when named commander in chief in 1775—and told her to burn it, while saving the historic one drawn up in July, which freed his slaves. That Washington had preserved both wills may suggest some last-minute wavering on the manumission issue. It said much about his lifelong dependence on slavery that he was now attended by four slaves—Caroline, Charlotte, Molly, and Christopher Sheels. Sadly, the four slaves assigned to this deathwatch were all dower slaves who would reap no benefit from the emancipation section of the will.

Though he never complained, Washington was expiring in a particularly gruesome fashion and constantly gasped for air. Climbing into bed bedside him, Lear kept gingerly turning him over to try to relieve the congestion. "He appeared penetrated with gratitude for my attentions and often said, 'I am afraid I shall fatigue you too much.' And upon my assuring him that I could feel nothing but a wish to give him ease, he replied, 'Well! It is a debt we must pay to each other and I hope when you want aid of this kind, you will find it."[19] Even in death, Washington never lapsed into self-absorption and remained singularly attuned to other people's moods, showing the same sensitivity that had made him a uniquely effective political leader. At one point, noticing that Christopher Sheels had been standing since morning, Washington urged the young slave to sit down.

Handicapped by the benighted state of medical knowledge, the three doctors were utterly perplexed about what to do, and Washington showed compassion for their bafflement. "I feel myself going," he told them early in the evening. "I thank you for your attentions, but I pray you to take no more trouble about me. Let me go off quietly. I cannot last long."[20] A couple of hours later they applied blisters and wheat bran poultices to his legs and throat, though they harbored little hope of an improvement. Washington had a horror of being buried alive, and around ten o'clock he conveyed this to Lear: "Have me decently buried and do not let my body be put into the vault in less than three days after I am dead."[21] Lear promised to honor his wish, which consoled Washington, making his breathing a trifle easier. This fear of premature burial was common at the time; Elizabeth Powel, for instance, left instructions in her will that the lid of her coffin should not be screwed on until minutes before it was lowered into the earth.

While retaining complete control of his faculties, as best we can tell, Washington never sought religious solace or offered any prayers as he lay dying. That no minister was summoned may also reflect the doctors' misjudgment of the proximity of death. With his stoic toughness, somber gallantry, and clear conscience, the patient was reconciled to his own mortality. Several times this most punctual of men asked what hour it was. Orchestrating matters until the very end, he had the presence of mind to take his own pulse and felt the life suddenly ebbing from his body. At that moment he perished. "The general's hand fell from his wrist," wrote Tobias Lear. "I took it in mine and put it into my bosom. Dr. Craik put his hands over his eyes." Washington, he said, had "expired without a struggle or a sigh!"[22] Christopher Sheels stood by the bedside, with Caroline, Charlotte, and Molly gazing nearby. Performing one final service for his master, Sheels emptied the keys from his pockets and passed them to Tobias Lear. It was December 14, 1799. Washington had died at age sixty-seven, long-lived by the tragically short standards of the men in his family.

All the while, at the foot of the bed, Martha Washington had sat in a motionless vigil, very much the Roman matron with her marble composure. "Is he gone?" she asked. With his hand, Lear indicated that Washington had died. "'Tis well," Martha replied, repeating her husband's last words. "All is now over. I shall soon follow him! I have no more trials to pass through."[23] This last line speaks volumes about the suffering she had silently withstood, the perpetual sacrifices she had made for her husband and her country. Haunted by this moment, she never slept in that bedroom again.

Washington died in a manner that befit his life: with grace, dignity, self-possession, and a manifest regard for others. He never yielded to shrieks, hysteria, or unseemly complaints. His doctors had treated him as if he were suffering from "quinsy," or a throat inflammation. From a modern vantage point, it seems likely that a bacterial infection had caused his epiglottis—the flexible cartilage at the entrance to the voice box—to become grossly inflamed and swollen, shutting off the windpipe and making breathing and swallowing an agonizing ordeal. Along with the rounds of debilitating bleedings, Washington's final hours must have been hellish, yet he had endured them with exemplary composure.

The day after Washington died, Tobias Lear sent instructions to Alexandria for a mahogany coffin to house Washington's remains. In all likelihood, Christopher Sheels performed the solemn rite of washing and readying his master's cadaver. Abiding by Washington's wishes, the funeral at Mount Vernon did not take place until four days after his death, on December 18, 1799. From beyond the grave, Washington was still stage-managing events, having stipulated in his will a desire to be "interred in a private manner, without parade or funeral oration."[24] After suffering through many tedious tributes, he wanted to temper public adulation, although he must have suspected that his humble wish would be ignored by a devoted public.

Instead of a lavish funeral, he had a simple military burial. At three P.M., a schooner anchored in the Potomac began firing minute guns, and the funeral cortège shuffled across the lawn, then swept down the hillside to the family vault.

The mourners stepped softly to the muffled hush of drums and mournful, ele-giac music. A Virginia cavalry unit led the march, trailed by infantry, a band, and four clergymen in black suits. Then came two slaves, Cyrus and Wilson, leading the general's horse, which was plainly outfitted with a saddle and pistols stuffed in their holsters—an apt image for a legendary horseman who had always looked magnificent astride a mount. The coffin was borne by six pallbearers, five of them Masons, followed by the mayor of Alexandria and the chief Mount Vernon employ-ees. Conspicuously absent was Martha Washington, who likely stayed hidden in an upstairs bedroom, too traumatized to venture forth. For once, her sense of public duty deserted her. As a remembrance of her husband, she asked Tobias Lear to snip locks of hair from the corpse before it was deposited in the coffin. At the burial vault, the Reverend Thomas Davis pronounced the Order of Burial from the Epis-copal Prayer Book. Then, testifying to Washington's deep faith in the brotherhood of Freemasonry, Dr. Elisha Dick stepped forward and, in his capacity as Worshipful Master of Masonic Lodge No. 22 in Alexandria, officiated over rituals performed by Masons garbed in their customary aprons. As the coffin was stored in the vault overlooking the Potomac, eleven cannon fired volleys into the air, and infantry dis-charged their muskets.

Free of grandiosity or false sentiment, the funeral was restricted to family, friends, neighbors, and associates—exactly as Washington might have wished. He had always been civic-minded, and the strong institutional presence—the govern-ment, the military, the church, the Masons—mirrored the priorities of his life. No less appropriate was the symbolic presence of the invisible workers who had made his epic success story possible: eight slaves, clad in black, all but one of them dower slaves with nothing to gain from Washington's will. For the slaves, the sole immedi-ate benefit of the funeral was that, after all the guests had departed, the "remains of the provisions" were circulated in their quarters.

The family vault where Washington was entombed had been dug into a grassy slope, topped by a knoll with juniper, willow, chestnut, and cypress trees. This crypt was so overgrown with vegetation that it seemed to disappear into the hillside and breathed a damp, moldy air of decay, causing Washington to leave instructions for a new brick vault. It speaks to Washington's humility that the greatest man of his age was laid to rest in a communal tomb where nobody could single out his grave or honor him separately. All visitors could do was peer through the slats of a rough oak door into a gloomy, malodorous den of ancient coffins. Some souvenir hunters later reached in and tore swatches from the black velvet pall covering Washing-ton's coffin until it grew ragged with neglect. In 1818 an appalled traveler objected that Washington had been "permitted to remain in obscurity and neglect, without a mausoleum, monument, inscription, a stone, or anything else to point [where] the hero and statesman repose or any evidence of his country's gratitude."[25] Another visitor left a still more horrifying description, comparing the vault to a "bake oven" and condemning it as "a low damp little place that is crammed with coffins, some of which are moldered to ashes and the bones are strewed on the pavement." When this visitor spotted a skull on the ground, a gardener told him it belonged to Lawrence Washington, the beloved older half brother of the first president. In later years, after a new tomb was built at Mount Vernon, the coffins of George and Martha Washington were transferred to marble sarcophagi.

After his death, Washington's will was made public and quickly became available in pamphlet form. If he had hoped that other slave masters would emulate his example in liberating his slaves, he was cruelly mistaken. Not only had the slave population of the United States grown rapidly for forty years, but the introduction of the cotton gin was ushering in a vast and terrifying expansion of slavery. By 1804 all the northern states had enacted laws for terminating slavery, but it persisted in the South in an entrenched form.

As soon as word of Washington's death spread, church bells pealed in every city and business wound to a standstill. "Each man, when he heard that Washington was dead, shut his store as a matter of course, without consultation," one Bostonian recalled, "and in two hours all business was stopped."[26] Starting with President Adams, government officials wore black clothing, army officers donned crape on their left arms, naval vessels flew their colors at half-mast, and the hall of Congress was draped in black. At her receptions Abigail Adams demanded that ladies restrict themselves to black gloves and fans.

No political figure felt more bereft than Alexander Hamilton, who owed so much to the older man's steadfast patronage and understanding. "Perhaps no friend of his has more cause to lament on personal account than myself," he told an associate, saying that Washington had been "an aegis very essential to me."[27] Such deep grief was not universal. Unable to conquer his envy, President Adams quietly recoiled at the Washington adoration and later griped that the Federalists had "done themselves and their country invaluable injury by making Washington their military, political, religious, and even moral Pope and ascribing everything to him."[28] It was all a plot, he insinuated, "to cast into the background and the shade all others who had been concerned in the service of their country in the revolution."[29]

On December 19 John Marshall rose in the House to register the formal notification of Washington's death. A week later a huge, subdued funeral procession snaked from Congress Hall to the German Lutheran Church. There General Henry Lee delivered his famous funeral oration in which he eulogized Washington as "First in war, first in peace, and first in the hearts of his countrymen," while further noting that the deceased was "second to none in the humble and endearing scenes of private life."[30] For all the fervor in commemorating Washington's death, Congress never made good on its intention to transfer Washington's remains to a marble crypt in the Capitol, as he had perhaps expected.

By the time of his death, Washington had poured his last ounce of passion into the creation of his country. Never a perfect man, he always had a normal quota of human frailty, including a craving for money, status, and fame. Ambitious and self-promoting in his formative years, he had remained a tightfisted, sharp-elbowed businessman and a hard-driving slave master. But over the years, this man of deep emotions and strong opinions had learned to subordinate his personal dreams and aspirations to the service of a larger cause, evolving into a statesman with a prodigious mastery of political skills and an unwavering sense of America's future greatness. In the things that mattered most for his country, he had shown himself capable of constant growth and self-improvement.

George Washington possessed the gift of inspired simplicity, a clarity and purity of vision that never failed him. Whatever petty partisan disputes swirled around him, he kept his eyes fixed on the transcendent goals that motivated his quest. As sensitive to criticism as any other man, he never allowed personal attacks or threats to distract him, following an inner compass that charted the way ahead. For a quarter century, he had stuck to an undeviating path that led straight to the creation of an independent republic, the enactment of the Constitution, and the formation of the federal government. History records few examples of a leader who so earnestly wanted to do the right thing, not just for himself but for his country. Avoiding moral shortcuts, he consistently upheld such high ethical standards that he seemed larger than any other figure on the political scene. Again and again the American people had entrusted him with power, secure in the knowledge that he would exercise it fairly and ably and surrender it when his term of office was up. He had shown that the president and commander in chief of a republic could possess a grandeur surpassing that of all the crowned heads of Europe. He brought maturity, sobriety, judgment, and integrity to a political experiment that could easily have grown giddy with its own vaunted success, and he avoided the backbiting, envy, and intrigue that detracted from the achievements of other founders. He had indeed been the indispensable man of the American Revolution.

Washington had dominated American political life for so long that many Americans could not conceive of life without him. A widespread fear arose that, deprived of his guiding hand, the Republic itself might founder. One preacher wondered, "Will not darkness now gather in our land? . . . Who knows but [his death] is the loud harbinger of approaching calamity."[31] Perhaps as an antidote to such apprehension, Washington was smothered beneath national piety, and it became difficult for biographers to reclaim the complex human being. The man immediately began to merge into the myth. As the subject of more than four hundred printed orations, Washington was converted into an exemplar of moral values, the person chosen to tutor posterity in patriotism, even a civic deity. In one eulogy Timothy Dwight compared Washington to Moses and noted, "Comparison with him is become almost proverbial."[32] Washington's transformation into a sacred figure erased his tough, often moody nature, stressing only his serene composure and making it more difficult for future generations to fathom his achievements. Abigail Adams justly rebelled at the idealized portrait: "Simple truth is his best, his greatest eulogy."[33] She was certainly correct that, to be convincing, Washington's greatness did not need to be cleaned up or sanitized, only honestly presented.

A popular print called the *Apotheosis of Washington* showed him ascending to heaven above Mount Vernon. Seated on a throne, resting on a cloud, and caught in a thick shaft of celestial light, he was clad in white robes with an outstretched arm as a winged angel received him. As the Father of His Country evolved into a divinity, some clergymen wanted to insert his farewell address into the Bible as an epilogue. The departed leader's image sprouted everywhere. "Every American considers it his sacred duty to have a likeness of Washington in his home, just as we have images of God's saints," observed a European traveler.[34] Later deploring the "idolatrous worship" of Washington, Dr. Benjamin Rush saw it "manifested in the impious application of names and epithets to him which are ascribed in Scripture only to God and to Jesus Christ," and he mentioned "our Savior" and "our Redeemer" as examples.[35]

Hagiographic biographies poured from the presses with indecent haste. The first and most influential was by Parson Mason L. Weems, an itinerant book peddler and Episcopal priest who had once been introduced to Washington by Dr. Craik. Weems had already published tracts on the perils of everything from gambling to masturbation. Eager to cash in on Washington mania, he wrote to his publisher in mid-January 1800, "Washington, you know is gone! Millions are gaping to read something about him."[36] Weems rushed out the first edition of *The Life of Washington* in pamphlet form that year. In that and succeeding editions, he manufactured enduring myths about Washington refusing to lie about chopping down the cherry tree, hurling a silver dollar across the Rappahannock, and praying at Valley Forge. Weems imagined future schoolchildren asking, "What was it that raised Washington to his godlike height of glory?"[37] Perhaps sensing something too stern and difficult about the real Washington, Weems tried to humanize him through treacly fables designed to inculcate patriotism and morality. He showed no scruples about inventing scenes whole cloth. Weems claimed that when Washington's father died, George "fell upon his father's neck . . . kissed him a thousand and a thousand times and bathed his clay-cold face with scalding tears."[38] To improve sales and with an eye on the main chance, Weems deleted all partisan references, boasting to his publisher, "Adams and Jefferson both will approve our little piece."[39]

If Parson Weems foisted a false image of a stiff, priggish Washington on American schoolchildren, Washington did not fare much better at first with more serious biographers. Bushrod Washington had inherited Washington's papers and knew they would be the ideal source material for a biography. To write an authorized life, he wooed one of Washington's foremost admirers, John Marshall, who wrote the book after he became chief justice and joined Bushrod on the Supreme Court. Marshall devoted five volumes to inflating Washington into a figure sculpted from marble. For all his deep knowledge of Washington, however, he could not make his old friend come alive, prompting one disgruntled critic to grumble, "We look in vain . . . for any sketch or anecdote that might fix a distinguishing feature of private character in the memory."[40] Like Weems, Marshall edited out Washington's more turbulent, unruly emotions. John Adams mocked the biography as "a mausoleum, 100 feet square at the base and 200 feet high."[41] The public didn't warm to the Marshall biography, which presented Washington as a distant figure, and sales flagged. In the 1820s Jared Sparks, later president of Harvard, prevailed upon Bushrod Washington and John Marshall to let him publish the first edition of Washington's papers, which ran to twelve volumes. So began the scholarly process of disinterring Washington from the many legends that had already encrusted his life.

MARTHA WASHINGTON HAD SACRIFICED so much privacy during her married life that after her husband died, she evened the score by burning their personal correspondence—to the everlasting chagrin of historians. By the standards of her day, her act was neither unusual nor wanton. After Alexander Hamilton died in a duel in 1804, Elizabeth Hamilton burned all her letters to him, although she did take care to preserve, with loving fidelity, his letters to her.

However much Martha sought to be a brave, cheerful widow, she was inconsolable in her grief. "I listened with tender interest to a sorrow, which she said was truly breaking her heart," reported a British companion.[42] A miniature portrait by Robert Field shows her pale, round face closely framed by a frilly white cap and surrounded by the black ribbon that betokened widowhood. Martha was not so much learning to live with bereavement as marking time until she could rejoin her husband. She refused to enter his study or the bedroom they had shared; she took up residence in a tiny attic chamber on the third floor at Mount Vernon, where she met with her sewing circle of slaves. Since Washington Custis kept a room on the same floor, she enjoyed some distraction by doting anxiously on her grandson. She haunted the narrow footpath that ran down to the family vault and often sounded a despairing note. "I always have one complaint or another," she told a correspondent. "I never expect to be well as long as I live in this world."[43]

Always warmly hospitable to visitors, Martha made no effort to mask her bottomless sadness and distributed locks of her husband's hair like so many saintly relics. Sally Foster Otis detected the contradiction when Martha spoke "of death as a pleasant journey which is in contemplation," while at the same time being "cheerful [and] anxious to perform the most minute civility and unerring in every duty."[44] Having buried two husbands, four children, and seven siblings, she saw herself as living on borrowed time. When the Reverend Manasseh Cutler visited, she reminisced about her husband with tremendous affection while "viewing herself as left alone, and her life protracted, until she had become a stranger in the world . . . She longed for the time to follow her departed friend."[45]

One insuperable problem that shadowed her was the fate of more than 120 slaves designated for freedom by her husband. Because Washington had not consulted her about his will, some scholars have speculated that she did not share his critical views about slavery. Impatient to claim their promised freedom, some of Washington's own slaves decided to escape at once: the remainder knew that the second Martha died, they could cast off their shackles. Unnerved by the situation, Martha admitted to a confidant that she "was made unhappy by the talk in the [slave] quarters of the good time coming to the ones to be freed as soon as she died."[46] For all his thoroughness, Washington had committed this one glaring oversight, thrusting Martha into a nightmarish situation. On a visit to Mount Vernon, Abigail Adams observed Martha's extreme distress as she confided that "she did not feel as though her life was safe in [the slaves'] hands," since many of them "would be told that it was their interest to get rid of her."[47] A suspicious event may have settled things for Martha. "There had been at least one alarming incident, when Judge Bushrod Washington was urgently called from the circuit court . . . because there had been an attempt to set fire to Mount Vernon," writes biographer Helen Bryan. "It was widely believed that some of the Mount Vernon slaves were implicated."[48] To quiet his aunt's fears, Bushrod Washington recommended that she get "clear of her negroes" by freeing them at once, and she decided to heed his advice.[49]

A year after George Washington's death, on January 1, 1801, Martha Washington signed an order freeing his slaves. Even this move did not entirely end her troubles, since at least one dower slave tried to escape by portraying himself as one of Washington's freed slaves. Many of the emancipated slaves, having never strayed far from Mount Vernon, were naturally reluctant to try their luck elsewhere. Some refused to abandon spouses or children still held as dower slaves and stayed at or near the estate. Following Washington's instructions, funds were used to feed and clothe the young, aged, and sickly slaves until the early 1830s.

Even though he had received his freedom and an annuity under Washington's will, Billy Lee stayed on at Mount Vernon, residing in his own house, working as a shoemaker, and emerging as something of a local tourist attraction. He remained a voluble raconteur about the war and its generals, and when one British baronet stopped by, Lee inquired "very earnestly after Lord Cornwallis."[50] Despite his apparent drinking problem, Lee managed to survive until 1810.

Politically, Martha had become a vocal Federalist and kept up her husband's antipathy to Thomas Jefferson. Even as he sat in the Senate chamber in a chair cloaked in black, Jefferson nursed private grievances against Washington and stayed away from the memorial service for him in December 1799, an action that may have embittered Martha. In private, Jefferson predicted a "resuscitation" of the "republican spirit" because the Federalists would no longer be able to hide behind Washington's stature and popularity.[51]

In early January 1801 Jefferson made a pilgrimage to Mount Vernon to see Martha, a visit with an unspoken political agenda. A few weeks earlier it had become clear in the presidential race that Aaron Burr would tie him in the Electoral College, throwing the race into a House of Representatives dominated by Federalists. Jefferson may have thought a well-publicized trip to Mount Vernon would curry favor with Federalist congressmen. If he did, he got precious little thanks from Martha, who fully shared her husband's cynicism about Jefferson. A friend recalled, "She assured a party of gentlemen, of which I was one . . . that next to the loss of her husband, [the visit] was the most painful occurrence of her life. He must have known, she observed, that we then had the evidence of [Jefferson's] perfidy in the house."[52]

Taking the high road in his first inaugural address, President Jefferson named Washington as "our first and greatest revolutionary character, whose preeminent services had entitled him to the first place in his country's love."[53] Martha Washington was not assuaged. "Her remarks were frequently pointed and sometimes very sarcastic on the new order of things and the present administration," wrote Manasseh Cutler. "She spoke of the election of Mr. Jefferson, whom she considered as one of the most detestable of mankind, as the greatest misfortune our country has ever experienced. Her unfriendly feelings toward him were naturally to be expected from the abuse he offered to Gen. Washington while living, and to his memory since his decease."[54]

For many years Martha had been plagued by a stomach disorder termed bilious fever, which recurred in early May 1802. This time, despite the careful ministrations of Dr. Craik, it proved fatal. On May 22, 1802, Martha Washington breathed her last, just short of her seventy-first birthday. She died with courage and an uncomplaining acceptance of her fate, which had been her trademarks since her husband rode off to Cambridge to take command of the Continental Army in June 1775, transforming her life forever. "Fortitude and resignation were displayed throughout," wrote a relative, who said that Martha had called for a clergyman to administer the sacrament. "She met death as a relief from the infirmities and melancholy of old age."[55] In accordance with her wishes, her coffin was placed in the dim, gloomy vault next to the illustrious husband whose fortunes she had so intimately shared and whose success she had so conspicuously aided. Finally, after many detours, many wanderings, and many triumphs, George and Martha Washington had come home to rest at Mount Vernon for good.

Acknowledgments

Any biographer of George Washington must stand in awe of the scholarly feat accomplished by the eminent team of editors at the Papers of George Washington project, which operates out of the University of Virginia at Charlottesville. By gathering 130,000 relevant documents from around the globe, they have produced a modern edition of Washington's papers that eclipses the far more modest edition published by John C. Fitzpatrick back in the 1930s and early 1940s. Whereas Fitzpatrick, in his thirty-nine volumes, limited himself to letters written by Washington, the new edition—sixty volumes of letters and diaries and still counting—includes letters written to him as well as excerpts from contemporary letters, diaries, and newspapers. Expert commentary appears at every step along the way. Strange as it may seem, George Washington's life has now been so minutely documented that we know far more about him than did his own friends, family, and contemporaries.

I am grateful to the community of Washington scholars for being receptive to a biography written by someone outside their professional ranks. Theodore J. Crackel, editor in chief of the Washington papers, was kind enough to vet the early chapters of the book and give me a sneak preview of two forthcoming volumes. Two of the best Washington scholars agreed to give the manuscript a sharp-eyed and tough-minded critique. Peter R. Henriques, author of *Realistic Visionary: A Portrait of George Washington* and emeritus professor of history at George Mason University, gave early encouragement to the book and closely reviewed the chapters dealing with Washington's pre– and post–Revolutionary War years. Edward G. Lengel, senior editor of the Washington papers and author of *General George Washington*, generously scrutinized the many chapters dealing with the Revolutionary War and gave copious commentary. Caroline Weber, a biographer of Marie-Antoinette and a professor of French and comparative literature at Columbia University, trained her erudite eye on the sections dealing with Washington and the French Revolution. All four scholars rescued me from errors of fact and interpretation and added subtlety and shading to the book. I thank them all sincerely. Any remaining errors are my sole responsibility.

Starting with president James C. Rees, the superb staff at Mount Vernon has been exemplary in providing help for the book. I was lucky to benefit from the new visitors' center and museum that opened as I labored. Stephen McLeod handled the arrangements for my visit to Mount Vernon, and John Marshall set up an early tour of the Mansion House before the crowds started piling in for the day. Mary V. Thompson, a major resource for any Washington scholar, enhanced my understanding of Washington's views on religion, slavery, and many other central issues. Carol Borchert Cadou lent welcome expertise on the hitherto-neglected subjects of Washington's furnishings and objets d'art. Dawn Bonner helped with illustrative material for the book. I was especially pleased to tour the grounds with J. Dean Norton, who expounded on Washington's talents as a gardener, and Dennis Pogue, who unlocked the mysteries of the distillery, gristmill, and pioneer farm. Gay Gaines, the former head of the Mount Vernon Ladies' Association, was a warm early supporter of this project.

In trying to retrace Washington's footsteps at Revolutionary War battlefields, I encountered many informative guides, curators, and park rangers. At Washington Crossing Historic Park on the Pennsylvania side of the Delaware River, and at Washington Crossing State Park on the New Jersey side, I profited from discussions with Jennifer April and W. Clay Craighead. At Cliveden, the former home of Benjamin Chew, Fred Achenbach gave me a superb tour of the house and a knowledgeable review of the Battle of Germantown. I enjoyed a long, stimulating chat with Jim Raleigh, president of the Friends of the Monmouth Battlefield, about the conflict fought at that lovely spot. The enthusiastic staff at the Old Barracks Museum in Trenton made Washington's two battles there come alive. At Yorktown, Tim Gorde gave a fine overview of the historic victory. Special thanks as well to two valued friends who accompanied me on my research journeys: Bruce McCall (to Princeton and Valley Forge) and Arthur Hirsch (Washington Crossing and Monmouth).

George Washington slept, ate, and worked at so many places that I was kept busy moving up and down the eastern seaboard. At Colonial Williamsburg, I enjoyed the intelligent commentary of Lisa Epton, Joe Spruill, Louise Lareau, and Jared Lorio. I am especially grateful to Linda Baumgarten, curator for textiles and costumes there, who educated me on eighteenth-century dress and shed light on Washington's height, hair, and clothing. At Ferry Farm in Fredericksburg, Linda Westerman and Noelle Hall patiently answered my many questions. I profited greatly from a talk with Paul M. Nasca, staff archaeologist for the George Washington Foundation, who recounted the exciting discovery of the archaeological remains of Washington's boyhood home and how it has transformed our understanding of his boyhood. At Kenmore Plantation, the residence of Betty and Fielding Lewis, Jane Huffman gave a most informative tour. I thank Lindsey Hobbs and Carla Wing for their hospitable reception at the Mary Washington House.

At the Powel House in Philadelphia, Kathie Dunn helped to re-create the world of Washington's social life with Elizabeth Willing Powel. David W. Maxey was especially helpful in deepening my understanding of that remarkable woman. In Washington, Ellen McCallister Clark, library director at the Society of the Cincinnati, gave me the benefit of her prodigious knowledge of Washington's library. In New York, Steve Laise of the National Park Service helped to unearth some Washington materials still in storage. Michael Amato and Michael Callahan provided guidance at Federal Hall National Memorial, the site of Washington's first inauguration. At the Morgan Library and Museum, curator Jennifer Tonkovich not only allowed me to examine the Houdon life mask of Washington but helped me to ponder its mysteries. Suzanne Prabucki, the curator at the Fraunces Tavern Museum, supplied information about Washington's famous farewell to his officers and biographical information about Sam Fraunces. At the New-York Historical Society, curator Kathleen Hulser gave me a splendid backstage tour of Washington paintings and memorabilia, arranged by society president Louise Mirrer. Pam Schafler and Sandra Tenholm provided me with a notebook of highlights from the George Washington and Henry Knox Collection, part of the Gilder-Lehrman Collection housed at the society. Thanks also to the staff at the Morris Jumel mansion in upper Manhattan, one of Washington's wartime residences. In Boston, Anita Israel conducted me on a private tour of the Vassall house, now the Longfellow National Historic Site, which was Washington's principal residence during the siege of Boston. Edward A. Smyk, the Passaic County historian, let me see a draft of his paper on the Dey Mansion in Wayne Township, New Jersey. Andrew Connell, a history teacher at the Appleby Grammar School in England, supplied invaluable information about the Washington's family's association with that school. Jeffrey H. Schwartz, a physical anthropologist at the University of Pittsburgh who re-created Washington's appearance for Mount Vernon, gave helpful hints for the book. Dick Scully, a Washington family descendant, kindly answered questions for me.

Many librarians and archivists contributed to the creation of this book. At the Massachusetts Historical Society, Peter Drummey and Stephen T. Riley led me through relevant collections, and I was especially pleased to handle there Washington's historic Newburgh address to his officers. At the Boston Athenaeum, Stanley Ellis Cushing and Mary Warnement provided guidance to a collection rich in nineteenth-century printed matter about Washington. Diane Windham Shaw at the Skillman Library at Lafayette College gave me a personal tour of an exhibition on the Marquis de Lafayette and helped with material about him. At the New York Public Library, Thomas Lannon offered direction to the Washington Irving materials. Bruce Kirby at the Library of Congress in Washington steered me through John Marshall's papers related to his early Washington biography. Special thanks to John Overholt at the Houghton Library at Harvard University, where I examined firsthand George Washington's personal copy of James Monroe's *A View of the Conduct of the Executive . . . ,* complete with his venomous marginal comments. At the Earl Gregg Swem Library at the College of William and Mary, Anne Johnson answered queries about special collections. Nelson D. Lankford, editor of the *Virginia Magazine of History and Biography,* rushed into my hands a copy of the magazine's excellent bicentennial issue on George Washington.

Washington's medical and dental history offered an especially fertile field for investigation. I was delighted to encounter dentist Dr. John Tosi, who tutored me in the fine points of eighteenth-century dentistry and described the torments of Washington's dentures. At the New York Academy of Medicine Library, Arlene Shaner gave me access to Washington's dentures, shepherded me through esoteric dental journals, and showed me, encased in a glass locket, Washington's last remaining tooth. My brother, Dr. Bart Chernow, and good friend Dr. Jerome Groopman answered numerous medical queries during the research.

Struck by recurrent mentions of Washington's trembling hands, I decided to explore the possibility that he suffered from Parkinson's disease, a disorder that was not named and identified until after his death. I consulted three renowned neurologists, supplied them with a comprehensive medical history of Washington, and asked them to diagnose his condition. While they agreed that Washington suffered from a movement disorder, there was no general agreement as to what it was. One expert opted for Parkinson's disease, a second for essential tremor, and a third for enhanced physiological tremor. In the absence of a medical consensus, I omitted the issue from the text of the book, but I was vastly impressed by the informed opinions submitted by the three experts: Dr. Stanley Fahn, professor of neurology at the Columbia University Medical Center; Dr. Daniel Tarsy, professor of neurology at the Harvard Medical School; and Dr. Carlos Singer, professor of neurology at the Leonard M. Miller School of Medicine at the University of Miami. It turned out to be a fascinating, if inconclusive, exercise, and I am indebted to the neurologists in question for their generous cooperation.

Late in the writing of this book, I suffered a severe orthopedic injury that nearly derailed the project. For that reason, I would like to extend my warmest thanks to Dr. Jonathan Deland at the Hospital for Special Surgery in New York, who is a veritable wizard at repairing feet and ankles. During this period, when I had to vacate my brownstone, Margo Lion and Helen and Roger Lowenstein extended welcome asylum that enabled me to go on researching the book. This was friendship of a high and special order.

As I have noted in previous acknowledgments, I am singularly blessed in my agent, Melanie Jackson, and my editor, Ann Godoff of The Penguin Press. With deep faith in this project, both women provided consistently intelligent commentary and as much encouragement as any author could possibly want. Their unfailing warmth, immense integrity, and personal kindness to me have made my long-standing business and literary collaboration with them a pure joy. Their respective assistants, Caitlin McKenna and Lindsay Whalen, steadily helped to move this project along. I have also appreciated the fantastic support of the entire team at The Penguin Press, especially Tracy Locke and Sarah Hutson, who have always been models of cheerful efficiency. Janet Biehl did a fine, judicious copyedit of the manuscript under the always vigilant guidance of Bruce Giffords. In the early stages of this book, I profited from the excellent research assistance of Kate Daloz, who tracked down many interesting books and articles and then helped to assemble the picture section of the work.

Finally, I must acknowledge the inexpressible debt that I owe to my late wife, Valerie Chernow, who died during the composition of this work. She encouraged me to undertake the project and discussed it with me nightly until the end. For more than twenty-seven years, Valerie was my muse, my in-house editor, my delightful confidante. To this beautiful human being, I owe simply everything.

Notes

Abbreviations

Diaries. Donald Jackson and Dorothy Twohig, eds. *The Diaries of George Washington*, 6 vols. Charlottesville, Va., 1976–79.

DiariesA. Dorothy Twohig, ed. *George Washington's Diaries: An Abridgment.* Charlottesville, Va., 1999.

MTV Library of the Mount Vernon Ladies' Association, Mount Vernon, Va.

PWC. W. W. Abbot, Dorothy Twohig, and Philander D. Chase, eds. *The Papers of George Washington: Colonial Series,* 10 vols. Charlottesville, Va., 1983–95.

PWCF. W. W. Abbot and Dorothy Twohig, eds. *The Papers of George Washington: Confederation Series*, 6 vols. Charlottesville, Va., 1992–97.

PWP. W. W. Abbot, Dorothy Twohig, Philander D. Chase, David R. Hoth, Christine Sternberg Patrick, and Theodore J. Crackel, eds. *The Papers of George Washington: Presidential Series,* 15 vols. Charlottesville, Va., 1987–.

PWR. W. W. Abbot, Dorothy Twohig, Philander D. Chase, Edward G. Lengel, Theodore J. Crackel, and David R. Hoth, eds. *The Papers of George Washington: Revolutionary War Series,* 18 vols. Charlottesville, Va., 1985–.

PWRT. W. W. Abbot and Dorothy Twohig, eds. *The Papers of George Washington: Retirement Series,* 4 vols. Charlottesville, Va., 1998–99.

WWF. John C. Fitzpatrick, ed. *The Writings of George Washington*, 39 vols. Washington, D.C., 1931–44.

WWR. John Rhodehamel, ed. *George Washington, Writings.* New York, 1997.

Prelude: The Portrait Artist
1. Barratt and Miles, *Gilbert Stuart,* 78–79.
2. Longmore, *Invention of George Washington,* 181.
3. Chernow, *Alexander Hamilton,* 89.
4. Burns and Dunn, *George Washington,* 58.
5. Barratt and Miles, *Gilbert Stuart,* 137.
6. Jefferson, *Writings,* 1319.
7. Schutz and Adair, *Spur of Fame,* 98.
8. Custis, *Recollections and Private Memoirs of Washington,* 418.
9. Higginbotham, *George Washington Reconsidered,* 282.

Chapter One: A Short-Lived Family
1. *PWP,* 10:333.
2. Higginbotham, *George Washington Reconsidered,* 20.
3. Anderson, *George Washington Remembers,* 31.
4. Wiencek, *Imperfect God,* 31.
5. Ibid., 34.
6. Wills, *Cincinnatus,* 68.
7. Freeman, *George Washington,* 1:58.
8. Ibid., 1:69.
9. *PWCF,* 2:175. Letter to the Marquis de Lafayette, December 8, 1784.
10. Freeman, *George Washington,* 1:193.
11. Conkling, *Memoirs of Mother and Wife of Washington,* 22.
12. Hervey, *Memory of Washington,* 45.
13. Felder, *Fielding Lewis and Washington Family,* 34.
14. Ramsay, *Life of George Washington,* 3.
15. *PWP,* 7:32. Letter to George Steptoe Washington, December 5, 1790.

16. Brookhiser, *Founding Father,* 137.
17. Abbot, "Uncommon Awareness."
18. *WWF,* 35:341. Letter to George Washington Parke Custis, December 19, 1796.
19. Henriques, *Realistic Visionary,* 188.
20. *WWR,* 3. "Rules of Civility," 1747.
21. Ibid., 10.
22. Ibid., 5.
23. Ibid., 6.
24. Sayen, "George Washington's 'Unmannerly' Behavior."
25. *WWF,* 35:295. Letter to George Washington Parke Custis, November 28, 1796.
26. *PWRT,* 1:169. Letter to George Washington Parke Custis, June 4, 1797.

Chapter Two: Fortune's Favorite
1. *PWRT,* 4:507.
2. Freeman, *George Washington,* 1:76–77.
3. *WWF,* 35:329–30. Letter to Sir John Sinclair, December 11, 1796.
4. Flexner, *George Washington,* 1:30.
5. *PWC,* 1:289–90. Letter to John Augustine Washington, May 28, 1755.
6. Ibid., 4:119. Letter from William Fairfax, March 22, 1757.
7. *WWR,* 720. Letter to George Steptoe Washington, March 23, 1789.
8. Flexner, *George Washington,* 1:27.
9. Palmer, *George Washington and Benedict Arnold,* 43–44.
10. Flexner, *George Washington,* 1:30.

11. *PWCF*, 5:515. "Comments on David Humphreys' Biography of George Washington."

12. Flexner, *George Washington*, 1:30.

13. Freeman, *George Washington*, 1:195.

14. Ibid., 1:199.

15. *PWCF*, 6:423. Letter to James Craik, August 4, 1788.

16. *WWR*, 142. Letter to Jonathan Boucher, July 9, 1771.

17. Ibid., 11. "A Journal of My Journey over the Mountains," March 15, 1747/8.

18. Ibid., 13. "A Journal of My Journey over the Mountains," March 23, 1747/8.

19. Ibid., 14. "A Journal of My Journey over the Mountains," April 4, 1747/8.

20. *PWC*, 1:44. Letter to Richard [no last name], ca. 1749–50.

21. *WWR*, 14. "A Journal of My Journey over the Mountains," April 3, 1747/8.

22. Lengel, *General George Washington*, 14.

23. *PWC*, 1:39.

24. Ibid., 1:45–46. Memorandum, ca. 1749–50.

25. Irving, *Life of George Washington*, 16.

26. Felder, *Fielding Lewis and Washington Family*, 33.

27. *PWC*, 1:41. Letter to Robin [no last name], ca. 1749–50.

28. Ibid., 1:47. "Poetry," ca. 1749–50.

29. Unger, *Unexpected George Washington*, 18.

30. Cunliffe, *George Washington*, 42.

31. *PWC*, 1:44. Letter to Richard, ca. 1749–50

32. *DiariesA*, xvi.

33. *PWC*, 1:6. Letter to Lawrence Washington, May 5, 1749.

34. Ibid., 1:38. Letter to Ann Fairfax Washington, ca. September–November 1749.

35. Flexner, *George Washington*, 1:47.

36. *DiariesA*, 12. Entry for November 5, 1751.

37. Lengel, *General George Washington*, 16.

38. Freeman, *George Washington*, 1:250.

39. *DiariesA*, 14. Entry for December 12, 1751.

40. Ibid., 15. Entry for December 22, 1751.

41. Ibid., 14. Entry for November 17, 1751.

42. Ibid.

43. Freeman, *George Washington*, 1:263.

44. Ibid., 1:51.

45. *PWC*, 1:49. Letter to William Fauntleroy, May 20, 1752.

46. Lengel, *General George Washington*, 16.

47. Unger, *Unexpected George Washington*, 19.

48. *WWR*, 1113.

49. *PWC*, 1:50. Letter to Robert Dinwiddie, June 10, 1752.

50. *PWRT*, 3:188. Letter to Maryland Masons, November 8, 1798.

51. *PWP*, 12:76. Letter to the Massachusetts Masons, January 1793.

CHAPTER THREE: WILDERNESS MISSION

1. Cadou, *George Washington Collection*, 212.

2. *PWC*, 1:199. Letter from Allan Macrae, September 3, 1754.

3. Freeman, *George Washington*, 3:6.

4. Lengel, *General George Washington*, 8.

5. *PWC*, 1:277. Letter to John Augustine Washington, May 14, 1755.

6. Wiencek, *Imperfect God*, 65–66.

7. Anderson, *George Washington Remembers*, 71.

8. Longmore, *Invention of George Washington*, 18.

9. *PWC*, 1:57.

10. Ibid., 1:352. Letter to Augustine Washington, August 2, 1755.

11. Flexner, *George Washington*, 1:55.

12. *PWC*, 2:151. Letter from Robert Hunter Morris, October 31, 1755.

13. *PWCF*, 5:516. "Comments on David Humphreys' Biography of George Washington."

14. *PWC*, 1:57.

15. *WWR*, 17. "Journey to the French Commandant," 1753.

16. Ibid., 18.

17. Ibid.

18. Lengel, *General George Washington*, 20.

19. *PWC*, 5:117. Letter to John Stanwix, April 10, 1758.

20. *WWR*, 19. "Journey to the French Commandant," 1753.

21. Lengel, *General George Washington*, 23.

22. *PWCF*, 5:516. "Comments on David Humphreys' Biography of George Washington."

23. *WWR*, 22. "Journey to the French Commandant," 1753.

24. Ibid., 25.

25. Ibid., 26.

26. Ibid., 28.

27. Flexner, *George Washington*, 1:68.

28. Ibid., 69.

29. *WWR*, 30. "Journey to the French Commandant," 1753.

30. Ibid., 32.

31. Ibid.

32. Freeman, *George Washington*, 1:320.

33. Lengel, *General George Washington*, 28.

34. *WWR*, 33. "Journey to the French Commandant," 1753.

35. Flexner, *George Washington*, 1:76.

36. *WWR*, 34. "Journey to the French Commandant," 1753.

37. *DiariesA*, 32.

38. *PWC*, 1:352. Letter to Augustine Washington, August 2, 1755.

39. *WWR*, 35. Letter to Richard Corbin, January 28, 1754.

CHAPTER FOUR: BLOODBATH

1. *DiariesA*, 38.

2. *PWC*, 1:72, Letter to Robert Dinwiddie, March 7, 1754.

3. Ibid.

4. Flexner, *George Washington*, 1:81.

5. Ibid., 1:82.

6. Lengel, *General George Washington*, 33.

7. Freeman, *George Washington*, 1:354.

8. *PWC*, 1:86. Letter to Governor Horatio Sharpe, April 24, 1754.

9. *WWR*, 39. Letter to Robert Dinwiddie, May 18, 1754.

10. *DiariesA*, 45.

11. Ibid., 47.

12. Lengel, *General George Washington*, 35.

13. *DiariesA*, 49–50.

14. Flexner, *George Washington*, 1:89.

15. *DiariesA*, 49.

16. *WWR*, 42. Letter to Robert Dinwiddie, May 29, 1754.

17. Ibid., 44.

18. Ibid., 48. Letter to John Augustine Washington, May 31, 1754.

19. Lengel, *General George Washington*, 39.

20. *PWC*, 1:117. Letter to Joshua Fry, May 29, 1754.

21. Ibid., 1:119. Letter from Robert Dinwiddie, June 1, 1754.

22. Ibid., 1:114–15.

23. Leibiger, "'To Judge of Washington's Conduct.'"

24. Henriques, *Realistic Visionary*, 6.

25. *PWC*, 1:129–30. Letter to Robert Dinwiddie, June 10, 1754.

26. Flexner, *George Washington,* 1:100.

27. Anderson, *George Washington Remembers,* 37.

28. Flexner, *George Washington,* 1:100.

29. *PWCF,* 5:517. "Comments on David Humphreys' Biography of George Washington."

30. Flexner, *George Washington,* 1:101.

31. *PWCF,* 5:518. "Comments on David Humphreys' Biography of George Washington."

32. Ibid.

33. Ibid.

34. *PWC,* 1:164.

35. Ibid., 1:170.

36. Ibid., 1:168.

37. Ibid., 1:169–70.

38. Ibid., 1:160.

39. Lengel, *General George Washington,* 46.

40. Flexner, *George Washington,* 1:107.

41. Lengel, *General George Washington,* 48.

42. *PWC,* 1:136. Letter to Robert Dinwiddie, June 10, 1754.

43. Callahan, *Henry Knox,* 320.

44. Flexner, *George Washington,* 1:5.

45. Freeman, *George Washington,* 1:416.

46. Lengel, *General George Washington,* 49.

47. Freeman, *George Washington,* 1:420.

48. Ibid., 1:432.

49. *PWC,* 1:216. Letter from Horatio Sharpe, October 1, 1754.

50. Ibid., 1:226. Letter to William Fitzhugh, November 15, 1754.

51. Ibid.

52. Cadou, *George Washington Collection,* 26.

CHAPTER FIVE: SHADES OF DEATH

1. *PWC,* 6:381.

2. Ibid., 1:243. Letter to Robert Orme, March 15, 1755.

3. Ibid., 1:246.

4. Ibid., 1:278. Letter to John Augustine Washington, May 14, 1755.

5. Ibid., 1:255. Letter to John Robinson, April 20, 1755.

6. Ibid., 1:246. Letter to Robert Orme, April 2, 1755.

7. Ibid., 1:278. Letter to John Augustine Washington, May 14, 1755.

8. *PWCF,* 5:522. "Comments on David Humphreys' Biography of George Washington."

9. *PWC,* 2:11.

10. Ibid., 1:299. Letter to William Fairfax, June 7, 1755.

11. Isaacson, *Benjamin Franklin,* 166.

12. *PWC,* 1:268. Letter to Mary Ball Washington, May 6, 1755.

13. Ibid.

14. Irving, *Life of George Washington,* 558.

15. *PWC,* 1:304. Letter to Mary Ball Washington, June 7, 1755.

16. Ibid., 1:261. Letter to Sarah Cary Fairfax, April 30, 1755.

17. Ibid., 1:265. Letter to Thomas, Lord Fairfax, May 6, 1755.

18. *WWR,* 54. Letter to Sarah Cary Fairfax, June 7, 1755.

19. Ibid., 53. Letter to John Augustine Washington, May 28, 1755.

20. *PWC,* 1:319. Letter to John Augustine Washington, June 28–July 2, 1755.

21. Lengel, *General George Washington,* 55.

22. Freeman, *George Washington,* 2:51.

23. *WWR,* 54. Letter to John Augustine Washington, June 28, 1755.

24. Cunliffe, *George Washington,* 49.

25. *PWCF,* 5:520. "Comments on David Humphreys' Biography of George Washington."

26. *PWC,* 1:332.

27. *PWCF,* 5:520–21. "Comments on David Humphreys' Biography of George Washington."

28. Marshall, *Life of George Washington,* 10.

29. *WWR,* 58. Letter to Robert Dinwiddie, July 18, 1755.

30. Flexner, *George Washington,* 1:129.

31. *PWCF,* 5:522. "Comments on David Humphreys' Biography of George Washington."

32. *PWC,* 1:340. Letter to Robert Dinwiddie, July 18, 1755. First draft.

33. Wiencek, *Imperfect God,* 64.

34. Freeman, *George Washington,* 2:82.

35. Ibid.

36. *PWCF,* 5:522. "Comments on David Humphreys' Biography of George Washington."

37. *PWC,* 3:181.

38. Cunliffe, *George Washington,* 49.

39. Flexner, *George Washington,* 1:134.

40. *PWC,* 1:346. Letter from Sarah Cary Fairfax, Ann Spearing, and Elizabeth Dent, July 26, 1755.

41. Ibid., 1:343. Letter to John Augustine Washington, July 18, 1755. First draft.

42. Longmore, *Invention of George Washington,* 30.

43. Irving, *Life of George Washington,* 83.

44. Longmore, *Invention of George Washington,* 29.

CHAPTER SIX: THE SOUL OF AN ARMY

1. *PWC,* 1:359. Letter to Mary Ball Washington, August 14, 1755.

2. Ibid., 3:416. Letter to Robert Dinwiddie, September 23, 1756.

3. Ibid., 2:208. Letter to Richard Washington, December 6, 1755.

4. *WWR,* 61. "General Orders," October 6, 1755.

5. Wiencek, *Imperfect God,* 64.

6. *WWR,* 64. Letter to Robert Dinwiddie, October 14, 1755.

7. *PWC,* 2:176. Letter to Denis McCarty, November 22, 1755.

8. Ibid., 2:102. Letter to Robert Dinwiddie, October 11, 1755.

9. Morgan, *Genius of George Washington,* 29.

10. *PWC,* 3:171. Letter to Robert Dinwiddie, May 23, 1756.

11. Ibid., 4:406. Letter to Robert Dinwiddie, September 17, 1757.

12. Fischer, *Washington's Crossing,* 15.

13. *PWC,* 3:417. Letter to Robert Dinwiddie, September 23, 1756.

14. Ibid., 5:130. Letter to John Blair, April 17, 1758.

15. *PWR,* 8:124. Letter to John Parke Custis, January 22, 1777.

16. Flexner, *George Washington,* 1:159.

17. Marshall, "National Treasure," *New Yorker,* May 23, 2005.

18. *PWCF,* 5:523. "Comments on David Humphreys' Biography of George Washington."

19. *PWC,* 2:226. Letter from Adam Stephen, December 23, 1755.

20. Ibid., 6:439. Letter from Andrew Burnaby, June 23, 1760.

21. Irving, *Life of George Washington,* 91.

22. Longmore, *Invention of George Washington,* 37.

23. Flexner, *George Washington,* 1:148.

24. *PWC,* 2:333. Letter to Robert Dinwiddie, April 7, 1756.

25. Ibid., 2:345. Letter to Robert Hunter Morris, April 9, 1756.

26. Ibid., 3:33–34. Letter to Robert Dinwiddie, April 22, 1756.

27. Flexner, *George Washington,* 1:154.

28. *WWR,* 73. Letter to Robert Dinwiddie, April 18, 1756.

29. Henriques, *Realistic Visionary,* 28.

30. *PWC,* 3:57. Letter from William Fairfax, April 27, 1756.

31. Ibid., 3:354. "Proclamation."

32. Ibid., 3:294. Letter to John Campbell, Earl of Loudoun, July 25, 1756.

33. Ibid., 4:86. Letter to the Earl of Loudoun, January 10, 1757.

34. Longmore, *Invention of George Washington,* 42.

35. Henriques, *Realistic Visionary,* 11.

36. *PWC,* 4:89. Letter to the Earl of Loudoun, January 10, 1757.

37. Higginbotham, *George Washington Reconsidered,* 59.

38. *PWC,* 4:89. Letter to the Earl of Loudoun, January 10, 1757.

39. Ibid., 4:90.

40. *WWR,* 86. Letter to Robert Dinwiddie, March 10, 1757.

41. *PWC,* 4:132. Letter to Richard Washington, April 15, 1757.

42. Ibid., 4:163. Letter to Robert Dinwiddie, May 24, 1757.

43. Anderson, "Hinge of the Revolution."

44. *PWC,* 4:306. Letter to John Stanwix, July 15, 1757.

45. Ibid., 4:360. Letter to Robert Dinwiddie, August 3, 1757.

46. Ibid., 4:199. Letter to John Robinson, June 10, 1757.

47. Ibid., 4:422. Letter from Robert Dinwiddie, September 24, 1757.

48. Ibid., 5:3. Letter to Robert Dinwiddie, October 5, 1757.

49. Ibid., 5:25. Letter to Robert Dinwiddie, October 24, 1757.

50. Ibid., 5:63.

51. Ibid., 5:64. Letter from James Craik, November 25, 1757.

52. Ibid., 5:56. Letter to Sarah Cary Fairfax, November 15, 1757.

53. Ibid., 5:92. Letter from Robert Carter Nicholas, February 6, 1758.

54. Ibid., 5:102. Letter to John Stanwix, March 4, 1758.

55. Ibid.

CHAPTER SEVEN: A VOTARY TO LOVE

1. Cadou, *George Washington Collection,* 29.

2. Ibid.

3. Ibid.

4. *PWC,* 5:447. Letter from Humphrey Knight, September 2, 1758.

5. Brady, *Martha Washington,* 55.

6. *PWC,* 5:112. Letter to Richard Washington, April 5, 1758.

7. Freeman, *Washington,* 2:302.

8. Cadou, *George Washington Collection,* 254.

9. Henriques, *Realistic Visionary,* 88.

10. MTV. "Early Descriptions Ante 1800." Nicholas Crosswell journal, 1774–77.

11. Henriques, *Realistic Visionary,* 101.

12. *PWRT,* 2:239.

13. Wiencek, *Imperfect God,* 84.

14. Bryan, *First Lady of Liberty,* 239; Wiencek, ibid., 85.

15. Custis, *Recollections and Private Memoirs of Washington,* 509.

16. Henriques, *Realistic Visionary,* 90.

17. Brady, *Martha Washington,* 30.

18. Wiencek, *Imperfect God,* 75.

19. Ibid., 73.

20. Ibid.

21. Ibid., 76.

22. *PWC,* 6:10. Letter to Sarah Cary Fairfax, September 12, 1758.

23. Ibid., 6:11.

24. Ibid.

25. Ibid., 6:41. Letter to Sarah Cary Fairfax, September 25, 1758.

26. *WWR,* 901–2.

CHAPTER EIGHT: DARLING OF A GRATEFUL COUNTRY

1. Higginbotham, *George Washington Reconsidered,* 54.

2. *PWC,* 5:117.

3. Lengel, *General George Washington,* 70.

4. *PWC,* 5:258. Letter to Henry Bouquet, July 3, 1758. *PWC,* 5:282. Letter to Henry Bouquet, July 13, 1758.

5. Henriques, *Realistic Visionary,* 33.

6. *PWC,* 5:271. Letter from James Wood, July 7, 1758.

7. Ibid., 5:305–6. Letter from Robert Rutherford, July 20, 1758.

8. Flexner, *George Washington,* 1:211.

9. *PWC,* 5:330. Letter from Robert Rutherford, July 26, 1758.

10. Ibid., 5:349. Letter to James Wood, ca. July 28, 1758.

11. Ibid.

12. *WWR,* 96. Letter to Francis Halkett, August 2, 1758.

13. Henriques, *Realistic Visionary,* 13.

14. Lengel, *General George Washington,* 71.

15. *PWC,* 5:424. Letter to Henry Bouquet, August 28, 1758.

16. Ibid., 5:433. Letter to John Robinson, September 1, 1758.

17. Flexner, *George Washington,* 1:215.

18. *PWC,* 7:205. Letter to Robert Stewart, April 27, 1763.

19. Flexner, *George Washington,* 1:220.

20. *PWCF,* 5:525. "Comments on David Humphreys' Biography of George Washington."

21. *PWC,* 6:177. Letter from Robert Stewart, December 31, 1758.

22. Ibid.

23. Ibid., 6:179. "Address from the Officers of the Virginia Regiment," December 31, 1758.

24. *PWCF,* 5:525. "Comments on David Humphreys' Biography of George Washington."

25. *PWC,* 6:186. "To the Officers of the Virginia Regiment," January 10, 1759.

26. Ibid., 6:187.

CHAPTER NINE: THE MAN OF MODE

1. Cadou, *George Washington Collection,* 244.

2. *PWC,* 6:283ff.

3. Brady, *Martha Washington,* 70.

4. *DiariesA,* 65. Diary entry for January 16, 1760.

5. Ibid., 58.

6. Burns and Dunn, *George Washington,* 12.

7. *PWC,* 6:359. Letter to Richard Washington, September 20, 1759.

8. Burns and Dunn, *George Washington,* 13.

9. Freeman, *George Washington,* 3:7.

10. Brookhiser, *Founding Father*, 66.
11. *WWR*, 417. Letter to John Parke Custis, February 28, 1781.
12. *PWC*, 6:200. Letter to John Alton, April 5, 1759.
13. Fields, "Worthy Partner," 129.
14. Unger, *Unexpected George Washington*, 41.
15. Wiencek, *Imperfect God*, 83.
16. Thompson, *Statements Regarding the Physical Appearance*, 74.
17. Irving, *Life of George Washington*, 615.
18. Fields, "Worthy Partner," 147.
19. Thompson, *Memorandum for the Martha Washington Anniversary Committee*, 24.
20. *PWR*, 1:3–4. Letter to Martha Washington, June 18, 1775.
21. *WWR*, 881. Letter to Elizabeth Parke Custis, September 14, 1794.
22. MTV. "Early Descriptions Ante 1800." Lieutenant John Enys visit to Mount Vernon, February 12, 1788.
23. Flexner, *George Washington*, 2:519.
24. Cunliffe, *George Washington*, 124.
25. *WWR*, 597. Letter to the Marquis de Lafayette, May 10, 1786.
26. Ibid., 599. Letter to William Fitzhugh, May 15, 1786.
27. Ibid., 570. Letter to William Gordon, December 20, 1784.
28. Flexner, *George Washington*, 1:269.
29. *WWR*, 706. "Draft of First Inaugural," ca. January 1789.
30. Furstenberg, *In the Name of the Father*, 75.
31. *PWC*, 6:315. Letter to Robert Cary & Co., May 1, 1759.
32. Ibid., 6:317. "Enclosure Invoice to Robert Cary & Co.," May 1, 1759.
33. Ibid., 6:453. Letter to Richard Washington, August 10, 1760.
34. Cadou, *George Washington Collection*, 212.
35. Ibid.
36. *PWC*, 6:375. Letter to Robert Cary & Co., November 30, 1759.
37. Ibid., 6:459. Undated typescript of a letter to an unidentified tailor.
38. Cadou, *George Washington Collection*, 238.
39. Hague, *William Pitt the Younger*, 4.
40. *PWC*, 6:359. Letter to Richard Washington, September 20, 1759.
41. *DiariesA*, 90.
42. *PWC*, 6:449. Letter to Robert Cary & Co., August 10, 1760.
43. Ibid., 6:459–60. Letter to Robert Cary & Co., September 28, 1760.
44. Wood, "The Shopper's Revolution."
45. *WWR*, 109. Letter to Robert Stewart, April 27, 1763.
46. Ibid., 111. Letter to Robert Cary & Co., August 10, 1764.
47. Ibid., 113–14. Letter to Robert Cary & Co., September 20, 1765.
48. *PWRT*, 1:248. Letter to Samuel Washington, July 12, 1797.

CHAPTER TEN: A CERTAIN SPECIES OF PROPERTY
1. Flexner, *George Washington*, 1:274.
2. *PWC*, 7:140. Letter to Robert Cary & Co., June 20, 1762.
3. Ibid., 7:385. Letter to Burwell Bassett, August 2, 1765.
4. Wiencek, *Imperfect God*, 45.
5. *PWC*, 9:70. Letter to Daniel Jenifer Adams, July 20, 1772.
6. Ibid., 8:256. Letter to Hector Ross, October 9, 1769.
7. Ibid., 8:3. Letter to John Posey, June 24, 1767.

8. *WWR*, 158. Letter to Bryan Fairfax, August 24, 1774.
9. *DiariesA*, 83. Diary entry for May 7, 1760.
10. *PWC*, 7:148. "Agreement with Nelson Kelly," September 1, 1762.
11. *PWP*, 11:229. Letter to Anthony Whitting, October 14, 1792.
12. *WWF*, 33:242. Letter to William Pearce, January 12, 1794.
13. Thompson, "'They Appear to Live Comfortable Together.'"
14. Higginbotham, *George Washington Reconsidered*, 117.
15. Thompson, "Lives of Enslaved Workers on Washington's Outlying Farms."
16. Adams, *Life and Writings of Jared Sparks*, 2:28.
17. Thompson, *Statements Regarding the Physical Appearance*, 56.
18. *PWP*, 13:225. "Circular to William Stuart, Hiland Crow, and Henry McCoy," July 14, 1793.
19. Ibid., 12:524. Letter to Anthony Whitting, May 5, 1793.
20. Lee, *Experiencing Mount Vernon*, 68.
21. Brady, *George Washington's Beautiful Nelly*, 134.
22. Decatur, *Private Affairs of George Washington*, 315.
23. Longmore, *Invention of George Washington*, 181.
24. Massachusetts Historical Society, Timothy Pickering Papers, Reel 52, p. 54.
25. Henriques, *Realistic Visionary*, 150.
26. Lee, *Experiencing Mount Vernon*, 23.
27. *PWP*, 1:223. Letter to John Fairfax, January 1, 1789.
28. *WWF*, 33:275. Letter to William Pearce, February 22, 1794.
29. *PWP*, 9:439.
30. *DiariesA*, 69–70. Diary entry for February 5, 1760.
31. Lee, *Experiencing Mount Vernon*, 77.
32. *PWP*, 12:634. Letter to Anthony Whitting, May 26, 1793.
33. Thompson, "'The Only Unavoidable Subject of Regret.'"
34. *PWC*, 8:521.
35. Morgan, "'To Get Quit of Negroes.'"
36. Wiencek, *Imperfect God*, 100.
37. Ibid.
38. *WWR*, 102. "Reward for Runaway Slaves," August 11, 1761.
39. Ibid., 103.
40. Ibid.
41. Ibid., 102.
42. *WWR*, 118. Letter to Joseph Thompson, July 2, 1766.
43. Ibid.
44. Wiencek, *Imperfect God*, 188.
45. *PWC*, 7:179.
46. Lee, *Experiencing Mount Vernon*, 23.
47. MTV. "Early Descriptions Ante 1800." Joseph Hatfield, 1787.
48. Wiencek, *Imperfect God*, 282.
49. *PWRT*, 4:133. Letter to William Roberts, June 17, 1799.
50. Chinard, *George Washington as the French Knew Him*, 118.
51. *PWRT*, 1:525. Letter to James Anderson, December 21, 1797.
52. Schwarz, *Slavery at the Home of George Washington*, 25.
53. *WWR*, 845. Letter to William Pearce, October 6, 1793.
54. *WWF*, 33:390. Letter to James Germain, June 1, 1794.
55. *PWCF*, 5:526.
56. MTV. "Early Descriptions Ante 1800." John Hancock, 1799.

CHAPTER ELEVEN: THE PRODIGY

1. *PWC*, 8:98. Letter to Charles Lawrence, June 20, 1768.
2. Fischer, *Washington's Crossing*, 431.
3. Unger, *Lafayette*, 39.
4. Flexner, *George Washington*, 1:234.
5. Burns and Dunn, *George Washington*, 127.
6. Marshall, *Life of George Washington*, 466.
7. Henriques, *Realistic Visionary*, 205.
8. Brookhiser, *Founding Father*, 116.
9. Thompson, *Statements Regarding the Physical Appearance*, 71.
10. Adams, *Life and Writings of Jared Sparks*, 1:558.
11. Thompson, *Statements Regarding the Physical Appearance*, 88.
12. *PWC*, 7:257. Letter to Richard Washington, September 27, 1763.
13. Brookhiser, *Founding Father*, 127.
14. *WWR*, 483. Letter to Bushrod Washington, January 15, 1783.
15. Unger, *Unexpected George Washington*, 87–88.
16. Lengel, *General George Washington*, 8.
17. Jefferson, *Writings*, 1319.
18. Flexner, *George Washington*, 2:401.
19. Lee, *Experiencing Mount Vernon*, 71.
20. *PWP*, 2:415. Letter to John Campbell, May 31, 1789.
21. *DiariesA*, 105. Diary entry for March 2, 1768.
22. Hervey, *Memory of Washington*, 93.
23. Irving, *Life of George Washington*, 124.
24. *WWF*, 35:341. Letter to George Washington Parke Custis, December 19, 1796.
25. Cadou, *George Washington Collection*, 33.
26. *PWC*, 7:260. Letter to George William Fairfax, September 29, 1763.

CHAPTER TWELVE: PROVIDENCE

1. Meade, "Gov. Fauquier."
2. Wiencek, *Imperfect God*, 140.
3. *DiariesA*, 110.
4. Freeman, *George Washington*, 3:49.
5. Schutz and Adair, *Spur of Fame*, 207.
6. *PWC*, 7:43. Letter to Van Swearingen, May 15, 1761.
7. Flexner, *George Washington*, 1:256. *PWC*, 7:13. Letter from Robert Stewart, February 15, 1761.
8. *PWC*, 7:43. Letter to Van Swearingen, May 15, 1761.
9. Wiencek, *Imperfect God*, 152.
10. *PWC*, 7:59. Letter to Andrew Burnaby, July 27, 1761.
11. Ibid., 7:68. Letter to Charles Green, August 26, 1761.
12. Ibid., 7:80. Letter to Richard Washington, October 20, 1761.
13. Ibid., 6:415. Letter from Augustine Washington, ca. April 1760.
14. Thompson, "*In the Hands of a Good Providence*," 1.
15. Henriques, *Realistic Visionary*, 183.
16. Ibid., 246.
17. Thompson, "*In the Hands of a Good Providence*," 20.
18. *PWRT*, 1:407. Letter to William Gordon, October 15, 1797.
19. Marshall, *Life of George Washington*, 466.
20. Thompson, "*In the Hands of a Good Providence*," 52.
21. Ibid., 94.
22. Ibid., 92.
23. Ibid., 9.
24. *PWCF*, 1:232. Letter to Tench Tilghman, March 24, 1784.
25. Decatur, *Private Affairs of George Washington*, 231.

26. *WWR*, 834. Letter to the Members of the New Church in Baltimore, January 27, 1793.
27. *PWP*, 10:493. Letter to Edward Newenham, June 22, 1792.
28. *WWR*, 590. Letter to George Mason, October 3, 1785.
29. Ibid., 971. "Farewell Address," September 19, 1796.
30. *PWP*, 2:420. Letter to the General Assembly of the Presbyterian Church, ca. May 1789.
31. Thompson, "*In the Hands of a Good Providence*," 124.
32. Freeman, *George Washington*, 3:211.
33. Ibid.
34. *PWRT*, 2:37. Letter to David Stuart, January 22, 1798.
35. *PWC*, 7:297.
36. Wiencek, *Imperfect God*, 144.
37. *WWR*, 483. Letter to Bushrod Washington, January 15, 1783.
38. Wiencek, *Imperfect God*, 144.
39. Chinard, *George Washington as the French Knew Him*, 88.
40. Smith, "Surprising George Washington."

CHAPTER THIRTEEN: A WORLD OF HIS OWN

1. Flexner, *George Washington*, 1:310.
2. Ellis, *His Excellency*, 55.
3. Freeman, *George Washington*, 3:123.
4. Ibid., 3:132.
5. Ibid., 3:136.
6. Ibid.
7. Ibid., 3:142.
8. *PWC*, 7:401. Letter to Robert Cary & Co., September 20, 1765.
9. Isaacson, *Benjamin Franklin*, 230.
10. *PWC*, 7:457. Letter to Robert Cary & Co., July 21, 1766.
11. Ibid., 7:206. Letter to Robert Stewart, April 27, 1763.
12. Ibid., 7:323. Letter to Robert Cary & Co., August 10, 1764.
13. Ibid., 7:324.
14. Ibid., 7:191. Invoice from Robert Cary & Co., April 13, 1763.
15. Ibid., 8:93. Letter to Robert Cary & Co., June 6, 1768.
16. Ibid., 8:92.
17. Ibid., 8:370. Letter to Robert Cary & Co., August 20, 1770.
18. Wiencek, *Imperfect God*, 8.
19. Custis, *Recollections and Private Memoirs of Washington*, 153.
20. MTV. "Early Descriptions Ante 1800." Chevalier de Chastellux, 1780–82.
21. *Diaries*, 2:146. Diary entry for April 11, 1769.
22. Lee, *Experiencing Mount Vernon*, 83.
23. Ibid., 33.
24. *PWP*, 9:438 and 8:401.
25. *PWC*, 10:135.
26. Ibid., 7:495. Letter from Martha Washington, March 30, 1767.
27. Longmore, *Invention of George Washington*, 88.
28. *PWC*, 8:179. Letter to George Mason, April 5, 1769.
29. Ibid.
30. Ibid., 178.
31. Wiencek, *Imperfect God*, 150.
32. *DiariesA*, 128.
33. Ibid.
34. Ibid., 129. Diary entry for May 19, 1769.
35. Ibid.

36. *WWR*, 133. Letter to Robert Cary & Co., July 25, 1769.
37. Flexner, *George Washington,* 1:315.
38. Longmore, *Invention of George Washington,* 97.
39. *WWR*, 121. Letter to John Posey, June 24, 1767.
40. Longmore, *Invention of George Washington,* 104.
41. Freeman, *George Washington,* 3:246–47.
42. Flexner, *George Washington,* 1:289.
43. Ellis, *His Excellency,* 56.
44. *DiariesA,* 151. Diary entry for October 19, 1770.
45. Ibid., 150. Diary entry for October 14, 1770.
46. *PWC,* 9:460. Letter to George Muse, January 29, 1774.
47. Ibid., 9:461.
48. *WWR*, 139. Letter to Thomas Johnson, July 20, 1770.
49. Ibid., 138.
50. Ibid.
51. Unger, *Unexpected George Washington,* 77.

CHAPTER FOURTEEN: THE ASIATIC PRINCE
1. MTV. "Early Descriptions Ante 1800." Journal of Nathanael Greene, September 12, 1783.
2. Griswold, *Washington's Gardens at Mount Vernon,* 20.
3. Brady, *Martha Washington,* 185.
4. *Diaries,* 2:141. Diary entry for April 14, 1769.
5. *PWC,* 8:240. Letter to John Armstrong, August 18, 1769.
6. Ibid., 8:496. Letter to Jonathan Boucher, July 9, 1771.
7. Ibid., 8:89–90. Letter to Jonathan Boucher, May 30, 1768.
8. Ibid., 8:96. Letter from Jonathan Boucher, June 16, 1768.
9. Ibid., 8:122–24. Letter from Jonathan Boucher, August 2, 1768.
10. Ibid., 8:227. Letter from Jonathan Boucher, July 20, 1769.
11. Ibid., 8:339. Letter from Jonathan Boucher, May 21, 1770.
12. Ibid., 8:412. Letter to Jonathan Boucher, December 16, 1770.
13. Ibid., 8:414. Letter from Jonathan Boucher, December 18, 1770.
14. Ibid., 8:426. Letter to Jonathan Boucher, January 2, 1771.
15. Ibid., 8:348. Letter to Jonathan Boucher, June 2, 1770.
16. Freeman, *George Washington,* 3:312.
17. *PWC,* 8:415. Letter from Jonathan Boucher, December 18, 1770.
18. *WWR*, 144. Letter to Benedict Calvert, April 3, 1773.
19. Flexner, *George Washington,* 1:228.
20. *PWC,* 10:349.
21. *PWR,* 3:189.
22. *PWC,* 9:49. Letter to Jonathan Boucher, May 21, 1772.
23. Custis, *Recollections and Private Memoirs of Washington,* 528.
24. Chernow, *Alexander Hamilton,* 56.
25. *Diaries,* 3:182.
26. *PWC,* 9:266.
27. Unger, *Unexpected George Washington,* 84.
28. MTV. "Early Descriptions 1801–1841." Charles Willson Peale Journal, May–June 1804.
29. *PWC,* 9:243. Letter to Burwell Bassett, June 20, 1773.
30. Thompson, *"In the Hands of a Good Providence,"* 94.
31. Ibid., 121.
32. Flexner, *George Washington,* 1:247.
33. Wiencek, *Imperfect God,* 10.
34. *PWC,* 10:109. Letter to Bryan Fairfax, July 4, 1774.
35. Dalzell and Dalzell, *George Washington's Mount Vernon,* 79.

36. *PWC,* 9:326. Letter from Dr. Myles Cooper, September 20, 1773.
37. Ibid., 9:406–7. Letter to Myles Cooper, December 15, 1773.
38. Ibid., 9:212. Letter from Jonathan Boucher, April 8, 1773.

CHAPTER FIFTEEN: A SHOCK OF ELECTRICITY
1. *Diaries,* 3:166.
2. Stoll, *Samuel Adams,* 115.
3. Ferling, "Myths of the American Revolution."
4. *PWC,* 2:179. Letter from Thomas Gage, November 23, 1755.
5. Palmer, *George Washington and Benedict Arnold,* 69.
6. Flexner, *George Washington,* 1:320.
7. Ellis, *His Excellency,* 58.
8. Longmore, *Invention of George Washington,* 123.
9. *DiariesA,* 189.
10. *PWC,* 10:119–25. "Fairfax County Resolves," July 18, 1774.
11. *WWR*, 154. Letter to Bryan Fairfax, July 20,1774.
12. Flexner, *George Washington,* 1:322.
13. Ellis, *His Excellency,* 64.
14. *PWC,* 10:96–97. Letter to George William Fairfax, June 10, 1774.
15. Ibid., 10:96.
16. Ibid., 10:97.
17. Ibid., 10:109–10. Letter to Bryan Fairfax, July 4, 1774.
18. Ibid., 10:110.
19. *WWR*, 155–56. Letter to Bryan Fairfax, July 20, 1774.
20. Ibid.
21. Ibid., 156.
22. Ibid., 157. Letter to Bryan Fairfax, August 24, 1774.
23. *DiariesA,* 190.
24. Burns and Dunn, *George Washington,* 21.
25. Longmore, *Invention of George Washington,* 132.
26. Brady, *Martha Washington,* 92.
27. McCullough, *John Adams,* 86.
28. Wiencek, *Imperfect God,* 193.
29. Flexner, *George Washington,* 1:324.
30. Longmore, *Invention of George Washington,* 138.
31. *WWR*, 159. Letter to Robert McKenzie, October 9, 1774.
32. Burns and Dunn, *George Washington,* 22.
33. Unger, *Unexpected George Washington,* 95.
34. *PWC,* 10:172. Letter to Robert McKenzie, October 9, 1774.
35. Unger, *Unexpected George Washington,* 95.
36. *Diaries,* 3:285.
37. *DiariesA,* ix.
38. *Diaries,* 3:280.
39. *WWR*, 160. Letter to Robert McKenzie, October 9, 1774.
40. Stoll, *Samuel Adams,* 138.
41. *PWC,* 10:191. Letter to John Tayloe, November 30, 1774.
42. Ibid., 10:269.
43. Longmore, *Invention of George Washington,* 149.
44. Flexner, *George Washington,* 1:328.
45. Longmore, *Invention of George Washington,* 148.
46. Flexner, *George Washington,* 1:329.
47. Irving, *Life of George Washington,* 154.
48. Longmore, *Invention of George Washington,* 149.
49. Freeman, *George Washington,* 3:404.
50. Ibid., 3:405.
51. Ibid., 3:406.

52. *PWC*, 10:308. Letter to John Augustine Washington, March 25, 1775.
53. Ibid., 10:292. Letter to John Washington, March 6, 1775.
54. Freeman, *George Washington*, 3:409.
55. *PWC*, 10:320. Letter to Lord Dunmore, April 3, 1775.
56. Freeman, *George Washington*, 3:409.
57. Flexner, *George Washington*, 1:330.
58. Ibid., 1:335.

CHAPTER SIXTEEN: THE GLORIOUS CAUSE
1. Stoll, *Samuel Adams*, 157.
2. *PWC*, 10:368. Letter to George William Fairfax, May 31, 1775.
3. Smith, *John Marshall*, 44.
4. *Diaries*, 3:327. Diary entry for May 4, 1775.
5. *DiariesA*, 197.
6. Longmore, *Invention of George Washington*, 162.
7. Ibid., 182.
8. Flexner, *George Washington*, 1:333.
9. *WWR*, 164. Letter to George William Fairfax, May 31, 1775.
10. Longmore, *Invention of George Washington*, 162.
11. Flexner, *George Washington*, 1:334.
12. Schutz and Adair, *Spur of Fame*, 97.
13. Ibid., 98.
14. Ibid.
15. Ibid., 97.
16. Henriques, *Realistic Visionary*, 22.
17. Flexner, *George Washington*, 1:343.
18. *PWR*, 13:322. Letter to William Gordon, January 23, 1778.
19. Longmore, *Invention of George Washington*, 163.
20. Grant, *John Adams*, 156.
21. Ibid.
22. *DiariesA*, 198.
23. Flexner, *George Washington*, 1:338.
24. Ibid., 2:9.
25. *Diaries*, 3:336. Diary entry for June 15, 1775.
26. *DiariesA*, 198.
27. *PWR*, 1:1. "Address to the Continental Congress," June 16, 1775.
28. Ibid., 1:2–3.
29. Flexner, *George Washington*, 1:342.
30. Longmore, *Invention of George Washington*, 177.
31. Freeman, *George Washington*, 3:439–40.
32. *WWR*, 167–68. Letter to Martha Washington, June 18, 1775.
33. Ibid., 168.
34. *PWR*, 1:15. Letter to John Parke Custis, June 19, 1775.
35. *WWR*, 168. Letter to Martha Washington, June 18, 1775. Ibid., 170. Letter to Burwell Bassett, June 19, 1775.
36. Ibid., 170. Letter to Burwell Bassett, June 19, 1775.
37. Cadou, *George Washington Collection*, 213.
38. McCullough, *1776*, 57.
39. Ibid., 44.
40. *PWR*, 1:56.
41. *WWF*, 14:385. Letter to John Jay, April 14, 1779.
42. *WWR*, 222. Letter to John Augustine Washington, March 31, 1776.
43. Cunliffe, *George Washington*, 75.
44. *PWR*, 1:95.
45. Ibid., 1:16. Letter to the Officers of Five Virginia Independent Companies, June 20, 1775.
46. *WWR*, 173. Letter to Martha Washington, June 23, 1775.

47. *PWR*, 1:33.
48. Ibid., 1:34.
49. Golway, *Washington's General*, 55.
50. *PWR*, 1:135. Letter to Samuel Washington, July 20, 1775.
51. *WWR*, 184–85. Letter to Lund Washington, August 20, 1775.
52. *PWR*, 1:41. "Address to the New York Provincial Congress," June 26, 1775.
53. Freeman, *George Washington*, 3:470.
54. Flexner, *George Washington*, 2:27.
55. Decatur, *Private Affairs of George Washington*, xxi.
56. Longmore, *Invention of George Washington*, 182.

CHAPTER SEVENTEEN: MAGNIFICENT BLUFF
1. Batchelder, "Col. Henry Vassall."
2. *WWR*, 178. Letter to Richard Henry Lee, July 10, 1775.
3. *PWR*, 1:54. "General Orders," July 4, 1775.
4. Cadou, *George Washington Collection*, 213–14.
5. Anderson, "Hinge of Revolution."
6. Palmer, *George Washington and Benedict Arnold*, 111.
7. Ibid.
8. Longmore, *Invention of George Washington*, 196.
9. Freeman, *George Washington*, 3:504–5.
10. *PWR*, 1:135. Letter to Samuel Washington, July 20, 1775.
11. Fischer, *Washington's Crossing*, 11.
12. Gaines, *For Liberty and Glory*, 105.
13. *PWR*, 6:482. Letter to Patrick Henry, October 5, 1776.
14. Gaines, *For Liberty and Glory*, 69.
15. Anderson, "Hinge of Revolution."
16. Cadou, *George Washington Collection*, 214.
17. *WWF*, 20:489. Letter to John Sullivan, December 17, 1780.
18. McCullough, *1776*, 31.
19. *PWR*, 1:55. "General Orders," July 4, 1775.
20. Ibid., 1:93.
21. McCullough, *1776*, 32.
22. Flexner, *George Washington*, 2:36.
23. Thompson, *Statements Regarding the Physical Appearance*, 4.
24. *PWR*, 1:104. Letter to James Warren, July 10, 1775.
25. Stephenson, *Patriot Battles*, 136.
26. Palmer, *George Washington and Benedict Arnold*, 111.
27. Flexner, *George Washington*, 2:541.
28. Massachusetts Historical Society. Timothy Pickering Papers, P-31, Reel 51, p. 228.
29. *PWR*, 1:140. Letter to John Hancock, July 21, 1775.
30. *WWR*, 195–96. Letter to Joseph Reed, December 15, 1775.
31. McCullough, *1776*, 62.
32. Stephenson, *Patriot Battles*, 175.
33. Flexner, *George Washington*, 2:36.
34. *PWR*, 1:221. Letter to Nicholas Cooke, August 4, 1775.
35. Ibid., 1:218. "General Orders," August 4, 1775.
36. *WWR*, 181. Letter to Thomas Gage, August 11, 1775.
37. *PWR*, 1:302. Letter from Thomas Gage, August 13, 1775.
38. *WWR*, 182–83. Letter to Thomas Gage, August 19, 1775.
39. *PWR*, 1:372. Letter to Richard Henry Lee, August 29, 1775.
40. *WWR*, 184. Letter to Lund Washington, August 20, 1775.
41. Flexner, *George Washington*, 2:37.
42. Ibid., 2:49.
43. Higginbotham, *George Washington Reconsidered*, 278.
44. McCullough, *1776*, 22.

45. Golway, *Washington's General*, 45.
46. Ibid., 54.
47. *WWF*, 20:241. Letter to George Mason, October 22, 1780.
48. Golway, *Washington's General*, 67.
49. Massachusetts Historical Society. Timothy Pickering Papers, P-31, Reel 51, p. 139.
50. Chinard, *George Washington as the French Knew Him*, 53.
51. Callahan, *Henry Knox*, 20.
52. *DiariesA*, 361.
53. Callahan, *Henry Knox*, 271.
54. Ibid., 32.
55. Ibid., 227.
56. *PWRT*, 3:42. Letter to John Adams, September 25, 1798.
57. Stephenson, *Patriot Battles*, 65.

CHAPTER EIGHTEEN: LAND OF FREEDOM
1. Rosenfeld, *American Aurora*, 276.
2. McCullough, *1776*, 51.
3. Ibid., 39.
4. Rosenfeld, *American Aurora*, 260.
5. *PWR*, 2:29. Letter to John Hancock, September 21, 1775.
6. Stephenson, *Patriot Battles*, 15.
7. Palmer, *George Washington and Benedict Arnold*, 133.
8. Brookhiser, *Founding Father*, 115.
9. Flexner, *George Washington*, 2:50.
10. *WWF*, 22:161. Letter to the Marquis de Lafayette, June 4, 1781.
11. *WWR*, 1011. Letter to John Adams, September 25, 1798.
12. Freeman, *George Washington*, 3:553.
13. Ibid., 3:556.
14. *PWR*, 2:239. Letter to Major General Philip Schuyler, October 26, 1775.
15. McCullough, *1776*, 56.
16. Flexner, *George Washington*, 2:53.
17. *PWR*, 1:399. "Instructions to Captain Nicholas Broughton," September 2, 1775.
18. Ibid., 2:463. Letter to Lieutenant Colonel Joseph Reed, November 30, 1775.
19. *PWP*, 10:74–75. "Memorandum on General Officers," Philadelphia, March 9, 1792.
20. Fund, "Whiskey Entrepreneur."
21. *PWR*, 2:300. "General Orders," November 5, 1775.
22. Ibid., 1:287. "General Orders," August 11, 1775.
23. Ibid., 1:321. "General Orders," August 18, 1775.
24. Ibid., 1:346. "General Orders," August 22, 1775.
25. Ibid., 2:493. Letter to Colonel Benedict Arnold, December 5, 1775.
26. Ibid., 2:498. Letter to Major General Philip Schuyler, December 5, 1775.
27. Ibid., 3:78. Letter from Major General Philip Schuyler, January 13, 1776.
28. Morgan, *Genius of George Washington*, 10.
29. *PWR*, 1:169. "General Orders," July 25, 1775.
30. Cunliffe, *George Washington*, 78.
31. McCullough, *1776*, 64.
32. Stephenson, *Patriot Battles*, 185.
33. McCullough, *1776*, 36.
34. Wiencek, *Imperfect God*, 200.
35. *PWR*, 2:125. "Council of War," October 8, 1775.
36. Ibid., 2:354. "General Orders," November 12, 1775.
37. Hochschild, *Bury the Chains*, 98.
38. *PWR*, 2:436. Letter to Richard Henry Lee, November 27, 1775.

39. Ibid., 2:611. Letter to Richard Henry Lee, December 26, 1775.
40. *WWR*, 195. Letter to Joseph Reed, December 15, 1775.
41. *PWR*, 2:623. Letter to John Hancock, December 31, 1775.
42. Ellis, *American Creation*, 35.
43. McCullough, *1776*, 65.
44. *PWR*, 2:614. "General Orders," December 28, 1775.
45. *WWR*, 196. "General Orders," January 1, 1776.
46. *PWR*, 3:19. Letter to John Hancock, January 4, 1776.
47. *WWR*, 203. Letter to Joseph Reed, January 14, 1776.
48. Ibid.
49. Smith, *John Marshall*, 51.
50. *WWR*, 206. Letter to Joseph Reed, January 31, 1776.
51. Cunliffe, *George Washington*, 75.
52. Nelson, *Thomas Paine*, 88.
53. *PWR*, 3:183. Letter from Major General Charles Lee, January 24, 1776.
54. Ibid., 3:419. Letter from Fielding Lewis, March 6, 1776.
55. *WWR*, 206. Letter to Joseph Reed, January 31, 1776.
56. *PWCF*, 1:445. Letter to James Madison, June 12, 1784.
57. *PWR*, 2:74. Letter to Samuel Washington, September 30, 1775.
58. Ibid., 2:72.
59. Ibid., 2:162. Letter to John Augustine Washington, October 13, 1775.
60. Fields, "*Worthy Partner*," 164.
61. Brady, *Martha Washington*, 104.
62. Thompson, "'As If I had Been a Very Great Somebody.'"
63. Henriques, *Realistic Visionary*, 91.
64. *PWR*, 3:172. Letter to Lieutenant Colonel Joseph Reed, January 23, 1776.
65. Ibid., 2:252. Letter to Richard Henry Lee, October 29, 1775.
66. Ibid., 3:173. Letter to Lieutenant Colonel Joseph Reed, January 23, 1776.
67. Flexner, *George Washington*, 2:60.
68. Fields, "*Worthy Partner*," 164.
69. Henriques, *Realistic Visionary*, 94.
70. Unger, *Unexpected George Washington*, 110.
71. Fischer, *Washington's Crossing*, 19.
72. Flexner, *George Washington*, 2:59.
73. Golway, *Washington's General*, 74.
74. Thompson, "'As If I had Been a Very Great Somebody.'"
75. Brookhiser, *Founding Father*, 159.
76. *WWR*, 207. Letter to Joseph Reed, January 31, 1776.
77. *PWR*, 2:243. "Poem by Phillis Wheatley."
78. *WWR*, 216. Letter to Phillis Wheatley, February 28, 1776.
79. Ibid.
80. Thompson, "'As If I had Been a Very Great Somebody.'"

CHAPTER NINETEEN: THE HEIGHTS
1. Flexner, *George Washington*, 2:427.
2. *PWR*, 3:449. "General Orders," March 11, 1776.
3. Ibid., 9:315. Letter to Colonels Alexander Spotswood et al., April 30, 1777.
4. Ibid.
5. Custis, *Recollections and Private Memoirs*, 258.
6. *PWR*, 3:27. "General Orders," January 5, 1776.
7. *WWF*, 24:110–11. Letter to the Secretary at War, April 10, 1782.
8. Ibid., 254. "General Orders," May 14, 1782.

9. *PWR*, 3:85. Letter to John Hancock, January 14, 1776.

10. Rosenfeld, *American Aurora*, 274.

11. *PWR*, 3:287. Letter to Joseph Reed, February 10, 1776.

12. Ibid., 3:336. Letter to John Hancock, February 18, 1776.

13. Ibid., 3:335.

14. Ibid., 3:370. Letter to Lieutenant Colonel Joseph Reed, February 26, 1776.

15. McCullough, *1776*, 87.

16. *PWR*, 3:379. "General Orders," February 17, 1776.

17. McCullough, *1776*, 92.

18. Ibid., 92.

19. Ibid., 93.

20. Ibid., 95.

21. Ibid.

22. Trumbull, *Autobiography of Colonel John Trumbull*, 24.

23. *PWR*, 3:467. Letter to Major General Charles Lee, March 14, 1776.

24. Flexner, *George Washington*, 2:77.

25. *WWR*, 221. Letter to John Augustine Washington, March 31, 1776.

26. McCullough, *1776*, 105.

27. Freeman, *George Washington*, 4:55.

28. *PWR*, 3:494. Letter to Lieutenant Colonel Joseph Reed, March 19, 1776.

29. *WWR*, 217. Letter to John Hancock, March 19, 1776.

30. *PWR*, 3:501–2. "Proclamation on the Occupation of Boston," March 21, 1776.

31. Ibid., 3:514. Letter to John Morgan, March 22, 1776.

32. Ibid., 3:566–69. Letter to John Augustine Washington, March 31, 1776.

33. Stahr, *John Jay*, 58.

34. Freeman, *George Washington*, 4:91.

35. *PWR*, 3:508. Letter from Josiah Quincy, March 21, 1776.

36. Ibid., 3:528. Letter to Josiah Quincy, March 24, 1776.

37. Fischer, *Washington's Crossing*, 11.

38. *WWR*, 220. Letter to John Augustine Washington, March 31, 1776.

39. Golway, *Washington's General*, 80.

40. Stephenson, *Patriot Battles*, 230.

41. *PWR*, 4:75. "General Orders," April 17, 1776.

42. McCullough, *1776*, 125.

43. Freeman, *George Washington*, 4:5.

44. *WWR*, 224. Letter to John Augustine Washington, May 31, 1776.

45. Flexner, *George Washington*, 2:93.

46. *PWR*, 4:485. Letter from John Parke Custis, June 10, 1776.

47. Ibid., 5:74.

48. Ibid., 5:134. Letter to John Hancock, June 28, 1776.

49. Chernow, *Alexander Hamilton*, 75.

50. *PWR*, 5:129. "General Orders," June 28, 1776.

51. Ibid.

CHAPTER TWENTY: ALL LONDON AFLOAT

1. McCullough, *1776*, 142.

2. Ibid., 6.

3. Ibid., 19.

4. Ibid., 131.

5. Callahan, *Henry Knox*, 64.

6. *PWR*, 5:266. Letter to John Hancock, July 11, 1776.

7. McCullough, *1776*, 135.

8. Fischer, *Washington's Crossing*, 31.

9. *PWR*, 5:180. "General Orders," July 2, 1776.

10. Ibid., 5:181.

11. Ibid., 5:191–93. Letter to John Hancock, July 3, 1776.

12. *PWR*, 4:11. Letter to Joseph Reed, April 1, 1776.

13. Darnton, *George Washington's False Teeth*, 98.

14. Winik, *Great Upheaval*, 76.

15. Gaines, *For Liberty and Glory*, 44.

16. Flexner, *George Washington*, 2:14.

17. Wills, *Cincinnatus*, 187.

18. *PWR*, 3:386. Letter to Burwell Bassett, February 28, 1776.

19. Ibid., 5:246. "General Orders," July 9, 1776.

20. Ibid.

21. Fischer, *Washington's Crossing*, 29.

22. *PWR*, 5:258. Letter to John Hancock, July 10, 1776.

23. McCullough, *1776*, 141.

24. *PWR*, 5:256–57. "General Orders," July 10, 1776.

25. Ibid., 5:260. Letter to John Hancock, July 10, 1776.

26. Ibid., 6:54. Letter to the New York Convention, August 17, 1776.

27. Freeman, *George Washington*, 4:136–37.

28. *PWR*, 10:410. Letter to John Hancock, July 25, 1777.

29. Flexner, *George Washington*, 1:156.

30. McCullough, *1776*, 75.

31. Irving, *Life of George Washington*, 219.

32. *PWR*, 5:296. Letter from Lord Howe, July 13, 1776.

33. Ibid., 4:11. Letter to Joseph Reed, April 1, 1776.

34. Ibid., 5:297.

35. Freeman, *George Washington*, 4:139.

36. *PWR*, 5:306. Letter to John Hancock, July 14, 1776.

37. Thompson, *Statements Regarding the Physical Appearance*, 6.

38. Ibid.

39. Ibid., 7.

40. McCullough, *1776*, 145.

41. Callahan, *Henry Knox*, 66.

42. Ibid., 65.

43. Ibid.

44. *PWR*, 5:400–401. "Memorandum of an Interview with Lieutenant Colonel James Paterson," July 20, 1776.

45. Ibid., 5:401.

46. Ibid., 5:408. Letter to Colonel Adam Stephen, July 20, 1776.

47. Ibid., 5:424. Letter to John Hancock, July 22, 1776.

48. McCullough, *1776*, 147.

49. Fischer, *Washington's Crossing*, 87.

50. McCullough, *1776*, 151.

51. Stephenson, *Patriot Battles*, 20.

52. Golway, *Washington's General*, 90.

53. McCullough, *1776*, 153.

54. Ibid., 148.

55. Ibid.

56. *WWR*, 236. Letter to Lund Washington, August 19, 1776.

CHAPTER TWENTY-ONE: DISASTER

1. *PWR*, 5:610. Letter to Jesse Root, August 7, 1776.

2. Ibid., 5:632. Letter to Brigadier General William Livingston, August 8, 1776.

3. Ibid., 6:18. "General Orders," August 14, 1776.

4. McCullough, *1776*, 155–56.

5. *WWR*, 234. Letter to Lund Washington, August 19, 1776.

6. Fischer, *Washington's Crossing*, 90.

7. *WWR*, 239. "General Orders," August 23, 1776.

8. McCullough, *1776*, 161.

9. *PWR*, 16:490. Letter from Major General Israel Putnam, September 2, 1778.

10. Ibid., 6:129. Letter to John Hancock, August 26, 1776.
11. Ibid., 6:137. Letter to Lund Washington, August 26, 1776.
12. Flexner, *George Washington,* 2:110.
13. Ibid.
14. *PWR,* 6:162.
15. Stephenson, *Patriot Battles,* 239.
16. Fischer, *Washington's Crossing,* 98.
17. Freeman, *George Washington,* 4:178.
18. Palmer, *George Washington and Benedict Arnold,* 186.
19. McCullough, *1776,* 178.
20. Flexner, *George Washington,* 2:112.
21. Ibid., 2:114.
22. Stephenson, *Patriot Battles,* 243.
23. McCullough, *1776,* 190.
24. Fischer, *Washington's Crossing,* 101.
25. Schecter, *Battle for New York,* 165.
26. *PWR,* 6:495. Letter to Lund Washington, October 6, 1776.
27. Ibid., 6:164.
28. Ibid., 6:364. "General Orders," September 22, 1776.
29. Flexner, *George Washington,* 2:121.
30. *PWR,* 6:494. Letter to Lund Washington, October 6, 1776.
31. Ibid., 6:114. Letter to the New York Convention, August 23, 1776.
32. Ibid., 6:207. Letter from John Hancock, September 3, 1776.
33. McCullough, *1776,* 204.
34. Flexner, *George Washington,* 2:119.
35. *PWR,* 6:249. Letter to John Hancock, September 8, 1776.
36. Ibid.
37. Ibid., 6:251.
38. Stephenson, *Patriot Battles,* 245.
39. McCullough, *1776,* 211.
40. Brookhiser, *Founding Father,* 19.
41. Stephenson, *Patriot Battles,* 245.
42. *PWR,* 6:313. Letter to John Hancock, September 16, 1776.
43. Thompson, *Statements Regarding the Physical Appearance,* 8.
44. *PWR,* 6:316.
45. Flexner, *George Washington,* 2:123.
46. *PWR,* 6:313. Letter to John Hancock, September 16, 1776.
47. Ibid., 6:316.
48. Flexner, *George Washington,* 2:123.
49. Fischer, *Washington's Crossing,* 104.
50. *PWR,* 6:334.
51. Flexner, *George Washington,* 2:129.
52. Lengel, *General George Washington,* 157.
53. *PWR,* 6:320. "General Orders," September 17, 1776.
54. Ibid., 6:348. "General Orders," September 20, 1776.
55. Chernow, *Alexander Hamilton,* 81.
56. Golway, *Washington's General,* 96.
57. Fischer, *Washington's Crossing,* 106.
58. *PWR,* 6:370.
59. Ibid., 6:400. Letter to John Hancock, September 25, 1776.
60. Freeman, *George Washington,* 4:208.
61. Callahan, *Henry Knox,* 73.
62. *WWR,* 255. Letter to John Augustine Washington, November 6, 1776.
63. Ibid., 249. Letter to Lund Washington, September 30, 1776.
64. Ibid., 250.

CHAPTER TWENTY-TWO: AN INDECISIVE MIND
1. McCullough, *1776,* 230.
2. *PWR,* 7:57.
3. Flexner, *George Washington,* 2:136.
4. *PWR,* 7:52.
5. Flexner, *George Washington,* 2:140.
6. Lengel, *General George Washington,* 163.
7. Ibid., 228.
8. *PWR,* 7:115–16. Letter to Major General Nathanael Greene, November 8, 1776.
9. Fischer, *Washington's Crossing,* 113.
10. Freeman, *George Washington,* 4:235.
11. Flexner, *George Washington,* 2:145.
12. Ibid., 2:148.
13. *PWR,* 7:106.
14. Ibid., 7:154. Letter to John Hancock, November 14, 1776.
15. McCullough, *1776,* 239.
16. *PWR,* 7:163. Letter to John Hancock, November 16, 1776.
17. McCullough, *1776,* 240.
18. Lengel, *General George Washington,* 167.
19. Irving, *Life of George Washington,* 274.
20. Stephenson, *Patriot Battles,* 250.
21. McCullough, *1776,* 243.
22. Callahan, *Henry Knox,* 75.
23. *PWR,* 7:104. Letter to John Augustine Washington, November 19, 1776.
24. Freeman, *George Washington,* 4:293.
25. Ibid., 4:264.
26. Lengel, *General George Washington,* 168.
27. Stephenson, *Patriot Battles,* 250.
28. Golway, *Washington's General,* 105.
29. Fischer, *Washington's Crossing,* 125.
30. Flexner, *George Washington,* 2:157.
31. McCullough, *1776,* 247.
32. Flexner, *George Washington,* 2:171.
33. Grizzard, *George!,* 267.
34. *PWR,* 7:238.
35. Ibid., 7:237.
36. Ibid., 7:237. Letter to Colonel Joseph Reed, November 30, 1776.
37. Ibid., 8:542. Letter from Joseph Reed, March 8, 1777.
38. Ibid., 10:4. Letter to Joseph Reed, June 11, 1777.
39. Ibid., 7:235. Letter from Charles Lee, November 30, 1776.
40. Ibid., 7:256. Letter to John Hancock, December 3, 1776.
41. Flexner, *George Washington,* 2:167.
42. *PWR,* 7:371. Letter to Samuel Washington, December 18, 1776.
43. Ibid., 7:365. Letter to James Bowdoin, December 18, 1776.

CHAPTER TWENTY-THREE: THE CROSSING
1. *PWR,* 7:321. Letter to Jonathan Trumbull, Sr., December 12, 1776.
2. *WWF,* 19:408. Letter to the President of Congress, August 20, 1780.
3. *WWR,* 257. Letter to John Hancock, December 5, 1776.
4. McCullough, *1776,* 262.

5. Fischer, *Washington's Crossing*, 133.

6. McCullough, *1776*, 272.

7. *PWR*, 7:370. Letter to Samuel Washington, December 18, 1776.

8. Ibid., 7:415. Letter from Colonel Joseph Reed, December 22, 1776.

9. Irving, *Life of George Washington*, 283.

10. Fischer, *Washington's Crossing*, 196.

11. Nelson, *Thomas Paine*, 113.

12. Ibid., 114.

13. *PWR*, 7:423. Letter to Colonel Joseph Reed, December 23, 1776.

14. McCullough, *1776*, 168.

15. Fischer, *Washington's Crossing*, 220.

16. Ibid., 203.

17. *PWR*, 7:436. "General Orders," December 25, 1776.

18. Fischer, *Washington's Crossing*, 218.

19. McCullough, *1776*, 271.

20. Fischer, *Washington's Crossing*, 212.

21. Ibid., 218.

22. McCullough, *1776*, 276.

23. Fischer, *Washington's Crossing*, 228.

24. McCullough, *1776*, 277.

25. Fischer, *Washington's Crossing*, 231.

26. Ibid., 232.

27. Ibid., 190.

28. Ibid., 204.

29. *WWR*, 264. Letter to John Hancock, December 27, 1776.

30. Fischer, *Washington's Crossing*, 248.

31. Ibid., 249.

32. Irving, *Life of George Washington*, 287.

33. Flexner, *George Washington*, 2:188.

34. *PWR*, 7:448. "General Orders," December 27, 1776.

35. Fischer, *Washington's Crossing*, 266.

36. Ibid., 266.

37. Ibid., 144.

38. Ibid.

39. *WWR*, 265. Letter to Robert Morris, George Clymer, and George Walton, January 1, 1777.

40. Fischer, *Washington's Crossing*, 272.

41. *PWR*, 8:123. Letter to John Parke Custis, January 22, 1777.

42. Fischer, *Washington's Crossing*, 272–73.

43. Callahan, *Henry Knox*, 91.

44. Fischer, *Washington's Crossing*, 300–301.

45. Ibid., 307.

46. Flexner, *George Washington*, 2:183.

47. Fischer, *Washington's Crossing*, 314.

48. Ibid., 315.

49. Ibid., 318.

50. Ibid., 324.

51. McCullough, *1776*, 288.

52. Fischer, *Washington's Crossing*, 333.

53. *PWR*, 7:528.

54. Flexner, *George Washington*, 2:185.

55. Irving, *Life of George Washington*, 293.

56. McCullough, *1776*, 289.

57. Flexner, *George Washington*, 2:187.

58. Lengel, *General George Washington*, 204.

59. Fischer, *Washington's Crossing*, 379.

60. *PWR*, 8:37. Letter to Jonathan Trumbull, Sr., January 10, 1777.

61. Fischer, *Washington's Crossing*, 259.

62. Ibid., 289.

63. Flexner, *George Washington*, 2:189.

64. Callahan, *Henry Knox*, 98.

65. McCullough, *1776*, 291.

66. *PWR*, 7:529.

CHAPTER TWENTY-FOUR: THE BUSY SCENES OF A CAMP

1. *PWR*, 8:123. Letter to John Parke Custis, January 22, 1777.

2. Palmer, *George Washington and Benedict Arnold*, 203.

3. *WWF*, 19:408. Letter to the President of Congress, August 20, 1780.

4. Flexner, *George Washington*, 2:191.

5. *PWR*, 8:61. Letter to Robert Morris, January 13, 1777.

6. Brady, *Martha Washington*, 114.

7. Flexner, *George Washington*, 2:198.

8. Ibid., 2:533.

9. *WWF*, 13:139. "General Orders," October 23, 1778.

10. Longmore, *Invention of George Washington*, 193.

11. *WWR*, 269. "Proclamation Concerning Loyalists," January 25, 1777.

12. Flexner, *George Washington*, 2:193. Fischer, *Washington's Crossing*, 353.

13. Golway, *Washington's General*, 120.

14. Palmer, *George Washington and Benedict Arnold*, 202.

15. *WWF*, 16:58. Letter to Major General Robert Howe, August 6, 1779.

16. *WWR*, 344. Letter to Elias Boudinot, May 3, 1779.

17. *WWF*, 14:277. Letter to Major Benjamin Tallmadge, March 21, 1779.

18. Ibid.

19. *PWR*, 7:489. Letter to Robert Morris, December 30, 1776.

20. Weintraub, *General Washington's Christmas Farewell*, 120.

21. *PWR*, 9:9. Letter to Elisha Boudinot, March 29, 1777.

22. Ibid., 79. Letter to Joseph Reed, April 7, 1777.

23. Ibid.

24. *WWF*, 14:291. Letter to Major General Alexander McDougall, March 25, 1779.

25. *PWR*, 4:112–13. Letter to John Hancock, April 23, 1776.

26. Ibid., 8:584. Letter to Samuel Washington, March 15, 1777.

27. Ibid., 5:462. Letter to John Hancock, July 25, 1776.

28. Jefferson, *Writings*, 1319.

29. Flexner, *George Washington*, 2:401.

30. Lee, *Experiencing Mount Vernon*, 30.

31. Golway, *Washington's General*, 118.

32. Flexner, *George Washington*, 2:302.

33. Chernow, *Alexander Hamilton*, 89. *PWR*, 2:407. Letter to Lieutenant Colonel Joseph Reed, November 20, 1775.

34. *PWRT*, 2:41. Letter to John Adams, September 25, 1798.

35. Massachusetts Historical Society. Timothy Pickering Papers, P-31, Reel 52, p. 27.

36. Ibid., P-31, Reel 51, p. 106.

37. *WWR*, 200. Letter to Joseph Reed, January 14, 1776.

38. *WWF*, 20:293. Letter to the President of Congress, November 5, 1780.

39. Freeman, *George Washington*, 4:210.

40. *WWR*, 190. Letter to William Woodford, November 10, 1775.

41. *WWF*, 18:45. Letter to the Board of War, February 23, 1780.

42. Ibid., 14:400. "General Orders," April 17, 1779.

43. Ibid., 24:261. "General Orders," May 16, 1782.

44. *PWR*, 15:82. "General Orders," May 9, 1778.
45. *WWF*, 16:13. "General Orders," July 29, 1779.
46. *WWR*, 228. "General Orders," July 9, 1779.
47. *PWR*, 2:74. Letter to Samuel Washington, September 30, 1775.
48. *WWF*, 24:432. Letter to James McHenry, July 18, 1782.
49. Thompson, *Statements Regarding the Physical Appearance*, 12.
50. Thompson, "'As If I had Been a Very Great Somebody.'"
51. *PWR*, 9:322.
52. Ibid.
53. Ibid., 9:321–22.
54. Ibid., 9:321.
55. *WWR*, 413. Letter to Sarah Bache, January 15, 1781.
56. Stephenson, *Patriot Battles*, 177.
57. Ibid.
58. *PWCF*, 2:412. Letter to William Gordon, March 8, 1785.
59. Gaines, *For Liberty and Glory*, 15.
60. Grant, *John Adams*, 304.
61. *WWF*, 22:353. Letter to Joseph Jones, July 10, 1781.
62. Unger, *Lafayette*, 4.
63. Ibid., 7.
64. Gaines, *For Liberty and Glory*, 36.
65. Ibid., 37.
66. Unger, *Lafayette*, 30.
67. Gaines, *For Liberty and Glory*, 63.
68. Ibid., 67.
69. *PWR*, 10:602.
70. Gaines, *For Liberty and Glory*, 6.
71. Ibid., 93.
72. Ibid., 70.
73. Ibid.
74. Flexner, *George Washington*, 2:215.
75. Ibid.
76. Schiff, *Great Improvisation*, 55.
77. *PWR*, 8:382. Letter to John Hancock, February 20, 1777.
78. Isaacson, *Benjamin Franklin*, 341.

CHAPTER TWENTY-FIVE: DARKNESS VISIBLE
1. Palmer, *George Washington and Benedict Arnold*, 223.
2. Flexner, *George Washington*, 2:211.
3. *PWR*, 10:290. Letter to Major General Philip Schuyler, July 15, 1777.
4. Ibid., 10:410. Letter to John Hancock, July 25, 1777.
5. Ibid., 10:506. Letter to Jonathan Trumbull, Sr., August 4, 1777.
6. Palmer, *George Washington and Benedict Arnold*, 231.
7. Ibid., 232.
8. *PWR*, 11:52. Letter to John Hancock, August 23, 1777.
9. Ibid., 11:53.
10. Ibid., 11:51. "General Orders," August 23, 1777.
11. Gaines, *For Liberty and Glory*, 71–72.
12. *PWR*, 11:148. "General Orders," September 7, 1777.
13. Ibid., 11:157. "General Orders," September 6, 1777.
14. Lengel, *General George Washington*, 232.
15. *PWR*, 11:190.
16. Gaines, *For Liberty and Glory*, 74.
17. *PWR*, 11:199. Letter to John Hancock, September 11, 1777.
18. Freeman, *George Washington*, 4:485.
19. Flexner, *George Washington*, 2:224.
20. Unger, *Lafayette*, 50.
21. Lengel, *General George Washington*, 241.

22. *PWR*, 11:200. Letter to John Hancock, September 11, 1777.
23. Ibid.
24. *PWR*, 11:332. Letter to Brigadier General Thomas Nelson, Jr., September 27, 1777.
25. Gaines, *For Liberty and Glory*, 75.
26. Jefferson, *Writings*, 1318.
27. Rosenfeld, *American Aurora*, 336.
28. Flexner, *George Washington*, 2:229.
29. Ibid., 2:226.
30. Gaines, *For Liberty and Glory*, 75.
31. Chernow, *Alexander Hamilton*, 99.
32. Rosenfeld, *American Aurora*, 335.
33. Lengel, *General George Washington*, 247.
34. Ibid., 250.
35. Morgan, *Genius of George Washington*, 9.
36. Lengel, *General George Washington*, 251.
37. Ellis, *His Excellency*, 107.
38. *PWR*, 11:336.
39. Lengel, *General George Washington*, 254.
40. Flexner, *George Washington*, 2:233.
41. Lengel, *General George Washington*, 255.
42. Flexner, *George Washington*, 2:234.
43. Lengel, *General George Washington*, 257.
44. Custis, *Recollections and Private Memoirs of Washington*, 200.
45. *PWR*, 11:397.
46. Palmer, *George Washington and Benedict Arnold*, 245.
47. Nelson, *Thomas Paine*, 120.
48. *WWR*, 278. Letter to John Augustine Washington, October 18, 1777.
49. *PWR*, 11:409. Letter to General William Howe, October 6, 1777.
50. Ibid., 11:410.
51. Palmer, *George Washington and Benedict Arnold*, 244.
52. Wiencek, *Imperfect God*, 239.
53. *PWR*, 11:487. Letter to John Page, October 11, 1777.
54. Ibid., 11:394. Letter to John Hancock, October 5, 1777.
55. Palmer, *George Washington and Benedict Arnold*, 245.

CHAPTER TWENTY-SIX: RAPPING A DEMIGOD OVER THE KNUCKLES
1. Nelson, *Thomas Paine*, 127.
2. Golway, *Washington's General*, 148.
3. Gaines, *For Liberty and Glory*, 78.
4. Flexner, *George Washington*, 2:238.
5. Ibid., 2:212.
6. *PWR*, 10:240. Letter to John Hancock, July 10, 1777.
7. Palmer, *George Washington and Benedict Arnold*, 238.
8. Flexner, *George Washington*, 2:247.
9. *PWR*, 11:512–13. "General Orders," October 15, 1777.
10. Cunliffe, *George Washington*, 109.
11. *PWR*, 11:541. "General Orders," October 18, 1777.
12. Ibid., 11:596. Letter to John Hancock, October 24, 1777.
13. Ibid., 11:614. Letter from John Hancock, October 25, 1777.
14. Ibid., 12:21. Letter to Major General Israel Putnam, October 26, 1777.
15. Ibid., 12:93. Letter from Major General Horatio Gates, November 2, 1777.
16. Ibid., 12:27. Letter to Landon Carter, October 27, 1777.
17. Ibid., 12:243. Letter to Patrick Henry, November 13, 1777.
18. Fields, *"Worthy Partner,"* 177.

19. Ketchum, *Victory at Yorktown*, 21.
20. Schiff, *Great Improvisation*, 109.
21. *PWR*, 12:60–61. Letter to Lieutenant Colonel Alexander Hamilton, October 30, 1777.
22. Chernow, *Alexander Hamilton*, 102.
23. *PWR*, 12:141. Letter from Lieutenant Colonel Alexander Hamilton, November 6, 1777.
24. Rosenfeld, *American Aurora*, 338.
25. Unger, *Lafayette*, 61.
26. Palmer, *George Washington and Benedict Arnold*, 276.
27. Freeman, *George Washington*, 4:597.
28. Ibid., 4:547.
29. Flexner, *George Washington*, 2:241.
30. *WWR*, 275. Letter to Richard Henry Lee, October 17, 1777.
31. Ibid.
32. Ibid., 276.
33. *PWP*, 10:75. "Memorandum on General Officers," March 9, 1792.
34. Flexner, *George Washington*, 2:248.
35. *PWR*, 13:139.
36. Flexner, *George Washington*, 2:258.
37. Freeman, *George Washington*, 4:556.
38. *PWR*, 12:276. Letter from Brigadier General Thomas Conway, November 16, 1777.
39. Flexner, *George Washington*, 2:258.
40. *PWR*, 12:577. Letter from Major General Horatio Gates, December 8, 1777.
41. Flexner, *George Washington*, 2:267.
42. Ibid., 2:263.
43. Rosenfeld, *American Aurora*, 339.
44. Ibid., 340.
45. Ibid., 341.
46. Flexner, *George Washington*, 2:251.
47. *PWR*, 13:360. Letter from Major General Thomas Conway, January 27, 1778.
48. Grizzard, *George!*, 57.
49. *PWR*, 13:195–96. Letter from Major General Thomas Conway, January 10, 1778.
50. Flexner, *George Washington*, 2:265.
51. Palmer, *George Washington and Benedict Arnold*, 278.
52. *PWR*, 14:329. Letter to Patrick Henry, March 27, 1778.
53. Flexner, *George Washington*, 2:266.
54. Schutz and Adair, *Spur of Fame*, 212.
55. *WWF*, 14:385. Letter to John Jay, April 14, 1779.
56. Gaines, *For Liberty and Glory*, 100.
57. *PWR*, 16:140. Letter from Thomas Conway, July 23, 1778.

CHAPTER TWENTY-SEVEN: A DREARY KIND OF PLACE
1. Brady, *Martha Washington*, 120.
2. *PWR*, 12:669. Letter to Henry Laurens, December 22, 1777.
3. Ibid., 13:435. Letter to John Parke Custis, February 1, 1778.
4. *WWR*, 284. Letter to Henry Laurens, December 23, 1777.
5. Grizzard, *George!*, 319.
6. *WWR*, 281. "General Orders," December 17, 1777.
7. Callahan, *Henry Knox*, 127.
8. Nelson, *Thomas Paine*, 121.
9. Flexner, *George Washington*, 2:261.
10. Chinard, *George Washington as the French Knew Him*, 27.
11. Flexner, *George Washington*, 2:282.
12. Golway, *Washington's General*, 165.
13. Chinard, *George Washington as the French Knew Him*, 13.

14. Flexner, *George Washington*, 2:277.
15. Ellis, *American Creation*, 69.
16. Flexner, *George Washington*, 2:277.
17. Rosenfeld, *American Aurora*, 341.
18. Stephenson, *Patriot Battles*, 96.
19. Schutz and Adair, *Spur of Fame*, 207.
20. Smith, *John Marshall*, 63.
21. *WWR*, 282. Letter to Henry Laurens, December 23, 1777.
22. *PWR*, 18:448. Letter to Benjamin Harrison, December 18, 1778.
23. Freeman, *George Washington*, 4:571.
24. *WWR*, 299–300. Letter to John Banister, April 21, 1778.
25. *PWR*, 13:323. Letter to Brigadier General John Lacey, Jr., January 23, 1778.
26. *WWR*, 292. Letter to George Clinton, February 16, 1778.
27. Ibid., 342. Letter to James Warren, March 31, 1779.
28. Ibid., 340. Letter to George Mason, March 27, 1779.
29. Fields, *"Worthy Partner,"* 175–76.
30. Unger, *Unexpected George Washington*, 122.
31. Chernow, *Alexander Hamilton*, 107.
32. Unger, *Unexpected George Washington*, 122.
33. Flexner, *George Washington*, 2:283.
34. Fields, *"Worthy Partner,"* 177.
35. Zinoman, "Leadership and Honor, Noble and Not So," *New York Times*, October 24, 2008.
36. Addison, *Cato*, 14.
37. Ibid., 31, 87.
38. Ibid., 87, 84.
39. Unger, *Lafayette*, 55.
40. Ibid.
41. Schiff, *Great Improvisation*, 227–28.
42. Chernow, *Alexander Hamilton*, 110.
43. Stephenson, *Patriot Battles*, 148.
44. *PWR*, 12:567. Letter from Baron von Steuben, December 6, 1777.
45. Gaines, *For Liberty and Glory*, 104.
46. Flexner, *George Washington*, 2:288.
47. *PWR*, 14:287. Letter to Lieutenant Colonels Francis Barber and John Brooks, March 24, 1778.
48. Ibid., 16:152. Letter to Henry Laurens, July 24, 1778.
49. *PWP*, 10:74. "Memorandum on General Officers," March 9, 1792.
50. Wiencek, *Imperfect God*, 128.
51. Ibid., 218.
52. Ibid., 244.
53. *PWR*, 14:429. Letter from Lund Washington, April 8, 1778.
54. Ibid., 16:315. Letter to Lund Washington, August 15, 1778.
55. Ibid., 14:1. "General Orders," March 1, 1778.
56. Flexner, *George Washington*, 2:289.
57. *PWR*, 15:38–39. "General Orders," May 5, 1778.
58. Ibid., 15:39.
59. Gaines, *For Liberty and Glory*, 108.
60. Unger, *Unexpected George Washington*, 124.
61. Thompson, *"In the Hands of a Good Providence,"* 151.
62. *PWR*, 15:221. Letter to Robert Morris, May 25, 1778.

CHAPTER TWENTY-EIGHT: THE LONG RETREAT
1. *PWR*, 12:27. Letter to Landon Carter, October 27, 1777.
2. Wood, "The Making of a Disaster."
3. *PWR*, 15:262. Letter to Gouverneur Morris, May 29, 1778.
4. Ibid., 15:261.

5. Ibid., 8:289. Letter from Major General Charles Lee, February 9, 1777.

6. Rosenfeld, *American Aurora*, 345.

7. Lengel, *General George Washington*, 289.

8. Ibid., 290.

9. Flexner, *George Washington*, 2:294.

10. *PWR*, 15:403. Letter from Major General Charles Lee, June 15, 1778.

11. Ibid., 14:325. "General Orders," March 27, 1778.

12. Callahan, *Henry Knox*, 143.

13. Lengel, *General George Washington*, 291.

14. Freeman, *George Washington*, 5:16.

15. Chernow, *Alexander Hamilton*, 113.

16. *PWR*, 15:526. Letter from Major General Nathanael Greene, June 24, 1778.

17. Lengel, *General George Washington*, 293.

18. Ibid., 294.

19. *PWR*, 15:536. "General Orders," June 25, 1778.

20. Ibid., 15:541. Letter from Major General Charles Lee, June 25, 1778.

21. Ibid., 15:560.

22. Ibid., 16:4. Letter to Henry Laurens, July 1, 1778.

23. Martin, *Private Yankee Doodle*, 127.

24. Lengel, *General George Washington*, 300.

25. Flexner, *George Washington*, 2:304.

26. Chernow, *Alexander Hamilton*, 114.

27. Flexner, *George Washington*, 2:305.

28. Chernow, *Alexander Hamilton*, 114.

29. Lengel, *General George Washington*, 300.

30. Flexner, *George Washington*, 2:305.

31. Ibid.

32. Grizzard, *George!*, 184.

33. Flexner, *George Washington*, 2:306.

34. Ibid.

35. Chernow, *Alexander Hamilton*, 114.

36. *PWR*, 16:5. Letter to Henry Laurens, July 1, 1778.

37. Ibid., 16:25. Letter to John Augustine Washington, July 4, 1778.

38. Ibid., 15:583. "General Orders," June 29, 1778.

39. Flexner, *George Washington*, 2:310.

40. *PWR*, 16:35. Letter from Henry Laurens, July 7, 1778.

41. *WWF*, 13:15. Letter to Henry Laurens, October 3, 1778.

42. Flexner, *George Washington*, 2:311.

43. Ibid.

44. *PWR*, 15:594–95. Letter from Major General Charles Lee, ca. June 30, 1778.

45. Ibid., 15:595–96. Letter to Major General Charles Lee, June 30, 1778.

46. Flexner, *George Washington*, 2:312.

47. *WWF*, 13:334. Letter to John Augustine Washington, November 26, 1778.

48. Flexner, *George Washington*, 2:314.

49. *WWF*, 13:384. Letter to President Joseph Reed, December 12, 1778.

50. Wiencek, *Imperfect God*, 225.

51. Flexner, *George Washington*, 2:327.

52. Gaines, *For Liberty and Glory*, 117.

CHAPTER TWENTY-NINE: PESTS OF SOCIETY

1. Gaines, *For Liberty and Glory*, 119.

2. *PWR*, 16:38. Letter from Vice Admiral d'Estaing, July 8, 1778.

3. *WWR*, 320. Letter to Thomas Nelson, August 20, 1778.

4. Freeman, *George Washington*, 5:54.

5. *PWR*, 8:580. Letter to Major General John Sullivan, March 15, 1777.

6. Ibid., 17:111. Letter to John Augustine Washington, September 23, 1778.

7. Ibid., 16:464. Letter to Major General John Sullivan, September 1, 1778.

8. *WWR*, 321. Letter to Count d'Estaing, September 11, 1778.

9. Unger, *Lafayette*, 86.

10. Flexner, *George Washington*, 2:327.

11. *WWF*, 20:350. "General Orders," November 15, 1780.

12. Ketchum, *Victory at Yorktown*, 169.

13. *WWR*, 329. Letter to Henry Laurens, November 14, 1778.

14. Schiff, *Great Improvisation*, 247.

15. *WWR*, 329. Letter to Henry Laurens, November 14, 1778.

16. Ibid., 330.

17. Ibid., 328.

18. Ibid.

19. Morgan, *Genius of George Washington*, 15.

20. Flexner, *George Washington*, 2:330.

21. *PWR*, 18:521.

22. *WWF*, 13:336. Letter to John Augustine Washington, November 26, 1778.

23. Schiff, *Great Improvisation*, 195.

24. *WWF*, 13:383. Letter to President Joseph Reed, December 12, 1778.

25. Ibid., 13:348. Letter to President Joseph Reed, November 27, 1778.

26. Stahr, *John Jay*, 109.

27. Chinard, *George Washington as the French Knew Him*, 73.

28. Golway, *Washington's General*, 197.

29. Flexner, *George Washington*, 2:336.

30. Palmer, *George Washington and Benedict Arnold*, 291.

31. *WWF*, 13:385. Letter to President Joseph Reed, December 12, 1778.

32. Cadou, *George Washington Collection*, 75.

33. Thompson, "'As If I had Been a Very Great Somebody.'"

34. Golway, *Washington's General*, 196.

35. Callahan, *Henry Knox*, 154.

36. *WWF*, 14:27. Letter to the Committee of Conference, January 20, 1779.

37. Wiencek, *Imperfect God*, 223.

38. Ibid.

39. Stephenson, *Patriot Battles*, 188.

40. Wiencek, *Imperfect God*, 224.

41. *WWR*, 1102.

42. *WWF*, 20:341. Letter to Lieutenant Colonel John Laurens, November 12, 1780.

43. *WWR*, 338. Letter to Henry Laurens, March 20, 1779.

44. Wiencek, *Imperfect God*, 232.

45. *WWF*, 24:421. Letter to Lieutenant Colonel John Laurens, July 10, 1782.

46. *PWC*, 10:330. Letter to Edward Montagu, April 5, 1775.

47. *WWF*, 335. Letter to Lund Washington, February 24, 1779.

CHAPTER THIRTY: THE STORM THICKENS

1. Flexner, *George Washington*, 1:323.

2. *WWR*, 540. Letter to James Duane, September 7, 1783.

3. *PWR*, 18:166. Letter to Brigadier General Edward Hand, November 16, 1778.

4. Grant, *John Adams*, 163.

5. Cadou, *George Washington Collection*, 75.

6. *WWF*, 14:199. Letter to Major General Horatio Gates, March 6, 1779.

7. Ibid., 14:484. Letter to the President of Congress, May 3, 1779.

8. *WWR*, 350. "Speech to the Delaware Chiefs," May 12, 1779.

9. Ibid.

10. Ibid, 351.

11. Fields, *"Worthy Partner,"* 182.

12. *WWF*, 15:189. Letter to Major General John Sullivan, May 31, 1779.

13. *WWR*, 365. Letter to the Marquis de Lafayette, September 30, 1779.

14. Ibid.

15. *WWF*, 17:465. Letter to Philip Schuyler, January 30, 1780.

16. Lengel, *General George Washington*, 307.

17. Grizzard, *George!*, 341–42.

18. Flexner, *George Washington*, 2:229.

19. *PWP*, 10:74. "Memorandum on General Officers," March 9, 1792.

20. Wood, *Empire of Liberty*, 130.

21. Grizzard, *George!*, 344.

22. Ketchum, *Victory at Yorktown*, 47.

23. Irving, *Life of George Washington*, 413.

24. *WWF*, 15:447. Letter to the President of Congress, July 21, 1779.

25. *WWR*, 363. Letter to the Marquis de Lafayette, September 30, 1779.

26. Ibid., 374. Letter to Joseph Reed, May 28, 1780.

27. Unger, *Lafayette*, 104.

28. Cadou, *George Washington Collection*, 75.

29. Chinard, *George Washington as the French Knew Him*, 75.

30. Ibid., 74.

31. Ibid., 75.

32. Ibid.

33. *WWR*, 362–63. Letter to the Marquis de Lafayette, September 30, 1779.

34. Chinard, *George Washington as the French Knew Him*, 75.

35. Ibid.

36. Cadou, *George Washington Collection*, 76.

37. Chinard, *George Washington as the French Knew Him*, 77.

38. *WWR*, 361–63. Letter to the Marquis de Lafayette, September 30, 1779.

39. Ibid., 361.

40. Ibid., 366.

41. Ibid.

42. Ibid.

43. *WWF*, 16:274. Letter to Count d'Estaing, September 13, 1779.

44. Ibid., 17:91. Letter to John Parke Custis, November 10, 1779.

45. Ketchum, *Victory at Yorktown*, 172.

46. *WWF*, 17:423. Letter to Major General Nathanael Greene, January 22, 1780.

47. Stahr, *John Jay*, 105.

48. *WWF*, 13:21. Letter to Gouverneur Morris, October 4, 1778.

49. Ibid., 14:432. Letter to Burwell Bassett, April 22, 1779.

50. Flexner, *George Washington*, 2:359.

51. *WWF*, 17:315. Letter to Philip Schuyler, December 25, 1779.

52. Ibid., 17:293. Letter to Governor William Livingston, December 21, 1779.

53. Ibid., 17:272. Letter to John Jay, December 15, 1779.

54. Golway, *Washington's General*, 212.

55. *WWF*, 17:460. "General Orders," January 28, 1780.

56. Ketchum, *Victory at Yorktown*, 8.

57. Chernow, *Alexander Hamilton*, 127.

58. Freeman, *George Washington*, 5:144.

59. Ibid., 5:156.

60. Grant, *John Adams*, 228.

61. Thompson, *Memorandum for the Martha Washington Anniversary Committee*, 7.

62. *WWF*, 18:453. Letter to Joseph Jones, May 31, 1780.

63. Ibid.

64. Ibid., 18:436. Letter to President Joseph Reed, May 28, 1780.

65. Flexner, *George Washington*, 2:356.

66. Ibid., 2:357.

67. Ibid.

68. Brady, *Martha Washington*, 134.

69. Flexner, *George Washington*, 2:357.

70. Ibid.

71. *WWR*, 380. Letter to John Augustine Washington, July 6, 1780.

Chapter Thirty-one: The Traitor

1. Grizzard, *George!*, 201.

2. *WWF*, 18:164. "Council of War," March 27, 1780.

3. *Diaries*, 6:130–31.

4. *WWF*, 18:509. Letter to Governor Jonathan Trumbull, Sr., June 11, 1780.

5. Unger, *Lafayette*, 111.

6. Unger, *Unexpected George Washington*, 133.

7. *WWF*, 19:36. Letter to the President of Congress, June 20, 1780.

8. Ibid., 19:131. Letter to Fielding Lewis, July 6, 1780.

9. Ibid., 19:481–82. Letter to Samuel Washington, August 31, 1780.

10. Flexner, *George Washington*, 2:365.

11. Gaines, *For Liberty and Glory*, 138.

12. Flexner, *George Washington*, 2:366.

13. Stahr, *John Jay*, 110.

14. *WWF*, 14:385. Letter to John Jay, April 14, 1779.

15. Hochschild, *Bury the Chains*, 184.

16. Ibid.

17. Chernow, *Alexander Hamilton*, 138.

18. *WWF*, 20:50. Letter to the President of Congress, September 15, 1780.

19. Golway, *Washington's General*, 183.

20. Ibid., 140.

21. Ibid., 182.

22. Ibid., 183.

23. Callahan, *Henry Knox*, 165.

24. *WWF*, 20:238. "Instructions to Major General Nathanael Greene," October 22, 1780.

25. Golway, *Washington's General*, 242.

26. *WWF*, 19:236. Letter to the Marquis de Lafayette, July 22, 1780.

27. Ibid., 19:403. Letter to the President of Congress, August 20, 1780.

28. Ibid., 19:405.

29. Ketchum, *Victory at Yorktown*, 141.

30. Chinard, *George Washington as the French Knew Him*, 63.
31. Flexner, *George Washington*, 2:371.
32. Ibid., 2:371–72.
33. Palmer, *George Washington and Benedict Arnold*, 354.
34. Chinard, *George Washington as the French Knew Him*, 40.
35. *WWR*, 390. Letter to John Cadwalader, October 5, 1780.
36. Rosenfeld, *American Aurora*, 397.
37. Wetherell, "On the Trail of Benedict Arnold."
38. Palmer, *George Washington and Benedict Arnold*, 212.
39. Ibid., 249.
40. Ibid., 301.
41. Ibid., 321.
42. *PWCF*, 4:175.
43. Ibid.
44. Palmer, *George Washington and Benedict Arnold*, 326.
45. Flexner, *George Washington*, 2:383.
46. Cooper, "Out of the Spy's Stocking and into the Wash," *New York Times*, September 8, 2005.
47. Palmer, *George Washington and Benedict Arnold*, 361.
48. Flexner, *George Washington*, 2:384.
49. Ibid., 2:386.
50. Ibid.
51. Ibid., 2:388.
52. Ibid. 2:389.
53. Ibid.
54. Ibid., 2:390.
55. Chernow, *Alexander Hamilton*, 142.
56. Flexner, *George Washington*, 2:388.
57. *WWF*, 20:95. "General Orders," September 26, 1780.
58. *WWR*, 392. Letter to John Laurens, October 13, 1780.
59. Chernow, *Alexander Hamilton*, 141.
60. Flexner, *George Washington*, 2:390.
61. Ibid.
62. Chernow, *Alexander Hamilton*, 143.
63. Flexner, *George Washington*, 2:387.
64. *WWF*, 20:87. Letter to Lieutenant Colonel John Jameson, September 25, 1780.
65. Ketchum, *Victory at Yorktown*, 66.
66. Ibid., 67.
67. Flexner, *George Washington*, 2:394.
68. Chernow, *Alexander Hamilton*, 144.
69. Ketchum, *Victory at Yorktown*, 68.
70. Stephenson, *Patriot Battles*, 73.
71. Ibid.
72. Ibid.
73. Unger, *Lafayette*, 125.
74. *WWR*, 392. Letter to John Laurens, October 13, 1780.
75. *WWF*, 20:95. "General Orders," September 26, 1780.
76. Ibid., 20:151. Letter to Count de Rochambeau, October 10, 1780.
77. *WWR*, 393. Letter to John Laurens, October 13, 1780.
78. *WWF*, 20:223. Letter to Major Henry Lee, October 20, 1780.
79. Ibid., 21:255. "Instructions to Marquis de Lafayette," February 20, 1781.
80. Brookhiser, *Founding Father*, 37.

CHAPTER THIRTY-TWO: MUTINY
1. *WWF*, 20:303. "General Orders," November 6, 1780.
2. Ibid., 20:314. Letter to the President of Congress, November 7, 1780.
3. Freeman, *George Washington*, 5:232.

4. Flexner, *George Washington*, 2:398.
5. *WWF*, 20:431. "Plan for Attack on New York," November 1780.
6. Ibid., 21:62. "Circular to the New England States," January 5, 1781.
7. Gaines, *For Liberty and Glory*, 150.
8. Stephenson, *Patriot Battles*, 99.
9. *WWF*, 22:191. Letter to Brigadier General Anthony Wayne, June 9, 1781.
10. *WWR*, 414. Letter to Robert Howe at West Point, January 22, 1781.
11. *WWF*, 21:136. Letter to the President of Congress, January 23, 1781.
12. Nelson, *Thomas Paine*, 157.
13. *WWR*, 409. Letter to John Laurens, January 15, 1781.
14. Grant, *John Adams*, 267.
15. *WWF*, 21:181. Letter to John Sullivan, February 4, 1781.
16. Chernow, *Alexander Hamilton*, 151.
17. Ibid.
18. Flexner, *George Washington*, 2:411.
19. Chernow, *Alexander Hamilton*, 152.
20. Flexner, *George Washington*, 2:412.
21. Chernow, *Alexander Hamilton*, 152.
22. Flexner, *George Washington*, 2:412.
23. Ibid.
24. Ibid.
25. *WWF*, 21:491. Letter to the Marquis de Lafayette, April 22, 1781.
26. Ibid., 22:3. Letter to Lieutenant Colonel Alexander Hamilton, April 27, 1781.
27. Ibid.
28. Schutz and Adair, *Spur of Fame*, 34.
29. Ibid., 47.
30. Flexner, *George Washington*, 2:494.
31. Ibid.
32. *WWF*, 21:411. Letter to the President of Congress, April 4, 1781.
33. Flexner, *George Washington*, 2:427.
34. Higginbotham, *George Washington Reconsidered*, 280.
35. Ramsay, *Life of George Washington*, 2.
36. Flexner, *George Washington*, 2:417.
37. Freeman, *George Washington*, 5:491.
38. MTV. "Early Descriptions Ante 1800." Reminiscence of Ludwig Baron von Closen.
39. *WWF*, 21:341. Letter from Benjamin Harrison, February 25, 1781.
40. Ibid., 21:341–42. Letter to Benjamin Harrison, March 21, 1781.

CHAPTER THIRTY-THREE: PLUNDERING SCOUNDRELS
1. Wiencek, *Imperfect God*, 241.
2. Golway, *Washington's General*, 260.
3. Middlekauff, *Glorious Cause*, 494.
4. *WWF*, 21:470–71. Letter to Nathanael Greene, April 18, 1781.
5. Flexner, *George Washington*, 2:421.
6. Ibid.
7. Ibid.
8. *WWF*, 21:332. Letter to the Reverend William Gordon, March 9, 1781.
9. Ibid., 21:386. Letter to Lund Washington, March 28, 1781.
10. Freeman, *George Washington*, 5:282–83.
11. *WWR*, 420. Letter to Lund Washington, April 30, 1781.

12. Ibid.
13. Ibid., 421.
14. *WWR*, 422. "Journal of the Yorktown Campaign," n.d.
15. *WWF*, 21:378. Letter to Major General John Armstrong, March 26, 1781.
16. Unger, *Lafayette*, 134.
17. Flexner, *George Washington*, 2:429.
18. Ibid., 2:399.
19. Ibid., 2:429–30.
20. *WWR*, 402. Letter to Benjamin Franklin, December 20, 1780.
21. Flexner, *George Washington*, 2:402.
22. Ibid.
23. Ibid., 2:399.
24. Ibid.
25. Ibid.
26. Ibid., 2:401.
27. Ibid., 2:431.
28. *WWR*, 429. "Journal of Yorktown Campaign," May 31, 1781.
29. *DiariesA*, 214.
30. *WWF*, 22:171. Letter to Count de Rochambeau, June 7, 1781.
31. Ibid., 22:208. Letter to Count de Rochambeau, June 13, 1781.
32. *PWCF*, 6:415. Letter to Noah Webster, July 31, 1788.
33. Ibid., 6:414.
34. Ibid., 6:415.
35. Flexner, *George Washington*, 2:434–35.
36. Ketchum, *Victory at Yorktown*, 14.
37. Ibid., 146.
38. Chinard, *George Washington as the French Knew Him*, 65.
39. Flexner, *George Washington*, 2:435.
40. *WWR*, 440. "Journal of Yorktown Campaign," July 18, 1781.
41. *WWF*, 22:396. "Conference at Dobbs Ferry," July 19, 1781.
42. *WWR*, 442. "Journal of the Yorktown Campaign," July 20, 1781.
43. *WWF*, 22:401. Letter to the Count de Grasse, July 21, 1781.
44. Ibid., 22:402.

CHAPTER THIRTY-FOUR: THE WORLD TURNED UPSIDE DOWN
1. *WWF*, 22:450. Letter to Robert Morris, August 2, 1781.
2. Ibid., 22:457. Letter to the Count de Barras, August 3, 1781.
3. Chinard, *George Washington as the French Knew Him*, 69.
4. Ibid., 68.
5. *WWR*, 451. "Journal of Yorktown Campaign," August 14, 1781.
6. Morgan, *Genius of George Washington*, 8.
7. Ketchum, *Victory at Yorktown*, 159.
8. Rosenfeld, *American Aurora*, 415.
9. Ketchum, *Victory at Yorktown*, 162.
10. Gaines, *For Liberty and Glory*, 157.
11. Flexner, *George Washington*, 2:443.
12. Stephenson, *Patriot Battles*, 35.
13. Chinard, *George Washington as the French Knew Him*, 42.
14. Ketchum, *Victory at Yorktown*, 16.
15. Wiencek, *Imperfect God*, 250.

16. Flexner, *George Washington*, 2:446.
17. MTV. "Early Descriptions Ante 1800."
18. Chinard, *George Washington as the French Knew Him*, 67.
19. MTV. "Early Descriptions Ante 1800."
20. Unger, *Unexpected George Washington*, 135.
21. *DiariesA*, 232.
22. Ibid.
23. Ketchum, *Victory at Yorktown*, 186.
24. Ibid.
25. Flexner, *George Washington*, 2:449.
26. Ketchum, *Victory at Yorktown*, 180.
27. Ibid., 209.
28. Flexner, *George Washington*, 2:449.
29. Ibid.
30. Stephenson, *Patriot Battles*, 349.
31. Flexner, *George Washington*, 2:451.
32. Ibid.
33. Ibid., 2:452.
34. Ketchum, *Victory at Yorktown*, 208.
35. Unger, *Lafayette*, 153.
36. Flexner, *George Washington*, 2:454.
37. Freeman, *George Washington*, 5:356.
38. *DiariesA*, 243.
39. Ketchum, *Victory at Yorktown*, 227.
40. Callahan, *Henry Knox*, 185.
41. Ketchum, *Victory at Yorktown*, 235.
42. Schutz and Adair, *Spur of Fame*, 45.
43. Wiencek, *Imperfect God*, 245.
44. Flexner, *George Washington*, 2:456.
45. Stephenson, *Patriot Battles*, 72.
46. *WWR*, 459.
47. Callahan, *Henry Knox*, 176.
48. Ketchum, *Victory at Yorktown*, 194.
49. Flexner, *George Washington*, 2:457.
50. Hague, *William Pitt the Younger*, 67.
51. Callahan, *Henry Knox*, 187.
52. Stephenson, *Patriot Battles*, 352.
53. Martin, *Private Yankee Doodle*, 241.
54. Fields, *"Worthy Partner,"* 187.
55. Freeman, *George Washington*, 5:377.
56. Flexner, *George Washington*, 2:458.
57. *WWR*, 464. Letter to Charles Cornwallis, October 17, 1781.
58. Ketchum, *Victory at Yorktown*, 242.
59. Wiencek, *Imperfect God*, 247.
60. Flexner, *George Washington*, 2:460.
61. *DiariesA*, 240.
62. *WWR*, 464. Letter to Thomas McKean, October 19, 1781.
63. Ibid., 468. Letter to Thomas McKean, November 15, 1781.
64. Callahan, *Henry Knox*, 188.
65. Flexner, *George Washington*, 2:469.
66. Unger, *Lafayette*, 162.
67. Ibid., 164.
68. Unger, *Unexpected George Washington*, 138.
69. Thompson, *"In the Hands of a Good Providence,"* 116.
70. Flexner, *George Washington*, 2:471.
71. *PWRT*, 4:489. "George Washington's Last Will and Testament," July 9, 1799.
72. Brady, *George Washington's Beautiful Nelly*, 21.
73. Flexner, *George Washington*, 2:446.
74. Ibid., 471.

75. Ibid.

76. Irving, *Life of George Washington*, 558.

77. Henriques, "Saint or Shrew?"

78. Felder, *Fielding Lewis and Washington Family*, 295.

79. Conkling, *Memoirs of Mother and Wife of Washington*, 51.

CHAPTER THIRTY-FIVE: MAN OF MODERATION

1. Flexner, *George Washington*, 2:474.

2. *WWF*, 24:495–96. Letter to Chevalier de Chastellux, August 10, 1782.

3. Flexner, *George Washington*, 2:475.

4. *WWF*, 24:271. Letter to the Secretary for Foreign Affairs, May 22, 1782.

5. Ibid., 24:91. Letter to Colonel Matthias Ogden, March 28, 1782.

6. Ibid.

7. Wood, "The Making of a Disaster."

8. Grizzard, *George Washington*, 18.

9. Ibid.

10. Ibid., 19.

11. Callahan, *Henry Knox*, 193.

12. *WWF*, 24:307. Letter to Brigadier General Elias Dayton, June 4, 1782.

13. Isaacson, *Benjamin Franklin*, 413.

14. *WWF*, 24:313–14. "The Address of the Commander in Chief . . . on the Banks of the Hudson, June 5, 1782."

15. Ibid., 24:273. Letter from Colonel Lewis Nicola, May 22, 1782.

16. *WWR*, 468–69. Letter to Colonel Lewis Nicola, May 22, 1782.

17. Ibid.

18. *WWF*, 25:37. Letter to the Reverend William Smith, August 18, 1782.

19. Ibid., 25:151. Letter to James McHenry, September 12, 1782.

20. Ibid., 25:176. Letter to Thomas Paine, September 18, 1782.

21. Ibid., 25:273. Letter to Benjamin Franklin, October 18, 1782.

22. Ibid., 25:142. "General Orders," September 9, 1782.

23. Ibid., 25:179. "General Orders," September 18, 1782.

24. Ibid., 25:303. "General Orders," October 28, 1782.

25. Ibid., 24:488. "General Orders," August 7, 1782.

26. Ibid., 25:281. Letter to the Marquis de Lafayette, October 20, 1782.

27. *WWR*, 484. Letter to Nathanael Greene, February 6, 1783.

28. *WWF*, 22:497. Letter to George Walton and Richard Howley, August 13, 1781.

29. *WWR*, 479. Letter to Joseph Jones, December 14, 1782.

30. *WWF*, 25:270. Letter to James McHenry, October 17, 1782.

31. *WWR*, 481. Letter to Tench Tilghman, January 10, 1783.

32. *WWF*, 26:97. Letter to Major General William Heath, February 5, 1783.

33. Ibid., 26:26. Letter to Major General John Armstrong, January 10, 1783.

34. Ibid., 25:465. Letter to Colonel Timothy Pickering, December 25, 1782.

35. *WWR*, 473. Letter to Benjamin Lincoln, October 7, 1782.

36. *WWF*, 25:227. Letter to the Secretary at War, October 2, 1782.

37. Ibid., 26:42. Letter to John Augustine Washington, January 16, 1783.

38. Ibid., 26:43.

39. Ibid., 26:44.

40. Ibid.

41. Ibid., 26:137. Letter to David Rittenhouse, February 16, 1783.

42. Chernow, *Alexander Hamilton*, 176.

43. Ibid., 177.

44. Ibid.

45. *WWR*, 488. Letter to Alexander Hamilton, March 4, 1783.

46. Ibid., 489.

47. Chernow, *Alexander Hamilton*, 179.

48. *WWR*, 1108.

49. Ibid.

50. Flexner, *George Washington*, 2:503.

51. *WWR*, 490. "General Orders," March 11, 1783.

52. Ibid., 492. Letter to Alexander Hamilton, March 12, 1783.

53. *WWF*, 26:229.

54. *WWR*, 497. "Speech to the Officers of the Army," March 15, 1783.

55. Ibid., 498.

56. Ibid., 500.

57. Ibid.

58. Freeman, *George Washington*, 5:435.

59. Brookhiser, *Founding Father*, 45.

60. *WWR*, 501. Letter to Joseph Jones, March 18, 1783.

61. Cadou, *George Washington Collection*, 78.

62. Ibid., 215.

CHAPTER THIRTY-SIX: CLOSING THE DRAMA WITH APPLAUSE

1. Thompson, *Statements Regarding the Physical Appearance*, 32.

2. Flexner, *George Washington*, 1:192.

3. Ibid, 2:432.

4. Ibid., 2:499.

5. Brown, "The Antiquities of Dental Prothesis," *Dental Cosmos*, November 1934.

6. Flexner, *George Washington*, 2:500.

7. Henriques, *Realistic Visionary*, 154.

8. Unger, *Unexpected George Washington*, 163.

9. *WWR*, 513. "General Orders," April 18, 1783.

10. Ibid.

11. Ibid.

12. *WWF*, 26:274. Letter to Theodorick Bland, March 31, 1783.

13. Ibid., 26:370. Letter to Governor Benjamin Harrison, April 30, 1783.

14. Ibid., 26:364. Letter to Daniel Parker, April 28, 1783.

15. Hochschild, *Bury the Chains*, 102.

16. *WWF*, 26:402. "Substance of a Conference between General Washington and Sir Guy Carleton," May 6, 1783.

17. Hochschild, *Bury the Chains*, 102.

18. Wiencek, *Imperfect God*, 257.

19. Hochschild, *Bury the Chains*, 102.

20. *WWF*, 26:404. "Substance of a Conference between General Washington and Sir Guy Carleton," May 6, 1783.

21. Hochschild, *Bury the Chains*, 104.

22. Ibid., 102.

23. Wiencek, *Imperfect God*, 256.

24. *WWR*, 505. Letter to Alexander Hamilton, March 31, 1783.

25. Ibid., 509. Letter to the Marquis de Lafayette, April 5, 1783.

26. Ibid., 516. "Circular to State Governments," June 8, 1783.
27. Ibid., 516–17.
28. Ibid., 517.
29. Ibid., 517–18.
30. Ibid., 518.
31. Ibid., 520.
32. Ibid., 526.
33. Ibid.
34. *PWCF*, 1:329. Letter to Henry Knox, September 23, 1783.
35. *WWF*, 27:57. Letter to George William Fairfax, July 10, 1783.
36. Flexner, *George Washington*, 2:517.
37. Ibid.
38. *PWCF*, 1:2. Letter to Richard Varick, January 1, 1784.
39. Brady, *Martha Washington*, 143.
40. Flexner, *George Washington*, 2:519.
41. Ibid.
42. Nelson, *Thomas Paine*, 174.
43. Ibid., 175.

CHAPTER THIRTY-SEVEN: CINCINNATUS

1. Schiff, *Great Improvisation*, 317.
2. *WWR*, 543–44. "Farewell Address to the Armies of the United States," November 2, 1783.
3. Ibid., 543.
4. Brady, *Martha Washington*, 151.
5. Lee, *Experiencing Mount Vernon*, 34.
6. Weintraub, *General Washington's Christmas Farewell*, 22.
7. Flexner, *George Washington*, 2:478.
8. Freeman, *George Washington*, 5:462–63.
9. Weintraub, *General Washington's Christmas Farewell*, 69.
10. *WWF*, 27:254. Letter to Sir Guy Carleton, December 2, 1783.
11. Ibid., 27:111. Letter to Samuel Fraunces, August 18, 1783.
12. Weintraub, *General Washington's Christmas Farewell*, 85.
13. Ibid.
14. Ibid.
15. Flexner, *George Washington*, 2:524.
16. Weintraub, *General Washington's Christmas Farewell*, 86.
17. *PWCF*, 1:195.
18. Ibid.
19. Ibid., 1:196.
20. Ibid.
21. Weintraub, *General Washington's Christmas Farewell*, 131.
22. Ibid., 130.
23. Ibid., 107.
24. Ibid., 138.
25. *WWF*, 27:285.
26. Ibid., 27:286.
27. Ibid.
28. Ibid., 27:283. Letter to Baron von Steuben, December 23, 1783.
29. Flexner, *George Washington*, 2:526.
30. *WWR*, 547. "Address to Congress on Resigning Commission," December 23, 1783.
31. Flexner, *George Washington*, 2:526.
32. *WWR*, 548. "Address to Congress on Resigning Commission," December 23, 1783.
33. MTV. "Early Descriptions Ante 1800." Letter from Mary Ridout to Anne Tasker Ogle, June 16, 1784.
34. Wood, *Revolutionary Characters*, 42.

35. Weintraub, *General Washington's Christmas Farewell*, 164.
36. Kaminski, *Great and Good Man*, 28.
37. Evans, *Genius of Gilbert Stuart*, 141.
38. Burns and Dunn, *George Washington*, 27.

CHAPTER THIRTY-EIGHT: AMERICAN CELEBRITY

1. *PWCF*, 1:88. Letter to the Marquis de Lafayette, February 1, 1784.
2. Ibid., 88.
3. Ibid., 1:138. Letter to Henry Knox, February 20, 1784.
4. Ibid., 1:137–38.
5. *WWF*, 27:287–88. Letter to Governor George Clinton, December 28, 1783.
6. *PWCF*, 1:87–89. Letter to the Marquis de Lafayette, February 1, 1784.
7. Ibid., 1:121.
8. Ibid., 1:123. "To the Citizens of Fredericksburg," ca. February 14, 1784.
9. *WWR*, 552. Letter to Benjamin Harrison, January 18, 1784.
10. Ibid.
11. Brady, *Martha Washington*, 147.
12. Unger, *Unexpected George Washington*, 155.
13. *WWR*, 578. Letter to Tench Tilghman, June 2, 1785.
14. Thompson, *"In the Hands of a Good Providence,"* 9.
15. Fields, *"Worthy Partner,"* 201.
16. *PWP*, 6:547. Letter to Tobias Lear, October 10, 1790.
17. Fields, *"Worthy Partner,"* 200.
18. Unger, *Unexpected George Washington*, 141.
19. Thompson, *Memorandum for the Martha Washington Anniversary Committee*, 11.
20. Weintraub, *General Washington's Christmas*, 172.
21. *PWCF*, 3:296. Letter to Armand, October 7, 1785.
22. Ibid., 1:161. Letter to Fielding Lewis, Jr., February 24, 1784.
23. *WWR*, 555. Letter to the Marquis de Lafayette, February 1, 1784.
24. *PWCF*, 2:253. Letter to Henry Knox, January 5, 1785.
25. *WWF*, 27:2. Letter to Lund Washington, June 11, 1783.
26. *Diaries*, 4:255.
27. Lee, *Experiencing Mount Vernon*, 93.
28. *PWRT*, 3:112. Letter to Mildred Thornton Washington, October 18, 1798.
29. Chinard, *George Washington as the French Knew Him*, 83.
30. *Diaries*, 4:157. Diary entry for June 30, 1785.
31. *PWCF*, 3:275. Letter to Benjamin Franklin, September 26, 1785.
32. Schiff, *Great Improvisation*, 360.
33. *DiariesA*, 300. Diary entry for March 19, 1786.
34. MTV. "Early Descriptions Ante 1800." Isaac Weld, Jr., ca. 1796.
35. Lee, *Experiencing Mount Vernon*, 27.
36. Ibid., 28.
37. Ibid.
38. Ibid.
39. Ibid.
40. Ibid., 31.
41. Ibid.
42. Cunliffe, *George Washington*, 161.
43. Ibid.
44. Chinard, *George Washington as the French Knew Him*, 86.
45. MTV. "Early Descriptions Ante 1800."

46. Cadou, *George Washington Collection*, 240.
47. Hervey, *Memory of Washington*, 88.
48. *PWCF*, 3:381. Letter to Elizabeth French Dulany, November 23, 1785.
49. Brookhiser, *Founding Father*, 47.
50. Thompson, *"In the Hands of a Good Providence,"* 80.
51. *PWCF*, 3:63. Letter to Henry Knox, June 18, 1785.
52. Ibid., 31:71. Letter to Richard Henry Lee, June 22, 1785.
53. *DiariesA*, 280. Diary entry for June 8, 1785.
54. *WWR*, 680. Letter to the Marquis de Lafayette, May 28, 1788.
55. Ibid., 680–81.
56. Ibid., 681.
57. *WWF*, 27:238. Letter to Lieutenant Bezaleel Howe, November 9, 1783.
58. *PWCF*, 1:235. Letter to James Craik, March 25, 1784.
59. Ibid., 1:178.
60. Ibid., 2:415. Letter to John Witherspoon, March 8, 1785.
61. Ibid.
62. Ibid., 2:332. Letter to Richard Henry Lee, February 8, 1785.
63. Ibid., 2:253. Letter to Henry Knox, January 5, 1785.
64. Ibid.
65. Grizzard, *George!*, 154.
66. *WWR*, 580. Letter to David Humphreys, July 25, 1785.
67. Ibid.
68. Lee, *Experiencing Mount Vernon*, 54.
69. *WWR*, 579–80. Letter to David Humphreys, July 25, 1785.
70. *PWCF*, 3:547. Letter to Benjamin Lincoln, February 6, 1786.
71. Brady, *Martha Washington*, 151.

CHAPTER THIRTY-NINE: GENTLEMAN FARMER
1. *Diaries*, 4:184. Diary entry for August 18, 1785.
2. *WWF*, 27:305. Letter to Clement Biddle, January 17, 1784.
3. *DiariesA*, 275.
4. Lee, *Experiencing Mount Vernon*, 34.
5. Ibid., 52.
6. *WWF*, 27:298. Letter to Samuel Vaughan, January 14, 1784.
7. Freeman, *George Washington*, 6:44.
8. Ibid.
9. Maclay, *Diary of William Maclay*, 258.
10. *WWF*, 21:248. Letter to James Duane, February 19, 1781.
11. Weintraub, *General Washington's Christmas Farewell*, 115.
12. *DiariesA*, 250. Diary entry for September 12, 1784.
13. *PWCF*, 2:78. Letter to Thomas Freeman, September 23, 1784.
14. Ibid., 2:119. Letter to Jacob Read, November 3, 1784.
15. *DiariesA*, 252.
16. Unger, *Lafayette*, 260.
17. *DiariesA*, 251. Diary entry for September 14, 1784.
18. Ibid., 254.
19. Ibid., 265. Diary entry for October 4, 1784.
20. Ibid.
21. *PWCF*, 6:111. Letter to Alexander Spotswood, February 13, 1788.
22. Jackman, "Young Englishman Reports."
23. *PWCF*, 3:90. Letter to George William Fairfax, June 30, 1785.

24. *DiariesA*, xvii.
25. *PWP*, 1:161. Letter to Arthur Young, December 4, 1788.
26. Ibid.
27. Unger, *Unexpected George Washington*, 171.

CHAPTER FORTY: DEVIL'S BARGAIN
1. Hochschild, *Bury the Chains*, 156.
2. Ibid.
3. *WWR*, 1110. Letter from the Marquis de Lafayette, February 5, 1783.
4. Ibid.
5. Unger, *Lafayette*, 173.
6. Ibid., 174.
7. *PWCF*, 1:27. Letter from the Marquis de Lafayette, January 10, 1784.
8. Ibid., 2:72. Letter from La Luzerne, September 12, 1784.
9. Ibid., 2:172. Letter to La Luzerne, December 5, 1784.
10. Ibid., 1:258. Letter to Adrienne, Marquise de Lafayette, April 4, 1784.
11. Unger, *Unexpected George Washington*, 157.
12. *PWCF*, 1:189. Letter from the Marquis de Lafayette, March 9, 1784.
13. Unger, *Unexpected George Washington*, 159.
14. *PWCF*, 2:64. Letter from William Gordon, August 30, 1784.
15. Unger, *Lafayette*, 198.
16. Ibid.
17. Ibid., 200.
18. *PWCF*, 2:175. Letter to the Marquis de Lafayette, December 8, 1784.
19. Ibid., 4:43. Letter to the Marquis de Lafayette, May 10, 1786.
20. Ibid., 4:44.
21. Higginbotham, *George Washington Reconsidered*, 122.
22. *PWCF*, 3:356. Letter from James Madison, November 11, 1785.
23. *DiariesA*, 301.
24. *WWR*, 593. Letter to Robert Morris, April 12, 1786.
25. Ibid., 593–94.
26. Ibid., 594.
27. *WWR*, 607. Letter to John Francis Mercer, September 9, 1786.
28. Ibid., 608.
29. Decatur, *Private Affairs of George Washington*, 316.
30. *PWCF*, 4:465. Letter to John Francis Mercer, December 19, 1786.
31. Ibid., 5:2. Letter to John Francis Mercer, February 1, 1787.
32. Ibid., 5:10. Letter to Henry Lee, Jr., February 4, 1787.
33. *WWR*, 701–2.
34. Henriques, *Realistic Visionary*, 148.
35. Lee, *Experiencing Mount Vernon*, 68.
36. *DiariesA*, 313.
37. *Diaries*, 4:277. Diary entry for February 17, 1786.
38. *PWCF*, 2:14. Letter to Clement Biddle, July 28, 1784.
39. Wiencek, *Imperfect God*, 349.
40. Henriques, *Realistic Visionary*, 148.
41. Wiencek, *Imperfect God*, 120.
42. *PWCF*, 6:88. Letter to Henry Knox, February 5, 1788.
43. *Diaries*, 5:260. Diary entries for January 3 and 4, 1788.
44. *PWCF*, 6:88. Letter to Henry Knox, February 5, 1788.
45. *Diaries*, 5:273. Diary entry for February 6, 1788.
46. Ibid.

47. *Diaries*, 4:259. Diary entry for January 4, 1786.

CHAPTER FORTY-ONE: THE RUINS OF THE PAST
1. *PWCF*, 6:502. Letter to William Barton, September 7, 1788.
2. Flexner, *George Washington*, 2:513.
3. Isaacson, *Benjamin Franklin*, 422.
4. Callahan, *Henry Knox*, 222.
5. *PWCF*, 1:142–43. Letter from Henry Knox, February 21, 1784.
6. Ibid., 1:190. Letter from the Marquis de Lafayette, March 9, 1784.
7. Ibid., 1:260. Letter to Jonathan Trumbull, Jr., April 4, 1784.
8. Ibid., 1:288–89. Letter from Thomas Jefferson, April 16, 1784.
9. Ibid., 6:502. Letter to William Barton, September 7, 1788.
10. Ibid., 1:330. "Observations on the Institution of the Society," ca. May 4, 1784.
11. Wills, *Cincinnatus*, 144.
12. *PWCF*, 4:378. Letter to Theodorick Bland, November 18, 1786.
13. Ibid., 3:213. Letter to Arthur St. Clair, August 31, 1785.
14. *WWF*, 24:497. Letter to Elkanah Watson, August 10, 1782.
15. McCammant, *George Washington the Mason*, 5.
16. *PWCF*, 2:233. Letter to James Madison, December 28, 1784.
17. Unger, *Unexpected George Washington*, 164.
18. *WWR*, 569. Letter to Richard Henry Lee, December 14, 1784.
19. Lee, *Experiencing Mount Vernon*, 24.
20. Ibid., 25.
21. *WWR*, 571. Letter to Benjamin Harrison, January 22, 1785.
22. Ibid.
23. Ibid., 572.
24. *PWCF*, 2:399. Letter to Henry Knox, February 28, 1785.
25. Ibid., 2:163. Letter to Edmund Randolph, July 30, 1785.
26. Lee, *Experiencing Mount Vernon*, 28–29.
27. *PWCF*, 6:491. Letter to Thomas Jefferson, August 31, 1788.
28. *PWR*, 14:140. Letter to George William Fairfax, March 11, 1778.
29. Ibid., 16:235. Letter from George William Fairfax, August 3, 1778.
30. *WWR*, 573–74. Letter to George William Fairfax, February 27, 1785.
31. *PWCF*, 3:78. Letter from George William Fairfax, June 23, 1785.
32. Ibid., 4:127. Letter to George William Fairfax, June 25, 1786.
33. *WWR*, 542. Letter to Lund Washington, September 20, 1783.
34. *PWCF*, 3:374. Letter to Lund Washington, November 20, 1785.
35. *WWF*, 26:29. Letter to Lieutenant Colonel Tench Tilghman, January 10, 1783.
36. *WWR*, 602. Letter to Thomas Jefferson, August 1, 1786.
37. *PWCF*, 2:60. Letter from Nathanael Greene, August 29, 1784.
38. Ibid., 2:59.
39. Ibid.

40. Ibid., 4:283. Letter from Jeremiah Wadsworth, October 1, 1786.
41. Golway, *Washington's General*, 314.

CHAPTER FORTY-TWO: A MASTERLY HAND
1. *PWCF*, 1:8. Letter to Solms, January 3, 1784.
2. Ibid.
3. Weintraub, *General Washington's Christmas Farewell*, 125.
4. *PWCF*, 2:52. Letter from George William Fairfax, August 23, 1784.
5. Ibid., 2:53.
6. *WWR*, 576. Letter to Francis Hopkinson, May 16, 1785.
7. *PWCF*, 1:387.
8. Ibid.
9. *PWCF*, 2:177. Letter from Thomas Jefferson, December 10, 1884.
10. Cadou, *George Washington Collection*, 120.
11. *PWCF*, 3:112. Letter from Thomas Jefferson, July 10, 1785.
12. Ibid., 3:279. Letter to Jean-Antoine Houdon, September 26, 1785.
13. Cadou, *George Washington Collection*, 120.
14. Ketchum, *Victory at Yorktown*, 3.
15. *PWCF*, 3:344. Letter to the Marquis de Lafayette, November 8, 1785.
16. *WWR*, 601. Letter to Thomas Jefferson, August 1, 1786.
17. Ellis, *His Excellency: George Washington*, 169.
18. *WWR*, 588. Letter to James McHenry, August 22, 1785.
19. Chernow, *Alexander Hamilton*, 222.
20. *PWCF*, 3:423. Letter to David Stuart, November 30, 1785.
21. Ibid., 4:216. Letter to the Marquis de Lafayette, August 15, 1786.
22. *WWR*, 606. Letter to John Jay, August 15, 1786.
23. Ibid., 621. Letter to James Madison, November 5, 1786.
24. Ibid., 588. Letter to James McHenry, August 22, 1785.
25. Ibid., 606–7. Letter to John Jay, August 15, 1786.
26. Ibid., 601. Letter to Thomas Jefferson, August 1, 1786.
27. *PWCF*, 4:56. Letter to John Jay, May 18, 1786.
28. Ibid., 4:169. Letter to William Grayson, July 26, 1786.
29. *WWR*, 4:605. Letter to John Jay, August 15, 1786.
30. Chernow, *Alexander Hamilton*, 174.
31. Adams, *Life and Writings of Jared Sparks*, 1:567.
32. Chernow, *Alexander Hamilton*, 223.
33. *WWR*, 1114.
34. *PWCF*, 4:295. Letter from Henry Lee, Jr., October 17, 1786.
35. Ibid., 4:297. Letter to David Humphreys, October 22, 1786.
36. Ibid.
37. Ibid., 4:300. Letter from Henry Knox, October 23, 1786.
38. Ibid., 4:325. Letter from David Humphreys, November 1, 1786.
39. Ibid., 4:332. Letter to James Madison, November 5, 1786.
40. *WWR*, 631. Letter to David Humphreys, December 26, 1786.
41. Callahan, *Henry Knox*, 242.

CHAPTER FORTY-THREE: A HOUSE ON FIRE
1. *WWR*, 705. "Fragments of a Draft of the First Inaugural Address," January 1789.
2. *PWCF*, 4:316. Letter to the Society of the Cincinnati, October 31, 1786.
3. *WWR*, 623. Letter to James Madison, November 18, 1786.

4. Ibid., 645. Letter to Edmund Randolph, March 28, 1787.

5. Freeman, *George Washington*, 6:62.

6. *DiariesA*, 313. Diary entry for January 10, 1787.

7. *WWR*, 624. Letter to James Madison, November 18, 1786.

8. *PWCF*, 4:448. Letter from James Madison, December 7, 1786.

9. *WWR*, 624. Letter to James Madison, December 16, 1786.

10. *PWCF*, 4:474–75. Letter from James Madison, December 24, 1786.

11. *WWR*, 644. Letter to John Jay, March 10, 1787.

12. Higginbotham, *George Washington Reconsidered*, 276.

13. *WWR*, 633. Letter to David Humphreys, December 26, 1786.

14. *PWCF*, 4:529. Letter from David Humphreys, January 20, 1787.

15. Stahr, *John Jay*, 242.

16. *WWR*, 635. Letter to Henry Knox, February 3, 1787.

17. Freeman, *Washington*, 537.

18. *PWCF*, 5:52. Letter to Henry Knox, February 25, 1787.

19. *WWR*, 642. Letter to Henry Knox, March 8, 1787.

20. *PWCF*, 5:96. Letter from Henry Knox, March 19, 1787.

21. Ibid., 5:97

22. *WWR*, 645. Letter to Edmund Randolph, March 28, 1787.

23. Ibid.

24. Wood, *Revolutionary Characters*, 45.

25. *PWCF*, 5:119. Letter to Henry Knox, April 2, 1787.

26. Ibid., 5:36.

27. Ibid.

28. Conkling, *Memoirs of Mother and Wife of Washington*, 57.

29. *PWCF*, 5:33. Letter to Mary Ball Washington, February 15, 1787.

30. Ibid., 5:34.

31. Ibid., 5:35.

32. Freeman, *Washington*, 558.

33. *PWCF*, 5:157. Letter to Henry Knox, April 27, 1787.

34. Ibid., 5:171. Letter to Robert Morris, May 5, 1787.

35. Ibid.

36. Ibid., 158.

37. Ibid., 171. Letter to Robert Morris, May 5, 1787.

38. Wiencek, *Imperfect God*, 265.

39. Kaminski and McCaughan, *Great and Good Man*, 83.

40. *WWR*, 413. Letter to Sarah Bache, January 15, 1781.

41. Schiff, *A Great Improvisation*, 359.

42. *PWCF*, 5:189. Letter to George Augustine Washington, May 17, 1787.

43. Unger, *Unexpected George Washington*, 178.

44. *PWCF*, 5:186.

45. *DiariesA*, 315. Diary entry for May 18, 1787.

46. Ibid., 316. Diary entry for May 23, 1787.

47. Maxey, *Portrait of Elizabeth Willing Powel*, 26.

48. Ibid., 21.

49. *WWR*, 224. Letter to John Augustine Washington, May 31, 1776.

50. *DiariesA*, 315.

51. Isaacson, *Benjamin Franklin*, 446.

52. *DiariesA*, 317.

53. *WWR*, 708. "Fragments of a Draft of the First Inaugural Address," ca. January 1789.

54. Burns and Dunn, *George Washington*, 37.

55. Wills, *Cincinnatus*, 107.

56. *PWCF*, 5:208. Letter to Thomas Jefferson, May 30, 1787.

57. Morgan, *Genius of George Washington*, 5.

58. Kaminski and McCaughan, *Great and Good Man*, 87.

59. *PWCF*, 5:219.

CHAPTER FORTY-FOUR: RISING SUN

1. *PWCF*, 5:219. Letter to George Augustine Washington, June 3, 1787.

2. Ketcham, *James Madison*, 210.

3. Chernow, *Alexander Hamilton*, 235.

4. Ibid., 236.

5. *WWR*, 653. Letter to Alexander Hamilton, July 10, 1787.

6. *Diaries*, 5:177. Diary entry for July 22, 1787.

7. Ibid., 5:179. Diary entry for July 31, 1787.

8. Ibid.

9. *DiariesA*, 324. Diary entry for August 19, 1787.

10. *Diaries*, 5:172. Diary entry for June 30, 1787.

11. *PWCF*, 5:269. Letter to Elizabeth Willing Powel, July 23, 1787.

12. Ibid., 5:280. Letter to Elizabeth Willing Powel, July 30, 1787.

13. Callahan, *General Knox*, 262.

14. Higginbotham, *George Washington Reconsidered*, 124.

15. Wiencek, *Imperfect God*, 266.

16. Wood, "Reading the Founders' Minds."

17. Morgan, "Problem of Slavery."

18. Ibid.

19. Wood, *Empire of Liberty*, 73.

20. Ibid., 119.

21. Burns and Dunn, *George Washington*, 42.

22. *PWCF*, 5:321. Letter to George Augustine Washington, September 9, 1787.

23. Ibid., 5:400. Letter from Gouverneur Morris, October 30, 1787.

24. Monroe, *View of the Conduct of the Executive*, iv. *WWR*, 800. Letter to Gouverneur Morris, January 28, 1792.

25. *WWR*, 932. Letter to the House of Representatives, March 30, 1796.

26. Ibid., 668. Letter to the Marquis de Lafayette, February 7, 1788.

27. Ibid., 695. Letter to Edward Newenham, August 29, 1788.

28. Ibid., 669. Letter to the Marquis de Lafayette, February 7, 1788.

29. *PWP*, 2:245. Letter to Philip Schuyler, May 9, 1789.

30. Fahim, "George Washington Letter Found in Scrapbook." *New York Times*, April 27, 2007.

31. Maxey, *Portrait of Elizabeth Willing Powel*, 30.

32. Ibid.

33. Goldwin, *From Parchment to Power*, 34.

34. Brookhiser, *Founding Father*, 66.

35. Goldwin, *From Parchment to Power*, 59.

36. Cappon, *Adams-Jefferson Letters*, 196.

37. Van Doren, *Benjamin Franklin*, 753.

38. *PWCF*, 5:331. Letter to the President of Congress, September 17, 1787.

39. *Diaries*, 5:186. Diary entry for September 19, 1787.

40. *DiariesA*, 325. Diary entry for September 22, 1787.

41. *WWR*, 671. Letter to John Armstrong, April 25, 1788.

42. Ibid., 658. Letter to Henry Knox, October 15, 1787.

CHAPTER FORTY-FIVE: MOUNTING THE SEAT

1. *PWCF*, 5:425.

2. Ibid.

3. Ibid., 5:399–400. Letter from Gouverneur Morris, October 30, 1787.

4. Van Doren, *Benjamin Franklin,* 756.

5. Wills, *Cincinnatus,* 157.

6. Ibid., 173.

7. *PWCF,* 6:448. Letter to Charles Pettit, August 16, 1788.

8. *WWR,* 667. Letter to the Marquis de Lafayette, February 7, 1788.

9. Ibid., 662. Letter to Bushrod Washington, November 9, 1787.

10. MTV. "Early Descriptions Ante 1800."

11. *PWCF,* 5:383. Letter from James Madison, October 18, 1787.

12. Ibid., 5:369–70.

13. Ibid. Letter from Alexander Hamilton, October 11, 1787.

14. Ibid., 5:380. Letter to Alexander Hamilton, October 18, 1787.

15. *WWR,* 657. Letter to David Humphreys, October 10, 1787.

16. *PWCF,* 5:426. Letter to Alexander Hamilton, November 10, 1787.

17. *WWR,* 692. Letter to Alexander Hamilton, August 28, 1788.

18. *PWCF,* 5:467. Letter to David Stuart, November 30, 1787.

19. Ibid., 5:500. Letter from James Madison, December 20, 1787.

20. Ibid., 6:150. Letter from Henry Knox, March 10, 1778.

21. *WWR,* 667. Letter to Edmund Randolph, January 8, 1788.

22. Ibid., 684. Letter to the Marquis de Lafayette, June 19, 1788.

23. Ibid., 681–82. Letter to the Marquis de Lafayette, May 28, 1788.

24. *PWCF,* 6:351. Letter to James Madison, June 23, 1788.

25. Ibid., 6:339. Letter from James Madison, June 18, 1788.

26. Ibid., 6:316. Letter from Bushrod Washington, June 7, 1788.

27. Burns and Dunn, *George Washington,* 45.

28. *DiariesA,* 330.

29. *PWP,* 10:631. Letter from Edmund Randolph, August 5, 1792.

30. Ibid., 4:1. Letter to James Craik, September 8, 1789.

31. Ibid.

32. *PWP,* 10:351. "Madison's Conversations with Washington," 5[–25] May 1792.

33. *WWR,* 679. Letter to the Marquis de Lafayette, April 28, 1788.

34. *PWCF,* 5:425.

35. Kaminski and McCaughan, *Great and Good Man,* 39.

36. *WWR,* 696–97. Letter to Alexander Hamilton, October 3, 1788.

37. *PWCF,* 5:400. Letter from Gouverneur Morris, October 30, 1787.

38. Unger, *Lafayette,* 226.

39. *PWCF,* 6:444. Letter from Alexander Hamilton, August 13, 1788.

40. *WWR,* 692. Letter to Alexander Hamilton, August 28, 1788.

41. Ibid., 697. Letter to Alexander Hamilton, October 3, 1788.

42. Ibid.

43. *PWP,* 1:24. Letter from Alexander Hamilton, September 1788.

44. Ibid., 119. Letter from Alexander Hamilton, November 18, 1788.

45. *WWR,* 671. Letter to John Armstrong, April 25, 1788.

46. *PWCF,* 6:534. Letter to James Madison, September 23, 1788.

47. Ibid., 6:470. Letter from James Madison, August 24, 1788.

48. *PWP,* 1:72. Letter to Benjamin Lincoln, October 26, 1788.

49. Kaminski and McCaughan, *Great and Good Man,* 99.

50. Ibid., 97.

51. Cappon, *Adams-Jefferson Letters,* 202.

52. *PWP,* 1:166. Letter from Gouverneur Morris, December 6, 1788.

53. *PWCF,* 6:531. Letter to Henry Lee, Jr., September 22, 1788.

54. *WWR,* 717. Letter to the Marquis de Lafayette, January 29, 1789.

55. Ibid., 697. Letter to Alexander Hamilton, October 3, 1788.

56. *PWP,* 10:535. "Jefferson's Conversation with Washington," July 10, 1792.

57. Ibid., 1:262. Letter to the Marquis de Lafayette, January 29, 1789.

58. Ibid., 1:226. Letter to Henry Knox, January 1, 1789.

59. Callahan, *Henry Knox,* 273.

60. *PWCF,* 5:43. Letter to Bridget Kirk, February 20, 1787.

61. Ibid., 5:173. Letter to Lund Washington, May 7, 1787.

62. Ibid., 5:288. Letter to George Augustine Washington, August 12, 1787.

63. Ibid., 5:325. Letter to John Cannon, September 16, 1787.

64. Ibid., 6:198. Letter to Charles Lee, April 4, 1788.

65. Ibid.

66. Ibid., 6:285. Letter to Thomas Lewis, May 19, 1788.

67. Ibid., 6:352–53. Letter to David Stuart, June 23, 1788.

68. Ibid., 6:423. Letter to James Craik, August 4, 1788.

69. *PWP,* 1:203. Letter to John Cannon, December 26, 1788.

70. Ibid., 1:361–62. Letter to Richard Conway, March 4, 1789.

71. Ibid., 1:368. Letter to Richard Conway, March 6, 1789.

72. *PWCF,* 2:317. Letter to Robert Lewis & Sons, February 1, 1785.

73. *WWR,* 724. Letter to Thomas Green, March 31, 1789.

74. Ibid., 725.

CHAPTER FORTY-SIX: THE PLACE OF EXECUTION

1. *PWP,* 2:2. Letter to Henry Knox, April 1, 1789.

2. Ibid.

3. *WWR,* 735. Letter to Edward Rutledge, May 5, 1789.

4. *PWP,* 1:424. Letter to Samuel Vaughan, March 21, 1789.

5. *DiariesA,* 337.

6. *PWP,* 3:317. Letter from Charles Thomson, July 25, 1789.

7. Ibid., 2:54. "Address by Charles Thomson," April 14, 1789.

8. Ibid. p. 2:29. Letter from John Langdon, April 6, 1789.

9. Ibid., 2:56. "Address to Charles Thomson," April 14, 1789.

10. *WWR,* 730. Diary entry for April 16, 1789.

11. Fields, *"Worthy Partner,"* 213.

12. Freeman, *George Washington,* 6:166.

13. *PWP,* 2:78. "To the Delaware Society for Promoting Domestic Manufacturers," April 19–20, 1789.

14. Wood, *Revolutionary Characters*, 50.
15. Kaminski and McCaughan, *Great and Good Man*, 104.
16. Ibid., 109.
17. *PWP*, 2:102.
18. Freeman, *George Washington*, 6:175.
19. *PWP*, 2:108. "To the Ladies of Trenton," April 21, 1789.
20. *WWR*, 735. Letter to Edward Rutledge, May 5, 1789.
21. *PWP*, 2:133.
22. Ibid., 2:134.
23. Ibid.
24. Ibid.
25. Ibid.
26. *PWP*, 1:444. Letter to George Clinton, March 25, 1789.
27. *DiariesA*, 338.
28. Callahan, *Henry Knox*, 274.
29. *DiariesA*, 338. Diary entry for April 23, 1780.
30. Freeman, *George Washington*, 6:182.
31. *PWP*, 2:114.
32. Wood, *Empire of Liberty*, 56.
33. Stoll, *Samuel Adams*, 131.
34. Winik, *Great Upheaval*, 67.
35. Isenberg, *Fallen Founder*, 233.
36. *WWR*, 706. "Fragments of a Draft of the First Inaugural Address," ca. January 1789.
37. Ibid.
38. Ibid., 708.
39. Ibid., 707.
40. *WWR*, 734. Letter to James Madison, May 5, 1789.
41. Cadou, *George Washington Collection*, 216.
42. *WWR*, 718. Letter to the Marquis de Lafayette, January 29, 1789.
43. Freeman, *George Washington*, 6:191.
44. Stahr, *John Jay*, 269.
45. Freeman, *George Washington*, 6:195.
46. Burns and Dunn, *George Washington*, 47.
47. Ketcham, *James Madison*, 283.
48. Callahan, *Henry Knox*, 275.
49. Wood, *Empire of Liberty*, 64.
50. *PWP*, 2:155.
51. Ibid.
52. Cunliffe, *George Washington*, 130.
53. Ketcham, *James Madison*, 283.
54. *WWR*, 730. "First Inaugural Address," April 30, 1789.
55. Ibid., 731.
56. Ibid.
57. Ibid., 730–31.
58. *WWR*, 704. "Fragments of a Draft of the First Inaugural Address," ca. January 1789.
59. Ibid., 732. "First Inaugural Address," April 30, 1789.
60. Ibid., 733.
61. Ibid.
62. Decatur, *Private Affairs of George Washington*, 8.
63. *PWP*, 1:253. Letter from Samuel Powel, January 26, 1789.
64. Ibid., 1:281. Letter to Samuel Powel, February 5, 1789.
65. Ibid., 1:338–39. Letter from Gouverneur Morris, February 23, 1789.
66. Fields, "*Worthy Partner*," 205.
67. Ibid., 223.
68. Decatur, *Private Affairs of George Washington*, 23.
69. Brady, *Martha Washington*, 3.
70. Ibid.
71. *PWP*, 2:205.
72. Brady, *Martha Washington*, 10.

73. Decatur, *Private Affairs of George Washington*, 21.
74. Fields, "*Worthy Partner*," 215.
75. Ibid.
76. Freeman, *George Washington*, 6:213.
77. Ibid., 6:213–14.
78. Fields, "*Worthy Partner*," 220.
79. Ibid., 219.
80. Thompson, "'As If I had Been a Very Great Somebody.'"
81. Fields, "*Worthy Partner*," p.223.
82. Ibid., 224.
83. Lossing, *Martha Washington*, 22.

CHAPTER FORTY-SEVEN: ACTING THE PRESIDENCY
1. Decatur, *Private Affairs of George Washington*, 56.
2. Ibid., 333.
3. Fields, "*Worthy Partner*," 250.
4. *PWP*, 2:246–47. Letter to John Adams, May 10, 1789.
5. Henriques, *Realistic Visionary*, 51.
6. Wood, *Revolutionary Characters*, 54.
7. Hitchens, *Thomas Jefferson*, 76.
8. Burns and Dunn, *George Washington*, 56.
9. *PWP*, 3:199. Letter from David Stuart, July 14, 1789.
10. McDonald, *Presidency of George Washington*, 25–26.
11. *PWP*, 5:526. Letter to David Stuart, June 15, 1790.
12. Ibid., 3:322. Letter to David Stuart, July 26, 1789.
13. Ibid., 3:323.
14. Ibid., 2:282. Letter to James Madison, May 12, 1789.
15. Ibid., 2:213. Letter from Alexander Hamilton, May 5, 1789.
16. Ibid., 10:655. Letter to James McHenry, August 13, 1792.
17. Ibid., 2:247.
18. Schutz and Adair, *Spur of Fame*, 101.
19. Sullivan, *Public Men of the Revolution*, 120.
20. Decatur, *Private Affairs of George Washington*, 68.
21. *WWR*, 763. Letter to David Stuart, June 15, 1790.
22. Chernow, *Alexander Hamilton*, 279.
23. Brady, *Martha Washington*, 167.
24. Cadou, *George Washington Collection*, 129.
25. Sullivan, *Public Men of the Revolution*, 117.
26. Chinard, *George Washington as the French Knew Him*, 120.
27. *Diaries*, 6:54. Diary entry for March 26, 1790.
28. Unger, *Unexpected George Washington*, 245.
29. Decatur, *Private Affairs of George Washington*, 45.
30. Maclay, *Diary of William Maclay*, 83.
31. Ibid., 74.
32. Ibid., 258.
33. Ibid., 137.
34. Ibid.
35. Ibid., 212.
36. Ibid.
37. Decatur, *Private Affairs of George Washington*, 123.
38. Maclay, *Diary of William Maclay*, 261.
39. Ibid., 365–66.
40. *WWR*, 762–63. Letter to David Stuart, June 15, 1790.
41. *PWP*, 11:182. "Thomas Jefferson's Conversation with Washington," October 1, 1792.
42. Ibid., 12:107. "Thomas Jefferson's Notes on a Conversation with Washington," February 7, 1793.
43. Ibid., 2:248. Letter to George Augustine Washington, May 3, 1789.
44. Decatur, *Private Affairs of George Washington*, 51.
45. Ibid., 116.
46. *PWP*, 2:248.

47. Decatur, *Private Affairs of George Washington*, 116.
48. *PWP*, 4:336.
49. Cadou, *George Washington Collection*, 144.
50. *PWRT*, 2:490. Letter to William Fitzhugh, August 5, 1798.
51. Wood, *Revolutionary Characters*, 52.
52. Burstein, *Original Knickerbocker*, 7.
53. *PWP*, 3:199. Letter from David Stuart, July 14, 1789.
54. Stahr, *John Jay*, 226.
55. Maclay, *Diary of William Maclay*, 34.

CHAPTER FORTY-EIGHT: THE CARES OF OFFICE
1. *DiariesA*, 297.
2. Flexner, *George Washington*, 3:212.
3. Ibid.
4. Ibid.
5. *PWP*, 3:77.
6. Ibid., 3:112. Letter to James McHenry, July 3, 1789.
7. Brady, *Martha Washington*, 167.
8. *PWP*, 4:1. Letter to James Craik, September 8, 1789.
9. Thompson, *Memorandum for the Martha Washington Anniversary Committee*, 15.
10. *PWP*, 4:1. Letter to James Craik, September 8, 1789.
11. Ibid.
12. Henriques, "Saint or Shrew?"
13. *WWR*, 740. Letter to Betty Washington Lewis, September 13, 1789.
14. *PWP*, 1:368. Letter to Richard Conway, March 6, 1789.
15. Adams, *Life and Writings of Jared Sparks*, 2:28.
16. *WWR*, 741. Letter to Betty Washington Lewis, September 13, 1789.
17. Ibid.
18. *PWP*, 4:35.
19. Maclay, *Diary of William Maclay*, 121.
20. Decatur, *Private Affairs of George Washington*, 59.
21. Ibid.
22. Maclay, *Diary of William Maclay*, 128.
23. Ibid., 129.
24. Ibid., 130.
25. Ibid.
26. Ibid., 386.
27. Guerrero, *John Adams' Vice-Presidency*, 183.
28. Ibid., 185.
29. Wood, *Revolutionary Characters*, 175.
30. Cunliffe, *George Washington*, 175.
31. Irving, *Life of George Washington*, 575.

CHAPTER FORTY-NINE: RAYS OF GENIUS
1. Maclay, *Diary of William Maclay*, 353.
2. Burns and Dunn, *George Washington*, 74.
3. Ibid.
4. *PWP*, 1:352. Letter to Thomas Barclay, March 2, 1789.
5. Ketcham, *James Madison*, 286.
6. McDonald, *Presidency of George Washington*, 27.
7. Chernow, *Alexander Hamilton*, 289.
8. Ellis, *His Excellency: George Washington*, 198.
9. Burns and Dunn, *George Washington*, 74.
10. *PWCF*, 2:253. Letter to Henry Knox, January 5, 1785.
11. Callahan, *Henry Knox*, 287.
12. Ibid., 281.
13. Ketcham, *James Madison*, 287.
14. *PWP*, 1:441. Letter from H.Z., March 24, 1789.
15. Adams, *Life and Writings of Jared Sparks*, 1:560.
16. *WWR*, 597. Letter to the Marquis de Lafayette, May 10, 1786.

17. *PWP*, 4:413. Letter from Thomas Jefferson, December 15, 1787.
18. *WWR*, 754–55. Letter to Thomas Jefferson, January 21, 1790.
19. Hitchens, *Thomas Jefferson*, 70
20. *PWCF*, 6:256. Letter from Thomas Jefferson, May 2, 1788.
21. Wills, *Cincinnatus*, 199.
22. Jefferson, *Writings*, 1319.
23. Ibid., 1321.
24. Thompson, *Memorandum for the Martha Washington Anniversary Committee*, 20.
25. Jefferson, *Writings*, 1319.
26. Ibid., 1320.
27. Schiff, *Great Improvisation*, 403.
28. Jackman, "Young Englishman Reports."
29. Burns and Dunn, *George Washington*, 55.
30. *PWP*, 4:67. Letter to James Madison, ca. September 23, 1789.
31. *PWCF*, 6:316. Letter from Bushrod Washington, June 7, 1788.
32. Burns and Dunn, *George Washington*, 72.
33. Ibid.
34. *PWP*, 4:78. Letter to John Jay, October 5, 1789.
35. *WWF*, 25:274. Letter to John Jay, October 18, 1782.
36. *PWP*, 4:137. Letter to John Jay, October 5, 1789.
37. McDonald, *Presidency of George Washington*, 40.
38. Wood, *Empire of Liberty*, 86.
39. Burns and Dunn, *George Washington*, 70.
40. *PWP*, 10:455. Letter from Henry Lee, June 15, 1792.
41. Flexner, *George Washington*, 2:550.
42. Decatur, *Private Affairs of George Washington*, 268.
43. *PWP*, 2:248.
44. *WWR*, 752. Letter to Catharine Macaulay Graham, January 9, 1790.
45. Chernow, *Alexander Hamilton*, 290.
46. Marshall, *Life of George Washington*, 467.
47. Wiencek, *Imperfect God*, 188.
48. Jefferson, *Writings*, 1318.
49. Ibid.
50. *WWF*, 35:138. Letter to the Secretary of War, July 13, 1796.
51. Brookhiser, *Founding Father*, 78–79.
52. *WWF*, 35:296. Letter to George Washington Parke Custis, November 28, 1796.
53. Wills, *Cincinnatus*, 100.
54. *WWR*, 662–63. Letter to Bushrod Washington, November 9, 1787.
55. Thompson, "*In the Hands of a Good Providence*," 8.
56. *WWF*, 33:319. Letter to James McHenry, April 8, 1794.
57. *PWCF*, 4:211. Letter to Theodorick Bland, August 15, 1786.
58. Freeman, *George Washington*, 7:493.
59. *PWRT*, 1:219. Letter to David Humphreys, June 26, 1797.
60. *WWR*, 823. Letter to John Francis Mercer, September 26, 1792.
61. Ibid., 699. Letter to Benjamin Lincoln, October 26, 1788.
62. Ibid., 712. "Fragments of a Draft of the First Inaugural Address," ca. January 1789.
63. *PWP*, 1:244. Letter from James Madison, January 14, 1789.
64. Ibid., 2:419. Letter to James Madison, ca. May 31, 1789.

65. Leibiger, *Founding Friendship*, 121.
66. *PWP*, 4:176. Letter to Gouverneur Morris, October 13, 1789.

CHAPTER FIFTY: THE TRAVELING PRESIDENCY
1. *WWR*, 737–38. Letter to John Adams, May 10, 1789.
2. *PWP*, 4:132. "Thanksgiving Proclamation," October 3, 1789.
3. Jefferson, *Writings*, 1319.
4. *Diaries*, 5:464. Diary entry for October 17, 1789.
5. *DiariesA*, 348. Diary entry for October 21, 1789.
6. Ibid., 349. Diary entry for October 23, 1789.
7. Irving, *Life of George Washington*, 562.
8. Ibid., 563.
9. *DiariesA*, 350. Diary entry for October 24, 1789.
10. *Diaries*, 5:475.
11. *DiariesA*, 351. Diary entry for October 25, 1789.
12. *PWP*, 4:228. Letter from John Hancock, October 26, 1789.
13. Ibid., 162. Letter to Betty Washington Lewis, October 12, 1789.
14. Ibid., 162–63.
15. Decatur, *Private Affairs of George Washington*, 83.
16. Miles, *George and Martha Washington*, 21.
17. *DiariesA*, 352.
18. Ibid. Diary entry for October 28, 1789.
19. Thompson, *Statements Regarding the Physical Appearance*, 48.
20. *Diaries*, 5:480–81.
21. Chernow, *Alexander Hamilton*, 278.
22. *DiariesA*, 353. Diary entry for October 29, 1789.
23. Ibid.
24. Ibid., 356. Diary entry for November 3, 1789.
25. Ibid., Diary entry for November 5, 1789.
26. Ibid., 357. Diary entry for November 6, 1789.
27. Freeman, *George Washington*, 6:245.
28. *DiariesA*, 358. Diary entry for November 13, 1789.
29. Ibid., 333.
30. Ibid., 341.
31. *PWP*, 9:217. Letter to Lafayette, November 21, 1791.
32. Miles, *George and Martha Washington*, 25.
33. Cadou, *George Washington Collection*, 134.
34. Custis, *Recollections and Private Memoirs of Washington*, 408.
35. Irving, *Life of George Washington*, 617.
36. Miles, *George and Martha Washington*, 17.
37. Barratt and Miles, *Gilbert Stuart*, 191.
38. Brookhiser, *Founding Father*, 165.
39. Wiencek, *Imperfect God*, 7.
40. Decatur, *Private Affairs of George Washington*, 310.
41. Custis, *Recollections and Private Memoirs of Washington*, 41.
42. *PWRT*, 2:324. Letter to George Washington Parke Custis, June 13, 1798.
43. *PWP*, 8:52.
44. *Diaries*, 6:26.
45. *PWP*, 5:193. Letter to Gouverneur Morris, March 1, 1790.

CHAPTER FIFTY-ONE: THE STATE OF THE PRESIDENT
1. Maclay, *Diary of William Maclay*, 179.
2. *WWR*, 749. "First Annual Message to Congress," January 8, 1790.
3. Maclay, *Diary of William Maclay*, 182.

4. Irving, *Life of George Washington*, 572.
5. *WWR*, 503. Letter to Lund Washington, March 19, 1783.
6. *PWCF*, 5:411–12. Letter to David Stuart, November 5, 1787.
7. Chernow, *Alexander Hamilton*, 297.
8. Burns and Dunn, *George Washington*, 79.
9. Adams, *Life and Writings of Jared Sparks*, 1:565.
10. *WWR*, 502. Letter to Joseph Jones, March 18, 1783.
11. *WWF*, 26:446–47. "General Orders," May 21, 1783.
12. *WWR*, 757. Letter to David Stuart, March 28, 1790.
13. Ibid., 756.
14. Ibid., 760. Letter to David Stuart, June 15, 1780.
15. *PWP*, 4:266. "To the Society of Quakers," ca. October 1789.
16. *WWR*, 1118.
17. Bordewich, *Washington*, 39.
18. Winik, *Great Upheaval*, 277.
19. *DiariesA*, 367. Diary entry for March 16, 1790.
20. *WWR*, 758. Letter to David Stuart, March 28, 1790.
21. Ibid., 761. Letter to David Stuart, June 15, 1790.
22. Fountain, "Observatory," *New York Times*, January 17, 2006.
23. *PWP*, 5:388. Letter from Henry Hill, May 7, 1790.
24. Van Doren, *Benjamin Franklin*, 780.
25. Schiff, *Great Improvisation*, 403.
26. *Diaries*, 6:56. Diary entry for April 4, 1790.
27. *PWP*, 5:394.
28. Ibid.
29. Ibid.
30. Ibid., 5:395.
31. Ibid., 5:393.
32. Ibid., 5:394.
33. Ibid.
34. *DiariesA*, 373.
35. Ibid.
36. Unger, *Unexpected Washington*, 200.
37. *DiariesA*, 373.
38. *PWP*, 5:397.
39. Ibid., 5:469. Letter to the Marquis de Lafayette, June 3, 1790.
40. Fields, *"Worthy Partner,"* 226.
41. *PWP*, 5:396.
42. Ibid., 5:397.
43. Chernow, *Alexander Hamilton*, 323.
44. *PWP*, 5:527. Letter to David Stuart, June 15, 1790.
45. Ibid.
46. Ibid., 5:469. Letter to the Marquis de Lafayette, June 3, 1790.
47. Decatur, *Private Affairs of George Washington*, 133.
48. *PWP*, 8:327.
49. Unger, *Unexpected George Washington*, 201.

CHAPTER FIFTY-TWO: CAPITAL MATTERS
1. *WWR*, 796–97. Letter to Arthur Young, December 5, 1791.
2. Ketcham, *James Madison*, 309.
3. *WWR*, 761. Letter to David Stuart, June 15, 1790.
4. Ibid.
5. Bordewich, *Washington*, 29.
6. Maclay, *Diary of William Maclay*, 257.
7. Chernow, *Alexander Hamilton*, 319.
8. Ibid., 328.
9. *PWP*, 11:98. Letter from Thomas Jefferson, September 9, 1792.

10. Maclay, *Diary of William Maclay*, 21.
11. *PWP*, 6:72.
12. Schutz and Adair, *Spur of Fame*, 105.
13. Maclay, *Diary of William Maclay*, 368.
14. Thompson, *"In the Hands of a Good Providence,"* 159.
15. Ibid.
16. *PWP*, 6:285. "To the Hebrew Congregation in Newport, Rhode Island," August 18, 1790.
17. Ibid., 5:448. Letter to the Savannah, Georgia, Hebrew Congregation, ca. May 1790.
18. Ibid., 6:303.
19. Freeman, *George Washington*, 6:279.
20. *PWP*, 6:681. Letter from Tobias Lear, November 21, 1790.
21. Ibid., 6:105. Letter to Clement Biddle, July 20, 1790.
22. Decatur, *Private Affairs of George Washington*, 169.
23. Cadou, *George Washington Collection*, 154.
24. *WWR*, 768. "Second Annual Message to Congress," December 8, 1790.
25. Chernow, *Alexander Hamilton*, 342.
26. Maclay, *Diary of William Maclay*, 377.
27. Decatur, *Private Affairs of George Washington*, 136.
28. *PWP*, 6:606. Letter from Tobias Lear, October 31, 1790.
29. Ibid., 6:409. Letter to Tobias Lear, September 9, 1790.
30. Ibid., 6:682. Letter to Tobias Lear, November 22, 1790.
31. Ibid., 8:85. Letter to Tobias Lear, April 12, 1791.
32. Ibid.
33. Ibid.
34. Fields, *"Worthy Partner,"* 230.
35. *PWP*, 8:85. Letter to Tobias Lear, April 12, 1791.
36. Ibid., 8:132. Letter from Tobias Lear, April 24, 1791.
37. Ibid.
38. Ibid., 8:232. Letter from Tobias Lear, June 5, 1791.
39. Schwarz, *Slavery at the Home of George Washington*, 36.
40. Decatur, *Private Affairs of George Washington*, 254.
41. *PWP*, 11:229. Letter to Anthony Whitting, October 14, 1792.
42. Ibid., 10:461. Letter to Arthur Young, June 18, 1792.
43. Henriques, *Realistic Visionary*, 151.
44. Fields, *"Worthy Partner,"* 233.
45. Henriques, *Realistic Visionary*, 150.
46. *PWP*, 11:229. Letter to Anthony Whitting, October 14, 1792.
47. Ibid., 11:333. Letter to Anthony Whitting, November 4, 1792.
48. Ibid., 11:401. Letter to Anthony Whitting, November 18, 1792.
49. *WWF*, 34:12. Letter to William Pearce, November 2, 1794.
50. Ibid., 35:34. Letter to William Pearce, May 1, 1796.
51. Henriques, *Realistic Visionary*, 149.
52. *PWP*, 11:461. Letter to Anthony Whitting, December 2, 1792.
53. Henriques, *Realistic Visionary*, 154.

CHAPTER FIFTY-THREE: SOUTHERN EXPOSURE
1. *Diaries*, 6:9. Diary entry for January 18, 1790.
2. *PWP*, 7:355. Letter to John Greenwood, February 16, 1791.
3. Ibid., 8:515. Letter from John Greenwood, September 10, 1791.
4. *WWR*, 985. Letter to John Greenwood, January 20, 1797.
5. Ibid., 986.
6. *PWRT*, 3:245. Letter to John Greenwood, December 7, 1798.

7. Ibid.
8. *PWRT*, 3:289. Letter from John Greenwood, December 28, 1798.
9. Ketchum, *Victory at Yorktown*, 166.
10. Decatur, *Private Affairs of George Washington*, 195.
11. Chernow, *Alexander Hamilton*, 362.
12. Decatur, *Private Affairs of George Washington*, 179.
13. Ibid., 177.
14. Ibid., 200.
15. Ibid., 173.
16. Chinard, *George Washington as the French Knew Him*, 94.
17. Miles, *George and Martha Washington*, 20.
18. *PWRT*, 3:243. Letter to Elizabeth Willing Powel, December 4, 1798.
19. Ibid., 3:242. Letter from Elizabeth Willing Powel, December 3, 1798.
20. Decatur, *Private Affairs of George Washington*, 311.
21. *PWRT*, 1:130. Letter to Mary White Morris, May 1, 1797.
22. *WWR*, 824. Letter to Elizabeth Washington Lewis, October 7, 1792.
23. Burns and Dunn, *George Washington*, 81.
24. Cappon, *Adams-Jefferson Letters*, 401.
25. *PWRT*, 1:392. Letter to Elizabeth Foote Washington, October 8, 1797.
26. *PWP*, 7:396.
27. Ibid., 7:357. Letter to Alexander Hamilton, February 16, 1791.
28. Freeman, *George Washington*, 6:293.
29. Cappon, *Adams-Jefferson Letters*, 363.
30. *PWP*, 8:359. Letter to David Humphreys, July 20, 1791.
31. Ibid., 5:236. Letter from David Stuart, March 15, 1790.
32. Ibid., 6:274.
33. Freeman, *George Washington*, 6:307.
34. *PWP*, 8:277. Letter to Tobias Lear, June 19, 1791.
35. *Diaries*, 6:107.
36. Ibid., 6:112. Diary entry for April 15, 1791.
37. Ibid., 6:113. Diary entry for April 16, 1791.
38. Ibid., 112.
39. *DiariesA*, 383. Diary entry for April 20, 1791.
40. *PWP*, 8:73–74.
41. *Diaries*, 6:120.
42. McCammant, *George Washington the Mason*, 11.
43. *Diaries*, 6:128.
44. Chinard, *George Washington as the French Knew Him*, xvi.
45. *DiariesA*, 385. Diary entry for May 3, 1791.
46. Ibid., 385–86. Diary entry for May 5, 1791.
47. *Diaries*, 6:125.
48. *PWP*, 8:183. Letter to Tobias Lear, May 14, 1791.
49. *DiariesA*, 387.
50. *Diaries*, 6:142.
51. *DiariesA*, 387. Diary entry for May 19, 1791.
52. *Diaries*, 6:154. Diary entry for June 2, 1791.
53. *DiariesA*, 391. Diary entry for June 4, 1791.
54. *PWP*, 8:357–58. Letter to Catharine Sawbridge Macaulay Graham, July 19, 1791.
55. Ibid., 8:358. Letter to David Humphreys, July 20, 1791.
56. Ibid., 8:415. Letter to William Moultrie, August 9, 1791.
57. Ibid., 8:327.

CHAPTER FIFTY-FOUR: RUNNING INTO EXTREMES
1. *WWR*, 589. Letter to James McHenry, August 22, 1785.
2. Grant, *John Adams*, 366.

3. Chernow, *Alexander Hamilton*, 294.
4. *Diaries*, 6:87–88. Diary entry for July 8, 1790.
5. *DiariesA*, 377. Diary entry for July 14, 1790.
6. *PWP*, 6:83.
7. Jackman, "Young Englishman Reports."
8. *PWCF*, 5:359. Letter from the Marquis de Lafayette, October 9, 1787.
9. Ketchum, *Victory at Yorktown*, 49.
10. *WWR*, 375. Letter to Joseph Reed, May 28, 1780.
11. *PWCF*, 6:137. Letter to James Madison, March 2, 1788.
12. *WWR*, 683. Letter to the Marquis de Lafayette, June 19, 1788.
13. Unger, *Lafayette*, 234.
14. Weber, *Queen of Fashion*, 200.
15. *PWP*, 5:241. Letter from the Marquis de Lafayette, March 17, 1790.
16. Ibid., 5:243.
17. *WWR*, 746. Letter to Gouverneur Morris, October 13, 1789.
18. *PWP*, 4:567. Letter from the Marquis de Lafayette, January 12, 1790.
19. Ibid., 6:231. Letter to Rochambeau, August 10, 1790.
20. Ibid., 6:233. Letter to Lafayette, August 11, 1790.
21. Unger, *Lafayette*, 263.
22. *PWP*, 6:317. Letter from Lafayette, August 23, 1790.
23. Nelson, *Thomas Paine*, 210.
24. Hitchens, *Thomas Jefferson*, 84.
25. Nelson, *Thomas Paine*, 217.
26. Ibid., 216.
27. *PWP*, 10:88.
28. Weber, *Queen of Fashion*, 239.
29. *WWR*, 780. Letter to Lafayette, July 28, 1791.
30. Unger, *Lafayette*, 277
31. *PWP*, 8:24. "Agreement of the Proprietors of the Federal District," March 30, 1791.
32. Berg, *Grand Avenues*, 103.
33. Bordewich, *Washington*, 73.
34. *PWP*, 8:288. Letter from Pierre-Charles L'Enfant, June 22, 1791.
35. Ibid., 4:15. Letter from Pierre-Charles L'Enfant, September 11, 1789.
36. Berg, *Grand Avenues*, 103.
37. MTV. "Early Descriptions Ante 1800."
38. *WWR*, 785. Letter to Tobias Lear, October 14, 1791.
39. Ibid., 787. "Third Annual Message to Congress," October 25, 1791.
40. *PWP*, 9:239. Letter to Thomas Jefferson, November 30, 1791.
41. Ibid., 245. Letter to Pierre-Charles L'Enfant, December 2, 1791.
42. Berg, *Grand Avenues*, 175.
43. *PWP*, 9:469. Letter to Thomas Jefferson, January 18, 1792.
44. Schutz and Adair, *Spur of Fame*, 103.
45. *PWP*, 10:18. Letter to Thomas Jefferson, March 4, 1792.
46. Bordewich, *Washington*, 101.
47. *WWR*, 745. Letter to Arthur St.Clair, October 6, 1789.
48. Callahan, *Henry Knox*, 317.
49. *WWR*, 768. Letter to Henry Knox, November 19, 1790.
50. *PWP*, 8:275.
51. Ibid., 360. Letter to David Humphreys, July 20, 1791.
52. *WWR*, 774. "To the Chiefs of the Seneca Nation," December 29, 1790.
53. Callahan, *Henry Knox*, 319.

54. *WWR*, 687. Letter to Richard Henderson, June 19, 1788.
55. Kohn, *Eagle and Sword*, 115.
56. Ibid.
57. Freeman, *George Washington*, 6:336.
58. *PWP*, 9:275.
59. Ibid., 10:71. "Thomas Jefferson's Memorandum of a Meeting of the Heads of the Executive Departments," March 9, 1792.
60. Ibid., 10:156.
61. Kohn, *Eagle and Sword*, 116.
62. *PWP*, 9:505.
63. Ibid., 10:169.
64. Ibid.
65. Callahan, *Henry Knox*, 322.

CHAPTER FIFTY-FIVE: A TISSUE OF MACHINATIONS
1. *PWP*, 5:468. Letter to the Marquis de Lafayette, June 3, 1790.
2. Ellis, *American Creation*, 165.
3. Ibid., 173.
4. *PWP*, 8:185. Letter from Thomas Jefferson, May 15, 1791.
5. Wilentz, *Rise of American Democracy*, 49.
6. McDonald, *Presidency of George Washington*, 92.
7. *Diaries*, 6:12. Diary entry for January 22, 1790.
8. Decatur, *Private Affairs of George Washington*, 266.
9. Burns and Dunn, *George Washington*, 84.
10. Ibid., 87.
11. Ibid.
12. *PWP*, 8:359. Letter to David Humphreys, July 20, 1791.
13. Chernow, *Alexander Hamilton*, 357.
14. Ibid., 358.
15. Ibid., 359.
16. Ibid.
17. Ibid.
18. Ibid., 380.
19. Ibid., 381.
20. Ibid.
21. Ibid., 382.
22. Fleming, "Wall Street's First Collapse."
23. *PWP*, 5:355. Letter from Lund Washington, April 28, 1790.
24. Berg, *Grand Avenues*, 188.
25. *PWP*, 9:483. Letter from "Anonymous," ca. January 1792.
26. Ibid., 10:174. Letter from "Anonymous," March 1792.
27. Ibid.
28. *PWP*, 10:6–7. "Thomas Jefferson's Memorandum of Conversations with Washington," March 1, 1792.
29. Ibid., 10:8.
30. Ellis, *American Creation*, 192.
31. *PWP*, 10:8. "Thomas Jefferson's Memorandum of Conversations with Washington," March 1, 1792.
32. Ibid.
33. Chernow, *Alexander Hamilton*, 400.
34. Decatur, *Private Affairs of George Washington*, 268.
35. Wiencek, *Imperfect God*, 362.
36. *PWP*, 10:314. Letter to Elizabeth Willing Powel, April 23, 1792.
37. Ibid., 10:349. "Madison's Conversations with Washington," May 5, 1792.
38. Ibid., 10:350.
39. Ibid., 10:352.
40. Ibid., 10:351.

41. Ibid., 10:400. Letter to James Madison, May 20, 1792.
42. Ibid., 10:401.
43. Brookhiser, *Founding Father*, 84.
44. *PWP*, 10:410. Letter from Thomas Jefferson, May 23, 1792.
45. Ibid., 10:412.
46. Chernow, *Alexander Hamilton*, 401.
47. *PWP*, 10:479. Letter from James Madison, June 20, 1792.
48. Chernow, *Alexander Hamilton*, 402.
49. *PWP*, 10:535. "Jefferson's Conversation with Washington," July 10, 1792.
50. Ibid., 10:536.
51. Ibid., 558. Letter from Tobias Lear, July 21, 1792.
52. Ibid., 10:624. Letter from Tobias Lear, August 5, 1792.
53. Ibid., 10:631. Letter from Edmund Randolph, August 5, 1792.
54. Chernow, *Alexander Hamilton*, 403.
55. *WWR*, 809. Letter to Alexander Hamilton, July 29, 1792.
56. Ibid., 811.
57. *PWP*, 10:594. Letter from Alexander Hamilton, July 30, 1792.
58. Ibid., 11:12–13. Letter from Alexander Hamilton, August 18, 1792.
59. Ibid., 11:45–46. Letter to Edmund Randolph, August 26, 1792.
60. *WWR*, 819. Letter to Alexander Hamilton, August 26, 1792.
61. Ibid.
62. Ibid., 820.
63. Ibid., 818. Letter to Thomas Jefferson, August 23, 1792.
64. *PWP*, 11:92. Letter from Alexander Hamilton, September 9, 1792.
65. Ibid.
66. Ibid., 11:104. Letter from Thomas Jefferson, September 9, 1792.
67. Ibid., 11:182. "Thomas Jefferson's Conversation with Washington," October 1, 1792.
68. Ibid., 11:183.
69. Ibid.
70. Ibid. 11:183–84.
71. Ibid., 11:184.
72. Ibid.
73. Ibid., 11:185.
74. Ibid.
75. Chernow, *Alexander Hamilton*, 408.
76. *PWP*, 11:396. Letter from Elizabeth Willing Powel, November 17, 1792.

CHAPTER FIFTY-SIX: CITIZEN GENET

1. *PWP*, 12:30. Letter to Henry Lee, January 20, 1793.
2. Ibid., 11:511. "Thomas Jefferson's Conversations with Washington," December 13, 1792.
3. Ibid., 13:472. Letter from William Gordon, August 17, 1793.
4. Chernow, *Alexander Hamilton*, 424.
5. *PWCF*, 6:355. Letter to Mathew Carey, June 25, 1788.
6. *PWP*, 11:245. Letter to Gouverneur Morris, October 20, 1792.
7. Decatur, *Private Affairs of George Washington*, 302.
8. *PWP*, 12:106. "Thomas Jefferson's Notes on a Conversation with Washington," February 7, 1793.
9. Schiff, *Great Improvisation*, 406.
10. Rosenfeld, *American Aurora*, 30.
11. *PWRT*, 1:408. Letter to William Gordon, October 15, 1797.
12. *WWF*, 17:225. Letter to Governor William Livingston, December 7, 1779.
13. *PWP*, 13:261. Letter to Henry Lee, July 21, 1793.
14. *WWR*, 834–35. Letter to Frances Bassett Washington, February 24, 1793.
15. *PWP*, 12:363. Letter to David Humphreys, March 23, 1793.
16. Unger, *Unexpected George Washington*, 217.
17. *PWP*, 12:242. "Cabinet Opinion on the Administration of the Presidential Oath," March 1, 1793.
18. Ibid., 12:265.
19. Ibid., 10:115–16. Letter from Lafayette, March 15, 1792.
20. Unger, *Lafayette*, 281.
21. Ibid., 285.
22. *PWP*, 11:205. Letter from Madame de Lafayette, October 8, 1792.
23. Unger, *Lafayette*, 292.
24. *PWP*, 12:331. Letter to Madame Lafayette, March 16, 1793.
25. Burns and Dunn, *George Washington*, 108–9.
26. Ellis, *American Creation*, 189.
27. Ibid.
28. Ketcham, *James Madison*, 339.
29. *WWF*, 33:414. Letter to Gouverneur Morris, June 25, 1794.
30. *WWR*, 836. Letter to Gouverneur Morris, March 25, 1793.
31. Ibid., 837. Letter to Thomas Jefferson, April 12, 1793.
32. *PWP*, 12:529. "Thomas Jefferson's Notes on a Cabinet Meeting," May 6, 1793.
33. Ibid.
34. Ibid., 12:472–73. "Neutrality Proclamation," April 22, 1793.
35. Chernow, *Alexander Hamilton*, 436.
36. Adam Cohen, "Congress, the Constitution and War," *New York Times*, January 29, 2007.
37. Ellis, *American Creation*, 191.
38. Ibid., 188.
39. *PWP*, 11:593. Letter from Gouverneur Morris, January 6, 1793.
40. Ibid., 12:393. "Thomas Jefferson's Notes on the Opinions Regarding the Reception of Edmond Genet," March 30, 1793.
41. Wills, *Cincinnatus*, 95.
42. *PWP*, 12:648.
43. Ibid., 13:19.
44. Ellis, *American Creation*, 183.
45. Burns and Dunn, *George Washington*, 125.
46. *PWP*, 13:145. Letter from Gouverneur Morris, June 25, 1793.
47. Ellis, *American Creation*, 192.
48. Chinard, *George Washington as the French Knew Him*, 105.
49. *PWP*, 13:187. "Memorandum from Alexander Hamilton and Henry Knox," July 8, 1793.
50. Chinard, *George Washington as the French Knew Him*, 105.
51. *PWP*, 13:175.
52. *WWR*, 841. Letter to Henry Lee, July 21, 1793.
53. *PWP*, 13:211. Letter to Thomas Jefferson, July 11, 1793.
54. *WWR*, 841. Letter to Henry Lee, July 21, 1793.

55. *PWP*, 13:392. "From Supreme Court Justices," August 8, 1793.
56. Unger, *Unexpected George Washington*, 219.
57. Cappon, *Adams-Jefferson Letters*, 346.
58. Chernow, *Alexander Hamilton*, 444.
59. Ellis, *American Creation*, 191.
60. Ketcham, *James Madison*, 343.
61. Chernow, *Alexander Hamilton*, 445.
62. Callahan, *Henry Knox*, 294.
63. *PWP* 13:312.
64. Ibid.
65. Ibid.
66. Freeman, *George Washington*, 7:131.
67. *WWR*, 553. Letter to Benjamin Harrison, January 18, 1784.
68. McDonald, *Presidency of George Washington*, 132.

CHAPTER FIFTY-SEVEN: BRING OUT YOUR DEAD
1. Cappon, *Adams-Jefferson Letters*, 347.
2. *PWP*, 13:297. Letter to Frances Bassett Washington, July 29, 1793.
3. Unger, *Unexpected George Washington*, 221.
4. Brady, *Martha Washington*, 198.
5. *PWP*, 14:54. Letter from Elizabeth Willing Powel, September 9, 1793.
6. Maxey, *Portrait of Elizabeth Willing Powel*, 36.
7. *PWP*, 14:113. Letter from Henry Knox, September 18, 1793.
8. *WWF*, 33:125. Letter to James Madison, October 14, 1793.
9. Chernow, *Alexander Hamilton*, 452.
10. Unger, *Unexpected George Washington*, 222.
11. *WWR*, 848. "Fifth Annual Message to Congress," December 3, 1793.
12. Bordewich, *Washington*, 105.
13. *PWP*, 10:562. Letter to the Commissioners for the District of Columbia, July 23, 1792.
14. *WWR*, 815. Letter to Tobias Lear, July 30, 1792.
15. *PWP*, 12:250–51. Letter to the Commissioners for the District of Columbia, March 3, 1793.
16. Bordewich, *Washington*, 151
17. McCammant, *George Washington the Mason*, 13.
18. *WWF*, 33:441. Letter to Thomas Sim Lee, July 25, 1794.
19. Wood, *Empire of Liberty*, 143.
20. *PWP*, 11:489. Letter to Anthony Whitting, December 9, 1792.
21. Ibid., 11:595. Letter to Anthony Whitting, January 6, 1793.
22. Ibid., 12:339. Letter to Frances Bassett Washington, March 17, 1793.
23. Ibid., 12:352. Letter from Anthony Whitting, March 20, 1793.
24. Ibid., 13:108. Letter from Tobias Lear, June 19, 1793.
25. Ibid., 13:263. Letter to William Tilghman, July 21, 1793.
26. *WWF*, 33:192. Letter to William Pearce, December 18, 1793.
27. Ibid., 33:240. Letter to William Pearce, January 12, 1794.
28. Ibid., 33:191. Letter to William Pearce, December 18, 1793.
29. Ibid., 33:193.
30. Ibid., 33:194.
31. Ibid., 33:132. Letter to Governor Henry Lee, October 16, 1793.
32. *PWP*, 14:595–96. Letter to Hiland Crow, December 23, 1793.
33. Wiencek, *Imperfect God*, 125.

34. *PWP*, 14:605. Letter to Henry McCoy, December 23, 1793.
35. Ibid., 14:605–6.
36. *PWP*, 14:598–99. Letter to Thomas Green, December 23, 1793.
37. *PWP*, 14:597. Letter to John Christian Ehlers, December 23, 1793.
38. *WWR*, 868. Letter to Tobias Lear, May 6, 1794.
39. Ibid., 856. Letter to Arthur Young, December 12, 1793.
40. Ibid., 852.
41. Ibid, 1120. Letter to Arthur Young, November 9, 1794.
42. Ibid., 868. Letter to Tobias Lear, May 6, 1794.
43. Ibid., 900. Letter to Alexander Spotswood, November 23, 1794.
44. Ibid.
45. Ibid.
46. *PWP*, 9:156. Letter to Charles Pinckney, November 8, 1791.
47. Hochschild, *Bury the Chains*, 263.
48. Hitchens, *Thomas Jefferson*, 100.

CHAPTER FIFTY-EIGHT: HERCULES IN THE FIELD
1. Brady, *Martha Washington*, 200.
2. Ellis, *American Creation*, 192.
3. Chernow, *Alexander Hamilton*, 453.
4. McDonald, *Presidency of George Washington*, 137.
5. Ellis, *American Creation*, 196.
6. Chernow, *Alexander Hamilton*, 454.
7. Nelson, *Thomas Paine*, 216.
8. Schutz and Adair, *Spur of Fame*, 93.
9. Ellis, *His Excellency: George Washington*, 150.
10. Callahan, *Henry Knox*, 343.
11. Chernow, *Alexander Hamilton*, 453.
12. *WWR*, 1121.
13. Ibid., 878. Letter to Henry Lee, August 26, 1794.
14. Ibid., 952. Letter to Thomas Jefferson, July 6, 1796.
15. Custis, *Recollections and Private Memoirs of Washington*, 216.
16. Oren, "How to Deal with Pirates," *Wall Street Journal*, November 22–23, 2008.
17. Schama, *Citizens*, 791.
18. *PWP*, 14:229. Letter from Gouverneur Morris, October 18, 1793.
19. Winik, *Great Upheaval*, 512.
20. Gilmour, "Liberty, Equality, Fratricide," *New York Times Book Review*, May 7, 2006.
21. Burr, *Political Correspondence and Public Papers*, 1:236.
22. *WWF*, 33:310. Letter to Governor George Clinton, March 31, 1794.
23. Wood, *Empire of Liberty*, 196.
24. Burr, *Political Correspondence and Public Papers*, 1:177.
25. *WWR*, 880. Letter to John Jay, August 30, 1794.
26. *WWF*, 33:411. Letter to the Secretary of War, June 25, 1794.
27. Fields, *"Worthy Partner,"* 271.
28. Decatur, *Private Affairs of George Washington*, 174.
29. Thompson, *Memorandum for the Martha Washington Anniversary Committee*, 16.
30. Callahan, *Henry Knox*, 324.
31. *WWR*, 893. "Sixth Annual Message to Congress," November 19, 1794.
32. Callahan, *Henry Knox*, 336.
33. *WWR*, 904. Letter to Edmund Pendleton, January 22, 1795.

3 4 . Ibid., 957. "Address to the Cherokee Nation," August 29, 1796.

3 5 . *PWP*, 11:76. Letter to Alexander Hamilton, September 7, 1792.

3 6 . *WWR*, 874. Letter to Charles Mynn Thruston, August 10, 1794.

3 7 . Brookhiser, *Founding Father*, 86.

3 8 . *WWF*, 33:461. "Proclamation," August 7, 1794.

3 9 . Chernow, *Alexander Hamilton*, 471.

4 0 . Ibid.

4 1 . *WWR*, 876. Letter to Henry Lee, August 26, 1794.

4 2 . Ibid.

4 3 . *PWP*, 11:59. Letter from Alexander Hamilton, September 1, 1792.

4 4 . Miles, *George and Martha Washington*, 29.

4 5 . *WWF*, 33:507–8. "Proclamation," September 25, 1794.

4 6 . Ibid., 33:508.

4 7 . Fields, "*Worthy Partner*," 277.

4 8 . WFF, 33:516–17. Letter to the Secretary of War, September 30, 1794.

4 9 . Chernow, *Alexander Hamilton*, 471.

5 0 . McDonald, *Presidency of George Washington*, 147.

CHAPTER FIFTY-NINE: CROWNS AND CORONETS

1 . *Diaries*, 6:180. Diary entry for October 3, 1794.

2 . Ibid. 6:182.

3 . Ibid.

4 . *WWF*, 33:521. Letter to the Secretary of State, October 6, 1794.

5 . Chernow, *Alexander Hamilton*, 475.

6 . Callahan, *Henry Knox*, 309.

7 . *WWF*, 33:524. Letter to the Secretary of War, October 9, 1794.

8 . Ibid., 519. "To the Inhabitants of the Borough of Carlisle," October 6, 1794.

9 . *Diaries*, 6:188.

1 0 . *DiariesA*, 396. Diary entry for October 6–12, 1794.

1 1 . Ibid., 397.

1 2 . *WWR*, 886. Letter to Edmund Randolph, October 16, 1794.

1 3 . *Diaries*, 6:190. Diary entry for October 13, 1794.

1 4 . *DiariesA*, 398. Diary entry for October 17–18, 1794.

1 5 . *Diaries*, 6:194.

1 6 . Ibid., 6:196.

1 7 . Chernow, *Alexander Hamilton*, 475.

1 8 . *WWR*, 888. "Sixth Annual Message to Congress," November 19, 1794.

1 9 . Ketcham, *James Madison*, 354.

2 0 . Brookhiser, *Founding Father*, 89.

2 1 . Ketcham, *James Madison*, 355.

2 2 . Ibid.

2 3 . Hitchens, *Thomas Jefferson*, 105.

2 4 . *WWF*, 34:109. Letter to Alexander Hamilton, February 2, 1795.

2 5 . Callahan, *Henry Knox*, 311.

2 6 . Ibid.

2 7 . Ibid., 312.

2 8 . *WWR*, 903. Letter to Edmund Pendleton, January 22, 1795.

CHAPTER SIXTY: MAD DOG

1 . *WWF*, 34:16. Letter to John Jay, November 1, 1794.

2 . Ibid.

3 . *WWR*, 913. Letter to Alexander Hamilton, July 3, 1795.

4 . Freeman, *George Washington*, 7:257.

5 . Stahr, *John Jay*, 336.

6 . Chernow, *Alexander Hamilton*, 487.

7 . Ibid.

8 . *WWF*, 34:254. "Letter Book," August 1 and 25, 1795.

9 . Ibid., 262. Letter to Alexander Hamilton, July 29, 1795.

1 0 . Unger, *Unexpected George Washington*, 227.

1 1 . *WWF*, 34:251. Letter to the Secretary of War, July 27, 1795.

1 2 . Ibid., 264. Letter to Alexander Hamilton, July 29, 1795.

1 3 . Ibid., 262.

1 4 . *Diaries*, 6:208.

1 5 . Freeman, *George Washington*, 7:282.

1 6 . McDonald, *Presidency of George Washington*, 164.

1 7 . Freeman, *George Washington*, 7:279.

1 8 . *WWF* 34:276. Letter to the Secretaries of the Treasury and War, August 12–18, 1795.

1 9 . Freeman, *George Washington*, 7:293.

2 0 . Randolph, *Vindication of Edmund Randolph*, 1.

2 1 . Freeman, *George Washington*, 7:294–95.

2 2 . Randolph, *Vindication of Edmund Randolph*, 2.

2 3 . *WWF*, 34:321. Letter to the Secretary of the Treasury, October 2, 1795.

2 4 . Ibid., 34:340. Letter to Edmund Randolph, October 21, 1795.

2 5 . Ibid., 34:344. Letter to Edmund Randolph, October 25, 1795.

2 6 . Malone, *Jefferson and His Time*, 3:263.

2 7 . Brookhiser, *Founding Father*, 117.

2 8 . *WWF*, 34:404. Letter from Alexander Hamilton, December 24, 1795.

2 9 . Freeman, *George Washington*, 7:335.

3 0 . *WWF*, 34:279. Letter to John Adams, August 20, 1795.

3 1 . Burns and Dunn, *George Washington*, 115.

3 2 . *WWR*, 918. Letter to Patrick Henry, October 9, 1795.

3 3 . Chernow, *Alexander Hamilton*, 504.

3 4 . Ibid.

3 5 . *WWF*, 26:349. Letter to James Madison, April 22, 1783.

3 6 . *PWRT*, 2:500. Letter to Alexander Hamilton, August 9, 1798.

3 7 . Malone, *Jefferson and His Time*, 3:263.

3 8 . Smith, *John Marshall*, 598.

3 9 . *WWF*, 34:288. Letter to John Marshall, August 26, 1795.

4 0 . Ibid., 34:318. Letter to Edward Carrington, September 28, 1795.

4 1 . Ibid., 35:277. Letter to Charles Lee, November 14, 1796.

4 2 . Ibid., 34:375. Letter to Alexander Hamilton, November 23, 1795.

4 3 . Ibid., 34:299–300. Letter to George Cabot, September 7, 1795.

4 4 . Freeman, *George Washington*, 7:304.

4 5 . Unger, *Unexpected George Washington*, 230.

4 6 . *WWF*, 34:404. Letter to Alexander Hamilton, December 22, 1795.

4 7 . Ibid., 34:425. Letter to James Madison, January 22, 1796.

4 8 . Ibid., 34:462. Letter to Alexander Hamilton, February 13, 1796.

4 9 . Unger, *Unexpected George Washington*, 231.

5 0 . *WWF*, 34:473. Letter to Thomas Pinckney, February 20, 1796.

5 1 . Ibid., 34:486. Letter to James Madison, March 6, 1796.

5 2 . Ibid., 35:62. Letter to Thomas Pinckney, May 22, 1796.

5 3 . *PWRT*, 1:209. Letter to Ségur, June 24, 1797.

54. Lee, *Experiencing Mount Vernon*, 62.
55. Ibid.
56. Unger, *Lafayette*, 245.

CHAPTER SIXTY-ONE: THE COLOSSUS OF THE PEOPLE
1. *WWR*, 933. Letter to Alexander Hamilton, March 31, 1796.
2. Ibid., 934.
3. Ibid., 931. " To the House of Representatives," March 30, 1796.
4. Freeman, *George Washington*, 7:376.
5. *WWF*, 35:62. Letter to Thomas Pinckney, May 22, 1796.
6. McDonald, *Presidency of George Washington*, 173.
7. Ellis, *American Creation*, 200.
8. Chernow, *Alexander Hamilton*, 499.
9. Ellis, *American Creation*, 200.
10. Ibid.
11. *WWF*, 35:30. Letter to Charles Carroll, May 1, 1796.
12. Chernow, *Alexander Hamilton*, 499.
13. Malone, *Jefferson and His Time*, 3:269.
14. Ibid., 268.
15. *WWR*, 952. Letter to Thomas Jefferson, July 6, 1796.
16. Ibid., 952.
17. Malone, *Jefferson and His Time*, 3:270.
18. *WWR*, 951–52. Letter to Thomas Jefferson, July 6, 1796.
19. Ibid., 952.
20. Thompson, *Memorandum for the Martha Washington Anniversary Committee*, 18.
21. PWRT, 2:176. "Comments on Monroe's *A View of the Conduct of the Executive in the Foreign Affairs of the United States*," ca. March 1798.
22. *WWR*, 936. Letter to Alexander Hamilton, May 8, 1796.
23. *WWF*, 15:199. Letter to Archibald Cary, ca. May 1779.
24. Rosenfeld, *American Aurora*, 34.
25. Henriques, *Realistic Visionary*, 121.
26. Monroe, *View of the Conduct of the Executive*, liv.
27. Ibid., xlviii.
28. Ibid., xxx.
29. Paine, *Complete Writings of Thomas Paine*, 705.
30. Ibid.
31. Ibid., 695.
32. Rosenfeld, *American Aurora*, 33.
33. Nelson, *Thomas Paine*, 305.
34. *WWF*, 35:359.
35. Rosenfeld, *American Aurora*, 33.
36. Miles, *George and Martha Washington*, 39.
37. Ibid., 42.
38. Barratt and Miles, *Gilbert Stuart*, 139.
39. MTV. "Early Descriptions, 1800–1841."
40. Unger, *Unexpected Washington*, 232.
41. Fields, "Worthy Partner," 276.
42. Flexner, *George Washington*, 3:196.
43. Barratt and Miles, *Gilbert Stuart*, 191.
44. Ibid.
45. Ibid., 193.
46. Ibid.
47. Ibid., 191.
48. Ibid.
49. *WWF*, 34:458. Letter to Elizabeth Parke Custis, February 10, 1796.
50. Barratt and Miles, *Gilbert Stuart*, 192.
51. Lee, *Experiencing Mount Vernon*, 62.
52. *DiariesA*, 415.

53. Ibid., 413.
54. *PWRT*, 1:266. Letter to George Washington Parke Custis, July 23, 1797.
55. *WWF*, 35:295. Letter to George Washington Parke Custis, November 28, 1796.
56. *PWRT*, 1:153. Letter to Samuel Stanhope Smith, May 24, 1797.
57. Ibid., 1:159. Letter from George Washington Parke Custis, May 29, 1797.
58. *WWR*, 907. Letter to Charles Carter, March 10, 1795.
59. *WWF*, 34:502. Letter to William Pearce, March 20, 1796.
60. Ibid., 34:451. Letter to William Pearce, February 7, 1796.
61. Wiencek, *Imperfect God*, 308.
62. *WWR*, 911. Letter to William Pearce, May 10, 1795.
63. Wiencek, *Imperfect God*, 349.
64. *WWF*, 34:453. Letter to David Stuart, February 7, 1796.
65. Ibid., 35:182. Letter to James Anderson, August 18, 1796.

CHAPTER SIXTY-TWO: THE MASTER OF FAREWELLS
1. Thompson, *Statements Regarding the Physical Appearance*, 47.
2. Wright, "Pickering's Letter."
3. Stahr, *John Jay*, 358.
4. *WWF*, 35:37. Letter to Governor John Jay, May 8, 1796.
5. Chernow, *Alexander Hamilton*, 505.
6. *WWR*, 938. Letter to Alexander Hamilton, May 15, 1796.
7. Ibid., 946. "Draft of the Farewell Address," May 15, 1796.
8. Ibid., 948.
9. Ibid., 950. Letter to Alexander Hamilton, June 26, 1796.
10. *WWF*, 35:104. Letter from Alexander Hamilton, July 5, 1796.
11. Ibid., 35:126. Letter to the Secretary of the Treasury, July 6, 1796.
12. Ibid., 35:178. Letter to Alexander Hamilton, August 10, 1796.
13. Ibid., 35:190. Letter to Alexander Hamilton, August 25, 1796.
14. Freeman, *George Washington*, 7:403.
15. *WWR*, 962. "Farewell Address," September 19, 1796.
16. Ibid., 963.
17. Ibid.
18. Ibid., 965.
19. Ibid., 968.
20. Ellis, *His Excellency: George Washington*, 237.
21. *WWR*, 968. "Farewell Address," September 19, 1796.
22. Ibid., 969.
23. Ibid., 973.
24. Ibid.
25. Ibid.
26. Ibid., 975.
27. Ibid., 977.
28. Thompson, *Statements Regarding the Physical Appearance*, 54. Chernow, *Alexander Hamilton*, 507.
29. Ketcham, *James Madison*, 366.
30. Ibid.
31. Schutz and Adair, *Spur of Fame*, 37.
32. Chernow, *Alexander Hamilton*, 508.
33. Schutz and Adair, *Spur of Fame*, 226.
34. Cappon, *Adams-Jefferson Letters*, 349.
35. Schutz and Adair, *Spur of Fame*, 226.
36. Brookhiser, *Founding Father*, 103.
37. *WWF*, 34:154. Letter to William Pearce, March 22, 1795.

38. Ibid., 34:476. Letter to William Pearce, February 21, 1796.
39. Wilentz, *Rise of American Democracy*, 62.
40. Rosenfeld, *American Aurora*, 30.
41. Schutz and Adair, *Spur of Fame*, 224.
42. Brookhiser, *Founding Father*, 177.
43. *WWR*, 594. Letter to Robert Morris, April 12, 1786.
44. Decatur, *Private Affairs of George Washington*, 268.
45. Cadou, *George Washington Collection*, 204.
46. Harvey and O'Brien, *George Washington's South*, 202.
47. Ibid.
48. Wiencek, *Imperfect God*, 323.
49. Harvey and O'Brien, *George Washington's South*, 202.
50. Fields, "Worthy Partner," 287.
51. *WWF*, 35:201. Letter to the Secretary of the Treasury, September 1, 1796.
52. Ibid., 35:202.
53. Ibid.
54. Wiencek, *Imperfect God*, 326.
55. Ibid.
56. *WWF*, 35:297. Letter to Joseph Whipple, November 28, 1796.
57. Ibid.
58. Ibid.
59. Ibid., 35:298.
60. Ibid.
61. *PWRT*, 4:237. Letter to Burwell Bassett, Jr., August 11, 1799.
62. Wiencek, *Imperfect God*, 332.
63. Lee, *Experiencing Mount Vernon*, 204.
64. *PWRT*, 2:60. Letter to Frederick Kitt, January 29, 1798.
65. Ibid., 2:16. Letter to Frederick Kitt, January 10, 1798.
66. Harvey and O'Brien, *George Washington's South*, 203.
67. *PWRT*, 1:83.
68. Ibid., 1:422. Letter to Bushrod Washington, October 23, 1797.
69. *PWRT*, 1:469. Letter to George Lewis, November 13, 1797.

CHAPTER SIXTY-THREE: EXITING THE STAGE
1. Freeman, *George Washington*, 7:420.
2. *WWR*, 985. "Eighth Annual Message to Congress," December 7, 1796.
3. Unger, *Unexpected George Washington*, 236.
4. Sullivan, *Public Men of the Revolution*, 145.
5. Smith, *John Marshall*, 182.
6. Grant, *John Adams*, 384.
7. Freeman, *George Washington*, 7:425.
8. Nelson, *Thomas Paine*, 304.
9. Jefferson, *Writings*, 1319.
10. *DiariesA*, 404.
11. Brady, *Martha Washington*, 211.
12. Unger, *Unexpected George Washington*, 237.
13. *WWF*, 35:409. Letter to Henry Knox, March 2, 1797.
14. Ibid., 35:412. Letter to Jonathan Trumbull, March 3, 1797.
15. Ibid.
16. *Diaries*, 6:236. Diary entry for March 4, 1797.
17. Freeman, *George Washington*, 7:437.
18. Ibid.
19. Custis, *Recollections and Private Memoirs of Washington*, 434.
20. Irving, *Life of George Washington*, 613.
21. Henriques, *Realistic Visionary*, 64.
22. Ibid.

23. Malone, *Jefferson and His Time*, 3:298.
24. Ibid., 3:307.
25. Rosenfeld, *American Aurora*, 35.
26. Ibid., 31.
27. Ibid., 31–32.
28. Grant, *John Adams* 387.
29. *PWRT*, 1:130. Letter to Mary White Morris, May 1, 1797.
30. Ibid., 1:28. Letter from Elizabeth Willing Powel, March 11, 1797.
31. Ibid., 1:29.
32. Ibid., 1:52. Letter to Elizabeth Willing Powel, March 26, 1797.
33. Ibid., 1:25. Letter to Tobias Lear, March 9, 1797.
34. Unger, *Unexpected George Washington*, 241.
35. *PWRT*, 1:71. Letter to James McHenry, April 3, 1797.
36. Wood, *Empire of Liberty*, 85.
37. Magnet, "Alexander Hamilton," *City Journal*, Winter 2009.
38. Schutz and Adair, *Spur of Fame*, 108.

CHAPTER SIXTY-FOUR: SAMSON AND SOLOMON
1. Brady, *George Washington's Beautiful Nelly*, 31.
2. Ibid.
3. Unger, *Unexpected George Washington*, 240–41.
4. *PWRT*, 1:79. Letter to James Anderson, April 7, 1797.
5. Ibid., 1:335. Letter to Lawrence Augustine Washington, September 3, 1797.
6. Freeman, *George Washington*, 7:453.
7. *WWR*, 1002–3. Letter to Lawrence Lewis, August 4, 1797.
8. Ibid.
9. *PWRT*, 1:53. Letter to Elizabeth Willing Powel, March 26, 1797.
10. *WWR*, 998. Letter to David Humphreys, June 26, 1797.
11. Freeman, *George Washington*, 7:469.
12. *WWR*, 996. Letter to James McHenry, May 29, 1797
13. Cadou, *George Washington Collection*, 173.
14. Brady, *Martha Washington*, 215.
15. *WWR*, 996. Letter to James McHenry, May 29, 1797.
16. Ibid., 996–97.
17. Lee, *Experiencing Mount Vernon*, 84.
18. *PWRT*, 1:495. Letter to Bartholomew Dandridge, Jr., December 3, 1797.
19. Lee, *Experiencing Mount Vernon*, 57.
20. *PWRT*, 2:273. Letter to Sarah Cary Fairfax, May 16, 1798.
21. Ibid., 2:272.
22. Ibid., 2:274.
23. Ibid., 1:79. Letter to James Anderson (of Scotland), April 7, 1797.
24. Ibid., 2:74. Letter to James Anderson, February 6, 1798.
25. Ibid., 1:378–79. Letter to Thomas Law, October 2, 1797.
26. *WWF*, 35:369. Letter to George Dunnington, January 15, 1797.
27. *PWRT*, 1:247. Letter to Samuel Washington, July 12, 1797.
28. Freeman, *George Washington*, 7:493.
29. Malone, *Jefferson and His Time*, 3:267.
30. Ibid., 3:305.
31. Wood, *Empire of Liberty*, 235–36.
32. Henriques, *Realistic Visionary*, 123.
33. Malone, *Jefferson and His Time*, 3:310.
34. Callahan, *Henry Knox*, 361.
35. *PWRT*, 1:313. Letter to Alexander Hamilton, August 21, 1797.
36. Ibid., 1:158. Letter to Thomas Pinckney, May 28, 1797.

37. Ibid., 1:384. Letter from Lafayette, October 6, 1797.

38. Ibid., 3:282. Letter to Lafayette, December 25, 1798.

39. Freeman, *George Washington,* 7:496.

40. *PWRT,* 2:241. Letter to James Lloyd, April 15, 1798.

41. Wood, *Empire of Liberty,* 245.

42. Brady, *George Washington's Beautiful Nelly,* 52.

43. *PWRT,* 2:280. Letter from Alexander Hamilton, May 19, 1798.

44. Ibid.

45. Ibid.

46. Ibid., 2:298. Letter to Alexander Hamilton, May 27, 1798.

47. Ibid.

48. Ibid.

49. Ibid., 3:284. Letter to Lafayette, December 25, 1798.

50. Ibid., 2:310. Letter from Alexander Hamilton, June 2, 1798.

51. Lee, *Experiencing Mount Vernon,* 86.

52. Ibid.

53. Ibid., 87.

54. *PWRT,* 2:352. Letter from John Adams, June 22, 1798.

55. Ibid.

56. Ibid., 2:369. Letter to John Adams, July 4, 1798.

57. Ibid., 2:370.

58. Ibid., 2:457. Letter to John Trumbull, July 25, 1798.

59. Ibid., 2:383. Letter to James McHenry, July 5, 1798.

60. Ibid., 2:387. Letter from Timothy Pickering, July 6, 1798.

61. Chernow, *Alexander Hamilton,* 556.

62. Schutz and Adair, *Spur of Fame,* 93.

63. *WWR,* 1006. Letter to John Adams, July 13, 1798.

64. Chernow, *Alexander Hamilton,* 558.

65. Ibid.

66. *PWRT,* 2:425. Letter to Henry Knox, July 16, 1798.

67. Callahan, *Henry Knox,* 363.

68. *PWRT,* 2:469. Letter from Henry Knox, July 29, 1798.

69. Ibid., 2:506. Letter to Henry Knox, August 9, 1798.

70. Callahan, *Henry Knox,* 368.

71. *PWRT,* 2:563. Letter from Henry Knox, August 26, 1798.

72. Smith, *John Marshall,* 240.

73. *PWRT,* 3:59. Letter to James McHenry, September 30, 1798.

74. Ibid.

75. Smith, *John Marshall,* 241.

76. *PWRT,* 3:21. Letter from James McHenry, September 19, 1798.

77. Ibid., 2:589. Letter from James McHenry, September 7, 1798.

78. Ibid., 2:609. Letter from Timothy Pickering, September 13, 1798.

79. Chernow, *Alexander Hamilton,* 560.

80. *PWRT,* 3:37. Letter to John Adams, September 25, 1798.

81. Ibid., 3:38.

82. Ibid., 3:41–42.

83. Ibid., 3:42.

84. Ibid., 3:43.

85. *PWRT,* 3:123. Letter to Henry Knox, October 21, 1798.

86. Callahan, *Henry Knox,* 372.

87. *PWRT,* 3:241. Letter to Lawrence Lewis, December 2, 1798.

88. Ibid., 3:298. Letter to David Stuart, December 30, 1798.

89. Unger, *Unexpected George Washington,* 253.

90. *PWRT,* 3:246. Letter from Elizabeth Willing Powel, December 7, 1798.

91. Ibid., 3:247.

92. Bordewich, *Washington,* 61.

93. Cappon, *Adams-Jefferson Letters,* 346.

94. Chernow, *Alexander Hamilton,* 593.

CHAPTER SIXTY-FIVE: A MIND ON THE STRETCH

1. Chernow, *Alexander Hamilton,* 570.

2. *WWR,* 1016. Letter to Alexander Spotswood, November 22, 1798.

3. *PWRT,* 3:287. Letter to William Vans Murray, December 26, 1798.

4. Ibid., 3:398. Letter to Alexander Hamilton, February 25, 1799.

5. *PWRT,* 4:51. Letter to Bushrod Washington, May 5, 1799.

6. Bordewich, *Washington,* 209.

7. *PWRT,* 1:220. Letter to David Humphreys, June 26, 1797.

8. Bordewich, *Washington,* 211.

9. Ibid., 98.

10. Wiencek, *Imperfect God,* 346.

11. Thompson, "They Appear to Live Comfortable Together."

12. *PWRT,* 2:119. Letter to John McDowell, March 5, 1798.

13. Ibid., 2:448–49. Letter to George Washington Parke Custis, July 24, 1798.

14. Ibid., 3:179. Letter to Henry Lee, Jr., November 4, 1798.

15. Ibid., 3:291. Letter to Richard Raynal Keene, December 28, 1798.

16. Ibid., 3:471. Letter to James Welch, April 7, 1799.

17. Ibid., 4:423. Letter to Alexander Addison, November 24, 1799.

18. Ibid., 4:296. Letter to James McHenry, September 14, 1799.

19. Ibid., 4:297.

20. Ibid., 4:109. Letter to William Augustine Washington, February 27, 1798.

21. Ibid., 4:292. Letter to James Anderson, September 10, 1799.

22. Ibid., 4:144. Letter from Jonathan Trumbull, Jr., June 22, 1799.

23. *WWR,* 1044. Letter to Jonathan Trumbull, Jr., July 21, 1799.

24. Ibid.

25. Ibid.

26. Ibid., 1045.

27. Ibid.

28. *PWRT,* 4:275–76. Letter to Jonathan Trumbull, Jr., August 30, 1799.

29. Ibid., 4:276.

30. Ibid.

31. Ibid., 4:373. Letter to Alexander Hamilton, October 27, 1799.

32. Ibid., 4:401. Letter from James McHenry, November 10, 1799.

33. Ibid., 4:410. Letter to James McHenry, November 17, 1799.

34. Ibid., 4:453. Letter from Gouverneur Morris, December 9, 1799.

35. Ibid.

CHAPTER SIXTY-SIX: FREEDOM

1. Lee, *Experiencing Mount Vernon,* 68.

2. Wiencek, *Imperfect God,* 348.

3. Lee, *Experiencing Mount Vernon,* 79.

4. Ibid.

5. Wiencek, *Imperfect God,* 351.
6. Ibid., 352.
7. *PWRT,* 2:613. Letter to Alexander Spotswood, September 14, 1798.
8. Ibid., 4:256. Letter to Robert Lewis, August 17, 1799.
9. Ibid., 4:256–57.
10. Ibid., 2:615.
11. Ibid., 1:404. Letter to William Stoy, October 14, 1797.
12. Harvey and O'Brien, *George Washington's South,* 197.
13. Freeman, *George Washington,* 7:583.
14. *PWRT,* 4:491. "George Washington's Last Will and Testament," July 9, 1799.
15. Ibid., 4:479.
16. Ibid., 4:480.
17. Ibid.
18. Ibid.
19. Ibid.
20. Ibid.
21. Ibid., 4:480–81.
22. Ibid., 4:482.
23. Ibid., 4:489.
24. *DiariesA,* 426.
25. *WWR,* 1050. Letter to Burges Ball, September 22, 1799.

CHAPTER SIXTY-SEVEN: HOMECOMING
1. *PWRT,* 1:520. Letter from Martha Washington to Elizabeth Willing Powel, December 17, 1797.
2. Lee, *Experiencing Mount Vernon,* 89.
3. MTV. "Early Descriptions Ante 1800." Howell Lewis, December 9, 1799.
4. Burns and Dunn, *George Washington,* 136.
5. *WWR,* 1051. Letter to Alexander Hamilton, December 12, 1799.
6. Henriques, *Realistic Visionary,* 192.
7. *DiariesA,* 428. Diary entry for December 12, 1799.
8. *WWR,* 1052. Letter to James Anderson, December 13, 1799.
9. *PWRT,* 4:548.
10. *DiariesA,* 428.
11. Ibid., 429.
12. Ibid.
13. Ibid.
14. Henriques, *Realistic Visionary,* 202.
15. Ibid.
16. *DiariesA,* 430.
17. Ibid., 430.
18. *PWRT,* 4:545.

19. *DiariesA,* 430.
20. Ibid.
21. Ibid., 431.
22. Ibid.
23. Ibid.
24. *PWRT* 4:491. "George Washington's Last Will and Testament," July 9, 1799.
25. Lee, *Experiencing Mount Vernon,* 104.
26. Furstenberg, *In the Name of the Father,* 26.
27. Chernow, *Alexander Hamilton,* 601.
28. Ibid.
29. Cappon, *Adams-Jefferson Letters,* 488.
30. *DiariesA,* 423.
31. Furstenberg, *In the Name of the Father,* 32.
32. Wills, *Cincinnatus,* 32.
33. Unger, *Unexpected George Washington,* 266.
34. Weintraub, *George Washington's Christmas Farewell,* 66.
35. Schutz and Adair, *Spur of Fame,* 229.
36. Neely, "Mason Locke Weems's *Life.*"
37. Furstenberg, "Spinning the Revolution," *New York Times,* July 4, 2006.
38. Furstenberg, *In the Name of the Father,* 135.
39. Ibid., 121.
40. Smith, *John Marshall,* 331.
41. Ibid.
42. Brady, *Martha Washington,* 226.
43. Decatur, *Private Affairs of George Washington,* 306.
44. MTV. "Early Descriptions 1800–1841." Letter from Sally Foster Otis to Mrs. Charles W. Apthorp, January 13, 1801.
45. MTV. "Early Descriptions 1800–1841." Diary of Manasseh Cutler, January 2, 1802.
46. *PWRT,* 4:494.
47. MTV. "Early Descriptions 1800–1841." Abigail Adams letter, December 21, 1800.
48. Bryan, *First Lady of Liberty,* 378.
49. *PWRT,* 4:494.
50. MTV. "Early Descriptions 1800–1841." Undated letter by Sir Augustus John Foster.
51. Malone, *Jefferson and the Ordeal of Liberty,* 3:443.
52. Smith, *Correspondence and Miscellanies of the Hon. John Cotton Smith,* 224.
53. Smith, *John Marshall,* 19.
54. MTV. "Early Descriptions 1800–1841." Diary of Manasseh Cutler, January 2, 1802.
55. Brady, *Martha Washington,* 229.

BIBLIOGRAPHY

BOOKS

Adams, Herbert Baxter. *The Life and Writings of Jared Sparks.* 2 vols. Boston: Houghton Mifflin, 1893.

Addison, Joseph. *Cato: A Tragedy, and Selected Essays.* Reprint, Indianapolis: Liberty Fund, 2004.

Anderson, Fred. *Crucible of War: The Seven Years' War and the Fate of Empire in British North America, 1754–1766.* Reprint, New York: Vintage Books, 2001.

———. *George Washington Remembers: Reflections on the French & Indian War.* Lanham, Md.: Rowman & Littlefield, 2004.

Barratt, Carrie Rebora, and Ellen G. Miles. *Gilbert Stuart.* New York: Metropolitan Museum of Art; New Haven, Conn.: Yale University Press, 2004.

Baxter, Katharine Schuyler. *A Godchild of Washington: A Picture of the Past.* New York: F. Tennyson Neely, 1898.

Berg, Scott W. *Grand Avenues: The Story of Pierre Charles L'Enfant, the French Visionary Who Designed Washington, D.C.* New York: Pantheon Books, 2007.

Blassingame, J. W., ed. *Slave Testimony: Two Centuries of Letters, Speeches, Interviews, and Autobiographies.* Baton Rouge: Louisiana State University Press, 1977.

Bordewich, Fergus M. *Washington: The Making of the American Capital.* New York: Amistad / HarperCollins, 2008.

Brady, Patricia. *Martha Washington: An American Life.* New York: Viking, 2005.

———, ed. *George Washington's Beautiful Nelly: The Letters of Eleanor Parke Custis Lewis to Elizabeth Bordley Gibson, 1794–1851.* Columbia: University of South Carolina Press, 1991.

Brookhiser, Richard. *Founding Father: Rediscovering George Washington.* New York: Free Press, 1996.

Bryan, Helen. *Martha Washington: First Lady of Liberty.* New York: John Wiley & Sons, 2002.

Burns, James MacGregor, and Susan Dunn. *George Washington.* New York: Times Books / Henry Holt, 2004.

Burr, Aaron. *Political Correspondence and Public Papers of Aaron Burr.* 2 vols. Edited by Mary-Jo Kline. Princeton, N.J.: Princeton University Press, 1983.

Burstein, Andrew. *The Original Knickerbocker: The Life of Washington Irving.* New York: Basic Books, 2006.

Cadou, Carol Borchert. *The George Washington Collection: Fine and Decorative Arts at Mount Vernon.* Manchester, N.Y.: Mount Vernon Ladies' Association / Hudson Hills Press, 2006.

Callahan, North. *Henry Knox: General Washington's General.* New York: Rinehart, 1958.

Cappon, Lester J., ed. *The Adams-Jefferson Letters: The Complete Correspondence Between Thomas Jefferson and Abigail and John Adams.* Reprint, Chapel Hill and London:

Published for the Omohundro Institute of Early American History and Culture at Williamsburg, Virginia, 1959.

Casper, Scott E. *Sarah Johnson's Mount Vernon: The Forgotten History of an American Shrine*. New York: Hill & Wang, 2008.

Chernow, Ron. *Alexander Hamilton*. New York: Penguin Press, 2004.

Chinard, Gilbert. *George Washington as the French Knew Him*. Princeton, N.J.: Princeton University Press, 1940.

Conkling, Margaret C. *Memoirs of the Mother and Wife of Washington*. Auburn, N.Y.: Derby, Miller, 1850.

Conway, Moncure Daniel. *Omitted Chapters of History Disclosed in the Life and Papers of Edmund Randolph*. New York: G. P. Putnam's Sons, 1888.

Cunliffe, Marcus. *George Washington: Man and Monument*. Reprint, New York: New American Library, 1958.

Custis, George Washington Parke. *Recollections and Private Memoirs of Washington*. New York: Derby & Jackson, 1860.

Dalzell, Robert F., Jr., and Lee Baldwin Dalzell. *George Washington's Mount Vernon: At Home in Revolutionary America*. New York: Oxford University Press, 1998.

Darnton, Robert. *George Washington's False Teeth: An Unconventional Guide to the Eighteenth Century*. New York: W. W. Norton, 2003.

Decatur, Stephen, Jr. *Private Affairs of George Washington: From the Records and Accounts of Tobias Lear, Esquire, His Secretary*. Boston: Houghton Mifflin, 1933.

Elkins, Stanley, and Eric McKitrick. *The Age of Federalism: The Early American Republic, 1788–1800*. New York: Oxford University Press, 1993.

Ellis, Joseph. *His Excellency: George Washington*. New York: Alfred A. Knopf, 2004.

———. *American Creation: Triumphs and Tragedies at the Founding of the Republic*. New York: Alfred A. Knopf, 2007.

Evans, Dorinda. *The Genius of Gilbert Stuart*. Princeton, N.J.: Princeton University Press, 1999.

Felder, Paula S. *Fielding Lewis and the Washington Family: A Chronicle of 18th Century Fredericksburg*. Fredericksburg, Va.: The American History Company, 1998.

Ferling, John E. *The Ascent of George Washington: The Hidden Political Genius of an American Icon*. New York: Bloomsbury Press, 2009.

Fields, Joseph E., ed. *"Worthy Partner": The Papers of Martha Washington*. Westport, Conn.: Greenwood Press, 1994.

Fischer, David Hackett. *Washington's Crossing*. New York: Oxford University Press, 2004.

Fitzpatrick, John C., ed. *The Writings of George Washington*. Washington, D.C.: U.S. Government Printing Office, 1931–44.

Flexner, James Thomas. *George Washington*. 4 vols. Boston: Little, Brown, 1965–72.

Freeman, Douglas Southall. *George Washington: A Biography*. 7 vols. New York: Charles Scribner's Sons, 1948–57. Volume 7 completed by John A. Carroll and Mary W. Ashworth.

Fulford, Roger. *Hanover to Windsor*. London: B. T. Batsford, 1960.

Furstenberg, François. *In the Name of the Father: Washington's Legacy, Slavery, and the Making of a Nation*. New York: Penguin Press, 2006.

Gaines, James R. *For Liberty and Glory: Washington, Lafayette, and Their Revolutions.* New York: W. W. Norton, 2007.

Goldwin, Robert A. *From Parchment to Power: How James Madison Used the Bill of Rights to Save the Constitution.* Washington, D.C.: AEI Press, 1997.

Golway, Terry. *Washington's General: Nathanael Greene and the Triumph of the American Revolution.* New York: Henry Holt, 2005.

Gordon-Reed, Annette. *The Hemingses of Monticello: An American Family.* New York: W. W. Norton, 2008.

Grant, James. *John Adams: Party of One.* New York: Farrar, Straus & Giroux, 2005.

Griswold, Mac. *Washington's Gardens at Mount Vernon: Landscape of the Inner Man.* Boston: Houghton Mifflin, 1999.

Grizzard, Frank E., Jr. *George! A Guide to All Things Washington.* Charlottesville, Va.: Mariner, 2005.

Guerrero, Linda Dudik. *John Adams' Vice-Presidency, 1789–1797: The Neglected Man in the Forgotten Office.* New York: Arno Press, 1982.

Hague, William. *William Pitt the Younger: A Biography.* New York: Alfred A. Knopf, 2005.

Harvey, Tamara, and Greg O'Brien, eds. *George Washington's South.* Gainesville: University Press of Florida, 2003.

Hayden, Sidney. *Washington and His Masonic Compeers.* New York: Masonic Publishing and Manufacturing Co., 1866.

Henriques, Peter R. *Realistic Visionary: A Portrait of George Washington.* Charlottesville: University of Virginia Press, 2006.

Hervey, N. *The Memory of Washington with Biographical Sketches of His Mother and Wife.* Boston: James Munroe, 1852.

Higginbotham, Don, ed. *George Washington Reconsidered.* Charlottesville: University of Virginia Press, 2001.

Hitchens, Christopher. *Thomas Jefferson: Author of America.* New York: Atlas Books / HarperCollins, 2005.

Hochschild, Adam. *Bury the Chains: Prophets and Rebels in the Fight to Free an Empire's Slaves.* Boston: Houghton Mifflin, 2004.

Humphreys, David. *The Conduct of General Washington Respecting the Confinement of Capt. Asgill.* New York: Holland Club, 1859.

Irving, Washington. *The Life of George Washington.* New York: William L. Allison Co., 1859.

Isaac, Rhys. *Landon Carter's Uneasy Kingdom: Revolution and Rebellion on a Virginia Plantation.* Reprint, New York: Oxford University Press, 2004.

Isaacson, Walter. *Benjamin Franklin: An American Life.* New York: Simon & Schuster, 2003.

Isenberg, Nancy. *Fallen Founder: The Life of Aaron Burr.* New York: Viking, 2007.

Jefferson, Thomas. *Writings.* Edited by Merrill D. Peterson. New York: Library of America, 1984.

Kagan, Robert. *Dangerous Nation: America's Place in the World from Its Earliest Days to the Dawn of the Twentieth Century.* New York: Alfred A. Knopf, 2006.

Kaminski, John P., and Jill Adair McCaughan, eds. *A Great and Good Man: George Washington in the Eyes of His Contemporaries.* Reprint, Lanham, Md.: Rowman & Littlefield, 2007.

Ketcham, Ralph. *James Madison: A Biography*. Charlottesville: University of Virginia Press, 1971.

Ketchum, Richard M. *Victory at Yorktown: The Campaign That Won the Revolution*. New York: Henry Holt, 2004.

Kohn, Richard H. *Eagle and Sword: The Federalists and the Creation of the Military Establishment in America, 1783–1802*. New York: Free Press, 1975.

Lee, Jean B. *Experiencing Mount Vernon: Eyewitness Accounts, 1784–1865*. Charlottesville and London: University of Virginia Press, 2006.

Leibiger, Stuart. *Founding Friendship: George Washington, James Madison, and the Creation of the American Republic*. Reprint, Charlottesville: University of Virginia Press, 2001.

Lengel, Edward G. *General George Washington: A Military Life*. New York: Random House, 2005.

Longmore, Paul K. *The Invention of George Washington*. Berkeley: University of California Press, 1988.

Lossing, Benson J. *Martha Washington*. New York: J. C. Buttre, 1861.

McCammant, Wallace. *George Washington the Mason*. N.p.: Kessinger Publishing, n.d.

McCullough, David. *John Adams*. New York: Simon & Schuster, 2001.

———. *1776*. New York: Simon & Schuster, 2005.

McDonald, Forrest. *The Presidency of George Washington*. Lawrence: University Press of Kansas, 1974.

Maclay, William. *The Diary of William Maclay and Other Notes on Senate Debates*. Edited by Kenneth R. Bowling and Helen E. Veit. Reprint, Baltimore and London: Johns Hopkins University Press, 1988.

McVickar, John. *A Domestic Narrative of the Life of Samuel Bard, M.D.* New York: A. Paul, 1822.

Malone, Dumas. *Jefferson and His Time*. Vol. 3, *Jefferson and the Ordeal of Liberty*. Boston: Little, Brown, 1962.

Marshall, John. *The Life of George Washington*. Reprint, Indianapolis: Liberty Fund, 2000.

Martin, Joseph Plumb. *Private Yankee Doodle: Being a Narrative of Some of the Adventures, Dangers and Sufferings of a Revolutionary Soldier*. Edited by George E. Scheer. Reprint, N.p.: Eastern National, 2006.

Maxey, David W. *A Portrait of Elizabeth Willing Powel*. Philadelphia: American Philosophical Society, 2006.

Middlekauff, Robert. *The Glorious Cause: The American Revolution, 1763–1789*. Reprint, New York: Oxford University Press, 2005.

Miles, Ellen G. *George and Martha Washington: Portraits from the Presidential Years*. Washington, D.C.: Smithsonian Institution, National Portrait Gallery, in association with the University Press of Virginia, 1999.

Monroe, James. *A View of the Conduct of the Executive in the Foreign Affairs of the United States, Connected with the Mission to the French Republic During the Years 1794, 5, & 6*. Philadelphia: Benjamin Franklin Bache, 1797. (George Washington's personal copy in the Houghton Library, Harvard University.)

Morgan, Edmund S. *The Genius of George Washington*. New York: W. W. Norton, 1980.

————. *American Heroes: Profiles of Men and Women Who Shaped Early America.* New York: W. W. Norton, 2009.

Nelson, Craig. *Thomas Paine: Enlightenment, Revolution, and the Birth of Modern Nations.* New York: Viking, 2006.

Paine, Thomas. *The Complete Writings of Thomas Paine.* Vol. 2. Edited by Phillip S. Foner. New York: Citadel Press, 1945.

Palmer, Dave R. *George Washington and Benedict Arnold: A Tale of Two Patriots.* Washington, D.C.: Regnery, 2006.

Puls, Mark. *Samuel Adams: Father of the American Revolution.* New York: Palgrave Macmillan, 2006.

Rakove, Jack N. *Original Meanings: Politics and Ideas in the Making of the Constitution.* New York: Alfred A. Knopf, 1996.

Ramsay, David. *The Life of George Washington.* London: T. Cadell & W. Davies, 1807.

Randolph, Edmund. *A Vindication of Edmund Randolph.* Richmond: Charles H. Wynne, 1855.

Randolph, John [Supposed author of forgeries]. *Epistles domestic, confidential, and official from General Washington.* New York: G. Robinson & J. Pull, 1796.

Reardon, John J. *Edmund Randolph: A Biography.* New York: Macmillan, 1974.

Rosenfeld, Richard N. *American Aurora: A Democratic Republican Returns.* New York: St. Martin's / Griffin, 1997.

Schama, Simon. *Citizens: A Chronicle of the French Revolution.* New York: Alfred A. Knopf, 1989.

Schecter, Barnet. *The Battle for New York: The City at the Heart of the American Revolution.* New York: Walker, 2002.

Schiff, Stacy. *A Great Improvisation: Franklin, France, and the Birth of America.* New York: Henry Holt, 2005.

Schutz, John A., and Douglass Adair, eds. *The Spur of Fame: Dialogues of John Adams and Benjamin Rush, 1805–1813.* San Marino, Calif.: Huntington Library, 1966.

Schwarz, Philip J., ed. *Slavery at the Home of George Washington.* Mount Vernon, Va.: Mount Vernon Ladies' Association, 2002.

Smith, Jean Edward. *John Marshall: Definer of a Nation.* Reprint, New York: Henry Holt, 1996.

Smith, John Cotton. *The Correspondence and Miscellanies of the Hon. John Cotton Smith, LLD.* New York: Harper & Brothers, 1847.

Smith, Richard Norton. *Patriarch: George Washington and the New American Nation.* Boston: Houghton Mifflin, 1993.

Stahr, Walter. *John Jay: Founding Father.* New York and London: Hambledon & London, 2005.

Stephenson, Michael. *Patriot Battles: How the War of Independence Was Fought.* New York: HarperCollins, 2007.

Stoll, Ira. *Samuel Adams: A Life.* New York: Free Press, 2008.

Sullivan, William. *The Public Men of the Revolution.* Philadelphia: Carey & Hart, 1847.

Thompson, Mary V. *"In the Hands of a Good Providence": Religion in the Life of George Washington.* Charlottesville: University of Virginia Press, 2008.

————, ed. *Memorandum for the Martha Washington Anniversary Committee.* Compiled for Mount Vernon Ladies' Association between 7/31/2001 and 4/7/2008. Typescript at Mount Vernon Library.

———, ed. *Statements Regarding the Physical Appearance, Traits and Personal Characteristics of George Washington (1732–1799)*. Compiled for Mount Vernon Ladies' Association between 1/31/2005 and 2/5/2008. Typescript at Mount Vernon Library.

Trumbull, John. *The Autobiography of Colonel John Trumbull*. New Haven, Conn.: Yale University Press, 1958.

Unger, Harlow Giles. *Lafayette*. Hoboken, N.J.: John Wiley & Sons, 2002.

———. *The Unexpected George Washington: His Private Life*. Hoboken, N.J.: John Wiley & Sons, 2006.

Van Doren, Carl. *Benjamin Franklin*. New York: Viking Press, 1938.

Washington, George. *George Washington, Writings*. Edited by John Rhodehamel. New York: Library of America, 1997.

———. *George Washington's Diaries: An Abridgment*. Edited by Dorothy Twohig. Charlottesville: University of Virginia Press, 1999.

Weber, Caroline. *Queen of Fashion: What Marie Antoinette Wore to the Revolution*. Reprint: New York: Picador / Henry Holt, 2006.

Weems, Mason L. *The Life of Washington*. Reprint, Cambridge, Mass.: Belknap Press of Harvard University Press, 1962.

Weintraub, Stanley. *General Washington's Christmas Farewell: A Mount Vernon Homecoming, 1783*. New York: Penguin Group, 2004.

Wiencek, Henry. *An Imperfect God: George Washington, His Slaves, and the Creation of America*. New York: Farrar, Straus & Giroux, 2003.

Wilentz, Sean. *The Rise of American Democracy: Jefferson to Lincoln*. New York: W. W. Norton, 2005.

Wills, Garry. *Cincinnatus: George Washington and the Enlightenment*. Garden City, N.Y.: Doubleday, 1984.

Winik, Jay. *The Great Upheaval: America and the Birth of the Modern World, 1788–1800*. New York: HarperCollins, 2007.

Wood, Gordon S. *Revolutionary Characters: What Made the Founders Different*. New York: Penguin Press, 2006.

———. *Empire of Liberty: A History of the Early Republic, 1789–1815*. New York: Oxford University Press, 2009.

Zimmerman, Jean. *The Women of the House: How a Colonial She-Merchant Built a Mansion, a Fortune, and a Dynasty*. Orlando, Fla.: Harcourt, 2006.

ARTICLES

Abbot, W. W. "An Uncommon Awareness of Self: The Papers of George Washington." *Prologue: Quarterly of the National Archives,* Spring 1989.

Anderson, Fred W. "The Hinge of the Revolution: George Washington Confronts a People's Army, July 3, 1775." *Massachusetts Historical Review* 1 (1999).

————. "The Lost Founders." *New York Review of Books,* September 21, 2006.

Barratt, Carrie Rebora. "Faces of a New Nation: American Portraits of the 18th and Early 19th Centuries." *Metropolitan Museum of Art Bulletin*, Summer 2003.

Batchelder, Samuel. "Col. Henry Vassall and His Wife Penelope Vassall with Some Account of His Slaves." *Proceedings of the Cambridge Historical Society* 10 (January 26–October 26, 1915).

Bickham, Troy. "Sympathizing with Sedition? George Washington, the British Press, and British Attitudes during the American War of Independence." *William and Mary Quarterly* 59, no. 1 (January 2002).

Brookhiser, Richard. "George Washington, Founding CEO." *American Heritage*, Spring–Summer 2008.

Brown, Lawrence Parmly. "The Antiquities of Dental Prosthesis: Part III, Section 2, Eighteenth Century." *Dental Cosmos* 76, no. 11 (November 1934).

Bryan, Mark Evans. "'Slideing into Monarchical Extravagance': *Cato* at Valley Forge and the Testimony of William Bradford Jr." *William and Mary Quarterly,* 3rd ser., 67, no. 1 (January 2010).

Burrows, Edwin G. "Patriots or Terrorists?" *American Heritage*, Fall 2008.

Conway, Stephen. "The British Army, 'Military Europe,' and the American War of Independence." *William and Mary Quarterly,* 3rd ser., 67, no. 1 (January 2010).

Desportes, Ulysse. "Giuseppe Ceracchi in America and His Busts of George Washington." *Art Quarterly* 26, no. 2 (1963).

Ferling, John. "Myths of the American Revolution." *Smithsonian*, January 2010.

Fleming, Thomas. "George Washington in Love." *American Heritage*, Fall 2009.

————. "Wall Street's First Collapse." *American Heritage*, Winter 2009.

Fund, John H. "George Washington, Whiskey Entrepreneur." *Wall Street Journal*, February 21, 2007.

Henriques, Peter R. "The Final Struggle Between George Washington and the Grim King: Washington's Attitude Toward Death and an Afterlife." *Virginia Magazine of History and Biography* 107, no. 1 (Winter 1999).

————. "Another Sally Hemings Case? The Relationship Between George Washington and West Ford." Unpublished talk, April 26, 2005. Copy in possession of the author.

————. "Saint or Shrew? George Washington's Controversial Relationship with His Mother, Mary Ball Washington." Unpublished talk, February 12, 2008. Copy in possession of the author.

Jackman, S. W. "A Young Englishman Reports on the New Nation: Edward Thornton to James Bland Burges, 1791–1793." *William and Mary Quarterly*, 3rd ser., 18, no. 1 (January 1961).

Kail, Wendy. "The Correspondence of George and Martha Washington." Papers of George Washington, http://gwpapers.virginia.edu/articles.

Kelly, Catherine E. "Face Value: George Washington and Portrait Prints." *Common-place* 7, no. 3 (April 2007).

Kennicott, Philip. "Plain as Dirt: History Without Gimmickry." *Washington Post*, July 4, 2007.

Killian, Tom. "Mount Vernon: Elite & Vernacular." *Material Culture*, Fall 2005.

Leibiger, Stuart. "'To Judge of Washington's Conduct': Illuminating George Washington's Appearance on the World Stage." *Virginia Magazine of History and Biography* 107, no. 1 (Winter 1999).

Lepore, Jill. "Back Issues." *New Yorker*, January 26, 2009.

———. "I.O.U." *New Yorker*, April 13, 2009.

Lipset, Seymour Martin. "George Washington and the Founding of Democracy." *Journal of Democracy* 9, no. 4 (October 1988).

Lombardi, Michael J. "Taking the Measure of Washington . . . Once More." *Colonial Williamsburg*, Summer 2005.

Magnet, Myron. "Alexander Hamilton, Modern America's Founding Father." *City Journal*, Winter 2009.

Meade, Robert Douthat. "Gov. Fauquier—Friend of Jefferson." *Richmond Times-Dispatch*, July 7, 1935.

Morgan, Edmund S. "Jefferson & Betrayal." *New York Review of Books*, June 26, 2008.

Morgan, Kenneth. "George Washington and the Problem of Slavery." *Journal of American Studies* 34 (2000).

Morgan, Marie, and Edmund S. Morgan. "Jefferson's Concubine." *New York Review of Books*, October 9, 2008.

Morgan, Philip D. "'To Get Quit of Negroes': George Washington and Slavery." *Journal of American Studies* 39, no. 3 (2005).

Neely, Sylvia. "Mason Locke Weems's *Life of George Washington* and the Myth of Braddock's Defeat." *Virginia Magazine of History and Biography* 107, no. 1 (Winter 1999).

Pogue, Dennis J. "Slave Lifeways at Mount Vernon: An Archaeological Perspective." Presentation to the symposium "Slavery in the Age of George Washington," Mount Vernon, November 3, 1994. Mount Vernon Web site.

———. "The Domestic Architecture of Slavery at George Washington's Mount Vernon." Henry Francis du Pont Winterthur Museum, 2002.

Riley, John P. "'Written with My Own Hand': George Washington's Last Will and Testament," *Virginia Cavalcade* 48, no. 4 (Autumn 1999).

Sayen, William Guthrie. "George Washington's 'Unmannerly' Behavior: The Clash Between Civility and Honor." *Virginia Magazine of History and Biography,* 107, no. 1 (Winter 1999).

Scheer, George F. "Why Washington Stood Up in the Boat." *American Heritage*, December 1964.

Schulte, Brigid. "Fresh Look at Martha Washington: Less First Frump, More Foxy Lady." *Washington Post*, February 2, 2009.

Schwartz, Jeffrey H. "Putting a Face on the First President." *Scientific American*, February 2006.

Shaw, Diane Windham. "Lafayette and Slavery." *Lafayette Alumni News Magazine*, Winter 2007.

Smith, Richard Norton. "The Surprising George Washington, Part 2." *Prologue: Quarterly of the National Archives,* Spring 1994.

Smyk, Edward A., ed. "Washington and the Dey Mansion." Wayne, N.J.: Passaic County Board of Chosen Freeholders for the Dey Mansion, 2009.

Sognnaes, Reidar F. "America's Most Famous Teeth: The Truth at Last About George Washington's Dentures Can Be Made 'A Parade of.'" *Smithsonian* 3, no. 11 (February 1973).

Thompson, Mary V. "'They Appear to Live Comfortable Together': Private Life of the Mount Vernon Slaves." Presentation to the symposium "Slavery in the Age of Washington," Mount Vernon, November 3, 1994. Mount Vernon Web site.

———. "'The Only Unavoidable Subject of Regret': George Washington and Slavery." Presentation to symposium "George Washington and Alexandria, Virginia: Ties That Bind," Alexandria, February 20, 1999. Mount Vernon Web site.

———. "The Lives of Enslaved Workers on George Washington's Outlying Farms." Presentation to the Neighborhood Friends of Mount Vernon, June 16, 1999. Mount Vernon Web site.

———. "Houdon's Bust of Washington." *Mount Vernon Annual Report*, 2000.

———. "'More to dread . . . than from the Sword of the Enemy.'" *Mount Vernon Annual Report*, 2000.

———. "'As If I had Been a Very Great Somebody': Martha Washington in the American Revolution; Becoming the New Nation's First Lady." Presentation to the Annual George Washington Symposium, Mount Vernon, November 9, 2002. Mount Vernon Web site.

Toner, J. M. "The Youth of George Washington." *Magazine of American History* 27 (May 1892).

———. "Washington and His Mother." *Magazine of American History* 28 (November 1892).

Wallenborn, White McKenzie. "George Washington's Terminal Illness: A Modern Medical Analysis of the Last Illness and Death of George Washington." 1999. Papers of George Washington, http://www.gwpapers.virginia.edu/documents/index.html.

Warren, Jack D. "Books at Mount Vernon." Papers of George Washington, http://gwpapers .virginia.edu/articles/warren.html.

Wetherell, W. D. "On the Trail of Benedict Arnold." *American Heritage,* April–May 2007.

Wilford, John Noble. "Archaeologists Agree: Young Washington Slept Here." *New York Times*, July 3, 2008.

Wood, Gordon S. "The Shopper's Revolution." *New York Review of Books,* June 10, 2004.

———. "The Making of a Disaster." *New York Review of Books,* April 28, 2005.

———. "American Religion: The Great Retreat." *New York Review of Books*, June 8, 2006.

———. "Reading the Founders' Minds." *New York Review of Books*, June 28, 2007.

Wright, John Womack. "Pickering's Letter on Washington." *Tyler's Quarterly Magazine* 7 (July 1925).

Zax, David. "Washington's Boyhood Home." *Smithsonian*, September 2008.

Illustration Permissions

In order of appearance

FRONTISPIECE

George Washington (1732–1799), by Charles Willson Peale (1741–1827)
Oil on canvas, 1787
Courtesy of the Pennsylvania Academy of the Fine Arts, Philadelphia. Bequest of Mrs.
    Sarah Harrison (The Joseph Harrison, Jr., Collection)

PART TITLE PAGES

George Washington in the Uniform of a British Colonial Colonel, by Charles Willson Peale
    (1741–1827)
Oil on canvas, 1772
Washington-Custis-Lee Collection, Washington and Lee University, Lexington, Virginia

Martha Dandridge Custis (1731–1802), by John Wollaston (active 1742–1775)
Oil on canvas, 1757
Washington-Custis-Lee Collection, Washington and Lee University, Lexington, Virginia

George Washington at Princeton, by Charles Willson Peale (1741–1827)
Oil on canvas, 1779
Courtesy of the Pennsylvania Academy of the Fine Arts, Philadelphia. Bequest of Mrs.
    Sarah Harrison (The Joseph Harrison, Jr., Collection)

Bust of George Washington, by Jean-Antoine Houdon (1741–1828)
Terra-cotta, 1785
Courtesy of the Mount Vernon Ladies' Association

George Washington, by Gilbert Stuart (1755–1828)
Oil on canvas, 1795–1796
Copyright the Frick Collection, New York

Apotheosis of Washington, by David Edwin (1776–1841), after Rembrandt Peale
    (1778–1860)
Stipple engraving on paper, ca. 1800
National Portrait Gallery, Smithsonian Institution / Art Resource, NY

ILLUSTRATION INSERT

Lawrence Washington (ca. 1718–1752), possibly by John Wollaston (active 1742–1775)
Oil on canvas, ca. 1743
Courtesy of the Mount Vernon Ladies' Association

Lieutenant Governor Robert Dinwiddie (1693–1770), by an unknown artist
Oil on canvas, ca. 1760–1765
© National Portrait Gallery, London

Sarah "Sally" Cary Fairfax (ca. 1730–1811), by Duncan Smith (1877–1934)
Oil on canvas, early twentieth century
The Virginia Historical Society

George William Fairfax (1724–1787), by an unknown artist
Oil on wood panel, 1773 or after
© Trustees of Leeds Castle Foundation, Maidstone, Kent, UK

Martha Washington (1731–1802), by Charles Willson Peale (1741–1827)
Miniature, watercolor on ivory, 1772
Courtesy of the Mount Vernon Ladies' Association

John Parke "Jacky" Custis (1754–1781), by Charles Willson Peale (1741–1827)
Miniature, watercolor on ivory, 1772
Courtesy of an anonymous lender

Martha Parke "Patsy" Custis (1756–1773), by Charles Willson Peale (1741–1827)
Miniature, watercolor on ivory, 1772
Courtesy of the Mount Vernon Ladies' Association

George Washington, by John Trumbull (1756–1843)
Oil on canvas, 1780
The Metropolitan Museum of Art / Art Resource, NY

General Charles Lee (1732–1782), by I. Neagle
Engraving, n.d.
Emmet Collection, Miriam and Ira D. Wallach Division of Art, Prints and Photographs,
     The New York Public Library, Astor, Lenox and Tilden Foundations

General Horatio Gates (1727–1806), by Gilbert Stuart (1755–1828)
Oil on canvas, ca. 1793–1794
The Metropolitan Museum of Art / Art Resource, NY

Henry Knox (1750–1806), by Gilbert Stuart (1755–1828)
Oil on panel, ca. 1805
121.6 x 98.11 cm (47⅞ x 38⅝ in.)
Museum of Fine Arts, Boston. Deposited by the City of Boston, L-R 30.76b. Photograph ©
    2010 Museum of Fine Arts, Boston

Nathanael Greene (1742–1786), by Charles Willson Peale (1741–1827)
Oil on canvas, from life, ca. 1783
Independence National Historical Park

Phillis Wheatley (ca. 1753–1784), by Scipio Moorhead
Engraving, frontispiece from Phillis Wheatley, *Poems on Various Subjects, Religious and
    Moral* (London: A. Bell, 1773)
Courtesy of the Library of Congress

John Adams (1735–1826), by Charles Willson Peale (1741–1827)
Oil on canvas, from life, ca. 1791–1794
Independence National Historical Park

Sir Henry Clinton (ca. 1730–1795), by Thomas Day (active 1768–1788)
Miniature, watercolor on ivory, 1787
Courtesy of the R. W. Norton Art Gallery, Shreveport, Louisiana

Charles Cornwallis, First Marquess Cornwallis (1738–1805), by Thomas Gainsborough
    (ca. 1727–1788)
Oil on canvas, feigned oval, 1783
© National Portrait Gallery, London

Benedict Arnold (1741–1801), after John Trumbull (1756–1843)
Engraving, ca. 1894
Courtesy of the Library of Congress

Margaret "Peggy" Shippen (Mrs. Benedict Arnold) (1760–1804), by John André
    (1750–1780)
Graphite on paper, 1778
Yale University Art Gallery

Washington, Lafayette, and Tilghman at Yorktown, by Charles Willson Peale (1741–1827)
Oil on canvas, 1784
93″ x 64″
Accession number: MSA SC 1545–1120. Collection of the Maryland State Archives

Alexander Hamilton (1755–1804), after Charles Willson Peale (1741–1827)
Oil on canvas, late eighteenth or early nineteenth century
Collection of the New-York Historical Society, 1841.2

"Baron" von Steuben (1730–1794), by Ralph Earl (1751–1801)
Oil on canvas, ca. 1786
Yale University Art Gallery. Gift of Mrs. Paul Moore in memory of her nephew Howard
    Melville Hanna, Jr., B.S. 1931

Mrs. Samuel Powel (née Elizabeth Willing, 1743–1830), by Matthew Pratt (1734–1805)
Oil on canvas, ca. 1793
Courtesy of the Pennsylvania Academy of the Fine Arts, Philadelphia. Henry D. Gilpin
    Fund

James Madison (1751–1836), by Gilbert Stuart (1755–1828)
Oil on canvas, ca. 1805–1807
Bowdoin College Museum of Art, Brunswick, Maine. Bequest of the Honorable James
    Bowdoin III

Thomas Jefferson (1743–1826), by Charles Willson Peale (1741–1827)
Oil on canvas, from life, ca. 1791–1792
Independence National Historical Park

Thomas Paine (1737–1809), by William Sharp after George Romney
Engraving, 1793
© National Portrait Gallery, London

Philip Morin Freneau (1752–1832)
Reprinted from Philip Morin Freneau, *Poems Relating to the American Revolution* (New
    York: W. J. Widdleton, 1865)

Martha Washington (1731–1802), by James Peale (1749–1831)
Miniature, watercolor on ivory, 1796
Courtesy of the Mount Vernon Ladies' Association

Frances "Fanny" Bassett (1767–1796), by Robert Edge Pine (ca. 1730–1788)
Oil on canvas, 1785
Courtesy of the Mount Vernon Ladies' Association

The Washington Family, by David Edwin (1776–1841) after Edward Savage (1761–1817)
Stipple engraving, 1798
National Portrait Gallery, Smithsonian Institution / Art Resource, NY

George Washington, by Charles Willson Peale (1741–1827)
Oil on canvas, 1795
Collection of the New-York Historical Society, 1867.299

INDEX

Page numbers in *italics* refer to illustrations.

industriousness of, 81, 118–19, 152, 218, 330, 410
and Jacky's death, 421, 424
Jefferson and, 816
kindness and generosity of, 133, 369
Mary Washington's relationship with, 97–98, 423
modesty of, 81, 97, 152, 218, 369, 410, 469, 573
as mother and grandmother, 101, 153–55, 156, 163, 231, 421, 463, 463–64, 473, 486, 526, 573, 615–16, 814
on Native Americans, 360
Patsy mourned by, 162, 164
Philadelphia social life and, 644, 645
politics of, 330, 571, 816
portraits of, 80, *95*, 106, 159–60, 217, 494, 509, 764, 814
religious observances by, 83, 131, 152, 816
on return to Mount Vernon, 770, 766, 775
Sally Fairfax and, 84–86
on Saratoga victory, 315
smallpox inoculation of, 231–32
sociability of, 80–81, 122, 152, 219, 295, 410, 469, 573, 578–79, 748, 776–77, 799, 814–15
strength and practical nature of, 80, 81, 216, 573, 816
Stuart's portraits criticized by, 747
support and devotion of, 80, 81, 101, 143, 294
wartime activities of, 215–19
wedding of, 97
widowhood and grief of, 814–16
yellow fever epidemic and, 701
Washington, Mary Ball (mother), 5–7, 461, 462, 545–46
critical nature of, 7, 11, 15, 80, 395–97, 422–23, 588
death of, 588–90
GW's wedding boycotted by, 97–98
pension requested by, 396–97, 431–32, 590
religious observances by, 131
as rumored Loyalist, 396, 423
stubborn and difficult personality of, 6, 10–11, 98, 113, 157–58, 423, 524–26, 589
thwarting of GW's career attempted by, 17–18, 53–54, 55, 63, 157, 189
Washington, Mildred (sister), 7, 8
Washington, Mildred Warner, 4–5
Washington, Richard, 64, 76, 99, 104, 106, 122–23, 129
Washington, Samuel (brother), 7, 129, 158, 192, 216, 267, 271, 289, 294, 373, 647
death of, 464
Washington, Samuel (nephew), 779
Washington, Sarah (niece), 52

Washington, William Augustine (nephew), 493
Washington administration, 608, 676, 677–78, 681, 691, 724, 733, 764, 770, 780
Madison's anonymous assault on, 672, 677
revolt against, 670–71
Washington and Lee University (Liberty Hall Academy), 803
Washington College, 428–29
Washington Family, The, 494, 503
"Washington's Legacy," 442–43
"Washington's March," 633
Watson, Elkanah, 489, 501
Wayne, Anthony "Mad Anthony," 307, 309, 310, 339, 340, 343, 361–62, 389–90, 413
in Northwest Territory, 668, 717–18
Wealth of Nations (Smith), 491
Webb, Samuel Blachley, 225, 236, 237, 240
Weber, Paul, 326
Webster, Noah, 403–4, 470, 780
Wedgwood, Josiah, 140
Weedon, George, 254, 375
Weems, Mason L., 326, 813–14
Wentworth, Thomas, 9
West, Benjamin, 159, 454, 508, 512, 614
Westchester Light Dragoons, 450
West Indies, 142, 337, 347, 401, 505, 640, 710
British, 730
French, 715
markets shut to Americans in, 465, 514, 656
West Point, 361, 377, 378, 380–85, 388, 390, 400
military academy at, 764, 805
Wethersfield, Conn., 401–3
Wheatley, John, 220
Wheatley, Phillis (slave), 219–21
Whigs, 427, 443, 470, 590
Whipple, Joseph, 761–62
whiskey, tax on, 636, 654, 718–20, 756
Whiskey Rebellion, 718–28, 755, 767, 786
White, Joseph, 218, 280
White, Philip, 426
White, William, 130, 132, 605
White House, 466, 584, 634, 703, 770, 794, 795
White House (Martha Washington's home), 78
White Mingo, 149
White Plains, N.Y., 257, 258, 266, 291, 348
Whitting, Anthony, 640–41, 663, 694, 705–6
Wiencek, Henry, 82, 117–18
Wilkinson, James, 273, 276, 313, 317–18, 480
Willard, Joseph, 614
William III, king of England, 239
William IV, king of England, 425–26
Williams, Henry, 12
Williams, William Joseph, 720–21